YOURS ALWAYS

"We never lose the friends about whose lives beautiful memories linger with us."
[20170724-7 Henry to Bertha, circa 1896]

"Forty-two years ago, I began this book. It does not seem possible. Still less does it seem possible that I have lived twenty-four of those years without Henry. And yet, he seems as vividly alive to me today as he did then. I know now that you never lose those whom you really love."
[Bertha 1893 Diary, February 14, 1935]

TABLE OF CONTENTS

PREFACE: The Other True Story

I have been thinking about the story of Bertha and Henry Scott ever since I was a boy. My father, Hugh Scott Jr., who knew my great grandmother, Bertha Warburton Drake, very well, used to relate the story of how Bertha came to be married to my great grandfather, Henry Clarkson Scott. I must have first heard this story when I was about 5 years old and over many years since then, and the story always seemed to get better and better. As I have since learned, the story was not based entirely on fact. Nevertheless, this was the story that captivated my mind when I was young and continues to captivate it today. In this book, I have set out to relate the actual story, which is more rich, intriguing and complicated than the one that was related to me as a boy. But, here below, I shall relate my father's story.

Bertha and Henry, as two young adults, fell in love and decided that they wished to marry. Their fault of rushing into an engagement without following various proper protocols might normally be excused as a product of their youth but this was 1890. When Henry went to Bertha's father, George Silas Drake, a man of great social standing and wealth, to broach the news of their decision to engage, there were various difficulties to overcome which George immediately recognized. First, Henry did not have a lot of money at the time and George, knowing his daughter, knew that she was accustomed to a life of luxury. Second, the Drakes were practically royalty, being descended from Edward III's lineage, ancient King of England, and the Scott's did not appear to have any such claim to a high pedigree. Third, Henry was a Southern boy raised in Fredericksburg Virginia and had only recently moved to Saint Louis, while the Drakes were New England Yankees and then well established in the St. Louis elite. The year 1890 was less than 30 years after the Civil War and "The War" was never far from anyone's mind. And you could tell from a man's accent whose side he came from.

So, George put various impediments in the way of their marriage. The first went something like this: "Mr. Scott, I will consider your proposal regarding my daughter as soon as you can afford to keep her in the style to which she is accustomed." Since Henry was relatively new to Saint Louis business and did not start with the advantages of various connections that would have been forthcoming had he grown up there, George felt that this impediment should end the matter. But Henry, with the prize held fast in his heart, worked tirelessly to build his businesses in gas and electricity and rail in order to be able to return to his future father-in-law with the means to secure his blessing for the marriage.

As Henry became more prosperous, George became increasingly concerned. And so the second impediment was to avoid Henry whenever possible and to avoid any discussion of the engagement. If the "enemy" approached with a superior position, avoidance was called for. And this went on for years, 10 years in my father's story. So, there came at last a time when Bertha and Henry's love could wait no longer. And they formed a plan which, they believed, would at last gain George's consent.

It was customary for the Drakes to summer in Rye Beach, New Hampshire, since St. Louis was far too hot in those summers to bear with no air conditioning. And during one such summer, Henry went to visit Bertha in Rye Beach. As was proper in those times among young ladies of social stature, Bertha would have always been with chaperons who could vouch for her continued virtue and this practice would certainly have been observed in Rye Beach. But Bertha and Henry had a plan.

There was a ferry which operated during daylight hours, the nighttime being too dangerous; it could transport persons from Rye Beach to the Isle of the Shoals, a small group of islands several miles offshore. Visitors could go there during the day and return by ferry before nightfall. However, should one miss the final ferry, one would stay overnight in the hotel which was on the island. This was a popular get away, especially for the young adults.

On the chosen day, Bertha and her chaperons, friends, and Henry left on the morning ferry. I am sure that the day was glorious and, by dusk, the day trippers were worn but pleased from their island activities. So, the last ferry of the day left for Rye Beach with all aboard, except for Bertha and Henry, who were "inadvertently" left behind. As a consequence and by necessity, the couple had no choice but to stay, unchaperoned, at the hotel on the island.

When George heard the news and recognized the implications, that his daughter's virtue had been compromised, he was furious. But he had no choice but to relent to Bertha's marriage to Henry. But in time, the father would come to admire Henry and treat him as a true son-in-law, so much so that toward the end of his life, he took up his residence at Bertha and Henry's home.

My father's story still guides my continuing interest in the actual story of Bertha & Henry. As I have worked on this book, I have come to believe that my father's story may hold more truth than the actual facts would suggest. Perhaps, sometimes, art captures certain essentials that facts may miss. Nevertheless, the actual story, which will take much more time to tell, is every bit as fascinating and more complex, about a world which is long past, and about Bertha, Henry and close friends, whose own stories are told in their own words from their letters and diaries.

I originally thought that their story was principally about Henry. Henry was an enormously successful businessman—one of the very significant movers and shakers of the late 19th century and early 20th. The businesses that Henry helped to create and the wealth that he earned over a very short time frame and from very modest beginnings, speak to his great ingenuity and drive.

But when reading their letters and the account of their lives, it became apparent to me that, between these two extraordinary people, Bertha was the more so. Bertha wrote many beautiful and insightful words which helped reveal much about her.

On February 14, 1935, she wrote in her diary:
> ... Love is worth everything that it costs and nothing is of any value beside it. The people are happy who are able to love, and I think that comes before the joy of being loved... With that gift, comes, the more one understands it, the knowledge of God ... With that knowledge too, comes an unshakable belief in immortality, for love cannot die. "Death is only an horizon, and an horizon is only the limit of our sight."

And, shortly before she died, she wrote:
> I started to write of myself, but one's own life is so small a thing, but it has been well worth living it, and I would gladly live it over. [April 30, 1942]

It is easy for modern society to underappreciate how significant were the contributions made by women to their husbands, families and their societies in the past, women of great aptitude and wisdom, and the strength, courage, and ability to accomplish great things with modesty and self-effacement. Henry grasped Bertha's character, writing to her in 1904:
> What experiences you women go through for men, Bert. And the best among us doesn't half appreciate your patience and courage and unselfishness. I try to, dearest, but I don't seem to develop much capacity for showing it. I know I have the best wife that ever a man was blessed with and yet, as far as I have ever been able to get in recognizing all I owe to her is an occasional indulgence in idle wonder that she should seem content with a life partnership to which she is

almost the sole real contributor. I can't give you back very much that is worthwhile but my love, dearest, but that must count for something and, since you are its inspiration, it can't be entirely worthless.
[20180328-1 (1904-06-29) Henry to Bertha]

Bertha's *"patience and courage and unselfishness"* are revealed in this book, not because she demanded attention to herself but in spite of making any such demand. She is the example we would do well to emulate. Bertha, therefore, is the main character in this book and it is well deserved. From what I have learned from their story, Henry would have agreed.

Bertha and Henry included the valediction *"yours always"* on virtually every letter that they wrote to each other from their engagement in 1892 until Henry's death in 1911, nearly 1500 letters in all. In her last letter to Henry before their marriage, she wrote: *"... there is another greater reason why I do not fear the future, my dearest. I believe that you and I truly belong to those "whom God hath joined together" and I am not afraid, my dearest, to promise "in the sight of God and of this company" to be yours always."* As one reads their letters and comes to know them, *"yours always"* embodies the faith and love that Bertha and Henry shared for each other.

Henry Clarkson Scott
Potomac, Maryland
Hcscott332@gmail.com
September 1, 2021

ABOUT THE BOOK

The contents of this book are derived from over 1,500 letters and over a dozen diaries of Bertha Warburton Drake and Henry Clarkson Scott that I received from my dad, (Hugh Scott Jr.), over 30 years ago. My dad, undoubtedly, received those same letters and diaries from my great grandmother, Bertha. From her writing, Bertha revealed the intention to set down Henry and her story for their family and posterity. However, it is also clear that this became emotionally too difficult for her to accomplish. Due to her very affectionate relationship with her grandson, I can only assume that she thought that she could pass on this work to him.

My dad, at various times in his life, worked to organize all of these letters and diaries and put together a 20-page booklet, the 1984 "Scott Booklet". The Scott Booklet principally related the ancestry of the Drakes and the Scotts, much of this based on my father's research of this ancestry which took a great deal of time, including travel to the places where ancestral records were kept, in an era before Ancestry.com. I vaguely recall that on one family trip to London, Dad disappeared for a good part of a day to try to locate genealogic records of our family.

Although my dad was generally loath to reveal his feelings, I know that they were profound and deep in his heart, so much so that I cannot but think that it was very difficult for him to spend the time necessary to thoroughly review these letters and diaries which reveal so much about his grandmother whom he knew and loved so well. Oddly, even though I never knew my great grandmother or great grandfather, they having predeceased me by many, many years, these letters and diaries could tear at my feelings in a way that made long exposure to reading them, at times, very difficult for me. Perhaps that is a reason that this project has taken me 30 years to resolve to start and over 5 years of pretty continuous effort to complete.

In transcribing these letters and diaries, the following should be taken into account when reading the "quotations". It was often the case that it was difficult for me to read all of the words. Notwithstanding, I have tried to "guess" at words if I had a pretty good idea based on the context. Where I was still uncertain but could read some of a word, I would generally write the word as best I understood it, regardless of sense, and follow it with "(?)" or "(??)" if there were multiple words of which I was unsure. If there were several words or a sentence which I could not understand, I used "…" or "… … …" etc. In addition, I have used "…" to indicate that several words or sentences were left out where such words/sentences may not have been relevant to the rest of the citation. Due to my use of "(?)", whenever Henry used either "(?)" or "(!)" in his letters, I have left out the parentheses to avoid confusion with my own notations.

All of the letters are referenced by either the letter's date, when that could be ascertained (i.e. "1892-06-25 Henry to Bertha" for June 25, 1892) or, if the date could not be ascertained, by a code for the date when I transcribed the letter (e.g. "20180625-1 Henry to Bertha" – for the first letter that I transcribed on June 25, 2018 from Henry to Bertha). Where the date could be partially surmised, especially by context, I have sometimes used both date codes. The dates given are generally the postmark dates which were often one or more days after the letter was actually written. It is possible, in rare cases, that a letter may have been returned to the wrong envelope so some of the dates recorded could be incorrect. Where a day of the week is given (Monday, Tuesday, etc.), generally this is the day of the week written on the letter which should be correct. Historical background footnotes, newspaper articles and photographs have been added by me where such additional background seemed helpful or interesting. All of Bertha and Henry's transcribed letters and diaries are available to view, as are the actual letters and diaries themselves. I have used "bold" type in the transcribed letters and diaries to show any text that I have used in this book.

I have tried to report only what I could glean from these letters, diaries, newspaper articles and my research in order to remain as faithful as possible to what is true. However, not surprisingly, this is often difficult to achieve regarding any persons, especially who lived so long ago. For example, there were many newspaper reports regarding the circumstances of Henry's death and each contained slightly different accounts. None were materially different but, in order to tell one story, judgment was used to determine the most likely series of individual events of that day.

I have no illusions that this story will interest more than a limited audience. I know, as I now have come to the end of the project, that this was never my goal any more than it was my dad's or Bertha's. It is a family story which is mostly told by Bertha and Henry in their own words, written in their letters from long ago, in a time that was different from ours. But, even in that distant time, their human experiences share much in common with ours. I hope that my siblings and cousins will enjoy this and, perhaps, others who are curious about two very extraordinary people. But, for me, I know that I have now preserved that which was passed down to me as faithfully as I was able.

HCS

To My Dad

It was due to the stories that my dad told me about Bertha and Henry that formed my desire to pursue this work. Perhaps the story that most held my fascination was Dad's telling of how Bertha and Henry finally convinced Bertha's father to consent to their marriage (which is related in the preface). I will always treasure this story. Notwithstanding that the story appears to contain some art, I believe that this art conveys its own special truth.

There is an interesting parallel to Bertha & Henry with my father's life. When my parents were discussing marriage, my mother's father had concerns about my dad who he thought was "a playboy". Bertha's father and mother likewise, for reasons which unfold in this story, had their "doubts" about Bertha marrying Henry.

One of the extraordinary things about my father is how he earned people's trust. In my opinion, the best example of this is with regard to Dad's father-in-law, who went from distrusting him, to bestowing him with his final trust. When my grandfather died, he made my father an executor of his estate.

I love and admire my dad. He was one of the most extraordinary people I have known, from his military service, a staunch competitor in sports and life, and a loving husband and father. Although he was very protective of revealing certain inward feelings of love and hurt, over his lifetime, one could see glimpses and know that they were there.

Growing up, my room was just above our driveway. Often, early in the morning and before dawn when Dad had a long day scheduled at work, I could hear the car start in the driveway and the sound of the engine, and see the headlights dart around in the trees until the sound and the lights had gone. This is a memory that I often relive.

I tried years ago to express my feelings to my father in a poem which I gave to him on Father's Day twenty years ago. Perhaps, not surprisingly, this poem has some relevance to this story since it includes something which Bertha said to her own son, Hugh. Bertha and Henry were concerned at times that my grandfather, Hugh, lacked drive and persistence in his work. I understand from my father that Bertha made her views on this subject very clear.

To My Dad

I love you Dad, with love that grows,
From early years from birth arose,
And through my life, and to its close,
To where such perfect loves repose.

I loved you when I heard you rise
While safe in bed and small in size,
Before the dawn to darkened skies
Your work begin, and day apprise.

And through the day, I knew you'd be
Hard at your work, supporting me;
"A gentleman shall work" said she
"He must, it is his pedigree".

Your suits you wore, so smart and right,
Your shoulders broad and stomach tight,
With shoes spit shined and polished bright
That boys could see their smiles light.

I knew you learned your shoes to shine
In service to this country fine;
What recompense could I design
To equal such a gift divine?

And at days end you homeward flew,
I was so glad to be with you.
For at bedtime, I always knew,
One whiskey rub I'd get, or two.

I'd fast to sleep, in my warm nest,
No harm could come to my sweet rest,
My father's love, my heart attest,
Would keep me safe and always blest.

Henry
Father's Day, June 18, 2000

DESCENDANTS OF BERTHA AND HENRY SCOTT
(First Through Fourth Generations[1])

BERTHA WARBURTON DRAKE & HENRY CLARKSON SCOTT

a) Hugh Scott
  i) Hugh Scott, Jr.
    (1) Hugh Scott, III
      (a) Hugh Scott IV
      (b) Sara Cady Scott Seabaugh
    (2) Phoebe Mercer Scott Burke
      (a) McAfee Scott Burke
      (b) Susanna Spencer Menees
      (c) Morgan Baker Burke
    (3) James Wesley McAfee Scott
      (a) Samuel McAfee Scott
      (b) Elizabeth Bates Scott
      (c) Madeline McBride Scott
    (4) Henry Clarkson Scott
      (a) Henry Clarkson Scott Jr.
      (b) Drake Anthony Scott
  ii) Nancy Boteler Scott Riesmeyer
    (1) Nancy Riesmeyer
      (a) Sarah A. Eisenstein
      (b) Paul D. Eisenstein
      (c) Benjamin E. Eisenstein
    (2) Fredrick H. (Fritz) Riesmeyer
      (a) Wesley David Riesmeyer
      (b) Mark Haase Riesmeyer
      (c) Emily Anne Riesmeyer Crupper
      (d) Daniel Scott Riesmeyer
    (3) Amanda Riesmeyer Seiffert
      (a) Leah Evelyn Seiffert
      (b) Elena Nancy Seiffert
    (4) David Riesmeyer
      (a) Samantha C. Riesmeyer
      (b) David W.L. Riesmeyer
  iii) Bertha Scott Perry
    (1) George Perry
      (a) Paxton Perry
      (b) Ashley Perry
    (2) Anne Perry Henson
      (a) Margaret Henson
      (b) Elizabeth Henson
      (c) Gail Henson
      (d) Katherine Henson

---

[1] This was the most complete listing that I was able to obtain at the time this book was printed. My apology to any of Bertha and Henry's descendants who were not included or whose names are not correctly listed.

b) Anne (Nancy) Warburton Scott Blumer
   i) Nancy Scott Blumer Hovey II
      (1) Chandler Hovey III
      (2) Thomas Blumer Hovey
         (a) William Chandler Hovey
      (3) Nancy Scott Hovey Cooper
         (a) Chandler Hovey Cooper
         (b) Charles Lockwood Cooper
   ii) Priscilla Alder Blumer Hornblower
      (1) Rosalie Hornblower
         (a) Doris Catlin
         (b) Laine Catlin Fletcher
         (c) Amy Catlin Haklisch
         (d) Tracy Catlin, MD
      (2) Ralph (Ray) Hornblower III
         (a) Samuel Roosevelt Hornblower
         (b) Luke Roosevelt Hornblower
         (c) Natalie Morgan Hornblower
      (3) Paul Skinner Hornblower
      (4) Priscilla Hornblower
c) George Drake Scott
   i) George D. Scott, Jr.
   ii) Henry Clarkson Scott
   iii) Thomas Scott
d) Alice Marion Scott Gross
   i) Patricia Gross Parker
      (1) Thomas Dempsey Parker
      (2) David Scott Parker
      (3) John Edward Parker Jr.
      (4) Victoria Parker Lombardo
      (5) Elizabeth Parker Cruz
   ii) Joan Scott Gross Canepa
      (1) Allya Francesca Canepa
      (2) Adam Kevin Canepa
   iii) Francis Linton Gross, Jr.
      (1) Joseph Gross
      (2) Matthew Gross

CHAPTER 1 – AN UNTIMELY END

"Nothing, I fear, can be done which will give me rest."

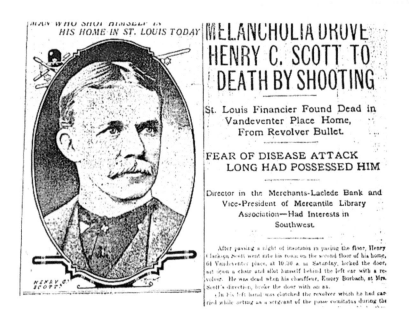

MAN WHO SHOT HIMSELF IN HIS HOME IN ST. LOUIS TODAY

MELANCHOLIA DROVE HENRY C. SCOTT TO DEATH BY SHOOTING

St. Louis Financier Found Dead in Vandeventer Place Home, From Revolver Bullet.

FEAR OF DISEASE ATTACK LONG HAD POSSESSED HIM

Director in the Merchants-Laclede Bank and Vice-President of Mercantile Library Association—Had Interests in Southwest.

After passing a night of insomnia in pacing the floor, Henry Clarkson Scott went into his room on the second floor of his home, 64 Vandeventer place, at 10:30 a. m. Saturday, locked the door, sat upon a chair and shot himself behind the left ear with a revolver. He was dead when his chauffeur, Emory Borbach, at Mrs. Scott's direction, broke the door with an ax.

In his left hand was clutched the revolver which he had carried while acting as a sergeant of the posse comitatus during the

Henry Clarkson Scott died on January 14, 1911 at age 52. His death was sudden and untimely. Henry left behind his fortune, his various business interests, board memberships, his four children and his wife, Bertha Warburton Drake Scott. Bertha would live another 34 years and would have a great deal of time for reflection.

A. NEWSPAPER ACCOUNTS

Many newspapers in St. Louis and across the country reported Henry's death. Bertha kept newspaper clippings from three newspapers in an envelope. But in addition to these articles, there were over 100 newspapers that reported the details of Henry's life and his passing, including the St. Louis Globe Democrat, St. Louis Post Dispatch and St. Louis Star, the Washington Post, the Baltimore Sun, the Free Lance in Fredericksburg, The Fort Worth Record & Register, The Chicago Inter Ocean, the Alexandria Gazette, the Philadelphia Inquirer, etc.

One newspaper quoted Henry's last words to Bertha, "*'I have an unaccountable feeling this morning', he told Mrs. Scott, 'a foreboding of something dreadful going to happen, as if my mind were going to fail me. Nothing, I fear, can be done which will give me rest.'*"

The article in the St. Louis Star on January 15, 1911 included the following about Henry: "*He returned home from his office Friday evening, more melancholy than usual, the disagreeable weather apparently having aggravated his indisposition. He ate little at supper and retired early to spend a night of sleepless tossing. Wherein, as he had been heard to remark, he would have given all his fortune to regain the ability to sleep as he once had done and as thousands of those who so much envied him his wealth, did daily without stopping to consider the value of it.*"

B. MELANCHOLY

That morning started like any other, perhaps better given the prospects of Henry and Bertha's planned trip to New York City which would combine recreation and business. They had planned to start east the next day. Henry had always lamented that his business trips often took him away from Bertha and often left him in a state of loneliness. This trip would be different.

But Henry had passed a sleepless and *"miserable"* night, perhaps arising from his ill health and depression with which he had struggled for years. Henry dressed, ate breakfast, and summoned his automobile which was waiting in front of the house to take him and Bertha downtown together. But Henry then returned to his room. When Bertha entered his room, he told her he had not slept all night. *"'I can't stand it any longer', he said."* Bertha sought to soothe him and left the room, advising him to lie down for a few minutes to rest while she finished making ready for their trip.

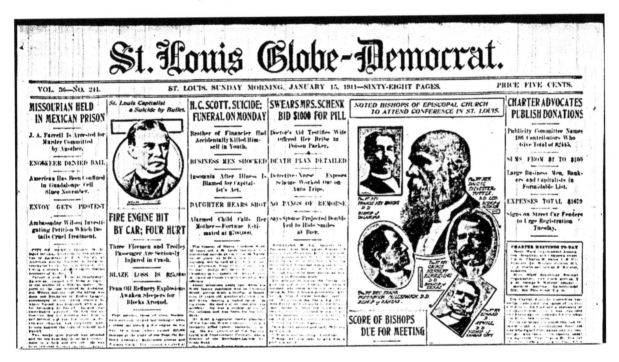

Bertha called to their 8-year-old daughter, Alice, to read to Henry. *"Alice started to her father's room and when she reached the door, which was locked, she heard the pistol shot within."*

Hearing the gun shot, Bertha ran to his room and found the door locked. Her screams summoned Emory Burbach, the chauffeur, who tried in vain to burst the door open with his shoulder. He was compelled to break a panel in the door with an ax from the garage to gain entrance. Henry had fallen from his chair and was lying partly on the bed, on his left side, the revolver in his hand, a bullet wound in the right side of the head, in back of the ear.

Bertha recognized the pistol. Henry had bought it at the time of the St. Louis street-car strike 10 years before when he volunteered for service acting as a sergeant of the *posse comitatus*. Bertha had often urged him to empty it of the cartridges and put it away but, on each occasion, he sought to reassure her by saying there was no use in his owning a revolver *"if it could not be kept in a handy place."*

Henry's brother-in-law, Dr. George S. Drake, was called to the house and pronounced Scott dead. George, speaking for Bertha, said the only motive they could assign for the suicide was the ill health of Henry who had suffered for six months from acute attacks of melancholia and a morbid dread of appendicitis with the prospect of an operation to remove it. George worried over his sister who was prostrated by the tragedy and feared that she may suffer a serious breakdown as the result of Henry's death.

Henry's daughter Alice was the only one of the children in the house. His son, Hugh, 17 years old, was attending the Hill School at Pottstown, Pa., his son, George, 13 years old, was a student in the preparatory department of Washington University and his daughter, Anne, 15 years old, was a student at Mary Institute.

Isaac H. Lionberger, a lawyer and a cousin of Bertha, was summoned by George. Isaac learned from Bertha everything pertaining to Henry's actions before his death and for a week past. It was he who first learned from her that Bertha feared his mind was giving way. At the request of Bertha, Isaac made the following statement:

> *About a year ago, Scott was in danger of appendicitis and his physicians recommended an operation which he refused to undergo. The thought of the disease, however, plunged him into melancholy which a recent attack of the grip deepened.*

Henry's friend, John ("Jack") Shepley said, "*He killed himself in a moment of aberration due to melancholia. His family relations were happy and his business circumstances prosperous.*" And Henry's next-door neighbor and long-time friend, Churchill Whittemore, said that Henry seemed in unusually good spirits a few days before and remarked: "*Isn't it fine when a man gets old and is rid of all his troubles and can enjoy himself?*"

Henry's fellow directors in the Merchants Laclede Bank wrote the following about Henry which seemed to capture what Henry's other business associates and directors felt:

> *Combined with ripe experience, wisdom and foresight that insured a splendid success and prosperity to whatever business devoted, he possessed such courteous manners, such charming social qualities and generosity of heart, as endeared him to all his friends and make his loss irreparable.*

The Centennial History of Missouri wrote the following of Henry:

> *All who knew him felt that a good man had been called to his reward. He held with Abraham Lincoln that "there is something better than making a living— making a life," and his contribution to the world's work was indeed valuable along the lines of cultural and moral progress. Well descended and well-bred the innate refinement of his nature was opposed to anything gross or common and the high ideals which he cherished were transmitted as a priceless legacy to his family.*
> [Centennial History of Missouri, One Hundred Years in the Union, 1820-1921, Vol. V, Published 1921]

C. FINAL INSTRUCTIONS

Henry must have known that his own frailties could bring him to his ending so he left detailed and complete instructions for Bertha in such event. He wrote the following on January 8, 1909, one year before he died.

> *Janry 8th, 1909*
> *My darling Wife,*
>
> *Mindful as I am of the uncertainty of life and wishing you to have all the bonds of every kind that I may buy or became possessed of, I confirm what I have repeatedly told you that I consider all the bonds which I have or may secure in the future as your property. The only condition I make to this gift is that I may use the income from these bonds in lieu of the regular and other payments which I make to you and deposit to your credit from time to time. I carry many of these bonds on my books merely because they represent the growth in part of property which I have tried to accumulate for our future wants and because it is convenient to thus carry the bonds with my other property. But as both the ledger Accts showing the cost of the bonds and the packages of bonds*

themselves show that they have all been given to you there can be no doubt about your ownership of them and should you survive me I do not wish any of said bonds listed in my estate.

You have a key to my safe deposit box, the duplicate of the one I always carry with my other keys and as you have power to enter my box when you wish, you can in case of my death or illness have access to the box and take into your own keeping all of said bonds.

The small package of bonds with the name of my sister, Marion Scott Carter, plainly marked on it will be delivered by you to her or kept in our box for safe keeping as she and you may prefer.

My will leaves all my property of every kind & nature to you because I have implicit confidence in you and know that you will provide for our four children or any other children that may be born to us hereafter.

Yours always,
Henry C Scott
[1909-01-08 Henry (StL) to Bertha]

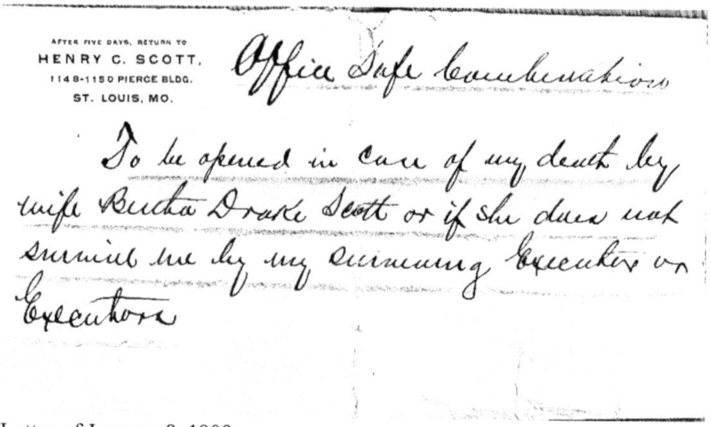

Office Safe Combinations

To be opened in case of my death by wife Bertha Drake Scott or if she does not survive me by my surviving Executor or Executors

Letter of January 8, 1909

Henry also left a second letter of instructions to Bertha written on June 24, 1909. Presumably, he wanted to be certain that she would be able to manage everything when he was gone.

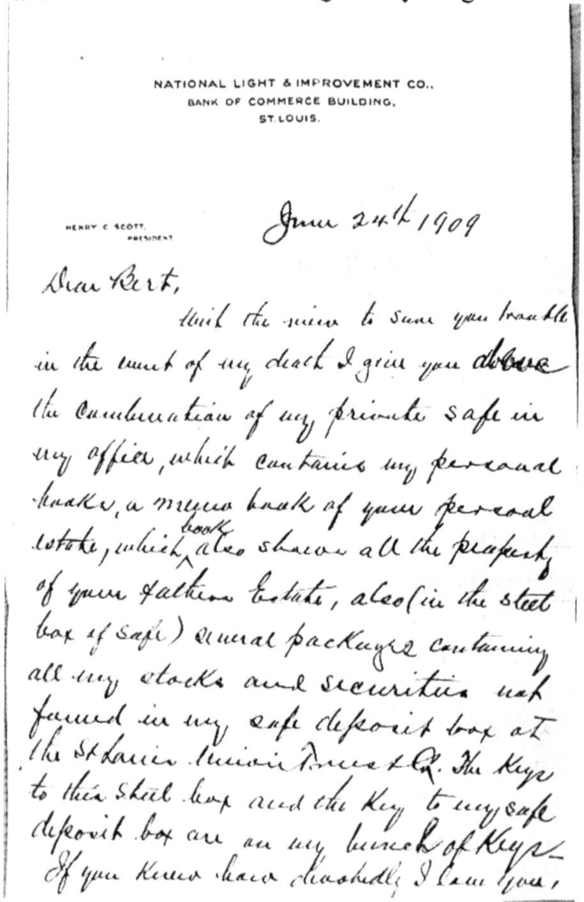

NATIONAL LIGHT & IMPROVEMENT CO.,
BANK OF COMMERCE BUILDING,
ST. LOUIS.

HENRY C. SCOTT,
PRESIDENT

June 24th 1909

Dear Bert,

Until the time to save you trouble in the event of my death I give you above the combination of my private safe in my office, which contains my personal books, a memo book of your personal estate, which book also shows all the property of your father's estate, also (in the steel box of safe) several packages containing all my stocks and securities not found in my safe deposit box at the St. Louis Union Trust & Co. The keys to this steel box and the key to my safe deposit box are on my bunch of keys— If you know how absolutely, I am Your,

June 24th, 1909

Dear Bert,
With the view to save you trouble in the event of my death, I give you above the combination of my private safe in my office which contains my personal books, a memo book of your personal estate which book also shows all the property of your father's estate, also (in the steel box of safe) several packages containing all my stocks and securities not found in my safe deposit box at the St. Louis Union Trust Co. The keys to this steel box and the key to my safe deposit box are on my bunch of keys.

If you knew how devotedly I love you as I write this memorandum, you would understand how strong is my wish that, should I be taken away before the boys are old enough to help you, you be spared all possible trouble in looking after my estate. It is because of this wish to save you unnecessary worry that I have with your full approval associated with you in the administering of my estate the St. Louis Union Trust Co whose management of estates deserves the highest praise and in whose directory are several of my closest friends who will, I am sure, always gladly help and assist you with sound advice when you stand in need of it.

As everything I have or whatever good there may be in me is due to the influence of your strong, pure life, I have left all my affairs in your hands and have tried to make the burden of their care as light as possible.

Yours always,
Henry C Scott
[1909-06-24 Henry (StL) to Bertha]

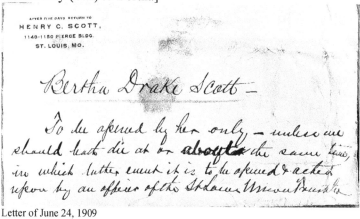

Letter of June 24, 1909

Henry executed his final Will and Testament on March 15, 1909.

D. HENRY'S ESTATE

On May 7, 1911, the St. Louis Globe Democrat reported the value of Henry's estate at $1.4 million.

SCOTT ESTATE IS $1,405,156.

Stocks of $30,000 to $40,000 Par Value Are Called Worthless.

An inventory of the estate of Henry C. Scott, who shot himself at his residence, 64 Vandeventer place, January 14, was filed in the Probate Court yesterday. The estate consists principally of personalty, and is valued at $1,405,156.22. Notation is made that $30,000 to $40,000 of stocks, par value, are worthless, and omitted from the inventory. Stocks owned by the estate are listed at $1,-316,057, and cash $85,713.58. There is an item of $600 insurance, $1282.50 in notes and $100 in bonds, the residue being goods and chattels and accounts.

E. LOOSE ENDS

Although Henry provided careful and detailed instructions to Bertha in the event of his death, it is peculiar that he did not leave a final note. And it is also peculiar that the reports and articles about his suicide made no mention that there was no such final note.

It is possible that Henry did leave a final note to Bertha which was very personal and very private, intended for her eyes only and which she kept to herself. Bertha was the first to enter Henry's room and may not

Page 18

have wanted such a note to become known. Although Henry's chauffeur broke into the room with her, it is unlikely that he would have said anything about this. It is also possible that there was a note that may have contained something scandalous or not "appropriate" for other than immediate family and necessary authorities. In that age of greater gentility, it may be reasonable to assume that the persons who were privy to such a note would have wanted to keep its contents secret.

But the real reason simply may have been that Henry believed that he had already explained all that needed to be explained and had already said all that could be said. As the reports of his death reveal, no one seemed surprised at the depth of Henry's depression and the then realization that this could drive him to one last desperate act. No doctor or investigator was needed to explain this to his friends and family.

And Henry so often said to Bertha what he needed to say from his heart. As he wrote in his letter to her on June 24, 1909, less than a year before his death (cited above), *"If you knew how devotedly I love you as I write this memorandum, you would understand how strong is my wish that, should I be taken away before the boys are old enough to help you, you be spared all possible trouble in looking after my estate."* He concluded this letter as virtually all of his letters to Bertha with the valediction, *"Yours always"*. [1909-06-24 Henry (StL) to Bertha]

That valediction was the all in all: *"Yours always"*.

F. HENRY'S FINAL WILL & TESTAMENT

I, Henry C Scott, of the city of St. Louis and State of Missouri, do make, publish and declare this as and for my last will and testament, that is to say:

FIRST: I hereby authorize and empower my executors, hereinafter mentioned, to pay, as soon as may be after my death, all my just debts and funeral expenses.

SECOND: I give and bequeath unto my oldest son, Hugh Scott, the portrait of his grand-father, John Scott; and I give and devise to him, subject to a life estate therein in my wife, my lot in Bellefontaine Cemetery.

THIRD: I give and bequeath unto St. Luke's Hospital in the said city of St. Louis, the sum of Five Thousand Dollars ($5,000.00).

FOURTH: I give and bequeath unto my sister, Margaret L. Scott, if she shall survive me, the sum of Fifteen Thousand Dollars ($15,000.00).

FIFTH: I give and bequeath unto my sister, Mrs. Marian S. Carter, the sum of Five Thousand Dollars ($5,000.00). I make this provision for her smaller than that made for her sister because of the fact that the latter has other means of her own.

SIXTH: I give and bequeath unto my brother, W.S. Scott, the sum of Five Thousand Dollars ($5,000.00), as trustee, to be held in trust and invested by him and the income derived therefrom to be used by him at this discretion for the benefit of his oldest son, my namesake, Henry C. Scott, second, until the latter shall have reached the age of twenty-one (21) years. When said son shall have reached such age, the principal of said sum shall be turned over to him absolutely.

If, however, said son shall not reach the age of twenty-one (21 years, then at his death said sum shall be distributed among the heirs at law of said W.S. Scott.

SEVENTH: I have four children, Hugh, born December 24, 1893; Anne Warburton, born July 5, 1895; George Drake, born December 7, 1897; and Alice Marian, born February 20, 1903. To each of said children and to any child who may hereafter be born to me, I give and bequeath the sum of Two Hundred Dollars ($200.00); and I make no other provision for any of my said children having full confidence in the judgment of my beloved wife and her affection for them.

EIGHTH: I give and bequeath unto my wife, Bertha D. Scott, the sum of Five Thousand Dollars ($5,000.00).

NINTH: All the rest of residue of my property and estate, of every nature whatsoever and wheresoever situate, I give, devise and bequeath unto my beloved wife, Bertha D. Scott, if she shall survive me; but if she should die before the time of my death, I give, devise and bequeath all of said residuary property and estate to my surviving children, in equal shares.

TENTH: I hereby nominate and appoint my wife and the St. Louis Union Trust Company to be the executors of this my last will; and I request and direct that no bond be required of said executors or either of them.

IN TESTIMONY WHEREOF I have hereunto set my hand and seal, this 15th day of March, 1909.

Henry C. Scott (SEAL)

The undersigned hereby certify that the foregoing instrument was signed, sealed, published and declared as and for his last will and testament by the said Henry C. Scott, in the presence of us, who have, at his request, in his presence, and in the presence of each other, hereunto subscribed our names as witnesses this 15th day of March, 1909; and further certify that at the time the said testator was of sound and disposing mind.

WITNESSES:
Isaac H. Orr
John F. Shepley
Oscar R. Beneke

CHAPTER 2 – A RECONSTRUCTED YOUTH

From the Clyde and Old Dominion,
Restless footsteps left his art
Searching for love's companion
And peace for his beating heart.
HCS 8/14/2020

Shipping on the Clyde, by John Atkinson Grimshaw, 1881

The Wandering Sailor
By John Arthur Scott

The wandering sailor ploughs the main
A competence in life to gain
Undaunted braves the stormy seas
In hopes to find content & ease
In hopes when lost & dangers o'er
To anchor on his native shore
In hopes.

When winds blow hard & waters roll
And thunders shake from pole to pole
The dreadful waves surrounding foam
Will flatt'ring fancy wafts him home
In hopes.

When round the bowl the jovial crew
The early scenes of life renew
And each his favorite fair will boast
"This is the universal toast
May we.

A. COMING TO AMERICA: John Arthur Scott

Henry Clarkson Scott was born on May 5, 1859 in Fredericksburg Virginia, into a prosperous merchant family, with a rich family history. Henry's grandfather, John Arthur Scott (1772-1848), immigrated to Fredericksburg Virginia in 1788 when he was sixteen from Greenock Scotland where the Scott family were successful shipbuilders. The Scott Shipbuilding firm was located on the Clyde River which was the hub of shipbuilding in Scotland and in England at that time and continued to be into the 20th century.

In her diary, Bertha wrote the following about John Scott:

> Perhaps I ought to begin his life by a little account of Henry's progenitors, anyway. His grandfather, John Scott came to this country from Scotland (Greenock) in the early part of the last century, or the very end of the eighteenth. He never liked to talk of his reasons for coming or to allude to it in anyway. Yet, he sent one of his sons back to be educated as a medical doctor in Scotland at the University of Edinburgh, and he (William Samuel Scott) visited the family at Greenock, while there. He also visited Sir Walter Scott, who took an interest in all Americans, because of a brother of his who had immigrated to America. Sir Walter was one of his sponsors when he got his degree. His [William Samuel Scott's] theme was on tuberculosis[2]. He also paid a pound to be present at a public dinner where Sir Walter was present, and which, as good fortune would have it, was the one at which he announced his authorship of the Waverly novels, which had appeared anonymously.
>
> [June 27, 1911 (Rye Beach)]

Henry was interested in learning of his Scottish heritage and was able to locate his kinsman, John Scott of Greenock Scotland, who had become the senior partner in the Scott shipbuilding business.

In response to Henry's letter, John wrote in 1899:

> 7 Belgrave Crescent,
> Edinburgh, Scotland
> December 8th, 1899
>
> My Dear Sir:
>
> As the Senior Partner of Messrs. Scott & Co., of Greenock, I have pleasure in replying to your letter of November 15th and more so because I believe the supposition which you start of being my kinsman is very probably founded on fact. You will observe that I bear the same name as your Grandfather, who you tell me came from Greenock about the year 1785 or 1790. I know, as a family tradition (received from my father) that relatives of our family emigrated to Virginia at the end of last century and he told me that he had seen a member of this American branch at his father's house who had come to Scotland to pursue his studies as a medical student at Edinburgh University. This is your uncle, no doubt, William Samuel Scott, whose career there you mention. I have frequently made inquiries of American citizens whether they could give me any information regarding a Family of Scott resident in Virginia and coming from Scotland, but I have until the receipt of your letter, been unsuccessful in obtaining any trace. I am consequently very much interest in the communication which you have been good enough to send to my firm.
>
> Your branch of our Family cannot, from the name of your grandfather, spring from a common source to mine, earlier than two generations prior to your grandfather, and from what I know of the genealogy of my branch or the Family, I think that the common origin was in John Scott, who was the great great grandfather of my Grandfather. The John Scott of that period filled the office of Town Treasurer to the then very small town of Greenock and died about the year 1734, leaving

---

[2] William Samuel Scott, graduated at the University of Edinburgh as an M.D. The entry in the Official Books of the University being as follows: "Gulielmus S. Scott, Americanus" (Subject of Thesis – "Tuberculis", 1827).

sons: John, James and Samuel. I am descended from John(2) who was the founder of the business which is now carried on by myself and my brother, and has descended direct from father to son from that period.

I think the John of your family, who migrated to America in 1785, must be a descendant of one of the other sons I mentioned above, but I will be better able to judge of this if you will kindly transmit copies of the records which you say some members of your immediate family, living in Virginia, still possess.

In reference to what you say regarding Sir Walter Scott, though I believe we are descended from a Scotch Border stock as he was, I do not believe that any relationship exists between our family and that of Sir Walter and I think, therefore, that the kindness shown to your uncle by Sir Walter and Lady Scott must have sprung from personal liking to him, probably increased by his possessing the same name as their own and possibly from the fact that Sir Walter had two brothers settled in America or, rather, I think in Canada.

I am not aware that any public records, except those of Baptisms and Burials, will throw any light upon your genealogy but I will be better able to judge of this when I have your reply to this letter, which I shall await with interest.

The Drexel Yacht will, I hope, be a very fine one and do credit to our name. It is the first vessel we have built for a United States owner. You are aware, no doubt, that your Navigation laws do not permit construction here of ships for the American Flag, except for pleasure purposes.

I reside in Edinburgh for a few months in winter, but my home is at Halkshill, Largs, Ayrshire, a place acquired by my grandfather early in this century and I shall be obliged by our replying to that address. Two of my sons are with me in the Shipbuilding business, nearly six generation since the founder, John Scott(2).

With the salutation of a kinsman, I remain,
Yours faithfully,
John Scott

In 1907, Henry received the book, "*Two Centuries of Shipbuilding*" from his cousin, John Scott of Greenock. A later copy of this same book had the following cover page. Henry wrote back to John with the following:

Dear Mr. Scott:
I was very much delighted with "Two Centuries of Shipbuilding" which I received through the mail a day or two since and I assure you I have looked through its pages with the greatest possible pleasure at the achievements of my kinsmen across the sea. Two hundred years of useful and successful endeavor by one family and especially upon the broad lines of the great work which you and your brother have fallen heir to and are now carrying on, is no ordinary achievement and I am sure you must feel great pride in what has been done by your ancestors and great satisfaction in your won accomplishments which have made secure the fruits of their work and have so broadly extended the field of work of the Shipbuilding Co. I beg to offer my heartiest congratulations to you and your brother[3] and I feel no little pride that I can claim even distant kinship with those of your family of the past and present generations whose exertions have made possible this great work. [Henry 1907-04-20]

---

[3] Presumably Robert Sinclair Scott. John and Robert were both sons of Charles Cuningham Scott.

TWO HUNDRED
& FIFTY YEARS OF
SHIPBUILDING

BY THE SCOTTS
AT GREENOCK

Fourth Edition, the First under this title

'Take it all in all, a ship of the line is the most honourable thing
that man, as a gregarious animal, has ever produced... Into
that he has put as much of his human patience, common-sense,
forethought, experimental philosophy, self-control, habits of
order and obedience, thoroughly wrought hand-work, defiance
of brute elements, careless courage, careful patriotism, and calm
expectation of the judgment of God, as can well be put into a
space of 300 feet long by 80 feet broad.'—*Ruskin.*

1961

Produced by James Jack Advertising Limited, Glasgow   Printed by Tillotsons (Bolton) Ltd., Bolton, Glasgow and London

Ironically, this John Scott IV apparently died in 1903 and his brother, Robert Scott (to whom Henry refers), died in 1905. Presumably, John may have left instructions to mail the book to Henry and this request may have been fulfilled by Robert Lyons Scott, John's son and subsequent Chairman of the shipbuilding company (The book was first published in 1906).

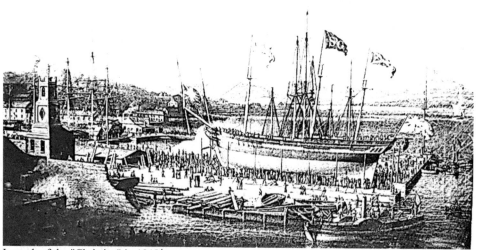

Launch of the "Christian" in 1818[4]

Henry also wrote the following to Bertha:

> *Did I tell you there is a long account in the Scientific American about the big works of Scott firm on the Clyde and that Robert Scott[5] had finally sent me the records showing the birth date of my grandfather's grandfather, a short family genealogy, the establishment of the ship building plant*

---

[4] I believe that the "SG" flag in the picture stands for Scotts of Greenock.
[5] Probably Robert Lyons Scott who was the son of John Scott.

in 1711 and closing with a very cordial invitation to visit him in Scotland. Wouldn't that be nice and wouldn't I have a fine proud time showing my pretty wife to the scotch kin!
[20180731-2 (1906--) Henry to Bertha]

Sometimes, Henry was mentioned in the papers, such as in Ft. Worth, which would describe his Scottish background.

LOOK WHO'S HERE
Henry C. Scott of St. Louis, president of the Fort Worth and Power Company, who is in the city for several days on business, is generally known for his connection with illumination plants but it is not so well know that he comes from the greatest family of shipbuilders in the world.

The Scotts of Scotland, which is the family from which Mr. Scott springs, have been building ships, men of war and every other kind of big floating craft on the River Clyde for nearly 200 years. The firm started in 1711 and the fifth consecutive John Scott is now its president, a son having succeeded his father in each case. The late Henry T. Scott, famous on all the Pacific coast and builder of the battleship Oregon, came from a branch of the same family.

Mr. Scott will be in Fort Worth longer than usual at this time, owing to the serious illness of Secretary Mountain, who is now at Fall River Wis., suffering from appendicitis.
[1900(-) 20180620-2 Ft Worth Newspaper Clipping]

As was common for a prosperous family in Virginia at that time, John Scott owned slaves which were passed on to his children when he died. Clause 6th of John's will provided special consideration for "Jack and Letty":

6th: My slaves Jack and Letty having by good conduct deserved particular indulgence, it is my desire that they together with the children of Letty & their descendants be not sold at the division of my estate but to go to such of my family as they may prefer to be valued however in proportion with my other slaves and it is my wish so far as it can conveniently be done that the rest of my slaves be not sold but divided.
[1846-07-29 Will of John Scott, Fredericksburg VA]

(This fact, that John Scott owned slaves, is solely intended to provide historical insight into the life and times in which the Scott family lived in Virginia prior to the Emancipation Proclamation and the enactment of the 14th Amendment to our Constitution.) John Scott died in 1848.

According to family history, Henry was a descendent of William Payne ("Captain Pepper", 1755-1837), who fought in the Revolutionary War and the War of 1812. Captain Payne was a Federalist of the strongest type and very forceful, intelligent and successful. He continued to dress in "colonial" attire until his last days, as described by Bishop Payne.

I visited a great-uncle, Captain William Payne, a venerable old gentleman and the grandfather of Richard Payne of Warrenton. He was dressed in knee pants, had served in the Revolution and was a fine specimen of the old Virginia gentleman.
[Excerpt from the 1984 "Scott Booklet"]

B. FREDERICKSBURG

Henry was born at an inauspicious time, in an inauspicious place. The Civil War started two years after his birth and its impact on southern cities, including Fredericksburg, was devastating. During the Civil War, Fredericksburg was the place of a major battle which destroyed parts of the city.

Fredericksburg played a major role in the Civil War, serving as the grounds for what was then the largest battle in America and the first urban battle since the Revolutionary War. On December 11, 1862, the Union Army of the Potomac, after bombarding the town with artillery fire, crossed the

Rappahannock River and landed at the foot of Hawke Street. The Union Army charged into town and ransacked homes and businesses searching for Confederate soldiers. Caroline Street became a stronghold for the Confederates and, thus, received the brunt of the battle which extended south to William Street. Several churches and dwellings, including Federal Hill at 501 Hanover Street, were used as makeshift military hospitals, and the basement of the town hall served as a refuge for slaves during the battle. By nightfall, the Confederate Army retreated to Marye's Heights to the south of the town. Two days later, on December 13, a second assault was mounted at Marye's Heights. Confederate soldiers were strategically placed behind a stone wall along the Sunken Road. The battle resulted in significant casualties for the Union Army. The entire Battle of Fredericksburg resulted in 12,653 Union casualties and 4,201 Confederate casualties.
[Fredericksburgva.gov]

The conclusion of the Civil War did not bring any immediate relief to Fredericksburg or its citizens. This was especially true due to southern resentment of US government policies to punish the South, including the quartering of Union Soldiers in many Southern cities to oversee these policies of "reconstruction".

The period of reconstruction in Fredericksburg following the Civil War is marked by a struggling economy and slow growth. The collapse of the plantation system severely impacted the city's economy, as it relied heavily on trade with the rural interior. Like other urban areas, Fredericksburg sought to establish a greater industrial base for the city. While the canal system that was expanded in the 1850s paved the way for water-powered mills and factories, it was not until the arrival of the railroad in Fredericksburg in 1872, along with capital from northern investors, that industrial activities began to surge and transform the city.
[Fredericksburgva.gov]

It is difficult to comprehend living in a defeated land where the many opportunities for success that were present just before the war almost entirely disappeared. Faced with such adversity, many undoubtedly became despondent and bitter. But that is not Henry's story.

Although Henry would adapt and progress with the times, there may have remained a "remnant" of the past. Bertha referred to this in jest in one of her letters to Henry.

George and mother and I went in this afternoon to see "Alabama" and very pretty it was, I thought, but I imagine my "unreconstructed" friend would not have cared for it.
[1893-01-05 (Wednesday) Bertha (Newton Centre) to Henry (StL)]

Fredericksburg offered the young Henry recreation by way of the Rappahannock River. In an 1892 letter to Bertha, Henry talks about his prowess as a swimmer. *"I have not the slightest dread of the water. Our home in Virginia was on one of the banks of the Rappahannock, the river you saw in the night as you were going from Richmond to Washington and, during the summers, I spent most of my time on the water…"*
[1892-08-02 Henry (StL) to Bertha (Farragut House, Rye Beach)]

C. FAMILY

Henry's family called their home in Fredericksburg, *Scotia*, presumably as homage to their former homeland of Scotland, "the land of the Gaels" as the Romans referred to it. My father described Scotia in the Scott Booklet, as follows:

Mr. & Mrs. Scott lived at "Scotia" on Charles Street between George and William (now Commerce) streets, and across the street from the Masonic Cemetery. It was a large frame building with a semi-basement, two full stories, and a half-story under the long gable roof. Two tall inside brick chimneys rose from each end. Seven large windows ornamented the second story of the front on Charles Street which were duplicated on the first floor, except that the center opening was occupied by a door covered by a small porch. Flanking the building were a small group of servants' quarters constructed of brick.

1. AUNT "FRANCES" SUSANNAH STONE SCOTT (1780–*1867*)

Henry's grandmother, Frances, William Payne's daughter, known as "Aunt Scott" and sometimes "Grandma Scott", was a great influence on the Scott family. Francis married John Arthur Scott in 1798, Hugh Scott's father and Henry's grandfather. In the Scott Booklet, my father related the following about Aunt Scott.

It is told of her that during the bombardment of Fredericksburg in the Civil War she walked with her son, Hugh, through a rain of bullets and shell to attend the birth of Hugh's child, constantly reproaching Hugh for dodging when a shot fell nearby.

This story is not entirely accurate since the battle for Fredericksburg was fought from December 11–15, 1862 while Hugh's son Samuel was born in early 1863. It is possible that the son in question was a cousin. Nevertheless, the story marked Aunt Scott as a woman of great strength and courage. She surely had a great influence on Henry.

Bertha wrote in her diary much later about Grandma "Frances" Scott and how Bertha's mother-in-law, Anne, was able to deal with her.

Henry's father's mother, Mrs. John Scott, known in the family as Grandma Scott, a woman of great strength of character, who ruled her family with a rod of iron, sent for her son Hugh (Henry's father) and told him that she considered it absolutely unsuitable that a son should live in a house, handsomer than that occupied by his mother. He submitted at once, though a man of notably strong character, sold the house and bought a frame house, very pleasant, but neither as large or as handsome as the family homestead owned by his mother and known as "Scotia". I suppose "Grandma" was satisfied, but I have sometimes wondered how my own sweet mother-in-law, Henry's mother, felt about it. She would never have opposed it if it made for family peace, I know, but sweet nature and true Christian as she was, I think she must have had some feeling about that.
[Bertha's Diary, June 27, 1911]

2. GRANDMA "ANNE" SCOTT (Annie Green Clarkson) (1833–1898) & HUGH SCOTT (1812–1877)

Henry was the second child born to Hugh and Anne Clarkson Scott. Hugh lost his first wife, Arabella J. Ritchie, in 1848 and married Annie Green around 1855. He was a captain in the Confederate Army during the Civil War and died on July 13, 1877 (as best we know). His wife, Anne, lived until 1898. Anne became very close to Bertha after her marriage to Henry. Perhaps because of Grandma Scott's relationship with her mother-in-law which was somewhat strained, she was loving and patient to her daughter-in-law. Her relationship with Bertha seems to contrast with the latter's relationship with her own mother of whom Bertha does not speak with the same affection that she expressed toward Grandma Scott.

Henry always showed great concern for his mother and her travails, as did Bertha. In 1893, Bertha wrote to Henry about his mother:

I likewise went over to see how your mother was. She was feeling better and said she believed, after all, Dr. Prosser was treating her tooth rightly, that the stuff he had put on it was to kill the nerve and, while she had suffered terribly up to ten o'clock Saturday, since then she had not had a twinge." [1893-10-10 Monday Bertha (StL) to Henry (Waco)] Henry's return letter revealed his concern. *"I am very sorry to know how much my mother has been suffering with her tooth. She is so frail that I am always alarmed when she is at all unwell. I do hope Dr. Prosser will settle the trouble for all time with his attempt to destroy the nerve for this tooth has always been troublesome. Give her my love when you see her, please.* [1893-10-11 Henry (Waco) to Bertha (StL)]

Grandma Scott seemed to fulfill her role as grandmother starting with her first grandchild, Hugh. *"Your mother spent the afternoon here playing with the boy and I think was perfectly blissful. She is looking better."* [1894-03-12 Bertha (StL) to Henry (Fort Worth)]

It seems that Bertha modeled her own later life after Grandma Scott. Bertha wrote in her diary when Grandma Scott died on November 12, 1898[6]: *"Dear, precious, Grandma Scott was taken home. It was the end of weeks of suffering and, to her, a great release. But to us, no one can know how great a loss. Ever since my marriage, the dearest, closest friend to me, never even one word of fault finding."* [1893 Diary]

3. HENRY'S SIBLINGS

Henry's siblings were Marion Clarkson ("Minnie") (1857–1938), William Samuel (1863–1940), Margaret ("Maggie") (1866–1943), and John Arthur (1870–1894). Minnie, Samuel, Maggie, and Arthur eventually followed Henry to St. Louis with Henry's mother where they made their home. Henry also had a half-sister, Frances P. Scott ("Fannie"). Fannie was the daughter of his father and Arabella (i.e. Hugh's first wife).

a. Frances P. ("Fannie") Scott (1839–1862)

There are limited historical records of Frances P. Scott, Henry's stepsister, who was the daughter of Hugh Scott and Arabella J. Ritchie and who died at age 22 in Fredericksburg in 1862. Some confusion arises due to the similarity in the name of Henry's cousin Frances ("Fannie") Stone Scott (1842-1893) who married Frank Carter (Frank later married Minnie Scott).Henry refers to this other Fannie as his cousin.

> *Dear, the reason I wished Mrs. Carter's name taken from my list is explained in a letter of my sister's, who told me she had written you of Mrs. Carter's death. You know she was a cousin of ours and, although I saw very little of her, I liked her very much indeed. I did not intend to tell you of her death, but Maggie tells me she wrote you about it, not knowing that I preferred not telling you. Cousin Tom's death was such a sad one that I did not wish to speak to you about it, now. Some people seem to be taken away when their lives are most useful and happy and I think few women were of more use to their families and friends than cousin Fannie was.*
> [1893-01-23 (Saturday) Henry (StL) to Bertha (Stancote MA)]

b. Marion Clarkson Scott ("Minnie") (1852/57–1938)

Minnie was born in Fredericksburg, birth date uncertain. She moved to St. Louis, sometime after Henry moved there, and married Frank Carter in 1895. Major Frank Carter (1838–1896 had served as a staff officer under General John Stevens Bowen. After Bowen's death at Vicksburg, Major Carter served on General Lee's staff. Frank had been widowed from Frances Stone Scott (Fannie), Henry's cousin, in 1893.

Minnie was only briefly married to Frank Carter who died on April 21, 1896, approximately one year after they were married. Bertha wrote very simply in her diary about Frank Carter:

> *April 21, 1896*
> *Frank Carter died. He has been quite ill all spring but grew suddenly worse at the last.*

Henry wrote to Bertha of Frank Carter's death and how happy Minnie had been with Frank, a man who could control her.

> *I agree with you that Minnie is a good woman, but when you speak of her happiness as a married woman, remember that if she had married a weak man who submitted to her caprices, she would have made herself and him as miserable as she and Frank were happy. Frank Carter controlled her and they both were most happy, but can you admit there would have been any chance of*

---

[6] Perhaps, because Grandma "Anne" Scott died on November 12, my birthday, my parents told me that they were going to name me "Anne" if I had been a girl.

happiness without that control? I am as sure that he found this the key to bringing out what was best in Minnie as I am of anything in life. Well, I have tried my best anyway and if I don't succeed, I shall be very sorry, but I shall not reproach myself.
[1896(-) 20170803-1 Henry to Bertha]

Early in the 1890's, Henry assumed the role of patriarch for his siblings and the person who resolved Minnie's frequent troubles.

The enclosed note from Minnie tells the tale of her recent silence. She is evidently getting ready for her annual blow up. It seems almost like the periodic sprees that some men go on. I don't know how much she owes but she has had ample money to run the house beside the cash she has undoubtedly been obtaining from her grocer. I am really at a loss to know what to do. If I continue to overlook these things, it simply means that they will recur more frequently and her physical breakdowns will be more frequent. I have asked her for a statement but I doubt if I get one. I shall try to have Sam look after her when I am away, but, just how to deal with this last broken promise, I can't see. I may get light(?) later on. Just now, I am partly sorry for her but largely angry because I can't get away from the thought that back of it all is her wish to again get into the center of the stage. I am not even certain whether I shall see her again before I leave for I am rather pressed and if I go out and come down hard on her, it will do her no good and if I overlook the whole thing, it will be the ruin of her. Truly, there are vexations in life, my dearest, but I should not complain for the sweetness of life is indeed mine in the deep abiding happiness of my life with you. ... And so I shall try to work out Minnie's trouble with the one thought that it is my responsibility to take care of in a way that will be best for her.
[20171215-7 Henry to Bertha]

Minnie seemed to understand that she could be a nuisance and wrote as much in a letter to Henry. *"I am ashamed to think you have such a sister. Pray for me is all I can ask."* [20170807-2 Minnie to Henry]

Since Henry was always very busy, it was not surprising that he would sometimes become frustrated with his sister and her lack of fiscal responsibility.

I think I shall have another siege with Minnie for I am morally sure she is in debt again. Maggie says so and she usually gets things pretty straight. Besides Scruggs(?) sent over to the office the other day and asked for Mrs. Carter's address and Peg[7] referred with awe(?) to a check the Trust Company returned marked "no funds". I think that is the reason she is not enjoying the summer. I hardly know what to do about it. It is disgraceful for her to run up bills and she has really no right to do that or check on the Trust Company when she knows she has no funds there and if I promptly came to the rescue there would be no limit to that sort of thing. It may be that the best way is to let her lose her credit as the only means of putting an end to the thing. Only I will do her the credit to admit that often she has endowed the church and run her bills to the limit and things begin to press down upon her she gets pretty miserable and I am afraid she is getting somewhat in that state now. I can't open the subject though and, until she does, I suppose I must wait for the crisis. If I took up and paid off these bills, which Maggie thinks are pretty large this time and for many unnecessary things, without another "understanding", it would simply mean a much worse state of affairs later and I am not sure that things might not get entirely beyond my power to correct. What do you think? I am not in my most cheerful mood and maybe I am harder on the girl than I should be, but I have never refused her money. I have only asked her to do her best and let me know what the bills are and that makes her actions this summer pretty trying.
[20170804-2 (1900-) Henry to Bertha]

In the following letter from Henry around 1902, Henry groused about paying Minnie's bills.

---

[7] i.e. Maggie, Henry and Minnie's sister.

I don't know what to say about Minnie. I finally rec'd a bundle of bills from her today and maybe I am too vexed to be fair with her but I think a saint would be slightly exasperated. There were some necessary bills but there were also many unnecessary ones - a silly expenditure of money to do no one good. I am writing her I shall pay them but I am really too angry to see her at once. I shall take up the sanitarium idea next week and see what it promises. I really am afraid of Rye for her and I think she is half right when she says it is unfortunate in that all her church friends are better off than she is. Somehow, I don't fancy the outcome of her summer with that Boars Head crowd of Episcopalians. But I shall consider your suggestions about Rye when I see Minnie.
[1902(-) 20170723-4 Henry to Bertha]

But Minnie did have her good qualities. When Bertha and Henry were moving into their new house in 1893 after they were first married, Bertha expressed her gratitude for the work that Minnie did in helping unpack all the furniture.

I had a letter from Nan today in which she condescended to approve very highly of our papers, her favorite being the dining room. I am afraid you have not given credit enough to your sister Minnie about the unpacking of the furniture. From your letters, I had quite a vision of yourself struggling single handed, whereas Nan says she found your sister nearly buried in excelsior and paper. It is very lovely of her.
[1893-01-07 (Saturday) Bertha (Newton Centre) to Henry (StL)]

After receiving the preceding letter from Bertha, Henry acknowledged Minnie's help and reproached himself for not being more grateful to his sister.

I felt reproached when you mentioned Minnie's activity at our house for I had intended to write you of the help both of the girls have given me. They seem to enjoy being over there and I don't know what I should do without them.
[1893-01-11 (Tuesday) Henry (StL) to Bertha (Stancote, Newton Centre, MA)]

Bertha also pitched in to assist Minnie. While Henry was away on business, sometime around 1905, she took Minnie around to look for an apartment, which experience, was trying.

I have just had two visits embodying the extreme of life. John Holliday and Marjorie, young, buoyant, radiant, with the world before them, and Madame Hoffman, who took dinner with me, looking pitifully old and broken, feeling too ill to begin with her private pupils and with only two thousand dollars in the world laid by. I would not help contrasting the pathetic insecurity of her life with Minnie's.

I have been seeing a great deal of Minnie lately for we have been apartment hunting together. I found Minnie was set against boarding and upon my soul, I could not blame her. I looked at the Berlin and Mona(?) Hotels (American plan). The stale odors around the Berlin were enough to make your heartsick. The Mona looked attractive but I hear the table is not good and the tales I hear of people hunting boarding places is not attractive. Miss Crump's is full. And Maggie Moore's remark "I think Mrs. Carter's pretty nervous to try boarding" brought to my mind visions of the way she behaved at the Yellow Sulphur and that place in Michigan and I thought for our sakes, perhaps, it might not be the pleasantest arrangement. Still, I laid the plan before her as persistently as I could but the trouble is she does not want to give up her furniture, her pictures, her belongings in general and Maggie Moore. She loves those thinks better than anything else in all the world. That's all there is, that is <u>her own</u>. And we have so much.

I just could not stand out against it, so I went apartment hunting with her from Dan to Beersheba[8]. *There was nothing we did not see. We saw them with janitors and without, with heat and without. The cheapest was the one on Maple Avenue, forty-five dollars, very bright and cheerful, second floor, no janitor. I did not care for the neighborhood. Those with janitor and heat were fifty-five and up. Finally, the last afternoon I said I am going up Cates and Clemens once more and on Cates just below Goodfellow, the same block with the Lockwoods, we saw a second floor sign. We went in, placard stated six room flat, forty-five dollars rent, hard wood floors, tiles bathroom. So we went up & found what I consider a model for the purpose. No janitor nor heat furnished however. Parlor, dining room, kitchen, maid's room, bathroom. Two bed rooms. A very pleasant lady in the lower apartment, with two grown daughters. Cellar, granitoid*[9], *divided in half, small furnace (takes about six tons of coals a year), laundry, lovely back yard. The people had just moved out. They were willing to let Minnie have it on a six-month lease so she can give it up in the spring if unsatisfactory. And she is going to move all her really good things & sell the trash.*

I hope this is satisfactory to you. If it isn't. I am awfully sorry. It seemed the best to me that could be done, short of absolute necessity. Madge Adams is downstairs.
[1905(-) 20180617-1 Bertha to Henry]

c. William Samuel Scott ("Sam") – (1862–1940).

Sam Scott attended Fredericksburg Military Academy and a youth and married Margaret Lytton ("Madge") on October 12, 1897 in St. Louis. Their children were Marjorie L., Henry C., and Samuel L. Sam was a grocery store clerk in Fredericksburg before he moved to St. Louis in 1882, one year after Henry moved. Sam had a variety of jobs including a post at Carondelet Gas Light Co. He was Vice President of T&H Mining Co. when it merged with Missouri & Illinois Coal Co, at which time he was made Vice President and General Manager of the newly merged company.[10]

Bertha mentioned Sam during her "engagement" with Henry, wondering who *Sam* was:
I had a package with some lovely Easter cards from your mother and sisters yesterday which I am going to write and acknowledge today. But this morning I received the daintiest possible white and silver copy of Phillips Brooke's Easter Carol from W.S. Scott . Please tell me if that is "Sam"? Or does your youngest brother sign himself W.S. Scott and is it an A and not a W? Now I put you on your honor not to tell about this, but won't you please find out which it was and let me know as quickly as you can so that I can thank him. Remember, I consider you as having promised not to tell the quandary I was put in. Whichever one it was, I appreciate it very much, and it was a lovely thing in itself.
[1892-04-19 Tuesday Bertha (NYC) to Henry (StL)]

Sam was helpful to Bertha and Henry during their move into their first house at 3337 Washington Ave. With Henry's busy schedule and Bertha in the east, he agreed to take care of the early arrival of a furniture shipment.
The "way bill" from Paine came Saturday afternoon. I only received it about two minutes before I left for the depot so I had no time to attend to caring for the furniture on its arrival. I gave the ticket to my brother Sam, though, and told him to have the boxes taken to 3337 and stored in the cellar if the car had to be emptied as I suppose it must be. I don't want it to go to one of the RR. Warehouses for I should not think it safe there and I am rather sorry Paine made the mistake in shipping so early. Sam laughed at my regret at not being there to receive the furniture. He said

---

[8] *From Dan to Beersheba* is a biblical phrase used nine times in the Hebrew Bible to refer to the settled areas of the Tribes of Israel between Dan in the North and Beersheba in the South.

[9] Granitoid - adjective form of granite

[10] From "The Book of St. Louisans: A Biographical Dictionary Of Leading Living Men Of The City Of St. Louis And Vicinity"

he thought he could take care of it as well as or better than I could and added philosophically "it's well enough to get my hand in on such matters anyway. I may need such information for my own uses one of these days."
[1892-12-15 (Monday 1892-12-12) Henry (Hotel Carey, Wichita KS) to Bertha (Stancote Newton Centre)]

However, Henry was sometimes disgruntled with Sam, especially when he would not leave Henry alone with Bertha when they otherwise could be together alone.

I had a very hot dusty trip down and I can see that it was best not to bring you with me but that thought does not make it easy to be away from you these long weary days. And I have grumbled a great deal about my last evening with you, dear. That brother of mine never was more in the way in all his life. I had thought of the hour I would have you all to myself and lo! That unnaturally stupid Sam spoiled all my plan. I hadn't the time even to thank you for packing up my things, you dear girl, "who takes such good care of" one that deserves a worse name than you gave me a very sleepy morning not long ago that I am ashamed almost to thank you now. [1893-10-11 Henry (Waco) to Bertha (StL)]

When Henry was away on business, Sam would often spend time watching over Bertha on her husband's instructions. In the following letter, Bertha revealed that she was also observant and watchful regarding Sam.

I have just had a long talk with Sam. How interesting you can judge from the fact that he came to breakfast at nine and when he finally said, "By the way, aren't you going to church this morning?" And looked at this watch, he discovered it was twelve o'clock. He thanked me for the morning service when he left. I gave him a great deal of good advice, which he probably won't take.

By the way, I must set you right on one point. That was not Miss Palmer that you saw him receiving in his shirt sleeves, that was a book agent or some sort of agent he was trying to get rid of. I did not mention Miss Palmer's name, I merely lectured him on general principles for receiving girls in his shirt sleeves, and he was puzzled at first, puzzled to know what I meant. Then he recollected this, and told me, and I said, "O, I'm relieved, I thought possibly you were setting up a rival to Clemens Avenue". And he said with some contempt, "I should think you might have known that I would not have had her calling on me in my office if I had!" I felt rather small, but decidedly relieved.

Then he talked to me of everything that has passed lately. He told me all about his quarrel with you, his engagement, his plans for the future, everything. I could not help feeling pretty sorry for the boy. He said there was one week he hardly slept at all. He said "It seemed to me, as if everything came on me at once. I am not saying I was not to blame for part of it. I am only telling you just what happened. I had quarreled with Henry. Things were all wrong with me out at 5911 Clemens Avenue. I got nothing from Maggie, but everlasting religion, and, with mother, it was worst of all, for when that anniversary came, she went over and over every detail of Arthur's death with me until I used to feel as if he were lying dead in the next room. In all my life, I have never had such a desperate feeling of loneliness."

Well, I have heard you say, it exasperated you when you thought Sam was dramatic. But he didn't try in the least to be dramatic, he just seemed to me like a boy that had had a hard time, whether through his own fault or not, did not matter. I have seen you when you thought nobody, not even your own wife, understood you, and you was "terrible based".
[1895-05-06 Bertha (StL) to Henry (Waco, TX)]

Bertha wrote to Henry that Sam was afraid of him because Sam cared so much for him.

> *Sam is evidently very anxious about your coming. He came up and spent an hour with me today and he said once very wistfully in the course of the conversation (I can't give you the whole talk, it would take too long) – "The only two people I have ever quarreled with have been Henry and --- (a break) and it's because they are the two people I care most about in the world. That's what makes anything from Henry hurt so. If I didn't care anything about him, it wouldn't make any difference."*
> [1895-11-06 Bertha (StL) to Henry (Wichita)]

Sam became engaged to Lily Palmer in 1895, the same woman, Henry thought, Sam had "received" in his shirt sleeves! (See above, 1895-05-06 Bertha (StL) to Henry). Bertha wrote in her diary: *"November 1895 - Sam announces to me his engagement to Lily Palmer."* [1893 Diary]

It is unclear what happened to this engagement which must have ended in 1896 since Sam married Margaret Lytton ("Madge") October 12, 1897. The only other entry concerning Lily Palmer:

> *Dec. 30, 1895*
> *Am telephoned by Sam that Lily Palmer is desperately ill. Go out there, but she has commenced to recuperate. Stanley Dwight comes to dinner. After he leaves, Henry goes again to the Palmer's, she is much better.*
> [1893 Diary]

Bertha wrote to Henry about Sam's wife, Madge, in a letter in 1898:

> *I meant to have begun my letter to you as soon as I came down this morning but one interruption after another came, the last being a visit from Madge who staid an hour and a half. It was curious for she had been on my mind and I felt that I ought to go and see her so when I heard she was down stairs, I made up my mind to be as nice as I could and the result was what it usually is, I believe. She was nicer than I ever saw her. I felt quite ashamed of myself. She was really very sweet and womanly about all that is coming to her and she spoke of how beautiful Sam had been to her through all her ill health and nervousness and fretfulness in a way that showed that whatever the past may have been, she is certainly learning to care for him now. She spoke in a perfectly simple, unaffected, way and said she had done everything on earth that was wearing, had cried for hours out of sheer nervousness, been impatient and fretful, and that his patience and tenderness had never once failed. It is a pretty high tribute to Sam, I think, and I really believe that you are right after all and they will be happy.*
> [1898-03-28 Bertha (StL) to Henry (Oriental Hotel, Dallas)]

At times, Henry was concerned that Sam was receiving bad advice from Madge.

> *I have seen nothing of Sam recently and I am not very well pleased with him just now. He says he tries to save me trouble but there are sometimes peculiar manifestations of that desire. I am afraid Madge is a poor adviser and that Sam gets many foolish ideas from her.*
> [20171206-2 (1902) Henry to Bertha; "Madge" – Margaret, his wife.]

And Henry's impressions of Madge were not always complimentary.

> *I have only been once to Sam & Madge. Because I had not been before, I purposely staid late but my impressions of my sister were quite the most unpleasant I have ever had of her. Perhaps the knowledge of her condition, which usually brings out the real sweetness in the natures of good women, made the impression stronger, but I never so fully realized how, with all her real cleverness, her character was mean and selfish and untrue to all the best things in life. I hope Sam will never see her as I did that night. It will cause him much suffering if he does. The house is pretty and very cleverly arranged and its mistress was in her most gracious mood, but I almost hated her*

before I left and I have never seen such an expression on a working woman in her condition. I am very glad you weren't with me.
[20180323-2 (1905-) Henry to Bertha]

Henry was paternalistic to his siblings. When Sam got himself into some financial trouble sometime around 1905, Henry acted like a father, scolding at first but, at the end, *"he is my brother."*

Sam took dinner with me last night at the Club. Poor fellow, he has been buying stock and is out about four thousand dollars and has been miserable. I first abused him roundly and then promised him I would try to help him out of the fix but just now it is not very easy to do. ...(?), of course, not sustain a loss but if I had not come to the rescue he would have had to let go yesterday. I think Madge is at the bottom of this last scrape, although I am not sure for I think she advised him to buy stocks & recoup his other losses. He is a nice, simple fellow with all his weakness and I am not going to forsake him in trouble. I am fond of him and he is my brother.
[1905(-) 20180425-1 Henry to Bertha]

And Henry was critical of Sam and his weakness in standing up to his wife.

I don't say it to cheer you up simply but I think there is far more hope for George then for Sam for Sam is not only weak and is becoming indirect but he has a bad advice[11], whose mentality is far stronger than his and who is gifted with abundant craft and as far as I can see not one atom of honesty. If a worse combination could be imagined for the righteous development of a dull weak but well-meaning man, I can't imagine it.
[1908-12-02 (20180419A-6) Henry (Ft. Worth) to Bertha (64 Vandeventer Place, Stl)]

Henry would periodically take an afternoon off to visit Sam and Madge at their Ferguson Missouri home. In the context of comments that Henry made of other friends, looking fat may not have been a bad thing since fat tended to go together with happy.

I spent three hours in busy toil down town and then went to the University Club for a late lunch then I called up Minnie and arranged for her to go out with me to see Sam and Madge. We had a beautiful run out and back, no bad roads except right in Ferguson where they were even worse than ever before and we really had a pleasant call. Madge was very nice and interested in the new house which is to be finished the first of October. Sam was playing tennis when we got there and appeared looking fatter and more perspiry than a galley slave. I suppose Minnie was unused to improvised tennis costumes for she remarked on the way home that Sam was certainly not as good looking as he was some years ago. They have a beautiful lot nearly two hundred and fifty feet square and with a wonderful view and I think the house and the whole place will be most attractive.
[1910-06-26 Henry (StL) to Bertha (Rye Beach)]

Sam and Madge had three children: Majorie Lytton Scott (1898–1989), Henry Clarkson Scott (1901–1979), and Samuel "Lytton" Scott (1904–?). My brother, Hugh Scott III, wrote of his connection with Sam Scott's family from his time at Yale.

WS Scott was "Sam", father of Lytton Scott and grandfather of Gene Scott[12], a well-known tennis player at Yale and elsewhere. When I was at Yale, Dad mentioned having had an Aunt Madge in New Haven when he was there. I assume that she was Sam's widow. While Who-Who[13] once mentioned that he knew Lytton slightly, there was never very much conversation among the Scotts

---

[11] Henry is probably referring to Sam's wife, Madge (Margaret Lytton).

[12] Eugene Lytton Scott: Born December 28, 1937, New York, U.S. Died March 20, 2006 (aged 68). Turned pro in 1968 (amateur tour from 1951), and retired in 1975. Highest ranking No. 11 (1965) Grand Slam Singles results Australian Open 2R (1964) French Open QF (1964) Wimbledon 3R (1964, 1965) US Open SF (1967) Doubles Career record 12–22 Grand Slam Doubles results Australian Open 2R (1964).

[13] James Wesley McAfee.

about the Sam Scott family. Lytton apparently had a brother named Henry Clarkson Scott who lived in Long Island and had a Yale connection but I don't know much about him.
[Hugh Scott III, email dated 8/2/2018]

d. Margaret L. Scott ("Maggie"; Henry sometimes called her "Peg") – (1866–1943)
Bertha wrote to Henry about Maggie and Minnie, after their congratulations on Bertha and Henry's engagement. This letter revealed now much Maggie admired Henry.

> *I am now regretting that penitent letter I wrote you yesterday. I ought to have scolded you for being a very unreasonable, foolish and exacting young man! And I now know part of the reason. As I told you before, I thought you were spoiled, but now I know it. The view your youngest sister takes of your character is enough to spoil anybody. I have had lovely letters from both your sisters, dear, and I wish I could see them and thank them for having written them. I don't believe you half appreciate your sisters.*
[1892-03-14 Bertha (Hotel Ponce de Leon, St. Augustine FL) to Henry]

On hearing how much Henry was talking about her to Maggie, Bertha scolded him, fearing that his family would become bored with her before they even met.

> *I had a very sweet letter from your sister Maggie today in which she mentioned a folly of yours of which I did not think you would be guilty. She said "he is always talking of you" and though she charitably adds "I do not blame him", I must say I do. You ought to be ashamed of yourself. Your family will be bored to death with me before I even reach St. Louis. Now, little boy, don't go and tell her I told you.*
[1892-12-20 (Monday 1892-12-19) Bertha (Newton Highlands, MA) to Henry (StL)]

Bertha wrote about a dinner at Henry's mother's house in 1895 with Sam, Minnie, Maggie, and Mr. Carter, Minnie's husband, when, apparently, Maggie was in a mood.

> *I dined at your mother's yesterday and, for sarcastic and biting viciousness, commend me to the deeply religious! I wonder there is anything left of Mr. Carter & myself, though I admit it was partly my fault. Maggie displayed a photograph of the lovely and beloved Mrs. Knapp. Well, I honestly did not like the picture. I hate to see a woman taken in a widow's veil, having it draped in the most coquettish & becoming style. It doesn't look as if it meant anything and I remarked, "Well, I think that is the most flirtatious picture I ever saw" and Mr. Carter chimed in briskly, "O, I don't think that lady is in the least averse to a flirtation if properly approached." Maggie said, "Mr. Carter thinks Mrs. Knapp is a flirt because she is a Presbyterian!" That settled him, and I forgot the thing & presently said, "Maggie, aren't you well, you really worry me, you have hardly spoken today", and she responded, "Nobody here is interested in the subjects I am, so it hardly seems worthwhile for me to talk." That settled me! Shortly after which, she retired from the uncongenial crowd and went to sleep, I believe, at all events, we did not see her again. Sam told me on the way home that was the way she treated them all at intervals and the worst of it is if any one does speak to her about it, she repeats in perfect floods of tears. He added, "I shall be devoutly thankful when you take her away from here."*
>
> ...
>
> *I am going to Minnie's to tea tonight for which I am very thankful. Last night was doleful.*
[1895-05-07 Bertha (StL) to Henry (Waco)]

Even when Henry was in Waco on business, his watchful eye was ever vigilant for his family.

> *I don't know what's to be done with Maggie. It seems to me she continues to make things uncommonly uncomfortable for mother. I hope she will get partially rid of the silly moods she drops in so easily now before she comes to us for, if she don't, there will be some mighty plain talk in the neighborhood of our cottage before the summer is over. You will not, perhaps agree with me but I am very glad she will be with us for a while and I shan't blame you a bit if you are not*

enthusiastic over the prospect because I consider it my Christian duty to let her know what I think of certain sorts of Christianity and I have an idea I can even make her understand some of my views. In any event, I shall try.
[1895-05-08 (2 letters) Henry (Waco) to Bertha (3337 Washington Ave, StL)]

In the summer of 1898, Maggie visited Bertha and her children at their summer cottage in Jamestown. Writing to Bertha, Henry expressed the following about Maggie:

If Maggie ever achieves heaven, I expect to hear from her. You observe I anticipate seeing her there if she is let in, filing a protest against the accepted order of things and, unless angels are powerfully long suffering, she will soon be the most unpopular seraph of the lot.
[1898-07-10 Henry (StL) to Bertha (Jamestown)]

A few days after this letter, Henry wrote:

Your accts of Maggie do not sound enticing. I am afraid she is making it interesting for cousin Marion. Unless she (Maggie) restrains herself, she will be like our cousin Betty in a year or two – a little hard to please.
[1898-07-11 Henry (StL) to Bertha (Jamestown)]

Maggie could put herself into a mood. One such occasion was 10 days after their mother had died and Bertha found Maggie "in a terrible state". Bertha seemed very deft at handling the situation, perhaps as a result of her practice with Henry?

I went over there this morning and found Maggie in a terrible state. She had locked herself in and when I insisted on coming in, I found her nearly in a condition of dumb hysteria. She said the devil was tempting her. She knew it could be nothing else. I knew it was an overwrought condition of body and soul but it was very painful. She said she could not feel that she had any belief and that worst of all she could not persuade herself that her mother was saved because she had not spoken or said anything that showed she was ready to die. I suppose I worked an hour and a half with her trying to show her what clear common sense should have showed her and also to persuade her that her condition was more illness of body than soul. She came down to lunch quite cheerily and brightly finally.
[1898-11-22 Bertha (StL) to Henry (Waco)]

Maggie and Minnie's appreciation for Henry can be seen in the following account from Bertha:

I really wish you could have heard Maggie talk about you today. I think I shall have to tell you a little about it at the risk of making you conceited. She began by telling me Minnie had said that you had been so lovely to her the other afternoon and then she went on. "But Henry always has been, all our lives. But I don't think I've ever cared for him as I have lately, I've always looked up to him but I've never felt as near to him. I think it began with our lovely visit last summer with him. It was just the most perfect time. There wasn't one jar or disturbance all the time, it was clear pleasure. And it was all Henry's doing. As for mother, I think her feeling for Henry was pretty near worship."
[1898-11-23 Bertha (StL) to Henry (Waco)]

Maggie apparently suffered from some kind of illness, which was never clearly explained in Bertha and Henry's letters. In one of his letters to Bertha, Henry wrote:

I have read your Saturday letter about Maggie most carefully and I think your last suggestion is the best – for her to remain at Waukesha during the summer then, if we don't see marked progress made, to try some other place. I did not mean that she should be forced to do things. My idea is that if there were a routine of duties which would occupy her waking hours, she would begin to develop capability for at least simple duties and amusements, and I am haunted by the thought that the lack of practice will make her prominently inert and useless. I think we must clearly try other

places this fall unless we discover by that time very marked improvement and this summer I shall try to post myself about other sanitaria.
[1905-07-10(-) 20170831-1 Henry to Bertha]

Henry wrote again about Maggie's condition and hoped that it would not make her helpless.
The reports from Maggie are about the same and this is most discouraging. She will not write a line to me and so I wish, if you think well of it, you would try a short note saying she really owes it to us to let us have a line to say how she is getting along and then tell her you know [how] hard it is to begin doing anything but, people after being ill, have to make a start or else they would get permanently helpless. Try your hand on her and see what your art can accomplish.
[1905(-) 20180626-1 Henry to Bertha]

In 1908, Henry was again concerned about Maggie ("Peg") and wrote Bertha to see if he should cut short his Texas business trip to be closer to her.
I was very much distressed about Maggie. Your telegram said there was no present danger but a ruptured appendix is a serious matter and that and the knowledge that Peg has no real stamina and very little strength makes me most uneasy. I telegraphed you I could return at once if you thought it wise but if it is not necessary, I may possibly save many future visits and avoid much anxiety if I can remain here until I complete my negotiations with the commissioners.

You know the old question laid over when Gordon[14] died last year has finally come up for settlement and though, as you may judge from the clipping sent you, I am by no means having it all my own way. I yet feel very hopeful that progress is being made and I should hate to have to go away in the midst of the most serious work where I am most needed. But this all counts for nothing if Peg is seriously ill and you must promptly let me know if she has any alarming set back. Poor child, she has never had any great pleasure in her whole life and now she is going through an ordeal that I think she dreaded more than death and to endure, which she seems physically and mentally so ill equipped. It is pitiful and I am very sorry and sad about it.
[1908-03-14 (20180419A-2 Bundle) Henry (Ft. Worth) to Bertha (64 Vandeventer Place, Stl)]

e. John Arthur Scott (1870–1894)
Arthur Scott died March 31, 1894 when he was 24 years old. Bertha and Henry wrote almost nothing about Henry's brother Arthur. When he died, Bertha simply wrote in her diary, "March 31 [1894], Arthur died." Arthur was buried on May 3, 1894 at Bellefontaine Cemetery.

At the time of his death, Arthur was living with his mother and his brother, Sam, at 8526 Chestnut Street. He was employed with Hydraulic Press Brick Company and was courting a woman. By all accounts on the night of his death, Arthur was in fine spirits and was preparing his "toilet" in his room before dinner. After hearing the pistol shot, Arthur's brother, Sam, gained entry to the locked room through the transom and the coroner was summoned. (The family explained that it was normal practice for family members to lock their doors when dressing.) Although originally believed to be a suicide, it was then concluded that the facts weighed in favor of an accident, including: no powder burns, the disposition of the pistol, and Arthur's positive state of mind. Arthur carried the pistol since he often carried cash for his employer to pay the payroll.

The details concerning Arthur's death were recorded in three articles by the St. Louis Post-Dispatch on April 2, April 3 and July 1, 1894. The July 1 article included the following:
Mr. Scott was seen to enter his room before supper and nothing more was known until the report of a pistol was heard about 7 o'clock. The entire family rushed to the room and found Arthur in a

---

[14] Charles Gordon Knox

dying condition with a pistol would in his right temple. He did not speak again. They said he had no cause to take his own life, being a steady businessman well thought of by everyone and without entanglements of any kind to cause so rash an act. They were convinced that the death was accidental resulting from unintentional discharge of the weapon. He had a habit of loading and unloading the pistol, keeping it always in prime condition. The possibility of suicide was, they maintained, excluded by the character of Mr. Scott and by the fact that there was no powder burn. They believed the latter fact proved the pistol had been discharged form some distance.

Dr. Wm. McPheeters, ..., was called in to attend the dying young man. All medical skill was unavailing and death resulted in about an hour. Mr. Scott did not speak. Dr. McPheeters ... found Mr. Scott lying forward with his head resting on the slop basin. He was before the mirror of the dressing case. The wound was very ugly. The young man lived only a few moments after he arrived.
[St. Louis Post-Dispatch, July 1, 1894]

Shortly after Arthur's death, Henry received a letter from Edward L. Adreon to extend his condolences. The letter revealed that Arthur had been engaged to Miss Josephine Adreon, Edward's daughter.
My dear Mr. Scott,

My family and myself understand and appreciate the spirit and suggestions of your kind letter and most sincerely reciprocate your generous expressions. Our love for and confidence in your noble brother were fully justified by his lovely character and could not have been more positively expressed than by our willingness to entrust to him the happiness of our precious daughter. Their engagement and tender mutual love reflected the dearest wishes of my child and ourselves. Her feelings are sacred and everything must be done to comfort her.

To yourself and family, our deepest and heartfelt sympathy is extended in this our mutual bereavement.

Very Truly Yours,
E.L. Adreon
[1894-04-03 Edward Lawrence Adreon to Henry]

Bertha always remembered significant events and recognized their importance to others. On the day before the one-year anniversary of Arthur's death, Betha wrote to Henry that she and her father had gone to Bellefontaine Cemetery to lay white lilies and ferns on Arthur's grave.
Father came by later in the afternoon, and we drove out to the cemetery. I took some beautiful white lilies and ferns out with me, dearest. Tomorrow is the thirty first of March and I thought some of your family would almost surely go out and would like to find them there. I ordered a few white roses and violets to be sent over to your mother tomorrow from us. Some people, I know, think it is better to let anniversaries pass unnoticed but I know she will not forget this one and I think she would like to know we remembered it too.
[1895-03-30 Bertha (3337 Washington Ave, Stl) to Henry (Light & Power Co, Waco TX)]

Bertha's thoughtfulness and care for Henry's mother and family was very touching.

The Flowers on Arthur's Grave
The eve before, the day he died,
She went to dress his youthful grave
That on the next, his mother came,
Would see there strewn the lilies brave.

What comfort did his mother find,
The flowers tenderly laid there,
And know an Angel had come down
To bless his resting place so fair.
[HCS August 7, 2019]

D. HENRY'S EDUCATION & EARLY CAREER

Henry rarely spoke about growing up in Fredericksburg but did provide some insights in a letter written to Bertha in early 1892.

> *Dear, as I came out, I read an article in the Century which interested me greatly: "The Mother and Birthplace of Washington"[15]. And as many of the incidents occurred in Fredericksburg, my old home, I thought you might like to read the articles which is interesting it itself so I send you the number. Those illustrations are excellent and I easily identify the funny little old house which was just two blocks from "Scotia", our old home, and the monument around which, as a very small youngster, I got my first lessons in shooting. And the church – St. George's – was the one in which I was baptized and learned to be such a good Episcopalian! "Kenmore" was the school house in which I had my big, best battle with Campbell Barton, a boy of my age, twelve, and, as I distinctly remember, a most viciously hard "biter". You will perhaps think I am drawing on my imagination but the corner window which I have worked I remember clearly opens into the room the fight occurred in.*
> [20180421-1 (1892-03--) Henry (NYC) to Bertha]

Henry attended public school in Fredericksburg which was then supplemented by a course of study in the Fredericksburg Military Institute from which he graduated with the rank of captain and adjutant. Henry did not attend University, a sore subject that he wrote to Bertha about 30 years later.

> *I dined with John at the University Club which we both agreed was on a grander scale than the Waldorf which is pretty high praise. The dining room is the finest room I have ever been in. I wish I were eligible to the University Club. It takes a college diploma and alas, my chance for any such privilege went as I told you with the unauthorized withdrawal by Uncle Sam Scott of the money - $2,500.00 – which mother had saved to give me the University course. I think it was the most crushing blow of my boyhood and I have hardly learned to forgive Uncle Sam to this day. I believe I have told you the story. I think it a pathetic one.*
> [20180204-1 (1899-09-19) Henry (New York) to Bertha]

Upon graduation from the Fredericksburg Military Institute, Henry went to work for J.B. Ficklen & Sons, who owned the Bridgewater Mills. (Henry may also have worked part time for J.B. Ficklen while he was in school.) The mill produced ten grades of flour, "Ficklen's Superlative" being the best. It also ground corn meals and animal feeds. *"No single industry located in Fredericksburg has done so much toward carrying the name and fame of the city to all parts of the world as the Bridgewater Milling Corporation,"* remarked a local newspaper in 1907.

Henry worked at the mill for 5 years. One can only speculate as to his initial job but it seems likely that it involved the hard labor of moving the raw and the milled grains to and from the mill and storehouses. During Henry's last year of employment with Ficklen, he held the job of bookkeeper and clerk, which was apparently considered a "professional" position.

---

[15] Article: "The Mother & Birthplace of Washington" published in *The Century Magazine* – January 1, 1892 by Ella Bassett Washington (Author)

Henry as a young man

It seemed clear that Henry became restless with his employment and opportunities in post-Civil War Fredericksburg and began to focus his attention on the growing opportunities in the west and in St. Louis in particular. Post-Civil War St. Louis was the fastest growing city in the United States and toward 1900 was the 4th largest city. For a man eager for opportunity, this was the place.

E. SAINT LOUIS: The Gateway of Opportunity

We occupy the most important point on this great circuit. If there were not a cabin or a white man from the Ohio to the Missouri; if our forests were still in pristine solitude, and our prairies untracked, save by the hoof of the buffalo and the moccasin of the Indian savage, I should still believe — considering the extent and richness of the valley, the number, length, and direction of its rivers, and its capacity to produce, in boundless plenty, all that can minister to the comfort, wealth, and power of man — I should still confidently believe that the greatest city upon the continent must be established within that span's length upon the map.
[Hon. Edward Bates (1793–1869), Lincoln.Net, 1155 http://lincoln-live.lib.niu.edu/islandora/object/niu-lincoln%3A37340]

St. Louis in the 19th Century was the "boom town" of the nation. Its growing importance is evident not only by its astounding population growth but also by its demographics: by 1880, 30% of St. Louis's residents were foreign born. During this century, there was a significant rise in western and north/south trade which passed through St. Louis, and manufacturing flourished there.

St. Louis being located in the heart of the Mississippi valley, in which are produced immense supplies of breadstuffs, meats, fruits, and vegetables, accessible by fifteen thousand miles of navigable rivers, with her grand network of railroads penetrating all portions of this vast valley, furnishing quick and cheap transportation for all the products of the soil, it must be apparent that at no other place in the world where labor is remunerative can staple provisions of the same quality be furnished cheaper than at St. Louis."
[Chapter XXV, 989. "St. Louis as a Center of Trade", Lincoln.net.]

Another indication of the rapid growth of St. Louis was evidenced by the high rents that were being charged to its residents. In 1839, Rev. Dr. Humphrey wrote, *"Rents are enormously high, higher than in any eastern city, not excepting New York itself, and I believe higher than anywhere else on the continent of America."* [Chapter XXV, 1008. "St. Louis as a Center of Trade", Lincoln.net.]

F. WESTWARD HO!

Henry had family connections in St. Louis. His aunt, Margaret Clarkson ("Aunt Mags", his mother's sister), was married to a very prominent and successful businessman in St. Louis, John R. Lionberger[16]. At this time, John was the Vice President of the Third National Bank of St. Louis and had extensive business connections around the city. Henry wrote to "Mr." Lionberger on January 21, 1881 to request his guidance and assistance. John sent him the following letter on March 3, 1881.

> *My dear Henry,*
> *Your letter of January 21ˢᵗ reached me by due course of mail but I have delayed answering it hoping I might be able to give you some encouragement in my reply. I have been unable, Henry, to procure for you employment but it has occurred to me that it would be well for you to visit St. Louis and possibly while here we may be able to find something for you to do. I would not advise severing your connection with Messrs. J.B. Ficklen & Sons but as you have been faithful in the discharge of your duties, they may be willing to grant you leave of absence with the understanding that if anything greatly to your advantage should offer when here you have permission to avail yourself of it. If you should fail to obtain employment, I will see, Henry, that you are not embarrassed on account of the expense of the trip. Your Aunt Mag & I will be delighted to see you & your expenses not not(??) be great.*
>
> *Should you conclude to come, I would advise coming at once as the spring business is now beginning. I again suggest that you get leave of absence from F & Sons as it may be impossible to find an opening. I should like to see you & to converse with you & know more of your qualifications so that if openings occur in the future, I could pass upon your fitness, etc., etc. So come if possible. Our no. is 1601 Olive Street.*
>
> *I hope this will find your mother, Aunt Marion well and all in good health. I am glad to say all are well, both at your Aunt Carrus(?) and at your Aunt Mags with much love to all.*
>
> *I am your affectionate Uncle,*
> *John R. Lionberger*
> [1881-03-03 John Lionberger (StL) to Henry (Fredericksburg)]

It appears that Henry's mind was so set on pursuing his opportunities in St. Louis that he had already begun to sever his ties with his employer and plan for his trip west. On March 15, not long after he would have received John Lionberger's somewhat cautionary letter about possible employment, Henry obtained a recommendation letter from J.B. Ficklen & Sons.

> *To whom it may concern,*
> *Mr. H.C. Scott, the bearer, has been in my employ for nearly 5 years & for over a year in ... Book Keeping & has surrendered his position with us for the purpose of going westward.*

---

[16] John R. Lionberger was the son of Elizabeth (Ashby) Tutt and a cousin of Thomas Edward Tutt who was the President of the Third National Bank. The Tutt and Lionberger families were natives of Virginia and were of Scotch-Irish descent.

We part with him with regret & it gives us pleasure to relate that he did his work well & understands it. He is a gentleman of energy & good ... & we cordially recommend him to any mercantile house in want of a ... & ... worthy clerk.

Very Respectfully,
J.B. Ficklen & Sons
[1881-03-15 JB Ficklen & Sons – Letter of Recommendation]

Henry also obtained sterling letters of recommendation from Robt. Knox, John Marye, Charles Wallace and Charles Herndon who were business owners in Fredericksburg and brought with him to St. Louis a recommendation from his pastor, J. Carmichael, who wrote the following letter to his "brother", the Rev. P.G. Robert, in St. Louis.

Rev. P.G. Robert
Rector of the Church of the Holy Communion
St. Louis, MO

Rev. & Dear Bro:
During the "sick furlough" of the Rector R.J. McBryde, I am in charge of this parish which sends you another of its members, Mr. Henry C. Scott, whose relations in St. Louis are already your parish sinners. I mean, Mr. Frank Carter and his mother. Hence, I need say nothing to you of Henry's social status. As an earnest, generous, faithful and loving child and communicant of the church, I desire to commend him to your special care & confidence, sincerely hoping that you will realize in him all that fastens him to us in love and respect.

Faithfully yours,
J. Carmichael D.D. (Doctor of Divinity)
Mar 16th/81
[1881-03-16 J. Carmichael Letter]

The die was cast. The Mississippi was crossed. There was no going back. Henry wrote to Bertha years later about his decision to try his fortune in St. Louis and leave Virginia on March 16, 1881.
I am reminded in looking at the date that just twenty-five years ago, a green lad started from Virginia to make fame and fortune in the west. He achieved neither but something far better, with which you have not a little to do, so you may imagine I am in rather a grateful mood, even though a rush of things, sundry and vexatious, is upon me.
[1906-03-16 Henry (Waco) to Bertha (StL)]

G. EARLY EMPLOYMENT IN ST. LOUIS

Henry's first position in St. Louis was as secretary of the Carondelet Gas Light Company in 1881 and was promoted to manager in 1884. John Lionberger was the President and Director of Carondelet Gas and presumably was influential in helping Henry obtain this position. At Carondelet Gas, Henry was able to associate with other businessmen who would become lifelong associates, including William & Joseph Taussig, George A. Madill, and Thomas E. Tutt. Later, Henry founded the Laclede Power Company and was elected to the presidency. He remained the president until the company was taken over by the North American Company around 1907.

Henry was very quickly able to form close business connections and connections that were not just about business. In 1891, he received the following letter from William Fitzhugh whose words revealed much more than just a business connection.

Vicksburg, Miss
Dece 25/91

My dear Henry,

I have waited for a day of leisure to thank you for the likeness of yourself and to express my gratification at being thus remembered.

Time and the cares of business seem to sit lightly on your shoulders. The only change I observe in your features is a little less hair about the forehead but they say a bald head indicates a quiet and contented mind and I think I can read between the lines that you are taking life more quietly now with less care and less work and less anxiety about the future. I infer too that like myself you are still "heart whole and fancy free". I trust the year just past has been a prosperous and successful one with you.

As for myself, I have changed very little since you saw me last. A trifle more gray and I trust wiser by a little. My pecuniary affairs have prospered too, so much so that on the first of January I am going into a new enterprise. I have a young friend here who has been very successful in the wholesale grain and provision business. He intends to leave here on the first of July next to live in Louisville Ky and I am going to take a half interest in his business. We will have an incorporated company with a capital of $50M paid in of which I shall own half. I am very much attached to the banking business and leave it with considerable reluctance but the other offers much larger compensation, less confinement and greater liberty and I am induced by these considerations to go into it. Time alone will decide whether I like it and can make a success of it but in any case, I shall feel that I have your blessing and your best wishes for my success. I shall not give up my interest in our two banks and by the way, Armistead Connay(?) is to be my successor here.

Tell me how all your various enterprises are doing. I want to know particularly something about the electric road at Waco. Isn't this your first experience in such an enterprise and how satisfactory is it? There is an exceptional opening here for such a line and I believe quite business enough to make it pay.

I hope to be in St. Louis during the spring or summer. Remember me very kindly to all the members of your household.

I hope the New Year may be full of good things for you.

Sincerely your friend,
W.H. Fitzhugh
[1891-12-25 William FitzHugh (Vicksburg) to Henry (StL)]

Henry was very congenial and seemed to make business and personal friends very quickly. He also enjoyed travel, at least in the early part of his business career. As evidenced by Bertha's comment in her diary when she was at Mrs. McKinley's house on February 9, 1889 attending the first meeting of the art club, Bertha wrote: "*Photographs of Mr. Scott & Mr. McKinley[17] on the Alps.*" [1888-11 Diary] Apparently, Henry was able to take time off to go to Europe with his buddies in those years. However, such lengthy European style travel soon became impossible as the demands of Henry's work increased over his career.

---

[17] Crittenden ("Kin") McKinley, (1854–1913), was a good friend of Henry and Bertha's. Mrs. McKinley was Kin's mother.

H. TIES TO THE PAST

While Henry made his fortune in St. Louis, he always remembered his past; and his past community of Fredericksburg always remembered him. In 1908, The Free Lance newspaper in Fredericksburg included the following article about Henry after he had received some notice by a Waco paper.

MR. HENRY C. SCOTT
A Fredericksburg Boy Prominent Business Man of St. Louis
The Waco Texas Tribune has a very complimentary article on Mr. Henry C. Scott, of St. Louis who has large investments in Waco. Mr. Scott is a Fredericksburg boy, son of the late Hugh Scott of this city. He went to St. Louis when a small boy, has been very successful, and is one of the prominent businessmen of St. Louis. It is with great pride that we refer to our boys who have gone away and made business successes. The most gratifying thing about it is that there are so many of them.
[The Fredericksburg Free Lance, October 24, 1908]

CHAPTER 3 – A PRIVILEGED CHILDHOOD

Richard Drake

A. THE DRAKES

Bertha Warburton Drake's pedigree was of the very best, being descended from the Drakes of England, a royal lineage. The *Centennial History of Missouri* included the following summary of George Sr.'s lineage:

> *In tracing the ancestral line from which he was descended, it is learned that through many centuries the Drake family has figured conspicuously in connection with the affairs of Great Britain. As early as 1272, John Drake held lands by grant of King Edward I and, in 1313, John Drake had permission of Edward II "to go beyond the sea." Many distinguished clergymen, martyrs, authors, and navigators have borne the name and among the most noted of the last mentioned class was Sir Francis Drake, prominent during the reign of Queen Elizabeth.*
>
> *In the year 1552 Richard Drake, the ancestor of the branch of the family to which George S. Drake belonged, was the high sheriff of Dublin, Ireland. This family was also represented by Robert Drake, Minister of Thundersly, in Essex England, who died a martyr at Smith-field during the reign of Queen Mary. When exhorted by Bishop Bonner to renounce his "heresy" he made this remarkable and courageous reply: "As for your Church of Rome, I utterly deny and defy it, with all the works thereof, as I deny the devil and all his works." In the year 1630 John Drake, of Devon, England, crossed the Atlantic and established his home in Connecticut, ten years after a landing was first made by the Pilgrims on Plymouth Rock on the completion of the first voyage of the Mayflower. In 1637, he took up his permanent abode at East Windsor, Connecticut, and to that place the ancestral line of the various branches of the family in America is traced. The name has long been a most honored one in various sections of the country for representatives of the family have been recognized as people of strong intellectual attainments and of marked ability in various lines.*
>
> [Centennial History of Missouri, One Hundred Years in the Union, 1820–1921, Vol. V, Published 1921]

After John Drake had settled in Windsor, Connecticut in 1630, the Drake family (of which this story is concerned) remained in Windsor for several generations. Of note, John Drake's son, John Drake Jr. (1708–1800) received some notoriety for his "hard headedness", true to family tradition.

[John Drake Jr.] Was Deacon in the Baptist Church at East Windsor. In that capacity and mind set, Nathaniel was punished from 1763 to 1767) for his religious opinions and resistance to the religious establishment of Connecticut, spending a lengthy period of time in jail at Hartford, Connecticut for refusing to pay taxes for the support of the ruling religious denomination in Windsor. In so doing, Nathaniel exhibited the martyr spirit which had characterized many of his ancestors.
[From *The Ancestors Of Almond Henry Drake*]

B. GEORGE SILAS DRAKE SR.

George Silas Drake, Sr.

We gathered flowers by the roadside. We wandered amid the groves, shrubs & flowers of Mr. Shaw's delightful place. It was the creaminess of delight to which ordinary pleasures are but the skim milk. [1863-05-11 George to Mary Roberts]

1. THE YOUNG GEORGE DRAKE & HIS 1ST MARRIAGE

Bertha's father, George Silas Drake ("George", "George Sr." or "The Pater") was born on October 11, 1825 in Hartford, Connecticut. George's parents were Silas and Elizabeth (Warburton) Drake who moved to St. Louis in 1827 when George was two years of age. George continued to reside in St. Louis until his death in 1908, although he continued to return east nearly every year and to Rye Beach New Hampshire in particular.

George had a private school education and attended Kemper College. After completing school at sixteen, he secured a clerkship in the dry goods house of Warburton & King and became a partner in the firm at twenty-two, then renamed Warburton, Rossiter & Drake. George was probably assisted in his early employment from his family connection to the Warburtons (his mother was Elizabeth Warburton). In 1852, he left this firm and then became a member of the firm Manny, Weld & Drake (later Manny, Drake & Company and Manny, Drake & Downing) which was a dealer in boots and shoes.

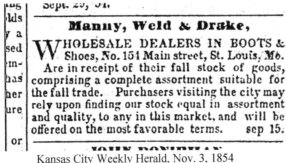
Kansas City Weekly Herald, Nov. 3, 1854

The Mannys were close friends of the Drakes, not only through their common business interest but also in their personal friendship. (Many of the correspondences with Mrs. John L. Manny, AKA Ellen E. Manny, during the 1869 Drake trip to Europe, can be found in Chapter 4.)

In 1865 when nearly 40 years old, George left this firm and devoted *"his attention entirely to the management of his invested interests"*[18]. He served on many boards of directors, especially the Boatmen's Bank in which he was involved from 1859 until his death.

George almost never spoke about his first wife, Alice Ingram, who died on March 4, 1852. In one of the few references made about her, George mentioned to Bertha in 1894 about Alice's death 42 years before. *"Father said, walking home yesterday, that it was the anniversary of his first wife's death, forty-two years ago. He did not however remind mother of the fact and keeps it as a solemn anniversary which is what Byron Sherman does."* [1893 Diary, March 6, 1894]

Based on Bertha's conversation and the Bellefontaine Cemetery records, George married Alice Ingram when she would have been a very young woman of around 17 years of age. Alice may have been pregnant at the time and delivered a daughter in February 1852 when she was still 17 years old. Alice apparently died from complications of childbirth since her death was on March 5, 1862, shortly after her daughter was born. Their child, Alice Ingram Drake, was named after her mother and died at age four on May 19, 1856. If this account is accurate, it is understandable why George did not wish to speak about his first wife and daughter, and why, after his loss, George carried a very heavy burden his entire life.[19]

2. GEORGE'S BUSINESS INTERESTS & THE CIVIL WAR

George wrote various, interesting, letters to his cousin, Mary Roberts, which reveal quite a bit of his character and wit, much of which clearly rubbed off on Bertha. In a letter to Mary, George wrote about his business in "dry goods" and uses the word "dull" repeatedly throughout the letter. *"Dull. It has a meaning in connection with a long, narrow, dark, sunless building ..., a store, filled with rows of boxes presenting their blank, expressionless sides in dreary gloominess. No customer so rich as to do them reverence or disturb their dreamless repose."* [1863-05-11 George to Mary Roberts]

---

[18] Centennial History of Missouri, One Hundred Years in the Union, 1820-1921, Vol. V, Published 1921

[19] The historical accounts of George Silas Drake, Bertha's father, such as in "The Book of St. Louisans", leave out any mention of George's first wife. It may be presumed that George wanted it so. However, it may be deduced from the Bellefontaine Cemetery records and Bertha's March 6, 1894 letter that his first wife was Alice Ingram. Specifically, Bertha recounts her father saying that his first wife died on March 5, 1852 and the Bellefontaine Cemetery recorded the death of Alice Drake, who is buried with the Drakes, as March 5, 1852. Alice Ingram was born in April 1834, according to "Find a Grave" so she would have been 17 years old at her death. Also, buried with the Drakes at Bellefontaine Cemetery is one Alice Ingram Drake who was born in February 1852 (according to Find-a-Grave) and the Bellefontaine records show that Alice Ingram Drake died at age four on May 19, 1856.

George continued in this letter to contrast his dull, work life with the spring outside.

> *First, the weather. How ... to a northern barbarian that happy blending of spring and summer when the melted snows with the chilling winds have passed away and ere yet the first of summer have been fully kindled? When the balmy breezes blow like gentle zephyrs fanning the delicious fragrance from the spring flowers and newly dressed trees & shrubs and, in the full enjoyment of it all, the escaped captives from the regions described, with a "pair in hand" and only half a pair beside them, drink in the delightful atmosphere together with intoxicating draughts of indescribable enjoyments from the bright eyes, thoughts and conversation of the companion of the drive. Dull.*
> [1863-05-11 George to Mary Roberts]

George concluded his letter, making sure Mary was reminded of his current plight. *"Kind regards to Mr. Roberts. Tell him trade is dull & as a place of business, St. Louis looks as if played out."* [1863-05-11 George to Mary Roberts]

Several of George's letters commented on the Civil War, such as this one in 1863 just after the Emancipation Proclamation:

> *Well, we are having a good time now since the Proclamation. The enemy have been sadly weakened having evacuated the Rappahannock & Vicksburg, left Galveston & Charleston and several other places are demoralized generally & we are swimming. All agreed among ourselves on the subject & confidence restored cotton & cotton goods down to nothing & gold a ... Gov't securities in demand and a fair prospect for Greely to be President, next time, I wish.*
> ...
> *If in New York, tell Mr. Roberts to be careful about Cotton goods. If Vicksburg is taken all right. If not taken, then will be peace, Southern Con'fed & all that. I hope it will be taken but we have no leader there, I'm afraid.* [1863-07-04 George Drake (StL) to Mr. J.W. Roberts (New York)]

Presumably, *"there is no leader"* in Vicksburg refers to General Grant whose army waged a two-month siege against Confederate Vicksburg. Regarding George's comment, ironically, the Confederates surrendered Vicksburg July 4, 1863, the day that this letter was written.

During the Civil War, George was employed by the government as a member of the Lyon Guards who successfully defended the state against the invasion of Price's army. He was also a member of the board of control in charge of Confederate prisoners, in which position, he related, he was *"managing the government finances and carrying on the war"*. In the following letter, George wrote to Mary of his trip down the Mississippi to Memphis and Cairo, not the cities of "antiquity":

> *I wrote my propensity to send dispatches from foreign countries strongly inclined me to let you hear from me when I was travelling in the "furrin countries" down in the Confederacy. It's a fact I have seen tho not felt the gorillas on the banks of the river & have stood amid the temples & columns of the Memphis, not of antiquities of the present age, and my experience on the matter leads me to the conclusion that I don't like antiquities.*
>
> *The hotel was modern but the meats were antiquated & I don't like antiquated meat & the sands of the desert had covered a great many things & ought to have been washed off. And Jews were too, plenty. And as I had two days at Cairo, another antiquity, I did not like that either, though the sands of the desert are all humbug, it was as muddy as the Slough of Despond[20]. Possibly John Bunyan had been there & in fact between mud, Jews, dirt, pick pockets, gamblers, gorillas etc., etc., I am decidedly of the opinion I don't like travelling on the lower Mississippi river at present.*
> [1863-12-08 George Drake]

---

[20] The Slough of Despond ("swamp of despair") is a fictional, deep bog in John Bunyan's allegory *The Pilgrim's Progress*, into which the protagonist Christian sinks under the weight of his sins and his sense of guilt for them.

In a lengthy account to Mary in a letter written on April 30, 1864 when George travelled to Memphis, then under Union control, he revealed more of his wit and humor.

> *I was down in this miserable country last fall but fortunately had to stay but a day or two. Now I am in for a longer siege. Fortunately, today the sun shines so I've taken a good look at the city. It must have been a right pretty place "before the war" – that's a stereotyped phrase here. But now, patched windows, broken down fences, neglected grounds and a scarcity of male protectors to the forlorn damsels that still remain at home, is the look of things at present.*
>
> *In the business part of the city, things look better. When trade is allowed, there is quite a business look about the place & the stores are equal to any place. If Jerusalem was in this neighborhood, you could readily imagine the restoration was about taking place as all the Jews I ever saw or heard of are here, occupying all the stores, &, for a wonder, not able to get rid of martial law, are members of the Enrolled Militia. On parade yesterday, I saw more Jews in the ranks than I ever saw in the military before altogether.*
>
> *The Gayoso House is a gay old home, sure enough, not a chair in the reading room or office, not a paper either, nor a tumbler, nor a drop of water. You have a decent bed & that's all that's decent about the premises. Small change is not much use. You can get rid of ten cents for a newspaper & by putting five with it get a glass of ale, but I know of nothing else they are used for.*
>
> *It's a happy place in the evening: five murders one night which, with a gentle intimation to me that unless my life was insured I'd better stay in nights, has kept me quietly at the Gayoso after dark. I learn that everybody foolish enough to be out by themselves expect to be robbed of course.*
>
> *I like this place. As I came down the river, the gorillas were in sight but they had no cannons & without them they can do nothing, except by surprise. Upon careful reflection, I've come to the conclusion that for a pleasure trip to spend some time, I'd prefer even New York to this city. St. Louis is of course better than either & I'm going back Thursday when I expect to wash out my mouth & task something clean.*
> [1864-04-05 George S Drake]

Even when traveling in Northern cities, George was not always enthusiastic.

> *I am on the road again, figuratively for just now I am in the 3rd story back of an Illinois hotel on a rainy Sunday afternoon with a musical young lady one story below who has a pretty fair piano for a pretty bad player.*
> [1865(-) 20180722-1 George Sr. In Bloomington IL to Mary Roberts]

As the Civil War was coming to an end, George wrote to Mary, briefly summarizing his military career, with tongue in cheek.

> *[T]hen I was a Lyon Guard and a fighting man and lived listening "anxiously" for the summons to the field and to glory and now "grim visaged war has smoothed her wrinkled front"[21] and peaceful times have intervened, not that it will last long ere another month after this. ... Well Mary, my military career, though glorious, was brief. I manned the inner door of the armory several times, eat oysters and drank ale at the expense of the Corporal. ... But peace has her victims as well as war. The sheriff got me vexed and for over four weeks daily I attended a constant votary at the shrine where the blind goddess weighs out justice. In other words, sat on a jury in an old land*

---

[21] Shakespeare, *Richard III*

case. ... In all human probability, when a monument is erected to me by my grateful fellow citizens, one side of the same are to be devoted to the record of civic virtues & another to my military achievements.
[1865-02-20 George Drake]

3. RENEWED INTEREST IN THE LADIES

Ten years after the death of his first wife, George wrote to Mary Roberts on April 22, 1862 that he had paid off his debts and became interested again in the ladies.

My business troubles so far as debts are concerned are over & I have little to do but growl about the Country debts. But there are minor comforts. For instance, I am to have three young ladies to take tea with here this evening. This & such like events help out the dull monotony.
[1862-04-22 (2 letters 1862) George Drake (StL) to Mary Roberts]

And, writing from Green Bay Wisconsin, August 19, 1863 to Mary, we learn more about George's pursuits which keep him "*half glad, half fond and wholly lunatic.*"

My dear Mary,
Almost at the end of the world and "en route" for the North Pole. My thoughts will travel eastward to you and, in spite of multifarious occupations, I must seize what may be my last chance of writing to you, for I have engaged to jump into Niagara Falls next Sunday with a young lady and I may not escape.
...
As you know, I am travelling with two charming ladies: Miss Ellen A. and Miss Nora M., and, in the society of either, I could find supreme delight but the varied perfections of both keep me in a state half glad, half fond and wholly lunatic.
[1863-08-19 George Drake]

George Silas Drake, Sr.

Two months later, George wrote Mary to grouse about his love life.

And talking of young ladies, it strikes me that your brothers are all provided for, lucky fellows all. I wonder why I'm left, such an isolated being. I think I'd like somebody to love me as well as anybody but it seems not so to be. Occasionally, I get quite desperate & resolve – I'll think about getting a wife so if you get "cards" someday, don't be surprised.
[1863-10-08 George]

In the following letter, George seemed to accept his bachelor status with an outward, self-assured, acceptance:

> *I am housekeeping on my own ..., put as much sugar as I please in my tea & have coffee if I like, with none to molest or make me afraid. I am inclined to borrow somebody sister to pour out my tea; however, as while being independent is abstractly very fine, practically, a little assistance does very well. I might mention in passing that I live very simply. Merely ... & green peas with strawberries for desert. Don't want much. Man wants but little here below. I drink ale for my health, being rather slim.*
> [1864-05-31 George Sr (StL) to Mary Roberts (New York)]

4. GEORGE MARRIES BERTHA MOLLOY

George remarried in 1865 to Bertha Molloy ("Bertha M") shortly after the war ended. Soon after their marriage, on April 30, 1866, Bertha M gave birth to Bertha Warburton Drake ("Bertha"). During the remainder of his life, George travelled extensively, including a one-year European tour in 1869–1870, another European tour in 1885, an 1890 trip to California, Tacoma Washington, and Yellowstone.

George and Bertha M were called Gruff and Muff by their grandson, Hugh Scott (Sr), at least for a time. It is not clear how active the two were in Hugh Scott's life; Bertha M was often ill and died in 1896 when Hugh was not yet three years old. But Bertha related one account in her diary:

> June 26, 1896
> "*Mother had brought presents for both children. Dear Mammie Muff and I go for a ride in the carriage with Hugh Scott through the Fens and all about and coming back, stop at the dairy for milk for the children and go buy our lunch at the woman's exchange. Then mother says goodbye to us in the station and as we go down the steps, Hugh Scott calls back "I will come back and see you Gruff".*"

5. HIS LATER LIFE

After his wife, Bertha M, died in 1896, George continued to engage his friends and business associates and continued his summer trips to Rye Beach. He also took a great interest in his family and grandchildren which seemed to infuse a new life in him. Writing from Morris Plains, NJ, to his grandchildren, Hugh, Nancy and George Scott, George wrote:

> *I looked at the little wrens this morning. They are almost ready to fly away. The rabbits & squirrels both run about and look very fine. But Saturday a new thing showed up. I saw down in the corner close by a hedge something running about & it was not a rabbit nor a squirrel. So I just walked down heading(?) behind the trees and when I was pretty close I saw two large muskrats eating away. So after looking at them I walked closer & away they went, down to the little brook, jumped right into the water and swam away, so I could not get my feet wet & I had to let them go.*
>
> *The little pussy kitten at the barn climbed up a tree this morning and, after playing up there, he did not know how to get down. It was so high & no branches so he did a little cat or kitten crying but that did no good. So finally, he ran down as far as he could hold on & down he jumped & was not hurt.*
>
> Grand Pa
> [1898-06-20 George – Father (Morris Plains NJ) to Bertha (64 Vandeventer Pl, StL)]

George Scott and George Silas Drake Sr.

George seemed to grow into his role as a widowed father, grandfather and protector of the widows in Rye Beach. In a letter to Henry, he even quotes Falstaff.

I have intended for some days to drop you a line but owing to my many cares and duties have not found the time. You see I have two children and three grandchildren here. Then there are sundry widows to be looked after which, with my other social and club duties, is wearing and as Falstaff said, worry & care puffed up a man. I'm afraid my avoirdupois is in ... Still as the children & the grandchildren are happy & well, I'm trying with patience to stand it.

The junior George, or is it 3 G, met me this AM as he came from the woods, a small basket well filled with raspberries which he thought he had gathered. So he took a fine one out to present me and soon after decorated me with two tiger lilies for a button hole bouquet. This PM I noticed Hugh, Nancy & Geo. just going it under the willows in front of our hotel with other children. I think the days are not long enough for them & they look well & happy.
[1900(-) 20180717-1 George Drake (Rye Beach) to Henry]

In the summer of 1903, Bertha describes going for a drive with her father with their two dogs.
... the atmosphere is so perfect that the mere sensation of living is rapture. The air is like wine – more like Dublin [NH] than Rye. Father and I had the pair and drove miles and miles this morning, just intoxicated with the glory of the day.
[1903-09-28 (2 letters) Bertha (NH) to Henry (Waco)]
("[T]*he mere sensation of living is rapture"!*)

George seldom expressed his true feelings except, perhaps, when cloaked with wit. But, he did express these feelings sometimes, as in letter to Bertha from Rye Beach. *"I shall be glad to see you & Henry, & I hope for pleasant weather. I feel sorry for the "chicks" and miss them very much, especially when I see little ones about their size about. ... Kiss the children for me."* [20180205-2 George Sr (Farragut House, Rye Beach) to Bertha]

6. GEORGE'S LAST SUMMER IN RYE BEACH

George declined in health over the course of 1908, so much so that it was noticed by his friends and associates. Henry wrote to Bertha of the concern of one younger business colleague.

> *Speaking of letters, I received a charming one from Louis Lemaine with a most sympathetic message to your father "Tell Mr. Drake to make haste and get well for the world can't spare such men from their accustomed places. He is a true gentleman of the old school and my earliest recollections of St. Louis are of him and men of his high type. We can't spare one of them for their example is a constant inspiration to us younger men." Tell your father this for I know it will please him.*
> [20171203-3 (1908) Henry (StL) to Bertha (Rye)]

In one letter, Bertha spoke of her father's decline while in Rye Beach with him. She said of him, "*As is always the case with him, he is much more courageous and cheerful in facing what is a real distress than an imaginary one.*" [1907(-) 20180725-1 Bertha (Rye Beach) to Henry]

During the summer of 1908, George was suffering from various ailments or "irritations" and it must have seemed clear to Bertha and Henry that the end was near. So that summer, Bertha left the boys with Henry and went with just the girls to Rye Beach to be with her father.

Henry's letter to Bertha that summer made their heartfelt concerns clear.

> *I am so sorry things are not going better. I had devotedly hoped that all your patient care and unselfish devotion would have its reward in your father's practical recovery and that he continues to be tortured by that relentless irritation is a horrible pity for him and for you, dear patient child. I don't know how he could ever have gotten along without you. In fact, I know he would not have improved at all but for you and I know he must understand and appreciate all your loving, intelligent, care. Ah, there never was anyone like you, dearie: no one who sees so quickly or so swiftly responds to real needs of those who are near you. But don't be discouraged because things will not right themselves more quickly. Your father is a very old man and his recuperative is not like yours or mine. He is better, that is plain, and you must accept that as good fortune and hope for still better things.*
>
> ...
>
> *In spite of your effort to hide it, I can see too that you are discouraged. Don't let the things that go wrong sadden you, dearest. We have a lot of little troubles, you and I, and you have many more than I, but we also have some big blessings, yes, a great many of them and come what may, as long as I can have health and brain to enjoy the consciousness of your life and your comradeship, the other things may sadden but they never can dismay me. You are my life, sweetheart, and I am selfish enough to want you all for myself but it is richer reward than any dessert of mine if you have to share with others much more even of your time and thought than you have in the fifteen years of our perfectly happy married life been able to give to*
>
> *Your husband,*
> *Henry*
> [1908-06-30 Henry (StL) to Bertha (Rye Beach)]

In the same letter to Bertha, Henry voiced his exasperation with Bertha's brother, George, who was not rising to the occasion in assisting Bertha with their father.

> *I have wasted a good deal of energy in indignation over that brother of yours that I might have applied to helping you and I admit that my criticism of his supinely sitting by and scarcely lifting a finger to help you and discouraging you often with brutal criticism of his own, would have had more force if I had not been equally innocent of any real aid in your time of stress. I can't waste much thought upon George for whom I see him idly lounging away his life giving no real aid or*

sympathy to his ill father and then, without the decency to get down on his knees and humbly thank you for taking all the burden which he should share, my indignation against him is at fierce heat and, but for you, I would have told him a few brutal facts long ago in manner and words that would left a distinct impression. But you need not fear that I shall do this. I would never think of so utter forgetfulness of you but don't think I do not see and understand, dearest, for I do. I am sorry you wrote him a letter of contrition for really I think that will help the boy to be duller and blinder to his real responsibilities than he is. When he told he had "some right to ask why he had not been more regularly posted", I had to close my lips hard not to inquire why he had not been cleverer in manifesting his deep solicitude than in the one scrawl of a few lines during ten days or two weeks. Please don't send him any more of that type of letters or I shall object and please forgive a hot-headed Virginian for boiling over in this fashion. I really would not do it even to you if I did not think you ought to see my point of view and to know better than I have been able to tell you how clearly I see and how deeply I appreciate your courage and devotion and unselfishness.
[1908-06-30 Henry (StL) to Bertha (Rye Beach)]]

Henry apologized to Bertha in his next letter for being so cross. Undoubtedly, he felt the strain that his wife was under.

I wrote you a rather stormy letter yesterday. Today, one of my old-time headaches has appeared and I am meek and apologetic. "The devil was sick, the devil a saint would be." I am both sick and repentant and so afraid of all strife that if I could lay my aching head somewhere near you and get the comfort and calm of your companionship, I think I should not mind whatever else happened in this wicked world.
[1908-07-01 Henry (StL) to Bertha (Rye Beach)]

Later in July, Bertha wrote to Henry of her father's decline.

Sarah took father and me [on] a most beautiful automobile ride today. Father's developing a new trouble which is quite distressing at times. He breathes hard as if he had asthma (the coughing relieves him somewhat) but at times he breathes so that you can hear him all over the house and he has twice had to sit up at night for an hour to get relief. In some ways it seems more like a bronchial trouble than like asthma. We have written to ask Dr. Christian, the advisability of consulting Dr. Otis, he being a lung specialist and on the spot.
[1908-07-18 Bertha (Rye Beach) to Henry]

George's condition worsened by the end of July.

I have written you about father's bronchitis and the sleeping bolstered up in bed but I have not written you exactly what Dr. Otis said. He said there was a slight (very slight) edema or filling of the lung caused by the kidney just as the swelling of the ankles was caused by the kidney. Dr. Christian wrote that about the ankles also. Dr. Otis said it was a condition which might continue indefinitely, years in fact, if no other disturbing cause came in. The filling of the bronchial tubes with phlegm threw more extra work on the lungs than usual and made the pumping of the blood through the heart harder and his heart did queer.

That was what frightened Miss Engelhardt and she did the only thing that I have not liked since she has been with me. She has been such an endless help and comfort and I have grown so to rely on her that I don't like to make even a criticism and though she did make a mistake that time, she did it from the kindest motives. She did not want to frighten me and so she didn't tell me. She wanted to call in Dr. Otis and father did not want him and I not knowing the reason agreed with father and said at least we should write to Dr. Christian first which we did and lost about three days. Of course, the condition was not very serious or she would have insisted but his pulse was much weaker and more fluttering and as soon as Dr. Otis was called in, he gave strychina and the thing straightened out in less than twenty four hours, I mean, as far as the heart was concerned.

The bronchitis continues though much relieved and he sleeps most of the night lying down once more. He is gaining again now but he so palpably lost ground for a week as for the first time during his whole illness to make me really worried. The more so as, when he was in real evident distress and discomfort, he was patient, courageous and cheerful, quite different from his ordinary way before small troubles of giving up completely.
[1908-07-25 (Saturday) Bertha to Henry]

When George died on July 27, 1908, The Republic, a very popular St. Louis periodical of the time, wrote the following obituary.

The death of George S. Drake announced in The Republic of yesterday removed one of the oldest residents of this city for Mr. Drake had lived here eight-one years. In that period, St. Louis grew from a frontier town to a great city of three quarters of a million people. George S. Drake grew as the city grew and to the day of his death was a factor of weight in its business and social life, in its enterprises and its philanthropies. Retiring from business many years ago, Mr. Drake continued to be associated with the activities of the community, his ripe judgment and wise counsel qualifying him in an exception degree for the many positions of trust in which he served. [20180719-2 (1908) Obituary for George S. Drake]

Bertha's diary entry was terse:
July 27, 1908
My father died.
[1893 Diary]

Bertha was very attached to her father with a fierce loyalty that almost scuttled her engagement with Henry. Her annual summer trips east to Rye Beach, although understandable given the St. Louis heat, were probably due just as much to her desire to spent time with her father at his "home". After her father's death, Bertha's interest in going to Rye Beach waned, since a principal impulse for going was no longer there.

C. BERTHA MOLLOY DRAKE

Bertha Molloy Drake

... My mother knew
My father not, yet married him and loved
And loves him still and will beyond the grave.
[Bertha's Poem #9, 1886 "Nausicaa". See Chapt. 6 for complete poem]

Bertha M was born on August 13, 1835 in Texas. Her father, William Molloy, was born in Ireland and moved to Texas. Her mother, Lydia Cronmiller, grew up in Pennsylvania. Bertha M's brother fought as a Confederate Major in the Civil War. When Bertha M was 14 years old, as attested by a Sunday School card from the St. Louis Centenary Methodist Episcopal Church, she came to St. Louis, apparently without her family (although her family resided in St. Louis at some point and then permanently settled in Texas). Bertha M may have come to St. Louis with little money and may have sought any employment to make ends meet.

Early in her life around 1857, Bertha M kept a daily diary in which she included short, inspiring, thoughts, some her own and others from various writers. One example from the pages January 19 to January 21, 1857, she wrote:

> *Monday, January 19, 1857*
> *Grief and sorrow ne'er depart,*
> *They only flit from heart to heart.*

> *Tuesday, January 20, 1857*
> *I'll love thee while there's light above,*
> *Or stars to stud the sky.*
> *I'll love thee till life's day is done*
> *And bless thee with my latest sigh.*

> *Wednesday, January 21, 1857*
> *And the heart makes angels of its friends.*

In another entry in which she was apparently quoting another, Bertha M included in her diary:

> *Wednesday, February 11, 1857*
> *"Commit thy trifles unto thy Lord,*
> *For to him is nothing trivial.*
> *And it is only the littleness of man*
> *That seeth no greatness in a trifle."*

The following entry was a loose quotation from John Bunyan, a popular English poet.

> *Sunday, June 14, 1857*
> *"Dark clouds bring the rain, bright ones never!"*
> *Bunyan[22]*

This theme, of dark clouds bringing forth rain and increase, must have inspired Bertha to write several of her poems on this subject.[23] At the very least, Bertha M's love of poetry was passed down to Bertha.

Bertha M must have met George sometime in the early 1860's when the Civil War was being fought. From Bertha M's diary (1870-05 Diary), it can be deduced that George married her on June 21, 1865 (i.e. Bertha M wrote in her diary that her *"wooden"* anniversary was on June 21, 1870). She also mentioned her anniversary in an 1870 letter (below) to Mrs. Ellen E. Manny[24].

---

[22] "Dark clouds bring waters, when the bright bring none." — John Bunyan, *The Pilgrim's Progress*
[23] See Chapter 6. From Bertha's poem, ***A Prayer** For K.S.B. on her birthday"*
  Not always sunshine fair,
  Ah nay, sweet Christ, not so,
  Shadowless light would be but pain,
  And sometimes there must come clouds and rain,
  Or the flowers would never grow.
[24] Mrs. Manny is Ellen Eliza Manny. (See 1897-02-13 Ellen E. Manny (Winchester MA) to Bertha (3337 Washington Ave, Stl))

Bertha M with Bertha

The next day was the anniversary of our wedding day and I received something which I probably never will again. My little girl picked a bouquet of alpine flowers at the summit of the Splugen & gave them to me with a wish for "many happy returns, dear Mamma." It comes over me so strangely sometimes to hear her use as familiar everyday terms, words which all my life have been synonyms with everything fair and beautiful, greatly to be desired, but far off and unattainable.

[1870-06-26 Bertha M Drake (Lucerne) to Mrs. Manny].

George and Bertha M didn't wait long to have their first child since their daughter, Bertha, was born on April 30, 1866. But, having children immediately upon getting married was common practice in those days. Very soon thereafter, they settled into a new, rented, house. In his January 15, 1866 letter to his cousin, Mary Roberts, George mentioned renting a new, expensive, house which he says he can't afford to buy (due to modesty?) but also mentioned the servants' rooms in describing the house.

George and Bertha M's courtship was complicated by the war. Bertha wrote to Henry about these years later. *"... you know my mother was a rebel, and the war prevented her marriage with my father. She staid by her own people and they did not become engaged until the close of the war, though he had asked her to marry him long before."* [1892-07-26 (Monday) Bertha (Rye Beach) to Henry (StL)] Since George was a "Connecticut" Yankee, George's family would have had some uneasiness with his Texas bride.

As Bertha wrote in a poem in 1886, *"my mother knew my father not"* is suggestive. Perhaps Bertha's father confided certain details to his daughter which gave rise to Bertha's poetic comment, but such details we do not know.

Bertha M left three diaries and a book of poems, as well as approximately 30 letters that Bertha M wrote to Mrs. Manny, describing her family trip to Europe in 1869–1870. Bertha M was very detailed in her descriptions and could spin a good story. So, their daughter had the good fortune on both her father and mother's side to be introduced to writing and literature.

Bertha M

Bertha M also introduced her daughter, Bertha, to religion. During her lifetime, Bertha M kept a prayer that her friend, Mary Nash gave to her (per Bertha's note).

Bertha M wrote down the prayer in her handwriting:

Protect me, oh Lord, from evil speaking and turn the hearts of mine enemies.
Let no evil come nigh me and mine, nor any plague come nigh our dwelling.
Have pity upon the sick who toss upon their sleepless couches and sigh after relief from pain,
And upon all the dying for whom this night will be their last.

[20190102-2 Prayer by Mary Nash and written down by BMD, Rye Beach]

During the Drakes' trip to Europe beginning in October 1869, Bertha M wrote to Mrs. Manny: "*Six or seven years ago I could have written such splendid letters to you with the material I have. But I declare I am too old to do more than scratch a few lines after a day's work. And I am very sorry for I am forgetting so many things you would be glad to hear & that I would be glad to keep for Dawtie[25].*" [1870-01-22 Bertha M (Naples) to Mrs. Manny]

Bertha did not write very much about her mother. However, in one letter to her father when she was 14 years old, Bertha wrote about a time when her mother "*made a good deal*" with her. It may be surmised that her mother was not excited about Bertha going to a party with boys and/or with having to buy her a $20 dress so Bertha M struck a deal with her.

Dec. 31, 1879
Papa

Happy New Year to you. I hope that you received George's letter. He took such pains with it and was so proud of it. I had a very merry Christmas and got about everything I wanted, ... diamond ring included. Thank you for the ... you told Mamma to give me.

I am going to spend the day at Nannie Shepley's with Helen Ernst.

Sam Ridgely is going to have a party and I am invited but Mamma said I could have either five dollars or the party and I chose the five dollars. She made a good deal, though, for my dress would have cost $20 at least, to say nothing of the time.

... got the catechism prize. I knew she would, although for the first fifty I did pretty well. Mamma was perfectly delighted with her album and George was also with his Noah's Ark. It took me a whole afternoon to set the animals up.

Give my love to Aunt Mary and Uncle William[26] if you are still with them.

---

[25] i.e. Bertha
[26] Mary and Jonathan William Roberts. Mary was George Drake's cousin.

Your loving daughter,
Bertie

P.S. I am afraid I did not spell Nannie's last name right or Helen's either.
[1879-12-31 Bertha (StL) to George Drake (5th Ave. Hotel, NYC)]

Bertha M never seemed to like St. Louis, either because of the summer heat or the dirt. As Bertha wrote to Henry, "*...tonight I am going to stay all night at my mother's. The house over there looks as if it had been struck by lightning. Carpets are all up already and mother in a rampant state of disgust over St. Louis dirt.*" [1893-10-10 Tuesday Bertha (StL) to Henry (Waco)]

Henry was no doubt aware of Bertha M's regard toward St. Louis and wrote in reply, "*I am glad to hear your family arrived safely and I hope St. Louis will not be so unbearable as your mother anticipates. How she must enjoy the hot weather? She considers it the light of the last straw, no doubt. I hope she will keep well.*" [1893-10-11 Henry (Waco) to Bertha (StL)]

We do not have letters or diaries from Bertha M for the last 20 years of her life and there were limited mentions of her in Bertha and Henry's letters. But we do have the following wherein Henry is able to praise Bertha by way of her sportsman like inheritance from her mother.

Writing to Bertha, Henry said:
Your other letter sounded as young and happy as a school girl and I have read and reread it. I had to even look up my smiling girl in white with the dog in her arms to emphasize the fact that when you are not ill and over tired, you are as young and as full of the joy of living as you ever were. And another memory came back to me, clear and strong as I caught your pride in your youngest son and it showed how much more there is in inheritance than the cynics concede. As I read your tennis battle it almost seemed to me I had heard the same story in the same terms and in the same spirit before. Then I remembered that it was your mother's baseball story which George second figured in and which she told so graphically to Gist and me at Newton Centre that Gist long afterwards said with enthusiasm. "My! Henry, she must have been a dead game sport when she was young!"
[20171203-3 (1908) Henry (StL) to Bertha (Rye)]

When Bertha's mother became ill and then died, Bertha recorded in her diary.
Oct. 1, 1896
Am told mother is ill.

Nov. 15, 1896
She has entered into rest. (I write this months after – but I find I cannot write more. I do not think she suffered.)
[1893 Diary]

Such passings are always hard, and so was this, especially on the next Christmas just a month later.
Dec. 25, 1896
Father, George, and Miss Jennie come to dinner with us, we go to tea there. We do our best to keep father cheerful. It is hard to.
[1893 Diary]

Mrs. Manny wrote to Bertha just after her mother's death. Her brief letter speaks of their history, not only with Bertha's mother but also with Bertha, and mentions the letters that she received from Bertha M over the years which were given over to her daughter.

My dear Bertie,

I don't believe you can quite understand the pleasure it is to me to have the picture of your little girl[27]. This might be the little girl of long, of long ago. Don't you think she looks like you? If only she had in her hands the worn old horas that you carried everywhere, I could quite think it was you. But this new dog belongs to another generation. What a dainty little darling she must be. I wish I could see her own self but its next best to have her picture. Thank you so much for sending it.

It was very good of you to tell me more of your dear mother. I cannot realize that she has gone even as I read your letter; I fail to comprehend it fully. I can only think of her as I remember her, full of life and beauty. You must find a sad pleasure in reading those letters – they delighted me years ago.

I am so glad to know that your father expects to be with you and interested in your brother's plans for the future. Whatever concerns you must always be of great interest to me. I can never forget my dear little girl, never.

"Miss Smith" was glad to be remembered. Frances sends love to you. Will you remember me to your father and believe me ever affectionately yours,

Ellen E Manny
[1897-02-13 Ellen E. Manny (Winchester MA) to Bertha (3337 Washington Ave, Stl)]

After Bertha M's death, Bertha wrote a letter to her mother's sister, Azula Burns[28], whom she mistakenly thought was Linnie, another sister of Bertha M. Although we do not have that letter, Azula's reply to Bertha provides a glimpse of Bertha M's youth. Azula's words also offered comfort at their shared grief at Bertha M's passing, quoting: *"Daughter, I Am. Can I suffice for heaven and not for earth?"*

My dear Child,

Your very kind letter was received and read with sad interest. I should have written sometime ago to thank you for it but my health is such that I cannot depend on myself at all and any extra exertion tries my strength very much. I thank you for the little incidents relating to your mother's life before her last illness.

I read with a warm feeling around my heart, the words a great pleasure in learning of so near a relative as my mother's sister[29] and I have written what I thought I should like to know myself.

My heart went out to you when I learned your dear mother had left you. I knew you were an only daughter and thought – what companionship there must have been and how sad and lonely you must be without it. I expect to "cross the river" soon myself and it is a great consolation to me to think my two daughters can comfort each other after I am gone.

---

[27] i.e. Anne ("Nancy"), born July 5, 1895.

[28] According to this letter, Azula M. Burns, was sister of Bertha Molloy Drake, Bertha's mother, who was the oldest of three sisters, Linnie, the middle, and Azula, the youngest. There was one brother, Philip. The Molloy family lived in Texas, except for Bertha M who came to St. Louis at a young age. Azula, born 1841, died 1909, was buried at Albany Cemetery, Albany, Texas.

[29] This letter makes clear that Azula is a younger sister to Bertha M. Azula may have meant "my mother's daughter", i.e. Bertha.

...

I have a book of your dear mother's and when I received your father's letter I thought I would send it to him knowing her children would prize it. Of late years, I have known nothing of you or your brother and was surprised to learn that Mrs. Scott was my sister's daughter.

Dear child, there are things that will never be explained in this world but I think there were no unkind feelings that caused the long silence.

No! I am not Linnie! She was the sister next your mother. She was away two years at school and married very early in life when she left home so that the sister younger than myself and I always felt as though we had but one sister and that was your mother. She superintended our early education & gave me my first music lessons. After we left Saint Louis, she directed my reading. The first book she read out aloud to me in my childhood days was the "Wide Wide World". I love that book yet and always have a copy in my library. When one is gone, I get another.

Your mother was my idol & the height of my ambition was "to be just like sister". She was beautiful. I was her little waiting maid when she dressed to go to parties and I can see her now turning around and asking in French if all is as it should be.

I am alone so much of the time that since your letter giving me so much to think of in your dear mother's last days, I have lived so much in the past and I would love to tell you all she was to us in our childhood days.

I think almost hourly of your loneliness not knowing how soon my dear ones may be called to the same trial and sorrow. I am so glad you have a dear family of your own for that in a measure will take your mind from your grief. Still, there is no one can take the place of "mother". After the poignancy of the grief has worn away, there will come that <u>longing</u> that nothing can fill. May the dear Father sooth that longing and you realize the voice that would say "Daughter, I Am. Can I suffice for heaven and not for earth?"[30] Once of my favorite verses is "Casting all your care on Him for He careth for you."[31] Sometimes it is hard to do. He is always sufficient if we are faithful.

---

[30] "Consolation", by Elizabeth Barrett Browning

[31] 1 Peter 4:7 – *4. And when the chief Shepherd shall appear, ye shall receive a crown of glory that fadeth not away. 5. Likewise, ye younger, submit yourselves unto the elder. Yea, all of you be subject one to another, and be clothed with humility: for God resisteth the proud, and giveth grace to the humble. 6Humble yourselves therefore under the mighty hand of God, that he may exalt you in due time: **7. Casting all your care upon him; for he careth for you**. 8. Be sober, be vigilant; because your adversary the devil, as a roaring lion, walketh about, seeking whom he may devour: 9. Whom resist steadfast in the faith, knowing that the same afflictions are accomplished in your brethren that are in the world. 10. But the God of all grace, who hath called us unto his eternal glory by Christ Jesus, after that ye have suffered a while, make you perfect, stablish, strengthen, settle you.*

Since I got your sweet letter I have had such a tenderness for you and I never fail to pray (and I believe in the efficacy of prayer) that the dear Lord may comfort you and keep you in his everlasting arms and that my dear sister's family, may be changed by looking forward to the time when they will meet her in the household He's preparing for them where they will be an unbroken circle. I love that verse "In my Father's house are many mansions."[32]

I did not intend to write so long a letter but I have not said half that my heart would dictate. Again, I thank you for the kind letter which, with your father's, has given us a great comfort in knowing so much of the last days of our dear sister.

Sincerely and with love, Yours

Azula M. Burns
Albany Texas
Feb. 12, 1897
[1897-02-12 Azula M. Burns (Albany, TX) to Bertha (3337 Washington Ave, Stl)]

D. BERTHA WARBURTON DRAKE

"the worst child on the beach"

Bertha Warburton Drake ("Bertha" or "Dawtie") was born on April 30, 1866 in St. Louis. For most of her childhood, Bertha was referred to by her parents and friends as "Dawtie", undoubtedly a more intimate form of "daughter" and some of her parents' generation continued to use this name into Bertha's later years.

Bertha

When this picture was sent to "Aunt Jennie", Bertha M wrote that she asked Bertha to put a kiss on the back. Bertha instead kissed the front and said, *"I think I will put it [the kiss] on the front & then Aunt Jennie could take it right off the little face."* [1870-06-08 Bertha M Drake to Aunt Jennie]

---

[32] John 14:2 "In my Father's house are many mansions: if it were not so, I would have told you. I go to prepare a place for you."

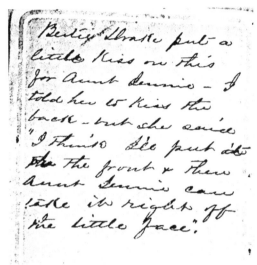
In the letter to Aunt Jennie

Her childhood was privileged, with all of the benefits and disadvantages that attend such beneficiaries. As Bertha said in her later letters, she was brought up by adults. She did not have virtually any childhood friends, probably due in part to travel including Rye Beach and Europe. Also, since her brother, George Silas Drake (George Jr.), was born on June 5, 1875 and more than 9 years her junior, he was hardly a suitable playmate, especially for a girl who was practically born into adulthood. Bertha became an avid reader, which is not surprising since her examples were adults who read. Perhaps other children would not have appreciated Bertha's interest in literature. Playtime without other children would have been a lonely experience so her refuge in books was not surprising.

Bertha

Even at a very young age, Bertha would be regarded as brave. Her mother described the sea sickness that the family encountered on their 1869 trip to Europe on a steamer and how three-year-old Bertha handled it.
Patient little thing. She was very sick for six days. But she never fretted or moaned, just lying in her berth as white as a sheet & every once in a while saying "I love you Mamma" or, if I closed my eyes, "are you dead Mamma?" And when I would have to attend to her when she was throwing up, in her little polite way "I'm sorry to trouble you Mamma." She is a splendid traveler.
[1869-10-29 Bertha M Drake (Paris) to Mrs. John L. Manny (Boston)]

Bertha grew quickly, and not only in her knowledge and intellect. In concluding her letter to Mrs. Manny in 1870 when Bertha was not yet 4 years old, Bertha M wrote: *"We all send love. Dawtie sends kisses to you all. She has grown two inches since we came over. I am very distressed. I am sure she will be a giantess."* [1870-02-14 Bertha M Drake (Naples, Rome) to Mrs. John Manny]

From her letters, it is clear that Bertha M took great delight in Bertha's "funny little sayings."

> *Last night she was rather wakeful and kept talking away, among other things she said she supposed "the angels were God's dear daughters". I said I didn't know. "Well, never mind, we can ask God all about it when we get to heaven."*

[1870-09-18 - 20170806-1 Bertha M Drake to Mrs. Manny]

Bertha

Bertha was precocious, daring and, perhaps, a little obnoxious. During their courtship in 1892, she wrote of her childhood to Henry and revealed her own insight of who she was as a child. In her words, she was a *"horrid little prig"*. As an adult, Bertha continued to be very self-aware.

> *You have not missed very much in not knowing me as a child, I think. Nan will tell you I was a horrid little prig. You see, I knew no children in St. Louis until I was sent to school when I was ten years old and, being an only child for so long – George is nine years younger – and associating with grown people altogether, the usual effect was produced: I was rather precocious, goody-goody and a prig. I think anyone would tell you that who knew me at home.*
>
> *The funny part of it is that my reputation at Rye is entirely different, for the reaction was so tremendous when I got away in the summer with other children that I was the greatest Tom boy on the place and led all the other children into mischief. And in all the years of my life, I have never had a compliment that filled my soul with such rapture as when Jon Dickey said I was the only girl he knew who couldn't be stumped! I suppose you know the difference between a stump and a dare, don't you? You have to do the stump first by yourself before you can challenge another.*
>
> *The crowning feat of that time of my life of which some of the old ladies here will still tell you with horror, was when I climbed to the top of the church on a rickety ladder and swung myself into the belfry by means of a small cord that was tied to something up there. It was not a very high church but some of the other children's nurses appeared upon the scene just as I was swinging myself through space and shrieked with alarm and dismay and I rather think that stamped me as the worst child on the beach. That was when I was ten years old.*

[1892-08-11 Bertha to Henry]

Henry observed that Bertha was prone to taking too many risks.

I can now understand, dear, where your propensity for dangerous performances comes from: your association in early life with those boys at Rye gave you a taste for all the venturesome experiments which are a large part of a boy's life. The difference between the boys I have known and an exceedingly bad grownup girl whom I have met, well, more than once, say, is that the boys have outgrown the habit of taking their lives in their hands on every convenient occasion while the girl I refer to seems at times to be as fond of tempting providence as when she was very little and didn't know any better.
[1892-08-12 Henry (StL) to Bertha (Rye Beach)]

Due to family travels, Bertha apparently was instructed by tutors in addition to the various times when she was able to attend schools. But it is clear that Bertha attended Mary Institute in St. Louis from the fall of 1880 through the spring of 1883, and possibly longer, based on her composition book which referred to this school.

After Mary Institute, Bertha attended Miss Porter's School[33] in Farmington, Connecticut, which she sometimes referred to as "Farmington". It appeared that Bertha attended Miss Porter's School for at least one year during the period from 1883 through 1885, completing her studies just prior to leaving on her second yearlong European trip in July 1885. Bertha attended Miss Porter's School with several other St. Louisans who became her close friends: Mary ("Mattie") McKittrick Stribling, Augusta ("Lutie") Blow Lemoine, Julia Shepley Coolidge, Cynthia ("Cynnie") Yeatman Sewall, Anne ("Nan") Shepley Nagel. Bertha wrote years later, "it is the dearest place in the world and I always look back to my year there as the happiest of my school life." [1892-07-29 (Thursday) Bertha (Rye Beach) to Henry (StL)]

Bertha kept her composition book from Mary Institute which contains some interesting and personally revealing compositions of Bertha from age 14 through 17. The following composition extols work and decries laziness: *"There are drones ... everywhere and none prosper."*

THE DRONES OF THE COMMUNITY
(Grade: 88)

Let us imagine ourselves in a beehive and watch the bees at their various employments for a while. It is a bright, sunny morning and many of the bees are already out in the air. Some come back, laden with pollen and honey, other go forward and, taking it from them, put into the little waxen cells which others still have prepared for it. The whole hive is full of bustle and confusion. One only is idle.

Do you see that great, lazy, black thing which rests idly on the side of the beehive? He is a drone. He will not be suffered to remain there long. Even now one of the busy working bees spies him. Summoning the rest, they crowd around the drone and sting him sharply. He refuses to move. They grow fiercer and fiercer. He lifts his wings for a moment, then drops from his place, dead. But the drones which we find in beehives are not the only drones. Were they, the world would be much happier and better. There are drones in court, drones in school, drones in society, drones everywhere and none prosper.

The Emperor of Russia is one of our human drones. Little would he care for or do to alleviate the sufferings of the working bees, his subjects, if he did not dread their stings. He has suffered so much from their attacks that he is perhaps less a drone than many of those who preceded him.

---

[33] *Miss Porter's School was established in 1843 by education reformer Sarah Porter, who recognized the importance of women's education. She was insistent that the school's curriculum include chemistry, physiology, botany, geology, and astronomy in addition to the more traditional Latin, French, German, spelling, reading, arithmetic, trigonometry, history, and geography. Also encouraged were such athletic opportunities as tennis, horseback riding...* (Wikipedia)

The drones in school, and there are many such, are those girls or boys who, while apparently good scholars, get help from another in every difficult lesson. If they cannot find a place on a map easily, they ask some friend who has found it to show it to them. If they cannot get an example right without working too hard, they borrow this friend's manuscript book and copy her examples and so they manage to get along. The drones of society are those young ladies who are continually complaining that they have nothing to do and who spend their time in reading novels and lying on the sofa.

The drones are not always the most disagreeable people, some of them are the very pleasantest people we know so we must always be on our guard against imitating them and remember to –
> *"Give every flying moment*
> *Something to keep in store;*
> *Work for the night is coming,*
> *When man works no more."*[34]

Oct. 29, 1880
Bertie W. Drake
[1880 BERTHA'S COMPOSITION BOOK: "The Drones of the Community"]

It is interesting to consider this youthful and cynical view, especially of the ladies "*who spend their time in reading novels*", when viewing Bertha's entire life. By her twenties, Bertha was a voracious reader who would finish long novels and other more "edifying" works in a day or two. While Bertha was always involved in church and charitable activities, she might not have written this composition in this same manner later in life. When she was twenty-two, she wrote in her diary, "*Esther, Daisy, Charlotte & I drive to Portsmouth and have an ideal, jolly, foolish time. O girls are so nice.*" [1888-05 Diary, August 4, 1888] And later, when Bertha was twenty-six, she wrote, "*A girl's life is a very happy care free life…*" [1892-09-08 (Wednesday) Bertha (Rye Beach) to Henry (StL)] How views are changed with the perspective of years!

Bertha's love of books was clearly evident at a young age. At 16, she wrote the following poem in her composition book which she read to her class at Mary Institute.

MY FAVORITE BOOKS
(Grade: 99)
Here while sitting in the twilight
As the shadows come and go,
I am thinking of the stories
That I loved so long ago.
When, with eager merry coaxing
I would say, "Please, mother dear,
Read the story of Prince Charming
Or of Snowdrop on her bier."

And again, as I grew older,
I could read a little then,
Came the days of "Dotty Dimple",
"Rollo Books", and "Little Men".
And of darling "Little Women"
With dear romping jolly, "Jo"
Pretty "Meg", and "Beth", so gentle,
"Amy", whom I long'd to know.

---

[34] *"Work for the Night is Coming"*, hymn text by Mrs. Harry Coghill.

Ah that book! Who has not read it?
It is dear to every child
Full of life and full of laughter
Yet gives moral lessons mild.
Then as boys and girls grew
Came the part not quite so gay,
Fears fell soft for "Laurie's" heart ache,
And when "Beth" passed calm away.

Then my taste grew more heroic
Reading Walter Scott, you know,
As I walked with Frank "Die Vernon",
Rode in state with "Ivanhoe".
"Richard Coeur de Lion", kingly,
Was the idol of my heart.
Though I wept for noble "Edith"
From knight "Kenneth" drawn apart.

O what gorgeous dreams these gave me
I would live for days and days
In my own most regal palace
Minstrels loudly sang my praise.
I was "Ovelyn" the lovely,
With "Rose Flammock by her side
And I saw the murdered "Vanda"
Rise before me in her pride.

And since I am growing older
Are the books I now love so
Half so pure or half so noble
As those tales of long ago?
Well, I next became romantic,
Mrs. Wister pleased me then
Orange blossoms fell around me
Wedding bells rang loud Amen.

Mourned I with unloved "Fiancé"(?)
Rich in gold but nought beside,
Till the gay young baron, "Marnau",
Rent him from his lofty pride.
Whispered as he clasped her closely,
"This shall our betrothal be,
And most fervently I'll woo thee
Till thou ownst that thou lov'st me."

Turning from the deeper story,
Next I read the "Duchess" books;
Lightly laughed with charming "Phyllis",
Basked in "Mrs. Geoffrey's" looks.
These were full of light and sunshine,
Brighter books you'll hardly find.
Though perhaps you'll say "Primora"(?)
How can school girls be so blind.

Best, while I have rambled onward,
I've omitted one most dear,
And of course you are astonished,
That you've not yet found him here.
Dickens, with his keen heart, reading,
Touching chords of joy and woe,
While he rouses smiles for "Veller"
Brings quick tears for little "Jo".

Buliver's(?) novels next enthralled me,
I, in trembling horror, read
Of the craft of dark "Arbaces",
And the "Witch's" curses dread.
Then I stood with royal "Harold"
Seemed myself to feel the dart,
When the stern monk brought the message
"Thou must crucify the heart."

Now that I have named so many
Seems a voice to slowly say,
"From all those that you have told me,
Which are favorites today?"
Out of all that I have mentioned,
There are five to me most dear,
Which, perhaps, I can't do better,
Than to name in order here.

They are contrasts, I acknowledge,
But that's not my fault, you know.
For you bade me tell you truly
Not what should be but what's so.
Now if books have any influence,
Will these make or mar my life,
"Rob Roy", "Phyllis", Buliver's "Harold",
"Bleak House", and the "Second Wife?"
[1880 BERTHA'S COMPOSITION BOOK: "My Favorite Books"]

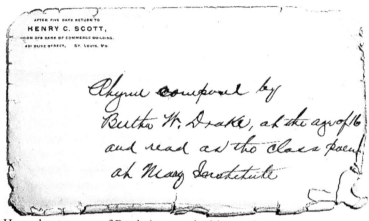

Henry kept a copy of Bertha's poem in this envelope.

Bertha developed very broad tastes in literature and poetry, the extent of which was not always shared by others, including Henry.

> O, I found Baudelaire. George[35] had seen it and, not knowing it belonged to anyone in especial and being absolutely fascinated by its binding and the fact that it was a subscription copy, for the young man has a very dainty taste in such things, had carried it off to his room. The edition is a gem, dear boy, but I am sadly afraid that your taste and mine do not agree in poetry. I laid it down on Mackay[36] and looked Aldrich[37] and Riley[38] with a sigh of relief to think what sunny, wholesome fellows they were and that you liked them anyway. [1892-01-29 Bertha (StL) to Henry (Wichita)]

As many of her letters show, Bertha always set aside several hours each day for reading the great literature of the day, especially when travelling.

> Was your advice to me to drop Swift and read the "Fair Maid of Perth"[39] dictated by the idea that I had never read the latter? If so, rassurez vous. I read it years ago. Once or twice you have spoken as if you thought the "Wizard of the North"[40] was unknown to me. Now as I have read all the poems except Rokeby[41] and, not only read them but re-read them over again and at least half the novels, that is an unfair charge. If I had ever owned a set of Scott, I should probably have read them all, those I did own I know almost by heart. The "Fair Maid of Perth" does not come in that

---

[35] George S. Drake Jr., Bertha's brother.

[36] Charles Mackay (27 March 1814 – 24 December 1889) was a Scottish poet, journalist, author, anthologist, novelist, and songwriter. Charles Mackay wrote the popular poem

> You have no enemies, you say?
> Alas, my friend, the boast is poor,
> He who has mingled in the fray
> Of duty, that the brave endure,
> Must have made foes.
> If you have none,
> Small is the work that you have done.
> You've hit no traitor on the hip,
> You've dashed no cup from perjured lip,
> You've never set the wrong to right.
> You've been a coward in the fight.

[37] Thomas Bailey Aldrich; November 11, 1836 – March 19, 1907) was an American writer, poet, critic, and editor.

[38] James Whitcomb Riley (October 7, 1849 – July 22, 1916) was an American writer, poet, and best-selling author.

[39] The Fair Maid of Perth (or St. Valentine's Day) is a novel by Sir Walter Scott.

[40] The Great Wizard of the North, January 1, 1989, by Constance Pole Bayer (Author). The book was written about the life of John Henry Anderson (1814–1874), a Scottish professional magician. Sir Walter Scott is said to have given him the stage name, "The Great Wizard of the North". [Wikipedia]

[41] Rokeby (1813) is a narrative poem in six cantos by Walter Scott. It is set in Teesdale during the English Civil War.

last category. I read that seven years ago in Scotland, just after having passed through Perth. While in Edinburgh, I read the "Heart of Midlothian" and just after leaving Carlisle, "Waverly". I always like if I can to read novels about a place while in that place. It makes them all seem so much more real. In fact, it adds interest to both place and novel.

...

Before I stopped talking books, I meant to tell you I am reading a perfectly fascinating novel now, "The Cloister and the Hearth" by Charles Reade, one of my Christmas presents, Times of Philip the Good of Burgundy, and extremely interesting. Have you ever read it? And I am diversifying that by reading Conan Doyle's detective stories aloud to George. Is that sufficiently frivolous for you?

[1893-01-10(-) (Monday 1893-01-09) Bertha (Newton Centre) to Henry (StL)]

Bertha must have inherited a love for letter writing from her mother, with words that could breathe life into old memories and shine a light toward the future. Bertha not only wrote letters and poetry but cut out poems and articles from newspapers, sometimes transcribing them, for her to always have near at hand. Bertha cut out the following poem from a newspaper in 1899.

FLORENCE, March 2, 1899.

My letters! all dead paper, . . . mute and white!
And yet they seem alive and quivering
Against my tremulous hands which loose the string
And let them drop down on my knee to-night.
This said, . . . he wished to have me in his
    sight
Once, as a friend: this fixed a day in spring
To come and touch my hand . . . a simple thing,
Yet I wept for it! this, . . . the paper's light,
Said, *Dear, I love thee;* and I sank and quailed
As if God's future thundered on my past.
This said, *I am thine*—and so its ink has paled
With lying at my heart that beat too fast.

And this . . . O Love, thy words have ill availed
If, what this said, I dared repeat at last!

Elizabeth Barrett Browning, 1806 – 1861

This preceding poem, "Florence", speaks to Bertha's passion for letters and the life she knew, that lives and breathes in these letters. And so, Bertha meticulously kept her letters and diaries throughout her life and passed them on to be kept and treasured, even unto today.

E. DR. GEORGE SILAS DRAKE JR.

Bertha's brother George was born on June 5, 1875 and died in October 1937. Perhaps because he was 9 years younger than Bertha, she spoke very little of him in his early years.

1. RYE BEACH, SUMMER OF 1892

"Put your hand on my shoulder and I'll take you in."

One of the first times that Bertha referred to her brother was during the summer of 1892 when they were in Rye Beach with the family. George was 17 at the time and had started to assume the male role of protector to his sister – the appropriate role for a young man at that time.

> *The bathing has been fine lately and, this morning, Charlotte and Miss Wilkes, Mr. Appleton and I swam way out. I can swim pretty well but I get tired more easily than the others. Consequently, I found myself just a little beyond my depth and completely blown. So, I turned over and began to float in order to rest myself when my hand was taken hold of and a voice said "put your hand on my shoulder and I'll take you in", most authoritatively. I obeyed and discovered that it was my brother who had taken possession of me, and, having swum in with me to where the water was not over my shoulders, he proceeded to deliver a lecture on my imprudence in going out so far. There was not the least danger; if there had been, Mr. Appleton is a beautiful swimmer, but I believe men like to bully their women kind and this taste develops in them very early.*
> [1892-07-29 (Friday) 20170724-4 Bertha (Farragut House) to Henry (StL)]

Bertha knew that Henry would be unhappy about the risks that she was taking with her safety. She tried to reassure him of the solicitousness of her brother in this regard – George was growing up. (Bertha also rebuked Henry for being a "hen".)

> *You will be very angry with me if I go out so far again!! Now suppose I say I will if I choose and I won't promise not to. That is clearly what I ought to do. George was not so heedless of my safety as you might think. I was quite amazed at the boy's solicitude. He actually went twice to my mother on the subject. I suppose I shall have to promise you – hen! Yes, hen! As Gordon Sherman once remarked when Edith called him one, "Edith where did you get that bar room expression?" I suppose you will make some remarks about my choice language in your next letter. If you were here, I am inclined to think I should defy you, but as you are away, I will try the effect of meekness upon you and promise to be a good little girl and not go out over my head anymore. Satisfied?*
> [1892-08-05 (Friday) (20170712) Bertha (Rye Beach) to Henry (StL)]

George became a very good athlete, starting with his tennis prowess while in Rye Beach.

> *The boys are having a tennis tournament ... George is in it so of course I am deeply interested, though I don't think he has any chance for the prize but he will probably be one of the last four left in.*

George Drake Jr.

Notwithstanding Bertha's modest comments about her brother, George was a very good tennis player and exceeded expectations in the Rye Beach Tennis tournament in 1892.

> *The tennis was wildly exciting yesterday. The cup was won by one of the younger married men, named Paton, whom everyone took for granted would have it. But to everyone's amazement, George was the other last man. Everyone expected Mr. Appleton to be. George played against him, and after he won the first set, the enthusiasm grew wild. The despised girls headed by Daisy Godfrey, led the applause, and I believe every soul on the place joined in. And when he finally won the second, the boys went mad. His chum, Norman Williams, embraced him publically and then nine of the fellows including some of the older men started to chair him. But he fought against them and escaped. Everyone knew he had no chance against Morton Paton, who is a noted player and has cups innumerable, so there was no surprise at his being beaten there. Though there was a great deal of sympathy. I was quite amazed to find how wide spread the popularity of the young man was.*
> [1892-08-12(-) Bertha (Rye) to Henry (StL)]

Concerning George's tennis success, Henry wrote of his developing interest in him.

> *I was very glad to hear of your brother's success at Tennis. What you have told me of him has greatly interested me and I have an idea that someday we may be rather good friends.*
> [1892-08-15 (Monday) Henry (StL) to Bertha (Farragut House, Rye Beach)]

After coming in second in the tennis tournament, George caught the favor of Daisy Godfrey. Bertha broached the subject with her brother; however, showing wisdom beyond his 17 years, George quickly changed the subject with, "*I wish you wouldn't wear that belt, it makes you look like a hayseed.*" So ended the discussion of Daisy Godfrey, for a time.

> *The tennis prizes were distributed yesterday, owing to rain and other things, they had not been able to play off the consolation prize before. The first prize was the orthodox silver cup, the second (George's) was one of the most beautiful racquets I ever saw. And I was amazed to see the ease and grace with which he took it. Daisy Godfrey threw a bunch of flowers after him as he went up – imp. And, I thought he would be rattled. Not at all. And when I asked him about it afterwards, he remarked with some scorn "If you think, after having to do things with three hundred boys looking on and ..., hall full of people is going to rattle me, you are mistaken", adding with a truly brotherly frankness "And I wish you wouldn't wear that belt, it makes you look like a hayseed."*

You really must not object to my using slang, I am getting such a choice collection from my younger brother, and if you do ever appear in a crimson and cream cravat, I shall certainly use that last lovely expression of his – it is so expressive.
[1892-08-18 Bertha (Farragut House, Rye Beach) to Henry (StL)]

During their 1892 summer in Rye Beach, Bertha wrote about her brother as having grown out of his childhood.

My brother scornfully declines to consider a horse as in any way to be compared to a bicycle, greatly to my disgust. He is a down right beauty, that boy. It is not because I am his sister, for the whole house is of that opinion and, for the last year or two, I have not thought him good looking, but he has grown out of that ugly age now. He has developed a great deal this year and it is really a good thing he does not like girls for they would spoil him if he could be persuaded to have anything to do with them.
[1892-07-07 Bertha (Rye Beach) to Henry (StL)]

In a letter during the early summer of 1892, Bertha related a story told by Bertha M about George's athleticism at school in the spring. It seemed that George was very modest about his achievements. The second part of this letter related a story from George's school which was quite amusing.

Mother came down from her trip to Concord, very well pleased in her mind about George. The young man had just won the school cricket belt for the cricketer making the most runs during the year. But he had not mentioned that in his letters. Shy, never to tell anything interesting in their letters, it takes a personal visit to get any information. He stands very well in his classes too, though not brilliantly. How is this for a specimen of schoolboy modesty?

The boys run a paper called the Horae for which they write the articles themselves. And the other day, one clever individual, by way of an experiment, copied a sonnet of Shelley's and sent it in as his own. The head editor rejected it on the ground that it had absolutely no merit of either form or idea to recommend it. Of course, when this came to the knowledge of the school, it roared with delight, whereupon, the editor defended himself by saying "Well, for that matter, Shelley and Shakespeare, too, had written a great many things that had no literary merit whatever"!!!!!
[1892-06-13 (Sunday) Bertha (Jaffrey NH) to Henry (StL)]

Bertha continued to wonder about George's seeming lack of interest in girls, including Daisy Godfrey.

You never can tell what men are going to like. George, after repelling all the advances of that fascinating little witch of a Daisy Godfrey, sits next to the plainest, most unattractive young girl in the hotel on a match party and comes home and says he had a very good time and she is a "right sweet little thing", while all the effect Miss Daisy had, after a prolonged conversation, was that George said to mother "I have been studying human nature, specially girls. And I have come to the conclusion that girls are a nuisance!!!" There is no accounting for tastes.
[1892-08-03 Bertha (Rye Beach) to Henry (StL)]

We are all rather amused over our young man George. I mean, he scorns girls in general and as in addition to this, he really is unusually handsome. The usual effect has been produced and they would rather have him bow to them than talk half an hour to any of the other boys. Daisy Godfrey, who is about fifteen and is the most fascinating little witch I ever saw, has every other boy on the place at her feet and yet it is for George that she lays herself out and the wretch won't have anything to do with her and flies round corners to get out of the way. The mothers are all much amused over the small drama. "Every lassie has her laddie" and today I happen to want mine more than usual.
[1892-07-29 (Friday) 20170724-4 Bertha (Farragut House) to Henry (StL)]

But as the summer vacation was coming to its end, George had a change of heart – "*It was the most sudden fall.*"

> *And speaking of affaires de coeurs, our family is convulsed over the sudden collapse of the woman hater. Far from scorning girls, within the last week, George has been discovered entertaining groups of them, without even a fellow man to sustain him. He is also known to have a photograph of two of them taken together in his possession. Which of the two is the particular charmer, I don't know, but that there is one, I have no doubt since George spent ten minutes brushing his hair for dinner the other day. It was the most sudden fall. Everybody is having an amused chuckle over it. They say George is like the cholera, there isn't time for him to do much this fall but look out for next year!!!! Older sisters and mothers tell me that the young crowd consider the young man the handsomest fellow down here, and I must say his athletics and his coat of auburn have made him even better to look at than when he came.*
> [1892-09-05 (Monday) Bertha (Rye Beach) to Henry (StL)]

When Daisy Godfrey left Rye Beach on her stage coach, George made sure not to miss her parting.

> *This must be a letter of scraps, dear boy, for news there is none. My sister in law departed this morning, Daisy Godfrey, I mean, for I really believe it was to her charms the boy succumbed at last. He ate about three mouthfuls of breakfast this morning in his mad haste to join her on the piazza, nor did he quit her side until the stage came. "How are the mighty fallen"? II Samuel, Chap. 1.*
> [1892-09-09 (Thursday) Bertha (Rye Beach) to Henry (StL)]

2. ST. PAUL'S SCHOOL

St. Paul's School, The Sheldon admissions building

George attended St. Paul's School[42] at Concord, New Hampshire, a boarding school, starting in September 1891, as preparation for college. Despite being a good student, George was not excited about school.

> *Poor George is very low in his mind over the prospect of school tomorrow, but I notice that when he met a school friend this morning, they both greeted each other with the most radiant smiles and, if he is equally delighted to see the rest of the "fellers", I doubt if life is such a tremendous hardship*

---

[42] St. Paul's School (also known as St. Paul's or SPS) is a highly selective college-preparatory, coeducational boarding school in Concord, New Hampshire, affiliated with the Episcopal Church. The 2,000-acre (8.1 km2) New Hampshire campus currently serves 534 students, who come from all over the United States and the world. In 1856, Harvard University-educated physician and Boston Brahmin George Cheyne Shattuck, inspired by the educational theories of Johann Heinrich Pestalozzi, turned his country home in the hamlet of Millville, New Hampshire, into a school for boys. Shattuck wanted his boys educated in the austere, bucolic countryside. Throughout the latter half of the 19th century, the school expanded. [Wikipedia]

at St. Paul's. I should be sorry though if he were eager to leave his family. But O!! What geese girls are! I have had several confidences from the young man on the subject and I find he goes back with his tintypes and a photograph, and another coming. However, people who live in glass houses - when I first knew any St. Paul boys, I was only fourteen myself and one of them carried my tintype in the locket on his watch chain for two years. So I suppose I need not say anything.
[1892-09-14 (Tuesday) Bertha (Backbay, Boston) to Henry (StL)]

George was thought to be immature for his age which led his parents to have a discussion as to whether he should stay an additional year at St. Paul's.

You asked me about George's going to college. He has passed his examinations but he seemed so boyish and immature that both father and Dr. Cort thought he had better stay at school another year. You see the fifth form prepares for college but there is a sixth form through which the boys can go who are not going to college or who, as in George's case, are too young. Several of his friends are going back with him. The sixth does not prepare for the sophomore but they review a good deal and do part of the freshman year work so the fellows start in very thoroughly prepared. George is seventeen but he is very young for his age.
[1892-09-23 (Tuesday) Bertha (East Jaffrey) to Henry (StL)]

George's last year at St. Paul's suited him and he was "*in a radiant good temper*" for the Drakes' Christmas 1892 in Stancote, just prior to Bertha and Henry's wedding the next February.

Well, the boy arrived yesterday in a radiant good temper with himself and the world in general. He has made quite a record for himself as a football player. O, he says the account you saw of St. Paul's versus Columbia referred to St. Paul's, Garden City. His St. Paul's is not allowed to play the colleges.
[1892-12-23 (Friday) Bertha (Newton Centre) to Henry (StL)]

George could be forgetful, as any young man. After a period when his parents were concerned about not having heard from their son, the father discovered the reason which Bertha conveyed to Henry. "*The mystery of their not hearing from George was explained by the fact that the young man had written & then carried the letter around in his pocket. It was discovered there when father went up.*" [1893-10-09 Bertha (StL) to Henry (Waco)]

3. COLLEGE, MEDICAL SCHOOL AND THE MEDICAL PROFESSION

George went to Yale University for college and matriculated in 1897. After graduating from Yale, he went to Johns Hopkins College of Medicine where he graduated in 1901. After completing his medical degree, George

...served for four years as house surgeon at the Union Protestant Infirmary in Baltimore and in 1905 returned to St. Louis, where he was made associate attending surgeon to the St. Louis Free Skin & Cancer Hospital and also associate attending surgeon to the St Louis Children's Hospital. He was associated with the former institution for five years and for two years with the latter. During the past fifteen years he has built up an extensive private practice and ranks high among the surgeons of the city, confining his attention solely to surgical practice. He keeps in touch with the most advanced methods and is thoroughly familiar with the latest scientific researches and discoveries having to do with the practice of surgery. He belongs to the St. Louis Medical Society, the Missouri State Medical Society and the American Medical Association. Dr. Drake enlisted for service in the European war and was assigned to duty at Camp Logan, Texas, in the Base Hospital Later he was transferred to Jefferson Barracks and afterwards to the Base Hospital at Camp Zachary Taylor, in Kentucky, being mustered out on the 19th of May, 1919, with the rank of captain.
[Centennial History of Missouri, One Hundred Years in the Union, 1820-1921, Vol. V, Published 1921]

George's prowess as a doctor caught the eye of various members of the medical profession. Henry, in a letter to Bertha (circa 1900), mentioned the following:

> *I had two pieces of good news at the breakfast table this morning. George's success I greatly rejoice over. I did not know about the University faculty although Houston asked me particularly about George and seemed greatly interested in the inquiries that both Apic(?) and Waring(?) made about him and Apic said rather bluntly that George ought to be helping the University. I don't know how well he knows George but he expressed open praise of his ability. It is really his opportunity and I believe he will make use of it. He may have been wise after all in going away although I can't exactly see why. But he has the chance and a big one for coming at this time it is specially an honor when they are picking choice men from all over the country.*
> [1900(-) 20171116 Henry to Bertha]

Bertha wrote in her diary on December 10, 1900 that George was operated on for an appendicitis. She visited George at the Hopkins Hospital on the 12th and wrote: "...*go see poor George at Johns Hopkins Hospital. He is doing very well.*" [1893 Diary] Bertha stayed in Baltimore until the 20th: "*I stay with father in Baltimore, and we visit George every day, make preparations for his Christmas, etc.*" [1893 Diary, December 16, 1900]

After George graduated with his medical degree from Johns Hopkins, he was sought after for his expertise.

> *I had a very interesting talk with Dr. Clapton today about George. He says he is very fond of George, believes in his ability and is most anxious to see him started in a useful busy life but that George almost positively thwarts his efforts in that direction and, when he calls him in to help him, has an engagement or some excuse for not meeting his request for aid but that he now has a real change to help George if the latter "will do his part." Clapton has been chosen as chief of the surgical department of the children's hospital and he wishes George to help him. He says he can't find George's address or he would telegraph him. I don't know where he is but, on the strength of your present from Atlantic City, I am writing him there asking him to telegraph when he will return. If you have the young man's address write and ask him to communicate with me for here is his opportunity if he will only take hold of it. I was much impressed by what Clapton said of his real strong friendship for George and his confidence in his ability.*
> [1905(-) 20170806-3 Henry to Bertha]

Henry seemed to more and more assume the role of patriarch, not only for his own family but also for the Drakes. In this regard, he periodically voiced his concerns for Bertha's little brother.

> *Speaking of those who do save themselves with a vengeance, I thought it cheeky of your little brother after all your hard journey to call on you to make the trip to & from Boston in order that he might go down to a carrousel which he had not even taken thought to provide for in making the plans which your father had to adjust himself to. He is a nice fellow but he has lived to and for himself so long that he really don't know what personal sacrifice is. I hope Doctor Mudd will go after him and the longer the club used the better it will be for George.*
> [20180416A-9 (Sunday) 1907-09- Henry to Bertha]

Shortly after writing the preceding letter, Henry conversed with Dr. Mudd who spoke highly of George.

> *I saw Dr. Mudd at the club and he didn't talk vaguely about George. He said George was a very able fellow but was neglecting his opportunities at the "Skin & Cancer" and he was going to tell him so on his return for he liked him too much to see him make such a blunder. He explained by saying that he frequently telephoned instead of going down & got his reports over the phone rather than by personal inspection. Of course, this is not to be mentioned to yr father or George.*
> [20180416A-13 (Friday) 1907-09- Henry to Bertha]

Henry followed up with another positive letter about George.

> *Don't worry about George. I, of course, did not encourage Mudd except in fun and there is no danger of a clash for Mudd is really very fond of George. I think Mudd expects George to take up several matters for him while he is away and he certainly speaks highly of his ability.*
> [20180416A-14 (1907-09-) Henry to Bertha]

In another letter, Henry wrote that George had performed an appendectomy with great success.

> *I have been very busy since our return and have scarcely seen anyone except George who seems very well. He has had quite an interesting amount of work at the "Cancer" and seems not to have minded the heat which must have been fierce enough for the most seasoned St. Louisan. He has also had an appendicitis case of a rich Baltimore man named Baldwin. The latter was so much pleased with George that he wishes him to take him, Baldwin, on to Baltimore where he goes to recuperate. George says he will not go if he can avoid it. I advised his doing so, especially as he is now ready to take his own vacation. George wishes to know about your plans for he thinks he will run up to Rye if you and your father are to remain much longer. I told him you would probably not leave before the twelfth to the fifteenth. He says he will go to New York and from there to Rye or will go to Rye direct if your father wishes it.*
> [20180416A-5 (1907-09-29) Henry to Bertha]

But Henry frequently worried that George was not applying his talents fully. Perhaps it was George's youthfulness at age 35?

> *I am ... with your brother George. I wrote him plainly that he was neglecting his interests in staying away and he writes, "I don't see why Clapton thinks I am indifferent for I told him I was deeply interested." And yet he stays on, loafing his life away, although I have written him plainly that both Mudd and Clapton have said that he ought not to have gone away during the ..., that he ought not to be away now when the men here are all striving to get on the children's hospital staff and he could get on "if he only showed he cared a d---n." Mudd said last night with bitterness "I am going to have one more talk with Doctor Drake when he returns and if that does no good, I shall feel hopeless." I don't think Mudd's talk is altogether unselfish for Doctor Asler's and John Truney's high praise of George were repeated here by Apie, Waring, Erlanger – three of the new W.U. men and they all asked me why George had to be away when they needed him to talk over the St. Louis situation with Opie, who is a nice fellow and very influential said "Mr. Scott, Drake is very able but, if he does not work, his ability won't save him for he will get so behind he will never catch up. The best work of the profession is improving and moving on to better things almost daily and the man who will not move with the procession will soon be lost for all time."*
> [1910-06-27 Henry (StL) to Bertha (Rye Beach)]

In one of his next letters, Henry again wrote of his concern for George's lack of drive.

> *Your worthless brother has not returned; I am going to give him the D- when I see him. Clapton and Mudd both wish to see him and he knows it and yet he loafs on at Atlantic City, probably amusing himself with some young woman of the stripe and worth of Miss Clark and doesn't even have the consideration to tell his friends when he will return. I suppose he thinks this indifference is smart but I think he is behaving like an idiot and is proclaiming his general worthlessness ...*
> [1910-07-12 (1st letter) Henry (StL) to Bertha (Rye Beach)]

4. MATRIMONY

George apparently became interested in matrimony at the time he was completing his medical degree at Johns Hopkins in Baltimore in 1900. On learning this, Henry offered his own advice for the young man.

> *I would like to meet George's girl myself. Tell him I expect to be presented in time to give them my blessing. Do you think it would be a bad scheme for him to marry when he gets through at*

Baltimore? If he is dead sure he knows his own mind, I think it would be well. The trouble is a fellow under thirty don't know what he wants. At least, I didn't until I approached that age.
[1900-08-07 Henry (StL) to Bertha (Rye or Dublin NH)]

Several days later, Henry followed up on the advice in his previous letter.

George's matrimonial dissertations sound like the speculations of a child. That young man will do well to go slow until he is very sure what he wants. I am glad you found your prospective sister even passably likeable for I know you viewed her with a critic's eye. I will tell you a story I heard today and then I must go to bed. "Smith, your wife has grossly insulted me, and I shall hold you accountable." "My dear Brown, my wife has grossly insulted me a thousand times, don't take it so hard, man." Brown – "You shall not evade the responsibility: your wife has grossly insulted me and I shall look to your redress." Smith – "my dear fellow, don't look to me. Why man, I am not even a blood relative of her's. She has two brothers in town and if you cannot be satisfied without reparation for the injury, go and get satisfaction from them!"
[1900-08-09 (Wednesday 1) Henry (StL) to Bertha (Dublin NH)]

George's love interest of 1900 did not last. Over the next ten years, there were comments written by Bertha and Henry about his love life but nothing progressed until George met Myrtle Clark who was the daughter of Henry Clark of Montgomery County, Missouri. George and Myrtle were married on June 3, 1911, shortly after Henry died. The details of the wedding were reported in the St. Louis Post-Dispatch on June 4th, including the fact that the wedding was held at Mrs. Henry Clark's house (Myrtle's mother) and was officiated by Rev. Dean Carroll M. Davis. After a reception in New York, the couple left on June 14th for a three-month tour of Europe.

During their honeymoon, the couple had arranged to take the White Star Line ship, the RMS Olympic[43], from Cherbourg back to New York. However, on its trip from Southampton to Cherbourg, the Olympic collided with the British Warship, Hawke, and was severely damaged and forced back to Belfast for repairs. The St. Louis Post Dispatch reported on September 20, 1911 that Dr. & Mrs. Drake were fortunate not to have boarded in Southampton, although they then had to find another ship to take them home.

MANY ST. LOUISANS ABOARD OLYMPIC

Three Escaped Accident by Arranging to Go on the Vessel at Cherbourg.

Several St. Louisans were booked for passage on the Olympic. At least three of these escaped the accident because they had arranged to go aboard at Cherbourg.

These are Dr. and Mrs. George. S. Drake, who was Miss Myrtle Clark, who have been spending their honeymoon abroad, and Miss Martha Hutchinson, a cousin of Mrs. Drake.

The St. Louis Post Dispatch, September 20, 1911

While George and Myrtle were fortunate to avoid traveling on the Olympic, one additional fact is also noteworthy. The Captain of the Olympic at that time was Edward John Smith (January 27, 1850 to April 15, 1912). Early the next year, when the White Star Line completed the construction of the RMS Titanic,

---

[43] Bertha went on the RMS Olympic to Europe on her 1925 trip (see chapter 24).

the sister ship to the Olympic, Captain Smith was its captain and whose life tragically ended on April 15, 1912 on the Titanic's maiden voyage.

The remaining details of George & Myrtle's relationship were not written about in Bertha and Henry's correspondences. What was related about Myrtle comes from a story that my father used to tell about her. Myrtle was apparently not a very good automobile driver and would sometimes mistake forward and reverse. After one such mistake when she ran the car through the back of the garage, the responding officer allegedly said, "Myrtle Drake, you take the cake!"

5. AT WAR AND AT PEACE

George served as a medical officer in World War I and practiced as a surgeon throughout his life. When he died in 1937, Bertha remembered her brother in her diary with the following poem written by Charlotte Yonge[44]:

Dr. George Silas Drake, Jr.

October 27, 1937
My brother, George Drake, died.
    "Seest thou the eastern dawn
    Hearest thou in the red morn
    The angel's song?
    O, raise thy drooping head,
    Thou who in sorrow dread
    Hast lain so long.

    Death comes to set thee free,
    O meet him cheerily,
    As thy true friend.
    Then shall thine anguish cease,
    And in eternal peace
    Thy penance end."

---

[44] From *The Heir of Redclyffe*, by Charlotte M. Yonge (a 19th Century English novelist), Chap. 35, Sintram's song.

Sintram's song seems to have been written for George, so I have copied it here. Surely peace came to him, after long suffering. This is what his physician, Dr. Cutler, wrote of him:

> *"I never knew a man who complained less in trouble or more fought his battle as a man would like to think he would act in similar circumstances. Would that all of us had more of the stuff that ran through his veins."*

[1893 Diary, October 27, 1937]

F. THE DRAKES' PLANS ARE A MOVABLE FEAST

> *You ask me when you think we will leave Rye. Well, you know the Drakes' plans are of the nature of a movable feast.*
> [1892-08-11 (Wednesday) Bertha (Rye Beach) to Henry (StL)]

Very early on, Henry seemed to understand the Drakes' concept of making plans.

> *You showed your usual penetration, my dear, in divining that we should not go to the "Ark" until Saturday. I see you are beginning to understand that where the Drakes say they are going on any particular day, it is safe to assume they will not. Tomorrow, however, I think we may be relied upon to go.*
> [1892-09-17 (Friday) Bertha (Brunswick Hotel, Boston) to Henry (StL)]

The history of the Drakes reveals courage in adversity, wit and humor, deep faith and great loyalty. But overriding all, was the Drakes' propensity not to stick to any schedule, which gave spontaneity to everything they did and showed their *joie de vivre*.

CHAPTER 4 – A THREE-YEAR-OLD IN EUROPE: 1869–1870

Bertha Warburton Drake (Dawtie)

Sometimes these warm days I braid Dawtie's hair up, much to her disgust. Yesterday morning, she sat still after the operation a minute & then said – "I think I look just like a snooks." I didn't answer & a few minutes after, "I think I look like the roses all off of a bush." Why how so, dear? "Well I think a bush looks abominable when the roses are all off."
[1870-06-05 Bertha M To Mrs. John L. Manny]

Bertha (or "Dawtie" as she was called then) was three when her mother (Bertha M), father (George) and Frances, their nanny/nurse, took her to Europe for a grand tour. Bertha's first European trip would take over one year and cover most European countries, including France, Italy, Germany, Holland, Belgium, England, and Ireland. Her mother wrote lengthy letters to her friend, Mrs. John Manny, and kept a daily diary of their travels and the details of the places visited. Bertha M's descriptions and stories provide a fascinating insight, not only of the times in which they lived, but also their personal opinions and views.

The following chapter recounts the many of the numerous details of the Drakes' 1869–1870 trip to Europe which may seem tedious and windy at times. However, one purpose of this account is to astound the reader as to the breadth and length of their journey, taken with two parents, a nanny and a three-year-old. Another purpose is to show Bertha as a very young girl. (Note: the quotations which follow are from Bertha M's letters to Mrs. John Manny and to the three Bertha M diaries recorded from 1869 to 1870 which are referenced by date.)

A. THE VOYAGE TO EUROPE, OCTOBER 1869

Bertha M, George and Bertha left for Europe from New York City after spending several months in the east. As Bertha M's diary revealed, the mother and daughter spent all of August (and probably the entire summer) in the east. The first entry in the diary was when they were in Portsmouth, R.I., where they briefly stayed at the "Sagamore", in Frost's Point. Of course, for most of the summer, they would have stayed at the Farragut House, their "summer home" in Rye Beach. Due to his business interests, Bertha M mentioned that George took trips to New York City and St. Louis. Most of Bertha M's time during this summer was spent socializing and traveling to other places, such as Boston, for shopping and cultural events (lectures and special events such as the Humboldt[45] Centennial celebration). Bertha spent most of her time with adults, such as the Manny's[46], and may have attended a school or had a tutor there (Bertha M mentions going to see Bertha in mid-September and that "*Dawtie came home*" on October 2nd).

MADAME AND MISS ALMA KRIEGE'S
German Kindergarten, to which an advanced class will be added, will re-open September 27, at 127 Charles st. The new course for the training of Kindergarten teachers, extending through six months, will begin at the same place October 1st. Early applications are desirable.
SW(s) 13t   au21

Newspaper Ad Kept in Bertha M Diary

By October 15th, the Drakes had finally made their way to New York City to spend four days before embarking on their trip.

The Drakes left for Europe on the on the steamer, SS Silesia, on October 19, 1869. The SS Silesia had just been launched on April 14, 1869, six months before their voyage, and was considered "state of the art".

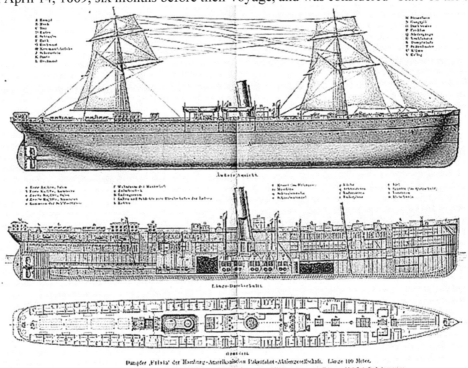

The SS Silesia

The SS Silesia was a late 19th-century Hamburg America Line passenger and cargo ship that ran between the European ports of Hamburg, Germany and Le Havre, France to Castle Garden and later Ellis Island, New York transporting European immigrants, primarily Russian, Prussian, Hungarian, German, Austrian, Italian, and Danish individuals and families. Most passengers on this route were manual laborers, including stonecutters, locksmiths, farmers, millers, upholsterers, confectioners, and tailors, though physicians and other professionals also bought passage on her. … With both a steam engine and a set of traditional masts, she was one of a brief but large category of "transitional" (wind-to-steam) vessels. Like many of these ships,

---

[45] Friedrich Wilhelm Heinrich Alexander von Humboldt; 14 September 1769 – 6 May 1859, was a Prussian polymath, geographer, naturalist, explorer, and influential proponent of Romantic philosophy and science. Humboldt's quantitative work on botanical geography laid the foundation for the field of biogeography. Humboldt's advocacy of long-term systematic geophysical measurement laid the foundation for modern geomagnetic and meteorological monitoring.

[46] Mr. & Mrs. John L Manny. John Manny was formerly George Sr.'s business partner in the firm Manny, Weld & Drake, wholesale boot and shoe.

the Silesia had a steel hull, two masts, and one steam funnel. … Twelve men shoveling coal continuously from her four coal bunkers kept her engines running around the clock, consuming 75 of her 1,100-ton capacity of coal per day. All of the steam generated in her boilers was recovered and reused during any given length of her journey. The smoke from the burning of coal quickly blackened many of her sails, … She began her maiden voyage from Hamburg to Le Havre and New York on 23 June 1869. [Wikipedia]

The SS Silesia was built for the Hamburg-Amerikanische Packetfahrt-Actien-Gesellschaft or HAPAG (often referred to as Hamburg America Line, literally Hamburg American Packet-shipping Joint-stock company). Although the ship was primarily used to carry immigrants to the U.S., it also had "luxury" accommodations. The ship could carry approximately 300 "regular" passengers in male, female or family compartments, and approximately 20 "cabin" passengers.

Bertha M described their departure in her diary entry on October 19, 1869. "*Started on Steamer Silesia for Europe. Rachie, Landreth, Ella, Mr. Kendace & … saw us off. Weather very raw & disagreeable, I, sea sick that eve.*" The next day, "*All sick. Poor little daughter, very ill. Ship making very fine run. Clear weather.*" And the next, "*Still sick. Very fine weather. Steamer running at rate of 336 miles a day.*" Finally, on the next day, October 22nd, "*Dawtie well. We are better, almost all are well. Fine weather.*"

The Drakes must have been relieved when their Atlantic crossing was completed based on Bertha M's letter to Mrs. Manny on the day they arrived in France which described the voyage in much more positive terms.

October 29, 1869 Letter to Mrs. Manny, onionskin paper written on both sides (only top side showing here)

We left New York on a real raw, penetrating day & I supposed we should suffer very much from cold but after we got out to sea, it was very mild & warm. Our steamer was perfectly splendid, new within six months. The inside of the cabin is entirely lined with birds eye maple, polished like satin, … in beautiful panels. At the side of each state room, doors are very fine bronze statues, one

holding a shield with the arms of Hamburg, the other with a shield with H A / P / A G and everything – spoons, china, linen etc. were marked the same way. The carpet is ... with the same shields on it in crimson & gold & united by chains. One kind of shield with one kind of chain, the other with another kind. On every panel between the state room doors hang fine oil paintings, ... in Germany. Each one cost 700 dollars in gold. The table I believe was considered very fine & everything was scrupulously clean. Our stateroom has two windows open all the time so we had all the fresh air we needed.
[1869-10-29 Bertha M (Paris) to Mrs. Manny (Boston)]

Regarding the Atlantic crossing, Bertha M wrote in her letter on October 29th that they had exceptionally calms seas. *"We had a remarkable trip for this season of the year. Ocean smooth, skies clear, weather warm. ... The chief engineer had crossed 160 times & he said he never had made a better passage."* But, in spite of such a *"good passage"*, they were all mostly sea sick during the voyage. *"[W]e were very sick. I don't know what would have become us if it had been stormy. We were not out of our berths for four days. Then we felt pretty well for two days and then retired into private life for the rest of the voyage. I didn't eat anything but tea & toast all the time and very little of that."* [1869-10-29 Bertha M (Paris) to Mrs. Manny (Boston)]

The SS Silesia arrived in Cherbourg, France, at 5 AM on October 29, 1869. The relief upon arriving in France is best expressed by Bertha M: *"We are at last in France & feel very much better this afternoon than I ever thought I should feel again."* [1869-10-29 Bertha M (Paris) to Mrs. Manny (Boston)]

B. OCTOBER – DECEMBER, 1869
1. CHERBOURG, OCTOBER 29, 1869
The Drakes had intended to go immediately to Paris but, due to a delay in getting their tender to shore, they missed their train. So, they stayed in Hotel L'Aigle in Cherbourg on the 29th of October and left for Paris the next day.

We went to the funniest little old-fashioned hotel – painted floors, basins like soup plates, high beds with curtains, down beds for quilts, a grown up man to empty the slops & make the beds & a woman to order the carriage & omnibus & make out the bills. Some of the people went on that afternoon but ... of us stayed until the next day & were more than repaid. The cooking was the best I ever tasted in my life – no French fancy dishes but perfection, service. Recommend you to the Hotel L'Aigle. Then the drive & the views! You would have stood on your head & danced. [1869-10-29 Bertha M (Paris) to Mrs. Manny (Boston)]

Their thankfulness for being off the ship increased when a storm blew in the next day.

We just left our steamer in time to miss a great storm that stressed the coast with wrecks. The Silesia went rocking away out of the harbor & how thankful we were not to be on her. That day the harbor was sufficiently smooth, studded with vessels of every sort, iron clads & all, some of them perfectly beautiful, and outside the break water the waves were dashing in fury. It looked exactly like some naval battle. The waves dashed against the breakwater & broke into clouds of white smoke (apparently) as high as a church steeple. Words can't describe that scene to you. And the queer old town with its noise, the clapping of the sabots, the rattling of wheels, the squealing of pigs, the chattering of old women in capes, its soldiers & sailors in all sorts of picturesque uniforms.
[1869-10-29 Bertha M (Paris) to Mrs. Manny (Boston)]

2. PARIS, OCTOBER 30, 1869
The Drakes arrived in Paris on October 30th and stayed for one month until November 30th. During their stay, they saw virtually everything there was to see in Paris, as Bertha M's diary related in great detail.

We are regular French folks now. Breakfast at 10 ½ A.M. Dine at 6 P.M. Dawtie at 6:30 P.M. It is astonishing how much French the child knows already but I don't know whether she ever will converse in it because we don't . She ordered the "dyenner" today. I told her in English & she told the waiter in French "café au lait pour deux, les muffins grille, magneseau grille pour un et pommes de terres à la maître d'hôtel." Her pap at breakfast said "grille" with his American brogue and she immediately corrected him, "grilyã" papa. Her "bonne" is satisfactory, excepting her uncontrollable flow of tongue. The other day Dawt looked at her "à minute" & then with the grandest air said, "Frances stop talking!!! Your tongue wattles (rattles), wattles, wattles just like a rail road trail." Of course I reproved her but not with a very good grace for she had so truly expressed my own feelings.

Today we walked the "Jardin des Plantes". She was perfectly delighted with the lions, tigers, bears, monkeys etc., etc., etc., and she informed Miss Richardson that this was the beautiful garden where God put Adam & Eve & forbade them to eat of the tree in the middle of it. ... She is as fat as she can be & never still one minute.
[1869-11-25 BMD (Paris) to Mrs. Manny]

Bertha M wrote a moving story of her visit to Père Lachaise Cemetery[47] in Paris.
We saw the decoration of the tombs in Père Lachaise on that day. I believe all Paris was there. Thousands of wreaths & bouquets of fresh flowers & immortelles of beads & paper, and statues & candles were for sale on the streets leading to the cemetery. None seemed too poor to buy. Some graves had as many as 40 wreaths. Inside the tombs were candles burning, fresh flowers etc. All sorts of inscriptions were made of black flowers in the wreaths of yellow immortelles "To my mother", "To our grandparents", etc., "To thee our tears", "For thee our sighs", "Our hearts are buried with thee", etc. etc.
[1869-11-25 BMD (Paris) to Mrs. Manny (Boston)]

3. DIJON, MARSEILLES, NICE & MONACO, NOVEMBER 30, 1869
The Drakes arrived in Dijon on November 30th and stayed there until December 2nd when they left for Lyon and then Marseilles, arriving in Marseilles on the 3rd. They left Marseille after 3 days for Nice where they stayed 3 days before leaving on December 9th for Monaco.

Bertha M described the view from her hotel in Nice to Mrs. Manny.
From the portico at our windows we could look on the blue Mediterranean, not as far off as your front fence from your front door. There is no tide & no sandy beach. A little strip of pebbles where the wash women dry their clothes, then orange trees, palms, etc. Then the beautiful English promenade, then our hotel. In the distance the Maritime Alps. Picture to yourself the sunlight falling on the sea, gilding twenty or more fishing smacks & luggers[48], just out before my window. The promenade thronged with most elegant equipages of every style. The little park on one side of our hotel, full of merry children dressed in picturesque costumes of every sort, with their bonnes[49], a band of music in the pavilion in the centre, discoursing sweetest music, people in elegant costumes everywhere & of every grade from the duchess to a flower girl, roses, violets & many new and beautiful flowers in bloom. Windows wide open, balmy air, etc. and you may have some idea of what we saw & where we were last week.
[1869-12-15 (2 letters) BMD (Genoa, Italy) to Mrs. Manny]

---

[47] Père Lachaise Cemetery – formerly Cimetière de l'Est, "Cemetery of the East") is the largest cemetery in Paris, France (44 hectares or 110 acres).[1] With more than 3.5 million visitors annually, it is the most visited necropolis in the world.
[48] Smacks and luggars are two types of sailing vessels used in fishing.
[49] Bonne – a French nursemaid or maidservant

Bertha M also wrote to a "Miss Smith" about her impressions of Nice.

> *I intended writing to you from Nice so got this paper. The dark streaks are fish nets, sardines, etc. Those for sardines look as fine as our hair nets. The white spots are clothes drying on the beach. The washerwomen are characteristic parts of every landscape in France and Italy. They wash in the gutters, in the brooks, & at the fountains. They empty the clothes out of the baskets and get into them (the baskets) themselves and it is an everyday sight. To see 30 or 40 of them tucked in their baskets, pounding away at the clothes and chattering like magpies, as far as the eye or glass can reach at Nice. The clothes on the beach look like sea foam.*

[1869-12-27 Bertha M (Florence) to Miss Smith]

4. SAN REMO & SAVONA, DECEMBER 15, 1869

The Drakes left Monaco for Savona on December 15th. Apparently, the trip to Savona from Monaco was too long to be completed in one day and they stopped for the night "*at Finale Marina*" in San Remo. The next day they continued to Savona.

> *Our carriage was quite new & handsome, open or shut at pleasure but for the baggage behind, just like one of your handsome barouches[50]. We had 4 horses driver & footman & a handsome black dog named Fidele keeping guard on top of the baggage. The drive was splendid, the views magnificent. We wanted to reach San Remo the first night so we rode by moon light. I couldn't tell you how beautiful it was. … Tomorrow night we hope to be in Genoa. We have seen olive gatherers all day getting in the second crop. Donkeys with the strange wooden saddles & huge panniers each side & a man riding on top & a woman holding on to the tail behind, steering the animal I suppose. We saw women carrying great stones as big as two water buckets on their heads and big copper kettles of mortar on their heads, helping to build railroads. If there is anyway worse or more awkward than any other to do anything, these Italians take that way. But they build finer roads & railways & all kinds of stone work than we do. It is utterly astounding to see the entire mountain slopes terraced. It does not seem possible for human hands to have accomplished so much. Everywhere we see priests, crosses, churches, shrines & consequently beggars. Today while waiting for the carriage, I took a short walk & was chased back when I reached the others (I was surrounded by 13 of different ages – beggars I mean).*

[1869-12-15 BMD to Mrs. Manny]

Bertha M described the trip to Savona in her letter to Mrs. Manny.

> *… we drove to Savona, a glorious drive, through the wildest, boldest scenery we have yet seen. The day was perfect. The waves of the sea broke as beautifully on the coast as old Atlantic does on New England's shore. The road winds along lofty and beautiful cliffs overhanging it & gigantic aloes & cacti, growing vigorously in the rifts. Ruins of castles & abbeys on many of the heights. In one place on our left, the rocks rose precipitously to the height of 1500 ft. and on our right the descent as precipitous to the sea of about 150 ft. only the carriage road between. The waves of the most exquisite blue you can imagine dashed against the rocks & once the spray sprinkled our faces. I couldn't help thinking of you all, all the way, how you would have enjoyed it.*

[1869-12-15 Bertha M to Mrs. Manny]

---

50 50 Barouche – a four-wheeled carriage with a driver's seat high in front, two double seats inside facing each other, and a folding top over the back seat

19th Century Carriage

Travel by carriage in 1869 was not a particularly comfortable undertaking, especially for a 3-year-old. Nevertheless, Bertha M speaks of Dawtie as being a perfect traveler in her letter to Mrs. Manny. *"Dawtie would send many kisses I know but she is sound asleep. She is splendid. Wakes at 5:30 A.M., rides all day stopping only for dinner(?) until 6:30 P.M. & never frets or is any trouble."* [1869-12-15 BMD to Mrs. John Manny]

Bertha was precocious and seemed well able to occupy herself during long travels. In this regard, Bertha M speaks of her daughter's grasp of the places to which they were traveling. *"It sounds so funny to hear Dawtie talking of Genoa, Rome, Florence, Venice, Naples, as Charlie does of Boston. She knows what she expects to see in every place."* [1869-12-15 BMD to Mrs. John Manny]

From Savona, the Drakes proceeded to Genoa by train, passing 42 tunnels in the 30-mile trip.
> *At Savona, we took the rail. I can't say much about the scenery for we passed through 42 tunnels in 30 miles. It was funny we didn't know we were as near & we came into Genoa, singing our old hymn "On the Mountain Tops Appearing".*
[1869-12-15 (2nd letter) BMD (Genoa, Italy) to Mrs. John Manny]

5. GENOA, DECEMBER 17, 1869
The Drakes spent 4 days from the 17th through the 21st in Genoa and did a considerable amount of sightseeing. (Bertha M's diary contained voluminous notations on where they went in Genoa.) In her letter to Mrs. Manny, however, Bertha M focused more on her hotel room and her overall impressions.
> *We came to Hotel Feder and I never saw such a perfectly splendid room as ours in my life. The room is 25 feet high, most beautifully proportioned & frescoed. The furniture, we have two beds, 2 large tables, small work stand, an étagère, a high ..., 2 large bureaus, a dressing table, a large full length swinging glass in a frame, 4 arm chairs, 4 small ones, a sofa, all of the most exquisitely inlaid wood, 4 silver candlesticks, 2 large bronze candelabras holding 6 candles each, elegant clock & vases, commodes, folding screen, etc. The beds are hung with curtains & a coronet over the head. The windows with crimson silk. But the most beautiful thing is the continuation of our room which is the loveliest oratory about the size of your guest room only higher, finished in gilding(?), an altar of white marble inlaid with colored marbles fills one side, the floor is mosaic marble. Crucifixes etc., etc. We look from our windows on the gulf, overlook the pool, etc.*
> *...*
> *One strange thing is everyone looks dirty & yet you see everywhere & all the time women washing. In the gutters, at the fountains, in every brook & mountain spring, 30 or 40 at a time. It is a peculiar characteristic of French & Italian scenery.*
[1869-12-16 Bertha M to Mrs. John Manny]

6. LA SPEZIA, DECEMBER 21, 1869

The Drakes went to La Spezia Italy from Genoa on December 21st.

I didn't lose my senses at Genoa but it was a wonder I didn't. We started from Genoa at 6 A.M. by rail only taking some coffee as we expected to breakfast at Chiaveri. We arrived there at 9, took a private carriage – our party took two – but found there was no breakfast. We could only find three loaves of bread and some figs. We saved one loaf as we did not know when we would get dinner, but as we were wandering our way, surrounded by beggars of all ages & sizes, up a steep hill, out rolled our bread into the road. I hope the beggars were better off for it but we had nothing to eat until 5:30 P.M. when we had a dinner, very scant it was too. (We were all hungry when we got up) at Borghetto.

The rain was pouring in torrents but on we went until 9:30 when we reached Spezia. The road would round the mountains on the brink of steep precipices with the mountain torrents rushing furiously with poor drivers, poorer carriages & worse horses. Brother Drake & Mr. Merrill were in torture almost & they say they never will take that risk again. Little Dawtie had nothing to eat or drink until 5:30 & of course went sound asleep & had to be waked when we reached the place but she didn't cry or fret once all the time.

We had telegraphed for rooms at the best hotel but our drivers were in league with the hotel of Milan and told us the "Cross of Malta" was full and far off & our poor horses were so "dead beat" that out of mercy to them, fearing we would have to return to the "Milan", we concluded to remain there. While we were eating, our supper, in walked the Secretary of the "Cross of Malta". We had telegraphed for rooms etc., etc., & we must pay for them. We were willing to do what was right & he asked 40 francs. We laughed him to scorn, paid him 20 francs & he went off satisfied. The next morning we found the "Cross of Malta" was just one square from the "Milan", so they go. One cannot believe a word an Italian says.
[1869-12-27 Bertha M (Florence) to Miss Smith]

7. PISA, DECEMBER 22, 1869

Their next stop was Pisa on December 22nd which they reached by train.

From Spezia to Pisa, more than delighted there. Disappointed in the leaning tower at first but the Duomo & Baptistery are magnificent. Saw then the lamp, the swinging of the which first led Galileo to think of the principles that govern the movements of the pendulum. I did not ascend the tower. Dawtie went to the top & kissed her hand to me from there. She don't go sightseeing much but her papa said if she wanted to climb that, she should. In the Baptistery she was greatly pleased with a marble lioness & "baby lion" that supports one of the columns of the pulpit and we were amused to find her astride of the beautiful lion, riding away, as if it was an everyday hobby horse.
[1869-12-27 Bertha M to Miss Smith]

8. LEGHORN, DECEMBER 23, 1869

From Pisa the Drakes travelled to Leghorn Italy on December 23rd. Bertha M described the effect of the rain and flooding that they encountered in her diary writing: "*Arno in a full teaming rage.*"

From Pisa, we went to Leghorn. Nothing there to see or do. We had very fine weather for a week and since then it has been rainy & cold. The Arno has been higher than it has been for 92 years. The whole country has been inundated & travel stopped. Christmas day we went to see a picture peculiarly believed to have been painted by the Angels which is only uncovered for great occasions. This time, it was for the benefit of the Pisan sufferers by the flood, first time for 8 years. Such a jam. We have to take our turn mixed up with dirty Italians suggestive of fleas & other vermin. We decided the Angels were very poor painters but the Virgin in the picture was very fine, having on a crown which lately cost 40,0000 dollars, set with precious stones. About her neck were elegant

pearls, diamonds etc. I don't know how they were fastened on, for there was a wire grating before it(??). They devout kissed the marble slab before it & handed up their rosaries, prayer books, etc. which a priest rubbed on this grating & thereby sanctified.
[1869-12-27 Bertha M to Miss Smith]

9. FLORENCE, DECEMBER 24, 1869

The Drakes left for Florence on December 24th and stayed there until the 29th. It rained all day on the 24th and so they had a pretty dreary Christmas eve. They spent much of the rest of their time in Florence going sightseeing and were able to visit an incredible number of the museums and attractions. There was, of course, time for shopping too, as Bertha M's diary relates. *"December 27, 1869: Very hard snow storm. Went shopping much to the disgust of Messrs. Merrill & Drake. Saw many pretty things but couldn't decide on anything. Tired out."*

10. PERRUGIA, DECEMBER 29, 1869

Perrugia:

Left Florence at 12, M. for Perrugia. Uninteresting ride through valleys surrounded by snow clad hills. Little town built of stone almost all of the snow still perched on the top of the hills. Present picturesque views to us as we pass. Reach Perrugia at 8 P.M. very long drive up a steep hill to hotel which we found very much better than we expected. Funny old halls, tiled & marble, rag carpets in rooms. Water pitchers like heavy porcelain... pots. [Bertha M Diary]

11. ROME, DECEMBER 30, 1869

The Drakes travelled to Rome on December 30th by train. Bertha M described the trip in her diary: *"Very hard ride until 11 o'clock at night. Were behind train so had to wait every station for other trains."* They stayed in Rome for 22 days before going on to Naples.

The time spent travelling provided Bertha M time to describe to her daughter the places they were visiting. When going to Rome, little Bertha took great interest in learning about the coliseum.

I told Dawtie a story about the Coliseum on the way in which she was much interested. The next day I stayed in the house all day & Dawtie went out with her nurse. In the evening when we were gathered around our wood fire, I said, "Well Dawtie, where have you been today?" "Oh, I've been to the coliseum to see where the lions & tigers tore up the Christians" with as matter of fact air as if she had been saying to you she had been to Mrs. Skilling's. We looked at each other & smiled at the ridiculousness of the idea. I wanted to see what she had seen and she said "It was a great, big place with very many doors & windows all around and the place where the lions used to be are all filled up with dirt & stones. And my dear Mamma in the middle is a beautiful green yard with large stones lying all round & there are very high steps to go up & on top there are all bushes & trees growing & there is a fountain where they used to wash." "You may depend upon it", said Mr. Merrill. "That child has been out there."
[1870-01-07 Bertha M (Rome) to Mrs. Manny]

During their stay in Rome, the Drakes seemed to have been able to visit virtually every sight, museum, and special place that Rome has to offer, and Bertha M listed in detail many of the specific works of art and attractions that they saw. The list was too numerous to recount. The following account of their shopping, however, deserves mention.

One thing troubles me. I always wondered why people didn't bring more things home when they went abroad. But I shall come home with just as few as anybody you even saw. In the first place, things are not cheap. They are perhaps, compared with the prices of the same things in the states. Everybody said – "Be sure & bring back lots of Roman sashes!" But Roman sashes are 9 dollars in gold a piece. We have no more money to spend than we had at home & should not very often

spend that much for a sash at home. And everything else is the same way. I have not seen anything cheap yet. Then here is Italy, they don't allow you a pound of baggage on the railways so we have the smallest of trunks & no room to carry anything. Then it will be such a nuisance to carry things round for the next year & a half. Then Mr. Drake says I must make a list of everything & pay duty, so I think my chances are small of bringing pretty things home.
[1870-01-07 Bertha M (Rome) to Mrs. Manny]

C. JANUARY – MARCH, 1870
1. NAPLES, JANUARY 21, 1870

The Drakes left Rome for Naples on January 21st. From Bertha M's diary: "*Beautiful ride but I was quite sick. George S. mashed his fingers. Saw more people at work in the fields than we have yet done. People much better looking as we left the Papal States. Reached Naples late. Had some trouble getting a room. Went at last to United States. Poor rooms, poor fare, no fire but good organ grinders. Before daylight, at 3 or 4 A.M., the view from the window was most glorious.*"

In Bertha M's letter to Mrs. Manny, she further expounded on the trip from Rome and their arrival in Naples.

> *It was a most glorious day & the road bounded by mountains snowy peaks on either side. It is winter yet so we saw not flowers or luxuriant vegetation, also though there was much verdure everywhere. It seems so funny to me that distances that looked so short on the maps at home should be so long. It took two days to get from Florence to Rome. We stopped at night of course and we were all day coming from Rome to Naples by railway.*

> *We reached Naples after dark, chilled & tired. Poor little Dawt, very thirsty and no way of getting a drink. We went to two or three hotels, all full and at last found rooms without a fireplace & not at all comfortable. I had been quite sick all day & was glad to get Dawtie & myself to sleep anywhere. Next day however we succeeded in getting the very best suite of rooms in the very best hotel – the Grande Bretagne, and we are just as comfortable as it is possible to be. We have all our meals served in our own parlor & very nice ones they are.*

> *We heard everywhere that when we got to Italy we would have only some black bread but we have the best bread we have had at all here. Opposite our windows is the beautiful Villa Reale, a public park for the gentry & nobility. Dawtie, I suppose, comes under the last head. Outside of that is the beautiful Bay of Naples, Capri & Ischia in full view. Vesuvius is just out of view round the corner of the street. The old fellow has an inveterate habit of smoking. I do wish he could get up some fireworks for our edification.*
[1870-01-22 Bertha M (Naples) to Mrs. Manny]
(Did the Drakes really want to see an eruption to become more edified?)

On January 26, 1870, the Drakes traveled from Naples to Pompeii, a very cold day trip which Bertha M described in her letter to Mrs. Manny.

> *Had a perfectly? horrid day, although I enjoyed myself after a fashion. Just think, Mrs. Manny, of my saying that after a day spent in Pompeii! We started from our hotel in the bright sunshine & I thought it was a nice warm day, wore only my waterproof suit, without any cloak & only a small shawl thrown over my arm. After we turned out of our sunny street, the wind struck us and I don't know that I ever suffered so much, certainly never from cold. We had an open carriage and the wind was the most intense, piercing, disagreeable, cutting wind I ever felt.*

> *When we reached Pompeii, I was completely used up. We entered the gate and I found I could scarcely move my limbs. My blood felt like ice water coursing through my veins. There was no*

place to warm. I knew there was four hours walk before me in a cold, desolate ruin. I was not properly clothed. I was already completely exhausted and the accumulated evils were too much for me, and I am sorry to say I boohooed right out loud. That seemed to strike consternation into the folks and the guide rushed round to find some fire. The wine & provisions had gone in the carriages round the walls of the city. Some soldiers had a pan of charcoal over which I warmed my feet & in a few minutes was ready to go. I do wish it had been a pleasant day. As it was, I could not be there without intellectual pleasure but the body hardly endured.

What impressed me the most was the lovely desolate aspect of the streets. Streets entirely paved with regular blocks of marble(?) with sidewalks & stepping stones across the streets. The ruts worn by the old chariot wheels are there, ... anywhere in the streets. It looks as if it had just been washed out. It seems as if the people must step out from their houses into their old familiar tramping grounds. In the houses, ruins, ruins, everywhere. But in the streets, only loveliness. I cannot tell you how it impressed me. Sometimes, going home very late on a bright moonlight night, I have felt something like it. This whole volcanic region is a constant wonder to me. The upturning, the heavings & contortions, the forces in action, the forces extinct are all marvelous.
[1870-01-22 Bertha M (Naples) to Mrs. Manny]

Bertha M wrote in great detail about a funeral procession that they witnessed between Pompeii and Naples and her observation on how Italians mourned their dead.

The day at Pompeii satisfied me. I shall try no more excursions on cold days. We have always heard of the crowds of beggars at Pompeii but we only saw one. We found out the reason on our way home. There was a grand funeral at which the Beggars were all assisting. We were delighted to have been free from the beggars & to see the funeral. First, came a procession of penitents in blue gowns & white caps pulled over their faces with holes to see & breathe through & lighted candles in their hands. Then more with red gowns & white caps & candles. Then an immense bier borne on men's shoulders covered with a magnificent red velvet pall absolutely covered with the most gorgeous gold embroidery, the velvet only occasionally peeping out between. On it was a huge sarcophagus of gold & red velvet, coronet, coat of arms, etc., on it. Then came another sarcophagus, gold & red but less gorgeous than the other. Then came another one of beautifully polished olive wood, brass clamped, etc. The first was that in which the body had lain in state in the church. The second the coffin was being carried in through the streets. The third was that in which the coffin would be placed in the grave.

I forgot, before these sarcophagi marched thirty or forty priests dressed in purple silk gowns & white ermine caps bawling away at the top of their voices part of the time & stopping when they felt like it to laugh & talk to each other or to someone in the crowd.

After the body came a band of music playing "Ah! I have sighed to rest me", an operatic air but appropriate. Then all the raggedest, blear eyed, horrid old rascals you can imagine dressed in shiny black oil cloth hats & caps with little old black banners, about a hundred or more. I suppose they got a little more for that than they could have begged. Then followed a long procession of coroneted carriages, coachmen & footmen in livery but not a single person inside of one of them. And even the coachmen in mourning on the family carriage laughing and joking with his acquaintances in the crowd. I never saw such a heartless piece of mummery. But no one cares for the dead here.

I saw a man walking along the street the other day with a gilt sarcophagus on his head, containing the body of a child about six or seven years old, a white veil over it & a wreath of flowers on it, and he walked along stopping to chat with those he knew. As Mrs. Merrill says every day, "I am so glad I wasn't born an Italian."

I saw four men walking along the street with a grand piano on their heads, a man following with the legs in a basket on his head. If there is a worse way to do anything than any other, these Italians do it that way. We saw them loading a ship with stone one day to our amazement saw six stout girls stepping briskly off with a large building stone on their heads. They keep perfect time but I can't tell how they got it on their heads or how they took it off.

I am sorry that we are here in this cold spell. Naples must be glorious in May. Today even, the Villa Reale opposite us is crowded with the youth & fashion of the city. Carriages are rushing to & fro in the Strada between us & the Park. There is an avenue between the Strada & us for horsemen and there are scores of officers in full uniform, little ladies & their grooms & young Italian dandies, riding their prettiest & casting sheep's eyes at the carriages to see if the ladies are admiring them. Now they all raise their hats as a carriage with the royal arms pass. Prince Humbert & his wife are in it. We saw the "Host" being carried to some dying person I suppose. The priest had on a very elegant vestment of silver cloth & roses embroidered on it, one end of which he put over the vessel that held the consecrated wafer. A dirty young chap carried an open faded red silk umbrella over him & six of the very dirtiest nosed, smeardiest faced, horridest headed and raggedest clothed boys you can imagine, carried a lighted candles by me. A most disgusting sight, I assure you & the poor people taking off their hats & kneeling to the "Sacred Presence". I should think if it was so sacred they would have cleaner people round it? They certainly don't believe cleanliness bears any relation to godliness here.
[1870-01-30 Bertha M (Naples) to Mrs. Manny]

Certainly, one of the lingering impressions that Bertha M had about Naples was how "filthy" it was. *"Naples is beautiful but so filthy. The worst looking specimens of humanity we have seen anywhere are here: dirty, deformed, degraded, disgusting, dowdies are the women of the lowest class and the men are, if possible, worse."* [1870-02-13 Bertha M (Naples) to Mrs. Manny]

While in Naples, the Drakes also visited Herculaneum and its various attractions. They remained in the city for 20 days. It sounded from Bertha M's letters that such a long stay was not planned. "We have stayed at Naples longer than we expected for Mr. Merrill was taken with lumbago & was confined to his bed for ten days. I think it was all right for the rest of us for we were going north too soon I think. I wanted to wait for spring." [1870-02-13 Bertha M (Naples) to Mrs. Manny] Evidently European trips in those times permitted great flexibility on travel dates, although this "flexibility" came at a price, having to exchange their rooms for ones which were not as nice.

A disadvantage for us was the necessary change of rooms. We had a large room next to our parlor and when we first came to Naples, they from choice went into a top story. Mr. Merrill has some whim about getting above the Italian atmosphere. Afterwards the house filled rapidly and when he was taken, of course, he couldn't get upstairs, we had to take their room for there was no other. I have to travel up seven flights, & long ones they are too, white marble ones all the way. The halls are of white & black tiling, pretty pattern. I seem to be walking on china, I am afraid I'll fall all the time, and by the time I reach my domicile or whatever you may call it, I am completely worn out. They used to come down to breakfast and not go up until bed time at night but on Dawtie's account I have to travel up & down half a dozen times a day and frequently when I go up at her bedtime I stay up & take my tea by myself up there & two or three times I haven't had any. Now this is a long tirade about nothing, filling up my letter with such stuff. We are thankful Mr. M. is up & will probably be able to start for Rome in two or three days.
[1870-02-13 Bertha M (Naples) to Mrs. Manny]

2. SORRENTO, FEBRUARY 11, 1870

The Drakes left Naples for Sorrento on February 11th. *"Mrs. Merrill, Dawtie, Mr. Drake & I went by car to Castellemare. Took carriage & drove to Sorrento. Had 8 horses abreast and a nice boy behind. Beautiful drive. View of Bay of Naples & Vesuvius. Great seamed mountain sides along our road, boat loads of oranges, men standing up to row. Were caught in a slight rain. Went to Hotel Framontara. Took luncheon. Afterwards, drove to Massa, which drive ended in an orange grove. Bought. Road work. After tea, the night was glorious. Our piazzas overlooked the bay."* [Bertha M's Diary, 1870-02-11]

Bertha M described Sorrento to Mrs. Manny in a letter:

> *Sorrento is the most beautiful spot on earth. And it is very, very beautiful. The road from Naples there is the finest we have yet travelled. Our hotel was on the cliff that makes an abrupt descent right straight into the bay. We stood on the little piazza of our rooms & lost ourselves in wonder & admiration. The beautiful bay was covered with white caps, for the wind blew briskly, everywhere boat loads of oranges were being propelled by men standing & rowing (they always stand here to row). Vesuvius loomed up right in front across the bay and all along the coast (we were in a crescent & could see both ways) were cunning villages, snuggled cozily at the foot of tremendous cliffs, seamed & scarred by volcanic action & earthquakes. We saw a scarlet geranium there, the trunk of which was twelve inches round, a beautiful little tree. The orange trees at Sorrento are large trees like our largest apple trees, covered with great golden oranges, fine to look at but very sour. I haven't tasted a sweet orange in Italy excepting the little mandarins, a little orange we don't see in America.* [1870-02-13 Bertha M (Naples) to Mrs. Manny]

And in her diary, *"Walked about Sorrento. Dawtie & her papa had a donkey ride. The view from the pension. The huge geranium. Band of music played during dinner - Star Spangled Banner, Yankee Doodle, Hail Columbia, etc."* [Bertha M's Diary, 1870-02-12] Bertha M wrote to Mrs. Manny about the "donkey ride".

> *Dawtie & her Papa had a grand donkey ride. He went for the animals & returned mounted on one, with a driver hanging to its tail and another for ... with a driver ditto! Papa loomed up so tall on the little animal & looked so comically that Dawtie shouted & danced & finally went off in an inward shaking laugh that set us all off. I never saw her so tickled. Father looked like Don Quixote. He & the little girl went off & had a good time. The drivers industriously twisting the poor donkey's tails. I would hate to be a donkey or a woman here.*
> [1870-02-13 Bertha M (Naples) to Mrs. Manny]

3. NAPLES, FEBRUARY 12, 1870

Bertha M wrote on February 12th, *"[H]ad the grandest drive home from Sorrento to Naples, wind so strong it blew the water like dust along the bay. Reached the hotel safely. Found all right."* [Bertha M Diary, 1870-02-12]

Bertha M painted a beautiful picture of the Mediterranean, *"Scarcely less restless than that of human life".*

> *We are having a great treat. Then has been a heavy wind storm this week and the waves of the tideless Mediterranean are as high & glorious as those of old Atlantic. They roll in & break & dash up twenty feet or more. Just imagine it. We sit in our comfortable parlor with windows to the floor & look over this ever surging Riviera di Chiaja across the villa Reale which is very narrow (but long), see all the fashion & the world right into this tempestuous sea. Scarcely less restless than that of human life under our windows. The waves are breaking so beautifully about as far from us as Mr. Skilling's house is from you, only we are elevated & look right down on it.*
> [1870-02-13 Bertha M (Naples) to Mrs. Manny]

Bertha M wrote again the next day to Mrs. Manny of the beautiful experience on the Mediterranean.

After I finished my letter to you, we walked down to the shore and it was magnificent. Just as furious as old ocean in a great storm only the wind was warm and balmy & we stood on a high parapet against which the waves broke, sprinkling us with the spray.

I don't think I told you of a very singular effect we saw on our way home from Sorrento. We were pretty high on the mountain road so that we couldn't see the roughness of the waves but there must have been some and the wind would sweep along over the surface & break the crest of the wave (I suppose) into light spray so that it looked exactly like a windy day at home rolling up clouds of dust from the road. It was very curious & new. We enjoyed it all the way home.
[1870-02-14 Bertha M (Naples, Rome) to Mrs. John Manny]

4. ROME, FEBRUARY 15, 1870

On February 15th, "*Left Naples at 9:30 A.M. Didn't feel well and yet had a pleasant ride. Lunched in cars. Changed cars at Isoletto. Had some very beautiful affects of sunlight & shade. Arrived in Rome at 8:00 P.M. and had our old rooms in Hotel de Romo.*"

The Drakes returned to Rome and, clearly, this second visit was very much to their liking.

Here we are again and it was very nice to find ourselves located in the same rooms. We didn't expect it. We telegraphed for rooms & the waiter and chambermaids were standing smiling at the door. Fires were lit in each room and we felt as if we had come home. We have a private parlor with a piano in it, so I opened it & played a tune & the rest danced a jig while the supper was being brought up. Our waiters everywhere are the most immaculate young men in black dress coat & pants, spotless shirt fronts and cravats, hair and mustache faultless.

I am even more pleased this time with Rome than I was before. I thought we had done it pretty thoroughly, but today we have seen several new things. Yesterday, we went to the top of the Capitol, a place we did not succeed in reaching before. Mr. Van Metes(?) obtained a permit some way and we all went up on the strength of it. The grandest view of Rome that can possibly be had. The Capitol stands on an eminence and, on one side, we looked upon the Rome of the Caesars, on the other, the Rome of the Popes. The surrounding campagna, the nearer range of mountains of classic fame, the farther peaks of the Apennines, old father Tiber winding round & the blue sky above combined to form an unsurpassable panorama. There is a great bell in the Capitol that is rung only at the beginning of carnival or at the death of the Pope.
[1870-02-14 Bertha M (Naples, Rome) to Mrs. John Manny]

Bertha M wrote of the unique experience of receiving the Pope's blessing, a Pope with "*a beautiful expression.*"

I am almost sanctified having received the blessing of the Pope eight times. Today we have a very fine view of him. He went in state to open an Ecclesiastical Art Exhibition, attended by his Cardinals in their magnificent carriages and by his full companies of cavalry, the Gardia Nobile, & his chamberlains. They passed us as they went and when they returned, we happened to be coming out of the Vatican just at his private entrance. There is a large courtyard paved with stone & a company of infantry was drawn up in line. With a whirl & clatter and dash, in rolled the dozen or more elegant carriages with four horses, two or three footmen (some two, some three) & coachmen lining, in galloped the horsemen in circles, then they drew up on either side, rattle went the drums, down tumbled the soldiery on their knees and enter the carriage of this holiness, scarlet & gold drawn by six black horses. There were only 5 or 6 of us there and I didn't quite know whether to go down on my knees or not. But he blessed us and descended from the carriage. He passed into a little anteroom with glass from floor to ceiling & we went nearer expecting to see his back going up stairs but lo! He stepped to the window & bestowed another blessing on us. He

looked straight into my eyes and I was so astonished that I made him a most profound courtesy. Watts Merrill saw it all & he was very much tickled. He said he "thought that astonishing courtesy of Mrs. Drake rather overcame the Pope." Joking aside, we greet him always with thorough respect. He has a beautiful expression.
[1870-02-14 Bertha M (Naples, Rome) to Mrs. John Manny]

5. VENICE, FEBRUARY 26, 1870

After visiting Rome, the Drakes went to Florence at 7 P.M. in the evening on February 18th riding all night by train and reaching Florence at 7:30 A.M. the next morning. From Bertha M's extensive diary entries, they were very busily engaged in their extensive sightseeing.

After one week in Florence, the Drakes left at 4 P.M. on February 26th for Venice. Regarding their trip to Venice, Bertha M recorded, "*Had a rather hard ride. Had to change cars. Reached Venice at 10:30. Our rooms not ready at Damili. Had to go to Beau Rivage. Beautiful rooms. Excellent fare. Came from depot in gondolas. Not at all disappointed in Venice.*" She was very taken in by Venice, as her next diary entry reveals.

> *Beautiful Venice, far surpasses all my expectations. In afternoon, walked to Piazza San Marco. Saw Ducal Palace, St. Mark's Lion, the colosius, Tombola, the Rialto Bridge of Light. Came home in Gondola. Peaceful & beautiful, the gliding motion. Saw crowds pass to the carnival ball. Went out for a few minutes in evening to see the Piazza. The most brilliant scene I ever saw. Mask, colored lamps, pagodas, cluster of gas lamps, bands of music, crowds of people, girl water carriers.*
> [Bertha M Diary]

6. TRIESTE, MARCH 3, 1870 & ADELBERG, MARCH 7, 1870

Left Venice for Trieste at 8 A.M. Rode to depot in a gondola. Rode in cars all day until 9 P.M., 133 miles. Reached Trieste safely. Hotel de La Ville. [Bertha M Diary]
Got up at 5 A.M. Started at 7 for Adelberg. Left a roaring, furious wind storm, broke our window. Reached Adelberg in a driving snow storm. [Bertha M Diary]

7. VIENNA, MARCH 8, 1870

Left Adelberg at 9 A.M. for Vienna. Had a long day's ride until 9:30 P.M. but most beautiful cliffs, mountains, gorges, churches, villages, castles, sometimes summer, sometimes winter.

Bertha M wrote of her visit to the Emperor's stable in Vienna. "*Instead of doing churches & antiquities, we went to riding schools, Emperor's stables, harness rooms, carriage rooms, etc., etc. The Emperor has 600 horses and about 300 carriages. I can't conceive what he does with them all. But we saw in the Lichtenstein gallery & the Belvidere some of the finest pictures we have yet seen, real gems.*" [1870-03-18 Bertha M (Munich) to Mrs. Manny]

8. SALZBURG, MARCH 15, 1870

Bertha included in her diary: "*Started at 9 A.M. for Salzburg. Had a glorious ride through mountains & vales. Reached Salzburg at 5:30 P.M. Took a beautiful long walk. Heard the bell chime. Saw a glorious sunset & moonrise. Good supper – fried trout. Fine hotel. Nice rooms.*" [Bertha M Diary]

Bertha M was more effusive about Salzburg in her letter to Mrs. Manny.

> *But Salzburg! I can't begin to tell you how beautiful it is. We saw it differently from most travelers. It is a favorite summer resort but we saw it wrapped in its winter mantle of white. A very pretty town snuggled down in the midst of the Salzburg Alps. We were enchanted. Mountains all around us from 4000 to 8000 feet high covered with snow from foundation to summit. A clear pebbly bedded river winding through the town. Chimes of bells playing Mozart's music and the most*

glorious sunset & moonrise. These were some of the things we enjoyed there. And added to these was the best hotel we have had. An immense summer palace beautifully furnished & no one in it but ourselves & the proprietor & servants. And trout! Trout every meal! Splendid trout!! If we live we are going there again next summer when we take our Swiss trip.
[1870-03-18 Bertha M (Munich) to Mrs. Manny]

Bertha M mentioned that the gentlemen took their leave of the ladies to visit the mines near Salzburg.
Mr. Drake & Mr. Watts Merrill visited the salt mines near Salzburg but as it necessitated putting on a sort of male attire, fastening on a leather apron behind & sliding down (sitting down) 1800 feet!!!, & after visiting the salt lakes, riding straddle a narrow wooden horse 6000 feet in order to get out! I concluded not to go, although ladies do frequently. Don't you think I was wise that time?
[1870-03-18 Bertha M (Munich) to Mrs. Manny]

9. MUNICH, MARCH 17, 1870

Left Salzburg at 9:30 A.M. for Munich. Snowed nearly all day but finally turned to a settled rain. Reached Munich at 4:15 P.M.

Bertha M 1870-03-18 letter from Munich

It was cold and snowy when the Drakes arrived in Munich on March 17th. But, it appears, they held their own during their trip.
We came through the driving snow to Munich, the seat of the Fine Arts. We are at the "Four Seasons" very comfortably located, handsome rooms, good fare, which is a blessing for it has poured down rain all day & I have had a raging headache. Indeed, I have scarcely been free from one since we left Trieste. But I am gaining flesh & Dawtie is "immense", as our valet, a Venetian, styled everything to which he called our attention.
[1870-03-18 Bertha M (Munich) to Mrs. Manny]

While in Munich, Bertha M got some shopping in – *"Mrs. Merrill & I had a little rampage in morning."*
But, otherwise, Munich was cold and dreary.

10. RATISBON/REGENSBERG, MARCH 25, 1870

Annunciation day. Left Munich at 9 for Ratisbon. Reached Ratisbon or Regensberg at 3:45 P.M. Dined & went out with Valet de Place. Our hotel, the Golden Cusp(??), is 500 years old. Don John of Austria was born here. Charles 5th stayed here 1546 A.D. Went to see the Rath haus or City Hall. Old conference room, old window glass. Emperor's chair 600 years old. Gallery in corner for ladies. Room with old portraits & emperor's canopy & flag. Room with old gobelin tapestry & needle work of 14 centaurs. Medallions representing scenes in man's life – one with a bridle in his mouth, jealousy, etc. Then the room filled with beautiful models of churches, houses, etc. then room lined with Irish art or curled maple, very fine. Then to the prison & the torture chamber. The rack, the triangle, the Spanish ass. The chair with spikes ... I was put in mind of Giovannie Cassani who said "the man died of anger or rather of want to have his dinner." [Bertha M Diary]

In her letter to Mrs. Manny, Bertha M described in more detail the trip to the Rath Haus.

At Ratisbon we looked from our hotel windows right into the open square where formerly the tournaments were held. The hotel itself is 800 years old. Emperor Charles 5th once staid there and ... John of Austria was born there in room no. 15. We had 20. In the old rath haus we saw the torture chamber, saw a rack, ladder on which the victim was pulled up and down, revolving triangular ... (if you may call them so) to tear the flesh of the back a triangle, a Spanish ass, a chair filled with spikes in which the sufferer sat with a heavy weight in his lap and one on each foot. I sat, in it a minute, but as the valet said, "you could not perceive the sentiment of it at first."
[1870-04-02 Bertha M (Dresden) to Mrs. Manny]

11. NUREMBURG, MARCH 26, 1870

Place of tournaments just before the hotel. Market place now. Can see that from our window & the spires of the old cathedral. One of the old towns where the patricians used to watch their enemies & to which they retreated in time of danger. Drove to Walhalla, a temple of fame. Snow everywhere on our way out. All gone on our way back. It really seems as if spring had begun. Rode all afternoon to Nuremburg. Reached Nuremburg at 7:30 P.M. Bavarian hotel. [Bertha M Diary]

On their trip to Wallhalla from Ratisbon, Bertha M wrote*: "The ground was so covered with snow on our way out that it dazzled my eyes so I could not look out at all and on our way home, there was not a vestige of snow anywhere. I never saw such a sudden & entire disappearance."* [1870-04-02 Bertha M (Dresden) to Mrs. Manny]

12. PRAGUE, MARCH 29, 1870

Rose 5:30. Left at 5 A.M. for Prague. Very long & tedious ride. Rached Prague at 7:30. All day the road lay through fields of snow. Poor supper but good bed. [Bertha M Diary]

Rose at 5:30. Left at 7. Rode all day until 9:30 P.M. with very poor dinner & reached Prague very tired, poor little girl used up. Prague has 160,000 inhabitants and is very old & queer. The church pointed as the new cathedral, the last one built is 300 years old. The oldest church is a synagogue 1300 years old. [1870-04-02 Bertha M (Dresden) to Mrs. Manny]

13. DRESDEN, MARCH 31, 1870

Writing from Dresden, Bertha M describes her views of Munich and Dresden, especially the team that was drawing the stone coal, *"a dog and a woman harnessed together."*

> *One of the curious sights [in Munich], there was bands of old women cleaning the streets with shovels – mud scrapers & brooms, instead of men. Dresses up to their knees, big shoes & coarse yarn stockings, 30 or 40 in a row. They worked, no matter what the weather. I also saw a woman sawing a load of wood at a front door and another carrying it in, in a great basket, on her back. Here in Dresden, we see everywhere wagons of stone coal, drawn by a dog and a woman harnessed together. I have tried to get a picture of it but was told that government would not allow that team to be photographed.*
> [1870-04-02 Bertha M (Dresden) to Mrs. Manny]

During their stay in Dresden, Bertha M and Bertha had their "quiet moments", interspersed with Bertha's insightful remarks, *"Mamma, did you have that kind of a face when I was a baby?"* Evidently, Bertha M looked cross.

> *This morning I wasn't very well pleased & I guess I looked cross. Dawt said, "Mamma, did you have that kind of a face when I was a baby?" I knew what she meant but wanted to see what she would say. "What kind of a face, Dawtie, how does it look?" She stopped a few seconds & said, "Well! I should call it - - - rather remarkable." Then said she didn't love me to plague her. She said, "That is a fairy tale I think." "How is it a fairy tale?" "Well! You know, a fairy tale - - is not altogether true is it?" That was putting the matter modestly I think.*
> [1870-04-02 Bertha M (Dresden) to Mrs. Manny]

D. APRIL – JUNE, 1870

1. LEIPZIG, APRIL 6, 1870

The Drakes arrived at Leipzig 10 P.M. on April 6th but were up for breakfast and out sightseeing in the new morning. (The pace of their travels never seemed to wane very much.)

2. BERLIN, APRIL 9, 1870

Left Leipzig at 8:30 A.M. Had a pleasant ride to Wietenberg at 10:30 and then to Berlin
The highlight in Berlin was the Berlin Aquarium, which Bertha M described in great detail.

> *It is a very large building several stories high, laid out as immense grottoes going downhill gradually & ascending again. First, we came to the snake room, through which we passed as fast as my feet could put me. The others lingered to look. I don't see how they could. Then we came to the bird room, every variety you ever heard of there. Many of them building their nests and others sitting on their eggs. So you could see all the habits & customs of any bird you wished. They were all singing and chattering, such a noise! But some of the notes were so exquisite that I could hardly tear myself away. The view I send you shows a little arrangement for the fishes. These bright places are the tanks for the fishes. Right in the rocky walls (made so naturally that you can hardly believe that they are artificial walls) are sets of plate glass (you can see how that is) through which you look and see fish of every variety. A picture of the fish in the tank with its name etc. on the sill of the window. The water is as clear as crystal with fresh air supplied all the time and salt water when necessary. Eels, frogs, codfish, every kind of fish are here in perfection. We saw a cod making a supper of a cunner.*
>
> *The tanks of gold fish are particularly fine and there was one tank of the loveliest fish – blue, red, gold, green, the rarest variegated colors. The prettiest fish possible. Then the anemones!!!! It isn't of any use to use words in describing them you know I can't do the thing justice. The delicacy, the difference of colors and of form. I came near staying there. I do believe all of you would have stayed there a month. There were beavers in full operation. Crocodiles, etc. At our turning, we*

came upon a grotto of white stalactites, illuminated by a red light - very pretty. And at another was an exact representation of the Blue Grotto at Capri. As we could not enter the real one, on account of storms when at Naples, this was a very good substitute. [1870-04-19 Bertha M (Berlin) to Mrs. Manny]

Just prior to leaving Berlin with the intention of eventually going to Paris, Bertha M wrote that they were all getting vaccinations against smallpox. The smallpox pandemic was believed to have started in Paris in 1870 and continued until 1874.

We were all vaccinated this afternoon. We hear 100 are dying a week of small pox in Paris. And as it is imperative for some of the party to go and we want to spend May there, so we have been cut, 7 places in my arm.
[1870-04-19 Bertha M (Berlin) to Mrs. Manny]
Getting vaccinated in 1870 was an unpleasant experience.

3. POTTSDAM, APRIL 15, 1870

Went at 8:00 to Pottsdam. Cold & cloudy. Saw rooms of Fritz the Great just as he left them. Picture of Barberini measuring standard for Fredrick Wilhelm 1st grenadiers, these all in winter palace. Piano, flutes & music written by Fred. Great. Beautiful comfortable rooms. One filled with silver ornamentation. Wrote at the King's own table. ... Wrote this on the desk where Humboldt wrote most of his cosmos at Charlottenhof, residence of the crown prince afterwards King William 1st. [Bertha M Diary]

4. AMSTERDAM, APRIL 28, 1870

After Pottsdam, the Drakes visited Hamburg (April 16th) and Hanover (April 22nd). The Drakes arrived in Amsterdam on April 28th and had a royal welcome two days later. In her diary on April 30, Bertha M wrote: "*Went to see docks and accidentally stumbled on to a ship launch. Saw King of Holland and all his principal officers, splendid launch.*" What a serendipitous experience!

At Amsterdam we went to the museum and on our way noticed that flags were flying everywhere. On our arrival at the museum, we found the king & queen of Holland was visiting Amsterdam and that the queen was expected at the gallery in a few minutes but, as we were an American party, we might enter provided we kept out of her sight. So the officials in full costume and white kidgloves, kept us moving from one room to another in a manner rather inglorious than otherwise. But I think her majesty wanted to see the western barbarians for, as we were comfortable seated in a room she had already visited, she entered attended only by her chamberlain. We all rose (10 of us), she made us a profound curtsey, told her chamberlain in French to tell us not to disturb ourselves & went out. She is apparently a nice lady but taking the queen, her lords & ladies all together, I think we were the best looking party, although we didn't have on our other dresses.

The next day Mr. Merrill & son went to look at pictures. Mrs. Sawyer & daughter wanted to write letters, so the rest of us decided to go & look at the locks. There was a crowd about the door but we drove grandly up, were received by bowing officials, we walked innocently in, but the courier was stopped for our tickets! Of course, we had none but, as it was an American party, we were politely shown to good places. We found we had stumbled on a launch of a man of war to be presided over by the King and we had entered at the door for the state dignitaries etc., "where ignorance is bliss", etc. The marine guard and ourselves were the only ones in the courtyard & we had a good view of the King, Crown Prince, High Admirals, Generals, etc. We joined their procession and went along out in full view of the assembled multitudes across a bridge etc. I wonder what the folks thought of us. It looked like rain(?) & we didn't have on our other dresses again, while the King and officers were in their fullest, grandest uniforms. Soon we came to the sanctum sanctorum and their the man insisted on our tickets but a gentleman high in authority came up said something in Dutch about Americans and assisted us up the steps to a good place

again. We heard the King make his speech, in good Dutch I guess, saw him with his royal hand knock away the last prop & safely & majestically the fine vessel glided out into the harbor amid the cheers of all. Were we not fortunate?
[1870-05-05 Bertha M (Brussels) to Mrs. Manny]

5. HAARLEM, APRIL 29, 1870

Between Hanover and the Hague, the Drakes visited Haarlem and saw the tulips.

I believe I did not tell you of our trip to Haarlem to see the famous tulips. We went by carriage and on the way stopped at a model farm belonging to the Burgomaster of Haarlem Lake. Ploughing, harrowing & almost everything else is done by a steam engine. I believe they do not yet milk cows by steam. We saw them sawing wood by steam but I don't think they cut as much as they consumed during the process. We visited the dairy, the cheese rooms, the stables, the chicken yard etc. The cows, 75 in number, had been sent out to pasture for the summer. They all had coats on like the fine horses at home to protect them from the chill of the spring nights and from the flies of summer.

When we reached Haarlem and the tulip garden, the first sight really dazzled the eyes, not mine only but the stronger ones of our party. Imagine a circular bed about 23 feet in diameter almost a solid mass of the brightest scarlet except the centre which was of white tulips, the petals edged with the most delicate pink, then another bed of scarlet & of canary colored tulips, then another of variegated magenta & white called the standard silver. These were the rarest bulbs. But there were acres of tulips & 50 varieties. And acres of hyacinths & lilies of the valley!!! & jonquils & every other species of bulb. Then the green house, it was fairy land. One deep pink azalea had over 5000 blossoms. They were so close that we could not see a green leaf or branch of tree. Another of violet color & one of white were almost as perfect. It was a most beautiful sight. Don't you think you would all have liked to see it?
[1870-05-05 Bertha M (Brussels) to Mrs. Manny]

6. HAGUE, APRIL 30, 1870

Little Dawtie four years old today. Raining. ... In afternoon, at 4:30, we started for the Hague. Very nice ride in cars. Reached the Hague at 6:30. [Bertha M Diary]

7. ROTTERDAM, MAY 2, 1870

Huis ten Bosch (House in the Woods)

Went to "house in the woods", private residence of the Queen of Holland. Japanese rooms, with wall paper & furniture all embroidered by hand. Beautiful ornaments on ceiling. Japanese children. On that wall large birds, etc., in high relief. Drove to royal bazaar. Japanese & Chinese curiosities. Left at 5:35 for Rotterdam. Very nice ride. At one time saw 73 windmills at once. Reached Rotterdam at 7:00 P.M. [Bertha M Diary]

8. ANTWERP, MAY 3, 1870 & BRUSSELS, MAY 5, 1870

Dined on board. Reached somewhere at 2:50 P.M. Took cars & arrived at Antwerp at 5:30.
Left Antwerp at 4:50 P.M. for Brussels. Reached there at 5:50.
On May 9, 1870, Went to Waterloo. [Bertha M Diary]

9. PARIS, MAY 10, 1870

Started at 9:30 for Paris. Peasant trip. Reached Paris 5 P.M. Wagram Hotel. Most exquisite
sunset. Beautiful view of Tuileries. [Bertha M Diary]

Returning to Paris, the Drakes focused a portion of their time shopping for the latest fashions with Bertha M going out on several rampages. This lengthy letter certainly conveyed the frustrations of 19th century shopping for ladies attire.

This has been the hardest two weeks. We haven't seen anything or done anything excepting one day at Versailles – since we came to Paris excepting climb stairs and hunt up despicable, abominable, not to be trusted for an instant, trades people, who take up ones time, perjure themselves without the slightest compunction & put everyone who comes in contact with them in a perfect fever of vexation and disappointment. Just to give you an idea, we expected to leave tomorrow, can't until Wednesday just because things won't come home!

The other ladies are getting up their "return home" wardrobe so of course it takes their dressmakers some time but I only have two travelling dresses that were faithfully promised for last Wednesday. None came. Saturday morning, Brother Drake and I took a carriage. Drove to my dress maker – then to Dawtie's travelling costume maker, then to hurry up Mrs. Sawyer's hoop skirts, then to Dawtie's dress maker (she is having buff linen dresses made for the warm weather). Then to her underclothing woman. There to her shoemaker, then to my shoe maker, then to Mr. Drake's hatter, his tailor, his bootmaker, his shirt maker, to the glove maker, to the letter paper stamper (with monogram): nothing ready would be sent home at 12M – positively. Waited until half past ... then took another carriage & went the round again. This is no exaggeration. Things won't all be at the hotel before we were.

Back we went & in about an hour, they began to come. Bootmans. All the men 6 of them had about two pairs apiece – and every single pair was too tight. Such stamping! & among the young men such raving! Boston young fellows that wanted their boots long & wide - & all made in the tightest style. Coats off, perspiration pouring off their brows, pants rolled up to their knees, & new boots slaving(?) round the room. I have to laugh now at the remembrance & I often shall. Poor Frenchie couldn't understand a word of English & I had to do the talking for all but Mr. Watts. "Bless me! If I only could talk French for only a few minutes, wouldn't I blow him higher than a kite!"

In the midst of the commotion in came the shirtmaker. Then all six rushed to try on their "chemises" as the French have it. Here was confusion worse confounded. Mr. Arthur rampant. "Ms. Drake just tell that man my 'chemise' is too low in the neck or this unfortunate young man will be found standing up in it, dead of a sore throat." Man insists it is the latest fashion, so Arthur gets a turn down collar & one of his sister's beautiful lilac crape cravat & shows himself as a "sweet young miss" just out of her governesses hands.

Ring, ring – the tailor - Mr. Drake puts himself into his new suit & light grey overcoat with a black velvet collar & looks as if he had just stepped out of a fashion plato(?) – very becoming indeed, but decidedly having the "odeur de Boulevard."

Ring – Mad. Amadie's man with fifteen new ... & over dresses will send the waists(?) Sunday morning, & the rest of the dresses. I wish you could see the dresses. 2 velvet trimmed with elegant lace, a satin, a black silk trimmed with feathers tetete(?).

Ring. Mrs. Drake's modest parcel – one dress won't do at all. Down the five stories I race again, hail a passing carriage & go to the dressmaker. "Madame" is desolee but Madame shall have the dress at ten o'clock Monday without fail. We shall see!

Back to the hotel, no clothes for Miss Drake. Frantically, I tear away to Mad. Van Kaeker. "Oh, Madame, I assume I have just been crying about it myself! They will be ready without fail tonight." They did not come & I am afraid they won't. Sunday morning, all the time we were at breakfast, packages kept coming. I've piled them all up ready for fussing Monday morning.
[1870-05-29 Bertha M. Drake (London?) to Mrs. Manny]
(Exhausting just to read about this!)

While the Drakes were in Paris in May, they received news of their friend, Mr. Hodgman's, death. This took some pleasure out of the remembrances that they were to bring home from this trip.
Mr. Hodgman's death has taken all the heart out of Mr. Drake and he thinks, beside, that he may be needed at the "Boatman's" or may be able to be of use to Mrs. Hodgman. I felt very sorry for him yesterday. We were looking over our photographs, putting the names of places on them & packing them to leave in Paris. Everywhere in choosing them, Mr. Drake has said if no one else cared for them, he knew Charlie Hodgman would and anticipated so much pleasure in showing them to him & talking of the places where they were taken. And now, that joy in anticipation is gone. I am afraid he will hardly take any more comfort in them.
[1870-05-20 Bertha M (Paris) to Mrs. Manny]

Bertha M commented during this latest Paris stay that Bertha was under the weather and "*demoralized*" and quoted Bertha as saying "*I am very much disorder.*" (This from a four year old?)
Little Dawtie was quite under the weather for several days, but she is quite well again. She said this morning "I think Auntie Thebis(?) is wondering if I am not coming home soon & I think she wants to see me very much." A few minutes after "I do wish we lived in Winchester, don't you Mamma? Charlie has boys to play with but he likes to play with me too." I don't know whether I told you of her sitting in the corner rather cross & saying "I am very much disorder! Distressed! Disappointed!!" She is very much demoralized.
[1870-05-20 Bertha M (Paris) to Mrs. Manny]

After nearly one month there, Bertha M was ready to leave Paris. "*The past two days have been spent in vexation of spirit over dress makers, linen women, shirt makers, boot makers, etc. And now we are all packed, ready for a start.*" [Bertha M Diary] The Drakes then travelled to Geneva on June 5th, Chamonix on June 12, Brieg on June 13th, Lugano on June 15th, Menaggio (on Lake Como) on June 17th, and Colico (on Lake Como) on June 19th.

10. GENEVA, JUNE 5, 1870
Geneva is beautiful. From our windows we look directly on the Lake as blue as the summer sky & the mountains are just across the lake in full view. Mt Blanc is there & Friday we had a glorious view of the "Monarch". We have not seen his majesty since & we were very fortunate, for they say he can be seen from here only about 60 times a year.
[1869/1870-06-5/12 Bertha M to Mrs. Manny]

Mr. Joseph Lawyer wanted us to go out sailing with him on Lake Geneva yesterday, but the wind was very high - & Mr. Drake said he was afraid he would be sea sick. "Why no, papa, you would be Lake sick – not sea sick." She is beginning to be herself again but she has been quite unwell for the past three weeks. [1870-06-05 Bertha M To Mrs. Manny]

11. CHAMONIX, JUNE 12, 1870

I believe I said we were to start for Chamonix. It was so windy & stormy we waited until Tuesday. Then with our two carriages & our hand baggage we left Geneva leaving Frances there & our baggage. I was afraid I should have to miss the Mer de Glace on Dawtie's account – but I thought that was less of a disappointment than the nuisance would be to have Frances sitting opposite me for three days, listening to all we had to say & putting in her remarks as she invariably does on all occasions. We had a very delightful ride through beautiful scenery, shopped for an hour for the houses at Bonneville, a miserable little French Swiss village, but situated among the mountains, God's works around, perfect, excepting the men, and they are poor, unintelligent, deformed, undressed, dirty, beggars, most of them I mean. We took dinner at St. Martin's, on the Rhone and a waiter poured the gravy all down Dawtie's back spoiling her cloak & dress - fortunately, not her newest ones, but the only ones we had with us.

Without any other mishap, we reached Chamonix. Right before our windows in all its majesty was Mt. Blanc. Mountains snowcapped all around. The Arve River, a mountain torrent fed by a glacier, rushed noisily under our salon windows and I should have been content to have staid there all summer. The next morning we went to the Mer de Glace to my great delight, Dawtie went too. The rest of us on donkeys (each lady had a guide) and the little girl had a chair; a low chair with a place to rest her feet in front – placed securely on two stout poles. A guide before & behind carried it – the ends of the poles resting in loops at the end of steady leather straps passed round the guide's necks so the motion is very regular. They went as fast and even faster than the mules with a smooth even pace, and it was a very pretty sight (to at least) to see the little girl in her broad brimmed mountain hat with her sunny face, her little alpenstock[51] across her lap, mounting up, up, up, just ahead of us all the way. She wanted to ride a donkey very much so the last half hour her papa took her on his, and then there was at least one perfectly happy person in this world. Not expecting her to take this excursion, I only had her dainty Paris boots with her. So took a guide to carry her from Montanvert down to the Mer de Glace.

Mr. Drake & the young men left us & crossing the Mer de Glace went down the other side the "Mauvais Pas" as it is called. It is reported very dangerous, but Mr. Drake thinks the accounts very exaggerated. To be sure if one should slip one would be dashed to pieces but he says with ordinary care one need not slip. The descent is by steps cut in the face of the precipice with only a hand rail fastened to the rock, and nothing on the side next the falling down place. They put great nails in their shoes – for sometimes there is ice on the steps. How would you like to let Charlie try it? Dawtie wouldn't be carried down the mountain (It was so hard Mrs. Sawyer gave it up & went back) but her shoes were so thin that I insisted on her being carried on the ice. I poked up some of it with my alpenstock and she did enjoy eating it. Coming down to Chamonix again, I walked most of the way & it was well I did for one of the handles of Dawtie's chair slipped out of the bed & gave her a pretty hard bump. If she had not been strapped in, it would have been dangerous, for she would have tumbled over the steep .... If I had been on mule back she could not possibly have reached her, but as it was, the little maiden was soon solaced. We went, the rest of the way, safely, found Father Drake there before us.

...

Little Dawtie's mountain trip benefitted her wonderfully – restored her to her normal condition. She is performing monkey just now & squealing at a tremendous rate. You are all perfectly well

---

[51] An alpenstock is a long wooden pole with an iron spike tip, used by shepherds for travel on snowfields and glaciers in the Alps since the Middle Ages. It is the antecedent of the modern ice axe.

assured of our loves so no need to mention it. Only my little pet lamb sends you very many kisses.
[1870-06-05 Bertha M To Mrs. Manny]

12. BRIEG, JUNE 13, 1870

Brieg! A little old, dirty, Swiss village, situated in the midst of the loveliest scenery. After tea, Mr. Drake & I took a walk over the river to another village & enjoyed it much. About nine, the moon was flooding the whole scene with magical beauty. My front windows looked up a narrow street to the gateway of an old place built in the Moorish style, square with a great court in the centre, a dome & minaret on each corner. A post carriage came up, dashing up, hostess moving round with lanterns, bells on the horses jingling. The old gateway & a few looking Swiss Italians, made it seem like one of the splendid pictures of Wouvermans. Then from my side window I looked across to my little white village nestling among the alpine hills, sweeter & fairer a great deal by moonlight than daylight. I hope the exquisite beauty of the picture will never fade in my memory.
[1870-06-19 Bertha M (Lake Como) to Mrs. Manny]

13. LUGANO, JUNE 15, 1870

Lugano, Switzerland

Took steamer, steamed down Lake Maggiore to Luino. Carriage to Lugano. Perfectly splendid. Reached Lugano at 8 P.M. Hotel de Pare. View mountains & lake. Rains. ... Beautiful lake Lugano. [BMD Dirary]

14. MENAGGIO, JUNE 17, 1870

I am sitting at a window in Menaggio which looks right onto the mountain side. There is a small garden between but I think I could throw a stone across. The other side of the house is too sunny in the morning but most glorious in the afternoon. The walls of the garden go right down into the water. The steps are built out into the water and lead to the pretty row boats. Thus far, it is very like Venice. But the scenery is most beautiful. Lake Como has not been too much praised. Lake Lugano is almost, perhaps, quite as fine in a different style, being much wilder.
[1870-06-19 Bertha M (Lake Como) to Mrs. Manny]

Bertha M always seemed to have a keen eye for beauty and details, as she related. *"The bouquets on our dinner table are composed of oleander & magnolia grandiflora. Just beside our windows are two magnolia trees as large as large maple trees, covered with the most perfect creamy white flowers when fully open as large as dinner plates, perfume of a delicate lemon flavor. The oleanders are great trees, masses of bloom. I wish I could, by any magic, have you just look at the garden I saw yesterday at Bellagio. Cherries! No words in which to tell you of them..."* [1870-06-19 Bertha M (Lake Como) to Mrs. Manny]

And Bertha always seemed to be a source of joy and entertainment, *"Eyes open & sparkling"* with her toy horse, flowers, and pocket full of stones.

[1870-06-19 Bertha M (Lake Como) to Mrs. Manny]

P.S. If you could just see the child this minute. She has come in from a walk, her toy horse decorated with flowers & her pocket full of stones which she collects for me everywhere. Eyes open & sparkling. All the emphasis possible to be put in, "Well Mamma!! Beautiful butterflys flying wound and birds singing & lizards playing around & splendid cherry trees, splendid! Do you hear, Mamma? Splendid!!! It was just like a picnic and we ought to have taken our dinner & you with Papa & me, and here's the kinds house & he's a very dear old horse. And it was splendid Mamma just like a fair." Much she knows of fairs.
[1870-06-19 Bertha M (Lake Como) to Mrs. Manny]

15. COLICO, JUNE 19, 1870
After dinner, we climbed the terrace belonging to the old palace, pretty hard climb, but the view more than paid for heat & weariness. We looked right down into the nicest old monastery with its well-kept orchard and fields, beautifully laid out garden, luxuriant barn yard & the grand old cloisters surrounding a court from the centre of which rose the lofty campanile, filled with its chime of bells whose soft music fell on the summer evening air at the "angelus" hour. On the other side we overlooked the lovely valley Bregaglia while all around the mountains seemed almost to bend in protection. Valley & mountain dotted everywhere with the graceful Campaniles which you know from a distinctive feature of Statrass(?) scenery. This Italian Switzerland is very fair.
[1870-06-26 Bertha M (Lucerne) to Mrs. Manny]

16. SPLUGEN PASS, APRIL 21, 1870
The Drakes left Lake Como, going north over the Splugen Pass on April 21st and arriving at Zurich on June 24th and then Lucerne on June 26th.

Anniversary of wedding day – wooden. Left Chiavenna at 7 A.M. Had a most glorious ride through or over the Splugen Pass. Loveliest flowers of every shape & hue. Deep blue gentians, light blue cunning little flowers. Mountain pink, etc. Dawtie presented me with a pretty bouquet of violet flowers, picked on top of the Splugen & wished me many happy returns. [Bertha M Diary]

17. ZURICH, JUNE 24, 1870

Went to Schaffhausen to Falls of Rhine. Felt very miserable all the way but after going down at the falls & getting lunch, felt better. Rain came up & cooled air. Pleasant ride home. Scenery looked like the prettiest New England views. I hope I shall never forget the beautiful storm of today as it came down on Lake Zurich, the lake blue green covered with white caps. The distant hills covered with a dark purple veil. Then the rain began like a cloud of dust reaching down to the river bank. Then spreading along the shore. Then the rainbow on the hill over the village. The clouds lifting afterwards & the sunshine following. Beautiful smiling lake of Zurich.
[Bertha M Diary]

18. LUCERNE, JUNE 26, 1870

In the Rheinthal on our way to Regatz at one time the(?) ruined castles were in view, perched on every apparently inaccessible point there was. How they were ever built or how people lived there is more than I can imagine. Then to Regatz, wonderful gorge & hot baths. Then to Zurich, on the margin of fair Zurich's waters. Each place now as we reach it seems the most beautiful we have seen. But I suppose we shall reach the climax at Interlachen, our next stopping place.

Here at the Schweizer Hof we have same rooms occupied by Emperor Napoleon when he was here. I am afraid they will make us pay Imperial prices for them.

Mt. Pilatus & Lake Lucerne

The Lake Lucerne is directly before us, Mt. Rigi to the left, Mt. Pilatus to the right and all between the rugged snow clad alp peaks. The gentlemen excepting Mr. Sawyer intend making the ascent of Rigi tomorrow. I have about decided not to go but steam down the lake instead to see the places made famous by Tell & his compatriots. Mt. Pilatus tradition reports is so called because Pilate, driven by remorse, found relief by throwing himself into a lake at its summit and, as it is the outlier of the alps, it catches & holds all the storm clouds from North & West so that its head is almost always veiled which the natives said was caused by the unquiet spirit of the lost Pilate. Just now it is grand with its bold bald crags against a crimson sky.

We have been to Scotch service today in a roman Catholic church with all its decorations and it looked so queer to see over the protestant minister's head a shield with great white letters Hilf Maria Hilf!! (Help, Mary, Help!)
[1870-06-26 Bertha M (Lucerne) to Mrs. Manny]

E. JULY – SEPTEMBER, 1870

From July through September, the Drakes had a very busy travel schedule in which they visited: Brienz, Interlaken, Fribourg, Baden Baden, Wiesbaden, Cologne, Paris, London, Oxford, Leamington, Edinburgh, Ireland, and England.

1. BRIENZ & INTERLAKEN, JULY 1, 1870

We reached Brienz at 5:30 P.M., rowed across Brienz Lake to Giessbach. I had put Dawtie to sleep in the carriage so as to keep her awake at night for the illumination. We climbed the hill for twenty minutes to the hotel & if I had not used up all my superlatives, I should use them now. The Lake below, the mountains either side, the beautiful cascade, a most lovely garden with flowers of all sorts, walks shady retreats, arbors, swings, etc., and a first class hotel and by that I mean better than any hotel I was ever at in America. We managed to keep the little girl awake until 10 P.M. when the waterfall was illuminated. I can't describe that but it is called the prettiest sight in Europe & I believe it is. I'll have to try & tell you about it when I see you.

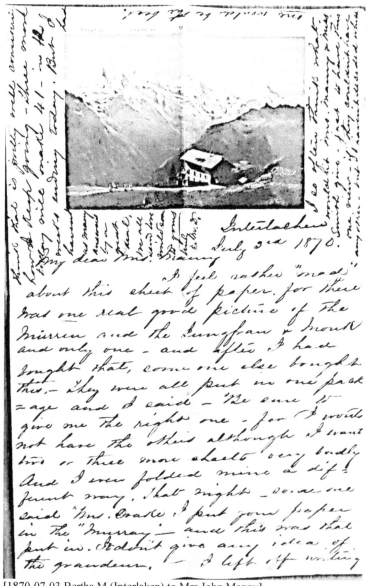

[1870-07-03 Bertha M (Interlaken) to Mrs John Manny]

The next day we came down the lake to Interlaken and here we are, the beautiful Jungfrau directly opposite my window, clothed in her silvery dress, just now a soft bridal veil floating about her brow. The Wengern Alp , the black monk in view, the Heimwehfluh also, so called because the view from it is so lovely that one having once seen it, is "homesick" to get back to it.

Friday, Mr. Drake, Mr. Joseph, Mr. Arthur & I made the ascent of the Murren, the house you see in the picture is situated 5000 ft. above the surface of the valley. The ascent is much steeper than Rigi. We had a glorious view going up but at dinner it commenced to rain and we came down in a pouring storm. As it was so dreadfully wet, muddy & slippery, I had to ride down instead of walking as I intended and it was very hard indeed. The gentlemen walked and, as we, none of us took cold. I am glad of the experience.
[1870-07-03 Bertha M (Interlaken) to Mrs John Manny]

2. FRIBOURG, JULY 5, 1870
"Went to H. de Freibourg. Had a perfectly glorious ride over a fine road between shady trees to Viaduct de Grand Fey , finest railroad bridge I ever saw." [Bertha M Diary]

Grand Fey Viaduct, 1862

3. BADEN BADEN, JULY 9, 1870
The Drakes' travel schedule continued through the hot July weather, *"a regular crusade"* to use Bertha's words.

It is dreadfully, furiously hot. Dawtie, you know, has been seeing pictures & hearing stories of crusaders exposed to the heat of Syria, their sufferings there etc. Yesterday we were out driving, went to see a cascade and I was thinking how awfully dreadful it was but wouldn't speak for fear of raising complaints that otherwise the little one might not think of, when with a great sigh she said, "Mamma, I think this is a regular crusade." They say it is warmer than it has been for 12 years. Rather funny isn't it that we should catch the cold so unusual last winter & the heat this summer? I am getting so very fleshy too that I can't stand the heat at all. This week we have been to Thun, Berne, Freibourg, back to Berne, on to Basle, thence to Baden Baden, where it is beautiful & hot & mainly vile.
[1870-07-09 Bertha M (Baden Baden) to Mrs. Manny]

In Baden Baden and the environs, Bertha M continued to observe and write about the local population during their tours. Her account on this 4th of July day, in Germany, was amusing.

After breakfast, Misses Lily, Lizzie & Emma Wilson, Mr. Drake, I & their courier made an excursion to the Grindelwald glacier, a two-hour drive through the beautiful valley of Lichenthal, great alps each side, river flowing down center, smiling fields & orchards everywhere, brought us to the Hotel of the Bear where we took our chairs & guides. It is a much easier & more agreeable way than riding up on a mule or climbing on foot. We all sat down, except bro. D., were lifted by our porters & merrily off we went. I felt very sorry for my men on account of my weight but they were glad to get it to do and I met as I came down, a lady being carried up who didn't weigh less than 200 pounds.

You know these people over here, are up to all dodgers at getting money out of good-natured travelers like myself and so when we went round a corner, there stood two little maidens of about 5 & 8, one light haired, the other dark. Their arms about each other in a picturesque attitude. The little one holding a bunch of alpine roses, both singing "America", the tune I mean. I could not understand the words. It was very pretty and we gave them some pennies but we went on a few yards further and there were two more maidens exactly the same only not so pretty. We laughed at them & went on until we saw perched upon a rock a dirty faced boy of 5 or 6 as broad as he was long in his Dutch pantaloons. His feet as far apart as he could get them, his dirty hands folded over his little fat stomach with an expression of agony, howling through his nose The Star-Spangled Banner. Imagine this image on the side of a grand old glacier. It was so ridiculous that even our solid guides broke into a laugh but he won his pennies at least.

We reached the grotto out into the solid glacier for 120 feet, hundreds of feet of solid ice below us and hundreds of feet ice all above & around. It is of the most exquisite blue color. Indeed, down in the crevices & chasms of the glacier, it is the same only if you take the ice out it is like any other. Indeed, the ice houses of Paris are supplied from this glacier. It was illuminated with lamps & we followed sounds of music heard in the distance. At last, we reached in an alcove, two old women smiling as much as possible, bowing, playing on an old zither & trying to sing Yankee Doodle which they did with variations. The ludicrous old creatures, the sight was worth the francs we gave them.
[1870-07-09 Bertha M (Baden Baden) to Mrs. Manny]

The most enjoyable part of the Drakes' 4th of July day in Baden Baden was the playing of patriotic American songs.

I think I will devote the rest of this sheet to our 4th of July. It was a glorious day and we were startled at breakfast by salutes by cannon & band playing Star Spangled Banner, Pop Goes the Weasel, Dixie and other national airs. ...

We dined at the Bear, drank to the health of the President & absent friends, drove home, found three big stars & stripes floating in the summer air. At 10 P.M., another salute by cannon, playing by band, firing of rockets, very fine indeed. It closed by the band playing "Hail Columbia". When the 3 fountains in front of the hotel were turned on full force, the water reaching to the third story windows, one was illuminated with white, one with red, one with blue fire, it was really splendid. At the same time, from each corner of the grounds, red, white & blue Roman candles shot forth & from each side, rockets alternately & continually ascended, while the explosions echoed & re-echoed from the Jungfrau, Scheinegeplatz (Stechelberg?) & other mountains, making in all I suspect, the finest Hail Columbia that was played in that day in the world. The entire population of the Canton was there & believe & the grounds were filled with guests from the other hotels. It was enthusiastically applauded but there was no "encore". We supposed the Landlord did it and thought all the Americans would join in reimbursing him but we found the whole affair was gotten up by one American family. It must have been very expensive & was very fine.
[1870-07-09 Bertha M (Baden Baden) to Mrs. Manny]

4. WIESBADEN, JULY 16, 1870

The Drakes encountered some unexpected events which, it may be said, upset their travel plans (even though they did not seem particularly upset). "*All excitement. Napoleon has declared war on Prussia. All French & Germans have left Wiesbaden. Napoleon must bear all the responsibility of this war.*" [Bertha M Diary] Bertha M wrote to Mrs. Manny the next day about the chaos this caused.

> *France has declared war against Prussia, Russia against France. But I guess I won't discuss that for Mr. Drake will say what he has to, to Mr. Manny. There has been a regular stampede, every one gone from here – French one way, Prussians & Germans another. It will be a war of enthusiasm with the Prussians. As our waiter said today, "Not a Prussian would stay out of the army if he could." I think L. N.[52] stands a chance of being "wiped out." And we have to suffer, for instead of going to Paris as we intended, we have to go to Rotterdam & sail to England. So we have to be made sea sick because L.N. wants a row with Prussia.*

> *Last week we visited Strasbourg and as I looked at the magnificent fortifications, I wondered if it worthwhile to spend so much money on them and whether they even would be needed again. Today "the troops are marching on Strasbourg." I went to Strasbourg Monday, found the great clock a "big thing" but, if you are ever over there on a very scorching hot day, the hottest day you ever felt, and you have to ride 2 hours in the cars there & 2 hours back, don't go. It won't pay, even if you do see the stork's nests on top of the high old chimneys everywhere, big as a big basket with the storks & their young in full view and the tomb of Marshal Saxe representing him "descending with intrepid steps in the open grave awaiting him" & erected by Louis 15.*
> [1870-07-17 Bertha M (Brussels) to Mrs. Manny]

It seems clear from Bertha M's letter that no one believed that France stood a chance against the Germans, which is one reason why the idea of leaving the continent through Germany (instead of France) seemed prudent. Also, for a major war, there is no hint that the Drakes felt that they were in any particular danger. Bertha M wrote in her Diary on April 17, "*Russia declares war against France. Sunday. Pleasant & cool.*"

5. COLOGNE, JULY 18, 1870

Left Wiesbaden at 8:30 for sail down the Rhine. Horses of coachmen etc. all passing muster. Most delightful steaming down the river until 6 P.M., crowds on board. At Cologne, went to Hotel Disch. Everybody in confusion. Waiters all ordered to the army. Hotel keepers having laid in stores, ... to be ruined. A party of French were surrounded by the people & danced around. Took a walk, excited populace singing etc. all night. [Bertha M Diary]

6. PARIS, JULY 25, 1870

In spite of the commencement of the Franco-Prussian War, the Drakes decided to return to Paris.

> *I don't want you to think we're here because we ran away from the war. No, Ma'am! We followed the stampeders. Our trip was entirely completed according to plan laid down. Only we had not quite decided whether or not we should come to Paris before going to England. But as no one knows what complications may arise & we may not want to be here in October, we decided we had better come & look after Mr. Drake's money and my trunks which were here.*

> *Paris is very empty. No one here hardly in the streets & Champs Elysees. Mr. Skillings is not reported here yet. I do wish we could go home on the Liberia to Boston but I am afraid all the berths are taken. Mrs. Skillings only has three, just what we want. They may however have obtained some others since.*

---

[52] Charles-Louis Napoléon Bonaparte, i.e. Louis Napoléon (or Napoléon III).

One thing I gained by the war. I have always wanted to go to Aix la Chapelle but Mr. Drake couldn't see it. He didn't care to go & there wasn't enough there to go out of the way. I didn't urge it at all and lo! The other day the only way to get along free from troops etc. was through Aix. So we stopped there one night & until 2 the next day. And I wondered what you would give just to have that morning's experience.
[1870-07-25 Bertha M (Paris) to Mrs. Manny]

The war was also noticed by Bertha, who commented about it to her mother, who was certainly "amused".
She amused me the other day when we reached Brussels. She seated herself as soon as we got to our room & said "Well, I'm glad to be in this Brussels where the good Germans or the good Belgians, I don't know which exactly, keep the country in order. The King of Belgium says you can't come fighting on my land and I am very glad of that. For now the old emperor has only a very narrow place to send his army to battle." These are exactly her words & I supposed her nurse had been telling her all that & I asked her who told her it. "Oh! I hear you all talking in the cars." Of course, the war is the staple topic and who would think of a four-year-old taking in the situation.
[1870-07-25 Bertha M (Paris) to Mrs. Manny]

In her letter to Mrs. Manny, Bertha M included the following information about the suicide of Mr. Pope, a St. Louisan who was spending time in Paris. It was striking how Bertha M related this news.
Letters are opened so I make no remarks on passing events. Mr. Chas A Pope, a prominent St. Louis man who married Miss A. Fallon, committed suicide here the other day by cutting his jugular vein. A man less likely to do such a thing you can hardly imagine. I suppose Mr. Manny knows him. We were chatting with him last time we were here.
[1870-07-25 Bertha M (Paris) to Mrs. Manny]

Their return to Paris, "for the last time", necessitated some additional shopping for Bertha M and Bertha. George expressed "appropriate" interest in the shopping, as befitting a gentleman.
As this is my last visit here, I am getting 5 dresses made (moderate am I not?) & doing other shopping for Dawtie & self. Though I am having her dresses made after the same pattern I brought from home as I don't see anything here I like for her. When he [George] goes with me, he looks so a martyr that it is dreadful to see him & yesterday morning he asked my plans for the day. I sketched the day's work: dress maker, milliner, "Bon Marche" (that's a big store you know), etc. & said he might do himself the honor & pleasure of going with me. He looked at me a few seconds & said "from plague & famine, from sudden death, etc., etc., etc." I excused him.
[1870-07-31 Bertha M (Paris) to Mrs. Manny]

7. LONDON, AUGUST 6, 1870
Bertha M's shopping continued in London, with George continuing to be a nuisance.
And Mr. Drake!!! It is as much as he can stand when you want a particular thing & he always asked "what are you going for!" Of course, that was what I didn't know. I wanted to see what there was & I didn't do that. I made some mistakes by going with him – he looked so utterly miserable that I took the first thing I saw so as to get out of the store.
[1870-08-06 Bertha M (London) to Mrs. Manny]

Since Bertha M "discharged" her nurse/maid in Paris, she retained a new one in London, to take care of Bertha when George and Bertha M would go out. Of the new maid, she wrote: "*My new maid I like pretty well, although today she is dressed in a trail light blue silk dress & scalloped in big waves & trimmed with quillings of blue ribbons. And she is very large.*" [1870-08-14 Bertha to Mrs. Manny]

8. OXFORD & LEAMINGTON, AUGUST 13, 1870

Sunday. Went to Service at English church. The intoning nearly set me crazy. Wrote in afternoon. Dear little Dawt, very good all day. Blessed are the pure in heart, etc. She thinks King William of Prussia will go to heaven but Napoleon!! [Bertha M Diary, 1870-08-14]

While in Oxford, the Drakes went to the Bedleian Library where Bertha M made specific mention of seeing *"Sir Francis Drake's chair, made of his ship."* But, perhaps, more amusing is her notice and recording in her diary of the following verse:

> *If thou bee old,*
> *Thou hast more wytt.*
> *The younge menns wyves*
> *Will not be taught.*
> *And olde menn's wyves*
> *bee goode for naught.*

9. EDINBURGH & SCOTLAND, AUGUST 22 1870

[1870-08-22 Bertha M (Edinburgh) to Mrs. Manny]

You will think we are like the boy who liked each season the best as it came, for we almost say "Edinbro" is the prettiest place we have been. Naples with its bay & Capri, Interlaken with the ... & Monk, Geneva with its lake & wooded hill slopes – are each beautiful & each so different one cannot compare them. In front of our windows here is a garden which descends to a ravine, formerly a loch, now the railroad. We can see the smoke above the trees but not the cars. Then

there is an abrupt ascent covered mist trees & green grass. On the heights, Edinbro' Castle, really magnificent. Free church of Scotland College, Bank of England, Art galleries, and Old Edinburgh with its lofty houses and funny gables. The drives about are very beautiful, and the view from Arthur's seat extended & varied & fine.
[1870-08-22 Bertha (Edinburgh) to Mrs. Manny]

The Drakes travelled to various attractions while in Edinburgh. Bertha M provided the following account of their visit to Warwick castle.

Warwick Castle is just what you dream an old Baronial Hall should be. In perfect preservation, grand & stately. The reception room would put you in ecstasies. A perfectly proportioned room very large lofty floor walls & ceiling of age darkened oak, almost like mahogany; floor polished like glass. A few life size old portraits. Suits of armor shinning like gold & silver mounted in pedestals; Every variety of ancient weapons arranged with great taste on the walls. A magnificent fireplace that would just about fill the Skillings side of your parlor, 12 great high backed carved arm chairs on each side extending out into the room, to a massive old table making a cozy spot about the fire, yet not taking any perceptive space in the room. Stained glass windows & grouped banners in the corner. Shut your eyes & picture that. Next the Red Velvet room, the Cedar room, the gilt room, the chapel & so on. We saw the mace & armor of Warwick, the King Maker.
[1870-08-22 Bertha M (Edinburgh) to Mrs. Manny]

While in Scotland, the Drakes visited many cities and towns, including Inverness and Glasgow. Also, George was able to take time to go to Greenock and perhaps saw the Scott shipbuilding business. (He could not have imagined then what future son-in-law came out of Greenock!)

10. IRELAND, SEPTEMBER 6, 1870

The Drakes left Glasgow on September 5th by steamer to Belfast. It seemed that every new place that the Drakes visited was better than the last and opened their eyes to some new wonderful world. But, as beautiful as Ireland was to them, Bertha M wrote: "*Here we are at the loveliest spot in Ireland but it does not compare with Scotland, we think.*" [1870-09-13(-) (2 letters) Bertha M (Ireland) to Mrs. Manny]

Bertha M recounted going to Killarney, checking into their lodging, and hearing "*a regular blessing*" from one English "*lady?*".

Monday we came to Killarney. It was a pretty long ride. We reached here at 7 P.M. in company with a good many others. Mr. Drake had written from Dublin for a room so we had the exquisite pleasure of hearing, "Mr. Drake? Yes, show Mr. Drake to No. 14." And no one else could get a room. One English lady? gave them a regular blessing. She said they should have sent word to the station that they could not accommodate people for they all had to ride back 4 miles to the railway hotel (which seemed to be a very fine one). It was very hard but I was not at all sorry for her, for she had behaved very impolitely, had run & pushed & packed herself & bundles & husband in such a way that none of us inside the coach could get out until her husband had a chance at the innkeeper. I took it very philosophically as I knew our rooms were engaged but under other circumstances I think I should have lifted her into the middle of the road.
[1870-09-13(-) (2 letters) Bertha M (Ireland) to Mrs. Manny]

While in Belfast, the Drakes made the carriage ride to see the Giant Causeway. In her diary, Bertha M described it as follows: "*Day began most beautifully. Took open carriage & went to Giants Causeway. Had very good driver. Saw Dawtie's white calf. She was so excited tears came to her eyes.*" [Bertha M Diary, 1870-09-07]

The Drakes went to Dublin on September 9th. As they often did on this trip, they attended church on Sunday which provided them additional insights into the local ways.

We went Sabbath morning to hear Dr. Hall's(?) (of New York) successor in Rutland square church, Dublin. The congregation thinks he is fully equal to the Doctor. We were not fortunate enough to hear him but heard a hifalutin young fellow who chose his text (Moses burial(?) for the sake of introducing - "On Nebo's(?) lovely mountains") which he repeated entirely at different times during his sermon & he made several mistakes too. He did not improve the original.

I was more struck with the trying frying pans they passed round for the collection. They would fit a medium sized charter oak, were made of copper with wooden handles. I don't know what the collection was for but every man, woman & child seemed to put in a penny. Our shillings looked quite pale with fright at finding themselves in such a dark assemblage. The frying pans were nearly full when I saw them & as they were not careful in putting in the money but threw or dropped them in, there was a continual clink, clank, clink that was a novel effect to me. It sounded as if someone was rattling a chain in the church as there were 4 skillets.
[1870-09-13(-) (2 letters) Bertha M (Ireland) to Mrs. Manny]

Bertha M in her letter from Ireland to Mrs. Manny commented about the Irish Jaunting car and certain Irish customs regarding the prohibition against disturbing the flora, apparently unheard of in the U.S.

The Irish Jaunting Car: a light two-wheeled carriage for a single horse, in its most common form with seats for two or four persons placed back to back, with the foot-boards projecting over the wheels. It was the typical conveyance for persons in Ireland at one time.

Today again looked dubious but I donned my cloak & hood, took our jaunting car & went the other direction from that which we took yesterday. Though the domains of Lord Castlerosse are very lovely, they are to ... Cascade. It is a pretty waterfall, coming down between rocks & mountain sides, covered with a wilderness of ferns and all about is a wild forest of tangled vines & under growth. Yet the lovely proprietor of this place sent two messages to the hotel & came last night himself to say not a single leaf or fern must be plucked by tourists. Isn't he a sweet scented geranium? That is perfectly fair in gardens, cemeteries or lawns, but such a prohibition in a regular wild wood is, well, I won't say all I think. I knew the game & fish were preserved in this country but it is the first time I have heard of preserving herbs & ferns.
[1870-09-13(-) (2 letters) Bertha M (Ireland) to Mrs. John Manny]

Bertha M described another "outing" which included a number of different modes of transport.

We went in a jaunting car several miles through wild scenery, rode on horses 6 miles farther through wilderness, heard marvelous echoes of bugles, cannons, violins & Hindonan's(?) songs, drank mountain dew & goats milk, saw Kate Kearney & her daughter, bought the photograph of the "Colleen Bawn", were persecuted by bardegged "mountain Dew" girls & at last took the boat. We had two very good rowers & a ..., & again had echoes ruins, legends etc., until a storm came on. We had 15 miles to go and by the time we reached the lower lake 7 miles wide, it looked something like the ocean. I never imagined that I should ever enjoy pitching up & down on a stormy wave but it was grand fun & I was thoroughly waterproof with my cloak, hood & big boots. We got in safely, found Dawtie sitting on the hall sofa cross legged, a little puppy named Midge in her arms & as happy as a clam at high tide, I thought.
[1870-09-13(-) (2 letters) Bertha M (Ireland) to Mrs. John Manny]

When they departed Ireland, Bertha M wrote: "*The last morning ... - Killarney, we could hardly bear to leave it. It was so surpassingly lovely. But even there we did not see it in its beauty for we had not a clear day and did not see the mountain tops at all.*" [1870-09-17 (2 letters) Bertha M (London) to Mrs. John Manny (Boston)]

11. ENGLAND, SEPTEMBER 17, 1870

The passage back to England was difficult in the rough Irish Sea waters. "*Oh! It is awful to be upon the sea.*"

I forgot to say we went from Dublin to Kingston to take the steamer. We were very sea sick coming over to Holy Head & it made our hearts go down into our boots at the thoughts of enduring that for ten days & I declare I don't think anything but search of health would bring me back here again, although I was already beginning to long to see Italy etc. again. The poor little girl was very sick. She kept saying "Oh! It is awful to be upon the sea." "I feel so sadly to be upon the sea."
[1870-09-17 (2 letters) Bertha M (London) to Mrs. John Manny (Boston)]

From the Holy Head harbor, the Drakes took the train to Chester. During their stay there, Bertha M described the new bridge over the River Dee and Eaton Hall, the Marquis of Westminster's residence. (The Marquis apparently had more money than he knew how to spend.)

We saw a beautiful bridge. They call its arch the longest span in the world – 200 feet a single arch & perfect – Grosvenor Bridge over the river Dee. We drove to Eaton Hall residence of the Marquis of Westminster whose income is 500,000 pounds!! I should think the Hall was nearly perfect before but he has torn it all to pieces so we only saw it in a state of upsidedown-at-ness. It is to be finished by the time the heir shall be of age. He is 18 now. To give you a slight idea, clue room, not a large one, which cost 18,000 pounds, (90,000 dollars) only 15 years ago, is all torn to pieces. I don't mean the furnishings. Simply the decorating of walls & ceiling, etc., cost that much. The walls were painted in oil by the best masters and he has barbarously knocked every particle of plastering off. I don't know how it is to be finished. But I suppose the matter with him is, he has so much money he don't know what to do with it! [1870-09-17 (2 letters) Bertha M (London) to Mrs. John Manny (Boston)]

From Chester, they next went to Liverpool, "*a big, dingy, busy, ugly city.*" [1870-09-17 (2 letters) Bertha M (London) to Mrs. John Manny (Boston)]

The Drakes arrived in London on September 24th and attended to their remaining shopping and sightseeing.

F. THE TRIP HOME, OCTOBER 1870

The Drakes returned to Liverpool from London on October 18, 1870 to catch their steamer, the SS Abyssinia, a ship that was just recently launched in that year.

SS Abyssinia, launched in 1870, was a British mail liner operated by the Cunard Line on the Liverpool–New York route.

Although the Drakes were now very accustomed to taking a steamer over various waterways, the return to America was not pleasant, as Bertha M tersely described in her diary.

Reached Steamer Abyssinia safely, but found we had not a very pleasant room, just beside the pantry. Mr. Jones & I had pretty good dinners. Bad night.

October 19, 1870
Stormy, sick!

October 20, 1870
Stormy, sick!!

October 21, 1870
Stormy, sick!!!

October 22, 1870
Dreadful! Ship only made 64 miles. We have the incessant clatter of crockery, scolding & quarrelling of waiters. Not very good attendance & my sofa bed is as hard as a board. Fortunately, Tom Harrison put the side in or I could not have kept in bed at all.

October 23, 1870
Still stormy. Head winds all the way.

October 24, 1870
No hope yet of clearing. We shall be out several days longer than we expected.

October 25, 1870
A little sun but still head winds.

October 26, 1870
Very rough. Get 170 miles only today. Mr. Jones & I had a little sing to comfort ourselves.

October 27, 1870
Still rough. Very hard trip. Miss Oliver keeps up & cheerful & Mr. Jones makes little calls which cheer us up.

October 28, 1870
No comfort still. Haven't had anything to eat but beef tea & tea & crackers.

October 29, 1870
Today, if we had good weather, we should have been sailing into New York harbor. As it is, we are miserable. Stewardess Mrs. Maham(??) is quite attentive but the swearing & quarreling of waiters & the breakage of crockery at our doors is dreadful.

October 30, 1870
Sunday. Tolerably smooth but dreary & disconsolate. Had a nice little slice of buttered toast for lunch. Signaled at night for pilot.

November 1, 1870
Rather smooth night but very rough morning. A great storm raging outdoors. Cleared up. Pilot came on board but we cannot get to New York today. Had first news for two weeks. Paris in statis quo. Prussians ditto. Heard the Cambria[53] went down with 200 souls on board, 1 only saved, about 150 miles from us, the night we sailed on the Irish coast. Also that several vessels have been lost on the American coast during the late storm. Hope we shall reach New York tonight, though we shall not go up till tomorrow morning.

The Drakes' European trip ended in November 1870, more than one year after they began on October 19, 1869. It remains difficult to conceive not only how they planned such a trip of this length but also how they were able to remain steadfast to its conclusion, especially in view of the difficulties of travel in 1869–1870, the outbreak of a war, and the avoidance of ship wreck, such as befell the Cambia which was travelling the North Atlantic on the same seas. This was a trip that left America with a three-year-old child and returned to America with a four-year-old adult. A wonder.

---

[53] SS Cambria was a British cargo-passenger steamship wrecked off the north-west of Ireland on October 19, 1870 with the loss of 178 lives.

CHAPTER 5 – A SECOND EUROPEAN TRIP

Bertha was 19 years old when her parents took her and her brother George Jr. who was 10 years old, on a second, grand trip to Europe, leaving in July 1885 and returning in the fall in 1886. Bertha's mother, Bertha M, kept a diary of the events of this trip [Bertha M Diary, 1885-07] but this diary was much less detailed than the three diaries in which she recorded their 1869–1870 European trip. Also, she did not keep any letters to/from her friends regarding the various trip events, which is unfortunate since such prior letters were very descriptive and fascinating. Therefore, the available history principally reveals their itinerary. Nevertheless, there are interesting observations that Bertha M makes in her diary. Also, the fact that the Drakes wanted to pursue a second, more than one-year long trip to Europe with their children, is pretty amazing.

Bertha began to write poetry in earnest during this trip. She wrote 27 poems which were often about the places that she visited, such as the following poem about Heidelberg.

> ### *Heidelberg*
> *Heidelberg, thou worn old castle*
> *In a thousand loving lays,*
> *Has been sung thy fame and beauty*
> *In the dreamy bye gone days.*
>
> *Surely t'is not much to ask thee*
> *From thy laurel crown to spare*
> *One leaf for the unknown poets*
> *Who have sung thy glory rare.*
>
> *With my dream eyes I can see them*
> *Trooping thickly, hand in hand,*
> *Sunny, blue eyed, bright haired, brave souled,*
> *Students of the fatherland.*
>
> *Bringing to your shrines, their tribute.*
> *Mingling with their dreams of fame*
> *Other sweeter dreams and fancies,*
> *Twining round some "Liebchen's" name.*
>
> *Loving Von der Vogelweide,*
> *Worshipping Von Eschenbach,*
> *I can hear them through the stillness*
> *With their "weindersch" on and "ach".*
>
> *Where have they all passed, the singers,*
> *Very few have won their crown.*
> *Many have in life's long journey*
> *Sadly thrown their lyres down.*
>
> *They have filled your ruined hallways*
> *Full of knights and squires gay,*
> *Ladies laughing at the windows*
> *But I see not them today.*

No troops from the middle ages
Greet me with their battle cries,
But the shades of bye gone singers
And the dreamy poet eyes.
[Bertha's Poem #23, 1886, Heidelberg]

A. THE SAIL TO IRELAND

The Drakes left New York City on the S.S. Etruria, on July 4, 1885. The Etruria had a service speed 19 knots and accommodations for 550 passengers in 1st class, 160 in intermediate class, and 800 in steerage.

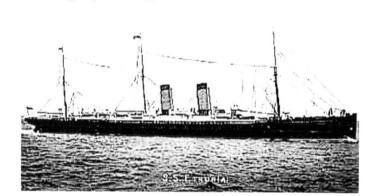

After seven days at sea, they arrived on July 11th at Queenstown (Cobh), Cork, Ireland, where they took a tender to shore and then to their hotel, the Queens Hotel.

> *Queens Hotel – French air of all the outside surroundings. Tiptop breakfast. Mutton cutlets, ham*
> *& eggs, potatoes, strawberries, marmalade, white & brown bread, tea & coffee & butter. Beautiful*
> *drive, hedges filled with white, wild roses, honeysuckle, foxglove etc., etc. Old castle, best kept*
> *place in Ireland. Lovely sail up the Lee. Black Rock Castle, etc.*
> [1885-7 BMD Diary]

After three days in Cobh, the Drakes took the train to Bantry and then the "wagonettes" to Glengariff, which lies on the southwest coast of Ireland, at the northern head of Glengarriff Bay. Notwithstanding that this was summer, Bertha M commented: "*English & Irish call it warm. I find it very cold. Wear my ulster all the time.*" During this stay (and whenever the chance permitted), George Sr., Bertha and George Jr. would go for a "*row*".

The Drakes traveled in Ireland until July 31st. During this twenty-day period, the Drakes visited Killarney, Limerick, Galway, Dublin, Kilkenny, Greystones, and Belfast, and toured the various castles (Rosa, North & Dunluce). The Drakes also went to the Giant Causeway which Bertha did not visit during their prior, 1869–1870, European trip. (Bertha M included the full legend of Finn McCool in the letters that she wrote to Mrs. Manny during her 1870 visit to the Giant Causeway.) In their trip from Limerick to Galway, Bertha M writes in her diary of their taking the Irish jaunting car. Bertha undoubtedly enjoyed the "jaunting" ride and perhaps had fond memories of the jaunting car when she was three years old, for she penned the following poem shortly after this trip.

> ### Ode to the Irish
> *You may ride in a phaeton as much as you please*
> *Or disport yourself proud in a little dog cart*
> *Or say you consider a coach "quite the cheese"*
> *But the gay jaunting car's the delight of my heart.*

You may talk of your broughams whenever you like
And say you prefer them wherever you are,
Or boast of a bicycle or of a "trike",
But I shall still cling to the old jaunting car.

You may say you consider it healthy to walk
And your health, I am sure, I would be loth to mar,
But I fear these precautions are most of them talk
And you never have driven the brave jaunting car.

So if you'll permit me to give you a toast,
Here's one you may drink with a hearty hurrah,
And one of which all of you proudly may boast,
T'is erin go bragh and the gay jaunting car.
[Bertha's Poem, #1, Ireland, 1886]

B. SCOTLAND & ENGLAND

The Drakes sailed to Glasgow in the evening on July 31, 1885. The weather during their passage was apparently very good. Bertha M wrote in her diary: "*Crossed to Glasgow. Sat up on deck all night.*"
They traveled through England and Scotland for the next 9 weeks until October 6th. While in Scotland, they visited Glasgow, Oban ("*horrid Americans*"), Ben Arie, Inverness ("*2 horrid men dined at one table*"), Edinburgh ("*Edinburgh, dear beautiful Edinburgh*"), and Aberfoyle. While in Edinburgh, Bertha wrote the following poem:

To E. J.[54]
Shall I paint you a saint for a shrine,
With a face, human still, made divine?
Let me first show the shrine, for its holding,
T's a soft rainbow light her enfolding.

And the bow is made up first of tears,
Then of smiles, interwov'n hopes and fears,
Sorrow's shade, gladness' light, round her play,
With a gleam as of fire seen through spray.

But not they can disturb her sweet face,
That rests calm in sereneness and grace,
Rising up in a pure atmosphere,
With no smile but a look soft and clear.

Ah but wait! Neath the shrine kneeleth one
With his face still in shade and unknown,
When his face he shall lift up and pray,
Saint no more, but a maid, answers –
Tell me, sweet, is the word yea or nay?
[Bertha's Poem #2, Edinburgh 1885]

---

[54] E.J. may have been Edith January, Janet January's sister, who were both close friends of Bertha.

The Drakes saw Ben Nevis covered in snow, took a steamer for Caledonian Canal with the Shepley family[55], rowed and sailed on various lakes (they "sailed" to Penrith) and visited the various castles. While in Edinburgh, the Drakes visited Abbottsford and Melrose. Bertha mentions that, while in Melrose, they saw the *Pirates of Penzance*. Bertha M remarked that on their trip to Ambleside and Bowness, there were "three Berthas in the wagonette of 5 women." While in Bowness on Windemere, the Drakes rowed on the lake, went to Wordsworth's grave, and visited the marketplaces and sites. And they ate fish. George Jr. asked Bertha M, "*Are the fish good to eat? - They are when they're cooked. - I don't know, I'm shoore.*" [Bertha M Diary 1870-05, August 24, 1885]

The Drakes' travel through England included stays in York, Llandudno Wales, Caernarfon, Snowdonia, Chester (visited the Warburton Chapel), Hereford (and Tintern Abbey), Gloucester ("*poor supper. Worse rooms*"), and London ("*Gorgeous rooms.*"). They spent nearly a month in London. Bertha M mentions, in addition to diverse sightseeing, that they heard Charles Spurgeon[56] speak and that "*Georgie sat in Prince of Wales seat*" in Temple Church.

C. FRANCE

On October 6, 1885, the family departed Dover for Calais. Bertha M wrote the following in her diary:
> *Sunny morning. Left Dover for Calais. Sick in Channel. Reached Calais. New sights & scenery for Georgie & Dawt. Pleasant ride to Paris. Young officer. Rainy & dark. Went to Continental Palatial apartments.*

They stayed in Paris until October 26th, and had plenty of time for driving around Paris and for sightseeing, including the Pantheon, Jardin du Luxembourg, Bois de Boulogne, the Louvre, the Catacombs, Arc de Triomphe, Saint Chapelle, Notre Dame, Tomb of Napoleon, Madeleines, Versailles, sewers of Paris, and concert in Trocadero. Shopping was also attended to and, as Bertha M commented that they "*prowled in the boulevards.*"

On October 26th, the Drakes left for Mâcon and Aix Les Bains. Bertha M described Aix Les Bains as follows: "*Mountains all about, powdered with snow. Beautiful little lake. Roman baths. Water running all the time. Washer women. Roman Arch of 3rd century.*" And on the 29th, "*Early in morning, the mountains powdered with snow. Lovely. ... Had goldfish & larks for dinner.*"

D. ITALY

They continued to Turin on October 30, 1885: "*Left early for Turin. Most glorious day. Snow covered mountains. Yellow & red trees against snow. Market day. Picturesque groups with donkeys, grey cows & black pigs.*" And the next day, "*Red letter day. Clearest, freshest day. ... Drove round city. Very beautiful – more like Paris than any other. No mean houses. ... Military everywhere. Gorgeous uniforms.*"

On November 2nd, the Drakes left for Milan which "*doesn't compare with Turin.*"

The Drakes went on to Venice on November 4th, arriving in the "*pouring rain at 7:30*". In addition to the usual sights, Bertha M mentioned that she: "*Saw grand funeral in golden gondola. Boatman in black & gold,*" and "*Rowed on canal in the sunsetting. Singing again.*"

---

[55] Presumably the "Shepleys" include John Foster Shepley (born 1858) who married Sarah Hitchcock Shepley in 1893 and "Jack's" siblings who were Mary Louise (Shepley) Lionberger, George Foster Shepley and Julie (Shepley) Coolidge. The Shepley family were well known to Bertha's family and Jack's wife, Sarah Hitchcock Shepley, became one of Bertha's closest friends thorough Bertha's life.

[56] Charles Haddon Spurgeon (19 June 1834 – 31 January 1892) was an English Particular Baptist preacher. Spurgeon remains highly influential among Christians of various denominations, among whom he is known as the "Prince of Preachers". He was a strong figure in the Reformed Baptist tradition, defending the Church in agreement with the 1689 London Baptist Confession of Faith understanding, and opposing the liberal and pragmatic theological tendencies in the Church of his day.

The Drakes were then in Florence from November 9th to 15th and saw the usual sights: Duomo, San Lorenzo, Giotto's tower, Uffizi Gallery, Pitti Palace, St. Maria Novella, Boboli Gardens, Belle Academia di Arti, among others.

The Drakes were in Pisa on November 16th and then traveled to Rome on the 17th where they stayed until December 8th. They went several times to St. Peters, which was "*rededicated*" on the 18th, and went to various churches and church services, including the Armenian Episcopal Church where Bertha M says: "*saw the Queen & King.*" As usual, their sightseeing schedule was crowded, at least on days that they were not unwell, and shopping was never ignored.

They continued south to Naples, Sorrento and Capri on December 9th. During this time, they saw Pompeii and Vesuvius: "*Vesuvius brilliant. Boats with beacons. Sky, stormy waves, clear gold. Silver. Silver grey sky, sea, islands.*" And they shopped: "*December 18: wasted in shops.*"

The Drakes returned to Rome on December 23rd and stayed through the 29th where they took their last "*Drive of farewell to Rome.*"
To commemorate her stay in Rome, Bertha wrote:

> ### ROME
> *Tones of deep bells slow sounding through the air,*
> *Dim faded shrines, an atmosphere of prayer.*
> *The sound of falling water everywhere*
> *And far above all else, a golden dome.*
> *You need no words to tell you this is Rome.*
>
> *Rome of the gods! Whose great white statues still*
> *Stand at the base of every crowded hill,*
> *Or silent guard some chattering fountain rill,*
> *And yet, they are but statues after all,*
> *Rome dragged her white gods with her, in her fall.*
>
> *Rome of the saints! Whose pictured faces calm*
> *By halves crowned or with some wreath of palm,*
> *Seem silent hymning some triumphant psalm.*
> *Who pauses now their lives to muse upon?*
> *The saints are dead, the world must hurry on.*
>
> *Rome of the poets! Thou hast passed away,*
> *No minstrel harp thy praises sounds today.*
> *The lights burn dim, t'is but a mourner's lay,*
> *Weeping as exile who hath lost his home.*
> *For Rome is dead, and buried, here in Rome.*
> [Bertha's Poem, #8 – 1885 – Rome]

The family returned to Florence on December 30th, staying at the same hotel as before (Hotel d'Italia) where they "*Moved into our old rooms.*" During this stay, Bertha M hired a music teacher and an Italian tutor for Bertha: "*Dawt looked hard at music & Italian.*"

The Drakes started for Genoa on January 20, 1886, and visited Nice, Monte Carlo, Marseilles on the succeeding days. On February 4th, they returned to Paris by "*sleeping car.*"

After their return to Paris, they were able to "move into old rooms" at the Hotel Maurice. *"February 8,9,10,11,12,13, - Shopped for dresses. Quelle horreur!!"* Bertha M's entry on February 15th was curious: *"Fencing lessons. Boxing lessons. Dressmakers."* Presumably, Bertha had the fencing lessons and Georgie the boxing lessons?

E. GERMANY & THE LOWLANDS

On March 2, 1886, the Drakes left for Cologne and their three-month travels through Germany and the lowlands. They visited Berlin, Prague, Vienna, Munich, Bavaria, Ratisbon, Walhalla, Einsenach, Hanover, Dusseldorf, Amsterdam, Hague, Antwerp, Brussels, Weisbaden, Frankfort, and Heidelberg. Bertha M may have become more fatigued at that point in their European trip since her daily diary entries became increasingly terse and many days are simply missing. Bertha M's diary ends on June 13, 1886, apparently when they were in the City of Heidelberg. Although there were numerous empty pages left in her diary, one can only surmise that she needed a break from her daily commitment. It was not clear from the available accounts when they returned to St. Louis. However, based on Bertha's poem which she recorded as having been written in Geneva in October 1886, it may be that the Drakes remained in Europe through the fall of 1886.

CHAPTER 6 – THE ROMANTIC

Bertha Warburton Drake

While Bertha's mother wrote beautiful descriptions with great detail, Bertha was a passionate writer and seemed more inclined to romanticism. In addition to her lifetime of letter writing, Bertha wrote delightful poetry and prose which seemed her outlet to express herself. Her poetry was romantic, sometimes with pathos, especially in her later years, but generally revealed her optimism.

A. EARLY ROMANTICISM

Some of Bertha's romanticism can be seen in her writings from her high school essay book. When she was 13 years old, she was assigned to write an essay about the Lord Byron poem, "The Eve of Waterloo". While the exact nature of the assignment is not known, Bertha chose to write the poem into prose, a clever way to show that she understood the poem while freeing herself from turning in a boring essay.

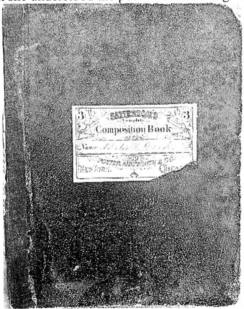

Bertha's Composition Book

The Eve Before Waterloo

Sounds of revelry came from a building brilliantly illuminated by hundreds of lamps for Brussels had gathered together her fairest daughters and her bravest sons to do honor to the Duchess of Richmond. Soft music swelled through the rooms while many a brave young officer told the story of his love that night to those soft eyes which but, too plainly, told their own in return.

All went merrily till a sound as of distant thunder startled all into sudden silence. Then, with light laughter at their own fright they said that it was nothing but the wind or the car on the stony street.

The dance goes on, joy reigns supreme. Who cares for weariness or thinks of sleep when youth is met by pleasure and they together, with flying feet, chase the glowing hours? Again that heavy sound breaks in as if echoed from the clouds now nearer and more distinct than before. It is the roar of the cannon! To arms! To arms! Ah, then and there was hurrying to and fro.

Cheeks, whose blushes but a short time ago had been called forth at the praise of their beauty, grew pale, tears gathered and young forms trembled with anguish. Then came farewells, pressing the life out of those young hearts. Farewells between those whose eyes might never meet again. Alas! That a morning so full of suffering could follow a night so sweet.

Steeds are mounted in hot haste while horse and foot, officers and common soldiers, hasten to form in the ranks of battle, watched by the citizens who with trembling lips and terror stricken hearts, announce the approach of the foe.

The "Cameron's Gathering"[57], the war-note of Lochiel, rises high above all other war cries. That cry which has so often wakened Briton and Saxon to the knowledge that death was near.

The pibroch thrills loudly and as the breath of the Scotch fills their mountain pipes so their hearts are filled with that fierce daring which recalls to them the stirring memories of thousands of years and the deeds of their most famous chieftains come back to them.

As they pass through the forest of Ardennes, still wet with the early dew, it seems to weep for those who will never more return. This fiery mass of valor, now advancing boldly on the foe, filled with high hope and burning courage, will alas!, ere evening, be trodden under foot like the grass on which they now tread but which shall grow again when they lie cold and low.

The day before, they were filled with life and love. The midnight brought the call to arms. The morning saw the marshalling, the noon brings the battle. The field is covered with smoke which, when it has cleared away, will show the earth covered with the slain, over which it, in its turn, will be thrown.

"Rider and horse, friend, foe, in one red burial blent."

[1880-01-07 *The Eve Before Waterloo*]

---

[57] The Clan Cameron has a long military history. At the battle of Waterloo (which is near Brussels), Donald Cameron the XXIII Chief fought with distinction with his clansmen.

"The Cameron's Gathering": several tunes have had the title "The Cameron's Gathering," one of them called "Chlanna nan con, thigibh a seo 's gheibh sibh feòil" (Sons of dogs, come here and get meat), which is the slogan or war cry of Clan Cameron. Another tune is "Pibroch of Donald Dubh," composed for Sir Walter Scott's air/quickstep march, which is based on the old piobaireachd tune "Piobaireachd Dhomnuill Duibh," also known as "Lochiel's March" or "Camerons' Gathering". The Chief of the Clan Cameron is customarily referred to as simply "Lochiel". "Pibroch" is a piece of music for the bagpipe, consisting of a series of variations on a basic theme, usually martial in character, but sometimes used as a dirge. [David Murray, *Music of the Scottish Regiments*]

Bertha wrote the following in her composition book in 1881:

A Trip to the Moon

I was sitting one evening at my window, watching the moon as it passed in and out from the fleecy clouds, leaving me in darkness or light accordingly, when I saw something fluttering down the long trail of moonlight and, when it came nearer, it proved to be the loveliest maiden I had ever seen. Her golden hair fell in clouds around her and her large blue eyes sparkled merrily as she held out her hand to me, saying in a clear musical voice, "come up, come up to the moon with me." At the same moment she gave me a gentle pull and I found myself in the air beside her where, to my surprise, I was not in the least danger of falling.

As we floated along, I said wonderingly, "Do you really live in the moon? I thought it was not inhabited." "That is all a mistake," she answered, laughing. "Your stupid old astronomers with their long telescopes have never seen but one side of the moon in spite of all their trying. They don't know anything about the other side, not even of its light. Why, the side they know nothing of is the side where our Queen lives and yet they say that no one can breathe on the moon, p'shaw!"

She was silent for a few moments and then on my questioning her, she told me that her name was Selene and that she was one of the nymphs who attended the Queen of the moon, Luna, the sister of the sun-god, Phoebus. Suddenly interrupting herself, she exclaimed, "Here we are!"

We were at the edge of the moon. Never had I seen anything half so beautiful as that which now met my eye. Everything was of the same form as on our earth but made of the finest, frosted gold and delicately finished off even to the tiniest blade of grass, while over all was poured the clearest, purest, most silvery radiance imaginable. Nymphs like Selene were flitting around everywhere but I could see no men. Presently I said something of this to my companion but immediately her eyes flashed indignantly and she said angrily, "How dare you! Don't you know that our Queen is the virgin goddess!" I begged her pardon, adding however, "But she loved Orion, did she not?" "Hush!", she said softly. "That is our Queen's great sorrow. When you have a stormy night on earth, with the wind moaning drearily and the rain falling heavily, you did not know that the rain drops were our Queen's tear drops and the moaning of the wind her moaning as she mourns for the lover, killed by her own hand."

At this moment I heard the sound of a soft footstep and the Queen of Night and Moonlight stood before me. Far, far above that of earth was her beauty, her raven hair, unbound, save by a golden circlet in which blazed a brilliant star, fell over her robe of silver tissue which floated softly about her and seemed to bear her up, but her face, though of wondrous loveliness, seemed always saddened by some deep sorrow. I stood watching her for a moment then I felt her presence by its spell of might, stoop over me from above. There was a soft touch on my forehead and she was gone.

I felt as if I could bear no more just then so I begged Selene to send me home. She was very unwilling to do so at first but finally she placed me in a chariot. "Of clouds condensed, a sable car", and the next moment I was in my window seat again, watching the last faint beams of moonlight die away as the sun rose gloriously in the eastern sky.

April 1, 1881 Bertie Warburton Drake
[1881-04-01 Bertha's Composition Book – A Trip to the Moon]

B. THE 1885 EUROPEAN TRIP

In 1885, Bertha started recording her poems in a book containing 33 of her poems, 27 of which were written during her 1885–1886 European trip. Only a few of the poems from this book are included in this chapter.

Bertha's book of poems

Bertha wrote the following poem when she was in Pallanza, Italy (Currently known as Verbania).

A Flower's Breath
The soft south wind blows heavily.
A fragrant breath, though full to me.
I deem each loving soul that is
Knows scents that hold deep mysteries.

For some bear songs in their sweet breath
As soft as summer, as grand as death,
And some paint pictures gloriously
That live in the heart's depths wondrously.

Perhaps t'is white magnolias bring
An anguish of remembering
Or winds across the new mown hay
Hold laughter long since passed away.

Or one dear dream of life's romance
T'is wakened by the rale La France.
Blow on, thou fair wind, murmuringly,
Touch weary hearts right tenderly.

And charm from fretted brows the line
By fair dreams brought from days long syne.
[Bertha's Poem #3, Pallanza, Italy 1886]

Bertha wrote a number of poems which dealt with her feelings about her gender, such as: "The Kissing Bridge" ("*She pauses a moment with roguish eyes, Mouth pursed like a rosy clover*") included in Chapter 8, "The Awakening" ("Love kissed her and she woke") in Chapter 9, and "A Woman's Love" ("*That he might find in me always delight*") in Chapter 13. Although Bertha sometimes railed against her womanly lot, her poems revealed an understanding and acceptance of her gender role, perhaps in the nature of Kate in *The Taming of the Shrew*. The following poems give more insight into what she felt as a woman and the patience for which she prayed.

Nausicaa[58]

The gods are cruel! Ay me that I should be
The first of women who hath dared so speak.
A man might curse, it is a woman's fate
To pray and to submit and so methinks
Might I, for other grief but this, but who
Can tell his strength or weakness till the test
Hath come, and what seems hardest is his own.
Why should I suffer thus? Who to the gods
Am guiltless of all sin. My mother knew
My father not, yet married him and loved
And loves him still and will beyond the grave.
And so, I thought to do, to him who claimed
My hand for his, and so I might have done.
But for the stranger of the glorious brows
A man, a man in very sooth, yet fair,
And like to god head in his strength and truth,
I was a child that morn, who played with flowers
Upon the sand where bleached my marriage clothes
And happy, nay not that, but light of heart
As babes are and the dragon flies that love
The sunshine and know nothing more beyond.
I would not have that childhood back again.
Ah no, this pain is sweeter though it burns
As noonday light after the sunrise dew.
But not for that I mourn, not my lost dreams,
But the gray future where he never comes
And where another holds this hand of mine
He touched once with his own, I feel it still.

That strong calm touch, that could both soothe a weak
Sick child and govern and constrain wild beasts.
To do his pleasure, love hath such, I think.
I may not break my oath and yet to bear
Another's words of love when all my heart
Is gone far hence on sunny waters cruel!
Am I so guilty? Let me speak but once
And after, die perhaps so happier, aray(?),
It may not be, my life is fixed for me.
I must live smiling on. Yes, why weep I,
I whom the gods have blessed with gold
And beauty and a strong man's love, but yet
My children ne'er shall wear his steady smile
To greet mine with and shall to meet my kiss
Turn(?) but another's eyes. Ah me, there waits
For him another woman, with a shrewd
Clear glance and skillful hands and heart so strong
To bear his absence as I could not do
Knowing he loved me. I am all too weak,
Aye sinful too, the gods know best who will
That I, as other women, sacrifice
Myself, so differing thus alone that they
Their loved ones serve, I one unloved, suff'ring,
They can to death look forward, so not I,
In death, as life, he would be hers, not mine.
I cannot pray for death. What then? Ye gods,
I ask but patience, evermore, but this,
The woman's great prayer, patience, grant it me.
[Bertha's Poem #9, 1886]

Similarly, "To Madeleine de Scudéry", a poem Bertha wrote to the French writer and novelist Madeleine de Scudéry, spoke of a women's love: *"We are foolish things, we women, we do not merely mourn, when our life's one crown of glory, Proves to be a crown of thorn."* But as Bertha writes, your warnings are useless, *"Still we seek that country rare"* and your *"fairest picture"*.

---

[58] Nausicaa is a character in Homer's Odyssey. She is the daughter of King Alcinous and Queen Arete of Phaeacia. Her name literally means "burner of ships". Homer gives a literary account of love never expressed (possibly one of the earliest examples of unrequited love in literature). While she is presented as a potential love interest to Odysseus – she says to her friend that she would like her husband to be like him, and her father tells Odysseus that he would let him marry her – no romantic relationship takes place between the pair. Nausicaä is also a mother figure for Odysseus; she ensures Odysseus' return home, and thus says "Never forget me, for I gave you life," indicating her status as a "new mother" in Odysseus' rebirth. Odysseus never tells Penelope about his encounter with Nausicaä, out of all the women he met on his long journey home. Some suggest this indicates a deeper level of feeling for the young woman." [Wikipedia]

Madeleine de Scudéry

To Madeleine de Scudéry

Ah, ce beau pays de tendre
Madeleine de Scudery.
You have drawn for us a country
That is very fair to see.

Was it just from seeing others
That you painted it so fair?
Ah no sweetheart, that you could not
You yourself had wandered there.

You had plucked the fruit bright golden
Gathered fern and perfumed flower
But to find that all to ashes
They had turned within an hour.

Was a handclasp, dear, so precious,
Or a smile, sweet Madeleine?
As to make those fluting moments
Worth the after years of pain?

You have told us what must follow
The deep waters of despair,
But we never heed the warning
Still we seek that country rare.

We are foolish things, we women,
And we do not merely mourn

When our life's one crown of glory
Proves to be a crown of thorn

When the thorn branch tears our
forehead,
Still it is not only woe.
It recalls to us the roses
That once bloomed there long ago.

Bear we every after discord
Just to hear though faint in tone,
Echoes from those long lost joy bells
In that fair land, once well known.

Does not one outweigh the other
Greatly, sweet de Scudery
You to paid the after sadness
Gladly for ce beau pays.

And we follow in your footsteps,
We must see that lovely shore,
And when we have left its roses
There will be as many more.

So your warning is all useless,
It was written but in vain,
But for this, your fairest picture,
Thanks, gentle Madeleine.
[Bertha's Poem #11, 1886]

In her poem, "Fantasy", Bertha sketched out the life of a maiden, from a child until death, weaving the story of the witch mother who counsels for the flowers of each of life's stages until the end where the witch's work is done and *"Angel fingers wind it yonder, where the work goes on for aye"*.

Fantasy

Weird witch mother, binding blossoms,
Weave a woman's wreath for me.
Tell me what the fittest flowers
For her sad and joyous hours
As I name them now to thee.

Sweet witch mother, weaving swiftly,
What her flow'rets when a child?
"White anemones, scarce lasting
Till the cold north wind them blasting
Leaves them scattered on the wild."

Dear witch mother, weaving swiftly,
What shall suit her when a maid?
"Bluebells, buttercups and daisies,
As her nature's changing phases
Pass from sunshine into shade."

Kind witch mother, weaving swiftly,
What with love's first lesson learned?
"Those are always fresh wild roses,
Filled with fragrance, sweetest posies,
Deep with radiant color burned."

Stern witch mother, weaving swiftly,
What when love has passed away?
"When a maiden's heart is broken
There is ever but one token,
Leaves of willow, cold and gray."

Sad witch mother, weaving swiftly,
What then hath she when at rest?
"Purple passion flowers blowing
Where the grasses sweet are growing,
O'er her pure and tender breast."

Calm witch mother, weaving swiftly,
What the emblems of her peace?
"Easter lilies, tall and slender,
Speak the spirit's message tender
From that home where partings cease."

Wise witch mother, you cease weaving.
Is the wreath complete today?
"Nay, but I no longer ponder,
Angel fingers wind it yonder,
Where the work goes on for aye."
[Bertha's Poem #24, 1886]

In "Rex's Love Song", Bertha wrote from the perspective of a man, the King who, in worship of his maiden, states *"Thou art my queen, thy subject I"*.

Rex's Love Song

Thou art my queen, thy subject I,
And bear my chains right willingly.
Nor ever do for freedom sigh
As thou dost guide me lovingly.

Thou art my sunshine, dull and gray
Without thee were my life's long day,
And lost and desolate my way.
Let thy dear light shine on, I pray.

Thou art my gospel, without thee
Our Lord himself were strange to me.

But in thy love hath he blessed me
And I cry benedicite.

Thou art my all, these songs I frame
Are feeble, halting, weak and lame,
But if my singing thou dost blame,
By great love, I pardon, claim.

Love me a little back again
And all life's weariness and pain
Transfigured by that greatest gain
Shall radiant shine, like sun kissed rain.
[Bertha's Poem #26, 1886]

The last verse rings with *"Love me a little back again, And all life's weariness and pain, Transfigured by that greatest gain, Shall radiant shine, like sun kissed rain."*

Similarly, In "Friedel's Love Song", Bertha wrote from the perspective of Friedel, the "peaceful ruler", who speaks of the virtues of a maiden whom he admires most of all things: "*best of all, Is the love of my maiden dear.*"

Friedel's Love Song

What is the fairest light on earth?
The sheen of the white moonshine?
Or the silvery star beam as it falls
Alight on the gloomy brine?
Or the rosy color that tints the sky
When the dewy sun doth rise?
Nay, these are fair, but fairer far
Is the light in my maiden's eyes.

What is the softest touch on earth?
A snow flake that's fluttering past?
Or a butterfly's wing against your cheek?
Or rose leaves afloat on the blast?
Or the thistle down that scattering light
By the farmer's curse is banned?
Nay, these are soft, but softer far
Is the clasp of my maiden's hand.

What is the sweetest sound on earth?
The wind in the dreamy pines?
Or the flash of the sea waves as they break
In foamy and wavering lines?
Or the plaintive note of the nightingale
As she sings in the warm soft south?
Nay, these are sweet, but sweeter far
Is a word from my maiden's mouth.

What is the best thing in the world?
The hope in a boy's brave heart?
Or the first faint smile on a baby's lips?
Or stately enjoyments of art?
Or the plaintive pleasures of memory?
Or the loss of a grinding fear?
Nay, these are good, but best of all,
Is the love of my maiden dear.
[Bertha's Poem #27, Germany, 1886]

Bertha wrote a number of poems about friendship to her close friends. The next poem is "To F.P." (?) who was far away when Bertha wrote this from Dresden. Her poem concludes, "*A friend's praise sweeter than a symphony, That I can give thee, keep that place for me.*"

To F.P.

Thou climbest high upon a mountain vast,
I, in the valley far below, must stand
Where echoes of thy footsteps come to me.
Thou meet'st the spirits of the masters old.

To thee they bare the secrets of their souls,
Whisper their love reams, tell their agonies,
When such as these surround thee, is there place
For humbler mem'ries, yea, I trust me so.

The masters speak to thee, but thou not yet
Can'st answer, hangs a heavy veil between.
They from the past down to the present speak,

Thou, haply to the future, that were sweet.

Yet twere cold converse ever but to hear
And never to reply, or when one spoke
No answer back to gain. Your world of sound
Is grand, but, though to you are clear,

Voices that dim and distant are to me.
Yet thou may'st find, sweetheart, in tired hours
A friend's praise sweeter than a symphony.
That I can give thee, keep that place for me.
[Bertha #13, Dresden 1886]

Janet January, who married Howard Elliott in 1892, was a very close friend of Bertha during her life. Bertha's friendship and regard for Janet was amply revealed in the following two poems which Bertha wrote, one from Rome and the other from Dresden during the 1885–1886 European trip.

To J.J. [Janet January]
A Christmas Greeting

As we wander about in this foreign place
I have seen many pictures full of grace,
But they're nothing sweeter than your sweet face
*   In their collection.*

I have seen such statues as prices prize
And most beautiful saints, before me rise,
But I'd give for one look into your deep eyes
*   All their perfection.*

They have fair Madonnas without an end
And your head with a reverent awe may bend,
But there's nothing so fair as the face of a friend,
*   To your heart's true lover.*

nd I deem it no sin at the Christmas hour
When surely petitions have fuller power,
If I call on the saints to bless my flower
*   As they bend above her.*

And this prayer I would make if so I may,
That your life shall be one long Christmas day,
And your joys be sweeter than flowers in May,
*   And stronger than granite.*

And that every year, you may hear again
The Christmas bells in their sweet refrain
Bid angels brush every shadow of pain
*   From bonny Janet.*
[Bertha # 16, Rome 1885]

To J.J. *[Janet January]*
How does the rosebud grow to a rose?
*   Who is't that knows?*
How comes the blue in the bonny bluebell?
*   Who is't can tell?*
How does the winter change into spring?
*   Who is't can sing?*
How comes first love in a young maid's way?
*   Who is't can say?*
Answer me, maiden and winter and rose,
*   Nobody knows!*
[Bertha's Poem # 14, 1886 Dresden]

Bertha's poems also revealed her faith and deep reverence for God. She wrote that the following poem was *"for K.S.B. on her birthday."* It is not clear who K.S.B was. and not entirely clear why the tone is so morose. But it may be surmised that this was written after a loss and was intended as spiritual comfort.

A Prayer
For K.S.B. on her birthday

I dare not ask rich gifts
Thou, fair Lord, knowest best,
Whether by her, be better borne
The lily wreath or the crown of thorn
For the doing of thy behest.

Not always sunshine fair,
Ah nay, sweet Christ, not so,
Shadowless light would be but pain,
And sometimes there must come clouds and rain,
Or the flowers would never grow.[59]

Grant thou but this one thing
When grief shall come and loss
Across all suffering weariness
Let fall the light from the dear Christ face
And the shadow of his cross.

So shall grief be to her
No simple scourging rod,
But like the Levite's wand of might
Bearing bright flow'rets in the night,
A mystery of God.
[Bertha's Poem #15, 1886 Dresden]

C. WEE MARGARET

In 1887, Bertha wrote a poem to her "adopted niece", Margaret. "Wee Margaret" was the daughter of Ethan and Margaret Hitchcock, who were very close friends of Bertha. Obviously, Bertha took a keen interest in the young girl. But the poem was also very personal as Bertha, even at age 21, feels the passage of time and how Wee Margaret will soon take Bertha's youthful place and Bertha will take her place *"Among the sages"*.

A Promise – to my adopted niece
O Margaret, wee Margaret,
To you our life is strange as yet
The height of your ambition's met
            In downy pillows.
Tis hard for us to realize
That time will come when those blue eyes
Shall learn to study with surprise
            Life's stormy billows

---

[59] This theme of light and dark is echoed in Bertha's poem, Weltschmerz, in Chapter 24.

And stranger still to think that when
Our Margaret reaches girlhood, then
We shall have passed beyond its ken
  Among the sages –
While she will claim as rightful due
To hear some stories "really true"
Of times when we were maidens too,
  (In long past ages.)

Then hear my promise, little one,
If sometimes when the day is done
You'll come to "dear Aunt Warburton"
  And plead for stories –
I'll use a real enchanter's art
Bring back your mother's girlish heart,
And make forgotten blushes start
  O'er old-time glories.

And tell how grave and staid Aunt Anne
Was simply known as willful Nan
While I recall as best I can
  Our merry courses –
You'll scarce believe the quiet face

Where life begins deep lines to trace
Was once as full of laughing grace
  As, well, as yours is.

T'is hard to think it is but truth
That when this bond is claimed, forsooth,
New names shall claim this land of youth
  We have our lot in.
And what now bounds our widest zone
We'll smile at as a thing outgrown
If so be that the fought for throne
  Is not forgotten.

But lest we learn too harsh a creed
And deem the present fills our need
Sweet Margaret be then our speed
  With low words pressing
That at the word of her gourmand
All gates shall ope in mem'ry's land
And past joys freed by that soft hand
  Come back in blessing.
[Bertha's Poem #29, October 1887]

The optimist at the end, Bertha concludes her poem that, through Wee Margaret, "*All gates shall ope in mem'ry's land, And past joys freed by that soft hand, Come back in blessing.*"

Bertha's devotion to Wee Margaret can be seen in her letters and diary, including this reference to a visit to the Hitchcock's house.

> *Miss Margaret, sweeter than ever and brimming over with mischief. She admires her Aunt Warburton's gambols, the only person who ever did.*
> [1888-05 Diary, May 24, 1888]

Wee or, sometimes, "small", Margaret had various names for Bertha: often Aunty Bert but also Bahpoo. "*Margaret has the measles and it is the first time I have ever seen her cross to her "Bahpoo.""* [1888-11 Diary, March 5, 1889] Bertha commented at the McPherson wedding, "*Margaret Hitchcock and the little McPherson girl make very cunning bridesmaids.*" [1888-11 Diary, March 23, 1889]

In her letters, Bertha periodically mentions Wee Margaret in amusing situations, such as the following involving Nan Shepley who was still single and unattached at the time.

> *We had lots of fun with Nan and she was mighty scornful. It seems Margaret pitied poor Nan before she came east because "you have no white ring like Mamma and Aunty Edith Knox." By the white ring, she meant their diamond engagement rings as you may guess and she was very anxious to know if there was no way in which Nan could get one."* [1892-05-30(-) 20180308-1 Bertha (Backbay Boston) to Henry (StL)]

As the preceding letter revealed, Bertha had a keen ear for a child's innocent humor.

D. LATER POETRY

Bertha continued to write poetry throughout her life. Sometimes, she would dash off a poem in short order. In the following, she composed a poem on a postcard in the summer of 1910 as she was making her connection in Boston on her way to Rye Beach.

> *We have arrived in Boston city*
> *We've all been car sick, more's the pity!*
> *We had no flask to make us well,*
> *But who forgot it, I won't tell.*
> *We've but one hour more to go,*
> *Praise God, from whom all blessings flow!*

[1910-06-09 Bertha – Postcard (Boston) to Henry (Price Bldg, StL)]

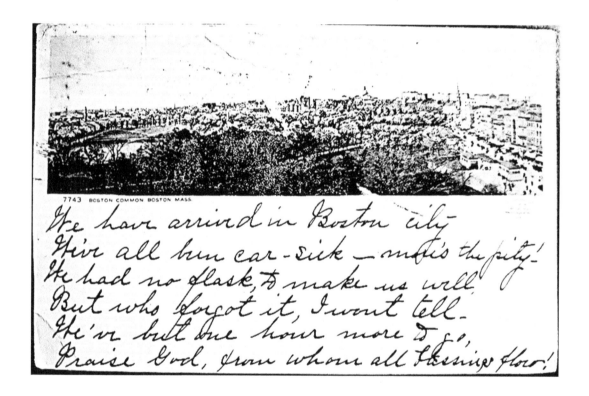

Bertha wrote the following poem in 1918 which explained her view of a woman's right to change her mind. This poem seemed to take her back to the time when she was a debutant.

Lo

Were you angry, sir, last night
When you went away?
You were scarce, I thought, polite.
I was not, you say?

Pardon, tis a woman's right
Oft to change her mind.
If I took another's side,
I was not unkind.

Were you aught but dull, my friend,
You'd have long since guessed,
Woman never aids that cause
Which she hold the best.
[Bertha's Poem #32, May 2, 2018]

To use one of her favorite adjectives, Bertha's poetry is delicious!

CHAPTER 7 – BERTHA'S FIRST DIARIES (1888–1889)

Bertha kept a diary (actually three diaries running consecutively) of her activities for exactly one full year from May 1, 1888 through April 30, 1889. These diaries are referenced as: 1888-05 Diary (which begins May 1, 1888), 1888-11 Diary (which begins on November 1, 1888), 1889-04 Diary (which begins on April 1, 1889). It is not clear why she kept a diary for just this one year. It is possible that her mother, who kept diaries, suggested it as a useful exercise or, alternatively, Bertha may have decided that such a record of her activities would be interesting to her later in her life.[60]

A. 1888-05 DIARY

The first of Bertha's diaries began on May 1, 1888 (the 1888-05 Diary[61]).

To make it "official", Bertha dutifully signed her name on the first inside page.

---

[60] As the readers of CHAPTER 4, "A Three-Year-Old In Europe", understand, the review of daily diary entries can be tedious. Nevertheless, some readers will find interest in the activities of a 23-year-old debutant during the late 19th century. Also, it is hoped that the selected excerpts may be of particular interest so that the reader can be spared the more mundane daily recitations. For enthusiasts, the entire diaries have been transcribed and are available to read.

[61] If not otherwise stated, the quotations under each daily date included in this section refer to this 1888-05 Diary.

1. EACH DAY'S ACTIVITIES

Bertha's 1888-89 diary contained pretty complete summaries of each day's activities and, periodically, some more interesting "snippets". For example, after the church wedding rehearsal for Tom McKittrick and Hildegarde Sterling (who were married on May 9, 1888), Bertha wrote of a discussion among her female friends as to who would be next to marry.

> *May 7, 1888*
>
> *... The rehearsal of the wedding at the church. It thunders, lightning, pours. The party adjourns to our house. George Choate. The pianist is late and E.[62] plays a couple of waltzes. We ballot for the girl to be next married. Mattie McKittrick[63] has the most votes. For the man – a tie between George Fishback and Henry Scott. Tom and Hildegarde both very quiet. "When 'neath her dimpled chin, she tucked her violin."*

Two days later, Bertha described the wedding, which was then the topic of conversation at the succeeding day's Topic Club.

> *May 9, 1888*
>
> *Hildegarde's wedding day. ... The wedding is prompt. The first on record. At the most solemn part of the service, the sun comes out radiantly. The reception. "One of the prettiest weddings ever seen." "The prettiest bridesmaids dresses we ever saw." "The pink roses give just the touch of color needed." Etc. Etc. For fear of forgetting, though, I don't think there is much danger, I will name over the wedding party in the order in which they walked out of church. Hildegarde Sterling and Tom McKittrick, Alma Sterling and George Leighton, Edith Sterling and Henry Scott, Mattie McKittrick and Dick Kennett, Janet January & Eben Richards, Isabel Vallé & Edward Dameron, Charlotte Kayser & John Shepley, Edith January and George Fishback, Bertie Drake & Wayman Cushman, Anne Shepley and Gist Blair.*
>
> *May 10, 1888*
>
> *The unfortunate Topics which discussed the wedding only.*

But the Topic Club did have its moments. "*Topic Club. Almost our first really rational meeting. Chinese Exclusion Bill. French Government.*" [1888-11 Diary, January 10, 1889]
Another of the topics discussed was immigration. [see 1888-11 Diary, February 21, 1889]

Much of Bertha's diary entries included the various house calls that she made, often with one of her friend's, such as Nan Shepley; the walks and rides through the park; her German studies; the games of tennis & whist; and the other evening events including music and poetry reading. One pretty typical day was:

> *May 22, 1888*
>
> *Alma, Edith Sterling, Mattie & I take the last named's cart and go to the park which is looking its prettiest, with lunch and a novel. After reaching the park, grand debate as to how to dispose of the horse. Finally, after careful study of the various buckles, we unharness him from the shafts and fasten him by us with some trouble. I take grape vine swing, they take rug. We become so interested in our novel "Criss Cross", that we drive in slowly so as to be able to read aloud as we go & finish it, and we, none of us, like the ending. It threatens rain. I reach home barely in time to dress for a horseback ride.*
> [1888-05 Diary]

---

[62] Possibly Edward Dameron who courted Bertha.
[63] Mattie McKittrick married Will Stribling on November 6, 1889, 1 ½ years later. It is certainly possible that Tom and Hildegarde McKittrick, who married on May 9th, two days after this event, knew something about this romance.

2. TRIP TO NEW YORK

Bertha wrote in her diary about the Drakes' trip to New York City (i.e. George Sr., Bertha M, George Jr. and Bertha), leaving St. Louis on May 24, 1888. The sendoff was grand, with various people joining them at the train station for their departure. H.C.S. sent a "*box of roses and maidenhair fern ... One of the prettiest boxed I ever saw.*"

Train travel must have been tiresome. The family left for New York on May 24th and arrived on the 26th. "*Mamma utterly miserable. Self, ditto, but less so. O for seven feet of earth for a grave! Except for our own feelings, journey peasant, weather cool in fact. "Every prospect pleases and only man (or woman) is vile!*" [Diary 1888-05, May 25, 1888]

Bertha took in the sights in New York City, including going to the Metropolitan Museum where she regarded a portrait of the woman who she aspired to be.

> *Drive through park looking its prettiest to Metropolitan Museum. The Wolfe Collection. Beautiful. "Last Token" by Gabriel Max. Superb portrait of Catherine Wolfe. She is just the type of woman I should like to look like.* [May 28, 1888]

Catharine Lorillard Wolfe (8 March 1828 – 4 April 1887) was an American philanthropist and art collector.

Bertha wrote of the Drakes trips to the theater. "*Lyceum Theater. "The Wife." One of the best society plays I ever saw. And admirably put on the stage. The hero and the old general especially fine. "George, men were made especially for the use of women." Indignant G. "Well, I'd like to know if men weren't made before women."* [1888-05 Diary, May 30, 1888] And "*Wallack's "The Lady and the Tiger." Not so good as I expected. DeWolf Hopper the best thing in it."* [1888-05 Diary, June 2, 1888]

One play, which didn't go over so well was *Lady of Lyons*. Bertha wrote: "*Went with Mamma to see Mrs. Potter in the "Lady of Lyons", and I must say I never saw anything quite so poor in my life. How people's tastes have changed since that play was the rage. Although I will say the play might have been better if it had not been so wretchedly given. Poor Mrs. Potter! She had to face a hostile audience too, who laughed at and criticized her the whole time.*" [1888-05 Diary, June 6, 1888] One historical account of this period in Mrs. Potter's acting career was: "*Her reception [in NYC] varied from chilly to little more than kind, but she persisted for a number of years, even taking her troupe overseas.*"

On some days, Bertha went to two theater performances, such as on June 7th: "*Went to theatrical performance at Wallack's with Mamma & George. So so. Evening – Went to see "Nadjy"[64] at the Casino with the same. Very good!*" [1888-05 Diary, June 7, 1888] The New Times wrote after the opening on May 14, 1888, "*Nadjy" is the title of the latest production in comic opera. The work was made known last night at the Casino to an audience which crowded the large auditorium and displayed a most suggestive eagerness to applaud on the slightest provocation.*"

It seemed that hardly a day went by without the theater. On June 9th, the Drakes went to The Broadway theater to see *The Queen's Mate*. "*Very good.*"

Being in New York provided ample opportunities for shopping. "*Was fitted at Altman's, ordered four dresses, blue, white, strawberry roan and dark red.*" [1888-05 Diary, May 31, 1888] And "expeditions":
> *An expedition to Stern's for Milward's needles[65] and much loss of time and temper. ... A pleasant day as far as weather goes, but have discovered that my temper is an extremely uncertain quantity.* [1888-05 Diary, June 1, 1888]

3. READING
While on her New York trip as she was always wont to do, Bertha read books, many books: *Story of Colette & A Life's Mistake, Beautiful Jim* by John Strange Winter, *Indian Summer* by William Dean Howells, *A Bachelor's Blunder* by W.E. Norris (one of the main characters is named "Bertie"), *A Teacher of the Violin & other Stories* by J.H. Shorthouse. After reading the first volume of *Clarissa's Ordeal*[66] Bertha wrote: "*Vanity of vanities, all is vanity.*[67]" [1888-05 Diary, June 3, 1888]),

Reading was not always for pleasure and amusement. As Bertha wrote, "*Read. Finished "Clarissa's Ordeal" and "A Family Fend." Read aloud "Leslie Goldwaits" to Mamma in the afternoon while she worked. My mind is running to waste. I must do some solid reading.*" [1888-05 Diary, June 5, 1888] Other books were: *Two Generations, Signa's Sweetheart*. One Diary entry was about *A Woman's Reason* by William Dean Howells: "*I enjoy Howells just at present. He suits me. It is photography not art, I suppose, but it is very fine photography and I feel in reading the books as I do when talking to a person who thoroughly understands me.*" [1888-05 Diary, June 21, 1888].

Bertha read these and many other books over a period of a little more than one month.

4. UNCLE WILLIAM AND AUNT MARY
On June 12, 1888, the Drakes went to visit Uncle William and Aunt Mary Roberts[68]. "*Papa, George and I go out to Morristown. Everything looks beautiful. Uncle William and Aunt Mary, the same as ever. Nothing gives me the same feeling of tranquility as sitting on that porch looking off across the brook and lawn to the hills.*" [1888-05 Diary]

---

[64] Nadjy refers to an operetta of the same name which opened at the Casio Theater on Broadway on May 14, 1888. In this operetta, the title character of 'Nadjy' appears in at least one scene in an all-black ballerina costume including a hat."

[65] Milward's Needles: The earliest reference to the Milward family in connection with needle making is a James Milward who was a needle maker on Fish Hill in 1676. Symon Milward created the company of Henry Milward & Sons aka Milward's Needles (Milward's) in 1730 at the age of 40, in Redditch, United Kingdom. It was, however, his son Henry who takes credit for the foundation of the company as the company was registered in his name during the first year of his birth.[see Redditch Museum Family tree] From the first half of the 18th century, the name of Henry Milward and Sons became well known as the makers of good quality needles. At one point, they were the largest manufacturer of its type in the world, producing knitting needles, surgical needles, and fishing tackle, from a number of factories both in the UK and globally, such as Murcia, Spain.

[66] Probably - *Clarissa, or, the History of a Young Lady* - an epistolary novel by English writer Samuel Richardson, published in 1748.

[67] Ecclesiastes 1:2

[68] Mary Roberts was George Sr.'s cousin. [See 1862-04 Letters of George Drake Sr.]

From Morristown NJ, the Drakes went to Boston on June 15, 1888. The following diary entry was written on June 18th:

> Scorching! The hottest day we have had. Papa and George go to see the procession for Bunker Hill Day in Charlestown. Mamma & I read aloud, etc. Afternoon – We all struggle to keep cool. Evening – We go down to see sunset on the river. I understand what Lowell meant.
> > "And Boston shows a soft Venetian side
> > In that Arcadian light when roof & tree,
> > Hard prose by day light, dream in Italy."
> Went to Public Garden afterwards. Like a scene from fairyland or Germany. Electric lights across the water. We plebeians take a swan boat ride.
> [1888-05 Diary, June 18, 1888]

The 1888 Boston Beaneaters

While in Boston on the 19th, Bertha rowed in the public gardens: "*I am glad I am a stranger who can do it.*" [1888-05 Diary, June 19, 1888] The men attended the baseball game which featured the Boston Beaneaters against the New York Giants. Boston won 8 to 7.

5. RYE BEACH

The Drakes went from Boston to the Farragut House in Rye Beach on June 20, 1888. Bertha described the trip and her arrival in her diary:

> June 20, 1888
> Pours floods!! Finish rereading Leslie Goldthwaite[69]. Feel pretty miserable but pack anyway. We take the train for Northampton, gradually glide out of the rain. I had forgotten how pretty the road was. The people interest me too, but it is warm. Meet Mr. Carter and Mr. Sawyer. Arrive at station, cordial welcomes, frightened horse. Handsome Phonny Batchelder and his late of true love. O the air, the air, the air!!! New mown hay & ocean breezes. The Farragut & geraniums. Mrs. Frank. Uncle Gus. His theories on wine drinking. The new ballroom. Moonlight on the sea!!

---

[69] *A Summer In Leslie Goldthwaite's Life,* By Mrs. A. D. T. Whitney, 1866.

a. Rye Beach Activities

Bertha's days in Rye Beach were often spent reading, going on walks, ocean baths, visits to friends in nearby towns such as Portsmouth, driving a carriage, watching baseball, tennis, afternoon tea, music, singing & dancing at night, and church on Sunday.

The Starrs, friends of the Drakes, arrived in Rye Beach two days after the Drakes, as well as various other couples for the summer. Bertha was disappointed with the "*improvements*" to their Rye Beach Episcopal church, St. Andrew's-by-the-Sea.

> *June 22, 1888*
> *... The Starrs came today and Pepper came with them. Esther, Pepper and I took a walk up the beach and Pepper thought those nice-looking pods were fresh water. Poor old doggie. We met several couples!!! What is Rye coming to? We inspected the church. The improvements have disimproved it very much. It looks like the outside of a checker board. Met Mrs. Lewis who has been at the head of the work and tactfully said it looked so <u>fresh</u>. It does!!! She said the head painter wanted to paint the doors green but she stopped him. For all small mercies! Moonlight. Esther plays on the autotroph(?).*

Esther Starr's arrival gave Bertha a chance to play tennis – Bertha's first game of the season. Bertha recorded in her diary: "*Fairly well matched! That is, we play equally badly.*" [June 25, 1888, 1888-05 Diary]

Bertha wrote of her first sea bath of the season on June 27th as "gorgeous". In the evening, "*Ike sings, Mrs. Starr sings, Mr. Starr and Mamma sing duets.*"

On Sundays, Bertha was generally in charge of arranging flowers at the church.

> *July 1, 1888*
> *Sunday. Arise very early to arrange the flowers in the church. O the deliciousness of that early morning and the ferns, flags and daisies in the dear quiet of the little church. Esther joins me later. We ask the clergyman, Mr. Cook, about the hymns. Service. I do not receive the message about the choir. The music goes like seat(?). I am unchristian, but delighted. Read to the boys. Afternoon, service. The Bordmans. A quiet time on the rocks. The rain. Read to the boys again.*

She also wrote of the 4th of July and the fireworks – "*What disappointing things they are.*"

> *July 4, 1888*
> *Arise very late. A most glorious sea bath, Miss Sherwood and I outstay all comers. Piazza talk, the richest woman in America, etc. Call on the Bordmans, the Whites & Miss Morse, also on Mrs. Jenness. "I want to(?) know." Fireworks! What disappointing things they are. First appearance of the strawberry roses(?).*

A few days later, there was a ball at the Farragut. Due to the scarcity of men, Bertha and some friends fill in. "*... A ball!! Charlotte, Daisy Jones and I acted as men. Ike Starr being the only real man available.*" [July 7, 1888]

b. The Reading Club, Choir, Plays

Throughout Bertha's life, she was always involved in reading, church choir and play acting. Being in Rye Beach was no exception and, during the summer of 1888, Bertha was active in all three.

> *July 14, 1888*
> *First meeting of the reading club. Begin "Marzio's Crucifix" by F. Marion Crawford. Members: Sarah and Mary Andrew (Boston), Bessie and Annie Shober, Charlotte Siter and Esther Starr (Philadelphia), Daisy Jones, Maud and Lorni(?) Leland, (New York), Martha Dana (Boston), Sarah Liblitts (Troy), Miss Guinar (New Haven(?)), Lulie Abbot (Boston), Mamie Cumming*

(Milton), Queenie Cabot (Stamford), & myself. Afternoon – Drive & tea with Myra, Mrs. Ogden & Miss Jones. Evening – They come down with me to Farragut & dance.

July 15, 1888
Sunday. Family make disagreeable remarks on the subject of my late rising. Arrange flowers in church. Delicious early morning in the church. Service. Row about the hymns; Mr. Hoffmann wins. Much vexation of spirit in consequence. Afternoon – Charlotte, Daisy, Esther and I go sit on the rocks. Then to church. I am the only member of the Farragut choir faithful to my post. Go sit on the rocks with Myra & Miss Jones. Evening – Walk with Papa to see Myra. Then around the square. Walk with Miss Andrews & Esther on the porch until I am weary.

July 20, 1888
Reading Club met in the little parlor because of the theatrical people in the hall. Rehearse the play. A game of pool with the Andrews and Miss Shimmin. Evening – Daisy & I go together to the entertainment. One play very poor, one rather good by the Pluto Thespians – recitations by George Belford, really unusually good, though some thought them too long. My first & last appearance "Aux Italiens", "The Pemberton Mill", "How Ruiby(?) Played."

July 21, 1888
Keep the Reading Club waiting because I could not find "Marzio". Linger and talk on the porch. Rehearse the play with Miss Shimmin for critic Ike does not like the play. Rex is going to do beautifully. Afternoon – Drive to Portsmouth with Mamie Cummins, Daisy Jones, Esther Starr. What jolly foolish times girls can have together. So much more fun than when men are around. "You is the ladies that came last year." Evening – Farragut ball of the usual ... Though I did have one dance with Tommy O'Tumble(?). Mr. Hotchkiss's roses.

July 22, 1888
Another Sunday morning in the little church. A fairly good choir. Afternoon – It poured floods. Had a quiet comfortable reading and writing time. Evening – Wrote out the answers to questions for the psychological society which Miss Shimmin had. Sang hymns. Sat in the room until half past eleven reading and never saw the eclipse. Stupid object! Why did I not raise the curtain and see that the rain was over. Esther's bad behavior in choir. "Ha! Ha! What have we here!"

July 23, 1888
Reading Club. Put out the wash. Am late to rehearsal of play but so is almost everyone. Postpone it until after dinner. After second rehearsal, Esther and I take books, papers, writing materials and chocolate creams and spend a long lazy afternoon on the rocks, joined later by Daisy Jones with her banjo and Maud Leland. Evening – Miss S. Andrews and I go to see Magician together. Then to the rocks. O the spray, the moonlight. College songs! The most perfect beautiful night!

July 24, 1888
Reading Club finishes "Marzio's Crucifix" and is rather disappointed. An invitation from the Januarys to go to Jamestown for a week. Rehearse the play. Are improving. Afternoon – Drive to Portsmouth with Mrs. Hotchkiss. The receiving basin. Spend all my money. Drive home on seat with Miss Guinar. "Put yourself in her place." Evening – Wear my red and gold shirt. Dance. Various maneuvers to escape from M.L., otherwise the "burr". Daisy, Esther and I go down on the rocks in the moonlight.

July 25, 1888

Reading Club. Sallie Tibbits reads selections from "The Life of a Girl Eighty Years Ago."[70] Bathing delicious – 60°. Rehearsal of play. Not so good as yesterday. Write. A glorious sunset on the rocks. Browning. Wonderful effects of color in the water. Esther joins me for a while. Evening – Mrs. Hotchkiss secures Daisy, Miss Tibbitts and myself to entertain the Morses! Miss Guinar, Miss Abbot and Ike Starr sing. More exquisite moonlight effects on the water from the rocks.

July 26, 1888

Reading Club. Letters on the subject of love very interesting. Bathing 68°. Rehearsal of play. Better than yesterday. Afternoon – Write a joint letter to Janie Seldon and have tea in Charlotte's room, Miss Andrews and I having given up our walk. Esther and I sit on the rocks, watch the sunset, read scraps of Browning. Evening – Meet Mr. Descamps. Pace up and down the piazza with him. "Warburton is not quite dead, I find." Mr. D. has met Mattie Wadsworth. A ball night of the same type as usual. I think it must be far more tiring to dance a man's part than a lady's for it never used to tire me so at home.

July 27, 1888

Reading Club. Bathing. Rehearsal. Rehearse again. Bowling Club. Play very badly. My mind is a chaos. I can think of nothing but play. Took a walk in afternoon with Daisy, Esther, Charlotte and Miss Tibbitts. Escaped from maudlin to do it. ... an uncharitable thing.

July 28, 1888

Reading Club. Bathing. Rehearsal. Afternoon – A very uncomfortable walk in blowing wind with Esther, Daisy & Miss Tibbitts. My red hat! Practicing at the church with Mr. Hoffmann. Evening – A hop night. Flowers from Mrs. Hyde & Mr. Hotchkiss. My black gown. Ike's compliment!

July 29, 1888

Sunday. The usual delicious early morning in the church. Struggles with the geraniums in the font. A thoroughly good enjoyable sermon from Phillips Brooke's brother John on the story of Joseph. Self-sacrifice. "There is no gain except by loss." That is not quoted from the sermon but that was the idea. A lovely afternoon on the rocks with Esther, Daisy & part of the time Mr. Hotchkiss. Superb spray. Evening service. Talk with the Bents. Then rejoin the girls on rocks. Evening - Music. Mrs. Lundell's friend & Miss Guinar.

July 30, 1888

Reading Club. Finish Eliza Bowne's letters. Superb bathing. Rehearse. Afternoon – Put out the waste. Then take my writing materials and books down to the willows where Esther is in her hammock. Write to Nan, then read "Annie Kilburn" aloud to Esther & to Ike who joins us and smokes a cigarette in peace on a corner of my shawl. Glorious sunset. Evening – Rehearsal. Miss Beale criticizes. The two men give an amateur operatic exhibition. "I'll go and propose to the maid, do you hear, to the maid?"

August 3, 1888

Morning – Arrange the stage. Rex! A call from Miss Morse. More arranging. Good stage effect. The last rehearsal. Rest and read on the rocks. Take a walk with Mr. Descamps. The play. "Who is to win him?"[71] "Mrs. Brushleigh." Myself. "Rose" Lousita Leland. "Musidora" Darcy Jones. "Sylvia" Charlotte Siter. "Minuetta" Esther Starr. "Arabella" Mary Andrews. "Maid" Mary

---

[70] *A girl's life eighty years ago*; selections from the letters of Eliza Southgate Bowne (1783–1809).
[71] *Who's to Win Him* – Thomas J Williams. A farce in one act.

Cummins. "Cyril Dashwood" Ike Starr. "Prattleton Primrose" Rex Sholer. "Dog(?) to Mrs. Brushleigh" Pepper. A wild success, could not have been greater. It certainly was an unusually pretty effective play but over it all to Miss Stimmin. Lemonade in Esther's room. Mr. Arnold & the flowers.

c. A Girl's Life

Bertha enjoyed being a girl, especially during the summers in Rye Beach. On August 4, 1888, Bertha again wrote in her diary about having *"an ideal, jolly, foolish time. O girls are so nice."*

August 8, 1888

Ada Eliot, Emma and I walk down to the chasm, sit there and talk, are joined by G.M.B.[72] Walk home. Mr. Babson is there. Try some Requiem. Afternoon – Watch tennis playing & read "Confessions of a Frivolous Girl" aloud. Say goodbye to Mr. Babson. Evening – A hop at the casino. Mr. Stoddard. Delicious dance. A long talk with Mattie. A chocolate cake & watermelon party at the McKittrick's. Holiday. Hodgman cottage. Ada Eliot's song & stories. "Over the Banisters." John Davis' bite. I know now why. Emma and I talk until the small hours.

August 9, 1888

... Evening – the whole party come to the Lanes. We bake vinegar squares[73] and nut taffy, sing a college book of songs halfway through, beside attempting some Lassen[74] songs. A very jolly time. Emma and I talk until one o'clock.

August 10, 1888

... Evening – Mattie & Emma make experiments with candy but fail because we all become absorbed in Lassen's songs & the candy burns too long.

August 11, 1888

Pack my trunk. Pull candy for the fair with Em, Myra, Lucy, Mattie, Mr. Harding & Hugh. Succeed very well. Afternoon - Go to the fair, buy a tray cover and work bag for mother's birthday, then bid goodbye to them all and, with Mr. Lane's flowers in my hand, drive off with Mattie & G.M.B. to Beverly. What a good time I have had. Take the train at Beverly, after some trouble about my trunk check and arrive at Rye, safely met by Mamma & Miss Grace who have just had a very narrow escape of being run over by the engine. We climb stage but get down again & are driven home by Papa. Return to my room but receive a visit & cordial welcome from Bessie Shober & the Andrews. A leader(?) "Woe be unto you when all men speak well of you." Visit from Belle Doolittle.

August 12, 1888

Sunday. A stormy day spent in my room, on the bed. Hold a regular reception, am hardly left alone at all. It is very pleasant to have such a warm welcome back. It is a nice day to spend in the room with a cozy wood fire but I am sorry to miss Percy Brown's sermon.

---

[72] GMB: George Morey Bartlett (See 1888-11 Diary)

[73] "Salt & Vinegar Squares" were like vinegar potato chips

[74] Eduard Lassen (13 April 1830 – 15 January 1904) was a Belgian-Danish composer and conductor. Despite being of Danish birth, he spent most of his career working as the music director at the court in Weimar. A moderately prolific composer, Lassen produced music in a variety of genres including operas, symphonic works, piano works, lieder, and choral works among others. His most successful pieces were his fine vocal art songs for solo voice and piano which often used elements of German and Belgian folk music.

August 16, 1888

... Come up for one dance, then Sallie treats to lemonades in a corner of the porch. Mr. Deacon joins us and gently "burbles" Wordsworth, Lowell, etc. in my ear until nearly half past eleven when we are amazed to discover the time.

August 17, 1888

We discuss costumes. Mr. Deacon shows me the curtains he has brought down for me. "You must not mind your mother." Start to get ready for bathing but it thunders, lightens and pours. Give up our call to the Wendells on that account. Start to walk. It rains and we take refuge in the carriage house. Walk again, three cents worth of candy. Rains again, take refuge in the casino, ice cream soda water. Wonderful effects of sea and sky. Evening – Meet to drape and discuss tableaux in my room. Lemonade.

August 18, 1888

Mr. Deacon exhibits his photographs on the piazza. Mr. Gillilan, Rex & I have a great deal of fun over them. Delicious bath, choir practice, Miss Blake playing the organ. Drive to call on the Wendells with Daisy and the two Bordmans. They are out. Go on to Portsmouth. Peach ice cream! Come home rather late. "Gilkooly's"(?) anxiety. Dr. Dickey has arrived. G.M. Bartlett also. The concert. Carrie Philbrick sings quite well. Esther behaves very badly. A talk on the piazza. "Mrs. Drake says you will please come upstairs very soon."

August 23, 1888

Evening – We have a little dance in the hall. Then adjourn to our room for a parting spree for Daisy. Invite all the girls who were in the tableaux. Lemonade & orange cake. Turn down the gas, light a fire & let in floods of moonlight. O, the light on the sea.

August 26, 1888

Miss Andrews and I arrange the flowers in the church. Esther not being well enough to. Mr. Hovey preaches. The music does not go very well. Mr. Shimmin thinks it a good sermon and we disagree. Afternoon – under the trees after seeing the Haywards off. Afternoon service. Then read aloud "Annie Kilburn"[75] to Sallie, Esther & Ike. We become so thrilled over the scene where Putney becomes intoxicated that we sat there until it was quite dark. Evening – Bessie, Miss Andrews, Miss Mary ..., Esther, Mr. Deacon, Mr. Paul & I sit talking on the porch, principally about love. We see from Mr. Gillilan's expression that Miss B. has refused him(?). Miss Andrews & I try to escape from the Deacon but he pursues.

August 29, 1888

We read aloud, beginning a story called "The Village Genius" in a book most exquisitely bound which Mr. Deacon lends me. Bathing 58°. Talk about "the girl who would like to marry" & "the man who would like to marry" and plan off the pictures to suit people in the house.

d. The Tableaux.

On August 14, 1888, Bertha wrote of the preparation for "The Tableaux". Apparently, the ladies and gentlemen who were lodging at the Farragut House would put on various costumes to represent a famous painting. In this particular case, the tableaux was of a painting by John Singleton Copley[76]. This was a big event and many of the Farragut House lodgers participated, including Bertha, her mother and her father.

---

[75] *Annie Kilburn* by William Dean Howells. Originally published in a serialized format in *Harper's New Monthly Magazine*, Vol. 77, nos. 457-462 (June-November 1888)

[76] John Singleton Copley (1738 – September 9, 1815) was an Anglo-American painter, active in both colonial America and England.

August 14, 1888
Afternoon – Discuss tableaux, I am to be Santa Barbara a Palma Vecchio. "A tangerine figurine", "Agribbins". Question. Has Miss Blake any sense of humor?

August 20, 1888
A Copley portrait. Sallie Tibbitts - St. Barbara; B. Drake - Mme. Lebrun et sa fille; M. Dana & E. McKenzie - L'Etoile; L. Leland – Richeleu; Mr. Tibbitts - A connoisseur; Rez Shober – a Russian exile; Mr. Godwin – monk & warrior; Mr. An(?) – a Greek girl; Miss Miller Drews & Mr. McKenzie - ... Veronexe; S. Andrews & H. Osborne – the daughter the Duch of Devon'shr & Sist.; B. Shober & M. Andrews – of the Niobe(?); M. Cummins – Rajahs; E. Starr – a figure de tannagre [tanagre?]; D. Jones – figures from a Sobieski; Mr. Deacon – Greek frieze; M. Dana – cowboy; I. Starr, L. Abbot, A. Lewis & M. Cummins - monk & choir boys; I. Cummins, G. Drake & W. Smith. Arranged by M... Blake & Miss Shimmin. Announced by Arnold. Pronounced by all to be the most genuinely artistic tableaux they had ever seen. Lemonade in E's room.
[1888-05 Diary, August 20, 1888]

August 21, 1888
Walked on the porch and talked about the tableaux, saw Mary Andrews off and went in bathing 62°. Afternoon – Drove to Portsmouth with Bessie Shober. Bessie, Rex, Esther & I. Rex's views of college life. Evening – Sit on porch with Sadie Andrews, a group forms around us. Lulie Abbot's tact. A Virginia Reel. I dance with Miss Shimmin. Mr. Deacon & Mr. Gillilan. "The Festive Goat & the Sportive Cow." A lemonade & orange cake party for Miss Leland, a farewell banquet at which Miss Leland, Miss Shimmin, Sallie Tibbitts, Daisy Jones, Esther Starr & I assisted.

August 27, 1888 (Monday)
... Afternoon – Sit on the rocklets with Sallie & Esther, after having a vigorous discussion on the subject of the tableaux with Mrs. Peabody who changes her requirements for my costume at a few hours' notice. The Deacon joins us and we have a very pleasant talk. Mr. D. Tells my fortune. Not a very happy one. Evening – the tableaux. I am attired entirely in black as a Spanish Lady, rhinestones, diamonds, pink roses, etc. Take part in Artist's dream - at sight of me the Artist wakes. These tableaux are a miserable failure compared with the others. We knew they would be. "Very well, I will reserve my compliments in future." Stupid.

e. Games & Story Telling

The Farragut House residents played various games, especially when it rained. – "*Again it rains. We play twenty questions ...*"
The question:

September 1, 1888
I think I've guessed your secret, though the truth from me was holden,
For you said it had no substance, and the Greek's have called it golden.
...
The answer to the twenty questions was silence.

August 30, 1888
Sit on the porch with Miss Shimmin, Sallie & Esther, the latter two playing "hoppity" while I write. I tell them my dream about the evil eyed raven. It gives me a shudder to think of it now.

September 1, 1888
Sit on the piazza and tell interesting tales about ghosts & insane people.

September 2, 1888
Evening – We sit in a group by the fire, while Miss Shimmin, Sallie and Mr. Deacon rival each other in burglar stories.

f. The Drakes Go To Maplewood

The Drakes and some of their Farragut friends decided to lodge at the Maplewood Hotel/Inn in Bethlehem NH for several days and take a vacation from their vacation. Bethlehem is due North from Rye Beach and very near Mt. Washington.

September 4, 1888
Sallie Tibbitts, Martha Dana, Esther & I depart on to the coach, father & Mr. Starr also on top, ...
... Sallie & her father have a final discussion where to go. We are separated when we find our seats. Aromatic spirits of ammonia. Engine off track ahead of us at North Conway. All join & walk up & down platform. Leave the Tibbitts & Danas at Glen Station. Arrive at Maplewood. The first person we see is Powers Harris. I room with Esther. Rex's cordial welcome. The poor boy has been pretty homesick. "Please promise to talk to me all the evening." Rex's sweet peas. Walk up & down the piazza, I with Rex, Esther with Powers.

The Maplewood Hotel, Bethlehem NH

September 5, 1888
Ride down to village & walk back. Afternoon – Drive to Sunset Hill. Papa, Mr. & Mrs. Starr & Esther in buckboard, Rex & I in a buggy with the best pair of horses in the stable. How we flew. Such a delicious drive. Rex is the dearest boy I ever saw. See Sugar Hill House & Mrs. & Miss Larduer. Evening – We sit in the ball room with Mrs. Harris, Powers & Rex. The mountain air does make one sleepy & hungry. Rex's lemonades. How sweet Mrs. Harris is!!

September 6, 1888
Arise at 6:15 and prepare for an expedition to Mt. Washington. Esther, father & I. Very cold. Different interesting people at Fabian's wonderful views. Good natured man who tries to open window. Superb view from top. Can see ocean. My usual luck about weather – one of the four clear days that month. Very cold but could not have had a better day otherwise. Lester O. Peck & wife. Bridgeport. Edwin Banks. Father meets Mr. Fisher & Miss Miller. Meet Mr. Harris. Evening – Do not dress but go to the ball room. Talk to Powers Harris all the evening. Say goodbye to Rex.

September 7, 1888
Esther & I coming down the stairs to our astonishment see Rex Shober ahead of us. He tells us he has been detained by the news of the death of Mr. Bradly, old Mrs. Shober's brother, Luly Abbotts grandfather. I go for a delicious three hour & a half drive through the mountains with Powers Harris. What a sweet boy he is. Give up the drive to the Profile House but Papa & Mr. Starr & meet Miss Dater(?) go. Esther, Mrs. Starr & I hunt for a place among the boulders where we read all the afternoon. Start for a walk to the observatory but it looks so cold we give it up. Evening – Desperately dull. The Bulgarian lecturer. Read aloud. Pack.

September 8, 1888
Give up trip to Centre Harbor[77] on account of storm and have Maplewood at eight o'clock AM. Meet Sallie Tibbitts & her father at Fabian's at Glen Station.

Fabian House [http://whitemountainhistory.org/Fabyan_House.html]

See Martha Dana & Luly Abbot gets on(?) at Intervale Mr. Shober joins her, both on their way to Mr. Bradley's funeral.(??) Mr. Bhober tells us they did make a plan to drive from Intervale up Mt. Washington the same day we did but gave it up because Anne was not well enough to go. Arrive at Farragut. Pretty well deserted. A telegram from Alma[78]. Pouring rain. Unpack, sew & read. Evening – Talk to Miss Anne & Kitty Jones, then retire to my room & finish "The Queen of the County", which is one of the sweetest novels I ever read.

g. Leaving Rye Beach
September 9, 1888
The last Sunday in the little church. Do not arrange flowers as not expecting to be back. I had told Mr. Childs he need have none & I did not change the order not having the heart to do it alone. Mr. Ward. A sermon on Robert Elsmere[79]. Trouble about the collection. Poor Mr. Sheldon. Afternoon – Write. Church. The parting sermon. Hymns #85, 341. Sit on the rocks with Mrs. Wilmerding, 100 B'dway. Evening – Talk to Mamma & Miss Grace.

September 10, 1888
My last day. Such a beautiful one. The golden rod is glorious. Pack nearly all day & write. Then escape to the rocks where I am now. Mamma & Papa have gone with Miss Grace & Miss Anne

---

[77] Center Harbor NH is approx.. 60 miles south of Bethlehem NH on the way to Rye Beach.
[78] Alma Canfield Sterling
[79] *Robert Elsmere* is a novel by Mrs. Humphry Ward published in 1888. It was immediately successful, quickly selling over a million copies and gaining the admiration of Henry James. Bertha refers to this novel elsewhere in her letters.

Wilkes to Portsmouth. There is water in the rock sofa so I take Miss Grace's seat. It is just as well. I should be more lonely in the other. A lovely sunset. See new moon over my right shoulder but it cannot bring me such a lovely month as the last. My beautiful summer, goodbye, goodbye. Evening – The Portsmouth althletics come to dine. Meet the Armours & bowl with them & Kitty Jones. Miss Anne's pansies.

September 11, 1888
Leave Rye on seven o'clock stage. Mr. Leighton's roses. A beautiful day. Arrive in Boston for breakfast. Meet Mr. Shober there. Afternoon – Mamma and I wander among book stores, china stores, etc. Lunch at Parker's, search for Wareham St. & find it not, buy shoes, etc. On train coming down from Rye was introduced to Miss Marguand(?).

6. NEW YORK CITY

The Drakes next went to New York City where they arrived on September 12, 1888. They stayed for two weeks, departing on September 27, 1888. New York City trips always involved shopping for dresses and theater.

September 13, 1888
Go to Altman's and select gowns. A dark red net dinner dress. Brown cloth suit. Green house dress, dark blue silk trimmed with steel passementerie[80]. Superb reception dress of shaded dull blues, silk & plush. Black jetted waist to wear with my old black net skirt.

September 14, 1888
Go for fitting to Altman's. Select two ball dresses, one white net embroidered with wild roses to be trimmed with wild roses. One exquisite pale pink. My opera wrap's gray & silver. Select two hats & a bonnet to wear with my reception dress.

September 15, 1888
Go for fitting to Altman's. Stop at Sterns on my way back. I like the people at Altman's. Miss Dwyer, head woman, Miss Smith, my fitter, and Miss Odorus, all of them.

Another fitting at Altman's "September 19, 1888 - *Fitting at Altman's.*" Additional fitting in PM.
Another fitting at Altman's September 22, 1888.
Another fitting at Altman's September 24, 1888
"*Fitting at Altman's. Three hours & a half standing.*" September 26, 1888

"September 21, 1888
Shopping. Bronze low shoes, black slippers, garnet set rhinestone hairpin, try on bonnets and jacket. Afternoon, try on dresses for three hours without stopping. Very wearying!! Get home quite late."

Being in New York City provided the opportunity to see the theater. Bertha always seemed to avail herself of any such opportunity, seeing many performances during her stay and some more than once. She would even take in two performances in one day.

September 22, 1888
Daisy comes to lunch. Then she takes me to the matinee to see "Lord Chumley", the most delicious play. Sothern's[81] acting is perfection. Caramels.

---

[80] Passementerie - :an ornamental edging or trimming (such as tassels) made of braid, cord, gimp, beading, or metallic thread.

[81] Edward Hugh Sothern (December 6, 1859 – October 28, 1933) was an American actor who specialized in dashing, romantic leading roles and particularly in Shakespeare roles. His greatest success came in the dual roles of the real Prince Rudolf and his look-alike impostor in The Prisoner of Zenda (1895).

E.H. Sothern as Lord Chumley

Evening – Mamma, George & I go to see "A Legal Wreck" [82]. Not bad but not particularly good. Lawyer, the best thing in it.

From New York City, the Drakes were able to visit various friends who lived nearby, such as the Stockwell's, who lived in Montclair, NJ. *"Afternoon – Go down to Hoboken with Papa, take a walk while waiting with Papa. Do not find Mr. Stockwell. Take train for Montclair. Train delayed by weakness of engine. Edith Stockwell meets me."* [1888-05 Diary, September 24, 1888]

Bertha always took advantage of her free time to read and often recently published books. Apparently, she read *"Robert Elsmere"* (a book of 604 pages in its original form) over a two-day period while in New York: *"Read Robert Elsmere. Glorious book!"* [1888-05 Diary, September 15, 1888]

And next, she read *John Ward, Preacher* by Margaret Deland, which provided her with insights into the current religious discussions around Anglican orthodoxy and the new liberal theologies. Bertha would refer to this ongoing debate in her diary many times over the next several weeks and months.

Even on her trips, Bertha and her family rarely missed Church on Sunday. Bertha shows her enlightenment, being able to discern the old orthodoxies from the newer theologies from her reading of *"Robert Elsmere"*, etc.

> *Went to Dr. Taylor's church. Heard Dr. Vincent preach. Afternoon – Read & wrote. Evening – Start to hear Dr. Parkhurst, no church there. Dr. Crosby, no church there. Join the Stanard's and go to a Methodist church. Had the orthodox doctrine good and strong. No new pernicious philosophies to creep into that church.*
> [1888-05 Diary, September 23, 1888]

7. ST. LOUIS

The Drakes returned home to St. Louis by train from New York City which took three days, from evening of September 27th to the morning of the 29th. After their return to St. Louis, the Drakes resumed their usual routines of dinners, house calls, intellectual discussions, church on Sundays and club meetings. Bertha also began to see more of Henry.

---

[82] *A Legal Wreck*, written by William Hooker Gillette (July 24, 1853 – April 29, 1937) was an American actor-manager, playwright, and stage-manager in the late 19th and early 20th centuries. He is best remembered for portraying Sherlock Holmes on stage and in a 1916 silent film thought to be lost until it was rediscovered in 2014.

On the evening of September 29, 1888, Bertha dined with Tom and Hildegarde McKittrick who were married in May, earlier that year. (Hildegarde Sterling McKittrick was a lifelong friend of Bertha's.) Bertha mentions "*Mr. S.'s beard*", of which there are no photographs. (One can only imagine.)

> *Go to Hildegarde's & have a perfectly charming time. Tom's miniature. The house is so cunning & they are so sweet together. At dinner, I sit between Mr. Scott & Tom, Lallie & Mr. Kent opposite. Mr. S.'s beard. Mr. Chauvenet calls after dinner. A violent tariff – free trade discussion. I support Mr. Kent against Tom.*
> [1888-05 Diary, September 29, 1888]

On Sundays, Bertha often taught Sunday School.

> *Go down for the first time to my Sunday School class. Annie McRoy and Lottie are watching for me. A warm welcome. Stella's illness. Dear children.*
> [1888-05 Diary, October 7, 1888]

Bertha made frequent "house calls" on friends and acquaintances. After one visit to an ailing older friend, she wrote "*O, the suffering! It is a good thing for one to see the other side of the shield sometimes, perhaps.*" [1888-05 Diary, October 9, 1888]

Bertha often wrote funny comments about various acquaintances in her diary. "*Meet Margaret, Ives' cousin, Miss Parker there. The debutantes!! Brother Dameron! "Gazing into vacancy".*" [1888-05 Diary, October 12, 1888]

Bertha wrote of her harmony classes. From the available information, Bertha was a good singer.

> *Evening – Harmony class under Professor Poppin. Mrs. McKittrick, Tom, Hugh & Hildegarde McK, Florence Hayward, the J's, Edith Sterling, Miss Clark, Rose Eliot, Nan & myself belong. Miss Strong directress. Harmony is going to be hard!!!!!*
> [1888-05 Diary, October 17, 1888]

Another class: "*Evening – Harmony class. First steps in composing.*" [1888-05 Diary, October 20, 1888]

Bertha participated in various clubs including: Topics, Sewing, German and Greek Dramatists, to name a few.

The sewing club had meetings at different days and times. Consequently, their meeting plans were sometimes thwarted: "*… to Mattie's for Sewing Club. Tom has forgotten the flannel again, so we do nothing but embroider & talk.*" [1888-05 Diary, October 30, 1888] Regarding another sewing club meeting: "*Sewing club at Nan's without any sewing. ["Wee"] Margaret comes in and I cannot tear myself away.*" [1888-11 Diary, February 26, 1889]

Bertha had weekly German Club meetings in addition to her German Class with Miss Hagen. On one occasion, Bertha confided that she doubted its seriousness. "*German Club at Isabel's. Very frivolous club which speaks English principally.*" [1888-11 Diary, January 7, 1889] That same evening, Bertha made an amusing comment about seeing an Italian opera after her German class. "*Go with G.M.B. to hear Trovatori. I must confess, Italian opera does seem rather funny after the German school.*" [1888-11 Diary, January 7, 1889] (Perhaps, any opera would seem funny after German school!)

Regarding her Greek Dramatists Club, Bertha recorded:

> *First meeting of the club for the study of Greek dramatists at Mrs. Green's. Members: Nan Shepley, Maud Reber, Myra & Emma Lane, Frances and Madge Markham, Margie Emmons, Sarah Hitchcock & myself. We begin with the Prometheus of Aeschylus.*
> [1888-11 Diary, February 25, 1889]

Although Bertha generally received her callers graciously, she did make exceptions. "*Evening – read aloud. Excused to callers and so miss Mr. Brookings and, O reward of virtue, Mr. Kendricks.*" [1888-05 diary, October 30, 1888] Bertha was apparently not very high on Mr. Kendricks! "*O reward of virtue!*"

In October, Bertha wrote of attending a teachers' meeting and wondering if there were more interesting endeavors.

> *Evening – Go to a teachers' meeting at the Shepley's. I do know things that are more exciting and interesting than teachers' meetings, strange as it may seem.*
> [1888-05 Diary, October 18, 1888]

When she concluded this first of her three 1888-1889 diaries, Bertha reflected on how she changed since starting this diary in May. "*I think my womanhood is begun.*"

> *So six months of my life are over. On the whole, they have been even unusually happy months and I know they have been very important ones. I can feel the change in myself and I think my womanhood is begun.*
> [1888-05 Diary, October 31, 1888]

The last pages of this 1888-05 diary included the signatures of certain people that she met.

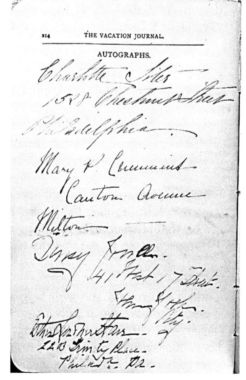

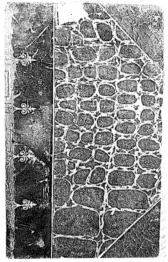

B. 1888-11 DIARY

Bertha's second diary ("1888-11 Diary"[83]) was from the period November 1, 1888 through March 31, 1889.

---

[83] If not otherwise stated, the quotations under each daily date included in this section refer to this 1888-11 Diary.

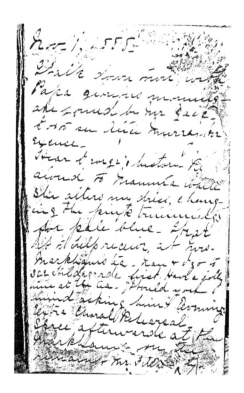

As in her prior diary, Bertha wrote down all of the events of each day, such as - *"Walk downtown with Papa"* (above on November 1, 1888). Much of her daily activities remained the same: calls on friends at their houses, receiving calls, attending her clubs (sewing, etc.), German class, helping brother George with homework, reading out loud to mama, reading her books, shopping, political discussions, concerts and church on Sundays, including teaching Sunday school.

1. NOVEMBER & DECEMBER 1888

The November 7, 1888 entry combined both politics and sorrow.

> *Sewing Club at Hildegarde's[84]. Tom comes home in a state of uproarious delight over Cleveland's defeat & Harrison's election - Triumphs over the despondent club & counts up his ill-gotten gains in a most insulting manner. Afternoon – Edith, Janet & I go to Mrs. Leighton's[85] funeral. It is terribly sad and, O, such a terrible day for a funeral, pouring in torrents.*
> (1888-11 Diary)

Receiving callers at her house was sufficiently commonly place that Bertha was surprised to have none on November 11, 1888: *"Sunday School & church. For a wonder, not a caller. Wondering."* (1888-11 Diary)

Bertha recounted a story of receiving a caller, Mr. Wiggins, on November 9 and *"I nearly fall asleep & think I see a little boy over his shoulder, while he is talking."* (1888-11 Diary) Apparently Bertha related this story to her friends since the story got out, to Bertha's embarrassment. At tea on November 12, *"Mattie told the story about falling asleep at home while Mr. Wiggins was calling on me & seeing a little boy over his shoulder, not knowing Mr. W. was the man at Sunday. Evening tea when Mr. W. was there. I shall never hear the end of it."* (1888-11 Diary) (A little boy on Mr. Wiggen's shoulder??? Undoubtedly a good laugh at Bertha's expense, but she seemed to find it funny too.)

---

[84] Hildegarde and Tom McKittrick.

[85] Isabella Bridge Leighton was Colonel George Leighton's wife (both very good friends of the Drakes).

While Bertha received calls from a number of men, Henry at this time already seemed to have a special place. On November 13, she included an entry at the end regarding the party that she attended that night: "*Note: with H.C.S. of course.*" (1888-11 Diary) Of course?? The party evidently lasted into the late evening based on Bertha's entry on the following day: "*Having slept but two hours, I appear at breakfast to the intense astonishment of the family.*" (1888-11 Diary, November 14) It may be surmised that Bertha would often sleep in especially after such occasions, as seen from her November 16 entry: "*Do not appear downstairs until after eleven.*" (1888-11 Diary)

Bertha went to nurses training on November 15 and "*toil nobly all morning.*" (1888-11 Diary) Also on that day, Bertha wrote candidly about her views of herself as a 22-year-old attending Mrs. Mackay's luncheon: "*Mattie, Nan, Maud & I depraved older girls, sit together.*" (Feeling old and depraved at 22!)

Bertha again remarked about her age on November 16: "*I feel I am growing old. Receptions bore me. Go to see Margaret afterwards. Blessed girl! How she does worship her "boppa".*" (1888-11 Diary) Interestingly, Bertha found relief by visiting Wee Margaret Hitchcock who was 10 years old at this time.

Planning and attending the social events took time and attention. On November 23 & 24, 1888, Bertha seemed to have a very busy schedule. "*Afternoon – Help receive at Mrs. Hitchcock's reception. Evening – My dinner & theater party. Mr. Lionberger & Lutie chaperoning. Katie, Lucy & myself, Mr. Scott, Mr. Chauvenet & Mr. Adams. ... Capital! Have a delicious time! Striking resemblance. I do like Mr. Zack so much. Lutie is a perfect vision in gray.*" [1888-11 Diary, November 23, 1888] Then on the next day, "*Afternoon – My chocolate party. A reception, but all the girls who help me to receive with the exception of the three debutants, Madge, Margie & Sarah, are dressed after the costume of La Belle Chocolatière. More men come than I had expected.*" [1888-11 Diary, November 24, 1888]

Bertha generally noted who were the escorts and chaperons for each occasion since having one was *de riguer* for unmarried ladies. December 3, 1888 includes the following comment: "*Dress for Mrs. Eply Catlin's party. Nan, the J's, Sarah, Margie & I go together in two carriages. Our alarm at not having escorts. One of the stupidest parties I ever went to, too crowded to dance with any comfort & none of the men I knew best there.*" [1888-11 Diary]

The ladies enjoyed their clubs, the sewing club especially. "*Sewing Club meets at the J's. Unutterable silliness!!! "Why, Bertie, you always seem so bright and gay, more so than ever."*" [1888-11 Diary, December 5, 1888] Then on December 10, "*Sewing Club at Mattie's. ... Unlimited laughter and nonsense.*" [1888-11 Diary]

Betha went to the theater on December 6, 1888 with her friends and with Zack and Lute Lionberger chaperoning. "*Evening – Go to dinner at the Shepley's. Then to see Fron-Fran(?), Mr. Zack, Lutie, Jule, Nan & I. Marvelous acting. Mr. Zack & I both moved to tears. Between acts, a great deal of laughing & nonsense. Have I ever been more gay? "But I tell you, ... as the play of life, and that woman played despair."* Years later, Bertha D. Scott included the additional comment: "*H.C.S. took Edith J. to the theater that night & sat in front of us.*"

Bertha would periodically insert some intriguing questions in her diary, such as on December 1, 1888, which Bertha wrote in quotations: "*'Have you really never been in love, Bertha?'*" [1888-11 Diary] It is not clear if this is being asked by a friend, possible Maud Turner, mentioned just previously in the Diary, or whether Bertha is asking this of herself. During a period when she increasingly saw her friends falling in love and marrying, she may have wondered. On December 16, 1888, Bertha wrote of Henry, "*Afternoon*

– H.C.S. called. "For heaven's sake, don't change. If I lose my faith in you, I don't know what will become of me.""[86]

Bertha often walked with her father downtown. Most of the time, there was no record of their conversations but, this one-time, Bertha specifically mentioned it. *"Walk downtown with Papa. A discourse on matrimony. Relieve his mind."* [1888-11 Diary, December 14, 1888] Bertha was obviously "of age" and was being caught up in the normal social affairs of young men and women. Her father, as we shall see more later, was very protective of Bertha so it is not surprising that he would raise this topic, probably with the intention of discouraging her getting too close to a man. Bertha clearly understood her father's intentions and, for the moment, put his mind at ease. Throughout, Bertha's love for her father was certain: *"Walk downtown with Papa. ... Such mud! Have a jolly Christmasy time. The world is a good place when one has a father like mine."* [1888-11 Diary, December 17, 1888]

Rumors were sometimes spread. *"Go to see the J's [Januarys], find them furious over the report that three engagements are to be announced that evening at Mattie's: Mattie's to George Fishback, Edith's [January] to Henry Scott, & Janet's [January] to Will Stribling, both [i.e. Januarys] deny theirs absolutely."* [1888-11 Diary, December 24, 1888]

Bertha described her 1888 Christmas starting with brother George, who was 13, going through the *"usual ceremonies"*.

> *George comes in very early & goes through all the usual ceremonies of asking about Santa Claus & the reindeer. Then we open our stockings. Then Miss Jennie comes to breakfast. My presents are perfectly lovely. Everyone I know, almost, has remembered me & I have thirty-five presents, besides Christmas cards, a beautiful black lynx boa and muff, among other things. It pours rain but I go to church with Nan, and into Mrs. Henry Hitchcock's afterwards. Evening – Nan, Miss Jule, Mrs. Treat, Mamma, Sara Hitchcock, George Hitchcock, Annie H., Arthur, Deck, George & I, all go to the theater to see "Lord Chumley" as do also Mattie & Mr. Downman, Janet and Mr. Stribling, Edith & Mr. Scott. All of them, except the children come to our house for a supper afterward, also Mr. Fishback & Bobby Markham. Janet's indignation: thirteen at the table.*
> [1888-11 Diary, December 25, 1888]

Bertha's 1888 Christmas was very busy. Bertha described one day just after Christmas: *"Go downtown, then fix the tête à tête room at the Imperial. Rush home & dress for Mrs. George Tausig's lunch to meet Mrs. Lawson, the soprano soloist of the Messiah. Go home & lie down. Go to the Harvard Glee Club, come home & put on my wild rose dress. Go to the Imperial with Mr. Stribling. O, the mad, wild, delicious, excitement of it. Shall I ever be as happy again? "Indeed you have no idea what I think of you." The flowers. "Mr. Schoen, you must play one more waltz.""* [1888-11 Diary, December 28, 1888]

The next day, Bertha seemed to not feel any ill effects of the previous day's partying. *"Having slept only two hours, appear at breakfast and walk downtown with Papa in wild spirits. Walk so fast and am so excited that I fairly worry him & he gives me a serious talk on the subject of the injury I am doing my nerves."* [1888-11 Diary, December 29, 1888] But on the 30th, her partying caught up with her: *"Tired nature takes her revenge and I feel as if I never could wake up. Get down very late to mission school."* [1888-11 Diary, December 30, 1888]

2. JANUARY, FEBRUARY & MARCH 1889

Bertha was courted and escorted out by various different men who generally became lifelong friends. Crittenden McKinley was one such escort who, early on, did not seem to greatly impress Bertha.

---

[86] Henry's words echo the Sting song *"If I Ever Lose My Faith in You, There'd be nothing left for me to do"*.

Crittenden McKinley comes to call. His first call. I am not quite sure that I like him very much, but I should like to make him like me. He is decidedly blunt."
[1888-11 Diary, January 6, 1889]

Crittenden was also Bertha's escort several days later.

Evening – Mrs. Jesse January's[87] party. One of the prettiest ball's I have ever seen. The room looked like some old-fashioned picture, entirely lighted by candles. Mamie Cummins was there. Crittenden McKinley as my escort. "Indeed, I will come again. I want to know you better."
[1888-11 Diary, January 10, 1889]

Henry demonstrated his patience, at least, at times:

Afternoon – H.C.S. comes to call - "I thought it must be nearly time for you to be at home." Mr. Stribling & Mr. Mitchell Scott come in. H.C.S. patiently sits them out and just as we begin to discuss interesting things, enter Mr. Ledlie. Botheration! Evening – G.M.B. calls. Stays until quarter past eleven discussing theology.
[1888-11 Diary, January 20, 1889]

Botheration! Perhaps that applied not only to Mr. Ledlie but also to the theology discussion later.

The following entry was suggestive of a deeper relationship with Henry, as are many of Bertha's diary entries.

Afternoon – H.C.S. and I go to see Mamie Cummins. She is out but we have a pleasant little talk with Mrs. Allen. It is snowing when we come out but we walk out to the park. It stops snowing, but the views are lovely. Go to see the Lanes. "Do stay to tea." Discovering it to be five minutes to six, we do so. Lula sings & Em plays. When we finally leave, "You can't be in any deeper than you are. Let's pay another call." Go see Lallie, make an appointment for tomorrow. "Can't I stand on the corner & you whistle when you are safe?"
[1888-11 Diary, January 27, 1889]

"*You can't be in any deeper than you are.*" Is it clear what Henry meant? Perhaps the answer lies in Bertha's history and in that, we have a good idea.

Bertha still had other gentlemen callers, such as Mr. Guy. "*Evening – Mr. Guy comes to call. "Please don't think I am very conceited, because I have talked so much about myself."* [1888-11 Diary, January 29, 1889] (Talking too much about yourself to Bertha was perhaps not the best approach!)

Although the escorts might change from night to night, the entertainment – the plays, etc. – often remained the same.

Evening – France, Maud, Nan & I go to Mrs. Sherman's to dinner. Afterwards with Mr. Sherman to see the "Erminie"[88]. Lutie & Mr. Zack chaperoning. "You frivolous society girls!"
[1888-11 Diary, January 24, 1889]

Erminie was evidently popular and Bertha was taken to it a second time, the next night.

Evening – Go to the Theater with Mr. Stribling to see "Erminie". A discussion as to how a man should act when reported engaged to a girl to whom he is not engaged.
[1888-11 Diary, January 25, 1889]

---

[87] Grace Valle January (1852-1919). Her husband, Jesse January, died in 1883 at the age of 33. Jesse was Janet and Edith January's brother, one of the many "J's".

[88] *Erminie* is a comic opera in two acts composed by Edward Jakobowski with a libretto by Claxson Bellamy and Harry Paulton, based loosely on Charles Selby's 1834 English translation of the French melodrama, *Robert Macaire*. The piece first played in Birmingham, England, and then in London in 1885, and enjoyed unusual international success that endured well into the twentieth century.

(That must have been an interesting discussion: "*how a man should act when reported engaged to a girl to whom he is not engaged*"!!)

Bertha was not superstitious but she clearly delighted in finding in her past the presentment of what was to come. Of one such event, Bertha writes about the throwing of apple seeds over the shoulder to divine the future. Coincidences?

> *Evening – Go to the Theater to see "Dorothy", cunning little opera, with Mr. Scott. Mr. Stribling & Mattie, spree at Mattie's afterward. Apple seeds.*
> *Note [written into her diary years later] – We cut the peeling and it fell when thrown over our shoulders in the shape of the letter S for both of us. She married Will Stribling later and I Henry Scott.*
> [1888-11 Diary, February 5, 1889]

Bertha took note at evening parties if the proportion of men to women was inappropriate – or not. "*Evening – Mrs. Lane's party. There are barely enough men to go around...*" [1888-11 Diary, January 9, 1889] Men, after all, did have some importance for a woman's self-confidence and having multiple future engagements with them provided some comfort. "*Evening – My third evening alone, but I thoroughly enjoy it and the blissful feeling that I have five invitations ahead keeps me from worrying.*" [1888-11 Diary, February 12, 1889]

Several nights later, Bertha went to the Imperial, the most splendid ball of the year. Even though Bertha was "*very blue*" in anticipating the evening, her mood changed when she received "*three invitations*" from men at the ball: she was a hit. Bertha recounted the glorious occasion in her diary.

> *Afternoon – Rest & read. Nan comes in. We are both very blue, she because she has had to give up the Imperial, I because I am going. Evening – Dress in my wild rose dress and go to the Imperial with H.C.S. Judge Breckinridge. My reaction from the blues has come and I feel radiantly happy. I have three invitations. Mr. Blair asks me to walk with him, Mr. Stribling to go see "Pygmalion & Galatea", and Mr. Crittenden McKinley for the Bachelor's Ball, but for the last, I am engaged. It is a pure joy to be alive when one feels like this. "Don't you consider it a compliment when I tell you the entire pleasure of my evening came from you?" "Five times!"*
> [1888-11 Diary, February 15, 1889]

When Bertha saw Mary Anderson in "*Pygmalion*", she remarked in her diary, "*the most beautiful woman I ever saw...*"

> *Evening – Go to the theater with Mr. Stribling to see Mary Anderson[89] in "Pygmalion and Galatea". The first time I ever saw her. She certainly is the most beautiful woman I ever saw and perfectly enchanting.*
> [1888-11 Diary, February 20, 1889]

---

[89] Mary Antoinette Anderson (July 28, 1859, Sacramento, California – May 29, 1940, Broadway, Worcestershire, U.K.) was an American stage actress. She was also billed as Mary Navarro during her silent film career. In 1883, after starring in an American production of W. S. Gilbert's Pygmalion and Galatea, she went on the London stage at the Lyceum Theatre, remaining in England for six years to perform to much acclaim including at the Shakespeare Memorial Theatre in Stratford-on-Avon.

Mary Antoinette Anderson

Interestingly, Bertha went to the theater on the next night to see who else? Mary Anderson in the "Winter's Tale".

Evening – Mr. McKinley's and Mr. Scott's theater party. Edith January & Mr. Blair, Janet & Mr. C. McKinley, myself & Mr. Stribling in front, Nan & Mr. Scott behind, to see Mary Anderson in "Winter's Tale." She is charming and it is beautifully set on the stage. We have a violent discussion as we are driving up as to whether she is awkward in the dance or not.
[1888-11 Diary, February 21, 1889]

And, Bertha went out again to see the "Winter's Tale" on the succeeding night with Henry and their friends. Bertha commented, *"She is no actress but she is beautiful."* [1888-11 Diary, February 22, 1889]

That Bertha was still under her mother's care cannot be doubted. After waiting *"in the cold for three quarters of an hour"* and then returning home, Bertha M asserted herself over her daughter.

Mamma sets her foot down. "You will go to your room and lie down all the afternoon or you cannot go to the Bachelor's Ball." Evening – The Bachelor's Ball. I go with Mr. Stribling in the carriage with Mattie and Mr. Scott. A radiant time until near the end. A rose stolen & thrown away. "Good night."
[1888-11 Diary, March 4, 1889]

The Bachelor's Ball was, apparently, a big success for Bertha was able to get little sleep that night.

I have not slept at all and Mamma will not let me get up until eleven. A lovely box of flowers comes for me with no name but it is not hard to guess who sent it. Is it a peace offering? Exquisite white tulips turning pale pink at the edges, a tiny bunch of pansies and white heather & one superb American beauty. Go to the sewing club in high spirits.
[1888-11 Diary, March 5, 1889]

One can only guess at what Bertha meant by her March 4 comment, *"A rose stolen & thrown away",* and then her March 5 entry regarding the receipt of flowers the next day, *"Is it a peace offering."* Bertha's diary does not explain but the mystery seemed to have Henry's fingerprints all over it.

At the end of this second diary, Bertha provided her opinion of men and lectures.

> *Go to dinner at the Markham's. Then France, Madge, G. Markham, G. Bartlett & I go to hear Benny's lecture on Child Labor & Factory Legislation. We decide never to go with men again. We had almost as soon go with tombstones.*
> [1888-11 Diary, March 22, 1889]

Bertha's remark about going out with men in priceless: *"We had almost as soon go with tombstones."*

C. 1889-04 DIARY

Bertha ended her one-year account of her life with this 1889-04 Diary[90], which encompassed the events of April 1889.

Based on what preceded, April was pretty normal. *"Sewing Club meets at my house, stupider than usual."* [1889-04 Diary, April 2, 1889]

April was filled with the usual calls and events – concerts and operas, parties, lectures. Bertha generally took careful note of who she heard at concerts, such as on April 4, 1889: *"Evening – Go with Mr. Brookings to Albani concert – Superb!!! Albani, Grace Damian, Massimi & Barrington Foote.[91]"* [1889-04 Diary]

And the lectures: April 9th, *"… we go to Fiske's lecture on Alexander Hamilton. Fine!!"* [1889-04 Diary] Apparently the Fiske lecture left an impression. As Bertha wrote the next day, *"Feel very tired, too tired*

---

[90] If not otherwise stated, the quotations under each daily date included in this section refer to this 1889-04 Diary.
[91] Albani, Grace Damian, Massimi & Barrington Foote – Opera singers: Soprano, contralto, tenor & bass. Ref: Pittsburg Dispatch January 6, 1889.

even to oppose Papa's views on the subject of Alexander Hamilton in which he becomes so interested that he forgets church time." [1889-04 Diary, April 10, 1889]

Bertha often chose to sleep late after her night outs. After going a second time to the Albani concert on April 5, Bertha wrote: "*April 6: Stay in my room until one.*" [1889-04 Diary] But Bertha might also sleep in if no one called the night before. On the evening of April 6th, she wrote, "*Evening – No one comes in, retire early.*" [1889-04 Diary]. And the next day, "*April 7: Stay in bed until dinner time.*" [1889-04 Diary] Life had its highs and lows.

Once Bertha admitted to falling asleep during a performance. "*Evening – Go to hear Mr. Hannibal Williams read "Julius Caesar". Laura Durkee goes with Papa & myself. Disgrace myself by going fast asleep.*" [1889-04 Diary, April 27, 1889]

Bertha noted in her diary the engagements of her friends which were announced in April, although it is not entirely clear from her diary what her feelings were about them. Bertha remarked about the announcement of Carrie Louise Richards engagement to Charles Claflin Allen on April 8, 1889 and, shortly thereafter, wrote on April 11: "*Carrie positively likes to be congratulated on her engagement.*" [1889-04 Diary] And then on April 18th came the announcement of George Markham's engagement to Mary Dameron[92].

Bertha enjoyed intellectual conversation. As she wrote after an evening "musicale" for Professor Fiske, "*I like to meet people who have brains.*" [1889-04 Diary, April 15, 1889]

There were moonlight walks (April 16th) and drives with Henry. "*H.C.S. comes for me to go to drive. It rains for about ten minutes but we refuse to turn back. Such a beautiful drive!*" [1889-04 Diary, April 17, 1889]

After this April 17th drive in the rain, Bertha's father asserts himself: ""*You do not understand & I cannot explain." Get in at quarter to eight. Papa's displeasure.*" [1889-04 Diary, April 17, 1889]

Bertha's April 23, 1889 entry was very short. "*A drive. Barbed wire. The last of the Fiske reunions: Daniel Webster.*" [1889-04 Diary]. However, 46 years later, Bertha went back to make an additional entry:
This was the day I became engaged to Henry Scott. Written April 23, 1935.
[1889-04 Diary, April 23, 1889]

Although August 25, 1891 was the "official" date that Bertha and Henry were engaged and the date that was engraved in Bertha's wedding ring, it was reasonably clear from their letters that Henry proposed to Bertha on April 23, 1889 and that Bertha accepted. Although Bertha's diary entry on that date implied no special event, it seems that "*a drive*" on this date was much more significant. This engagement was never made public, to anyone including Bertha's parents, and was, within three months, broken off. [This is a discussion left for Chapter 9.]

---

[92] This engagement must have been broken off since Mary Dameron married Count Reventlow in 1892 and George Markham married Mary McKittrick in 1902.

[1889-04 Diary, April 23, 1889]

The last day of Bertha's diary was April 30, 1889, her 23rd birthday.

Washington's inauguration day. Also my birthday. Twenty-three years old. Go with Tom, Hildegarde, Mary McK., & Ralph(?) to baseball match, St. Louis wins against Louisville 3-2. Pretty cold weather. Come home. My birthday presents: $160 in gold, $10 from G, $50 from Mamma & $100 from Papa to buy a present in Europe; flowers, hundred year old plate, cup & saucer from Mamma; the most superb flowers I ever saw from H.C.S.; silver pen from Nan. Afternoon – Go over to University Club with the Shepleys to see the procession pass. It takes over three, nearly four, hours to pass & is very interesting. The Card Expert. Evening – The crowd comes to our house to see the procession pass. Crowd consists of Myra & Emma Lane, Miss Violet Brown, Cynnie Yeatman, Jule & Nan Shepley, Miss Mary Richardson, Hildegarde & Tom McKittrick, ... Shepley, E.C. Dameron, G.M. Bartlett, W.M. Chauvenet, H.C. Scott & Blair Lee. The bicycle procession is most gorgeous, Japanese lanterns ad lib. Afterwards we sing, chat, etc. Then the great Inauguration Day & my birthday are over.

Then Bertha concludes with her thoughts about the past year.

[Continuing] I have kept my diary for one year as I said I should & I am very glad. It has been a strange year. I think I have known more pain in it than I have ever known before and yet in many ways it has been the happiest year of my life. I have learned some things and I believe I am more of a woman now than I was at the beginning. God help me to be a better and a truer one.
[1889-04 Diary, April 30, 1889]

What wonderful concluding words about her past year and her own personal journey. Bertha's words reflected an understanding of the change in her life from being a girl to being a woman. *"God help me to be a better and a truer one."*

CHAPTER 8 - THE LOVE CHASE

"A summer sonnet, that the author dares not show in St. Louis, as it is hot enough for him already with the thermometer at 98 in the shade and every member of the One Hundred at fever heat."

THE LOVE CHASE (by The Poet)

A Queen there dwelt in our town
Of beauty, wealth and pride,
Before her many suppliants knelt
And prayed she'd quick decide
To which of them as Prince Consort
She'd give herself as bride.

One held the place of merchant king
Had goodly substance too.
In sooth he seemed in all respects
A suitor fit to woo.
So fair a maid and well 'twas thought
That not in vain he'd sue.

Another bore ancestral name
He'd long been on the list
Of those who plead most earnestly
And did his plea assist
With argument and depths profound
Of law, the very Gist.

But in this matter must he field
To other one, intent
On bearing off this beauteous dance
One who most surely meant
To cull his wealth of flowery talk
Not from Blackstone, but Kent.

Still others trimmed their hopeful sails
And tacked from port to lee
Hard as the fitful favors chanced
On this uncertain sea
While one stood jealously to Mark -
'Em, who so ere they be!

Wealth, wit and wisdom, love untold
All to her feet they brought.
Alas! For them, not with such things
Can modern girl be caught.
She must in other ways be moved
With other wiles be sought.

There came that way a student new
Of Aesculapin's art
Who'd left the tedious marts of trade
And fain would bear a part
In curing ills, especially,
Affections of the heart!

Aha, said he, I'll try my hand
On this most doubtful case.
I'll bring to bear theosophy
Put science in the race
With unsuspected weight but sure
Try "fad" in this love chase.

(As all great writers now leave off just when they ought to go on, this poem will proceed no further. There is a moral but should the writer set it down in verse, he might be accused of plagiarizing that

great poet who has written so beautifully of the successful but wingless June bug.) [Poem5[93], (1891?), *"The Love Chase"* Poem sent to Bertha from "The Poet"]

"The Poet", AKA William Marc Chauvenet, and Bertha corresponded with poetry for many years from 1885 until 1892 when Bertha was officially engaged to Henry. In the preceding poem, we can surmise who were many of the persons to which The Poet referred.
- Bertha, of course, was the sought-after Queen of beauty, wealth and pride in verse 1.
- Henry may have been considered the *"merchant king"* in verse 2 since, by 1891, he was well on the way of becoming a very successful businessman.
- The Poet gave us the name of the gentleman in verse 3, Gist Blair, who became a lifelong friend of Henry and was Henry's best man.
- The suitor in verse 4 may have been Ed Dameron who stood to inherited money and land as did James Kent who was a proponent of private property rights over Sir William Blackstone's objections. (Blackstone believed in a communal right of people to all property.)
- The Poet also gave us the name in verse 5, "Mark – 'em", i.e. George Markham, a friend of Henry's who found business success in insurance.
- Verse 7 apparently referred to a doctor, name unknown.
- Verse 8 may be referring to the Poet himself who could be thought of as both a scientist and philosopher/theologian.
-

That the Poet would commemorate this courtship, this "Love Chase", with a poem said much about this era and this unique St. Louis society of the late nineteenth century romantic period. From her correspondences, we know that Bertha was pursued by an assortment of suitors in addition to the ones mentioned above. Three of these suitors are highlighted below.

A. THE "POET"

William Marc Chauvenet, or "Will", was called the "Poet" by his friends somewhat teasingly, although it was clear that he was respected. He was a highly admired geologist and may have been bookish, especially considering his interest in poetry and the arts, so the name The Poet stuck. In a biography, Hermann Von Schrenk wrote the following of him.

> *He was a most versatile man and, aside from his mining and chemical work, was a poet of no ordinary ability and his watercolor paintings were excellent. His circle of friends and acquaintances was worldwide, and no more charming companion could be found than he.* [Hermann Von Schrenk, https://vdocuments.site/documents/william-marc-chauvenet.html]

The Poet was certainly the object of teasing as Henry wrote in a letter to Bertha.

> *... the Poet who, if that were possible, was more of an ass than he usually is. They were talking of doctors and Will praised Fischel in language both fulsome and poetic and ended up by characterizing Rably as the most ignorant and useless member of the profession. With the memory of the old man's skill very present with me, I arose in my wrath and smote William with the sharpest words my tongue is capable of and he grew so quiet under my attack that Mrs. Graham suggested to me that Will didn't seem to mind opposition. The Poet in his most suave manner replied "O, I don't mind criticism; I am used to it." I replied "One has to get used to it if one is often wrong."* [1900(-) 20170724-3 Henry (StL) to Bertha]

Bertha and The Poet both enjoyed poetry. Bertha kept 8 poems which The Poet gave her during his "courtship" of her, and Bertha kept 2 poems that she wrote for the Poet. These poems were carefully written

---

[93] This poem, together with the other poems in this chapter, have been kept in a separate, white, 9" x 12" white envelope.

out on heavy bond paper which strongly suggests that the authors wanted these poems to be preserved. The Poet and Bertha wrote in the romantic style of the Victorian age, a time of gentlemen, ladies and courtesy.

In an early poem written by The Poet, he wrote of "*the old trysting place*" which no longer held "*a trace of your face.*"

ALL DAY LONG

All day long have my thoughts clung about you
And my lips have been surging of thee
And my heart has been sighing without you
As the inland wind sighs for the sea.
Like a ship or a star
You seem floating afar
And my world seems to end with the land.
Not a trace of your face
In the old trysting place
Nor a touch of your dear friendly hand.
[From Poem7 – 1885-1888(-) All Day Long – William Chauvenet]

In a more hopeful vein, The Poet expressed his wishes for a future relationship, the "*rose twill soon be growing.*"

But now that in my heart I find
The lamp of youth still glowing
And the old joy within my mind
In spite of cold and snowing.
I make that thine which once was lost
And swallowed up by space and frost
A little seed that now is tossed
Into thy life, it has not cost
Much labor in the sowing.
But let it find at length the place
Where it may spring and see thy face
        A rose twill soon be growing.
W.M.C.
Jan 3, 1888
[From Poem2, "Wasted Lines"]

Bertha could be "stand-offish". In the following excerpt from "*A Photograph*", Bertha gives some hope to The Poet but also fair warning.

Alas! for him who dares to come
Too near this sacred grove.
Although these pictured lips be dumb
These eyes that watch so well above
Can shoot forth other fire than love
Who feels it must succumb.

But I who write am passion tossed
My eyes see other years
When all the calm of these is lost
When something of life's loss and tears
And thronging doubts and pallid fears
Come creeping like a frost.

Such wealth of purpose here is set
Such brave resolve, such power,
Such thought that shall new thought beget
Such strength to wait the telling hour.
Such love to burst to sudden flower
And pay love's utmost debt.

Apr. 28th, 1888
B.W.D.
[Poem3 - 1888-04-28 Bertha to William Chauvenet – "A Photograph"]

Bertha expressed her feelings for The Poet in the following poem entitled "*Her Photograph*". At the end of this poem, Bertha wrote:

Put out your hand from the picture sweet,
Come, I will help you down
With my cheeks aglow & my heart abeat
Here I stand waiting your smile to meet
Waiting with word and glance to greet.
Your two eyes soft and brown.

May 3, 1888
B.W.D.
[from Poem6 - 1888-05-03 Bertha to William Chauvenet – "Her Photograph"]

The Poet, in turn, expressed his own feelings in his poem, "*I Know a Man*", thusly:

Where did we learn such discords? Tell me where.
In my fond heart I hold one woman fair
Set all my days, lean toward her, give my dreams
To floating little ventures down the streams
That wash her garden, plant new seeds of thought
That shall one day to joy for her be brought.
Give my fond foolish heart full rein to run
Down the swift years till all its hopes are won.
[from Poem4 - 1888(--) William Chauvenet to Bertha]

("*Give my fond foolish heart full rein to run, Down the swift years till all its hopes are won*"!)

In the next poem, "One Word More", the Poet may have begun to see that his heartfelt pursuit of Bertha may be losing to the allures of the world. Still, the Poet concluded, "*Grant me this, I ask it ere your going, Though you sing to others all your world songs, Keep one heart song all for me…*"

ONE WORD MORE

To – B.W.D. May 8, 1889

Once before in that long vanished May-time
Once before when June was leaning earthward
You and I stood hand in hand at parting
Full of spring, for in your heart was Spring-time.
Since that day three times has May returning
Kissed the earth with lips that promised summer
Now again 'tis May and this the fourth time.

Once again your eyes are turning seaward
Once again the restless sea winds call you
And you go, so absence fills your lifetime
Fills the little space Earth grants for living.
Fills the time of homely joys and sorrows
Fills the time for friendship, ah! That even.

Must the deeper raptures and emotions
Only known where hearts beat close together
Be to you like voices from afar off,
Heard but faintly, little comprehended?
While you roam 'twix shrines and fallen temples.

You and I have talked of those emotions
Talked together late into the darkness
Sent our eyes and thoughts to one another
Shut the whole world out and the world noises.
You and I have lived our lives together
Sometimes lived the same unnamed emotion
For a moment's space our two thoughts one
thought.

You and I shall talk no more together
When the deep world's waste is tolled between us,
When the winds from Capricorn divide us.
But your thoughts – alas! I fear in going
Where your heart is must your thoughts be also.

One last word, I beg, or since it happens
That I have no one word so to fashion
Many words in one may you grant me.
Where my thought goes, let my verse go also.
Where my verse goes, there my heart must follow.

If you had a friend who was a poet
In an age when poets sing unheeded
And one day, you said to him, "O, poet,
Sing for me the sweetest song you've written."
Did he sing you then the world song only
Pomp of place and noisy acclamation
Heard where pride shouts loud in praise of
Princes?
Would you not be sorry he had chosen
Thus to sing to you the world song only
Leaving all his heart's deep songs unuttered?

This I ask you then, since you are going
Where I learned of yore dwells only silence,
Where your lips are stony like the sphinxes
Since no word of any past escapes them.
Though the centuries have made us human,
Though the human heart should scorn
conventions
Made by timid men and timid races
Pale in heart and pale in comprehension.

This I ask of you, who are a poet
That you lift the curtain of your future.
Look with fateful eyes that do not falter,
See your heart's great needs and inspirations
Written high where poet's needs are written.
Let no voice, however sweet its singing
Woo you with the world songs tempting measure
With the lure that men waste life pursuing.
Give thy world song freely, men demand it.
Be to them the yet uncomprehended
Till some eye more deeply seeing, clearly,
Looks beyond the echo of thy world song,
Till some ear more tuned and more prophetic
Hears, in silence even, all your heart songs.

This I ask you, you who are a poet
With your heart's most tender songs unuttered.
Grant me this, I ask it ere your going
Though you sing to others all your world songs
Keep one heart song all for me and
--------------- Silence.

Yours,
W.M.C.
[Poem1 - 1889-05-08 William M Chauvenet to BWD]

The preceding poem captured so much of Bertha and the romanticism of the age. The poem was written to Bertha just before the summer of 1889. The Poet recalled his past Springs with Bertha and then the summers where the Rye Beach "*restless sea winds call you*" and "*the winds from Capricorn divide us.*" His poet's plea to Bertha was to look past "*the world songs tempting measure with the lure that men waste life pursuing*" until -

> *... some eye more deeply seeing, clearly,*
> *Looks beyond the echo of thy world song*
> *Till some ear more tuned and more prophetic*
> *Hears, in silence even, all your heart songs.*

The Poet's plea to Bertha was to listen to her heart songs and, in so doing, turn to his more deeply seeing eye and more tuned ear, that longed to hear her heart songs.

The Poet wrote the next poem in 1891, the last one that he sent to Bertha when he must have realized that his suit for Bertha's hand was coming to its end. After writing of "*his ride*" with Bertha when his "*spring was a heaven with love at the gate*", he wrote at the end, "*Once we rode the night down, only once in a life, Twas a dream so my lifetime goes spinning away. Love has nothing to do in this toil and this strife, And the street is still dark and the skies are still gray.*" His suit, "*Twas a dream*".

THE LOST RIDE

So this spring that to me has brought only the cold?
Given cloud, given smoke of the desolate street,
For that promise of joy which her laughing lips told
The heath of the mountain, the green of the wheat.
'Twas a vision of life like the opening way
Love alone can prepare, for his chosen to tread
With the soft kiss of April that leans unto May
With the world under foot and the sun overhead.

"We shall ride", she had said and my heart at the word
Was away at a run and my blood was a tide
And my soul was a river of song when I heard
And my life was a gallop with her by my side.
Need I measure the past? It was over and done
And the present was only a winter to wait.
All my fears were at rest, all my hopes were as one
And my spring was a heaven with love at the gate.

So I said, "We shall ride" and the mountain shall ring
To the clatter of hoofs on the shingle below
And the thicket shall bend to embrace as we sing
Through the glades of the wood where the wild asters blow.
So I dreamed and I rode through the pine lands with her
Let my past be the past that I needed no more.
She alone for the sign of the place where we were
With nothing behind her and nothing before.

We two riding alone with the world out of sight
With the souls in our eyes each for other. The day
Just kissing the tops of the mountains good night
And fading and blushing and dyeing away.
Would I care then for fame with this uttermost gain?
What had glory to bring me that this would not shame?

Was she really my own? Ah, beloved, draw rein,
Let me look in your eyes, if I doubt, can you blame?

Was not love once a phantom that never would stay?
However found him at last in the glades of a land
Where we ride through the heart of the spring for a day?
Close, crupper to crupper and hand in hand
We were sad, my beloved, too sad, you and I
In the years that extinguished hope's uttermost spark
Is our joy aught the less for that sorrow put by?

As we ride in the twilight that dips into dark
I am freed from the pain of the wound which was mine
While I toiled in the dark, till my days were a lie
And my soul is a river that mingles with thine
As we ride with this flood of the moon in the sky.
All the dreams of my youth that were builded amiss
All the hopes of my manhood, cold tinctured with scorn
Are garnered and blended and metted in this
As we ride in the starlight that dips into morn.

Shake the rein for a moment, we gallop aware
How the stars speed away o'er the tops of the pine
And the night wind is caught in the stands of your hair
While your heart beats aloud in this hand that is mine.
Who had thought in those years that were empty of joy
That the world had for me such an hour to bring?
That my heart should again be the heart of a boy
And that we thus together should ride through the spring.

See the meadows are white where the pale mists arise
And the flowers are hid in a mantle of white
So the world looked to me e're I found in your eyes
The love that could banish the phantoms of night.
How I toiled through the years as if life had to give
Something better than love, something stronger than truth
Now the thought that you love me has taught me to live
And I laugh at the phantoms that troubled my youth.

What? A dream did you say? Yes, old fellow, a dream
And the sound in my ears is the noise of the street
And the toil and confusion of life's murky stream
The old task for my brain, the old path for my feet.
I was off in the hills and from daylight to dark
Rode the wild way with her for a pledge I had won.

And we saw the long roof of the Battery Park
Glow red in the light of the vanishing sun.
Once we rode the night down, only once in a life
"Twas a dream" so my lifetime goes spinning away.
Love has nothing to do in this toil and this strife

And the street is still dark and the skies are still gray.

> *April 1891*
> *"Who know but the world will end tonight?"*
> [Poem10 - 1891-04—William Chauvenet to Bertha]

Thus The Poet wrote in his dream: *"Would I care then for fame with this uttermost gain?, What had glory to bring me that this would not shame? Was she really my own? Ah, beloved, draw rein, Let me look in your eyes, if I doubt, can you blame?"* A dream? *"Yes, old fellow, a dream."*

The news of Bertha's engagement to Henry reached The Poet in the Spring of 1892. Ed Dameron wrote to Bertha about the Poet's reaction: *"that our agony was of no further use"*. [see letter below]

Henry mentions the Poet (i.e. Will Chauvenet) after the announcement of his engagement to Bertha. I imagine that the Poet was trying to put on a good face but perhaps not too convincingly.

> *Oh, speaking of prophetic spirits, did I mention that Will Chauvenet in congratulating me said that he had long since felt that it was a foregone conclusion and that, as soon as you returned, he had told Miss Nan that "one would be blind not to see and know what was going on!" Can't you hear him getting off this nonsense? If you can't, you can easily imagine how exceedingly weary this emulation of Ananias[94] made me.*
> [20170823-6 (1892-06--) Henry to Bertha]

B. EDWARD CASWELL DAMERON

That Ed Dameron was courting Bertha was clear from his feeling *"broken hearted"* when "Scotty" won "The Love Chase". Ed Dameron wrote to Bertha after learning about the engagement and its impact on himself as well as The Poet. Ed also concluded his letter with a most cordial endorsement of Henry, writing *"the world is all the better for possessing some like him rather than them of my ilk."*

> *My dear Miss Bertha,*
> *I'm broken hearted because I was unable to extend my trip & meet you on neutral ground - Florida. That is to say, I was broken hearted until I met the Poet today who informed me that our agony was of no further use because your engagement to Scotty, alias "Henry C Scott" has been announced.*
>
> *Seriously, though, Miss Bertha, I take this first chance I have to send you my heartiest & warmest congratulations. I honestly believe that you're the loveliest girl I know and, as for Scott, while he "riles" me occasionally, I have sense enough to appreciate his sterling quality and to know that the world is all the better for possessing some like him rather than them of my ilk.*
>
> *Goodbye! Sweet Miss Bertha, always think of me as*
> *Faithfully,*
> *E.C. Dameron*
> [1892(-) 20180720-2 Ed Dameron to Bertha]

Ed was from a prominent St. Louis family and certainly an eligible suitor. But, from Henry and Bertha's letters to each other after their engagement was announced, it was clear that Ed took the news hard in spite of the "good face" that he tried to put on. Bertha and Henry's letters provide a fascinating insight into Ed, their friend, and into Bertha and Henry's attitudes about courtship and finances.

---

[94] Henry referred to Acts 9:18 when Ananias went to Saul (St. Paul). When Ananias laid his hands on him, the "scales" of dead tissue on the surface of his eyes fell off and St. Paul gained his sight.

Within a relatively short time after the announcement, Ed traveled to Europe. The entourage included Mary Dameron, Count Reventlow, the *"Count's mother and sister"*, and Ed. (Mary Dameron was Ed's cousin who was recently engaged to Count Reventlow.) Bertha's next letter shows an obvious interest in a couple's "financial status".

> *O, I had a long letter from Emma Lane yesterday principally about all she had heard of Mary Dameron's young man. She has not met him yet however as he, his mother and sister, Mary and Edward, have all gone to Lucerne together. Miss Hagen told me in Boston that she came from the same part of the country as the Reventlows and that their reputation stands very high. In the first place, they are the real old nobility and then they have the name of being men of the highest honor. She says it is in all probability a love match that the Reventlows, though not what Americans would call rich, have land and money of their own and are not in the least of the fortune hunting type of impecunious young officers with which Germany is over run.*
> [1892-06-20 Bertha to Henry]

During Ed's trip to Europe with the entourage, Ed became engaged to Francis Tootle who, in Bertha's words, was *"a stranger"*. [1892-07-18 Bertha to Henry] Bertha and Henry were surprised at the alacrity with which Ed got engaged so shortly after his quest for Bertha had ended. Bertha's next letter to Henry covered more details of the bride, Miss Tootle, including her wealth which, it was suspected, may have been a motivating factor, in addition to her moonlighting as "Florence Nightingale" to the ill Ed.

> *I wish you could hear Mrs. Lane on the subject of the Dameron marriages. Miss Tootle, it seems, is the possessor of two millions and a half. I am very much afraid that had something to do with it for Mrs. Lane says that the Dameron property was all Mary's, her mother having been the rich one while Edward's mother had nothing. And it seems Edward in one of his moments of confidence once told Emma that "if sister ever married, he would be very hard up." This was news to me as I always supposed that when old Mr. Dameron died, the money was evenly divided and I know he left more than anyone expected. However, this is all conjecture. Edward was sick in Nice and Frances Tootle (O quelle name!) entertained him during his convalescence, so it may have been a case of affinities. But I am a worldly minded old thing and I don't believe it. Mrs. Lane also informed me that the Reventlow estates are heavily mortgaged. She says the old castle is near Dresden and is one of the most beautiful places in Saxony but the family are poor. O, life is not long enough to tell you all she told me.*
> [1892-07-21 Bertha to Henry]

Bertha wrote back to Henry with her own news about the couple.

> *Mrs. Brookes, the cousin whom Emma is visiting, has seen a great deal of her [Francis Tootle, Edward's fiancée] and says she is very quiet and unassuming in spite of her millions, sweet natured apparently, but with little or no education. Her brother, they say, is odiously common, but not the girl. Still, this does not sound attractive. Was our Eddy hard up? Dr. Lane said he thought not, that he thought on the contrary he was rather better off than he had been for some time. Don't tell me you think I am developing into a gossip, I assure you, I have told you half the gossip I have heard. But it is nearly all from Mrs. Lane, the girls talk very little of that sort.*
> [1892-07-23 Bertha (Kennebunkport PO) to Henry (Stl or Wichita)]

Bertha also related to Henry, *"Did I tell you Charlie Hodgman told me he knew Miss Tootle quite well and that she was the young woman whose mother presented her with a million-dollar check as a birthday present."* [1892-08-03 Bertha (Rye Beach) to Henry (StL)]

The rumors of Ed's wealth or lack thereof was disputed by Henry who also decried the rumor mongering by their friends. *"Your friends do Ed Dameron injustice, Bert; I know something about his affairs and he is quite well off in his own right. I don't know anything about Miss Tootle but, if I did and was sure Ed married her for her money, I would not say so as long as I admitted he was still my friend and, privately, I don't at all admire Mrs. Lane's method of talking about people generally and, in particular, about a man whom she has always welcomed to her own home."* [1892-07-25 Henry (Hotel Cary, Wichita KS) To Bertha (Rye Beach)].

Henry continued the subject of Ed's wealth in his next letter to Bertha.

> *... Carr was right about Ed Dameron, for he is not only not 'hard up" but his property is much larger than that of his sister. I have heard the affair discussed here by Ed's friends and I am surprised to learn from men who ought to know that the young man had already as much money as was good for him for if he puts on airs now, Miss Tootle's money will spoil a really good, though often extremely silly, fellow.*
> [1892-07-30(?) (Wednesday) Henry (StL) to Bertha (Farragut House, Rye Beach)]

But, after putting up some defense for his friend, Henry's next letter to Bertha revealed that he was not very enthusiastic over Ed's engagement. Henry speaks of a letter that he received from Ed. *"It was a peculiar letter to me, full of enthusiastic expressions but as free from any real feeling as if he had been discussing a new fad and, after reading the letter, I confess, I did not feel at all charitably toward Ed.*
[1892-08-02 Henry (StL) to Bertha]

Henry's succeeding letter reveals his disapproval not only of the hasty wedding but also the rumors that were being spread. So even though Henry's opinion of Ed was diminished, Henry especially disliked Ed's supposed friends who were making *"disagreeable speeches"* about him.

> *Ed Dameron was married today in London. We had this cable-gram from him at the club, dated London "Married here today. Please announce." This affair was carried through without much loss of time, was it not? I am undergoing a change of opinion of Edward, I am afraid. The whole thing has much too business like an appearance to suit my notions and I shall have to acknowledge that I am not quite as ready to defend Ed as I have been. Although I shall not fail to do so to anyone but you, for I dislike, as much now as I did at first, the disagreeable speeches that are being made over the affair. One of the fools that spend the best part of their lives loafing at the Club said "Well, Mitchell, Scott has been distanced." I felt like kicking him out of the Club for he is one of the men who has always professed greatest attachment for Dameron.* [1892-08-04 Henry to Bertha]

Henry remained concerned about the spread of rumors by *"people who are all more or less ignorant of the object of their violent attacks."* Henry was hopeful that the St. Louis crowd would give Ed and his bride a fair chance.

> *The Comptess Von Reventlow evidently holds the common estimate of Miss Tootle as a fair one. I hope she is too careful to give her opinion to any but her closest friends, for it seems as pity to cut off any chance Ed's wife may have for making a good impression upon his friends. Give a dog a bad name, you know, and I hope people will suspend judgment until Mrs. Dameron gives them a better chance to value her than can be had from the gossip of people who are all more or less ignorant of the object of their violent attacks.*
> [1892-08-15 Henry to Bertha]

When Bertha heard the news of Ed's speedy marriage, she wrote of her surprise.

> *So Mr. Dameron is married!! Nan has lost her bet with him. Do you imagine he had any thought of this when he bet her he would be married within the year? Had he ever met Miss Tootle before? I must say I don't like anything about the proceeding very much as far as this exceedingly hasty marriage is concerned. I think she is to blame and not he, for I have yet to meet the man who does not think the proper time to be married is on the spot and there may have been reasons too, similar to those in Mary's own case, why Miss T. preferred being married abroad. But as I do not know anything about her, whether she has a father or mother living or not, this is all pure surmise. Only I cannot somehow believe that Mr. Dameron's heart was in it and I am very sorry if it is so for it*

has always seemed to me, with him more than the majority of men, that his marriage would either make or mar him entirely.
[1892-08-08 (Saturday) Bertha (Rye Beach) to Henry (StL)]

Bertha echoed Henry's sentiments that the engagement and wedding seemed unduly rushed, especially since Ed had not met Miss Tootle until he arrived in Europe in the Spring. Bertha also wrote that she heard from Charles Hodgman, Ed's best man, that *"it was the most mournful wedding he ever assisted at in his life."* [1892-08-22 Bertha to Henry]

After the wedding, Ed returned to his friends, fat and happy. Evidently, Ed had so increased in size that Alf Kennett remarked, *"gentlemen, the largest ever grown in captivity!!""*

Ed Dameron has returned without Mrs. D, happily, and the men at the Club seem not sorry to have him back. I have not seen him but you may judge from the following greeting which Kennett gave him that the nightingale is not looking very badly. As he came into the Club, Alf was so struck with his enormous increase in bulk that he climbed on a chair and shouted "gentlemen, the largest ever grown in captivity!!"
[1892-11-27 (Friday) Henry (StL) to Bertha Hotel Brunswick, Back Bay, Boston)]

Notwithstanding the vagaries of the love chase, Bertha and Henry remained good friends with Ed. Henry related the following news to Bertha in 1906. *"I saw Eddie tonight. He is fat, rich and prosperous. I am emaciated, poor and unprosperous but we swapped highballs and lies and enjoyed the evening."* [1906(-) 20180709-1 Henry to Bertha]

Ed sent a letter to Bertha in 1908 with miscellaneous news but mostly, it seemed, to relate his continuing affections. *"Except for a brief moment, I haven't seen you for years, such a number of them too and yet, I think of you very often. And it is such a nice thing to be able to talk of you with Fan because she, you know, thinks quite as much of you as I do, and bids me tell you so. You were always such a nice girl and I've always been very fond of you."* [1908-08-12 E.C. Dameron (Clarksville MO) to Bertha (StL)] According to Ed's letter, his wife, Fan, was also very fond of Bertha; but one cannot know this with certainty based on a man's viewpoint.

C. GIST BLAIR

Gist Blair

Gist Blair was born to a politically prominent family. His father, Montgomery Blair, was a former U.S. Postmaster General, and his grandfather, Francis Preston Blair, was the Editor-in-Chief of the Washington Globe and a confidant to Presidents Jackson and Lincoln, among others. Gist Blair's uncle, Francis Preston Blair Jr., was the Democrat party's nominee for vice president in the 1868 election in which he lost to the Republican, General Grant. Gist was born in 1860 in Washington DC, Montgomery Blair's second son. Gist spent most of his life in the east, including Washington DC and Bar Harbor Maine (where he died in 1940). But he did spend part of his young adulthood in St. Louis where he met Bertha and Henry.

In the Love Chase, there was little written about Gist Blair other than that he was "in the hunt". In fact, Henry and Gist were already good friends during the Love Chase as Henry's following letter around May 1892 reveals:

I must tell you about an experience I had with Gist which rather amused me. He came up and asked me to dine with him and when we arrived at the club, I had to listen for an hour or more to the most reproachful harangue I have heard in a long time. He started by asking me to go away with him to Lebanon or Eureka for two or three weeks and, when I told him I was much too busy for any such loafing arrangement, he pitched into me and abused me roundly. In fact, turned the tables on me completely for usually I am kept occupied laying down the law to him for some one of his inconsistencies and you would have thought because I preferred to stay at home and attend to my affairs, I was committing a crime. I did not tell him I expected to go to see you the end of this week or he might have behaved better, although I think he enjoyed taking advantage of me, for I was not as belligerent as usual and did not shut him up very promptly as is the case generally when he attempts to imitate my treatment of him by delivering a lecture (for, whereas I know my reproaches and admonitions do him good, his attempts to pose as an adviser only greatly fatigue me, not to mention my preference for lecturing others rather than being lectured by them.)
[1892(-05) 20170811-6 Henry to Bertha]

Prior to their wedding, Henry consulted with Gist about Bertha's concern about obtaining their wedding license.

O, I told Gist about your panic on account of the marriage license. I knew you would like me to tell him!!! He replied "Tell her not to grieve about it too much" and then added, very thoughtfully, "it is much easier to do than to undo, my dear boy".
[1892-11-27 (Friday) Henry (StL) to Bertha Hotel Brunswick, Back Bay, Boston)]

Bertha was none too happy about the discussion of the marriage license and quipped, "*I am very sorry I am engaged to you*"!

Henry Clarkson Scott, you are a horrid old thing!!! You promised you would not tell anyone about that license story. When you said you meant to ask someone, I kindly advised you not to get yourself laughed at, telling you it was unpleasant. So you took my advice and offered me up instead. I shall not blame Gist for repeating that story, for it can be made exceedingly funny and I should do it myself in his place. And I have not decided what clergyman I want, just at present. I don't feel as if I wished for any clergyman or any wedding at all. I am very sorry I am engaged to you. And I have been sick with a heavy cold for two days.
[1892-11-29 (Monday) Bertha (Backbay Boston) to Henry (StL)]

Gist was Henry's best man at Bertha and Henry's wedding and remained a good friend to both throughout their lives. Henry and Gist even had a bet that the other would marry first: Henry lost but must have been very happy to have done so. [Ref. 1893 Diary, June 23, 1893]

One incident, which Bertha described in her diary shortly after Bertha and Henry's marriage, demonstrated Gist's fortitude.

July 16th, 1893
Henry, Mr. Blair and I go out to the Country Club. Find Mr. R. Frost on the train going out. Mr. Frost and Mr. Blair go to ride, Henry and I go shooting. On our return, find Mr. Hodgman there, we wait for the others to have tea. After a long wait, hear their coming in. Mr. Hodgman goes to meet them and does not return. Henry goes and does not return. I wait and wait and grow more and more anxious. Finally, they come back and tell me Mr. Blair's pony fell with him and rolled over on him – and they were needed to assist the doctor.

July 17th, 1893
Spent the morning lazily trying to cheer up Mr. Blair, in the afternoon, he insisted on going in with us, after a jolting ride to the station. Find we have just missed the car and have to take another jolting ride to the other station, Mr. Blair suffering tortures. Are deterred in every imaginable way, going in, stop train to put a man off, etc., but finally reach home in time for tea...
[1893 Diary]

One can surmise from Bertha's letter (below) that Gist was a frequent guest at the Scotts, so much so that he might come by to tea, somewhat unexpectedly.

Did Gist consider himself invited here to tea tonight? I mean, did he have any right to so consider himself? For he arrived & I, expecting no one, was calmly settled upstairs in my tea gown with my tea on a tray beside me and a novel and excused to everybody. I shall have to crawl tomorrow night but it never entered my head he would come while you were away & I shall ask him to come next Sunday and ask Mary or someone to make it more festive.
[1894-03-10 (Tuesday) Bertha (StL) to Henry (Waco)]

Henry did not seem terribly surprised by Bertha's comment about Gist coming to tea and responded:

I have long since concluded that Gist considers 3337 [Bertha and Henry's house] his Sunday evening headquarters and we must either put him out or endure him at least for the present. I guess he is a lonely duffer and thinks he has a right to drop in on a certain well satisfied & complacent couple once a week to take water on the affirmative side of his matrimonial investigations or maybe he is simply carried away with my very manifest ability to make you supremely happy!!! If this latter is the case, let's humor him, dear, for the picture of such bliss will be good for him.
[1894-03-10 Henry (Waco) to Bertha (3337 Washington Ave, Stl)]

When George Drake Scott was born December 7, 1897, Gist was named as his godfather. Gist was living at that time in Washington DC where he wrote the following letter to Henry.

Dear Henry,

Yours received several days ago and I felt quite badly over not seeing more of you while west and particularly since the probabilities of my going to St. Louis frequently do not seem as great as I thought they would be when I first removed here to live.

I send you for my little god-son a small remembrance with his initials marked on it. Please tell Mrs. Scott that I trust she will select some real good woman for his god mother, one whose keenest pleasure will be the instructing him in that sacred lore which opens the future for all good boys along the right road of honest living and as to the giving of which instructions I may be forgiven for confessing I am not well prepared. Indeed, so illy able am I to instruct him in his ... & good books that I cannot but see what the dangers are which you both have incurred for him in having selected me as his godfather. However if this good fairy god-mother of his will undertake to instruct our little son in those most important and necessary matter as he older grows, you both may put more confidence in my performing my share of these pleasant duties – i.e. of instructing him - and it will not be unlikely that your old bachelor friend may be able to aid him in acquiring a true &

proper appreciation of society of the class in life to which he has been born, even of the world itself so that he will become not only an ornament to all of these & a strong & generous support for both his parents but he may even be something of an aid to others who shall know & like him. For I have always believed that the goodness of every man's heart is only a little thing unless he have some keenness of intellect and sound judgment with which to supplement and perfect this true emotion.

And to conclude, if the good godmother of your young gentleman will but duly inspire in him this same goodness of heart, for it springs from early teaching as well as from our beloved parents, then I shall feel if incumbent upon me and look forward to the great pleasure which may be mine in attempting to train and to guide this in my own poor way & where circumstances shall bring it to pass as within my power, so he shall use this same goodness, govern it and develop it with a true worldly knowledge without which every man must needs fail & with which, if he be good, he is a blessing to everyone who comes near to him.

Many kind wishes for Mrs. Scott, Mr. Drake & yourself.

Affly,
Gist Blair
[1898-02-04 Gist Blair (Washington DC) to Henry]

Although Gist was living far away from St. Louis, he seemed to be very attentive to his role as a god father.
I have sent from New York City some tin soldiers express paid which I hope my little god son will find the time & inclination to enjoy together with his many other Xmas gifts and that he will be reminded of his god father's having a constant pleasure in wishing him well.
[1900-12-24 Gist Blair (DC) to Henry (StL)]

As much as Henry liked Gist, there were times when their methods diverged, such as in 1896 over some investments.
I believe I did not tell you that Miss Tutt's nephew, Monroe, confirmed all my suspicions about Gist. He said Gist had been to Frazer and advised him not to take the new stock but to try to make a trade upon it which the other stockholders would not share in. Frazer feels very bitterly about it. Says Gist deceived him entirely and he is to stop here on his way west to talk to me about it. He simply despises Gist for that young man's acts in the transaction and I think is really too hard upon him. I am over my anger about it and merely attribute Gist's very indirect and unmanly action to his desire to pose with his brother and Frazer as a man of affairs. When I see him I shall tell him, if it were not for that charitable construction, I would cut him dead.
[20171118-1 1896(-) Henry (StL) to Bertha (Jamestown)]

In 1898, Gist apparently moved back east from St. Louis. Writing to Henry from Bar Harbor Maine, Gist waxes philosophical and somewhat sentimental about St. Louis.
I sometimes wonder how it is St. Louis with its great wealth & large population manages to avoid such beautiful & dashing surroundings as one finds here. But our dear old town was ever conservative & domestic in its taste and its adoption of your humble servant was only to give him some education of the true and solemn beauties which crown the rightly constructed mind whose fortune carries the him or the her into that real idealism – domesticity & sober earnest purposes for daily thought. If I am just a bit touched by the appreciation of these things, I suppose you will excuse me for I have no doubt I will recover my philosophy tinted with its other tints. At the same time, I fear I have seen so much more of the worldly side to life since leaving you that it may be as well to cultivate sentiment.
[1898-08-10 Gist Blair (Bar Harbor, ME) to Henry]

Gist corresponded often with Henry and Bertha over the years and he was close enough to both to proffer his advice, as he did to Henry about business pursuits, "*one pays a great price for it if one loses everything else to secure it.*"

> *Give my love to Bertha & the boy & remember old friend we only live one life & are a long time dead. If love of business success is the game giving greatest pleasure, I have nothing to say. If it is not, then one pays a great price for it if one loses everything else to secure it & when the time for enjoyment is gone, no charm or talisman can bring it back.* [1906-09-09 Henry (StL) to Bertha – letter enclosed from Gist]

Back in his natal city of Washington D.C., Gist would marry Laura Ellis Lawson in 1912 and serve as a major in the US Army in World War I.

D. BERTHA: A FLIRT OR SIMPLY ROMANTIC?

Bertha played the role of debutant very well and enjoyed it. The best expression of her feelings about The Love Chase can be seen in a poem that she wrote when she was 20.

The Kissing Bridge

Across the valley and over the hill
Stands a bridge that is old and shaken
But many a time in the years gone by
Have wooers that pathway taken.

For a penalty dire for crossing the bridge
Reads thus that a maiden slender
Unwarily caught by her true love there
Must a kiss for a forfeit render.

Over the fields that are heaped with hay
And the meads that the workers are mowing
A gracious couple is passing today
And straight toward the old bridge going.

He is a bonny and brave eyed lad,
With bright hair, soft and curly,
And she, but a tiny maid of swen(?),
A wee, dainty, winsome girlie.

They scarce would come with a statelier head
Or a mien more grave and royal,
Were she a lady of olden time
And he, her fayre knight loyal.

But ere they gain to the brooklet side
Her eyes grow alight with laughter
Like a startled fawn she has sped away
And left him to follow after.

Now gaining the spot, past danger's line
She waits for her tardy lover,
Till all too late he attains her side
And reproachful, bends above her.

She pauses a moment with roguish eyes
Mouth pursed like a rosy clover,
Then "Ah, she whispers, that wasn't quite fair,
Let's go back and do it over."

Geneva, October 1886
[Bertha's Poem #25, 1886, The Kissing Bridge]

Bertha clearly liked being a woman who could flirt and was always entitled to change her mind.

Pardon, T'is a woman's right,
Oft to change her mind.
[Excerpt from her poem, 1891-11-27(-) Bertha (StL) to Henry (Lebanon, MO)]

During the love chase, Bertha truly came into her own: beautiful, wise and worldly.

CHAPTER 9 – THE COURTSHIP

The Awakening

God Hermes just in sport, they say,
Made women long ago
To plague the men Apollo made
(And still she's doing so.)

He made a net for sunbeams
And caught them in her hair
He searched the deep for sea shells
And formed her ear when there.

He robbed the midmost heaven
Of the stars to make her eyes
But he hid them under curtains
That could lift in sweet surprise.

And on her cheeks he placed the
Sweetest roses from the south
And from red clover blossoms
Stole the sweetness of her mouth.

He blessed her with all sorts of charms
To win from man his rest,
And then he gave her patience
The sweetest gift and best.

But a new and startling trouble
Now rose upon his view
For to wake his new creation
He knew not how to do.

It was he whose hand had formed her
Who had spent his strength and skill
But for him she would not waken
(Ah! She is ungrateful still!)

One day as he was musing
O'er his unawakened maid,
God Eros came upon him
As 'mid the woods he played.

The puzzled god upraised his face
But, err a word he spoke,
The Gordian knot was cut in twain
Love kissed her and she woke.
[Bertha's Poem #4, 1886]

A. PHOTOGRAPHS

Henry: pictures taken in St. Louis by Guerin

From the time that they because serious, Bertha and Henry kept photographs of each other, and it mattered to each if the photographs were well done.

> *Will you do something for me, dear friend? You will find it a horrid bore too. But won't you please go to one of the really good photographers in New York and have your picture taken for me? I do not really like either of the two I have with me and they do such good work there. I like Roseti, 297 5th Avenue very well but King and Mendelsohn and Cox and Sarony – O, any of them are better than our home workers and would you very much mind wearing either a white cravat or a dark one without white spots. I believe I prefer the white but I am not sure so I leave you the option of that. Only, the white dashes on a dark ground do not look well in your other photographs. Please, dear boy, have it taken. I think I ought to have a really good picture of you now that I am away from you. You told me in one of your last letters that I might command you to do anything I choose but I only ask you to be "kind".*
>
> [1892-04-06 Bertha (Port Comfort, VA) to Henry (Holland House, NYC)]

After Bertha's preceding request, Henry went to Roseti in NYC. Henry wrote:

> *The Roseti photographs were not good, dear. Shall I send you one? Or will you wait until I can have another chance to sit in New York? The trouble is, dear, not with the photographer but with the subject and I doubt if Roseti's work will be greatly improved upon and anything like a likeness secured.*
>
> [1892-03-28-6 (6 letters) Henry to Bertha – partial letter (circa 4-20-1892)]

The photographs taken by Rosetti

When Bertha received the Rosetti photographs, she wrote back to Henry, *"I cannot say it flatters you."*

Your picture has come. I cannot say it flatters you, my son, and those turned down collars which are now the proper thing, gives decolleté effect which somehow adds to the somewhat worn, staid, out-all-night expression of the picture. In some ways, I rather like it but I must honestly confess it comes far off from being the likeness I want of you. I wish I could combine the three pictures I have of you; they each have something I would like to retain and together would make a fine likeness. However, I am glad to have this one, I look at the three and brings you to my mind in different moods.
[1892-04-21 Bertha (-) to Henry (StL)]

After Henry had diligently performed his duty of providing the requested photograph of himself, he requested the same from Bertha. In her letter back to Henry, she is clearly annoyed that Henry waited until Bertha was in Boston to make the request since *"they are notoriously poor"* in Boston. Obviously, Bertha knew things of which Henry was oblivious.

When I read your letter asking me to have my picture taken for you, I said to myself, "this is the perversity of mankind". I have been three weeks in New York, where they have the best photographers in the country and he waits until I come to Boston, where they are notoriously poor, to ask me to have my picture taken. I suppose I shall have to submit to fate, however, and struggle with a Boston artist.
[1892-05-08 Bertha (Boston) to Henry (StL)]

And just as Bertha did not find Henry's photographs flattering, Henry likewise did not find Bertha's photographs anywhere near the likeness that he loved.

I can't say, dear, that either of the pictures please me as I had hoped they would. The half-length isn't the happy, bright face of my darling at all and the troubled expression of the eyes almost makes me blue. The Roseti girl with all her sadness was a face that could smile and this one, well, it isn't a happy or contented face, dear, and it recalls the struggle you made that hot day in Boston to please me. You look at me from the picture as if you meant to tell me what a bother I was. I like the other much better, although it is much too grave and has somewhat the fault of the standing one, as if sitting for a photograph was not very pleasant occupation, but, like other duties, must be endured with becoming fortitude. It recalls however my last sight of you very clearly, dear, and if it did not look tired and a little perplexed, I should like it better than any I have. I don't like to admit that the Roseti is the least sad of the three pictures but I am afraid I must do so.

It was an unreasonable conceit I know, dear, but I wished to see that beautiful expression of hope in the future which so often came into your face when we were last together and, because the photographs do not redeem this foolish demand, I am a little disappointed. But I ought to have known that no artist however good would give me all that I asked for as I know quite well none will be able to give me a "counterfeit presentment" that will, in the least, satisfy my demand for a true copy of the original. I am very much obliged, dear, for all this trouble you have taken for me and if it gratifies you to know what pleasure I have taken in the arrival of two new friends to be added to my little collection. You have the only return I can give you for your sweet thought of me for I don't know how to thank you, dear child.
[1892-06-21 Henry (StL) to Bertha (The Ark, East Jaffrey)]

Bertha responded to Henry's preceding letter: *"I call it extreme humble mindedness that you should imagine I could look at a camera as I do you"*. (Priceless!)

I am sorry you were disappointed in the pictures. I did not expect you to like the three-quarter length, nobody does. And I am sorry I ordered any struck off. But I like the other very much. It is grave but I do not see why you think it either sad or perplexed. I think it rather decided looking, myself. I don't call it "unreasonable conceit" in you to have expected the expression you did in the picture, I call it extreme humble mindedness that you should imagine I could look at a camera

as I do at you. Consider for a moment all the surroundings, including the photographer himself, in a photograph gallery, and the wonder to me is that we succeed as well as we do, especially after being told to look natural and pleasant.
[1892-06-27 Bertha (East Jaffrey) to Henry (StL)]

Henry responded that he was glad that Bertha's dour countenance was not due to her having been thinking about him.

Your explanation of the gravity of countenance in the photographs induced me to immediately go off and have them framed. I was so glad the photographer and not I was in your thoughts for the reflection that I was in some way the direct cause of that distressed, uncertain and most dejected expression was not comforting, I assure you.
[1892-06-29 (Wednesday) 20170828-1 Henry (StL) to Bertha (Farragut House, Rye Beach)]

Bertha worried that Henry was going to litter his house with Bertha's photographs, which would have been "*unpardonable.*"

I am glad you liked the picture, for it is the last one you will ever receive. I was mortified when I read of how you adorned your room, you foolish, <u>foolish</u> boy! Put at least four of those pictures away directly. You might have three out, though, even that would be very absurd, but seven is unpardonable.
[1892-07-12 Bertha (Rye Beach) to Henry (StL)]

Under the circumstances with Bertha in the east, Henry was unmoved by Bertha's request to put away at least 4 of the 7 photographs of her. "*Now, don't you see you have had all your worry about me for no cause, dearest? The only person who can take those pictures from my room is away and, as she does not expect to come back for a long time, I think they will remain where they are for the present – <u>all the seven</u>.*"
[1892-07-14 (Thursday) Henry (StL) to Bertha (Farragut House, Rye Beach)]

B. THE FRIENDSHIP BEGINS WITH FLOWERS AND GIFTS

Bertha first met Henry in 1886[95]. However, she never mentioned the particulars of their early friendship and only later wrote obliquely about it. One early diary comment in October 1888: "*Mr. Zack and his cousin come in.*" (Henry and Zack Lionberger were cousins.) What seemed clear from the available history was that Bertha liked Henry a great deal but was conflicted about entering into a more permanent relationship. Henry mentioned in an 1892 letter to Bertha that, years before, he had met the "sweetest girl" at Miss [Laura] Durkee's card party[96] but nothing further. Henry was clearly the steadfast suiter who rarely seemed to tire or show frustration in his suit. Bertha was the often-reluctant object of Henry's affections, who vacillated between feelings of love for Henry and of wariness that the relationship would draw her away from her parents and her foolish and carefree life as a girl.

The earliest letter which we have from Bertha to Henry was dated December 21, 1887, to thank Henry for the flowers sent by Henry. These early letters were written with formality and decorum. Flowers were special to Bertha and Henry was eager to please.

My dear Mr. Scott,

When I received that delicious box of flowers last Friday, I thought I should see you in a day or two and be able to thank you in person, but as that has not happened, I must write just a line to tell you how very much I have enjoyed them and, indeed, enjoy them, for some of them are fresh still.

---

[95] See 1889-09-05 Bertha to Henry, "*I shall try to arrange not to come home before January as I think that will make it easier to meet simply as the friends we have been for three years.*"
[96] See 1892-09-10 (Friday) Henry (StL) to Bertha (The Brunswick hotel, Boston)

With many thanks, Yours cordially,
Bertha Warburton Drake
[1887-12-21 Bertha to Henry]

In another early letter, Bertha was similarly formal and cryptic.
My dear Mr. Scott,

My friends have come so I shall claim your promise for Friday evening. Mrs. Knox had an engagement so Mrs. Lionberger has undertaken the duty of chaperoning the party. Please be tactful and, if you should hear your cousin[97] speak of it, do not say that I asked anyone else first. I shall expect you at six.

Always cordially yours,
Bertha Warburton Drake

Wednesday Ev'g
[1888-11-22 Bertha (StL) to Henry]

Sending flowers to Bertha always gave Henry the opportunity to enclose a card with his sentiments.
If I could group together beautiful ideas as gracefully as these flowers will be clustered when they come into your hands, I would try to tell you how happy I am this morning. I cannot do this but I can at least thank you, my darling, for what you are to me and say again I love you.
[20190929-9 (1891-) Henry to Bertha (StL)]

Bertha clearly enjoyed getting flowers from Henry and would also write back a kind note, including the following done in verse.
BWD
My dear Mr. Scott,

This morning when I first awoke, my headache almost passed away.
I will not say what time it was, but not too early in the day.

They told me you had been to see if I, this morn, could ride with you
Then sadly sank my spirits down, and all the world looked very blue.

I cannot say how long I might have stayed in this exceeding gloom,
Then suddenly from somewhere near there came a fragrance through the room.

Those flowers raised my spirits high, the world has gaily changed its hue.
I've sought my best most antique jug to give to them the honor due.

I thank you, sir, with all my heart, I wish that I could say it better.
But "thank you" says it all, I think, and I must haste to end this letter.

I hope your journey may be gay,
That you in it will pleasure take.
Your friends all wish this,

---

[97] The "*cousin*" was probably Zack Lionberger. It is not clear who "*Mrs. Lionberger*" was. (Henry's aunt, Margaret Clarkson Lionberger died in 1881, seven years before these events.)

But none more than –

Truly yours,
B. Drake
[20180508-3 (1891-) Bertha to Henry]

On another occasion when Bertha was in New York City less than one year before they would be married, Bertha wrote Henry of the flowers he had sent and included the compliment – the flower arrangement was *"very beautiful"* but *"not so beautifully arranged as when you do it yourself."*

> *I have had a beautiful Easter, my dearest. This morning I found on my table a beautiful bunch of jonquils and an exquisite madonna, the latter a facsimile in beautiful soft colors that I shall have framed some day from my mother. Then this nice letter of Mrs. Tiffany's which I enclose and this afternoon a few moments ago, came my last and dearest greeting. Do you ever forget anything that you think will make me happier, dear friend? I thought of your roses last Easter and have how much more these mean to me. They are very beautiful in themselves too, but I will pay you a compliment, my son, not so beautifully arranged as when you do it yourself.*
> [1892-04-17 Easter Sunday Bertha (Fifth Ave Hotel, NYC) to Henry (StL)]

Henry had the ability to surprise Bertha with his gifts. On Bertha's 26th birthday in 1892, Henry sent Bertha a pin which was magnificent. Perhaps most revealing was Bertha's praise of Henry: *"you have the most exquisite taste of any man I ever knew."*

> *O Henry Clarkson, you dear, generous, extravagant, foolish, lovely boy! I never saw anything so lovely or rather, I did, I saw one something like it in England three years ago and was crazy for it. Only this one is prettier; it is one of the most perfect ornaments I ever saw! At the risk of spoiling you, I must say you have the most exquisite taste of any man I ever knew and the box was so dainty. I don't know how to thank you, dear friend, you do so many lovely things for me. I can hardly wait to show it to Nan.*
>
> *I have been watching it quiver on the wire in the hair pin, it is the most brilliant thing! It is your thought for me, my dearest, that makes it dearer to me than anything I ever owned before. But I love it for itself too. And my roses did you remember that they were white roses which you sent me on my birthday three years ago?*
>
> *Dear, I feel as if you gave me so much joy and so often I give you only disappointment. The very day you were planning all these lovely things for me, you say you had no letter. I am so sorry. I remember I was very busy Monday and did not write, and now I feel so reproached.*
>
> *You say you want to see me wear my beautiful pin some time. My dearest, when will that be? I want to wear it for you. Don't think it is only because it is so beautiful that I am glad today. If you know how dear everything is to me that you do for me, because you do it, if you knew how proud I am because of your care for me. But I cannot write these things, dear love, you know them. I will make this birthday the starting point for a year which shall be a happy one, you do not need to tell me that when I am sure of your help and friendship. My darling, there may be hard things in store for us, but I feel today as if nothing could be very hard now that we have learned what we can be to each other.*
>
> *God bless you, my dearest. Yours always,*
> *Bert*
> [1892-04-30 Bertha (NYC) to Henry (StL)]

Bertha's words are poignant: *"My darling, there may be hard things in store for us, but I feel today as if nothing could be very hard now that we have learned what we can be to each other."*

Bertha was still thinking about Henry's birthday gift of the pin six days later when it was Henry's birthday on May 5, 1892; Bertha was anxiously awaiting Henry's return so that she could wear the pin.

> *It is your birthday, my dearest, and it has made me think again of how good you were to me on mine. I wonder if I half made you understand how I appreciated your gift. I love to go and look at it and watch it flash, though I shall not wear it until I can do so for you. It is the most beautiful ornament I have ever owned, so rich and yet so delicate, and the case is a gem in itself. I have almost hesitated to say as much as I wanted to about it, for what you may think a foolish reason and yet I think you may understand me. I dreaded to say anything which could make you fancy for an instant that you could make yourself dearer to me by means of any gift, however lovely. Dear love, that could not be but I think you know that.*
> [1892-05-05 Bertha (Boston) to Henry (Wichita)]

Bertha often wrote to Henry of the *fragrance* and *perfume* of his flowers in a way that Henry would have almost been able to smell them.

> *I have had a very pleasant day, beginning with something which made all the rest of the day bright. It was hardly ten when your flowers came. I would say the sweetest you ever sent me, only, I will make a confession to you. I think that of so many of your boxes. But you may judge of their fragrance when I tell you that, before I reached my door when I came home from church while I was still in the outside hall, the perfume of violets reached me, and it was not imagination for I was not thinking of them. The room has been delicious with them all day. Thank you, dear boy. I enjoyed the message enclosed with them too, just a little bit. Mother and I had dinner in our sitting room. It seemed so much more cosy than to go into the big dining room on Thanksgiving Day. And I took a photograph of the room with the table set for dinner and decorated with your flowers. The red chrysanthemums are still pretty.*
> *...*
> *Indeed you said very little, dear, but you are quite right when you say that I am glad to be missed. Quite right!!*
> [1892-11-25 Bertha (Backbay Boston) to Henry (StL)]

On one occasion, Henry's flowers didn't exactly get delivered on time. Bertha wrote that, when she opened the boxes of the now dead flowers, "*I nearly wept over them.*"

> *I have opened my letter to tell you of a very melancholy thing. An extremely apologetic expressman has just arrived with two boxes which he says have been at his place since the week before New Year's. On both boxes was written very clearly – "Be sure to deliver this evening", so it was not the sender's fault. I opened them: out of one came a bunch of dry shriveled stalks which once were lilies of the valley; out of the other appeared the brown ghosts of some roses. I nearly wept over them. You dear boy, you spend your time and thought trying to give me pleasure and get no thanks. But you did give me a great deal of pleasure, my dearest, even those withered flowers had more sweetness about them than many fresh ones I have had. Thank you, dear, again and again.*
> [1893-01-17 (Tuesday) Bertha (Newton Centre, MA) to Henry (StL)]

Bertha's refreshing words were able to restore any such "*brown ghosts*". As Bertha wrote, "*even those withered flowers had more sweetness about them than many fresh ones I have had.*"

Eight months after Bertha and Henry's marriage, when he was away on business, Henry had flowers delivered to Bertha to commemorate their wedding day on February 14th, much to Bertha's delight.

> *You are the best and dearest friend in the world. I tell you this because I know you have never heard it before. I am afraid your florist did not obey instructions when he sent me those gorgeous roses this morning with the card October fourteenth inside. Weren't they meant for next Saturday? But I loved them just as much today. You would not have said I was indifferent to flowers if you could have seen the delight I took in fixing these. It made me late to church by the way.*

...

All the news was Rye Beach news so I have nothing to tell you, my sweetheart, except that I love you [even] if it is eight months after date for such expressions, & to thank you over & over again for my beauty, beauty roses.
[1893-10-09 Bertha (StL) to Henry (Waco)]

While flowers were virtually always what Bertha wanted, it was also clear that Bertha wanted the proper sentiments to be delivered with them. On one occasion, Bertha reproached Henry when he sent a "*disagreeable*" message with the flowers.

Your flowers were perfectly beautiful but the next time you want to write me a note of that sort, my son, don't send it in flowers. I used, even as a child, to prefer taking disagreeable things straight to taking them in sugar. And you know you meant to be disagreeable. Still, I forgive you.
[20180415-3 (1892-) Bertha to Henry]

C. FRIENDSHIP

During their early courtship, Bertha generally concluded her letters to Henry with "*your friend*" and often seemed to emphasize that they were "just" friends. And as friends, Bertha could be distant and formal. Henry wrote to Bertha about one such occasion:

I felt last night that I had embarrassed you in asking you to go to the opera with me. Why this should be, I cannot understand but believe me I have no wish that you do anything for my pleasure which will not be a like pleasure to you. If consideration for me alone prompted you to suggest you're going in a party with me, I would rather you would not go. But if you care to go, let me know and I will ask you to select another couple whom you would like to have make up the party. Or, if you care to join a party of our friends whom I shall ask Mrs. McKittrick to chaperon for me during the week, you know how much pleasure it will give me to have you do so. Let me know what evening you can go with me if you care to go at all and be perfectly frank with me, Miss Drake, for I am indeed your friend.
[1890(-) 20180526-2 Henry (StL) to Bertha (2807 Locust St, Stl)]

Regarding the problem of the "chaperon" in the previous letter, Henry apparently resolved this shortly thereafter, as he wrote to Bertha:

My dear Miss Drake,

I have found as you suggested that Mrs. McKittrick was engaged for Wednesday evening and so I have asked her to go with us on Monday. I too would have chosen Wednesday evening for I will not soon forget the last time I saw Carmen and the idea that a pleasant memory of the same evening suggested the Opera to you is more to me than I can express. I thank you for your kind note.

Your friend,
Henry C. Scott
[1890(-) 20180527-1 Henry to Bertha]

As the preceding letter revealed, Henry was a stickler for the proper form and accepted the way things must be done. (But, what 29-year-old male arranges for a chaperone for his date?)

During this period around the year 1888 (the exact dates of these letters are unknown), Bertha kept 13 letters from Henry whose principal purpose was to schedule times for Henry to go out with Bertha. While these letters were all short, Henry was able to incorporate some humor and sophistication.

There seems a reasonable prospect that it will not rain within a few hours and, although my experience lately with the weather has not inspired me with the hope that it arranges itself with

much regard to any of my purposes, I think it safe to trust it today and I therefore hope you will be able to give me this evening.
[1888(-) Early Letters (13) Henry to Bertha (StL), #3]

I am going out of town this evening and hope to return Sunday morning. I will see you Sunday evening if nothing prevents my plans working out as arranged. Entrenched as you will be with Mr. Spenser's opinions and conclusions, you will no doubt be a formidable opponent to the few simple yet wholesome truths which I upheld. But I engage to maintain my much abused ideas as earnestly as I have done, if not entirely prostrated by my journey.
[1888(-) Early Letters (13) Henry to Bertha (StL), #4]

This afternoon will be one of the distressingly rare occasions in which my owners will not claim an undivided interest in my time. I cannot suggest a more profitable & pleasant disposition of the leisure hours than a drive with you would bring, so if you have made no engagement and would like to ramble through the park, I will call for you at four or later, if you desire it.
[1888(-) Early Letters (13) Henry to Bertha (StL), #6]

You will, no doubt, be greatly disappointed on learning that the number of your companions will be reduced to one and, that one, myself. But I hope this sad fact will not interfere greatly with your enjoyment of the ride.
[1888(-) Early Letters (13) Henry to Bertha (StL), #7]

D. NEW FEELINGS

During the years 1888 and 1889, Bertha and Henry's friendship became something greater. They both enjoyed the arts and music, and carriage rides in the park. As a 22-year-old woman, Bertha must have begun to feel that she was ready for the next chapter in her life and, at 29, Henry may have been getting impatient. Some of Henry's early letters were revealing.

I shall see you this evening, my darling, and I do not think I shall, as usual, be able to stay away until I can safely rely upon being the last caller, in order that I may see you alone. You must give me the whole evening, dear, if you can, for I must know what you have been doing this week. Besides, this will be my only chance to see you this week, dear child.
[20171212-3 (1889-) Henry to Bertha]

Perhaps if I cared less, my dear child, you wouldn't have to discipline me with reproaches as you do. But, dear, it is far better to be thought moody and sensitive than to forfeit one memory I have of you, and every thought of you is beautiful. No doubt I poorly express what I try to tell you of my love for you. I am very happy, dear, and you must not think otherwise, no matter how many selfish wishes I make known to you. Remember I told you that all men were selfish and you must begin to understand that I did not intend to except myself from a share in this common fault of men. You must see that I am selfish about you, my darling, for I am never satisfied, no matter how good you are. What is worse, I don't wish to be satisfied, child. Do you understand this feeling?

You were very beautiful last night and very good to me. The gown was so pretty and my rose was pretty too, Bert. You do make me think of my "mercies" my darling.

With devoted love,
HCS
[20170528 (1889-) Henry to Bertha]

E. THE "UNOFFICIAL" ENGAGEMENT

The actual date that Henry first proposed to Bertha was only made apparent from Bertha's entry in her 1889-04 Diary[98]: "*This was the day I became engaged to Henry Scott. Written April 23, 1935.*" To explain, Bertha periodically went back to prior diary pages to include additional entries. On April 23, 1935, 24 years after Henry had died, Bertha must have been reminiscing about the past and was reminded of the happy time when they were "first" engaged on April 23, 1889.

This April 23 date was also referenced in Bertha's letter to Henry of April 23, 1892: "*My blessed boy, You are quite the dearest and best friend in the world. Your roses have just reached me, so you did not forget the twenty third any more than I did. And my favorite roses too. It is superfluous to say "thank you". You know how much they mean to me.*" [1892-04-23 Saturday Bertha (New York) to Henry (StL)]

Bertha also mentioned this April 23 anniversary on the next day when Henry's letter arrived a day late: "*your letter for our April anniversary came a little late but it was none the less dear to me. Sweetheart, a great deal has happened in those three years.*" [1892-04-24(-) Sunday Bertha (NYC) to Henry (StL)]

From Bertha and Henry's correspondences in the summer of 1889, it seemed clear that promises of engagement were made between them. But it was not clear why Bertha went back in 1935 to write the date of this first engagement in her 1889-04 diary, which event was originally left out. Bertha and Henry were "officially" engaged on August 25, 1891 and that was the date that the world knew. Perhaps because she broke off their first engagement, Bertha remained somewhat embarrassed by her own ambivalence toward the man she loved and was not able to accept her inner conflict until so many years later when the passage of time made such things trivial. Of course, since this engagement was a secret (Bertha's father and mother would have strongly disapproved), Bertha may have worried lest someone should see in her diary more than she was willing to openly divulge. Regardless, while Bertha mentioned the various times when she saw Henry in her diary, she did not express any special happiness or mention anything specific about her engagement. What Bertha did express in her concluding entry in this 1889-04 Diary: "*It has been a strange year. I think I have known more pain in it than I have ever known before and yet in many ways it has been the happiest year of my life.*"
[Bertha Diary 1889-04, April 30, 1889]

F. SECOND THOUGHTS

Bertha had second thoughts about their April 23, 1889 engagement very soon thereafter. There may have been various reasons for change of heart. The principal reason that Bertha consistently gave for breaking off their engagement was due to her obligations to her parents and her parents increasing need of her help and assistance as they grew older. It also became increasingly apparent that her parents did not approve of her relationship to Henry. In one letter, Bertha mentioned that her father felt that she should not marry at all. Bertha was well studied in the Bible and would have known Ruth's words to her stepmother: "*where you go, I will go.*"[99]

One question which Bertha does not mention but may have been in her mind: was she ready to make this commitment? Bertha was 23 years old in 1889 and had been sheltered throughout her life. She had limited interaction with her St. Louis peer group due to her European travels, summers in Rye Beach and boarding schools, and it is not clear that she was given very much latitude by her parents for romance. Although never mentioned in her letters and her diaries, it is easy to imagine that Bertha may have wondered whether she had been too impulsive in accepting Henry's engagement proposal and, therefore, may have been more and more reluctant to proceed, especially in response to Henry's ardent desire to move forward.

---

[98] Bertha's Diary 1889-04, April 23.
[99] The Book of Ruth, 1-16.

Bertha's parents took her to Europe within several weeks of this first engagement as evidenced by a letter written to Bertha by William Chauvenet on May 28, 1889[100]. One may surmise that Bertha's parents may have intuited (or discovered) what had happened that Spring. On July 27, 1889, Bertha wrote to Henry from Heidelberg, Germany, to ask him "*to give me back my promise*".

> *My dear friend,*
>
> *I am going to ask you to give me back my promise. I say that because, though you were most generously, tenderly considerate for me in helping me to respect my father's wishes, still I was in honor bound to you. And, though I tried to keep my promise to my father honestly, indeed, I never had a thought but that I should renew my promise to you when I came home. You must have known that. But it never can be. I have seen the change in my father every day, looking older and more worn and a little while ago my mother told me she was afraid his health was giving way and that it came simply from grieving about me. I knew he had been grieved and disappointed but I never dreamed he felt like that or I should not have wronged you as I have done.*
>
> *I should have told you before I went away that it could not be. He has been everything, done everything for me all my life long and the most that I can do could never repay him. Be generous to me, dear friend, do as I ask without urging me to change. Do you think I could write this if I were not sure? I have not done it hastily, I have thought over it night after night and I cannot do anything else. I should like to keep your friendship still but I do not know if it would be possible or best. If you could come as you came last winter, simply as my friend and asking nothing in return but my friendship, expecting nothing beyond it. But if you cannot do that, put me absolutely out of your life. Knowing you, I cannot help knowing that this is giving you pain. But, dear friend, you will not let it spoil your life, you are too truly strong for that. And some time too, after a little while, you will make some woman's life a beautiful one.*
>
> *It is no use to write any more, it would only be the same thing. I have not said it the right way, I know, but I cannot write it over. You have always understood me, you will understand me now and forgive me.*
>
> *Your friend always,*
> *Bertha Warburton Drake*
> [1889-07-27 Bertha (Heidelberg) to Henry (StL)]

Bertha stated in this letter and the several letters that follow that her promise to Henry must yield to her promise to her father (and mother). Given that Bertha was in Heidelberg under the care of her parents, Henry's influence was severely diminished. Perhaps, then, it was no surprise that, during Bertha and Henry's courtship over the next three years, Bertha's parents took Bertha away from St. Louis and Henry on a regular basis.

Henry responded to this letter from Bertha a week later when she was then in London. Henry was, at first, very conciliatory and understanding of Bertha's concerns for her father's feelings; however, Henry's concluding remarks made clear that he had not given up: "*you have asked me to forget you – do you not know I cannot?*"

> *My dear friend,*
>
> *I have just read your brave, sweet, letter, so full of thought for me, so forgetful of yourself that, if I were not moved by it to banish every other feeling than that of consideration for you, I would indeed*

---

[100] i.e. 1889-05-28 William Chauvenet.

be unworthy of your friendship and basely ungrateful for the happy days which I owe to you and which, believe me, will be a blessing to me all through my life. I have read your letter many times, dear, and, if I give you pain by anything I shall say to you now, try to think that I wish not to do so and that I wish only to do what is best for you.

When you were with me last, I let you go away with scarcely a word of farewell, because I was sure I would not be able to speak to you and hide my feelings, and I wished you not see how much it cost me to have you go, lest I should mar the happiness of your summer and make it less easy for you to be a comfort to those who are so dear to you. And I can forget myself now, I trust, my darling, and think only of you.

You cannot tell how it grieves me to know I have made you so sad and that I have brought sadness into your father's life and, oh, believe me, my darling, that I would have never told you of my love for you if I could have guessed that your father's sanction, which is necessary to your happiness, would not be given me if I won your regard; for I know he is your dearest friend and that his every thought is for you and that he must think me more unworthy than I know myself to be, or he would not so plead with you to consider his case of your future happiness and to put me away from your thoughts.

God knows, my darling, how unworthy I am of you and how humbly thankful I have been for the blessing of your friendship, which is so much more than I deserve, but can it be possible that your father thinks me even less worthy than I am? I ask you this, and I must speak to you very plainly, dear, because this means much to us both. If it is clear to you that your happiness would be perfectly safe in my keeping, if you are very sure that my love for you would drive away every fear, then I beg you to give me opportunity to show your father that I am not utterly unworthy of his esteem and that my life has been of some value to those who have come under my care. All the pride which I felt when I knew that, partly from my own efforts and because providence greatly aided me, I could surround you with many blessings and could therefore look into the future without fear if I could earn your love, has all gone now and I now see clearly that I have done little to mark my way among men and nothing to justify me in asking for a precious gift which no man could deserve. But your father is just, dear. We both feel this, and that he looks only to your happiness. May it not be possible that I shall be able to induce him to think better of me? I was too proud to talk to you of my hopes & expectations for the future. I do not fear that I can make it plain that my efforts are receiving that reward which men reckon each other's capacity by, and, all unworthy as I am, I cannot but see that I have been cruelly unfortunate in making any impression upon your father when I have talked to him, and I think, if opportunity is given me in time to come, I can persuade him that I am not utterly unworthy of his esteem.

Then I ask my dear friend that you will speak to your father plainly. Tell him what I ask. That you owe me nothing; are bound by no promise to me, but only ask for me that he will not refuse to listen to me. If, after a long while, he has found me not without, as he now must think me, qualities that recommend me to him. If I did not think myself able to change your father's opinion of me, I would think he is right and that I have been all wrong in this matter!

Think only of your own happiness and what is best for you, my darling. Do not grieve for me. There is something higher & better than this for us both to consider? If it does not seem perfectly clear to you that God, to whom you so trustingly carry your troubles, will bless our lives if you give your life to me, that, although others may not know how much we need each other, there can never come a doubt to us that we will be blessed in our love, then I bid you turn away from me and give me no hope for the future. But if you do care for me, my darling, rest the matter in God's hands, feeling very sure that, if I am what I ought to be, all will yet be well. I can wait for you, dear. Can you do as much for me?

I have tried to answer your letter as you would have me speak to you if you were here tonight, and every goodbye, you have asked me to forget you – do you not know I cannot?

You will write to me? I am sure I need not ask you to do so and I trust that God will put it into your heart to treat this matter as I wish. For your sake and mine, and may He watch over and keep you from all harm, my darling, and direct you to do that which is best for your future happiness.

Devotedly yours,
Henry C Scott
[1889-08-04 Henry (StL) to Bertha (London, England)]

Bertha wrote to Henry several more times over the course of this summer while in Europe with more insistent requests for Henry to yield to her desire to end their engagement and remain, as before, friends.
My dear friend,

I have your letter and I cannot tell you how I thank you for it. It was like you, and I am not worthy of such generous love as you have given me. But, I have made you misunderstand me. It is hard to realize when one understands a thing so clearly oneself to see that it is not equally clear to another who cannot know all that has passed before. I have made you believe that I did not act of my own free will or at least that I was very strongly influenced by others & that is not so. I cannot recall exactly the words I wrote but I think I did say to you that it was a terrible disappointment to my father that I should have thought of becoming engaged at all. It had been his great hope and wish for so long that I should never marry but should always remain at home that he had begun to believe anything else impossible. But he was not selfish about it and he always tried to be just to you, yourself, for he thoroughly respects you. He did not forbid my engagement, on the contrary, he had promised to give his consent if my mind was unchanged when we came home.

All this you knew before we left but what you could not know was this: that after leaving home, he did leave it entirely to my own choice. He never spoke of you or tried to influence me in any way. It was only the change I saw in him myself and what my mother finally told me that decided me. If she had not spoken, I might have fancied that it was my own vanity that made me think myself so necessary but I could not doubt after that.

Do you remember one of the drives we took last spring? That day when the trees were all in blossom and it rained? I said to you that I was of no particular use to any one and you answered, "I believe you are the greatest joy of your father's life". I did not know then how very true it was but it is so, he cannot spare me. It is not as if they had other daughters, it is not right that I should leave them. More than that, I have been slowly learning to see this summer that they stand first with me.

It is hard to write that when you have been so unspeakably good to me but I must be honest both with myself and you. And I mean that apart form the question of right or duty, they are dearer to me than anyone else can ever be. I did not realize this when I wrote to you before or I should have told you then but I did not mean to give that as an excuse, for I ought to have known. You see, I cannot do what you ask. I told you, I was unworthy of you.

Neither my father nor my mother know what has passed between us this summer beyond the mere fact that everything is over. Although my mother must know what led to that, still she does not know that I told you and perhaps I ought not to have done so but I could not let you think that it came from a mere caprice on my part. Though I believe my father does think that and I wish that he should. No one else need ever know anything of this. (I meant to have written that before.) I think both of us can be spared that for I have told no one and I know without asking that you have kept your promise.

I have been asked to spend the winter over here. That I cannot do but if it be in any way possible, I shall try to arrange not to come home before January as I think that will make it easier to meet simply as the friends we have been for three years. I think I was foolish to have ever thought it possible that our friendship could be really broken, we shall be dear friends all our lives, I hope. I cannot help again thanking you for the goodness and tender thoughtfulness you have always shown to me. I shall be a better woman all my life, I think, for having known you loved me, and I know I shall always hold it as having been my dearest honor.

But let this be a real goodbye now. I am in earnest when I say you must put any thought but friendship aside. I spoke truthfully when I said you were not first with me. You must not let me be first with you. Dear friend, do not make me feel that I have spoiled your life. Once more, goodbye. God bless you always,

Your friend,
Bertha Warburton Drake
[1889-09-05 Bertha (Buckingham Palace Hotel, London) to Henry]

It is difficult today not to be struck by Bertha's words, "*…it was a terrible disappointment to my father that I should have thought of becoming engaged at all. It had been his great hope and wish for so long that I should never marry but should always remain at home that he had begun to believe anything else impossible.*" Perhaps these words reflected the mores of a different age.

We do not have Henry's response to Bertha's preceding letter but Bertha's next letter made it clear that Henry had not given up his hope for their future together. In response, Bertha became increasingly resolute in her decision and blunt in her expression.

My dear Mr. Scott,
You must have misunderstood me indeed to write to me as you have done. My first letter must have been very far from clear. I see now that I was so sure of being perfectly understood that I wrote too little and I blame myself bitterly but I never dreamed, I can hardly believe it possible now, that you would think I could have been influenced in the slightest degree by the considerations you have spoken of.

The letter I wrote in answer to your last will have shown you how utterly unworthy of you such a thought is and it must also have proved to you that my decision is unalterable. I have failed in my plan for staying over here and shall be at home before the first of November. You ask me to keep my promise to wait until then to give you my final answer.

I do not want to act unfairly and, if you still wish that, I will not break my word but I think you must see now that it would be useless and only cause needless pain to both.

Sincerely your friend,
Bertha Warburton Drake
Sept. 15, 1889
[1889-09-15 Bertha (London) to Henry]

When Bertha returned to St. Louis in November 1889 after 6 months in Europe, she again reiterated her position to Henry with the admonition: "*I forbid you to answer this letter."*

Wednesday

My dear friend,

I am going to write a few words to you which ought to have been said last night and they are to be the last between us on this subject for I forbid you to answer this letter.

We have spoken to each other very fully and clearly and you know now that I have no other answer to give you than the one I have already given. But you asked me if there was any way in which you could help me. You can do so, if you will meet this, which I cannot help knowing is a grief to you, like a brave man and a strong one, such as I know you to be.

Whether it is best and bravest for you to go away or to stay here, I cannot tell. You are the only one who can know that. But I beg you to be honest with yourself about the decision. Do not spoil your whole future life for the sake of avoiding present suffering. You are not the only man who has had to conquer pain and make his life a noble one in spite of it. If you ever want my friendship, now or, if not now, at some future time, you know that it is yours and I can be a true friend. Prove that you really wish to help me now by meeting me as if nothing had happened between us and by being strong enough not to refer to what is past.

If this letter sounds cold and hard to you, you understand me well enough to know I have not meant it so. And if I have hurt you, I know that I am sure of your forgiveness.

Your friend always,
Bertha Warburton Drake
Wednesday morning
[1889-11-13 Bertha (2807 Locust St., StL) to Henry]

How Henry was not devasted by these letters from Bertha was a mystery. Perhaps, through his force of will, which was certainly manifested in all of his business endeavors, Henry only knew how to persevere. And his perseverance would be tested again and again.

G. BERTHA IS CONFLICTED

Bertha's 1889 "winter frost" gave way to a brighter Spring for Henry. By April of 1890, Bertha's feelings seemed to warm to Henry, especially on her birthday which Henry remembered with flowers.

You have beautiful weather for your birthday and I am very glad for you. I hope the flowers I send will add a little to the sweet happy thoughts which should be yours this morning and that you will include me among those who wish for you in the coming year all the happiness you so richly deserve.

Your friend,
Henry C. Scott
[1890-04-30 Henry to Bertha]

Bertha's obvious pleasure in receiving Henry's flowers would not have gone unnoticed by Henry.

My dear Mr. Scott,

When you spoke of my birthday, I did not think you were going to remember it in such a pleasant way. Indeed, I understood from what you said then that you expected to have gone away before now. But, whatever cause has kept you, the effect has certainly been a delicious one for me this morning.

One of the birthday flowers kept by Bertha with Henry's letter.

Some good fairy must help you in choosing flowers – you send me those I like best, although I could not have told beforehand which those would be myself.

Thank you.

Sincerely your friend,
Bertha Warburton Drake
April 30, 1890
[1890-04-30 Bertha (StL) to Henry]
(Of the flowers sent by Henry, *"you send me those I like best, although I could not have told beforehand which those would be myself"!)*

During the months of May and June, Bertha's father and mother traveled west to California and visited Yosemite, Yellowstone, Tacoma Washington, a grand tour of the west. Their absence from St. Louis may have greatly influenced their daughter's destiny.

Bertha's parents returned in time to take Bertha to Rye Beach for the rest of that summer and Henry's prospects for additional progress in his suit waned. Henry wrote the following letter was probably written on the eve of Bertha's trip east to Rye Beach when he felt most alone.

You go away this evening and I shall not see you again. I bid you goodbye with the earnest hope that your summer may full of happy hours and beautiful experiences. You will not misunderstand my thanking you at this time for your sweet thought of me during the last few happy days. I cannot help telling you how I bless you for all you have done for me and, although you should never think of me in the future as I wish, I shall always know you have been the best influence of my life.

You know how I am tempted to write to you now. I cannot restrain myself and, lest I give you cause for sorrow or regret by betraying the feelings which I fear I cannot even for your dear sake repress, I bid you goodbye.

Your friend,
Henry C. Scott
[1890(-) 20180527-3 Henry to Bertha]

Soon after the preceding letter, Henry again wrote to Bertha with a final, "stated", wish that Bertha will not carry a sadness away with her from their parting. Unstated, Henry undoubtedly hoped that Bertha would think of him.

I am going to ask a favor of you, my dear friend, one that you can grant if you try, for you can do anything, make any sacrifice for those who you care for. It is not very much for me to ask, I think, and I am going to assume that you will do what I wish for.

You seemed unhappy last night, and so sad, that I went away with the thought that you will spoil your summer in dwelling upon a subject that had best be discussed now that you are not clear what to do or when your duty calls you. Now I ask that you will promise not to be sad, not to think of things that give you pain and that you will let me believe you are not suffering. You will do this for me; you will make your life bright and happy, my dear friend, because I ask it, will you not? And may God bless you and keep you from all harm.
[1890-08 or 09-?? Fragment Henry to Bertha]

Once Bertha was back in Rye Beach under the guidance of her parents, Bertha's withdrawal of her affection for Henry was made brutally clear. The next letter that Bertha wrote to Henry on August 23, 1890 from Rye Beach was lengthy and reiterated her resolve from the prior year to break off the relationship.

August 23, 1890
Farragut House,
Rye Beach, N.H.

My dear Mr. Scott,

It has been finally decided that we are to stay in the east until Christmas and perhaps for the whole winter, so I think I ought to write to you at once. The note you sent me the day I left home was a kind one and I thanked you for the feeling which I knew had led you to write it but I did not misunderstand you. I knew you had written because you thought me ill and tired, morbid, perhaps, in no fit state to judge clearly but I cannot claim that excuse now and I know you meant what you said the last evening I saw you.

You told me then that I must make a decision that I had had abundant time and that I would have blamed others severely for such weakness and vacillation as I had shown. You were quite just. I am going to set you free now. I was in earnest then when I said I held you free but you did not feel yourself so. I must write a longer explanation than you will perhaps think necessary but without it you might think I had been unfair as well as weak.

When my father talked to me last fall, he said that people were often honestly mistaken in themselves, that nothing but time could prove this and that if they were, it would be far better even at the cost of pain and mortification to learn the truth. He asked m then to leave myself absolutely free from any engagement until after I should be twenty five. I promised him unconditionally and he, himself, has never spoken to me on the subject since. I had no thought then of your ever undertaking this test but, when you came to me in the spring as you honestly wanted to, I decided that it would not be unfair and, though I knew it was hard, I did not know how hard you would find it for I did not realize then how differently you and I look at certain things.

What I meant then was that the subject of the future should be absolutely dropped between us and that we should try by a frank, fair friendship, which bound neither of us to anything, to prove whether the feeling between us was so true a one that it would only grow stronger and more beautiful as time went on. That I failed in what I wanted was, I think, more my fault than yours. I know you meant to help me. I felt that, even when you hurt me sometimes, and this feeling led me to yield my judgment to yours once or twice when I ought not to have done so.

In the spring, you asked whether one reason I hesitated was that I was not sure of myself. I refused to answer you because I thought the question unfair after what I had told you of my promise to my father. I will tell you now. Then, I had no doubt of myself but I did doubt whether, in following my own wishes, I was not doing a self-willed and selfish thing. But I do not think so now. My father asked of me only what was wise and fair, that he should, and I know I was right in trying to do what he wished. But no one has a right to entirely surrender his own judgment to anyone else and, if a woman believes that the happiness of her own life and that of another is dependent on her decision, I believe she would be doing wrong to sacrifice that to the prejudices of others, even of those dearest to her.

So you must not think it is that motive which influences me now, but I am not sure of myself, as I was then, and I think you are right in saying if I am not now, I never shall be. If you and I, both meaning, as I know we did, not to think of ourselves but help each other, could fail so entirely in three months that instead of the perfect confidence and understanding there should have been between us, there should be nothing but doubt, misunderstanding and pain, there could be no hope for our happiness in the future.

Do not misunderstand me. This is my final answer. For anyway in which I have hurt or grieved you, indeed, you cannot blame me more bitterly than I blame myself. Think of me kindly as you can.

Always your friend,
Bertha Warburton Drake
[1890-08-23 Bertha (Farragut House, Rye Beach) to Henry (StL)]

"*This is my final answer,*" Bertha concluded. Once again, Henry had to face the end of his dreams. After this letter, Henry seemed to accept what now appeared to be inevitable and, accordingly, wrote to Bertha that he was accepting her decision.

My Dear Friend,

Your letter came to me last evening and I have spent the night in anxious thought of all you have said. For I made you misunderstand me greatly, for I only spoke to you as I did because you looked so ill and worn that I was afraid if everything was not done you would be made seriously ill; and although it tried all my courage when I saw how I hurt you, although I knew what I risked in speaking to you and did, I thought it was right and best for you and I even tried to make you feel that I did not care because I would have done anything to drive away a sadness which I knew was doing you irreparable harm.

And I did not try to make you break your promise to your father, my dear friend, I never dreamed you would, but I thought as this promise was made, was asked of you for your own sake against a safe guard against hasty or ill-advised action, that you would be released, if you acted it, when you were very sure of yourself.

Do not think that I did not understand you; I know that I did, and not a thought of reproaching you occurred to me. My vanity I suppose must have convinced me that I could help you, and that I ought to do so even if I gave you pain. I felt so sure of the future, so sure of my use to you that I knew I could in devoting my life to you show that I never meant to wound you. Your happiness it seemed to me was at stake and if I failed to help you secure it when you leaned upon me for help I would not be worthy of you.

Your letter has not been written hastily. I know you have given it calm thought, and I ask you not to dismiss me now. Remember I ask only a place among your friends and the right someday to ask you again to be my wife. You are bound by no conditions and I know that you released me from any claim save that of friendship a year ago. Will you be happy now and leave the rest with your God? I cannot think that I have only given you pain when you have made my life so full of beautiful thoughts. I must have given something in return and how beautifully you tell me this in your letter. I know, my friend, that I have your confidence and that someday, it may be after many years, you will see how dearly I have valued your esteem.

You tell me you will not return home this winter. I am very sorry but you know what is best and, if you think you will be happier where you are than in your home and among your friends, I will be glad although I shall miss you. Goodbye,

Your Friend
Henry C Scott
[1890-08-27 Henry (StL) to Bertha (Farragut House, NH)]

Although Henry wrote that he hoped in time to have "*the right someday to ask you again to be my wife*", Henry's goodbye in this letter could have been the end of this story. Bertha seemed to have achieved her aim of making Henry understand that the relationship was over and that they needed to move on.

However, almost as soon as Bertha received Henry's letter, she wrote back to Henry. Apparently, not everything had been spoken and resolved between them.

August 31, 1890
My dear friend,

I have been hesitating for a day or two over my answer to your letter but I believe I have no right to refuse what you ask. I will let everything rest as you wish but this is to be a long goodbye. You must not write to me, now, even to answer this, and I do not know when I shall see you again. You were mistaken in thinking it was my choice to stay away this winter. I had no voice in the decision and we are to be away all winter for we are going south after Christmas. The future is not clear to me at all. But I do believe that as long as you and I are true to what is best and highest in ourselves, we cannot really harm each other though we may give pain. If I did not feel sure of that, I could not have yielded, even this far.

Goodbye, Your friend,
Bertha Warburton Drake

Dear friend, you must not think I do not understand how hard it is for a proud man to do what you have done. I wish that I could help you, but I cannot.
[1890-08-31 Bertha (Rye Beach) to Henry (3526 Chestnut St, Stl)]

It is interesting that Bertha, after being so definitive, states "*the future is not clear to me at all.*" Henry did not need any additional encouragement to resume his quest and wrote to Bertha less than one week later.
My dear Miss Drake,

Without waiting for a reply to my letter, I have come here, to go from here to see you if you will permit me to do so. You will understand I know the feeling which restrains me from seeing you without your consent and I am sure you will let me come. Do not refuse me this because you think our meeting will be painful. I will only remain a little while to ask you about your letter which becomes less plain as I think it over from day to day and, without referring to the past, I will leave you. Let me come if you can and remember you trust to me that nothing shall be said which will give you pain.

Your friend,
Henry C Scott
[1890-09-05 Henry (Young's Hotel Boston) to Bertha]

Under the circumstances, Henry's letter was impulsive and did not achieve its aim. In response to Henry's continued pursuit of her, Bertha, again, resisted and specifically wrote of her parents' opposition to Henry.

Sept. 6, 1890
My dear Mr. Scott,

I am sorry you have done what you have done. If you had waited until you received my letter you would have understood this. You must know how my mother and father are opposed to you: prejudiced, unfair, it may be, but it is true. I thought all this ground had been gone over and I thought, as long as I was not sure of myself, now the only fair thing that I could do toward you was to tell you that I considered you free of any bond toward me. I think so still. My mother does not wish me to see you here and I cannot do so. It is unlike you to have done this and, though I understand that you believed it would be better for me as well as yourself to have an explanation face to face, it was a mistake. This had better be our goodbye.

I know that this must seem unkind after your long journey but I cannot act otherwise. You must remember that really we ought never to have spoken of this subject until after I was twenty five but as I saw that you felt bound, I thought that as soon as I felt the end uncertain, I ought to release you. I do so now fully and entirely.

Forgive me for the pain I know I am giving you.

Sincerely your friend,
Bertha Warburton Drake
[1890-09-06 Bertha (Rye Beach) to Henry (Young's Hotel, Boston)]

To emphasize her message, Bertha telegraphed Henry on the same day: "*Do not come. Have written. BWD*"

Bertha's preceding letter and telegraph were blunt and must have surprised Henry. While Henry was undoubtedly aware by now of Bertha's parents dislike for him, it was another matter to have this expressed to him in so forward a way by the very object of his affections. Further, in nearly all of her correspondences, she spoke of her promise to her father and her father's wishes for her. In one of the only times that she spoke of her mother's opposition, Bertha states: "*My mother does not wish me to see you here and I cannot do so.*" In the continuing drama that unfolded hereafter, it appeared increasingly that Bertha's father had found himself trapped between his wife and his daughter, a place in which he seemed increasingly uncomfortable. And, Bertha was also very uncomfortable.

Once again, Henry was conciliatory. He stated that he understood "*both your mother and father are opposed to me*" and that he accepted Bertha's wishes. However, Henry still wrote of his fleeting hope that "*you will one day bring your troubles to me and in the fullness of that faith which casteth out fear.*"

My Dear Miss Drake,

I received your telegram yesterday; your letter came this morning. The telegram was unnecessary for I had no thought of seeing you unless you wished me to come. My only regret in coming here is that I have alarmed you and made you think that I would do what was not sanctioned by you. You ought not to have thought this, for you know I would not go to see you in your own house if I doubted that you would be glad to welcome me. Your mother and father have a clear right to my seeing you, if they know it is your wish that I should not do so, and I wonder you think it necessary to remind me of this.

I understand that both your mother and father are opposed to me. I have known this for a long time, and although I have never felt any unkindness because of it. I have been sure that, if your father had reason to think I could not make your life happy, that there was anything that he could offer as a reason which any fair man could give another, he would have spoken to me long ago.

I know that one in my position does many things to strengthen opposition and little to relieve it, but I have always believed that, if the time ever came when your decision would depend upon your father's ability to satisfy you, there was some good reason for your not trusting your happiness to me, I could meet your decision without fear.

Do not think this is vanity, my friend, you and I feel alike about this, for you have told me so in your letter, and we both know that a woman should decide this question uninfluenced by others, only any considerations which do not establish the unworthiness of the man who asked her for her love. For we have discussed this matter so often it is not necessary to return to it now. You seal my lips in telling me you are uncertain about yourself and you must understand that, if you cannot give me your love as freely, as unreservedly, as I offer mine to you, you would not be doing right to let me make you my wife.

Now let me ask you to do what I wrote you I wished you to do just before you left St. Louis. Dismiss this matter for the present. Try to be happy and useful to your friends and be comforted in the hope that if, after a while, you can be clear as to what is best for your happiness. I will help you to do your duty to yourself and to me.

And, my friend, do not think I am going to be unhappy about this. I know you will do what is best for you and is not that enough to make me happy? And you must not reproach yourself for that would hurt me very much and that would be unkind to another. Make me feel you are going to be well and strong and happy, and when we meet again, let me see in your face no care or sorrow, dear. Remember this is my dearest wish, dearer than the hope that you will one day bring your troubles to me and in the fullness of that faith which casteth out fear, you will let me hear them for you.

I return to St. Louis tonight ready to take up my work where I left it a few days ago, and I am not gloomy or sad, dear, because since I asked it of you, you are going to be happy and this will make me content. You have a stronger friend than I and he will help you and be nearer you now and bless your life as you have made mine beautiful.

Your Friend
Henry C Scott

PS Read the little book I send. You will like it, I am sure.
[1890-09-07 Henry (Youngs Hotel, Boston) to Bertha (Farragut House)]

What was most interesting in this preceding letter was that Henry seemed to show a newfound confidence: "*And, my friend, do not think I am going to be unhappy about this.*" First, Henry commented that Bertha's father had not given any reason for not allowing Henry's suit. "*I have been sure that, if your father had reason to think I could not make your life happy, that there was anything that he could offer as a reason which any fair man could give another, he would have spoken to me long ago.*" Previously, Henry had been extremely deferential regarding Bertha's father and resisted any urge to even remotely criticize him. Now, Henry's words suggested that Bertha's father had no reason to withhold his consent. Second, Henry believed that Bertha had already agreed that the decision to engage was hers alone: "*… we both know that a woman should decide this question uninfluenced by others...*" Third, in less than one year, Bertha would turn 25 years old, at which time her father had promised that she was free to make her own decisions. Finally, Henry seemed very comfortable in stating that this matter should rest and that he was returning to "*St. Louis tonight ready to take up my work…*" (In Latin, Henry might have said: "*Vale puella, iam Catullus obdurate!*"[101])

H. LOVE REKINDLED

During the remainder of 1890 and the beginning of the next year, it became increasingly clear that Bertha began to change her allegiances, especially after her twenty-fifth birthday, and started to work more "on" her father than "with" him. Even if the main impedance to Henry was from her mother, Bertha seemed to prefer to deal with her father and to let her father deal with his wife. In a letter from Bertha to Henry, probably in the fall of 1890 (the exact date is uncertain), Bertha revealed such a change.

> *You are coming to see me tonight but I must write this to you first so that I can tell you quite clearly all that I wish, say things that you will not let me say when you are with me. Before I made any decision, I had to have another talk with my father since then the subject has been dropped with them as with you. My father pleaded with me very, very earnestly not to marry ever, never to leave him. Then he asked me at least to leave the subject for the present, to have no definite engagement until spring, not to refuse to go out with you entirely as I did a year ago, but to see you and go out with you no more than with any other man to let the engagement be in abeyance. In short, to be on those terms that we have been on this last week.*

> *In the spring, this house is to be sold. That will be done anyway, no matter what happened and then my mother is to spend the winter east. My father cannot be with her then. There is too much here which he cannot heave even if he wished it, all at once and she cannot stay alone. I must be with her. I cannot tell you all the reasons here it would take too long but I will tell you and I can see myself that there is no question there of what I ought to do. It is hard for you to realize just how dependent my family are on me but if you think of your own mother and sister, you will understand a little. You said to me the other day that my first duty was to myself. I cannot see that. I could not be happy even as your wife if I felt that I had failed in what I owed them, that I had not made a hard thing as easy as I could for them, and for the present, they absolutely cannot spare me.*

> *This, or at least, the fear that my mother would be ill and need me, was what made me write to you in the spring as I did. You see what this would mean that I could not come to you until a year from next spring at the very earliest and this was not what you meant or hoped for when you asked me to be your wife. You have waited a long, long time already, it would mean another waiting almost as long. Four years altogether. We talked of spoiled lives the other day. There is nothing that could spoil mine so utterly as to feel that where you wanted me as a help to you, I had brought nothing but pain and weariness into your life. I have given you too much already and rather a*

---

[101] "*Goodbye girl, already Catullus endures*". Poetry of Gaius Catullus.

thousand times rather than that, I would say goodbye to you tonight. There is nothing more to write. I am,

Always your friend,
B.W.D.
[1890(-) 20180508-1 Bertha (StL) to Henry (StL)]

By the winter of 1890, Henry was seeing more of Bertha.
My Darling,
After we have spent an evening together, I think of very little the next day that is not in one way or another associated with our last meeting. Even if this were not true, I would be ungenerous indeed if after last night I should say or write anything to you that will be disagreeable now. I do intend to find fault a little, dear.

My protest is that I do not see enough of you; and really, Bert, I don't see how criticism can be better invited than in following out what seems to be your present plan of seeing or going out with me at long intervals. Perhaps I see my side of the case more clearly because I feel so cheated out of what has become my only great pleasure, but when I think of your long absence from home and how I shall have to wait on again so long without you, I don't think you are very good to me, dearest; do you?
[1890-12(-) Henry to Bertha - *No Date – Around December, 1890*]

In the preceding letter, Henry advised Bertha "*not carry your "discretionary measures" too far*". While it was not exactly clear what these measures may have been, it seemed clear that Bertha was now working to reconcile her parents to Henry's suit, and Henry was actively aiding and abetting the cause.

In February of 1891, Henry requested an audience with Bertha's father to request his blessing. The timing of this request was interesting since the intended engagement, while spoken about, was apparently not entirely settled, as will be seen later. Nevertheless, Henry requested such a meeting and then received the following, frosty, reply from George.
St. Louis, Feby 24th
Mr. Henry C Scott,
In reply to your note received last evening, I have to decline the meeting you ask for.

My daughter is acting independently for herself. If the reasons I present to her for a given course of conduct are not sufficient & satisfactory to her, I do not wish to discuss the question with anyone else. I must abide by her decision and she takes the responsibility of her action.

Yours truly,
Geo. S. Drake

We do not need to correspond further on this subject.
[1891-02-24(-) George Drake, father (StL) to Henry (StL)]

While Bertha's father may have been put off by Henry's persistence, he may also have been annoyed at having to deal with his wife's animosity toward Henry. The fact that Bertha's father would have known Henry's rising star in St. Louis business and would become much closer to Henry later in his life suggested that he was an unwilling participant in this matter. Perhaps his comment was telling: "*My daughter is acting independently for herself*" – i.e. I wash my hands of this.

Henry seemed to have made some progress with Bertha in the Spring of 1891 and must have been encouraged by the fact that Bertha had her 25th birthday in April 1891. As her father promised, Bertha was then entitled to make her own decisions about marriage. Nevertheless, Bertha's parents were unrelenting and, under their influence, Bertha questioned her own judgment. Bertha wrote the following letter to Henry in May of 1891 wherein she said that any decision must be put off for at least the remainder of the year but added, *"I cannot see that my decision will be any different then from what it is now."*

Hotel Brunswick Boston to St. Louis
Dear Friend,

I have your letter, and I have thought most earnestly over what you have asked, but I cannot see you now. I have had two long talks with my father and I will try to tell you exactly what he said to me this morning after he had thought of it all night. It will explain to you better than anything else I can say just how I am situated. "Your mother and I have always thought that your promise to wait two years, meant to wait until next fall, two years from the time the promise was given. But I would put that aside as far as you are concerned, you are a woman, now, old enough to judge what is right and best for you to do. But, I cannot have the subject opened with your mother in her present state of health. You must not let Mr. Scott come, delicate as your mother is now. I cannot answer for the consequences if she has any more trouble or anxiety of any sort. The question might not be brought up. Wait until she has had a summers rest and we are at home."

My mother is very delicate just now, I have given up my visit to Chicago, because I do not like to have her alone – and I think I realized she must not have the excitement, though it seemed hard to refuse to see you when you have waited so patiently. But I have written all this, only to explain why I cannot let you come on. I do not expect we shall ever open this question again. I have tried to face everything clearly and to see what it will be right for me to do. Last Christmas, when I was at home, I expected to be able to give you a different answer now – but all spring, I have been learning to see differently. I am afraid my mother's health is breaking absolutely, if it should do so, my place will be with her, you must see that dear. I think you will say perhaps then why not tell her now. But my father judges differently. He does not want the subject touched upon in any way, being sure that whatever was said or done could only be not good for her now and hoping that she will be stronger at the end of the summer. I hope that too but I am afraid it will not be a permanent thing and I cannot see that my decision will be any different then from what it is now. And I cannot stand this waiting. Or for you, with what I know will only be disappointment at last. Dear, let this be the end, indeed, it is best.

Goodbye, God bless you,
Your friend,
Bertha Warburton Drake
[1891-05-17 Bertha (Boston) to Henry (StL)]

The illness of Bertha's mother and the concerted influence of both parents made it very difficult for Bertha to be decisive, especially when Henry could not plead his case in person. But once again, Henry recognized that his position was untenable and bluntly wrote: *"I can see now what I should have known before that the real cause of your indecision has been that the interest you have felt was not strong enough to enable you to make the sacrifice I asked of you"* and *"I cannot longer blind myself to the real cause of your indecision and so I meet the issue as you wish."*

Saint Louis
May 21 -1891

My dear Miss Drake,

Your letter explains to me, as I have never understood it before, just why it has been so hard for you to know what it was best to do with the question upon which I have asked you to finally decide. I can see now what I should have known before that the real cause of your indecision has been that the interest you have felt was not strong enough to enable you to make the sacrifice I asked of you. I do not intend to be harsh with you but I know it is best that I speak to you plainly. The feeling you have had was not what you thought it was or what I really believe you hoped it was or you could not have subordinated it to any other consideration.

You wrote me some time ago how clearly you felt it to be a woman's duty to give her first thought to one for whom she cared, even if in so doing she gave pain to her nearest friends and, although in that letter you wounded me deeply by references which I could not misunderstand, I forgot everything else save that you knew I was right in what I had said to you on this subject. And I felt only glad because I thought I saw I had helped you. Although I never for a moment thought you were acting wisely in deferring your decision to do what you believed to right and best for you, I learned to think you were trying to be very gentle with your friends and, to save them from any doubt of what your true feeling was, you permitted time to lapse before giving me your answer to convince them that this was not a passing fancy but your highest hope of happiness.

That I misapprehended the true cause of your trouble will be a regret as deep as any sorrow I have ever known. Your parents' opposition, bitter and unreasonable as I thought it, now seems well justified for, in seeing what I was not able to comprehend, they did nothing less than what was right in trying to persuade you there were other things you cared more for than that which seemed to me everything to you. That your decision once made would be accepted by your parents, I cannot think you doubted. Neither do I doubt that you were clear that what was best for you would in the end bring them most happiness and comfort. I also feel it is clear to you that your friends would have neither have been quite fair to you nor to me in trying to influence you against your judgment of what was not only your wish but your duty.

The despair I so often felt when I saw how grieved you seemed to be, with no one to help you without the aid I had learned to think a girl's parents would always be ready to give her in solving such a problem, was no doubt the cause of much of the folly and weakness I have so often been guilty of. I thought you did not see that effort was being made to keep you from following your own judgment. I did not believe until your last letter came that your friend's efforts were continued and that you hesitated because you doubted yourself. But I understand it all now and I know quite well how to act.

When first one reason and then another is urged by you as a barrier to the realization of my hopes and wishes, I cannot longer blind myself to the real cause of your indecision and so I meet the issue as you wish. You hardly meant, I think, to suggest that I could not understand your desire to be near your mother while she is unwell and I shall forget that part of your letter.

You ask that this shall be the end and it shall be so. I accept your decision as final and with the hope that you will forget the trouble and anxiety which I am sure I have given you many times.

I am sincerely yours,
Henry C Scott
[1891-05-21 Henry (StL) to Bertha (Hotel Brunswick, Boston)]

"You ask that this shall be the end and it shall be so", Henry wrote. However, it was not clear that Henry had abandoned all hope. In stating his acceptance of Bertha's request to end their relationship, Henry was the spurned lover to one whose heart could not requite his love, whose *"interest you have felt"* was not

strong enough. Among persons who previously voiced love for each other, "*interest*" was cold indeed and Bertha must have been struck by that word. Already, Henry seemed to know how to find the right way back into Bertha's heart.

By that summer of 1891, Bertha and Henry were again communicating by letter as before. In a letter written by Bertha around June 5, 1891, Bertha made fun of Henry's hoping that Bertha would not become ill until he was there to take care of her: "*… you would not begin to take as good care of me as my mother would and more than that, being a man, it would bore you awfully.*" [1891-06-05(-) Bertha (the Ark, East Jaffrey) to Henry (StL)] In spite of her protests, Bertha knew that she did not want Henry to stop pursuing her.

I. ACCEPTANCE

In August 1891, Henry went to visit Bertha when she was staying in Rye Beach. Their tryst was arranged by Helen Ernst who played the role of cupid for the "estranged" lovers. In order to avoid the disapproving eyes of Bertha's parents, Helen separately invited both Bertha and Henry to visit her at the Appledore House on Appledore Island. (Appledore Island is part of the Isles of the Shoals, a group of islands approximately 6 miles offshore from Rye Beach.)

The Appledore House in 1901. The hotel was built in 1847. (Wikipedia)

In a letter, dated August 17[102], Bertha wrote to Henry, "*I had a letter from Helen Ernst this morning saying she is coming down to the Shoals next week and asking me to come over and spend the day again with her, adding 'possibly I may see something of you this time.'*" [20180218-1 (- -08-17) Bertha (Rye Beach) to Henry (StL)]

In a letter one year after this event, Henry wrote to Bertha of his "*profound obligation*" to Helen Ernst, without whose intervention in arranging their meeting on the Isles of the Shoals in August 1891, "*I think we should have never met again.*"

> *You speak of the Isles of Shoals. Will you see Miss Ernst this summer? You know I sometimes am led to think that if she had never lived, I should not have met you last summer. And if I had not met you then, I think we should have never met again, dear. And if we had not met at all - well, this train of reasoning usually leaves me with a sense of profound obligation to that girl, even though I distinctly remember she called me a name that does not imply wisdom.*
> [1892-08-15 (Monday) Henry (StL) to Bertha (Farragut House, Rye Beach)]

One can imagine that Helen Ernst may have called Henry a fool for his mad pursuit of Bertha. But, if so, was there ever a better commendation of someone's love?

On August 25, 1891 on the Isles of the Shoals, Henry was waiting for Bertha and her entourage when they arrived on the ferry to Appledore Island. At some point during the day, Henry was able to secret Bertha

---

[102] The year was not included in the letter but, based on the content, it must have been 1891.

away from the watching eyes of her friends and take Bertha to a private place among "the rocks" where he proposed anew and Bertha accepted.

Henry wrote the next year to commemorate the very happy one-year anniversary of their engagement in a letter to arrive on August 25, 1892. However, being away from Bertha on business, Henry was lonely and was *"occupied mainly with my own thoughts, the most comfortless companions."*

> *Hotel Ryan*
> *St. Paul, Minn. Aug. 23rd, 1892*
> *I have been indulging in some very wise reflections today, dear, and the most important conclusion I have arrived at is that I am never going away from home again unless you are with me or unless I am compelled to go on business for this trip, since I left Chicago, has been a dead failure and I am served just right for coming here. I was not obliged to come but thought it would help me to see some new construction work which has been done in St. Paul and as I could spare one or two days I concluded I could turn them to good account here, but I don't think I have gained any new ideas from the work I have seen here. It is rather behind than in advance of the work done in the states farther south and at any rate I finished up early today.*
>
> *And then I tried to amuse myself by looking up several friends but finding after one or two trials that they did not help me to kill the time. I left the last man promising most enthusiastically to "see you later". I hope I shall never set eyes on the man again and turned my steps towards the hotel which I have not left since, having been occupied mainly with my own thoughts, the most comfortless companions.*
>
> *I have tried to look this town and Minneapolis over while I was waiting for the letters I expected to get here today but which do not come until tomorrow but this, like my other attempts to be festive, is a hopeless failure. I would not give a fig to see all the beauties of creation if I had to do so without a really congenial companion and, dear, I am fast coming to the conclusion that you are the only really congenial companion I have, for whatever pleasure comes to me now, I think my enjoyment of it is almost nothing so greatly does it accentuate the feeling of loneliness which never seems to entirely leave me.*
>
> *I did not intend to write you a gloomy letter, dear. I would rather leave you think of what has been in my thoughts a great deal for the last few days. This letter will reach you, I hope, on the morning of the 25th, just a year, my darling, from the day you promised to be my wife and, dearest, I want the day to be a happy one for you. I shall think of you on Thursday morning and I shall wonder if your beautiful influence in my life will continue to increase the capacity for happiness which I have received from you since you blessed me with the promise to be my wife, dear. I say, I wonder if my happiness in you will grow as it has done because it seems now that no greater happiness is possible than mine would be if I had you near me and knew that I could keep you all through my life and yet after thinking this I have many times during the last year seen that, through a new light which I received of the pure spirit of my darling, new and greater power seemed to be given me to bless her and each day something seemed to be added to the great love I have for her. I wonder too, dear, if it comes into the lives of many people to know that they have gained the love of the one person on earth who can give them the greatest help in their lives, who can make the best things so well worth striving for. My darling, you have made life so beautiful to me that I feel ashamed of yielding as I have today to the sense of loneliness because you are so far away and I shall turn from all such gloomy reflections and think only of the beautiful period when we , you and I dear, will be one.*
>
> *God bless you now and always, my own beloved. Henry*
> [1892-08-23 Henry (St. Paul, MN) to Bertha (Farragut House, Rye Beach)]

At the same time, Bertha was writing to Henry about this anniversary: *"Can you guess why I wanted to spend Thursday there [at the Shoals]? The date will correspond to one engraved inside my ring[103]."* [1892-08-22 Bertha (Farragut House, Rye Beach) to Henry]

Two days later, Henry telegraphed Bertha:
> *To: Miss Bertha W. Drake, Marion*
> *I hope this will be among your happiest anniversaries.*
> *H.C.S.*
> [1892-08-25 Henry (Chicago) – telegram to Bertha (Marion, MA)]

Henry also wrote about this event around 1900 in a letter to Bertha when she was at Rye Beach. Henry was reminiscing about *"the day that you finally decided to rescue me…"* when they went to *"those rocks"* at the Shoals, away from their friends.
> *How I would like to be there with you just for one day or, while I am wishing, for two days – for we might, if we had nothing better to do, the second day, leave the chicks and go over to the shoals and after lunch stroll down to those rocks and try to find the original two which sheltered us from the gaze of our friends that day you finally decided to rescue me from my unhappy condition. I think it would make me feel like a boy again, climb[ing] over those big fellows with you.*
> [1900(-) 20170724-12 Henry to Bertha]

Appledore Island circa 1890 [from Portsmouth Athenaeum website]

Henry remembered the details of their engagement for the rest of his life and was jealous if Bertha went to the Isles of the Shoals without him, as he wrote in two letters to Bertha in July 1908.
> *I don't see how you have the courage to go over to the Shoals without me! Don't you dare to go down to those rocks! But if you do, it may mitigate the depths of your present sorrows if you will go there alone and contemplate in rapt silence the ecstatic moments you enjoyed there. Let's see - this coming twenty fifth of August seventeen years ago!*
> [1908-07-17 Henry (StL) to Bertha (Rye Beach)]

---

[103] i.e. August 25, 1891.

...what must have been your meditations as the boat drew near Appledore and your eager glance saw no kidnapper in the guise of a nice young man to rush off with you to the rocks in order that you might be given the chance to show him how a good woman loved him!
[1908-07-18 Henry (StL) to Bertha (Rye Beach)]

J. THEIR LIVES ARE FOREVER CHANGED

Bertha and Henry's engagement changed them and even their friends, as Bertha wrote.

> *The other day I would write to you what Miss Hagen said and forgot it. She came to see me in Boston and begged me "to tell her a little of what a good time I had when der Herr Scott was here." I told her a little of what we had done, possibly my expression said more than I did, for she listened with such eager wistful eyes and said at the end "O, I am so glad, so glad. You do not know how beautiful it is to me to think that there is such happiness in the world." Just think of always standing on the outside, and only being able to be glad about other people! Dear old boy, don't think you are so very conceited in thinking we have a better time together than most people do. And, after all, I doubt if we could have come so near to each other if we had always had smooth sailing. And 'tis the way of the world, son, if Mr. Shakespeare is to be believed, we are not the first by ever so many – "the course of true love never did" you know[104]. And I don't suppose it will to the end of time.*
> [1892-06-12 Bertha (East Jaffrey) to Henry (StL)]

In 1892, Bertha wrote to Henry of how much she had learned of unhappiness and happiness and to accept both in her life since they were first engaged three-years before.

> *Sweetheart, a great deal has happened in those three years. I told you then I did not know what it meant to be unhappy. I might have told you just as truly, though I did not know it, that I did not know what real happiness meant. I have learned both of those things since then, dear, and I would not give up the one if it obliged me to sacrifice the other. The joy of a girl's life is not half so beautiful ...*
> [1892-04-24 (Sunday) Bertha (-) to Henry (StL)]

As a young lady, Bertha wrote of joys of being a girl: *"What jolly foolish times girls can have together. So much more fun than when men are around."* [1888-05 Diary, July 21, 1888] This was a time when Bertha could say that she did not know unhappiness. But during the time of her engagement to Henry, she discovered that she never before knew *"real happiness"*. Perhaps, it was just as she wrote in her poem, "Love kissed her and she woke"[105]. Bertha woke to the knowledge of great happiness and, also, unhappiness. Henry certainly had the same awakening. The price of their newfound happiness was joined with some bitter unhappiness.

---

[104] "*the course of true love never did run smooth.*" William Shakespeare, from *A Midsummer Night's Dream*.
[105] This poem by Bertha is included in Chapter 9.

CHAPTER 10 – THE FATHER OF THE BRIDE

George S. Drake, Sr.

Henry's relationship with his father-in-law to be, George Silas Drake, did not get off to a good start. But, these troubles at the start may have paved the way for a more solid relationship later.

A. REQUESTING HIS DAUGHTER'S HAND

After Bertha and Henry's "official" engagement of August 25, 1891, the main obstacles to their nuptials were Bertha's father and mother. Bertha and Henry did not want to make the announcement until George had given his blessing, which blessing was not forthcoming. Still, Henry was surely comforted that Bertha was now resolutely on his side and, as she wrote in her letter (below), was actively advocating for Henry.

> *I have just heard the result of your attempt today. I am sorry for I did the best I could to make it otherwise. But I am glad you made me have that talk with my father and I think I can succeed in making you not feel bitterly about his refusal to see you when you come to me Wednesday. I am only sorry that I cannot see you before then but it is not possible, I am engaged every minute.*
>
> *As always,*
> *B.W.D.*
> [1891-11-18(-year) Bertha (StL) to Henry (StL)]

By December 1891, Bertha was becoming bolder in communicating with her father.

> *I had another talk with my father which relieved me as to his being in any doubt as to how we stand toward one another. I felt worried after you left me and wondered if he could have misunderstood me but he understands perfectly.*
> [1891-12-04 Bertha (StL) to Henry]

Henry seemed well aware of Bertha's struggles and continually offered his support. Henry also wrote, *"Trouble brings those who care for each other nearer"*, a silver lining.

> *I hope the bad cold has disappeared this morning, my darling, and that you are quite well again. And don't be blue, dear, because things don't work out as quickly & as happily as we wish. Our lives will be all the happier, after a while, because you made it hard for yourself in your brave effort to consider others before taking thought of your own future. We will make up the lost time, dear, and it may be that I will become a better man because I shall have more to make you forget than if matters had seemed clear from the start. Trouble brings those who care for each other nearer, you know, & I try to think that some of the beauty of your life would have been hid from me if it had been easier for you to give me your life.*

God bless you, dear, and may my blessing be the strength to help you whenever you need my aid.

Devotedly,
Henry
[1891-xx-xx(-) Henry to Bertha]

Similarly, in the following letter to Bertha, Henry expressed his desire to help Bertha through this difficult period. *"If our future happiness costs us something now, will it not be sweeter?"*, Henry reassured.

I hope, my dear, dear child, that what you did for me last night will not bring any trouble to you this morning. It seems mean of me to request your doing anything for me that will result in annoyance to you at times when I cannot be near to answer, as I should be able to, any unkind words that may be said to you. I am writing you this from home this morning in the hope that it may reach you in time to help you, and oh, my darling, I do so wish to help you and shield you from care. Do you know, Bertha, the hardest thing to bear is that you do sweet, unselfish things for me and then I cannot protect you from being destressed in consequence of this care for our love. But we can't be made sad by these things, my darling, can we? If our future happiness costs us something now, will it not be sweeter, dear? I only plead for my share of the price you are paying for what we hold so dear and this is added evidence of my selfishness, dear child, for if I do not contribute equally, can I claim an equal share in the reward?

Yours always,
Henry
[1891-xx-xx Henry to Bertha 20190223-1]

As the months of fall and winter of 1891 passed, Henry redoubled his efforts to meet with George to allow him the opportunity to properly request for Bertha's hand in marriage. With Bertha fully committed to this end, she too spoke with her father to help arrange the meeting. But Bertha's dealings with her father could try her spirits, as reflected by the following letter. In January 1892, Bertha wrote to Henry of her decision to have an additional delay in the public announcement and, in turn, the date that they would be married. Bertha still held to her desire to make peace among all the parties. And Bertha made clear that this was her decision, not influenced by her friends, such as Nan Shepley.

I have been looking at your beautiful ring. It is so beautiful, it gives me an aching feeling too think how little I thanked you for it after all, the time and trouble you had taken to give me pleasure. It is the most beautiful one I ever saw. I have thought a good deal of what we said that night too. You did hurt me, dear. It always hurts to think I have failed in what you expected of me. But I do not think you were quite just. I have thought of it carefully, trying to decide as I would for another woman and I am quite sure I should say to her "Never let go of your main purpose, never let others think that you mean to do so, but don't increase bitterness of feeling by a series of petty struggles, don't embitter feeling where you might avoid doing so by little concessions." I may have carried this too far, I know, indeed that it was the easier thing to do and that was why I thought you might be right when you said that I was weak in yielding. But, dear, when I have made them unhappy, do you think it is either the best or the wisest to go on inflicting a series of petty annoyances? It would make life unbearable and I have tried hard to make the winter a pleasant one. There is my defense and my honest opinion, dear boy, uninfluenced by anyone else. For you have not been spoken of since your departure; I have not even seen Nan alone.
[1892-01-19 Bertha (StL) to Henry (Ft. Worth)]

In spite of Bertha and Henry's efforts, George's refusal to see Henry continued, as Bertha wrote:

Mr. H.C. Scott, Present

Dear friend,

I am sorry my father would not see you today as I especially asked him to do so. I do not know what to do. I told you I was sure of what was right and I am not sure anymore.

Yes, come tonight, I shall be excused to everyone and I must see you.
As always,
B.W.D.
[20180507-1 (1892-) Bertha (StL) to Henry (StL)]

Henry clearly did not wish to have Bertha be responsible for arranging the meeting between George and himself. But there was no other way, given George's recalcitrance.

I have just read, in reply to my second request to meet and talk with your father, his statement that he had talked with you last evening and that he waited to hear your decision before meeting me. I would have greatly preferred your father seeing me today but I shall not attempt to meet him until he has again seen you as I imagine this course accords with your wishes.

You must not be troubled, my dear friend, at this delay. This matter will work out all right, I am very sure. And if you can only let me feel you are following my wishes and are not making yourself anxious about a trouble which will soon be over, I shall be happier than I can ever tell you. I think of you always, dear, and this delay would pain me inexpressibly if I did not remember your promise to be bright & happy until I should see you again.

I have restrained every impulse to go & see you and you must know how hard this is. I haven't even sent you a flower to bear a message for me. But I must see you tonight, dear, & I shall do so for I know that it is right that we should see each other. We won't talk of our affair, dear, for that is really already settled and we will not even think of it, for surely we will not have time to think of gloomy things when I have so much to say to you about the glad thoughts that are in my heart, that you, my darling, have given me. How can I be other than
Yours always, Henry
[20170716-1 (1892-) Henry (StL) to Bertha]

Certainly, Henry appreciated Bertha's efforts with her father in the "*bitter struggles.*"

You know I do not ask you ever to let me come unless, beside being glad to see me, you think I can help you some. I do help you a little, do I not Bertha? We need courage, dear, to do anything where opposition is to be dealt with and I wish so much, my darling, that I had the power of expression to convince you that all of us must get stronger from the efforts we make to do what we think is right, even if these efforts are sometimes bitter struggles. Isn't this what some wise man calls the necessary exercise for moral development?
[20180425-4 (1892-) Henry to Bertha]

Notwithstanding his view that this period of waiting would make their relationship stronger, Henry's patience had reached its limit. So Henry proposed taking bold action "*I have determined to call on him and insist upon his seeing me.*"

My dearest Bertha,
All day I have been looking for a reply to my note to your father. I especially asked that he reply without delay, saying when I should have opportunity to talk with him. Now my judgment was that I could best show my disposition to be entirely fair by giving your father an opportunity to think over what I wrote him before meeting me. He has, however, had time enough for that now and I am not willing you shall be kept longer in suspense as to the result of our interview, so I have determined to call on him and insist upon his seeing me before I meet you this evening.

I write you my determination because I wish to keep you posted and because it has occurred to me it will help you a little, dearest, to know that I shall not say anything to your father that will unnecessarily wound him and that I only shall insist upon his talking with me to hear what he has to say against the time fixed for our marriage. I left no doubt in his mind as to our full determination to carry out our arrangement for I was sure it would unnecessarily involve matters if I was not very positive. But I stated that I wished to hear his side of the question between us to be very sure that no consideration bearing upon the matter should be lost sight of by us.

I do not anticipate that your father will decline to see me today but, if he does, I shall at once advise him by letter that the matter will not be discussed by you or me any further and that, exercising the right you have given me, I must advise him that nothing will prevent our marriage at the time we have agreed upon.

You must let me be positive with your father, dear, because I think it will ultimately be best for him as for you and try to think that I will not forget he is your father in anything I shall say to him.

I have told the boy to ask for an answer to this in the event you may care to send one. Be brave, my precious child and I promise to work out this problem so that it shall not trouble you any more, dear. Can't you trust me to do that, my darling?

Devotedly,
HCS
[20170711a -1891 or 92(?) Henry (StL) to Bertha (StL)]

Although Henry was resolute in his letter, i.e., "*I must advise him that nothing will prevent our marriage at the time we have agreed upon*", Henry could not prevent the further delays in their wedding plans.

It was clear that Bertha wanted to avoid a dispute between her father and Henry and was willing to make additional accommodations to her father. Since Bertha knew him well, this was undoubtedly the wise course of action.

> *As you have not seen my father, I would rather you not come to see me tonight. I have not had a chance to talk with him yet and, until both I and you have done so, I think it would be better for you not to come to see me. This evening I must give to him and we have someone to dinner so I cannot see him until quite late. Please do not think me unkind.*
> [20170611 – (1891-) Bertha (StL) to Henry (3526 Chestnut St. Stl)]

Henry endured the seemingly endless wait for his suit to move forward, made more difficult by his other friends who seemed to easily become married.

> *Mattie says Janet [January] is the happiest girl she has seen in a long time and that his[106] beaming countenance is the most refreshing thing she has seen in a long time. Dear, Miss Nan's prophecies have, thus far, come true, for we will not be married until long after Miss Janet.*
> *I suppose it is mean spirited but their happiness, coming so much sooner than ours made me blue and I could not help contrasting the ease with which some people seem to get what they most desire in life and the disappointments that have beset me on all sides. I think they much deserve happiness, more than I do or – no, I don't think this, dearest. I have to struggle harder because I have aimed higher, because I shall gain more, and if, as we think, the disappointments at first will make the future any dearer to us it is well worth the while, even though in our gloomy hours the troubles were very hard to bear.*
> [1892-01-20(-) Henry to Bertha StL. to East Jaffrey, NH]

---

[106] Howard Elliott who married Janet January on October 12, 1892.

Bertha was very aware of how difficult it was for Henry to accept the delays with only muted complaints.

> *We have not left very much to say to each other but I am vain enough to think you will be a little*
> *blue tomorrow morning so I am writing this as a greeting. Dear, I wonder sometimes if you know*
> *how fully I understand how bitterly hard certain things have been to you that you have done for my*
> *sake without a word of complaint. I do know and I believe the remembrance of your gentle*
> *consideration for me now when I needed it so much will be a help to me all through my life.*
> [1892-03-03 (-day) Bertha (StL) to Henry (StL)]

George kept Henry waiting to have an audience with him through the end of April 1892. Bertha wrote that she had insisted that her father speak to Henry as soon as he returned to St. Louis.

> *By the time you receive this, if all has gone well, my father will have been to see you. I want you*
> *to know now that I insisted upon this before I would make any promise of delay. I felt that due to*
> *myself as much as to you. I want you to know that I would never have allowed last winter to pass*
> *as it did if I had not supposed that he would see you in the spring. I was as much surprised as you*
> *could have been. We had no argument about it. I told him just how I felt and he promised to go.*
> *I only write all this now because I do not wish you to feel, as I fear you have sometimes, that your*
> *dignity is any less dear to me than my own.*
> [1892-04-26 Tuesday Bertha (New York) to Henry (StL)]

The preceding letter was the last to mention Henry's request to George of Bertha's hand in marriage. One can only presume that the two met within the several weeks of this letter and that this formality was finally performed.

B. THE ENGAGEMENT WAS FINALLY ANNOUNCED

Bertha and Henry officially announced their engagement around the end of January 1892 when Bertha had already gone back east with her parents. At that time, Henry had still been unable to meet with George and would not be able to do so for many more months. George and Bertha M were still pulling Bertha's "strings" and may have gotten some satisfaction by arranging this announcement to proceed without the couple being together. One can only imagine that George was being pressured by Bertha M to try to put a stop to this marriage while George may have become tired over the whole ordeal and simply wanted to bring the matter to its conclusion. So George and Bertha M permitted the announcement to be made, after which, George became noticeably *"stronger"* and *"more like his old sunny self"*. Contrarily, Bertha M became more ill, as Bertha explained in her letter.

> *My father has gone off to Ormand on a fishing excursion. I think this trip has done him no end of*
> *good and, I think, though he probably does not realize it, that the fact of the announcement being*
> *over and done with has something to do with it. At all events, whether it is that or the meeting his*
> *cousin or the bright weather or the entire change of scene and occupation, he looks much stronger*
> *and seems to a great extent to have shaken off his gloomy depression and to be more like his old*
> *sunny self. This gives me great hopes for the future.*
>
> *My mother is very unwell. She suffered intensely in her rheumatic attack, does still to some extent*
> *and of course the constant pain wears on her. I do not think we could have come back to St. Louis*
> *even if we had meant to for the railway traveling will be so painful that we shall probably go north*
> *by short stages, stopping at Savannah, Charlestown, Richmond, every good place, we can in fact.*
>
> *O, I must tell you a conversation I had with the Bryans. They had come over from Pass Christian*
> *and had had no letters for some time so they had not heard the all-important news of our*
> *engagement. Nor did I tell them at first but, by some odd chance, they began talking about their*
> *own engagement and of course the trepidation John went through when he had to go speak to Mrs.*

Turner. Susie said her mother at first positively refused to see him, said she had nothing to say to him, did not wish to see him and did not see what good could be obtained by her seeing him. When she finally did, she said, "I know what you have come for, Dr. Bryan, Susie has told me but she must give her own answer." Whereupon the embarrassed doctor responded "well, she says it's all right." "Well, I have nothing to say about it. Susie is of age, she must decide for herself. I have nothing to do, you must arrange everything as she wishes." With which she turned her back on him and left the room and John sent the maid upstairs to Susie for a fan. This reminds me a little bit of some other people's experiences. I have told them since about ourselves, and they were very nice, especially the doctor.
[1892-03-16(a) Bertha (St. Augustine) to Henry (StL)]

The story of Mrs. Turner's refusing to see her daughter's suitor and then dismissing him with "*Well, I have nothing to say about it*", mirrored the approach taken by Bertha's father. And, more profoundly, both examples showed how parental authority over daughters' decision to marry was changing, leaving parents uncertain of their prerogatives and of the correct course of action. In both cases, hands were washed and any parental decision avoided.

The announcement of Bertha and Henry's engagement brought many words and letters of congratulation. Bertha wrote to Henry that her father had broached the subject of their impending marriage with old friends which was a sure sign of his acceptance and consent.

I must tell you what happened this morning. My father came upstairs saying he had met the Sawyers. Mr. and Mrs. Sawyer are Boston people and old friends of ours. They travelled all through Europe with my father and mother twenty years ago. Well, on our way to church -- This has nothing to do with the case but I must tell you that I wore one of your roses and a spray of rose geranium that was a very carefully ordered box, dear boy, with its maiden hair fern and rose geranium, You don't know how I have enjoyed it. --- To go back, on our way to church, we met the Sawyers and after a little chat, Mrs. Sawyer said to me, "Your father has told us of the new life ahead for you, you must let me give you our very warmest good wishes and congratulations." I was surprised; there is nothing my father could have done to set his seal more emphatically to the fact that his opposition is withdrawn. He had had to receive congratulations before but this was different, he deliberately announced it of his own accord to old friends who were not in the way of hearing it otherwise. It is a great advance for him and I must tell you also that I do not think you will have any further discourtesy to resent from him.
[1892-04-24(-) (Sunday) Bertha (NYC) to Henry (StL)]

Bertha found additional support from her father's lawyer, Samuel Holliday, who took Bertha to a play in New York City and gave her his own "fatherly" counsel. Mr. Holliday told Bertha, "*A woman possesses no more unalienable right on this earth than that of marrying... and I never knew anything but harm come of thwarting it.*"

I had such a lark yesterday evening. Mr. Holliday took me to see "Colonel Carter. .... Do you know him at all? Samuel Holliday, the lawyer? Well he is my father's lawyer, one of his co-trustees in the Allen Estate and one of his most trusted friends and advisers. Father thinks he has one of the clearest heads of any man he knows and I think he proves it by being exceedingly fond of me.

He began to congratulate me last night and went on thus, "I have always had an idea that your father wished you never to marry, wanted you to stay at home with him, yes? Mother too, perhaps? We don't think any man good enough for you, of course. Well, it is natural enough, God knows." (His only daughter, whom he simply idolized, died when she was seventeen.) "But it's not right all the same. I want to tell you that I think you have acted just exactly right. Parents have a great many rights, there is no man on earth believes that more strongly than I do, but there's a point where they stop. A woman possesses no more unalienable right on this earth than that of marrying.

I have had a good deal of experience in sixty years and I never knew anything but harm come of thwarting it. I was just thoroughly and heartily glad from the bottom of my heart when I heard your decision."

You may judge whether I loved Mr. Holliday or not after that. You once asked me if I could not get some outsider's opinion. I have it without asking from my father's most trusted adviser. We had a very gay time.
[1892-04-29 Friday Bertha (NYC) to Henry (StL)]

During the summer of 1892, Bertha and her parents visited Colonel Leighton in Dublin, NH, where, after her impulsive prompting, Bertha received Colonel Leighton's sincere congratulations, "*most sincerely!*" It was like "*a sun beam breaking through a cloud.*"
Friday
I had no letter from you last night but I do not on that account conclude that you did not write on Tuesday, only that you probably mailed the letter up town.

My father came and this morning he drove Miss Hobart, Miss Going and myself over to Dublin. We met Charlotte Kayser, Mr. Catlin and Colonel Leighton. They all asked us to get out but we declined and then the Colonel told us to drive up to his place to see the view. We did so and he presently left the Catlins and ran up to his house by a short cut so as to meet us. He took us on his piazza to look at the view which is perfectly magnificent of the lake and mountains, reminds me of Scotland. Then as we stood on the porch, he went up and gathered one of his prettiest white roses and handed it to me, saying "I want you to wear a Dublin rose for me, Miss Bertie." Miss Going laughed and said "That's a bride's rose." "Indeed, it is," said Mr. Leighton, still with a little hesitation, though he smiled at me. Then I said "Aren't you going to let me have your congratulations, Colonel Leighton, I have never had a chance before to have them." I wish you could have seen his face, have you ever seen him in his gracious moods, really the hackneyed remark about a sun beam breaking through a cloud is the only thing that compares to it. He took my hand in both his and said "My dear, I do congratulate most sincerely." Then raising his voice a little, he repeated with a marked emphasis "most sincerely."

Don't you think I ought to have done this? It was done impulsively but it seemed to me the simplest, most direct mode of placing things in their right position and there was no awkwardness at all. Father did not say anything but there was no reason that he should. I thanked the Colonel and then he showed us his house, invited father to dine with him and we parted on the most cordial terms all round.
[1892-06-02(-) Bertha (-) to Henry (StL)]

C. PLANNING FOR A NOVEMBER WEDDING

Bertha and Henry originally planned that they should be married no later than November 1892 and this had been agreed to by all concerned. Still, Bertha felt an obligation to her parents from whom "*absolutely nothing has been denied to me*" and this was manifest in her letter to Henry.

Dear, I hope that in some way we shall be able to meet before next November and I shall do my best to bring it about for we cannot be married before that. November has been definitely agreed to and I think it would be unwise and unkind to open the subject again. My promise to you and the fact that I am absolutely positive in my own mind that another winter like the last would be a mistake for all concerned made me hold to November. But I cannot come to you sooner. I know that you sometimes think I yield too much but I do not, dear. There is one thing that it would be wrong for me to yield but, outside that, there is <u>nothing</u> that would be too much to show my love and gratitude to them for all that they have been to me. It has not simply been the ordinary *relationship between parent and child but absolutely nothing has been denied to me. What hope of happiness could there be for me in my new life if I failed in what was the right thing for me in the old. Not much self-denial has been asked of me; to practice a little now will not make me less fit to be your wife, your help mate, as I hope to be, my darling. Don't you like that word? And I do so want to be that in its fullest sense.*

You grieve me when you tell me of your tired, worn-out feeling. I have not helped you as I should in some way. Let me tell you one thing about myself. Until this trip, I have never really missed you when I have gone away from you. I have wanted to see you sometimes but it has not been the constant want of your presence, the need of your sympathy in every interest I have, that there has been this time. But I would not go back to the old feeling, dear, would you like to have me? And yet, if I did not feel that I could not only do something for my family but make my own life a happy one, I should be afraid of what life might bring to me.

Dearest, forgive me but I do not think it is right to make one's happiness all dependent on one thing. It does not make me stronger and you are so much stronger than I in every other way that it almost frightens me to have you write to me as you do sometimes. And yet, it is not that I want to be less dear to you.
[1892-04-02 Bertha (Old Point Comfort, VA) to Henry]

Bertha's words must have warmly greeted Henry: "*Until this trip, I have never really missed you...*" However, Henry bristled that Bertha felt that her obligation to her parents superseded her obligations to herself and to her own happiness. With the "wind at his back", Henry wrote that "*there is no obligation to parents*" but "*our care for each other is ... the first consideration, the first duty.*"

Dear, it has occurred to me if, in matters that are to be decided governing the time of our marriage or any other question concerned with our future, you would treat our relationship as you expressed it to me – "we cannot more absolutely belong to each other, even after marriage" - I think it would help you in deciding certain questions that you are in doubt about as nothing else would. In your sweet unselfishness, dearest, you are apt to treat as a secondary matter that which we both know should stand first. I know this from the manner in which you put your obligation to parents. Dear, there is no obligation to parents, to anyone in a matter of this kind. It must stand above every other thing or it is nothing. You and I see this so plainly when we talk of it apart from other things that I know it will ultimately hold its own place with you in its relation to other considerations.

Dear, for the reason that our care for each other is not only "the sweetest thing on earth" but, because it is the first consideration, the first duty. I did not like the sentiment of "Sir Hugo's Choice"[107]. That seems maudlin sentiment to me and it is not sustained by the last thought of any age of true enlightenment. Your Bible does not teach you this, child. And, while I am lecturing, I must dissent from what you told me in the "moral discourse" letter about your obligation to your parents. You are all wrong about the existence of that sort of obligation to parents, the existence of any obligation to them, save that which should make you use all the opportunities they give you for making your life most useful. What a wretchedly unhappy man I would be if I thought my mother's care of me imposed an obligation! And how unhappy parents would be, dear, if they felt they were imposing obligations on their children by their care of them. It is sweet of you to think you have had greater care and I don't wish to rob you of such generous thought of those whom you love but do you not think other girls believe themselves especially blest? Not in perhaps the same things that have made your life happy but in the indulgencies which naturally became the dearest pleasures because they came from the hand of a parent.

---

[107] "Sir Hugo's Choice*"* - Poem by James Jeffrey Roche. In the poem, Sir Hugo dies for duty and not for love. "*To do thy duty, whate'er its worth, Is better than life with love forever— And love is the sweetest thing on earth*."

...
Dear, don't let your talk with your father worry you. You will do what is best and right and I will be your true friend and help mate in carrying out whatever plan is decided upon, only don't worry if you wish to be very good to

Yours until death us do part,
Henry
[1892-03-28-5 (6 letters) Henry to Bertha]

Bertha and Henry's hopes of seeing each other during the summer of 1892 were dashed. To Henry's chagrin, Bertha wrote on April 7th that she would not be returning to St. Louis during that summer. So from the announcement of their engagement to the agreed to time for their marriage, there was no scheduled time for the couple to see one another.

Dearest,

I cannot come to St. Louis. I am so glad that you wrote me you were prepared for that for, if you had been counting upon it as a certainly, I should have felt it so much harder. I knew my going with you was out of the question but I had not entirely given up a faint hope of going until yesterday. Myra Lane wrote to me that she wanted me to come visit her at the time of Lallie's wedding and then Cynnie was going to ask Emma, Janet, Edith and myself to stay with her in Joplin for the wedding. It was rather a delicious plan, was it not? But the opposition was of a kind that I had to yield to, at least I thought so, and there are many things I feel bound to yield. Anyway, for the other reasons you will find in some one of the letters you have not yet received, I think you rather expected this result. It did not much surprise me and that you wrote it would not surprise you so as to help me.
[1892-04-07 Bertha (Hygeia Hotel, Pt. Comfort VA) to Henry (NYC)]

Bertha wrote to Henry the next day to try to arrange for them to meet in New York City in April, even though Bertha was wary of seeing Henry for too long due to her parents' feelings.

So you have been tired and ill, dear friend! Well, I have a suggestion to make to you. How would you like to call on me Tuesday evening? Will you find it worthwhile to stay in New York two days longer for two hours? My father has had news from St. Louis which makes him anxious to get home sooner than he expected and Mamma prefers being left in New York to staying here. So Tuesday we shall arrive at the Fifth Avenue Hotel and Tuesday evening I shall hope to see you. Do not stay over longer than that for I could not see anything of you to speak of. Indeed, I may go out to Morristown immediately to look at those places there as my father's time in New York will be limited now. But Tuesday evening shall be all yours.
[1892-04-08 Bertha (Old Pt. Comfort, VA) to Henry (Holland House, 5th Ave & 30th, NYC)]

On the following day, Bertha wrote that her parents would not object to their meeting in New York City.

I send you a very short letter yesterday being principally occupied by the news I had to tell you. To tell the truth, I have not much doubt of your acceptation[sic] of my invitation so I will write on the idea that you will do so. I told my family I expected to see you and there was no objection made of any kind. We shall arrive in New York some time Tuesday morning but I shall require some short time for arranging things and resting or you will not find me entertaining and I have no wish to bore you so I will not invite you to visit me until the afternoon when you may come as early as you please. That is, unless you have some previous engagement when I will excuse you, especially if it be a visit to our next President. I was very much interested in your account of your visit to him and I was not disappointed in what you said, I mean, I was prepared for it. Having a father who is inclined to be skeptical on the subject of public men's utterances, at least so far as office seeking goes, I have very little change of idealizing my political favorites. Who was the western politician who took you? And what brought you east, dear friend? Is that one of the things in which a woman is expected to take no interest? You must remember, there is no part of your life and ambitions in which I do not take an interest and if it is outside my comprehension, why you must try to overcome my stupidity.

[1892-04-09 Bertha (Old Pt. Comfort, VA) to Henry (NYC)]

As Bertha mentioned in this letter, Henry was to have a meeting with a presidential candidate while he was in New York City. Henry was actively supporting Grover Cleveland and was apparently introduced to Cleveland by a fellow westerner. Cleveland won the presidential election later that year.

From their correspondences, it appears that Bertha & Henry were able to meet in New York City on April 11 & 12, 1892, probably for just a part of each day. No longer visit was possible since Henry had to return to St. Louis on the next day and since the ever-watchful eyes of Bertha's parents were upon them. After this tryst, Bertha was very sad at Henry's leaving; even her mother said that she looked like a *"wreck"*. Since they had not seen each other in months and were not expected to see each other for many more months thereafter, their meeting must have been very emotional. But the next day, with Henry's flowers, Bertha wrote of her full recovery.

I did not fulfil your prediction and write to you yesterday and it is just as well for your peace of mind that I did not. I never remember to have been so overcome with a feeling of blank loneliness as beset me after your departure yesterday. Then if I brought good weather with me, you certainly took it away with you, for it rained and snowed alternately all the afternoon. And toward evening, I developed a mild sore throat and slight headache, neither violent but combined enough to not exactly raise one's spirits so that by nine o'clock after playing whist with a dummy for an hour and a half, mother suddenly broke off the game, told me she had rarely seen such a specimen of a total wreck and to retire immediately thereupon, which I did.

...

You do not know how beautiful your flowers have been as a rule. Tulips are not so pretty when they open but I have never seen such splendor of coloring as there is in there. As my mother said, "they make a perfect glory in the room." They say that scent is one of the most powerful things in recalling memories and making associations. Dear, I am certain that I can never smell the fragrance of rose geranium again without it recalling these two beautiful days, days that I feel have brought us nearer together than we have ever been before.

Take care of yourself, dear friend, after the weather became so decidedly stormy, I worried a good deal about you, your trip, for your cold was anything but gone.

[1892-04-15 Friday Bertha (Fifth Ave Hotel, NYC) to Henry (StL)]

D. THE WEDDING WAS POSTPONED AGAIN

After the exhilaration of seeing Bertha in New York for 2 days, Henry learned around April 15th that George and Bertha M had decided that the November 1892 wedding date should be postponed. Henry was exasperated.

... my darling, it did hurt to know that what I gave up when I saw you last was under a misapprehension of the true condition of things. For if, as you state, November had positively been agreed upon by your father, I know it was a grave error in me to have sanctioned your yielding to this last demand for a postponement of our marriage. Dear, I cannot better show you how little I understood the situation than in reminding you of the fact that we talked it over in the light of your never having made matters quite plain to your father whereas you tell me in your letter "November has positively been agreed upon and I think it would be unwise and unkind to open the subject again. My promise to you and the fact that I am absolutely positive in my own mind that another winter like the last would be a mistake for <u>all</u> concerned made me hold to November."

Now, darling, I know you did not mean it so but your failure to tell me this was a great mistake and it seems to rob the sacrifice we agreed to make of any of the help it may have been to us to know that good ought to come out of our giving up that which meant so much to us both. Do I make my meaning clear, child? This is what I am trying to tell you. If you and your father, as your letter makes clear, had gone over this ground and, after fully talking it over, you had given him your decision so that he fully understood it, a great mistake was made in yielding after this. For harm, not good, can alone come from yielding in matters once decided. What I so much hoped for, dearest, was that, in meeting your father after I left you for going over his wish for a postponement, you would, if you conceded what he asked, make your concession a means of good for the future. Now, dear, it will I think do more harm than good for it will only seem to be yielding under pressure when a decision previously announced so positively is abandoned. I have agreed to trust you in this matter entirely, dearest, and, in spite of the very different view I now hold from the one I held when I saw you, I still entirely rest the matter with you, only adding to what I have said that with a fuller knowledge of what you have previously said to your father I very much fear your yielding will be entirely misunderstood and, dear, it is bitterly hard to give up what is so dear to me when I cannot see that the least good or happiness can come to you because of the sacrifice.

Dear, I am going to rest the matter entirely in your hands and you must not think that I do not fully understand how much you wish to do what is right and best and I wish you to try and forget anything I may have said when I was last with you about my own feeling of bitterness because of certain things. In my great anxiety to have you meet your father with a clear idea of all the questions involved in your decision to be reached after you talked with him, I may have said too much about his attitude to me. Now, dear, save the effect of your father's actions towards me, upon you and your life, I wish you not to think of me at all, for you know I rest perfectly content in my love for you and shall always be happy in it provided I can be sure of your happiness. You will I am sure write me fully as soon as you have talked with your father and meanwhile, although I could not forbear telling you how my view of our future actions was affected by the knowledge your letter gave, remember my trust in you is implicit, dear, and, if you decide to grant your father's request, I will help to make it a means for good as earnestly as if I approved the wisdom of the concession.

And, my darling, don't think I have allowed this trouble to dim to any extent the beautiful memory of the few hours I have had with you. Ah, what did you not do to make me happy while I was with you, child? I am afraid I do not show you always how fully I understand your sweet consideration of everything that I care most for. You seem to read my thoughts, dear, and to respond to my every wish for I am constantly wondering why it is that you do and say what gives me most pride in you and what seems most responsive to my love for you. Darling, those short meetings seemed to bring us closer together than ever before and I think, dear, you were never so fully in control of my every thought. It is good to love so dearly, child, that in every thought and action a place seems made for your loved one. And you can hardly imagine how promptly the questions comes to me in everything great or small that I do - "will she like this?" or "will this bring our lives closer together?" Try, my darling, not to let what I have written you trouble you. It is not meant for that. I wish to make you see clearly what is before us and remember a mistake made now will work as much harm to your father and mother as to us. And, child, every moment that we can concede to the time of our married life is going to increase the period of our use to others as well as to ourselves. We cannot too soon begin the work of healing the trouble with your parents and you know, dear, by bitter experience, that your father does not yield because you concede to him. It only serves to make him harder to deal with.

O my God, if I could only make you trust me enough to rest this matter with me! I could not hold you to a promise you seemed so anxious to withdraw and, in yielding to you, I tried to do so in a way that would help you most but I feel now it would have been better to have hurt you a little now rather than concede that which promises no good to anyone.

You must not think darling, whatever your conclusion may be, that I shall worry more than I can help. You know I can't be very happy without you. You know also how much I need you every day of my life. I try hard dear not to let this trouble wear me and make me careworn for I know this will make me less useful to you and I shall be content to wait if I can see good to come from it but I do not think anyone can make this plain to me.

[1892-03-28-4 ("The Friday Letter", 4/15/1892) Henry to Bertha

Henry's angst at the latest delay was palpable: "*O my God, if I could only make you trust me enough to rest this matter with me!*" But in the end, Henry concluded, "*I will help to make it a means for good as earnestly as if I approved the wisdom of the concession.*"

Bertha tried to explain the wedding delay more fully in her April 18th letter (below). In this letter, Bertha wrote that her father had not exactly agreed to a November wedding. In addition, due to her mother's current condition and the necessity that Bertha stay with her mother all winter in the east, the wedding date had to be delayed. The twin pricks of George not having agreed to the date and Bertha M being "*too much of an invalid*", burst the November wedding balloon.

Dearest,
I received your Friday letter just this minute and I am hurrying to answer it.

I am very sorry that the Pt. Comfort letter[108] turned up. When I wrote that the question was settled for November, I supposed that it was. When in St. Louis, I had told my father of my promise to you and my intention to keep it. He had made no comment except that I had chosen to decide for myself and, as he had never alluded to it afterward, I thought he had accepted my decision. But at Pt. comfort, he said he had not done so, that I, of course, could do what I wished but that he had meant to have another conversation with me putting considerations before me which he thought I had overlooked. He had intended to wait until just before he went home but, as I was going to see you, he thought it better and more just that I should have the opportunity of discussing it with you.

It was then that he told me that he was in these positions of trust which he would either have to resign outright or be able to devote a large amount of his time to next winter and the latter he could not do if I did not stay with my mother, as she is too much of an invalid for both of us to be away from her. For him to resign these things means the breaking of the only business connections he still keeps and giving up what are among the greatest interests of his life. Whether it is necessary for him to give them up, it is impossible for me to know, but of one thing I am absolutely convinced and that is that he deceives himself if it is not so – that he feels convinced in his own mind that he should resign them.

Had the question concerned only myself, I should have yielded; he has been too dear, too good to me in every way for me to have hesitated. Indeed, if I were to marry you in November at the cost of his giving up these things, I think I should have felt as if there were a mar on my whole married life, as if what I should have wished to have entered with the purest and holiest feelings would always have had the shadow of a selfishness over it. I should have felt too as, if in refusing this at the end, all the good of the three years sacrificed would have been thrown away.

But it was not entirely a question of myself. I felt that you had never been treated fairly and that is the only thing for which I have ever felt any resentment toward my father. So I told you that I had made you the promise and that I left the matter in your hands. I felt that I owed that to you but, if

---

[108] See above in this Chapter, 1892-04-02 Bertha (Old Point Comfort, VA) to Henry

you had held me to it, it would have been a grief to me. It would have taken away from the joy I look forward to, my darling, if you could have known how I felt when you gave me your generous answer. How I loved and blessed you. I think it might have repaid you. Still, you must not think from all this that I do not intend to be perfectly firm when the discussion comes. I will not make a useless sacrifice. I will not have any possibility of having this struggle over again. And if I feel it best to yield, I will show him very clearly what a sacrifice it will be to both you and me. I feel that you trust me, dearest, do you think that I wish to prove unworthy of that trust more than that. I know it will be of no good to them otherwise. Have faith in me, indeed, I will try to justify it.

Yours always,
Bertha Warburton Drake
[1892-04-18 Monday Bertha (NYC) to Henry (StL)]

It is interesting that Bertha signed this preceding letter with her full name which was very unusual for her at this point in her relationship with Henry. Perhaps Bertha was subconsciously emphasizing her family ties and wanted to add gravitas to her words, "*Have faith in me, indeed, I will try to justify it.*"

Bertha wrote to Henry three days later about how she signed her name: "*I signed my full name to a letter I wrote you the other day without thinking and laughed at it afterward. I was amused to see that you punctiliously did the same thing in the answer or was it unintentional on your part?*" [1892-04-24(-) Sunday Bertha (NYC) to Henry (StL)]

Henry wrote of his bitter disappointment that their wedding would be delayed again. As discussed in Chapter 14, "The Scott Homes", Henry had already begun to search and make all of the necessary plans for their new home house after their marriage. But, Henry understood and accepted the decision.

Saturday
I did not write to you yesterday, my darling, for I knew the letter you wrote Wednesday meant that you had spoken with your father and that I should have your decision in your next letter. You ask me to give you my "real opinion." I shall do so and keep back no part of it.

I confess then it was hard at first to know that you would not come to me in November for all my plans seemed to have shaped themselves to that time and, although I often have very selfishly brooded over the separation from you, lately it has not been quite so hard for I felt that it was only waiting a little beyond the summer season and that it would give me time to prepare your home for you. And the disappointment, I suppose, brought up all the old arguments against further delay, the probability of your mother's feeling being embittered by the increased time she would have for looking forward to an unpleasant thing, the shorter time you would have in which to remove this feeling. All these things came back to me, dear, and then, in spite of them, I saw that if you had come to me after you had talked with your father and had asked me what answer you should give him, I would have told you to yield to his wish, for hard as it was for me to see it, I know it was best now. I doubt, dear, whether it will be best for the happiness of your mother or your father either in the immediate future but your father will, in recognizing what you have sacrificed, be of more help to you with your mother than he could have otherwise been and the best thought of all is that you will now feel you have done everything in your power to make matters as easy for your parents as possible.

I confess that I was not quite fair in assuming your father would think your willingness to yield a trivial concession and, knowing the position he has now taken, I can tell you, not because I wish to help you only but because I believe it: you have done what was best. I am sorry, dear, that my letters hurt you. I did not mean that they should. I only wished you not to make, what would be more than a useless sacrifice, a source of positive harm. I confess too I did not think you could be as brave about it as you have been, dear. Do you forgive me for not having faith in you sufficient to be sure you would do all I asked before yielding?

We must put all this trouble behind us now. I will do all in my power to make you forget it, dear, and, if we look back upon it at all, it must only serve to show that you have made a sacrifice that is easier because we agree that good may come out of it. And you must not worry about me, dear. I am very well and I shall have your letters, you know, to cheer me up if I am at times not very happy without you, and, in helping each other to make the waiting easier, we will grow even nearer than we now are. And it may be I shall learn better how to help you, my own beloved.

I can't write any more now, dear. You know how I love you. God bless you now and ever.

Yours always,
HCS
[1892-04(-) (Saturday) 20170823-3 Henry to Bertha]

Bertha's response to Henry's letters made clearer her reasons regarding the postponement of their wedding. *It was just as well that your Saturday letter arrived just now, dear, for it was all that saved you from a very stern one from me. I had been thinking over your Friday letter and had come to the conclusion that you ought not to have let my letter from Old Point, written before I had that talk with my father, over weigh with you all the conversations we had together after I had had it, both because I had new light on the subject then and because it is all but impossible to make a letter absolutely full & clear, while in talking, we could and did discuss every point. My mistake in the letter evidently was in saying "that the arrangement had been agreed to." It had not been agreed to. It had simply been allowed to pass with the protest that that had not been what I had at first said I would do. But we have gone all over this ground.*

I assure you I will not yield except it be with the arrangements we agreed upon. I agree with you in thinking it would do them no good. Indeed, I should not think waiting would do any good, except that I cannot feel it would be right to let my father break with all his interests at home for any reason, be it real or fancied. There, I think until I have had my talk with my father, I will lay this subject aside and talk of something else.
[1892-04-19 Tuesday Bertha (NYC) to Henry (StL)]

Bertha had her discussion with her father and wrote the following very lengthy letter explaining the details. Two of Bertha's comments about the wedding delays stood out: "*He has never treated me so much as a woman before*" and "*he did not ask it as a duty I owed him at all.*" Her father was finally realizing that his little girl was a woman whose destiny should be in her own hands and not his. In another notable comment, Bertha wrote, "*I think you know that my mother is absolutely implacable about this and regards my marriage with you as separating me from her.*" Although her mother's feelings about Bertha and Henry's marriage are rarely mentioned, this letter and a few others make clear her opposition. Since her mother grew up as a Southerner (in Texas) of moderate means, perhaps she had an innate distrust for this Southern boy from Virginia. And perhaps it was just that she wanted Bertha to take care of her in her old age. Nevertheless, the result of Bertha's discussion with her father was that Bertha agreed to postpone the wedding until February 1893 and her father and mother agreed to drop all objections.
My dearest,
I did not write you but a line yesterday, for I had no time to write a long letter and I wanted to write very fully when I wrote. Your letter distressed me somewhat. It came after my talk with my father, of which I will tell you the result first and the steps which led to it, afterward.

I agreed to wait until the Wednesday before Lent or, if Lent should come unusually late, until the middle of February and he "agreed to put no further opposition in the way of our marriage, to recognize the matter as finally settled and agreed to, and that the arrangement is to be changed for no reason whatever." I quote from your letter of Saturday in which you said that must be agreed to and it has been.

Now, to go over all that led to it. I could not stand what seemed to me absolutely useless, purposeless, waiting any longer and I brought about the conversation. At the same time, I knew perfectly well my own weakness in argument, I forget what I want to say to make my position most strong and allow others to think it a weak one and to make their own points when I know I am in the right. And besides, I have twice lost control of myself when talking to my father and cried so as to put an end to anything like reasonableness. Don't think I am the kind of a woman that cries for everything, Henry. I very seldom do, Nan could tell you, and I despise myself utterly for having been so weak, but still it had happened and I made up my mind it should not again.

So I wrote out all my side very clearly and positively and told him that I wanted to talk to him but that I wished him to read that and think over it first. He waited a night before he did talk to me and then he was very kind. He has never treated me so much as a woman before. He said he had no right to ask me to wait any longer, that he realized that fully, that if I wished to be married in November, he would throw no obstacle in my way but, if I could not stay east next winter, then he must and he should resign from all the different positions he held when he goes back next week.

I must tell you, though I hate it, but I think you know that my mother is absolutely implacable about this and regards my marriage with you as separating me from her. But she has said she would not interfere again and she keeps her word. We leave the subject alone and try to make life as pleasant as we can for each other. I think as you do that when it is once settled and over, she will change – she cares too much for me not to and she is lovelier than I can say to me in every other way. My father agrees with me in thinking it a question of time but he knows that it may be a long time.

Next winter, she will not come home and he or I must be with her. I told him I did not see what obliged him to give up these places and he said it was not like regular business which a man can put in order and leave for a year. He is entirely out of business and these different committees he serves on for instance, they put men on who are not in regular business because they are the men who have time to attend to them and, if he is not going to attend to them, he is in honor bound to resign them to those who can. He went over a number of things to me which need constant close supervision and it is the winter time and the fall when these things are done.

He says "If I were a younger man, it would make no difference. I could pick up fresh interests and start again. But as it is, I cannot. Being away so much as I have been already in these last years has broken off my connection with a great many things. If I give up these, I leave myself without occupation or interests of any kind & a dreary existence of that kind would be terrible to me. Even now", he said, "being so long without regular occupation, I find myself brooding over little worries and troubles as if they were great ones. A man of my age cannot break into his customary interests in this way and not suffer. I am longing to get back next week."

You see, if I do not give up next winter, the responsibility of his doing this will lie with me. He did not say this, but I can see it. After that, it will not be my responsibility and I do not think he will be asked to do it. You know enough of older men to know how I should dread the effect on his health.

But I have not finished all he said. He said he had withdrawn all his opposition to my marriage, that he looked upon it as a settled thing, he would not ask me to postpone it again - he did not think it would be right or best. He would not ask me to postpone it now but I had said last fall that I would wait until over next winter and it would be such a very, very great boon to him if I would do so. He said very frankly that any personal objection he had to you had long since gone, that in fact, if you had wanted to marry anyone else's daughter, he would have seen nothing against you. His opposition lately had been on account of my mother's feeling and his own dislike to giving me up. I must add he did say he thought he could have made me happier than you would but he allowed me the right of private judgment. He said he regretted that any bitterness of feeling should have grown up between you and himself, spoke of having seen you downstairs and said he was glad to have had a chance to shake hands with you and said he would have sat down and talked to you if he had not been sure you would have talked of this and he said he did not want to talk of this. He had withdrawn all his opposition and considered the matter settled.

As a matter of fact, dear, I think he does regret very much that is past and, if he could only blot that out, he would like to be friends with you. But that matter, I cannot settle. The future must determine those things and the first advance, I understand perfectly, must come from him. It cannot be right otherwise.

Perhaps you will think all this does not amount to very much but it means a great deal to me. It is the beginning of what I have been hoping for. He promised positively not to ask me to wait again, to make all his business arrangements, looking towards the middle of February as the time. And he did not ask it as a duty I owed him at all. Nor ought I to have spoken of all these things as "obligations" in my letter to you, it gave you a wrong impression. I ought to have said that out of my love for him, I was willing to do anything to make a hard thing easier for him that would not be a wrong to you.

So far I had acted remembering that I must not wrong your faith in me, that I must not yield under any other; understanding this, but, having made all these things fully understood and seeing what the cost of my holding to November would be, I did yield. I thought I had your full approval, hard as it was for you. I remembered your saying "Selfishness now will not help our lives in the future, while the thought that we have not thought of ourselves now, may come back to us to help us through many a hard place, will strengthen our trust in each other and in our love for each other." I know how hard it had been for you to come to that decision. The sacrifice is not a light one to me, as I told my father, nor do I wish you to think it was an easy thing for me to lay aside all my plans for our home and our life together next winter. I have never told you half my beautiful dreams about it. But still, my sacrifice was for those who are very dear to me and that made my part the easier than yours but the fact that you had seen it as you did helped me so much, for I could not have asked you to do it against your judgment of what was right.

Your letter yesterday troubled me a great deal. In both the others, though you urged so much against yielding, you still allowed that, if all these things were granted in fact, if I could see that it would do good and not harm, you would not try to keep me from doing it. It is not that I am afraid of your blaming me. You are too kind for that. But I feel now as if, while I have done as I thought and think the right thing for me to do, you will not agree with me and will bear it for my sake indeed but feeling it wrong and unnecessary and so made far more unhappy by it. Write to me honestly what you think. If you feel that I have made a mistake, tell me so; it will not help me for you not to tell me your real opinion or even to have you keep back part.

I do not feel as if I could have done otherwise and I have tried to show you my reasons fully but, even if you agree with me, I know I shall have given you a great deal of pain and for that, I ask you to forgive me.

Yours always,
BWD
[1892-04-21 (Thursday) Bertha (NYC) to Henry (StL)]

In the preceding letter, one of the memorable comments that Bertha made in speaking of her father was how his views of Henry were changing. *"He said very frankly that any personal objection he had to you had long since gone that, in fact, if you had wanted to marry anyone else's daughter, he would have seen nothing against you. His opposition lately had been on account of my mother's feeling and his own dislike to giving me up."* George was becoming fonder of Henry, although true affection would take more time.

Henry had no choice but to accept the delay and express his disappointment. Bertha wrote to him that she appreciated his concession and understood that he was hurt by the delay.

Thank you for your letter. It was just what I wanted and needed. If you had said you had accepted the decision with no doubt or questioning, I doubt if I should have believed you. If it had given you no pain, I think that would have hurt my feelings. That is just the mean spirited individual I am. Being just what it was, it gave me just the help I needed that I have learned to look to you for. And you have never yet disappointed me. It gives me such a feeling of restfulness that I have your strength to lean against. I feel as if I could write to you again. I have not written a natural letter since you left, looking forward to the struggle, then to your decision and feeling as if I could not get in touch with you at all, somehow I cannot explain why, for it was totally unreasonable. But all my letters have been more or less forced and I am afraid they sounded so. Now I feel like writing a volume. But a volume of writing would not take the place of half an hour's talk.
[1892-04-27 Wednesday Bertha (NYC) to Henry (StL)]

Although Henry now seemed to accept the delay in their marriage, his subsequent letter voices an edge – *"even if you are not as good as you ought to be"*.

Your letter, Bert, makes me so wish to be near you again that I become blue even in writing to you. I know I cannot stay away from you much longer and, if that Wichita work does not get into proper order soon, I believe I will disgrace myself and run away from it to see you, which offence will be properly chargeable to you for going away and leaving me when I most need you to best accomplish whatever lies before me in the way of usefulness. You are very dear to me, my love, even if you are not as good as you ought to be and, someday under my good influence!, your thought of every one – for me too – will be such that you will be well-nigh perfect – a development, I apprehend, you are by no means ambitious to attain to.
[1892-05-01 Henry (NYC) to Bertha (Hotel Brunswick, Boston)]

Bertha next wrote that her mother was feeling better and that, after three years of waiting, an additional three months until February 1893 was not such a long time.

Mother seems to improve steadily in this atmosphere. She said today that she never knew what it meant to feel as well for an hour at home as she has here for the past week and, indeed, she is a different person. It reconciles me more than anything else to being so much away from home; reconciles me to the thought of next winter, that, and the feeling that, at whatever cost, I could not let my father separate himself from those interests which really serve to keep him as well as he is at his age. I have seen too much of the effect on older men of breaking off all business ties.

I did not mean to go into this tonight, I don't know why I did except that it troubles me something to think that this waiting all seems useless and wrong to you. Only this you can see if we had not yielded the extra three months, all the work of the last three years would have been rendered of no use. I have not been talking this over with anyone, dear, I have not spoken of it since you left. Only tonight, it seemed to me as if I could see the good it was doing others so plainly and it troubled me

that it should seem to you as if I were not giving what I hoped for and wished to you; it is all hard, I wish I could help you. Don't think I am worrying I am not. I only don't want you to.
[1892-05-31 (Tuesday) Bertha (Backbay Boston) to Henry (StL)]

E. RUMORS ABOUT "STRONG OPPOSITION"

Even as Bertha and Henry were making their wedding plans, the rumors began to circulate about *"strong opposition"* to the marriage, especially during the summer of 1892 when Henry was diligently trying to acquire a suitable house for rent and then undertake the necessary renovations. Bertha wrote to Henry in April about her annoyance with these rumors.

I am of course terribly annoyed and pained at the gossip which you say is afloat. I do not know how it started. Mother heard a little the other day and was very indignant. She says that she had never spoken of all that is past to anyone and I know nothing could be more unlike her. Neither you nor I have of course but gossip seems to start from absolutely unpalpable things. We must let it wear itself out, I suppose. But I do wish one could be let alone. I long ago made up my mind that if one is to be happy, one must not mind what other people say about them. But I am afraid I am not equally philosophical on your behalf. I think my father will do what he can to prevent further talk when he returns.
[1892-04-24(-) (Sunday) Bertha (NYC) to Henry (StL)]

By June, the rumors were not abating. Henry wrote to Bertha that some of his acquaintances felt that Henry should delay his house search to avoid more gossip.

On my return I spoke to my people at home about our plan to select our house at once and I suppose in this way my purpose became known to outsiders, for one of my best friends came to me a day or two afterwards and said. "Look here, this is none of my affair and you may resent what I say as an impertinence if you like but, as my interest in you prompts me, I shall try to tell you what I wish to unless you stop me. Now if I were you, I would not at this time do anything to add an item to the gossip that is afloat. I have heard you were thinking of securing your house and I wish to say to you that, unless you can do so without anyone knowing of the arrangement, don't take any such step at this time. It is well known that there is strong opposition of some kind to your marriage and, as no specific reason has been assigned for it, I will frankly say to you that much curiosity has been shown by people to know the real cause of your trouble. You know how prone society is to busy itself with the affairs of engaged people at all times. Now you have not asked my advice but I merely suggest that you think carefully before you do anything that will prolong the impertinent attention which certain persons have given to your personal affairs."

You can imagine that this was not a pleasant thing for me to know but you must not think I permitted it to distress me. I have known ever since my return that your father has not only persisted in acting in a manner that made comment a natural result but that he had positively invited attention to the awkwardness of our situation by declining to acknowledge our engagement when he was spoken to about it. I did not expect this, I must in fairness to you tell you, but I concluded to say nothing to you about it until the circumstance that I have given you made it necessary. I do not wish you to write your father again on the subject. I expressly desire that you will not do so. I have thought I fair and right however to put the whole situation before you and then ask you to let me know whether it may not be wise not to make any plans just now which will possibly cause additional annoyance to either of us.

I wrote perfectly frankly when I said I was not permitting this matter to distress me but I must also add that I am becoming indignant at the manner in which your father is treating us and I believe I am not quite as generous about it as I should be, for in the last day or two I have become thoroughly angry on my own account as well as yours and I do not doubt, if you understood the matter as I do,

that you would consider my feelings natural, even if you concluded I was not as considerate of you as I should be in permitting myself to indulge in anger when I ought, perhaps, to ignore these things altogether for you sake. I do try to help you, my dear Bert, but it is pretty hard to bear sometimes and, recently, I have not treated the delay in itself as a burden. We both agreed to this and should both abide by our decision cheerfully but to find this period is made on means of embarrassment and constant annoyance is pretty taxing at times. I would not have written all this if I had not thought it necessary to do so, dear, and, if I find that you worry over what I have written, I shall not think it right to speak to you again so plainly. Let me know what you think about securing the house and, dear, don't do so until you have thought the matter over carefully.
[1892-06-04 (Thursday) Henry (StL) to Bertha]

Bertha wrote back to Henry that it was probably best to delay the house hunting until summer when most of the gossipers would be vacationing in the east.

About going on with getting the house, you can tell better than I, dear. I should think your friend would not have spoken without very good reason. But perhaps it would be better to wait a little but I should think the town, the gossip loving community at least, would be starting east very soon and you could do what you wanted in the comparative quiet of the summer. Only I am afraid you will go west at the same time. It seems a pity to lose a good opportunity for silly vulgarity! But I am sure that warning would not have been given without good cause & we don't want to make ourselves talked about more than necessary.
[1892-06-07 20170829-9 Bertha (East Jaffrey) to Henry (StL)]

The crux of the gossip was that Bertha's father still did not approve of the marriage. Bertha wrote to Henry of her helpless feeling of dealing with her father and how *"bitterly angry"* she was over what Henry had to endure.

Your Friday letter came last night and perhaps it was just as well I could not answer it then. I don't think I have suffered so acutely since our engagement was announced and I could not be reasonable about it at all. This morning was glorious and I have been for a long ramble through the woods so I have calmed down a little bit. I will try not to worry, dear, but I don't think you would believe me if I told you I was not intensely pained and grieved. It is not the gossip so much, that is disagreeable enough, and it does not make it any easier to bear to know that you have to face the full brunt of it while I escape the worst. But I try to remember that everyone is more or less gossiped about and that this will die down as other gossip does.

But I cannot understand my father. I have always looked up to him so in everything. You don't know what a helpless, hopeless feeling it gave me - for it was not only I but my mother who spoke to him about the desirability of avoiding gossip. Indeed, he said he did not wish anything that had passed to run any risk of being gossiped over. Are you sure he has refused to acknowledge it? Is not that some exaggeration of his saying he did not care to accept congratulations or something of that sort? That would have been inconsiderate enough but the other, why, what motive could he have had? He knows that you have been on to visit me, that mother has told all our friends in the east.

O Henry, I don't think I can be very calm about it. It makes me so bitterly angry to think what you have had to stand. I have never wanted so much to be at home. I shall not write to my father as you do not wish it. Indeed I do not know what I could say for every bit of this ground was gone over in New York.
[1892-06-07 Tuesday 20170829-9 Bertha (East Jaffrey) to Henry (StL)]

Bertha was somewhat more optimistic in her next letter, writing that she thought that her father's opposition was going to cease.

I am rather afraid that you meant to show me that all I had done had not succeeded in conciliating my father but I hardly think, though he is acting most unlike himself in this matter, that we will have any more active opposition. At all events, if we do, he cannot but feel himself that it is unjust while, if I am obliged to oppose, I shall at least have the knowledge that I have made every concession possible, done everything in my power to prevent it. Still, I hope and trust that trouble will not come & if it does, I am not afraid to meet it. The hard thing about the whole matter is that all the worst of the annoyance falls on you where it certainly does not belong.

Dear, you need not have told me that you had tried to help me. You are the best and truest friend a woman ever had and do you think I do not know it? I am glad too that you said to me yourself that you knew this was not like my father. Indeed, it is most unlike him.
[1892-06-08 (Wednesday) Bertha (NH) to Henry (StL)]

Even before Bertha's letter, Henry was aware of the rumors that George was either denying the engagement or, at least, declining to admit to it. Henry viewed this as a serious blunder on George's part.

Dear, your father has undeniably made some serious blunders but I am sure he does not realize the full effect of this – thoughtlessness I shall call it – upon others or, on his own account, he would have acted very differently. He is not a young man and I think whoever cares for you or me will remember this if disagreeable things come to them. Thus, there is no question but all these things grow as they are passed about from one person to another and this particular matter may have been exaggerated somewhat, although I am obliged to say there can be no doubt in the main points about what I wrote you. It is not necessary, is it, dear, to tell you how the matter was brought to my attention? You can understand that there is good reason for my wishing you should not know the person who spoke to me and, unless you ask it, I shall not tell.
[1892-06-09 (Thursday) Henry (StL) to Bertha (The Ark)]

During this period, George apparently backtracked on some of his promises to Bertha (and Henry) and was not speaking to his friends of the engagement. When confronted by her father's *"failure"* to keep his agreements, Bertha nevertheless felt that she must abide by hers. Henry must have found comfort in the following letter in which Bertha used the word "Mizpah" which implied not only for God to watch over them while they were away from each other but also for God to be a witness to their agreement.

I do not see that my father's failure to keep his agreement releases me from mine. I agreed to make this next year as easy as possible for him and my mother and that I shall do. But he has made a terrible mistake. There are somethings one may learn to forgive, indeed, I try not to be bitter, but they will be very hard to forget. It is not his action as it relates to me, between a father and daughter, those things may be passed over but the position in which he has placed you. I have not written to him, but I must speak to him when he comes out. He must not maintain this position next fall when he goes home.

...

Dear love, you do not know how grateful I am to you, for not pressing me to act as if released from my agreement and make our marriage earlier. I understand just how perfect your generosity is in this and thank you for it, more than I can say. For you are right in thinking I should not think it right. Only my father must make me very certain that he will not again deny our engagement in the fall. Has he actually denied its existence, Henry? Dear, you know he does not act like this in his agreements with others, you know he does not. And I cannot understand it.

You write again as if you were worried over having told me this. You must not, dear friend, it was my right to know. I had to know. And you must not think I let this make me bitter. I fight against that. I go back to what I know my father is and to all he has been to me and remember that this is only one thing on one side against numberless things on the other.

....

Now, I positively am not going to write on this subject again, it does not do either you or myself a bit of good to brood over it, rather a great deal of harm. And so, goodbye, best friend, and "mizpah".[109]
[1892-06-12 Bertha (East Jaffrey) to Henry (StL)]

Henry voiced his opinion that George's behavior in this matter was foolish and that it was probably for the best that he had not seen George then since he would have had little patience.

Dearest,

I am very glad you are so happy at Jaffrey and that you are not fretting about what I wrote you. I am very glad now that I decided to write you about your father, for sooner or later you would have heard of it and it is much better you should have learned about it from me. I am glad your father is going away so soon, for I think he is harming himself as well as you by his very foolish behavior. If I had asked you to express my own views of the effect of this little trouble upon you, you could not have more directly voiced them than you have done and, dear, when your father does realize what he has been doing, I think, for his own sake, he will take a very different course.

I am very glad he has not spoken to me for I would be much too angry to be as patient with him as I hope to be after I have had a little time to get over my indignation, which I must do for your dear sake, my darling. If I had not been forbidden to, I would indulge in one of those choice expressions you reproached me for when I was in Boston for, in my attempt to discuss a disagreeable matter with some show of generosity, I have wound up with some bitterness. But I will not tear up this letter for you bid me write very plainly and I suppose you may as well find out now what a disagreeable fellow you will have to deal with. You know I have often told you that my only hope in my future attempts to redeem your expectations of my thought of you lies in the good influence you will have over my life. If you cannot save me from a life of uninterrupted failure and uselessness, I shall know I am past redemption, dear, and not worth saving.
[1892-06-13 (Sunday) Henry (StL) to Bertha (the Ark, East Jaffrey)]

Several days later, Bertha responded to Henry's letter and took some comfort in Henry's admission of being *"a disagreeable fellow"* in the previous letter.

Dearest, I was very glad you said at the end of your letter that you would not tear it up but let me know just how you felt and "what a disagreeable fellow I will have to deal with." It is clearly your duty to let me know the latter fact in every way you can so that I shall not be too much disappointed in the future and it was just as clearly your duty to let me know just now you felt for who has a better right than I to know? It would grieve me beyond words if you kept your feeling to yourself and shut me outside.

My darling, we belong to each other and we cannot divide our lives in that way. I am not so unreasonable as to think that you and I are never going to be obliged to be patient with each other. I may have my doubts as to your being such a disagreeable individual as you think yourself but don't flatter yourself for an instant that I think you are perfection. And I only wish you knew how very far off from it I am. You have some terrible disappointments in store for you.

But I am sure of one thing, that you and I have a fund of mutual understanding and sympathy that will make it easier for us to bear with each other than for a great many who really do care very much too. And there is another thing I am very sure of, though I don't often write it, and that is

---

[109] "Mizpah" - Hebrew for " The Lord watch between me and thee, when we are absent one from another". It marked an agreement between two people, with God as their witness. From Genesis 31:49. (Bertha also referred to mizpah in Chapter 19.E)

*that you are dearer to me than anything else in the world and that my love and trust grow deeper
every day.*

God bless you, dear, dear friend.

[1892-06-16(-) Bertha (East Jaffrey) to Henry (StL)]

In his next letter, Henry explained in more detail what he had heard: that George would not admit to the
existence of their engagement, although, apparently, George did not deny it.

*Dear, you do not clearly recall what I said about your father. I wrote that he declined to admit the
existence of our engagement, not that he denied it. This is equivalent, almost, to denying it but not
quite that bad. Several of his friends have tried to speak to him about it and he has simply declined
to answer anything that was said to him on the subject. You say in one of your letters you will
speak to your father about this when you see him. Do this if you wish, dear, but don't ask anything
for me, as I do not think now any good would come from my meeting your father. I think you have
a right to insist that you shall not again be put in the position you have been placed in recently but,
having raised and insisted on this point, say nothing more unless you may find it wise to recall your
agreement, in which event, you can make it plain that, while I do not ask you to come to me before
February, I will claim you as soon as you will come. And bless you too for every day you can see
fit to discard of this long and weary period of waiting. And yet, you must not act in any manner
that will seem a concession to my anxious thought about the delay. I shall be happy in my love for
you if I can only be sure you will keep well.*

[1892-06-13 (Monday) Henry (StL) to Bertha (The Ark, Jaffrey)]

Bertha tried to find some solace in Henry's letter from the fact that her father had not denied the engagement
but had simply refused to acknowledge it.

*I do not intend to bring up any of the old issues with my father and I regard my promise to him to
wait until February as a settled thing which I cannot break because of any failure on his part. But
I think it only just to you and myself and to him also to put before him very clearly and forcibly the
effect of what he has done and to get his promise that we shall not be put in such a position again.
That was all I intended to do.*

*I am glad you wrote me that he did not absolutely deny it for that was how I had understood you
and I really believe he cannot have realized the effect he was producing. But there! I said I would
not speak of this again and I will not. My father arrives this evening and some time before we leave
here I shall have this talk with him. I hope that, with his departure and the general summer exodus,
that the most exasperating of the annoyances you have suffered will be over.*

[1892-06-17 Bertha (Jaffrey, NH) to Henry (StL)]

George's apparent indecisiveness about the marriage was inconsistent with his life as a very successful
businessman and trusted advisor. Again, this may suggest that Bertha M was exerting considerable
influence on George which disturbed his normal decision making and presented him with a seemingly
irreconcilable conflict.

While Bertha M may have been the main impediment to Henry's marriage plans, Henry never focused his
attention on her, which was undoubtedly wise. Instead, Henry solely focused on George with his
inconsistencies and his failures to abide by his agreements. In the following letter, Henry again mentioned
that he had heard from an unnamed source that George was again *"refusing to acknowledge the existence
of our engagement."* But there was little that Henry could do other than wait since Bertha's mother was ill
and the decision had already been made to postpone the wedding.

*I have thought more than once I had given you some reason to reproach me in writing you last
week about our plans, not that I regret writing you plainly, but I think I could have been gentler
about it if I had tried more not to hurt you. You must not think I was worried at the arrangement*

you made in New York, for you will be doing me injustice if you imagine I still felt rebellious about your last agreement. It was the palpable failure of Mr. Drake to carry out this agreement (I do not mean his failure to see me, for this I do not wish) that I grew bitter about, for I held then as I now maintain that, instead of doing what he could to remove chance for a continuance of all this gossip, he has distinctly in violation of his understanding with you provoked it by refusing to acknowledge the existence of our engagement. And, although angered and annoyed as I naturally have been at what I have heard of this, I have not even asked you to put a stop to it in the only way that this would be possible because I knew you had a duty to perform in the care of your mother for the time of your promise (or that you thought this your duty) and, although I consider you entirely released from your agreement because of your father's failure to comply with the conditions you made and which he assented to, I would not ask you now to change your plans for our marriage because I cannot convince you, even with the fulfillment of some of the troubles which I was apprehensive of, that this delay will not bring the good you hoped to secure by it.
[1892-06-28 (Sunday) Henry (StL) to Bertha (The Ark, East Jaffrey)]

Undoubtedly Bertha was frustrated with her father. But, like Henry, Bertha must have realized that there was also little that she could do. So, in the following letter, she simply thanked Henry from shielding her from knowing who told Henry of her father's behavior.

I have your Thursday letter and I thank you for it very much. You always know best how to help me. But I said I should not take up that subject again and I shall not. I have ceased to let it annoy me as I told you I should. I shall not ask you to tell me who told you. I purposely did not do so. I know you would tell me if I made a point of it but I would rather not know for while I realize and even am grateful for the kindness meant, I have just that ill regulated kind of mind which would be unable to meet that person without an unpleasant association. And you were quite right in thinking I should not wish to know.
[1892-06-13 (Sunday) Bertha (Jaffrey NH) to Henry (StL)]

During the next few days, Bertha spoke directly to her father about the rumor that George had refused to acknowledge the engagement. George was "*indignant*" and said that he did not do such thing. Instead, George told Bertha that his actions were intended to avoid gossip about the marriage.

Dear,
I have had my talk with my father. I never saw anyone so amazed and indignant in my life. He said that the whole thing was utterly untrue, that he had never either by word or manner given anyone to understand that he was opposed. He said "On the contrary, I was careful not to. The thing that I especially wished avoided on every one's account was such gossip as this. Do you think I want my private affairs discussed by the world?" I asked him if he had not said something impatiently which might have been misconstrued but he repeated "No, I did not, for I was particularly anxious that no such impression should get about. In the first place, very few people spoke to me about it and from those who did, I accepted their congratulations. I may perhaps have said to one or two that losing a daughter was hardly a subject for congratulation but I did not say that in a disagreeable way or intend it so. The thing is inconceivable; I gave no foundation even for any such report." He ran over the few people who had spoken to him about it, mentioning Ben Graham particularly as having said very nice things of you. And then he paced up and down the porch saying "It is the last thing I wanted to have happen, the thing I most wanted to guard against. And I cannot see how it happened over and over again." Then he stopped and said "Mr. Scott must have been very much annoyed. He had a perfect right to be so. I wish you would write to him at once and tell him that I neither said or did anything which could ever give a foundation to such a report."

I felt ashamed to think I had believed the story. From the beginning, if anyone but you had told it me, I should have dismissed it without question as untrue. It was so utterly unlike him. But I was sure you would not write me a thing which you knew would give me such pain without being very sure. Do not misunderstand me, I did not mean that as a reproach, though I see that it sounds so. But I have no doubt not only that you believed it but that whoever repeated the story to you believed it. I can imagine perfectly how, if anyone had a previous idea that there was some opposition as some people had, how that sentence about being sorry to lose a daughter could be misreported and distorted. I am afraid there are some people who would do it maliciously and, if a thing gets started, there is no stopping. I know only too well that a thing is not the less believed because it is untrue. But for me, the bitterness has gone. I am sure you can quite understand how I suffered at the idea that my father should have done this - should have done it at all in the first place. And after all that had passed between him and myself in the second. I am so thankful for that, that just now, I cannot even mind the gossip. That is, on my own account. On yours, I do, and I know that this does not make that less hard for you. But I think you must be glad to know this, to have my father not only deny it, but be nearly as angry about it as you were. I am going up the mountain today and have no time to write more.

Always yours,
BWD
[1892-06-22 Bertha (Jaffrey, NH) to Henry (StL)]

Henry's bitterness must have been partially assuaged by George's comment, *"Mr. Scott must have been very much annoyed. He had a perfect right to be so."*

Since Bertha had fully accepted her father's explanation, Henry had no choice but to abide. So Henry apologized, sort of - i.e. it was a mistake to write about it.

You make it very clear that I made a mistake in writing to you about the unpleasant gossip that came to me about your father. As I wrote you, I doubted the wisdom of annoying you about it and I only decided to do so because I did not see that it would be possible for it to escape you. I then concluded it was best that you hear of it from me. I was perfectly sure that what I wrote you on this subject would give you pain. I could not fail to understand that it would be annoying and, now that you are quite sure there was no reason for the circulation of this exceedingly disagreeable gossip, it is a matter of deep regret to me that I wrote you about it. I shall certainly try to forget the whole matter, dear, and I hope you will give it no further thought. And let us not refer to it again.
[1892-07-24 Henry (StL) to Bertha (Farragut House, Rye Beach)]

F. APART AND WAITING

Bertha and Henry discussed trying to see each other during the summer and fall of 1892 and Bertha wanted Henry to meet her Rye friends whom she had known her entire life. However, given the sensitivity of her parents and inability not to be noticed by others, Bertha discouraged Henry from visiting her in Rye Beach since the situation would be *"almost too cruel to be borne."*

Now comes the hardest question. You say that you think you can get away for a few days in August and want to know if you cannot come on to me. Dear, do you know anything of the life of these hotels? Not a large hotel where no one is noticed but the outdoor piazza life, doing everything together & all known and commented on so that not even a stranger like Miss Cushman can be here two days without being noticed. Then remember that all these people are old friends of mine who have known me since I was a child. And all of them eager and anxious to know you. Dear, don't you see that, while my family maintains the relations they do toward you, you could not come here without you and myself being placed in a position almost too cruel to be borne. The hardest part is that it is what I should most like, to have you meet my friends & see all my old haunts and I

do so want to see you. When I thought you could not get away, it did not seem so hard but, now when I know you could, it makes me feel bitter & sad. Dear, when shall I be able to give you anything but pain? I am so sad today that I can hardly enjoy the thought of my visit.
[1892-07-12 (Tuesday) Bertha (Boston) to Henry (StL)]

Once again, Henry had to accept and cope with the long wait.

Two letters came today, one dated Monday and the other Tuesday. The latter posted at Salem. When I read the first letter, well, I wanted to put my arms around you and thank you for making me so glad. It was one of the sweetest letters a man could ever get, dear, and he would be a poor fellow indeed whose life would not be made brighter and better with messages like those you have just sent me.

Then I read the other letter, my darling, and it made me reproach myself rather bitterly for thoughtlessly making you sad. Dear, I don't mind not seeing you now. There were times when I could not have truthfully told you I could patiently wait for you. But I can say it now and I wish you to feel that the attitude of your parents is no longer a cause for worry. We agreed to forget about these disagreeable things. We both know that whatever of pain this may have cost us in the past, we will suffer much less from the wrong they are doing you from this time than they will. And about the few days I asked for, that is a very little thing to give up and, as dearly as I should prize a few hours with you, I count it a slight disappointment and a circumstance to be quickly forgotten that I cannot see you now. My darling, do you not see how your love makes me stronger and happier each day? I hardly need to tell you that a disappointment of this kind a few months ago would have been hard to bear and now it seems a trifle, dear.
[1892-07-14 (Thursday) Henry (StL) to Bertha (Farragut House, Rye Beach)]

The 1892 summer in Rye Beach was undoubtedly good for the Drakes as the irritant of the marriage to the hard-shelled parents could be slowly pearled over. As Bertha corresponded to Henry, there was no talk of "*any opposition*" in Rye Beach.

You know, dear, no one here has the faintest idea that there has been any opposition and they speak of my engagement and chatter and laugh over it when my father and mother are about without the shadow of an arrière pensée, which is very nice. Charlotte remarked the other day "Well, we are all dying to see him but I should think you and he would really be rather glad he could not get away for everybody on the place for miles round would want to meet him and I should think he would find it rather trying to say the least," in which remark there was some truth.
[1892-07-18 Bertha (Rye Beach - mailed from Portsmouth NH) to Henry (Ft. Worth)]

By the end of the summer of 1892, Henry was reconciled to the new wedding plans.

You see, Bert, I want to help make your promise to your parents the easier because you will know that, although I can't hide the loneliness which separation from you makes inevitable, I can make you see that losing you for a few months is nothing and a sacrifice I am glad to make if it brings you one comforting thought to be added to all our bright hopes for the time when our lives will be joined together.
[1892-09-19 (Sunday) Henry (StL) to Bertha (The Ark, E. Jaffrey)]

G. HENRY & GEORGE RECONCILED

Years after Bertha and Henry were married, it was increasingly clear that George grew to trust Henry more and more, even to the point of asking Henry to attend to his affairs.

Tell your father I got his letter, will be delighted to attend to his little commissions and will answer his letter in a day or two. His letter was a very bright and happy one and I am very glad he is so

well. *I think your being there has much to do with his fine spirits. Who would not be happy near you?*
[1895(-) 20170822-7 Henry to Bertha]

Similarly, Henry voiced his care for George in the same manner as for any one of "his own".

I think your father is making a mistake in taking no exercise. If he doesn't get some exercise, he is not apt to keep well and it seems to me he ought to gradually try to get back to his old active habits. If he doesn't do this too suddenly, I don't see how it can possibly aggravate his trouble and without the exercise, he surely will not be as strong and vigorous.
[1897-07-15 Henry (StL) to Bertha (Jamestown)]

Perhaps the clearest indication of the reconciliation of George and Henry is when George decided to live with Bertha and Henry after Bertha M died. Henry's letter to him in July 1897 makes apparent that both George and George Drake Jr. would be taking up residence in Bertha and Henry's new house in Vandeventer Place.

Mr. Geo. S Drake
Jamestown, RI
July 24, 1897

My dear Mr. Drake,
I am just in rect of your note. The H2500.00 sent will not be needed for some time as I still have a considerable balance to pay the builder his last order before I leave. I shall therefore put the dft in the safe and keep it there until it may be needed in the fall.

You have certainly made most generous provision in this whole matter and I hope very much that the pleasure and comfort you and George will get out of the house and Bertie's happiness there will in some measure repay you.

I will hand the amts named to Wilmer and Brown and will see that Brown pays the Water license. Brown reported that the carrier had been delivering your mail regularly to Whittake Hodgman so I thought as I was going to be absent so soon it would be well not to disturb this arrangement.

Tell George[110] only one box has as yet arrived and, as I left word with W.& H. to send in any notices of expressed articles, I assume he only sent one parcel or that the other shipments have tarried on the way. I am sorry to learn that George has not been well. Tell him I have lately been in a position to deeply sympathize with him.

It is getting hot here again and, as my hopes at the prospect of leaving here are rising with the thermometer, I think I shall be able to stand the heat until the time fixed for my departure but I don't like the heat. It becomes harder to endure each day.

Yours Truly,
Henry C. Scott

I suppose you have observed from the papers the fortune I have lost on sugar!
[1897-07-24 Henry to George Sr.]

On December 22, 1897, George moved into the upstairs rooms in Bertha and Henry's mansion at 64 Vandeventer Place.

---

[110] George S. Drake Jr., Bertha's brother.

Dec. 22, 1897
Father moves up.
[1893 Diary]

George developed a fatherly concern for Henry. While in Rye Beach in 1898, George wrote to Bertha who was in Jamestown of his concern for Henry after hearing that Henry's vacation from work may have suffered a setback due to his illness.

> *I have just rec'd your letter and am so very sorry Henry's had so bad a vacation. I am sure he ought not to go back now. He needs to get well first and then have some vacation and then days extra time now will save him possibly weeks of time in the future. Anyhow, his health is the first consideration and nothing short of absolute necessity should take him back. We are breaking up rapidly. I judge you will keep Henry a while longer and go back together. That's the most sensible plan.*
> [1898-09 (20181214-1) George Sr (Farragut House) to Bertha]

In George's next letter to Bertha, he reiterated his concerns for Henry's health and his recommendation that Henry stay in Jamestown longer. (George almost sounded like Henry on health issues.) *"The more I think of it, the more I hope Henry will stay another week. The weather continues hot out west & I believe he will save time & ability to work by waiting."* [1898-09-07 George Drake Sr. (Farragut House) to Bertha (Jamestown)]

George again voiced his concerns in his succeeding letter. *"I feel anxious to hear what you decide upon. … [PS] Am anxious to hear about Henry, was what I intended to say as I know your decision [to remain in Jamestown] rests upon that. Regards to all."* [1898-09-10 George Drake (Rye Beach) to Bertha (Jamestown)]

After the rocky start of George and Henry's relationship, George's newfound fatherly affection for Henry was touching. There were also glimpses of this affection in Bertha's letters. *"I went [to church] with Pater and he told me I ought to have gone with you to Texas."* [1898-11-21 Bertha (StL) to Henry (Waco)] Bertha reflected on her father's sentiments and wrote: *"nothing ought to have kept me at home".*

George had come to realize that his daughter had grown up and that she had started her own family with Henry. And George also realized that their family was his also.

CHAPTER 11 – THE DRAKES 1892 TRAVELS

For nearly the entire 1892 year prior to their wedding, Bertha and Henry were apart. It seemed clear that Bertha's parents wanted their daughter for themselves during this time and so they made travel plans for virtually the entire year, one new plan after the next. Bertha was accepting of her familial obligations and Henry was forced to abide until he could claim his reward.

A. THE DRAKES' SPRING TRAVELS
My pen is poor, my ink is pale,
My love for you will never fail.[111]

1. ST. AUGUSTINE – March 1892
The Drakes spent approximately three weeks at the Ponce de Leon Hotel in St. Augustine during March 1892, a good place to be, away from the cold northern winters.

The Ponce de Leon Hotel, circa 1909

Now, to tell you a little of what goes on here, of how we would spend a day, for instance, if you were down here with me. It is warm sunshiny spring weather, and I have on the dress I wore to the shoals last summer and a blue sailor hat. Do you think you would like my appearance? I think if you had been here yesterday, we should have gone over to the Casino in the morning, and listened to the band, and watched the boys swim, for one hour, so – and then we would have come back in to these lovely cloisters, looking out on the tropical garden, of which I am going to send you a photograph, and have read "David Grieve". In the afternoon, it was gayer than usual. There was actually a "tournament", you know. I told you I had never seen one. And the riding was really beautiful. Some of the men from the hotel rode and some of the officers from the barracks. But it was an English officer who carried away the prize – would you have stayed with me or would you have left me with pretty Mrs. Frank Ogden, a New York woman, a friend of Myra Lane's, and have ridden yourself? In the evening, there was a ball but I do not think we should have gone, not with the moon more than half full outdoors. But as it was, I went to look on simply with some cousins of my father's. One of the pleasant things of our coming was meeting them. There has been an estrangement for several years but now it is all made up and father has had a lovely time with them. Write to me all about yourself and tell me all you do, dear boy, you know how it interests me.
[1892-03-12 Bertha to Henry]

---

[111] Bertha's letter: 1893-01-25 (Sunday) Bertha (Stancote MA) to Henry (StL). Traditional valediction at the end of a letter.

Bertha could always tell a good story for Henry, such as the following.

We went to another tournament yesterday. Susie and John Bryan joined us and it was great fun! The winner chose a queen this time. He was a very handsome man. I don't know who but I have admired him for some time ever since I have been here in fact. And when the wreath of roses was given him, he rode down the whole line and presented it to a little girl about seven years old, one of the prettiest children I ever saw in my life, and then took her on his horse and rode back with her. You never [saw] such radiant happiness in a face in your life and, of course, the grandstand fairly shook with applause. It was very pretty.
[1892-03-21 Bertha (Augustine) to Henry (StL)]

The weather in St. Augustine was splendid in March 1892 allowing everyone to wear their "whites".

Yesterday morning I took a long tramp with father and, in the afternoon, I went to the tennis tournament. I wore a white dress, Edith a lilac summer silk, and, when Powers Harris joined us, he had on his white flannels; none of us wore wraps of any kind. This may serve to give you an idea of the weather. The playing was sufficiently good, nothing remarkable. In the evening, Emma Shursby(?) gave a concert at the casino and mother and I went over to hear her.
[1892-03-23 Bertha (St. Augustine) to Henry (StL)]

I have been taking observations of the men here. They are all exceedingly well set up looking set, New York and Philadelphia principally, and I wish to assure that I have not seen a single red or even red spotted cravat and that they all wear three studs with their dress suits. I don't wish to say I told you so, but you may happen to remember I did.
[1892-03-24 Bertha (St. Augustine FL) To Henry (StL)]

Over the course of the next two months, Bertha wrote to Henry of the events of her trip from St. Augustine to Savannah Georgia, Charleston South Carolina, Richmond Virginia, Port Comfort Virginia and New York City. The newly engaged and separated couple had plenty of time to think and then write to each other about their future.

2. SAVANNAH GEORGIA – March 24

I have decided to be buried in Savannah. Do not be alarmed, I have no immediate intention of doing so, only ultimately. There is the most beautiful cemetery here I ever saw: magnificent trees with curtains of southern moss hanging from it. They say the one at Charleston is even finer but it is hard to believe it. So if the elevator breaks the next time I go up, I hope you will remember my parting wishes. I mention this as an extremely likely contingency for the rope is so nearly worn out that I feel I take my life in my hands every time I go up in it. And I am obliged to go up in it for the hotel is so crowded we can only get rooms on the fourth floor. Why it is crowded I would like to have someone explain to me for apart from being buried, I see nothing in Savannah to do. There might have been once before everybody died or went to sleep, for some of the old houses with immense gardens full of roses already in bloom look charming.
We arrived here Friday night and we go on tomorrow. We spent yesterday exploring the city which really is a quaint old place and driving out to the cemetery and an old plantation which I expect is as fine a specimen of an old fashioned southern plantation as we shall see. Even the old slave quarters, little brick cabins, are still standing though gone to ruin.
[1892-03-27 Bertha (The Desoto, Savannah GA) to Henry (StL)]

While in Savannah at the end of March 1892, Bertha wondered how nice it would have been to go riding with Henry, although she made clear that she didn't want Henry to pick her horse – undoubtedly Henry would choose a nag to keep Bertha safe.

I wish you were here to take me horseback riding. Not today, but it is a wish I have often had since I came south. The girls ride so much and I see such nice looking horses. There were some capital ones at St. Augustine, only I assure you, I should not have let you choose the horse I was to ride. There were some painfully meek looking beasts there whose looks I am afraid would have attracted you.

[1892-03-27 Bertha (The Desoto, Savannah GA) to Henry (StL)]

3. CHARLESTON SOUTH CAROLINA – March 27

Bertha was not impressed with the trip to Charleston or the City itself which was "*broken down*".

We met a most unpleasant surprise on reaching here. Instead of going on tonight as we expected, everything was engaged until Friday and Charleston is by no means a place in which one would care to spend a week. However, much to our relief, someone gave up their sections for tomorrow night so we are only detained a day. This is only slightly a bore but we have already seen all there is to see of Charleston. Undeniably it is an interesting place to see once and I am almost tempted to wish I had been alive before the war and lived here. Have you ever been here? Such houses! I did not know there were such in this country; palaces would be a better description. But it is the most broken down place I ever saw. It is far more melancholy than Savannah, though it must once have been far more magnificent than Savannah ever dreamed of being. I wish, strange as it may seem, that you were with me. I think exploring these quaint old places would have the same charm for you that it has for me. One of the things I most enjoy, I think I said before, are the colored folk. The intense sympathetic interest they take in everything you do is delicious. And the children! The fat black pickaninnies! Words fail to describe them.

...

I went to hear another colored brother Sunday night and I wish I could have preserved a copy of the sermon. It was on the Fall and I much regret to say, the preacher said the serpent waited until Adam was out of the way for he knew the man would have kept her from getting into any such trouble!!

[1892-03-29 Bertha (Charleston) to Henry (StL)]

4. RICHMOND VIRGINIA – April 1

Concerning Bertha's visit to Richmond, Henry wrote of his regret that he was not there to show Bertha around a city that he had known well as a child.

It is too bad that you are going to Virginia now. I wished to take you there and, although I imagine Richmond has changed very greatly since I was there thirteen years ago!, I think it would not be hard to find a few of the old crowd left. I started to send a dispatch to Sam Wallace, a man I have known for twenty-five years, to call upon you. Then I concluded that it probably would not be pleasant for you or for him and so I did not do so. (It may be necessary to add that Wallace and I knew each other as boys when our friendship began.) When I was in Richmond, Franklin and Grace streets were the prettier residence streets. The Westmoreland Club was the popular rendezvous for men from all parts of the south and its membership ran into the thousands. The drives around the city are fine and I hope you will be able to take them. That is what I wished to do with you, Bert. But it makes me gloomy to think of these things now.

[1892-03-28-1 (5 letters) Henry to Bertha]

I am very anxious to know your impressions of Richmond and I hope you will conclude to remain there several days. I have some cousins there, the daughters of Judge Robert Scott, whom I would so like you to meet. Their brother too is in Richmond now, I think filling the office of State's Attorney General. I would have telegraphed some of my friends to call on you if I had thought you would like it but, as you have said nothing about remaining in Richmond, even for a few days, and have not even given me your hotel there, I assume it would not be giving you any pleasure to turn you over to the tender mercies of a lot of Virginians whom you had never seen before.

[1892-03-28-3 (6 letters) Henry to Bertha]

Bertha also felt that it would have been good had Henry been with her to show her around Richmond.

> *I thought of you constantly all through our drive yesterday thinking how familiar all these places must be to you or most of them, for the club house is new and you have never seen General Lee's monument. I quite love the hotel. It reminds me of English hotels, big, old fashioned and comfortable, but you must forgive me if I think the sign I saw in the hall very characteristic of your native state. "Gentlemen will please not smoke in the Ladies' Parlor." I am rather glad you did not send Mr. Wallace to call on me. I am always glad to meet any friend of yours, you know, I do not need to tell you that. But I think I would rather meet them with you.*

[1892-04-01 Bertha (Richmond VA) to Henry (StL)]

5. OLD PORT COMFORT, VA – April 2 to April 9

The Drakes stayed approximately one week at the Hygeia Hotel in Old Port Comfort. While in Old Port Comfort, Bertha became agitated about the letter that she had written to Henry the day before. She wrote that her fears would subside if Henry told her how much he was missing her.

> *After writing you that extremely moral letter yesterday, I went up and staid awake for ages with the worst fit of the blues I have had since I left home. Our beloved Mr. Pennell used to say after a lesson in experimental chemistry, "though the experiment has failed, the principle remains the same", but I am not even strong minded enough for that. For among other woes that beset me, was the fear that you would not write again that you missed me. Please write at once and tell me that you miss me very much and cannot get along without me, and then you may lecture me on caprice as much as you choose.*

[1892-04-03 Bertha (Old Port Comfort VA) to Henry]

Bertha often lectured Henry too about being too gloomy. Bertha could also provide some humor as she did in recounting a dream from which she was very glad to wake after Henry came in and *"the agreeable part ended just there."*

> *I am afraid I gave you the benefit of the bad temper. ... See what we have to look forward to in the future. Having begun finding fault with you, however, I think I'll keep on.*
>
> *Why did you say you might not to have written to me about feeling gloomy and depressed? I entirely approve of your feeling ashamed of being so but not having written to me about it. Who has a better right to know, I wonder? Or to lecture you about it? I am quite sure, at all events, that no one exercises the latter right so freely.*
>
> ...
>
> *I have had such a pleasant dream, last night, at least, part of it was pleasant. I dreamt I was arranging a house, our home, dear boy, and I can see a great many of the details still. I must say it was built in a most curious fashion, unlike any mortal house, but the rooms were so pleasant and cozy, one in especial was charming, with books and pictures, my sea piece was there and I had just finished lighting the lamps and the fire when you came in. I am sorry to say the agreeable part*

ended just there. You came in with an expression of the utmost annoyance and said "what on earth did you do all this for? I had just decided not to take this house." I assure you, I woke up with the greatest sensation of relief to find it was a dream. And I hope at least some of it will go "by contraries".

[1892-04-05 Bertha (Port Comfort VA) to Henry (NYC)]

6. NEW YORK CITY – April 10 to April 30

Henry was able to attend to business in New York City when the Drakes were there. After their brief visit of two afternoons together, Henry wrote to Bertha, *"I shall have the light which has shone in your beautiful face these last blessed days to comfort me."*

University Club
Tuesday evening

Just having left you, with the joy and hope you always give me, strong in my heart, the thought has come to me that I can help you a little in the long time of our separation by telling you once more, before you go away, of the help and influence for good you have been in my life during this last winter. I say I can help you, my beloved, for do I not know that, in knowing your helpfulness in my life, you are more strongly appealed to in looking forward to the future, which we wish to make beautiful for each other, than in any promise I can make for bringing into your life such happiness as I may be able to give you.

In the many doubts and fears which came to you when you were trying to see where your highest duty lay, before you could tell me what you could be in my life, you were sorely tried, dear, and God knows I sorrowed for you then but you bore all the burden alone and you did not spare yourself until you saw clearly what was the true cause for you to pursue. Will you let me tell you that in all that time you did nothing that did not show me more clearly each day the beauty and truth in your life and that now, save the care it cost you, I can think only of your treatment of my cause with feelings of thankfulness, that in the doubt and sad uncertainty then I learned of the strength and beauty of your life as I should not have known it if there had been no hours of sadness and trial.

Let me think that you go away from me to be happy until we meet again. You will be made so, dear, by the faith you have in a power that orders all for the best. And I will not murmur because I shall have the light which has shone in your beautiful face these last blessed days to comfort me; because you have given me a courage that is as great as is my faith in you and because my life seems so blessed in your confidence and friendship. I shall count myself more bountifully dealt with than would have been possible had your generosity not been great in the extent of my unworthiness.

May God protect and bless you and may no harm or sorrow come to you. Goodbye,

Henry
[20180322-3 (1892-) Henry to Bertha]

From May through September 1892, Bertha's parents kept her with them in the east. After they left New York City, the Drakes went to Boston, Jaffrey NH, Magnolia MA, Kennebunkport ME, and Rye Beach.

B. HOTEL BRUNSWICK, BOSTON MA, May 1892

The Drakes left New York City and arrived in Boston on May 2, 1892 where they stayed for a month at the Hotel Brunswick.

The Hotel Brunswick

Bertha's letters often seemed to find a balance between offering words of affection and trying to avoid "*spoiling*" Henry.

> *I came in from Marion at half past seven and thought I had a whole long evening to write to you when who should march in but my doctor for a friendly visit, if you please, and he stayed until quarter to ten. He told me I was looking extremely well and my beloved Miss Hagen informed me that she wished der Herr Scott could have stayed twice as long for I looked like a different creature from when I reached Boston. There is a testimony to your power as a caretaker.*
>
> *I must also tell you at the risk of making you extremely vain that your admiration for Mrs. Hitchcock was reciprocated. She wrote a note to Julia Coolidge in which she devoted two pages to you which I can only describe by the word: fulsome. Jule gave me the note to read apparently under the impression that I should enjoy it.*
>
> ...
>
> *Have I missed you at all? I shall not answer that question, you are too spoiled now. But let me tell you that your roses are perfectly beautiful, the white are lovely but the red are simply superb. They are beginning to open now and they make the room glorious with their fragrance and color. As for your "hyderange", it is doing itself proud, one flower has sent out a side shoot and made a great double blossom of itself and the other two are beautiful.*
>
> *My dearest, I hope you did not find that extra holiday made much confusion and extra work. Tell me just how you found things. If they were very bad, I give you leave to relieve your feelings on condition you do not say, "doggone!!" That is worse than wicked.*
> [1892-05-03 Bertha (Back Bay, Boston--) to Henry (StL)]

In the following letter, Bertha was very direct with Henry, although she insisted that she did not wish to "*abuse*" him.

> *Don't you think you are a little bit unjust in your description of my indifference as to you coming? Do you possibly remember how you spoke of coming? If you need me, I can manage to spare a few days. Did you expect much urgency after that? I do not mean that you spoke as if you did not wish to come, I am not quite so unjust as that, dear friend, and such an idea never entered my head. But certainly, unintentionally or not, you did give me the impression that it would be a very great*

inconvenience and I did not want you to do that. I had an idea too that this would be an easier time for you to come than later for, when you were with me, you spoke of being away from St. Louis toward the end of May? What changed your plan? We were going up to Jaffrey either the twenty first or the twenty eight of May according to the weather for my mother is anxious to get into the country as soon as possible. But from your letter, I am afraid that you will not be free to come east before then. Write to me as nearly as you can when you think you will be able to come and I will make arrangements to stay. I do not take much account of your reproaches. You know whether I want to see you or not.

Dear, I will follow your directives and confess that I have the blues tonight or am cross or something. My nerves are just in that delicious condition when to have someone shake a jigglety table makes you long to throw an inkstand at their heads. Perhaps I had better stop for fear I may abuse you, who certainly do not deserve it.
[1892-05-04 (Tuesday) Bertha (Hotel Brunswick, Boston MA)]

The next day, Bertha wrote to apologize for being hard on Henry.
I am very much afraid you did not get an agreeable letter last night. An old Bostonian who dropped into call last evening said the wind had been in the east all day and had made him feel like a wreck. Will you kindly put my letter down to the east wind?

Since writing it, I have been afflicted with the idea that it might be the last you received before you went to Wichita. So I hasten to write this morning instead of waiting until evening again in the hope of this overtaking the other. I say before you go to Wichita for of course you are going at once in spite of the letter I just this minute received. Do you think, after that glittering, gilt edged, complement you received in New York on the management of your company, I am going to let you run away and throw the blame on me? No sir!! Observe how I make a virtue of necessity for I know very well that, if urgent necessity called you to Wichita and I called you the other way for no reason at all, what the result would be. But, I like to preserve a semblance of power. Come when you can, dear boy.
[1892-05-04 (Wednesday) Bertha (Hotel Brunswick, Boston) to Henry (StL)]

Bertha was sometimes petulant. This was certainly true when she came down with the mumps while in Boston.
Possibly you may think I might occasionally write you something agreeable but I am just not going to, I am going to be as disagreeable as I like and you can't fire back for I am a poor sick girl and have to be spoiled! Now! I am considerable spoiled. Did I tell you about old Mrs. Rockwell last year? my friend of eighty-seven who said I was the most congenial person she had met for a long time. She sent me a magnificent rose this morning and sends her maid regularly to inquire after my health!!
[1892-05-10 Bertha (Boston MA) to Henry (StL)]

Henry wrote of his concern that Bertha was becoming spoiled by all of the compliments being paid.
I am just a little afraid too you are becoming unruly, for praise such as you have been receiving from Miss Hagen is calculated to spoil you. No one can spend "three hours and a half" in telling you what a fine girl you are without doing you a great deal of harm. I mean, of course, no one except myself for when I tell you what a good girl you are, I can see that it improves you or I would not do so. You will therefore be good enough to tell Miss Hagan that such is your susceptibility to turn from flattery; you can allow no one to indulge in it with you except the one individual who can praise you without destroying the small amount of humble mindedness which has survived the blandishments which have been so freely poured out to you by everyone recently.
[1892-05-11 Henry (StL) to Bertha (Hotel Brunswick, Boston)]

C. THE "ARK", JAFFREY NH

The Drakes returned to the Ark in Jaffrey New Hampshire during June 1892 and stayed there for most of that month. The Drakes were frequent visitors at the Ark.

Joel Hobart Poole, a grandnephew of Joseph Cutter Jr., bought the house and 100 acres of land for $1500. He and Mrs. Poole, gradually restored the farmhouse, which by then, had been vacant for a number of years and neglected.

In 1874, Dr. and Mrs. William P. Wesselhoeft of Boston, delighted by the place and it's location, asked to rent part of the house for the summer. It is said that Mr. Poole named an exorbitant price in hopes of driving them away. His terms were accepted, however, and for the next six seasons the Wesselhoefts occupied the easterly side of the house and also had two guest cottages built. Within ten years, the Pooles had summer boarders. Despite the protests of the Pooles, "The Ark" had become a business!

Poole's son, Arthur, was later taken into partnership. Accommodations expanded in 1895 when the annex (now the Carlson Manor) was built close by. Arthur E. Poole died in 1912, and after the death of the elder in 1926, Charles Bacon, a member of the operating staff of "The Ark" for twenty years, became manager for Mrs. Poole. At the time it cost guest twenty-five cents to take a bath in "The Ark's" one bathtub. The key to the bathroom hung with the bunch of household keys at Mrs. Poole's waist. [from: History of the Ark, East Jaffrey NH]

Bertha loved her visits to The Ark. The Drakes would sometimes drop in for a few days or, as they did in June 1892, for an entire month.

1. THE ARK & THE POOLES

Bertha wrote Henry a description of the Ark and its inhabitants which was vivid and alive with her personal feelings.

Cof Mr. Poole, "The Ark", East Jaffrey NH
Friday
My dearest,

Here we are and so comfortable. The heat in town was perfectly unbearable the last few days and up here everything is in its fullest beauty; the spring being a little later here, apple blossoms and lilacs are just running riot. I don't believe I gave you any idea of how beautiful Jaffrey is, especially that part where we are. You know we are four miles from the village and a mile and a half from any other house, except Dr. Wesselhoeft's little "camp" which hardly deserve the name, being six rooms. They take their meals at the "Ark". We are just at the beginning of the slope of the mountain and literally in the midst of the woods, for you have only to cross a not very wide meadow on either side of the house to be in the woods, pine one side, birch, the other, and jolly little mountain brooks all through them.

The drive from the station is too beautiful for words, you come out of bits of road where the trees literally meet overhead, on views that take your breath away, slopes of hills with great snowy apply orchards in full bloom.

There, I've finished attempting to describe scenery, and now I will make a confession. All the way up from the station, I was overpowered with a feeling of homesickness for you. It was all so beautiful and I knew you would love it so and it would be so much better for you than that hot stuffy old town. We had a most cordial welcome from the Pooles. There are only two other people staying here at present, a Miss Schafer(?), who has a very strong sensible face. I think I shall like her. And a Miss Hobart, who was here last year, a semi-invalid and student of Emerson. Mrs. Wesselhoeft and her friend Miss Spicer were over at the Camp and we had a jolly evening with them. Do you know the Wesselhoefts did see us that evening at the theater and, at the close of the play, Dr. Will (the son) hurried round to try to intercept us coming out but missed us in some way. Mrs. Wesselhoeft and Miss Spicer had only come up to get the camp in order and went back this morning but Dr. Will Wesselhoeft, his wife and their two children come up tomorrow to stay all June and I expect to have a very good time with them. I have never met her but he is charming, a friend of Charlie Coolidge's by the way, and they say she is just as nice as she can be.

Mrs. Wesselhoeft was much interested to hear of my engagement, and promptly inquired if you and I were old friends or not. On hearing we were, she heaved a sign of satisfaction. "O, she said, you'll have so much better time together than if you had only known each other a short time." Of course, I was pleased to have my mind relieved on that point but really she is one who can speak with authority for they have an ideally charming home life and she and the doctor are a living contradiction to cynical remarks about life not being worth living, etc., etc.

Mr. Poole and his wife are another example of a happy married life. It is beautiful to see the courtesy with which he treats her and not at all one's idea of the way farmers treat their wives. I wish you could see them. They are an interesting study. He is such a splendid specimen of the "back force(?) of the country". He is about forty-eight, she I imagine about forty-two and the prettiest woman! He is an autocrat in his way, very well off and a power in the country. He is not obliged to take boarders and, if he does not life any of them, they never come back: he simply never has a room disengaged. But those they do take, they do make gloriously comfortable.

Then there is Arthur, the son, a boy of twenty-three, clever as he can be too. He claimed my attention for quite a while last evening to tell us about his winter. It was awfully gay. He said, "lots going on. The minister had a set of lectures for young men Sunday evenings, and then there was another set of lectures in the village with stereopticon view, and a secret society and the chess club, and the sociables to the church and extras(?). Something going on most every night."

There! Now call yourself dissipated after listening to that list of gaieties. You must be pretty bored with this letter by this time. Of course, this cannot interest you as it does me here in the thick of it & coming on Monday morning too. If only I can hear you say "O, I suppose I must finish this letter but I've lots of work to do, I wish she had cut it sort." So goodbye,

Yours Always,
BWD
[1892-06-05 Bertha (East Jaffrey NH) To Henry (StL)]

Bertha described the Jaffrey air as *"like wine"* and the Ark was *"a haven of refuge"*.

> *It was good of you not to write until I reached Jaffrey, for no one could be blue long who is out of doors all the time in this glorious air. It is like wine, exhilarating all day long. In the evenings, still cool enough for a fire.*

[1892-06-08 (Wednesday) Bertha (NH) to Henry (StL)]

> *As you perceive, dear boy, we did not go. We held on to the Ark as a haven of refuge from the deluge. It poured in floods. There was no use in our going to Boston – we could not have done any of the things we wanted to.*
>
> *...*
>
> *I spent yesterday morning after I wrote to you over at the Camp and enjoyed myself in spite of the fact that the children behaved like - well, what did you behave like in those very very long ago days when you were young and shut up in the house on a wet day?*
>
> *In the afternoon, I wrote letters and played whist. I believe it is a mistake ever to let rain or anything else stop you when your trunks are packed and you are ready to go. We might not have done what we wanted in Boston but it would have been no worse than the sensation of killing time we enjoyed yesterday. After all, you and I managed rainy days in Boston very profitably.*

[1892-06-28 Bertha (The Ark, East Jaffrey) to Henry (StL)]

And Bertha always had time to read a good book.

> *You ask me how I spend my time. I am outdoors nearly all day either walking or driving and in the evening, we get round the fire and either read aloud or play cards. Just at present for my own private enjoyment, I am going through my annual reading of "Middlemarch". I enjoy it better each year. I read somewhere the other day that George Eliot was the Bible of the young people of today. I don't think that but I hope you will not think me irreverent if I say you find a good deal of sound practical advice about modern life in her which are of such great use that one might almost call her inspired.*
>
> *I read a conversation last night between Caleb and Mrs. Garth [from Middlemarch] that came home to me with a keen enjoyment. When Caleb answered a remark of Mrs. Garth's about what the Vincys would say of a certain action of theirs, "Life's a poor tale if it is to be settled by nonsense of that sort. There's no sort of work that could ever be done well if you minded what fools say." That sounds a little hackneyed now that it's written down, but the whole chapter was charming.*

[1892-07-01x (Friday) Bertha (Jaffrey NH) to Henry (StL)]

2. "MARGETTA" & THE WILLS

Bertha often kept an eye out for new arrivals. When the Wills arrived at the Ark, Bertha met Dr. & Mrs. Will's maid, Mary, who harbored a keen eye for the ludicrous and mischievous wit for the humorous.

> *We have two new arrivals beside Dr. Will and his wife. Mary, the maid, told me about them yesterday. She is, as you often see up here, much more a friend than a servant of Mrs. Poole who depends upon her as her right hand. Mary met me in the hall yesterday and said "O, Miss Drake, t'is the handsome couple is come this day." I knew they were expecting two sisters from Boston someday soon, so concluding they had arrived, I said "Are they? How nice". "They are that!" said Mary with much enthusiasm.*

So I came down to the table with my mind made up to meeting a pair of elegant Boston girls. Henry, if you could have seen them! Side by side, at the table, a man and his wife, the man looking like the Presbyterian ministers of fifty years ago: long, thin, gray beard, high forehead, gold spectacles, long tailed coat. The woman with a gown all of one piece, a kerchief around her neck and fastened in front with a large gold pin, hair parted in the middle, and brought down almost over her ears. You never have seen anything like them, unless among your grandmother's daguerreotypes or some pictures in the magazine of people in the early part of the century. In the doorway, going out to the kitchen was Mary who turned around to watch the effect on me with her eyes simply dancing with regular Irish fun.

I got to the table shaking inwardly and made some weak little joke to Miss Hobart to account for going off into a fit of laughing. I interviewed Mary afterward in the woodshed on the iniquity of her conduct, but I don't think I made much impression, for she simply shook all over at the remembrance and said "O, but Miss Drake, if ye'd only come in two minutes sooner and seen him wid the plaid shawl around his shoulders, ye wud a died entirely, ye wud!" But you cannot judge people by their appearances. [1892-06-06 Bertha (East Jaffrey) to Henry (StL)]

Bertha wrote of going for rides with Mrs. Will. Perhaps to tease Henry over his great concern for her safety, Bertha sometimes wrote about the horses that they would take, including *"the backer and the kicker"*.

We drove eighteen miles yesterday afternoon and shall go as far today if it does not rain. The Giles's and Dr. Will have departed, so we are entirely a household of women and I must say Mrs. Will is much nicer now that one absorbing object of interest is gone. Also, she has a cousin, a girl, come to visit her, who has roused her up. It is Mrs. Will who is going to drive us this afternoon, us consisting of Miss Hobart, myself, and Miss Bradley (the cousin). She is going to drive the doctor's horses, who are familiarly known as the backer and the kicker, and I think mother rather expects to see me come back in small pieces. I think it will sufficiently relieve your mind, though, to know that I have declined to drive though. Mrs. Will offered to share the responsibility with me. I am not sure enough of my driving to undertake a spirited pair (are you surprised?) though Grover Cleveland (I believe I told you that Mr. Poole, though a member of the G.A.R., is a mugwump) whom I drive in the buggy when I take mother, is not at all a meek, superannuated beast of the type you admire.
[1892-06-08 (Wednesday) Bertha (NH) to Henry (StL)]

Henry was not amused by incidents involving wild horses and Bertha, so he tried to put his foot down.

Please remind Arthur Poole that there will be a death in the Poole household if he is careless in permitting you to drive his horses.
[1892-06-13 Henry (StL) to Bertha (The Ark, Jaffrey)]

Bertha took great delight in spending time with Margetta, *"as she calls herself"*, the four-year-old daughter of Dr. & Mrs. Will with whom the Drakes were good friends. During this June 1892 visit, Bertha recounted many stories of Margetta.

Margetta and I have been feeding the squirrels. I don't know whether I told you that among the attractions of the "Ark" was a cage with four squirrels. Margetta, as she calls herself, otherwise Margaret, is Dr. Will's small daughter aged about four, I suppose. I am free to confess that Mrs. Will was a disappointment. She is totally absorbed in her husband and children, a beautiful feminine trait which commands your highest admiration in the abstract I know. In the concrete, I think, you would be as much bored by Mrs. Will as I am, but you would like Margetta though I must say she is spoiled. But she and the squirrels together were a pretty picture. I went down to the village to get some peanuts for the latter this morning & I felt repaid.

What do you think was the last thing at which I assisted? The Ark is a place for new experiences, certainly. Last evening being Sunday evening, our Baptist brother and sister brought in some hymn books, I think with a view to preventing light and frivolous conversation and suggested singing. There is not an instrument of any kind in the house but the rest of us consisting of mother, Miss Hobart, & myself agreed. Brother Giles prefaced each selection by a short account of the author of the hymn, how it came to be written or something of the sort, and then sister Giles would start it. Such singing!!! What she sang, I am not quite sure, but I think it was what brother Bartlett used to call "counter" i.e. alto an octave above. In the end, I had to lead, no one else sang soprano, so little Bertha led with great dignity but I did not dare look at mother. Every now and then the situation was almost too much for me as it was. Mr. and Mrs. Giles go tomorrow and some new people come to fill their places so I may have some more new experiences but I doubt anyone else's coming who will be so totally different from the people we ordinarily know. [20180404-1 (1892-) Bertha (The Ark, East Jaffrey) to Henry (StL)]

In spite of her comments about Mrs. Will in the preceding letter, Bertha wrote of growing fond of her. Bertha also admired Dr. & Mrs. Will's deep affection for each other which, after five years of marriage, defied the *"opinion of all sensible people"*.

I did not walk to the post office or mail your letter yesterday after all. Mrs. Will came by in her trap and drove me down & Margetta insisted on mailing my letters. She insisted also on standing up on the seat going back with one arm tightly around my neck subjecting me to frequent violent embracings in addition which, like Yolanthe's youthful appearance, "had its inconvenient side". But she is a lovable little thing. I wish you could see her magnificent eyes.

I have grown to really like Mrs. Will very much. She is not one bit clever but she is a thoroughly sweet woman. Dr. Will came up last night to spend Sunday and it was rather pretty to see the expression in his eyes when he looked at her. Only it is absurd. People who have been married five years are not expected to be so much in love with each other. At least, that is the opinion of all sensible people. Dr. Will is going to take us the twenty-mile drive around the mountain this afternoon. Us meaning Mrs. Will her cousin Miss Bradley & myself and it is a perfect day for it.

I went to church this morning. They took out the big wagon and took the whole house. But I sat on the driver's seat with Arthur Poole and discussed the political situation with him all the way down. He is very clever and the absolutely unfeigned admiration with which I saw him survey my gown and gloves was balm unto my soul.
[1892-06-13 (Sunday) Bertha (Jaffrey NH) to Henry (StL)]

Regarding the Will's sentimentality in their marriage, Henry came to the defense of sentimentality: those couples are the *"only really happy individuals that I ever meet"*.

I entirely agree with your remarks against the evidences of sentiment you have observed in the Dr. "after five years of married life", for I of course agree that both Dr. Will and his better half should have long since emancipated themselves from anything so "absurd" as sentiment. I can add, however, that "absurd" people of this particular ilk are the only really happy individuals that I ever meet, and thinking that I may prefer the criticisms of worldly minded people, like you for instance, you bad girl, to forfeiture of what may possibly make me happier than anything else in life, I shall remember what you reminded me of about people who live in glass houses and refrain from my natural inclination to ridicule the highly unnatural attachment of your medical friend and his wife. [1892-06-15 Henry (StL) to Bertha (East Jaffrey NH)]

On the following day, Bertha went for a "drive" with the doctor. When they found a turtle on the road which they brought home, Margetta exclaimed: *"O, who lost it?"*.

> *We had a superb drive yesterday, the doctor drives like Jehu, and we went up the hills like the wind. I don't know why, it is the horses seem to know the touch of a man's hand on the reins, but they went from the very beginning differently from what they do with Mrs. Will, and yet, I don't think he used the whip as much as she does.*
>
> *We came back with great masses of pink swamp azalea, which Dr. Will got out and picked under protest, that it was a judgment on him for taking a wagon load of girls along. He groaned further when we met a large turtle in the road, and Mrs. Will asked him to get it to take home to Margetta, but he got it and we wrapped it up in the dust cloth, and had a lively time keeping it there on our way home.*
>
> *Margetta was crazy over it. "Where did you get it, Mamma?" "Found it in the road dear." "O, who lost it?"*
>
> *I am getting very vain of Margetta's devotion to me. Her mother says it is one of the strongest fancies she has ever seen her take to anyone. And she is a very stately little lady and rejects Miss Curtis's overtures with scorn.*
>
> *I don't know whether all this bores you, son, but the life we lead here, while it is most enjoyable, is very simple and there is not much to write about.*
>
> *We had quite an exodus from the house this morning. The two Miss Curtises & their friend, Miss Hales (three old [maids] belonging to all the first families of Boston) & Miss Bradley, left for good and the doctor went down to the city again. Of course, the two latter do not belong to the Ark proper, but they take their meals here & are over here so much that they might as well. So we are about reduced to our original numbers.*
>
> *Today is the first really warm day we have had, and it is a beautiful kind of a day to do nothing in. It makes me appreciate more what you miserable individuals in St. Louis are enduring. Only you cannot take life as leisurely as we do.*
>
> *It has just occurred to me now foolish I was to send you those specimen wildflowers. If anyone was in your office, I am afraid you found it difficult to persuade them that that was a business letter. Was anyone there?*
> [1892-06-14 Bertha (Jaffrey NH) to Henry (StL)]

It was not clear if Henry was jealous of Margetta. Perhaps a little since she could spend such time with Bertha when he could not. The St. Louis heat did not help.

> *I have the key to Margetta's devotion to you, dearest. You told me she was capricious. Now, with this strong vein of congeniality between you and that young lady, how could it be otherwise than that you should beget strong admiration for each other, I will wager, though, I could cut you out, if I had a fair chance to divide Miss Margetta's time with you.*
>
> *Don't stop sending the wildflowers in your letter, dear. They give me such an idea of cooler, pleasanter places than this hot town, that it is common charity to send them. And when will the photograph come, Bert? Send two will you? That is, if you can spare me more than one for I have an especial use for number two which I will write you about later.*

Just now, I have only time to tell you I love you, my darling, and goodbye. [1892-06-17 (Friday) Henry (StL) to Bertha (The Ark, East Jaffrey)]

In his letter 3 days later, Henry more clearly expressed his jealously for the people who were able to be with Bertha when he could not. His daily letters to Bertha were then his only outlet.

Next to the pleasure your letters give me, the chief enjoyment of the day is writing to you.

...

..., let me explain that "the last part of my life" is that which I pass in writing to you for your letters are apt to arouse contending emotions. They are so dear, so like my darling, that the happiness they give me is mingled with a fierce longing to brush away all the obstacles that keep us apart and make you in name what is reality you are: my closest friend, my companion, my wife. Does this feeling of longing every day come to you my child? Tell me if it does and I shall know that there is good cause for my being very, very impatient.

...

I am very glad you have been having such a pleasant time with your friends at Rye. I feel a little "jealous" of those people who can see my darling every day while I cannot speak to her for a moment when sometimes I would almost give up my life for one look into her beautiful eyes.
[1892-06-20 Henry (StL) to Bertha (the Ark, East Jaffrey, c/o Mr. Poole)]

Bertha wrote to Henry again about Mrs. Will and her "admiration" for her character. The only exception Bertha made was for her view that engaged women were uninterested in men and uninteresting to men.

I spent this morning over at the camp playing with Margetta and baby Susie and I am more than ever convinced that you would admire Mrs. Wills' character. What do you think she said this morning apropos of a mutual friend of hers and mine in Boston who is engaged? "Why, I don't see why it is any temptation to her to flirt. I know when I was engaged, so far from that, other men really did not interest me a particle, rather bored me in fact." I realized that I could not say that last. And then I thought how much you would approve of such sentiment, and then I thought how very uninteresting she must have been to other people when she was engaged.
[1892-06-17 Bertha (Jaffrey, NH) to Henry (StL)]

Some of Bertha's letters were more businesslike – did you get the "photographs?". Otherwise, life in Jaffrey was a frolic.

I expect you got the photographs Tuesday, for I mailed them yesterday and they usually take a day longer than a letter. I wonder how you will like them. I sat six or seven times (all the same day though) but all the others were awful. The man told me to look pleasant and the result was such a maudlin looking individual as to make me resolve never to look pleasant again. I like them but opinion here is very much divided. Mrs. Will took one of the profiles when I first opened the package and has since had to put it on a high shelf to be out of reach of Margetta who insisted on carrying it round with her everywhere because it is "so beautiful, Mamma." You will have hard work to beat that compliment, son, and I know it was honest.

...

I am perfectly well and growing more vigorous every day. You ought to see me, I am as black as an Indian. Nobody dresses much up here and I have all day in a cheviot blouse and plain skirt, russet shoes and a cap like the one in the picture you like with the dog, outdoors all the time and retire at half past ten. You are perfectly silly to worry about my health, dear friend, it is the last thing you need have on your mind.

I spent this morning over at the camp. Have I ever described the camp to you? It is a cottage, built in the most primitive style that is at all consistent with comfort in the woods on the slope of the hill behind the Ark. Its principal attractions are a wide hall with a big fireplace in it and a broad piazza. It was on the latter that Mrs. Will and I established ourselves with the children. Mrs. Will had asked one to bring my mending over and have a mending morning. Though not fond of sewing, as you know, I am still not so utterly graceless as not to do my own mending. I am growing very fond of her. She is two months younger than I am and she has been married five years. She told me this morning that there was not a day in the whole time that she would not be glad to live over again. We had a very pleasant morning.

Henry, I have made an awful discovery. I am afraid I am a terribly commonplace woman! I am interested in such commonplace things!!
[1892-06-20 (Saturday) Bertha (Jaffrey) to Henry (StL) (6-18-92)]

As Bertha wrote in this letter regarding Mrs. Will's sentiments about her marriage: "*there was not a day in the whole time that she would not be glad to live over again...*" In a similar vein, Bertha wrote in her diary in 1942 about her own life, "*it has been well worth living it, and I would gladly live it over.*"

Regarding Mrs. Will, Henry offered his own comments. "*Mrs. Will*" improves steadily as I grow more familiar with her character. I hold her up to you as a shining example of true womanhood and I am not at all deceived by your affected scorn of certain of her qualities. I am beginning to see how very much you resemble her in these things!!"
[1892-06-22 Henry (StL) to Bertha (The Ark, Jaffrey)]

Bertha was not particularly pleased with Henry's comments about Mrs. Will and let him know.
After your conceited remarks about my affection for Mrs. Will, having grown from your approbation, I seriously thought of quarrelling with her, but she is too nice. The doctor is up here today again and he is pretty nice too. I would like to hold him up as a model to you. The other evening when we were talking in the firelight, Mrs. Will said "You can't know less about housekeeping than I did", by which you may guess what part of the foregoing conversation had been. "I did not know one thing, and I don't know what I should have done if Will had minded all the things that happened but he did not, he always saw the funny side and that helped me through. We had lots of real good times over scrapes that might have been terrible." That is one thing that will be so hard for us, you and I never see the funny side of things, you know!
[1892-06-27 (Sunday) Bertha (Jaffrey NH) to Henry (StL)]

Leaving Jaffrey that June 1892 for Rye Beach was difficult for Bertha for she knew that the future summers would never be the same. And Bertha must have felt some regret after their last climb up Mt. Monadnock[112] which was *"delightful to the people who go but not very much to tell about."* This was something that she could not share in a meaningful way with Henry.

> *I shall really be very, very sorry to leave Jaffrey. I like our pleasant, thoroughly informal outdoor life here. And I grow fonder of Mrs. Will and the children every day. I spend a great deal of time at the Camp. Yesterday evening after supper, I went over with Mrs. Will and we lit the fire in the great hall fireplace and sat there in the dark with only the firelight after the babies went to sleep and made popcorn and had a jolly cozy time all by ourselves. I took the lantern when I went back to the Ark but it was pretty late and a cloudy night and the little path through the woods, though perfectly safe, is pitchy black and I think I would rather have had your company than the lantern even.*
>
> *I did not tell you about our day on the mountain, when we climbed Monadnock and flashed telegrams with looking glasses from the top down to the Ark and had a picnic lunch. But there really was not much to tell. Such expeditions are very much alike: delightful to the people who go, but not very much to tell about.* [1892-06-25 Bertha (The Ark, Jaffrey) to Henry (StL)]

3. SEPTEMBER RETURN TO THE ARK

The Drakes returned to the Ark in September after their stay in Rye Beach and a brief stay in Boston during the summer of 1892.

> *I am enjoying the drives here very much but I do not need to engage Arthur Poole to drive me when father is here. He drives us everywhere and each drive is more beautiful than the last, for every day the leaves change more gloriously. We take tramps through the woods too and come home laden with boughs and gentian and golden rod. Father, by long training, has come to be very skillful and usually succeeds in finding the finest of all.* [1892-09-20 (Sunday) Bertha (Jaffrey) to Henry (StL)]

Bertha wrote upon her return in September that the air was *"like wine"*, just as she had written in June.

> *Henry, excuse slang, for real excellent weather and beauty that makes you glad you are alive, give me the spring and the fall. The air is just like wine.*
>
> ...
>
> *I must finish my letter but as I put the ferns in, I cannot help wishing you had been with me to see all that wonderful tracery of light and shadow up in the woods where I got them.* [1892-09-23 (Tuesday) Bertha (East Jaffrey) to Henry (StL)]

---

[112] Mount Monadnock, or Grand Monadnock, is a mountain in the New England state of New Hampshire, known for its presence in the writings of Ralph Waldo Emerson and Henry David Thoreau. It is the most prominent mountain peak in southern New Hampshire and is the highest point in Cheshire County, New Hampshire. It has long been known as one of the most frequently climbed mountains in the world.

The gentian flower[113] was sought after in the fall, especially by Bertha who knew her botany.

Now, I am enjoying simple country joys in the same placid way I have all along. I enclose you a gentian. Mrs. Wesselhoeft and I went on a gentian hunt yesterday tramping through bogs and we got quantities. Mrs. Wesselhoeft is the most charming woman and the youngest seeming. You never would dream she was a grandmother, not that a little thing like that would disturb me as far as companionableness goes. There are only those two girls here and three or four old ladies and I really think I prefer the old ladies. We play grabouge(?)[114] every evening and have a lovely time. Of course, most of the day I am out of doors. You would never accuse me of not being fond of the country if you could see me here. I enjoy everything about it. I love the "Ark" dearly, especially in fall. Perhaps too much of it would bore me but I have never known that sensation here yet.
[1892-09-23 (Thursday) Bertha (the Ark, East Jaffrey) to Henry (StL)]

There always seemed to be some old friends who were at the Ark during summers and Bertha always seemed to elicit complements: *"I adore being liked."*

Well, I have had a headache. I have been worried and <u>cross,</u> especially the last with a double underscoring for the whole week. And now in one day, I feel like a different person and I think this is a pretty nice world after all. I am sorry to have to show myself to you in such a disagreeable light but facts is facts and it is just as well that you should be thoroughly acquainted with me and my limitations. But I will just try to describe the contrast to you.

Out of this noise and rattle and dust and heat, we came up here yesterday evening. We got here just at sundown and the air was all full of a soft damp coolness. Dr. Wesselhoeft[115] the elder came up on the train with us, his wife & Mrs. Perry who was here with us last fall, met him and they carried mother off in their carriage. Arthur Poole met us with the big wagon and a broad beam of welcome. Then we drove the three and a half miles up through the woods, cool and quiet fully expresses it. And coming out on bits of road where you could see the afterglow (the sun was down) turning the air flame color. It was quite dark when we got up to the Ark but Mrs. Poole was waiting on the porch and she fairly put her arms around me when I arrived.

There are not many people here, Mrs. Will, I regret to say has gone, but only one party of strangers. The others were all here either last fall or last spring. And we sat down at Mrs. Perry's table (we

---

[113] Gentian: a plant of temperate and mountainous regions, typically with violet or vivid blue trumpet-shaped flowers.
[114] Grabuge?? - French word meaning "trouble".
[115] Dr. and Mrs. William P. Wesselhoeft of Boston.

had a very good supper by the way) feeling more as if we had reached home than anything else. Then this morning, Mrs. Poole sent in to know if I would drive down to church with her which I gladly accepted. I was the only one who went; the others were either too orthodox or too lazy. So Arthur drove his mother and me down alone. I hope you haven't forgotten about that Universalist Church and preacher. I took such pains to tell all about them last spring. It is a heavenly day to drive and the fall more beautiful than the spring even. The borders of the road just lined with golden rod and the leaves have only just begun to turn. Here and there a solid crimson tree stands out and the swamps are simply magnificent.

We staid after church of course while Arthur went to hitch up and the minister came up to speak to me. I told him I hardly expected him to remember me. To which he responded "O, I could never forget your face, your name I might but not your face. It is not the kind that one forgets, if, if I may say so", looking terribly embarrassed. I don't believe he ever paid a girl a compliment in his life before, not that, after diligently studying the faces of his congregation, one could take it as so very great a compliment. Then Mrs. Poole informed me that she would like to have me meet some of her friends and she introduced me to some old ladies with whom I had a lovely time.

I do love Jaffrey. I like the place and the people <u>and</u> I adore being liked myself. If you think you can pay me as nice a compliment as that young minister did, I shall give you free permission to try it. Seems to me, I told you I liked the sea better than the mountains and I believe I do. But still, Mt. Monadnock is a very grand restful old thing. O, and these bright spots of color are enough to drive one wild with delight. There is only one girl here, the other eight are all considerable advanced in years and the girl and her mother are the strangers, but she looks nice and I expect to have a lovely ten days here.
[1892-09-29 (Sunday) Bertha (The Ark, East Jaffrey) to Henry (StL)]

During the cold, Boston, winter of December 1892, Bertha was reminded of Margetta and her summer at the Ark after looking at the photograph of Bertha which Margetta referred to as *"My pretty Mrs. Drake"*.

> *There was also a picture of myself on the mantel piece (that won't be in our parlor) which Mrs. Will tells me, Margetta introduces to people as "My pretty Mrs. Drake". She never calls anyone Miss. I went upstairs to see the children and then staid in her room and chatted while she sewed on some doll clothes for Margetta's Christmas present. I am so sorry that you were here just at the time her grandmother died, for you would have enjoyed meeting Mrs. Will. She is a womanly woman, if you like.*
[1892-12-08 (Wednesday) Bertha (Backbay, Boston) to Henry (StL)]

D. FARRAGUT HOUSE, RYE BEACH, Summer 1892
"My foot is on my native heath, my name Macgregor"[116]
After leaving the Ark toward the end of June, the Drakes went to the Farragut House in Rye Beach on June 28th, their summer home away from home.

---

[116] Bertha quoted Walter Scott in her letter to Henry [1892-07-11 Sunday Bertha (Rye Beach) to Henry (StL)] - *"Don't mister me nor Campbell me! My foot is on my native heath, and my name is MacGregor!"* These words, put into the mouth of the cateran, Rob Roy, by Sir Walter Scott, express in a nutshell much of the spirit and history of this famous clan. Strangely enough, no tribe of the Highlands was more proud of its ancient name than the MacGregors, and no tribe had to suffer more for bearing that name, or was more cruelly compelled to abandon it. *"Is Rioghal ma dhream"* - my race is royal - was and is the proud boast of the MacGregors, and no more bitter fate could be imposed upon them than to give up the evidence of that descent. [Wikipedia]

DRAKE HOUSE,
RYE BEACH, N. H.

MENU.

SOUP
Macedoine

FISH
Boiled Salmon. Holandaise Style

BOILED

ROAST
Chicken with Currant Jelly
Lamb " Mint Sauce.

ENTREES
Banana Fritters with Vanilla Sauce

VEGETABLES
Potatoes. Asparagus on Toast
Green Peas — Stewed Tomatoes

PASTRY AND DESSERT
Washington, Squash, Apple Pie.

TEA *Strawberry. Ice Cream* COFFEE
Plums

Meals served in rooms and fruit or lunch taken from the table will be charged extra.

1. SUMMER HOME

Bertha's parents seemed to have been most at home in New England in general and at the Farragut House in Rye Beach in particular. From the available accounts, George and Bertha M spent virtually every summer in Rye Beach from the time that Bertha was seven years old until the end of their lives. George Drake was summering in Rye Beach when he died in 1908.

Bertha also spent all of her summers before her marriage in Rye Beach and many in later years. Bertha was very well acquainted with Rye Beach and loved her time there, being very active in the outdoors: walking, riding, cold sea baths, and tennis, to name a few of her activities.

Bertha included the following newspaper story in a letter to Henry in 1892:

> *"One of the most attractive and graceful tennis players at Rye Beach is Miss Bertha Drake, a charming St. Louis girl, who is a guest at the Farragut. Mr. George S. Blake[sic] and family are at this house for the season. The Nonantum House at Kennebunkport, Me., has as guests from St. Louis: Mr. John Beach Lane, Mrs. Francis Adams Lane, Miss Josephine Lane."*
> [1892-07-21 Bertha (Kennebunkport NH) to Henry (StL)]

In the following letter to Henry during the summer of 1892, Bertha described her days in Rye Beach and her Daily "Programme".

> *Now, as I have nothing of yours to answer, it occurs to me that you might like a sort of programme of the way our days are spent. It will give you a better idea of our very delightful, very lazy time here than I can do in any other way.*

In the first place, I don't think I am quite as bad as your friend Miss Ernst at breakfast but I like your friend, Mr. Blair's ideas on the subject much better than I do yours and I never under any circumstances get down earlier than quarter past nine and, when I even accomplish that, I am sorry because I then get through so much earlier than the rest of the crowd. After breakfast, everybody congregates on the piazza and gather into their own particular and congenial groups, with their work if they have any, and just prepared to talk if they have not. If anyone has a call to pay, this is usually the time they may expect to do it or receive it as, for instance, when Cherry Bent drops in occasionally. But calls are a rarity. At eleven o'clock, the mail comes in and the bathing bus comes round and everyone gets their letters and starts for the beach.

After bathing, people go to their rooms generally and that is my time for writing to you. I write between one and two generally so if, making allowance for difference in time, you should ever happen to think of me between twelve and one, you may be reasonably sure that you are occupying a large share of my thought at that time. I do not however believe that that is the time of the day you generally have the time to think about me or anything outside the work which I know has to take up so much of your life. Dinner at two and, in the afternoon, we drive, walk, or read aloud. We are very fond of adjourning to the rocks and reading aloud. And sometimes we play tennis. At quarter to seven, the evening mail comes in and that is the one in which your letters always arrive. I never get them in the morning, except on Monday, when as there is no mail on Sunday, the letters which would have come on Sunday evening naturally arrive in the morning mail.

In the evenings, Tuesday, Thursday and Saturday, there is a hop. There are no men here but there are a quantity of young people about George's age and a year or two older who keep up these hops with great vigor. And we girls go in and dance together or with Mr. Appleton. I did wrong to say there were no men, there is one man, Mr. Appleton, a young fellow of about twenty eight who comes here summer after summer, no mortal knows why, and Saturday evening there are occasional men who rundown to spend Sunday or come up to spend a week with their families. This last is very occasional. Other evenings, we bowl or play whist.

Now, from all this, I can see you drawing the conclusion "no wonder they say Rye is stupid." Well, it is for men. As I said, no mortal know why Mr. Appleton comes but the charm for the rest of us lies in an exceptionally pleasant set of people. Our crowd of girls is thoroughly congenial and we like to do things together, as I have told you. I have some friends here, almost as dear as I have at home and the same is true of all the rest of the family. George has a set of boys he has grown up with and they live on the tennis ground and on their bicycles. And, of course, for older people, the place is perfection for with a beautiful place, lovely drives, comfortable hotel, and a set of old friends, what more could you ask? But for younger men, there is nothing to do and they don't come. But I enjoy it thoroughly, every minute of it, though I would like to transport the Kennebunkport river here.
[1892-07-27 (Tuesday) Bertha (MA/NH) to Henry (StL)]

The summer rains never deterred Bertha from her outdoor activities – picking flowers and going for drives in a horse drawn carriage.

I went for a drive yesterday and took Cherry Bent about three miles from home. We were caught by the rain, not a gentle shower, but a pouring flood. Fortunately, she had her rubber coat but I had not so I reached home drenched through. This morning, I woke with a very slight cold and stiffness which was getting off better than I deserved. You may judge how little it amounted to from the fact that I went down to fix the flowers as usual and plunged through some very wet swamp to get some especially pretty elder while Janie Seldon stood on the edge and jeered at me. Jane is a very attractive member of our crowd and Charlotte is coming tomorrow. Charlotte Siter is just

splendid. She and I have been here for nine summers together and when we get together, we run the place to suit ourselves.
[1892-07-11 (Sunday) Bertha (Rye Beach) to Henry (StL)]

2. THE FARRAGUT HOUSE

The perennial summer abode for the Drakes in Rye Beach was the Farragut House, named after the U.S. Admiral who won fame in the 1812 war in Mobile Bay (among his other claims to notoriety).

FARRAGUT HOUSE, RYE BEACH, N. H.

Owner John Colby Philbrick pulled out all the stops for his guests, even carrying them into the surf to dunk their oilskin-covered heads before they exposed their entire bodies to the Atlantic chill. Originally known as the Philbrick Hotel by John Colby Philbrick in 1865, Philbrick, along with others at Rye Beach, was so overcome with excitement at the visit of Admiral Farragut to his Atlantic House (located just behind the Farragut site) in 1866, that he renamed his new hotel after the great man.

The hotel's front lawn and tennis court stretched right to the rocky shore, until Ocean Boulevard cut through them in 1902. A gazebo was built on the rocks for ocean views and a willow shaded path lead to St. Andrews Episcopal Church, then beyond to Philbricks Beach, a small crescent reserved for the exclusive summer guests.

After the new hotel was built a multi-purpose building across the road was added for all manner of occasion -- from religious services, dancing, parties, theater (and later film) – as well as gambling. Mr. Welds hall was the top entertainment center of Rye Beach.
[from: "*Remembering The Farragut*", By Alex Herlihy]

Bertha often wrote to Henry about the Farragut House and its attractions. Initially, this may have been to persuade Henry to take his summer vacations there but by 1892 the Farragut House and Rye Beach were special to both of them. As for Bertha, "*I love every stone on the place.*"

I send you the Roseti today, and also a picture of the Farragut which will give you some little idea of how it looks about here. In the round town at the right end of the house, second floor, is mother's room and mine is the one next with two windows, both with shutters closed. My view is lovely. Only the wide lawn and stone wall separate the hotel from the sea and I look straight across under those willows to it. It is high tide this afternoon and the waves are just dashing up spray on the rocks which unfortunately are not included in that little view of the beach. Rye is beautiful! It is the only place I know in which you have both the trees and the water. I am sorry that view of the willows is taken in winter instead of summer. You may have heard me abuse Rye as a summer resort but never said anything against the place itself. I love every stone on the place.

The Farragut Hotel, Rye Beach, New Hampshire

You see we have been coming here ever since I was seven years old and every corner has its association. I know the position of every rock on the beach, every bough on the apple orchard, where to find the first wild roses and iris, and the best place for blueberries in season. And I know all the natives from the bathing house man from whom I bought the photographs, who does some work in the photographing line himself, to the Indian woman who sells baskets who congratulated me yesterday, having just heard of my engagement. I know them all and I like them all.

The people who bore me sometimes are the civilized individuals who come here. As a matter of fact, my only objection to Rye at all is that I am not very fond of hotel life. The Farragut is much better than the majority of summer hotels in this way. It is small and so many of the same people come each year, that there is always a colony of old friends, so it has many of the advantages of cottage life. But it is not quite the same, you cannot be as independent. You may say you will but you cannot, unless you mean to shut yourself out entirely which is a physical impossibility for me. Why, certain courtesies are demanded of you and sometimes these are a great bore. I am quite aware that this is a selfish view to take of it but I am just telling you what I consider the only drawback to the place. I don't mind it's not being a gay place for I honestly do not care for that kind of thing in summer, if one could only be quiet in one's own independent way.
[1892-07-07 Bertha (Farragut house, East Jaffrey) to Henry (StL)]

The owners of the Farragut House, Lizzie and John Philbrick, became very well acquainted with George and Bertha M who had stayed there over so many years. Lizzie Philbrick wrote to Bertha M upon learning of the birth of Hugh, "*I received your note and was very much surprised to hear that your daughter had a little son. I am so pleased. For I know she will be such a sweet mother. I can fancy how happy she is and I know with you and Mr. Drake are very proud of it. I congratulate you. Do give her my love and tell her I shall want her to come to Rye more than ever to see the baby.*" [1894-01-15 Lizzie B Philbrick to Bertha M]

Page 257

In the evenings at the Farragut House, music was a regular feature. It seemed that, among its guests, there were always musicians ready to play.

> *After supper last night, we walked over a mile to hear Mr. Hoffmann play. That is one of the pleasantest things we do at Rye. Every Sunday evening, Mr. Hoffmann who stays at one of the cottages, plays for two hours and there are a great many of us who have a standing invitation to come over. He plays with all the windows open and people come over in little groups to sit on the piazza, look at the ocean and listen. All that is required of you is not to talk and it is the most delightful way of spending Sunday evening that you can possibly imagine. He has the most exquisitely delicate touch and he always plays the most beautiful music: Chopin, Wagner, Mendelssohn, Schubert, gliding from one thing into another.*
> [1892-07-02 Bertha (Rye Beach) to Henry (Wichita)]

3. THE BEAUTY OF RYE BEACH

Bertha never seemed to tire in writing to Henry of the beauty of Rye Beach and her words always seemed to convey the feel and scents in the sea breeze and the peace that she felt being there.

> *Someday, I am going to tell you a little about Rye but I must finish this letter to catch the mails. But I wish I could give you a breath of the air that comes in my window. They have just cut the hay and it is lying in heaps on the lawn and the salt breeze from the sea sweeps across that. The fragrance is indescribable. I enclose a spray of bay berry leaves to give you a breath from the country. I never go down the lane that leads to the church without picking a handful, just for their delicious fragrance.*
> [1892-07-01 Bertha (Rye Beach) to Henry (Wichita)]

> *This the most magnificent air, clear and bracing and salt! I have not been able to wear a thin dress yet and today it is enough to make one feel like dancing reels all over the place. If it were not for that, tis a low-spirited girl I should be this day.*
> [1892-07-06 Bertha (Rye Beach) to Henry (StL)]

And Bertha spoke of the moonlight whose beauty could only be slightly diminished by a "*horrid old bore*".

> *O, we did have the most gorgeous moonlight night yesterday and we all went down on the rocks to watch the spray dash up. There are times when I feel the want of you more than others and when old Mr. Hotchkiss said "don't you wish he was here, Miss Bertie?" I felt a strong inclination to push him off his rock backwards. Horrid old bore; what did he know about it?*
> [1892-08-11 (Monday) Bertha (Rye Beach) to Henry (StL)]

Over ten years later in in 1903, Bertha still wrote of her joy being in Rye Beach where "*the atmosphere is so perfect that the mere sensation of living is rapture.*"

> *You will get this in the midst of worries at Waco which may make you question whether this life is worth the trouble of living it. And here the atmosphere is so perfect that the mere sensation of living is rapture. The air is like wine – more like Dublin than Rye. Father and I had the pair and drove miles and miles this morning, just intoxicated with the glory of the day. My one feeling is - if you were only here but I suppose that would be too much.*
> *...*
> *I took the puppy off for a long walk with me alone over Perkins' land yesterday, father having gone to drive, and he was a great companion. That land on the opposite side from the cottages, on Perkins' own side, is perfectly beautiful. I walked it from end to end and it has beautiful pine woods on it and the loveliest pastures, orchards and farm lands back of it. I believe I told you it is here that the Deweys are so taken with the property and there is no comparison between it and the property we looked at on the other side of the road. This is much prettier.*
> [1903-09-28 Bertha (Rye, NH) to Henry (Waco)]

Bertha and her four children celebrated the *"the nicest fourth we ever had"* during their summer in Rye Beach in 1904.

> *We wound up the fourth of July in a blaze of glory. Sidney Allen told his mother that the Scotts had spent just loads of money on fireworks and couldn't they bring them over to the bonfire and set them off there. "How much money did you say?" "O, loads! I think it was almost three dollars!" So the entire family, Grandpa, mother and children went to the Allens to supper and the loads of fireworks were set off around the bonfire. And, "It was much the nicest fourth we ever had, mother!"*
> [1904-07-06 Bertha (Rye Beach) to Henry]

On rare occasions, the Rye Beach weather was hot. This provoked a fair amount of consternation since Rye Beach weather was expected to be cool in the summer. But, at least, the Rye Beach guests could find some solace in reading the even worse weather reports from Washington and other places.

> *The hot-wave which is all over the country has struck Rye also and the only way in which we keep even comparatively cool is by reading the weather reports from Washington and such places. But still it is very warm and today, the hottest of the season. Anna Lewis (One of the cottagers) is giving a luncheon. Now, a luncheon at Rye is an event. About twice in the season they occur and ordinarily, we would look forward to them with considerably more pleasure than we should in town. But today, the very thought of the Lewis's small dining room with fourteen girls in it gives me a shudder & as soon as I finish this letter, I have got to dress for it. I am going to wear the coolest thing I have which is a combination of white and pale blue and your favorite black hat with the white lilacs. But I don't think anything will really feel cool in that room.*
> [1892-07-28 Bertha (Rye Beach) to Henry (StL)]

By the next day after the preceding letter, cooler weather prevailed. *"You see, I survived the lunch and had a very good time too, though I felt less ashamed of having complained of the heat when I found it was 95° in the shade on the porch. The beauty of the seashore is, however, that it does not last long. Today is gloriously cool."* [1892-07-29 Bertha (Rye Beach) to Henry (StL)]

After hearing of some very bad weather after Bertha's arrival in Rye Beach, Henry remarked: *"The weather has been treating you so shabbily that I shall never have any respect for it again, no matter how worthily it may behave hereafter."* [1905(-) 20170831-3 Henry (StL) to Bertha (Rye)]

4. BATHING

Rye Beach

Bertha greatly enjoyed her sea baths in the cold Rye Beach waters. Her 1888-05 Diary recorded the following entries from her 1888 summer in Rye Beach.

June 27: *"The first sea bath of the season! Gorgeous!!! 62°."*
July 6: *"Bathing 57°, wind freezing."*
July 7 – *"Bathing 55°."*
July 12: *"Cold bathing, but they laugh at me and I go in, resolved to do or die."*
July 13: *"Bathing. Record says 55°. It is really fifty and bitterly cold."*
August 4: *"Bathing 58°."*
August 30: *"Bathing 53°, really cold."*

Four years later in 1892, Bertha was still enjoying her sea baths. Although she wrote to Henry of declining to bathe when the waters were 53°, on other occasions when the waters were similarly cold, she was undaunted.

I have not begun to bathe yet, the water was only fifty-three degrees this morning and I am waiting until it shall have warmed up a little bit, though it is never much over sixty here.
[1892-07-06 Bertha (Rye Beach) to Henry (StL)]

The next week when the waters were 61°, it was "*magnificent*".

I have just come up from my first sea bath this season. Do you like sea bathing, Henry? If you do, you know just what an exhilaration I have been through and I am indeed still feeling. The water was 61° and a good many people don't like Rye on account of its cold bathing. Nothing would induce Nan to go in when she was here last summer but I love it. At Marion, the water is always 70° or over, and I am chilly all the time I am in for there is no reaction but here, after the first icy shock, the reaction is perfectly magnificent and I come out feeling like a queen!
[1892-07-12 Bertha (Rye Beach) to Henry (StL)]

The waters got colder over the next few days that summer but Bertha was unstoppable and got "*some sand*".

The water was 57° this morning and Charlotte said to me as we went shivering in, "Why do we bathe, O why do we?" And I said "Because", as Carlyle remarked, "the English nation is composed of millions of people, mostly fools. I am going out." To which Charlotte responded "O dive down Bertie and get some sand!" Which remark had a double meaning but, as you don't know any slang, I suppose you would not understand it. However, I did not(?) go out and I enjoyed it immensely afterward.

…

Dear boy, I don't like your being in Fort Worth one bit, and I do not believe you do. I know that 57° water sounded pleasant to you. Please tell me if you still feel perfectly well. I was so very, very glad that you did before you left.
[1892-07-18 (Saturday) Bertha (Rye Beach) to Henry (Ft. Worth)]

Although bathing was always a pleasure to Bertha, one of her swims in the cold water in early September 1892 gave her second thoughts. When she was tired and cold from her swim and thinking of getting into the nearby boat, she wondered if, in the cold wind, it would be "*out of the water into the refrigerator.*"

You are right about me, not attempting to drive vicious horses or swim in deep waters after my promise to you. I only wish I could make you think my freeze out (literal) on Friday was due to my devotion to my promise. The way it happened was lately they have had a life boat go out with some of the more venturesome swimmers and they let a rope hang behind, to which we girls lately have had a habit of clinging & letting ourselves be towed out & back. Friday, we started on this expedition when we had already been in some time and the swimmer, who chanced to be an unusually venturesome one, was some distance ahead of the boat, and swam as though intending

to reach the shoals[117]. Of course, the boat had to follow the swimmer and we had to follow the boat. It was when I first began to get chilled that I thought of letting go the boat and swimming back. And I would like to say that nothing but my promise to you not to swim in water over my head restrained me. But though I did think of that and it settled the question without any further debating, still candor compels me to state that I doubt if I should have dared to anyway. Ordinarily, we would have gotten into the boat but the wind was so bitter that day that, to get in in our wet clothes, would have been not exactly out of the frying pan into the fire but out of the water into the refrigerator. So we shivered at the rear of the boat until we got within hailing distance of the swimmers and then induced them to turn back. O, it was idiotic, the only thing was that we had no idea we were going so far when we started. I am all right now, there is no earthly reason I should not go in today but the family won't hear of it and, of course, everybody makes a point of saying as they come up that it was "quite the best bath of the season." I don't believe a word of it now!
[1892-09-05 (Monday) Bertha (Rye Beach) to Henry (StL)]

In spite of this icy sea bath experience, Bertha wrote five days later calling Henry a "*goose*" for being so concerned about the cold water.

I think your description of yourself in your Monday letter quite correct. And you are a goose besides. The idea of inveighing against sea bathing as foolish when it is the thing that best agrees with me when I am not kept too long in perforce. I haven't stayed out – I defied my family and went in again when the temperature of the water rose to 64%. I have just come from a splendid bath and I again feel like a "winner".
[1892-09-10 (Friday) Bertha (Rye Beach) to Henry (StL)]

5. THE ROCKS

The "rocks" near the Farragut House were a very special place for Bertha. She went to the rocks almost every day when she was there: it was her joy and refuge, a place to meet her friends and a place for contemplation. Bertha and her friends had various names for the rocks, such "turtle rock" and each person had their own particular rock seat.

Bertha wrote about the rocks in her 1888-05 Diary: "*More reading and dreaming on the rocks. The surf is glorious.*" [1888-05 Diary, July 2, 1888]

July 3
After tea, the surf is magnificent. Watch it first alone, then with Esther. I wonder if I am hypercritical. Likewise, I wonder how disagreeable I was when I left school and whether I thought what I did not know was born out. I suppose I did. [1888-05 Diary, July 3, 1888]

August 15 –
Discover that I have lost my purse. Have the astonishing good fortune to find it where I left it – on the rocks where it has been all night. Go to see Daisy who is ill to celebrate having found my purse. I treat to lemonade, etc. Afternoon – Esther, Daisy, Sallie Tibbetts, and I read aloud under the willows. S. leaves us and we three adjourn to the rocks where we are joined by Mr. Deacon who reads Browning & other poems to us in a voice like a buzz saw. Also gives us description of the passion play as he saw it. Evening – A large group of us collect on the piazza. Ike & Tom with banjos & all sing college songs. One of the two most beautiful religious pictures in the "world".
[1888-05 Diary, August 15, 1888]

---

[117] The Isles of the Shoals refer to a grouping of islands approximately 6 miles offshore from Rye Beach.

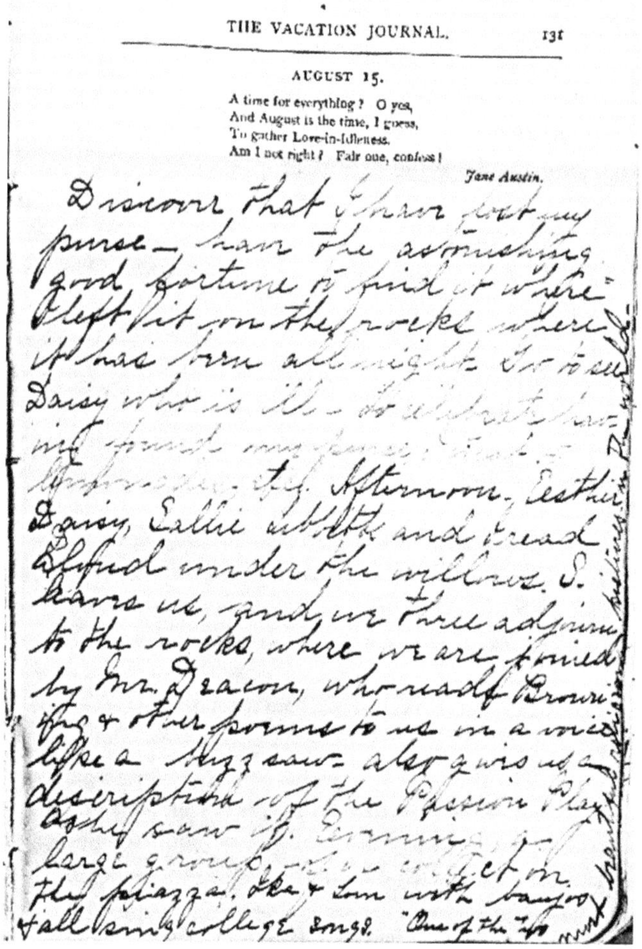

AUGUST 15.

A time for everything? O yes,
And August is the time, I guess,
To gather Love-in-Idleness.
Am I not right? Fair one, confess!

Jane Austin.

[handwritten journal entry, largely illegible cursive]

August 16, 1888
Evening – Sallie, Daisy, Esther, Johnny Tibbitts and Ike with his guitar go down on the rocks in the moonlight and sing.

August 29, 1888
... In the afternoon, we go down on the rocks and Mr. Deacon reads aloud to Miss Andrews, her cousin & myself, the rest of "The Village Genius" & can hardly control his voice. It is the most exquisite little story and O, the wonderful effects of sea and sky in the sunset while he is reading. Perhaps Homer meant some sea like that when he said "wine colored". These are surely halcyon days. I wonder what storm is coming? Evening – We all get together and read the pound of love letters which Miss Shimmin took to the pound party & Sallie tells our fortunes with cards.

When summer of 1888 drew to a close, Bertha returned to the rocks. "*How I hate the breaking up of pleasant summers. We sit on the rocks until closely shut in by the mist.*" [September 3, 1888]

In her diary on September 3rd, Bertha included a flower.

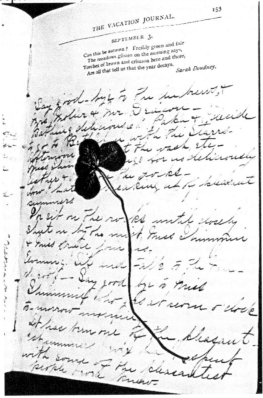

On the day that Bertha departed Rye Beach at the end of the summer of 1888, she wrote of going to the rocks for that last time and, being alone, sat in *"Miss Grace's seat"* instead of the *"rock sofa"* that she would normally sit in with her friends. *"My beautiful summer, goodbye, goodbye."*

> *There is water in the rock sofa so I take Miss Grace's seat. It is just as well. I should be more lonely in the other. A lovely sunset. See new moon over my right shoulder but it cannot bring me such a lovely month as the last. My beautiful summer, goodbye, goodbye.*

[September 10, 1888]

6. A SUNDAY RIDE TO PORTSMOUTH

In July 1892, Bertha decided to drive the horse cart with her girlfriends to Portsmouth, a drive that proved to be very eventful in way that was sure to make Henry nervous. Bertha, being mindful of Henry's protectiveness, didn't broach the details of the ride until after writing of the *"mournfulness"* of their separations.

> *I received your Tuesday letter last night, dearest, and the mournfulness of it recalled to me a conversation I had with Myra. "O, poor boy," she said, referring to Nat. "I would just give anything if I could be back. I know it is right for me to be away, I am getting so much stronger but it is awfully hard on him, you don't know what homesick letters I've had from him." I said "Yes, I do too", whereupon she regarded me with calm scorn and said "No, you don't either, being apart before is just nothing to what it is afterward." I am undecided now as to the best way of preventing this: whether it would be wiser for us never to be married at all or never to be separated afterward. If the latter should be the alternative, I cannot be too thankful that they have built a good hotel at Fort Worth. But possibly you would prefer the former.*
>
> *Which reminds me that you came within an ace of attaining that blissful possibility. I did not tell you about it at the time for I really did not know what a narrow escape it was. But in the light of*

later events, I will tell you about it. Did you receive a letter at Fort Worth post marked Portsmouth? Well, I mailed it there a week ago yesterday when Jane, Charlotte, Esther and I drove over to Portsmouth, I acting as driver. Just before we got into Portsmouth, our horse suddenly shied violently and ran upon the path by the roadside, nearly knocking down two old ladies. I tried to make him go back, whereupon he shied still more violently and nearly went into the stone wall. Then I let him stand still for a minute and Jane said "Bertie, there is nothing for that horse to shy at. I believe part of his harness is caught and you are pulling him to one side without knowing it. Do get out and see." I said I knew it wasn't but Janie, who is very nervous about horses, implored me so to get out and look that I gave the reins to Esther and got out. No sooner had I done this than the horse started rapidly for the other side of the road apparently with the intention of climbing the wall there but, just before he got there, he tried to turn round and go home, this last maneuver so alarming Janie that she jumped out of the carriage and barely escaped getting caught between the wheels. Then the horse stopped & Charlotte rapidly followed Jane. Poor Esther said meekly that she would like to get out too but we told her not to stir. Then my somewhat scattered wits returned and I said "girls, there is nothing the matter with that horse. He was startled at first and we have frightened him more by acting like idiots. Let's get back." But neither for love nor money would they do it until they had seen for themselves that he was not going to shy again. So I got in on the left side, for the carriage was turned that way, and Esther said, if I did not mind, she would rather not pull on these reins again so I took the reins, addressed some very stern language to the horse and he went off as good as gold, trotted to the top of the hill where we waited for Charlotte and Jane and they got in. He behaved perfectly for the rest of the drive, except that he shied rather badly once or twice.

Now to confess the whole truth, at that time, I thought that Esther had caused this. I blamed myself for ever having gotten out of the wagon for I knew Esther did not like to drive and I thought she had gotten nervous & pulled the wrong rein. Now, I know she did not and she was the pluckiest of the whole lot for she staid in the carriage while she was afraid. Naturally, I never said I thought it was her fault, though.

Well, yesterday, an old clergyman and his wife took this same horse and a drive from the stable to drive him. About a mile from here, he shied in the same way, rushed at a fence and behaved so badly that Mrs. Lewis got frightened and her husband made the driver go to the horse's head and hold him while they got out and the beast then broke loose and tore madly round and round and kicked the wagon into smithereens. Dr. Lewis says he thinks it was a fit of blind staggers but we have not heard the report from the stable yet.

But the worst of it is that father and Mr. Rogers (Janie's brother in law) now pace the piazza indignantly and talk about the iniquity of giving young girls a horse like that and say they never will allow us to drive alone again which, I think, shows the lack of logic in the masculine mind. The man did not know he was giving us a bad horse. It was a new one and had so far behaved perfectly well and he probably would take especial care we had a safe one in future. And as it was all caused by the horse and not by our bad driving, I cannot see why we cannot go again. Those drives were among our greatest sprees and they would be no fun at all with a driver and it is not sensible anyway. We've driven summer after summer with no accident and this was no fault of ours.

[1892-07-25 (Sunday) Bertha (Rye Beach) to Henry (StL)]

Bertha knew very well Henry's mind when it came to Bertha being exposed to any risk and, perhaps, she welcomed Henry's scolding as a protective balm and the spreading of the blame: *"those matters ought to be looked after for you."*

The hurry I was in yesterday saved you the very stern lecture I intended to give you for driving a horse you did not know all about. And I cannot blame you very much, dear, because I think those matters ought to be looked after for you. I will only add that, since you have driven very little in your life and have not had as much to do with horses as some girls have, will you not promise not to go out again without a driver unless your horse is one that your father or some other man whom you can trust to be cautious in giving his opinion knows to be perfectly safe? I ask you this, my darling, for the reason that your want of experience with horses makes it impossible for you to understand how very dangerous an unreliable horse is. Some of the most distressing accidents have occurred to persons whom I have known well from trusting to unreliable and strange horses and, if you knew how the account of your adventure frightened me as I read it, I am very sure you would satisfy me that there is no chance for a repetition of a similar experience. I don't want to say anything that will interfere with your driving when you can go with perfect safety but, dearest, you will promise me what I ask, will you not? If I ask you more than is reasonable, I should think it natural for you to rebel so I only beg that you won't drive again unless you yourself know the horse is entirely reliable.
[1892-07-28 (Thursday) Henry (StL) to Bertha (Farragut House, Rye Beach)]

Bertha was able to pretty quickly recover from her sense of contrition in her prior letter and wrote in the next letter that she felt *"rather revengeful"* about Henry's criticisms.

Esther, Daisy, Miss Cartwright & I are going up to Portsmouth this afternoon, and we have engaged the gentlest old sheep on the place to take us. I confess, I still feel rather revengeful at your criticisms on my driving.
[1892-09-(-) (Monday) Bertha to Henry (StL)]

7. SPORTS & GAMES

a. Card Games:

Bertha loved playing cards and would regularly play whist or euchre. Generally, the card games were a delight but, sometimes, not so much.

I expected to feel tired tonight but I don't. I went to a progressive Euchre party last night at the Farragut and had the Allen party at dinner today. The progressive Euchre was, between ourselves, of the nature of a bore. I was informed this morning that I was the life of the occasion. It needed life badly enough. It was like lifting ton weights.
[1902-07-30 Bertha (Rye Beach) to Henry (StL)]

b. Other Games: identify the flower

It is difficult to imagine that Bertha's mind ever remained still: her mind seemed to always be engaged in some new endeavor. So it was that she devised a game of "identify the flower".

I tried a new scheme, I made six bouquets of six different kinds of wildflowers all of which grow in our immediate neighborhood and offered a prize to the girl who could name the greatest number correctly. I had yarrow, wild carrot, sour grass blossoms, wild mustard, meadow rue, wild spirea and self-heal. Every single flower was familiar by sight to all of them but the prize went to Mary Allen for naming two correctly – sour grass and wild mustard. Frances knew the spirea and one of the others knew the wild carrot but we had a great deal of fun over it. But do you know Mary Allen and Miss Knapp were infinitely the most entertaining? Emily Wickham is pretty good fun but Emily Catlin!
[1902-07-30 Bertha (Rye Beach) to Henry (StL)]

c. Tennis

It may be surmised that Bertha was a good tennis player and very competitive – of course, within the bounds of womanly modesty of the time. In her letter to Henry during the summer of 1892, she wrote of a match that she was to play in the afternoon.

> *I am engaged to play tennis with one this afternoon, against Mr. Appleton and Miss Nash, or I am to play with Mr. Appleton, I am not sure which. The latter young man, I think, regards an engaged girl as an exceedingly uninteresting being except on the tennis field and there he generally prefers my society to that of the unengaged who don't play as strong a game. Miss Nash and I are considered the best girl players here. I tell you that without any particular conceit about it for there is not a girl here who really plays a good game, such a game as Mattie used to play in the old tennis club days for instance. I don't begin to play the game I used to. George Fishback drilled certain things into me so that I never could forget them. But I have hardly played at all for three years and am just beginning to get back into practice. And I do enjoy it immensely. Both the men we are going to play with, Mr. Wright and Mr. Appleton, play a splendid game.*
> [1892-08-03 (Wednesday) Bertha (Rye Beach) to Henry (StL)]

Henry understood that Bertha was a good tennis player and simply summarized: "*You are a vain child, dear.*"

> *I am rather glad you were defeated in the match against Mr. Appleton and Miss Nash, for you did not at all fail to impress me with your pride in your game. Even though you started out by saying you were only "fairly good", it was easy to see that I was not to take account of your opening statement but rather bear in mind that you had not forgotten the drilling you received from Fishback whom I remember to have been our best player out here. You are a vain child, dear, and I am not sure that you should not be so for I have an idea that, where one is as sweet and dear and gentle as my darling is, one is justified in having a large amount of this essentially feminine quality.*
> [1892-08-09PM (Tuesday) Henry (StL) to Bertha (Farragut House, Rye Beach)]

Well, Bertha certainly did not like being called "*vain*" and stiffly asserted her "humbleness".

> *… I don't like to be called vain, a humble minded person like myself!! And I did mean what I said about only playing a fair game of tennis & I don't even think that anymore, for since Esther came, I have been beaten steadily.*
> [1892-08-13 (Friday 1892-08-12) Bertha (Rye Beach) to Henry (StL)]

d. Whist & Baseball

As Bertha related, she liked whist and baseball: whist to play and baseball to watch. From other letters, it was clear that Bertha was a competent whist player; nevertheless, in order to show her modesty to Henry (after he accused her of vanity), she professed that she would never grasp the game.

> *It has been pretty warm here the last few days and we have done little except sit under the trees or down on the rocks, indulging in eminently instructive conversation or playing whist on the piazza which last science, I have finally made up my mind, I shall never grasp if I live to be a hundred though I shall still continue to like it.*

> *This afternoon, they have a baseball game here. The married men of the Farragut, having challenged the young men, otherwise boys. George[118] is one of the enthusiasts on the latter side, being on the nine up at school. Baseball is one of the games I most thoroughly enjoy watching. I don't like football and I think cricket deadly stupid. So I am prepared to cheer myself hoarse this afternoon.*
> [1892-08-19 (Friday) Bertha (Farragut House, Rye Beach) to Henry (StL)]

---

[118] George S. Drake, Jr., Bertha's brother.

8. THE LADIES JAPANESE FAIR

The ladies of the Farragut House held a Japanese Fair during the summer of 1892 for the benefit of their church and Bertha was an enthusiastic participant.

We are using the Japanese lady (do you remember her?) as a model for our Japanese tea. Just at present, we are living and breathing Japanese tea. We are going to have it Saturday afternoon and evening from five until ten and, by the time this reaches you, I shall probably be in the last agonies of preparation. We are to have three booths on the dancing hall: a fan booth, a candy booth, and a tea booth where you buy the cup and the tea at the same time. And all the girls are going to be dressed in Japanese costumes and I am morally convinced we shall look like frights, my dear, but it is for the benefit of the church so let us sacrifice ourselves nobly in the cause thereof. It is Mrs. Jones' idea. She saw one in California last year and it has the merit of being slightly different from the everlasting fair. Daisy has a Japanese costume which is serving us as model to cut out by but your lady showed us exactly how the sashes were arranged and we hoped at first her hair might be an assistance but I am afraid that way of dressing it is beyond the power of occidentals. We sent for the material to Boston, Mrs. Jones and mother cut out, and we have to make the costumes ourselves. They are decidedly simple to make, not like an American girl's tailor-made gown but you know how I love sewing of any kind and can realize how delighted I am over the prospect of spending tomorrow at this kind of work. Do you think you can imagine me as a Japanese girl? If your imagination fails you, buy a Japanese fan with a lady in a flowered gown of deep crimson and cream color and you may be able to form some slight conception of how ravishingly hideous I am going to look. But we are all in the same boat and I rather think the general effect will be pretty gorgeous.

[1892-08-11 (Wednesday) Bertha (Rye Beach) to Henry (StL)]

Picture kept by Bertha

Henry wrote of his confidence that the fair would be a "*magnificent financial success*" due to the "*money-making power of a lot of attractive females with no consciences*". (How did Henry get away with writing this?!)

The fair must have been pretty, dear, and you are a very dear child to tell me all about it. How I should like to have seen my darling! You were very pretty, I know dearest, and your eyes were very bright and soft and, yes, I have a very good picture of you in your pretty gown. As to the fair itself I can easily imagine it was "stunning" and the magnificent financial success fills me with profound admiration for the money-making power of a lot of attractive looking females with no consciences and with the end justifies the means theory to sustain them in their attacks upon their helpless friends. I had not one doubt that the fair would be pretty and that it would make money – I once attended a fair!!

I have a theory which may account for the hopeless confusion of the church music on Sunday. I think the members of the choir, having been likewise fellow conspirators in the fair piracy when Sunday came, were much too busy with their sins to have thought for songs of praise. A part of the Litany which especially applies to hardened sinners might have been chanted with effect! Your friend's suggestion that you were going to marry a Christian (I am much pleased to know, dear child, that thou hast told thy friends of my piety) ought to be full of comfort to you for you must look forward with much joy to the comforting influence of a pious man.
[1892-08-07 (Wednesday) Henry (University Club) to Bertha (Farragut House)]

The Japanese Fair was an exhausting event for Bertha which may have partially averted Bertha's focus away from Henry's previous disparaging remarks about *"females with no consciences"*. But Bertha concluded with her own rejoinder to Henry about not appreciating *"the serving women of the country, poor souls!"*

I am a wreck and, the next time I get myself let in for a Japanese tea, I'll know it and I don't care if that is slang! I served four hours on that awful thing and you cannot have a long letter because my eyes ache. I put this in with malice intent because I know you think so highly of a woman who sits serving for hours and I want to show you the other side and I want to go immediately and do something for the benefit of the serving women of the country, poor souls!
I came within an ace of sending you a scrap of my dress (I decided on a different one, not the crimson, less startling) when I suddenly recollected that, nice as you are in many respects, you are not another girl and would not have appreciated it at all.
[1892-08-13 (Friday 1892-08-12) Bertha (Rye Beach) to Henry (StL)]

Henry tried to smooth everything over in his next letter.

I wish I had known about your Japanese tea sooner for I think it would have occurred to me to send you one of the photographs which Smith sent out here last week. I never have seen such a pretty collection of photographs before (except one I own). The prettiest, daintiest, little Japanese girls, dressed in the most attractive costumes of the pretty, bright colors I like to see in cravats. And this reminds me that a cravat to match that Japanese dress of yours would be a joy forever!!
[1892-08-15(-) Henry (StL) to Bertha (Farragut House, Rye Beach)]

9. THE RYE BEACH SPINSTERS

The summer of 1892 would be Bertha's last as a spinster. Bertha had spent nearly 20 summers there as a girl and then a young woman, and had formed life-long friendships with the other ladies of her age. So the news of her engagement and impending marriage to Henry was a blow to her friends' thoughts of future summer camaraderie.

Charlotte, Esther, Jane and I are going to drive to Portsmouth this afternoon and I will give a thought to your lonely wanderings there, poor boy. They are all very interested in you and rather indignant at you, to tell the truth, for breaking the ranks of the Rye spinsters.
[1892-07-18 Bertha (Rye Beach) to Henry (Ft. Worth)]

Henry's response to Bertha's letter was terse.

It's high time the spinster ranks were broken, for it is quite clear each young woman of that most choice band is in need of a guardian.
[1892-07-21 Henry (Ye Arlington Inn, Fort Worth TX) To Bertha – Farragut House, Rye Beach, NH]

Bertha's spinster group were all in the early to mid-twenties and clearly considered themselves in a different class than the girls in their late teens. Bertha wondered if she was even "*as silly*" when she was that age.

> *I had some of the cottage girls over to tea with me last night, those who gave the lunch the other day. And I have been wondering ever since if I could have been as silly as that when I was nineteen. Charlotte & I think we were not but I suppose it is impossible to put ourselves in their position now.*
> [1892-08-03 Bertha (Rye Beach) to Henry (StL)]

Bertha wrote to Henry about how her friend, Esther, had a "*lively hatred*" toward Henry.

> *Daisy and Esther are constantly sending you messages but I have declined to deliver them because I do not think it is proper. Esther, I think, is inclined to regard you with a lively hatred. She is one of the best friends I have anywhere and here we do everything together. She always saves a place for me, waits for me if I am late, etc. I doubt if a man can appreciate this but girls hate to do things alone. Esther remarked yesterday on the rock, pensively, "I am so glad one cannot see a year ahead, what one will be doing." And when I asked why specially, "Because I am morally certain I should see myself seated on this selfsame rock! There is a fatal charm about Rye; you've broken it. But I never shall and, as long as you were here, I did not care." I suggested that I might return but she declared that she did not want me. "No, I know just what it will be like; I would as soon not have you here at all as absorbed in somebody else. And you needn't tell me you wouldn't be. I've met just your kind before." And yet, the illogical young woman abuses me terribly for having kept you waiting so long. She dates things back to that telegram and declares I treat you very badly. Do you think I treat you badly? It is hard enough to have all my friends at home take your part. If these begin too, I am in an evil case indeed.*
> [1892-08-11 (Monday) Bertha (Rye Beach) to Henry (StL)]

When Janie (Jane Seldon) was leaving toward the end of summer of 1892, there was the loss that the spinsters felt for her but it also gave them occasion to mourn the future loss of Bertha as a spinster.

> *Janie went away this morning and she will be a great loss to us all here. A great gal in the spinster group. Last night Charlotte and I went out to tea at the Nichol's and when we came home found Jane, Esther, Daisy and Belle seated in a group on the piazza. As we came up, Jane said "Bertie, Esther says she's never coming back here after you leave and we're all been mourning over your departure. When I think we shall never have any more whist together, I am ready to weep." I said "girls, I do wish you would not all talk as if I were going to be buried. I may come back here." "Oh, but you won't be any good, you'll be married." "But I don't see how that is going to affect my playing whist." Jane said "but, Bertie, you don't seem to understand, you won't be free to do as you please, you'll have to stay with him or see that he is having a good time, anyway, before you can play." I tried vainly to imagine you acting in this tyrannical way, which was an exact description of the way Janie's brother in law behaves, but I only said "well if the worst comes to the worst, I'll make him play whist too." Chorus. "We don't want him." Esther came in just as I was writing this and I gave her your message which she greatly enjoyed, and she said to thank you for it, adding "give him my very best love this time and tell him I hate him for taking you away." With which not at all contradictory statement, she departed. You see you are not exactly in favor with the spinsters.*
> [1892-08-16 (Monday) Bertha (Rye Beach) to Henry (StL)]

Henry's response to Bertha about the spinsters simply focused on the natural order of things and on their avoiding the "*irretraceable single blessedness*".

> *The spinsters, by the way, think I shall require a vast amount of your time and attention, don't they? I am inclined to think they have quite proper ideas as to a woman's duties and, if I came across a man who is good enough to marry a friend of yours, I shall tell him to go to Rye and make himself known to the a crowd of some twenty young women who are on the danger line of irretraceable single blessedness.* [1892-08-18 Henry (StL) to Bertha (Farragut House)]

As the summer of 1892 was nearing its end, Bertha not only felt the usual remorse at its passing but also the additional anticipation of being married to Henry.

> *I begin to feel very much as though the summer was going. So many people have left this week, most of them to be sure on their way to the mountains, not home, but it gives a feeling of breaking up. And the golden rod is coming out beautifully, another sign of the end of summer.*
>
> *We had another small card party last night to celebrate Belle's departure and I again won the prize. We have had a great deal of card parties this summer and this is the third time I have won a prize. My luck is becoming proverbial. The funny part of it last night was that Esther and I and Mr. Doolittle were playing against Belle and Daisy and Mr. Huling(?) (the latter is a man who used to be devoted to Lallie Newman; he is in mourning (not for her) and came here because it was quiet; just arrived). Mr. Doolittle is an engaged man who had run down to see his family for a few days. (He is an old habitual here.) Of course, when he and I won, there was a chorus of "lucky at cards, unlucky in the other thing, better take care." And Belle inquired if I had a letter that day. Not having had one for two nights, this question was trying but I simply told her not to be impertinent.*
>
> *You observe I am not allowed to forget you but I more often hear of you under an alias. I don't think I told you of how the girls began calling you Mr. Foster, did I? When Charlotte first came, she could not remember what your name was and could only think of Foster, which I told her was like Mrs. Nickleby calling Smike – Slammons , because of the remarkable similarity of their being an S in both names. So the girls really, I think, because they feel a little shy of being playful with your real name, generally speak of you as Mr. Foster, except Charlotte and Esther who now both call you Henry in the most intimate way.*
>
> [1892-08-18 (Wednesday) Bertha (Farragut house) to Henry (StL)]

Bertha expressed some of the anticipation she felt about becoming a married woman writing, "*it is very nice to be a girl*".

> *It was just as well for me to see these girls this morning. Esther, Daisy, Charlotte and I took that drive yesterday. Charlotte is going next Monday and I shall not get back until Saturday night so it was our last drive and on the way home we grew so mournful over it that, when Esther asked me if I did not want to change my mind at the eleventh hour, it is a wonder I did not say yes. Henry, it is very nice to be a girl and we have had lots of good times together.*
>
> [1892-08-24 (Tuesday) Bertha (Farragut House, Rye Beach) to Henry (StL)]

The successive days brought the end of the 1892 Rye Beach summer even closer, with more departures and fewer friends to participate in the St. Andrew's-by-the-Sea Church Sunday service, leaving Bertha as the lone chorister.

> *We have been spending the afternoon on the rocks and we went from there to the afternoon service, whereas Esther said "I expected to feel very pathetic and sentimental the end of the summer, we three going to say goodbye tomorrow, Bertie going to leave our ranks forever." But we didn't. Mr. Hoffmann has gone and a strange organist played and, as I was the only member of the choir left, I had decided not to go up and we were not going to have the chants sung, just the hymns, and to have very familiar ones everyone knew. This morning all went well but this afternoon, some enterprising ladies from the Sauer(?) house as the new organist, volunteered to lead the chants if he would play, which he did. He was not at all familiar with the pointing[119] or rather, he was familiar with one and they with another. And the result was chaos. Instead of pensive thoughts, we had all we could do to keep our faces straight and were shaken by that horrible painful silent laughter. I don't know whether men ever are attacked by it and what made the matter worse was*

---

[119] Bertha may be referring to the organ point or pedal point.

that the clergyman had a broad Irish accent which made the psalms simply indescribably funny. Well, of course, I don't mean we laughed all through the service. We got control of ourselves and I really think we carried the hymns through but it was not in the least what we had expected.
[1892-09-13 (Sunday) Bertha (Rye Beach) to Henry (StL)]
(*"Instead of pensive thoughts, we had all we could do to keep our faces straight and were shaken by that horrible painful silent laughter."* Yes, men are also attacked by this!)

In one of her last letters from Rye Beach that summer, Bertha spoke of watching her remaining friends leave and of her feelings of no longer being called *"Bertie Drake"*.

We have been seeing stage load after stage load of people off. I hate last days and I feel very mournful. You know too well with what hope and trust I look forward to the future. Don't misunderstand me when I say I cannot help grieving over these last times – for it never will be quite the same again. A girl's life is a very happy care free life and mine has been especially so and to go about among the old places and feel that that life is over makes me feel very sad. Possibly you are a strange confidant to choose for these feelings but you see I'm used to telling you things.

Mrs. Philbrick said yesterday "Why, to think that Bertie Drake will never be about the place again. I can't fancy it. The place won't be natural and you won't seem the same under another name." Mrs. Philbrick is our landlord's wife and I had been coming here for eleven summers before she married him.
[1892-09-08 (Wednesday) Bertha (Rye Beach) to Henry (StL)]

E. KENNEBUNKPORT

Bertha left Rye Beach toward the end of July 1892 to visit her friend, Myra Lane, in Kennebunkport ME for several days.

Nonantum House

Myra met me at the station yesterday and she and Mrs. Ben Taussig rowed me up to the Nonantum House which is on the river though very near its outlet into the sea. Kennebunkport is not really as pretty as Magnolia but there is a great deal more to do. The river is a never-failing source of occupation and last evening, coming up in the sunset with the river covered with boats and canoes, with the girls in their summer gowns, and men in flannels, it was just as pretty as it could be. And the Lanes are the dearest family to visit. From Mr. Lane down to Beach, they all make you feel as if you were their own personal guest and a most welcome one. It is a great gift to be able to make one feel as comfortable and at home.

Myra looks very well and belies her reputation of not having been well, though she is still taking care of herself. She and Belle[120] and I rowed down to the village and back this morning. I tried to remember your riverside instructions but Belle was a much more severe critic than you are. K'port does not compare with Rye in beauty but I do envy them the river. I should like to be able to do some rowing; ...

We are going to row a long way up the river this evening and take our supper on picnic rock from which I believe there is supposed to be a very fine view of the country. Myra is to be the chaperon of the party.
[1892-07-21 Bertha (Kennebunkport ME) to Henry (StL)]

Kennebunkport

The day after her arrival, Bertha went on a canoe trip with Myra who had been asked to chaperon some sixteen and seventeen-year-old girls who were to be with boys a year or so older. It was clear that Bertha didn't much like this role, *"knowing we were regarded as antediluvian…"* But Bertha greatly enjoyed her time there and regretted having to leave so soon.

We had the most ideal time on that picnic yesterday. We were canoed six miles up the river to a most beautiful place in the woods. Beach[121] managed to run our canoe on some very sharp rocks once or twice so that it was leaking when we got there and the first thing we had to do was to roam the woods looking for pitch on the pines to fix it with.

Then we had supper on a bluff overhanging the river. We had devilled chicken sandwiches, doughnuts, watermelon, mince pie, bananas and marshmallows. And I ate them all! I don't mean all the marshmallows, but all the varieties of eatables.

After supper, Myra and I went off by ourselves. She had been asked to chaperon the party and I only because I was her friend, for the others were all girls of sixteen and seventeen and boys a year or two older. So knowing we were regarded as antediluvian, we went over to where a huge tree had been uprooted and fallen over and Myra sat up among the roots and I on the trunk at her feet while we watched the most gorgeous sunset over the river. I told Myra she made a picture of an ideal summer girl in her pretty gown and blazer and white cap with a visor, leaning back against those great roots. And so she did. I suppose we stayed there an hour and a half and she was guilty of the sentimental suggestion: would not this be absolute perfection if we only had our best young men here? I did not, of course, think anything could have made it pleasanter.

Then, when it grew pitch dark and the tide had turned so that we could go back with it, the boys lighted Chinese lanterns and hung them at the prow of the canoes (if canoes have a prow) and we

[120] Belle Lane was Myra Lane's sister in law.
[121] John Beach Lane (1875-1972) was Myra's brother in law, the brother of her husband, Nat Lane.

went back. Our canoe was the last and the boats ahead with their gay lanterns made the prettiest effect. And to crown it all, we had the most magnificent display of the northern lights. This seems to be a fine year for them.

I am in love with Kennebunkport. I think it unites more advantages than any seashore place I ever stayed at. And I am having the most gorgeous time. I shall leave here Saturday with the utmost regret. But I shall leave, though they asked me to stay until next Tuesday. Myra says "Some summer we'll take a cottage here together, Bert, & we'll have a lovely time, Nat and Henry & you and I."

...

Myra Lane is certainly one of the sweetest women I know and I don't wonder Nat sits up and worships the ground she walks on. She sends you her very best love - the way in which girls feel privileged to send you messages for that kind, now, is perfectly amazing. I must say goodbye now. Shall I add myself to the list of girls and send you my very best love?
[1892-07-22 (Thursday) Bertha (Kennebunkport, ME) to Henry (Wichita)]

I am very sorry my visit is drawing to a close. I have enjoyed every minute of it and I am more convinced all the time that this is the nicest sea shore place I ever stayed at. Bar Harbor is of course far more beautiful but I would just as soon stay at home as live the life they do at Bar harbor and Newport. I like the climate better than I do Marion, Mattapoisett or any of those places on the south shore of Cape Cod, and there is more to do than there is at Rye or Magnolia. More to do and less formality. You can live in your blazer and cap from early morn until dewy eve and the same dress every day. But it is distinctly a young people's place. Mrs. Lane pines for the comforts and civilization of Magnolia and I know mother would not stay here a day.
[1892-07-23 Bertha (Kennebunkport PO) to Henry (Stl or Wichita)]

F. THE SHEPLEYS & LIONBERGERS IN MARION MA

Bertha went to visit the Shepleys and Lionbergers in Marion Massachusetts for several days at the end of August 1892. (Marion is a very small town approximately 50 miles south of Boston.) The following was Bertha's account of one afternoon.

[drawing] This is a kiss from Jack[122] made by himself with much difficulty.

...

I am writing this somewhat under difficulties as I am setting in what is supposed to be the rear car of a train and Jack demands my ticket every other second. It is rather a stormy day and we are confined to the house and have just finished an exciting duplicate game of baseball in which Nan and I acted as batters with tennis rackets, Jack and Peg[123] were pitchers and Winston Churchill[124], stretched full length upon the ground, acted as catcher and fielder for both sides. Uncle Jack[125] was enthusiastic audience, umpire and referee. The latter does not look very well, I think, though they all declare he is much stronger. He went peacefully off to sleep on the sofa last night at about half past eight and he looked like a tired boy of sixteen but, by daylight and awake, he looks both old and worn. He has just departed to the village to see Sarah[126] despite the weather, strange as such indifference to outward circumstances may seem. Jack gave utterance to one of the most sentimental sentences I ever heard from the lips of man yesterday and from him it was especially funny. [1892-08-27 (Saturday) Bertha (Marion MA) to Henry (StL)]

---

[122] John Shepley Lionberger ("Little Jack") (1889-1966)

[123] Margaret Lionberger ("Peg") (1889-1963)

[124] Winston Churchill (November 10, 1871 – March 12, 1947) was an American best-selling novelist of the early 20th century. In 1906 he unsuccessfully sought the Republican nomination for governor of New Hampshire.

[125] John ("Jack") Foster Shepley (1858-1930)

[126] Sarah Hitchcock (1870-1957). Married Jack Shepley in 1893, the year after this summer.

Henry responded to Bertha's letter that he was not keen on women playing baseball.

Your "busy day" Wednesday did not excite my admiration as you imaged it would, dear, for apart from the fact that it is not a mark of one's wisdom to try one's energies and tax one's strength merely because one may for the time being feel perfectly well, I entirely agree with your brother about the wisdom of young ladies refraining from games which are usually left to men. This no doubt sounds very disagreeable, dear, and I don't mean to be that. But I will be frank and say very positively that I don't think baseball very elegant amusement for girls, especially when there are people looking on who may not know the young ladies well enough to understand. Well I shall not provoke a defense from you and I think I shall reserve my opinion as you are apt to think it less reasonable than I do and, at any rate, I am not particularly pleased with any of my notions or opinions today. A bad headache generally gives me a most humble opinion of myself and this one is sufficiently effective to have taken away quite a large part of my normal supply of pride and obstinacy.
[1892-08-29 (Monday) Henry (StL) to Bertha (Farragut House)]

While in Marion, Bertha developed a great fondness for little Jack.

Henry, you ought to have been there with us. I mean all the time. I wanted you and we would have had a good time. O, we would. Even my precious Jack was a poor substitute, dear little lad! I told him I was going and he informed me "Jack will go with you, Aunty Bert!" And really believed he was until the last minute. Of all my nieces and nephews, Tom, Fick(?) and Mildred included, there is not one I care about as I do for him. He is not like other children at all. I took a picture of Nan carrying Jack on her back yesterday and then they pranced off on their way to Julie while I shut up the camera. I saw a "halt" called but I did not know the reason until I caught up and a very soft whisper told me that "Jack wouldn't leave you behind for anything", so afraid my feelings would be hurt.
[1892-08-31 (Monday) Bertha (Rye Beach) to Henry (StL)]

Henry knew of Bertha's very intimate relationship with the Shepley women and did not doubt that the *"affairs of men and things"* would surely be adjusted by their opinions.

Your control over the weather does not seem as absolute as it has been and I am afraid the stormy days at Marion prevented your enjoying your visit as greatly as would have been the case had you been able to go out more. Still I cannot think of you and "those Shepleys" having a very poor time together no matter how badly the weather may behave and the days indoors were no doubt turned to most profitable account through your mutual exchange of confidences and also I have not the slightest doubt in the adjustment of all the affairs of men and things which in the opinion of that tribunal of three required attention.
[1892-09-02 (Thursday 1892-09-01) Henry (StL) to Bertha (Farragut House)]

G. THE DRAKES STAY IN BOSTON FOR THE FALL 1892

The Drakes remained in the east for the remainder of the year and principally in Boston where they resided at the Brunswick Hotel from September through early December. Although Bertha did return to St. Louis for approximately two weeks to attend the Howard Elliott and Janet January wedding on October 12, 1892, the principal task for the Drakes was to find a house near Boston for the winter.

You ask me to tell you of our plans for the winter and indeed I will as soon as I know them myself. The difficulty is in finding a house. But we shall be in or near Boston. So far, when people have asked me when my family will be at home, I have simply said that mother has been forbidden to go west until really cold weather sets in. She suffered so much from malaria last year, which statement is perfectly true. But I think by the time I come out, I shall be able to tell not only you but anyone who is interested of our arrangements. I don't look forward to the winter very enthusiastically,

dear. I would rather talk of that lovely time which is nearer at hand, my own visit home. It is now fully settled that I am to come with the Shepleys and we will probably start the twenty eighth of September. We are going by way of Chicago in order to see Julia and her baby safely home and be in St. Louis the morning of the first of October. And I shall stay until the day after Janet's wedding.
[1892-08-31 (Tuesday) Bertha (Rye Beach) to Henry (StL)]

1. ANOTHER FALL AND WINTER APART

Bertha realized that her staying away from St. Louis would be a big disappointment for Henry, as well as it was to herself.

We have been searching diligently for houses in Newton, Longwood, etc., but found none that suited, so yesterday the family decided to take a suite of rooms at the Brunswick for the winter. You said they would do this last year but I did not believe you and I did everything I could to prevent it. I feel more badly about it because I think, in spite of the fact that you did expect it somewhat, it will be a disappointment to you as well as to me. I don't believe I have got myself enough in hand to talk about it yet, so I will write about other things. Only I am very very sorry, dear. I looked up promising advertisements and dragged the family out to inspect them but there really was nothing very nice or comfortable.

...

Dear, I did not mean to imply that I was the only member of my family interested in getting a house. For it was a very great disappointment to my mother that we could find nothing suitable. The rooms here are much pleasanter than those we had before: on the ground floor with a very pretty little private parlor & perhaps it may be better for her. The summer has not been nearly so beneficial as we hoped, the last month she has been very unwell, though I hope the change to the mountain air will do her good. But she ought not to have any care or worry of any kind and at the same time, she needs entertainment. It would not do for her to be at some of those places where she has no friends and no convenient way of getting into town. That was the great drawback. There was one house, I think, we should have taken but it was a mile from either station or electric train.
[1892-09-17 (Friday) Bertha (Brunswick Hotel, Boston) to Henry (StL)]

Henry seemed to take the news of the Drakes remaining in the east for the remainder of the year quite well. He wrote that he was not surprised by the *"determination"* of Bertha's parents and that Bertha should not worry.

My darling child,

I shall try to return the help you gave me last week when I was so tired and worn by cheering you this morning. If I can summon the art to put in a letter what I want to say, I shall be sure of doing some good, for no woman could fail to receive some comfort from one for whom she cared, if he could make her see such love and pride and happiness in her pure, strong life as I have for you today my beloved.

The determination of your family was no surprise to me. You must have known that, dear. All along it seemed clear to me they had no fixed or well-defined purpose ahead and I waited patiently to be informed that you would spend another winter at the Brunswick. And, if you were not very blue and disappointed, dear, I should boast of my very superior discerning powers and point the finger of warning at you, to make you repose that blissful and implicit confidence in your future lord which will save you such disappointments in future. But, dearest, you are made sad by this turn in the family plans and that makes, what I would have passed over as trivial, a serious matter. So I am going to tell you why you should not worry about the winter at the Brunswick.

Let me see. There are so many reasons I hardly know just where to begin. I am almost tempted to number them as the diviners do in the knock-down arguments which usually bring up the rear in the ordinary exhortations one hears for the pulpits of the dissenters. In the first place, dear, I don't believe you would have as pleasant a winter in one of the suburbs of Boston as in the city proper and certain am I that I should see less of you than at the Brunswick. To which I wish you to know I am much attached by associations about which I shall tell you nothing until you acknowledge that it is not half so stupid as your letter pictures it.

Don't you think too, dear, that the little shopping and preparations you will want to attend to can be better done if you are in the city? Then think of those lovely things we saw at the theater in Boston. You would weep, I know, if you found the distance in to town were so great that, when I came, I could not take you to see "1492"! And think of – O, think of Bunker Hill!!

Dear, all this nonsense would be ignoring the fact that you are distressed at abandoning the idea of the house in the suburbs if it did not show you that it really seems a little matter to me. The real reason I cannot be greatly troubled by it, dear, and you must not think I overlook some of the disagreeable results of your remaining at a hotel until we are married, dearest, - indeed, I have thought of all that – is because the day has been left far behind that could bring any serious trouble to me when made so rich and proud in the love of the bravest, truest woman that God ever made. No, this must not be cause for sorrow and disappointment, my darling. Keep your promise bravely and faithfully, and, dear, I really believe these little troubles will help you to bear with the many faults you will find in my life.

If everything had gone perfectly smoothly with us, dear, you might have expected more of me – more perfect rest in the new life just a little beyond us and soon to be realized, dear, than it would have been in my power to give you. Don't you see, dear, how the little sorrows and vexing cares increase my power to help and comfort, my darling? We could not care so much if we did not need each other so, my own beloved, my wife. For you are as much my wife as if we had always lived with and for each other. You have made me forget sorrow and trouble very often, dear. Can I hope that I have once at least done as much for you?

Yours always,
Henry
[1892-09-19 (Monday) Henry (StL) to Bertha (The Ark, E. Jaffrey)]

2. RETURN TO THE BRUNSWICK

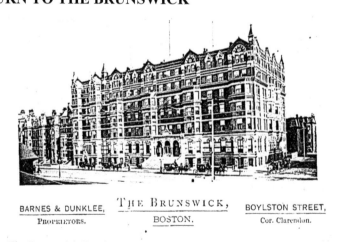

BARNES & DUNKLEE, PROPRIETORS.   THE BRUNSWICK, BOSTON.   BOYLSTON STREET, Cor. Clarendon.

The Brunswick Hotel

During their stay at the Brunswick Hotel, Bertha had a chance meeting with a new mother with child who was left stranded at the Brunswick by her working husband. This led Bertha to warn Henry about trying to make a business home in Wichita.

> *I have just been talking to a very forlorn girl. I have meant to speak to her for some time but other things have taken up my attention lately. She and her husband sit at the next table to us and she is very attractive looking and has a dear baby about eight months old that I see in the halls sometimes. I thought she seemed lonely and tonight I began to talk to her and discovered, poor thing, that she was pining for a girl to talk to. She is about three years younger than I, I should judge from her speaking of a Farmington mate of mine: "O yes, I knew her slightly, but she was married and went away the year I came out." She came from Washington where she knows everyone and is in everything, to Boston where she doesn't know anyone. Her husband was offered a good position here and a few of his business acquaintances have called on her, that is all. Next year, they expect to keep house but this year they thought it better to board. So here she is at the hilarious Brunswick and he is away most of the day. Poor child! Henry, I hope your prospects in Wichita are not such that you will begin to think it necessary to live out there to look after them. I told her I thought she was in luck to be exiled to Boston but she did not seem to see it.*
> [1892-11-26 (Friday) Bertha (Backbay Boston) to Henry (StL)]

In a December letter to Henry, Bertha described the unfortunate result of using "soft coal" which apparently produces lots of smoke. (The things that we can learn from the past!)

> *We are having a heavy snow storm here & I am housed in consequence having added slightly to my cold yesterday. No, not by going out, Grandpa, I will tell you how, as thereby hangs a tale and some instructions about the house. At dinner time, I changed my cloth dress for a thinner one as I usually do. And, the room seeming a little chilly, mother told the fireman to put on a little soft coal to make a little warmer fire but not too much of one. Well, when we came back from dinner, the room was filled with smoke. It seems that chimney won't carry soft coal and the regular fireman knew but he was off duty and a new hand had done it. Well, the fire had to be all put out, the windows opened and, in the melee, I took fresh cold. And the room was covered with soot. It was a job to get it clean! It was this that led mother to advise me to "tell Mr. Scott" that it would be a wise thing to have the chimneys all tried to see if they drew perfectly and likewise to see if they had been cleaned, for a couple of hours of a smoking chimney would take all the first freshness of everything there! Now, I won't say house again in this letter for you must be tired of hearing it.*
>
> *...*
> *I wish I had you here this afternoon, the snow is just whirling outside and there is a cozy fire inside and it is almost time to light the gas. Don't you think we could have rather a pleasant talk?*
> [1892-12-01 (Wednesday) Bertha (BackBay, Boston) to Henry (StL)]

Bertha was very aware of the people around her and seemed well able to discern the worthy from the "*the abomination of desolation*".

> *I have just finished a note declining a luncheon invitation next week from Luly Abbott, horrid girl! They live on Commonwealth Avenue and her mother is an old friend of mother's and a very attractive old lady, but Luly is unto me the abomination of desolation mentioned in Daniel the Prophet. I never could bear her and two years ago she justified my opinion of her. She was engaged to a very nice fellow, very rich too. He lost his money and she discovered her feeling for him had not been what she thought it and broke her engagement. There were men in town, Charlie Coolidge among them, who said the man was in luck to lose his money.*
> [1892-12-10(?) (Sunday) Bertha (Newton Centre MA) to Henry (StL)]

3. FINDING THEIR WINTER HOUSE

The Drakes managed to find the Pulsifer's house, called "Stancote", in Newton Massachusetts which was offered for rent starting in December. It was in this house that Bertha and Henry would be married.

> *Mrs. Pulsifer wrote mother this morning saying she and Mr. Pulsifer want to go to California for the winter and the trouble in the way has been getting their house taken care of. And, if we would rent it, servants and all, it would be just what they wanted. And, O Henry, it is just what we want. It is in the prettiest part of the prettiest of the Newtons - not a large house - in lovely grounds and you are only one block from the station and the trains run in and out every hour. You know it is the same road Riverside is on, only Newton is nearer Boston. And everything is in beautiful order for us just to take possession and then mother can see if it's the climate and life she likes. It is just what she has always dreamed of and there is the most beautiful room where we could be married, dear, or else in the little country church. You don't know how I dreaded having my wedding from a hotel but I might have known things don't just happen. It is all just what I most wanted. Please don't speak of all this just yet for father and Mr. Pulsifer have to talk things over and, naturally, we don't want things discussed until everything is settled. I think we cannot have it until December though, so perhaps when you come on for your visit I shall still be at the Brunswick. But perhaps that will be even more convenient. You won't mind anyway because you are the best and kindest friend a woman ever had and the truest helper. I am so glad today and so thankful.*
> [1892-09-22 (Wednesday) Bertha (Jaffrey NH) to Henry (StL)]

Bertha later confirmed that the Drakes were to take possession of the Pulsifer house in mid-December. "*We are to have possession of the Pulsifer house on the tenth of December, probably, certainly between that and the seventeenth. And it is everything that can be desired.*" [1892-10-26 (Wednesday) Bertha (Boston, MA) to Henry (StL)]

4. BOSTON MEMORIES

Bertha and Henry had many experiences individually and together in Boston. These are a few of their accounts.

> *George Shepley sent me a message to the effect that, if I galloped so madly through the suburbs of Boston, he really would not like to be responsible for the damage caused by runaways. It seems he saw Snowball in one of her mad careers up hill and, though I went by too fast for him to recognize, he knew you when you followed.*
> [1892-05-03 Bertha (Back Bay, Boston--) to Henry (StL)]

On a drive through Boston with her mother, Bertha recalled being with Henry through these remembered streets.

> *Mother and I took a drive afterward and I discovered one of the places where you and I must have made a wrong turn for it took you and me a long time to get home from this spot and our driver did it in very brief time. But I am glad it did take us a long time. I wish it had taken us longer. Every step of the ground we went over today you have given an association for – or no, not quite all. Our driver took us through one or two of the places you wanted to go into so much, saying they were show places and people were allowed both to drive and walk through. I never saw anything to compare with them except some places in England. And then he drove us home through a part of Brookline that we missed, past the Richardson place and the Country Club where the races were going on. It is a pity you did not see the latter; you might have compared it with the one at home.*
> [20180308-1 (1892-05-30(-)Bertha (Backbay Boston) to Henry (StL)]

When Bertha wrote to Henry of the places that they had been to together in Boston, Henry's remembrances of them also returned.

> *Dear, I had a queer, abused feeling this morning when I thought of your return to Boston and that you were so near many of the beautiful spots of which you have given me memories that I think will always stand out very clear and beautiful. I thought of four rides through Cambridge, of our drives and rides through Newton and Milton and Brookline and, you may imagine, dear, I did not fail to recall those beautiful days at Riverside. It makes me blue almost to think of the loss I sustain these days because of this distance that lies between us.*
> [1892-09-13 (Tuesday) Henry (StL) to Bertha (The Brunswick Hotel, Boston)]

The sensation of shared memories was expressed by Bertha, her feelings being very much the same as Henry. *"I feel very kindly affectioned to you today for some reason or other. Possibly because everything about Boston brings you so vividly to my mind."* [1892-09-14 (Tuesday) Bertha (Backbay, Boston) to Henry (StL)]

However, Boston did have its drawbacks: it was loud and hot, in stark contrast to the country.

> *You cannot imagine the restful sensation it is to be here. Boston was horrid. It was still warm, too warm to have one's windows closed and the rattle that arose through those open windows was simply deafening, especially after the quiet at Rye. Then the city was crowded with people on their way home, the shops thronged with them, everything was dusty.*
> [1892-09-29 (Sunday) Bertha (The Ark, East Jaffrey) to Henry (StL)]

5. A TRIP TO HILTON MA

In November, Bertha took a short trip to Hilton Massachusetts, a town near Boston, to visit the Lewises. The trip itself was not particularly remarkable; however, Bertha's account of meeting Ross Turner at the Lewises was special as was Bertha's closing sentiments.

> *I had a lovely time at the Lewises. Hilton is a beautiful place in the same mountainous country as Jaffrey though nearer Boston and they have a lovely place there. There the air was gorgeously clear and bracing, the views magnificent, the sunlight on the yellow leaves (the red ones were all gone) most exquisite, and Ross Turner was there, the watercolor artist. You know him by reputation of course and I have never met a more absolutely fascinating man: handsome, brilliant, original, and a man of the world in the most charming sense of the phrase. I told Mrs. Lewis this morning after he went that my heart was gone and she said "It seems to have been reciprocated. He told me four separate times yesterday a propos of nothing, how charming he thought you." A man of fine appreciation, you observe. Alas, there is a Mrs. Turner and a Henry Scott but then neither of them were there.*

Ross Turner, The Mussel Gatherers, 1879

> *Seriously, though, I think you would have been as delighted as I. He was so quick and so responsive and so clever. The Lewises tried to make me stay the rest of the week and, as I would not, demanded that you and I should spend a day or two at least with them next summer. If this goes on, you and*

I will have no time for Canada: two invitations within a week and the way they accept you on faith is amazing. People must think I have very good taste but they don't know.

We drove and drove - such gorgeous drives - and that whiff of mountain air made me feel like a new creature.
...
One thing I need not tell my dearest friend is, that whenever he comes, I shall be so glad, O so very, very glad to see him.
[1892-11-01 (Monday) Berth (Boston) to Henry (StL)]

Bertha's preceding letter was written three months before her wedding, during a year when Bertha had scarcely seen Henry. As Bertha wrote: "*whenever he comes, I shall be so glad, O so very, very glad to see him.*"

CHAPTER 12 – THE ENGAGEMENT

O, Henry, my best friend, I am writing nonsense to you as usual and the thought deep down in my heart tonight is that I thank God for having brought us together.
[1892-07-18 Bertha (Rye Beach) to Henry (Ft. Worth)]

... never before have I felt such deep recognition of the governing hand that has wrought all these changes and I wished that I knew how to thank God for bringing you into my life.
[1892-08-05 Henry (StL) to Bertha (Farragut House, Rye Beach)]

H. THE GOVERNING HAND

"You do not know how beautiful it is to me to think that there is such happiness in the world."
[Bertha quoting her friend, Miss Hagen, 1892-06-12]

Was it fate that Henry should find Bertha in St. Louis and that the two should find their true love? True love often seems like a distant dream but perhaps it is not always so distant. Years after Bertha and Henry were married, Henry spoke in New York City regarding the work to complete St. John the Divine Cathedral. His words at this occasion also seem relevant here: *"Let down your anchor where you are."*

There is a story told of a coasting vessel which was going out to sea from the great Amazon River. It was found when just outside the river's mouth that the ship's supply of fresh water had become exhausted. A heavy gale was sweeping the small craft out to sea in spite of its crew's frantic efforts to put back into the river to obtain fresh water, without which those aboard the little vessel must perish. The captain, sweeping the horizon line with his glass saw a passing ship and sent it a distress signal. Back came the answer, "Let down your anchor where you are." The small vessel, though far from land, was not outside the freshwater lien of the great river's mouth and the needed relief was within easy reach.
[20180803-5 Henry(-)]

During the summer before they were married, Bertha and Henry had a great deal of time to reflect on their past and to consider their futures together. In many of their letters, there is an understanding of their imperfections but an even stronger sense of a deeper purpose. In the following, although Bertha wrote that knowledge only comes in *"by sad experience"*, she concluded: *"I thank God for having brought us together."*

I must thank you, my dearest, for one of the letters I found waiting. They are all dear to me but this ought to help me to be a better woman. Dear, your faith in me almost frightens me sometimes. You think me so much better than I am. But, my darling, you cannot think I love you better than I do. I felt almost tonight, when I got back to my own room and read your three letters, as if I were having a little visit with you after having been away a long time and I was so glad to get back and have you to myself. I don't like to talk about you very much or to hear even very dear friends talk much about you and they have a good deal these last few days. Not that I did not enjoy my visit for I did most thoroughly and it was so nice to talk to someone who was really sympathetically enthusiastically interested in all the plans about the house and everything. But Mattie says very truly that you have a sad awakening ahead of you, "for you really know less than any of us did, Bert, you have not had a bit of experience and Henry just sits up and thinks you know everything."

Now, dear old boy, I wish you would note, for what she says is true. Mother never would let me do anything and, even when she was ill, Wilma (our cook), having lived with us seventeen years, knew how to manage as well as mother did and I have had no experience at all. And if you think the knowledge comes in anyway except by sad experience, you are mistaken. And another great trial in store for me is that all my friends, instead of sympathizing with me, all take your part. You saw how Nan behaved in Boston and Mattie does the same thing. I don't know what is to become of me. I shall have to fall back on Will Stribling; I think he might think you were wrong sometimes.

O, Henry, my best friend, I am writing nonsense to you as usual and the thought deep down in my heart tonight is that I thank God for having brought us together.
[1892-07-18 (Friday) Bertha (Rye Beach) to Henry (Ft. Worth)]

Henry was elated with the certainty of his marriage to Bertha, making him *"the vainest, most stuck up ... man in this or any other country."* As to Bertha's worries about her faults, without them, Henry wrote, *"you never could bear with mine."*

Dear, when I had read your letters through this morning, I felt strong enough and confident enough to undertake anything, however difficult, and I serve notice upon you now that you are the direct cause of my being the vainest, most stuck up (I use slang because I know how much you like it) man in this or any other country; and why shouldn't I? Have I not won you, my darling, and is not that more than any other man can accomplish? And let me tell you, dear, you are not to mind the foolish things Mattie and the other girls say to you, for I don't expect any such ridiculous perfection as they credit me with looking forward to. If they mean that I know, I don't think anything about it - you are the sweetest, gentlest, dearest woman in the world - they understand me perfectly. But if they mean that I think you will make no mistakes, I would like for them to tell me how I ever expect you to sympathize with all the fruitless efforts of my life, with all my mistakes and short comings. Why, my darling, that's the beautiful thing about our love, our friendship. I don't wish you to be free from faults, for if you were, you never could bear with mine, and I have a great many, dear, and then, too, we never could live in such sympathy or work together as we shall, all through our lives, my darling.

...

No, dear, we will make a great many mistakes and we can't expect not to have our share of troubles but that is the sweet part of it all to me, my darling: you will make me so much more patient, so much stronger to deal with disappointments, that when they come, dear, I shall forget them as soon as they have been dealt with. For the happy house you will give me will be too many and they will come too often for me to waste more time on the disappointments I must anticipate, in spite of all your love and care, than is required to wake them as light to my darling as my power to shield her will give me.
[1892-07-20 Henry (Ye Arlington Inn, Ft. Worth TX) To Bertha (Rye Beach, NH]

In a letter to Bertha two weeks later, Henry reflected on the past and wrote that, compared with the love that had entered his life, *"I have nothing before me worth remembering."* Henry also wondered at all of the changes and events that brought Bertha and him together: *"never before have I felt such deep recognition of the governing hand that has wrought all these changes."*

Do you know, dear, one of the things that I greatly feel the loss of is some knowledge of you when you were a child. No one has spoken to me about you then and I do not know many persons who knew you when you were a little girl so I have no help in the attempts I often make to bring you before me as a child. You must remember what I have lost in this way, dear, and some day you must try to recall more of the incidents of your childhood and give them to me.
The date of your first unhappy experience in driving your seventh birthday nineteen years ago, caused me to do some reminiscing on my own account and I tried to remember some event in my life in that year[127]. But, apart from the fact that I wore an officer's sword and uniform that year for the first time as the insignia of my Cadet captaincy at school and thought myself on this account quite the most important individual in the world, I have nothing before me worth remembering. I then began to wonder at the many and great changes which became necessary in your life and mine

[127] Henry was 14 years old in that year, 1873.

to make it possible for us to have been brought together and never before have I felt such deep recognition of the governing hand that has wrought all these changes and I wished that I knew how to thank God for bringing you into my life.
[1892-08-05 Henry (StL) to Bertha (Farragut House, Rye Beach)]

Three days before the one-year anniversary of their engagement when Bertha was in a particularly reflective mood, she wrote to Henry about their engagement and her feelings back then and at the present: *"I felt ... that my struggle with myself was over. It seemed almost as if I had laid my own responsibility aside and had left it in someone else's hands."* This feeling of peace, Bertha concluded, was *"because her hand is clasped in God's."*
Farragut House, Rye Beach
Monday

My dearest,
I have your Friday letter and I am glad beyond measure that you are going away to get those few day's rest and change. I was very much afraid you would change your mind at the last minute. It is strange how you and I think of the same persons and things at the same times. I often notice too how your mood corresponds to mine in letters written on the same day.

I was sorry at first I could not manage to see Helen [at the Shoals]. I had rather a fancy to go over to spend next Thursday, the day I expect you to get this letter, dear, and now I shall be at Marion on that day. But after all, it would have been a lonely trip to take alone. I would rather go some other summer.

Can you guess why I wanted to spend Thursday there? The date will correspond to one engraved inside my ring[128]. I have been recalling all the incidents of that day. Anne and I drove over to Portsmouth on the stage, Nan enlivening the way with a discussion as to the iniquity of a girl's yielding her own individual rights too entirely to her family – a purely abstract discussion. Then we sailed over and I saw you on the landing. Nan said afterwards that she was not in the least surprised that it seemed to her as if she had known it all along. I did not feel that. I was surprised so much so that I felt faint for a moment.

Afterward, when we went for that walk, I felt as we started that my struggle with myself was over. It seemed almost as if I had laid my own responsibility aside and had left it in someone else's hands. I have always had that feeling about that day, dear. It is quite different from any other of my life, as if in the midst of all my own trying and struggling to bring things about, do the thing that would be right for all, a stronger will than mine had put all the puzzles aside and had marked a path for a little way which I had nothing to do but follow. It was that day which made me understand that sentence in the "Little Minister" about the safety of a woman's doing right at that time "because her hand is clasped in God's." That feeling stayed with me all day.

Nan and I hardly spoke on the way home and everything was so still. It was a gray day, if you remember, the sky was overcast and the water was like polished steel with hardly a ripple. And there was not a doubt or a question in my mind, I never had felt so absolutely at rest. I lost that afterward, you know, and had all sorts of doubts and questions that I ought not to have had and made you suffer a great deal and suffered a little myself, but that is over. I don't want to go back to that today. Take all that the year has had in it and has it not been a beautiful one?

---

[128] August 25, 1891, the date of the "second" proposal when Bertha finally resolved to marry Henry.

Henry, dear friend, the more I see and know of other's lives, the more I know that what has been hard for us has been more than made up, that our happiness is much greater than that of others who to the outside world seem to have had the easier time.

I don't think I can write anymore. I meant to write you a long letter but there are some things one cannot write and I cannot talk about frivolous things today.

God bless you, my own.
Yours always,
Bert
[1892-08-22 Bertha (Farragut House, Rye Beach) to Henry]
("*[T]here was not a doubt or a question in my mind, I never had felt so absolutely at rest*".)

The many letters that Bertha and Henry wrote during 1892 before their wedding not only revealed their need to be together but also their steadfast faith in the "*governing hand*" that had united them.

I. THE ANNOUNCEMENT & CONGRATULATIONS

There are times when I am quite convinced that you are the best friend any girl ever had and today is one of them.
[1892-01-31 Bertha (Newton Centre, MA) to Henry (StL)]

Bertha's engagement to Henry was announced in early February 1892. Bertha's parents had taken her back east so the announcement was made when Bertha and Henry were apart. Over their lives, Bertha and Henry would have to get used to not being together on many important occasions. There was no official date for the announcement since Bertha wanted to let her closest friends and relatives hear the news from her first. But the news leaked out and spread quickly so Bertha was unable to announce the news as she wished. Bertha reprimanded Henry, "*You did not lose anytime about telling people, did you? I confess to a little surprise at the rapidity with which the news was told.*" [1892-03-07 Bertha (St. Augustine FL) to Henry (StL)]

Henry responded: "*You hurt me, dear, in what you say of the announcement of our engagement. I spoke of it the evening you left to Mattie and to Miss Hildegarde[129]. The next day I told Mary and some of my older friends. Since then I have answered the inquiries of my friends without evasion. Did you wish otherwise?*"
[1892-03-05(-) 20170828-3 Henry to Bertha]

Bertha tried to smooth things over in her next letter:
> *... you said in your Wednesday letter that you were hurt by what I said of the announcement of our engagement. I did not mean to hurt you, dear. I was a little annoyed that the news had spread so quickly, for I had given Nan special messages to certain people whom I wanted to have hear it first, but I did not blame you for that. It is the nature of such news to fly and I am very glad now that everyone does know it.*
> [1892-03-13 Bertha (St. Augustine) to Henry (StL)]

In a later letter to Henry, Bertha confided that she was glad that she was not in St. Louis when their engagement was announced. "*Henry, dear old boy, do you know I am rather glad I was not at home when my engagement was announced.*" Bertha did not need or want all of the attention. [1892-07-14 Bertha (Magnolia MA) to Henry (StL)]

---

[129] Mattie - Mary Martha McKittrick Stribling, married Will Stribling in 1889; Hildegarde Sterling McKittrick married Mattie's brother, Tom McKittrick in 1888; Mary McKittrick Markham, the sister of Mattie and Tom, married George Markham in 1902.

As soon as the word of their engagement was out, Bertha and Henry received numerous congratulations. Alma Sterling wrote to Henry:

> *Hildegarde's letter containing the splendid news has this moment reached me, and I write at once to offer my heartiest and sincerest congratulations. The words sound so formal but in my heart I am saying harrah! I am so happy and delighted. I love her dearly and I know the story will be "and happy ever after that", so of course I am delighted.*
> [1892-03-03 Alma Sterling to Henry]

Louise Richards Allen wrote to Bertha of her hopes that Henry would be "good enough" for her.

> *Mr. Scott will have to be an archangel to live up to our idea of a man good enough for you. I hope I shall know him better someday, for everyone says he is such a splendid fellow and in every way worthy of his good fortune.*
> [1892-03-06 Louise Richards Allen to Bertha

Especially during the time after the announcement of their engagement, Henry was generally very self-effacing and even admitted to not being the "archangel" that Mrs. Allen was hoping for.

> *I am sorry you will be compelled to prompt Mrs. Allen with the disappointing announcement that, so far from my being what she thinks I should be to deserve the happiness you have given me, you have my own confession in "black and white" that I am not even one of the lesser angels. Perhaps though she will understand that I could not be as proud of you or as happy as I am if I felt I in the least degree deserved you.*
> [20170823-6 (1892-06--) Henry to Bertha]

Bertha understood how difficult it would be to be married to an archangel. During the summer, when she became impatient and angry over a waylaid post, she wrote to Henry about her frustration about a telegram that had been sent to her from Mattie Stribling inquiring whether Bertha would like to visit her in Magnolia, Massachusetss. The telegram was waylaid by "some clerk" and Bertha did not get to see Mattie then.

> *Last night if you had been here, you would have changed your mind about my not being able to get angry. Perhaps you have done so already but you did tell me once in a moment of delirium that you did not think I knew how. But, I put it to you, if it was not an exasperating case.*

> *Last evening, I received a telegram by mail. It had been telegraphed to the Brunswick, which had mailed it to Jaffrey, <u>although we had been in the hotel that very morning on our way to Rye</u>. I suppose some clerk had directed it who did not know we had been there. The Jaffrey people had directed it here but, as no mail goes out from there on Sunday, it did not reach me until last evening, July fourth. It was dated Magnolia, June twenty ninth, and was from Mattie Stribling asking me to come there for the rest of the week and stay over the fourth with her. And I know the reason. I was asked then was because Mary McKittrick[130] was away and they had her room free, for their cottage has not unlimited space, so they are not likely to repeat the invitation. And I do want to see a girl from home so badly and specially Mattie. Just think how much she could tell me about the house!! Was it not enough to exasperate a saint? At least, I don't think I should like to know the saint it would not have exasperated.*

> *I am so very glad, my son, that you are not a saint or even an archangel. For you never would be able to sympathize with earthly annoyances. Gertrude Dillon says Mr. Macdonald is one and I am very sorry for her.*
> [1892-07-06 (Tuesday) Bertha (Rye Beach) to Henry (StL)]

---

[130] Mary McKittrick was Mattie McKittrick Stribling's sister.

Lucy Bent[131] and her fiancé, Crittenden McKinley, each wrote to Henry and Bertha to congratulate them.

In acknowledging your kind note to me, I did not dream that I should so soon have the pleasure of congratulating you upon your engagement which I have hoped for. I admire Miss Drake so much and have so enjoyed knowing her better that I can ... heartily congratulate you, feeling that happiness in your future is assured. And yet, I quite realize that the good fortune is not all yours. You have as much admiration in my little household that this news was received with earnest interest, each one of us realizing that Miss Drake's good fortune is quite equal to your one. The kind wishes you expressed for my future I sincerely share for your own, hoping that in it we may all be better friends.
[1892-03-06 Lucy Bent (StL) to Henry (StL)]

Bertha wrote to Henry of Kin's (Crittenden McKinley) letter to her.

I must tell you I had a note of congratulation from Kin the other day. I am sure Lucy had told him he ought to do it. He apologized for not having written before on the score of his being "not much of a hand with his pen". But on the strength our future intimacy called me "Miss Bert" which, as he never ventured anything but the formal "Miss Drake" before, was thought lovely.
[1892-04-09 Bertha (Old Pt. Comfort, VA) to Henry (NYC)]

Will Stribling told Henry that he was to marry *"one of the finest women I have ever known."*

Mattie has just advised me of the announcement of your engagement to Miss Bertha. My dear fellow, I want to extend to you my heartiest congratulations. You have certainly great cause for thankfulness as you are to marry one of the finest women I have ever known. I have hoped for some time that this pleasant piece of news would be given out and it pleases me more than anything I have heard for many many days. Mattie seems about as much pleased as you can be. With best wishes for your happiness.
[1892-03-06 William Stribling to Henry]

Tom McKittrick wrote to Bertha and Henry:

Hurrah! Hurrah!! Hurrah!!! Another good man gone wrong but I haven't stopped hurrahing yet; and yours truly will here record that he is mighty pleased and that he will dance at the wedding in the most hilarious frame of mind possible. You ought not to have gone away however, as we are all ready to celebrate and cannot more than half do so without you.
[1892-03-07 Bertha (St. Augustine FL) to Henry – with the letter from Tom McKittrick]

Henry apparently wrote to Maggie Rollins, Henry's cousin, of his great fortune and Maggie repaid Henry with a very kind complement in her return letter.

After receiving your letter, I shall first have to scold you a little before congratulating. The idea of your deprecating yourself as some vulture who had seized upon its prey only to destroy it! I think Miss Drake will be quite as fortunate as Mr. Scott, thank you. In this affair and when I see her I shall tell her so. If there even was a man who deserved a sweet lovely woman to preside over his heart & home, you are the man. Have you not wasted all these years to deserve such a fate! And now, dear boy, I am glad you have met it, a thousand congratulations & good wishes. We all discussed your prospects, ... & ..., when I was in St. Louis and they all agreed that you would get a charming woman for a wife & that you deserved her. That charming face in the locket spoke volumes to me, I know all was well or it would not have been there.

If your life has been a happy one up to this time, you are fortunate. For I can reassure you that in the married state, there is happiness you have little dreamed of and far greater than any you have even felt. With your affectionate nature, you have your fortune in your own hands for any man who

[131] Crittenden McKinley ("Kin"), married Lucy Bent on April 19, 1892, just one month after she wrote this letter.

knows <u>how</u> to <u>love</u> a woman can make her happy. Be as considerate as a husband as I am sure you will be as a lover and all will be well. I shall feel much interest in knowing the date of your wedding and hope it is not far off for long engagements are the most wearing and trying of all things.

Cousin Marion wrote me of the announcement of your engagement about a week ago. She is so sweet and lovely in always remembering to write me of you all and what you are doing. I hope your mother is pleased, though she must feel sad at the thought of giving you up to someone else. Give my love to her and to all. Wishing you many years of unalloyed happiness, Henry, in which Mr. R joins me. I am yours lovingly,

Maggie R.

Papa thinks you deserve anything you ask in this life so you may be assured of his hearty approval.
[1892-03-09 Maggie (Columbia MO) to Henry]
("*That charming face in the locket spoke volumes to me, I know all was well or it would not have been there.*" Henry kept a locket with Bertha's picture, always close to him.)

Henry received very nice compliments from Helen Ernst and Gertrude Dillon.
Helen Ernst said she had telegraphed you her congratulations as soon as she heard of the engagement but not knowing your address had sent it to the St. Louis Club thinking you were a member. She also tenderly inquired if you wore your new clothes all the time now, for she said you had made yourself so gorgeous to behold the day I came over to the Shoals[132]. I will just mention in passing that I remember admiring that suit myself. Gertrude Dillon also sent you a message which I can assure you, I shall be very particular to deliver. She said she did not know you, but to tell you that "a very wise and discerning girl" had said she thought you "in danger of the jealously of the gods."
[1892-03-14 Bertha (Hotel Ponce de Leon, St. Augustine FL) to Henry]

Myra & Jane Tutt wrote:
No, Mr. Scott you need not say that we deserted you and left you when we came away to school. I think your mind was made up long before then and even if we had stayed at home you would have acted just the same way. Miss Drake is too sweet for anything and one of the very few people who are good enough for you. Now, please don't think this flattery for I mean it all in earnest because Jane and I are awfully fond of you and send you every good wish possible.
[1892-03-15 Myra Tutt (Dobbs Ferry NY) to Henry]

Miss Lupper sent an amusing message to Bertha which said that she thought Henry very "*presumptuous*" to think that he was "*good enough*" for Bertha. Bertha, of course, passed this message on to Henry.
I must give you a message Miss Lupper sent you. Miss Lupper was a very clever little old maid who came to the Ark, whom I played whist with so much. She was just as bright as she could be and a <u>most excellent</u> judge of character. You will see why I am so careful to tell you this when you receive the message. "I suppose" she said, as we were saying goodbye "that I shall never see Miss Drake again?" I told her I thought that was possible. "Well", she said, "if you come to New York on your wedding trip, you might send me your new card over to Brooklyn and I will come to see you. I know you will be so anxious to see me under those circumstances. However, I should like to see that young man who thinks he is good enough for you. The next time you write, you may tell him from me that your friends here think he is very presumptuous." I hope you do not think self-

---

[132] Henry proposed to Bertha on the Isles of the Shoals, after Helen Ernst arranged the tryst on August 25, 1892. Undoubtedly, Henry wanted to look his best on that occasion.

depreciation the great fault in my character. [1892-07-01 (Friday) Bertha (Rye Beach) to Henry (StL)]

Bertha received a compliment about Henry from Cherry Bent who spoke of Henry's "*astonishing*" knowledge of the hymnal. Bertha wondered at Henry's accomplishments and which of the two of them were being "*presumptuous*" in thinking that they were worthy to marry the other.

My dear Henry Clarkson, what a paragon I am engaged to! I humbly apologize for not having duly appreciated you before, you model of all the virtues!!

No, I am not going out of my mind or any little thing of that kind. I have only been talking to Cherry Bent for an hour. Mrs. Bent began it. Then she said she knew Cherry wished to talk to me and she left me whereupon Cherry took up the strain and, really, I am beginning to have serious doubts as to which one of us is the "presumptuous" one. How did you manage to produce such an effect! I thought I knew you pretty well but some of your accomplishments you have concealed from me.

For instance, Cherry said "I must tell you of our way in which Mr. Scott has had a good influence over me, though he does not know it. Sister said that he was not only so very well read, so well acquainted with all the poets, but that his knowledge of hymns was something astonishing. And the other day in church while I was waiting for service to begin, I thought of that and what a shame it was for me not to know more of them so I have begun learning hymns in my idle moments in church." Henry, this is truly touching. Why have you concealed this "astonishing knowledge" of yours so long from me?
[1892-07-01 (Saturday) Bertha (Rye Beach) to Henry (Wichita)]

Henry's responded to Bertha, tongue in cheek, about Miss Bent's ability to judge of character.
Well, when Miss Bent one evening was talking about the hymns of our church, I asked her about one or two of Dr. Watts' that I had learned at about four years of age, there finding that she knew less on this subject than about Ruskin. I took advantage of her ignorance, that's all. I wish it understood, though, that Miss Bent is mighty accurate and reliable when it comes to judging human character.
[1892-07-06 Henry (StL) to Bertha (Farragut House, Rye Beach)]

Just prior to their wedding when Henry was attending one of the St. Louis balls of the season, Henry was paid a very nice compliment from one of Bertha's friends which he related to Bertha.
You see I enjoyed my evening, darling. I might add that there were other things said to me by everyone I met that made me wish for the time to talk with everyone in the room. "Mr. Scott, you will see Bert very soon and we won't see her for a long time. And we don't like you very much for keeping her away, and please won't you bring her back very, very soon, and tell her we all miss her tonight, and that we shall be as glad to see her, as you are even, for we can't get along without her either."
[1893-02-04 (Saturday) Henry (StL) to Bertha (Stancote)]

J. THE ENGAGEMENT RING
Bertha was delighted with her engagement ring and was anxious for the day when she would be able to wear it.

I want to write to you - perhaps it is I who am foolish this time, about that ring. Just to tell you that I never did wear a ring on that finger from the time I spoke of until you gave me my own. I shall be glad not to do so again until the time when I not only own my ring but can wear it. You say that you are foolish. Well, perhaps, but, when you think I did that first just for my own feeling, don't you think it will be a dearer thing to me now that I know you notice and care. [1892-02-05(-) Bertha (StL) to Henry (StL)]

By June, Bertha was wearing her ring and clearly enjoyed telling Henry about the complements that she received.

She [Mrs. Catlin] and Mr. Catlin gave my engagement ring proper admiration too. You do not know how much that ring has been admired; so many people speak of the unusual beauty of the stone and I do not know how many from Mrs. Harry Bridge to Mrs. Will Wesselhoeft have told me it was the most beautiful engagement ring they have ever seen. I think people who do not know you really accept you on the strength of its beauty. They seem to think a man who has such good taste must necessarily be attractive. But that does not follow at all! Mrs. Harry Bridge has a very beautiful ring herself.
[1892-06-25 Bertha (The Ark, Jaffrey) to Henry (StL)]

When visiting Mattie Stribling and the McKittricks in Magnolia MA during the summer of 1892, Bertha was able to compare rings.

We compared rings, Hildegarde, Mattie and I, and mine was much the prettiest. Mattie's is very strikingly like mine, only the stone is a little smaller. She said Janet[133] compared hers to Mattie's one day and on finding hers was the smallest, said "Yours is bigger than mine, I won't play". And Mattie felt much the same way on matching with me. She says Mrs. January gave the casting vote, so to speak, about Janet's engagement. Janet could not make up her mind and her mother finally told her that as long as she cared for Mr. Elliott as much as she did and thoroughly respected him, she ought to accept him. This is strictly between ourselves, of course. And she says too that there is no doubt about Janet's feeling now.
[1892-07-18 Bertha (Rye Beach - mailed from Portsmouth NH) to Henry (Ft. Worth)]

Bertha continued to show off her "diamond star" and "diamond solitaire" during the summer of 1892.

Did I tell you that I wore your diamond star for the first time to a card party the other night. It is the first occasion which has been full dress enough for it and it was immensely admired. Only I wanted you to hear what people said of it. Just as I feel it is a pity you cannot see how much more beautiful my ring is than any other solitaire in the house, as their owners frankly acknowledge. Someday, though, you will hear all that anyone can say of anything of mine in those beautiful days when we shall be together always, my dear love, my best friend.
[1892-08-05 (Friday) (20170712) Bertha (Rye Beach) to Henry (StL)]

I wore your diamond star again the other night or sun, as I am told I should call it, and you would be surprised to know how many people spoke to me of it, admiring the delicate beauty of the setting and the brilliancy of the stones. I told those who were intimate enough to be interested that you had given it to me but I could tell no one what it is that makes it dearer to me than any ornament I ever owned. The day you told me, dear, that it was the first token of success in a work in which you were interested and I knew that you had cared to give it to me. You made me a very proud woman, my darling, and the gladness I felt then comes back to me again when I wear it.
[1892-08-11 (Wednesday) Bertha (Rye Beach) to Henry (StL)]

Bertha very much appreciated Henry's good taste in his gifts to her, something that undoubtedly made each gift special. Bertha received another gift from Henry for their second anniversary of their August 25, 1891 engagement. Her compliment in her letter to Henry was endearing: "*you really have far and away the best taste of any man I know.*"

---

[133] Janet January who married Howard Elliott October 12, 1892.

Sometimes I think no woman was ever quite as happy as I. That is a lovely gift of yours, mother and Esther, and Daisy, the only people who have seen it all exclaimed over its beauty and "perfect taste". And I know all that and I love its dainty perfection and am proud of the taste that selected it. Do you know, dear boy, you really have far and away the best taste of any man I know. But I am gladder of something else. I want you very much tonight, I want to be able to tell you as I never can on paper what you are to me, my best friend, what the feeling of trust in a care that never fails me is, and how much I care, dear. I have felt rather shy about telling you a remark of small Margaret's[134] which Julia reported to me after many questions concerning the nature of an engagement. "Do you think, Dudy, that? That Uncle Henry loves Aunty Bert quite as much as she loves him?"
[1892-08-31 (Monday) Bertha (Rye Beach) to Henry (StL)]

K. WHAT SHOULD I CALL YOU

Dear Henry, I am going to try to accustom myself to the use of your name, so that you shall not laugh at the stiffness with which I do it." [1892-01-10(?) Bertha (StL) to Henry (Wichita)]

Henry was flattered that Bertha was "*experimenting*" with his name.

I am glad to see you are experimenting with my name, dear. You don't know how precious you made that letter by beginning it as you did, or what a thrill of joy came over me when I saw the heading. ... It isn't to be wondered at, that you grow more precious to me every day or that I am becoming so dependent upon you for my happiness that I am made sad when away from you?

...

My only cause of complaint is that I shall not see you for so many days. Do you miss me as I do you, Bertha? I hope not, dear, for I wish you to be bright & happy always and I am sure I shall not find much comfort or interest in things that I cannot in some way associate with you. Ah! I do love you, my child, and every day of my life you grow more precious to me; and I don't think now it is weakness to give way to this feeling. Should I attempt to shut out of my life any of the joy that you have given me, my darling? Think how few men are so blessed, dear, and then you will count me ungrateful if I did not yield absolutely to the sweet influences of your care for me and my devotion to you.
[1892-01-20 (Tuesday) Henry (Wichita KS) to Bertha]

Bertha's friends also took delight that Bertha would soon be, "*Mrs. Henry Clarkson Scott*". Emma Lane wrote:

How is my dear Mrs. Henry Clarkson Scott! Have you yet become accustomed to your new name? At the sewing this morning at Hildegarde's, you were the only topic of conversation. We all longed to see you and, if any person who ever got married before had so many lovely things laid on them, I should be glad to know them.
[1893-02-15 Emma Lane (StL) to Bertha (Tampa-)]

During this time of name experimentation, Bertha tried out the title "*Esquire*" in addressing Henry.

The reason I addressed you as Esquire was because I discovered every other girl addressed her letters so. Years ago I read an article declaring it an affectation and that plain Mr. was all that an American citizen could claim. And since then I have always addressed all my letters Mr. But I find I am unique. The question came up at Marion and I carried it back with me to Rye. Nan informed me that Matthew Arnold was on my side but Mat does not begin to have the same influence over me that Nan does. [1892-09-15 Bertha (The Brunswick, Boston) to Henry (StL)]

---

[134] Margaret is presumably Margaret Shepley, George & Lula Shepley's daughter who was 5 or 6 years old at this time. Julia Shepley was Margaret's aunt. (It is also possible that this refers to "Wee" Margaret Hitchcock who was 13 or 14 at this time or Margaret Lionberger, 5 or 6 years old, the daughter of Zack and Lute Shepley Lionberger – Julia and Lute were sisters.)

Henry would have nothing to do with such "provincial" titles.

> *I am sorry, very sorry to challenge the accuracy of so high an authority as Miss Nan, especially as you acquiesce in her conclusions. But, my dear child, Esquire is the most palpable provincialism and, if you knew as many men about town as I do who flatter themselves that all such matters are important and who regard Esquire in the use made of it as they do, the title Honorable applied to a police justice and, further, if you could hear the aforesaid authorities wonder when they receive letters addressed esquire, why the heads of households don't teach their daughters not to make such breaks, I think you would in this case agree that our friend Miss Nan has blundered. It is worse than seeing a man's visiting card with Esquire after instead of Mr. before the name and your friend Miss Ernst could tell you, I think, that in Boston or Washington, this latter would be thought scarcely less extraordinary. But I did not intend to write an essay on the subject, only please remember that in the use of Mr., you are not "unique".*
> [1892-09-19 (Sunday) Henry (StL) to Bertha (The Ark, E. Jaffrey)]

L. ENGAGED AND ALONE

During 1892, Bertha and Henry were together less than 25 days. So, notwithstanding their elation that their engagement was officially announced, 1892 was a very lonely and difficult year, especially for Henry.

1. ABOUT LETTER WRITING

By necessity, Bertha and Henry became accustomed to having their letters be their primary means of communication. During 1892, Bertha and Henry had to "*talk*" to each other by letter, writing over 450 letters to each other that year. The volume of their letters and the range of issues addressed is so prodigious that these letters have been incorporated into this, the prior three chapters and in the next.

Given the importance of letter writing and of receiving the other's written words, Bertha and Henry became very sensitive as to whether the other person was fulfilling his/her responsibilities. For example, in response to a letter from Henry complaining about her letters, Bertha expressed her dim view of Henry's sometime ingratitude in not writing more.

> *If you are not an impersonation of the ingratitude of man, I don't know who is. I write you an eight-page letter and you spend four lines in thanking me for having done so and a whole page in scolding because I have not done it oftener, only write four pages yourself and excuse it because you went to the Thomas Concert with Nan, and then growl at my calls from Powers Harris. O logical minded individual, there is a lovely text about specks in your brother's eye and beams in your own[135] that it would be well for you to study.*
> [1892-03-18 Bertha (St. Augustine) To Henry (StL)]

Henry's response to Bertha's March 18 letter was a bit defensive.

> *I have been reading over your Friday's letter this evening and for the second time my hair stood on end at the terrific storm I brought upon myself for meekly petitioning for longer letters. You wind up by quoting scripture to me and thus imply that I deserve Heaven's wrath as well as yours. Now, instead of misapplying "a lovely text", you should have thought of that which promises "the meek shall inherit the earth". You then would have done all in your power to fulfill the prophesy by adding to my greatest blessings, your sweet letters, dear child.*
> [1892-03-28-2 (5 letters) Henry to Bertha]

---

[135] Matthew 7:3.

In another letter, Bertha compared Henry's complaints of her insufficient letter writing to Talleyrand's letters to Madame de Récamier. But Bertha knew the best way to end a letter: "*I am just glad I am alive and want you to be.*"

> *I am beginning to understand Talleyrand a little better. Did you even have the bad luck to read Talleyrand's letters to Madame Récamier? I did when I was about eighteen and I thought I had never read anything so stupid in my life. It was a succession of "Why do you not write to me?" "I think some of your letters have gone astray. Number them in future that I may know if any are lost." "You write me a tiny note on the smallest of paper in answer to pages upon pages from me. Well, it is quite true that a line from you is worth volumes of mine, but I wish you would be more generous." Etc. etc. ad infinitum, until I was so bored that I don't know why I ever finished them except that, being far more conscientious then than I am now, I usually finished a book if I began it. Well, it has just begun to dawn on me that, perhaps, that all interested Madame Récamier more than it did me. I wish <u>her</u> letters had been preserved; I should like to have read all her excuses for not writing.*

> *There is nothing new under the sun but the old things are very lovely, are they not, dear? I liked your cousin's letter. I think I might lay it to heart as well as you. You don't know how beautiful life looks to me this morning. It is perfectly glorious spring weather and it seems to me as if there were so much to live for and to look forward to. It is not worthwhile to be blue, my dearest. One misses all the "little things by the way." That sounds more like a copy book than my usual style of writing but I don't feel copy booky, I am just glad I am alive and want you to be.*
> [1892-03-22 Bertha (St. Augustine FL) to Henry (StL)]

Bertha could assert herself and decided in the next letter to set Henry straight about letter writing.

> *I am writing today from a stern sense of duty. The poet[136] once asked me to write too. I declined but said he might write to me if he liked which he declined in his turn, saying it was as impossible for him to write when his letters were not answered as it would be for him to talk if his remarks were not responded to. I have a little of that feeling today but I know it will be impossible for me to write tomorrow and that probably I cannot before Sunday. But this time, dear friend, remember that I have positively promised to telegraph if anything goes wrong so you are not to worry. If you were not such a very unreasonable boy, I should not go into such minute details.*
> [1892-03-24 Bertha (St. Augustine FL) To Henry (StL)]

In spite of their sometime complaints, Bertha and Henry often seemed to anticipate what the other person was thinking, as Bertha commented in the following letters.

> *In your second letter, you said if I did not come West you might come east. I told you yesterday what your welcome would be my dearest. In fact, I practically answered these two letters yesterday. It is a little habit we both have, dear boy, of answering each other's letters before we received them. I am inclined to believe in this new science of telepathy on that very account.*
> [1892-04-28(-) (Thursday) Bertha (5th Ave Hotel, NYC?) to Henry (StL)]

> *It is strange how you and I think of the same persons and things at the same times. I often notice too how your mood corresponds to mine in letters written on the same day.*
> [1892-08-22 Bertha (Farragut House, Rye Beach) to Henry]

Henry was not alone in complaining about not receiving longer letters. Perhaps to shame Henry, Bertha wrote that Nat Lane wrote long letters even after 3 years of marriage!

> *I enjoyed the description of the private car very much. Only I felt I had wasted a great deal of pity on a young man for hard travelling when he certainly was in no need of it. Such luxury! And why*

---

[136] William Chauvenet, called "The Poet" by his friends.

did you say you thought I should be bored in hearing about it? Does it bore you to hear of where I am and what I am doing? If so, I shall shorten my letters considerably! And I don't think much of your letters anyway. Myra has just had one from Nat – six sheets of big business paper, written on both sides, equal to twenty-four pages of your sized paper. Pretty well for a man who has been married nearly three years, though Myra declares that it is only his Sunday letters that are as long as that, that his every day ones are shorter. And she writes on smaller paper than I do.
[1892-07-21 Bertha (Kennebunkport NH) to Henry (StL)]

Henry did not like being compared to another man, especially with regard to letter writing.
I am disposed to resent your comparison of my letters with Nat Lane's to Mrs. Nat, and not because your comparison was one that I suffered by but simply because I am shocked at your assuming that three years of married life necessarily means comparative indifference. Is it your prediction that this state of affairs will naturally result from your treatment of me? If this is your conclusion, I must make up my mind to look for nothing else, although it is decidedly contrary to my theory that, in spite of all I can do to prevent it, you will be nearer and dearer to me every day of my life. Which do you think the true prophet, my darling, and which prophesies the best future? And as to the length of Nat's letters, that's of small consequence. Think of the volumes of thought that I am capable of condensing within a few sentences!!! And you may also wake up your mind that, when the same Nathaniel is his own master, he will not have quite as much time for twenty-four page letters. He may then perhaps develop my astonishing aptitude for economizing space or words.
[1892-07-25 Henry (Hotel Cary, Wichita KS) To Bertha (Rye Beach)]
(Henry's excuse for shorter letters: "*Think of the volumes of thought that I am capable of condensing within a few sentences!!!*")

Bertha shrugged off Henry's comment and wrote that she was only "*getting a rise out of you.*"
I put in that remark about Nat Lane and three years married life for the express purpose of "getting a rise" out of you, my son, as you possibly surmised and I succeeded beautifully. But all your remarks about his being unable to write such long letters were he his own master had nothing to do with the case, my dear Henry, for that particular letter was written on Sunday!
[1892-08-06 (Saturday) Bertha (Rye Beach) to Henry (StL)]

Bertha sometimes questioned whether it made sense to write every day, especially if she did not have very much to write about.
Your last letter fully convinced me, dear boy, that a woman ought to follow her instincts. And when she feels that she has absolutely nothing to say, she had better not say it. I thought at first of answering your letter thus:

> *My dear friend,*
> *I have received your letter, which I greatly enjoyed, but as I have nothing to tell you of in return, will wait until something interesting occurs to write more.*
> *Sincerely yours,*
[1892-09-15 Bertha (The Brunswick, Boston) to Henry (StL)]

By the way, I forgot to tell you I have been seriously considering that I ought not to write to you so often. Mr. Dillon told Gertrude it was a very bad principle to write every day. You might tell me your ideas on the subject and help me to decide.
[1892-06-27 (Sunday) Bertha (Jaffrey NH) to Henry (StL)]

Henry always felt that daily letters were important and responded to Mr. Dillon's advice in the following.
Please remember in considering Mr. Dillon's advice about writing every day that, by the confession of his own child, he is "like all the rest" of his family "talented but of very little use in the world".

Now, when he begins to give advice about mother of which he knows nothing, he progresses backward from negative uselessness to a position of possible power for harm.
[1892-06-29 (Wednesday) 20170828-1 Henry (StL) to Bertha (Farragut House, Rye Beach)]

When Bertha's letters arrived at his work, Henry often dropped everything in favor of reading Bertha's letters.

I was so glad to get your letters that when they were given me I excused myself to a man who had come in to see me on business and went into the next office to read them. The man evidently thought he had encountered a lunatic but, when I returned and told him I was ready to go on with our talk, he had the wisdom to make no comments. I don't think I ever allowed your letters to interrupt my work before, dearest. On the contrary, I had rather prided myself on my ability to put them in my desk and not read them until whatever I was working at, when they arrived, reached a stopping place so to speak. But I had no letter yesterday and last night. I thought a great many times of a very bad girl who insisted upon doing all sorts of venturesome things, such as driving vicious horses, trying to swim across the ocean and attempting other very, very foolish experiments. So when I found no letter at the office this morning, I was really distracted about you and so that man had to wait until I knew you were well. Does this seem weak and foolish, my darling?
[1892-08(-) (Wednesday) 20170722-1 Henry to Bertha]

Bertha often requested that Henry write more about himself and his work (and less time lecturing her about *"her iniquities as a letter writer"*).

I am going to tell you a story. When Julia Coolidge was engaged, she told me she had never had such hard work in her life as finding material about which to write to Charles and Charles one day wrote to her – "your letters sound as if they were dragged out by main force. Don't write to me when you don't feel like it." She took him at his word and shortly afterwards received a telegram to know if she were ill and, not long after, Mrs. Coolidge wrote to her that she hoped she would not often allow days to elapse without writing, as Charles immediately thought she had changed her mind and was going to break the engagement and his family did not have a very good time in consequence.

I am going to tell you another story. There once was a young woman, who wrote to a young man that she wished he would write to her more about himself, the way he passed his time, the work he was interested in, and so forth, for that every bit of it was interesting to her. And the young man wrote back that she was mistaken in thinking the "details of a very hum drum office existence" would be anything but a bore to her. And the young woman, though still maintaining her own opinion that she would have liked to be able to form some picture of the young man's life day after day and to know more of his work, did not have her feelings hurt at all but realized that they must be rather stupid things to write about to the person who did the writing. The moral of this story is, that it is a poor rule that does not work both ways. The moral of the first story is that the young man in question has never had to write such a letter to the girl, as Charles did, because she has never tried to pump up material for him but has written just what her mind was full of and, if one wants spontaneous letters, one cannot dictate the number of words they are to contain. And furthermore, as regards the time said young woman has to spend on letters, be it remarked that she is in debt to all her friends for them and does not expect to have any one speak to her when she goes home. And of late, she has often been unable even to get in her half hour of solid reading, so that if anything happens to interfere with the hour before dinner, she is hard put to it. But that, she rarely allows to happen, not only because she wants her letters to be a help and pleasure if possible to somebody else, but because that quiet time which she has to give to her best friend is the pleasantest hour of her whole day.

And speaking of letters which are a help and comfort, she came home last night from a twenty mile drive rather tired and there was a card party in the evening to which all the guests of the house had subscribed and to which she had invited two guests from a cottage up the road, the two daughters of her beloved Dr. Nichols of Boston. She wanted to be feeling very fresh and bright and entertaining and she thought, under the circumstances, she was foolish to have taken the drive. But her spirits went up when she found a letter in her box. Now she had not expected a letter for she had had two in the morning mail, and that made it all the more delightful and she carried it off to her own room to enjoy by herself. And when she opened it, it was four pages of the smallest sized University Club note paper and consisted entirely of a lecture on her iniquities as a letter writer. And on that, there is no further need of comment.
[1892-08-02(?) Bertha (Rye Beach NH) to Henry (StL)]

Bertha knew that Henry, like their friend, Charles Coolidge, was always anxious if he did not receive a letter each day from Bertha. So, like a mother instructing an absent-minded child, Bertha sometimes wrote to remind Henry – there will be no letter on *"Tuesday"*.

Remember that you never get a letter Tuesday, so that the silence will not be caused by any other reason. I assure you if I am maimed or killed, I will telegraph you. Likewise, if I am drowned in bathing, I will leave instructions with the family to that effect. I mention all this to cheer you, knowing that Tuesday is apt to be an anxious day and as I am evidently much too young to take proper care of myself, I wish to have your mind relieved from all care on the subject.
[1892-08-20 Bertha (Rye Beach) to Henry (StL)]

Through the course of their letter writing, Bertha and Henry found the ability to communicate their most personal feelings, even when they were being scolded. Henry wrote one such letter when he was exasperated at a reprimand from Bertha: La donna è mobile! But he appreciated the scolding.

What a capricious child you are! One day you write a very meek, subdued letter, full of melancholy thoughts, then you send me a message so sweet that I cannot measure the gladness it brings with it, and after this, your third letter comes and I am bullied and called names and abused, and for what? Why all because I conscientiously corrected a slight fault in a dear girl who, for the first time in her whole life, made a slight mistake. My most honored and respected friend, I most humbly crave forgiveness and upon my pardon being secured, I promise to make no further suggestions which can possibly be interpreted as accusing you of "bad form". Will it mollify your wrath if I add that I thought perhaps you wished me to acknowledge the first presents that arrived, in order that you might adopt my graceful style in writing the other acknowledgements!!!!

...

... you will no doubt be surprised to know that, of the three letters, I liked best the scolding one, for that told me most unmistakably that you had entirely recovered. No sick girl could have written such a belligerent letter!
[1893-02-03 (Thursday) Henry (StL) to Bertha (Stancote, MA)]

2. HENRY HAS THE BLUES
It was hardly surprising that Henry, who suffered from depression, would find the 1892 year particularly difficult and it was certainly made even more difficult since the object of his dreams awaited him but would not materialize during 1892. Henry's letters showed his elation when he was with Bertha or received her letters, but also his despondency over the seemingly endless wait.

After Henry saw Bertha in New York City in April 1892 for two days (as permitted by Bertha's parents), he began to miss Bertha almost immediately.

If you knew how sad I was yesterday and have been up to the time of the arrival of your letter this morning, you would not have to be assured that I miss you and need you in my life all the while if

it is to be made happy. My God, how I have missed you these last few days! I kept it out of my letter yesterday, darling, because, fail as often as I may, I am really trying all the time not to burden you with the sorrow, the separation from you gives me. But yesterday and today, due to a most foolish piece of imprudence, I caught a wretched cold and then, with no word from you, I went down into the depths it seems to me, deeper than I have gone since you shut out all the sunshine by leaving me. I did not get the Saturday letter at all, dear, and it must be lost for your Sunday letter written before you got my telegram was forwarded from St. Louis. Repeat what you said in the last letter, won't you dearest? I shall need that moral letter more than you may imagine and I promise not to scold or to criticize, no matter how severe you were. Severe! You can't be, Bert, for you care too, darling. But I want that lost letter! Will you write it over or as near as may be and sent it to me? ... This head is too bad to be cured by anything but a long walk and I am going out to take it and think of what a happy man I ought to be because I lie in my love for you.
[1892-04-16(-) 20180403-1 Henry (NYC) to Bertha]

Even after one month had elapsed since their New York City *rendez vous*, Henry still clung to that memory.
Dear, if the thousand and one beautiful memories you have given me could be forgotten and I could only recall this last visit and the beautiful days we passed together, I think I should be so deeply in your debt I never could repay you. And, dearest, you do not know how sweet is the thought that I owe all the happy memories to you. I seem almost to have been in a dream, darling, and I think this is partly why I did not do more for you while I was with you. When I was preparing for my meeting with you, my thoughts were full of our plans for the future and there were many things which I intended to talk over with you and lo, when I saw you, every thought seemed to leave me save the consciousness that we were together once more and that I loved you more dearly than ever before.
[1892-05-29 Henry (StL) to Bertha (Hotel Brunswick, Boston)]

Henry often wondered why they were apart and pledged to never "*leave you for a single minute again*".
I don't think I shall ever leave you for a single minute again for I just figured it out that, in the "doctrine of chances", I shall not have time to see enough of you on earth by half to fit myself for your companionship in heaven where, I am told, those who dwell together must be alike and fashioned after the angels. Will you be able to metamorphose me or will you smuggle me in as Dolly did her last friend?
[1902-07-25 Thursday Henry (StL) to Bertha (Rye Beach)]

Henry was also frustrated that all of his feelings and thoughts had to be put in writing when what he most desired was to speak with Bertha face to face and share his joys with her.
I think, dear, it is hard to put on paper our best, our most sacred thoughts and so, even in writing to you whom I wish to know every thought, every hope of my life, I cannot write as fully, as freely as I feel and as freely as I can talk to you, for when we are together, dearest, we seem so near, so absolutely one that I never think of holding from you whatever thoughts come to me. There is more sadness, more of one's life lost in long separations than anyone can estimate save those who suffer such privations and, try as I may, it is sometimes impossible for me to think of remaining away from you so long without. Why do I permit myself to write to you in this vein? I start out all right and with a firm determination to keep all such disagreeable reflections to myself and, before I am aware of it, I am mourning to you as if I were being tortured.
[1892-07-30 (Saturday) Henry (StL) to Bertha (Farragut House, Rye Beach)]

I had to go to the "south side" this morning in the part of the city just south of Lafayette Park and when the cars got that far with me I got off and walked through the park. It was perfectly beautiful, dearest, and I thought, if I could have looked into your face for one instant and have caught your expression of delight at the exquisite flowers and beautiful grass and trees that almost made it fairy land, I would have been perfectly, absolutely, happy.

[1892-08-18 (Thursday) Henry (StL) to Bertha (Farragut House)]

When Henry's business trips were dull or worse, such as one such trip to St. Paul, Minnesota in August 1892, Henry could not help but express his loneliness.

I had four letters from you this morning, dear, and I am quite sure you would not be displeased if you knew the effect they have had on my spirits which have been drooping these last two days. I don't think I have ever been so lonely in all my life, Bert, and I hope this melancholy condition will excuse an unusually inane letter I wrote you yesterday. Next year, if business calls me to any place where there is chance of my having much leisure between times, I am afraid you will have to go with me for being alone in a place where one has nothing but business friends is next to perdition.

I can understand Tom McKittrick's statement that he almost has nervous prostration when he goes east. Tom has few acquaintances in New York except those whom he knows in a business way and he told me the other day that his visits to New York were, by far, the most disagreeable exactions of his business. He should try St. Paul if he would know what it is to be in a truly happy frame of mind! I don't like a single man I have met here. The natives of Texas are Chesterfields beside them. I think I have been asked to take a drink by every man I have met and, as far as I can see, this innocent occupation constitutes the single form of amusement of the male portion of the population and the women! You should see some of the toilets. They would, indeed, make you green with envy.

[1892-08-24 Henry (St. Paul, MN) to Bertha (Farragut House, Rye Beach)]

After Bertha's October 1892 visit to St. Louis for the Elliott-January wedding, Henry was gloomy again, writing "*I have not been very contented since I caught a last glimpse of my darling last night...*"

Last night it began to rain and all day. It is six o'clock P.M. now. The floods have descended and people who have been obliged to go out today have had a mournful time wading about the muddy streets which have been converted into lakes of mire. I did not start out this morning alarmingly hilarious and my numerous tramps through the mud and wet have not improved my spirits. To be very honest, dear, I have not been very contented since I caught a last glimpse of my darling last night as she disappeared in the car which I stood watching until it was hidden in the darkness. I miss you Bert!

[1892-10-18 (Tuesday) Henry (StL) to Bertha (William H. Benton, Chicago IL)]

The next day, "*The effect of your departure...*" was still weighing on Henry.

The effect of your departure was so plainly shown in my very dismal letter yesterday that further description of my utterly collapsed condition does not seem necessary. I think, partly because I am very much ashamed of myself for moping around and making yesterday such a burden to everyone I came in contact with (for it seemed to me that all the bright cordial faces I had been meeting for two weeks past had disappeared and that everyone whom I met was wearing a most funereal expression of countenance, which I attributed to their having come in contact with me), I am in a little more hopeful frame of mind, but there is a vast difference between your being here and being away, my darling, and it is rather hard to be cheerful and contented without you. You are entirely right in thinking me spoiled, dear. It would spoil anyone, for any other companionship than yours who could know you as I do. I do not mean though to make this letter one long story of sorrow because you have gone away. You like to be missed, I know, but I am sure you wish my letters to tell you of other things than my sorrow in your absence and I shall try to think to write of other matters.

[1892-10-19 (Wednesday) Henry (StL) to Bertha (C/O Mr. Wm. W.H. Benton, 5021 Washington Ave, Chicago IL)]

Even though they had been apart for over a month since Bertha's October visit to St. Louis, Bertha wrote to Henry in late November: *"I have never felt you were so near to me as I have these last few days…"*.

> *Dearest, I have never felt you were so near to me as I have these last few days. You asked me not to grow away from you. Don't grow away from me. Write to me of all your interests, dear boy, your ambitions and your disappointments, even when you come in second at the races and the pool tournaments, I will try not to be too stern with you. I shall think of you tomorrow, spending a mournful thanksgiving on the cars.*
>
> …
>
> *I hope you are not very, very tired, son. I know how these long journeys take the life out of you and I do not want you to have such a mournful ending to your visit. Give my love to your mother and sisters and you may keep a very little for yourself.*
> [1892-11-24 (Wednesday) Bertha (Boston) to Henry (StL)]

Henry wrote back to Bertha about being with her in the prior month: *"When I was with you, our wedding day seemed not far away; now, it seems a lifetime before the fourteenth of February."*

> *I shall never be content until I can have you near me again, my dear. In a flippant style, which makes me hate myself now, I told you when we were last together, how I needed you in my life but O, my darling, if I had made known to you the extent of my loneliness when I am away from you, I do not believe you would be as patient in waiting for that far off reunion as you are. When I was with you, our wedding day seemed not far away; now, it seems a lifetime before the fourteenth of February. My dearest, just as you thought me a boy in the perfectly happy condition I was in when I came into the charm of your presence and an old man "with lines of coal" when I know I shortly must go away from you, so is my life made full of joy or sorrow as I look to an early reunion or look forward to a period of weary separation. And, Bert, two months and nineteen days is a long time to be separated. I am glad that I shall be so busy this winter. It will help some to make the time seem not so long. I shall try to be content in waiting, dear, for I know it seems like a want of thankfulness to you, for all the happiness you give me, to be so utterly disconsolate when I am away from you. If you think me very ungrateful for the joy of those last beautiful days with you, try to remember, darling, that we think the lesser light darkness when we have just stood in the splendor of the clear sunlight. Was it not all beautiful darling? There was a time when I treasured a particular drive or horseback ride with you or one of those many beautiful talks with you. Now, I only remember that I was near you for a few short days and that every moment of the time was one of happiness. But, I did not intend to write all of this. Why should I tell you what you know so well that every thought of my life which brings me joy is because of you.*
> [1892-11-27 (Friday) Henry (StL) to Bertha Hotel Brunswick, Back Bay, Boston)]

Henry's explanation of being *"utterly disconsolate when I am away from you"* rings true: *"we think the lesser light darkness when we have just stood in the splendor of the clear sunlight."*

3. HAVE FAITH & BUCK UP

Although Henry was desperate to see Bertha during March 1892, Bertha would have none of Henry's *"pathos"*. Bertha wrote to Henry of the Lenten discipline!

> *No, dear boy, I do not think it would be wise or best for you to come and see me, though the pathos of your having been without seeing me for the greater part of a week was too deep for words. I sympathize with you, but my dear Henry, it is extremely fine Lenten discipline for you.*
> [1892-03-12 Bertha to Henry]

Bertha seemed well aware that Henry could become morose and would encourage Henry to "snap out of it". In the following letter, Bertha wrote that Henry was acting like her younger brother, George.

I don't like to have you say that you are always sad when you are away from me, though I like to have you miss me, dear boy. But I will confess that I am a little suspicious of that sadness. When George first went away to school, he never wrote home except when he was feeling terribly homesick, so we got the impression that he was homesick all the time. Do you see any resemblance?
[1892-01-23 Bertha (StL) to Henry (Fort Worth)]

On one hand, Bertha wanted Henry to miss her: "*Dearest, I cannot feel very sorry that you were "particularly dismal" when you reached home. If you had been particularly jolly, I should have sat down and wept. I want you to miss me.*" [1892-05-29 (Saturday) Bertha (Boston MA) to Henry (StL)]

However, Bertha seemed wary of letting Henry give in to his melancholy when Bertha was away. Perhaps the problem was Henry's work?

Dear boy, after my concerted assumption yesterday that you were "particularly dismal" because of my absence, it occurred to me that possibly that [I] had nothing to [do] with it, but that you had returned to find the Laclede Power House flooded, that Mr. Blair had not sold the Grand Avenue property, that the plans for the Wichita works were all wrong, that, according to some formality you had overlooked, you were responsible for all those notes that went to protest, and that even Fort Worth was not the comfort you had hoped to find it. If any or all of these misfortunes was the cause of the blues, let me offer you my sincere condolences but I cannot feel half the sympathy I should if they were caused by your absence from me. Did you not once quote to me that "a fellow feeling makes us wondrous kind."
[1892-05-29 (Sunday) Bertha (Boston) to Henry (StL)]

Of their current trials during the 1892 separation, Bertha wrote that their love would make the time pass and would surely make their relationship stronger. So Bertha wrote to Henry with the Bible quotation, "*And Jacob served seven years for Rachel, and they seemed unto him but a few days, for the love he had to her.*"

First a quotation went through my mind and kept running there – "And Jacob served seven years for Rachel, and they seemed unto him but a few days, for the love he had to her." And then I thought how very long ago that was and how times had changed. And then I remembered a man I once knew who, beginning when he was thirty-three years old, waited five years, not for a certainty, not even for a great hope, but for the bare chance that something might happen to change a woman's mind toward him. And he did not have to go to Edith Knox to learn to admire the woman he loved either. And then, I wondered what it was in a woman that made her pass by a man like that and care about another who wrote her letters which made her blue and even kept her awake at night sometimes, wondering how she could help to keep him from becoming bitter.

I was rather blue, myself, the other day, of course from none of the foregoing causes, and I took up my Thomas a Kempis – I am not much given to religious literature but I always carry Thomas with me and am rather fond of him for Thomas was by no means a saint by nature, whatever he became by grace, and he understands human nature uncommonly well. I enclose here a quotation from a chapter of his on patience and please do not understand that it has any personal reference, I merely thought you might think of some other person to whom it would apply, at least, that was the effect it had on me.

"Thou oughtest therefore to call to mind the more heavy sufferings of others, that so thou mayest the more easily bear thine own very small troubles. And if they seem unto thee not very small, then

beware lest thine impatience be the cause thereof. He is not truly patient who is willing to suffer only so much as he thinks good and from whom he pleases."[137]
[1892-06-23 Bertha (East Jaffrey) to Henry (StL)]

Henry understood Bertha's reprimand to him for being blue and for the need to be patient. However, as Henry wrote in response, it was not within his power to hide his feelings from Bertha.

I did not mind your holding up Jacob as a model. I would be greatly improved in patterning after him. Nor did the quotation from Thomas A Kempis particularly disturb me but I would have omitted the reference to the man you "once knew" for there you place me in unfortunate contrast with an ordinary individual, neither a saint nor a religious teacher, and I naturally resent the comparison. I wish it was in my power to tell you that I have been annoyed at things I should not have noticed. I can say with perfect truth that they no longer influence me but to have told you it would have been possible for me to be insensible to these things would have simply been deceiving you and I do not remember having done this yet and I hope I shall never try to.
[1892-06-27 (Saturday) Henry (StL) to Bertha (Farragut House, Rye Beach)]

In his next letter on the following day, Henry tried to be philosophical about the waiting and clung to the thought, *"she cares"*.

Often when I am tired and perhaps not very strong I can rest a little while and think "she cares" though and, while this is so, nothing can make me unhappy" and then I know, if you were here, dear, it would be all sunshine for me and this brings me to the conclusion which I always reach, that it is because I miss you so that I am so often unspeakably lonely and sad. You will think, dear, that I am gloomy now but I do not think that I am for I see as clearly as I have ever done that, notwithstanding we have had to bear unusual troubles, sometimes to endure almost humiliation, we have much more happiness in store for us than is the lot of many others, even among those who join their lives together because they care. For, dear, I do not think many persons are as happy together as we are. Is not that conceited?
[1892-06-28 (Sunday) Henry (StL) to Bertha (The Ark, East Jaffrey)]

During that summer of 1892, Bertha recounted one of Henry's letters in which he wrote that being apart was becoming less hard. Bertha wrote that this was *"a far greater proof of your love than all your mournful letters."*

I have your first letter from Wichita, dear, and your decision about Marion did not surprise me very much for I was prepared for it. And I understood your feeling but I could not help having a little rebellion all to myself at certain things in our lot which seem pretty hard, though I do not dwell on them very much. And another thing, dearest, I feel as if I were really the cause of your not taking a much needed summer vacation and that is harder than not seeing you. If I thought the Oregon trip would be a rest, I think I should be tempted to beg you to go but I don't believe anything which involves so much car riding is very resting to you.

Well the hard things are not the things which we like to talk about, are they, my own love. I cannot thank you but you help me all the time. But you are right in saying as you did a little while ago

---

[137] Thomas a Kempis, *The Imitation of Christ*: Book 3:

3. He is not truly patient who will only suffer as far as seemeth right to himself and from whom he pleaseth. But the truly patient an considereth not by what man he is tried, whether by one above him, or by an equal or inferior, whether by a good and holy man, or a perverse and unworthy; but indifferently from every creature, whatsoever or how often soever adversity happeneth to him, he gratefully accepteth all from the hand of God and counteth it great gain: for with God nothing which is borne for His sake, however small, shall lose its reward.

that being apart is not as hard as it used to be. I wonder if many people would understand that I felt that a far greater proof of your love than all your mournful letters to Florida. It is not because we care less, is it, dear friend?

[1892-07-29 (Thursday) Bertha (Rye Beach) to Henry (StL)]

While Bertha and Henry wrote such things, deep down, their separations were always very hard on them and seemed to become more difficult over time.

4. ABOUT LONG ENGAGEMENTS

Henry definitely felt that long engagements were a bad idea and frequently tried to argue his case with Bertha. To buttress his opinion, he referred to the views of Mrs. Knox who *"loves you dearly"* and who pressed home *"her argument ... against long engagements..."*

I went to call on Mrs. Knox and, as Gordon did not come in for some time after I arrived, she took the opportunity to speak of you. She is one of the few people whom I like to hear speak of you, dear, for she is not flippant and it is easy to see that she loves you very dearly. I think she was trying to press home her argument of Sunday evening against long engagements for, without saying anything definitely on that subject, she so earnestly and sadly referred to all you are losing and have lost in remaining away from home so long. How she and other friends of yours had noticed you were much less strong than you were a few years ago, when "Bert was the strongest of all the girls, Mr. Scott", that I could hardly sit still and listen to her so bitterly did I reproach myself for not trying harder to be more helpful to you, to make you see certain things as they seemed best to me. And then she spoke of the place you held among your friends. How dear you were to them all and I, well, I thought if my care for you had even been as great as hers I should have saved you much of the worry and trouble you have endured. But I do not intend to be tragic, dearest. It is high time I should be learning that certain subjects are best avoided when - But enough of this.

[1892-06-17 (Friday) Henry (StL) to Bertha (The Ark, East Jaffrey) – The "Friday" letter]

Bertha was "troubled" by Henry's "Friday" letter (above) but still asserted the view that they must wait and to not struggle against what was then decided.

I have your Friday letter and it has troubled me a little. All your last letters seem to me as if, instead of regarding certain things as settled, you were fighting against them. And dear, if it were on your own account that you did this, I don't think I should be able to blame you because I know and realize so fully how patient you have been. But you speak of all this as being harmful for me and that it is not. I am growing stronger every day and nothing helps me more, except the knowledge of your love, than the fact that I am no longer in rebellion against my family.

The reason I have been so worn out, as I have been the last year or two for it would be foolish to say that I have not been, is because I have been in a constant state of nervous tension, either struggling against my own feeling for you or against their wishes. Now this is all over, there is no struggling, I feel perfectly calm and I look forward to a beautiful life ahead for which I do not mind a little waiting.

To have come in November, to have had to leave my family in defiance after all I had tried to bring about differently, would have made this six months a much more wearing strain than this nine months. And the feeling that I had not done everything to make it easier for them would have been a worrying pain all the time. Now I know that I have done all I could. The only thing that grieves me now, dear, and, it does grieve me very much, is that all this has been made so hard for you when you have helped me so bravely and so tenderly. But I am sure I can prevent your being so annoyed again. I have not yet opened the subject with my father but I will. The waiting I cannot help but at least it is only to a certain date and there is no fear of any more opposition there. Every arrangement is being made with a view to my marriage in February.

[1892-06-23 (Monday) Bertha (Jaffrey) to Henry (StL)]

In June, Henry attended the Taylor-Lohman wedding which was held on a very hot St. Louis summer day. Henry, of course, wanted to let Bertha know how he was suffering and not only from the heat. In the following letter, Henry was able to call attention to comments that he had received about marriage and Mrs. Crittenden's comment: *"Mr. Scott, I don't believe you are as determined as Crittenden was."*

I went to the Taylor Lohman wedding yesterday and hot! The men all wore dress suites and, if the distress in their faces had been less acute, they would have been sufficiently funny looking to amuse me even with the thermometer above one hundred F.H.!

I met George Bartlett in one of the rooms trying to talk to the oldest Miss Garey and, at the same time, to bolster up his collar which had wilted until I was not sure he wore one. When his back was turned and when I took a front view to reassure myself that he had not been absent minded in making his toilet and forgotten a part of his toggery, the front was so absolutely forlorn that I collapsed and, to protect myself from his wrath, I retired to another part of the house. His collar and cravat had melted together completely, his hair was dripping and I graphically describe him in asking you to imagine our esteemed friend dipped head first in a tub of water and there exposed to the admiring gaga of an audience that had the appearance of having been similarly treated.

Don't think I refer particularly to Bartlett because he was worse off than the other men. Not at all! I only make him serve as an illustration. And, indeed, the girls looked very little better. I arranged to meet Mary Lionberger there and she had escaped before my arrival which desertion I was inclined to resent but, when I saw the other females, I not only forgave her but blessed her for going, for I should not have enjoyed seeing her look like most of the girls whom I met.
...
After the wedding, I called on Crittenden and Mrs. C.[138] and, you will not believe it, I know they are the happiest couple I have seen in a long time. Madam Lucy sent you no end of messages about wasting your life and mine when we ought to be having "such a good time." I even received a lecture from her: "Mr. Scott, I don't believe you are as determined as Crittenden was. I would have made him wait if I could and, if he had yielded, I should have spent the rest of my life reproaching him for permitting a whim to cheat me out of a great many days of happiness." You don't think I yielded from weakness, do you, my darling? If you do, raise the question as to whether you have acted wisely and see how I will struggle to make you come to me now. I am approaching a dangerous subject and the most reasonable treatment I can give it is perfect silence so goodbye.
[1892-06-17 (Thursday) Henry (StL) to Bertha (The Ark, East Jaffrey)]

Bertha wasted no time in her rejoinder to Henry's Thursday letter (above). Time wasted? Bahh.

I have received your Thursday letter, dear boy, and I wish to state here that, if you send me any more messages of Lucy McKinley's, I won't answer your letter. Of course, she and Crittenden did not wait – they had no time to lose. What is the difference between my age and hers – and yours and Crittenden's?[139] You and I wanted to enjoy society a little longer! Also, I have no patience with people who talk about time being wasted that is not spent together. Did she consider the five or six years of her life after she was twenty-six and before she was married wasted? I do not see any reasonableness in that at all. I mean that really. And don't write to me anymore about married people. I am tired to death of hearing about them and seeing them. They are the most self-satisfied people on the face of the earth and I do not see that they are a bit more useful than unmarried people.
...

[138] Lucy Bent married Crittenden McKinley April 19, 1892, two months before this letter was written.
[139] Lucy was 5 or 6 six years older than Bertha and Crittenden was 5 years older than Henry.

My dear boy, if you think the beginning of my letter stern, I must refer you to Mary Garth for a reason when she said she married Fred Finey "because she never could have enjoyed scolding anybody else so well." And you really have not a well-disciplined mind at all.
[1892-06-20 (Sunday) Bertha (East Jaffrey, NH) to Henry (StL)]

Undoubtedly due to Henry's persistence about their friends not waiting to get married, Bertha reiterated her position that these couples were all older.

I know you feel tired and don't want to be lectured but I am just cross grained enough to do it anyway. "I grow more impatient with others - - -, And I know this is because I am growing older." I just wish to remind you dear old boy that Zack was almost thirty-three when he married, a year advantage of you, after a year and a half's engagement and a much longer time trying to become so. That Gordon Knox and Will Stribling were both over thirty-six and that the former spent eight of the ten months he was engaged away from Edith. I do not know ...'s age but I do know Professor Potter's and I know that, the year of their engagement, he spent in St. Louis while Agnes was in Germany with her mother. Hardly any of your own especial "crowd" are married yet but I do not on that account doubt that they will and even be very happy. No, my son, there are undeniable hardships in our lot but I do not think them very unusual nor do I count your age & increasing incapacity for enjoyment among them. Possibly if your "impatience" grows, I may someday have to consider that a hardship.
[[20180125-3 (1892-) Bertha (-) to Henry]

5. HENRY TRIES TO BE MORE POSITIVE
Henry often tried to see the "silver lining" in their separations which would make him more worthy in Bertha's eyes.

Bert, what is it that makes me love you more and more each day? You are not here with me and yet you are near to help me, every hour, and every hour and every day my love grows stronger. It is, I think, the growth of what is best I me. You gave me this care for, this thought and love for you my darling, then you went away to let it grow and develop, to make me more worthy of you when you came back, to be with me always. God grant that I may use this waiting time to best insure your happiness in the future which you will make so beautiful for me. [1892-07-08 (Thursday) Henry (StL) to Bertha (Farragut House, Rye Beach)]

You spoiled that Thursday letter for I am yet foolish enough, as you will perhaps think it, to believe that your letters will be among my dearest treasures all my life, my darling. I have kept every one you have ever written me, dear, and, if you could see how many of them are almost worn away, it would not be hard to conclude that they had been read over a great many times.
[1892-07-09 Henry (StL) to Bertha (Farragut House, Rye Beach)]

Of course, Henry was always very upbeat when he thought about how they would soon be together: "*there will be joy as of heaven.*"

... for I do love you, dearest, and I don't like to live apart from you. It seems such a little while that we have ahead of us that it seems wrong to be separated, apart from the pain of it. I have missed you so this time that it was almost like another grief in my life to look for ahead and know that I must wait day after day with no cheer from your sweet face near me. I have not liked it, my darling, and we must some way fashion our lives that you may not be away from me so very, very long. There will be rejoicing in this lonely house as if you were here, almost, when I can write you that I know when we shall meet and when we do meet, there will be joy as of heaven...
[20180802-5 (2nd page only) Henry to Bertha]

When your letters came this morning, there were two. I could have cried out because of the thrill of happiness they gave me. The thought that you are mine, to be near me always, to be my helper, my companion, my nearest friend in every act of my life, to be the best part of my very existence, is the most beautiful realization that I am capable of. I call it a realization, dearest, because I know now what is, will be, to have you all my own. There is nothing vague now in the beautiful thought of you as my wife. As I think of it now, I seem almost to have the power to bring you here, so strong is my love, my darling, and I have the power, dear, for you are with me now, else how is it that I am filled with the feeling of perfect joy which comes to me only when your hand is in mine which never came to me before I knew and loved you, as now, and which never could have come into my life if you had not joined your life with mine.

Do I wound you in telling you all this, my love? If I speak too strongly or too plainly and of things you would have me only tell you when I can whisper my thoughts. So near will your heart be to mine if I write of those things which are too sacred to be told you except when you are near me. How very near, sometimes, my darling! You must forget what I write and forgive me. [1892-08-15 (Monday) Henry (StL) to Bertha (Farragut House, Rye Beach)]

Toward the end of the summer of 1892, Henry wrote optimistically since he would see Bertha in early October in St. Louis and then there were only four months until their wedding. Since the waiting period was almost half over, Henry looked forward to the next period, one of preparation.

After we are married! Does that thought thrill you with joy as it does me, my darling child? I thought today that, not only had "more than half the time passed", but that in a little while it would seem no longer a period of waiting but one of preparation for the beautiful lives we shall live together. You see, dear, you will be here in a month and from that time, four months, dearest, just half the time I counted so dismally that morning in Boston when you would not let me cheat myself into making the eight months seven, dear. We will have so much to plan and so many beautiful things to think of that I know the time will pass more quickly than it has. And, dear, I shall be so helped by your visit in October!! And you need not count upon my letting the four months after that go by without my seeing you.

When your visit to Miss Nan is over, you must let me go to see you in the east as soon as I can get away, for I could not stand another long separation like this last, Bert, unless you especially asked it, dear, and I don't think you will do this for certainly no good can be done by my staying away from you now. I will not write any more now, dear. There are times when I cannot write all that I feel. Some thoughts, ... put into words, seem robbed of their deepest meaning, do they not, my darling?
[1892-08-29 (Sunday) Henry (StL) to Bertha (Farragut House, Rye Beach)]

Henry knew how much Bertha would miss Rye Beach and her Rye Beach friends at summer's end. Henry wrote to Bertha of his gratitude for Bertha's friends with that *"peculiar feeling of pleasure we often have when we think of those who prize the treasures one cares most for"*.

This is the last letter I shall write you at Rye, dear. When I knew at first how long you were to be there without my being able to see you, a little of the bitterness I felt at the separation from you must have made me hold the place in some degree responsible for my gloom. But the picture you have given me of your summer there have robbed me of this feeling entirely and, apart from your attachment for it, I shall always think of it and of the friends who have made your summer so bright and happy with the peculiar feeling of pleasure we often have when we think of those who prize the treasures one cares most for.
[1892-09-07 (Thursday) Henry (StL) to Bertha (Farragut House, Rye Beach)]

Henry's praises for Bertha was heartfelt.

When I read your letter through, I sat thinking of you for quite a long time, dear. Considering the rush I and the whole office force were in all day, it seemed strange even to me that I could so

absolutely forget every worry and care and dwell upon the sweet memories of my darling, which thought of her always brings back to me. And, Bert, I wondered if there was ever a man who, beside the care he had for the woman he loved, so honored and worshiped her for making the world seem better, for making all his thoughts higher and better, for blessing him in freely unfolding to him a life so strong and pure that he makes it a standard by which to judge and value all the best and highest ambitions of his life. Yes, I wondered, my darling, if any other woman even held such a place with her best friend, and I could not believe any other man so blest, dear, for there is no other woman in all the world like my darling.
[1892-10-30 (Saturday) Henry (StL) to Bertha (Miss Bertha W Drake, Hotel Brunswick, Boston MA)]

6. BERTHA'S EXPRESSIONS OF LOVE

Writing to Henry after he had left New York City where they saw each other for two days in April 1892, Bertha reflected on their now three-year relationship and how the *"joy of a girl's life"* is not half as beautiful as the happiness that she now found.

Bertha's summers at the Farragut House in Rye Beach provided plenty of time for reading and writing letters. Becoming philosophical, Bertha started a letter to Henry by stating how important it was to have *"pleasant surroundings"* on Sunday to make the rest of the week bearable. But she quickly concluded, however, *"The needful thing was companionship"*.

> *This morning, I started out with the idea that Sunday wasn't much of a day unless one had all the pleasant surroundings to make rest bearable and it was not until I got your letter from the post office that I suddenly found my theory was a sham and that one wanted every quiet moment that could be honestly taken for developing a true appreciation of some of the things that make life so beautiful. On second thought, my theory was not so faulty after all. The needful thing was companionship and I found it in your letter, dear.*
[1892-06-30(-) Henry (StL) to Bertha (Farragut House, Rye Beach)]

Bertha reiterated her feelings about companionship two weeks later, quoting from Henry David Thoreau about *"the cost of a thing"* from her calendar.

> *July 11 Monday: The cost of a thing is the amount of what I will call life which is required to be exchanged for it, immediately or in the long run. Thoreau*
> *Indeed, I do like that word "companionship" and I think you and I have learned the definition of it pretty well already, while it takes some people a good part of a lifetime. Don't you think it is worth what, according to the calendar quotation I enclose, is its cost.*
[1892-07-12 Bertha (Rye Beach) to Henry (StL)]

Although Bertha had many reasons to be nervous about her future married life, a life completely different than any life she had ever known, Bertha wrote in response to Henry's questioning regarding the future, *"I am not at all afraid."*

> *I don't mind being scolded, dear boy, but to feel that I have said anything that makes you shut any part of your life away from me, that hurts. It makes me feel as if I had disappointed you in something. It did make me want so to see you for a moment and ask you to forgive me if I had hurt you. You see, I have no fear of what your answer would be. No, I have no fear of there ever being a serious misunderstanding between us, nothing that being together for a little while will not set right, though I don't doubt that two slightly quick-tempered people will quarrel occasionally. But when I am asked, as I have been once or twice, if I am not afraid of the future, of the great change, the new life, it is no affectation to say that I am not at all afraid. This may be presumptuous on my part but, it is not that I do not expect to make blunders, it is only - what is it that "casts out fear", my dear, - love. You don't know how beautiful the world looks to me today and the life ahead. I*

am glad that you really have chosen our house at last. I like to be able to think of it. [1892-07-01 Bertha (Farragut House) to Henry (StL)]

In an August 1892 letter, Bertha wrote: *"it is as impossible for me to picture any life without you ..."*

O, my dearest, you do not know how much I want to see you. There is not a thing that I do, not a pleasure that I have, that I don't want you with me. I never make a plan that the thought does not come if only Henry were here to plan it with me. And although we are apart and have been apart so much, it is as impossible for me to picture any life without you in the years to come as it is impossible for me to picture death.
[1892-08-11 (Wednesday) Bertha (Rye Beach) to Henry (StL)]

Although Bertha's letters often contained various small reprimands to Henry, more than anything else, they showed that Bertha was nurturing person and wanted to be Henry's helpmeet: *"I like the word and I want to be that needful help to you so much."*

You said you would let it rest with me, whether you should tell me more of your daily struggles or not - and if I want to know about them. I am a woman, dear, not a child, though I like to have you call me your child. And more than that I am, as you said the other day, in everything but name, your wife. And that gives me the right to share things, does it not? Write to me what is a relief to you to write for if, on the other hand, you would rather escape from the whole atmosphere for a while, why throw it aside. But remember that I do care to know and make me as much your helpmeet as you can until I can come to you. Helpmeet means the right help, doesn't it? As I told you before, I like the word and I want to be that needful help to you so much.
[1892-08-16 (Monday) Bertha (Rye Beach) to Henry (StL)]

After a letter from Henry in which Henry apologized for speaking "too plainly"[140], Bertha was very sweet in her reply.

My darling, I have not said anything about the rest of your letter because I could not, though I shall never forget it. And you need not ask to be forgiven for telling me the sweetest thing that I shall ever hear. God bless you, dearest, best friend.
[1892-08-18 (Thursday) Bertha (Farragut House, Rye Beach) to Henry (StL)]

7. BERTHA ASSERTS HERSELF

Henry often felt gloomy being apart from Bertha during their engagement in 1892 and continually expressed his need to be with her. Perhaps since Henry's happiness so much depended on Bertha, he may have thought that Bertha was likewise dependent on him for her happiness. In response to one such letter from Henry, Bertha's response was indignant and self-affirming. Essentially, "I don't need you to be happy".

Your letter, reaching me after my blue mood was over, dear, did not receive the sympathetic reading it deserved. You are mistaken, my friend, in thinking I am seldom happy except with you. I am almost always happy. My blue moods are the exception and I am very sorry you happened in on one last night. No, I do not at all approve of your plan of seeing me oftener. Thursday night is quite soon enough and indeed, I do wish you would take some other girl sleigh riding! Why don't you take Cynnie?
[1892-01-13 Bertha (StL) to Henry (StL)]

Bertha soon regretted her suggestion that Henry take Cynnie Yeatman out for a drive.

I notice you lost no time in taking my advice to drive with other girls. Hildegarde told me she met you at Mattie's.
[1892-03-05 Bertha (Ponce de Leon, St Augustine FL) to Henry (StL)]

---

[140] See Henry's 1892-08-15 letter above, Par. E.5.

In spite of her bluster, Bertha could display some jealousy.

> *Emma told me more of your doings than you do yourself. Pray, when you told me of your goodness in going to the Cathedral Easter, did you not tell me of your having the service early and of your walk home? It is not the walk I mind, but this intense secretiveness. Can you not see the green eyed monster rising?*

[1892-04-27 Wednesday Bertha (NYC) to Henry (StL)]

After their April 1892 New York City visit, Henry presumptuously wrote of his concern that Bertha was "blue" over Henry's departure. Henry was feeling blue himself and must have thought it reasonable to ascribe the same feelings to Bertha. *"I call it impertinent to understand more than is told you!"* Bertha wrote.

> *The rest of your letter was just what I needed too, but I highly disapprove of your method of reading between the lines of my letters. What right had you to know I was blue the early part of this week when I did not tell you so? I call it impertinent to understand more than is told you, and then the outrageous conceit of thinking it was all due to you. No, my son, I have not yet reached the point which brought Margaret Ives home to the professor in the depths of July to weep upon his shoulder that she "could not live without him". Tradition says the Professor was not pleased and I doubt if you would be more so if I summoned you east at this season of the year.*

> *No, dear boy, glad as I should be to see you at any time, just now you would bother me as much as I should bother you, for I am busy every minute with shopping, etc., and shall be until I go on to Boston. Moreover, my blues were not all due to your departure by any means. Partly, perhaps, I wonder how you would like it if it made no difference to me whatever. But in addition, having a strong resemblance to that gentleman in Shakespeare who "in his time, dies many deaths", I was dreading the talk with my father, my mother was confined to the room two days with sciatica suffering very much, I had a cold myself - not bad enough to warrant sympathy but annoying, the weather was awful, and George had chosen that particular time not to write for two weeks and so worry mother nearly to pieces. (The German measles accounted for a short part of the time, the rest was because he was born a boy, I suppose.) That did not worry me, except reflectively. But was not that enough to make anyone blue?*

[1892-04-23 (Saturday) Bertha (New York) to Henry (StL)]

Bertha and Henry discussed the numerous topics of the day and it seemed pretty clear that Henry could be labeled as argumentative. While Bertha accepted this character trait in Henry, she gently pushed back in the following letter and requested that Henry respect *"my firm beliefs"*.

> *That reminds me that I don't think I did myself justice with you in our discussion afterwards or in one or two others. I think I made you think me more foolish than I really am. I cannot argue. I do not need you to tell me that and I never seem stupider than when I try to, for I always get thrown off my own line of thought and forget all the really good points I have on my side until afterward. You might not consider the points good but I could at least have shown you my reasons for my stand point. Don't be alarmed, I am not going into a theological discussion with you, I only want to say this in my own defense. There are certain things I do believe very positively, there are others that are only matters of speculative interest to me and you attacked them as if they were all alike – my firm beliefs.*

[1892-05-29 (Sunday) Bertha (Boston) to Henry (StL)]

In response to Henry's "*growling*" over not receiving a letter, Bertha wrote of how spoiled Henry was.

> *My dear Henry Clarkson,*
> *You are too spoiled to live! To take up two pages of a four-page letter, growling because I had not written as you supposed on Saturday. I hope you felt properly ashamed when the Saturday letter arrived. I am going to pay you off now (that is not slang, is it?) by writing you all about the Jaffrey postal arrangements which will bore you nicely but I hope it will prevent any more complaints.*
> [1892-07-01x (Friday) Bertha (Jaffrey NH) to Henry (StL)]

> *Myra and I composed it* [the telegram] *together, only she strongly objected to my saying "don't you wish you were here." That will make him feel so badly, Bert, why don't you say "we wish you were here." But I thought you were too spoiled as it was.*
> [1892-07-22 (Thursday) Bertha (Kennebunkport, ME) to Henry (Wichita)]

Many times, Bertha was able to communicate a reprimand, followed by loving words which was surely a balm to any sting.

> *... you insinuate that the men I like are "Miss Nancyish". Presumably you do not include yourself in that category. I was at first inclined to be very indignant at such a remark but then I remembered that I did have two friends who might come under that appellation and I suppose that is enough to give a man excuse for a general accusation. And then you lost your equanimity over my playful remarks about the Ozark scenery, cross grained old thing, what a poor look out I have for any kind of a time with you! And yet, just at present, I would give almost any of my most valuable possessions for an hour of that kind of a time with you. You do not need to have me tell you again that I love you better, far better than anything else in the world, my dearest.*
> [1892-08-08 (Wednesday) Bertha (Farragut house, Rye Beach) to Henry (StL)]

When Bertha felt that Henry was hiding his feelings from her, she called Henry a brick.

> *Your note written Saturday afternoon came last night and the gladness you felt, dear boy, showed what a weight had gone. Knowing you as I do, I knew you must feel all this but you never showed a word of it in your letters and that was one reason I said you were a brick and you are.*
> [1892-09-20 (Tuesday) Bertha (Jaffrey) to Henry (StL)]

And in Bertha's letter three days later, "*Henry, you are a brick!!*"

> *Henry Scott, you are a brick!! I know you don't like terms of that kind but, even if you "have not been a boy since you were seventeen", perhaps you can remember that very far away time just enough to know what a compliment that is. You say that perhaps if things had always gone smoothly, I might have expected too much of you in the future. I don't know about that, dear boy, I do know that if ever there comes a time in the future when I want help from you and do not get it, there will be a woefully surprised and disappointed woman in this world.*
> [1892-09-23 (Thursday) Bertha (the Ark, East Jaffrey) to Henry (StL)]

Bertha was never afraid to let Henry know when his self-assurance of being "*absolutely right*" was annoying. As Bertha wrote, "*I have yet to meet you when you are convinced of anything else.*"

> *I have not teased you yet about your delightfully self-satisfied frame of mind over the Waco affair[141]. What was it your handwriting said about a "slight tendency to inflation?" I have no doubt that, determined altogether, Napoleon's policy was the very best possible, but you need not have assured me, my dear, that you were conscious of being absolutely right. I have yet to meet you when you are convinced of anything else. It is a shame to do this, however. To whom can a man toast if not*

---

[141] Bertha was referring to Henry's letter – [1892-12-19 (Monday)] – in Chapter 18. – "*I really believe we have won our fight at Waco.*"

to his female relatives. I am not a relative exactly but I shall be a connection soon and I feel it my duty to keep you from being spoiled by those individuals who had such absolute confidence in your power to set things right, you know.
[1892-12-27 (Monday 1892-12-26) Bertha (Newton Centre) to Henry (StL)]

Bertha and Henry felt a need through their letters to warn the other of their faults and lower the other's expectations. Bertha wrote to Henry about her childhood in another letter as being a "*horrid little prig*" and in the following, as being "*a spoiled and indulged child*". Bertha warned Henry about trying to spoil her further. "*I loathe people who are "kind" to me.*"

I received your Saturday letter last evening, dear friend, and it is the first letter I have ever had from you that has provoked me, that is, lately. My dear boy, my whole life I have been a spoiled and indulged child and always, excepting one particular, I am so still. I know, at least, I am afraid that nothing would give you greater satisfaction than to think of me as a martyr but I am not at all. To have a headache and be forced to travel a week after all traces thereof have passed away, one could scarcely call that hardship and to travel in this way, breaking the trip at short intervals is a perfect delight to me. I love seeing new places; it is only the getting to them that tires me. While, as for being less well than usual, Edith tells me I have not begun to look as well all winter and, as Nan tells me, the same of you. It shows plainly what a good effect separation has on both of us.

But I have not finished my lecture, not nearly! Do not think I am one bit grateful for your having expressed the intention of "being kind" to me. I loathe people who are "kind" to me. If you are kind to me, I think I shall treat you well. How would you like that? No, my friend, people are kind to children and dogs and inferiors generally. (I am not sure that children are inferiors, by the way.) But fancy yourself saying you would be kind to Gist! Having recently discovered his pugilistic qualities, I am quite sure he would use that lovely expression of his, if he did not hit you and I hope he would do the latter.
[1892-03-22 Bertha (St. Augustine FL) to Henry (StL)]

Obviously, Bertha felt that being kind was condescending and she would not stand for condescension: "*people are kind to children and dogs and inferiors...*" One can imagine that, in 1892, men often treated women in such manner and Bertha wanted nothing of that. When Bertha felt that Henry was flattering her excessively, she would rebuke him.

I received your Monday letter today. My son, you have gotten into a very bad habit of complimenting me. Now, though I like a really good spontaneous compliment sometimes, I do not like them when they are written with evident and palpable effort, so unless you really feel very complimentary, do not try to be so.
[1892-10-27 (Thursday) Bertha (Boston) to Henry (StL) on Wedding Plans, etc.]

Henry was generally used to having his compliments well received and expressed surprise at Bertha's rebuke. But, was Henry actually surprised?

I don't think I ever said or wrote you a word or a line in all the time of our friendship, dear, that did not at the time mean to express my thought of you. I thought I had been pretty frank with you, often I have felt that I spoke to you too plainly. So you can imagine I was not prepared for your criticism on my sincerity. I expect, though, it is pretty tiresome to receive the same compliments so often and with as little variation as I offer them, so I shall try to spare you a little in future, dearest.
[1892-10-31 (Sunday) Henry (StL) to Bertha (Hotel Brunswick, Boston)]

Summers in St. Louis must have been boring for the few men that were obliged to remain at their posts. So, when St. Louisans began returning in mid-September 1892, Henry's social life improved immensely, as he communicated to Bertha. In response to an upbeat letter from Henry, however, Bertha wrote that his letter was "*positively uncomplimentary.*"

My dear gregarious friend, the increase of cheerfulness in your letters since people got back to town is positively uncomplimentary. If you had any kind of tact, you would at least have kept up some pretense of blues until my return and not broken out into such absolutely wild hilarity as that invitation to the Lane's and the Gary's produced.
[1892-09-23 (Thursday) Bertha (the Ark, East Jaffrey) to Henry (StL)]

After Bertha's St. Louis visit for the Howard Elliott-Janet January wedding on October 12, Bertha continued to Chicago to visit the Bentons, Bents and Buckinghams. Due to its proximity to St. Louis, Bertha tried to arrange for Henry come up on his "free" Sunday. At the last minute, Henry declined.

You make me blue, Bert, about next Sunday. I simply can't get away from here. I am obliged to be in the office early on Monday and I have made up my mind to put up with the disappointment as best I can but I am not very reasonable about it yet, dear. It seems sometimes as though everything combines against me to keep me away from you as much as possible. But I am very glad you are to remain in Chicago over Sunday and you must think of me sometimes that day, for I shall need the thought that, even if I can't be near you, I am not altogether banished from your thoughts.
[1892-10-20 (Thursday) Henry (StL) to Bertha (5021 Washington Ave, Chicago)]

Henry's refusal to make the round trip from St. Louis to Chicago brought scorn from Bertha. As an additional "bonus" to Henry, Bertha apparently read to "the girls" (possibly Kate & Lucy Benton and Lucy Bent) the part of Henry's Wednesday letter explaining that he could not travel to Chicago to see Bertha because he needed to be in the office early on Monday. This caused "*a perfect howl from the girls. 'What does he call early?'*"

I have just received your Thursday letter as we had no mails yesterday. I read your reason for not coming up Sunday aloud – vis that you had to be at your office early Monday morning and there was a perfect howl from the girls. "What does he call early?" As the train from Chicago gets into St. Louis at six forty, I thought that excuse a little transparent, myself. I did not blame you for not wishing to travel twenty four hours for three hours conversation (the time the family was at church was all you could have had to yourself) but I did think you might have sent a more plausible excuse for the girls evidently considered that my charms were being wasted on a very unappreciative individual.
[1892-10-24 (Saturday) Bertha (Chicago) to Henry (StL)]

Henry was hurt by Bertha's letter implying his lack of sufficient interest in not visiting her in Chicago and wrote as much. Bertha's penitence in her reply to Henry's letter was sincere.

I don't believe I ever was disagreeable to you in my life without being sorry for it. Your letter written Friday evening came this morning and made me feel very penitent for the letters I have sent you. Forgive me, dear old boy. I won't do it again.
[1892-10-24 (Monday) Bertha (Chicago) to Henry (StL)]

(Bertha's sentiment, "*I don't believe I ever was disagreeable to you in my life without being sorry for it*", surely put this matter to rest.)

8. BERTHA'S HEALTH

Bertha was always very cautious about writing about her health because of Henry's sensitivity. But in one letter, Bertha was able to write about a cold in a humorous fashion which seemed an effective way to avoid a reproach from Henry.

I am a miserable sinner and not in the prayer book sense either. Did you ever play consequences? Well, Miss Drake met the sun on 5th Avenue. He said, "why aren't you too warm in a winter dress and fur cape when I am shining so brightly?" She said "Yes, I think I am, I'll go home and put on a thinner dress and a summer coat directly." The consequences were a very bad cold in the head and the entire metamorphoses of all her m's and n's into b's & d's. And the world said, "Served her right, what did she do such an idiotic thing for?" Do you know the utter miserableness of a

cold in the head? Nothing dangerous, nothing interesting and nothing more trying to your temper. That is to say, my temper.
[1892-04-28(-) Thursday Bertha (5th Ave Hotel, NYC?) to Henry (StL)]

When Henry lectured Bertha about her health, she took offense at the implied condescension. In numerous letters, Henry would express his worry about Bertha not taking care of her health. Bertha knew that Henry was concerned even if *"my little finger aches"* and so she would sometimes not speak of an illness until it had nearly passed. Such was certainly the case when she contracted the mumps while in Boston in May 1892.

My dear friend, I have the mumps. I did not say anything about it yesterday for I was not sure until after I saw the doctor, whom I could not get hold of until late in the afternoon after I had written you, and there was no use bothering you. I would not write now, knowing your tendency to worry if my little finger aches, if it is were not that I had promised you solemnly to let you know if I were ill and that I should feel you treated me badly if in like case you did not tell me. By the time you get this, I shall probably be out, as my doctor assures me, mumps are only a matter of three days and that by Tuesday or Wednesday at the latest, I may go out.

My doctor (Dr. Nichols) is, in addition to being one of the leading doctors here [in Boston], a very old friend. He has a cottage at Rye and has attended me through two sprained ankles and various minor ills in the past fifteen years and I don't think he fully realizes yet that I am grown up. He spent an hour chatting with me today and we were joined by Gertrude Dillon who was not afraid of the contagion and who spent the whole afternoon. One of the meanest things about it is that I am cut off entirely from Nan who has never had them. I only hope she did not catch them Friday, for of course, it was in its early stages then and indeed my cheek felt a little sore and stiff but I only thought I had bruised it on the arm of the sofa for I had not been feeling perfectly fine owing, I suppose, to the approach of this and had been lying down. All I entreat of you is do not laugh at me! Everybody does at(??) mumps, for they are not an atom dangerous, and they are undoubtedly absurd. But I assure you they are literally no laughing matter, for I had to beg Dr. Nichols to stop telling funny stories yesterday, my enjoyment was too painful.

I am much better today, and I have been occupying myself with being devoutly thankful that you had to go to Wichita this week. Just supposing you had been in the city and unable to see me.
...
I do not suppose you are in the least afraid of contagion but I assure you, this letter shall be fumigated before it goes.
[1892-05-08 Bertha (Boston) to Henry (StL)]

It is rather a bore, its having lasted so long and now that I am decidedly on the mend, I will confess I have been quite miserable. I developed what the doctor called a sympathetic sore throat. How could Grapho[142] say I had narrow sympathies! Would that they were less broad – fever, pain, sleeplessness!!! I shall never laugh again at people who have the mumps! Don't you dare to laugh at me! I am writing all this so that you shall give me an immense amount of sympathy. But it is all over, I have nothing to tell you, however, for of course my days are absolutely monotonous.
[1892-05-11 Bertha (Boston MA) to Henry (StL)]

True to form, Henry was concerned and, then, angry at the doctor for not doing more.
You speak of going out today which is evidence that Dr. Nichols is not careful and, in spite of all your praise of him, I have little confidence in his prudence as an adviser, however agreeable he

---

[142] Apparently, the name of one of Bertha's doctors.

Page 311

may be as a companion which, I regret to say, seems a more important thing to most women than professional ability.
[1892-05-12 Henry (StL) to Bertha (Hotel Brunswick, Boston)]

Bertha's weight was a constant concern of Henry – that Bertha did not weigh enough. In the 1890's, it is possible that extra weight on a woman signified health. Regardless, throughout their engagement (and marriage), Henry would worry about Bertha being too thin.

I was thrown into a state of panic by your announcement that you only weight "twenty five pounds". Please correct this if it be an error or I shall go on immediately to see for myself. Seriously dear, one hundred and twenty-five is ten pounds less than you told me you weighed in Boston and I don't like to know you have lost since you left there at all. Try to take care of yourself for my sake, will you not, darling?
[1892-06-21 Henry (StL) to Bertha (The Ark, East Jaffrey)]

Bertha dismissed Henry's concerns about her weight, writing *"You are a dearly beloved goose."*

You are a dearly beloved goose, dear boy, to be worrying about my health. I am exceedingly proud of only weighing one hundred and twenty-five pounds and I only wish I might not gain any of it back but I am afraid I shall in this delicious place, living out doors all day and keeping the early hours we do.
[1892-06-17 Bertha (Jaffrey, NH) to Henry (StL)]

As an historical note, Bertha was always able to stay fit. In 1904, one year after Bertha delivered her fourth child, Alice, Bertha weighed 125 pounds. Henry was concerned anyway.

I am delighted to hear what you say about your health, although 125 ½ is not reassuring. You ought to weigh at least 150. How many pounds will you contract to gain by the middle of August? I shall not come on until you report you have gained at least ten pounds and may be not until you have added fifteen. Now, you have got to hustle or I shall not have any vacation and, if I don't see you soon, I shall not weigh even 125 ½! I shall be a pathetic example of the deserted husband.
[1904-07-(-) 20180630-2 Henry (StL) to Bertha (Rye Beach)])

During their brief time together in Boston in May 1892, Henry vigilantly watched for any signs that Bertha was becoming ill. In a June letter, Henry recounted the reasons for his concerns.

I hardly had time in yesterday's letter to lecture you for being playful on the subject of your health. I was not attempting to indulge in a mere formality in asking you to be more careful of yourself. Do you know, dearest, I was scared two or three times when you absolutely gave out in Boston during some of our excursions. I could hardly believe it was the same girl who had walked or ridden with me all the afternoon a few years ago without showing the slightest sign of fatigue. I think your power of endurance less than that of almost any girl I know, dear, and I tell you very frankly that if I could have my way about it, I would tyrannize over you to an extent that would insure your being more prudent. As it now is, I can only sit here and fret over it without being able to do the slightest good. And about the driving, this is a much less serious matter for the others who are with you will have sufficient regard for their own safety not to trust those horses to you without providing an assistant capable of managing that wonderful team in emergencies.
[1892-06-22 Henry (StL) to Bertha (The Ark, Jaffrey)]

Henry was clearly frustrated and anxious about Bertha taking unnecessary risks with her health and would periodically try to exercise his manly prerogative over Bertha. Bertha never reacted well to this approach and often rebuked Henry for his *"impertinence"*.

You command me to take care of my health, do you? I like your impertinence. You have not yet the legal right to do that yet, my lord, and, if you do not be very careful, I will follow Mary Bell

Rouauau's(?) example and have "obey left out"!!! A few weeks ago, I might have been meek and submissive but I have reached that state of health and spirits now, when I enjoy taking liberties with one self, a dangerous time to stir up a mutiny in the camp and the immediate effect of your letter was to create in me a wild desire to go out and take a walk through the wet grass in the pouring rain and come in and eat a supper of cheese and fruit cake!! I did not do it but I may do something like it yet, if only for the pleasure of finding out what those terrible effects of your wrath would be. And all this comes from a man who then writes calmly that his doctor tells him "you experiment with your health sufficiently to cause you great discomfort!" On the whole, your doctor's verdict was a great comfort to me, though. I cannot even be so very sorry that he forbade polo, in spite of the fact that it is a "much more innocent game than football", and I am so very very glad to know he thinks there is no reason you should not keep perfectly well through the hot weather. I do not like to know you are unwell and so far away from me, dearest.
[1892-06-27 (Sunday) Bertha (Jaffrey NH) to Henry (StL)]

In the following letter, Henry went even farther in asserting his prerogatives over Bertha when she had reported that she had been in deep water off of Rye Beach.[143]

University Club
Monday

Your reply to my threat began in such vigorous language that I began to wish I had said I should be "sorry" and not "angry" if you were a bad child again and attempted to disobey a very wise man's instructions by going out over your head. If you had not promised me, there would have been deep trouble for you, my dear, for I had made my plans as to what I should do if you declined to give me your promise. I should have left here by the next train with a minister and on my arrival at Rye I should have looked you up, introduced my companion to you and then have made known my further intentions as follows. "Attention! Mr. Minister, this child belongs to me. She is only temporarily in the care of others because I have been a very weak, yielding creature. I couldn't help being weak with her, Mr. Minister. She makes me yield to her by using a certain power which you know nothing about with all that wise look which your gospel agents wear as a work of your craft. Now I have found that this same young lady has been very bad, very unmanageable lately and so I have decided to cut off the holiday I have been generous enough to grant her and I have come here with you to claim her and take her home with me where, to punish her for being wicked, I shall not permit her to go out of my sight for a long time. Now, Mr. Minister, do your duty!"

How would you have like me to have appeared at your much beloved Rye and put in my claim before all those eminently proper and peaceable members of its society. The church riot would have passed out of notice so busy would have been its shining lights with this episode in the bright career of its choir leader. And the spinsters!! Never again would they lack a topic of common interest. It would last the length of their sweet but uneventful lives! But, my darling, you did promise. I asked your promise because I love you, darling and you gave it to me because, why dear? I admit that your epithet was not a favorite of mine but then what is the use of my trying to quarrel with you about it? I should simply forget as I always to when I try to quarrel with you, that I must be very angry and about the only thought I should be able to keep in mind would be that God had made a beautiful, sweet child and had given her to me for my own. And then I should take you in my arms, my darling and ask you to forgive me for being unkind to you.

Yours always,
Henry
[1892-08-08 (Monday) Henry (StL) to Bertha (Farragut House, Rye Beach)]

---

[143] See 1892-07-29 (Friday) 20170724-4 Bertha (Farragut House) to Henry (StL), in Chapter 3.

The winter of 1892 at the Brunswick Hotel in Boston gave Henry additional cause for concern for Bertha's health.[144]

> *Having acknowledged your letters, may I not now scold you a little for catching cold again? You frighten me, Bert, when you take cold in this way. I can't bear to think of your being so susceptible to colds and I think this would not be so were it not that you are neither as strong nor as well as you should be. You certainly made me see the importance of attending to the chimneys in our house. I might have forgotten to have them examined, even if by so doing the freshness of everything had thereby been endangered but I don't think there is much danger of my risking your catching cold from the same cause that your accident at the Brunswick cast you. I will not say anything more about your taking better care of yourself, dearest, but if you only knew how much harder it is to be separated from you when I am not sure that you are well, I think you would be rather sorry for me and try to be prudent. You will try, won't you, my darling?* [1892-12-07 (Tuesday, 1st letter) Henry (StL) to Bertha (Hotel Brunswick, Boston)]

Probably because the wedding was two months away, Bertha's responses to Henry's concerns for her health during December and January were more diplomatic.

> *My dearest, I have never thanked you for all the thoughtful consideration you have shown for all my wishes, not only about this but about all our plans. You are my best friend always, dear. But there is no need for you to lecture me on taking care of my health, my son, I assure you I take beautiful care of it and, out at Newton, I shall simply be a model. I wish I thought you would behave half as well. And now, goodbye, my own dear love. Think of me occasionally on your journey & once in a while I will send a thought to you.*
> [1892-12-08 (Wednesday) Bertha (Backbay, Boston) to Henry (StL)]

> *Please take care of yourself and don't send me anymore lectures about my health until you can take better care of yours.*
> [1893-01-03 (Monday) Bertha (Newton Centre) to Henry (StL)]

Bertha employed many techniques to rebuff Henry's constant concerns for her health which included the threat of bad behavior.

> *I have your Monday letter and I should think you ought to have learned wisdom by experience. Of course, the instant that I read that you forbade me to get tired, I wanted to go into Boston and tramp all day, shopping, etc. And nothing but the snowstorm prevented me. We are having a real old-fashioned snowstorm. It snowed all yesterday, all last night, and is still briskly at it. The snow is about a foot deep now and perfectly beautiful. There is a promise of gorgeous sleigh rides to come.*
> [1893-01-06 (Friday) Bertha (Boston) to Henry (StL)]

M. CHRISTMAS 1892
Bertha loved the Christmas celebration, including the rush and bustle of shoppers and the common feelings of good will.

> *I missed you today, my dearest. I was making up a package of Christmas things and I wanted your help in tying them up, you were such a useful boy last year. Do you remember what a jolly evening we had? This particular parcel was one I was sending out to Lute. It is a little too bulky to carry in my trunk to Newton Center so I shall ask her to keep it and not show the contents to the babes till Christmas day. She will think my Fall's work is still having an effect on me when she sees*

---

[144] Henry's letter was in response to Bertha's letter, 1892-12-01 (Wednesday), in Chapter 11, G.2.

Peggy's. The dearest wee set of furniture, my dear, the sofa, ours in miniature, except the color which really was what attracted me to the set at first, I think.

I really have thought very little about Christmas things until today when it began to dawn upon me that the day of our departure for Newton Center was approaching and that it would not be nearly so convenient to shop when I was out there as it is here. As a matter of fact, however, I should probably have left the little of this work that I have to do until near Christmas anyway for I love to shop with a Christmas crowd. To go months beforehand and select in a leisurely manner what one is going to give has no charms for me whatever. I love the whole swing and rush and general ... common ground feeling of a crowd at Christmas time, especially in the toy stores.
[1892-12-14 (Wednesday) Bertha (Boston) to Henry (StL to Waco)]

For Henry, the Christmas of 1892 meant that *"The waiting time has almost gone."*
You bring that evening last year back to me very vividly, dearest. We did have a good time at which I wonder greatly considering the poor times we usually have together. I wish I could interrupt the completion of this letter as I did the preparation of those Christmas remembrances, my darling. I want you here with me now, dear, very near with your hand in mine. It is a real sorrow to me. But to be away from you this Christmas tide and - But I did not intend to indulge in further complaints or regrets over this long separation from you. I have kept all these thoughts out of my letters recently and I mean not to refer to them anymore. The waiting time has almost gone and I ought to think only of the things that I can do to make your future a happy one and not waste my thought of you in vain regret of the time I have lost in being separated from you, O my darling.
[1892-12-19 (Monday) Henry (Ft. Worth) to Bertha (Newton Centre)]

Bertha sent Henry a Christmas gift from Boston and provided him with strict instructions that it should not be opened before Christmas.
I sent you a Christmas remembrance today but unfortunately there is no name in the package. I told them to lay it aside for me the other day and I would tell them when to send it and they not only did that but sealed it up ready to go so I had no chance to put in from whom it came. You will have to devise that for yourself. But you are to open no parcel that has the name of a Boston firm on it before Christmas or at the very earliest, Christmas Eve, do you understand?
[1892-12-20 (Monday 1892-12-19) Bertha (Newton Highlands, MA) to Henry (StL)]

Amid the anticipated joys of this Christmas, Bertha also remembered the past ones, including one about a certain man five years before, and all of the Christmases in between.
Merry Christmas, my dearest, and all best and loving wishes for you. I am writing this while I wait for George's arrival which gives me the feeling that Christmas has already begun almost.

Last night I ran over some of our Christmases in the years just past and they came in this order.

There was one where a certain man came to call and I said I was excused and then, on learning who it was, sent George to call him back, although that was five years ago. And he came back and then brother George and Bobby Markham came in and we all drank egg nogg & had a very good time.

Then came the one you say you do not remember when Mattie and Edith and Janet and you and Mr. Fishback and Mr. Downman all went to see Chumley[145] in one party and Mother, Mrs. Treat, six boys, George Hitchcock, Sarah, Jule, Nan and I went in another and we all met at our house for supper afterward.

---

[145] *Lord Chumley*, by David Belasco; Henry Churchill De Mille, [New York], [1888]

And then there was one when Mrs. Wainwright gave a reception and we did not speak to each other only bowed, although I will confess it now, I had broken my rule of not leaving my family on Christmas Day simply because I hoped that I might see you there, which was very wrong of me when everything was at an end between us.

The next was the one when dear Mattie[146] tried to bring things right by sending us home together. O, that miserable drive through the snow!

Then last year, when you did not come to see me but sent me beautiful roses and a pen, that I ran away and hid and was almost afraid to look at.

O, my dear, we are farther apart [this] Christmas than any of the others, but how much nearer, really. Dear, I thank God that this Christmas is what it is and not like the others.

I have only time for these few lines, I must go and get ready to meet the boy. Once more, a Merry Christmas and God bless you, my dear love. Yours gladly, now and always,
Bert
[1892-12-22 (Thursday) Bertha (Newton Centre) to Henry (StL)]

Henry was very taken by Bertha's recounting of the five years of Christmases past that she and Henry had shared and by "*the unspeakable joy your presence always brings to me.*"
My darling, I stopped to read over your record of the Christmas days of the past five years. That was a beautiful letter, my precious child. No, all your letters are that, but this one tells me of your care for me in a way that sends the hot blood into my face with the unspeakable joy your presence always brings to me. If you had been here, if you had come into my arms, my love, I doubt if I would feel more strongly the power and beauty of what you are to me than your letter gives me as I read it over and over again. Surely I shall be able to repay you for some of the happy thoughts and bright hopes you fill my life with, Bert. There will be strength given me when I am weakest, hope when I am most gloomy, all I most care for will come from you and I think I can hope to learn to return something of the helpfulness of your love, for do I not care very, very much, my darling?
[1892-12-28 (Tuesday, Wednesday) Henry (StL) to Bertha (Stancote, Newton Centre)]

When Henry's roses arrived on Christmas day, Bertha wrote that "*I felt almost as if you had spoken to me.*"
I was too busy to write to you yesterday and, when your violets came in the evening, I felt a pang of reproach. They were so lovely, dear. I thought of course that they were to be my Christmas flowers so it was another lovely surprise when the roses came this morning. I felt almost as if you had spoken to me. And your letter did come on Christmas Day. I thought I was to have no word from you for I had no letter yesterday and today was Sunday but, it being Christmas, they kept the post office open for an hour and we sent for our letters.
...
It has been an ideal Christmas Day. A beautiful snow storm outside and a magnificent fire of real yule logs inside and it has been a most delightful one. I think one appreciates other people's remembering them so very, very much when one is away from home. You don't know how near I feel to all these dear people who thought of me.

I am so glad, dear boy, that you feel encouraged about Waco. That Fort Worth letter was delightful from the hopefulness in it and the "cheered up" ring to it. Do you remember what a hard time you

---
[146] Mattie McKittrick Stribling.

had to write me a note last Christmas? I trust you will find it easier today. I have no time for any more. Next Christmas, perhaps, you will not have to make time to write to me or I to you.
[1892-12-25 (Sunday) Bertha (Newton Center, MA) to Henry StL)]

As much as Bertha thought of her own last Christmas with her parents as "a child", she also thought of what that Christmas must be like for Henry's mother.

I am glad you were going to make the effort to get home for Christmas Eve. I know your mother wanted you. I think I can just understand how she felt, that she would like to have you to herself for one more Christmas for, after this, there would always be someone else about whom she doesn't know very well and who will rather spoil things by being an outsider. I should feel just so in her place. My dear, it is very hard on families. But I hope and trust that the anticipation is the worst part for them.

...

We finished our Christmas Day in the same quiet pleasant way it began. I read Dicken's Christmas Carol aloud in the evening for the benefit of George who had never heard it but I think the others enjoyed it just as much. There is nothing else that has such a real ring of Christmas in it.
[1892-12-27 (Monday 1892-12-26) Bertha (Newton Centre) to Henry (StL)]

Bertha received an amethyst vase as Henry's Christmas gift to her. Henry greatly downplayed how pretty it was calling it a "*bric a brac*". "*You fraud!*', Bertha wrote.

So that is your idea of a very plain little vase!! You fraud! I never saw any piece of bric a brac of that sort that I thought compared with it. It is no description to call it bric a brac, it is a jewel and a most rare and exquisite one. I would far rather own it than a piece of jewelry. It has just this moment come and mother fairly lost her breath over it. You dear boy, it is getting hackneyed to tell you that you have the best taste of any man I ever knew and it is almost equally worn out to say that you spoil me. But they are both true and I do thank you dearest. That beautiful thing will be a joy to me always. How did you find time to spend so much time on me in that little bit of time you had in New York? Some time when we can put this amethyst gem into some corner of our house and I am where I can put my hand in yours, I will try to tell you the pleasure it has given me.

...

One more thing, I had a box of beautiful white carnations from someone who never forgets anything that will give me pleasure, someone whom I care a little bit more about than about any other human being.

Before I stop speaking of your present, I must tell you that another saw a piece of this amethyst glass for the first time at Briggs' this summer and she thought it so lovely that she made me walk by his window this fall just to look at it. But they did not have a single piece that began to be as beautiful as this one. Thank you once more, my own dear boy.
[1892-12-27 (Tuesday) Bertha (Newton Centre) to Henry (StL)]

Bertha received a compliment from her mother about of the amethyst vase which she related to Henry. (Henry must have been very pleased!)

The light is falling beautifully through your vase. Mother said yesterday "this is a comfortable house, but the only real gem in it is that amethyst vase of yours." You do not know what a constant pleasure it is to me, my dearest.
[1893-01-25 (Sunday) Bertha (Stancote MA) to Henry (StL)]

On hearing of the number of presents lavished upon Bertha during that Christmas, Henry could only write, "*What a popular girl you are, dearest*".

What a popular girl you are, dearest! You see, not knowing you very well, I am greatly surprised to know how very many people remembered you on Christmas morning. You dear child, I wonder

if there is a single St. Louis girl whose friends outnumber yours. Don't wonder, rather, I know there is not one.
[1892-12-30 (Thursday) Henry (StL) to Bertha (Stancote, Newton Centre, MA)]

N. WHAT COMES NEXT?

During the period of their engagement, Bertha and Henry reflected on what marriage would be to them. On her last trip to Rye Beach as a single woman, Bertha wrote of the joy of having twelve of her friends all in her room, knowing that such times were coming to an end.

> *I did not write at my usual time today because I had a spree in my room after we came up from the bathing beach. My room is not very large and I had twelve girls in it, all ages, and we drank – plain lemonade, soda lemonade, apollinaris lemonade and claret lemonade! And ate crackers and cheese and they said next door that it sounded as if we had a ball and a Fourth of July celebration. I don't know whether you know how much twelve girls can say if shut into one room together. I doubt if any man knows.*
> [1892-08-05 (Friday) (20170712) Bertha (Rye Beach) to Henry (StL)]

Bertha and Henry never failed to recognize important milestones in their relationship. On their first anniversary of their August 25, 1891 engagement, they exchanged telegrams, with Henry sending: "*I hope this will be among your happiest anniversaries. HCS*" Bertha responded, "*Your hope is not unfulfilled. BWD.*" [1892-08-25 Telegrams]

And so it was. Bertha gave up the life of a girl and Henry's hope was not unfulfilled!

CHAPTER 13 - THE WEDDING

Bertha & Henry

A WOMAN'S LOVE

I would I were a thousand times more fair,
     Just for his eyes,
That he might gaze on me with glad surprise.
I would my gifts were multiplied tenfold,
     Just for his sight,
That he might find in me always delight.

I am so true a woman, I would glad suffer all pain,
So might his days be bright and free from rain.
I would give up unmurm'ring every joy,
     Needed he me,
For him, I'd sacrifice eternity.

Look down upon me in thy tender grace, fair Lord in Heaven,
Pardon me, if such love must be forgiven.
That grace sufficeth me, for him I crave
     All blessedness,
Grant me that boon, dear Lord, his happiness.
[Bertha's Poem #6, 1886]

A. PLANNING THE WEDDING

Once the engagement was announced, Bertha turned to shopping.

> *This afternoon, I start on a wedding present hunt. It is rather fun in Boston and New York. One sees such quantities of beautiful things. In St. Louis, I think one always groans over the very small choice. Don't think, however, that I am abusing the latter place. I love it more and more. Neither shops, public garden, or even Riverside can ween me from my allegiance.*
> [1892-09-14 (Tuesday) Bertha (Backbay, Boston) to Henry (StL)]

It took Bertha and Henry a great deal of time to determine the date when their wedding should take place. Henry desperately wanted the earliest possible date, regardless of impediments and possible impracticalities. After having given up on a November wedding, Henry's last request was for the 8th of February 1893.

> *O, speaking of that time, dear, when we shall be nearer than we ever have been, when you will be my wife, my darling, have you been able to determine when we are to be married? I think it will be the 8th of February, will it not? Lent comes in on the fifteenth, I think, and we could be married on the first, for the month comes in on Wednesday. Dear, if you care to talk about this now, you can write me about it after you reach Jaffrey. I like to think of your dreaming of and planning about your wedding day in that beautiful and quiet spot which you seem to have grown so attached to. I shall of course say nothing about your family's plans and you must tell me about them as soon as you can for I shall want to know where you will be this winter, dear.*
> [1892-09-06 (Tuesday) Henry (StL) to Bertha (Farragut House)]

Bertha decided that another week's delay was reasonable and, so, they were to be married on Tuesday, February 14, 1893, St. Valentines Day.

> *And I will answer your question. I think our wedding day might be the fourteenth of February. I hesitated between that and the eighth. I have not talked to anyone about it but I think I like the fourteenth best for two reasons. In the first place, not expecting Lent to come in quite so early, I have always spoken of my wedding as coming about the middle of the month and I think my family have rather reconciled themselves to that. Then, instead of having a long Christmas holiday this year, George is to have his weeks at Christmas and two at Easter, so my mother would have only Lent to wait before he would be at home with her. Then, the second reason you will smile at perhaps, but it is a very real one, I have always said I wanted to be married on Wednesday but I should like the fourteenth of February, though it comes on Tuesday, even better, because it is St. Valentine's day and I should dearly like to be married on St. Valentine's day. It ought to be the most fortunate day of the whole year.*

Flowers enclosed in Bertha's letter to Henry.

I had thought of this many times, for I had not entirely forgotten it though you might think so, when one day Esther spoke it. "Married in February", she said, "O why don't you choose St. Valentine's day. I have always thought it would be the most beautiful day of the year. It alone ought to bring good fortune to you." But I did not even tell her I had thought of it. I had no wish to talk about what day it should be with any one until I should have done so with you. My only wish is that it shall be a day which shall be a glad anniversary to us all our lives. It is to be the special day in the year for us, is it not? And you must tell me if there is any other day at about that time you would prefer or if you dislike the fourteenth for any reason. For I do not want on any account to choose a day you would not like. And I want you to be as frank with me as I am with you, so I tell you now, I really could not have either Friday or the thirteenth, and you may tease me for being superstitious if you wish.

I have a magnificent bunch of Autumn sunshine on my table which I gathered this morning and I enclose a small spray to you. God bless you, dear.
[1892-09-05 (Monday) Bertha (Jaffrey) to Henry (StL)]

Henry continued to make his case for the 8th of February, writing: "*... a week counts for much when it is a difference for that period between absolute happiness and waiting and hoping for it.*"
And about our wedding day, dear, I would rather have the eighth because it is nearer, but if St. Valentines day is preferred by you, why then I can wait. But you must not forget that it is a week later, my darling, and a week counts for much when it is a difference for that period between absolute happiness and waiting and hoping for it. But, my child, you choose between the days. Not now, if you don't care to decide, but later when, if you wish it, you can have talked the matter over with me. And whatever you wish will be my choice, dear. I haven't your prejudice against the thirteenth or Friday or against any other day. I think I need you too much to have preference for any day but the nearest. And yes, I am very superstitious about delays, for once upon a time I wanted something more than I ever wished for anything in my life and postponement almost cost me what I wished for, dear. "What I wished for" does not express it, darling. It was what I could not live without. It was a need in my life my darling and I am frightened as I think of how many times I almost lost my treasure. Dear, do you think anything else but the knowledge that we could not live our lives apart could have given me the power to win you for my wife?
[1892-09-23 (&24) (Thursday-Friday) Two letters - Henry (StL) to Bertha (The Ark, East Jaffrey)]

By the end of September, Henry accepted the plan to have their wedding on February 14th at the Pulsifer's house, the Drakes' temporary residence in Newton With this resolved, Henry expressed renewed enthusiasm: "*I have seen some beautiful visions of our life together.*"
The more I think of your new plan for the winter the greater is my pleasure in it and it gives me very bright visions of our wedding day to think that I shall have your promises to be my wife in a spot which I can already see you are beginning to grow attached to. And, dear, I am sure all your anticipations of the place will be realized for I remember very well hearing you speak of the Pulsifer's house when I was in Boston and I thought then that it must very greatly resemble some of those quaint pretty places we found in our numerous exploring tours through the different suburbs of Boston. And, my darling, I am so glad for you, for I know this plan will give you much happiness. You were very dear and brave in meeting the first decision of your family to remain at the Brunswick. You only wrote me that you were angry and tried to make me believe it was only an irritation to you, but you did not deceive me, dear. I saw that it was a real grief to you to think of spending this last winter with your friends at a hotel and having our wedding from there and it hurt me so to think of your sorrowing about it that it did make me angry and I am afraid, as I had rather expected some such arrangement, I was not very fair in some of my conclusions.

...

When I got your letter this morning, I felt like going off where there would be no one to interrupt the many pleasant thoughts suggested by it. So, although I knew no one of the other men was coming out here, I decided to do so and, as soon as I left the office, I took the late train and, since I have been here, I have had a beautiful time for in the quiet of this superb night I have given all my thoughts to my child. And, Bert, I have seen some beautiful visions of our life together, of the journey, of our home, of the hours we shall pass together. O, my darling, this is indeed a beautiful world!
[1892-09-25 (Saturday Evening) Henry (Stl CC) to Bertha (The Ark, East Jaffrey)]

Henry next wrote: "*when you come dear, ... it will be happiness sweeter than anything I have dreamed of.*"

O, Bert, I didn't think in my wildest dreams it would all be as beautiful as this! I can scarcely take my thoughts from you long enough to do my work and, dear, your face seems mirrored in every object I look at. Bert, do you think we can grow any closer to each other than we are now? I have thought many times before, that the climax of my happiness had been reached only to find when little more time had passed that you were so much dearer and nearer to me that I felt like reproaching myself for not having appreciated and valued you before. But, I don't see how it can be any better than this, dear, even when we are <u>one</u> in name and in all the purposes and pleasures of our lives, and when you come dear, when I can hold you close in my arms. O, my darling, it will be happiness sweeter than anything I have dreamed of.
[1892-09-25 (Monday) Henry (StL) to Bertha (The Ark, East Jaffrey)]

Even after the wedding date was settled, Bertha's mother continued to advocate for an additional delay. It may be surmised that either she wanted to have more time with her daughter before she was no longer her child, or she thought (or hoped) that Bertha might still change her mind. Bertha, in her letter below, almost seemed ambivalent about another delay.

I have no news to tell you. Mother said the other day she did not see why you and I had not waited until May. She thought we had made a great mistake in selecting February. I did not say anything but I thought I would mention it to you and if you think it is a mistake, why, my friend, it can be most easily rectified. You have only to mention that you wish it deferred until May and your will is my law, you know.
[1892-12-12 (Sunday) Bertha (Boston) to Henry (Wichita)]

Bertha waited until the end of her four-page letter to slip in: "*I have no news to tell you. Mother said the other day...*" There was no doubt that the news that Bertha M was discussing an additional delay in the wedding date was significant and unpleasant news to Henry. However, the subject of any additional delay in the wedding was apparently dropped since there are no additional correspondences on this subject after this letter.

Perhaps to set the wedding date in concrete and with some bravado, Henry asked Bertha what time they would conduct their wedding ceremony so that he could have his "*railroad friends*" stop the "*through*" train at Newton to let him off. And, of course, the clergyman needed to be notified.

You have not answered my letter, dear, about the hour you would like to fix upon for our marriage, dear. May be you prefer not doing so just yet and I would not have bothered you about it only I thought that I might have to arrange about the train to New York and, it occurred to me, I might get one of my railroad friends to prevail on the Boston and Albany officials to stop the "through" train at Newton Centre. And, dear, you know I must write to the clergyman beforehand, at least, I imagine it is best to do so.
[1893-01-19 (Wednesday) Henry (StL) to Bertha (Stancote, Newton Centre)]

A week before their wedding, Henry tried to comfort Bertha for her sadness to be leaving her parents.

Dear, it would be strange if, in the few days which will pass before I can claim you for my wife, you were not made sad at the thought of leaving your parents. Now I want you to think of the real results of this change in your life, dear, and, if you have the care which I ought to give you, which I hope to give you, my darling, you will appear to your parents in a light which I think they have never been able to imagine. Your marriage, dear, will mean the real change from girlhood to womanhood to them and, knowing as I do how dearly they love you, I can easily see that they will be as proud of the woman and love her as dearly as they were tender and thoughtful of their child.
[1893-02-07 (Monday) Henry (StL) to Bertha (Stancote, Newton Centre)]

Henry's words to Bertha were touching, writing: *"your parents … will be as proud of the woman and love her as dearly as they were tender and thoughtful of their child."*

B. THE MARRIAGE LICENSE!

There are always last minute concerns.

O, before I forget it! That license! Father said today that there used to be a law in Massachusetts when he was a young man that three weeks' notice must be given. He said it might be obsolete and I told him what you said of Mr. Blair. But are you sure he knew? If not, had he not better write to his uncle? Father goes west Monday and he did not think of it until today when this suddenly flashed across him. He said he did not know exactly whom to ask about it anyway. So I write promptly to you though I know you will be amused at my reopening that subject.
[1893-01-11 (Friday) Bertha (Newton Centre) to Henry (StL)]

Henry's best man, Gist Blair, was tasked with ensuring that Bertha and Henry's Massachusetts marriage license was obtained.

I shall see Blair tomorrow and again broach the subject of our License. I shall impose upon him the important duty of quieting your fears on this subject and it may be that he will send you an official opinion.
[1893-01-13 (Tuesday) Henry (StL) to Bertha (Stancote, Newton Centre)]

O, about that license. Blair is deep in the study of the law of the Commonwealth of Massachusetts regulating marriage and he promises to see that no legal obstacle shall interfere with that ceremony.
[1893-01-19 (Wednesday) Henry (StL) to Bertha (Stancote, Newton Centre)]

C. STANCOTE (THE PULSIFER HOUSE)

We move a week from tomorrow so, if you stay in St. Louis, a letter written as late as Monday will find me at the Brunswick. Our address is: Stancote, Newton Center, Mass. Stancote, which I believe is the old English for Stone Cottage, is the name of the Pulsifer Place and the little station is Newton Center, not Newton, which is the one next beyond. I am afraid my letters will be later in reaching you and yours in reaching me after we go out there though I do not know. I do know that there are but two mails a day and no postman but that George, the Pulsifer's man whom we retain, goes for the mail. Perhaps I may do you the honor myself occasionally but that, I assure you, will be if your letters prove to come in the afternoon.
[1892-12-08 (Wednesday) Bertha (Backbay, Boston) to Henry (StL)]

Stancote was made even prettier for the Drakes by the first snow.

It is the most perfect day. When I woke, the air was full of soft snow flakes, not a blustering storm, a soft clinging snow and every tree and bush full of it. It is so beautiful that I cannot keep away from the window and at present I am almost inclined to think you are right in your belief in a life in the country being the only right one. So you look upon my life here as a sort of retreat? Do you mean that I ought to spend my time in fasting and meditation as a preparation for the ordeal of battle that lies before me?

It is a lovely house and, O, it is such a delight to be in a house instead of a hotel. You would be amused at the way in which I study all the minor objects in the house. The Pulsifers have old brass fixtures and the old brass is lovely and they have both straight and curved and the curved are ever so much the prettier. But I am very thankful we have not many rugs. I slide and tumble from one end of this house to the other and it is really changing my manner of walking.
[1892-12-20 (Tuesday) Bertha (Newton Centre) to Henry (StL)]

With each day, Bertha became even more charmed with the house.
I wish we had made time while you were here to go and see the Pulsifer's, that you might have seen what an utterly charming house this is. No, I don't. I cannot wish that visit of yours anyway different from what it was but I wish you might look in on me tonight in this delightful room – library and sitting room in one (there is no parlor), three sides of which are lined with books reaching to the ceiling while the other has an enormous fire place with logs in it, three feet long, and the windows – O Henry, the view from those windows! The ground has just a light covering of snow and you know we are up on quite a little hill and we look away off. And at night, it is almost prettier than in the day time, the lights in all the windows along that snowy ridge opposite and in a little church on another hill not far away, and every now [and] then a train just flashing along below us. And every room in the house is charming, the billiard room with a bay window full of plants, the dining room which is just the size of ours at 8887 and the lovely hall with a fire place into which the front door opens, opens into the hall, you know, not the fire place. Upstairs it's equally fascinating. And books, books, books all over the house.
[1892-12-21 (Friday) Bertha (Newton Centre) to Henry (Stl / Waco)]

D. NEWTON CENTRE

After another two weeks in Newton, Bertha's views of "country life" evolved.
My supply of news is running short though. Very little happens here, not that I mind that, I rather like it. But there is very little to write about. No, I don't think I should like a country life permanently. I like this, it is very beautiful and very restful, but I like it because I know it is only a way station, a temporary thing. I should not like it if I thought years of it stretched out ahead of me.
[1893-01-06(-) (Thursday) Bertha (Newton Centre) to Henry (StL)]

Newton Centre, MA

Bertha wrote of the next snow – "*magnificent*".

Today it was magnificent – father and I came out from church into the midst of it and it has lasted through the afternoon. And the snow does not melt at all so each successive storm packs down on top the rest. The sleighing is magnificent and everything is on runners, coupes, carriages, milk wagons, everything. It is an ideal winter, cold but not that bitter piercing cold, a clear bracing delightful cold and, when the snow is not actually falling, the sun is generally shining; we have had none of that lovely foggy damp weather of which there is usually such an abundance at home.
[1893-01-18 (Sunday) Bertha (Newton Centre) to Henry (StL)]

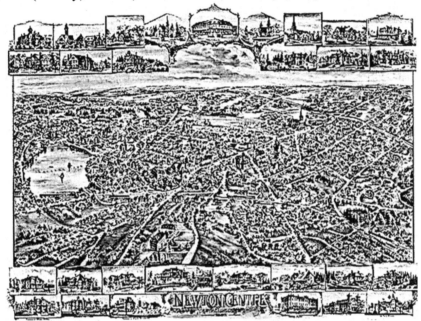

Map of Newton Centre

E. HENRY'S LAST DINNER WITH THE MEN BEFORE THE WEDDING AND OTHER FRIVOLITIES

Henry became very busy during his last month in St. Louis prior to his wedding and much of it was not about work.

I think this week will be the most dissipated I shall have before I leave here. There is something going on every evening and how I am going to find time to do my work and give up all my evenings to frivolity – which, strange to say, I feel obliged for various reasons not to miss – is past my finding out. I asked Miss Nancy some time ago to see Sothern with me and I am going to take her tomorrow night. Wednesday I have a business meeting. Thursday I am going to the theatre with Miss Allen. Friday is the night of Lil ... dinner, and Saturday the whist club meets at Miss Hitchcocks. I might wind up with a notice of the funeral on Sunday but, as I may survive, I withhold that item.
[1893-01-17 (Monday) Henry (StL) to Bertha (Stancote, MA)]

Henry's male friends arranged for a dinner at the St. Louis Country Club on Saturday, February 4, 1893, to toast his pending nuptials. Some of Henry and Bertha's comments about this dinner were notable. On hearing about the dinner for Henry, Bertha agreed to give her "*consent*" with the condition that Henry immediately write to her with all of the particulars.

I was not particularly surprised at hearing of the dinner offered you, but I do not know that it would not be wise for me to be as slow as Lute in consenting to your appearance there. However, I will let you go, on one condition! You are to write me a letter the next day. I should prefer its being written in the morning, and certainly no delay in its reaching me will be pardoned. And it is to

contain a full description of the dinner from the beginning clear to the end. I want to know everybody who was there, what the toasts were, who proposed them, what they said and what you said. And heavy will be the penalty if you fail.
[1893-01-17 (Monday) Bertha (Newton Centre, MA) to Henry (StL – Bank of Commerce Bldg)]

Henry promised to disclose everything about the men's dinner.
I faithfully promise to write you an account of the dinner on the fourth of February and I shall do so on the following day as evidence that I have not abused the freedom you have given me. My dear, why do you wish an account of the dinner even up to its last agonies? And suppose I rely that, an account "clear to the end" might not be entertaining, would you still insist on my giving you full particulars? I promise, however, to preserve a record of what is said by the fellow who are kind enough to take this opportunity for helping me to forget my many shortcomings and I shall give you the substance of any marked exaggerations which I may hear from the lips of any of those men who are temporarily enthused to an extent that will make them indulge in flattering remarks.
[1893-01-23 (Sunday) Henry (StL) to Bertha (Stancote, Newton Centre)]

Bertha was obviously curious about the dinner. Perhaps to better make her case, she teased Henry about marriage writing, *"I don't think I approve of it anymore."*
The reason I requested a description of the February Fourth dinner "clear to the end" was because I remembered Jack told Nan he "did not remember" about the end of "Kin's" & I wish to see if you "remember". When I recall a flaming argument you and Nan once had at my house on "woman's destiny", an argument in which I was not even allowed to get a word in sideways some two years and a half ago, I don't wonder you were slightly amused at the change. I was not surprised. It has been gradually coming ever since Julia's marriage and the engagement of one or two of her intimate friends but no, I have not been writing to her on the subject. If I had mentioned matrimony, it would not have been complementarily. I don't think I approve of it anymore. Being unmarried is a great deal pleasanter. I don't think I ever appreciated how very pleasant it was till now.
Yours always (I suppose I can't help it),
Bert
[1893-01-25 (Thursday) Bertha (Stancote, MA) to Henry (StL)]

Henry wrote to Bertha after the dinner, late that evening, but refused to recount what was said. Henry wrote that *"When a lot of men get together ... the less said about it the better."*
The dinner was very nice although, from the number of absentees, you will imagine that I am a very unpopular young man. A chapter of accidents kept a number of men away who had promised to be present. Mr. Lionberger is at home sick in bed with a very sharp attack of rheumatism. Mr. Tutt fell on the ice yesterday and is also laid up. Your guardian is in New York, Judge Madill was called away by business matters and is, I believe, in Jefferson City. Mr. Graham is in New York, Arthur Lee is in Boston. Elliott and McKinley were, of course, absent. So, with these good people absent from the festal board, the list narrowed down to John, Zack, Will, Lee Brookings, Blair, Smith, Al Shapleigh, Tom McKittrick, George and Ned Paramore!

You asked me to tell you what was said and I flatly refuse to do so, at the risk of being disciplined for disobedience. When a lot of men get together and agree that the occasion is one which justifies unlimited indulgence in flattering, flattering run amok(?), the less said about it the better. Zack and Will Lee were pretty tactful and said some very true things about my being a lucky fellow. Jack Shepley said he would be fully prepared to write my obituary but was incapable of giving any good advice or anything else than his blessing but the other fellows seemed to think that fulsome flattery was the program and acted accordingly.

An item of much more importance to you, dear, is that I have been able to sign myself so soon after a slightly hilarious affair.

[1893-02-06 (Sunday #1, 1893-02-04) Henry (StL) to Bertha (Stancote, Newton Centre, MA)]

In addition to Bertha's interest in what happened at the men's dinner, she wanted to know that Henry would not be incapacitated as a result. Henry addressed that concern in his next day letter.

I wrote you a few lines last night by way of evidence that I was not entirely prostrated by that dinner. I enjoyed the evening very much indeed but I believe men's dinners are not altogether delightful and in strict confidence I will tell you I don't altogether like them. I am very glad that Lute will not have cause to complain of Zack this time for I think I left him on his way home thoroughly convinced that the key hole had not fallen out of the door which I believe was his particular embarrassment the night of Crittenden's dinner.

[1893-02-06 (Sunday #2, 1893-02-05) Henry (StL) to Bertha (Stancote, Newton Centre MA)]

F. ABOUT ATTENDING A QUIET WEDDING; INVITATIONS?

On April 19, 1892, Henry attended the Lucy Bent - Crittenden McKinley wedding. Henry described it as a "gloomy" affair with only immediate family which made the house look *"almost vacant"*.

Tuesday

The wedding is over, Bert dear, and it was the most remarkable one I have known. No one but the immediate family was invited and the house, small as it is, looked almost vacant. Neither Mrs. January nor the young ladies were invited, nor was Mrs. Tyler, Miss T, Mrs. Davis or any of Mrs. Burt's relatives except Mr. Bacon there. I really felt provoked that the wedding was made so designedly a gloomy affair and, if Crittenden were around about this time, he should have my opinion on the subject without the trouble of asking for it. The J's were a good deal cut up, because they were not asked, and very properly so, I think.

My dear child, you should have seen Miss Lizzie McKinley!!! Her dress was made, as far as I could tell and you know I'm an expert, on the same idea little Mimi Tulley's was, and she was so coy and pleased with herself I could hardly keep my face straight whenever I caught sight of her. She told me she liked weddings but she would have enjoyed this one more if it had been from Christ's church. I guess she missed the opportunity to display that remarkable toilet to a larger number of people. After the ceremony, the whole McKinley family – Mrs. McK excepted – went to the depot to see them off and Mrs. Crittenden did <u>not</u> seem pleased at the innovation. As Kin's last man, I had to take Mrs. Tilley down to the depot and I never felt so ashamed of myself in my life for, when the procession of McKinleys appeared in the car, every passenger was advised in the most unmistakable manner that a bridal couple was on board and Mrs. T happily took this last opportunity to give "a young couple just starting out in life" her parting blessing, sandwiched with a few bits of advice. I did not know whether to cry "hear! Hear!!!" or to weep for the persecuted bride. Mrs. Crittenden asked me to write you they would expect to see you in New York and that she hoped you would come to see her at the "Plaza" where they would be until Saturday.

You asked me to tell you about the dinner, dear. I am afraid I can't tell you much except that I am very glad I was not there, for the men who were there have not yet been able to give a lucid account of it. Jack and Will spent three days at home after the affair. Zack has decided not to go to any more dinners and your guardian has been affording much amusement by his account of his own and Stribling's speeches - Will made fifteen by actual count and Judge Boyl delivered an oration with a basket of fruit on his head, held in position by two of the other men.

[1892(-) 20170720 Henry to Bertha]

Henry's observation about this wedding revealed quite a bit about his views of how a wedding should be done and not done. Although Henry never voiced any objection to his and Bertha's wedding being in Newton and to it being a "quiet" affair, it would be difficult not to suspect that he had some disappointment about the quiet part.

Bertha understood Henry's feeling about their own wedding, but nothing could be done about this given Bertha's mother's wishes.

> *She [Bertha's mother] and I talked over a great many things today and I must tell you she opposed the idea of wedding invitations very strongly. She said everyone knew that it was to be a quiet wedding with no one but the family there, and it would simply be a formal absurdity to send invitations. She had expected to send announcement cards and as she seems to prefer it so strongly, I don't like to insist on the other, though I shall be sorry if you are disappointed. You were prepared for the fact that it was to be absolutely quiet, were you not? I tried to make you understand that I really meant absolutely no one would be there but I was never quite sure that you understood it.*
>
> *Dear, I am very sorry that your wedding day will not be a gayer one. When you criticized Crittenden's wedding it made me feel sad instead of amusing me, for I knew your own would be even quieter. I don't like to write of disagreeable things, but when we are together, we always glide away from unpleasantnesses so quickly that discussion of them must be carried on a paper if at all. You must see why I did not urge Nan. It would have been no pleasure for her, indeed, I should not even have spoken to her about it if you had not seemed to wish it so strongly.*
> [1892-10-27 (Thursday) Bertha (Boston) to Henry (StL) on Wedding Plans, etc.]

Of course, Henry had to accede to the wishes of Bertha's parents regarding the wedding invitations and keeping the wedding to a very small number of people.

> *Now, about our wedding invitations, dear, I don't think you ought to permit any of these comparatively trivial details to worry you. I would have preferred and, under all the circumstances, I thought it best to issue the invitations although I thoroughly understood it was a mere formality. But, if you or your friends think differently, the other arrangement will do very well and it certainly is not a matter of sufficient importance for you to worry about, dearest.*
>
> *And you must not think that I anticipate that our wedding day will be a gloomy one, my darling. How can you suggest such an idea, Bert? Will it not be the day of all others to be cherished all my life as having given me my most priceless treasure, my best beloved, my own darling wife? No, dear, you overestimate the value I attach to the lesser incidents of our marriage. When you ask me about these things, I am perhaps led to speak too plainly through a desire to have you thoroughly understand me. And as a matter of choice, I would change certain of the plans for our marriage, but all these things are of secondary importance and are certainly not worth worrying about.*
>
> *Do you mean that you prefer I should not bring Gist and my brother with me when I come on to be married, dear? You must write me frankly about this, as freely as I have written to you and whatever you wish I shall do.*
> [1892-10-31 (Sunday) Henry (StL) to Bertha (Hotel Brunswick, Boston)]

In view of having a very small wedding with principally family, Bertha had broached the subject about whether Gist Blair should be the best man. But, since Henry had already spoken to Gist, this created a quandary and Bertha was equivocal.

> *And when you come on, we will talk about Mr. Blair. I would rather not have you withdraw that invitation if possible but it is a question in my mind whether it will be any pleasure to him, whether on the contrary, it will not be a very awkward position to be the only outsider brought in with a very small family, a harder position for him than for your brother [Sam] even. I ought to have*

thought of all this sooner but I did not seem to realize things before and, as I say I am very unwilling to have the invitation withdrawn, let us drop any further thought about that just now and when you come on we can talk it over at the same time with several other things which need not be settle at once.
[1892-11-02 (Thursday) Bertha (Boston) to Henry (StL)]

Wedding announcements were still *de rigeur* and Bertha requested that Henry obtain the latest copy of the St. Louis Blue Book.

... as soon as you can, dear boy, will you send me your list. I have a suggestion to make about the St. Louis people. If you will buy the newest edition of the blue book and mark every one you want, not with a little stroke but a good line out to the edge of the page, it will be much the best way as yours and mine will be very much the same and then I won't have to keep comparing my list with yours. I will just mark the rest of mine the same way. And then copy the addresses on to the envelopes directly from there. The list of people out of town, of course, will have to be written, there is no avoiding it, and be sure you mark those gentlemen who are to have no "at home" cards sent there.
[1892-11-27 (Sunday) Bertha (Boston) to Henry (StL)]

G. THE PRE-WEDDING SEPARATION

During the several weeks before their wedding, Bertha's steadfast loyalty to her parents kept her apart from Henry. While Henry was hoping to be able to see Bertha before the wedding, she wrote to him, "*I don't want you. ... you, my dear, will be rather in the way ...*"

My dearest,

I did not write yesterday when no letter from you arrived and today, as usual, I am repentant. I had a long lecture prepared on that subject but after this morning's letter, I cannot write it. My darling, I cannot say anything to you about that letter – I have read it over and over and the words in it have been in my heart all day – but I cannot answer it because there are some things one cannot put into words, only I pray to God that I may not fail in what you wish of me.

Dear, I do not feel as you do about those four years. They have been hard but I would not have them done away with. It seems to me that I can see their work so perfectly and, dear, things are much better with us than they would have been if it had all been smooth sailing. I have hesitated a good deal about writing what I am going to now but, having your strict commands to be frank with you to bring as an excuse, I shall say what I want at the risk of being called "hard hearted".

You said you should leave home on Monday. That will bring you here on Wednesday and to be absolutely honest, dear boy, I don't want you. It is my last week with my family, father indeed will probably be in St. Louis for the two weeks before that and just get back for that week. And you, my dear, will be rather in the way. I may be hard hearted but I fancy not more so than other girls for Gordon Knox did not come to Morristown until Saturday before, Charlie Coolidge did not come to St. Louis until the Sunday before. And I don't think that they came this late particularly of their own desire. But the time just before her wedding, a girl belongs pretty exclusively to her family. And if you can only be away from home a certain time, dear boy, I would so much rather have those three or four days at the other end. You are not hurt, dear? You cannot be while I sign myself –

Yours always,
Bert
[1893-01-11 (Wednesday) Bertha (Newton Centre MA) to Henry (StL)]

To say that Henry was disappointed would be an understatement: *"To be flatly told that I am not wanted settles the question..."* Henry was also annoyed at Bertha's assumption that his reason for coming to Boston earlier was solely because of her and not his business. (Henry and Bertha were much alike in this: they each did not like the other to assume too much about their inner motivations and feelings.)

> *Your refusal to see me earlier is so point blank that I haven't the courage to further argue with you. You might have heard my reasons for going on so very far ahead of the fourteenth before locking the door on further discussion of the matter. For instance, I might have had some business arrangements to make in Boston etc. However, I yield. To be flatly told that I am not wanted settles the question and I shall not appear in Boston until, until Saturday morning the eleventh. And if you decree that I shall not see you until the morning of the fourteenth, I shall even endure this command, although I humbly suggest that inasmuch as a few preliminaries must be talked over it may be well for you to desert your family for a short time on Saturday, Sunday and Monday and not leave me all this time to plunge into mad dissipation with my brother and the distinguished head of St. Louis' educational institutions.*
>
> [1893-01-14 (Friday) Henry (StL) to Bertha (Stancote, Newton Centre, MA)]

Bertha apologized to Henry writing, *"It was my unpardonable vanity that led me astray."* Bertha understood that, if the situation were reversed, she would have accused Henry of *"impertinence!"* However, she still suspected that Henry's local business affair was *"fluff"*.

> *I plead guilty to your accusation of not having inquired whether it might not be business that would have brought you to Boston earlier in the week preceding February fourteenth. It was my unpardonable vanity that led me astray. It never occurred to me that it was anything but a desire to see me. I must even confess that it had not occurred to me that you had intended to make this a partial business trip. For both my vanity and ignorance, I humbly crave your pardon and promise not to be so misled again.*
>
> *The second part of your letter, in which you said you would if I so wished not to intrude upon me until the morning of February fourteenth, I read with a calm sweet smile. It was very noble and lovely but it did not impose upon me one bit. For you to be within eight miles of my vicinity and not come to see me would be a physical impossibility my son and this is not conceit but what older people call wisdom gained by experience.*
>
> *I am very glad you are not coming until Saturday[147] (excuse me if I appear uncomplimentary) and I really am grateful to you for postponing your arrival, but I don't want to be unreasonable. If there is something really important you have to attend to, why you must come of course, but if it was as I surmise "fluff" (bar room?), I much prefer the present arrangement.*
>
> [1893-01-17 (Tuesday) Bertha (Newton Centre, MA) to Henry (StL)]

Henry wrote to Bertha of his views of the wedding, the planning of which was almost entirely done by Bertha and her mother. In Henry's view, it only was Bertha's *"responses"* that mattered.

> *I don't think of that wedding quite as you do. It seems very much my own but the details don't interest me, dear. This may be highly unnatural but it is true nevertheless. I only think of the ceremony, dear, and whether I shall hear your responses. You know I have not heard your voice for a very long time, my child, and the thought of it is like music to me. And so, I have almost heard you repeat some of those beautiful lines in our marriage ceremony.*
>
> [1893-01-30 (Sunday) Henry (StL) to Bertha (Stancote)]

---

[147] Saturday, February 11, 1893.

...

H. JITTERS & EMOTIONS

Although Bertha was a very confident woman and not accustomed to jitters, the lifelong commitment in marriage provided Bertha with the occasion to show some nervousness. During the period prior to their wedding, Bertha worried about Henry's expectations of her and whether she was enough of a *"womanly woman"* for him.

> *My dearest, I have not told you, at all, all your letter meant to me. Like Hildegarde, I think you have very bright visions and I am afraid you will have some bitter disappointments. I am not nearly so good as you think I am. But I do love you, dear, and I am not very much afraid of our friendship and trust being anything but strengthened as the years go by.*

[1892-09-05 (Monday) Bertha (Rye Beach) to Henry (StL)]

> *My dear, I am intimately acquainted with a man whose ideal is a "womanly woman", and I sometimes feel very sorry to think he will never see that ideal picture realized.*
>
> *[Bertha enclosed the following clipping from the NY Sun]*

> > *The Delusions about Ideals*
> >
> > *The ideal woman of every man is the "womanly woman". The ideal man of every woman is the "manly man." And the expression "a womanly woman" means pretty much the same to every man who uses it, just as the "manly man" of one woman expresses a certain combination of qualities well-known to every other woman. The man's "womanly woman" is gentle, amiable, quiet and domestic. She loves to sit upon a low chair and hem things, with the lamp-light falling over her hair. It is unnecessary to say that, although in theory this is the sort of a woman a man prefers, in practice he may choose one entirely her opposite. She does not exist in large quantities, which is lucky, as she might prove dreadfully insipid if she did.*
> >
> > *"My dear," asked the brunette, "I wonder if men know how women criticize their clothes? If they know how they abhor trousers that are too much creased, scarfs that are badly tied, handkerchiefs that are not fine, lawn shirts that do not fit well and are not well laundered, and coats that look as if they might have been made for any man and just happened to fall on this one. I know a girl who refused to marry a man because he called on her one evening wearing a colored shirt."*
> > *"She was quite right," said the blonde. "A man who would do such a thing as that would be capable of beating a woman." After this they had another cup of tea.*
> >
> > *[NY Sun, circa Nov. 1892]*

[1892-11-27 (Sunday) Bertha (Boston) to Henry (StL)]

(*"A man who would do such a thing as that [i.e. wear a colored shirt] would be capable of beating a woman."* Perfectly logical!]

On New Year's Day, 1893, Bertha had many thoughts on her mind which she expressed in the following letter to Henry. There was a selfish concern that Henry was having too good time in her absence (*"Man is a vain thing"*), the deep love for Henry (*"I am never going to be married again"*), the helpmeet's concern that Henry might forget his familial duties to his mother (that he not be *"undemonstrative"*), and the admonition against too much praise - *"you don't deserve it."*

> *No letter from you!! A nice way to begin the New Year and I am convinced that this same lack is occasioned by your having gone to the Dramatic Club. I do not observe in your actions that aversion to society or languidness in the enjoyment thereof which your words would give me to understand. I was for a short time complimented by your having left the Imperial at its height but, when on the fourth page I found the date Wednesday with the remark that you were too tired to finish the night before, I came to the conclusion that your weariness of the ball had not been occasioned by any absence as I had fondly imagined but from other causes. Man is a vain thing and put not your trust in him.*
>
> ...

My dear, I am never going to be married again, no matter what attractions are offered me. There is a New Year's resolution for you.

I hope you have persuaded your mother that you are not going to entirely forget her and that you have not been so "undemonstrative" as you say you are. I speak very feelingly on this subject for George has reached the age when he prides himself rather on being undemonstrative and bestows most of his confidence on father, regarding him as a man and therefore able to understand him, which feeble feminine intellects are not capable of and mother does not see the funny side of it.

I read in Deronda[148] the other day Mrs. Mayrick's explanation as to why mothers were inclined to think more of their sons than their daughters. "My dear, boys are so infinitely much more trouble that we never could stand them at all if we did not think they were worth more." Yes, I hear you, sir, "My mother thinks I am perfection." You conceited thing! I know she does but you don't deserve it and I assure you, I don't think so. This is a very wholesome truth for New Year's Day and so will suffice to end this letter.

Goodbye my own dear boy. God bless you.
[1893-01-01 (Sunday, New Year's Day) Bertha (Newton Centre) to Henry (StL)]

Bertha's worry about Henry's expectations of her were understandable in light of the pedestal on which Henry placed her, and Bertha worried about what Henry would think on their honeymoon when he might get to know her better, including some of her "*disagreeable characteristics*". She concluded that she did not want to be known better.

No, I have no wish to have you come on to scold and be disagreeable to me. Time enough for that afterward on that journey when you learn to know me better. That sentence frightened me a little. Knowing me better involves the discovery of several disagreeable characteristics of mine. I don't think I want to be known better. I prefer to be thought a good deal better than I am.
[1893-01-06(-) (Thursday) Bertha (Newton Centre) to Henry (StL)]

As the time for their wedding approached, Henry reflected on the "*sad period of struggle*" which almost ended their relationship. That their relationship survived must have given Henry renewed strength and permitted him to write, "*whatever there is of strength or worth in my life is all yours.*"

I ought to be very thoughtful of you now for, dear, just one month from next Monday I leave here to go and claim you for my wife. Bert, I often wonder that I can be as patient as I am now when I have almost immediately before me the unspeakable happiness of claiming you for my wife, for my friend and helper and companion all the days of my life.

Dear, do you look back at the last four years as I do and wonder at the happiness which has come to us out of a long, sad period of struggle and waiting? If you do, then you will understand how it frightens me as I recall how nearly I was to the end of all my hopes and prayers. What could I have done without you, darling. How could I have lived without your love? But now we are brought very near each other, dearest. One month more and we will have entered into that bond which the church and the world terms the "holy" bond. And does not this seem a proper and fitting term, my darling? You and I will promise to be each the other's friend and companion and helper in the hours of gladness, when the shadows of sorrow meet us, "in sickness and in health, until death us do part". O, my darling, it is the companionship of those who love each other better than all the world beside and the relation is the most beautiful conception of creation. Dear, if I fail to be all the help and comfort to you that I should be, if I fall short as I know I shall, of giving back to you as much help in the days you may need it, as you will bring to me in any of my disappointments by

---

[148] *David Deronda* by George Eliot.

the comfort of your sweet sympathy, remember O my darling that limited as is my power to aid you, whatever there is of strength or worth in my life is all yours and has long ago been devoted to the study of whatever seemed to promise greatest usefulness to the purest, sweetest woman that God ever made.

I can't write about other things now, my darling, my whole being seems filled with one wish. To be near you and bless you for what you are to me, for what you are to everyone who has ever known you, dear. It seems sometimes that the gift of your love is the trust of a treasure in which all your friends have a share. For have you not been a factor in their happiness and, as I shall become your guardian, I shall also be their trustee, shall I not? And, dear, I have only one friend to draw from, to fit me for your service, that of perfect love. Will that suffice, my child?
[1893-01-08 (Saturday) Henry (StL) to Bertha (Stancote, Newton Centre, MA)]

In spite of the ideal image that Henry had of her, Bertha wrote, as she had written before, "*I am not afraid of the future*".

Your letter reminded me of Captain Letterblair's answer to the old lawyer's homily about the "sweetest girl in all England". "But there never was any girl so sweet as Fanny." I do like it, I admit, my son, I am not in the least superior to these young women mentioned in Jerome's essay on flattery. But "it is a terrible responsibility, Mr. Scott", such an ideal to live up to. My dearest, it is very good of you to try to reassure me but I don't need it, not yet, though I will not promise you that my heart may not fail when the time comes. But just now I am not afraid of the future, dearest best friend.
[1893-01-09 (Sunday) Bertha (Newton Centre, MA) to Henry (StL)]

One week before their wedding in February 1893, Bertha wrote the following letter which expressed her apprehension of her new life with Henry and what his coming, this time, would mean for her. As she wrote, your coming "never meant quite so much before".

My dearest,

This is the last letter I shall write you so I shall answer some of your questions asked in the letter I received yesterday.

Yes, I think I shall feel a little shy with you when you come. Your coming never meant quite so much before. And yes, too, there are some things I am a little afraid of. I am almost afraid to meet you when I think of all your coming means and I am afraid when I let myself think of it, of the tremendous change of my whole life and the great responsibilities. And, most of all, I dread the parting with my family.

But there is one thing about which I have never been afraid for a moment and that is the future. It is the present strangeness of everything that is hard but, my dearest, I trust you absolutely, that there is nothing but that to fear. I sometimes think that my faith in you is greater even than my love for you. Do not misunderstand me. You know what that is in my life. But I can believe that when our lives and interests have grown even more closely together than they have now, that you may teach me to care for you even more deeply than I do, but you could not make me trust you more perfectly, dear. You cannot make a thing more than absolute.

And there is another greater reason why I do not fear the future, my dearest. I believe that you and I truly belong to those "whom God hath joined together" and I am not afraid, my dearest, to promise "in the sight of God and of this company" to be

Yours always,
Bert
[1893-02-06 (Sunday 1893-02-05) Bertha (Newton Centre, MA) to Henry (StL)]
Bertha's words revealed such a deep faith and trust in Henry: "*you could not make me trust you more perfectly, dear. You cannot make a thing more than absolute.*"

Henry also had a range of emotions before the wedding, which included joy in anticipation and a longing during the waiting period.

Four weeks from today, my darling! Are you not glad a little that we shall meet again and that this is our last separation for so long a time? Dear, I think there is no stronger desire in my heart tonight than that you will never leave me, for such a long weary life without you as the last three months have been.
[1893-01-13 (Tuesday) Henry (StL) to Bertha (Stancote, Newton Centre)]

Every day seems to leave an especial significance now, my darling, for the time is drawing near when I shall look into your beautiful eyes again. Today I know that I shall leave here in three weeks and think of it, Bert! You will be my wife within less than four weeks!
[1893-01-20 (Thursday) Henry (StL) to Bertha (Stancote, Newton MA)]

While Henry could be ecstatic just two weeks before the wedding, he also wrote of his loneliness and a choking sensation in his throat.

... dear, I love you more and more every day, that is what makes it all so beautiful. And there is only one drawback, I miss you terribly these last days. Let me tell you how I miss you, dear. Not many days ago I was in our house looking over the things and I must have been in a dreamy mood for somehow I felt that you were approving what I had done there and it seemed for a moment that I had won a smile from you, my darling, and then I realized that you were far away and, well, if I had been a child instead of a man, I would have thought the choking in my throat was caused by a sob.
[1893-01-30 (Sunday) Henry (StL) to Bertha (Stancote)]

I. THE WEDDING

Bertha commenced her "1893 Diary" at the time of her wedding to Henry and this was the diary that she kept throughout her lifetime.

Bertha had inscribed her BWD monogram, the date "August 25", and the year "1891" to the left and "1892" to the right. August 25, 1891 was the "official" date of Bertha and Henry's engagement and 1892 marked their first anniversary.

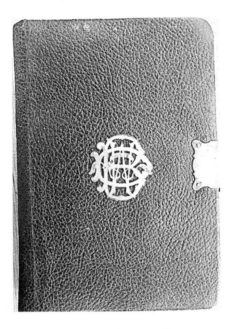

On the first page of the diary, Bertha proudly announced:

> *February Fourteenth*
> *Eighteen hundred and ninety-three*
> *Newton Centre,*
> *Massachusetts*
>
> *Rev. Edward Sullivan*
> *Married*
> *Henry Clarkson Scott*
> *Bertha Warburton Drake*

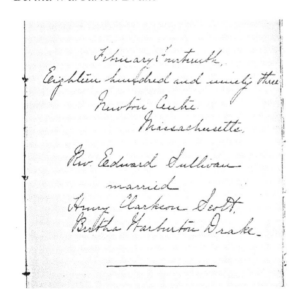

Following this, Bertha wrote on page 2 of her diary the list of guests:

> *Wedding Guests:*
> *Mr. & Mrs. George S. Drake [Bertha's parents]*
> *George S. Drake, Jr. [Bertha's brother]*

Mr. William Samuel Scott [Henry's brother]
Mr. Gist Blair (Best Man)
Mr. & Mrs. George Foster Shepley
Mr. O. J. Lewis
Miss Lewis
Mr. George C. Hitchcock
Rev. Edward Sullivan

It was a quiet wedding indeed.

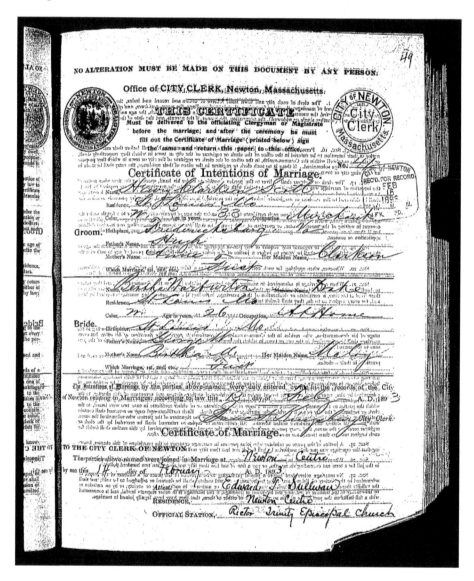

About her wedding day, Bertha wrote in the Diary:
> *After a snowstorm of twenty-four hours, the fourteenth itself was brilliant with sunshine. The wedding took place at ten o'clock in the hall at Stancote, which was decorated with flowers, many of which were sent by friends, including a box four feet long filled with roses from the directors of the Merchants National Bank.*
[1893 Diary1]

J. WEDDING GIFTS

One of the first gifts that Bertha received was a Nuremburg Wedding Cup[149]. Bertha recounted the history of it in her letter to Henry.

> *We have had our first wedding present. By that, I mean, not including Uncle William's and Mr. Durkee's which are really to buy us gifts in the future, but the first bonafide present. And it was from my dear Miss Hagen[150]. Do you remember once at a dinner at our house drinking out of a cup shaped like a woman holding another cup over her head, the object being when both cups were filled, to drink from one without spilling what was in the other. Let me illustrate by one of my beautiful drawings.*

[Bertha included two drawings of the German Bridal or Wedding Cup]

> *There are two attempts. Turn it upside down and it looks like this.*

[Bertha provided two additional drawings of the cup upside down]

A Nuremburg Wedding Cup

> *You see the cup she holds swings on a pivot though why you should see that from my drawing is a mystery, perhaps. Well the cup is an exact reproduction of an old German one in the green vaults at Dresden, and it is called a maiden cup. It was the custom in old times on a wedding day, to fill*

---

[149] Story of the Nuremburg Wedding Cup: Centuries ago, in old Nuernberg, the noble mistress Kunigunde fell in love with a young and ambitious goldsmith. Although Kunigunde's wealthy father (a powerful nobleman) did not approve of this pair, it was clear that she only wanted the goldsmith to be her husband as she refused many titled and rich suitors who asked for her hand in marriage. Her father became so enraged that he had the young goldsmith thrown into the darkest dungeon. Not even his daughter's bitter tears would change her father's mind. To her father's dismay, imprisoning the young man did not end his daughter's love for the goldsmith. Instead, he could only watch as his daughter grew paler and paler as a result of the separation from her true love. The wealthy nobleman reluctantly made the following proposal: He told his daughter, "If your goldsmith can make a chalice from which two people can drink at the same time without spilling one single drop, I will free him and you shall become his bride". Of course, he was certain nobody could perform such a task... Inspired by love and with skillful hands, the young goldsmith created a masterpiece. He sculpted a girl with a smile as beautiful as his own true love's. Her skirt was hollowed to serve as a cup. Her raised arms held a bucket that swivels so that it could be filled and then swung towards a second drinker. The challenge was met. The goldsmith and the nobleman's daughter joined hands in marriage and with the bridal cup set forth a romantic and memorable tradition as charming today as it was originally hundreds of years ago. To this day and to many couples the chalice remains a symbol. Love, faithfulness and good luck await the couple who drink from this cup.

[150] Miss Hagen was Bertha's German teacher.

both cups, then the groom was obliged to drink the large one empty without spilling what was in the smaller. The larger was then refilled and the bride had to drink the second one empty without spilling what was in the larger. If the feat was performed without either of the couple spilling a drop, it was held to be a token of great good luck. Miss Hagen got this for me in Germany last summer, and gave it to me with the request that we would follow the old custom on our wedding day.
[1892-12-31 (Friday 1892-12-30) Bertha (East Jaffrey NH) to Henry (StL)]

While Henry seemed upbeat about the wedding cup, he was not certain that the groom should be tasked with *"anything so difficult"*.

Good for Miss Hagen! But it seems to me the bride alone should test her future with the loving cup. You see, my dear, in this case, the groom will not need any assurances that the fates are propitious; he will defy the fates if need be and then too, of course, this is not my reason for making the above suggestion. Grooms are said to be rattled in most cases and a failure in this feat might be humiliating. Think of Tom or poor Will on their wedding days. Do you think either of them would have undertaken or could have achieved anything so difficult?
[1893-01-04 (Tuesday) Henry (StL) to Bertha (Stancote, Newton Centre)]

Bertha provided a nine-page listing of the wedding gifts in the Diary, meticulously recording each item and their benefactors.

Wedding Presents

GLASS
- *Two claret pitchers, two sherry decanters, one dozen finger bowls and saucers, one dozen goblets, one dozen claret glasses, one dozen champagne glasses, on dozen sherry glasses, one dozen liqueur glasses. Mr. John R. Lionberger*
- *One dozen hock glasses. Mary Lionberger .*
- *One dozen liqueur glasses. Eliza Carr.*
- *Cut glass pitcher. Mr. & Mrs. Samuel Wallace*
- *Cut glass ice cream dish. William C. Stribling*
- *Cut glass decanter. John Downman*
- *Cut glass bowl. William Wickham*
- *Cut glass punch bowl and stand. Mr. & Mrs. James Carpenter*
- *Cut glass bon bon dish and spoon. Mr. & Mrs. Onward Bates*
- *Cut glass claret pitcher with silver shaker. Mr. & Mrs. Howard Elliott.*
- *Cut glass bowl. William E. Guy*
- *Cut glass bowl and plate. Mrs. E. C. Sterling*
- *Cut glass toilet bottle, silver stopper. Mr. & Mrs. Henry S Potter*
- *Maiden cup. Miss Hagen*
- *Two carafes, cut glass. Mr. John Clarkson*
- *Cut glass sugar bowl and cream pitcher. Gertrude Dillon.*

SILVER
- *One dozen large forks, one dozen small forks, one dozen table spoons, one dozen dessert spoons, one dozen tea spoons, one soup ladle, two gravy ladles, one dozen pearl handled dinner knives, one dozen pearl handled breakfast knives. Mrs. Anne C. Scott [i.e. Anne Clarkson Scott, Henry's mother], Minnie, Maggie, Sam and Arthur Scott .*
- *Silver service, coffee pot, sugar bowl, cream pitcher. George Drake Jr.*
- *After Dinner Service: coffee pot, sugar bowl and cream pitcher (antique). Emma, Myra and Nat Lane.*
- *After Dinner Coffee Pot (repoussé), Colonel Leighton*
- *Water Pitcher: Mr. and Mrs. Hezekiah King*
- *Water Pitcher: Mrs. Merrill*
- *One Dozen Coffee Spoons: Sarah Hitchcock*
- *Candlestick: Maud Reber*
- *Bonbonnière: Anne Allen*
- *Cake Dish: Mr. & Mrs. Frank Ridgely*
- *Fruit Dish: Dr. and Mrs. S. J. Nicolls*

- Fruit Dish: Mr. & Mrs. Kendall
- 2 Salt Cellars: Mrs. Hugh Campbell
- 2 Salt Cellars: Mr. & Mrs. John D. Davis
- 2 Peppers: Irwin Z. Smith
- 2 Peppers: Mr. and Mrs. Watson
- Mustard Pot: Mr. & Mrs. William Gray
- Tea Strainer: Margaret D. Emmons
- Ice Cream Set, Slicer and one dozen forks: Gist Blair
- Silver Tea Strainer: Mr. & Mrs. John Bryan
- Hat Brush: Mary Lackland
- Olive Dish and fork: Kate and Maud Buckingham
- Bread Fork: Mr. & Mrs. James Garfield
- Break Dish: Judge and Mrs. Madill
- One Dozen Oyster Forks: Mrs. J. C. Philbrick
- Bonbonnière and spoon: Mr. & Mrs. Edwards Whittaker
- One dozen Antique Coffee Spoons: Helen Ernst
- Card Tray: George Leighton and Charlotte Kayser
- Pair of Boubonnières with spoons: Mr. & Mrs. Isaac Starr
- Tray: Mrs. Grace Wilkes
- Pair Gold Butter knives, enameled handles: Mrs. Charles Davis
- Four bon bon spoons: Mr. Jones and Margaret E. Jones
- One Gold Spoon (antique pattern), One Silver Spoon: (FARMINGTON - Edith Stockwell, Emma, Eddy, Anne Ward, Louise and Julia Carpenter)
- Berry Spoon: Mr. & Mrs. Richard Bowles
- Berry Spoon: Messrs. Frank and John Carter
- Gold bon bon Spoon: Clarence Buckingham
- Pie Knife: Miss Bent
- Berry Spoon: Mr. Y. Downman
- Spoon: Mrs. Skinner (my father's cousin)
- Spoon: Mr. & Mrs. Wayman Cushman
- Pen Tray: Mr. & Mrs. Seddon
- Pair Candlesticks: Mr. & Mrs. Coolidge
- Pair Candlesticks: Mr. & Mrs. Knox
- Pair Candelabra: Mrs. Charles Larrabee
- Bon Bon Spoon: Laura Richardson Wells
- Pair of Grape Scissors: Miss Laura Durkee
- One Half Dozen Nut Picks: Mrs. Richard Perkins

CHINA:
- Fish set (Limoges) – one dozen plates, one dish, one gravy boat, and ivory and gold fish knife and fork: Mr. and Mrs. George L. Allen
- Two marquise cups set in silver, and spoons: Mr. & Mrs. Hudson E. Bridge
- One dozen Limoges plates: Mr. James E. Yeatman
- One Dozen Bouillon Cups: Mr. & Mrs. Hugh McKittrick
- Limoges Berry Bowl and one dozen saucers: Mr. & Mrs. Edward B. King
- Dresden Plate: Mr. & Mrs. Siter
- Dresden Plate and Bowl: Mr. & Mrs. Frank Masters
- Dresden Tray: Miss Cynthia Yeatman
- Dresden Plaque: Edythe Wister
- Dresden Bowl: Miss Anne Blood
- One dozen Dresden Plates: Mrs. James McLane
- One Dozen Dresden Plates and one dozen Dresden after dinner coffee cups: Mr. & Mrs. I.H. Lionberger [Isaac H. Lionberger who married Mary Louise Shepley]
- Salt cellars (Dresden): Count and Countess Reventlow

CLOCKS
- Tall Hall Clock: Mr. Dwight Durkee
- Blue Sevres clock: Mr. & Mrs. Crittenden McKinley
- Clock (antique work): Mr. and Mrs. Byron Sherman
- Clock (gold and glass): Mr. Augustus Knight
- Clock (china): Mr. and Mrs. Thomas McKittrick

MISCELLANEOUS:
- *Looking Glass: Miss Broadhead*
- *Books: Mr. Landreth King*
- *Etching: Miss Frances Markham*
- *Etching: Mr. George D. Markham*
- *Etching: Mr. George Morey Bartlett*
- *Engraving: Mr. Robert S. Brookings*
- *Italic Color Facsimile: Mr. & Mrs. Harrison P. Bridge*
- *Etching: Mr. Hugh McKittrick Jr.*
- *Etching: Mr. & Mrs. George Wasson*
- *Etching: Mrs. Henry Hitchcock*
- *Rokewood Pitcher set in silver: Mr. & Mrs. J. Gilbert Chapman*
- *Doulton Pitcher: Mr. and Mrs. Alfred Shapleigh*
- *Glass Vase: Mr. & Mrs. Walker Hill*
- *Dresden Table Lamp: Mrs. Shepley*
- *Cut Glass Inkstand: Mr. J. F. Shepley*
- *Antique Table: Miss Anne Shepley*
- *Silver Cornered Blotter: Mr. Harry Hitchcock*
- *Cut Glass Vase & Flowers: Mrs. E. A. Hitchcock*
- *Cut Glass Vase & Flowers: Mrs. T. K. Skinker*
- *Mahogany Tea Table: Mrs. Benton*
- *Brass Tea Kettle: William H. Benton Jr.*
- *Tea Strainer (Silver): Julia Benton*
- *Sugar Tongs (Silver): Rita Benton*
- *One Dozen Dresden Tea Cups: Kate & Lucy Benton*
- *Doulton Jar: Mr. & Mrs. Newell Knight*
- *Cut Glass Vase: Mr. & Mrs. McKittrick Jones*
- *Carvers (Ivory, mounted in silver): Mrs. William P. Graves*
- *Vase (Doulton): Wichita Light & Power Co*
- *Vase (Doulton): Mr. Hamilton Downman*
- *Gilt Chair: Mr. & Mrs. Benjamin Adams*
- *Powder Box (glass & silver): Miss Charlotte Siter*
- *Pair of Blue Garters with Silver Buckles: Miss Esther Starr*
- *Vase: Mrs. Bailey and Mrs. Foster*
- *Vase (Crown Derby): Mrs. Daniel Catlin*
- *Afghan: Mr. & Mrs. Loughlin*
- *Lamp: Miss Edith January*
- *Lamp: Miss Alma Sterling*
- *Fan: Mrs. Sloss*
- *Fan: Mrs. Norris*
- *Mirror: Mr. & Mrs. Samuel Copp*
- *Book ("The Oregon Trail"): Mr. & Mrs. Fitzhugh Simon*
- *Vase: Miss Jane Seldon*
- *Mahogany Desk: Mr. and Mrs. Thomas E. Tutt*
- *Double Heart Scarf Pin: Mrs. George Shepley*
- *Live Photographs of Stancote: Mrs. William H. Pulsifer*

EMBROIDERIES:
- *Center Piece: Miss Pingree (?)*
- *Center piece: Miss Madge Markham*
- *Center Piece: Mrs. Scott*
- *One Dozen Doilies: Miss Scott*
- *One Dozen Doilies: Mrs. Samuel Treat*
- *Embroidered Table Cloth: Mrs. Frank Lane*
- *Tea Cozy: Mrs. Dexter Tiffany*
- *Bureau Scarf: Mrs. Charles Allen*
- *Bed Spread: Mrs. Emmeline Brown*

FLOWERS:
- *Roses: Merchants Bank*
- *Flowers: Miss Ida Pollard*
- *Roses: Mrs. O. B. Filley*

Page 340

-     *Roses: Mrs. & Miss Manny*
-     *Roses: Mr. O. J. Lewis*

OTHER:
-     *Diamond Necklace: Henry Clarkson Scott*
-     *One Hundred Dollars in Gold: Mr. & Mrs. Jonathan W. Roberts*
-     *Furniture, Carpets, Curtains, etc.: Mr. & Mrs. George Drake*

It goes without saying that Bertha wrote a personal letter to each and every person who was on this list. On April 19, 1893, Bertha wrote to Henry who was in Ft. Worth on business, "*I have just finished the last letter of thanks, eighteen at one fell swoop and I am weary in body and brain…*" [1893-04-19 Bertha (StL) to Henry (Fort Worth)] Bertha worked on her "thank yous" for many, many weeks.

K. HONEYMOON

Two months before the wedding, Henry was already dreaming of his honeymoon with Bertha.

> *I telegraphed you today to write your next letters to Wichita. I expect to leave here on Saturday evening and will reach Wichita Sunday. I remain there until Wednesday or Thursday and then go to Fort Worth, so after you get this, write to me, please, at Fort Worth for three days, then to Waco for three days and then to St. Louis again. I expect to have a pretty busy time of it on this trip for I shall rely upon the thoroughness of my adjustment of our affairs in the south to protect me against any interruption of business matters during that beautiful journey I am going to make with the sweetest girl in the world as my companion.*
>
> *Dearest, you have no idea of the beautiful visions I have of that journey! To have you near me all the time, to know that you will have to depend on me alone to take care of you. O, my darling, I shall never be able to make you see how perfectly happy those blissful days will be to me. But, dear, I think you will understand my feeling somewhat when I tell you that it seems to me when people, even our best friends, ask me where we are going and how long we will be away, that they are intruding upon the sacredness of a period which I wish to shut out from all the world and share even the thought of with my darling alone.*
>
> [1892-12-10 (Thursday) Henry (StL) to Bertha (Hotel Brunswick, Boston)]

Bertha provided limited details of her honeymoon trip in her Diary, but even these limited details provide some insights.

Memoranda (Wedding Trip)

Remember – Fairy Land & the queer old captain
Remember
-     *John, the waiter at Rock Ledge*
-     *Pete, the fisher boy*
-     *Our friend, the orange planter, the windy day we went bass fishing*
-     *The crow I shot at Lake Worth*
-     *Warren, our skipper at Lake Worth*
-     *Meeting the Godfreys at Lake Worth*
-     *Harold and the Turks at Rock Ledge*
-     *The Hows at Ormond*
-     *Mr. Peabody at St. Augustine*
-     *The horse that ran away at St. Augustine*
-     *Shooting fish at Lake Worth*
-     *Tangled fish lines and fishing at Rock Ledge*

- *"Both of you going to take a bath"*
- *The concert at Rock Ledge*
- *The ball at St. Augustine, "Our party"*
- *The Cuttingtons at Lake Worth*
- *The Brown Bride (Mr. Snow and wife)*
- *Reading "Sweet Bells Jangled out of Tune" and the "Mill on the Floss"*

Instead of writing the trip out in detail, I have made these memoranda, which will recall abundance to me, without its being necessary for anybody else ever to know the details of our wedding trip.

After the wedding, the bride and groom went in a sleigh into Boston, where they took the noon train to New York. Arrived in New York at five in the afternoon, Hotel Buckingham. Left New York February sixteenth for Florida. ...

February Seventeenth – changed cars at Savannah. Went up to the hotel for dinner.

February Eighteenth – Delayed by a wreck on the track ahead. Take lunch and spend several hours at Daytona – Arrive in the evening at Rock Ledge. Hotel Indian River. Manager – Andrew J. Lee.

March Seventh – Left Rock Ledge and went down the Indian River to Lake Worth

March Eight – On Indian River. Jupiter Narrows. Three Bridal couples. Arrive at Jupiter. Take train to Juno. Sail down Lake Worth to hotel. The friendly German.

March Twelfth – Return from Lake Worth via Indian River. Search light at night.

March Thirteenth – Arrive at Rock Ledge again. Miss King

March Fourteenth – Leave Rock Ledge for Ormond. Arrive at Ormond.

March Seventeenth – Leave Ormond. Arrive at St. Augustine, Ponce De Leon.

March Seventeenth – Leave Florida

March Twenty Second – Arrive in St. Louis, met at station by Sam. Raining. Arrive at 2807 Locust Street. Met by Brown and Emmeline. Go to inspect 3337 Washington Avenue and to visit 3526 Chestnut St. Evening. Dinner at the Ben Adams's.

March Twenty Third – Dinner at the St. Louis Club, given by Arthur Lee to Mr. and Mrs. Blair Lee.

March Twenty Sixth – Palm Sunday. B.W.D.S. and Sarah Hitchcock were confirmed together at Christ Church Cathedral. Dinner at the J.H. Lionberger's afterward. Tea at the Shepley's. During all this time, are arranging 3337 and gradually unpacking and inspecting wedding presents, most of which were waiting in St. Louis instead of being sent to Newton Centre.

L. POST WEDDING

Immediately after the wedding, Bertha's father sent her the following letter, which was mostly "business", but reveals some of George's wit and sentimentality at the end: *"Well, I hope you are having a good time, some people do on their "trial trip" south. Kind regards to Mr. Scott."*

Stancote
Feb. 17th

My dear daughter,
Your mother collapsed this morning and is now comfortable in bed enjoying her coffee, sun shining in her window and an implied promise that she will stay there today & enjoy herself. A day's rest & quiet will do her a great deal of good.

George went back Wednesday evening.

Your letters from Buckingham & Mr. Scott's dispatch all came to hand. I would have been glad to have you send the three telegrams enclosed to him were ... at the Buckingham as I suppose they were as they were mailed in time.

Now business first. The collars(?) are promised today or tomorrow & will be immediately forwarded to Indian River Hotel, Rockledge, Florida, and if that is not the correct address, inquire about it. French says the goods were sent all right and has a tracer to find out where they are. I am to remind you the "Carter" spoon was not ack.

Mrs. Menice(?) was at Manchester & did not get the letter in time. Glad she was invited and glad she was not at home. Proposes to send you a present.

Your mother says tell Mr. Scott the wedding cake was forwarded to his mother & she is afraid the parteboard box was not strong enough to take it safely. I think the discovery of a "board" box afterward "which would have been so much better" is the cause of the fear. Sundry other small boxes have been sent.

Mr. Hagan sent a nice note which is to be forwarded unless lost. And your mother wishes to know what the girls say about their dins(?). And that closes the business.

No, I'm opposed to sending your watch until we know exactly where to send it & as time is not valuable to you now. You may need the watch later. I say keep it. Still it may be sent with the collars.

Since you left, weather has been pleasant. Sunshine & melting. Today 10AM cooler – 15° above but clear sunshine & snow most gone. Of course, after your departure, everybody left and when George left, your mother & myself went back to first principles and had the house to ourselves. The next day, cake boxes, etc., filled the time with George on the afternoon. (Oh, I took the Hagan flowers, etc., and delivered them in the afternoon 14th. Yesterday visited the Pooles & Cubbage(?). The evening – by the bye. You will get the "Poole" letter to me as a copy. Corry you have already answered so many as this is superb in its way.

Well, I hope you are having a good time, some people do on their "trial trip" south. Kind regards to Mr. Scott.

I am affectionately
Your "Pater"
[1893-02-17(-) George Drake (father – Stancote) to Bertha (Florida)]

Bertha and Henry's honeymoon lasted about 6 weeks. Although Bertha and Henry purposely wrote nothing about their honeymoon (Henry considered their honeymoon strictly personal), with the arrival of Hugh Scott on December 24 that year, one can intuit that they had a *"good time"* and that it was a great success.

Bertha's father mentioned that her mother was sending the wedding cake, presumably to preserve it for Bertha and Henry's first wedding anniversary. Without further knowledge, we can only imagine that this may have been an interesting tradition before the advent of refrigeration. But Bertha's diary comment on this first wedding anniversary provides a clue. *"The wedding cake is so dried up that it has to be pounded to break it up."* [1893 Diary, February 14, 1894]

Thank goodness for today's refrigeration!

CHAPTER 14 – THE SCOTT HOMES

The New House

The new house is a stately house,
The old was naught to see,
But the new house has no memories,
It's not my home to me.

The new house is my own house,
We did but rent the old,
But in the old were pictures bright
That makes the new seem cold.

My mother chose the plenishing
To make it fine and fair,
She never saw the new house,
I cannot see her there.

I came a bride in that wee house,
It seemed all filled with light,
For youth's bright sunshine lit the way,
And all the world was bright.

And there I learned the woman's lot
Of suffering and pride,
For my first son was born to me
On the eve of Christmastide.

O, the new house, my own house,
Is grander far to see,
But the old house, the rented house,
That was my home to me.

[20180803-4 Bertha's Poem – "The New House" circa 1898]

Bertha wrote this poem during the time that Bertha and Henry moved from first home at 3337 Washington Avenue into their new home on Vandeventer Place in 1898. In a number of letters, Bertha expressed her nostalgia for places and people in the past and did so very poignantly in this poem about her first home with Henry. While Bertha was always fully able to move forward and welcomed her Vandeventer Place home, her past was always close to her heart.

A. THE ST. LOUIS SUMMER HEAT

The selection of a suitable home in St. Louis must take into account the torrid heat of the St. Louis summers. Bertha and Henry frequently wrote about this, as Henry did in the following letter.

> *The hot weather has come with a vengeance. It was one hundred even in the shade today and is waxing hotter every hour. Tonight promises to be very superior from a hot weather point of view and there is little likelihood of any one catching cold.*
> [20180424-2 (1893-) Henry to Bertha (Rye)]

> *It's hotter than – well, it is quite warm but I stand it beautifully although yesterday my high spirits were made to droop when on arriving at the office, I found two mails unopened and no*

stenographer, my chief of staff having sent word that sickness would prevent her from reporting for duty. Maybe there were a few fiercer men in town than I was for a short time, but I doubt it. If I had continued long to "furiously rage" as the heathen are said to, the office would have caught fire from the combined heat of the atmosphere and that created by my magnificent display of temper. When I had worked at the mail for a few hours and saw how little I had to grumble about, I repented and verily was filled with the true emanations of a contrite heart. I have been good since, although a whole day has past.
[1892-06-15 Henry (StL) to Bertha (East Jaffrey NH)]

Fortunately for Henry, toiling in St. Louis during the hot summer of 1892, Henry sometimes got a break from the heat.

I am sorry you have had a touch of the heat wave which seems to have extended throughout the whole country. We are having pleasant weather here now which is a God send for, if a change had not come, I don't think there would have been left enough people to write our histories.
[1892-07-30 (Saturday) Henry (StL) to Bertha (Farragut House, Rye Beach)]

During her entire life, Bertha was used to going to New England during the summer. Although Bertha claimed that she generally did not mind the heat, there were clearly times when the heat became unbearable. In one amusing letter to Henry in early May 1895, Bertha wrote to Henry that she had never suffered so much from the St. Louis heat and was very happy to learn from the Society Papers that she would soon be going to Jamestown (a trip of which she was apparently unaware).

I saw in the society items Sunday that Mrs. B. Drake Scott would close her residence in July & go to Jamestown for the summer where she had taken a cottage. I also saw that Miss Mary Lionberger & her brother Mr. Zack Lionberger would make a tour of Ireland on their wheels. I am very glad Mrs. B. Drake Scott is going somewhere. I never have suffered so in my life. You know I don't usually mind heat, but they tell me that everyone under these circumstances suffers like this. Poor things! It is only ten o'clock & I am sitting in a wrapper in the coolest place I can find but I have been out twice to put in water on my head and wrists, & my head feels now as if all the veins were bursting. It does not ache but it is a horrid sensation.
[1895-05-09 Bertha (StL) to Henry (Wichita)]

It is so hot (91° in my bedroom all yesterday afternoon) that nobody stirs in the daytime and when one has not one's best friend to fall back on in the evenings, life is not what it might be.
[1895-05-10 Bertha (StL) to Henry (Wichita)]

During one summer, Henry wrote that the St. Louis heat "*has taken the heart out of the most courageous.*"

I didn't write yesterday. It sounds feeble minded for a [veteran] of this equatorial season to complain of any new record of the weather dispenser but this last episode has taken the heart out of the most courageous. I fare better than the average for I keep well but it is hard to work, my dearest, and yesterday after an all-day struggle with a full day's work and that obstacle to all efficient work, a green and stupid stenographer, it would have been an effort to write even to you. I needed the rest and took it and neglected my best beloved. It was too hot when I got out here, seven o'clock, to play golf, so after dinner with the Nick Jones', Miss Edith, George Markham, Phil Scanlon, Hugh McKittrick, Jack Davis & Gordon, the two last and I sat on the piazza until twelve roasting and praising our world's fair climate. I should have excepted Jack for when I asked why he didn't evacuate the town he replied "Sam wants me to join him but I think it's more fun here!" You would think him a lunatic if it were not for his good fortune in his immediate companionships at the time. If I am writing incoherently, please attribute it not to the heat but to the fact that a rag time concert is going on behind me. It is of course too hot for golf, so the whole crowd has moved into the house and they are singing hymns which I have never yet heard in church or elsewhere, within about five feet of me! [20170725-2 (1895-) Henry to Bertha]

The St. Louis heat in May 1896 was apparently little better than in the prior year, as Bertha described in her letter.

> *Hot, hotter, hottest! I can't stand much more of this. I think when you come home you will find no wife, only a little pool.*
>
> [1896-05-09 (year?) Bertha (StL) to Henry (Light & Power Co, Fort Worth)]

Since Henry was in Ft. Worth Texas, he was probably experiencing much of the same!

Henry wrote to Bertha in another hot summer that he was keeping very clean, with all of the showers that he was taking.

> *I am very sorry you are having such bad weather. It is getting much warmer here, now 80° in the room, so I know it must be hot there! I admit that we haven't the salt baths and that they would be a luxury but we have a mighty fine shower at the club. Between Saturday afternoon and Sunday night, I am the cleanest thing in town. If I get out in the afternoon early, I take a shower before putting on my golf clothes. Then, when I come in from golf, another, after golf in the morning and another after playing in the afternoon. I shall soon be scrubbed through to the bone.*
>
> [1900-07-23 Henry (StL) to Bertha]

But Henry could take the St. Louis heat in stride and show a bit of humor about his predicament.

> *It has been hotter than either Texas or the other place[151] with which heat comparisons are often made, but I seem to be thriving. I can't take any exercise for I found that would not do, but I sail around in those thin things that you so admire and am really very comfortable.*
>
> [20170831-2 (1901-06-30) Henry to Bertha]

B. FINDING THEIR FIRST HOME

From the following letter that Bertha wrote to Henry in March of 1892 when she was travelling with her parents, it was clear that Henry had to do virtually all of the "leg work" on obtaining and fixing up their first house.

> *About the house, I was not surprised to hear you speak of taking one soon. I knew one often had to, to secure what they wanted. I am under the impression that Charlie Coolidge took his a year before he needed it. But do not ask me about it, dearest, it is your house and you must choose the one you like. If you are at sea about what a woman likes in the way of kitchens, pantries, laundries, etc., ask your sister Minnie's advice; she would know all about it. And tell me what she says. Tell me something about the inside of the different houses if you can. I should like to know your powers of description, dear boy, and you know how much you will interest me. And if there is anything I violently dislike and would be thoroughly uncomfortable with, I will tell you. But otherwise, I would far rather have it where it belongs – with you.* [1892-03-19 Bertha (St. Augustine) to Henry (StL)]

1. THE REBER HOUSE

One of the first houses that Henry inspected was the Reber house. Hildegard McKittrick wrote to Henry in March 1893 of this opportunity.

> *Miss [Maud] Reber has just told me, tho' they are not telling the public, that there is every reason to suppose they will give up this house in June. You had better come to see ours upstairs and down from garret to cellar. They are very superior houses, I assure you.*
>
> [1892-03-25 Hildegarde McKittrick (StL) to Henry (StL)]

---

[151] I.e. hades. (Referring to: "If I owned Texas and Hell, I would rent out Texas and live in Hell" — attributed to General Philip Henry Sheridan.)

Henry wrote that he was interested in the Reber house but was not convinced.

The Rebers, as I told you, are really decided upon the question of giving up their house and I think there is good chance of my securing it if we wish to. You know the house better than I do, although I carefully inspected every crack and corner of its duplicate, Tom's [Thomas McKittrick], yesterday. I confess I was not very much impressed and think it in some respects greatly inferior to the Cabanne mansion! Still I would like to have your advice. Now don't tell me again, dear, "it is your house" or "choose the one you like best" but give me any ideas you may have. They can't be more vague than mine and a combination of errors would be better than many of one kind. I will send a diagram of the next house that I try and at all approve of. Meanwhile, if you can think of any questions to ask about the two I have my eye on, speak or you may be sorry you have not done so later on.
[1892-03-28 (5 letters) Henry to Bertha]

Henry decided to call on the Rebers who were close, intimate, friends of Bertha and Henry.

I called on Miss Reber last night and enjoyed seeing her greatly. I don't know her as well as many of your other intimates but I have always thought her exceedingly attractive. She is different, yes, quite so, from any other girl I know and she is less shy in speaking of you to me than any of your friends. Miss Nan asks after you as if she expected me to deny that I knew anything about you save in a most vague and general way. Not so Miss Reber. She goes very fully into particulars!! She wishes to know when you are coming home, why you can be persuaded to stay away so very long, why I don't like Florida, etc., etc. She says too you are a poor correspondent and looks at me as if she expected me to prove the contrary. I think on the whole she enjoyed my call!
[1892-03-28 (5 letters) Henry to Bertha]

Bertha and Henry decided not to pursue renting the Reber house. Due to her close relationship with Maud Reber, Bertha mentioned her a number of times in her diary, especially regarding Bertha's various clubs in which she formed her closest friendships. In her diary entry in April, 1933 many years after Maud had died, Bertha remembered her fondly as one of the original members of the Topics Club.

[Some history. Maud Reber married Rev. Carroll Melvin Davis ("Dean Davis") on October 12, 1897. They tried to have a family but their first child, born in 1898, died at age 2 and was buried on May 5, 1901[152]. Their second child died at birth and buried on March 2, 1901. Their third child died at birth and was buried November 2, 1903. Maud died 9 days after the death of their third child and was buried November 11, 1903. Rev. Davis lived until 1932 and must have needed the faith of Job over his remaining lifetime.]

2. THE CABANNE STREET HOUSE

The next house that Henry considered was the Cabanne House.

Now I shall proceed to say that all that I meant to yesterday. First, about the house, I am like you inclined to prefer the Cabanne house though it is difficult for me to say as I know absolutely nothing about the inside except that Mrs. Whittaker thought very favorably of it and was only sorry that it was too small for the Kennetts and I know she would be apt to be critical. And then, it is new and the Reber house is old. I fancy it (the Reber's) is comfortable in many ways and I should not object to it. The location is pleasant, though even there I think Cabanne has the advantage. But I do think that there is one thing against it. I am not sure but I think it has a basement kitchen. You may be amused at my starting on housekeeping details already but, although I don't know much of trials with maids from actual experiences, the lady who rules our kitchen, having been in possession seventeen years, still I have not had so many of my friends marry without hearing of their experiences and I know that cooks violently object to going to houses where there is a basement

---

[152] The burial dates are from the Bellefontaine Cemetery, St. Louis MO, records.

kitchen and I must say I don't blame them in the least. Still, that is not an insuperable objection for one cannot expect perfection.
[1892-04-03 Bertha (Old Port Comfort VA) to Henry]

While he was in New York City, Henry sketched a diagram for Bertha of the Cabanne house floor plan.
Dearest,

I thought I would make this a strictly business letter and write about the house more definitely than I have hitherto.

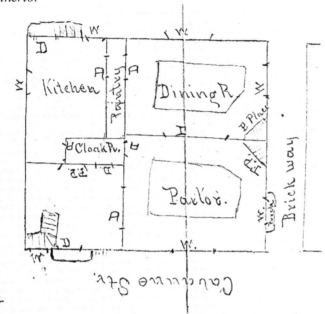

1st Floor, Cabanne Street House

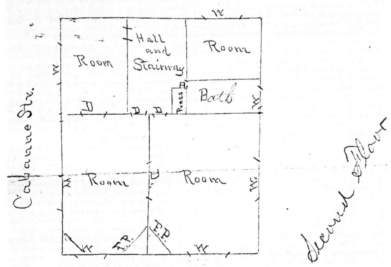

2nd Floor, Cabanne Street House

I have marked off the subdivisions of the first and second floors in something like the manner of their arrangement and I have tried to get the doors and windows in their proper places. I have not attempted to photograph! the basement or third story, as these are both cut up into such a number of small and irregularly shaped rooms as to defy my draughtsman's art. The basement, though, is quite convenient and has a fairly good laundry with the usual store and coal rooms. The third story has two very good rooms and the rest are small, answering well for either servants' or store rooms. The kitchen, you will see, is convenient to the dining room, communicating with it through the pantry.

The light in the house is very good indeed. There is one thing against all houses facing west, however. The afternoon sun is apt to be disagreeable. I have tried to show you that, south of the house a brick way opens these separating it from the houses south by an open space about half as wide as the street. This adds considerable to the attractiveness of the whole south side of the house. The presses etc. about the house are small but not more so than those in the other rented houses I have seen. Now would it do for me to ask Mattie to look the place over with me when I return? She has lately been struggling with problems of this nature and as she seems to have solved many in arranging their establishment, she may contribute some suggestions that will help us. My mother & sisters will of course do anything in the way of assisting with our selection but the view of a young housekeeper, a beginner in fact, would be more valuable don't you think so?

Now, darling, don't make this a matter of worry to you. We have plenty of time to make our selection and arrangements and I wish you to treat it as a matter to divert and entertain you rather than as a bother. Don't hesitate to speak to me perfectly plainly dear when I ask you questions or when you wish for especial items and we will make our home as comfortable as may be now and change it to suit you when you are installed as its mistress.

I wanted to suggest that I do not think it a drawback to have only one parlor for if this be made a comfortable "living room" such as Zack and Lutie have arranged theirs, I think it really answers better than the two rooms. I don't like the way Mattie has furnished her one parlor with the one room only. I would, I think, have made it more comfortable and easy, not in fact the reception room she has made of it.

You will laugh at my pronounced views on a subject of which I am so densely ignorant but I only give you the ideas as they come to me, not caring if they seem to start you on the way to telling me what yours are. You see, Bert, the work in our home is for you for you will make it so beautiful to me there that I shall not have place or thought for the surroundings save as they help me to make your life bright and happy. What would I not give now to wander through our own home with you, dearest, and hear your sweet voice tell me you never, never, will leave me again. Or to see in your beautiful eyes that the dream I have had for years had been fulfilled and that you were made happy in my care for you. Dear, we must not be gloomy at the little trials that beset us now. They will soon be over and then, if there is enough thought of you in my life to make you a happy woman, you cannot fail to find all the joy I ask for you.

Goodbye, my darling. God bless you always.
[1892-04-04(--) (Saturday) Henry (NYC – Holland House) to Bertha (-)]

3. **3331 WASHINGTON AVENUE**

Henry next looked at a Washington Avenue town house which immediately attracted his attention.

Dear, I can at last write you about the house and I think, if you approve, we will live at 3331. That is, if my arrangement with Mr. Clendenin is carried out. First let me say that Mrs. Knox and Mattie both condemned the Cabanne house. Mattie thought the arrangement much less convenient than hers and Mrs. Knox and Gordon who, it seems, went down on their own account to inspect it thought it would be so hot even in the early spring as to be unbearable. A new drawback which I had not been able to consider until recently is that, on the south side of the street (Olive) facing Cabanne, a very large and tall row of flats are going up and this so shuts out the breeze from the south that this, with the western sun, would make the house I am afraid very warm in the early

spring. And, as I don't intend to let you leave me in the summer as long as the weather is pleasant, you can see that the selfish man at once conceives to be a prejudice against it. Gordon Knox grew eloquent on the subject. He said they would like to be as near neighbors of ours but they both thought it a less comfortable situation for a house than any of those that it seemed possible for me to secure. I have seen Clendenin and, on Monday or Tuesday, I shall look the house over then, if he concludes to give it up and you approve, I think I shall take it, dear. You must write me fully and freely on the subject for you know I am quite uncertain of myself and will be glad to have you help me with any suggestions that occur to you. I have not sent you the plans of the Cabanne house because they cannot be found. If the owner can find them, I will send them to you with those of the Washington Ave. house and, maybe, you will find, by comparison of the two plans, which one you distinctly prefer.
[1892-06-20 Henry (StL) to Bertha (the Ark, East Jaffrey, c/o Mr. Poole)]

Henry was anxious to make a final inspection of 3331 Washington Avenue.

Dear, my prospective Hebrew landlord took himself off to the country today so I hadn't the pleasure of inspecting our new house as I had arranged to do but as he returns tomorrow or Thursday you can prepare yourself for no end of data on the subject of mantels, fireplaces, etc, etc, etc. I shall probably telegraph you as soon as I am satisfied that it is best to secure the house for, despite your willingness to give me entire charge in the matter, I don't intend to start out by relieving you of a full share of responsibility in my decisions. I think we can practically assume that the house is taken for your letter on the subject was clearly one of approval. Still, that was before you had the plans and you may not be so enthusiastic after seeing them.
[1892-06-29 Henry (StL) to Bertha (Farragut House, Rye Beach)]

Henry was enthusiastic about renting 3331 Washington Avenue and started to make plans for its renovation. He wrote that it is the most east of 4 houses on the plan, including Mattie's house[153].

Dear, I stopped before I could finish this to see the owner of the house I have decided to take unless you disapprove. I mean 3331. The arrangement is all but completed. That is, I have the refusal of it and tomorrow or Tuesday, I am going to look it over to stipulate the repairs I wish made before taking it. I had a long talk with the architect who built the house yesterday, and I satisfied myself as to the pluming and furnace arrangements and, if it does not bother you too much, dear, will you write me for any particulars you may wish as to the kitchen, the laundry or anything that you wish to know more about than you can learn from the plans which, of course, give you the dimensions of each room and the outlines drawn accurately "to scale". O, don't mistake the right house. There are four on the plans sent and ours is the east one of the four. You will notice too that it is a foot narrower than Mattie's, but this, I take it, is no drawback and, Bert, I did not say so before, for I wished first to be sure, I am delighted with it. I think it will suit us much better than any of the thousand and one which I have looked at. I am anxiously waiting to hear from you after you have looked over the plans, for as I shall take a lease for three years, I do not wish to conclude the transaction without feeling sure you approve. I may find it necessary to act before I hear from you. If I do, I will give you a chance to have your say against the selection by telegram, for it would not be fair to you and I don't wish to do anything without your positive approval. You see, dear, the house would not be half as attractive to me if you did not thoroughly like it.
[1892-06-30(-) Henry (StL) to Bertha (Farragut House, Rye Beach)]

One day later, the 3331 Washington Avenue house was still foremost in Henry's thoughts.

I sat up half the night studying the plans with the most intense delight. Of course, I understood them unusually well, that is, I understood what the effect would be from knowing Mattie's house. The only part entirely unfamiliar to me being the basement. I think the arrangements capital, I

---

[153] Mary Martha McKittrick Stribling.

have always thought Mattie's house most unusually comfortably arranged. I used to go by that row last winter and wish someone would move out, but I never really thought we would have such good fortune. Of course, I regretted that extra foot of width, especially when I saw how much more closet room it gave Mattie, but I think that a slight defect. I would far rather have less closet room and Mattie next door than have Mattie's house and a stranger next door.

...

You speak of some repairs being necessary and I suppose there are, but on the whole, I think it is rather nice for us that someone lived there first. You know the proverb, that if you build a house, you want your enemy to live in it the first year, your friend the second and yourself the third. Mr. Clendenin could probably tell you any needed thing in the house far better than I could. I think it is very nice that he is not to leave until November for I think to see the house standing empty and waiting would be a great trial to your patience.
[1892-07-01 Bertha (Farragut House) to Henry (StL)]

The planning for 3331 Washington Avenue continued for weeks with numerous back and forth letters between Bertha and Henry, with Bertha writing the following letters.

Dear, your scouting of the plans was very effective to my mind. I was grumbling because the one foot less width would take some of the wall space in the "living room", where we shall, no doubt, place our large library and the shelves for the books, and that the dining room would be smaller than Mattie's, and I did not follow this loss in width to the second story, so did not notice that the closets would be more shallow than those of the other house. I will try to remember about the stationary tubs in the laundry and any other items I am in doubt about, I will write you about the fixtures as soon as Mrs. Clendenin, who is unwell, can let me look the house over.
[1892-07-06 Henry (StL) to Bertha (Farragut House, Rye Beach)]

One thing I did mean to ask and forgot, will you be able to put the electric lights in this house? I know you said in the other that arrangements were all made for introducing the wires.
[1892-07-11 Bertha (Rye Beach) to Henry (StL)- the house, 3331 Washington]

Mattie says to tell you that all the windows leak and that Bernheimer has refused to fix any of them, except their parlor, and also that the tenant is entitled at the beginning of each lease to have the house repainted and some papering done (She says that is not a message, that you probably know it.) - that she and Will are going to see about that, when they re-lease their house. Further than that, she says she thinks there is nothing, that that is all that is needed in their house, and she supposes the Clendenin's have taken equally good care of theirs. As for the difference in size, she says that is so slight that the effect of the two houses is precisely the same. She says no one ever notices that Mrs. Clendenin's parlor is smaller than hers and that, as a matter of fact, she did not know it herself for some time, that the difference is not an appreciable drawback at all. She is radiant over the prospect of her new neighbors.
[1892-07-14 Bertha (Magnolia MA) to Henry (StL)]

You thought I hardly talked house enough to you. Mattie and I talk house all the time. She says to "tell Henry that those houses have the dirtiest furnaces in town, I mean, the furnace that make the most dirt. Perhaps Bernheimer may do something about them for him". But she added the not very consoling remark "I don't think there is the slightest possibility of his doing so, but still, Henry might try".

I deliver the message, but I should hardly think he would do anything. The more Mattie tells me about the houses, though she is very frank about the drawbacks, the more I like them. And I think there is nothing I don't know about from the fact that there are no stationary tubs in the laundry, to the difficulty of heating the servants' room in the second story, the fact that the back stairs lead

into it, and that the mantel pieces upstairs are marble. I am delighted with most of what she tells me thought and I am sure I shall like it better than I should have the other houses.
[1892-07-15 Bertha (Magnolia MA) to Henry (StL)]

Based on Bertha's comments and his own thoughts about the house, Henry had a talk with the landlord, Bernheimer.

I shall tell you now what I have done with Bernheimer. I found him a pretty fair sample of his race, inclined to "drive" a bargain without reference to what our needs or those of his property demanded but I encouraged to make him see that certain things must be done to preserve the house and, having scored this victory, I concluded I would prefer doing the other things to having him attend to them in indifferent manner. I will not bother you with all the details of the work now but when you come out we will discuss the painting, papering and all the other details. I think we can arrange for the electric lights when the house is being papered. I will have the laundry arranged and the stationary tubs put in. Then I shall want to ask no end of questions about the kitchen arrangements, etc., etc.
[1892-07-19 Henry (Ft. Worth TX) to Bertha (Farragut House, Rye Beach)]

Based on the reports about 3331 Washington Ave., Bertha wrote of being *"perfectly delighted"* with it.

I shall be perfectly delighted if you take 3331. In the beginning, when we first thought that Mattie might give up her house, I had a far stronger leaning toward that than toward Cabanne and now, when we have the opportunity of having almost the same house with Mattie and Janet for neighbors, I feel radiant about it. As far as I know, Mattie's house it is very convenient too and I suppose they are very much the same. I consider the accumulated testimony as to the heat of the Cabanne house conclusive and I think it would be foolish to take a house that you almost know would be uncomfortable for so large a part of the year. I think nothing could give me greater pleasure than to know you had taken 3331 and I believe if you write me that Mr. Clendenin won't give it up, I shall set down and weep for the first time since you left me. They want me to play whist (it is a fearfully rainy day) so I will say goodbye, my dearest, and God bless you.
[1892-07-24 Bertha (Jaffrey) to Henry (StL)]

In order to move the preparation of their house forward, Henry had additional conversations with Bernheimer and, apparently, had some success at having him make some repairs.

Our worthy landlord and I had another of our love-fests this morning and he tells me the furnace is being repaired and thoroughly over hauled and that those windows will be changed next week if he lives. I replied "if the windows are not fixed, you will probably not live long thereafter." And I think I cowed him sufficiently to ensure his attending to the work. I shall not mind though if it is not promptly done for as I must practice up a little for Jack Shepley[154], I shall get my hand in by punching our Israelite friend's head if he doesn't carry out his promises.
[1892-09-03 (Saturday) Henry (StL) to Bertha (Farragut House)]

C. 3337 WASHINGTON AVENUE – Bertha & Henry's First House

During Henry's inspections and planning for the 3331 Washington Avenue house, Henry became increasingly aware of the advantages of the neighboring house, 3337 Washington Avenue "town" house, which was the "corner" house.

---

[154] See John Foster Shepley, RELATIVES & FRIENDS Chapter 16. Jack jokingly threatened to beat up Henry.

1. HENRY AGREES TO RENT 3337

In October 1892, Henry was able to switch his rent contract to 3337 Washington Avenue instead of 3331 Washington Avenue. This required Henry to confirm the availability of 3337 and find a tenant for 3331.

> *I have tried to run down Shylock Bernheimer today but without success. I don't think, though, there is any doubt about our securing the corner house for Valle has agreed to take "our house" and this is the only condition that is required to secure the other house.*
> [1892-10-18 (Tuesday) Henry (StL) to Bertha (William H. Benton, Chicago IL)]

> *Let me tell you about the house first. Our Israelite friend behaved rather decently this morning and I have formally secured the corner house so you can prepare for the struggle with those windows and such other difficulties as we were warned against. I am surprised to find that having taken this house, I feel rather superior to and sorry for those three families who will be obliged to take their meals in dark dining rooms while we are rejoicing in the brilliant light let in by those numerous western openings.*
> [1892-10-19 (Wednesday) Henry (StL) to Bertha (C/O Mr. Wm. W.H. Benton, 5021 Washington Ave, Chicago IL)]

In the end, Henry wrote to Bertha of liking 3337 Washington Avenue better than 3331. *"Yes, I have transferred my attachment to 3337 completely and the discarded favorite 3331 is no longer thought of."* 1892-12-02 Henry (StL) to Bertha (Boston))

2. REFURBISHING 3337

Bertha and Henry wrote numerous letters about the refurbishing of 3337 Washington Ave. Excerpts from these letters are included below to provide a glimpse of how much time and attention Bertha and Henry spent on this task. Since nearly all of their many letters from the late summer through the end of the year contained their concepts, thoughts and wishes for their first home, only a small fraction of their comments are included here. Henry included the following comments in two October 1892 letters to Bertha.

> *I have been to look at our new house since I wrote you yesterday and you can credit yourself with being a very nice girl for, Bert, it is, to use your most enthusiastic expression, "far and away" better than any of the inside ... Besides having better and larger closets in all the rooms, it is better built, the dining room is furnished in hard wood, and, in both the first & second floor baths, the floors are of hard wood. The parlor floor is not laid in hard wood but the dining room has the hard wood border like that Cabanne St. house, and the dining room is a beauty, Bert! I will go over the house some day in the day time and write you more fully about it. I would not have time to further particulars now for I must stop.*
> [1892-10-20 (Thursday) Henry (StL) to Bertha (5021 Washington Ave, Chicago)]

> *Mr. Taylor, the former tenant, wishes to know if I can use his gas fixtures, awnings screens, shades and three sets of gas logs (in the parlor hall and dining room). I think I shall buy his awnings and screens if they are in good condition and if you approve, but I don't believe we will use the gas logs and the fixtures are not dreams of beauty. I think I shall get you to do about the fixtures for the lower part of the house and for your room as we arranged about the papering. You can look in at one of the stores in Boston and select some that you think will suit and when I go on I can get them. The other fixtures we can get here, I think.*
> [1892-10-23 (Sunday) Henry (StL) to Bertha (Wm H Benton, 5021 Washington Ave, Chicago)]

Since Bertha was in the east and could not personally inspect the house, she relied on "the plans" of the house in order to make her own choices.

> *I am waiting anxiously for my plans, for, I cannot begin to get anything until they come and I have the measurements. O I must tell you that my mother says she and father included the papers when they spoke of furnishing the house, so I shall get the papers myself and send them out to you as*

soon as possible. And my dear boy, you must choose the gas fixtures yourself, I positively decline to select them, and you have pretty good taste considering you are a man. I think that is a very happy thought about the screens and awnings. They are at all in good condition. It will save us a great deal of trouble. I think mother has definitely settled that I am to have Wilma and Louise too, which would save trouble also.
[1892-10-27 (Thursday) Bertha (Boston) to Henry (StL) on Wedding Plans, etc.]

Why don't you keep the gas log in the hall? I know artistically it is a great blemish and I should not think of leaving it in the parlor. But practically it is a great comfort to have one place where you can turn on a fire at any time if you need one without the bother of making it. And it is a great deal cleaner in a hall especially when dirt and ashes are more apt to fly up to the upper story. The Buckinghams have one and I realized its comfort especially coming home after the theater when we turned on a blaze to make things cheerful and then turned it off with no worry about leaving a fire blazing. This is all suggestion, you need not do it if you don't want to and remember I am not so lost to all artistic ideals as to want one in that sitting room of ours for I don't think them things of beauty.
[1892-10-28) (Friday) Bertha (Backbay, Boston) to Henry (StL)]

During this period, Henry's letters were generally full of various specifics about the house.
What do you think of putting in an electric button to call the kitchen from the dining room? These buttons hid under the carpet (near your place at the table, dearest, is where we would place ours) seem quite convenient. Then I have had several copies made of the floor designs of our house. I shall send you one or two copies for you may wish to have one with one of your shop keepers and in this event you will need an extra copy of the drawings. I still have the original plans and as you may want to see the side elevations of the house, I shall send back the original drawings and when you have finished using them you can give them to me while I am in Boston or mail them to me later.
[1892-10-29 (Friday) Henry (StL) to Bertha (Hotel Brunswick, Boston)]

Don't forget to take account of the register in the dining room - in fact, in all the rooms – in selecting the carpets or rugs for the floors. It occurred to me to mention this as the registers are all in the floors and I think not very conveniently located.
[1892-10-31 (Sunday) Henry (StL) to Bertha (Hotel Brunswick, Boston)]

It occurs to me in looking over the house that the best place for our servants will be the rear room in the third floor. The back room on the second floor is very small and for two servants it would be too small. The other room has a large closet and, beside its being roomier, would put the servants entirely off the second floor.
[1892-10-31 (Sunday) Henry (StL) to Bertha (Hotel Brunswick, Boston)]

"Where are my measurements? How high? How wide?" Bertha had numerous questions.
About things that do have to be settled at once, you will think I give you no rest about measurements but will you please measure the exact space in the dining room that is not covered by the hard wood. I think I will get a rug for that room and I want to have some idea of the size. And how high and how wide & broad are the steps, and how many are there? I think even if they are hard wood, I will have to have a stair carpet, not a wide one, but down the middle and the width of the landing? And in the third story, how far from the floor does that slope inward of the ceiling commence? I want to know about how high the furniture can stand against the wall, not that I intend to have the chairs standing in rows against the wall either. I believe that is all just now but I shall probably think of some more tomorrow. How tired you will get of these letters. No, you won't either. It is

our home and our future life we are planning, is it not, my dearest? And it cannot be anything but a happy home and a happy life with the love and trust we can bring to it.
[1892-11-02 (Thursday) Bertha (Boston) to Henry (StL)]

In addition to providing her thoughts on Henry's renovations, Bertha was also busy buying the furnishings for the house.

I am getting on with my work famously, the furniture is nearly all bought. The three bedrooms, parlor and dining room are about ready, except the sideboard, which now haunts me in my dreams. And a few odd chairs I intend to get at different places. A good deal of it was selected before you came on, only I had not quite made up my mind between certain different things. Mother gave me a dear little desk today, which can stand in the parlor at the right of the door, as you go in. It is not big enough to take much space and won't interfere with the other door at all. It looks like a real antique, and is very quaint and dainty, but it is thoroughly a woman's belonging, and you must not expect to be allowed to use it. I shall keep it locked!!!
[1892-11-26 (Friday) Bertha (Backbay Boston) to Henry (StL)]

I sent off the rest of the paper today. That is, I sent the paper for my room, your room, and the third story front room. The rest, that is, the girl's room and the hall, I have decided to let you do as you offered and get in St. Louis.

I have made several discoveries. One was that I could not prepay the expressage as they told me they could not find out what it was at this end. So I apologize to you for not having done it. Discovery number two was about the hall paper. I wanted to get cartridge paper of about the color of the sample I enclose, one of those shades, anyway, and it was fifteen cents a roll. I decided that, after thirty six rolls of that paper had been expressed out and taken out to the house, the expense and the bother would nearly equal the cost of the paper, a fact which you probably thought of when you spoke of getting the girl's room paper yourself but which I did not realize and I know you can get almost this same paper at home, if you like it. The other three papers I got, however, and will carry samples with me when I get the carpets. I don't believe you can make a mistake as to which is for which room for the quantities differ. There are thirty-two rolls for the upstairs room, nineteen for mine and fifteen for yours. But for fear of mistakes, I enclose these marked samples, not that I think you can judge very much from samples. Whenever I saw a paper I liked, I made the man unroll four strips and lay them side by side to give me some idea of what a wall would be like and several that I liked quite well in a strip simply would not look at after I saw the effect of a quantity.

You have no idea how hard it was to get pretty ones. The styles this year are all in very large patterns, which I dislike anyway and most especially upstairs. I tried nearly every place in town and I had to go back to Davenport in despair. I think you will find these unobjectionable. I am not sure that I do not like the spare room the best of the three, though it is not as nice a paper as the other two. You remember that the other two, the two sent first, the blue is for the parlor and the terra cotta for the dining room, and you will not forget, will you son? (I think I see your air of scorn at that remark.) I imagine that from these small samples you will think that the front and back room papers are very much alike, but they are not really. The effect of them in the piece is quite different. The last discovery I made was that he had sent those two other papers to Mrs. H.C.S. and I can only hope your family did not see the address.
[1892-11-27a (Sunday) Bertha (Boston) to Henry (StL)]

3. ABOUT INQUISITIVE FRIENDS

Bertha and Henry were very sensitive about inquiring friends who might start rumors about their affairs in general and their house hunting in particular. On finding out that his friend, Tom McKittrick, had not kept his promise to keep secret his house hunting, Henry vented his anger.

Now as to Tom, I have no such feeling and as soon as I return home, I shall kill two birds with one stone: show you that I am still a pretty healthy specimen of humanity and gratify my thirst for his gore for I shall most certainly punch the young man's head! I don't mind your knowing about the slip I made with Tom, in fact, I thought I had told you of it. But I do mind his breaking his word to me. After having caught me through some very thoughtless questions, I asked him about Mrs. Reber's house and then solemnly promising to mention nothing of what I told him. Just tell Madam Hildegarde[155] to buy her mourning clothes on east where she can make better selection of it; she will need it soon!!!

[1892-07-18 Henry (Ft Worth) to Bertha (Farragut House, Rye Beach)]

Not surprisingly, Bertha and Henry's work on their new home attracted the increased interest of their friends who felt at liberty to drop in and look around, as Henry commented to Bertha.

I have just come from the house. When I got there I found Mary and Lutie[156] in full possession. I asked them about the shades I had chosen for the ceilings and I was mightily set up over their unqualified approval of my good taste. They were either very much pleased with the general promise of things there or else they have uncommon talent for making people who are in doubt about their decisions feel comfortable. Lutie thought your room was going to be beautiful and I was so much flattered by her comments that I have once or twice concluded that perhaps my true vocation is house decorating.

[1892-12-07a (Tuesday, Wednesday) Henry (StL) to Bertha (Hotel Brunswick, Boston)]

Bertha was not particularly pleased at everyone seeing her house, before even she had seen it. There was obvious pride in being able to personally show off one's home for the first time.

... while we are speaking of furniture, dear old boy, there is a favor I want to ask. I am very glad of course that Lute and Mary admired the papers and ceilings, etc. But, after the carpets are down and the furniture in, would you mind very much not letting the girls go in. I do not mean Minnie and Maggie[157], of course, but none of the others, not even Nan[158]. It may be a foolish feeling on my part but I do not want other people, even dear friends, to look at my things and talk about them before I have seen myself how they look together and then I would like to have the pleasure of showing it myself. Don't you think you could manage that diplomatically and without offending anyone? Naturally, I would rather sacrifice a feeling of my own than hurt any of my friends. But it is a pretty strong feeling. Now, don't misunderstand me, dear, I do not mean your sisters at all. I hope they will look at the things and I most sincerely hope they will like them but I mean other people. It seems superfluous to ask you not to misunderstand me for I have rarely known that to happen. And please do not think I had any foolish feeling about Lutie and Mary. Of course I know, while the painters and paperers are there, that the house is open and any one can go in. This is only a little expression of what I should like after the furniture is in and you must do as you think best about it.

[1892-12-04(-) (Friday 1892-12-11) 20180405-1 Bertha (Newton Centre-) to Henry (Wichita)]

Henry did his best to make light of the renovations in order to not attract any unwanted interest.

I have just returned from Tom's house[159]. I have not seen them since my return home so, although those several million duties that I wrote you about have not all been attended to, I took holiday for an hour or two and spent a very pleasant evening with them. They were very much interested in our house and Hildegarde wanted to know the colors of the papers, about the carpets, furniture,

---

[155] Hildegard Sterling McKittrick was Tom's wife and close friends of Bertha and Henry.
[156] "Lutie" was Mary Louis Shepley Lionberger who was married to Isaac Henry ("Zack") Lionberger. There are many possible "Mary's" but it may have been Mary Lionberger who was Lutie's sister-in-law.
[157] Henry's sisters.
[158] Anne ("Nan") Shepley, one of Bertha's closest friends.
[159] Thomas and Hildegarde McKittrick

even the gas fixtures, and I "talked back" as if there had not been a problem or a doubt or hesitation about any of the work I am having done here, leaving out the times when I have been through the hair tearing process. And as a consequence, those two think I am simply having a little recreation in wrangling with those painters and paperers. You will observe my dearest, how I am learning to hide house troubles from the outside world. Are you not pleased with this evidence of progress in me?
[1892-12-09 (Wednesday) Henry (StL) to Bertha (Hotel Brunswick, Boston)]

Bertha wrote of having learned from her mother about how trying it is to have friends inspect your new house before it is finished.

You are quite the most satisfactory person I ever knew. There is never any need of explaining what I want to you because you know it beforehand. This is apropos of not letting the populace into our house. Mother had a very trying time when we moved into 2807 - Twice she found people calmly walking over the house and inspecting carpets, etc. Once it was Mrs. Treat & Mrs. Parsons who "thought she would not mind them", but the other time it was just some of the neighbors who seemed to consider a newly furnished house as public property. She says it is the part of wisdom just to say to the carpet men or whoever is at work in the house that you do not want people to come in, otherwise they feel they have no right to refuse.
[1892-12-17 (Saturday) Bertha (Stancote, Newton Centre) to Henry (StL)]

I can almost forgive you for Lute's invasion, though I cannot resist the temptation of saying "I told you so". Never mind, I accept your apologies on condition it does not happen again.
[1893-01-05 (Wednesday) Bertha (Newton Centre) to Henry (StL)]

Given her reprimands, Henry wondered if Bertha appreciated how difficult it was to keep their friends from entering their house.

You are by no means properly appreciative of my struggles with your friends to keep them out of that house or you would not be so sniffy about Lute's visit. My dear, your friends are simply terrible! As to Mrs. Knox, it required the combined effort of Gordon and myself to dissuade her from making 3337 her headquarters for the next two months and, when I announced that if she entered that house before your arrival it would be over my dead body, it strained a friendship which had been of a rather intimate nature. I don't think Miss Jennie Alexander will be on speaking terms with me if I remain in town much longer and you may say to your mother that, if Miss Treat has not taken as much interest in your house as she did in hers when it was being arranged, it is because the storm doors refused to yield to her attacks. My sister tells me she has a man at the door half the day, shouting to the applicants for admission his orders "am very sorry but the house is in disorder and I have instructions to admit no one".
[1893-01-10 (Monday) Henry (StL) to Bertha (Stancote, Newton Centre MA)]

4. FINAL HOUSE PREPARATIONS
a. Henry's Business Exigencies
Henry was obviously juggling the preparation of the 3337 Washington Avenue house around his work. Due to his trip to Wichita, Waco and Ft. Worth around December 9 until just before Christmas 1892, Henry's house preparations were paused; however, Henry was pleased at the progress he had made.

This will probably be my last letter from St. Louis until my return from the south, dearest, for I leave on the early train tomorrow and, between that house and the winding up performance at the office, I shall be fortunate if I catch my train.

You don't know how much I hate to leave that house now, Bert. It is beginning to look really attractive, unfurnished as it is and I shall miss the hours I have been spending there. Today as it was cold, I ordered in the hard coal and when it came, we made a fire in the furnace and it behaved beautifully. I have already tried all the chimneys where there are open fireplaces and I don't think the windows will have to be raised to drive out the smoke when the fires are lighted after our return. I also had the gas turned on today and I lit the gas logs in the hall to see how they would look and do you know, dear, the single trial has conquered all my prejudices. The fire is really a very pretty one and, remembering the reason you gave for wishing to keep them, I sat down before this bright fire and told myself a prettier story than ever came out of fairy land.

This evening I went over and had an illumination and inspected the day's work. The ceilings have all been tinted, the greater part of the papering has been done and the painters are almost ready to depart. On my return, I shall move in the carpets and the furniture which will be here probably by the first of next month. Then the kitchen stove will go in and the other little things in the laundry arranged and then, well, I shall have nothing to do but wait until I can go to my darling.

O, I intended to tell you that the parlor ceiling is tinted a sort of fawn color. The dining room is a deep cream and your room, the prettiest ceiling in the house, is the old rose color of the figure in your paper. Your room will be a perfectly beautiful place, dear. I have smiled more than once when I found that this room was the first that I found it necessary to inspect when I have been over the house day after day. I find myself there without realizing that it always happens to be the room that I am most anxious to have please you.
[1892-12-10 (Friday) Henry (StL) to Bertha (Hotel Brunswick, Boston)]

b. Bertha's Plans for the New House

Bertha always kept Henry fully informed of her ideas for the preparation of their house.

I told you that today I would write you a number of items and you might keep this letter by you for reference as I know you probably will not set to work on the carpets until after New Year's. Only my mind is full of it and has to be relieved.

The parlor carpet is the mahogany colored English Hilton(?). My room is the blue gray Brussels. The rugs for the hall are made rugs and the stair carpet from the first to the second story matches the center of these rugs. Your room carpet and the carpet for the second story hall are the same Brussels brown with a little leaf in it and the same makes the stair carpet from the second to the third story. The green carpet is for the spare room and I think it would be wise, dear boy, to have those shades you spoke of put up in that room before the carpet is put down for the sun will certainly fade it. As that room has no inside blinds, I think we will have to have a double set of shades there anyway – dark for inside and the same as the rest of the house outside. The dining room rug is a Turkish rug but it was impossible to get it the exact size of that space. They come in certain proportions you know and one that was wide enough was always too long for the room. Of course, I could have had one made like the hall rugs but I wanted that rug to be a genuine Turk. Well this rug is just a little too narrow for the space; there will be an inch and a half each side uncovered but the man said it would be a very simple matter to have another strip of wood of that width laid alongside. It need not be the same color even, a dark strip would look as if the floor were inlaid or, if that should prove impracticable, though he thought it would not if you have a painter paint a strip around the edge of the same color exactly as the wood, no one would notice the difference on an inch and a half and in this mother agreed with him and the rug is a beauty. Then there are the rug adjusters – strips of thin flexible iron shaped - - They are put on the underneath side of the rugs so.

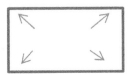

Not coming clear out to the corner and the effect thereof is that when the corner of a rug is pulled up or turned over, it snaps right back into place. You might have the men sew those on where they put down the carpets. I told him to put in a set for each rug and you must tell me if they are not there for they are a new patent and I don't know if you can get them at home yet. There is enough of each carpet to carpet the closet of our room and the linen closet and they are all shaped except the stair carpets but I told you of all that before.

I hope the furniture will arrive safely. It was all based in wooden boxes. I should imagine there was enough boxing to keep us in kindling wood for the remainder of our natural lives. But I was afraid of accidents.

One of the girls I went to see Wednesday told me of a mournful experience of a friend of hers who was married a year ago and went to live in New York. She got all her carpets, furniture, etc., in Boston, went off on her wedding trip and when she got back, as soon as her house was in order, sent for her things. They sent her family items by a sound steamer – furniture, carpets, ball dresses and wedding presents and it was that steamer that was run down by the ocean steamer. Do you remember the circumstance? The poor girl had to go to the wharf day after day as the things were fished up and try to identify them. But with the exception of her silver, she recovered literally nothing but unrecognizable pulp. Even the clocks were hopeless ruins. Fancy the long drawn out agony of it! At least, my things cannot be sunk.
[1892-12-17 (Saturday) Bertha (Stancote, Newton Centre) to Henry (StL)]

c. New Furniture

Bertha wrote of her father's concern about a furniture shipment to be sent to St. Louis from the east; her father apparently wanted to make sure that it would not unduly burden Henry.

O, before I go any farther, father is writing to you. He said, if he could have been sure of being in St. Louis, he would have had that furniture sent to him and he would have turned it over to you, and then he would not have had to arrange things in this way. But as he could not be there, he had to leave that trouble to you, although he was very sorry not to be able to arrange it all himself. But he is very anxious that you should not fail to let him know if he had not sent you the right amount. As he said to me, "that is included in my gift to you and Henry." I am ever so sorry, I always have been, that you should have had this bother yourself but I did not very well see how it could be avoided and you have not minded, have you? Father would have spoken to you about this in St. Louis only he thought the arrangements had all been made at this end and that we found we could not do. You will do as he says, dear, for you know these things are mine and you have not the right to hold yourself responsible for any debts as yet, though I believe that awful responsibility falls upon you later. He felt very badly about all this not having been arranged before and asked me to tell you so, although he was going to write also.
[1892-12-31 (Friday 1892-12-30) Bertha (East Jaffrey NH) to Henry StL]

The quantity of furniture delivered to their new house was prodigious, as Henry wrote to Bertha.

I have just come from 3337 and, before closing up the house, I had the pleasure of locking in it all the furniture, carpets, and fixtures. About half of the boxes have been unpacked and, my dear, I shall establish and operate a wood yard with the wood from those boxes. I filled the shed very early today and now I think the yard is about full, say even with the top of the fence. All the furniture which we have opened was well packed except the bookcase that was packed carelessly and narrowly escaped being smashed up. It was not scratched but when the box was opened there was nothing to protect the glass doors and that they were unharmed simply proves that the days of miracles are not over. This is the only article that was not beautifully protected in packing and as

it was unharmed, except a small piece which had come unglued, I don't think you can complain of the care used in preparing the furniture for shipment.
[1892-12-31 (ref: 1893-12-31) Henry (StL) to Bertha (Stancote, Newton Centre)]

Darling, that house is beginning to fill me with pride. It is lovely, Bert! And I say this notwithstanding a few disappointments I have had lately. My gas fixture man sent me the wrong fixtures for some parts for the house and so I started last week with a row with him. Then I could have paid a visit to Boston for the pleasure of killing your friend Paine for, on making closer examination of that bookcase, I found it so badly used up that I had to have it all taken to pieces - every door was broken in one or more places. And, until I found it could be mended and made as good as before it was injured, I was a very sad man for it is one of the prettiest cases I have ever seen. I am glad to say that the injuries can all be repaired and you will never know, I think, that it was at all hurt. The fixtures, I think, I shall leave as they are until you come, the others like them but I don't care particularly for the hall light and I think the side brackets are too severely plain. In fact, I would change several of the fixtures if you were here and I could therefore be sure I would not make another mistake. As it is, I shall wait until you pass on them and then make such changes as we may think necessary. The parlor pendant and side brackets are very good and the fixture in the dining room is very pretty as are the side lights in your room and the hall, but the other things are not very satisfactory.

Dear, you should have seen the house tonight! The parlor carpet is down and it is a beauty! That room looked almost as if you had peeped in and lighted it up with your smile. Your room – ah, I can't tell you about it, dearest. I think you will like it. I had already concluded that it would be best to put that sofa on the east side of the parlor and I think it will look very well there. In fact, I should have placed it there if you had not spoken of it for this seems much the best place for it.
[1893-01-10 (Monday) Henry (StL) to Bertha (Stancote, Newton Centre MA)]

Bertha confided to Henry that her mother didn't trust her with the final household purchases. (Her mother surely had much more experience with domestic matters than Bertha.)

You said the other day that, after the front part of the house was fixed, you would go to the kitchen. You will have to judge the number of the Charter Oak[160] by the size of the kitchen and by the way mother says that kettles and roasting pans are supposed to come with the stove as they have to fit. Possibly you knew this before but I did not and, on the chance of your being as ignorant as myself, I tell you. My other household goods are coming from here. Mother could not make up her mind to trust me with the choosing thereof. And I was very glad, having some doubt of my own knowledge and furthermore everything that is gotten now will make it easier for us to get promptly into the house and less time to be at the hotel.
[1893-01-11 (Friday) Bertha (Newton Centre) to Henry (StL)]

d. Servants Quarters

There was the matter of where the servants' quarters should be located, giving appropriate consideration to Bertha and Henry's privacy. Henry certainly had his own views about this as well as when they should move into their new house after their wedding.

I am afraid I must take up a large part of my letter as usual with business matters for I have a number of questions to ask. First, it has occurred to me to ask you to again go over the servants' room matter. You know I papered the third-floor back room with the intention of putting them in there because it was larger than the second-floor back room and because it had a large closet in it. There is no doubt that the room itself is the better of the two for the purpose but this idea has occurred to me. There are no back stairs to the third story hence the servants will be constantly

---

[160] Charter Oak made stoves.

passing the landing on the second floor and also that on the third floor whereas that back room on the second floor is absolutely cut off from the rest of the house. Now if you think my objection to using the room in the third story is a material one, look at your plans and tell me if we shall change to the second story room for the servants, provided you think it large enough. You know it has a closet in it but the plans will show that.

A great many people including your friend Mrs. Knox think you would be saved much bother if we could go straight to our house on our return and fix "from within", as one of these nice people puts it, and my sisters think they could have the house ready if you care to let them unpack such of your things as will be necessary the first few days and you know, dear, the shades and curtains could be put up just a day or two before our return. It seems to me a feasible matter but you know best, dear. Talk the matter over with your mother and ask her if you would not be saved some bother by going direct to the house. Of course, the servants' question must be considered but they could be arranged for very quickly, I should imagine.
[1893-01-13 (Tuesday) Henry (StL) to Bertha (Stancote, Newton Centre)]

After first deciding that the servants' quarters should be on the second-floor, Bertha changed her mind and felt that the third-floor room would be more suitable.

I am afraid you will think I am very changeable but I hope this letter will reach you before you have commenced operations on that little back room in the second story. I have decided to keep to the third for the servants' room. Mother and I have just measured off the space contained in the second story room and, when I thought of putting bed, bureau and washstand in that space and then two human beings over the kitchen too with spring and summer coming on, my heart failed me and mother agreed with me that it would be better to put up with the other inconveniences no matter how annoying. I think it would be better to put matting, good strong matting in that room than carpet. I hope that this change will not inconvenience you much and that you will agree with me.
[1893-01-25 (Wednesday) Bertha (Newton Centre, MA) to Henry (StL)]

Henry concurred and the third-floor room for the servants was decided.

I have both your Tuesday and Wednesday letter and I have arranged to prepare the third story room for the servants. All the carpets will be laid tomorrow and the matting for this room and, as I purchased our range today showing in its selection my great knowledge of kitchen operations, I am nearly through. I was advised by Mr. Tilly not to get the pans etc. for the stove. He said they could send them up at any time to fit. As the number of the stove would insure their being sent of the proper size and as there were several million things to choose from in making up the set, I thought I would leave that trifling duty to our cook that is to be who will no doubt be better able to tell what is wanted than either you or I.
[1893-01-29 (Friday 1893-01-27) Henry (StL) to Bertha (Stancote, MA)]

e.   The Mississippi Mud

St. Louis water in 1892 was not of the same quality as it is today and contained copious amounts of "Mississippi mud". This required Henry to purchase a "Pasteur filter".

Another purchase which I am making is a Pasteur filter[161]. Do you prefer this or any other device for extracting mud from the Mississippi's fluid? And don't you think an ice chest of size to fit a space left for it in the pantry will meet our requirements in this line?
[1893-02-03 (Tuesday 1893-01-31) Henry (StL) to Bertha (Stancote)]

---

[161] A **Chamberland filter**, also known as a Pasteur–Chamberland filter, is a porcelain water filter invented by Charles Chamberland in 1884.[1] It is similar to the Berkefeld filter in principle.

f. Final Plans

In spite of Henry's views to the contrary, Bertha did not like the idea of moving into their house immediately after their honeymoon.

Now, I hope you will not be very much disappointed when you find that I am strongly opposed to going straight into our house. I think, myself, that in two or three days' time we can have it sufficiently in order to move in and finish "from within". For instance, there is no need whatever of curtains and shades being put up before we go in. But those few days' work I want to do myself.

Please, dear boy, do not think me ungrateful to your sisters. Indeed, I am not. I feel perfectly overwhelmed with what they have done already. But I want to do part of the work and, dear, I do not want anyone to unpack my linen and china but myself. Please don't be hurt at that or let them be but I do not think they will be. I think possibly your mother would understand my feeling about that better than you. I think I would rather have none of these things that are coming now – linen, curtains, china and household things - opened until I get there. O, there is one box you might open – the andirons and steel basket from Jordan & Marsh's – if you would like to see them. But the others I would like to superintend myself. You don't disapprove of my wanting to do this, dear?

I have the highest respect for your friend Mrs. Knox as an authority on housekeeping when she speaks from personal experience but in this case she does not. She has forgotten that she and Gordon stayed six weeks at the Sherman house while they were getting their own in order.
[1893-01-23 (Saturday) Bertha (Newton Centre) to Henry (StL)]

5. MOVING IN

Bertha recorded in her diary, April First. (1893) – *"Easter Eve. Moved in and took possession of 3337 Washington Avenue."* [1893 Diary]

Bertha and Henry moved into their new home at 3337 Washington Avenue on April 1, 1893, shortly after they had returned from their honeymoon in mid-March. As Bertha recorded in her diary, they wasted no time in having their friends visit them.

Easter Sunday. First day spent at home. Went to church – took dinner at Mrs. Scott's but hurried home as we expected visitors. Mr. Otto Meysenburg, Mr. A. L. Kennett, Mr. Irwin Z. Smith, Mr. Charles Hodgman, and Mr. Gist Blair came to call and inspect the mansion. Mr. Meysenburg and Mrs. Filley sent flowers, the latter with a card saying "A greeting to the new home amid the myriad houses of earth." H.C.S. himself sent flowers. At that time our destinies are presided over by Miss Margaret O'Neil in the kitchen ("Miss, Honorably Miss" as she afterwards told me, "and not because I couldn't have had it different, if I'd wanted."). A veritable angel whose memory I shall always bless, who steered me through all my first entertainments with great care and pains and was always a stand by and comfort. Mr. James Brown also watched over our destinies as we had no housemaid at the time. And my being late to breakfast one morning, H.C.S. said to Brown, "Well Brown, we all have our trials." "Yes Mr. Scott, but some of us have far more fiery trials than others."
[1893 Diary]

Bertha was able to put her house in order very quickly as evidenced by her April 19th letter to Henry.

The household seems to be running all right. Nan said it seemed to her as if it had been running for years. And "Nan and I" have decided that you cannot have your little trays to put burnt matches on. I asked her what she thought of them and she remarked "Well, to speak frankly, nothing to mind looks so disorderly about a house as little trays of burnt matches," which was my opinion exactly.
[1893-04-19 Bertha (StL) to Henry (Fort Worth)]

Bertha included a description of her first home as a married couple in her May first 1893 diary entry:

Papa had arrived in St. Louis the very day we went to the World's Fair[162] and I had shown off my house to him with great pride. He pronounced it the prettiest little house he had ever seen. I believe I will here put in some slight description of my house. I don't think I shall ever forget just how it looked or even where every piece of furniture stood, yet I may be glad to have it all recalled someday.

The hall has a wood carpeting on which we laid thick made rugs of a beautiful terra cotta brown shade. The walls and ceiling clear up to the third story were terra cotta cartridge paper. In the parlor, the walls were a dull electric blue shade (old blue), mahogany furniture and mantelpiece, and a carpet that might almost be called mahogany too. The wood in the hall was oak. In the dining room, oak again, the floor has a hardwood border and a beautiful turkey rug. Walls terra cotta. The papers were all Davenport.

My room upstairs, everyone exclaims over when they enter, the wood work is painted ivory white and varnished, so is the mantel piece. The floor is dull shade of gray blue. The paper a lovely Cretonne pattern. The ceiling old rose. Furniture mahogany with a brass bed.

Henry's room is oak, with a brown carpet and Cretonne patterned paper.

My spare room has a pale green carpet and paper with daises on it and my own beautiful carved light furniture that I brought from home. It is a darling of a house and I love it. Here is a small imperfect sketch of the plan of the first and second stories [below].

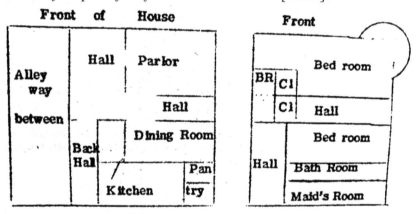

3337 Washington Avenue, [1893 Diary]

By their accounts, Bertha and Henry spent 5 very happy years at 3337 Washington Avenue.

D. 64 VANDEVENTER PLACE

"...it is the thought of your coming home at night that makes the pleasantness of the days. I listen always, all through the reading to the children for the sound of your key in the lock. At 3337 you used to shake the house when you came up the steps, but you don't anymore."
[Bertha reminiscing about their old house, 1902-11-09 Bertha (StL) to Henry (Waco)]

---

[162] The 1893 Chicago World's Fair.

Vandeventer Place, St. Louis

Vandeventer Place was once described as the grandest private street in St. Louis. It was a bold and confident statement to the country that St. Louis had arrived.

1. THEIR NEW HOUSE

64 Vandeventer Place, 1899
From the Catalogue of the Annual Exhibition of the Saint Louis Architecture Club (1899). This two-and-a-half story Elizabethan-style mansion was designed by Shepley, Rutan and Coolidge in 1898 for Henry C. Scott, a Confederate war veteran[163] and St. Louis capitalist. The H.C. Scott mansion stood at 64 Vandeventer until the 1950s city acquisition.

Vandeventer place! This was THE place to be. The homes were all magnificent and their owners were all the "movers and shakers" in St. Louis. If they had not "arrived" before, Bertha and Henry surely did then. But, while grand, the new house did not contain their history and live their memories. Bertha's mother had helped to decorate and furnish the old house and did not live to see the new one; and Bertha and Henry' first two children began their lives in the old.

The land on which their house was built was purchased by Bertha's father in 1891, presumably so that he could live there with his wife, Bertha M. After Bertha M died on November 15, 1896, George transferred the property to Bertha on January 19, 1897 and the house was built and completed by Bertha and Henry. George took up his residence there, with Bertha and Henry, sometime thereafter and remained until his death in 1908.

---

[163] "Confederate War Veteran"??? Henry was 6 years old when the civil war ended.

2. MOVING TO VANDEVENTER PLACE

Bertha and Henry were in Jamestown when their house was being completed and readied for them to move in. Bertha described their trip home from Jamestown in her diary.

> *Sept. 13, 1897*
>
> *Leave Jamestown for house on steamer "Priscilla". Go up to Fall River to take steamer. Children wild with excitement. Have two beautiful state rooms. Nancy quite capable of running whole boat.*

> *Sept. 14, 1897*
>
> *Arrive in New York. Go to Everett House. Uncle William [Roberts] comes to see us. Go buy carpet at Arnold Constable, and porcelain stove at Jacksons. Start home on New York Central – fearful trip, hot – 100° in dining car. Dust beyond bearing.*

Vandeventer Place

> *Sept. 15, 1897*
>
> *Arrive at home[164]. House shining clean. Bessie & Lizzie smiling to meet us and wild to meet the children.*

> *Sept. 16, 1897*
>
> *Go up to see the new house for the first time. Am perfectly amazed at the way it has grown but have studied the plans carefully that it all looks just as I expected. How beautiful it is! Our builder, Macfarland, is a trump, so is Charlie, the foreman. (Later we changed our opinion of Charlie but never of dear old Mac.) Go to see the house every day and work hard over it. Weather is fearfully hot.*
>
> [1893 Diary]

Bertha's letters to Henry always spoke of how much she was looking forwarding to moving into her new house. But her diary reveals another side which she may not have fully shown to Henry.

> *Nov. 22, 1897*
>
> *Our last night in our first house. Cry my eyes out.*

---

[164] The 3337 Washington Ave., soon to be their former home.

Nov. 23, 1897

Leave dear old 3337 Washington Avenue and move to 64 Vandeventer Place. Marion Davis comes down and drives me up. I sit at the head of the stairs and direct the New York storage company where to put each piece of furniture as it comes in. Myra Lane brings me some lunch. Marion Davis comes over with a cup of bouillon & some biscuits from her lunch. Mary Lionberger and Sarah both drop in. The children spend the day at their Grandmother Scott's. Bessie and Lizzie and Helen work like Trojans. We take dinner at father's. It has been a brilliantly sunshiny day.
[1893 Diary]

Perhaps no house was without its problems and the Vandeventer house was no exception. Evidently, as Henry wrote, some "varmints" got into the house.

I have also a better report about the varmint that got into the picture and wood work. We are treating the book case to a dose of gasoline daily and after a day or two will stoop up all the little holes with magnetic paste and I am sure that will exterminate the critters and really no serious harm has yet been done to the book case. Lizzie made the discovery and from the smell of the library she is doing her duty with the gasoline.
[1903-07-29 Henry (StL) to Bertha (Rye Beach)]

(Who knew for what use gasoline could be used.)

Other mishaps included Henry locking himself out one night.

I locked myself out tonight and, as it took an hour to get a ladder and climb in through a second story window, my time for writing has gone by as has my zeal. I am sorry and ashamed to add, for a really mad or angry man does not love anyone very dearly but thank God men don't remain angry long and already, I am beginning to love my wife again just as if I had not barked(?) my shins and spoiled my clothes and swore in volumes and in tenacity to make the medal(?) trooper envious.
[20180206-6 (1905-) Henry to Bertha]

And the new, big, house had some issues which caused annoyance.

I have been cussing Mauran steadily since reading your history of the last down pour from that leaky roof. I was wrong to assume that it would do no more harm and we must tear up the bad part and do it all over thoroughly. A leaky roof and smoking chimney ought to put an architect out of business but our friend seems to thrive on his reputation for numerous deficiencies. Don't worry over it, though, we will cuss Mauran and plan to rectify his neglect together. That sounds nice when I return as I hope to see you Saturday morning.
[1906-04-21 Henry (Wichita) to Bertha (StL)]

3. THE DEMISE OF VANDEVENTER PLACE

The remains of one of the Vandeventer houses.

Bertha moved from 64 Vandeventer Place to 31 Westmoreland Place several years after Henry died. This move was not mentioned in her Diary or letters which may have partially been due to the fact that Bertha was less diligent in keeping her diary after Henry's death. But alternatively, it may have been that the rise of Vandeventer Place marked a high point for St. Louis society and for the confidence that St. Louisans had in the city. The succeeding decline in Vandeventer Place was a sad harbinger of an overall decline which may have been apparent to many. Henry's business career followed the rise of wealth and business opportunities in St. Louis and Henry's untimely death spared him from seeing the decline of a city that he had helped to build.

The Vandeventer Place Gates, now in Forest Park (Photo by Chris Naffziger)

The following article by Chris Naffziger provides some insight into the rise and fall of Vandeventer Place.

Long before modern-day zoning and regulations, a segment of St. Louis high society chose to separate itself from the rest of the population, often living in the predecessors of modern suburbia designed by Julius Pitzman. Most of these private streets still exist, though some, such as Vandeventer Place, were annihilated in the mid-20th century. Today, these elite refuges for the wealthy are viewed by today's St. Louisans as wonderful reminders of the glory days—or as telling relics of unresolved class resentment. Regardless, it's interesting to see what the contemporary observer of these private streets, as the streets were being platted and sold, thought of these St. Louis inventions.

An interesting article from May 6, 1895, in the now-defunct St. Louis Republic offers insights into the institution of private streets around the year 1900, when most of the Pitzman designs opened. There is always a certain confidence in newspapers at the time, and the article opens with a humblebrag about the recently opened Union Station, which was the largest and busiest train station at the time. The author remarks that since all rail traffic passes through the terminal, out-of-town visitors do not have the opportunity to see any of the city while transferring to other rail depots, despite the fact most private streets are not located anywhere near downtown St. Louis.

But the reporter does go on to include an insightful quote from a driver who provided tours to visitors:

> *"Everyone is surprised and delighted at our private places, and notably Vandeventer, Westmoreland, and Portland; these being the three most convenient to include in a two hours' ride."*

The conversation later turned to the visitors' amazement at the well-tended boulevards that separated grand carriageways. A few wondered aloud how the money was raised in order to keep all the gardeners paid. Vandeventer Place was famous, of course, for requiring unanimous approval of all landowners for any change in the restrictions put in place at its founding. There are rumors that it's still difficult for the residents of some private streets in St. Louis to keep the bills paid for the large numbers of privately held streets or medians.

While the eventual demise of Vandeventer Place is famous—Grand Center transformed from an exclusive residential area after the Civil War into a second downtown in the early 20th Century, signs of its weaknesses were already showing in 1895:
> "To the impartial observer at the present time it appears as if the only mistake made by the projectors of Vandeventer Place was the overlooking, or rather the underestimating of the growth of the city. Vandeventer Avenue [the western border of the private street] is rapidly a retail street, and Grand Avenue [the eastern border] is putting away residential ideas with a pertinacity which, while sure evidence of the city's progress, is painful to the lover of old times. Vandeventer Place is now very largely hemmed in by street railroads and business houses, and in the course of a few years this is liable to prove quite a detriment."

View today of Vandeventer Place (Photo by Chris Naffziger)

These were prophetic words, as eventually the whole neighborhood around Vandeventer Place would either convert to office buildings, theaters, or relatively low-income housing. The grand private place was demolished in two parts, one half for the veterans' hospital and the other half for a juvenile detention facility.
["Behind the rise—and fall—of private streets in St Louis", by Chris Naffziger]

E. 31 WESTMORELAND PLACE

Bertha moved to her last home at 31 Westmoreland Place between 1913 and 1914 shortly after the house was built in 1912. (The Gould's Blue Book for the City of St. Louis for 1914 reports the owners of 31 Westmoreland Place as Mrs. H.C. Scott & dr. and Hugh Scott. Prior to 1914, Gould's does not list an owner for this property.) Bertha did not write about the acquisition of this home or about the move from 64 Vandeventer Place. Perhaps the Vandeventer house may have felt empty without the nearer presence of Henry and her father, and Bertha may have been aware that Vandeventer's glory years were already passing.

31 Westmoreland Place

31 Westmoreland Place would become the new home in which Bertha welcomed her children and grandchildren over the rest of her life. Of her home, my father wrote:

> *31 Westmoreland is where, for twenty years, we grandchildren shared in the joy, excitement and love that her name generated. It is a memory as fresh today as ever. From the minute William dropped us off to the at distinctive click of the front door, we knew we were entering a marvelous world. The stairway with the greatest "sliding" banisters, the cane rack, the library with all those books, the parlor, especially at Christmas with the tree, and so many places and items we loved are still vivid in our memory. In the games we played: parcheesi, mah jongg, backgammon, chess, bridge, twenty questions or whatever, Gami was always a willing teacher and an enthusiastic contestant. We all looked forward to the joy of those evening and days. And none of us can forget our friends in the back, especially Mary Cox.*
> [Hugh Scott Jr., The "Scott" Booklet]

F. THE STAFF

Bertha wrote in her diary on May 10, 1945, six months before her death, of her heartfelt gratitude toward all of the people that worked for Henry and her over their lives.

> *I would like to place here a tribute to the wonderful service I have had for which I can never show sufficient gratitude. This comes fifty-two years of housekeeping. First of all, Lizzie Haase, my cook, who came to me six months after I was married[165] and staid with me until her death, forty years later, a steadfast friend through every vicissitude, sickness, death, child birth, household, first of children, then of gay young people. The first to see my oldest son when he was born. The first person he told of the birth of his oldest son.*

> *William Burbach, my chauffeur, who lived with me for thirty years. He had driven my father in a Victoria from Marshall's livery stable for some years before that, and applied to us to have him trained as a chauffeur. Retired because he was too old to continue the work, living in California, still writes to me once a month and sends flowers on Christmas and my birthday.*

> *Mary Cox came from Ireland to succeed her sister, Katharine, who had lived with me nine years. Mary, faithful friend, has been with me thirty-two years and is still with me. Katherine left me to be married.*

---

[165] Bertha wrote on September 10, 1893: "*Mr. Vogel sends me a girl for cook, Lizzie Haase.*" [1893 Diary]

Page 370

William Campbell, my colored man succeeded Johnny Morgan, who had lived with me fifty-one years. When Johnny went to the hospital where he died, he recommended William. William lived with me twenty-five years until his death.

Cora who came as an accommodation, off and on, thirteen years ago is now living with me regularly.

Mary Moynihan came as accommodation, and has been away with me in summers, still accommodates, has for about ten years.

Mary, the laundress, for eight years.

Mollie Lavin worked for my mother, was with the family since mother's death in 1896 until her own death in 1937 – a faithful soul.

Mary Whitmore, my laundress for ten years, died while still with me, a self-denying saint.

It is a marvelous record of fine people & joy. I forgot Olga Scheperclaus who lived with me ten years and left to take care of a mother who was paralyzed.

Helen Curran who is my daughter Alice's cook and has been for many years, was my assistant nurse maid came to me at fourteen and staid until her marriage.

Maggie Moore came to me from my sister-in-law Minnie Carter as an assistant to Lizzie when the young people were in society, and there was constant entertaining. She lived with me until her death ten years later.

Very few left except for marriage. The waitresses whom I had for shorter periods than those I mentioned: Katie Lavin, Mary Mahan, Jennie Shields, Ester Rush, Katharine Cox (she was an upstairs maid), all left to be married. One or two, like my first cook of all, Maggie O'Neill, retired on account of age. But all those that I have mentioned, I can say honestly, were among the finest people I have ever known, with high standards of honor, faithfulness, almost all deeply religious, and having won the warm affection of my children as well as myself. They stood by me many times where it meant self-sacrifice and hard work, but they never failed. My gratitude to them is deeper than any words can express.

Bertha's May 10, 1945 diary entry was one of the last before her death later that year. Bertha's remembrance of the loyalty of those who worked for her and her gratitude toward them spoke volumes. *"My gratitude to them is deeper than any words can express."*

The new house is a stately house,
  The old was naught to see,
    But the new house has no memories,
      It's not my home to me.

The new house is my own house,
  We did but rent the old,
But in the old were pictures bright,
That make the new seem cold.

My mother chose the plenishing
  To make it fine and fair,
She never saw the new house,
I cannot see her there.

I was a bride in that wee house
It seemed all filled with light,
For youth's bright sunshine lit the way
  And all the world was bright.

And there, I learned the woman's lot
Of suffering and pride,
For my first son was born to me
  On the eve of Christmastide.

O, the new house, my brave house,
  Is grander far to see,
    But the old house, the rented house,
      That was my home to me.

CHAPTER 15 – THE SCOTT FAMILY

Hugh, Anne (Nancy), Bertha, Alice & George

When she married Henry, Bertha already loved children. Just prior to her marriage in January 1893, Bertha described a visit to George and Lula Shepley's home and her joy at having 3-month-old George Shepley Jr. entrusted to her.

> *But I believe the best time I had was this morning when Lula entrusted that soft bundle of a George Foster [Shepley] Jr. to my charge and I had him all to myself for a while and he was as good as a kitten and did not even make any effort to get back to her when she came for him. That was an enjoyment a man is incapable of appreciating.*
>
> [1893-01-18 Bertha (Newton MA) to Henry (StL)]

Bertha and Henry were married on February 14, 1893 and their first child, "Hugh Scott", was born December 24, 1893. Bertha and Henry were both ready to have a family and were devoted parents. In addition to writing to Bertha when they were apart, Henry would also write to his children just as they would sometimes write to him. One such letter was to Hugh, Nancy and George during the summer of 1901.

> *My dear Hugh, Nancy & George,*
> *Dad got three letters today and they came from the three sweetest children that ever were but I will not tell you their names for you must guess that. One was a girl and the other two were boys and I believe the girl has blue eyes and the boys have brown eyes but, mind, I am not going to tell you who they are. You can just sit down and guess.*
>
> *Dad went to a cat and dog show one night and it was a beautiful show. First, there was a big table and on it was a black cat, a grey cat, a brown cat, a black and white, and a light blue cat. The man stretched a rope high in the air between too tall trees and, will you believe it, the black cat climbed one tree and walked across to the other tree on the rope which was high in the air, and he was about to walk back when just as he got far out on the rope the white cat started up the tree and out on the rope and the black cat couldn't pass the white cat so old blackie gave a jump in the air over the white cat and landed safe on the rope without falling. Then the cats all stood on their hind legs and the man put little soldiers clothes on them and little guns in their paws and they marched around like real soldiers and when they saw any bad dogs coming they would point their little guns at them and go Bang!!!!! And the dogs would fall over and pretend they were dead. And when daddie sees his dear children he will tell them another story about those beautiful cats & dogs.*
>
> [1901-07-13 Henry (StL) to Kids (Rye Beach)]

A. HUGH SCOTT

"Hugh Scott", as Bertha called him as a baby, was born on Christmas Eve, December 24, 1893. There was, of course, great anticipation on the birth of their first child.

1. GREAT EXPECTATIONS

When she was pregnant, Bertha wrote to Henry about their unborn, first child.

> *...your son has taken to growing so rapidly this past that I have had to let out my skirt again. ... Minnie told me that, the day I showed my things to your mother, she (Minnie) came home and found our mother in a state of great enthusiasm, talking to Mattie "I don't know when I have had such a good time, they are the prettiest things I ever saw in my life and I just can't wait for that dear baby to come."*
> [1893-10-08 Bertha (StL) to Henry (Fort Worth)]

(It was touching that Bertha referred to Grandma Scott not just as "*your mother*" but also as "*our mother*".)

Henry was excited about the newly expected child and did not pass up an opportunity to show his affection for his wife.

> *So my son has been growing. I wonder if it is a boy, after all. Sometimes I think not very strongly. I imagine a little girl with a sweet small voice and a beautiful face and glorious eyes like her mother's. And maybe, some of the fine qualities of her father! Mother seems greatly excited over her grandchild.*
> [1893-10-14 Henry (Ft. Worth) to Bertha (3337 Washington Ave, Stl)]

The 1893 Christmas was a special one for Bertha and Henry. They were together for Christmas, for a change, it was their first Christmas as a married couple, and they were celebrating the Advent with their first child.

> *December Twenty Third, 1893*
> *Walk down to mother's in the afternoon – in the evening, decorate the whole house with Christmas greens. Henry wreathes chandelier, frames, mantel piece, with greens, and we hang holly wreathes in all the windows. Mother's present, a superb life size photograph of the Defregger [Franz Defregger] Madonna, framed in white and gold, arrives, and Henry hangs it over the mantel piece in my room.* [1893 Diary]

Madonna, by Franz DeFregger

(What euphoria! From the gift of the DeFregger Madonna from Bertha's mother, to Henry's hanging it over the mantel piece in Bertha's room. One wonders how long Bertha allowed it to remain there!)

2. THE FIRST CHRISTMAS & CONVALESCENCE

The birth of Hugh Scott on Christmas Eve brought happiness and cheer to family and friends.

December Twenty Fourth (1993)

At half past one in the morning, Hugh Scott is born. A Sunday child. Sunday is a beautiful day. First father and George come, then mother, then Mrs. Scott and Maggie. Ever so many people come to inquire, Mary Lionberger, Mr. Blair and Mr. Wiggens, etc., but as yet the news is not very generally known. In the afternoon, Henry goes off to deliver my Christmas presents and to take the news to Nan, the Lanes, etc. At Edith Knox's, he finds the truth already known and Edith falls upon his neck and embraces him, whereupon Gordon suggests it might be a good plan to pull down the curtains. I forgot to see that Mrs. Herbert and Dr. P.G. Robinson are at that time the two who preside over my destiny. Blessings on them both. [1893 Diary]

(The enthusiasm by Bertha and Henry's friends and family at this birth may have been best captured by the reaction of Edith Knox: *"Edith falls upon [Henry's] neck and embraces him, whereupon Gordon suggests it might be a good plan to pull down the curtains."*)

Christmas and the days that followed brought more cheer and blessings to Bertha and Henry: the *"the three most beautiful weeks of my life"*.

December Twenty Fifth, 1893

Christmas Day. Another beautiful day. Visitors crowd to inquire. The McNairs, the Adams, the Elliotts, the Valles, Tom, (Tom, Henry & the Doctor have a drink together to celebrate). Lute and Nan, the Knoxes, the Tutts, etc. My room is a bower of flowers, at least it would be if the perfume were not so strong. Magnificent roses from the Laclede Power Co and from Mr. Blair and many others. Loads of lovely presents. Henry gives me a Rookwood rose bowl set in silver and a dozen cut glass champagne cups. The family sends silver vegetable dishes to me, the French "salon" to Henry, a beautiful carved ivory cross to the baby to hang over his beautiful pink bassinette that Auntie Lutie Lionberger and Auntie Nan Shepley gave him. It is a perfect dream of a bassinette and my son sleeps serenely in it, while his father adores him. Sam sends me a dainty card receiver (porcelain), Arthur a cut glass bon bon dish. Grandma Scott and Anita's lovely things for the boy. Henry goes over to Christmas dinner at his mother's, after we look at the Christmas papers together.

Then follow the three most beautiful weeks of my life. I am not allowed to get up or to have a worry or trouble of any sort. Presents pour in on my boy. He has fifty-three presents, not counting his entire outfit which his Grandma Drake [Bertha M] gave him. She wishes to be called Muff by her grandson, as George [Bertha's brother] and I called her Muff. George one day is asked if he has ever seen anybody so small as his nephew, and indignantly answered "of course I have and smaller too. Pickled babies." In addition to his presents, I have sixteen boxes of flowers. The record of all those is to be found in Hugh's baby book. It is long before his name is decided upon. We vibrate long between George Drake and Hugh. Mamma Drake gives the casting vote in favor of Hugh. For ten days nobody is allowed to see him but the family. Then the girls pour in, Frances Markham first. For two weeks, I am allowed to see no one but the family – with the one exception of Myra Lane on the fifth of January, 1894.

[1893 Diary]

(What a beautiful picture: *"and my son sleeps serenely in [his bassinette] while his father adores him."*)

One may surmise that new mothers were treated differently in those days than today, at least mothers of means – three weeks in bed! On January 11, 1894, two and ½ weeks after Hugh's birth, Bertha wrote: *"On Thursday, the eleventh, I am allowed to sit up."* [1893 Diary] The Progress continues over the next two weeks, as Bertha wrote:

January 21, 1894
On Sunday, the twenty first, we have dinner served upstairs and I take dinner with Henry. Mary fixes the table so prettily with all my best china and glass.

January 28, 1894
On Sunday the twenty eighth, I am allowed to go downstairs and out for the first time. Henry takes me to drive in Forest Park in a closed carriage. Gist Blair comes to tea.
[1893 Diary]

From these diary entries, it appears that Bertha and Henry did not dine together until January 21st and Bertha did not leave the house until January 28th – more than 5 weeks after Hugh's birth. Bertha happily wrote on February 3rd, "*My first outing.*" [1893 Diary]

Hugh was a normal baby, including the sleepless nights. This always seems to come as a surprise to new parents.
February 1, 1894
On Thursday, February first, Mrs. Herbert is summoned in the middle of the night. Henry spends the rest of the night getting up and down with Hugh Scott, "you brat!"

February 2, 1894
Annie arrives and takes charge of my son.
[1893 Diary]

3. CONGRATULATIONS
Bertha and Henry received many letters of congratulation on the birth of Hugh. One such letter was from Bertha's friend, Alma Sterling Porter, who had just married Dr. William Porter in December 1893. Her letter revealed an unbridled joy. "*Oh the joy of him.*"
My dear Bertha,
I had been waiting until the new year came in to write to thank the good people who were good enough to add to my happiness on my wedding day whom I did not have the time or opportunity of thanking before leaving home.

On Friday of holiday week, Miss Hagen dined with me and I learned the joyful news of your Christmas boy. So I have waited until his fortnight's birthday in order that you may surely read my letter yourself. Oh, you happy, happy woman. Twice blessed wife and mother. My heart rejoices with you and over you. It is so beautiful to know there is such joy in the world. It makes one's own happiness seem even greater to grow conscious that it is a part of a great beautiful plan in which each one of the sons of man has his share.

You are the wisest woman – of course, he was a son with the fine training prepared for him. But what other woman ever chose to be married on St. Valentine's Day and to bring her baby into the world on Christmas Eve! Your sense of the fitness of things is simply overwhelming. We can only wonder.

I wish I could see you both and I am eagerly looking forward to a letter from Hildegarde who I hope will have seen Henry Clarkson Jr. by this time. And I wait to hear that you are well and growing stronger every day. But oh the joy of him. I can just fancy how your heart sings over him as you hold him in your arms. Your son. Your very own. And his father? Give him my love and congratulations. I should like to see his eyes shine with his happiness.
[1894-01-08 Alma Sterling Porter (Boston) to Bertha]
("*It is so beautiful to know there is such joy in the world.*")

4. POST PARTEM

After the excitement of Hugh's birth subsided, there was the normal lull. As Bertha wrote after her entry of February 14, 1894, "*Now comes a trying period. Try to do more than I really have strength for, at first, and am despondent and tired all the time. Henry is away for two weeks in March...*" [1893 Diary]

The birth of Hugh certainly affected Bertha's outlook. Bertha expressed some her dispirited feelings writing "*The scripture is not moving me*". She also decided to advise the 2 ½ month old Hugh about not getting married in an imaginary discussion.

> *I ought to go on "the scripture moveth us", but I won't. The scripture is not moving me. I went downtown today and bought a hat and there is nothing so hard to get in this town. My family pronounced favorably on this one but I am not sure that you will.*
>
> *I had a jolly time at the Lanes last night. They are an awfully nice family to visit, but my walk home with Nat was not madly exciting, possibly owing to his being a married man. I have been so gay lately, but I don't believe it was purely that, I am inclined to believe that, even when unmarried, Nat could never have been of the nature called thrilling. Still, he and I now have some very congenial tastes, we discussed nurses most of the way home.*
> ...
> *Dearest, I hate worse than I can say to have you away from me and not feeling well, but I hope soon to have you back here with me. Your son will also be pleased to see you. I regret to say he and I have already differed very essentially in our views on life. After brother Guy's wedding, I said to him "My son, I am never going to allow you to get married", and he responded very distinctly & positively "Are going to, are going to, are going to." And let nobody think I am imaginative.*

[1894-03-01 Bertha (StL) to Henry (Wichita)]

Henry clearly missed Bertha and Hugh, especially on this trip after Hugh was born, writing from Dallas:

> *I have been separated from you very often since our marriage and, if I had been properly disciplined by my hard luck in this respect, I would be reasonable or rather reconciled to this period of banishment. But I am very far from meek submission to fate just now and between my growls over what seems my very hard luck I will give an account of my wanderings since I said goodbye to my child, Saturday evening.*
>
> *We, Cunningham and I, had rather a pleasant trip down and since my arrival I have been busy with coal rates for Fort Worth, looking over "my railroad", getting data for electric equipment, etc., etc. The railroad is a regular sink hole. I think about four hundred thousand dollars has been spent on the property and I doubt if it is worth half that sum today. The rects from the road have dwindled during the hard times to about fifty dollars per day and how to increase them will be the problem I shall have to solve or give up the ship, which latter horn of the dilemma I don't propose to take.*
>
> *But business "be blowed", dearest. I want to know about you and "the family". Have you been resting lots since my departure? How does ten o'clock breakfast suit an industrious individual who has promptly? appeared for weeks back in the dinning row at eight? And who have you had to comfort in your loneliness? Has Emma been down yet? You must keep me informed about yourself and about the finest boy in the world, dearest. You have a double duty on your hands now and your letters will, I am sure, be very long ones. If I were at home, for instance and you were away, I think I could write all day about the wonderful daily or even hourly performances of that small Hugh Scott.*

[1894-03-03 Henry (Oriental Hotel, Dallas) to Bertha (StL)]

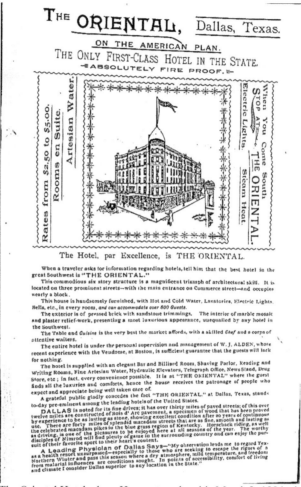

The Oriental Hotel where Henry stayed on his March 3, 1894 trip to Dallas

Henry was always interested to hear of his newborn son and Bertha kept him well informed.

> *You say you think I ought to be able to give hourly reports of the small Hugh Scott. Just at present I feel more than usually qualified to do that. For I let Anne go out this afternoon to see a friend who is dying and for the last two hours I have had the undivided attention of Mr. Hugh Scott who has been wide awake the whole time and good as a kitten, alighted & smiled and cooed but declined to be neglected for one instant and has just this minute gone off to sleep at about a second's warning with his old soft head nestled up against my silk sleeve. So I have consigned him to his bassinet and decided to devote a little time to his father.*

[1894-03-09 (Thursday) Bertha (StL) to Henry (Fort Worth)]

Bertha wrote to Henry how fond Hugh Scott (the "Buster") was of his father and how reproachful Hugh was if Bertha did not write to Henry. And the Buster was also very fond of his grandfather.

> *The Buster is very reproachful to me for having forgotten it [to write]. He is the best old thing! Father came this morning while Em and I were at breakfast & immediately afterwards I went up for the boy. He had just that instant waked up and he was a very sleepy baby with his eyelids dropping down but the moment he saw father, he went off in a series of rapturous smiles. Father, to use your expression "grinned like a possum" and Em was very much impressed with him.*
>
> *He only slept half an hour yesterday afternoon during which I wrote you. So with that exception, I had him from quarter of two until twenty minutes of seven and, though Nan was in and played*

with him a long time, still I confess I was glad to see Annie when those bright eyes remained popped open and the owner thereof refused to be held anywhere except by main strength up against my shoulder.

…

Annie [Nan Shepley] has just told me that the Buster wishes to know if his papa is not a little bit homesick for his boy. Em and I decided today that he had father's head & forehead, eyes, & your mouth & chin.
[1894-03-09 (Friday) Bertha (StL) to Henry (Ft. Worth)]

With Hugh at home, Henry had one more reason to worry when he was away on business.

I was very glad yesterday to get your telegram. I went to the telegraph office as soon after my arrival here as I found there were no letters here from you and wrote a dispatch asking if you were all right for I had become very anxious about you. When the boy took my message he turned to the desk and said "Mr. Scott, perhaps you will find this message unnecessary. Here is a dispatch for you from St. Louis", and your message was handed me. I am sorry I did not write out my Dallas address for you, dearest. I missed hearing from you there and, what with the worry of my work there and a very lame foot, I managed to imagine every possible ill had befallen my "family". I am very glad to know that you are both well – you and that baby boy – and I wish with all my heart I could see you both this morning.
[1894-03-09 Henry (Waco) to Bertha (3337 Washington Ave, Stl)]

Needless to say, a portion of Bertha's letters was always reserved for Hugh.

I went down to mother's and the Buster arrived shortly after in a most radiantly good humor and showing a very wide and beamy smile the moment his grandfather spoke to him. He had enough attention paid him to satisfy even him and sat a long time on my lap listening to mother play while his eyes nearly popped out of his head. I asked him just now if he had any message for you and he stated very distinctly "au-goo", which I trust you are able to translate.
[1894-03-10 (Tuesday) Bertha (StL) to Henry (Waco)]

And, of course, a portion of Henry's letters were addressed to his son.

You are very good to give me such interesting accounts of our boy, dearest. I enjoy his interviews with the people who have been at our house recently and have been especially entertained with the very decided cordiality of his greeting to your father. I wonder if the little lad will smile that enthusiastically at this own dad on his return.

…

Embrace the buster for me and tell him his dad is trying very hard to work his way home to the prettiest mama in the world.
[1894-03-11 Henry (Ft Worth TX) to Bertha (3337 Washington Ave, Stl)]

Bertha and Henry were clearly ecstatic about their new son and waited attentively for each new step and intellectual acquisition that he made as he grew. But, to avoid any sort of overconfidence in the matter, Bertha enclosed a newspaper commentary about babies: humorous but sobering.

BY AN OLD BACHELOR
(From the New York Ledger)

Babies are not the little know-nothings they are popularly supposed to be. Their intellectual gifts are underrated. They are as sly as opossums, cunning as red foxes and natural-born tyrants, every one of them. At the age of 4 months or thereabouts, the ocelot or tiger-cat instinct of babyhood begins to develop itself. The nails of infancy are at that age capable of scarification; but the "blessed little creature," aware that its weapons are as yet feeble and flexible, only attacks the eyes and other thin-skinned localities, where they are sure to make an impression, cunningly postponing their more general onslaught until the talons are equal to the work and the progress of dentition enables it to assail its mother and the general public with tooth and nail.

*But the craft of a baby is at least on a par with its cruelty. Give way never so little to a young hopeful in long clothes and, for every inch given, it will exact an **ell**[166]. Walk about with one for ten minutes in the middle of the night "just to quiet the poor little thing," and in a week you will be in good training to walk 1000 miles in 1000 hours. Trot one, twice or thrice on your knee, and the stimulated pony will thereafter be in continual request during the day until at last, between the equestrian exercise by daylight and the pedestrian feats by gaslight, you will be fit for the position of high private in the 7th Regiment. Cunning as malicious and malicious as cunning, there is nothing so gratifying to your baby as to travel at other people's expense and no full-grown Happy Jack ever practiced the art more successfully. There is but one way of escaping the infliction and, that is, never to begin. It were easier to shake off ten old men of the sea than one infant that has acquired a taste for mid-night excursions and diurnal trots. Babies are the most persistent young jockeys that ever rode a free horse to death.*

[Included with: 1894-03-10 (Saturday) Bertha (StL) to Henry (Fort Worth)]

After almost 3 months with Hugh Scott, Bertha and Henry's eyes were undoubtedly more open.

Hugh always seemed to miss his "Dad-Dad" and, whether Bertha imagined Hugh's feelings or not, Henry, no doubt, appreciated the thought that he was missed.

O, I must tell you, I really think the boy thought you had come back this morning. I took him down to see Sam and he gave a perfect leap in my arms and held out his arms, the first time he has ever done it. Sam was immensely flattered and took him but he did not hold him comfortably and there was a wail instantly & I had to take him back but I am sure he thought Sam was his Dad-Dad. And I suppose you will say I am very foolish to imagine such a thing.

[1894-03-15(-) Bertha (StL) to Henry Ft Worth)

5. THE TODDLER

From the very beginning, Bertha seemed to have wise, maternal instincts.

Just a line to say we are all right. One of us is progressing over a red shawl spread on the floor and evidently has a great deal of business on hand. He took breakfast with me this morning and put his fat hand right into the middle of my cream toast. When I took it away, he howled bloody murder so, fearing I was raising a second Baby Bernheimer, I turned my back on him. Finding nobody paid any attention, the howl ceased and I turned round to find him perfectly placid with a big tear on each check, solemnly regarding me. I gave him a spoon and napkin ring to play with and had an angel for the rest of breakfast time.

[1894-09-17 Bertha (StL) to Henry (NYC)]

Bertha needed to be a good parent since Henry was so frequently away on business. But Henry never forgot his family and expressed in his letters how much he missed his son and his wife.

I spent part of the day looking at the shops in remote streets & picked up another rubber addition to the buster's collection. Nice little boy! How I should like to hold him now and make him smile that wide smile of his. I thought the evening I left you that you had grounds for remonstrating at being left behind but now you seem far the more fortunate, dearest, for you have the dear boy for company while poor dad hasn't her nice little boy even to console him for separation from his sweetheart.

I hope I shall hear from you tomorrow, dear, for I want to know how you are. You looked tired and worn all day Saturday & I don't like to be away from you when I am not very sure you are well. Besides, I miss you, Bert, which is no news since you know I miss you always when you are

---

[166] An ell is a unit of measurement, originally a cubit, i.e., approximating the length of a man's arm from the elbow to the tip of the middle finger, or about 18 inches

not near me. We have pretty much all of our pleasure times together now, don't we? I wish you knew how happy I always am when I am near you, my darling, for then you would see how I wish for you now and how almost since I came here I have been planning what we would do together if only you were with me.
[1894-09-17 Henry (New York) to Bertha (3337 Washington Ave, Stl)]

Bertha was fond of calling the baby, "Hugh Scott", and did not take kindly when her very dear, life long friend, Nan Shepley, made some unflattering remarks about this name. And Bertha was sufficiently annoyed that she decided to reprimand Henry for sharing *"confidences"* with Nan about their past summer vacation. When so provoked, there were no exceptions for sharing such information even with the closest of friends.

I don't think much of you anyway. What did you go and run down the Highlands[167] to Nan for when I have been talking it up. I went up to Mary Lionberger's yesterday and found Nan and Edith January there, was expatiating on how I enjoyed my summer when Nan remarked sardonically, "Yes, Henry & I exchanged confidences on the subject of western watering places at the Exposition." After that, nobody believed me. I hate Nannie anyway. She said, "Why do you call him Hugh Scott? Why don't you call him Hugh? Hugh Scott always makes me think of a darkey." To which I responded "Why do you call little Louise, Louie? I think its one of the ugliest nicknames in the language." And we parted.
[1894-09-18 Bertha (StL) to Henry (New York)]

Bertha and Nan could never allow themselves to have a difference between them for very long. So, the very next day, *"Nan came to see me yesterday and we made it up…"* [1894-09-19 Bertha (StL) to Henry (Hotel Buckingham, NYC)]

Bertha was not always favorably inclined towards doctors, but she could make exceptions.

I fell from my high estate of scorning doctors this morning and sent for one, getting rather laughed at for my pains. But I was so worried about my poor buster. I told you yesterday he was sick with his teeth but I did not tell you that he was nauseated & droopy & that was the principal reason I came home early from mother's. Well, he had a restless night & when the same performance started again this morning, I telephoned Abbie. To my secret delight, he was out and I sent for Dr. Valle. Of course, by the time he got there, Master Hugh, who up to that time would not sleep and was fretful and nervous, had gone off into a perfectly sound sleep, nice moist hands and brow and looked as well and rosy as you please. Dr. Valle said he had had an attack of indigestion but the worst of it was over and it didn't amount to very much anyway, though he did say it was wise to send for a doctor as a good many diseases, measles, etc., began with those vomiting spells and the mother couldn't always know. I like Dr. Valle very much. He is willing to be asked questions about diet, etc., that Dr. Robinson sniffs at, and then he told me one or two simple remedies to keep in the house.
[1894-11-23 Bertha (StL) to Henry (Waco)]

Henry watched the weather in St. Louis vigilantly from his Texas outpost, cheering any good weather for his son and wife.

I also see that pleasant weather has been blessing the country in which Hugh Scott and his Mamma live from which I conclude that Hugh Scott travels many miles each day in his perambulator and is therefore flourishing. I hope you have been taking lots of open-air exercise, too, for you need it and you don't need any of those tiresome séances known as women's clubs. Take care of yourself until I return, dear.
[1895-04-04 Henry (Waco) to Bertha (3337 Washington Ave, Stl)]

---

[167] Bertha, Henry and Hugh (and visiting friends) spent the summer of 1894 at the Meramec Highlands.

And Henry was always aware if Hugh Scott was not up to snuff.

I am sorry the lord of our house is not very well. Dear little chap, I feel pretty sorry for him as I recall his scare that night and I hope that and the hot weather will not make him sick and that we will get him out of town before he begins to wilt from the hot weather.
[1895-05-07 Henry (Waco) to Bertha (3337 Washington Ave, StL)]

Hugh Scott could throw a tantrum, as Bertha wrote, often when something was taken away, including - *"Lairs dad dad?"*

Hugh Scott went to see the circus procession today. It went by Thirty-Fourth and Olive & he came back howling with rage because there was no more of it. The calliope and a large gilded wagon with bills on it were what specially attracted him and he told me over and over "choo-car moojik ding-ding", also "cam-ell." He was determined to go downstairs to see you this morning. "Lairs dad dad"? And when I insisted you were not there, he threw himself on the floor and wept in a real pitiful way too, not mad, just disappointed.
[1895-05-07 Bertha (StL) to Henry (Waco)]

Bertha's stories of Hugh Scott must have been entertaining to Henry.

The first thing I heard this morning was a voice like a silver bell saying "vide-car-car-car-car". His majesty came in very graciously – he would like to live on the car-car-car-car. He spent nearly the whole day at the park today and rode on the merry-go-round and had to be coaxed off it. There is a place Annie can stand & hold him on. He also made friends with the donkeyman and was lifted on the donkey back. I have a secret conviction he would have had a "vide" on the donkey if the money hadn't given out.
[1895-05-08 Bertha (StL) to Henry (Oriental Hotel, Dallas)]

The next day, Hugh Scott was back at the park.

Dear Hugh Scott spends most all day in the park. The "merry wound" man gave him a free ride yesterday after he had had two because he sat up like such a major & was so broken hearted when he had to leave.
[1895-05-09 Bertha (StL) to Henry (Wichita)]

Hugh Scott's comments always seemed to sparkle and shine to his parents. When Bertha asked Hugh, what does Henry call "Mutter"? *"He ca's her dearwy, I sink."*

Here is a conversation. "Mutter, ask me phat I call whisser?" "Well, what do you call whisser?" "I ca' her fergchen." "What do you call Mutter." "Mutter." "And Dad?" "I ca' him Dad-dy, on phat Dad ca' mutter." "What do you think he calls her?" "He ca's her dearwy, I sink."
[1896-03-05 Bertha (StL) to Henry (Fort Worth)]

Henry was almost as concerned for Hugh's health as he was for Bertha's and constantly advised her to get Hugh to take additional rest in order for him to lay away *"a supply of strength."*

Your reports of Hugh continue to be encouraging but I think you are letting him do too much. If he gets overtired many times, it will be a long time before he is strong again. Make him see that rest is another way of laying in a supply of strength and he will see that the surest way to get the most out of his summer is to wait until his storage battery is well supplied rather than to drain it of its last drop of energy. [1895(-) 20170817-3 Henry to Bertha]

Hugh could capture the mood when his father was gone to Texas, as Bertha related.

Your son says you have gone to Tektex and that sounds as if it were a place you would like to leave. ... Your son has been inquiring all over the place for dad-dad. Tektexs, while he says it as glibly as a parrot, conveys no particular idea. And he has finally made up his mind that you are gone "bye bye."

[1895-04-01 Bertha-Hugh (StL) to Henry (Ft. Worth)]

6. THE BOY

Henry encouraged the youthful Hugh to be brave, especially for his family.

I have heard a great deal of what a brave good boy you have been lately and I almost think Uncle Sam will be coming down to Jamestown to look for that little boy who is almost as brave as George Dewey. Dad thinks you will soon be getting so brave and big and strong that you will be taking care of mother and Nancy & George Drake and Auntie Minnie and Auntie Maggie, and they will not be afraid of anything because you will be their protector.

[20180129-4 (1898-) Henry to Hugh Scott]

Hugh had a proper Christian upbringing. But, as Bertha learned, this could lead children to startling insights, especially when they are not yet 5 years old.

Your son is certainly imbibing orthodox views. I heard him instructing Nancy this morning, "There ain't no night in heaven, Nancy. Do you want to know how you can sleep? Well, you don't never get tired in heaven, so now, what do you think of that?" It all slid off Nancy as cheerfully as water off a duck's back.

[1898-11-21 Bertha (StL) to Henry (Waco)]

(Tom Sawyer could not have said it better!)

Hugh always missed his Dad when he was away on business. *"Hugh Scott said when he kissed pater and myself goodnight, 'I am very sorry Dad is away.'"* [1899-03-28 (3 letters) Bertha (StL) to Henry (Ft. Worth)]

While in Jamestown in 1899 when Hugh was 6 years old, Bertha described one of Hugh's illnesses, Hugh's apparent desire to appear strong for his Dad, and the medicinal effect of whiskey.

Hugh has had a little attack of intestinal indigestion. Don't be alarmed at the length of the word, it's nothing serious but we were called up at twelve o'clock last night. The poor little lad had such a bad pain in his poor small stomach and it was some time before whiskey, paregoric, and hot water bags took effect. He finally went to sleep and was apparently all right this morning but had another and much more abstinent attack this afternoon so I sent for Dr. Birney who says he is the fifteenth child since Sunday morning with the same sort of an attack & thinks he will be all right tomorrow. (Change of weather giving colds.) He has had rather a hard time and has been as plucky as plucky could be. I told him I would write you that he had been the best and most patient little fellow I ever saw and he said "What kind of a cold will you tell Dad I have?" "A cold in your stomach". "No, I mean, will you tell him I have a violent cold?" he said in an access of misery today. "Everything always happens to me. But I am very glad Nancy has not got this, I know she would howl if she did." Don't worry about him. I tell you everything absolutely as you know and it is no thing but a childish attack that will be over tomorrow.

[1899-07-13 (1st letter) Bertha (Jamestown) to Henry (StL)]

Apparently, Hugh's little attack became a bit bigger and, not surprisingly, Hugh didn't like pain.

Well, dearest, we have had quite a little siege. The little chap is comfortable and contented as you please this morning lying in bed and greatly relieved at being taken off his milk diet. He says "tell Dad that I had an awful pain first, then a little pain came after and I haven't much of a pain today." The night after I last wrote you was awful. I was exceedingly glad you were not here. The boy woke every hour and just screamed with pain. "O, mother, mother, can't you stop this awful pain, can't that doctor do something for me?" And most pathetic of all, "I am trying not to cry the best I can but I just can't help it."

What I should have done without Minnie I don't know. I never was so thankful for anything as that I had her with me. The little chap did not want me to leave him and Minnie flew about and got remedies and did everything that could be done. She and Ellen and I were up nearly all night. Hugh slept between the pains just fell over exhausted and slept. But he woke each hour until four and I don't think the rest of us slept much until then. After that he rested and so did the rest. Yesterday, I staid in bed, he in his crib beside me, having occasional twinges but much relieved and last night he slept the night through. Today he is practically over the pain, some soreness remaining but he is allowed soup, rice & toast. I think he will be up tomorrow but am not sure.

I did not mean to mislead you when I last wrote saying the worst was over for I really thought so and was much surprise when it proved not to be. But Dr. Birney says it really is over now and he does not think he will be much the worse for the attack. He says it is by no means one of the worst he has had to treat. The child has been a regular soldier about taking his medicine & standing his pains. I think he would like it if you sent him some compliments.
[1899-07-13 (2nd letter) Bertha (Jamestown) to Henry (StL)]

Soon, Hugh recovered and his gratitude toward his caretakers was endearing.
To return to Dr. Birney, he pronounced Hugh quite over his attack this morning but advised care in his diet and not letting him do too much and keeping him quiet for a day or two. He certainly is the darlingest child I ever saw. He presented us each with a shell this evening, some shells he has been treasuring, and he came up to me afterwards to say very softly, "You has all been so awful good to me, I thought that was the best thing I could do."
[1899-07-13 (3rd letter) Bertha (Jamestown) to Henry (StL)]

Henry was very glad to receive a letter from his children and was certain to write back upon receiving one. Henry included a newspaper clipping (below) – the latest in boys' swimsuits – for Hugh who was then 6.

D FASHIONS FOR JUNE, 1

3634 **3634**

No. 3634.—BOYS' BATHING SUIT. The pattern is cut in 7 sizes, from 3 to 15 yrs. The 5-yr. size requires 2⅜ yds. 27, 1½ yds. 44, or 1¼ yds. 54 in. wide. As represented 1½ yds. blue serge 44 in. wide and 5½ yds. white braid to trim. This suit may be made of serge, flannel, stockinette, etc., and be trimmed as preferred. Price, 15 cents.

I found your Friday and Saturday letter here and the letter of my oldest son. Tell him that letter came to most the biggest town and was waiting for me in quite the biggest house I ever saw and this shows that Uncle Sam who carried the letter to Dad thought it was a very nice one. And tell him I am very proud of a little boy who is only six and can make such pretty letters. The little lad tries to be faithful to his friends, doesn't he?
[20171116-1 (1900-summer-)]

Given his concern for Bertha's welfare, Henry periodically wrote of his desire that his boys would grow up and be able to care for Bertha.

> *Tell Hugh I dreamed about him last night. I thought he was sleeping at the foot of my bed and when I awoke in the morning, I tried to coax him up nearer me but he sprang up and said "Dad, I haven't got time, nobody is with mother and I must go and take care of her." Bless their little hearts, how I would like to squeeze each one of them.*
> [20171214-1 (1901-) Henry to Bertha]

Sometimes, Henry worried that Hugh was "delicate" and "unmanly". Hugh's lack of weight gain was an additional worry, especially as his younger sister Nancy was "stocky".

> *I am a little uneasy about Hugh in spite of your assurances for he is a delicately made little lad and any set back must go hard with him.*
> [20180127-2 (1895-) Henry to Bertha]

> *Are you sure Nancy only weighs three pounds more than Hugh? If that is the only difference, she must have glue on her shoes for it's a heap harder to lift that stocky solid weight.*
> [20171214-1 (1901-) Henry to Bertha]

> *I hope you are sitting on Hugh hard. I think I have Christian grace enough to stand a pious daughter but a preaching, sniveling boy, never! I hope somebody with whom he may discuss the terrors of hell will introduce him to a few of its mysteries.*
> [20180206-6 (1905-) Henry to Bertha]

Bertha wrote a letter to Henry in 1903 of one of Hugh's curious questions about swearing and Bertha's tactful response.

> *Hugh has just asked me "Mother, is darn a polite word for damn and is it swearing?" I won't say what I said but I have got to stop and do that darned packing.*
> [1903-09-28 (Saturday) Bertha (Rye, NH) to Henry (Waco)]

7. THE YOUTH

Henry and Bertha had discussions around 1906 whether Hugh should go camping during the summer with John Shepley, Jack and Sarah's son. Henry wrote that he was *"against the plan"*.

> *Jack Shepley was in to say he and Sarah have about decided to send John up to a man who takes boys camping for July and August and he wishes to know if we will let Hugh go. They must be ready to go June 29th, are to be just outside of Chelsea, Mass, near Dublin and the man is so splendidly recommended, Jack thinks it a great chance for both boys. The charge is $150.00 for the two months. I thought it would be a fine thing for John but I doubt the experiment for Hugh but I may be wrong. What do you think?*
> [1906(-) 20180713-1 Henry to Bertha]

> *My own judgment, as I very plainly wrote you, is against the plan, at least for this year. Hugh, I think, needs his mother as much as she needs him. We have no problem to solve of an uncontrollable child and, while I fully understand as I distinctly wrote you that it is a wise move for John, I am by no means sure it will be a good plan for our boy. I think there are distinct benefits in the experiences & discipline of that camp life but our boy can well wait for it.*
>
> *...*
>
> *As to the conclusion the Shepleys may reach, I don't mean to put it rudely but I must make myself plain. I don't care the snap of my finger what they or anyone else thinks of our methods with our young people. We are deciding for them, for their own good, and not for the approval of other people and I hardly understand your embarrassment in meeting and discussing the matter with Mrs. Shepley. We are a weak minded old couple if any plan proposed for our boy is to be solved*

or dodged because it runs counter to the view of our friends and, to make myself very plain, I wish to add that whereas I shall acquiesce in whatever conclusion you have arrived at if you have not yet decided, I say no and I distinctly wish to take the entire responsibility of the decision.
[1906(-) 20180711-1 Henry to Bertha]

The decision not to let Hugh go to camp with John Shepley was a disappointment to Hugh. But Henry seemed particularly concerned that Bertha was being overly indulgent and causing Hugh to be "*morbid*" (or moody): "*… it is not a boy's or a man's part in life to indulge such tendencies.*" Henry wanted Hugh to toughen up.

I am glad you are feeling better and are not worrying over Hugh's camp disappointment, his rejection of heaven's charms or even over the possible whooping cough attack. You may not be worrying but you are making another mistake quite as serious. You are taking the boy far too seriously and, I think without realizing it, you are encouraging the morbid tendency in him. Sympathize with him always when there is strong and legitimate call for it but don't let him play upon your or his own feelings and, when he shows a tendency to morbidness, make him see that it is not a boy's or a man's part in life to indulge such tendencies. This sounds like a lecture, I know, but I only wish you not be too sympathetic for the boy's own good, for that sort of kindness really fosters morbidness. There is no danger of the boy feeling that you do not share his real troubles. You are far too nice with your offspring for any such possibility but, when Hugh works his nerves and imagination over time, a few short, save and even curt and abrupt words to exclude the melodramatic climax he has been working up to, will do him lots of good and without in the least degree lessening his mother's influence over him. My observation has been that not the mothers who always most deeply sympathize with their sons but those who judge their acts with unerring discrimination accomplish most in the way of influence and affectionate reverence. There!
[20180206-2 (1906-) Henry to Bertha]

I don't think you need be seriously concerned about Hugh. I went off on excursions of a far more serious nature when I was a youngster for I very distinctly wished to learn this wicked world and be an angel and with the angels stand. I don't know that you can exactly call it morbidness that a boy is having such a good time on earth he is in a panic over the possibility of heaven. I should say he was over tired and needed a resting spell for a few days.
[1906(-) 20180731-2 Henry to Bertha]

In the summer of 1906, Bertha and the children went east to Rye Beach. After Bertha's charity fair ended, she wrote to Henry of one of Hugh's nightmares.

The fair is over and successfully! The day has been rather a long one for me for I was wakened by something resembling a caterwaul[168] this morning and flew out of bed thinking someone was ill, to discover Hugh sobbing aloud for fear when he was a man he would do something wicked and be sent to Hell. Now really, at four o'clock A.M.!! If I ever wanted to tell a person to go where he particularly did not want to, it was at that instant. Christian grace enabled me to invite him into my bed where I rubbed his back until he went to sleep and so did I but it did not tend to make me feel that today would be the "gladdest day of all the glad New Year, mother."
[1906-07-27 Bertha (Rye Beach) to Henry (StL)]

Perhaps, out of frustration, Henry concluded that Hugh was simply lazy.

The truth about our son Hugh is that he is plain lazy. This with the cocky influence which comes from a certain direction makes him careless as well and I think you will make a mistake, if you don't tell him that because of his heedlessness and carelessness, he is already penalizing you and himself in being compelled to do the work he should have done in the regular school term, and that

---

[168] Caterwaul: (of a cat) make a shrill howling or wailing noise. "The caterwauling of a pair of bobcats"

he will assuredly fail the second examination and be sent home in disgrace if he does not turn in with a will and master thoroughly what, I believe I said before, was the ground work, the drudgery, of his different studies. I feel discouraged about the boy and not at all sorry for him for his insistence that he knows a study which, he must realize, he has not really worked hard over, has a note to it that I distinctly don't like or approve of! I have filled several pages of paper with disagreeable items and I am tempted to send them to the scrap basket.
[20171205-4 (1908-Saturday) Henry to Bertha]

8. THE HILL SCHOOL

Hugh entered the Hill (boarding) School in the fall of 1908. Given Bertha and Henry's position in society, getting Hugh into The Hill School should not have been difficult. However, both Bertha and Henry fretted about this for months.

I don't think Hugh should be overconfident about Hill. He has received what they call a warning and I understand that, when a boy has been given the kindly hint Hugh has received and does not profit by it and seriously try to make up the deficiency, they do not treat him with much consideration on the second trial. And I don't understand that Hugh will not have to be examined again in Latin as I recall that he must make up deficiencies and, if so, he will of course be examined to see if he has made up what is expected of him. I think Hugh must do some steadfast work in the drudgery end of Latin. He has little or no vocabulary, does his verbs very badly and, if he don't go at that end of his Latin with a will, he will be mighty sorry later. Ask Mr. Peabody if I am not right in this. I think Dr. Miya letter was equally urgent as to Hugh's work in English – and he must go after his grammar work...
[20171203-2 (1908-) Henry to Bertha]

"The Hill" (The Hill School): The Hill School in Pottstown PA was founded in 1851 by the Rev. Matthew Meigs as the Family Boarding School for Boys and Young Men. However, it has been known as the Hill School since at least 1874. The school opened on May 1, 1851, enrolling 25 boys for the first year. The Hill was the first to be founded as a "family boarding school" (a school where the students lived on campus), as opposed to boarding with families in the town. (Wikipedia)

Henry again approached the subject of Hugh getting into The Hill School with the following, "business letter", to Bertha.

You will notice that Hugh did not exactly cover himself with glory and that he must make up this summer his deficiencies. I don't know whether you will think I should have said more to Dr. Muggs but I thought my letter the best answer to send him. There is nothing for Hugh to do but get down to work under Mr. Peabody and, if he will really take interest, I believe he will get in all right but I think you must have a plain talk with him and tell him, if he is unwilling to do the work, he may as well come back and either go back to Miss Phillips or to Smith. I think his principle trouble is his lack of any really thorough work for the last two years.

I am as you know very rusty in Latin but that evening I spent going over the sample papers with Hugh convinced me that he had been very lazy and heedless about his work for he found not so much difficulty with the construction of sentences which is the hardest part of Latin but he had little or no vocabulary and, as to the irregular verbs, I doubt if he knew a half dozen thoroughly. And this with a boy of Hugh's memory means he has been learning to loaf and not to study. I think you must make it clear to him that, unless he is really interested in study, there is very little use in our attempting to carry out the Hill plan. If on the other hand he will cheerfully accept the fact that he must make up now what he should have acquired last year and what I know he could have easily acquired then if he had given a small part of his best efforts to his work, and will go cheerfully to work with Mr. Peabody with the same confidence in himself that you and I have in him, he will, I am sure, get through. But if he is not willing to do this, I think the plan to send him to Hill may as well be abandoned. I don't think Dr. Muggs' letter is altogether discouraging and as to Hugh's ability to qualify, I haven't the slightest doubt, <u>providing he is sufficiently interested</u>.

What I was particularly struck with, that night I went over the sample papers with him, was that the work which called for the graph at sight of a clear logical mind he had well mastered, but the vocabularies, the verb endings & conjugations, the rules, in fact, the drudgery but really the easier part for an industrious mind, he was badly deficient in. Pets and things are well enough and I would not have our boy with less strong affection for such treasures but, when it comes to the point of their blotting out everything that is difficult, then it were far better for him never to know or possess any such companions.

I know you will be distressed at the thought of the effect on Hugh's strength of the work he must do this summer and I confess I was disturbed about this at first, but I have thought matters over pretty seriously since Dr. Muggs' letter came and especially since I have seen Jack and learned of our boasting John's[169] hopeless failure, I have very clearly concluded that it will not hurt Hugh but will really do him good if he has to put in an hour or two a day in work. I think he ... too much all day at any rate and that the change and physical rest for an hour or two will not hurt but help him and I believe, moreover, if he takes up his task like the manly boy he is, realizing that he must make up for past neglect, he will not only get in but he will have learned a most useful lesson. John's failure, unless Jack overstated it, was complete and John Sr. said there was no assurance whatever from Dr. M. that the young man could possibly qualify later. You may judge that father John was heated when he referred to his hopeful's downfall, he said John had overwhelmed him with most confident and serene assurance that he had passed and that he felt inclined to send him back to Morristown until he at least learned to be a little better than a boasting little idiot.

I really don't think Hugh is as bad as that and I believe if he is sincere in his desire to go to Hill, he can do the necessary work to pass at a later examination. I feel so strongly and am so clear in this conclusion that, if you think it will, you may read Hugh such part of this letter as you think will aid in getting him into the attitude of mind which I think so absolutely essential to the successful result of the work he must take up pending this second examination.
Yours always,
Henry C Scott
[20171205-1 1908(-) Henry to Bertha]

---

[169] John Rutledge Shepley (1894-1990), the son of John Foster Shepley and Sarah Hitchcock Shepley.

Bertha was also concerned about Hugh's laziness and had her own, business, talk with him.

Dear Henry,

This being Sunday, I called your son into my room before church and had a very short talk with him. I had previously read him your letters as they came up but, to date, I had been somewhat disappointed in the way he took hold of things so I made one short speech which I here set down in practically the same words.

My dear son,

I want to say just a few words to you and I don't want to say them again. I don't believe in continual nagging and hammering at a fellow. I am going to say all I have to say now and let that finish it.

Your father has written to me again about you. He feels as I do very much distressed and anxious at the spirit in which you have taken up your school work this summer. There has been no real interest or ambition. Everything that is suggested is a grind or a bore and has to be so planned as not to interfere with any amusement or else you are a very ill-used boy.

Now I want to put one thing before you very plainly. <u>This is your chance!</u>

We want to give it to you and we have chosen an expensive school, one of the best in the country where the nicest fellows go. You have the opportunity to go there, have a splendid education, the best physical development, and will go down to college with a crowd of the nicest kind of boys and the starting college life under the best possible auspices.

Now your whole school and college career rests on <u>this summer's</u> work. You have not got an unreasonable amount to make up. Dr. Muggs wrote you a very different letter from what he wrote John, <u>but</u> you have go to work hard while you do work and you have got to work regularly. You must make up your mind that this summer will not be as pleasant as the other summers. You will miss a great many things and the boys will go off without you a great many times but all the years of your school and college life depend upon it.

I think John is a bad influence in the way he takes up his work and I do not want you to tell John but I think you ought to know that his school record was a bad one and a great disappointment to his father and mother. He was unpopular with the masters because he was a braggart and a shirk, and with the boys for the same reason.

Now, we don't feel that way about you. The reports of your character have been good and we trust you. But you <u>are</u> lacking in ambition and industry and those are what you have got to show this summer or fail. And it is no use to spend your time criticizing Mr. Peabody. He may not be the best or most inspiring of teachers and he may even make an occasional mistake in Latin but he knows abundance to oversee and direct your work and not teacher on earth can do your work for you. <u>You have to do that yourself.</u> And that is what we expect of you this summer. Do you think it is unfair or too much?

He seemed a good deal impressed, said it was not unfair and he would do it and he has hung around me most affectionately all day but the future effects remain to be seen.

It is hotter than I like to speak of.
Yours always,
Bert
[1908(-) 20180810-3 (see 20171205-1, 20171205-1) Bertha to Henry]

Henry devoted a significant part of a letter to Bertha in July of 1908 to address how Hugh was doing and his conclusions seemed brutally honest. Hugh stayed in St. Louis with Henry for part of the summer while Bertha had gone to Rye Beach to be with her father, the summer that he died.

> *I have written so fully about Hugh's examination that I shall make no further comment than to add that it is with the boy to steadfastly and deliberately determine whether he is really sufficiently interested to bravely and hopefully get at the task of making up for what his lack of real interest in the past has cost him. That he can do this, I have not the slightest doubt if he has real interest and without material draft upon his strength or his play time this summer. In fact, I believe if Hugh takes daily an hour or two for rest and study, he will come out of the summer physically stronger than if all his time is taken up in play. That his lack in his preparation is due to mere want of interest and application and not to any mental deficiency is also perfectly clear to me. My one session with him gave me great comfort in his clear strong grasp of the fundamental principles which had to do with his studies. But he showed hopeless want of application to the mere drudgery. Don't let him misunderstand my estimate of him and, if you can agree with me in that estimate, I shall be certain of its accuracy. To see that his cerebration, his power to think clearly and logically, is strong is most comforting. To know that, despite the aid of a really wonderful memory, he is not enough interested to master the details & to see that the dust is all cleaned out of the cracks and corners is, I admit, discouraging. But I have faith in the boy's fine spirit, in the interest, latent though it be, to make his life of some value and I believe he will take hold and that he will not grudgingly and rebelliously but loyally and hopefully take hold and pull up and you must say to him from me that if he takes hold with the same confidence in himself that I have in him, I am in no doubt that he will win out and enter school quite as well equipped as the average boy in his class.*
> [1908-07-03 Henry (StL) to Bertha (Rye Beach)]

In one of his next letters, Henry chided Bertha about being too soft on Hugh and stressed the need for Hugh to work hard.

> *I am afraid you are not strict enough with Hugh. I don't wish to be hard on the boy, but he must be made to see that he has been worthlessly indolent and that all this extra trouble to you and himself is due to his lazy and indolent habits at school. And that if he does not now turn to his work with a will, we will accept the fact that he is too indifferent to really care for the best education with attractive boys and must therefore be left with the more indifferent opportunities and like associates. I should think that John's unfailing flinchings and downfalls at every test would make some impression upon Hugh and I confess I am baffled at the boy's admiration for an associate who has so few qualities worthy of a nice boy's sympathy or admiration. I don't believe John will get through with a second trial and I think John Sr. has quite made up his mind that result for he talks hopelessly about his oldest son and I confess I am not very sorry this is the case.*
> [1908-07-09 (Wednesday) Henry (StL) to Bertha (Rye Beach)]

> *I think Hugh would have taken his set back better had it not been for the bravado attitude of his friend. We are trying to help him but he must help himself or he will, I am afraid, have a very unhappy life. As I saw it well put the other day, if the material can be removed from contaminating influences, fused in the furnace of hard work and kept in the mold until it has set, the best has been done that education can do for character. I don't know any boy to whom close training and hard work are so important if he is to be a useful, happy man, but we can only influence him and arose him and he will not respond unless he has the true prompting of loyalty to our wishes and some pride for his own future. I have not written to him and shall not do so unless you think it best. You are with him and understand him thoroughly and I shall not risk the too many cooks mistake unless you think I should do so. I shall of course have a full talk with him when I see him.*
> [1908-07-13 Henry (StL) to Bertha (Rye Beach)]

Toward the end of 1908, Bertha apparently expressed increased optimism over Hugh's progress. Henry, however, had a different point of view.

> *I think it takes a large amount of motherly pride and enthusiasm to enable one to take your view of Hugh's report per letter. John[170] has the largest number of demerits in the school, 36, and our hopeful is a good second with 26. Still much enthusiasm about Thanksgiving boxes, razors!, etc., and no apparent interest in his work except a dull regret over the consequences of his failure to do his tasks. He apparently has not had time to answer my letter suggesting a consultation with Mr. Briggs about his proposed drop to the second form. Do you still think he should be put back at once or that, in view of your encouragement from his letter, you think it better that he try on a little longer? I really would like your view as to this for, despite the fact that his case still discourages me greatly, I am inclined to defer to your view for I really think you understand the boy better than I do. When I tried to cheer up over the situation, I reread that letter which would have been barely creditably written by George and sank into gloom over our son's future prospects. The demand for a razor was a mere copy of John's similar plea and I distinctly argue that the requisition be declined. I think your box was a very nice one and I am very glad it was for, although I can't stand for the young man's lack of application, I am very glad his first Thanksgiving away from home will have a reminder that, even if he is a rather worthless urchin, his home people love him and miss him.*

[1908-11-26 (Wednesday) (20180419A-3) Henry (Ft. Worth) to Bertha (64 Vandeventer Place, StL)]

9. THE YOUNG MAN

Hugh Scott

After The Hill School, Hugh went to Yale University in 1913 but left in his senior year, in May 1917, to join the Three Hundred and Fortieth Field Artillery of the Eighty-ninth Division in World War 1. He graduated in absento.

Some of Hugh's WW1 history was recorded in the Centennial History of Missouri.

> *Mr. Scott's older son, Hugh, was a member of the Three Hundred and Fortieth Field Artillery of the Eighty-ninth Division. He left the senior class In Yale and was graduated in absento. In May, 1917, he enlisted and was sent to the officers' training camp at Fort Riley where he was under the*

---

[170] John Rutledge Shepley

instruction of General Wood for a year. He was made a lieutenant in August, 1917 and was sent to France the following June. He participated in the St. Mihiel offensive[171] and was on the Euvexans front at the time of the signing of the armistice, after which he was sent with the army of occupation into Germany where he remained until May, 1919. He then returned home and is now associated with Robert Gaylord, Incorporated, a paper box manufacturing company. On the 6th of October, 1920, he married Miss Anne Block, a daughter of Harry L. Block of St. Louis. (Centennial History of Missouri)

Hugh sent one letter to his sister Alice shortly after the St. Mihiel offensive. One can only assume that soldiers needed to have a good sense of humor at the front.

Hugh Scott
2nd Lt.
American Expeditionary Force

Dear Alice,
Might as well continue to you the letter which I wrote Nance the other day. Got Back to camp in fine style although some infantry right near us got shot up some. We saw them running like mad and I figured we had better stay where we were as the German artillery was evidently chasing them. Heard that they got home next morning.

Certainly enjoyed breakfast when I got back. It was steaming hot: bacon, biscuits, syrup, jam, coffee, canned milk and sugar. If you are urged to go light on food, you will know it's because Lt. Scott, Corp. Wild & Pvt. Sands ate all the food in France.

Certainly enjoyed life here for a while. My immediate commander was one of my closest friends if not the closest. Had the job which I wanted most and the finest battery on the front. When I think of the way those men have acted, it makes me think mighty deep. Clark's system is different from nearly every other executive around here. He has knocked off all courtesies, etc., since we got here. We sleep in the pits with the men, eat together, talk things over, swap stories and steal each other's property, all in one crowd. Whenever an order has been given, however, it's never been questioned. We have had the best results every way that could be hoped for. There is not many men that will work 48 hours at a stretch and work hard with only three hours off. Funny enough, Clark is the scaredest man here but no one knows how scared he is but me. They're not liable to either.

We were shelled the other day and he had everyone take shelter but himself and the gas non-com. They stayed out there and took it and I'll tell you it is not a pleasant job.

Roy sent me back to the house lines the other day so I am safe for some time, I guess forever. He told me that he had more confidence in me than any other man in the battery which is some consolation but I wish I knew less about horses and more about other things. This is sort of a top sergeant job here and, although it isn't my fault, I feel like a quitter.

---

[171] The Battle of Saint-Mihiel was a major World War I battle fought from 12–15 September 1918, involving the American Expeditionary Forces (AEF) and 110,000 French troops under the command of General John J. Pershing of the United States against German positions. The U.S. Army Air Service played a significant role in this action. This battle marked the first use of the terms "D-Day" and "H-Hour" by the Americans. The attack at the Saint-Mihiel salient was part of a plan by Pershing in which he hoped that the Americans would break through the German lines and capture the fortified city of Metz. It was the first large offensive launched mainly by the United States Army in World War I, and the attack caught the Germans in the process of retreating. This meant that their artillery was out of place and the American attack, coming up against disorganized German forces, proved more successful than expected. The Saint-Mihiel attack established the stature of the U.S. Army in the eyes of the French and British forces. [Wikipedia]

One thing tickles me to death. Artie W. was so worried for fear that we wouldn't be ready in time to go up with them and we arrived a long, long time first.

Love,
Hugh

News has just come in that someone found four bombs under Roy's blankets. He has been sleeping there for five days. Came in tired out in the dark and didn't notice where he went to sleep. I would like to see him when he found it.
[1918-09-28 Hugh Scott Sr. (Recon From Army, Bordeaux) to Alice Scott (Gadney Farm Hotel, White Plains, NY)]

10. ANNE MONTGOMERY BLOCK

Hugh married Anne Montgomery Block (1899-1974), the daughter of Harry L. Block (1863-1934) and Nancy ("Nannie") Boteler Livermore (1866-1946) around 1921 after the war. Grandma Scott, as we knew her, was a very fine sculptor and artist, and produced wonderful works of art. As a sculptor, my father always said that she was animated to find the shape that was already contained within the stone. Michelangelo wrote,

The best of artists hath no thought to show which the rough stone in its superfluous shell doth not include; to break the marble spell is all the hand that serves the brain can do.

In a similar vein, Henry Moore wrote: "*I had to think in the same way that Michelangelo might have done, so that one had to wait until an idea came that fitted the shape of the stone and that was seen, the idea, in that block.*"

Portrait of M.R. sculpted by Anne B. Scott[172]

THE SCULPTOR
The hard-stone head endures impassively
Many days of polish and chiseling.
She looks at the photograph absently
Then peers at the stone, silent and waiting.

---

[172] Grandma Scott sculpted this head on commission from M.R. Apparently, M.R. did not care for the representation and refused to pay for the sculpture. As a result, it has become a treasured item of the Scott family.

What mysterious shape have you concealed
From my inquiring hands and inner sight?
Is this the likeness that I see pictured?
And will it be recognized in this light?

She takes one step back, then two, uncertain,
And puts down her tools to regard anew,
Removes her glasses, opens the curtain,
"Ah, it is finished! I see what is true."
[HCS July 6, 2020]

ANN SCOTT
SCULPTOR

Grandma Scott with her dog, Claire, at her backyard studio in St. Louis.

The children of Anne & Hugh were: Hugh Scott Jr. (July 10, 1921 to January 8, 2015), Nancy Boteler (Scott) Riesmeyer (May 25, 1923 to July 10, 1999), and Bertha Drake (Scott) Perry (June 10, 1927 to August 1, 2002). I recall hearing that Margaret Boteler (McDonald) Priest ("Aunt Margie Priest") came to live with the Scott family as a girl when her mother, Margaret Boteler Block Hill/McDonald[173], Grandma Scott's sister, died in 1936 at age 38.

---

[173] It appears that Margaret Boteler Block married Walker Maury Hill Jr. (1892-1955) around 1920 but the marriage did not last long. She then married John Dillon McDonald (1894-1960) in 1923 and gave birth to their daughter, Margaret Boteler McDonald Priest in 1924. Walker Maury Hill Jr. remarried in 1935 to Adgate (Ellis) Gay who was a widow.

11. POPS' LATER YEARS: A REMINISCENCE

Hugh, as a grandfather, was known as "Pops". Pops died on March 2, 1970 after having lived 70 years. As an older man, he suffered from emphysema and would always be in a chair near the "oxygen lung", the big tank of oxygen from which he needed breath on a periodic basis. My Dad had explained that his condition was the result of being gassed in World War I when he fought with the American forces at the front. While there was certainly some truth in this, another part of the truth which I learned later is that Pops used to smoke a pack or more of cigarettes each day for much of his life. I imagine that contributed just a bit.

My Dad and Mom used to take my siblings and I to visit Pops and Grandma Scott periodically, often on a Sunday afternoon. Sometimes we would ride bikes downtown to his house on Maryland Avenue in St. Louis' Central West End, not far from where Bertha used to live in Westmoreland Place. On one such visit, several years before he died, Dad and I played chess with Pops. I believe that Pops was a good chess player but my Dad was a very good chess player. The game probably lasted about 30 minutes and I mostly watched as Dad pretty much took Pops' pieces to task. When the end was near and, I imagine, Pops was probably getting annoyed at losing to his son, I suggested a move which looked good. My Dad was just about to play another piece and would have won the game anyway in not too many more moves. However, as I found out (I did not realize the true worth of my move when I suggested it), my move was an immediate checkmate. I recall, whether imagined or not, that Pops was very pleased that the *coup-de-grace* was delivered by his grandson and not his son. To this day, I believe that this made Pops happy, and my Dad too. A true "*coup-de-grace.*"

B. ANNE WARBURTON SCOTT

Anne, who was called "Nancy", was born July 5, 1895 when Bertha and Henry were in Jamestown Rhode Island. Bertha wrote very little about the birth of Nancy in her diary. From her diary entry, this sounded like a pretty ho-hum day for Bertha.

> *July 5, 1895*
> *Get up at half past four, sun is already up but watch some sunrise effects - Come down stairs. Write a note thanks to Emma Lane. Finish stitching around bottom of Gertrude. Put the parlor in order & write up the last two days of my diary.*
>
> *Eleven o'clock AM on July 5, 1895, Anne Warburton Scott was born.*
> [1893 Diary]

In October that year, Bertha mentioned Nancy being ill and struggling to find a nurse.

> *Oct. 1, 1895*
> *Mrs. Hurley goes home. Immediately afterward Anne is taken ill. For three days, I hunt a nurse, being nurse in the meanwhile, myself. Then Lizzie comes to the rescue and offers to take the nursing and I get old Maggie to come and do the cooking. My dear old Maggie, my first cook.*
> [1893 Diary]

In a November 1895 letter to Henry, Bertha wrote to Henry how Bertha's mother selected the nickname "Nancy", for baby Anne. That name was certainly better than "sister".

> *I have not spoken of the babies for some time. Both are well. Mother has made a special request that we do not call the baby "sister" anymore. I told her as she had been meant to select the name and really had hardly done so she might select any nick name she liked and she chose "Nancy" & that is the favorite of all of us. It was a fortunate choice.*
> [1895-11-06 Bertha (StL) to Henry (Wichita)]

Bertha included little tidbits about the children in each letter and wrote the following funny stories about Nancy.

> *Now I will ask no more questions but will close with one anecdote of Nancy. I said "Nancy, get off that trunk, you'll fall". "No, I won't, not if God don't let me. He just has to say 'don't be falled off that trunk' and then I won't fall off."*
> [1899-07-13 (3ʳᵈ letter) Bertha (Jamestown) to Henry (StL)]

> *No fresh news about the chicks, except that Nancy cut off some of her front hair today & looks peculiar!!*
> [1899-07-19 Bertha (Jamestown RI) to Henry (StL)]

Nancy apparently had a very fine 5ᵗʰ birthday in Rye Beach, the summer of 1900. Although Henry was working in St. Louis at the time, he was apparently well informed of the goings on.

> *I am so glad to know Nancy had such a nice birthday. You know I think when things are going entirely her way, she is capable of more unalloyed bliss than either of the boys, and I have no doubt she will remember that birthday until she is able to tell it to chicks of her own.*
> [1900-07-10(-) Henry (StL) to Bertha]

Nancy married Thomas S. Blumer on June 12, 1918 and they resided in Boston, Massachusetts. Mr. Blumer was a first lieutenant in the Massachusetts Field Artillery during the First World war.

C. GEORGE DRAKE SCOTT

George Drake Scott ("Uncle George") was born December 7, 1897 and died December 15, 1978. Bertha first mentioned George in a very nonchalant manner.

> Dec. 7, 1897
> *George Drake Scott is born. Tuesday at ten o'clock in the evening. Mrs. Herbert and Dr. Robinson in charge.*
> [1893 Diary]

Being the third child, George is mentioned far less than Hugh but more than Nancy. The comments made about George are amusing, such as when George was 4 months old: "*The youngest has learned a new word. He says "out" when asked where anyone is who is not present.*" [1899-03-28 (3 letters) Bertha (StL) to Henry (Ft. Worth)]

Bertha mentioned George one time after he was bitten by their dog, Barry. It was striking that George, who was not yet 2 years old, exhibited a fair amount of courage through the event and the medical aftermath. In the end, George held "*no grudge of any kind*" toward the doctor, fortunately, or the dog, "*unfortunately*".

> *I am feeling rather jubilant today anyhow. I have been under a cloud but did not wish to tell you until it was all over. On Saturday last, the long expected happened & Barry bit George Drake. I was in bed collapsed when he came in. It was just before his bed time and I did not think it much of a bite, though it bled, and did not get the doctor. I sucked it, washed it in hot water & then in whiskey, Hildegarde having said that was antiseptic and let it go. The next morning there was a slight suppuration on the end of the little finger so I took him to Dr. Rhett (Birney had gone early in the morning to Dumpling) and could not be raised. Dr. Rhett looked at it and said it would have to be cauterized. I asked if it would have had to be done if I had brought him the night before and he said yes, it would have had to be done in any case but there would have been less danger of blood poisoning if I had brought him at once. I asked him if he would do it immediately and he said "the sooner the better but can you stand it?" I was alone. I told him if the baby could, I undoubtedly could so he did it. George was very plucky and did not scream until he literally had*

to. Then we went home and in half an hour he was placid as a kitten and went off to sleep. Then I did collapse for a little while, got rather sick and faint and had to have some whisky.

We have been down every other day since to have it dressed, the wound has been healing beautifully and cleanly while Dr. Rhett said all along, "I do not think you need worry, everything is going beautifully." He would not say until this morning that there was no further danger of blood poisoning, a beautiful clean healthy skin had formed & I could dress it myself until the skin had grown thick enough not to be injured. It was such a relief, almost the worst of all was that horrible feeling that, if harm did come, it would be my fault for not having taken him at once and I used to agonize over what might [have] happened. But Mr. George is an admirable patient, he never lost an hour's sleep or a meal and except for the actual bite and burn, apparently felt nothing.

Birney left Sunday night anyway so Dr. Rhett kept him and the two have become great chums. He says this baby & Mr. Eustis' are the two pluckiest patients he has and he cannot get over the way in which George marches into the office, holds out his fat hand and never fights or struggles a bit, although twice - the cauterization & the first dressing – he was hurt, and he loves the doctor & has no grudge of any kind. Nor, unfortunately, has he any toward the dog. We have just as hard work to keep him away as ever. There!

I hope you forgive me for not having had the sense to take him to a doctor at once. I don't forgive myself, though. Fortunately, no ill came of it.
[1899-09-21 Bertha (Jamestown, Newport) to Henry (StL)]

When Bertha took the family to Rye Beach when he was four years old, George conveyed emotions not usually associated with boys.
The hayride, I think, was an unqualified success. I will give you George Drake Scott's opinion. He said to me this morning, "Mother, I almost cried on that hayride." "Did you dear, why what was the matter?" "O, there was so much noise and so much music and it was all so joyful that I just felt as if I had to cry." Dear lad, he is a little young to feel that sensation, isn't he?
[1902-07-19 Bertha (Rye Beach) to Henry (StL)]

George had his scrapes in life, in addition to dog bites. When he was seven years old, Bertha wrote about George's "run in" with a rusty nail while they were in Rye Beach.
The fourth ended rather badly after all. In arranging the Allen bonfire, George ran a rusty nail into his foot. The doctor probed it and disinfected it promptly (a most unpleasant operation) but he probably bruised a nerve or perhaps sprained a small muscle for he was frantic with pain. The doctor relieved my mind promptly on one score for he said that, even if there were blood poison, which was most unlikely, it would not show for twenty-four hours so any pain would be from another cause. But poor old George. He tried to sit on the porch to watch the fireworks and gritted his teeth but the tears would spill over in spite of him and he could not sit still, the pain was so great. So I took him home & put him to bed with ice on it. After he finally got to sleep, he would sob in his sleep and cry out with pain and I would find the ice bag gone and renew it. About two o'clock the bromide the doctor had given him took effect and he slept peacefully. Today there was only a little ache left as long as he kept it up so I kept him in bed. He was pretty thoroughly done up after the two nights anyway.
[1905-07-05(-) 20180725-2 Bertha (Rye Beach)]

George Scott at Rye Beach

Since the Scott family was in Rye Beach when George received his rusty nail injury, Henry had to write of his concerns for George's health from a distance.

> *I am a little concerned about George. I don't suppose there can be the slightest danger of tetanus but rusty nails are pretty dangerous and I am almost sorry you permitted him to go off to Annie's. I suppose, of course, the doctor knows and that you consulted him but I shall not feel entirely comfortable for a day or two. ... I am just as sorry for the little man as I can be and I hope you will tell him that I think his pluck was very fine and manly.*
> [1905-07-10(-) 20170831-1 Henry to Bertha]

George loved the outdoors and he had great opportunities to explore while the family was in Rye Beach. Bertha provided Henry with one account of George's outdoor activities and the medical advice from Bertha's brother, George, who was a doctor at that time and approved these outdoor activities.

> *I am taking George's advice about not putting them to bed but letting them stay out so George third in the last two days has only fallen into the brook once, got soaked and dripping by the rain once and his feet absolutely drenched twice. Personally, I do not think it has improved his cold but doctors know best.*
> [1906-09-24 (Sunday) Bertha (Rye Beach) to Henry (StL)]

In the following letter, Bertha wrote to Henry of George's grit and tenacity, and the virtues of football.

> I believe your son George is really going to amount to something. He had a tooth ache the other day and I invited him to go and be relieved at Dr. Prosser's. *"No, I can stand it,"* he said, *"and I ought to play in a football match this afternoon. Make it tomorrow."* I am coming to the conclusion that the trainers are right: football is the only thing that teaches the sons of the upper classes self-control and endurance and a few of those other virtues which they so very much need."
> [1908(-) 20180801-1 Bertha]

Bertha observed that George had a mind of his own which led him to break rules from time to time, especially when he had some encouragement from his Shepley "cousins".

> *Your son George has not much conscience. I think I have not written you about the smoking spree that Sarah and I found out by chance. John bought the contraband supplies of course and he, Ethan and George, went on a smoking bat(?). And by a most unforeseen disposition of providence, not to say unfortunate, none of them were sick. It is needless to ask what George smoked, with that*

Irish mug(?), a pipe and Bull Durham tobacco!! His account of it when found out was convulsively funny. He readily agreed not to smoke again this summer but begged to keep the pipe.
[1908-07-22 (Wednesday) Bertha (Rye Beach) to Henry]

George Drake Scott

The Scott family had a very close friendship with the Shepleys. So it was not surprising that, while George's his brother Hugh was a good friend of John Rutledge Shepley (1894-1990), George took up with Ethan Allen Hitchcock Shepley (1896-1975), John's brother.

Henry wrote of one occasion when George and Ethan attended a football game together on Thanksgiving Day, November 26, 1908, when the Carlisle Indians defeated St. Louis University 17-0. The Carlisle Indian Industrial School in Carlisle, Pennsylvania, was a federally-funded, off-reservation Indian boarding school whose student body was composed of American Indians. Hence, the team name, "Indians", was very appropriate. The Indians had two not so secret weapons: Jim Thorpe and Glen "Pop" Warner (the coach). George & Ethan were 10 and 12 years old at the time.

> *I saw by the paper that the Indians won the football game so I infer George and Ethan enjoyed the game as I think neither of them would be likely to be partial to the St. L. U. team. And your son do like to have his side win out.*
> [1908-11-28 (20180419A-4) Henry (Ft. Worth) to Bertha (64 Vandeventer Place, Stl)]

The Indians went on to beat Nebraska in a rout on December 2, 2008.

George attended the Sheffield Scientific School but, like his brother Hugh, left school to join the military (the US Navy in George's case) in May 1917. Later, George was transferred to the naval aviation section and graduated from the Massachusetts School of Technology as an ensign in February 1918. He was then made instructor in aviation at Bay Shore, Long Island and left the service in April 1919, with the rank of junior grade lieutenant. He was associated with George Tiffany & Company, cotton brokers of St. Louis after he left the armed services.

D. MARY ROBERTA SCOTT

Mary Roberta Scott was named after Aunt Mary Roberts. She was born on September 29, 1901 and died five hours later[174]. Bertha wrote in her diary: "*St. Michael & All Angels Day. My baby girl was born and taken away – Mary Roberta Scott.*" Bertha did not make another diary entry until that Christmas.

---

[174] See 1901-10-03 Sarah H. Shepley (Monadnock, NH) to Bertha (Stl)

Many of the condolences that Bertha received spoke of the reassurance that she and her friends shared in God. The following letter from Rev. Carroll Davis, who had lost his wife and 3 children, was particularly poignant.

We cannot attempt to understand God's dealing with us. From our point of view, at times, it seems too hard. But we can only trust His love. Sometime, with longer vision, we shall see and know. But now, we can only know that these trials and sorrows are calls to us to stand firm in the storm and, in patience & trust, hold fast to Him, doing our duty, however hard it be. God bless and strengthen you is my earnest prayer. Give you courage and love until the time comes when our partings are over, and, in Christ Jesus, we shall meet again our loved ones.
[1901-10-06 Rev. Carroll Melvin Davis to Henry & Bertha]

Similarly, the following letter from Florence Boyle spoke of God's providence.

It seems so strange a thing that a little life should be permitted to come into this world only to pass out of it. Sometimes I think that, of all the mysteries of God's providence, that is the most impossible of human understanding. But surely our God, whose only begotten Son, when on this earth, held little children in His arms and blessed them, surely He held them so close in His love that not even a little new born baby can pass through the gates of death without fulfilling some wise and loving purpose. So, after all, in this, as in every other mystery of suffering, we can only rest our aching hearts and weary questioning minds upon faith in the "love of God which passeth knowledge."
[20191018-2 (1901-Fall-) Florence Boyle to Bertha]

Bertha also received a rather unusual letter of condolence from Mrs. William H. Benton who wrote about her own loss of a 3-day old baby and her hope that Bertha will be able to say, *"It is well."*

My dear Bertie,
Will you think me heartless when I tell you I congratulate you – a baby <u>forever</u> at the court of heaven. A baby safe in your mother's care. You cannot say I know nothing about the loss and the heartache. <u>I can feel for you</u> for years & years ago. I had a like experience – God lent me a baby for three days and then took him home. And to a home so much better than any I could provide for him. That thinking about <u>his infinite</u> gain, I forgot to mourn my loss, so it will be with you, dear Bertie. The time will come when you will not only be comforted but you will be able to say, "<u>It is well.</u>"

When you are as old as I am, you will rejoice as I do that you have one child waiting for you in the other home. Please do not think that I do not feel for you now in your sick room and with this disappointment in your heart. I am sorry for you but I am so glad for the baby – gone to God. What could a mother's prayer in all the wildest ecstasies of hope ask for her darling like the bliss of heaven?

I hope soon to hear that you are getting well and strong. The baby gone, does not need you anymore. The children <u>living here</u> demand your loving care, your <u>constant watchfulness.</u> Do you not think it would help you to regain your strength and cheerfulness <u>to come to us for a little while?</u> We would so gladly welcome you and will try and do you good.

Even yours with loving sympathy, your mother's friend,
K.L. Benton
[1901-10-10(-) K.L. Benton to Bertha (StL)]

The loss of Mary Roberta continued to cast a shadow over Bertha for some time. Henry wrote of having to modify their September plans the next year.

> *I couldn't distress you, Bert, by talking for the end of all our plans for September but I do hope you know that I understood what that sorrow was to you. I think I do understand, my darling, and while I know you and I can't forget, we must not let the shadow side of life keep us away from the enjoyment of all the happiness that may come to us. That is insane to me if my life is spared the ordinary span and you are saved from sickness and sorrow.*

[1902-07-02(-) 20180630-1 Henry (StL) to Bertha]

Henry wrote the preceding letter and others to Bertha to comfort her in "*that sorrow*" over the loss of their child and to express his understanding of Bertha's motherly devotion to their children who are a mother's glory. Henry apparently also wrote of his concern that Bertha may have become afraid to try to bring another child into the world. In response to these letters, Bertha wrote the following when she was expecting their fifth child, Alice Marion, who would be born 7 months later, on February 20, 1903. In this letter, Bertha showed her great inner strength and gently rebuked Henry for his concerns about her, writing: "*I am not afraid*" and "*This child shall have its own place but not hers.*"

> *Dearest,*
>
> *I hardly know how to answer your letter. It was different from what I expected. In some ways, it was a very comforting letter and in some ways it hurt. I know you did not mean that, you need not tell me that. It is strange how very near two people can be to each other and dearer than anything in the world and yet not quite understand.*
>
> *One thing, perhaps, I had better say first of all. I do not think there is any possibility of a mistake. The difference between the twelfth and the twenty second is only ten days and I have never expected anything else.*
>
> *There are other reasons too for thinking I am not mistaken. Dearest, do you think I am such a coward that you need ask me not to let my life be "clouded with dread"? I am not afraid. Or do you think that I, who have lost a child, needed to be asked to have a welcome for another? You hurt but you hurt worse when you ask me to look upon the new life coming as in place of the one taken away. Not that. That is mine for always, far beyond this life. It has taken even some of the dread of dying. I have never been afraid to die - I don't mean that. But I don't want to die. Life is intensely dear to me and death has always meant to me only an agony of separation. Now, when that time comes, there is one comfort in it, I shall have my baby who has never had any mother. This child shall have its own place but not hers.*
>
> *Then you will ask me, if those two things do not distress me, what it is? In the first place, I have not meant to be sad. You spoke of my sadness last winter in another letter. I had not meant to be. I am afraid I have been even less a help to you even than I had hoped, for I meant to be bright at home and keep that life for you, even if I could not go into the rest of life with you and be the companion I want to be in your work, plans, ambitions. It isn't easy to tell out one's inmost soul, but just once, I will try to tell something. I shall not bother you again.*
>
> *It is not always easy to submit to God's working with us. But I am more and more convinced as I grow older that He knows what is best for our special natures. I think the matter with me is that I am like friend Demas[175] in the Epistles who forsook Paul "having loved this present world". I should have gone along with Demas and found St. Paul uncongenial. I love this present world. Honestly, I love it more for your sake than for mine but I like it for my own well enough.*

---

[175] In Second Timothy 4:10, a letter traditionally ascribed to Paul, where it is mentioned that "...for Demas, because he loved this world, he has deserted me and has gone to Thessalonica."

But my ambitions are for you. And I was proud of being not only your wife but being able to live your life with you, and the bar of ill health has been very bitter to me. I have the long inaction, the being shut out, the incapacity to be your companion in anything that I dreaded. It has been so long since I could be to you what I want. I have fought that battle out I think, after all it is "this present world". The ambitions and hopes and striving aren't wrong but there is something better.

The greatest gift that God can give is a child. A year could be a pitifully small price to pay for the life of any one of those we have and why grudge to the one who will be as dear. When I look at other people, at Maud[176], at Sadie[177], I wonder that I am not ashamed to speak of even having a struggle. I have used big words for a small thing and smaller probably than I thought, like most of our bug bears, for I am gaining all the time. When you come, I think now I shall be entirely myself again. It is usually the time that is best of all with me.

One thing more, you speak of the children as having been the greatest joy of our married life. Dear as they are, they have not been that to me. The glory of my life is now what it has always been since your love first came into it, and even the children are second to it.

Yours always,
Bert
[1902-07-09 Bertha (Rye Beach) to Henry (StL)]

Bertha's closing words in this letter are poignant: "*you speak of the children as having been the greatest joy of our married life. Dear as they are, they have not been that to me. The glory of my life is now what it has always been since your love first came into it, and even the children are second to it.*"

Henry replied to Bertha's letter with: "*Our children are our chief blessing but they haven't made our love any sweeter or greater.*"

Dear Bert,
I don't think you quite understand my meaning. By this, I mean that you seem to think I look at these things from a point of view single and separate from yours. I know I cannot express the degree of sympathy which you put into your letter. I know I am not capable of that and I know also my capacity for sounding the depths of deepest feeling is far less than yours, just as I know, dear, that in the sweetest, the best things I turn to you now as I think I unconsciously did when I first began to know you for inspiration, for the help which always comes whenever I most need it. But I do not think our real view is different. I would hate to think this and when I wrote that letter which seemed to hurt, when I meant it should help you. I was trying to make you see our, not yours or my own, but our hope in the future if you should be called on devote again a part of your life to what seemed the greatest joy of our married life.

You compare the children with life itself, dear, for our married life is all, everything to me as it is to you, and I have never thought of that as a thing to be added to or changed while God spares our lives. Our children are our chief blessing but they haven't made our love any sweeter or greater. I doubt if I can make you see how even they are secondary to that which is everything that makes my life worth living. And I did not mean that another child could shut out forgetfulness of our baby girl but I did mean that, that another life to bless our love would soften as I think it will that other sorrow. The regret that I shall feel will rest safely upon the trial which will come to you for I know

---

[176] Maud Reber Davis (who was married to Rev. Carroll Davis) –had lost her two children as of the date of this letter, her first who was 3 years old and the second may have died in childbirth. Both children died in 1901. Maud was buried at Bellefontaine Cemetery on November 7, 1903, after having lost her third child who was buried November 2, 1903.

[177] Sarah ("Sadie") Knox Taussig whose husband died in 1898 at the age of 41, leaving two children.

in spite of what you say it will be a tax for, though I realize that nature fits women for such ordeals and that in the larger, far larger number of cases women who have children are the stronger for it, I did not wish you to be taxed now until you yourself felt you were fitted to the demand upon you and until it was your distinct wish. You didn't mean it, dearest, but your last statement that you have been in the past year less helpful, less my companion, is a morbid view which you would smile at as almost a jest if you were rested and strong. For if it were suggested that the past year with its bitter sorrow had been less happy, less really rich with the greatest blessing of our lives, our love and our companionship, you would pass it by as an idle thought.

I am afraid I don't make my meaning very plain to you for I seem unable to understand that there can be any different point of view between us. I do not think there is, my darling, if you keep in view my rougher nature which can never even under your hand, be wrought into even a mean imitation of your beautiful life.

I can't go on today with other things I meant to write about. Your letter has stirred me so my slow indolent nature has seldom been aroused even by you. I can only write on to bless you for all you have been to me in the past, for giving me the only real interest, the only motive I have ever had to do something with my life that will make me in the least degree worthy of you and of your love.

Yours always,
Henry
[1902-07-14 Henry (StL) to Bertha (Rye Beach)]

If there was any misunderstanding, it was then resolved. Although Bertha wrote that she deserved a reproach from Henry, she was glad that such a reproach from the "*master*" of the house was not "*in writing*".

I did not deserve that beautiful and tender letter which I really think made me love you even better than before. You are too much of a gentleman, sweetheart. Do you know how you should have answered what you justly called that morbid letter. "You are my wife and the husband is the head of the wife and what is his will, she should not dispute or question but accept as generations of women have done before her. And you, if you complain, shall learn your place and that I am your master." That is the answer I deserved.

You think I would have been angry? Maybe so, but I will tell you a secret that some men know and some men do not. I think it is the gentlemen who do not. In the old days, a man captured his wife by main force and had the power of life and death over her. And the women were proud of it and in every woman there is a faint survival of that primitive savagery. And you need not think because I was born in a Christian land and of puritan antecedents, that I am any less of a savage than any other woman. Possibly I should not liked it in writing though; those early heathen did not know how to write.
[1902-07-19 Bertha (Rye Beach) to Henry (StL)]

Henry picked up on the "savage nature" of man in his next letter.

I think, dear, I have never before realized, much as I have cherished you, what a beautiful nature yours is. Yes, I confess to enough of the savage nature to wish to be supreme with my wife, to be strong enough to help her and wise enough to guide her but I wish that domination because she knows she can trust me to think for her and for her good, - and call it weakness or what you will, the only limit to my happiness will be in my failure to govern and protect and guide and cherish you up to the measure of your trustful love. That isn't the ideal you say your sex has created. Maybe it is not yours. Well, then, it is what I am and we must make the best of what we or, rather, you have. [1902-07-22 Henry (StL) to Bertha (Rye Beach)]

Bertha never wrote again about Roberta. Yet it seemed clear from her faith that Bertha believed that one day she would be reunited with Roberta in God's heavenly kingdom.

E. ALICE MARION SCOTT

Alice Marion Scott ("Aunt Alice") was born February 20, 1903. Bertha was very "matter of fact" about the birth of each of her children after Hugh, and Alice was no exception. Her diary entry was simply:

> *February 20, 1903*
> *Alice Marion Scott is born, Friday at nine o'clock in the evening. Dr. Robinson, and Miss Kellar (the nurse who was Hugh's night nurse when he had typhoid fever) in charge. In the morning, I had been to reading club at Edith Knox's and to see Lute.*
> [1893 Diary]

Alice Marion Scott

Alice was clearly a willful child, even at two years old. Henry wrote:

> *... my dear Alice completes your chapter of accidents. I think that young lady needs a little more competent care, don't you? When about all the thinking is done by the two-year-old child and none by her nurse, it is time to think over the situation.*
> [1905-11-10 Henry (Citizens Railway Company, Waco Tx) to Bertha]

Alice was an interesting child. Bertha included the following comment to Henry when Alice was around 4 years old. "*Alice is holding a funeral service in the back yard over a dead mouse as she explained to me 'with candles and a cross like a real funeral.'*" [1906-02-08(-) Bertha (64 Vandeventer Place, Stl) to Henry]

Bertha often included comments about all of the children when they were in Rye Beach during the summers. Bertha made the following comment about Alice in one letter: "*Alice is perfectly happy with her kittens and is rarely seen without them. She generally has one on each shoulder and looks as if she had a fur boa around her neck.*" [1906-09-24 (Sunday) Bertha (Rye Beach) to Henry (StL)]

On Alice's 4th birthday, Henry was on his way to the Panama Canal construction project with a business delegation. Bertha diligently wrote several letters to Henry shortly after he left on February 19, 1907 so that he would have some letters on his trip. The letters sometimes took a week or more to arrive.

> *Today is Alice's birthday and a most satisfactory one up to date. I gave her a music box from you which she said she liked the best of all her presents. She unfolded all her bundles with solemn but*

rapturous interest. The party which is to come off, to come off this afternoon, is the next interesting thing on the programme.

...

This morning, I wanted to send you a telegram just so that you should know all was right with your family before sailing but father thought it so foolish that I thought maybe you would think so too, so I did not send it. But when your telegram was brought to me about ten minutes ago, I was so glad to get it that I think perhaps I made a mistake not to send to you. It is too late now for allowing for the difference in time, your ship should sail in half an hour. In fact, you will have been about half an hour under way when Alice's party begins.

...

[the next day]
The party was a radiant success. I never saw anything sweeter than the hostess – her eyes were like two stars and they grew bigger & brighter as each child came in with a small offering. She played all the games and sang "London Bridge is Falling Down" and "Chickamy, Chickamy, Craney Crow" as if her life depended on it. Then came a very thrilling time. A picture of Buster Brown minus his necktie was put on a sheet and every child had a very pretty paper mask like those in the Sunday papers tied on and was then blindfolded. The solemn little group of Japanese ladies, Indians, Spaniards, etc., were perfectly lovely. Each was given a necktie to pin on Buster while blindfolded, the nearest to the spot to get the prize. Irene Wallace Goddard got the prize, Arthur Lionberger the second and George Curtis Eaton the booby prize.

Then I had a fish pond (prizes bought at the 10 cent store). They fished with an Alpine stock behind the sofa and Edith Whittemore and Nancy fastened the prizes on the hook. Edith and Nancy and George and even Hugh turned in and were most efficient helpers in running the party. Then we had supper with a cake with four candles and ice cream animals. Alice had asked for an ice cream lion and she got it but her cup was too full. "I cannot eat but just the head of my lion", she said, and remained perfectly good and watching the others but absolutely unable to eat. That the party was a success may I think be judged from the parting speech of "Sister Smiff", "Mrs. Scott, it was the nicest party I have ever went to in my whole life, nicer than my own birthday that my own mother gave."

...

I asked Alice for a message to send to you. Here it is. [illegible letters] and Ellen says she prays for Daddy every night. Also, "please tell Daddy to send me a picture postal card just for myself."
[1907-02-20 Bertha (64 Vandeventer Place) to Henry]

Henry must have anticipated the request for postcards and letters from his family and wrote to them while his ship was still in Charleston. Henry's postcards and letters were a *"great success"*.

Your letter was almost a greater surprise for I had not expected you to have time to write from Charleston and the postal cards were a great success. I do not know who liked them best but I am inclined to think Alice Marion Scott. Her blue eyes watched so anxiously as I read each name in turn and looked so satisfied when hers came.
[1907-02-24 Bertha (StL) to Henry (Steamer "Prinz Joachim", Cuba)]

While Henry was on his trip to Panama in 1907, Bertha included the following comment about Alice who was admired by other fathers, including John Shepley. *"Alice sends her love and declined an offer of adoption from John Shepley yesterday, because she loved her daddy too much."* [1907-03-03 Bertha (StL) To Henry – Havana Cuba]

When Bertha was away with her ailing father in Rye Beach during the summer of 1908, Bertha took particular delight in little Alice. *"Alice Scott is nicer than ever. I put her to bed tonight and I'd like to do it every night for anything funnier and sweeter never lived, specially in her nightgown.*" [1908-07-16 Bertha (Rye Beach) to Henry (StL)]

When Alice was seven years old, Henry wrote the following note to her when she was in Rye Beach.

Dear Alice,

There is a pansy on my desk that I think is about the most beautiful pansy I ever saw because you can really see a great many interesting things when you look at it a long time that you don't see at first. Now, as I look at it this morning, I at first see the pink and blue and yellow and purple petals with the black hearts to those colored leaves. Then I look again and I see the brown head of a little girl. I am not saying what her name is for that is a secret which you must guess. Then I see that the little girl is looking at me and smiling. Then a wonderful change comes to that pansy for the leaves seem to be the border of a picture frame and the center of the picture is the same little girl only this time I can see all of her in her white dress sitting in church and looking like a very good girl.

Well, I look again and I see the same little girl in a blue frock playing with Marmian and Vlad and also looking very smilingly and good but what is this I see? One of the leaves is crumpled up and when I look closely, I see the face of the same little girl but this time she is not smiling. Would you believe it, the little girl is frowning and scolding Ellen! And this time, I am bound to say she does not look very good. At least, I think it can hardly be the same girl I saw a minute ago sitting so quietly and goodly in church but it may be the same little girl for she may change like the pansy – suddenly. Once more before I go to my work, I take a sly peep at my pansy and lo! The same little girl is there but this time the colored leaves and twisted stems are the rocks and the sand and the waves at Rye Beach and the little girl is sitting playing in the sand with the water now and then stealing up ever so gently and caressing her fat legs. She is a very happy little girl now for she is laughing aloud at the waves and at their tricks.

I shall not tell you who this little girl is for you must guess. And mind only ten guesses and I will help you a little for it is not Catherine Stiedman and it is not our beloved Doll. Now you must look for another wonderful pansy like mine for if you find the right kind and look at it very closely, you may be able to see the house in St. Louis and someone in it who loves his little daughter dearly.

Dad
[Henry to Alice, 1910-07-29]

Many years later during the summer of 1922, the Scott's and many of their friends toured Europe. During Alice's visit to Florence, Bertha wrote to her about purchasing some pearls that Bertha wanted. But as Bertha mentioned, they were to be Alice's in time. The letter contains a long discussion about how to select pearls, perhaps some good, old fashioned, motherly advice?

I don't suppose you ever do read letters abroad but be very careful about doing it, and don't read this because it is about the pearls. I honestly don't know what to say about them. Italy is so famous for fakes that it seems almost incredible that these can be true and I do feel as if any pearls in these days should be passed on by expert jewelers whom you could trust. That is no reflection on Miss Edith's ability to know for even people who own most beautiful ones and consider themselves experts are taken in. Yet it seems almost too wonderful a chance to lose. Nancy and Tom think it a great risk and Nancy has the address of a second hand place in Paris which she thinks would be safer as they could be tested by experts there. On the other hand, you may know something about it through Miss Edith (about their reliability) that I do not.

My outside price in Italy, I think, would be a thousand dollars. My imitation string has seventy-eight pearls and is nineteen inches long and, if you saw one that approached that for a thousand, I should be inclined to take it, I think. Would you have the nerve to bite one? That is one of the most unfailing tests. On the whole, I am inclined to think, perhaps, Paris is safer but if for any reason the others are going to look at necklaces, you might as well go along. The pearls are to be yours in the end and you have a voice in the matter. I prefer the white ones and a shorter string with less gradation in the size of the pearls, a little smaller at the back but not much. My imitation string is really about what I like. Most people like them longer. Also, of course, if there was simply marvelous difference between a thousand & an eleven hundred, I should not stand on a hundred. So there you are!

And you will probably be glad if you have left Florence when this arrives. I would not sacrifice the hour of seeing Florence for pearls either. (I have re-read your letter & I have to leave it to your judgment.) O, I hope you love it as I loved it.
[1922-07-15(-) Bertha (Dinard, France) to Alice (Hotel Grande-Bretagne, Florence)]

Alice was married to Francis Linton Gross (1897-1979) and lived with "Uncle Pip" until her death on June 26, 1978.

Alice Scott Gross on her wedding day

F. PARENTING

Bertha was devoted to her children. Although she acknowledged in her diary that she didn't always comment about them, they were always near to her thoughts.

February 15, 1903
The heaviest snowstorm of the season. It is curious that I should have written so little about the children in going over the last few months. I suppose it was because I was trying to write up the extra things rather than our daily life. They have all three developed very much. I read aloud every evening between our tea and their dinner, the last book being Kingsley's "Heroes" which roused a wild enthusiasm in George who is only five. I was afraid it would prove too old for him. We have had a Bible lesson every Sunday, and they have gone from "Joshua to Daniel" and seem to remember it well. Nancy at seven and a half can read almost any story she likes but Hugh does not read so well, though he has improved immensely, both in lessons and what is more important, general health and vigor. I have lessons with George every day. He is learning to read in words of these letters.
[1893 Diary]

And Bertha knew of how much their children meant to Henry.

> *I walked down from Dr. Nicoll's church this morning with Brother Guy and he told me an Arabian proverb. "The music of the lute is sweet to him who hath not heard the laughter of his own children." He undertook to explain the point to me which was a little saddening. I wish you could have heard that music today, poor lonely old boy. Your letter this morning gave me the blues. When I think of you not well and alone and in bad weather, I feel I ought to be with you and that nothing ought to have kept me at home. I want to be with you so much, dearie.*
> [1898-11-25 (3 letters) Bertha (StL) to Henry (Waco)]

Although Bertha wrote about writing so little about the children, her letters to Henry are filled with their stories and adventures and the sound of their voices. Perhaps, because her children were life itself to Bertha and Henry, no volume of words in a letter could scarcely have hoped to capture it.

CHAPTER 16 – RELATIVES & FRIENDS

A. THE SHEPLEYS

The Scotts and the Shepleys have had a close relationship going back generations. In part, this may have been due to the fact that they were relatives. The familial relationship began with the Lionbergers who married into the Shepley family. John Robert Lionberger was Henry's uncle on his mother's side and his son, Isaac Henry Lionberger ("Zack"), married Mary Louise Shepley ("Lute") around 1886.

1. JOHN ROBERT LIONBERGER

John Robert Lionberger was Henry's first significant business connection in St. Louis. The Centennial History of Missouri wrote the following about John R. Lionberger.

> *In the annals of St. Louis the name of John R. Lionberger figures prominently, for as merchant and banker he left the impress of his individuality and ability upon the history of city and state. He was born in Luray, Page county, Virginia, August 20, 1829, and was in the sixty-fifth year of his age when death ended his labors on the 20th of May, 1894.*
>
> *His ancestral history was one of close connection with a most picturesque and romantic epoch in the development of the new world. The Lionberger ancestors were of French Huguenot stock and came to the new world with William Penn. The great-grandmother of John R. Lionberger was killed in the Indian massacre at Luray Cave and the history of that cave is closely interwoven with the history of the family. It was toward the close of the eighteenth century that representatives of the name established their home in Page county, Virginia, where Isaac Lionberger, father of John R. Lionberger, was born and reared. In early manhood he sought the opportunities of the growing west and became one of the pioneer residents of Missouri in 1836, establishing his home in Boonville, Cooper county. There he followed general mercantile pursuits and was widely recognized as a man of affairs in that section of the state for many years. His fellow townsmen, appreciative of his worth and ability, called him to the office of sheriff and he also served as judge of the county court, while he was also a local director of the old State Bank of Missouri, which at that period was the most important banking house west of the Mississippi. Isaac Lionberger wedded Miss Mary Tutt, daughter of Philip and Elizabeth (Ashby) Tutt, who were also natives of Virginia and were of Scotch-Irish descent. The grandfather in the maternal line was Captain John Ashby, while the grandfather in the paternal line was Lieutenant Charles Tutt, both of whom were soldiers of the Revolutionary war, entering the army as representatives of the Virginia line.*
>
> *...*

The year 1855 witnessed the arrival of Mr. Lionberger in St. Louis. He was well equipped and well trained for life's practical and responsible duties and the field of commerce offered in the growing Missouri metropolis was to him an enticing one. Here he established, under the firm style of Lionberger & Shields, a wholesale boot and shoe business and almost immediately became recognized as one of the alert, wide-awake and progressive merchants of the city. After two years he purchased his partner's interest and for a time carried on business alone but afterward was joined by Junior partners under the firm style of J. R. Lionberger & Company. The house won a wide reputation, enjoying an extensive trade during the middle portion of the nineteenth century, Mr. Lionberger remaining an active factor in its control until 1868, when he sold his interest and retired from the mercantile field, ... He entered banking circles in 1857 as one of the organizers of the old Southern Bank, of which he served as a director and as vice president. Upon the reorganization of the bank in 1864 under the national banking law, and the adoption of the name of the Third National Bank of St. Louis, Mr. Lionberger continued to be a large shareholder and in 1867 was elected to the presidency, thus serving until 1876, when he resigned for the purpose of making an extended trip abroad. Upon his return to America Mr. Lionberger was elected vice president of the bank and he also became one of the founders of the St. Louis Clearing House Association, serving on its first committee of management, of which he was, made chairman. He was likewise a member and director of the Chamber of Commerce and was a member of the building committee which had in charge the erection of the Merchants Exchange. ... [The Centennial History of Missouri]

John married Margaret Clarkson ("Aunt Mags") in 1851 who was the sister of Henry's mother and daughter of Dr. Henry Clarkson, Henry's grandfather, from whom Henry received his name.

John R. Lionberger

John and Aunt Mags had four children:
- Marion Scott Lionberger Davis (1852-1908) who married John David Davis;
- Isaac ("Zack") Henry (1854-1948) who married Mary Louise ("Lute") Shepley;
- Margaret (Maggie) Lionberger Potter (died in 1906) who married Henry S. Potter; and
- Mary Lionberger.

Since Bertha was a lifelong friend of Lute, Zack's wife, the Scott and Shepley/Lionberger families were closely knit together. So, when Bertha and Henry referred to a Shepley or Lionberger as a "cousin", this was not an idle claim.

Zack and Lute's children, many of whom were known to our generation, were:
- Margaret Lionberger ("Peg" or "Peggy") (1887-1963));

- John Shepley Lionberger ("Little Jack") (1889-1966);
- Louise Shepley (Lionberger) Amory (1894-?);
- Annie Shepley (Lionberger) Lehmann ("Nan Lionberger") (1894-1991);
- Mary Ruth Lionberger (1899-1987); and
- Arthur David Lionberger (1903-2008).

2. ZACK & MARY LOUISE SHEPLEY ("LUTE") LIONBERGER

Isaac Henry ("Zack") Lionberger was a complex and fascinating person.

"Lawyer and economic authority. Born in Booneville, Missouri, Isaac and his family moved to St. Louis in 1855. After attending Washington University in St. Louis for a while, he completed his education at Princeton University. He then entered upon the study of law. After graduating from the St. Louis Law School he was admitted to the bar and began practice in 1879. Left $500,000 by his father, who died in 1894, Lionberger lost all of the money in the next three years. He then decided to learn something about economics and learned so well that he made $1,000,000 through investments in stocks and bonds on $100,000 he had borrowed. For several years he was a lecturer in the St. Louis Law School. During the years 1896 and 1897 he served as assistant Attorney General of the United States by appointment of President Cleveland. In 1899 he was elected president of the St. Louis Bar Association. He was also a member of the board of directors of Washington University."

[from GENi & "Find a Grave", online databases]

Isaac & Lute Lionberger's house, at 3630 Grandel Square in Midtown St. Louis, Missouri. It is the last private residence designed by noted American architect Henry Hobson Richardson.

Zack (1854-1948) was born 5 years before Henry. As cousins, they would normally have known each other from childhood However, since the first grew up in St. Louis and the second in Fredericksburg, a very great distance at that time, it does not appear that they knew each other personally until Henry moved to St. Louis in 1881.

Bertha knew Lute Shepley Lionberger (1863-1910) for most of her childhood and may have gotten to know Zack before Henry did. Bertha frequently mentioned being with Lute and sometimes with Lute and Zack in her 1888-1889 diaries. In October 17, 1888, Bertha wrote a suggestive comment in her diary, possibly referring to Henry: "*Mr. Zack and his cousin come in.*"

After Bertha and Henry's engagement was announced, Bertha related to Henry in a letter some comments that Zack had made about matrimony and about Henry being "*a pretty good sort.*"

I had another large batch of letters ... Zack's amused me immensely, it was intensely characteristic, he gave me a great deal of good advice, told me that you were a pretty good sort, but not too expect

too much of you – "a man is only a man" adding sadly, "that is the rock Lute split upon" – but he finished the letter by remarking that he hoped the wedding would be soon, for matrimony was perhaps the least foolish experiment there was in all this foolish life of ours. Only a man and not an archangel!
[1892-03-12 Bertha to Henry]

In the summer of 1892, Henry was at the Country Club and played polo with the other men, including Zack who could be a madman on horseback.

The Country Club was not sufficiently alluring this time to keep me until Monday and, when Zack and I announced that we intended to return this evening, I found that the others had already concluded to come in so the entire party returned by the late train. I think Zack and I would have remained until tomorrow but that enthusiastic young man tried to show us yesterday that a novice could play polo better than those who had received some knowledge of the game by pretty constant practice. As a consequence, he was pretty well played out today and I don't think he will feel, for a few days, very kindly towards the Club.

I have never seen anyone as excited as Zack was from the moment the game began until he was compelled to stop. As wild as Jack gets, he is coolness itself compared with Zack who, beside riding like a madman, seemed to have very little control over himself when the ball was in his part of the field. And it is a mystery to me that he didn't break his neck which he came very near doing once or twice. First, he was thrown pretty badly but not hurt much and then, just before the game closed, he ran in under one of the men as he was striking and received the stroke intended for the ball, the natural result of which was a very bad cut in the head. I was frightened pretty badly when he rolled off his horse and his shirt reminded me of what John Bryan said of Jack when he met him after his fall in the park. John said he thought for a minute that Zack was wearing a red shirt. Zack's appearance reminded me of this and for a little while, I had all sorts of uncomfortable sensations but when we had mopped his cranium with cold water, I was very glad to see that he had been only slightly hurt. The young man was mighty quiet all day about polo and I think he was glad to leave the Club this afternoon.
[1892-08-29 Henry (StL) to Bertha]
(It was interesting that Henry referred to Zack as a "*young man*" when Zack was nearly 38 years old and Henry only 33.)

Bertha always enjoyed being with young children. When Lute and Zack's son, John Shepley Lionberger ("Little Jack"), was three years old, Bertha wrote to Henry of the occasion which provides a glimpse at the closeness of the families.

Yesterday afternoon, the rain subsided into a heavy Scotch mist. And Nancy[178] and I went for a two hours tramp up the road and in the evening, as it rained again, Nan and I took turns reading aloud and then Jack[179] taught me how to play piquet[180]. We do have a mighty cozy time, especially with the children. I really am afraid to write any more about the children for fear you will be bored, but I never feel really thoroughly content unless little Jack[181] is about.
[1892-08-28 (Sunday) Bertha (Rye Beach) to Henry (StL)]

---

[178] Both Nancy and Nan apparently refer to Anne Shepley who married Charles Nagel in 1895.

[179] John Foster Shepley ("Jack Jr"), (1858-1930) married on May 18, 1893 to Sarah Hitchcock (1870-1957)

[180] PIQUET: Rules: Piquet is played with a 32-card deck, normally referred to as a *piquet deck*. The deck is composed of all of the 7s through to 10s, the face cards, and the aces in each suit, and can be created by removing all 2–6 values from a 52-card poker deck. Each game consists of a *partie* of six deals (partie meaning match in French). The player scoring the most points wins (see the scoring section for further details).

[181] John Shepley Lionberger ("Little Jack") (1889-1966)

Bertha was very fond of all of the Shepleys but, sometimes, not as fond of their spouses. However, Bertha's unintended snubs appeared to have a "*salutary effect*", at least in Zack's case.

> *Lute and Zack came down about eight o'clock yesterday evening and spent the evening with me. I am a weak-minded inconsistent woman. I don't like Zack one bit and yet, when I am with him, invariably succumb to that perfect charm of manner. I think I owed the visit to the fact that he thought I snubbed him at the Monday Club. At least, he told me that he went home very mad because he thought I meant to snub him and Lute said "Yes, he came home mad as hops about it." I really did not mean to but it had a most salutary effect on him for he came the next morning before I was up and asked to see the baby and, as he failed then, he came again last night. He did not see the Buster, though, he was asleep.*
> [1894-03-10 (Saturday) Bertha (StL) to Henry (Fort Worth)]

One of the reasons why Bertha may have had her differences with Zack could be found in the blunt manner in which he expressed himself and, especially, in his views about a woman's place.

> *Zack says "American women have no training in business and the last person with whom a businessman thinks of discussing his business difficulties is his wife."*
> [1895(-) 20180528-3 Bertha to Henry]

After Zack proudly related a Post-Dispatch newspaper article written about him to the men at the club, Henry wryly commented:

> *Zack was in his most garrulous mood and was very entertaining. He explained three times an interview in the Post Dispatch which I may send you and which sets forth Isaac's great wisdom. He declined positively to be interviewed, etc., so the reporter manufactured an article. If he did, reporters are very good guessers for it was an excellent account of Isaac's opinion of Isaac. I don't think his disclaimer impressed the crowd and I simply wondered how much he paid for the article.*
> [1903(-) 20170802-2 Henry to Bertha]

In another letter, Henry wrote of some of Zack's business affairs in a not too favorable light.

> *Wednesday*
> *Dear Bert,*
>
> *I dined with your cousin, Isaac, and heard all the world reviled for crimes innumerable. He was in a sweet humor and, as usual when he is in that state, his hatred centered on his brother-in-law, John[182], whom he called names unfit for print.*
>
> *I ran across another of his [in]accurate statements a day or two ago. He told one of the men that he was a large stockholder in our National Company, that he did not think much of the stock, that he knew our eastern stock holders and that he had written all our Philadelphia people and could not get any offer for this stock. The facts are he is small stockholder, he does not know a single one of our eastern people (who, by the way, are rather unwisely, considering Wichita, trying to buy more stock), he has not offered his stock to them but on the contrary has told me he proposes to hold it for much higher prices, and he is a born liar and sometimes a very malicious one. He was very friendly with me last night and, as his prevarication was treated as one of his highly polished yarns, I feel no present resentment but rather regret that a fellow of such really brilliant possibilities should have brought himself down to the Will Chauvenet class, for he is really quite as dangerous and undependable as Will.*
> [20180729-7 Henry to Bertha]

---

[182] John D. Davis who married Marion Scott Lionberger (1852-1908), Zack's sister.

Notwithstanding Henry's comments in the previous letter, Zack was a very successful St. Louis businessman and highly regarded. Perhaps Henry's opinion could be chalked up to Henry's unreasonably high standards?

In 1921 Zack Lionberger gave an address at his alma mater, Princeton, entitled "The College Man". The following are some excerpts from this address.

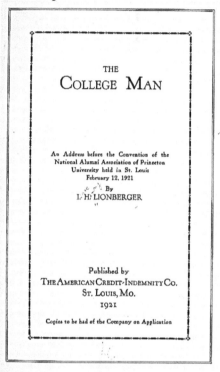

... we have the average schoolboy, who has somehow got it into his head that learning can be poured into him as we pour milk into a pitcher...

[The College Man] does not know so much as to offend, nor so little as to distress us. We trust him and like to associate with him. He can understand us and we him. If he is not wise, he is usually modest, for he is intelligent enough to know that he may also be ignorant.

[President] Wilson ... claimed for us the spiritual leadership of the world but he did not tell us on what ground he based his claim, nor to what goal we should lead the world. Peace, the right of self-determination, righteousness, are words, high-sounding perhaps but still mere words ... Such vague notions, eloquently expressed, captured our fancies and filled us with a comfortable self-complacency, for they required no thinking ...

Our system is wrong. It rests upon the notion that boys may be forced to learn. Enlightenment comes by loving.

These amazing historical events were the immediate results of the Greek method of instruction. It taught not what to think but how to think. It was at once interesting and stimulating, and none who felt it could resist its fascination.

When we graduate, we do not end but commence that real education which ends only with life.

If we ask why [President Lincoln] was so great, men will tell you he was humble-minded and wished to understand. To implant such a wish should be the object of a university.
[Isaac Henry Lionberger, "The College Man", 1921]

Clearly by the time of this speech in 1921, Zack acquired the wisdom to say that the past great historical events *"were the immediate results of the Greek method of instruction. It taught not what to think but how to think."* Well said.

3. THE DAVISES

In addition to their long friendships with Bertha and Henry, the Davises and the Scotts were related through the marriage of John David Davis (sometimes "Jack") (1851-1917) to Marion Scott Lionberger Davis (1858-1908) who was John R. Lionberger's daughter.

a. John David & Marion Davis

JOHN D. DAVIS.
Member of the Committee of Two Hundred and a director of the Exposition. Served on the Foreign Relations, Mines and Mining, and Reception and Entertainment Committees.

Due to their close family ties, Henry often had news about the Lionbergers and their mutual friends. Henry recounted to Bertha one interesting account was of an "adventure at sea" when the Lionbergers and friends were in Islesboro Maine[183] in the summer of 1892.

> *I heard a piece of news last night which will interest you. Your friend Miss Nancy and the other girls at Islesboro came within very little of being shipwrecked last week. Miss Nan, Marion Davis, Mary and I believe, Miss Sarah[184], went out for an hour's sail, were caught in a storm and were tossed about for <u>twelve</u> hours before they reached the shore which they finally did reach but in a most exhausted condition. Maggie Potter had a letter from Mary describing their adventure and it was evidently a pretty alarming one and a most trying experience to Mr. Lionberger and John Davis who were left at the hotel and who, when the storm came up before the party returned, waited for hours on the beach until they and the others at the hotel had concluded that the whole party had been lost. I don't like to make merry over so serious an affair but ye Gods! Think of being in a wreck with Marion Davis!!!!!!!!!!!!!!!!!!!!!!!!!!!!!!!!!!!!!!!*

[1892-08-18 (Thursday) Henry (StL) to Bertha (Farragut House)]

---

[183] Near Camden ME.

[184] Anne ("Nan") Shepley, Marion Davis (John David Davis' wife), Mary Shepley Lionberger (Isaac Lionberger's wife), and Sarah Hitchcock.

While Bertha was interested in Henry's details of the ladies' harrowing sail, she was not amused by Henry's lack of respect for cousin Marion Davis.

> *I was very much interested to hear of Nan and Mary's narrow escape and I am more anxious than ever to see Nan and get an account at first hand. I am amazed at the disrespect with which you speak of your cousin Marion. She is not a person to be treated with disrespect and in fact is, I believe, the person in your family of whom I stand most in awe.*
> [1892-08-22 (Sunday) Bertha (Farragut House) to Henry (StL)]

Henry was very close to Marion and John Davis and was very moved by Marion's death in 1908 at the age of 56. He was affected not only by the loss of a dear friend but also the impact that her death had on John. Henry wrote to Bertha regarding John: "*John was there standing his trouble like a man but looking worn and old.*"

> *I went to see Mary[185] last night and found her with Lion & Julie[186]. John was there standing his trouble like a man but looking worn and old. Mary looked better than I had expected to find her. She is leaving for Dublin [NH] tomorrow. John has no plans as yet and I think they all hold that his work is the best thing for him just now. When I can brace up a bit, I shall try to get him off in the country when he will go, for it seems that I ought to be able to help him a little.*
>
> *Henry Potter[187] tells me he did not return in time for the funeral. He had been to New Orleans and was on his way home on one of the river boats and could not get here until last night.*
>
> *The end came very suddenly for Marion. She and John had been talking Friday evening and John, seeing that she was very weak, said he would leave her and they would finish their talk in the morning. She told him that would do provided she lasted until morning which he considered was merely evidence of depression due to weakness. John went down to Mary's - this was about eight o'clock and he had hardly sat down when the telephone rang and the man told him to come home immediately, Mrs. Davis was dying. John ran all the way to the house but Marion was dead when he reached her. She had had a hemorrhage and was evidently too feeble to stand any strain and the nurse told John she passed away without the slightest pain or struggle. Her death must have been even more sudden than Gordon's[188] but that was a blessing, although it must have been a hideous shock to John and it seems bitter that, after all his faithful watching, he was not with her at the last. These wrenches are among the unfathomable mysteries of life and are without meaning or help except that we who have so much to live and strive for should never permit a bitter thought or gloomy moment. When I think of the blackness of John's life, I am almost inclined to contempt of my cowardly indulgence because my head happens to work rustily for a day or two.*
> [1908-06-26 Henry (StL) to Bertha (Rye Beach)]

To stand your trouble like a man may have been a mantra for Henry but it was a difficult one to follow. A short time later, when Henry was having dinner with John Davis at his house and the loss Marion was very present to everyone, Henry was moved to the point where, after he returned home, he wrote, "*I behaved like a child.*"

> *I came in rather tired and sad from dinner with John. He and I played golf together and he asked me to come in and dine with him at the house. Of course, I couldn't refuse but, though Lion[189] was there too, it was hard. When I went in, I could not rid myself of the idea that I should see Marion. She had so filled every part of that house with her strong personality that I could remember, really*

---

[185] Probably Mary Lionberger, Zack & Marion's sister.
[186] Julie M. Vietor who was married to John Lionberger Davis ("Lion") (1878 – 1973), John Davis Davis' son.
[187] Maggie Lionberger's husband.
[188] Gordon Knox died in March 11, 1907 at the end of the business trip to the Panama Canal (see Chapter 17).
[189] i.e. John's son, John Lionberger Davis.

recall, her at every turn, her call of greeting to the hall, the way she always met me in the library, how she ran her little dinners. All came back so vividly that I almost turned to find her at times. And when I left John alone in that desolate house, I came over to my own lonely home and behaved like a child.
[20171205-1 (1908) Henry to Bertha]

b. John Lionberger Davis ("Lion") & Julie M. Vietor

"Lion", John Lionberger Davis, was Marion and John D. Davis' only child, born October 2, 1878 and died April 13, 1973. The website, Find A Grave, provided this commentary on his life.

Civic leader. Mr. Davis retired in 1947 as chairman of the board of the old Security National Bank Savings and Trust Company. He also had interests in realty companies and was the chairman of many St. Louis and Missouri civic organizations and governmental reform committees. He made many gifts of art treasures to the St. Louis City Art Museum and the Museum of Science and Natural History as well as to museums in New York, New Jersey, Vassar College, Princeton and Syracuse Universities.

In 1959 he took part in dedication ceremonies for Davis Hall at the Museum of Science and Natural History. Mr. Davis donated $100,000 for the hall as a memorial to his father and grandfather, John David Davis and John Robert Lionberger. A well-known art collector, he gave a series of art works to the City Art Museum, including 52 art objects in 1956 and 70 art objects in 1957. He gave $50,000 for new galleries at the museum. He was chairman of the St. Louis Regional Planning Commission, the St. Louis chapter of the American Red Cross and the Community Council.

Mr. Davis was a friend of President Frank Delano Roosevelt. Mr. Roosevelt stayed at the Davis home during visit to St. Louis. Mr. Davis and Mr. Roosevelt met while they were trustees for Vassar College. Mr. Davis supported Roosevelt in his election campaigns and was reported in 1940 to have turned down an offer of a position in the Roosevelt cabinet.
[Find A Grave]

Lion married Julie M. Vietor on November 1, 1906, just two years before Lion's mother, Marion, died. Of the future "*Mrs. Lion*", Henry wrote: "*I saw Lion at the club and he was very nice but somewhat boastful. He is a good fellow though handicapped with rather bad manners which I hope the future Mrs. Lion will lick into shape.*" [1900(-) 20180728-1 Henry to Bertha]

Henry commented on Lion's bride in a letter to Bertha in 1906. Henry's comments revealed not only some of his views about Lion who needed to pass through his "*adolescent stage*" but also how Marion, Lion's mother, would likely have viewed the union.

I have not written you about Lion because they did not tell me of it but I shall write and congratulate him. It will be hard for Marion at first but she will soon get much pleasure from the daughter if she is a nice girl and I hear she is all that although not one of the four hundred or in fact a society young woman. This will be a disappointment to Marion at first but ultimately it will be for better for her as well as for Lion. I hope she is a strong minded person who will know when to assert herself for she will have need to if she would pass through Lion's adolescent stage with comfort.
[1906-08-(-) 20180729-3 Henry to Bertha]

While Henry very much liked Lion's father, John, he often found himself exasperated with Lion.

I dined with Henry Potter today. John and Lion were there and, really, L is a very opinionated, exasperating young man. I think he is really a nice boy but if either of my boys ever speaks to me as he spoke to his father today, I shall take a strap to them if they are fifty and feel that I am but doing my Christian duty to them!
[1908-07-13 Henry (StL) to Bertha (Rye Beach)]

c. Horatio Nelson Davis Jr. ("Ray")

Henry was also very close friends with John D. Davis's brother Horatio ("Ray") Nelson Davis Jr. (1853 - 1915). Henry liked Ray but could readily discern Ray's personal qualities which were trying to others.

> *Seriously, I forgave Ray for loitering when my eye fell on some of this choice and high priced stationary, which charity institutions, heavily in debt, are always lavishly supplied with, and realized that I could write you here and give him opportunity to say anew, for the millionth time, all his instructions to the engineer, the laundress, head nurse and each of the orderlies or other help who may be so unfortunate as to run into him. When Ray gets to heaven, if he arrives at all, I am perfectly sure he is going to take St. Peter aside, the moment he is let in, and tell him they ought to get things "organized" and I see the Rock of the church flying about breathlessly getting things in better shape, urged on by the new arrivals war cry "get busy".*
> [1908-07-19 (Sunday) Henry (StL) to Bertha (Rye Beach)]

4. THE HITCHCOCKS

The Hitchcocks were related to the Scotts by way of the marriage of Sarah Hitchcock (1870-1957) to John Foster ("Jack") Shepley (1858-1930). (Jack Shepley was the brother of Lute Shepley Lionberger who was married to Zack Lionberger, Henry's cousin.)

Ethan Allen Hitchcock

Sarah Hitchcock's father, Ethan Allen Hitchcock (1835-1909), came from an illustrious family and had a notable career.

> *Ethan Allen Hitchcock was born on September 19, 1835, in Mobile, Alabama, the son of Henry Hitchcock (1791 - 1839), a justice on the Alabama Supreme Court, and Anne Erwin Hitchcock. He was the brother of Henry Hitchcock, nephew of Major General Ethan Allen Hitchcock, grandson of Judge Samuel Hitchcock, and great-grandson of Ethan Allen. He was in mercantile business at Saint Louis, Missouri, 1855–60, then went to China to enter a commission house, of which firm he*

became a partner in 1866. He was married to Margaret Dwight Collier ("Maggie") on March 20, 1869. Ethan and Margaret Hitchcock had three daughters, Sarah, Anne and Margaret Hitchcock.
[Wikipedia]

Ethan married Margaret ("Maggie") Dwight Collier Hitchcock (1840-1912). Their children were:
- Sarah Hitchcock Shepley (1870-1957)
- Anne Erwin Hitchcock Sims (1875-1960)
- Margaret Dwight Hitchcock ("Wee Margaret") (1878-1926)

In 1906, Henry made a rare comment about Ethan and Maggie regarding their neglect of their daughter, Sarah, with whom Bertha and Henry were very close. Henry makes his feelings about her parents and Ethan's political aspirations abundantly clear.

> *I read your comment of Sarah's family's cool neglect of her with hot indignation. A stupid man raised above his merits or abilities is a very poor guide in a household. I am not surprised with all the honors that have come to Ethan that his head is turned for he was ever a dull fellow but that public life should make Mrs. Maggie forget the care which even animals are wont to give their offspring is only the be accounted for in the rather silly idea, if it be not true, that she deems her life also dedicated to her country's service. They are a badly spoiled lot as I see it which is the inevitable result when accident dumps little people into the places which are made for and which fit snug those of greater statue.*
> [1906(-) 20180714-1 Henry to Bertha]

Undoubtedly, Henry would never have openly said what he wrote (above) about Ethan Allen Hitchcock and his wife Maggie: *"They are a badly spoiled lot as I see it which is the inevitable result when accident dumps little people into the places which are made for and which fit snug those of greater statue."*

5. JOHN RUTLEDGE SHEPLEY & MARY AUGUSTA (CLAPP) SHEPLEY

Lute Shepley Lionberger was the daughter of John Rutledge Shepley (1817-1884) and Mary Augusta (Clapp) Shepley (1831-1908). While Lute and Zack's marriage provided "kinship" between the Shepleys and the Scotts, the Shepley family members were already very close with both Bertha and Henry even before this marriage. John and Mary Shepley had the following children.
- Julia Shepley Coolidge (1856-1935),
- John Foster ("Jack") Shepley (1858-1930),
- George Foster Shepley (1860-1903),
- Mary Louise Shepley ("Lute") Lionberger (1863-1910), and
- Anne Shepley ("Nan") Nagel (1866-1951).

Brig. Gen. George Foster Shepley

The name, Foster, apparently comes from John Rutledge Shepley's brother, Brigadier General George Foster Shepley (1819 – 1878) who was an officer in the Union Army during the American Civil War, military governor of Louisiana and a United States Circuit Judge of the United States Circuit Courts for the First Circuit.

6. JOHN FOSTER ("JACK" or "JACK Jr."[190]) SHEPLEY AND SARAH HITCHCOCK

Jack Shepley (1858-1930) married Sarah Hitchcock (1870-1957) on May 18, 1893, three months after Bertha and Henry were married. Jack was an attorney and worked for firm of Lionberger & Shepley until 1900 when he went to work for the old Union Trust Co which was consolidated with the St. Louis Trust Co. in 1903 to become the St. Louis Union Trust Co. Sarah and Jack lived at 60 Vandeventer Place, next door to 64 Vandeventer Place, Bertha and Henry's home for over 10 years.

Bertha was jealous over Sarah Hitchcock's union with Jack Shepley. This was not due to any jealously over Jack but due to the fact that Sarah would be close to Jack's sister, Nan Shepley. Bertha had always been particularly close to Nan Shepley dating back to when they both were attending the Miss Porter School.

> *I suppose you would be slightly astonished to learn that my first feeling when I heard about Jack and Sarah was one of overpowering jealousy, which had nothing to do with Jack however. Possibly you did not need to be assured of that. But Nan, think how near Jack's wife will be to Nan. O yes, I know, I ought to be very much ashamed of such an unworthy feeling and I am, and I give you leave to lecture just as much as you please, but the truth remains the same and I feel rather relieved that I have confessed it.*

[1892-08-05 (Friday) (20170712) Bertha (Rye Beach) to Henry (StL)]

Henry wrote that he did not understand Bertha's jealousy over Jack's marriage to Sarah. On the contrary, the groundwork for the marriage seemed to have been prepared by Jack's cousin, "Mrs. Dexter", i.e. Anne

---

[190] It may be surmised that Jack Shepley was called "Jack Jr." since Jack's father was also named John.

Hathaway (Shepley) Tiffany[191] (1850-1922), who was married to Dexter Pardon Tiffany (1846-1921). (Anne was 8 years older than Jack and obviously had familial motivations for her interest in the marriage.)

Jack Shepley went direct to Marion [MA] from here but the Islesboro [ME] trip had undoubtedly been arranged some time back for I heard Tiffany[192] reminding Jack of a promise made early in the spring to visit them, so Mrs. Dexter has no doubt been discussing ways and means to bring Jack and Miss Sarah together for some time. I did not quite understand your feeling of jealousy on account of the possible happy working out of this affair, for Jack is not the only member of the Shepley family who will have committed matrimony and possibly Mrs. Jack will no more interfere with that truly heavenly friendship than Mrs. George[193] of the respective husbands of Miss Nan's older sisters. My "logical mind" does not comprehend the cause of your jealousy. Now if you were moved by the possibility which is a reasonable one that Jack will be married <u>months</u> before we are, I accept as natural your unhappy thoughts and do herewith extend my most profound sympathy.

[1892-08-09PM (Tuesday) Henry (StL) to Bertha (Farragut House, Rye Beach)]

Bertha was annoyed that Henry could not understand her jealous feelings about Sarah (or "Mrs. Jack") and wrote him back to set him straight. Specifically, Mrs. George Shepley (i.e. Julia Richardson "Lula" Shepley), did not live in St. Louis and men *"do not come into a girl's life in at all the same way."*

Speaking of other girls, reminds me of the remark you made in your Tuesday letter about not understanding why I should be more jealous of Mrs. Jack than of Mrs. George or of Zack or Charles. Because, my dear, Mrs. George does not live in St. Louis and the other two are men and do not come into a girl's life in at all the same way. And you call vanity "distinctly a woman's failing" and then boast of your logical mind when you cannot even see so simple a thing as that! Nor do I think that it at all logically follows that they (Jack and Sarah) will be married so much sooner than you. For even if they are definitely engaged and I don't think they are yet, they evidently do not intend to announce it before fall and that can hardly mean a wedding until after Christmas.

[1892-08-13 (Friday 1892-08-12) Bertha (Rye Beach) to Henry (StL)]

Bertha and Henry traded stories about Jack Shepley in their letters. Henry wrote the following comments about Jack's virtues (and faults) in his letters to Bertha.

What you say of Shepley is quite true for, without in the least intending to be so, he is very thoughtless of others and he has less self-control than any man I have ever known. He has a splendid mind – he is much stronger intellectually than you think, then he has all the fine qualities that make up a first class man, but one – and that is the power to concentrate his thought and energies, and he is less able to apply himself in this way than many less worthy and much less attractive men than he is. I think, however, if Jack married, his restlessness would give way to the demand which the responsibility for another's happiness would make of him and I would greatly prefer seeing a woman I liked marry a man like Jack than the other man. For his (Jack's) faults, wearing and taxing to others as they are, could be pardoned and dealt with. The fault of the other man is unpardonable and knows no remedy.

[1892-08-05 Henry (StL) to Bertha (Farragut House, Rye Beach)]

I am glad Jack's affairs seem to promising and I sincerely hope that Miss Sarah and he will have solved their difficulties before he returns, for it will be a great thing for him if [he] can come home

---

[191] Anne Hathaway (Shepley) Tiffany (1850-1922), was the daughter of Brig. Gen. George F. Shepley, the brother of John Rutledge Shepley. John Rutledge Shepley was the father of Jack and Nan, mentioned above, as well as George Foster Shepley Jr., Mary Louise Shepley Lionberger, and Julia Shepley Coolidge.

[192] Dexter Pardon Tiffany, i.e. Anne Shepley's husband. (Dexter Pardon Tiffany was not a "Jr." since his father's name was Pardon Dexter Tiffany.)

[193] Julia Hayden ("Lula") Richardson (1867-1965) ("Mrs. George") married George Foster Shepley (1860-1903) in 1886.

well rid of a trouble which has evidently made him wretchedly dissatisfied with himself and the rest of the world for some time past. Don't think for a moment that Jack's movements are a secret here. I heard Zack telling Charlie Hodgman yesterday all the particulars of Jack's visit from the number of new flannel suits Jack purchased in New York to make his appearance in at Marion, to the minutest speculations of the family as to the prospect of an engagement. Nice man that to tell secrets to but I have heard that he is no worse than some other married men we know.
[1892-08-29 (Monday) Henry (StL) to Bertha (Farragut House)]

Bertha wrote the following about 8 months before Jack married Sarah when Bertha went to visit the Shepleys and the Hitchcocks in Marion Massachusetts. Jack was at the Hitchcock residence at the time and Sarah had *"a mighty proprietary air..."*

We have had an uncommonly stormy time but yesterday Nan and I got desperate and drove over to the village to see the Hitchcocks where we found Jack comfortably sconced in the sofa with Sarah bullying him. There is a mighty proprietary air about that young woman. In fact, as Lute said when she and I were discussing the matter this morning, "If it were any girl I didn't want, I'd be sure it was so."
[1892-08-28 (Sunday) Bertha (Rye Beach) to Henry (StL)]

During this time (i.e. August 1892), Jack (AKA "Jack Jr.") wanted to write Bertha a poem of congratulations on her engagement but apparently struggled with the composition and may not have liked the final result which he gave to Bertha.

Nan told me yesterday that Jack Jr. had used up a quire[194] and a half of note paper trying to write me a note of congratulations, so I chaffed him about it in the evening and he went on about his writing ability until he asked me what I would take to surrender that poem of his and I told him I was not waiting to get home to show it to you. "You show it to Henry, you just dare, all right for you. I'll take it out on Henry. I'm stronger than he is and I'll lick him, now!" So, you would better get up your muscle, son.
[1892-08-28 (Sunday) Bertha (Rye Beach) to Henry (StL)]

Henry, of course, heard of the threat made against him by Jack. Although Henry didn't take the threat particularly seriously, it was also clear that Henry didn't want a rumble with Jack.

I am glad Jack's affairs are flourishing and I know of no better evidence of his being in an exalted frame of mind than is shown in his threat which occurs to me is a somewhat reckless and enthusiastic venture to retaliate on me in the event of your showing me that poem. Please advise the young man through his sisters that, as I should dislike exceedingly to see one in his very hopeful state disappointed in a matter that he is so certain of, he might possibly be acting with wisdom if he conferred with some of the members of the Country Club before proceeding to revenge himself on the theory that he is the strongest. Zack or Al Shapleigh might give him some interesting information on this subject and I send Jack this message by his sisters that they may counsel him not to endanger his chances of success in another direction by undulating(?) two doubtful contracts at the same time. Although for Miss Sarah's sake, I should try to correct Jack's erroneous impression in this particular as gently as possible.
[1892-09-02 (Thursday 1892-09-01) Henry (StL) to Bertha (Farragut House)]

---

[194] Quire (plural quires): 1. One-twentieth of a ream of paper; a collection of twenty-four or twenty-five sheets of paper of the same size and quality, unfolded or having a single fold. 2. (bookbinding) A set of leaves which are stitched together, originally a set of four pieces of paper (eight leaves, sixteen pages). This is most often a single signature (i.e. group of four), but may be several nested signatures. 3. A book, poem, or pamphlet.

In another letter, Henry joked about the threatened brawl with Jack wondering if he would have to leave town before Jack returned.

> *Another incident today will, I think, interest you, for I am almost ready now to leave town when Jack Shepley returns because of a panic I took on hearing a story Sandford told this evening of Jack's muscular powers. Will[195] and I had supper together at the Club and I happened to mention Jack and then I said "Chief, is Jack stronger than the average man? I want to know because I may have to lick him or leave town one of these days, and I am thinking of the matter to determine which I can do most conveniently." He replied "You can do as you please, but if I were deciding for myself, I should leave town. I threw a boot at Shepley once and I am sorry, even now, that I was so hasty in resenting my wrongs. It has made me, this slight mistake, I mean, a much more peaceable and prudent man." I naturally wanted full particulars so he told me it was a great many years ago when the trips to Colorado were first made and, one rainy day, after he, Jack and A.Q. Kennett had been cooped up in the tent by bad weather for nearly a week during the latter part of which time no one of the three was on speaking terms with the others and each of the three was spoiling for a row, Jack said something unpleasant to Sandford who replied with his boot taking effect on Jack's eye. A row was the immediate result and Sandford continued his story by saying "I began to get the worst of it so, as we struggled past Kennett, I managed to give him a kick which from that time made the fight a three handed one but, notwithstanding that, Kennett thought Jack the one who had made him howl with pain and paid strict attention to him. I was a total wreck for a week." The Chief did himself proud in his account of the fight, for ridiculous as it may seem, it was no sham battle. And I haven't laughed so in a long time.*
> [20190929-2 (1892-09-(-) (Sunday) Henry (StL) to Bertha (Rye Beach)]

Bertha was glad that Henry withdrew from the challenge and did not read to Henry the poem that Jack had written.

> *Speaking of prize fights, I was glad to hear you withdraw your challenge. I had not sent it owing to the fact that I had not written to Nan in the interval between those letters. And as I have told you before, I think the buzz saw theory apples to Jack Shepley more than to most men.*
> [1892-09-09 (Thursday) Bertha (Rye Beach) to Henry (StL)]

Four months prior to Jack's wedding to Sarah, Henry was concerned about the happy couple.

> *I forgot to tell you yesterday that Jack was not at the whist meeting, pleading a bad cold as an excuse for not going and the cold or something else is the cause of another of his blue fits for I have seen him once or twice lately and he is altogether the most crushed and humble minded individual I have ever encountered. Miss Sarah also puzzles me not a little. I had quite a long talk with her last night – the others were playing and she had been showing me the new house and she suddenly asked after Will Stribling and then added that it seemed impossible to her some time ago that people could bear a trouble like that[196] but "Mr. Scott, I believe now that people adjust themselves to everything and if many hard things come to them, they grow not to mind after a little time." This does not sound like the reflections of a very happy person, does it dear? And her manner was so sad that I really felt very sorry for her. You may imagine that I am somewhat correct in my conclusions that everything is not moving smoothly with Miss S. when I add that more than one of her friends have spoken of her as seeming so depressed and tired all the time. I should like to have your diagnosis of the case, dear, for I admit I can't make it out.*
> [1893-01-23 (Sunday) Henry (StL) to Bertha (Stancote, Newton Centre)]

---

[195] Probably William Clarkson Stribling (1853-1929).

[196] William Clarkson Stribling (1853-1929) lost his wife, Mary Martha McKittrick ("Mattie") on November 5,1892 at age 26, two and ½ months before this letter. She left two young children. See below, E.4.

Two days after the preceding letter, Bertha voiced her concern about Sarah and Jack. Bertha's mother speculated that religion could be the issue but Bertha thought that it was probably Jack's lack of business prospects.

> *About John and Sarah, I am still more puzzled. Mother suggested a solution this morning, which seems possible, though not probable, as she herself said. She said "I cannot conceive of any objection unless it is religion. Maggie Hitchcock[197] belongs to the most rigid school of Presbyterians and she has brought Sarah up in the same views and, you know yourself, how almost morbidly religious Sarah is. It is just possible she may not think it right to marry a man, who is an out and out unbeliever." I can very readily believe that Mrs. Hitchcock would apply "Be ye not unequally yoked with unbelievers"[198] to just such a case as poor Jack's but I doubt if Sarah would go so far. Still, there is a morbid strain in Sarah which you have never probably come in contact with. I am more inclined to think it is John's health or business (lack of business, I should say) that is in the way, however.*
> [1893-01-25 (Thursday) Bertha (Stancote, MA) to Henry (StL)]

Regardless of Bertha and Henry's concerns, Jack and Sarah were married on April 12, 1893, and remained happily married throughout their lives. Sarah and Jack had three children: Margaret (?), John Rutledge (1894-1990) and Ethan Allen Hitchcock ("Ethan") Shepley (1896-1975). As discussed in Chapter 15, John and Ethan Shepley were good friends of Hugh and George Scott.

Ethan Shepley (1896-1975) was known to my generation in particular because of his political race as a Republican for Missouri Governor in 1964. That Ethan lost that race should not poorly reflect upon his good standing since, in 1964, Lyndon Johnson and Democrats won landslide victories across the country. Ethan was the chancellor of Washington University, served as a director of Anheuser-Busch, Inc., and Mallinckrodt, Inc.

7. GEORGE FOSTER SHEPLEY & JULIA HAYDEN RICHARDSON

George Foster Shepley (1860-1903) and Julia ("Lula") Hayden Richardson (1867-1965) were married on June 30, 1886. George had graduated from MIT in 1882, and had started to work for Henry Hobson Richardson, who was Lula's father and the architect of Zack & Lute Shepley Lionberger's house at 3630 Grandel Square in St. Louis. In June 1886, George joined with Charles Allerton Coolidge[199] (1858-1936) and Charles H. Rutan (1851-1914) to form Shepley, Rutan and Coolidge, an architecture firm based in Boston.

Bertha spoke of Lula and George Shepley's children in the following letter to Henry in 1893 which not only paints a beautiful picture of Lula and George but also Bertha's great enjoyment of children, an *"enjoyment a man is incapable of appreciating."*

> *I have just come back from Lula's and I did have the nicest time! She has the dearest children, Harry and Haydie (Julia Hayden) and Pet (Violet) and George Foster Jr. who is only three months old.[200] Harry, the oldest, is three months older than Margaret Lionberger ["Peg"] so you can see at what cunning ages they are. Lula and I heard perfect shrieks of delight as we came up the stairs and we went straight to the nursery where were three radiant individuals, dripping wet. "We washed our dollies' clothes, we washed all the dollies' clothes." And a most indignant individual in the shape of the nurse: "Ah, Mrs. Shepley, look at them! And I dressed them all nice and clean for Miss Drake and only was out of the room fifteen minutes!" It was the funniest picture.*

---

[197] i.e. Sarah's mother, Margaret Dwight Collier Hitchcock
[198] 2 Corinthians 6:14
[199] Charles Allerton Coolidge was George Shepley's brother in law (George's sister, Julia Shepley Coolidge, was Charles' wife).
[200] From the available records, George, the oldest, was 6 years, then Haydie and Violet ("Pet"), then George Jr. – 3 months.

Well, we got our things off and then I left Lula or rather she left me to attend to some household duties which I proceeded to make friends which did not take long with Harry and Haydie but Pet was shyer. I soon discovered that she was the unlucky one. Harry showed me the whole treasure of toys and, of every broken one, it was "this is Pet's." Then we began to play ball. I am afraid we romped, my dear, but I have not enjoyed anything so much in ages. Harry & Haydie danced and pranced and pitched the ball and shrieked with delight when Pet suddenly became fired with an ambition to join and pitched her contribution with might and main – a small china dog! Of course, the result was inevitable. Open door, enter George Shepley, a study of myself in the glass afterwards convinced me, my dear, that crazy Peg was a beauty compared with me. My hair was all coming down and I was scuttling over the floor like two forty[201] on a shell. I almost slid into his arms and we both laughed.

My dear, nobody knows what George Shepley is until they have seen him with his children. Pet flew to him with the broken dog for consolation and as I watched the sweetness in his face while he talked to her, I understood suddenly why Nan thinks there is no one like him. It is a revelation. We went on with the game and then the two little girls went off with him while Harry elected to come with me.

…
O, I must tell you a story George Hitchcock had told [of] George Shepley of his Christmas vacation. It seems George went to call on Sarah "at the sunset hour", says George, "the glowing, sweetest time of the day", found Sarah in parlor. Presently Mrs. Hitchcock's voice from the head of the stairs, "John!" No answer. "John!" No answer. In a surprised why who else can it be at this hour sort of tone, "Why John, isn't that you?" George meekly, "No, Aunt Maggie, it's I." Sarah (in an airy off hand way, but bright pink in countenance) "rather hard to be taken for a black man isn't it?" And George says that such is his devotion to the cause that he restrained his emotions and didn't even wink. Isn't that delicious and suspicious?

But I believe the best time I had was this morning when Lula entrusted that soft bundle of a George Foster Jr. to my charge and I had him all to myself for a while and he was as good as a kitten and did not even make any effort to get back to her when she came for him. That was an enjoyment a man is incapable of appreciating.
[1893-01-18 Bertha (Newton MA) to Henry (StL)]

8. ANNE ("NAN") SHEPLEY NAGEL AND CHARLES NAGEL
It may be easily surmised from the number of times that Bertha wrote of her that Nan was one of Bertha's closest lifelong friends.

Nan Shepley (1866-1951) married Charles Nagel (1849-1940) on May 1, 1895. Charles was widowed from Fannie Brandeis, his first wife, whom Charles had married in 1876 in Louisville KY. [See 20180321-3 (1903-07-17-)] Charles and Fannie had one daughter, Hildegard Nagel. Nan and Charles had the following children: Mary S (1896), Edith, Charles (1899) and Anne Dorothea.

Charles had a very interesting life and illustrious career. Some of the most noteworthy events in his life were: (1) In 1863, his family was forced to flee Texas and go to Mexico due to their Union sympathies during the Civil War. (2) Charles was an attorney at Nagel & Kirby and taught law for 24 years at St. Louis Law School. (3) Charles was Secretary of Commerce & Labor for President Taft from 1909 to 1913. (4) The Centennial History of Missouri wrote: "*He is usually found in those gatherings where men of*

---

[201] Two-Forty: a speed of a mile in two minutes and forty seconds; so called from its having once been a trotting record. [Webster]

intelligence are met for the discussion of vital problems, and it is well known that association with him means expansion and elevation."

Bertha related a story which their friend, the "Poet"[202], told about Nan. The Poet mused how long man would have to wait for Nan *"for so little a reward"*! (Certainly, Bertha didn't feel this way. Perhaps the Poet was the difficult person.)

> *She ["Cynnie"[203]] told us that the Poet had ceased going to see Nan because one evening he said to her, "Miss Nan, I should think you would be a hard woman to win, the old Bible seven years waiting would about suit you." Whereupon, says the Poet, "Miss Nan drew herself up very straight and said, "yes, indeed, I would not abate a jot of it and, if the man expected to be on at all intimate terms with me, then he'd be disappointed." And the Poet said he thought how long a wait that would be for how little a reward! I wish you had seen Nan's face when Cynnie told it.*
> [1892-01-03 Bertha (StL) to Henry (Wichita)]

Henry seemed very amused by Poet's story about Nan and was ready to tease Nan about it.

> *I liked the Poet's story but I would give a great deal to have heard it while Miss Nan was around. As it is, I promise myself, no little delight in asking her to recall the occasion. Don't you think she will enjoy my request for her version of the interview? Miss Nan will be pleased at this great interest which I show in her affairs and, apart from the fact that she may be curious to know where I heard the story, I don't see that there will be any harm in speaking to her about it, do you dear?*
> [1892-01-03 Henry (Wichita) to Bertha (2807 Locust St, StL)]

In another letter, Bertha defends her friend, writing *"now she is by all odds the nicest girl in St. Louis."*

> *I have just come from the Thomas concert which I went to hear with Miss Nan. It was splendid, dear, but it is like all the other nice things that happen to me, I wanted you here to really enjoy it. Not that Miss Nan wasn't as bright and charming as usual – she always is delightful and now she is by all odds the nicest girl in St. Louis. But, dearest, no man could know you as I do and not be missing you all the time you are away. And I miss you as much when the good things of life come to me as when the hard times are to be endured.*
> [1892-03-10(-) 20170823-4 Henry (StL) to Bertha (St. Augustine)]

Bertha wrote about corresponding with Nan about Henry's selection of an appropriate house and Bertha's dream about his selection that *"was something too awful to describe."*

> *I also had a letter from Nan which destroyed all the feelings of pity I have been wasting on you. She said you had been to see her, and that you looked much better than when I left. She said afterwards that she was not sure it was tactful of her to tell me that. She also remarked that she never had known anyone so hypercritical as you on the subject of houses, that you objected to one because the mantels did not suit your taste and added that if you went about the matter in that spirit, she was afraid you would not find anything in St. Louis to suit you. Whereupon I dreamed last night that you chose a house with carved wood mantel pieces inlaid with slabs of green malachite. The effect was something too awful to describe.*
> [1892-03-17 Bertha (St. Augustine) to Henry]

In May 1892 when she was staying at the Hotel Brunswick in Boston, Bertha spent several days visiting Nan who was in Marion Massachusetts with various Shepleys and Lionbergers. Henry had to appreciate what Nan said: that he and Bertha were the *"nicest engaged people she had ever known."*

> *If you had staid over, she did intend to ask you to go down to Marion with us, and O, I do wish you could have gone, as Nan said, "While I was interviewing workmen, etc., I would have turned you*

---

202 William Marc Chauvenet
203 Cynthia ("Cynnie") Pope Yeatman Sewall

Page 426

and Henry loose in the country." That would have been less charming than it sounds for it rained all the morning and the grass was pretty wet afterwards. But it was lovely after it stopped raining and I think you would have enjoyed seeing the places. The orchard back of Lutie's[204] house was a perfect mass of bloom and there was a great lilac bush in blossom at her side door.

Nan and I had a lovely time. We had the man build a big fire in the fireplace and then we watched the ocean and discussed all the affairs of the nation. We took our lunch down with us and had a picnic time over that and in the afternoon, we took a long tramp over the roads which were hardly even muddy, the soil is so sandy. Nan said she wrote home that you and I were the nicest engaged people she had ever known for we had no end of a good time together and yet we were not a bit silly and did not make other people feel a particle de trop. Don't you wish you could have been along today to justify her good opinion?
[1892-05-03 Bertha (Back Bay, Boston--) to Henry (StL)]

Nan could evidently be very direct. Henry wrote that Nan was quite indignant when Henry did not have a letter from Bertha for her.
My first greeting from Miss Nan was "give me my letter. I know you have one for me." When I denied having been made use of as your messenger, this time that young woman fell upon you and indulged in many retaliatory threats, so if you ever wish to hear from her again, you will profit by writing her at once ...
[1892-11-27a (Saturday) Henry (StL) to Bertha (Hotel Brunswick, Boston)]

Later, when Nan received the expected letter from Bertha, she was *"very gracious."* In the ensuing conversation, Henry's gloominess that he could not travel east to visit Bertha must have been obvious to Nan who had thought that Henry was going to visit Bertha in Boston. Henry wrote of Nan's own disappointment for them, *"now your explanation has spoiled all the pleasant reflections I have indulged in, Mr. Scott."*
I saw Miss Nan this afternoon and heard of the arrival of that letter. She was very gracious and you may be assured that she has forgotten her indignation at your tardiness. I was considerably amused at a mistake she made about my next trip to Texas. At the dinner she asked me when I was going away again and, thinking that she had heard me speak of the Texas journey, I told her I should probably leave here next Saturday the tenth. She then asked when I expected to return. I replied that I thought I should be away until Christmas and I was somewhat astonished at her exclaiming "O, how nice to be able to go away again so soon!" Today as I was leaving she said, "So you will be in Boston again in little more than a week," and when I told her I had no thought of any such good fortune but was looking forward to a rather dismal journey south, she told me it was a real disappointment to her and that she had many times thought how wonderfully fortunate I was to be able to return to you so soon and "now your explanation has spoiled all the pleasant reflections I have indulged in, Mr. Scott."
[1892-12-07 (Tuesday, 1st letter) Henry (StL) to Bertha (Hotel Brunswick, Boston)]

After Hugh Scott was born on December 31, 1893, Bertha wrote of spending the day at Nan's and of Bertha's great affection for Nan's mother. (The baby Hugh was not yet 3 months old.)
I went up to lunch at Nan's yesterday where were also Lute and Mrs. Tiffany & the small Hugh came by for me afterwards and was petted to his heart's content. I will say what you have never heard me say before that Mrs. Shepley[205] is one of the loveliest women I ever knew.
[1894-03-10 (Saturday) Bertha (StL) to Henry (Fort Worth)]

---

[204] Mary Louise "Lute" Shepley Lionberger was Nan's sister. Lute was married to Isaac ("Zack") Lionberger.
[205] Mary Augusta (Clapp) Shepley, Anne ("Nan") Shepley's mother.

Bertha attended Nan's wedding in 1895 while Henry was away on business. In her diary, she wrote:

Nan Shepley was married. It was a hot sultry day, and we had two thunderstorms, one in the middle of the day and one at night but none at the time of the wedding. She made a beautiful, stately, bride and he looked exceedingly well. A house wedding, only family and intimate friends present.
[1893 Diary, May 1, 1895]

Bertha visited Nan after she returned from her honeymoon. Their honeymoon was cut short by her husband's work and their new home seemed empty with his absence.

Nan having returned from her wedding trip the day before (it only lasted a week, owing to Mr. Nagel's being on the City Council and having to return.) I went over to see her in her new home, 2044 Lafayette Avenue. It is a nice house, Mr. Nagel's old house. But she does not seem at home in it nor does it seem natural to see her there. Last night was her first evening and he went to the City Council and Nan staid at home alone as Mrs. Shepley had grip and could not have her to dinner. Dr. & Mrs. Fischel called. I call that a dismal home evening. I was the first of her friends who had been over.
[1893 Diary, May 8, 1895]

B. FRIENDS

The following friends are included here, not only due to their close relationship with Bertha and Henry, but also due to the sometimes poignant comments that Bertha and Henry wrote about them in their letters.

1. COLONEL GEORGE ELIOT LEIGHTON AND ISABELLA BRIDGE

Bertha was introduced to Colonel Leighton at a young age since he was a good friend of Bertha's father. Bertha wrote of Col. Leighton and his son George throughout their lives and Henry also became an admirer of Colonel Leighton.

Col. George Eliot Leighton

a. Summer of 1892 in Dublin NH

Bertha wrote to Henry about spending part of her summer in 1892 at Colonel Leighton's house in Dublin New Hampshire.

... the Colonel told us to drive up to his place to see the view. We did so and he presently left the Catlins and ran up to his house by a short cut so as to meet us. He took us on his piazza to look at the view which is perfectly magnificent of the lake and mountains, reminds me of Scotland.

...

You asked me once how we got to Dublin. It is on the opposite side of Mt. Monadnock from Jaffrey but only six miles away and one of the prettiest drives there is. We drove over one of the hottest days we have had early this week and, just as we reached Dublin, a thunder shower came up. We drove into a barn and for the next hour, watched a magnificent combination of hail storm and thunder shower come out into a fresh coolness and drove home watching effects of rainbow and sunset, too beautiful to describe.

[1892-06-02(-) Bertha (-) to Henry (StL)]

In another letter to Henry, Bertha described at length the Colonel's farm in Dublin.

I went over with father to the Leighton's yesterday to a midday dinner and had a charming time. They have an absolutely ideal country place and the house is an idyll, a poem. It is so perfect in its taste and refinement. After I had gone through it, I told the Colonel I was really glad Mamma had not been able to come over, she would have broken the tenth commandment [thou shalt not covet] so badly and he answered, "Ah, Bertie, we all of us have something, some good thing in our lives. This <u>place</u> *is beautiful, it satisfies me perfectly but it lacks the mistress[206] who made it what it is." And the tears came into his eyes. They planned it all together and she only lived to spend one summer in it.*

We walked all over George's[207] farm afterwards. Such beautiful Alderney cows[208], Henry, and they rubbed their great soft heads up against me and let me stroke them in the most friendly way. It is a stock farm and he has all the modern improvements. His churning, skimming, fodder chopping is all done by machinery. He has a little Westernhaus engine[209] (is that the way to spell it?). Then we walked through the Colonel's pine woods and around his own little special pond which is not very little but called so in comparison with Dublin Lake. It was here the Colonel took occasion to say to me, after some little conversation leading up to it, "I don't know Mr. Scott personally, Bertie, but I know of course many of his friends and I have never heard from any person anything but praise spoken of him. Not from <u>any</u> *person and I am very, very glad." I don't know whether I ought to tell you this but you seem to have been low in your mind lately.*

I had a compliment myself too and I am sure it was a sincere one. See what you think. The dogs went with us on our walk, a lovely Irish setter and a beautiful mastiff, the dearest things, and when we came back, the mastiff came and stood in from of my chair and looked up at me. I talked to him but George said, "Get out, get out, go away and lie down." The great thing looked at him and then at me and then calmly walked a little closer, lay down and rested his splendid head on my russet books and there he staid until I went over to the Catlins...

[1892-06-24 Bertha (Jaffrey) to Henry (StL)]

Henry had heard about Colonel Leighton who was highly regarded by his friends.

I do not know Colonel Leighton at all but I have always heard him so highly spoken of by the older men here that I have conceived quite an admiration for him.

[1892-06-22 Henry (StL) to Bertha (The Ark, Jaffrey)]

---

[206] Colonel Leighton's first wife, Isabella Bridge, died in November 4, 1888. (See 1888-11 Diary, November 4, 1888)

[207] Colonel Leighton's son, George B. Leighton, married Charlotte Kayser. See letter Henry's letter 1893-01-04. Colonel Leighton's wife died on or just prior to Nov. 4, 1888 (see Bertha's diary entry on this date).

[208] Alderney cattle. The Alderney was a breed of dairy cattle originating from the British Channel Island of Alderney, though no longer found on the island. The pure breed is now extinct, though hybrids still exist.

[209] The Westinghouse Farm Engine was a small, vertical-boilered steam engine built by the Westinghouse Company that emerged in the late nineteenth century. In the transition from horses to machinery, small portable engines were hauled by horses from farm to farm to give power where it was needed. Many small workshops used them as well. As a side line to the airbrake products, George Westinghouse made these horse-drawn, vertical-boilered and horizontal-cylinder engines which looked like a coffee pot on wheels. It came in 6, 10 and 15 horsepower sizes. The engines were produced from 1886 to 1917 when they were superseded by larger, standard farm engines.

Henry wrote of how delighted he was at Bertha's great capacity to make friends.

> *I am glad you had such a pleasant day at the Leightons. Co. L develops into being quite a friend of yours or is he a recent capture? You make your friends very easily, dear, and so I am never surprised when the number is added to, through the acquisitions that inevitably follow your association with a new circle of people. Don't accuse me again of being gregarious, dear. Not satisfied with establishing yourself upon teams of closest intimacy with people of all ages here from that of wee Miss Lionberger to your boon companion Mrs. Campbell and of all conditions and kinds, as witness your predilection for clubs and organizations of every variety and character known to this part of the world, a madness only accounted for by the immense interest you manage to take in the remarkable people who "carry on" these resorts for the idle and dilettante of our population. But you must establish foreign relations on as generous a scale and, as a consequence, I have only to mention some place which you have explored. It seems not to signify whether you have dwelt in it for an hour or a year. And you introduce me to intimate friends and truly congenial spirits whose number is limited only by the population of the place. There is just a little spirit of coquetry in all this too, my dear, in your acquaintance, for instance, with Arthur Poole. Has it occurred to you he may miss you when you go away more than is good for him and that the attractions of those long winter evenings may not be as absorbing as they have been?*
> [1892-06-30(-) Henry (StL) to Bertha (Farragut House, Rye Beach)]

Bertha seemed to take some offense at Henry's remark about being able to make friends so quickly, writing that the Colonel "*is not a recent acquisition.*"

> *Colonel Leighton is not a "recent acquisition". He is the one of all my father's more intimate friends that I know best. When George Leighton[210] and I were children, I used to eat [at] the house a great deal. But I think the foundation of my friendship with the Colonel was really laid at Rye when he used to come here years ago and rather supported me in some wild pranks that were not looked upon with equal favor by the mothers and nurses about. As a matter of fact, in those days, I could run a great deal faster and jump a great deal farther than George Leighton could. But I am afraid I have lost those accomplishments now.*
>
> *There was something in your remarks about the instinct of a dog that did not savor to me of any extreme self-depreciation on your part. Perhaps you think I do not remember who the man was to whom Mrs. Lane's dog paid such especial attention. By the way, it was the mastiff, not the setter, who made such especial friends with me at Dublin. What made you think it the setter?[211]*
>
> *I scorn your jeers at my gregariousness. It is very well to talk of "friendships on very short acquaintance", but when you spend a month in the same house with a person, you know them much better than after an ordinary acquaintance of a year.*
> [1892-07-01 (Friday) Bertha (Rye Beach) to Henry (StL)]

---

[210] Colonel George Eliot Leighton (1835 – 1901) apparently had a son, George Leighton who was Bertha's contemporary.
[211] Bertha was referring to Henry's letter - 1892-06-30(-) Henry (StL) to Bertha (Farragut House, Rye Beach)
The intelligent preference of the Irish setter reminds me of the evening we spent at Mrs. Lane's when her small "fox" marked you out with his especial attentions. I do think the setter's "compliment" sincere for among men the dog instinct is most reliable. I never saw a mean fellow who could manage or attract dogs or children. This, I take it, is because they do not know how to be "kind" to them, which I am told, by most excellent authority, is the proper treatment for "inferiors".

b. The Colonel's Death

The death of Colonel Leighton in 1901 greatly affected Bertha and Henry. Henry wrote to Bertha of Colonel Leighton's death.

> *Colonel Leighton's death has depressed me as I did not imagine the death of one I knew so slightly could. I was really very much attached to him and I shall look back to that visit to his house in Dublin as one of the very pleasant experiences in a lifetime.*
> [1901-07-05 (20170822-2) Henry to Bertha]

Bertha did not write about the Colonel's death until the New Year's Eve after he died when she was reminded of her prior year New Year's Eves with the Colonel. From Bertha's diary:

> *Dec. 31, 1901*
>
> *Last year at this time, we were all together, a gay crowd, at Colonel Leighton's. Now, the brave Colonel, himself, has left us. The gallant fight with death that lasted so long, ended last summer. ... The verses Colonel Leighton read last year, have been ringing in my head all this evening:*
>
> > *"So each shall morn, in life's advance,*
> > *Dear hopes, dear friends, untimely killed;*
> > *Shall grieve for many a forfeit chance*
> > *And longing passion, unfulfilled.*
> > *Amen! Whatever fate be sent,*
> > *Pray God the heart may kindly glow*
> > *Although the head with cares be bent*
> > *And whitened with the winter snow –*
> > *Come wealth or want, come good or ill,*
> > *Let young and old accept their part,*
> > *And bow before the Awful Will,*
> > *And bear it with an honest heart"*
>
> [Quotation from "The End of Play" by William Makepeace Thackeray]

(Lest this ending seem sour, Thackeray wrote this last verse to the poem which is included below:

> > *My song, save this, is little worth;*
> > *I lay the weary pen aside,*
> > *And wish you health, and love, and mirth,*
> > *As fits the solemn Christmas-tide.*
> > *As fits the holy Christmas birth,*
> > *Be this, good friends, our carol still:*
> > *Be peace on earth, be peace on earth,*
> > *To men of gentle will.*
>
> ["The End of Play" by William Makepeace Thackeray])

2. GEORGE E. LEIGHTON JR. AND CHARLOTTE KAYSER

George Leighton Jr. wrote to Henry upon hearing of his engagement to Bertha. Because the Drakes were frequent guests at his father's house in Dublin NH, Bertha had a long history with George but Henry would have known George only slightly. George's letter to Henry must have been very touching since Henry wrote that his letter evoked a feeling that *"one has to go back to the toys one grew up with for that."*

> *I had a letter from George Leighton, the other day, which touched me a great deal. No man who has written to me has shown such warm personal feeling – one has to go back to the toys one grew up with for that. He asked me to send you his congratulations.*
> [1892-04-05 Bertha (Port Comfort VA) to Henry (NYC)]

Henry wrote to Bertha upon hearing of the engagement of George to Charlotte Kayser, a union which was predicted by the "*professional gossips*".

> *I have a piece of news tonight. The engagement of Miss Charlotte Kayser and George Leighton has been announced. It seems to negate the idea of the unexpected always happening, does it not, for this has been predicted by all the professional gossips for a year or two. So the prophets will have an inning, the sceptics will be put to rout, and mother Kayser will fall on her knees in her exuberance of joy that another extremely eligible man has "spoke" to her youngest daughter and has thus relieved her of her single remaining charge. May the old lady have the strength to fully enjoy the ecstasy which this good news will bring to her and may the Colonel have much pride in his buxom daughter-in-law.*
> [1893-01-04 (Tuesday) Henry (StL) to Bertha (Stancote, Newton Centre)]

Henry wrote a week later to Bertha about how "*mother Kayser*" received the news of the engagement – she "*was turning hand springs in the alley!*"

> *Your mention of your congratulatory letter to Leighton and Miss Kayser recalls a rather "fetching" story on your friend mother Kayser which in confidence I will tell you. It is said by someone who knows and therefore I vouch for the accuracy of the story that, shortly after Miss Charlotte had conveyed the joyful intelligence to mamma, the old lady disappeared and a diligent search failing to discover her, the household became alarmed and turned out en masse to find its missing chief. After a long and anxious inspection of the most remote corners of the house, someone was attracted by the rattle of tin cans in the rear of the house and, further investigation being made, it was found that Madam, having cleared away the ash barrels and tin cans, was turning hand springs in the alley!*
> [1893-01-12 Henry (StL) to Bertha (Stancote, Newton Centre, MA)]

Bertha wrote back to Henry of her and her father's assessments about George and Charlotte's engagement.

> *I have just finished writing my congratulations to Charlotte and George, very sincere congratulations in both cases for I think they will suit each other very well and be very happy. Rather to my surprise, my father differed with me and said he did not think any woman who married George Leighton would be happy. I was quite annoyed for father has always been rather fond of George but he maintained his opinion nevertheless. I think him wrong though; a more sensitive woman might be made unhappy but Charlotte is not sensitive and she is thoroughly sweet natured and I believe really fond of George. Indeed, I think they will both be very happy.*
> [1893-01-07 (Saturday) Bertha (Newton Centre) to Henry (StL)]

Henry was pleased to hear that Bertha felt the engagement was a good one since he thought George was a "*nice boy*" and Charlotte a "*nice girl*".

> *I am glad you approve of the engagement, dear. It seems an entirely convenient arrangement and I suppose will work out all right. I can't say that I was particularly enthusiastic but I know both of them very slightly and this circumstance, no doubt, partly accounts for my inability to fully appreciate the chances for happiness which you think are so well assured for this couple. George Leighton seems a nice boy but I had imagined it would take a stronger woman than Miss Charlotte to steer him clear of the inevitable pitfalls which will beset his career if he does not learn more to respect the opinions of others than he now does. I am very sure that I wish them both a great deal of happiness and she richly deserves a happy life for she is a nice girl.*
> [1893-01-11 (Tuesday) Henry (StL) to Bertha (Stancote, Newton Centre, MA)]

George and Charlotte wasted no time in setting a wedding date which was originally set for the same date that Bertha and Henry were married.

> *Have you heard that George Leighton and Miss Kayser were to be married the day before lent? I don't know that this is more than gossip but it would be amusing if they fixed upon the same day*

that we have chosen. It looks like hurrying matters a little but I suppose Mother Kayser wishes to chance no accident by delaying the marriage.
[1893-01-10 (Monday) Henry (StL) to Bertha (Stancote, Newton Centre MA)]

George Leighton married Charlotte Kayser in April 1893 and they wasted little time in starting a family. Bertha wrote in November, *"I saw Charlotte's boy. He is a magnificent healthy-looking child but so ugly – the image of George."* [1894-11-22 Bertha (StL) to Henry (Waco)]

3. THE MCKITTRICKS
Hugh McKittrick Sr. (1837-1895) and Mary Webber Cutter (1839-1909) had 9 children: Norman (1859-1863), Harrington (1861-1863), Thomas Harrington (1864-1930), Mary Martha ("Mattie") (1866-1892), Hugh Jr. (1870-1941), Allan (1871-1886), Walter (1873-1965), Mary McKittrick Markham (1875 - ?), and Ralph (1877-1923). Sadly, many of the McKittrick children died at a young age.

Bertha and Henry were good friends of the McKittrick family and were especially close with Thomas, Mattie, and Mary McKittrick.

a. Tom and Hildegarde (Sterling) McKittrick
Bertha and Henry formed interesting insights into the lives of Tom and Hildegarde. In a letter to Henry in 1892, Bertha wrote of the McKittrick family and Tom McKittrick in particular. Apparently, from Bertha's perspective, the McKittrick men relied heavily on their wives to take care of them.

You must not imply either that our friend Tom is not a hard worker, though I admit he had his work so cut out for him as to render the beginning exceedingly easy. I know you did not mean that, though it sounded so, for I have heard you speak of his work. I don't think he is as hard worked as you are but, if I were Hildegarde, I should be worried about Tom - his nerves go all to pieces at the slightest overstrain. In fact, I think she is from some things she said at Magnolia which came up apropos of Tom's trunk and had not even gotten home from some expedition. Hildegarde began wondering whether she had better pack it for him and Mattie[212] said "now Hildegarde, you just let it alone, you spoil Tom awfully, you just run round and wait on him all the time. Now in my family, Will waits on me." To which I remarked, "Yes, but you didn't marry into the McKittrick family, Nat and Hilda did." Mattie threw something at me and Hildegarde went on, "well, when we left home, I did not pack Tom's trunk and he came home only two hours before we started and had to hurry so and was so worried for fear we'd miss the train that it upset him so that he did not get over it for a week afterward. And I don't want to run the risk of that happening again." They came east purely on his account, you know, and left the children with Mrs. Sterling. The result of the conversation by the way was that Hilda got all his things together for him but I believe he did pack his trunk himself.
[1892-07-28 Bertha (Rye Beach) to Henry (StL)]

Henry wrote to Bertha before they were married of a conversation that he had with Hildegarde who told him, *"Bert has greater capacity for caring for another than any of us"*. This was a compliment that could be given only from a very dear friend.

Miss Hildegarde tactfully replied, "Well, you have pretty high ideas, but I am not in the least surprised to see you looking forward to so much happiness. Bert would make that in the life of any man she cared for", and then she said "Mr. Scott, all the girls in our crowd would tell you that Bert has greater capacity for caring for another than any of us. She is much more unselfish by nature than the other girls. Not that they are not all fine women but they are more like me and I care for and want too many things to think and feel as deeply as Bert does." That is just it, dear.
[1892-09-02 (Friday) Henry (StL) to Bertha (Farragut House, Rye Beach)]

---

[212] i.e. Mattie McKittrick who married to Will Stribling.

As was Bertha's wont, she could always befriend the children of her friends. Bertha wrote to Henry in 1892 of her encounter with Tom McKittrick Jr., age 2, an encounter that revealed the true Bertha.

Thomas H. McKittrick Jr.

You ask me to describe some of my days to you. Take yesterday for an example. I read aloud to mother while she worked until eleven, then I went over to the sewing club. We worked pretty steadily too, too steadily to please Tom McK[213] who wanted me to play with him and even appealed to Hildegarde, "Must Auntie Bert work, Mamma." He was deeply aggrieved and did not show an altruistic spirit when I told him about the poor children who were so cold and needed the things.
[1892-01-23 Bertha (StL) to Henry (Fort Worth)]

4. WILL & MATTIE MCKITTRICK STRIBLING

William Clarkson Stribling (1853-1929) married Mary Martha ("Mattie") McKittrick (1866-1892) November 6, 1889. Will and Mattie had two children: Mildred Clarkson (1890-1956) and William Clarkson (1892-1937).

Mattie sent a congratulatory letter to Bertha after the announcement of Bertha and Henry's engagement. In the letter, Mattie speaks understandingly of Henry's desire to not let other people spoil his time alone with Bertha.

I have had some very sweet letters. Mattie's especially was just as nice as it could be. She attributed your refusal to bring her down to me as unwillingness to have your "last remembrance spoiled by a third person's being about", and adds, "I have been through it myself and did not blame him a bit."
[1892-03-07 Bertha (St. Augustine FL) to Henry (StL)]

During the summer prior to Bertha and Henry's wedding, Bertha received a letter from Mattie in which Mattie offered Bertha her advice not to postpone their wedding. Not only was Bertha nonplussed about the advice, she called out the "iniquity" of Henry's conduct in confiding in Mattie.

I received a letter from Mattie yesterday ... I enclose a clipping from her letter on which I make no comments. My feelings at the iniquity of your conduct are too deep for words. The proper course for you would have been to say you preferred the postponement. Now, see what a lecture you have let me in for.

> *[from Mattie's letter] "I think it is a shame that you will not be married in the fall. I had planned it all you see to suit my own & Henry's pleasure. Poor fellow, I think you are very*

---

[213] i.e. Thomas Harrington McKittrick Jr. (1889–1970), the son of Tom Sr. and Hildegarde.

hard on him for he is so disappointed about it. He was on the verge of tears when he told me you had postponed it. Do change your mind."
[1892-07-09(-) Bertha (Rye Beach) to Henry (StL)]

Bertha did not let her annoyance with Mattie's wedding advice affect her intimate "visit" with Mattie when she came east in July 1892 with her brother Tom and Tom's wife Hildegarde. Bertha was delighted to catch up with Mattie – *"The dear old girl"*. Of course, that did not mean that Henry was off the hook – *"my confidence in you is sadly shaken."*

The dear old girl [Mattie] met me at the station yesterday and we have hardly stopped talking since. To my great surprise, Hildegarde and Tom were both here and it was awfully nice to see them and talk over everything but I never quite realized the difference in my own feeling toward Mattie and Hildegarde before. Of course, we discussed everything, past, present and to come, all of us together, but it was not until Mattie and I went up to our own room that the real confidences began. And we sat up until one o'clock watching the moonlight on the water and talking.

Let me tell you, son, that my confidence in you is sadly shaken. You told Mattie everything that happened up to the Isle of Shoals time! And you were ashamed to tell me! I should think you might have been! Though you did have the grace not to tell of our actual engagement until I gave you leave – that is, to tell her. But I know all about your house from the Imperial with Tom!! I would not have cared if you had told me but now, though I shall not scold, much as you deserve it, my confidence is seriously shaken.

...
Mattie sends you her love which I deliver under protest. She looks like another person, almost as well as she did before she was married. If you happen to mention to Will that she looks well, don't add the latter part or he might not feel complimented. Mildred is a shy little thing but she is getting slowly to be friends with me and the baby is simply dear.

Henry, dear old boy, do you know I am rather glad I was not at home when my engagement was announced. It has been such a beautiful thing to me and the things Hilda and Tom say are. It is not that I mind being teased, I mind nothing that Mattie says and you know the fun Jule and Nan had with me. But I think you can understand what I mean. And if I feel that, with Hildegarde, I should have disliked it much more from some other people. They are going tomorrow and, much as I honestly and truly like them, I believe I am rather glad that I shall have the other two days just with Mattie and the children. They have a lovely place here right on the sea, over windows looking straight out to sea. And Mattie and I are writing industriously, interrupting each other occasionally.

...
Tom and Mattie both say you are overworking yourself terribly, dear. Won't you please not? It is not fair to me.
[1892-07-14 Bertha (Magnolia MA) to Henry (StL)]

In his next letter in response, Henry got defensive about confiding in Mattie whose *"earnest and insistent questions"* could not be resisted, especially as they came from a woman who *"I hold to be worth more than that of a thousand girls of the ordinary type."*

Dearest, I am very glad you have been enjoying your visit to Magnolia and I am particularly pleased to see that you think of remaining a day or two longer than you at first expected to. I did not imagine you and Mattie would be particularly uncommunicative with each other but you have both exceeded my highest expectations for there is nothing you seem not to have discussed and, speaking of confidences, reminds me that I have no excuse to offer for telling Mattie about you, dear, although I don't think I told her as much as you imagine. To resist her earnest and insistent questions requires more strength than I am capable of. She always started in by speaking of you as no one else has ever done to me and this disarmed me in the start and made the thousand and one questions she asked seem to come solely from her affection for you and not to be resented as impertinence which would have been the case with anyone else. And I was often conscious that I let her talk and talked to her more freely than I liked. I still think though this most insinuating young woman may have captured more of your confidence than you may have otherwise given her through assuming many things that were more or less vague to her and I warn you against her because I have fallen into her snare. The worst of my experience is that I am never able to feel very sorry for talking to Mattie even though I am perfectly satisfied of her inability to keep a secret for she is so sweet with all her little designing ways that I invariably flatter myself that it is her way of showing her friendship which, by the way, I hold to be worth more than that of a thousand girls of the ordinary type.

[1892-07-18 Henry (Ft Worth) to Bertha (Farragut House, Rye Beach)]

Henry continued the defense of his breach of trust in a subsequent letter to Bertha. Henry explained that among all their friends, he likes Mattie because "*she likes me*".

I am very glad your heart is softened toward me on account of what I said to Mattie, but I am mean enough to think you would not have been half so forgiving if she had not interviewed you also. She is trying, there is no doubt about that and, unless a man hates a woman like that, he is in rather a helpless position when she begins to ply him with impertinent questions. His only defense is to keep out of her way and this I often did although, among all the girls, I believe I like her, Miss Nan excepted, the most. And this, perhaps, because I am sure she likes me.

[1892-07-30(?) (Wednesday) Henry (StL) to Bertha (Farragut House, Rye Beach)]

As usual for Bertha, she loved her time with the little people and found joy in playing with little Mildred who was two years old during Bertha's July 1892 visit to Magnolia Massachusetts.

I am feeling very jubilant over my capture of that small yellow haired thing called Mildred. She has adopted me entirely, follows me about and even told Mattie to go away this morning when she and I were playing together on the steps. But my proudest moment came when Mrs. McKittrick's cousin, who came the train after me, tried in vain to bribe her to come to her with candy. And Mildred shaking her yellow head defiantly, marched across the porch and (uninvited) hid her face in my lap and clung to my dress. I am mightily set up about it though Mattie says that last performance mortified her very much for Mrs. Whitin did not like it at all.

[1892-07-15 Bertha (Magnolia MA) to Henry (StL)]

Henry wrote of being favorably impressed with Bertha's success at befriending Mildred, something in which Henry did not often succeed.

I was glad to hear you had made such friends with Mildred, for having tried to establish friendly relations with her myself and having failed, I know how much tact is required to subdue her or win her over, rather.

[1892-07-21 Henry (Ye Arlington Inn, Fort Worth TX) To Bertha – Farragut House, Rye Beach, NH]

Toward the fall of 1892 when she was 26 years old, Mattie became very ill. Henry wrote to Bertha of his concern.

Mattie Stribling is quite sick. I saw Mr. McKittrick [her father] last night and he seemed very uneasy about her. He said she had taken deep cold, the result, no doubt, of her imprudence that evening of the V.P. parade.

[1892-10-29 (Friday) Henry (StL) to Bertha (Hotel Brunswick, Boston)]

At first, Bertha wrote of how Mattie's illness might stir up her husband, Will, in a good way, words that Bertha would soon regret.

> *I am so very sorry to hear Mattie is ill. She has had a pretty hard time lately and I am glad Will is anxious, it will do him good & stir him up a little. I think I see your reproachful expression but he does need stirring up, my dear, and you know it.*

[1892-11-03 (Thursday) Bertha (Boston) to Henry (StL)]

After this letter, Bertha learned that Mattie's illness was very serious.

> *I had no idea Mattie was really so ill or I would not have been so flippant about Will's anxiety. Poor little girl, I hope she is nearly well now.*

[1892-11-04 (Friday) Bertha (Boston) to Henry (StL)]

Four days after Bertha's previous letter, Henry wrote to Bertha about Mattie's death at age 26 and her funeral while Bertha was still in Boston with her parents. Mattie's death was completely unexpected and was very difficult for Bertha and Henry. Henry wrote that the funeral was *"so terribly sad."*

> *You will understand I think, why I could not write yesterday. Since Saturday night, I have been with Will almost all the time, in fact, I have arranged to remain with him for a few days until they can persuade him to go to the McKittricks. Mr. Mckittrick[214] is anxious to have him bring the children and live with him but Will seems unwilling to give up his home. He says he thinks Mattie would have preferred to have him remain in their house and take care of the children[215] himself and that, unless he finds he is unable to watch them as closely and take as good care of them as Mrs. McKittrick can, he will think it right to bring them up in a house of his own. He has become much calmer but it is sadder to be with him now than before. He talks about her all the time and seems to forget that he has spoken of certain things in her life, for he repeats the same incidents many times. The little girl[216] is a great help to him and she and Mrs. McKittrick are almost the only persons who can get him to talk about other things. Mildred has been the best child I have ever seen and so very sweet. I think she will be the greatest help her father has, for he seems devoted to her. The funeral was yesterday at three o'clock and it was so terribly sad. I was almost glad you could not be there, dear. I don't like to write about it, dear. If there is anything you wish to know about, let me know and I will write you as fully as I can.*
>
> ...
>
> *I can't write any more now, dear. I have tried not to go back to Mattie's death but it is before me all the time. Will we not miss the dear, dear, little girl when we come home? Do you know, Bert, I don't think any one of your friends or mine looked forward to our marriage with more delight than she did. She spoke of it every time I saw her and seemed so glad we were to be near her and now – But I don't know how to write to even you, dear, without a heart ache, which not all the memories I have of her or the evidences everywhere of the deep sorrow of her many friends which tell how dear she had made herself to so very many of those who know her can drive away. I suppose with each dear friend whom we lose we feel there is a vacant place which no new friend can ever fill and I am sure this will be true of the place which this poor little girl filled in your heart and mine, my darling.*

[1892-11-08 (Tuesday) Henry (StL) to Bertha (Hotel Brunswick)]

Bertha was clearly moved by Mattie's passing and her loss seemed to have more poignancy due her flippant remark made previously.

> *It has been a very, very sad time. Dear, I wrote some things last week I would give anything not to have written. I have thought since that they must have reached you Monday but you know that it*

---

[214] Hugh McKittrick, Mattie's father. Mrs. McKittrick refers to Mattie's mother.
[215] i.e. Mildred Clarkson (1890-1856) and William Clarkson (1892-1937).
[216] i.e. Mildred

Page 437

was written carelessly and in utter ignorance. It must have pained you as I think all my letters must have pained you, full of such utter nonsense and reaching you in the midst of all the heart-breaking trouble others were in. But you were not angry with me, were you? You knew I did not know. Perhaps it is foolish of me to write this but I cannot bear just now to think of any shadow coming between us and, if my thoughtlessness did give you pain, you must remember, dear, in what utter ignorance we all were of what was coming.
[1892-11-10 (Thursday) Bertha (Boston) to Henry (StL)]

Henry wrote about the week after Mattie's death that it was *"terrible to be there and see the breaking up of that home."*

I am still with Will and it is terrible to be there and see the breaking up of that home. He has finally decided to go down to the McKittricks and he is getting ready to move. Today he sent one or two of Mattie's things to Mother and, with them, one of the prettiest pieces of bric-a-brac Mattie had for you. He said he wanted us to keep it for you and give it to you with his love when you came home. I think this will be my last night there for tomorrow the furniture is to be moved and Will will go to Mr. McKittrick's to remain there at least for the present. I can't write you very clearly about it all, dear. When I see you I shall try to tell you anything you wish to know about Mattie's illness. I think I would rather not write about it now.
[1892-11-11 (Thursday) Henry (StL) to Bertha (Hotel Brunswick)]

One month after Mattie's death, Bertha still wrote of how much she missed her.

I do hope Will will come to see me when he comes on. I shall be out at Stancote then but I sincerely hope he will try to get out there anyway for I want to see him. I think of Mattie so much. I believe, except Nan, there is not one of the girls, unless perhaps Edith Knox, whom I should miss so much. I find myself thinking often - when Mattie and I can do this together or Mattie would not allow such and such a thing to be said of me. She is too loyal a friend and so I did not know how often unconsciously she was in my thoughts and plans until now when the reality breaks in to contradict what I am thinking.
[1892-12-12 (Sunday) Bertha (Boston) to Henry (Wichita)]

Bertha included one last remembrance of Mattie from a conversation with Mrs. McKittrick, Mattie's mother, six months after Mattie's death. Mrs. McKittrick had wanted to give Mattie a Christmas gift that year and it *"seemed natural"* for Bertha to have it.

O, I must tell you about Mrs. McKittrick. I was so touched. I met her the other day on the street and spoke to her of her presents & she said "The way I came to send bouillon cups to you was that Mattie always wanted them and I meant to give them to her this year for her Christmas gift, so when I thought of a present for you, it seemed natural that you should have those."
[1893-04-19 Bertha (StL) to Henry (Fort Worth)]

5. GEORGE DICKSON MARKHAM & MARY MCKITTRICK MARKHAM

Mary McKittrick (1875 - ?) was Mattie McKittrick Stribling's younger sister. Mary McKittrick married George Dickson Markham (1859-1947) on February 5, 1902.

George Markham was successful in the insurance business, eventually becoming the head of W. H. Markham & Co. which had been started by his father. George was active in improving building construction and in establishing just and equitable ratings for insurance premiums.

Henry was a good friend of George Markham and was aware of rumors in 1892 being spread about George's marital interest in Edith January, unfounded as they apparently were.

> *Mary Lionberger left tonight and she, I believe, is the last girl except Miss Edith January[217] that remains and, from the accounts I have from the club members whom I have met recently, George Markham is monopolizing Miss Edith to a sufficient extent to give rise to the rumor that Howard's best man and Miss Janet's maid of honor will move up from second to first place in a wedding party before the winter is over. Mary told mother a few days ago that she would not be at all surprised if there was good ground for the belief that these two are engaged. What do you think of it and how would you like the arrangement?*

[1892-07-13 Henry (StL) to Bertha (Farragut House, Rye Beach)]

George Dickson Markham

While Henry liked George, Henry was critical of some of his weaknesses.

> *Markham, Jim Blair, Tom McKittrick and several of the men you do not know came out with me today [to the Country Club] and we have had a very pleasant time. I am obliged to admit that George is a charming companion for this sort of thing. He is worth more than any of the other fellows in a crowd but, beside a peculiarity in some things which I distinctly do not like, he developed today a weakness which I have never before discovered in him and which will do him more harm than the other "peculiarity". You can't pin him down to one position in argument at all. We were discussing his church's doctrine of election and he started out to defend it and, if there was nothing else noteworthy in the discussion, his dodging and running from one position to another would have lent interest to it. He began by quoting Doctor Brooks who was not a great favorite of the crowd and, before George had concluded his discussion, he had so confused his own and the Doctor's creeds and standpoints that he finally cut off debate by stating that these questions could not be explained in argument but that a man's faith was his only reliance in accepting the doctrines of his church.*

[1892-08-15(-) Henry (StL) to Bertha (Farragut House, Rye Beach)]

Bertha also knew George and was not surprised at George's "*peculiar habits of arguing*".

> *I am surprised you never discovered Mr. [George] Markham's peculiar habits of arguing before. I expect it is because you never tried him on religious subjects before. I doubt if he argues the same way about anything else but he occupies a totally inconsistent position as far as religion goes and he can't uphold it. In other words, he accepts James Martineau[218] as his standard and wishes at the same time to be considered an orthodox Presbyterian and the thing "can't be did." You*

---

[217] Edith January (1867-1954), Janet January's sister, married to John Tilden Davis on April 30, 1902.

[218] James Martineau (21 April 1805 – 11 January 1900) was an English religious philosopher influential in the history of Unitarianism. Alfred, Lord Tennyson - who records that he "*regarded Martineau as the master mind of all the remarkable company with whom he engaged*". Prime Minister Gladstone said of Martineau; "*he is beyond question the greatest of living thinkers*".

remember when he once quoted James Martineau at George Bartlett and the latter inquired if he knew to what church Martineau belonged, G. M. responded "Well, I know the Unitarians claim him but I don't think he is one."
[1892-08-18 Bertha (Farragut House, Rye Beach) to Henry (StL)]

On one occasion when George was teasing Henry about Bertha just prior to their wedding, Henry took offense.

I shall tell you of a scrape I got into today. I met George Markham this morning with Ben Adams and Crittenden. It was just after I had read your letter and, well, I was thinking about some rather beautiful days that were to come into my life before very long when I heard George, whom I had not yet noticed, shout in my ear "see him smile, fellows, my, my. He doesn't look very sad!" I innocently replied "that's my Christmas smile, I've seen the star in the east." At which George tried to be very funny and asked me when I returned from the east, anyway. Of course, his two companions laughed as heartily as two fat, lazy boobies are able to laugh and I left the crowd much disgusted.
[1892-12-06 (Monday) Henry (StL) to Bertha (Hotel Brunswick, Boston)]

Bertha was not sympathetic to Henry's annoyance at George.

I am afraid you laid yourself open to Mr. Markham's jeers, my son, but allow me to say that it would be more fitting for you to blame yourself for imbecility than to vent your wrath by calling your esteemed friend Crittenden, whom frivolous girls are unable to appreciate, a "fat, lazy booby." Fie upon you! What would Madame Lucy[219] think of you?
[1892-12-09 (Thursday) Bertha (Backbay Boston) to Henry (Wichita)]

6. HOWARD ELLIOTT AND JANET JANUARY

WELL-KNOWN ST. LOUISANS.

Howard Elliott.
Howard Elliott is a young and successful railroad man. He entered the service of the Chicago, Burlington & Quincy in 1880, being employed as a level-rodman. He has been with the road ever since in various capacities. In 1891 he was made general freight agent of the entire Missouri system. Mr. Elliott's conduct in his position has led the management of his road to substantially appreciate the importance of St. Louis as a freight center.

[St. Louis Post-Dispatch, June 10, 1895]

---

[219] Lucy Bent married Crittenden McKinley April 19, 1892.

Howard Elliott (1860-1928) married Janet January (1865-1925) on October 12, 1892. Howard made his career in the railroad business and became President of the Northern Pacific Railway Co. in 1903.

Prior to Janet's engagement to Howard, Henry wrote of Janet's seeming ambivalence to the union.

The gossip column is very short this time, dear. Miss Janet seems no nearer a declaration, so to speak, than ever and I have been so often disappointed by her that I have lost interest and could see her settled as a member of that unhappy class whose lives are made wretched from a predilection for cats and tea without shedding a tear.

[1892-06-04 Henry (StL) to Bertha]

However, less than two weeks after Henry wrote the preceding letter, Howard and Janet's engagement was announced. Bertha wrote, "*It would be funny if her marriage were to come first*". It seems highly unlikely that Henry saw the humor in this, having been forced to wait for his own wedding for years.

Father has just written us the news of Howard Elliott and Janet's engagement, and I am, of course, greatly thrilled. I am eagerly expecting your letter to tell me a few particulars for I suppose you know rather more than he does. When are they to be married? Janet took her revenge on me by not writing me before the announcement, I suppose. Imagine it will not be a long engagement as I have heard Janet express her opinion on that subject. It would be funny if her marriage were to come first, after all.

Did I ever tell you about Nan's vision when we were all school girls? It was just after we had that first group of the seven taken and we had all been sentimentalizing a good deal, writing poetry, etc. And in the summer, Nan had this vision or rather second sight. She wrote to me that one day, she had suddenly had this intense impression of knowledge of what was going to happen in the future to our seven. Hildegarde was to be married first, a happy marriage. Then Janet, whose marriage was to be happy, but not so very. Then mine, which was to be the happiest of the whole seven. I have forgotten quite the order of the others but I have always said to Janet, I would not dare to marry until after she did for fear of the other part not coming true. I remember too that Nan's conviction was that Edith[220] would never marry.

[1892-06-15 Bertha (East Jaffrey) to Henry (StL)]

Since Tom McKittrick married Hildegarde Sterling on May 9, 1888 and Howard Elliott married Janet January on October 12, 1892, Nan's predictions regarding the first three ladies to be married came true, as well as the prediction that Bertha's marriage would be the happiest of all her friends!

Bertha must have immediately reconsidered writing of Janet January that it "*would be funny if her marriage were to come first…*" Bertha wrote in her next letter that she understood that these events must seem "*pretty bitter*" to Henry.

Howard Elliott's triumphant announcement of his engagement and the ease with which things seem to have arranged themselves for those two, even their wedding being at the time you wanted ours, must have made the contrast seem pretty bitter and you were a very dear boy not to say so. I confess that it seemed to me things were not always very justly divided when I heard the news and there may have been something of a fellow feeling that made the reading between the lines so easy.

But I felt a little more reconciled when I read Janet's letter to me this morning. It was a very sweet one but it was not a thoroughly happy one. Of course you are not to say I told you this. She talked a good deal about her flowers and the cups people sent her and the trip to Manitou, and then she told me of how hard it had been to decide to do it. No, I won't quote from her letter but she says that even now, when she thinks of leaving home, she feels as if she could never do it. I don't mean

---

[220] Probably Edith January (1867-1954) who married John Tilden ("Jack") Davis Jr. (1868-1937) on April 30, 1902, 2 months before Bertha's letter, so Nan's prediction was not entirely true.

that Janet's not being perfectly happy was what reconciled me, for it is only a stage and she will get over it. It was only that I realized that, with all the annoyances and deprivations I have had to face, I am a thousand times happier than she is. If only I could spare you these annoyances, and, just now, there is not even a way in which I can make up to you for them.
[1892-06-16(-) Bertha (East Jaffrey) to Henry (StL)]

Henry agreed with Bertha's opinion of Janet's disposition about her marriage to Howard, writing: *"unhappiness seems a family characteristic."*

I think you are right about Miss Janet. You know I have never thought hers a happy disposition. In fact, unhappiness seems a family characteristic. It certainly is so in the case of Mrs. J. and both of her daughters but, if any man can overcome this in Miss Janet, Elliott can. He seems to me singularly unselfish and she is much too nice a girl not to be greatly helped by the consideration I am sure he will always show her.
[1892-06-20 Henry (StL) to Bertha (the Ark, East Jaffrey, c/o Mr. Poole)]

After another two weeks, Bertha and Henry were still corresponding about Howard and Janet's engagement with a frankness that one doesn't normally hear. Bertha wrote that the engagement *"does not satisfy me"*. Clearly, these are thoughts that Bertha would not have expressed to anyone except Henry, writing, *"you are my other self and do not count."*

Did I tell you Julia's[221] suggestion for Janet's bridal trip? That she should take the whole wedding party within her private car. This, she said, might prevent that "being bored", which was one of the most serious fears Janet had expressed concerning matrimony when engaged in those serious discussions this spring. I don't know whether I am in that foolish state of mind they say engaged people are apt to be in when they cannot understand other people being as happy as they are. I don't think I am for I understand and sympathize perfectly with some other people. But somehow Janet's and Mr. Elliott's engagement does not satisfy me. It may be because I am not there and am only judging from the past. Certainly, I seem to be alone in my feeling. The only other people I have seen who know them seem to think it a "match made in heaven" and all that. And of course, it is distinctly suitable. Well, I may as well confess, too suitable by half. Am I wretchedly uncharitable or is it the externals, the excitement, the being entertained, the house, and the "going to be married" that are taking up Janet most? Remember, I am not there and it is not from Janet's letter I am judging for, or course, no woman writes or talks her deepest feelings.

I cannot exactly tell why I feel so but I do feel so distinctly a woman's reason. But I have not spoken so to anyone, not even to Nan or my own mother, for I fully agree with you in thinking it a cruel thing to criticize a woman at this time. Only you are my other self and do not count. Besides, I shall be only too glad to have you write back to me that I am very silly and altogether wrong.
[1892-07-05 Bertha (Rye Beach) to Henry (StL)]

Similarly, Henry commented on the engagement, *"of all the engaged girls whom I have known, she is the most unsatisfactory."*

I think I am glad you did not send Miss Janet's letter, although I can easily divine its contents. She has, since the engagement came out, done nothing but obey the promptings of what she has shown to think society considers to be the proper treatment of her engagement and, of all the engaged girls whom I have known, she is the most unsatisfactory. I think about half the people in town have been carefully informed that she had a most terrible experience in making up her mind and more foolish silly stories have been told about how faithfully Elliott waited all this time - they have known each other well about six months!!! - than I ever care to hear repeated. Don't think, dear,

---

[221] Julia Hayden Richardson ("Lula") who married Jack Shepley.

that I do not agree with you that Miss Janet is a very sweet girl, for I do, and it is because I really like her that I dislike her belittling what ought to be the best and most sacred thing in her life.
[1892-08-15 (Monday) Henry (StL) to Bertha (Farragut House, Rye Beach)]

Bertha heard from Janet that Howard was going to ask Henry to be one of his ushers at his wedding, news which gave Bertha great satisfaction to be able to share with Henry. (Bertha was one of Janet's bridesmaids.)
Janet told me in her letter yesterday that Mr. Elliott meant to ask you for one of his ushers. That was the piece of news that I would not tell you and that was such a satisfaction to me. It makes more difference to me than I shall flatter you by saying, mon ami, to have you in the wedding party, at the rehearsal and everything. Besides, I have never been in a wedding party but once without you (Edith Knox's) and I do not think that I shall be in any future wedding without you either.
[1892-09-(-) (Monday) Bertha (Jaffrey) to Henry (StL)]

Later, Henry received a note from Howard asking him to be an usher at his wedding and deduced that he had been included since Howard reached "*the limit to his more intimate friends.*"
I had a note[222] a few days since from Howard Elliott asking me to be one of the ushers at his wedding. I have been unable to see him and accept his invitation to be in his party. I was rather surprised at his asking me for I know him less intimately than many of the other men. But ten men – six groomsmen and four ushers – are a pretty large number and I suppose the limit to his more intimate friends had been reached.
[1892-09-09 (Thursday) Henry (StL) to Bertha (The Ark, East Jaffrey, NH)]

Henry received a nice letter from Janet while she and Howard were on their honeymoon in Asheville NC.
I had a very nice note from Mrs. Howard Elliott yesterday, dated Asheville. She starts out pretty well "I hope your wedding day will be as perfect as ours was. You will be so happy when you are married!" They have apparently settled down after a run through several of the Southern cities, for Asheville was the last place they had in view and I suppose they will return home about the middle of November.
[1892-10-23 (Saturday) Henry (StL) to Bertha (5021 Washington Ave, Chicago Il (c/o Mr. Wm. H. Benton)]

Henry's view of Howard and Janet's marriage seemed to change upon their settling into their new house.
Mr. & Mrs. Elliott were at last night's meeting and a more, well satisfied, couple I have not seen in a long time. I called on them on Friday and inspected their house and they are rather nicely fixed but, dear, that house is very ugly and I don't believe they will ever be able to make it very pretty or attractive. It is too early in the day to brag but I don't believe you will abuse me very roundly for my poor taste in selecting our gas fixtures when you have seen theirs. Maybe it's my own ignorance of the subject but I thought their fixtures the most remarkable I had ever seen.
[1892-11-28 (Sunday) Henry (StL) to Bertha (Hotel Brunswick, Boston)]

Henry wrote to Bertha about Janet's warning to him that neither she nor Bertha had any training in housekeeping: "*Poor Howard! And poor Henry!*".
... I found time to dine at Mrs. January's with Mr. & Mrs. Elliott. Miss Janet says she is very much in need of you these days – that she knows nothing about housekeeping and you know even less than she does and that she thinks you will sympathize with her difficulties and tribulations "and not fly at me when I ask questions with 'don't' you know even that? And then proceed to tell me a million easy ways of doing what I want to do, none of which I understand." Poor Howard! And poor Henry!!!!!!!!!!!!!!!!!!!!!!!!! Howard proposed an exchange of the articles on the "free list" of

---

[222] 1892-09-14 Howard Elliott (StL) to Henry (StL)

our households. A brewer friend of his supplies him with beer gratis and he suggests my putting in a gas pipe from our house to theirs, he reciprocating by running a beer pipe from their domicile to ours. I told him I referred all matters which were outside of the regular daily routine to my superior officer – that I would report his proposal and, if bidden to do so, would reply. I even intimated that his suggestion might be considered sufficiently valuable to call forth an official reply to it from the commander-in-chief, direct.

[1893-01-10 (Sunday 1893-01-08) Henry (StL) to Bertha (Stancote Newton Centre)]

Bertha expressed no pity to Henry for the lack of her housekeeping expertise, saying "*you have only yourself to blame.*"

As for the impertinence of your wasting pity on Howard Elliott and yourself, all I can say is you both of you brought it on your own heads. You in especial had several chances to escape so, if in the future I hear any complaints from you, I shall only repeat that delightful remark that all our pastors and masters have made us familiar with from our youth up "Well, my dear, you have only yourself to blame."

[1893-01-19 (Thursday) Bertha (Newton Centre) to Henry (StL)]

Bertha wrote to Henry of the birth of Janet & Howard's daughter, Janet Elliott (Hobart), born October 17, 1893 and Howard's joy – "*they say the house is not big enough to hold Howard.*"

Janet's baby was born last evening at half past five o'clock, a wee little girl, weighing seven pounds, with black hair all over its head. Mrs. January says it is exactly like all her babies so I suppose it will not take after its father. Janet is doing very well and they say the house is not big enough to hold Howard.

[1893-10-19 Bertha (StL) to Henry (Wichita)]

7. GORDON & EDITH SHERMAN KNOX

Bertha and Henry were very fond of Charles Gordon Knox (1852-1907) and his wife, Edith Sherman Knox (who died in 1935). Gordon was vice president of the St. Louis National Stock Yards and president of Stock Yard Bank and the St. Louis Cattle Loan Co., among his various business interests.

Charles Gordon Knox

Prior to the announcement of Bertha and Henry's engagement, Mrs. Knox already seemed to be rooting for the union by praising Henry. Bertha simply wrote, "*Mrs. Knox spent a great deal of wasted time in praising your character to me yesterday.*" [1892-01-29 Bertha (StL) to Henry (Wichita)]

When Edith Knox heard about Bertha and Henry's engagement, her letter to Bertha revealed her great pleasure for Bertha and Henry, writing:

I need hardly try to put into words all that is in my heart for you, my dear, dear infant. If you are half as smart a wife as you are a friend, you husband (how good that sounds, at last!) - will surely be the happiest man in the world, in my humble opinion. As for you, well, you know very well what I think of him already! We shall be thinking of you both all day next Tuesday, and if even half of our hopes for you both come true, you will have very little left to wish for here below – long life and lasting happiness for both, long may you wax and may your shadows never grow less![223] (This latter wish is truly fervent.)

[1892-02-09 Edith Knox to Bertha]

Gordon Knox included a postscript in the preceding letter. Understanding Bertha and Henry's long engagement, Gordon counseled, *"the best things in life are worth waiting for..."*

I cannot let this go to you without adding my wish for every possible happiness for you in the years to come. I fear we have been but a poor example for you since it is only after all these years that our first bridesmaid ventures to follow in our steps. But, at least, I can tell you from my own experience that the best things in life are worth waiting for and happiness sometimes all the more perfect though long delayed. With heartiest congratulations to you both. I am very sincerely your friend, C. Gordon Knox

[1892-02-09 Gordon Knox to Bertha]

Edith Knox wrote to Henry three weeks later to personally congratulate him *"on winning one of the sweetest women in the world for your wife."*

My dear Mr. Scott,

I was so very sorry to miss you last evening for I have really longed for the last two days to tell you a little what I think of the most joyful piece of good news that I have heard in many a day. I don't think I ever wrote a note of "congratulations" before and so I can't do it properly now. But I just want you to know that I rejoice with all my heart over the good fortune and coming happiness the girl whom I adopted for my "special own" years ago and have dearly loved over since. And that I can congratulate you (because I know!) on winning one of the sweetest women in the world for your wife. O, I am so glad for you both!

Mr. Knox joins me in cordial regards and every possible good wish for the future

[1892-02-28 Edith Sherman Knox (3617 Delmar Avenue, Stl) to Henry]

Bertha received a letter from Edith in August 1892 in which Edith seemed to be taking Henry's side about the long separations that Bertha and Henry endured.

I had a letter from Edith Knox yesterday in which she spoke of our long separation as if it were a positive grief to her and added that six weeks was as much as she could stand. It was a most characteristic letter, eleven pages long and four of them given up to humble apologies for not having written before. She sent her love to you and of course made a number of nice remarks about you but I shall not repeat them.

[1892-08-11 (Wednesday) Bertha (Rye Beach) to Henry (StL)]

---

[223] The length of your shadow depends on your height so the shorter you are the shorter your shadow. Our standing and reputation in the eyes of others depends on how they assess us. This metaphor is a simple way of praising someone but at the same time warning of the dangers of diminishing themselves by the wrong actions. People are often encouraged to walk tall in the metaphorical sense and this leads to the idea of a long shadow. (Web post by William Clark)

At times, Bertha got frustrated with Edith's praises for Henry and her thoughts about a woman's place.

> *As for Mrs. Knox, you cannot go to see her anymore. I forbid it. I disapproved of it before and now I disapprove of it more. Because she has no health herself and cannot stand an ordinary amount of work is no reason she should make herself a standard to judge women of ordinary strength and endurance by! Go to!!!! (That's Shakespearian – if you had been talking, you would probably have said – Go to thunder but I don't use bad language.)*
> [1892-11-04 (Friday) Bertha (Boston) to Henry (StL)]

Henry obviously liked Edith's views, especially in praising him. "*... dear, don't silence Mrs. Knox when she praises me. It will do her no harm, for I promise she shall never see the great mistake she is making and her praise may do me lots of good. On the whole, I think I need praise.*" [20170722-4 (Thursday 1892-11-10-) Henry (Wichita) to Bertha (StL)]

Henry wrote of his call at Edith's house and of the intimacy of their conversation.

> *I had a great disappointment in finding no letter from you this morning and, with this very poor beginning, I started in on a number of calls upon people with whom I had to make some business appointments for the coming week and this took up all my time except a very pleasant half hour which I managed to save for my own indulgence and which I passed most pleasantly with my friend, Mrs. Knox. So you will see that I can give an account of the day in a very few words for the call at Mrs. Knox's was about the only event of the entire day which would be worth repeating. Mrs. Knox asked a great many thousand questions in that half hour and, if I told you half of the particulars concerning the fourteenth of February about which she was curious, it would take me until that day without interruption or rest to write them out for you. Don't think I am criticizing your friend, dear, for I am not. What I would consider the mere promptings of idle curiosity in others I know to be evidence of strong, genuine interest with her. She is mighty confidential with me these days too and that flatters my vanity. She even asked my advice as to what she should give you for a bridal present. Of course, I told her!!!!*
> [1892-11-28 (Sunday) Henry (StL) to Bertha (Hotel Brunswick, Boston)]

Henry would get annoyed if Bertha wrote short letters to him. So, Henry threatened to "*pour out my woes to Mrs. Knox*", a prospect annoying to Bertha.

> *You are a bad girl, Bertie Drake. You write me letter after letter of only a few lines – me whom you look to "for your highest hope of happiness" – and then when Uncle Sam's mails will not carry my letters to you promptly, you decide "not to write tomorrow" and threaten me into the bargain. Perhaps I can make you feel a little remorseful if I tell you the hour I am writing to you now – half past twelve. And perhaps always assuming you to be a good girl, which you are not, you would be still more inclined to reproach yourself if I were to tell you what I have had to do since half past six this morning but you are a bad girl and you shall not have my confidence tonight. I think I shall go over and pour out my woes to Mrs. Knox and to let you see what a really nice friend she is and also to furnish a sample of a longer note than I have been receiving of late from my very bad child. I enclose one which I have just received from her. I had asked her to go to see Sothern in Captain Lettarblair , with Miss Allen and me.*
> [1893-01-17 (Monday) Henry (StL) to Bertha (Stancote, MA)]

Bertha was clearly miffed by Henry's letter and rejoined: boys "*are born bad and they do not improve.*"

> *Anyone would think you were big enough and old enough to have outgrown the love of teasing but I don't suppose boys ever do. They are born bad and they do not improve. Your last attempt was brilliantly successful. I was not at all pleased at having your letter to me laid aside that you might write to Mrs. Knox. It made my feelings against that lady assume a very virulent type. I thought I forbade you to go to see her anyway.*
> [1893-01-19 (Thursday) Bertha (Newton Centre) to Henry (StL)]

But, in a moment of self-reflection, Bertha wrote that she agreed with Edith's view that she was a spoiled woman.

> *Dearest, because I do not always speak it, don't think I don't notice your constant watchful care of me. I think Edith Knox was right when she wrote me the other day, "You are going to be the worst spoiled woman in town and all my noble efforts to the contrary in your education will have been fruitless."*
> [1893-01-18 (Sunday) Bertha (Newton Centre) to Henry (StL)]

After Bertha and Henry were married, Bertha wrote to Henry about her visit to Edith during a heat wave in October 1893. Bertha and Henry had grown very close to the slightly older couple but they were accustomed to addressing the Knox's with the customary formality of "Mrs." & "Mr." Edith told Bertha that Henry should stop calling her "Mrs."

> *I hope you are not having the weather we have here. It has turned scorching again. I was up at Mrs. Knox's this morning & coming home it was fearful. That lady is not yet supplied with a cook and is in pecks of trouble. The one she tried was anything but satisfactory. She sent her love to you however and said under no circumstances were you to call her Mrs. Knox or she would go back to calling you Mr. Scott.*
>
> ...
>
> *Edith said Gordon Knox said he thought you rather in luck to be away at this time, that he had discovered, when families first come home, husband's stock was very low.*
> [1893-10-10 (Monday) Bertha (StL) to Henry (Waco)]

Henry was in Waco when he received Bertha's letter about St. Louis heat and the advice of the Knoxes about a husband's stock after getting married. Writing, tongue in cheek, Henry observed: "*You say it has been hot in St. Louis. I am astonished! It has only been 100° F.H. in the shade with us here!!*" Henry added: "*Tell Gordon Knox he don't know anything about "husbands stock" that, in our house, it is always at a premium, cook or no cook, but why do I suggest your telling him this when you have no doubt indignantly denied that the head of some households could ever, for any cause, fall from their lofty places.*"
[1893-10-11 Henry (Waco) to Bertha (StL)]

Unlike many of their peers, the Knoxes were able to express their affections.

> *Edith Knox has just been here and left me in a really beaming state of mind. She is going on to Gordon's wedding and then she is coming back here to stay until the middle of July and she says if it is hot here she & Gordon will come out to Meramec for that time. Would not that be a scheme!! Sister Knox says wonders if you think her insane from the way in which she falls upon your neck whenever she meets you. Do you?*
> [1894-05-22 Bertha (StL) to Henry (Oriental Hotel, Dallas Tx)]

Henry was pleased to the be the recipient of Edith's affection.

> *I was much interested in what you said about the Knox family. That would be a bully scheme! And please tell Edith that I take very kindly to people who fall on my neck. If you give her this message, I shall be assured a cordial greeting when we next meet. You may tell her too that I am accustomed to a great amount of affectionate attention from my wife so that, coming from others, it seems only what I am entitled to.*
> [1894-05-25 Henry (Dallas) to Bertha (StL)]

Years later, Henry related a scrap between Gordon and Zack Lionberger concerning Edith, who had had a bit of a set-back.

> *Speaking of foolish things, Gordon and Zack had a friendly set-to at the club yesterday. It seems Margaret[224] wrote to Madelaine[225] about "Aunt" Edith's sunstroke where upon Sadie wrote in great anxiety to Gordon offering to come to St. Louis and nurse Edith, asking him to telegraph particulars to save mother anxiety, etc. Gordon was severe with Isaac and Isaac was mad at being sat on and we enjoyed the scrap. Gordon sticks to the malaria theory and I stick to my theory that a combination of torrid weather, much exercise in the sun and a sour lemonade immediately thereafter means a powerfully interesting stomachache. But it isn't good form to discuss the ailments of the wife of a friend with him, so I let it go at malaria in tearful silence.*
> [20171206-2 (1902) Henry to Bertha]

Gordon died on March 11, 1907. His passing was very difficult for Edith and Henry seemed to feel that she was misdirecting her grief toward others, including himself. Henry was with Gordon on the trip to Panama in 1907 when Gordon fell ill and died. Perhaps Edith felt that Henry was at fault or, perhaps, Henry felt some guilt?

> *I anticipated all you say of Edith's visit as you may judge from my earlier letters. I knew the visit would be a taxing, unsatisfactory, one and that you would sigh with relief when it was over. I have seen with sadness the bitterness growing in her lately, the feeling that no one appreciates her sorrow, that they, her friends, were politely sympathetic, perhaps genuinely so at first but that they soon grew so busy and preoccupied with their own affairs that they hadn't time for thought of Gordon or of her. She angered and hurt me once or twice by treating me as one who, though strangely attached to Gordon and grieved at his death, did not have a nature deep enough for this feeling to be long kept alive and I got entirely out of touch with her when there was a plain assumption that, while with good natured loyalty, I felt the loss of my friend, the finer appreciation of him, was quite beyond my grasp. I think the poor girl thinks I am honestly indifferent to her and her sorrow and only wish to do for her what would be expected of a man with decent instincts in my position. I suppose I have not been very tactful with her or I should have been of more help to her but she has almost repelled me whenever I have tried hardest. Still, Bert dear, neither you nor I must forget what her suffering has been and what it will be all the remaining days of her unhappy life. And because she does not help herself, our aid must not be withheld whenever the chance comes to us. I have only to think of you and the merciful providence which has spared you to me, of your companionship, your wise helpfulness, the perfectly happy life you have made for me and my daily joy and pride in you, to know that my hand should go out to help Edith when and where the change may come to me. And, although she may thwart and hinder and distress me, I know I should be an ingrate if I ever permitted that or anything ... to try to be of help to her when it is possible.* [1908-07-09 (Thursday) Henry (StL) to Bertha (Rye Beach)]

Henry felt a strong sense of loyalty to his departed friend, Gordon, and a duty to his widow.

> *Do make Edith stay until I come. I don't like the feeling that we never see her now. She really belongs to us, you know, and it makes me really sad and sometimes bitter that Gordon's wife is so little with us for I really believe, if he had known he must leave her, he would have made a compact that I should never let her get entirely from under my eye. I should have asked as much from Gordon in any danger of separation from you and I know he would have expected as much of me had he known. And I really care for Edith, little as she may realize it, for no one more thoroughly understands how little I have been able to do for her than I do myself. Get her to stay if she can.*
> [1910-07-12 (3rd Letter - partial) Henry (StL) to Bertha (Rye Beach)]

---

[224] Probably Margaret Lionberger, Zack's daughter.
[225] Madelaine Taussig is Sadie Taussig's daughter.

8. UNCLE WILLIAM AND AUNT MARY ROBERTS

Bertha "inherited" her very strong relationship with "Uncle William" and "Aunt Mary" from her father. George Drake's bond with his cousin Mary Roberts and her husband William was a lasting one for him as it was for Bertha. The Roberts lived in Morristown, New Jersey, in a house which they called "Glenbrook". Bertha was able to visit them on a number of occasions.

Prior to her wedding when she saw her Uncle and Aunt in Boston, Bertha wrote to Henry about their affection for the two of them.

> *Uncle William and Aunt Mary are here at the Vendome. And I had a very good time there today. During my visit, Uncle William said to me "Now, Bertie, your Aunt and I want to give you some remembrance of us when you are married. And I want to talk to you about it. We are getting old and we don't know much about selecting presents for young people. And if we did send you something, the probability would be you would get two or three others like it. When my own nieces married, I gave them each a check. Now, I have never had any difference of feeling between you and them. They are no nearer and no dearer to me than you are. So if you do not mind taking a gift in that form when the time comes, I want to give you the same that I gave them. Then when you see what you have, I want you get something that no one else has given you and that you really want and have it in your home to remember your Aunt and myself by. Mary here thought perhaps we had better go and choose something at Tiffany's but I told her you would not think any less affection went with it if we let you choose something that you really wanted for yourself."*

> *Dear Uncle William, I wish they had come before you left for I would like you to know him. He is the one of all my relations that I care most about and he is not really a relation at all; Aunt Mary is father's first cousin and father is Uncle William's dearest friend, that is all, but I feel as if he were my real uncle. They are going to be here for a week and then go south for the winter. Aunt Mary is very delicate and they usually shut up their Morristown house about this time and go south until the cold weather is over.*

[1892-12-04(-) (Friday) 20180405-1 Bertha (Newton Centre-) to Henry (Wichita)]

> *I have just come in from a walk with Uncle William. We walked up past the new old south on Boylston St., then across to Commonwealth, down by the Vendome, to the Public Garden and Common, and home again. Familiar ground to us, is it not, dear boy, only I never let you do as Uncle William did and put your arm around me as we stood on the Brunswick steps, trying to open the door, which you know is heavy and the boy was off somewhere, though I might have let you to say to me as he did just before, "Well, Bertie, I think there is no danger of our not being the best of friends always as long as we both live."*

[1892-12-12 (Sunday) Bertha (Boston) to Henry (Wichita)]

Bertha wrote to Henry of Uncle William's avuncular advice about marriage and his advice that "*no human being can profit by the experience of another*".

> *I said goodbye to Uncle William and Aunt Mary yesterday. I will repeat for your benefit some of the Uncle William's parting remarks to me and they may serve to reconcile you somewhat to my stay in Newton Centre.*

> *I had asked him if he did not have some good advice to give to a young person about to commit matrimony, to which he responded "You don't need any, and if you did, I should not give it to you. It has not taken me quite the whole of my life, though it took a good deal of it, to learn that no human being can profit by the experience of another, you have got to have your own experience, child, like the rest of us. But I would like to give you one bit of advice for just now. Don't tire yourself out with preparations! This going out to Newton Centre is the best thing that could have happened for you. Now make the most of it. Go to bed early, sleep late in the morning (nice Uncle!)*

and get rested. I have seen enough of worn out brides in my own case and others. Ella (my cousin who was married last week) came to see me the week before their wedding and I believe I should have passed her on the street without knowing her. There was not a trace of pretty rosy Ella. She was a thin pale girl, with deep hollow under her eyes. Now you don't look like that and my own opinion is that the tired look there is in your eyes occasionally would not be there if the distance between St. Louis and Boston were shorter. Girls are such unreasonable things. But I want you to keep well, let other things go and rest now. Don't save it all for Florida, you want to enjoy yourself then."

They will be south themselves long before February so they gave me their wedding present yesterday, a hundred dollars in gold to be kept until we see what else is given us and then buy someone special thing that we want and have not received. They want us to come visit them next summer and, whether we accomplish that or not, I do hope you will meet them sometime for they are very dear.

[1892-12-10(?) (Sunday) Bertha (Newton Centre MA) to Henry (StL)]

After Bertha gave birth to her first son who they christened "Hugh" after Henry's father, Aunt Mary's letter to Bertha was one of the first to be received.

Glen Brook
Dec. 26, 1893

My dear Bertie,

I hasten to acknowledge receipt of the message which brought its own joy with it and gave us truly a very Merry Christmas! We heartily rejoice in the joy of you all and trust that Henry Clarkson Scott Junior may be a worthy successor to the name and richly fulfil all that is expected of the son of his dear mother! We congratulate you that it is a son and pray that for all the blessings besought for him. He may prove a blessing to parents and friends in years to come. We wish you dear Bertie a speedy return to good health and a continuation of that unchanging happiness (now intensified) it has always been yours to enjoy.

The happiest of happy New Years to you.

Ever affectionately yours,
Aunt Mary
[1893-12-26 Mary (Roberts) to Bertha]

As noted in Chapter 15, Bertha named her second daughter Mary Roberta after her beloved Aunt. Sadly, Mary Roberta died shortly after her birth in 1901.

9. JAMES E. YEATMAN

Henry's various business interests gave him the opportunity to become friends with James Yeatman.

James E. Yeatman

I will start my letter to you by telling you of an incident that occurred today. Your first letter since your return to Rye came at eleven o'clock and, at half past twelve, I went over to the bank. In the director's room I found Mr. Yeatman sitting alone and writing. He turned from his work and shook hands with me in his usual cordial manner and I saw his face brighten as he said, "Mr. Scott, you seem unusually happy this morning. You must have had exceedingly pleasant news from the east?" You see, I could not hide the effect of your letter, dearest. It made everything seem to be in a beautiful clear sunlight, and the light shone deep down in my heart and made it very glad, my darling child. God grant that, your power for working good in me and for influencing me to higher, better things, will never be less than it is today. If there is enough of worthiness in me to always as fully understand you, to love and worship you as I do today, my life can't be an utterly useless one.
[1892-09-02 (Friday) Henry (StL) to Bertha (Farragut House, Rye Beach)]

Bertha also knew of Mr. Yeatman because of her friendship with his niece, Cynthia ("Cynnie") Pope Yeatman. (Of some interest, Cynnie's mother was Lucretia Leonis (Pope) Yeatman who was the sister to Maj. Gen. John Pope (1822-1892) of Civil War fame.)

Henry wrote to Bertha when Mr. Yeatman died with words that sounded like a eulogy.
I didn't have time to write yesterday. I left the office at five and as Mr. Guzzam(?) had just telephoned me that Mr. Yeatman was sinking rapidly I went by there on my way home and so was late to come out here to meet an engagement made earlier in the day. Mr. Yeatman died at one o'clock this morning, not having suffered greatly of late except on account of the heat. The operation was apparently successful and no complications of any kind had set in but the intense heat in his weakened condition brought on a bowel trouble which grew more aggravated daily and which ultimately caused his death. The papers will give you the particulars of his last hours as far as I know them.

James E. Yeatman

He seemed to have passed away in the same quiet dignity in which he had lived and, as I imagined, the people of St. Louis have at this late hour become conscious of the presence among them until now of one who did more to the honor of the community by his simple life of tireless usefulness than can be found in all the noisy and well noticed exploits of the remaining "first citizens". Another evidence is given me of how much I lose of the best things in life through my weak yielding to my petty business life in that I have seen so little of the last days of such a man who was big enough and generous enough to call me his friend.
[1901-07-07 (20170804-5) Henry (StlCC) to Bertha]

Henry's words are an appropriate conclusion to this chapter on relatives and friends: "*how much I lose of the best things in life through my weak yielding to my petty business life in that I have seen so little of the last days of such a man who was big enough and generous enough to call me his friend.*"

CHAPTER 17 – SOCIAL LIFE & EVENTS

A. THE BENTONS – CHICAGO TRIP, OCTOBER 1892

The Midwest was the economic growth region of the country in the 1890s and St. Louis and Chicago were the hubs. Given its proximity to St. Louis, Bertha and Henry had numerous friends who lived in Chicago and Henry periodically went there on business.

During the last two weeks of October 1892, Bertha visited her friends, the Bentons, in Chicago.

I have had a gorgeous time. I mailed Minnie a paper with an account of all the festivities in it. It may interest you to glance over it too. Then I was much interested at the Lunch Club yesterday. I waited on the girls from behind the counter, serving soup, sandwiches, etc., for an hour and a half and have made up my mind, if all other resources fail, I will become a saleslady. I feel I was cut out for it.

We came home and found Clarence waiting for us. He brought me a magnificent box of candy to take on the train with me tomorrow. Then he and Lucy and I raked leaves in the back yard (it is in the suburbs, you know) and quarreled over the relative size of our piles until we went to drive until supper time.

After supper, we made a bonfire of them. He came down again this morning with some lovely pansies for us and spent the day. We went down to the World's Fair and wandered about, admiring the buildings, which we did not enter, owing to its being Sunday (they are magnificent!) and towards evening, walked in halfway, took the elevated the rest, and went to the Buckinghams to tea. Their library is my ideal of what a room should be. Kate says to tell you missed the opportunity to make several warm friends in Chicago, they were all prepared to give you a most cordial welcome.

[1892-10-24 (Sunday) Bertha (Chicago) to Henry (StL)]

While Bertha was visiting the Bentons, Henry had intended to take the train to Chicago on Sunday to see Bertha, depending on his Monday morning business matters.

I missed you all day, dear, and I think if you were here now, I would not feel as melancholy and utterly used up as I seem to be. I am going to make a last effort tomorrow to go up and see you on Sunday and if I succeed, I shall telegraph you but I am not very hopeful. I simply must be here early on Monday morning unless I can make other arrangements than I now have. So, if I cannot see you, dear, will you be very sorry for me and for my ill luck? It does seem that everything goes wrong sometimes. My cold has been wretched since you left, my spirits have been, O so low, and it seems to me I shall not be content again until I can be near my darling one more. You see I can't yet write anything but mournful expression of my loss of you, so I shall say goodbye.

[1892-10-22(-) (Tuesday 1892-10-18) Henry (StL) to Miss Bertha W. Drake – C/O Mr William Burton 5021 Washington Ave, Chicago, IL]

By the end of the week, Henry concluded that he would not be able to make the trip to Chicago.

You can congratulate yourself that I did not go to see you in Chicago, dear. I have been laid up today and I don't think I could have made the journey, short as it is, and have been of any use to you tomorrow. I must have caught cold some days back for it has been impossible almost for me to get through with any of my work all this week without a struggle and I don't think I have been as uncomfortable in years – which is speaking strongly considering the numerous ailments I am constantly complaining of. You seem to have been away for years and I look back upon your visit as a dream for it hardly seems possible that you have been here for two weeks. I think, dearest, that I shall look back when I am old, upon my married life in much the same way. The time will

have passed so swiftly, so beautifully, that I shall hardly be able to realize that I have had you near me for years. It will be beautiful enough for dream land, will it not, dearest?
[1892-10-23 (Saturday) Henry (StL) to Bertha (5021 Washington Ave, Chicago Il (c/o Mr. Wm. H. Benton)]

Henry wrote to Bertha about his views that Chicago was a good place to hold the 1896 World's Fair since *"Bedlam never reigned as supreme in any city of any age as it does there…"*

… I am glad you did not write on Saturday but I shall not forgive you if [you] have tired yourself out in the attempt to keep up with the natives of the windy city in their pursuit of the various and sundry excitements of last week. Chicago seems a typical place for a fair. Bedlam never reigned as supreme in any city of any age as it does there and, in selecting it as the place to celebrate our four hundredth anniversary, Congress acted very wisely for it cannot be denied that the city and people are more in touch with a life of excitement and mad rush and hurry than any other people or city on earth.
[1892-10-25 (Monday) Henry (StL) to Bertha (Hotel Brunswick, Boston)]

Bertha very much enjoyed her visit with Bentons. Her only regret was that Henry was not able to join them.
I wish you could have come up to Chicago, dear, you would have liked it I am sure. About an hour before I left, two more of your letters came and Mr. Benton called to me that he had them. He is too lame with gout to come upstairs easily, so I ran to get them and thank him. "Ah, Miss Bertie, I have been there myself," he said, "And I want you to give a message to Mr. Scott from me. I am very sorry he did not come up Sunday. He would not have liked to have come straight here I suppose. But I meant to have met him at the hotel and given him a welcome and brought him back with me and tell him there is a cordial welcome waiting for him here whenever he comes to claim it."

As for Mrs. Benton, just before I left she said to me "Bertie, the first guests I mean to invite to the World's Fair are Mr. and Mrs. Scott. I want them to spend the first week in May with me. Will you give them that invitation when you meet them? And the Buckinghams are all so anxious to meet you and I know you would like them. Clarence[226] may be a rough diamond but the fact remains that I like him better and have had a pleasanter friendship with him than almost any man I know. Sunday evening he was saying that his pet castle in the air was to take a driving trip through England with a congenial party. "Let's go summer after next, Miss Drake, Sister Pat and Katie, and Lucy here, and yourself and Mr. Scott, and myself. And we might find one or two more." You see, they are all prepared to adopt you. My visits there have been almost the best times I ever had and both those families are very dear to me. I do so want you to know them. That you would like them, I have very little doubt. They are not a bit society people, you know, but just the dearest people in the world.
[1892-10-26 (Wednesday) Bertha (Boston, MA) to Henry (StL)]

---

[226] Clarence Buckingham. Bertha wrote that the Buckinghams were cousins of the Bentons.

B. THE COLUMBIAN CHICAGO WORLD'S FAIR (400TH Anniversary of Columbus' discovery of America)

Chicago World's Columbian Exposition 1893 [Photos are from Wikipedia]

1. DEDICATION OF THE CHICAGO WORLD'S FAIR

The Chicago World's Fair, "The Columbian Exposition", was held to celebrate Columbus' discovery of America and was dedicated on October 21, 1892. The Ohio Democrat newspaper described the scene as follows:

> *Chicago, Oct. 21. When the multitudes began pouring into the downtown district Thursday morning to view the great civic parade they saw stretching away in every direction, streets aglow with decorations till they looked like a gigantic flower garden. The national colors predominated, but with the red, white and blue were mingled the flags of all nations, and hero and there a streak of terra cotta, Chicago's newly chosen municipal color.*
>
> *...*
>
> *All Chicago was up with the lark in the morning. On the sidewalks along the line of the parade men, women, girls and boys began to secure positions of vantage almost with the break of day. The route of the parade was less than three miles in length and the head of the column had got back to the starting place and disbanded long before the center had begun to move. The extra ordinary shortness of the route, which had been selected by Gen. Miles in the face of the emphatic protests, naturally produced a congestion of the sight-seeing populace on the sidewalks and cross streets and, those who got into the center of the city even two or three hours before the time fixed for the head of the column to move, found themselves barely able to get within sighting distance of the tops of the largest flag-poles carried by the processionists.*
>
> *How the masses got into the parade district is a mystery. They seemed to sprout up like mushrooms out of the roadway and from between the cracks of the pavement. The steam and street railroads brought their entire equipment into requisition but even these facilities, ample enough at ordinary times, were painfully inadequate to meet the exigencies of the occasion and*
>
> *thousands of people, tens of thousands in fact, were compelled to tramp it from the residence district and in some cases even from the distant suburbs. Vehicular traffic was entirely prohibited in the business district after 10 o'clock.*
>
> [The Ohio Democrat, October 29, 1892]

Bertha attended the World's Fair dedication with an "*invitation*" for reserve seating (thus avoiding the huge crowds): "*we were all standing on chairs waving our handkerchiefs.*"

> *I am having a perfectly beautiful time. You know I feel more at home here than any other place on earth, except my own house. And I love every member of the family. And we are having such larks*

Page 455

now. The invitation you promised me for the dedication did not come. They are very difficult to get now, possibly that is why (possibly you forgot it!) but Clarence Buckingham secured a reserved seat for me with the other so I'm beautifully fixed. And we expect to spend the entire day tomorrow at the World's Fair Grounds. Have you read the programme? Just think of a chorus of six thousand singing the Hallelujah chorus!!!!!
[1892-10-21 (Thursday) Bertha (Hyde Park, Chicago) to Henry (StL)]

You must not blame your friend for not sending me an invitation. They were very difficult to get at this late date, almost impossible. I had one of the best seats in the house after those reserved for the guest of honor. And it was a very thrilling experience, one I would not have missed for a good deal. To hear six thousand people sing America and ninety thousand applauses rouses up your patriotism a good deal. And at the end of Chauncy Depew's speech we were all standing on chairs waving our handkerchiefs. The fireworks in the evening were magnificent too. Altogether it has been a time to remember.
[1892-10-24 (Saturday) Bertha (Chicago) to Henry (StL)]

The Ohio Democrat also described the speeches given at the World's Fair dedication:

At the concluding sentence of the Vice President's address and, as he pronounced the dedicatory words, the members of the foreign diplomatic corps arose simultaneously to their feet in graceful approval of the sentiment and the example, so delicately set by the representatives of foreign nations was instantly followed by all the thousands assembled beneath the vast roof. The "Hallelujah Chorus" that followed added to the deep solemnity of the scene and the true gravity of the moment was ineffaceably impressed on every mind and, when at its conclusion, Henry Watterson advanced to deliver the formal dedicatory ovation worthy to crown a lifetime of glory. A dead silence reigned over the acres of humanity as the orator of the day delivered his speech. Scarcely was the ovation ended when Chauncey M. Depew, of New York, advanced to deliver the Columbian oration. It was nearly a minute before the applause subsided and, when silence was finally restored, Mr. Depew delivered a masterly address, Mr. Depew ended with the following:

> *"All hail, Columbus, discoverer, dreamer,*
> *hero and apostle! We here, of every race and*
> *country, recognize the horizon which bounded*
> *his vision and the infinite scope of his genius.*
> *The voice of gratitude and praise for all the*
> *blessings which have been showered upon man-*
> *kind by his adventure Is limited to no language,*
> *but is uttered in every tongue. Neither marble*
> *nor brass can fitly form his statue. Continents*
> *are his monument and unnumbered millions,*
> *past, present and to come, who enjoy in their*
> *liberties and their happiness the fruits of his*
> *faith, will reverently guard and preserve,*
> *from century to century, his name and fame."*

[The Ohio Democrat, October 29, 1892]

2. BERTHA & HENRY'S VISIT TO THE CHICAGO WORLD'S FAIR IN 1893

The next year on April 29th, 1893 just after they were married, Bertha recorded in her diary that she and Henry went to Chicago to visit the Bentons and visit the World's Fair.

Left for Chicago to visit the Bentons and see the opening work of the World's Fair. Arrived on Illinois Central Train at Hyde Park, Sunday morning, April Thirteenth, in the rain. Were met at station by William and Lucy Benton, who had been there since early morning. Cordial welcome from the family. Went to tea at the Buckinghams. [1893 Diary]

Bertha and Henry went together to the World's Fair on May 1st.

The Manufactures and Liberal Arts Building

Opening of the World's Fair! Kate, Lucy, Julia, William and Rita Benton, and Henry and I went together. After waiting a long while for Clarence Buckingham to join us at the corner of the Manufactures and Liberal Arts Building, we gave him up and secure a very good place in the Court of Honor where we can see the platform with all the distinguished guests in front of the Administration Building. There probably will never be in the world anything more beautiful than that Court of Honor, looking out through the stately Peristyle to the lake beyond.

The Administration Building and Grand Court

At the proper time, Cleveland presses the button, the electric fountains fly up in the air, the cannon goes off, the band plays "Our Country T'is of Thee" and a million voices join in, everybody waves a handkerchief and the World's Fair is opened! It is one of the moments that stand out in a lifetime! And even the cold, raw day doesn't spoil it.

Then we go in search for lunch which we take at the Casino, almost freezing to death, as we do so. The men are obliged to keep on hats and overcoats. In the afternoon, Henry and Kate get separated from us and, we hear afterwards, spend the afternoon in the liberal Arts Building while the rest give a cursory glance through Machinery Hall, nothing going, Mines and Mining, Transportation, and Horticulture. Nothing is thoroughly in order yet, hardly.

Horticultural Building

In the week that follows, we spend every day at the World's Fair. See in addition to those already mentioned, the Woman's Building, Illinois State, Art Administration. Take ride in the electric launch around the canals. Ride on the elevated railway. Also visit Forestry Building, Convent of La Rabida, White Horse Inn, Libby Glass Co, Electricity, Fisheries, Manufactures and Liberal Arts. The Vienna department in the Liberal Arts I remember with especial pleasure. Such beautiful glass, tables of lilac, pink buff, white & gold, etc. The Ferris Wheel is not going yet and hardly any of the shows in the Midway Plaisance.

Midway Plaisance

Friday evening we leave. It is Henry's birthday and, in his honor, Mrs. Benton has a birthday cake and afterwards a little amateur play acted by Rita, the little Hunters, and a boy named Allen (surname unknown). They acted the "Children's Joke", dramatized and versified by Mrs. Benton. Also the "Kittens".
[1893 Diary]

3. ANOTHER VISIT TO THE CHICAGO WORLD'S FAIR

Bertha and Henry went back to Chicago on June 18, 1893 and stayed at "*Mr. O.W. Meysenburg's Astor Place, North side*". Bertha included in her diary all of the exhibits visited and interesting descriptions and details in her diary. Bertha's full account of this trip is included below.

June Eighteenth, 1893

Sunday evening – Very hot and close. We started for Chicago. Mrs. January and Edith on same train.

Next morning, June 19th, wait a long while in the station to secure our luggage. Then arrive very hungry and worn out at Mr. O.W. Meysenburg's Astor Place, North side. Perfect gem of a house, yellow brick entrance at the side. Are met by colored man, Tom, who presents Mr. Meysenburg's apologies at being unable to welcome us but he waited as long as he could before keeping an appointment down town.

Go through beautiful hall, up a wide stair case, into a perfectly beautiful room where a rosy cheeked chambermaid takes possession of us and says breakfast will be ready immediately. Our room is a gem, hard wood floor, beautiful rug, one or two exquisite pictures, beautiful little white tiled bath room belonging to it.

Came down stairs to a perfection of a breakfast table and find Mrs. Wright presiding over it. She is charming and so is the breakfast. Then we are introduced to Mrs. Block who is just leaving, and then Mrs. Wright tells us Mr. Meysenburg expected us to go out to the Fair.

We go over to the South Side and go down on the Whaleback (boat) to the Fair. Meet William Chauvenet[227] and Mrs. Holden on Board. Get the magnificent view of the lake front of the Fair. Go through Agriculture building. My mind is divided as to which is the most beautiful building – as a building, no reference to contents. Agriculture by the "McKim, Mead & White, or Art, by Atwater. Take lunch at the Vienna bakery and linger listening to the band. Take a ride in the electric launch and wind up with a fascinating glimpse into Liberal Arts and Manufactures.

Come home, dress for dinner, come down to find Mr. Meysenburg waiting for us. Sit with him on the little back porch overlooking the lake until dinner, then go walk along the lake wall to see the electric fountain its first night. Afterward, Mr. Meysenburg plays the piano delightfully until bed time.

June 20, 1893
Mr. Meysenburg takes us all over his beautiful house. Such gems of pictures. Then start for Fair again. Make for Electricity, take another glimpse of Liberal Arts. Lunch at Casino, then, when going to electric trainway, meet Mary Lionberger, George Bartlett, Edith January, Mrs. January and Mr. Brookings. They are starved and in search of lunch. We ride on the railway. Then go to the Midway Plaisance. Go to the Chinese Theater, Turkish Theater, etc. Go to see Venetian glass works, Irish Village, Street of Cairo. O delicious! Dinner in Old Vienna, enchanting Austrian band. Then it pours. We linger in old Vienna, making purchases, then try the Electric train again to get the effect of the illumination even in the rain. Glorious. To Electricity to see the illumination there. (Gorgeous). Return home very late and weary.

June 21, 1893
Go straight to the Art Building and then Liberal Arts, French section, and have a most enchanting time. See France, Germany, Sweden, Denmark, Switzerland, Holland, Italy (carved furniture) with another passing glimpse of England and Austria. Lunch in French section. Afternoon. Go to hear the United Choral Societies give the St. Paul. Again meet the January - Lionberger party. Have to leave early on account of the dinner to the German Ambassador. Arrive home, find Mr. Meysenburg went on the trial trip of the Ferris wheel and was stuck up there for four hours, the wheel refusing to go and he barely gets dressed in time for the dinner. It is a stag dinner. Mrs. Wright and I have a delicious little tea in the hall upstairs. Then go for a long delicious drive, she enlivening the way with reminiscences of her life. Come back to find delicious ices waiting for us. The dinner was given to the German Ambassador, the one to the country, not the delegate to the World's Fair, Von Hollenden or Von Hollenen, I forget the exact name. The guests were General Wilson who is staying in the house, Mr. Benton, Mr. McVeigh, General Black, and the Ambassador's private secretary, and Henry. He comes upstairs before all the guest leave.

---

[227] i.e. William Marc Chauvenet or "The Poet" (see Chapter 8)

June Twenty Second, 1893
Have a lingering, lazy breakfast, gorgeous cherries! Do not go to the Fair. Henry has business in town so I go down to the Bentons to spend the day. Find Rita has just been taken ill with scarlet fever but spend the day as her attack is very light. Edith January also comes in. Henry comes for me in the late afternoon. All this while I have never mentioned our breathless rushes back, always at the very last minute. Taking cab at the station and flying home. Evening – several people come to call. Mr. Meysenburg has the gout.

June Twenty Third, 1893
Immediately on entrance to the Fair, take two wheeled chairs. Go to the Virginia building. Go to the Midway, see the Alcazar, the Turkish and Algerian Bazaars, the Street of Cairo again (the camels and donkeys). The last time we had been to the temple, this time go to see the Egyptian Theater, having been told it was bad (AND IT WAS). Go see the outside of the Dahomey village. Lunch in New Vienna, Chinese band near. Have not time for the Ferris wheel. Go to the Japanese Tea House (fascinating) and pay a final visit to dear bewitching Liberal Arts and Manufactures and the beautiful Austrian glass. Buy Gist's present (the bet Henry lost by marrying first), pitcher, glasses and tray, a birthday present for another, and some champagne glasses for ourselves. Then back to Mr. Meysenburg's for last evening and we depart for home after what will always stand out in my recollection as one of the most radiantly beautiful weeks of my life. Not a cloud or annoyance of any kind. Clear delight all the way through. I shall never forget what I owe Mr. Meysenburg for a time of such unclouded happiness.
[1893 Diary]

Bertha and Henry returned to St. Louis on June 23rd , "*after what will always stand out in my recollection as one of the most radiantly beautiful weeks of my life.*" [1893 Diary, June 23, 1893]

C. **THE SOCIAL EVENTS OF APRIL & MAY 1893**

Bertha's next diary entry listed all of her social engagements during the months of April and May of 1893. Bertha periodically did this, it appears, not only as a record of what she had done but also to ensure that she wrote notes of thanks.

I here enclose a list of as many of the entertainments as I can remember that took place during April and May of 1893. Some may have been early in June also, but I know some have slipped away from me, a great proportion of them were in our honor.

Dinner at Mr. & Mrs. Ben Adams'
At The St. Louis Club, given by Mr. Arthur Lee
At Mrs. Lane's
At Edith January's
At Mr. KR. S. Brookings'
At Mrs. Daniel Catlin's
At Mrs. Thomas E. Tutt's
Sunday evening dinner at Anne Shepley's
Informal dinner at Mary Lionberger's, Graham Frost's lecture on Divorce at the Social Science Club afterwards.
At Zack and Louise Lionberger's
At Tom and Hildegarde McKittrick's
Mrs. Tiffany tried at three different dates to give a dinner to us and we were always engaged.
Ball at Mrs. John Whittaker's
Charlotte Kayser and George Leighton's wedding and reception

April Twelfth, 1893
Sarah Hitchcock and John Shepley's wedding and reception.

May Eighteenth, 1893
Concert party given by George Bartlett.
George Markham's concert party
George Bartlett's concert party to hear Boston Symphony Orchestra, supper at the University Club afterward.
The Shaw dinner (only HCS went to that – stag dinner)
Gist Blair and Irwin Smith's circus party, supper at Beer's afterwards
Charles Hodgman's party to the Country Club
Alma Sterling's open air supper at Bodeman's grove
Annie Wright's and Charlie Hazeltine's wedding,
Luncheon at Marion Davis's, Mrs. Judge Boyle's, Nan Broadhead's, Hildegarde McKittrick's, Edith Knox's, Lutie Lionberger's (Paderewski's concert afterward)
At Frances Markham's
Mary Copelin Day's
Mary Lionberger's
Reception at Mrs. William Lee's
Luncheon at Sarah Hitchcock's
Reception at Mrs. Copelin's
Reception at Mrs. Tom Skinker's
Field day at the Country Club
Reception at Agnes Farrar's
Reception at Mrs. Ray Davis'
Morning Choral concert (Sadie Taussig sent tickets)
George Markham's party to hear Alfred Robyn's operetta
Hildegarde and Tom McKittrick's wooden wedding
Whist club at Anne Shepley's
We ourselves gave a dinner to Sarah Hitchcock and Jack Shepley. Nan Shepley, Mary Lionberger, Mr. Hodgman and Mr. Blair were there.
Gave the lunch to Countess Reventlow before described.
Lunch to Topic Club – Edith Knox, Lutie Lionberger, Nan Shepley, Mary Lionberger, Frances Markham, Maud Reber, Lutie Kennett & Carrie Allen. Maud & Carrie could not come.
We also gave many informal things, such as those suppers before the concerts, mentioned before.
(It is exhausting just to read through all of these entries. Imagine attending them all and then writing thank you notes!)

Bertha and Henry's first separation after their wedding was on April 16th when Henry had to travel to Wichita, Ft. Worth, and Waco, spending about two days in each location to attend to his business matters. Bertha seemed to fare very well as her letter to Henry on the 19th confirmed. Bertha was constantly busy and her friends stayed with her overnight.

I am making all my plans for my luncheon for Madame La Countess. I have asked Nan, Hilda, Janet, Edith, Emma, Myra, Nan Broadhead, your sister Maggie, Mary & myself. I told Maggie the cook what I was going to do and she rose to the occasion with bouillon, fish coquilles, and everything that could be expected.

…, your mother arrived and, from then on, I have not had one minute. Then Maud and Mrs. Young came and staid until I had barely time to dress for Nan's lunch which she was giving for Annie Allen's Miss Tucker(??). Then from there drove over to Nan Broadhead's tea for Mary Day. Nan Broadhead is going to give me a luncheon next week and so is Frances Markham.

You see, as soon as you are safely disposed of, my friends take pity on me. Your sister Minnie stays with me tonight, Frances tomorrow night. Nancy was with me last night and we talked until nearly twelve. The nicest talk I have had with Nan since I came home, poor old thing, she is pretty blue over life in general.
[1893-04-19 Bertha (StL) to Henry (Waco)]

Concerning the luncheons, Bertha wrote: *"I have found my check book which, in view of the ruinous expenses I find involved in giving luncheons, is a fortunate thing."* [1893-04-20 Bertha (StL) to Henry (Ft. Worth)]

Bertha was evidently very adept at being a hostess for such affairs: *"That lunch was a gorgeous success, dear boy. I wish you might have heard the compliments your wife received. I am too modest to repeat them but, honestly, that table was a dream."* [1893-04-21 Bertha (StL) to Henry (Texas)]

Bertha related various other social gatherings and not without some wit. *"The Lane's dinner. I went to without Henry, he being away. We sang comic songs afterwards, ostensibly to show Count Reventlow what American college songs were like, really to entertain ourselves."* And *"At George Leighton's wedding, there was a tremendous fuss because the people were all assigned special seats instead of setting where they chose and the doors were tightly closed at a certain hour. Our seats were very good, so we were not among the fussers."* [1893 Diary, May 1893]

D. ST. LOUIS SUMMER OF 1893

Bertha and Henry's return to St. Louis on June 24th from their trip to the Chicago World's Fair did not go as planned.

Arrive in St. Louis. Could not get a cab. Go jogging up in a forlorn old omnibus to find that the girls did not expect us until Sunday and no breakfast is ready. Wait an hour for breakfast. Henry goes down town with a raging headache. That evening he departs for Texas – to San Antonio this time, and thence into the interior, off railway lines and out of reach of mail. ... I cannot remember who staid with me that week, but Frances did, and Minnie and Maggie. Henry was gone only a week which was less than he expected.
[1893 Diary, June 24, 1893]

Bertha and Henry had a splendid month of July 1893. Bertha wrote – *"We have a very pleasant July, go to Uhrig's Cave, have long delicious rambles in Forest Park, make acquaintance with its lake lit by Japanese lanterns, etc."* [1893 Diary, July 17, 1893] The only unfortunate event that Bertha relates is the injury caused to their friend, Gist Blair, when his *"pony fell with him and rolled over on him"*. Bertha described the next day of traveling with Mr. Blair who was not back to his true form. *"Spent the morning lazily trying to cheer up Mr. Blair, in the afternoon, he insisted on going in with us, after a jolting ride to the station. Find we have just missed the car and have to take another jolting ride to the other station, Mr. Blair suffering tortures."* [1893 diary, July 16-17, 1893 - full entry in Chap. 8]

E. 1893 VACATION IN THE EAST

On August 7, Bertha and Henry departed for Niagara Falls and the Northeast on their vacation, perhaps a second honeymoon?

Bertha and Henry only stayed at Niagara Falls for four hours where they *"Go under the Bridal Veil Fall, get a thorough drenching and cooling off. Have tea in a funny little restaurant."* [1893 Diary, August 8, 1893]

They then went by train to Clayton NY which is on the St. Lawrence River near Lake Ontario. They had intended to take a boat from Clayton to their next location but their plans changed when the boat had already left.

> Arrive at Clayton[228]. Porter has not waked us, and first boat is gone without us. So go up and take breakfast at inn which reminds us of English inns. Then explore Clayton, inquire about boats, fishing, etc. And decide Clayton would be a nice place to spend the summer.
> [1893 Diary, August 9, 1893]

Bertha and Henry decided to stay at the Crossman House and spent much of their time in Clayton fishing and rowing. On August 10, Bertha included the following in her diary.

> Take an early breakfast and start on our trip. Tom [Comstock] is a big strong fellow, said to be the best guide about. We have a large boat. My seat in the stern has a cane seat bottom and arms. We hire large farmer's hats which we tie down to shield ourselves from burning to a crisp. Fish all morning with but little success, though Tom catches enough pickerel to serve for our lunch. Then we land on an island for lunch. Tom fixes an impromptu table and starts a fire to cook the fish, chops potatoes, corn, etc., which we have brought with us and we wander off through the woods. The meal is perfectly delicious, in spite of the yellow jackets who will join us, and so is the lazy lounging time afterwards. So is the row home when, though we catch no fish, we have a magnificent sunset and Henry aids Tom in the rowing. In the evening, make the acquaintance of Mrs. Dubois of New Haven who chases the flies off me at the supper table and afterward, wander about exploring and admiring the illumination of the islands.
> [1893 Diary, August 10, 1893]

The next day, Bertha found "glory" in the waters.

> Another all-day fishing excursion under the same auspices. This time a German and his wife fishing near us add a little zest by rivalry. They are rowed by Tom's brother, a young fellow who doesn't enjoy his job. We have another delicious picknicky lunch. Coming home, I cover myself with glory. I catch a small mouthed black bass which, on being weighed, proves to be the largest bass of the season and I find myself the heroine of the hotel. (It weighed 4 ½ lbs.) Tom boasts of this achievement to all comers.
> [1893 Diary, August 11, 1893]

Bertha's achievement was noticed by more than their own party. As noted in her next diary entry, "Henry hears a dispute between two boatmen as to which hotel has made the largest catch. Finally hears the Crossman House man say 'look here! YOU KNOW the one the gal caught was the biggest.'" [1893 Diary, August 12, 1893]

On August 16, 1893, they left on a steamer for Montreal. "We have an exciting time shooting the rapids, but when we reach the Lachine Rapid, they decide it is too bad a day for it and we go up to Montreal by canal. Have some trouble getting our luggage but our cabman waits patiently and then we are whirled through the dark streets until we almost think we are being led astray. Finally reach the hotel & comfort." [1893 Diary]

Their next stop was the Westport Inn, Westport New York, on Lake Champlain. They arrived late on August 18, 1893 and the next day were greeted with the beautiful lake.

> Wake in an enchanted land. View of Lake Champlain perfectly beautiful, tree in front of us with one branch of leaves already turning. Ideal breakfast room. Wainscoted in wood, little corner cupboards by brick fireplace filled with sunflowers, and delicious breakfast. Twenty-five cent fine

---

[228]Clayton, NY. This is reached by train from Niagara Falls going around Lake Ontario, currently around the Northern/Canadian side, to the headwater of the St. Lawrence River.

if you take breakfast after nine. Hire a boat by the week. Go rowing, are caught in sudden storm. Take refuge in a fisherman's hut. We sit at table with the Whittemores and Miss King. Miss W. has a temper. [1893 Diary, August 19, 1893]

Bertha and Henry spent the next week in Westport, trout fishing, rowing, hunting (shooting turtles among other targets) and playing card games (whist & euchre). On August 25, 1893, Bertha wrote: "*Our anniversary. Do not remember it until we are perched on the turtle rock.*"

On August 31, Bertha wrote: "*While fishing, Henry has a strike, his reel falls off his rod. In the excitement, I lose a rowlock. After fruitless search for it, scull & sail with umbrella down to next boathouse where we borrow a rowlock.*" [1893 Diary] They left Westport on the next day.

> *Leave dear Westport. Everybody was down to the boat to see us off, we having previously bade a fond farewell to Mrs. Daniel and Mrs. Lyon. Mr. Cutting introduces us to the captain. We have a gorgeous trip through Lake Champlain and Lake George but we are sick of scenery. Take night boat at Albany for New York. Such a jam!*
> [1893 Diary, September 1, 1893]

Bertha and Henry were in New York City for a week which included theater, concerts, baseball, afternoons in the park and a trip to West Point. After a 24-hour train ride on the New York Central, they arrived home on September 7, to be greeted by Mary, their housekeeper.

F. SUMMER 1894 – MERAMEC HIGHLANDS

Instead of going east, Bertha and Henry spent their 1894 summer vacation at the Meramec Highlands.

Depiction of Meramec Highlands during its heyday.

By 1894, the wealthy were well acquainted with the lower Meramec River when the Meramec Highlands Inn and recreation complex was opened. Providing access to the river on a grander scale, the Meramec Highlands Inn provided its own depot, swimming beach, boathouse, rental cottages, a Pagoda dance pavilion, tennis courts, stables, croquet courts, and a mineral water bathhouse. Providing an excellent view of the Meramec River Valley, the Inn itself offered 125 stately rooms with "sanitary plumbing" and electric lights which made the resort the crown jewel of the summer resorts of the area. Numerous indoor amenities included a bowling alley, billiards, and chess rooms, a barbershop, bakery, wine cellar, restaurants, banquet rooms, a stage for plays, and large verandas, where guests congregated to view the beautiful scenery. Many affluent St. Louisans would stay at the resort while still commuting to work on the Frisco Railroad. By the time the resort was in full operation, 12 trains a day stopped at the station.
[www.legendsofamerica.com]

June 18, 1894
We took possession of Fairview Cottage, Meramec Highlands. We passed a quiet, delightful summer. The Treadways and Mr. Greeley took "Riverview Cottage" – the Bonsacks and Niedringhauses "Belleglade", the Harts "Oakwood", the Bernheimers "Elmwood". Henry comes out on the four o'clock train, reaching here at 4:50 every day, and we usually go straight to the Meramec river and row, sometimes we shoot instead.

July 1, 1894
Sam comes out. We go for a long drive, taking Hugh Scott and Annie on Sugar Creek road. Reaching the end at last, a farmer tells us the only way back is the way that we came. But he finally relents and tells us a shorter way. A thunderstorm is now threatening and we take refuge in a country store, almost immediately follows a terrific hail and thunder storm. Hugh Scott behaves like a brick all the way through and reaches home erect and sturdy holding on to the umbrella.

July 2, 1894
Nan and Sarah come out to spend the day but are telegraphed to return on account of the strike. The stations are all guarded by policemen. We suffer little from the strike. Only three of the suburban trains failing to run here. But elsewhere the excitement is terrible, especially in Chicago. No news except of tied up trains, strikes, wrecks, fires, etc.

August 1, 1894
My precious buster was sick, his first illness, cholera infantine – a very light attack, the doctor said, but scared us to death. Annie in especial, became terribly nervous.

August 2, 1894
Henry staid until the twelve o'clock train and we petted the poor buster who was still a pretty sick baby. Went to sleep in the afternoon and woke up all right.

August 25, 1894
A fox chase takes place led by Governor Stone[229], Bessie Kingsland, Eva Lemoine and I pursue the fox with a Kodak.

September 1, 1894
I simply said this summer had been delightful but I did not give many details. We have rowed, shot, driven, bowled with the Bullen's and Mr. Greely, played pool together, had various people out to dinner, and enjoyed ourselves generally but, of course, nothing could give us the sea breezes. Still my boy has thriven splendidly and I myself am a different person. I wish Henry could get away for a rest though.

September 12, 1894
Pouring rain. Henry takes trunks in, in the morning. Annie, Hugh Scott and I come in on the five-six train when it has stopped raining. Find Lizzie and black Lizzie waiting for us and the house looking spotless. Henry is utterly rejoiced to get home again but I pine a little for the Highlands.
[1893 Diary]

G. SUMMARY OF 1894-1895 ENTERTAINMENTS
Bertha provided a detailed listing of all of Henry's and her entertainment events for 1894 and 1895 which took up nine pages in her diary[230]. She also included a summary of these events as follows:
I have forgotten some entertainments we went to but in summing up what was accomplished during the winter and spring – it amounted to about this.
- *Attended over eighty five entertainments, about forty seven of them together,*

[229] William Joel Stone (1848 – 1918) was a Democratic politician from Missouri who represented his state in the United States House of Representatives from 1885 to 1891, and in the U.S. Senate from 1903 until his death; he also served as the 28th Governor of Missouri from 1893 to 1897.
[230] See the detailed listing at the end of this chapter 17.

- entertained over eighty different people at the house, sixty of them at formal entertainments – and many of them several times.
- Paid two hundred and sixty five calls, so that now all my wedding calls are returned except two in the country and all my entertainment calls paid.
- Organized a German Club with Mrs. Dwight Collier, and went faithfully every week, from the middle of January to the middle of April, missing but two meetings, both for good reasons, the work done included translating two German novels into English - besides English into German translations, German letters, etc. Members Mme. Hoffman, Conductress and teacher, Mrs. Dwight Collier, President. Self - Secretary and Treasurer. Mrs. Dan Catlin, Mrs. Mallinckrodt, Miss Florence Hayward, Miss Lily Irwin, Mrs. Edgar Lackland, Mrs. Jesse MacDonald, Mrs. Wayman Cushman, Miss Emma Lane, Mrs. George Leighton, Mrs. John Dyer, Mrs. Tracy, Mrs. Ephron Catlin, Mrs. Joseph Chambers.
- Belonged to a weekly French Club, which however, I attended less faithfully and did less work for.
- Went to the "Dorcas" every week until after Christmas.
- During Lent, went almost every week to another sewing society organized by Emma Lane.
- Was on the selection committee of the Review Club.
- Was on the collecting and distributing committee of the needlework guild – of which I was a Section President and collected one hundred and twelve garments for it.
- I took lunch with mother almost every day, never letting two days pass without being down there, and I presided over my boy's bath every day, no matter what happened, generally putting him to sleep afterward.

This may sound conceited, but I think when you consider that with all this, I kept my accounts, ran my house fairly smoothly, had no domestic upheavals and saw a good deal of my intimate friends, that it was a pretty successful winter. I went to church quite regularly too.
[1893 Diary, February 14, 1895]

H. CHRISTMAS 1895

Bertha and Henry's 1895 Christmas was very special.

Dec. 24, 1895

Hugh Scott's birthday and Christmas Eve. Go to mother's to lunch. George comes back and helps me fix tree. Evening. Grandma Scott, Uncle Sam, Aunt Maggie and cousin Hugh and Aunt Minnie and Uncle Frank Carter come to dinner. Have the tree and the presents first. Uncle Frank makes love to baby Nancy and she responds. Hugh Scott presides at the table and then goes to bed. A happy evening.

December 25, 1895

The happiest Christmas I have ever spent. Loads of presents in the morning. Henry gave a silver waiter. Father drops in to breakfast. He has had his but we are still at the table. Mother has sent Henry a beautiful liqueur set, glass set in silver – and to me a whole basket of things, but her real present to me was a superb flowered silk of which she brought the materials from New York, trimmings, linings and all, beautiful rhinestone buttons, but she gave it to me in time to have Miss Slater make it up for the Catlin ball. After looking at presents, we rush down to church. The service is beautiful. The dear old Dean Schuyler presiding. The last Christmas he was to be there, though we did not know it then, of course.

Then back to my precious mother's to dinner. Hugh Scott on a horse Gruff had given him. A jolly bright dinner. Take Hugh Scott to the Christmas tree at the Elliott Bridges, where he has a lovely time. Take him home and rush out to the Guy's (it has all been rush), to see the play performed the "Mouse Trap". Walk home with the Lanes. Meet Sam on our door step. He comes in and we have

a picnic supper. Servants all out. Then we go up to Minnie and Frank Carter's for some egg nog and imperial cake and wind the day up there. A happy, happy day – full of sunshine, with all the people we love the dearest and with good friends. There was not a cloud on that day. I shall look back to it often. With Christmas Eve and Christmas together, we saw all of both our families. A red letter day in life's calendar.
[1893 Diary]

I. 1896 ENTERTAINMENTS

Bertha kept very careful records of all of the social events that she attended and noted that Henry attended *"more than half"*. Her diary recorded the following summary:

[1896 SEASON RESUME]
To give a resume of the season, as I did last year, we entertained over a hundred people at the house, some of them many times, formally and informally. We went to over a hundred entertainments, more than half of them together. Was a member of the Dramatic Club Committee. Received at the Second Imperial. Received at the first Country Club Field Day. Was on Collecting and Distributing Committee of Needlework Club. Was on Selecting Committee of Review Club. Went to Sewing Club once a week. Went to mother's nearly every day. Paid ninety calls.
[1893 Diary]

J. 1899 EVENTS

The 1898 year ended on a somber mood. *"Have quiet, sad winter. Both Henry and I far from well."* [1893, November 12, 1898] Even Bertha's Christmas entry in 1898 seemed to lack enthusiasm. *"A quiet Christmas. George home. All the family come to us."* [1893 Diary]

But 1899 was a new year. The visit of Helen Ernst in April 1899 certainly was a delight to Bertha.
Helen Ernst came to me and staid two weeks. Such a happy time. All my girlhood comes back. Helen is unchanged in her own dear self and more charming than ever. So many friends of mine were away or in mourning that I had feared she might have a dull time but she is entertained on all hands. She was here two weeks and went to thirty five entertainments, almost all given in her honor. I am writing this some little time after and some may have escaped me, but I want to keep in mind those especially given for her, so I write those as nearly in order as I can remember, not trying to keep count of those not given especially for her.
- *Dinner at Mrs. Dexter Tiffany's*
- *Lunch at Myra Lane's,*
- *Lunch at Mrs. Henry Hitchcock's,*
- *Card party at Janet Elliott's*
- *Reception at Sarah Shepley's*
- *Dinner at our house,*
- *Lunch at Mrs. Shepley's*
- *Theater party and supper at St. Nicholas by Jack Davis,*
- *Lunch at Madge Scott's*
- *Dinner at Charlotte Leighton's*
- *Lunch at Country Club with Marion Davis*
- *Reception at Lucile Chouteau's*
- *Supper at Mrs. Campbell's (a charming everning)*
- *Lunch at my house,*
- *Dinner at Hildegarde McKittricks,*
- *Lunch with Frances Markham at Country Club,*
- *Reception at Bereiner Morrison-Fuller's*
- *Dinner at Mary Lionberger's,*

-       *Dinner at our house.*
[1893 Diary, April 5, 1899]

Bertha took a more serious interest in golf in May and June of 1899. She wrote in her Diary that she went for lessons at the St. Louis Country Club every other day. There was a trip to Chicago in June and she entertained the "summer widows" at her house. Bertha left for Jamestown on July 6 for a three month stay. Her father visited her there and Henry came for a full month during August & September.

As the following post attests, Bertha kept up with her shopping when she was in New York.
> *I expect you will think my next demand very exorbitant but it is only getting some in advance of October or November's dividend for I had to have some hats. I have not had a new winter hat for two years so, as Madame Smyth had her opening on Bellevue Avenue today and I had been informed by Shoreby Hill and others that she was one of the best places in New York, so I went and her hats were perfectly beautiful, the most becoming shapes to me that they have had in some years. And I bought a dress hat and an everyday hat – sixteen and ten dollars and sent them home C.O.D. That is not expensive for good hats, I was amazed to find a New York woman so reasonable – so will you please give Lizzie or Bessie the money to pay when they arrive. I know you don't mind the money, don't misunderstand me, I only hate to press you anymore just now but it is so hard to get a decent hat in St. L.*
[1899-09-21 Bertha (Jamestown, Newport) to Henry (StL)]

Although Hugh Scott came down with typhoid fever in early December, his recovery after several weeks led to a joyous Christmas.
> *Dec. 25, 1899*
> *Have a beautiful Christmas, so thankful the little lad is out of danger. George is home. Have family dinner – all the family. Decorate two little Christmas trees for dinner table. One is carried up to Hugh Scott in evening, one later taken to little Tom Skinker at Hospital. One of the gayest holiday weeks I ever spent.*
> *Country Club dinner. "Messiah" supper at Mary L's afterwards. Dinner for George at our house. Yale Glee Club & Imperial afterward. Beautiful Maud Turner! Dinner at Nan's, poetry party at the Harry January's.*
>
> *Dec. 31, 1899 & Jan. 1, 1900*
> *See the old year out and the New Year in at Colonel Leighton's. Colonel Leighton makes a speech that breaks all our hearts. Afterwards, everyone exerts themselves to the utmost. Gay Virginia reel, Col. Leighton leading off, Mr. Catlin in shirt sleeves. Sing "America" and "Auld Lang Syne".*
> [1893 Diary]

K. 1900

In her diary, Bertha gave a brief summary of the year leading up to her 34th birthday.
> *April 30, 1900*
> *Thirty-four years old. Have been looking back at the entries of thirty-one and thirty-two. How much younger, stronger, brighter in every way, I feel, than on those two anniversaries. And what has the year accomplished? Well, we have had much sickness, Minnie's nervous prostration, Hugh's typhoid fever, Nancy's grip, Miss Jennie's grip, and father's illness. But thanks to God's infinite mercy, there have been no breaks in our family circle and all are pretty well now, except over at Minnie's where she has just had another attack. Outside, we have lost many friends, I have hardly ever known such a winter. Dear Charlie Hodgman, Maud Turner, Tom Booth, Mary Young, Mrs. Lockwood, Charlie Moffitt, and dear little Elizabeth Smith, Nancy's friend.*

May 16, 1900

I would like to finish giving a resume of the year such as I have given other years but it is much mixed up. Out of thirty weeks, thirteen of illness, six of entertaining guest – i.e. Bishop Leonard, Gist Blair, my brother George and Emily Graves – takes much time. The French club lived a feeble life thru Lent. We have taken up social life again after three rather quiet years. Have paid over a hundred calls. Dorcas has flourished and I feel more and more at home and thoroughly in touch with the Home of the Friendless work. Henry has been elected by the board of directors at St. Luke's Hospital. In spite of the illnesses, we have entertained one hundred different people at the house, many of them many times. Hugh and Nancy have had their first year at school, that is, in the kindergarten – under Mrs. Collins.
[1893 Diary]

Bertha spent the first part of the summer of 1900 in Rye Beach and found it very hard to leave. (This was Bertha's first full summer back in Rye Beach since 1893, not including short visits to see her father.)

From June 27th to Aug. 7,

Have a perfect month. Golden weather, meet all my old friends, Siters, Lewises, Hotchkisses, Miss Grace, etc. Introduce the children to the Philbricks, Mrs. Seavey, etc. Visit all my old haunts and love it more every day. Our table in the dining room consists of Mrs. Knox and her daughter Bessie, Admiral and Mrs. Balch and their two daughters, Maisie and Grace. We grow very fond of each other. Esther Starr comes over from York and spends a day with me, and we go to the Farragut for claret punches and dinner, and I spend a day at York Harbor with her. Every day, I love my view over the beautiful salt marshes and out to sea more and, when we leave, I feel a little like my son Hugh who cries all the way to the station.
[1893 Diary]

From Rye Beach, Bertha took the family to Dublin New Hampshire. It was disappointing.

Aug. 7, 1900 (Dublin, NH))

Leave Rye. Minnie meets us and takes the ride from Lynn to Boston with us. Then we go to Dublin, each mile it gets hotter, it is so dusty when we reach there that even the lake looks dusty. The Nagels and we have taken a house together. Find they have arrived just two hours ahead of us. One of their rooms has been given to Mrs. Dawson of Baltimore; one of them is the general passageway for the whole house and is unusable. These were her two main rooms. Dining room infested with flies, children's worse, supper uneatable. Holy Moses! And I left paradise to come to this hole!
[1893 Diary]

Bertha was able to get away from Dublin the next week, thank goodness!

Aug. 16, 1900 (Boston)

Go down to meet Henry in Boston. Stay at Touraine.

Aug. 17, 1900 (Rye Beach)

Go down to Rye. Stay at the Farragut with father, have a perfect time dazzling weather. Play golf every morning, then take hot salt bath. After dinner, drive.

Aug. 29, 1900 (York Cliffs, NH)

Go to York Cliffs, spend day and night with the Fowlers. Knoxes come to lunch. After lunch, men play golf, we drive. Evening – meet the Shobers again at the Inn. Mrs. Shober and Bessie very little changed.

Aug. 30, 1900 (Walpole, NH)
Leave York Cliffs, go to Walpole. Spend two nights and a day with the Bridges. Beautiful place. In the time we are there, are served with fourteen fresh vegetables from their own farm and that by no means exhausts the list. Come very near buying a beautiful old place there in perfect colonial style, furnished throughout with old colonial furniture, has big trees, a brook, a lilac hedge eight feet high - the Knapp place. We might not have been able to get it, but it is under the lea of the hill and that settles it anyway.

Sept. 1, 1900 (Dublin, NH)
Return to Dublin – heat unspeakable. Henry nearly dies. After a few days, tho', get cooler weather, H.C. engages a team of horses for three times a week. We join the golf club, go to all the tennis tournaments, etc. But still we pine for Rye, though we frequently look at one farm which is for sale in Dublin with a longing eye. Marion and Maggie visit Mary during this time.

Sept. 20, 1900
Nan, Sarah, Henry & I drive around the mountain. Previous to that, Henry one day drove the same party over for Nan to inspect Shattuck's and the "Ark", and we had a nice chat with Mrs. Poole.

Sept. 22, 1900
Henry goes home.
[1893 Diary]

The 1900 year concluded with the Christmas and New Year's Eve festivities.
Dec. 25, 1900
Christmas Day, 1900. Nice day. It snowed yesterday so we had a beautiful white Christmas. Children very happy with their stockings. George Drake able to be up, though he was in bed all the day before. Miss Jennie, Maggie, Hugh and Preston come to dinner. After dinner, have the tree. Sam, Madge & Marjory come – Carr Meysenburg comes to call & stays to supper. A pleasant Christmas, a great joy to have father home again. Henry gives me some long needed sherry glasses, father - a fur for my neck. We have the house trimmed with greens and holly and the tree is the most gorgeous we ever had.

Dec. 31, 1900 & Jan 1, 1901
Go to Colonel Leighton's to see the old year out and the New Year in. First have the choir boys from Christ Church Cathedral sing Christmas carols. About thirty people there, all our nearest and dearest friends. This year, Colonel Leighton does not feel equal to a speech but made instead and most beautifully, Tennyson's "Ring out wild Bells" and part of Thackeray's "Actor's Farewell". Afterward, many speeches, much gaiety, sing Auld Laug Syne. After supper, Howard & I dance Cakewalk, followed by Laurie Mauran & Emily Wickham. Then we dance Virginia Reel, but this year, Colonel Leighton only watches us. Wind up as usual with Auld Lang Syne again and "America". A beautiful evening. New Year's Day – take mid-day dinner at the Country Club with almost the same crowd that were at the Leightons the night before. After dinner, play "Old Man's Out" and "Follow my Leader". Come in by way of the Dan Russell tea. Father took lunch with Col. Leighton and called on Mrs. Ridgely, where he got us usual glass of egg nog.
[1893 Diary]

L. 1901

Bertha must have liked to surprise. On her eighth wedding anniversary On February 14, 1901, she decided to wear her wedding dress to breakfast! After 8 years, Bertha wrote that it fit perfectly although, alas, it may have already gone out of style during those years. (Such changing fashions!)

*Our eighth wedding anniversary. Henry brings me violets and lilies of the valley – wear the dress
I was married in to breakfast. It fits perfectly, but O, it looks old fashioned.*
[1893 Diary, Feb. 14, 1901]

On the urging of Henry and her father, Bertha joined Henry on his business trip in February 1901. The trip
took Bertha to Wichita on February 18th, Ft. Worth on the 21st, Dallas on the 23rd and Waco on the 25th. In
each place, Henry had arranged for Bertha's entertainment while he was working, especially in arranging
for the wives of his business associates to take Bertha out. About Wichita, Bertha commented: *"Wichita
must be a pretty town in summer but February is no time to see it."* [1893 Diary, Feb. 21, 1901]

Bertha's visit to Ft. Worth seemed to go a little better than Wichita.
Feb. 21, 1901 (Fort Worth)
*Arrive at Fort Worth – Worth Hotel. Nice rooms, bath, etc. Mrs. Lord, wife of superintendent,
takes me to drive in the afternoon to see the city. Pretty place, spring weather. Meet Henry at Mrs.
Lord's, have sweet wine & cake. Darling baby John Lord Burke, Mr. Lord's grandson.*

Feb. 22, 1901
*Mrs. Brown, wife of secretary, calls. Take dinner at Mrs. Lord's. She cooked it herself. Afterward,
her daughter plays and son-in-law sings. Leaves a pleasant picture of a family group. It begins to
snow. Evening – go to tea at the Brown's, have pleasant evening. (Nice little girl, Elizabeth.)
Come home in heavy snow.*
[1893 Diary]

Dallas was the next stop and it seemed to agree with Bertha.
Feb. 23, 1901
... Go to Dallas. Oriental Hotel, pretentious, but not as well kept as Worth House.

Feb. 24, 1901 (Dallas)
*Sunday. Go to Church at very handsome cathedral, hear good sermon from man named Luck.
Take walk. Afternoon, go over Henry's [railroad] line to Oakcliff. After inspecting park & car
shed, walk in – have walked eight miles today. Dallas is a pretty place.*
[1893 Diary]

Lastly, Bertha went to Waco.
Feb. 26, 1901 (Waco)
*Nice walk. Spring weather, picturesque town. Afternoon – Beautiful drive. Would rather live in
Waco, I believe, than any place I've seen yet.*

March 1, 1901
*Ride over Henry's car line to University. Car-driver, on seeing my name on my pass, asks if I am
the President's wife and adds, confidentially, that he knows the "old man".*
[1893 Diary]

On her 35th birthday in 1901, Bertha included the following in her Diary.
April 30, 1901 (St. Louis)
*"Weary Heart, thou art halfway home[231]." Don't feel very weary. This year went to ninety-seven
entertainments, fifty-four together in the evening. Entertained ninety-six people at home, forty-six
formally, ran Dorcas, was Asst. Sec'y Home of the Friendless, Review Club, Book Committee.*

---

[231] From "The Years of a Man's Life Are Three Score and Ten", Poem by Nathaniel Parker Willis (January 20, 1806 – January
20, 1867), also known as N. P. Willis, was an American author, poet and editor.

June 19, 1901
Minnie, Maggie, Hugh, Nancy, George, Ellen, Helen, Lizzie and I leave St. Louis for Rye Beach.
Hot night, but cool afterward.

June 21, 1901 (Rye Beach)
Father meets us at Rye. Find the cottage more than our fondest dreams could have pictured it.
Miss Jenness waiting with the Russell Sawyers – and delicious supper ready. Every modern
convenience in house – and the house itself so dainty and exquisite. The view, the perfection of
peace and beauty. I have a fleeting glimpse of George Drake, now Dr. Drake, who is in for Francis
Dibblee's wedding. Month that follows is the hottest I have ever known at Rye but it seems cool in
comparison with the reports from home where the thermometer reaches 106 degrees constantly.
Minnie is ill a good deal, though plucky.
[1893 Diary]

Henry remained in St. Louis for the first part of the summer and was jealous of Bertha who was able to
leave for Rye Beach.
I am beginning to be jealous of Rye. I don't think I have ever known you to write in such enthusiasm
of any place. That letter from the woods was a very nice one, dearie, and I could almost see you
surrounded by your girlhood friends. The friends of our youth do appeal to us with uncommon
force and there is something in getting back to old haunts unlike in its pleasure any other
sensations.
[1901-06-- 20170807-3 Henry(StL) to Bertha]

But Bertha's 1901 summer ended too soon.
Sept. 1, 1901
Have been writing up the summer's record. Have had a beautiful, peaceful summer. Father comes
twice a day. Have had the children with me a great deal, particularly in the early part, teaching
them to read, reading aloud, etc. We have Sunday School together in the pine woods – on damp
mornings on the beach – until Mr. Tompkins comes and has a regular Sunday School, Sunday
afternoons at the little church. I am feeling very well now, though it took me a long while to gain
my strength. Everyone has been so kind and I feel as if I had been very unresponsive. I think the
children have had a lovely summer. Among other pleasures, they have had two kittens, one of
which, Whitetoes, a beautiful Maltese , with white feet. It will be a real grief to me to leave, myself.
We are to leave on the seventh – only one more week of paradise!
[1893 Diary]

On September 29, 1901 after returning to St. Louis, Bertha's lost her daughter, Mary Roberta Scott, in
childbirth. She made no other entries in her diary until that Christmas.
Dec. 25, 1901
A quiet happy Christmas. Go to church for the first time in months. The Bishop preaches a
beautiful but sad sermon. Henry and I go to see the Post-Dispatch dinner afterward, a sight well
worth seeing, seven thousand people fed, and all the children receive Christmas presents. Then
home to a family dinner, all the family as usual, Maggie absent, sick, and Dr. George, who has
been delayed on his trip south, does not get home until night. Christmas tree in the afternoon.

Dec. 31, 1901
Last year at this time, we were all together, a gay crowd, at Colonel Leighton's. Now, the brave
Colonel, himself, has left us, the gallant fight with death that lasted so long, ended last summer.

Hildegarde and Tom are in deep mourning for their youngest child, and my beautiful baby was given to me and taken from me again. Among the others who were there, I think there have been no bereavements – but among our other friends, what a year it has been. Otto Meysenburg, Mr. Yeatman, Judge Madill, those were the nearest to us, but my father counted ten among his friends who are gone.
[1893 Diary]

M. 1902

Bertha spent the summer of 1902 with the children in Rye Beach. And those summers in Rye Beach were always a pleasure.

June 20, 1902 (Rye Beach)
Leave for Rye. Take Nellie for house girl, Mary Whittemore for cook, Ellen as usual. In every way, one of the happiest and most successful summers I have ever spent. It was cold but we all gained in health, steadily. I had Marion Treadwell and her boy Abbot with me for a visit to the endless delight of the children who made a dear and intimate friend of him. Emma Lane Ward and Gist Blair also staid with us, and Helen Ernst and Cynnie Yeatman Sewall spent different days with us. Gave a straw ride to seventeen children.

[A postal card found tucked in the diary at this point addressed to H.C.Scott, St. Louis, reads as follows:
"Rye Beach, N.H.
Wednesday 1902
One hay-wagon! Sixteen children!! Three boxes of ginger snaps! Two boxes of candy! Sixteen American flags! Sixteen tin horns!! ME!!! Funeral tomorrow at half past nine. B.D.S."]

August 5, 1902
Henry came on.

August 10, 1902 (New York City)
We went to New York. Waldorf Astoria.

August 11, 1902
Louis Lemoine took dinner with us. We went to "Chinese Honeymoon" with him afterward.

Aug. 12, 1902 (Morris Plains, NJ)
Spent a most perfect and beautiful day with Uncle William and Altha at Morris Plains. The place has never looked more exquisite in its loveliness and our welcome was delightful. Drive to Washington Headquarters first, of course, after leaving Morris Plains.

Aug. 13, 1902
Evening – Take sound boat "Puritan". Notice the coal smoke in the harbor. Glorious sunset.

Aug. 14, 1902 (Marion, MA)
Arrive at Fall River. Take Trolley to Marion. Stay with Nan. Charming little house.

Aug. 15, 1902
Henry goes sailing in race with Jack Lionberger and Zack. Is nearly frozen and has violent attack of pain on return. Tea with Hildegarde and Alma.

Aug. 16, 1902 (Rye Beach)
Back to Rye by way of Boston.

Aug. 18, 1902
Hear of Florence Boyle's not being well. Dear Florence – being with her was one of the great pleasures of the early summer.

Aug. 22, 1902
Buy skiff with sail at Salisbury Point, name it "Nancy".

Aug. 30, 1902
Give my tea at the Golf Club. Esther Doolittle, Marion Treadwell, and Mary Batchelder help me make sandwiches in the morning. Maria Dickey helps pour tea in the afternoon.

Aug. 25, 1902
Spend day at the shoals[232] with Helen Ernst, being the eleventh anniversary of our engagement.

Aug. 26, 1902
Let maids go to shoals. Gave children & Abbot Treadwell a picnic in the woods.

Sept. 15, 1902
Spent day at York Harbor. Dinner with the Starrs. Henry went to see Mrs. Hitchcock. Mrs. Starr very ill.

During this last month, Florence Boyle went through her long painful illness, was finally taken home, and we received the news of her peaceful death, two days later.

Sept. 20, 1902
Father moved to our cottage. Hotel closed 22

Sept. 23, 1902
Drive to Exeter. Mrs. Ash Newell & sister at supper.

Sept. 24, 1902
Mazie Balch and her fiancé, Mr. Sears, come to dinner. Tried to get Mrs. Butler, wife of President of Columbia College with whom we have formed pleasant friendship, this year but she was away.

Sept. 26, 1902
Left for home. Ellen leaves children's basket of clothes. Joys on train.

Sept. 28, 1902 (St. Louis)
Arrive home. House in lovely order. Lizzie and Mary Mahan smiling to meet us.

Sept. 29, 1902
Children start to school again.
[1893 Diary]

---

[232] i.e. The Isles of the Shoals where Henry proposed to Bertha in August 1891.

N. CLUBS

Bertha and Henry joined many clubs – social, academic, professional, etc. Henry was a member of Academy of Science, Missouri Historical Society, St. Louis Commercial Club, St. Louis Club, University, Noonday, St. Louis Country, Florissant Valley, Contemporary clubs. [1911-01-15 Newspaper Reports of Henry's death]

Bertha also belonged to a variety of clubs over her lifetime, including: Topics, German, and Sewing (to mention just a few). Clubs were so central to social life that even their children had clubs.

1. KODAK CLUB

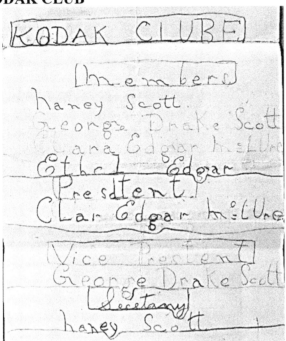

Belonging to one or more clubs was a matter of importance in St. Louis. So when Nancy and George Scott were very young, they joined the "*Kodak Clube*". George was elected Vice President and Nancy Secretary. Undoubtedly, these positions bestowed upon them great respect among the members!

2. ST. LOUIS COUNTRY CLUB
a. A Place of Refuge & Entertainment

The St. Louis Country Club was a place of refuge for Henry, especially when Bertha was out of town. It provided relief from the summer heat in the city, recreation, friendship and even a night's rest.

> *I cut the office and came out here because I was just played out and I hope to get a good night's sleep, for it is "coming to me". The last few nights I have slept poorly and altho' I am very well, I am tired beyond expression.*

[20180127-1 Henry (StL) to Bertha]

> *I came out here this morning, dearest, and I am very glad I concluded to come for already the Country air has helped me greatly and I am practically well again. There was no work pressing at the office so, after getting your two letters, the first received from Rye, I took the first train for the country. This is the first "field day" of the Country Club and I am really quite proud of it. We have entertained about fifty guests and have done it very well. The place itself is beautiful and the races, the polo games, the trap & bird shooting, have all been very interesting. When "our crowd"*

comes out next year, we will have fine fun. George Shepley is here. He and Jack have been living out here for several days. The whole party has left me, even Mr. Parsons and the elder Mr. Scudder, to see the second race of the day between Jack, Al Shapleigh and one of the Scudders. I am "out" of field sports for the time being and only participate as one of the audience.
[1892-07-05 Henry (StL) to Bertha (Farragut House, Rye Beach)]

Since Henry was friends with most of the members, he was made a director in 1892.

Dear, the Country Club has loaded me with honors. I am a director. The board of control consists of five members elected by ballot each year and the first selection are Jim Blair, Jack, Mr. Scudder, Al Shapleigh and one H.C.S. I am not by any means sure I am a permanency for I don't see what good I can be on the board so, as I had to leave the meeting before it adjourned, I asked one of the men to offer my resignation and urge in my place your guardian who would make a much better officer and would really, I think, like the work.
[1892-03-28 (6 letters) Henry to Bertha]

In October 1892, Henry planned a party at the club for Bertha when she returned for Howard Elliott and Janet January wedding.

Did I tell you that Jack and I have planned to have you and Miss Nan and one or two of the other girls out at the Country Club in October? When you come, I shall consult you about the selection of a chaperon of sufficient age and dignity to satisfy the demands of two very particular young women and, by that time, I think we shall have arranged to take care of a sufficient number of people to enable you to include any of your particular friends whom you may care to add to the party. I don't think I shall permit you to suggest any of the men – you would be sure to select some of your especial admirations and they would be in the way. Do you think you and I could stand my taking my holiday then and giving you the opportunity to become familiar with the Florissant valley under my guidance?
[1892-08(-) (Tuesday 1892-08-02) 20170828-4 Henry to Bertha]

Bertha responded to Henry's letter noting that she would be better at selecting the men for the affair; she acknowledged that Henry's selection of the women would be satisfactory.

I hope you will carry out your intention of moving out to the Country Club, Henry, for I think the city must be odious at present and the heat may be more bearable out there. Your plan for the fall there is perfection in all but on particular, I want to choose the men myself. You can choose the girls if you want to, I am sure your selection would be satisfactory. Your taste in girls is admirable but I am not sure that, as regards men, it is equally good. However, Kin is married!!!

Dear, I do not wish to criticize any letters which was as agreeable as your last but when you tell me you enjoyed the scenery of the Ozark Mountains because it made you think how beautiful the scenery of the Florissant Valley would be next fall, I become skeptical and think of Jerome K., Jerome's remarks in the subject of flattery. Still, slightly far-fetched as that seemed to me, it did not in the least interfere with my enjoyment of the remarks you made as to your taking your vacation at the Country Club when we were there.

"Do I think I could stand it?" If it referred to the superabundance of your society, I really think, if there were enough people there to break the monotony, of course. I really think I could. And, O, won't we have a good time, dear friend? Possibly the time may come when I may have too much of your society but so far that is not one of the tests to which I have been subjected.
[1892-08-06 (Saturday) Bertha (Rye Beach) to Henry (StL)]

Henry was obviously amused by Bertha's suggestion that Henry was not up to the task of inviting suitable men for the Country Club affair and by Bertha's remarks about the *"scenery of Florissant Valley"*.

> *I am glad you like the suggestion that we make up a party for the Country Club – even if, incidentally, my "taste in men" was found fault with. Now, I dislike to humble the pride of a young woman upon a matter too that she has especial pride in but frankness compels me to state that, as poor as is my "taste" in this particular, I tremble at the prospect of having the Club filled up with the men whom I am afraid not to accept as the proper "sort" but who will probably give it the appearance of being a female seminary rather than an athletic institution. However, I'm resigned to the inevitable and you may ask every "Miss Nancy" in St. Louis if you give me leave to turn them over to Jack who will be, you well know, delighted(!) to entertain them. And you were mighty funny about the "scenery of Florissant Valley"! I have not recovered my equanimity sufficiently to tell you how very amusing you were! I promise you however not to move you to excite me to any such alarming merriment for some time to come.*
> [1892-08(-) (Wednesday 1982-08-10) 20170722-1 Henry to Bertha]

Later in 1892 in October, Henry wrote about his race at the Country Club on Club Day and the *"ignominious failure of one of its members to achieve glory."*

> *The Country Club meeting "broke up" at seven this evening after a most successful day, generally, but having registered a most ignominious failure of one of its members to achieve glory. So instead of the telegram of exultation I promised to send you, I modestly record my defeat here. In the only straight race in which I was entered, I came out a very poor second and, as I had confidently expected to win, my disappointment was great but I bear up under my misfortunes reasonably well for the day was not less pleasant than it would have been had I won. I think everyone enjoyed the day. The weather was on its good behavior and we had a very fair attendance, although a number of people did not go out because of the storm Thursday. Miss Nan, Lute, Mattie, Mary, Miss Edith January and Mrs. Tom McK were the representatives of your crowd and all the men you know were there. Jack Shepley won his race but his side was defeated at polo. One of the races was won by China(?) Bachman and your guardian[233] won the cigar and umbrella race. Perhaps all these details are a bore but I thought they might possibly interest you. Miss Nan, by way of making me feel cheerful, wished for you several times during the day and Lute said "if Bert would only not run away from St. Louis as she does, she and we would have a much nicer time, wouldn't we?"*
> [1892-10-22(-) (Tuesday 1892-10-18) Henry (StL) to Bertha – C/O William Burton, Chicago, IL]

Bertha wrote that she was not *"sorry"* that Henry lost in the Club race, especially since she was not in St. Louis to *"quench you properly"* if he had won.

> *I have forgotten to sympathize with you on your losing the race. On the whole, I think I am not sorry. You were so dead sure of winning, son, that there would have been no living in the house with you if you had won and I not there to quench you properly.*
> [1892-10-26 (Wednesday) Bertha (Boston, MA) to Henry (StL)]

The Country Club was generally a good place to go to beat the St. Louis heat in the summer. During a particularly hot St. Louis summer day, when *"the men were sitting around grumbling and reviling their luck at being in town when Alf [Kennett] came in with: 'Some men were born great, some achieve greatness, while others leave a great thirst upon them. Gentlemen, what will you have?'"* [1897-07-13 Henry (StL) to Bertha (Jamestown)]

Sometimes, the Country Club was bedlam.

> *I could have written yesterday but for coming out here. But I will at least put in the claim that I thought I could do so from here and was not prepared for the bedlam that reigns here Saturday*

---

[233] Henry periodically refers to "Bertha's guardian". Unfortunately, Henry never mentions him by name.

evening and until well into Sunday morning and which makes writing about as impossible [as] preaching a sermon.
[20170725-1 (1900-) Henry (StL) to Bertha]

And the Club could be fun and games.

O, I forgot to tell you of our dinner last night. Gordon, John, Ray Davis, Bud Dozier, Shapleigh and I sat at my table. At the next table were the Nic Joneses, Dexter Tiffany, Jack Davis, the Howard Elliotts, Edith January, Geo Markham, Miss West. We noticed that the other table was drinking claret and that Jack and George were plunged into deepest gloom over their unhappy situation. We had ordered the regulation ... ..., but to complete the ... fortune of the two bachelors at the other table, we had our drinks sent in in champagne bottles with napkins tied around them and served in champagne glasses. Jack finally responded with alacrity to a ... from Dozier to a glass of wine and you should have seen his face when he gulped down a wine glass of whiskey and seltzer. He got the laugh on his own people though by announcing that, although it was a disappointment, it was a far better drink than he had got from his own table. They say that George M. is making a dead set at Carroll West. I am inclined to think he will go in there. She is rich.
[20170725-1 (1900-) Henry (StL) to Bertha]

Henry enjoyed playing bridge and, not surprisingly, he liked to win. *"We played bridge at the club, Gordon and I against Larry and John Davis and their bloody scalps are at our belts."* [1906-09-(-) 20180729-6 Henry to Bertha]

But, periodically, there was no fun at the Country Club due to a *"most uninteresting crowd."*

I went to the Country Club for tea yesterday evening. Found a most uninteresting crowd and did not enjoy it. I prefer work to that crowd. They don't suit me "not by no means."
[20170724-9 (1900-) Henry to Bertha]

b. Golf

Henry played golf frequently at the club and, like most golfers, was often unhappy with his game.

I went out to the Country Club again this morning and took a lesson from Mackael. I think my case is hopeless. I got in one good drive during the lesson. If all his pupils are equally stupid, I wonder Jimmy don't quit his avocation and go to breaking rock or something else that's easier.
[20180129-3 (1895-) Henry to Bertha]

I played golf this afternoon – horrible golf – 81.
[20180127-1 Henry (StL) to Bertha]

To his credit, Henry could look at his awkward moments with humor, such as the following when he slipped on muddy ground and *"got up looking like a mud bank."*

I took counsel with myself this morning and decided to go to the Country Club. I have been out all day and have just returned. It rained all morning but in the afternoon we had some fine golf and I think it has set me up no little. The Club is the only place I have seen since you left that looks alive, but the summer widowers are either enjoying life there or making a great presence. Will was out and exasperated me no little. He needed the exercise badly but did not play because it is naughty to break the <u>Sabbath</u> in that way. Jack Shepley, Duncan Mellier(?), Judge Priest, Al Shapleigh, Charlie Knapp, Lindell Gordon, Bud Dozier, Duncan Jug(?) & Dan Taylor made up the crowd or mixture as you may prefer to call it. We were caught in a thunderstorm during our last round and I distinguished myself in trying to leap the small gulley from no. two teeing off place and, as the ground was slippery, I landed flat on my back and got up looking like a mud bank.
[20171220-2 Henry to Bertha]

Henry did have his golf victories and they seemed to more than make up for the defeats.

We went out today, four of us – Gordon, Williams, Semple(?) and I – at five o'clock and played a foursome, Gordon and Semple vs. Williams and Scott. We agreed to play thirteen holes, the first nine then two, three and nine. My side started badly and at the fourth hole, we were three down. At the ninth, two down. At the tenth, three down. Eleven, twelve, thirteen, even and a tie, so we had to go back and play over nine. I drove up to the tree and Semple beyond it – not bad playing. Then we both got on the green in three, they missed and I made a twelve foot put – a sort of miracle in, we winning the match. Wager: high balls, dinner, caddies, golf balls, cigars, liqueurs for four. I am getting even up on my defeat last week.
[20171117-5 (1896-summer-) Henry (StL) to Bertha (Jamestown)]

Regardless of how well (or not) Henry played the game, Henry felt that he was able to advise Bertha about golf and the selection of her clubs.

Be sure to remember what I said about the length of your golf sticks. As you strike the ball, they should be flat on the ground – see illustration on the other side.

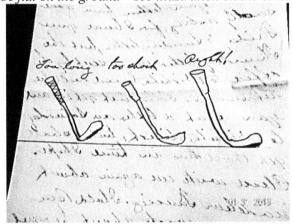

Hand written drawing of three clubs: first – too long (club toe off the ground); second – too short (club foot off the ground); third – right!

Henry clearly understood his limitations as a golfer. His comments in 1908 suggested that golf would never be his "day job" as his player companion that day was spotting him 2 strokes a hole.

Everyone is out of town so, if I don't find Jack Shepley, I may have to play golf tomorrow with my esteemed friend Mr. Stewart Stickney who, despite the fact that he gives me two strokes a hole, admires my game with the tact of an accomplished liar and shows Christian patience with me. That boy ought to get married. He is so meek and submissive that I know he would make a good husband. My! It's a far cry between a game with Mr. Haarstick and Stewart.
[1908-07-04 Henry (StL) to Bertha (Rye Beach)]

c. A St. Louis Cyclone

Being in tornado alley, St. Louis has always been subject to these severe storms, called "cyclones" back in the day. One particular cyclone struck the Country Club. (Apparently, this was not part of the massive 1896 cyclone which destroyed large parts of St. Louis.)

We had a most exciting time at the Country Club last night. A cyclone struck the house while we were at dinner, tore the porch railing down and took our dinner, plates, glass, etc., and scattered them over the grounds smashing them into bits. In a way, it was more alarming than my experience in the first cyclone for the velocity of the wind was so terrific that I really thought the club house would go down under its pressure. Apart, however, from the loss of all the china, glass and table furnishings on our end of the porch and the destruction of many of the best remaining trees, the survivors of the last cyclone and the fire, there were no losses or injuries except to Judge Bayle whose foot was slightly hurt by one of the tables which was blown over on it.

The Seldons had rather a thrilling experience. They were just driving up to the club when the storm struck and managed to get the horses up to the doorway where they were controlled by several of the servants but not before all the lamps in the driveway had been torn down and smashed over the horses. Anne Carter was rather shaken up over her experience and declined, after the storm was over, to drive home so they went back on the cars and as it had meanwhile turned cold, I lent her my golf coat to wear home. When she put it on, we had a good time with her over the fit. Mrs. O'Fallon was at the table next to us and retreated just in time to escape the storm which literally swept away everything at her table, including the table itself and the porch railing immediately behind it.
[20170810-1 Henry to Bertha]

d. An Unexpected Dinner Guest at the Club

Henry was unexpectedly roped into dinner with a visiting Texan, a prospect to which he did not look forward, especially when "*my first impressions confirmed my worst apprehensions of a sad evening.*"

I met another interesting person at the club last night. Dozier and I had been playing golf and, as we were late, ordered our dinners expecting to have no other companions. Just as we were going in to dinner, Mr. Hilliard who is Vice President of Gordon's bank rushed up and said "I have taken the liberty to countermand your dinner order, gentlemen. I want you to dine with me and meet a friend who is president of one of the best Texas banks and, withal, a most charming companion."

Dozier seemed charmed but I was not for I had met Texas bank presidents before. But I couldn't decline without being rude so we were taken up and introduced to the Texan. There were several other St. Louis men in the party and, as I was sitting next to them, I had nothing to say to the Texan for a while. In fact, my first impressions confirmed my worst apprehensions of a sad evening for I don't like jewelry as large as a he egg and moreover the Texan wore no coat! You may imagine my ill luck in being laid hold of and made to take my dinner where I didn't wish to go, with Mary Tilly's party at our table, Grace Jones at another and Mrs. Tracy just behind me.

I found out in a moment however that I had underestimated the Texan for the men on the other side of the table were simply absorbed in the Texan's story which was being told with a most absurd Spanish accent and the story itself proved a great hit. Before we were half way through our dinner, Judge Bayle, Tom and a half dozen other men left their tables and came over to ours and I found the Texan, who proved to be a commissioner of the World's Fair and had been here a week, was the rage and was held to be the most interesting stranger in town, which reputation was clearly well sustained in my case for I had really the time of my life and heard some of the best and best told stories in my experience.

You may imagine the crowd was carried away for the stranger called up a storm of protest by announcing an early return to Texas as necessary! I was hardly prepared however for the general announcement of nearly every St. Louis man present that they would go to the train and thus see the last of our guest and I was clearly not prepared for Dozier's quiet proposal that we should each send some flowers to the train and you will be more astonished than I was for I have not yet told you that the bank president was a woman! And a mighty good looking one too, in spite of the large coral(?) ornaments.
[1904-07-18 Henry (StL) to Bertha (Rye Beach)]

(Henry could definitely spin a good story!)

e. Polo at the Country Club

Henry wrote an amusing letter about playing polo in the heat of 1892.

I am afraid if you knew how I paid for another attempt I made to ride last Sunday, you would see that the doctor is wiser in this matter than you or I for it was made quite plain to me that headaches and horseback rides must be enjoyed together or I must give up the former during the hot season. I am very well but the first semblance of a head-ache I have had for a long time came on Monday and I attribute it to a very hard ride I took Sunday and a polo game played on Sunday afternoon.

(Newspaper cartoon from around 1900)

The doctor laughed when I told him about it and said "well, nothing hurts you very much, that's very plain, but you experiment with your health sufficiently to cause you a good deal of discomfort. Stop riding until cooler weather comes. You need quiet if you are going to work here all summer, at least when you leave your office, and, if you are reasonably careful, you will keep perfectly well for the hot weather seems to agree with you." So, although I shall not give up riding at the Club entirely, I shall abandon the gymnastic performances of the polo field for a short time. Compared to football, polo is a most innocent game. In fact, there is not the slightest danger to one who can ride at all. But it is the hottest amusement on earth in warm weather.

[1892-06-23 (Wednesday) Henry (StL) to Bertha (The Ark, East Jaffrey, NH)]

Bertha found out about this polo match from her friend, Miss Hagen.

Miss Hagen sent me a copy of St. Louis Life the other day because of some articles about the Mary Institute in it. And in reading it through, I came across this item which I cut out. I had been quite delighted over what you said of the Country Club and that you were willing to drop that hard work of yours for a while and go out. But since reading this, my enthusiasm is abating somewhat. Were you in it? And if no, which of your features did you lose? Please break it to me gently.

> *"From what I can hear, that last game of Polo at the Country Club must have been a terrible bloody affair, as scarcely a rider or pony escaped without a permanent scar. However, it is an exhilarating species of sport and should be encouraged even though the players do lose a few features now and then."*
>
> [Article clipping enclosed with Bertha's letter]

[1892-06-13 (Sunday) Bertha (Jaffrey NH) to Henry (StL)]

In an 1898 letter to his son, Hugh, Henry described one of the Club Polo matches.

Dad went to the country the other day and saw lots and lots of very beautiful ponies and some boys in red and white coats were riding the ponies and there was a big white ball and the boys in red coats were trying to hit the ball one way with sticks while they were on the ponies! And the boys in

white coats were trying to knock the ball another way and the ponies would rush at the ball and, if the boys who were riding the ponies did not hit the ball, those wonderful ponies would kick the ball for away on their side and then run after the ball and kick it again until Dad laughed until he most burst because those ponies kicking the ball and trying to play like boys were so awfully funny.
[20180129-4 (1898-) Henry's letter to son, Hugh Scott]

Likewise, in 1906, Henry wrote to Nancy and George about another Polo match.

This is the fourth of July and Dad is out in the country where the polo ponies are and the other men out here seem to be having a good time. It is not as quiet as at Rye. Last night a very nice man brought his friend who was sick out here where it was quiet and where he could have a good sleep but the other men didn't know this and they thought they ought to celebrate the Fourth as soon as it was twelve o'clock at night. So at that time, they began to sing and fire canon crackers and then about two o'clock they got a big drum and marched by every man's bed and woke him up and made him join the procession and when the procession found a very sleepy man, they would take him out and give him a shower bath to wake him up and, if he didn't like the shower bath, they made him stand on a chair and sing Yankee Doodle. Well, the sick man said this morning that it was [not] so very quiet out here after all and I don't think he likes his friend who brought him out here quite as much as he liked him yesterday.
[20180206-8 (1906-) Henry (StL) to Hugh, Nancy and George (Rye)]

f.   The Rackaboa Club

As Henry explained it to Bertha, the Rackaboa Club was formed from St. Louis Country Club members for the purpose of determining what to do with the gift to the Club of a sacred cow from Will McMillan after his hunting trip in Africa. (You can't make this stuff up!)

I believe I did not write you fully about the Rackaboa club, to whose dinner I am asked Friday. This is their second dinner since the club was formed. I could not go to the first as I had another engagement and Judge Boyle who was there tells me I missed the entertainment of the year. The club is new, having been recently formed, to celebrate the gift of Bixby to the Country Club of a sacred cow (only this time it's a he), Rackaboa, which Will McMillan killed in South Africa, had stuffed and shipped to Bixby. The thing looks as big as an elephant and the club directors, when they saw it, regarded the gift in the light of that arrival of the white variety. They put it at first in the largest room but, finding the studious "reading" munchers who haunt that room had all taken to the woods on account of the beast's odor, it was moved out on the porch where it was rained on for several weeks, the rain neither improving its looks or smell. Judge Boyle seemed obviously troubled because of Bixby's manifestations of his affectionate regard for the club but, like a brave man, he stoutly refused to burn the offering, this having been glibly suggested to him as a safe method of permanently removing a strong counter attraction to the other interests of the members. At last, someone suggested that an inner circle club be formed to determine the best disposition of the new member and the Rackaboa club, as they say in history, sprang into being. I shall go the second dinner, if I am alive.
[1908-07-19 (Sunday) Henry (StL) to Bertha (Rye Beach)]

3.   BERTHA'S CLUBS

Henry periodically teased Bertha about her clubs. Bertha would have none of this.

As for my unnecessary clubs, I don't belong to any and, of course, I go to the others.
[1892-01-29 Bertha (StL) to Henry (Wichita)]

I have shed many tears since reading your dismal account of the pool tournament – only third! And only second in the race! Really, my son, this is not what I expected of you, and I am mourning very deeply. Seriously, dear boy, I am sorry for your disappointment but don't you think after telling me of that it was a poor time to commence an attack on my clubs? Suppose I were to say

that I entirely disapproved of the University Club as tending to weaken the influence of home over men; that I could not endure the Country Club because it led to playing polo on Sunday; & that I must certainly request you not to join the Criterion because I disapprove of your joining in such festivities while I was away? Come now, what would you really do if I were to start an attack of that kind? And it would not be a particle more unjust than your attack on the innocent organizations to which I belong. In fact, I could defend mine with more justice for they are useful and yours are not!
[1892-11-04 (Friday) Bertha (Boston) to Henry (StL)]

Bertha wrote to Henry about her sewing club in an 1896 letter.
>   *Jan. 5, 1896*
>   *Sewing and lunch club at Carrie Allen's. This club formed in the fall, started by Nan, Charlotte and myself, is called the sewing clutch of '95. It is run on the plan of the Boston sewing circle – each member must finish two garments a month – and only two solids and a sweet, bread and butter, & tea, coffee or chocolate allowed for lunch.*
>   [1893 Diary]

Prior to her marriage, Bertha often said *"it is very nice to be a girl"*. Based on the extensive social activities and clubs that Bertha participated in after her marriage, it is hard to imagine that she had time to miss being a girl. And Henry never seemed to have any time not scheduled for work and his clubs.

O. COMPLETE DIARY LISTING OF 1894-1895 SOCIAL EVENTS

BALLS – SEASON 1894 – 1895

December 7 (1894)
Bachelor's Ball at the St. Nicholas Hotel. I was one of the receiving chaperons, wore pale blue and gold, danced the German [the Allemande] with Henry. Sat at supper with Lallie Gray, Mary Cushman, Fanita Hayward and their husbands.

December 10 (1894)
Mrs. Skinker's Ball. Wore rose colored brocade. Took Jane Tutt, Mary McKittrick & Mamie Mitchell.

December 14 (1894)
Mrs. Daniel Catlin's German. Wore white brocade and diamonds. Had a most charming time. German was danced in art gallery. The married people only invited to look on. The Dwight Colliers, Frank Hirschbergs, Edmund Wickhams, Wayman Cushmans, George Leightons, Tom McKittricks, Mrs. Whittaker, and ourselves. We dance while the young people are at supper. Afterward, have our own supper. Gist's rudeness to his partner, Jane Tutt.

December 21 (1894)
Mrs. Gilbert Chapman's Ball. Same dress as to the Catlin's. Beautiful ball. Take Hildegarde with us, Tom being away.

December 27 (1894)
The "Imperial". It takes place at the St. Nicholas, after a row that nearly breaks up the club.

January 1 (1895)
Did not go to second Bachelor's Ball.

January 23, 1895
The "Dramatic Club". Wear black lace. Go with Edith and Gordon Knox. Play, "The Dowager". Mary Boyle saves the play by her acting.

January 29 (1895)
Mrs. Jesse January's ball at Hotel Beers. Wear rose colored brocade. Beautiful ball. Go with Edith and Gordon Knox. They exasperate us greatly by talking about leaving all the time.

February 21, 1895
Second Imperial. Henry was away so I did not go.

February 26, 1895
Second "Dramatic". Henry was too ill with grip to go. They say the play was splendid: "two strings to a bow".

LUNCHEONS

November 21 (1894?)
Mrs. Gilbert Chapman's, Mrs. E.C. Dameron's, Mrs. Ralston's to meet Mrs. Madill.

November 28
Charlotte Leighton.

December 4
Mrs. Boyle's, Mrs. Louis Chauvenet's, Mrs. Gordon Knox's.

December 29
Mrs. Guy's – did not go

January (1895)
Mrs. Daniel Catlin's, Mrs. John Shepley's – (same day as Mrs. Catlin's – did not go).

Mary Cushman's, Mrs. Wayman Cushman's

Mrs. Breckenridge
Mrs. Howard Elliott
Mrs. William B. Potter (to meet Miss Yeatman)
Mrs. William B. Potter (to meet Mrs. Austen)
Miss Lane (to meet Mrs. Austen – did not go)
Mary Lionberger's – several times, informally

Topics – Maud Rebers' (2), Carrie Allen's, Lutie Lionberger's,
Edith Knox's, Annie Shepley's, Lute Kennett's

DINNERS

October (1894)
Oct. 1   Mrs. Shepley
Oct. 4   Mr. Bartlett's dinner and theater party
Oct. 11 – Men's dinner at Mr. Henry Hitchcock's
Oct.   Mr. and Mrs. Howard Elliott's

November (1894)
Mr. Bartlett's dinner to Miss Shepley & Mr. Nagel
Miss Edith January's
Mrs. Tom McKittrick's to meet Miss Shepley & Mr. Nagel
Mrs. William Gray's
Mrs. John D. Davis' wedding anniversary dinner

January (1895)
Jan 24 – Mrs. Dexter Tiffany's to meet Miss Shepley & Mr. Nagel
Jan 31 – Mrs. Henry Hitchcock's to meet the same (had another engagement, could not go)

Mrs. Henry S. Potter
Christmas dinner at mother's
New Year's dinner at Mrs. Scott's
Mrs. Halsey Ives to Miss Shepley –

RECEPTIONS

Mrs. B.S. Adams
Mrs. Breckenridge

Nov. 10 (1894) Miss Lemoine's

Dec. 12 – Mrs. Little (did not go)
Dec. 28 – Mrs. Orrick – to meet Mrs. Comey's (evening)
Dec. 28 – Mrs. Tennent – did not go
Dec. 25 – Mrs. Hugh McKittrick
Jan. 1 – Mrs. Wayman Cushman
Jan 1 – Mrs. Norris

Oct. 31 – Mrs. John Whittaker – to meet Mr. and Mrs. Taber (Julia Marlowe). They did not come.

Jan. 22 – Mrs. Huntington Smith
Nov. 23 – Mrs. Julius Pitzman (did not go)
Feb. 1 – Mrs. Boyle to meet Mrs. Forbes Leith
Feb. 1 – Evening – Mrs. Price Lane
Feb. 14 – Mrs. Simmon's (did not go)
Nov.   Mrs. Daniel Catlin's
Nov.   Mrs. Bryson
Dec.   Mrs. Dexter Tiffany. To meet the Harvard Glee Club

January
*   Mrs. Ethan Hitchcock*
*   Mrs. Clifford Richardson*
*   Mrs. George E. Leighton*
Mrs. Edger Lackland (did not go)
Mrs. Ephron Catlin's
Mrs. Clifford Richardson – to meet Mrs. Terhune – (Marion Harland).
Mrs. Robert McKittrick Jones (musical reception to meet the Mrs. Gary – did not go)
Miss Emma Lane's – to meet the Mrs. Gary
Mrs. George Hayward – to meet Mrs. Julian Story (Emma Eames)

May 15   - Mrs. E. A Hitchcock – to meet Mrs. Collier – (Did not go)
May 17 – Mr. and Mrs. Pascall Carr (evening, did not go)

Mrs. Edmund Wickham – to meet Mrs. Benedict – did not go.
Mrs. Tutt's – to meet the Misses Rensalaer – Henry went

MISCELLANEOUS

(including what was forgotten under other headings)

Review Club meeting at Mrs. Ethan Hitchcock's
Mr. Brookings box party to "Priscilla", supper after

Feb. 9 – Morning Choral – Compliments of Mrs. H.M. Semple
Dec. 31 – Supper at Mary Lionberger's – to see the old year out.
Theater – "Sowing the Wind" – just ourselves
Theater – Sothern in his new play. ..."A Way to Win a Woman"
Theater – John Drew in "Butterflies" – ourselves

Dec. 28 - "The Messiah"

Hagenbach's animals – ourselves
Mr. Blair's theater party – supper at Janet's afterwards.
Sunday Evening Tea at George Leighton's
Sunday Evening Tea at Mary Cushman's
Sunday evening tea at Edith Knox's to meet Nan & Mr. Nagel
Piano Club at Mrs. Ben Taussig's
Choral Symphony – Thomas Concert. Had seats next Zack & Lute
Clemence Garneau's wedding
Opera "Falstaff" – with Sam (Henry out of town)

April 22 – Tristan and Isolde – Went down in the carriage with Edith & Gordon Knox – all week, Alvari, Sucher, Bremer sang - but the opera was very heavy.

April 23 "Lohengrin": Rothmuhl, Gadski, Brenner. Magnificent. An experience of a lifetime.

April 26 – "Tanhauser" – fine!

April 27 – Two acts of "Gotterdammerung", second act of "Lohengrin". There has been a change which was made necessary by the recall of Vischer to New York on account of his wife's illness, but it was a magnificent evening. At the close, the audience stood still in their seats & shouted for Damrosch.

Jack Davis' Theater party to see "Rejane" – could not go.
Mrs. Wayman Cushman's Card Club
Mrs. George Leighton's Card Club (Henry went, not I)
Miss January's Card Club – did not go
Theater with Myra and Nat Lane to see Olga Nethersole.

April 20 – Maud's lunch for Nan.
May 1 – Nan's wedding. Anne Shepley and Charles Nagel were married. Hot, sultry day.
May 24 – Carrie Allen's topic lunch for Maud
May 30 – Edith Knox's lunch for Nan
– Janet's lunch for Nan.

OUR OWN ENTERTAINMENT

October – Luncheon to Irene Catlin
Nov. – Topic Lunch
December 5 – Dinner for Jane and Myra Tutt
Dec. 8 – Dinner for Nan and Mr. Nagel, (character by handwriting)

Jan. 3 – Luncheon for Cynthia Yeatman

Christmas Eve – Family dinner and Christmas tree for Hugh Scott's birthday. Eleven at the table including Hugh Scott who entertained the whole party. Cousin Yates' "moo cow".

Small dinner for Mr. Sherman
Sunday Evening tea for Uncle Hez & Landreth

Jan. 31 – Formal dinner for several friends
Feb. 14 – Wedding anniversary dinner
March – Dinners for the two Van Renssalaers girls from New York who were visiting the Tutts.
March – Dinner for Judge Madill and his bride
March – Card Club
May 17 – Topic lunch for Nan.

CHAPTER 18 – HENRY'S BUSINESSES

"Men die. Institutions live. And the good works of benevolence put into useful & helpful institutions has a flavor of sweetness & strength which endures throughout generations."
[1903-05-08 Letter from Daniel Sylvester Tuttle, Bishop of Missouri, to Henry]

Portrait of Henry commissioned after his death

In the year before they were married, Bertha enclosed the following quotation from her July 4th daily calendar to Henry, writing, *"Goodbye, dear friend, I enclose a quotation from my beloved calendar to you, which you may take as a compliment, if you like."*

> *"All true whole men succeed, for what is worth success's name unless it be the thought, the inward surety, to have carried out a noble purpose to a noble end."* [James Russell Lowell, *"The Nobly Born"*]
> [1892-07-05 Bertha (Rye Beach) to Henry (Stl)]

Henry's response to Bertha's preceding message was self-effacing:

> *The quotation from your calendar would be comforting if I, in anyway, deserved it. It is encouraging to know that my darling has enough faith in me to think that I am trying hard, even if what is commonly known as success seems, as it does so often to me, utterly unattainable. I do not grow dispirited at the very slight reward I have in other things, for if they were all failures, your love, my beloved, would much more than compensate me for whatever I have done that deserves praise.*
> [1892-07-08 Henry (StL) to Bertha (Farragut House, Rye Beach)]

A. DIVERSE BUSINESS INTERESTS

Henry managed and invested a diversity of businesses which were located in many different cities and communicated with financiers and business leaders in even more diverse locations. It is not clear how anyone would have been able to keep all of these businesses running at the same time and maintain one's sanity.

Henry's businesses included electrical generation and distribution, gas production and distribution, municipal water, railroads and coal mining. Henry's principal businesses were located in St. Louis, Dallas,

Ft. Worth, Waco, and Wichita. From his written accounts, Henry had an intimate understanding of each of his businesses, including knowledge of how the various business components functioned and were integrated, including technology and labor. Perhaps as a result of his unique understanding of these businesses, Henry was not able to delegate very much of his authority to others and so Henry was constantly traveling to resolve a plethora of business matters. In addition, Henry was always active in seeking out new business opportunities which led him to travel to many other locations including New York City, Paducah KY, Philadelphia, Sacramento, Shreveport LA and Mexico.

1. TRAVEL

Henry often had to travel to Texas and Wichita to manage his businesses and it was clear from their letters that neither Henry nor Bertha were too fond of Texas. In an 1892 letter, Bertha wrote the following.

> *You say you have been obliged to miss several days from your office lately. Did that mean Chicago, etc.? Or have you been ill and not told me? I fully agree with you that it is best to tell each other the worst of everything or we imagine it is worse than it is. I am glad it is Wichita you are going to and not Texas. I fairly dread those trips to Texas.*
> [1892-05-04 Bertha (Hotel Brunswick, Boston) to Henry (StL)]

Henry did have his good trips to Texas, so Texas was not all bad. As he commented in a letter to Bertha, *"hard work and obstinacy"* was rewarded, *"even in Texas"*.

> *I seem to be driven from one point to another with ever increasing pressure to urge me on and, what with the meetings and out of door examination work and the checking of the books and the hurried runs on sleeping cars from point to point, I am left with very little breathing time. I have one thing to comfort me though. I have been perfectly well since I left home and, up to today, I think I can count this the most successful trip I have ever made to Texas. It is beginning to look as if hard work and obstinacy was rewarded, even in Texas.*
> [1894-11-26 Henry (Waco) to Bertha (StL)]

Part of Henry's problem in managing his businesses were the distances between them and means of transportation. Although late nineteenth century transportation was vastly better than what came before it, nevertheless, Henry bemoaned the distances between Texas towns as well as Wichita and the time it took to travel between all of them.

> *Yesterday I had no time to write. I was in Fort Worth part of a day then I went to Waco and from there here and it seems to me all my time since Monday has been passed either on a train or in preparing to take one and I feel worn to a very, very thin thread tonight, my dear child. We think our distances magnificent in St. Louis. I mean, the distance to other places, but Texas defies comparison in this particular and, if a man can be found who has tried its slow trains for bridging the spaces of say a few hundred miles between each or any of its towns who does not appreciate that the world is large, in Texas he, in my opinion, is a queer calculator.*
>
> *I have managed so far well and my few hours in Waco ought to count for something. Here I have little hope for a comfortable time except that the hotel is good and the weather fairly cool for the south. Tomorrow I shall have an all-day siege of it with the lawyers in damage suits, construction contractors, lumber people, machinery cranks, etc., etc., so on the theory that idle hands find devilment, mine are likely to be kept out of mischief.*
> [1894-05-24 Henry (Dallas) to Bertha (3337 Washington Ave, Stl)]

Henry's principal business activities were in gas and electrical generation and distribution. Gas distribution became significant during the second half of the 19th century as gas was supplied not only for commercial and public/street lighting but also increasingly for private homes. As a consequence, obtaining supplies of natural gas and then providing the pipe distribution connections to the various consumers of gas was a very significant and lucrative business activity.

2. ELECTRICITY

Electrical generation and distribution started to become commercially significant in the 1890's. In additional to electricity's commercial use to power machinery, electricity was increasingly used to illuminate private homes. Although it was estimated that electricity was used in only 8% of private homes as of 1915, the trend toward electricity and away from gas for lighting was apparent by this time. Some of the inventions that made this transition to electricity possible was the invention of the dynamo in 1831, the first power station or "powerhouse" in 1882, and the first practical light bulb in 1876. (The first light bulb was invented by Faraday in 1821 but his invention was not commercially viable.)

A Dynamo - an electrical generator that produces direct current.

Henry wrote of his Ft. Worth plant:

Our works here are the best I think in the country and it really seems that all the troublesome problems have been solved. I thought of our day at the Brewery tonight as I watched our great engines and dynamos driving the machinery for lighting up this busy town. The weather here is really warm. We have been sitting in the office all day with the windows thrown up and such a thing as an overcoat is not seen on the streets.
[1892-01-24 Henry (Ft Worth) to Bertha]

Henry and Bertha wrote several letters about electricity which revealed its novelty and the growing awareness of its importance. In 1892, Bertha wrote to Henry to learn more about this new technology.

Now can you send me something to read about electricity? Don't laugh, I do not mean anything foolish. I don't want to go into the subject exhaustively. But the graduating class of Mary Institute (which class I did not go through, you know) take a course of electricity in connection with their natural philosophy. And I would like to know as much as those children know, enough at least to understand the terms of the work you are interested in. When I translated that German for you and could not believe but that "gurtel und shaft" must mean something besides "belts and shafts[234]" because I did not see what belts and shafts had to do with the case, you may see how dense my ignorance is. I suppose I could get about what I want by sending for some student's handbook of natural philosophy but I thought perhaps you might know of something a little more interesting on this subject, being, so to speak, "in the trade yourself." And I should be so very much obliged to you, dear boy.
[1892-06-28 Bertha (The Ark, East Jaffrey) to Henry (StL)]

---

[234] See infra, Subchapter E, History of Belts & Shafts

Henry was only too happy to oblige Bertha and had books ready at hand to send her.

I am going to send you one or perhaps two books on electricity today. I am afraid you will find the subject a pretty dry one but, by merely glancing through them, you will be able to understand the use if not the theory of the science. You asked once what "shafts and belts" have to do with the subject. Shafts and belts are the agencies of all machine power for, through the use of one or the other or both, the power is transmitted to the machinery which the engine or pump or, in electricity, the motor supplies.
[1892-07-08 Henry (StL) to Bertha (Farragut House, Rye Beach)]

Dear, I have just sent you the books on electricity. The smaller of the two gives you a very fair idea of the general subject and the other its application to modern uses. In the latter book you will see a notice of the "C&C" and "Cracker-Wheeler" motors which are the ones the Laclede Power Co. controls.
[1892-07-10 (Friday) Henry (StL) to Bertha (Farragut House, Rye Beach)]

The following article, "The Force of Electricity", was written during the period of the 1890's and is an interesting account of electricity and its uses. (It is unclear if Henry wrote this.)

On the twenty fifth of January, we had an electric motor set up merely by way of trial. The result has satisfied us so entirely and has proved the usefulness of the new motor to be so far beyond that of the old steam engine that we have resolved to adopt it as a permanent arrangement.

Some of our readers may be interested to hear how this electric force works and how many friends it has already gained in St. Louis. The usual system of the Laclede Power Company is, in their central station on Mound Street, to exchange steam power for electric power. This latter is carried by means of wires through the different parts of the city and wherever electric power is wanted a motor of the required size can be set up and then by means of branch wires can be connected with the head management. Whenever the electric force is wanted, it is only necessary to turn on the current and the power is there. In like manner, if the work is over, it is only necessary to turn off the current. There is no delay, no heat, no waiting, no danger of explosion. We see no dirt and no grease and added to this, the motor scarcely a tenth of the room required for the steam engines and boilers.

Instead of being obliged to furnish a foundation of solid stone for the motor, as is necessary for the steam engine and boiler, instead of being obliged to obtain the mechanical power through belts and shafts, whereby a great deal of the aforesaid power is lost, the motor is set directly on the press and so a great deal of power is saved.

Other establishments besides the "America" where this electric power is used are the Shelp(?) Wagon & Carriage Co, Carr Str. & Levery, which uses a fifteen horse power, B. Fischtel Planning Mill, 19 & Wash Str. Thirty horse power, ... Hammar, Paint C, 2 & Cedar Str. Forty five horse power, Loth ... Clothing Co 8 and Olive Str. Ten horse power. The Riverside Printing co Main and Olive Str. ten horse power. Herket & Meisel, trunk makes, 16 & Poplar 15 horsepower, J.B. Sickles, Saddler Co, 21 & Washington Ave 20 horsepower.(???)

Besides these, there are a great number of other motors in activity clear down to one eighth horse power. Everybody who has tried the electric apparatus discovered that it is the best thing they have ever made use of. We are convinced that this system will do much to diminish the smoke evil in fact to do away with it altogether. And, as the power is concentrated in one place, it will aim also at doing away with a great amount of hitherto necessary machinery. The motors themselves deserve special attention. Our experience has brought us to the conclusion that this system will in time be adopted in all the great cities on account of its economy, convenience, and general superiority. [20180720-1 "The Force of Electricity" – Henry(-)]

3. COAL & RAILROADS

Henry was involved in purchasing coal on an annual basis which he needed for electricity generation. Therefore, coal required his periodic attention and always seemed to be a nuisance. Due to the importance of coal in his business, Henry was at one time the president of Missouri and Illinois Coal Company and then was succeeded as president by his brother Sam.

> *I have been very much pressed all day which is a mercy for I haven't "lived the day in true spirit of contentment." My coal contracts look promising but I have been unable to close them up on a fair basis for our people and the uncertainty hangs over me like a pall. If those idiot miners in the east would quit striking and go back to work I could make a fine arrangement but the uncertainty of the market there makes the coal men out here afraid to quote prices and, although I planned this year better than ever before and have closed up a part of the work on a fine basis, the most important part is still open and there is a prospect that I may do as badly in the latter as I did well in the first part of this problem. Life in the business world is not a sinecure, Bert, and I wonder I have an idea for anything after all that is in me is threshed out in the daily grind. It is presumptuous for me to claim the possibility, I think.*
> [1902-07-12 Henry (StL) to Bertha (Rye Beach)]

But, as Henry wrote a week later, he generally seemed to be able to close a deal on his terms.

> *I am glad to say I have finally gotten one bug bear out of the way. I finally closed up my contract for next year's coal supply and at a small saving on last year's prices. I am glad it's over for the strike in the east made it almost impossible to do anything with the miners here and the anxiety over the miserable thing was wearing me to a thread. I think with a good Sabbath rest, I will be all right by Monday but just now I feel that I shall be tired all of my days.*
> [1902-07-18(-) Henry (StL) to Bertha (Rye Beach)]

Henry also had several railroad investments such as the Citizens Electric Street Railway Company in Waco, a Dallas City railway and the St. Louis, Brownsville & Mexico Railway. However, these never seemed to be among Henry's foremost concerns and do not appear prominently in his letters.

4. INDUSTRIAL PROGRESS

Henry was very proud to be a part of the industrial progress of his age and to contribute to the positive impact that innovation was having on people's lives.

> *I think I forgot to tell you that the Laclede Power Co. got a very large customer yesterday and of a kind that I think will interest you. You have heard of the shirt makers. Well, Hood's song of the shirt[235] does not exaggerate the labors of the shirt makers of St. Louis. We were called upon by a shirt maker who employs fifty women, each woman working a sewing machine for ten hours every day. The employer had heard of some of our work and his negotiations ended in our equipping or*

---

[235] "The Song of the Shirt" is a poem written by Thomas Hood in 1843. The following is the first stanza of the poem. [Wikipedia]

> *With fingers weary and worn,*
> *With eyelids heavy and red,*
> *A woman sat in unwomanly rags,*
> *Plying her needle and thread —*
> *Stitch! Stitch! Stitch!*
> *In poverty, hunger, and dirt,*
> *And still with a voice of dolorous pitch*
> *She sang 'The Song of the Shirt!'*

contracting to equip such of the machines with a small motor, invented by poor Lufkin[236] and as soon as the work is completed, those women will have nothing to do but guide their work. The man estimates that, besides the great physical relief from that tread mill strain, the women, through their ability to work more quickly, ought to earn a third larger wage. Such is the progress of science.
[20170724-5 Henry to Bertha]

Henry was in the right place and the right time: gas and electric businesses were expanding at a rapid pace at the end of the 19th century and St. Louis was the hub of the fastest growing part of the United States. It was a heady time.

B. HENRY'S BUSINESS ACTIVITIES

1. A DAY AT WORK

Henry rarely wrote to Bertha about his work. Generally, his excuse to Bertha was that his workdays were mundane and he did not wish to bore Bertha. It was also clear, from "reading between the lines", that Henry did not want Bertha to worry about his business matters about which Henry worried for the two of them. But Henry did periodically mention some things about his work as in the following letter.

Dear, you asked me in your last letter to tell you more about my movements and occupations. I have given you an account of half of this afternoon, now let me try to recall the rest of the day and make you regret your request for such information.

This was a duller day than usual for the first letter I usually read was not on the desk when I reached the office and I think my stenographer realized that something was wrong for the letters were mighty short and to the point. You know we don't write letters ourselves these days, all this work is done by dictation. I mean the business letters, of course. This letter is not dictated, so as soon as I am ready for work in the morning, I open the mail first and answer the letters as they are read then, while I am working at other things, the letters are put into type from the short hand notes and are ready for signing and the mail before the office is closed.

Is not all this thrilling? But you have shown a large amount of curiosity, dear, and I am going to punish you with further details of my thrilling everyday occupations. After the mail had been disposed of this morning, I spent an hour in the Laclede Power Co. office auditing bills and grumbling about expenses. Then I made up my report to the Library Board. I wrestled with three Corliss engine salesmen, each trying to show me his particular engine was the only pattern suited for our new Wichita "plant".

I next went over the plans for a small brick power house we are building, signed over a hundred vouchers, bought a small bill of supplies, went to the meeting of the discount committee at the bank, had to listen to a fool who was boasting of some new railway equipment until I almost put him out of the office, and then met Judge Madill. There, do you see what a charming life I am leading and how full of interest are my daily occupations? Aren't you sorry you asked any questions and, dear, aren't you sorry too you are not here to make my life less hard and dreary than it is?
[20170721-1 Henry (StL) to Bertha]

---

[236] The Lufkin motor company, originally named E.T. Lufkin Board and Log Rule Manufacturing Company, was founded by Edward Taylor Lufkin, an American Civil War veteran in Cleveland, Ohio 1869. The company was acquired in 1967 by Cooper Industries.

In another letter to Bertha in 1892 before they were married, Henry wrote to Bertha of some various business troubles in Wichita, including a gas war, labor issues, and "coaching" his Secretary.

> I have just received your last letter and, as you wish to know what I am doing here, I answer in a few words: I am trying to make a rather lazy lot of men do more work than they have been doing. Our company supplies the town with gas and electric light and we would do splendidly if I could only get the men stationed here to do their full duty. Sometimes I think I will make a "clean sweep" and employ all new men but other people, including our vice president, Judge Madill, tell me "we are doing very well" and practically advise me to be more reasonable so I try to be content, although quite sure in my own mind that being "more reasonable" means nothing less than permitting work to drag along for months that should be finished in a few weeks. You will think this another evidence of my obstinacy, won't you dear?
>
> We are just coming out of a "gas war" here and it is very helpful to know that we are going to win after a contest which has lasted nearly five years. You remember I told you about the Pine Bluff troubles? This is almost a repetition of our experience there and I am almost sure we have won here as we did there. I don't know that I can tell you much more of what I do here. Something is always getting out of "fix" and I have to mend it. I think that about comprehends my work. Our secretary is a real trial. He is much the ablest man I have but I think about the least interesting thing in all his life is his work and the "coaching" he requires would test the patience of an angel. And I am not an angel.

[1892-01-22 (Friday) Henry (Wichita Gas, Electric Light and Power Co) to Bertha]

During the period of Henry's aforementioned trip to Wichita in January 1892, Henry expressed some worry that speaking of his various business struggles would upset Bertha, especially when she would become "serious" in her letters. Bertha reproached Henry for suggesting that, when she was "serious", she was "sad or gloomy".

> You say "a man must speak seriously sometimes". Exactly! But then, he must not think that a woman is necessarily sad or gloomy because she answers seriously. Turnabout is fair play, my son. And why did you think your last letter from Wichita would not interest me? It did interest me very much. There is no part of your life that would not do that. But apart even from this feeling, business things always interest me. I have always liked to hear father talk about them. An inherited taste, I suppose it is, it certainly cannot be anything else.

[1892-01-29 Bertha (StL) to Henry (Waco)]

Henry rarely bragged about his businesses. However, when Henry was in particularly good spirits, he could brag, such as in the following (circa 1895).

> I am afraid I have been bragging about my work for your picture of my toiling existence is really pathetic and I am glad to say much overdone. I must reassure you so let me say that in many ways this is the least anxious summer I have had since we have been married – and I count nothing before that my darling, except the happy visions while I was trying to win you. There is much to do and there's no denying that but I think my work in past years is beginning to show, for not only are the earnings of our work greater to better enable me to push forward its development, but the organization is so much stronger and better that we advance more surely and smoothly and that helps me immeasurably in my part of the planning.
>
> The Laclede new station will be, I think, far the best electric works built in St. Louis or the west. Not the longest but I think clearly the best. It is not small either, as its cost, two hundred thousand dollars will be spent with care and economy. Then the Ft. Worth work runs well. My plant there at Waco and Wichita to give the poorest family the opportunity to cook by gas without greater charge than with more troublesome fuels, has really been a great success and we have almost doubled our business as a result. It has cost almost to the limit of our ability to bear but we are

beginning to reap a very satisfactory harvest. You know I found the poorer people couldn't afford to buy gas storage pipe their houses, etc., so I presented them with this equipment and the lesson has been thoroughly taught that the poorest man can better afford to use gas than the rich.

The Coal Co and St. Charles are the two bow strings which I am most worried about but I think even they with patience will ultimately find immunity from the troublous conditions which have beset them.

So you see, dear, I give you almost a complete rebuttal of your charge that I am overtaxed. Now, the less I am ready for sweet rest with you than I have ever been before, not because I am more tired or worn but because you have added to my education and I better understand what is the fullness of joy.
[1895(-) 20170822-7 Henry to Bertha (discusses gas business)]

Bertha also took great pride in the work of Henry's company. Bertha apparently saw the following article about Laclede Power Co. in Amerika, a German newspaper which was published in St. Louis from 1872 to 1924. The article entitled, "In Vier Stunden" ("In Four Hours"), was written in German and reported the successful repairs performed by the Laclede Power Company for the German newspaper – in four hours.

Bertha included the English translation with this newspaper clipping (Bertha was fluent in German).

A quick piece of work was carried out in the press room of the "America" last week. At the first trial to set the new press in motion, the steam engine which should have furnished the mechanical power, suddenly refused to work. As time pressed, it was necessary to send for speedy assistance. They sent for an agent of the Laclede Power Co. from the Bank of Commerce Building, who after he had surveyed the field, explained that "within four hours" he could furnish all the power that would be needed for the work. At the end of the third hour, he had a thousand pound "C.C" motor ready and set up, and in the course of the fourth hour, the press was in full swing, thanks to the electricity of the Laclede Power Co.
[1892-02-02 published in Amerika]

2. JUDGE GEORGE MADILL

Henry spoke many times of his business relationship with Judge Madill. After the announcement of Bertha and Henry's engagement, Henry wrote of Judge Madill's delightful conversation with him over lunch.

Judge Madill came over and took lunch with me yesterday and I would like for you to have heard what he had to say on the subject. No wonder he fascinates men, for his ability to say delightful things in the most felicitous way can't be surpassed.
[1892-03-05(-) 20170828-3 Henry to Bertha]

However, sometimes the Judge's visits to Henry's office got in the way of work, to Henry's chagrin.

I thought I should be unable to write you today for Judge Madill came in to inspect my new quarters this afternoon and, from the length of time he remained, he was evidently pleased with my selection for he arrived at three and left at half past five and, as a result, I had to make up part of the lost time after his departure. If I had been less busy I should have been flattered at the Judge's lengthy call for it is the first time since I have known him that he has come to see me to talk about anything but business matters but today he seated himself in the corner window where he could see the river and watch the throng of people on Broadway and Olive Street and spent the entire time chaffing me about my great care for "new fangled office paraphernalia" (his office looks like a second hand book store).

He wanted to know where it was proper to put his hat and if it made any difference if the chairs were moved a little to enable him to get at one of the windows. He thought he was very funny – I didn't – when he remarked "Scott, you are being disciplined. Now confess that you are on your good behavior and realize that you must have a watchful eye for appearances or expect trouble" and "that's right: practices, a knowledge of decorative art that will astonish a friend of yours someday. You remind me of the small boy who practiced "ball" in the back yard in order that his play might astonish his companions when they met in the field. The proper place, you know, for the display of that sort of skill."

The old fellow stayed so long and seemed to enjoy himself so much that I thought of proposing a permanent partnership only it seemed wicked extravagance to be willing to pool my magnificent income with his very moderate one!!! even if in so doing I secured the association of the most attractive man in St. Louis.
[20170721-1 Henry (StL) to Bertha]

In July 1899, Henry spoke of a tiff between Henry and Judge Madill and his immediate regret.

I did not write yesterday. I had my row out with Judge Madill in the afternoon and it consumed all the afternoon and nearly all of me. So I did not write. I am not even in a decent mood today, although I have been to the country all morning and have had a very good dinner at the McK Jones', when I remembered last night that Judge M was the first real friend I had made in St. Louis and realized that after eighteen years there was to be an end of it all. I very seriously raised the question as to whether I had any longer the capacity for either making or keeping friends. I don't see how I could have acted other than I did but I am in very serious doubt whether I might not have so managed as to avoid an open breach with an old friend.

I seem to have caught up the faculty of creating much trouble with those whom I see much of and this last experience has helped me to understand how much I must have hurt you more than once, dearie. I have thought today several times of the last night you were here and, if self-reproach can repair selfish and inconsiderate actions, I have made some slight amends for annoying and distressing you.
[20171219-3 (1899-) Henry to Bertha]

Henry apparently got into a dispute with Judge Madill that shook up their 18-year friendship. It appeared that the fault may have rested with Henry.

> *I am pretty tired today but well. That rumpus with Judge Madill has shaken me a good deal but I guess I will be all right in a day or two. I really think that my tactless and ill-considered treatment of a very dear friend of mine, that last night, has made me conclude that at the bottom there is some lack which makes me always take hold of things unkindly and I think I need one of your dear letters to enable me to even have hope again in my ability to be either fair or generous with others.*
> [1899-07-10 Henry (StL) to Bertha]

Bertha wrote back to Henry of her concern for how this quarrel was affecting Henry.

> *Your letters troubled and distressed me, sweetheart. I am very, very sorry that you have had the fresh trouble of a quarrel with Judge Madill. You say you might have avoided an open breach but I doubt if you could. Sooner or later this was bound to come. I am only very, very sorry for your sake that it has come now when you are ill & worn out. Please write me all about it.*
>
> *The distress it causes you makes me feel like giving you a little advice about Ben Taussig. Ever since you told me that John Davis and some of the others thought Ben might be innocent, it has come back upon me at intervals that perhaps you are wrong and he maybe only stupid. At all events, you cannot make back the money now and there are so many friends connected with us through Ben Taussig that, unless it becomes your positive duty (as it may be) to have an open breach with him, I don't think I would.*
>
> *As for me, dearie, that part of your letter distressed me more than all the rest. You and I belong, sweetheart, and, when things go wrong, I usually know that either you or I are ill and let it go. And to find you grieving over anything of that sort, distresses me terribly. I never should have cried if I had not been utterly worn out physically and it was very, very silly of me, it was not your fault, dear old boy, in anyway or shape. Please don't let that weigh on you after our beautiful sunshiny month together. I have not been as happy since my mother died and I really thought that you had shared it until these letters of yours.*
>
> *Dearie, you once said you would not hold the passing anger of a moment against me. You have not even that to blame yourself with and yet, you are brooding over it. Stop it, dearie, it means you are unwell and unreasonable. Try and get a more right, natural and cheery view of things.*
> [1899-07-19 Bertha (Jamestown RI) to Henry (StL)]

In short order, Henry wrote an apology to Judge Madill for his behavior and, shortly thereafter, received Judge Madill's reply.

> *I enclose a letter from Judge Madill in answer to a note I wrote him telling him I was sorry for the difference but that I had acted as I thought to be my duty to others and that in any event the matter seemed trifling compared with the severance of an association of eighteen years. Keep the letter, please, as I shall preserve it, and tell me what you think of it. I will show you a copy of mine to him someday.*
> [20180127-4 (1898-07-19-) Henry (StL) to Bertha]

Judge Madill's reply to Henry's apology showed a wisdom that comes from years of experience.

> *My dear Mr. Scott:*
> *Your letter, fully appreciated by me, came late for a reply in St. Louis. And, as I sail early this day, I can get time only to say that I shall be very glad to let the past be forgotten so far as it has unpleasant events in it but be remembered for its many most agreeable experiences to me. You are not as old as I am but, when you come to be, you will find you cannot carry "in the pack upon your back" much that earlier in life was hardly noticeable to you.*

Wishing you an agreeable summer where ever you may spent it, I remain,
Very sincerely yours,
Geo. A. Madill
[1899-07-19 Judge George A. Madill (New York) to Henry (StL)]
(What wise counsel: when you are as old as me, you cannot hold such trifling disagreements "*in the pack upon your back*".)

3. HENRY'S EMPLOYEES & BUSINESS ASSOCIATES

Henry seemed to have a very keen sense of the talents and abilities of his employees. Henry had noticed Preston who had started to work for Henry at a young age and Henry's observations are telling.

> *I ought not to pass the office work without telling you what a comfort Preston has been during Miss Grace's absence. The boy has really astonished me by his clearness and quickness. I have put on his desk work which men of mature age might be proud of doing well and the boy has responded splendidly to every added duty and responsibility. He has the making of a very useful and very fine man and, from a selfish point of view, it was no mistake to add him to the office force. You would smile if you could see his calm confidence in dictating letters to the stenographers. I looked over his letters today and concluded that some of mine were exceedingly bad!*
> [1895(-) 20170822-7 Henry to Bertha]

Henry also demonstrated great sympathy for his "*boys*" when tragedy befell them, especially "*because I cannot change certain things that seem so ill arranged*".

> *I lost one of my best boys on Thursday. The poor little fellow was drowned while swimming with some of his companions in the river. He was one of the brightest little fellows in our force and it shocked me greatly when I heard of the accident. Perhaps, my darling, these things seem to you the burdens that one should carry more easily than I do. You mistake me, though, in thinking that I worry greatly. I am often sad just a little but I would not change my nature in this respect if I could, dear. Only I will try not to let you see that it sometimes makes me blue because I cannot change certain things that seem so ill arranged.*
> [1892-06-27 Henry (StL) to Bertha (Farragut House, Rye Beach)]

And Henry felt great sadness from the loss of his business friends and associates.

> *I feel as though I had been in a battle and men had been killed all around me for I have just come from the University Club and on the board are the death notices of six of its members, Mr. Yeatman, Colonel Leighton, Ed Walsh, Mr. Foy, Mr. Lane and young Stone who, by the way, you will remember as the young man who put in our hot water system, Hughes & Stone was the firm you know. I have been wrestling today with St. Charles so you may know I am not very cheerful and on the whole the world doesn't seem as much worthwhile as I have sometimes been led to believe. If it were not for you and the chicks, I would feel like enlisting for the Philippines!* [20180319-5 (1900-) Henry to Bertha]

C. HENRY'S PLACES OF BUSINESS:
1. WICHITA

Although Wichita was the third largest city in Kansas in the 1890's, its population was only about 24,000. It was a prairie town which had depended heavily on the Texas cattle drives for much of its economic livelihood in the 1870s. The growth in its population during the 1880s was largely the result of rapid immigration and in a speculative land boom. After the land speculation bust in the 1890s, the city entered an economic recession and many of the original settlers went bankrupt. After the discovery of oil and gas in 1914, Wichita experienced another economic boom.

In a letter to Bertha two months before their marriage, Henry spoke of some of his business matters in Wichita, especially regarding the corrupt city council.

I have not had a very delightful journey thus far. In Wichita, I caught a slight cold which, notwithstanding our business prospects there show marked improvement, made me rather blue for a day or two. The cold has practically disappeared now but I have a number of rather vexing problems to unravel here and, as dealing with a corrupt city council is not a specialty of mine, I am by no means clear as to the happy ending of some of the obstacles that stand in the way of our accomplishing the ends we hope for. It is some slight consolation to know, however, that my associates here have pretty strong faith in my ability to secure the results I am working for, as it is to know that "our friends the enemy" are going through an experience compared to which our condition is <u>heavenly</u>.
[1892-12-10(-) (Thursday 1892-12-15) Henry (Waco) to Bertha (Stancote, Newton Centre)]

In a letter to Bertha in 1893, Henry expressed his feelings about Wichita which, at that time, were only slightly better than his feelings about Texas.

Dear, it is not very cheering to be out here alone and so far from you. My spirits go way down when I can stop to think of the particular reason for a very well-defined conclusion that Saint Louis is the blessedest spot on earth and that Wichita is the saddest place in all creation except Waco and Fort Worth. I don't have time for many reflections thought for I am very busy and I am somewhat consoled by the thought that I am doing some good here.
[1893-04-16 (two letters) Henry (Hotel Carey, Wichita) to Bertha (3337 Washington Ave, Stl)]

Carey Hotel, where Henry frequently stayed in Wichita

In 1898, Henry wrote about his struggles to conclude a contract in Wichita.

I got here yesterday evening and, as the trip utterly played me out, I did not write. I don't think my trip here has done much good. The Mayor says we will get the contract and he has agreed to my proposal but I doubt if he will be able to carry the Council with him and so the whole matter may go over until autumn. I thought this morning I would be able to take the contract home in my pocket but, on a vote of the Committee, action was postponed for ten days and I was asked if I would come out in August to finish up the matter and to yield "certain points" which the city might find it necessary to insist upon our conceding. I declined to come again in August and told them our proposal would remain good for ten days and, if not acted upon then, would be withdrawn.

So I arranged to return to St. Louis tomorrow, feeling that my hot, long journey has been a failure and that no confidence is to be placed in anyone, except you, Bert. I shall reach St. Louis or rather my train is due there Wednesday morning. It has been hot here and I expect it will be <u>delightful</u> on

the train. It has not rained for several days but I hope my bad luck will not follow me further and that it will either rain or grow cooler tomorrow.
[1898-07-18 Henry (Wichita) to Bertha (Jamestown)]

But the next day brought new hope and some contrition to Henry.

Although it is hotter than even today and I have no letter from you, my spirits have revived. I leave in five minutes for St. Louis and just now I have closed an interview which promises that my trip has done good after all. And this accounts for my seeing a ray of hope in things in general. Just think how I have deteriorated. A mere question of a little money gained or lost makes the who[le] world seem glad or cheerless. Wouldn't you greatly prefer a husband who was struggling on one of our ships in a great cause and for a high aim, to one who confines his efforts entirely to a humiliating struggle for money? – or bread would be putting it better?
[1898-07-19 Henry (Wichita) to Bertha]

Henry received better news from Wichita the next month when things turned in his favor.

I did not intend to be so busy toward the last but Mr. Lord's arrival from Fort Worth, the unexpected turn of all the Wichita papers in our favor and their demand that I write them for publication article "defining our position" which were used as editorials to help them out of the scrape they found themselves in for advocating an utterly irresponsible set of men who had viciously attacked us and whose rascally scheme became known finally to the public.
[1898-08-06 Henry (University Club, Stl) to Bertha (Jamestown, RI)]

In spite of the progress, Henry's frustrations with Wichita were never very far away.

I am not sure of being there when Father Sill arrives. Wichita is in trouble and I have no right to be here until it is either helped over the hill or until I find I can do nothing. I think I must go there in a few days and maybe I shall be lucky enough to heal the trouble but I doubt it.
[1905(-) 20180730-6 Henry to Bertha]

It was clear that around 1906, Henry became interested in the natural gas deposits which were found near Wichita. According to the history of Wichita, many of these discoveries were made around 1914 and 1915[237]; however, Henry's letters revealed that he was making business inquiries about these natural gas fields earlier than this and was aware of the competition from Standard Oil. In a 1906 letter to Bertha, Henry spoke of Rockefeller's (Standard Oil's) move into Wichita

As to business, I have not written you about it because so little has happened since you left. The coal strike is over and Waco is serene, but John D. Rockefeller is preparing to put Wichita into his capacious pocket and, although I shall probably get licked, I am going to give him a run for his money.
[20180206-7 (1906-07-01-) Henry to Bertha]

Henry went to Chicago in July 1906, apparently to try to resolve the Wichita problems. His frustration with Wichita was palpable.

I haven't accomplished anything by coming here again and it looks as though a fight at Wichita is inevitable. When I think of straying off here and trying to work out problems for that wild western town when the people are too perverted to care for honest dealing and too mean to appreciate the

---

[237] In 1914 and 1915, deposits of oil and natural gas were discovered in nearby Butler County. This triggered another economic boom in Wichita as producers established refineries, fueling stations, and headquarters in the city. By 1917, there were five operating refineries in Wichita with another seven built in the 1920s. The careers and fortunes of future oil moguls Archibald Derby, who later founded Derby Oil, and Fred C. Koch, who established what would become Koch Industries, both began in Wichita during this period. [Wikipedia]

immense obligation they are under to us when I might otherwise be with you and be enjoying perfect happiness, I call myself a fool with no little emphasis.
[1906-07-25 Henry (Chicago) to Bertha]

Bertha provided Henry with her own advice about the "Chicago-Wichita" matter.

I was surprised to see Chicago on your envelope for I got your letter saying you were going to Chicago in the same mail that I got that. You don't tell me how you are running the Chicago-Wichita matter but I surmise you are holding out for a big price and you will pay the price many times over in loss of strength, time, nerve force and gray brain matter, and this time, not improbably, in cash too. Remember St. Charles and take a friendly warning: take less and make more later in the free time you will have. I think this is good advice as regards your "constituents" as well as yourself but what do your directors say? Do you ever ask them or are you afraid to for fear they will give you the same advice I do? I expect you to say in answer to this what Jethro Bass did to Cynthia when she gave him advice on politics. "Do I meddle when you're dress-makin', Cynthy?"[238]
[1906-07-27 Bertha (Rye Beach) to Henry (StL)]

Henry again mentioned the Rockefeller & Standard Oil move in Wichita but recasted these problems in a good light since it would permit him to go east and see Bertha on the same trip. However, Henry didn't relish the prospect of meeting with "Thede" Barnsdale.

Theodore ("Thede") Newton Barnsdale

I have had a pipe dream myself today. I say this because it is altogether too heavenly to be true. You know I told you I would have some business in Boston during the summer. This was certain but I have been trying to put it over until August. Well, now comes the Standard Oil crowd that is

---

[238] This quote is probably from *Coniston*, a novel by Winston Churchill, the American writer, just published in 1906. A similar line from Chapter 2:

"*What is it?*" *she said anxiously.* "*Have you got rheumatism, too, like Cousin Eph? All old men seem to have rheumatism.*"
"*No, Cynthy, it hain't rheumatism,*" *he [Jethro Bass] managed to answer;* "*wimmen folks hadn't ought to mix up in politics. They—they don't understand 'em, Cynthy.*"

vexing my soul at Wichita and announces that its Royal Highness, Mr. Barnsdall, would like to see me in Pittsburg. I may go there the last of this week or the first of next and, if I do, I shall make the Boston trip at the same time and there I should see you!

I can only be gone a few days for I must come back here to buy my coal and oil and supplies for the coming year which work can't be done now but I suppose on such a hurry trip I could induce you to come down to Boston while I am finishing my business there for a day or two and then I can take you back to Rye and perhaps remain there a day or two before my return west. There is one complication. I may have to go from Pittsburg to New York for a day and New York is too far for you to come to meet me. But you will come to Boston, won't you? I shall telegraph you of course and don't count upon it, particularly for I may not be able to carry out my play and it really seems far too good to be true anyway.

[1906-09-(-) 20180729-4 Henry to Bertha]

Newspaper Article kept by Bertha

Henry met with "Thede"Barnsdall at the beginning of September 1906 in New York City, which meeting tired him out sufficiently that he took the wrong train out to try to meet Bertha.

I reached <u>New York</u> on time anyway! and have finished here and by a scratch will catch a train over the Pennsylvania for St. Louis which by schedule will arrive there at ten o'clock tomorrow *night. I hope you were not completely broken down when you and the young people reached Rye. I was rather humiliated with the double error I made in going to and from Taunton[239] until I reflected upon what I had been doing since Sunday night and I took comfort in the reflection that most tired people temporarily part with their intelligence.*

I did no harm coming here but I am afraid I cannot claim to have achieved any advantage, certainly for the present from my meeting with Barnsdall. However he promised to meet me in St. Louis next week with a definite plan for his withdrawal from Wichita and, if he were either truthful or honest, this would count for something but as he is neither I am treating him with my blandest smiles and preparing for a fight.
[1906-09-06 Henry (NYC) to Bertha]

In his letter to Bertha in September 1906, Henry specifically mentioned buying up natural gas properties.
In re: vacation topics, my fate as to my vacation is in Mr. Walsh's hands, our Wichita superintendent. He is ... natural gas lands and he thinks he wants me now but is not sure. I have replied that I imagine it will take him a month to acquire the five thousand acres we need and that one man can do the buying better than two since the price is fixed and it becomes a mere matter of selecting the best lands.
[1906-09-(-) 20180729-6 Henry to Bertha]

Henry wrote the following letter at some point during this period when he was "at war" with Rockefeller. However, since Henry was then older and wiser, he became more philosophical.
I assume our trials are accountable for our sweetness of character! and I try not to be very peevish even if my head now and then gets "soarer" that those of mine enemies. I wish I could go to Africa and slay them all in one hunt a la Teddy, but, alas, I grow older and they seem to keep their youth and strength monstrous well.
[20170721-4 Henry to Bertha]

2. FORT WORTH

In the mid-1800s, Ft. Worth was at the edge of civilization. Great herds of Longhorns were driven from South Texas to the railheads in Wichita Kansas and Fort Worth was on the main route — the Chisholm Trail. Lowing herds camped near the town and cowboys galloped into Fort Worth, firing their pistols into the air and even riding their horses into the saloons. The red-light district that sprang up there came to be known as "Hell's Half Acre." It was one of the most infamous and the basis for many caricatures of the Wild West. By the end of the 19th century, the city's population was booming. In 1880, the population was 6,663; the 1900 census counted 26,668. Since Ft. Worth was a livestock shipping center with significant railroad connections, Ft. Worth became a major meat packing city in the late 19th Century.

With the boom times came a variety of entertainments and related problems. Fort Worth had a knack for separating cattlemen from their money. Cowboys took full advantage of their last brush with civilization before the long drive on the Chisholm Trail from Fort Worth up north to Kansas. They stocked up on provisions from local merchants, visited saloons for a bit of gambling and carousing, then galloped northward with their cattle only to whoop it up again on their way back. The town soon became home to "Hell's Half-Acre", the biggest collection of saloons, dance halls, and bawdy houses south of Dodge City (the northern terminus of the Chisholm Trail), giving Fort Worth the nickname of "The Paris of the Plains".
[Wikipedia - Ft. Worth during the 1880s]

---

[239] Probably Taunton MA.

In the summer of 1892, Henry went to Ft. Worth and Waco with his friends, Judge Madill and Colonel Fordyce in the Colonel's railroad car, traveling "first class".

> *We go down in Colonel F's car so we shall be pretty well cared for. The car carries among other good things an excellent cook, is beautifully equipped, runs very easily, has a good bathroom, fine sleeping arrangements with a glass observation end and even a speed indicator which registers and records the speed the car is running at. In short, it is the sort of travelling companion which makes one see what a poor thing a "Pullman" is and how lucky a thing it is to be a railroad president. The "Gladys" is the most elaborate private car that runs out of Saint Louis.*
>
> *...*
>
> *I shall have two pleasantest companions. You know my opinion of Judge Madill. You have known it since that excursion to Montesano (how many years ago was that, dear?). And Colonel Fordyce is excellent company ...*

[1892-07-16 Henry (Country Club, Bridgeton Stl) to Bertha (Farragut House, Rye Beach)]

a. Ye Arlington Inn

When Henry travelled to Ft. Worth, he often stayed at the Ye Arlington Inn.

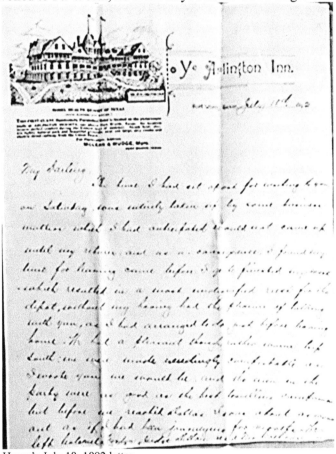

Henry's July 18, 1892 letter.

On his summer 1892 trip, Henry stayed at the Ye Old Arlington Inn with his companions, Judge Madill and Colonel Fordyce[240]. Henry clearly liked the hotel.

> *We had a pleasant though rather warm trip south. We were made exceedingly comfortable as I wrote you we would be and the men in the party were as good as the best travelling companions but, before we reached Dallas, I was about as worn out as if I had been journeying for months. We*

---

[240] Colonel Samuel Wesley Fordyce

left Colonel Fordyce, Judge Dillon and Mr. Cochran in Dallas and Judge Madill and I came over here. We are more comfortably situated than I have ever been in Texas. This hotel is new, having just been opened and it is excellently well kept, run by two typical Yankees who thoroughly understand their business and who are teaching the natives of some of the comforts that are to be gotten from living respectably, an art unknown to the greater portion of these people. The Judge is charmed and proposes that we remain a day or two after I get through. I am not quite as enthusiastic although the cool nights, the beautiful situation of the hotel – I can see from my window up the Trinity Valley for more than thirty miles and the view is a beautiful one and the really first class accommodations make life decidedly bearable and make me rather dread our stay in Waco which has no suburban resort to relieve one of the insufferable heat of the town.
[1892-07-18 Henry (Ft Worth) to Bertha (Farragut House, Rye Beach)]

On a second 1892 trip to Ft. Worth, Henry enclosed the Bill of Fare from the Ye Arlington Inn in his letter to Bertha (see below).

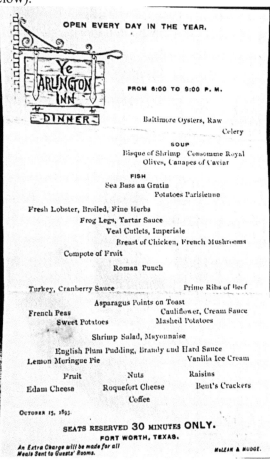

Ye Arlington Inn,
Fort Worth, Texas, Dec. 19th, 1892
It is a great comfort to be comfortable, dearest. And as this happens to be the first of the hotels I have been abiding in since I left home where thoroughly comfortable provision is made for travelers, I am all the more appreciative of my surroundings. This hotel has improved ever since last summer when we thought it excellently kept and really it could not be more thoroughly well equipped. It is very prettily furnished and the table is excellent. I was so enthusiastic over the dinner tonight that I should have sent you the menu card had I not been afraid you would accuse

me of the same weakness you were unkind enough to attack me about that day when I thoughtfully reminded you I would have to take you home in time for your luncheon.
[1892-12-19 (Monday) Henry (Ft. Worth) to Bertha (Newton Centre)]

Regardless of his other views about Texas, Henry found relief and comfort in the Ye Arlington Inn, especially after he had a frustrating trip to Waco in 1894.

I arrived last night, having escaped from Waco somewhat sooner than I imagined it would be possible to leave that hot, dusty town and a most hideously primitive hotel behind me. Here, life is infinitely more endurable. The hotel is excellent, the town is rather attractive and my work is most congenial. Our work here is simply fascinating and we have the prettiest station in all the land. I am very glad to see one of my undertakings give some evidence of all the care I have given it. It encourages me to bear more patiently with the unpromising children of my business household who seem so slow to respond to my training or entreaties. I have done very little here today but our work has grown so splendidly of late that a most casual glance at the business gives me very strong evidence of our growth and increased prosperity since my visit last fall.

... I have wished for you a great many times today and if this hotel continues open I think I must bring you and the small Hugh down to quarter here while I am working my next rounds though this "bla..sted" country. The weather here is simply perfect and the hotel can't be beat in this or any other country.

Just before I retired to my room, I ran across Mrs. McCord who lives on the heights near the hotel. She inquired particularly after you and your daughter and, after having received a very stern correction for such a blunder (I don't mean for her interest in you, my dear, but because of her mistaking that boy for a girl, ignorant woman!), she proceeded to ask any number of questions about your coming to Texas the next time I came, etc., which I wondered whether she loved you madly or was desperate for the society of a civilized female in this far off land.
[1894-03-11 Henry (Ft Worth TX) to Bertha (3337 Washington Ave, Stl)]

During the cattle convention in March 1894, Henry was clearly pleased that the "mob" stayed elsewhere and not in the Ye Arlington Inn in Ft. Worth. Given the historic reputation of cowboys from this period, the use of the word "*mob*" was probably very close to the mark.

I have arrived here with the cattle convention! You should see the mob! Nothing like it has ever been found or will ever be reproduced outside of Texas. The hotel [Ye Arlington Inn] is crowded but this hotel, which is the only decent one in Fort Worth, doesn't suit the tastes, God be thanked, of the more pronounced types so we are comparatively free from the horrible freaks of nature who swarm like bees around those execrable places which pass under the name "hotel" down town.
[1894-03-12 Henry (Ft. Worth) to Bertha (StL)]

b. About Fort Worth
Henry often spoke about the Texas heat even in the spring when the approaching warm weather made him anxious to leave.

It has turned warm and it seems torrid with my thickest winter clothing and I am rather anticipating that I shall find it more uncomfortable at Waco for it is usually much warmer there. If I telegraph for my white lawn – the one trimmed with blue ribbons and open in the neck - you will please express it for I may need it on the cars on the return trip! It looks like midsummer here and the flowers are in full bloom in all the yards so I congratulate myself that I did not have to delay my visit for if this weather continues, the Texas summer with all its terrors will arrive and I am devoutly hoping to escape before it breaks loose in full force.
[1903-03-18 Henry (Ft. Worth) to Bertha (StL)]

It was not only the heat that bothered Henry in Ft. Worth but also the mud after hard rains.

> *Has St. Louis been washed away? If it has rained there as it has here, I tremble for the safety of my family. I started from Waco in the rain. It "pored" all during the journey and its unceasing ejaculations all night and all of today have left me in a state of mind bordering desperation. I thought Boston in a storm was the most gloomy of earthly habitations but I was mistaken. Fort Worth with its streets running rivers of mud, the houses washed and wilted to sea sick pallor. The limp and dejected natives whose neglect of soap and water seems emphasized by the reeking moisture which Lord says "pervades my marrow". The ensemble is not cheering and I am right glad you are not along, which is one of my rare examples of unselfishness since it would be impossible to imagine any blessing that would bring such balm to my lacerated spirits.*
> [1906-03-18 Henry (Ft. Worth) to Bertha (StL)]

Even when the heat was not a problem, Henry's lack of enthusiasm for Ft. Worth was evident from his recalling General Sheridan's comment about preferring "Hades" over Texas (incorrectly ascribed to General Sherman). But, fortunately, at least one element of Hades was lacking on this trip: the heat.

> *As the enclosed clipping indicates, I have not been exactly idle since my arrival yesterday. To prepare for that meeting and dance(?) attendance to those grangers in one day is no small undertaking and, although I uttered none of the extravagances attributed to me in the "yellow" press, I felt like going much further and invoking the baseball bat. I am simply a fixture here as far as I can now see and I am seriously thinking of renting a house and asking the family down to visit me. There is absolutely no prospect of my escape before Tuesday or Wednesday of next week and it may be not even then and, as I have received three summons to Waco and must go there before I return, there is likelihood of your winning added renown as one of the bachelor wives. If you didn't have so many children and so many claims upon you which are prior to a husband's, I should telegraph you to come down and share my privations, for one of the prerequisites to that land General Sherman likened unfavorably to Hades is not lacking – the weather is fine and I have just spotted a decent restaurant. So if you were not otherwise occupied, you might be here doing chores instead of having impertinence fired at you in this fashion.*
> [20171121-2 1908-03-14(-) Henry (Ft. Worth) to Bertha]

Henry went back to Ft. Worth toward the end of 1908 to look into his natural gas business interests. Natural gas supply was a significant issue for the growing city and Henry wanted to make sure that Fort Worth Light and Power Company was a major player. While there, Henry wrote to Bertha and included two articles from the Telegram, the Fort Worth newspaper, about his activities. Henry wrote: "*I enclose some clippings just to let you know that I have something to keep me here and am not separating myself from you and home and friends because "I don't like" them.*" [1908-11-26 Henry (Fort Worth) to Bertha (StL)]

H.C. SCOTT HERE, SAYS "I'LL SELL NATURAL GAS!"
President of Company confirms Telegram's Story.

NOT WORRIED
"When natural gas is here, I guess you will find us in it", he says.

H. C. SCOTT HERE, SAYS "I'LL SELL NATURAL GAS!"

President of Company Confirms Telegram's Story

NOT WORRIED

"When Natural Gas Is Here I Guess You Will Find Us in It," He Says

CALLS ON MAYOR
W.J. Mackey, Attorney for
Navarro Gas co is now
in Fort Worth

Henry C. Scott, president of the Fort Worth Light and Power Company is in the city from St. Louis and confirms The Telegram's exclusive announcement that his company is ready to contest with others in Fort Worth with a natural gas supply.

"When the natural gas is here, I guess you will find us in it," said Mr. Scott almost fiercely.

"There is natural gas in both Palo Pinto and the other fields. It is foolish, however, to talk about gas in the millions of cubic feet. My advice is not to waste it. There is no good in going around making big claims at this time. Wait until we have something definite to propose and the public will have it."

Mr. Scott is beautifully noncommunicative in regard to the natural gas proposition. This is an encouraging sign.

In the course of an interview on Thanksgiving, weather and prosperity, this was all the natural gas information that could be secured by questing from various points of attack. Mr. Scott's smile displayed none of the worry that might be pictured on the countenance of the head of a corporation about to lose the demand for its product. It is evident that he has entire confidence in his own prediction that when natural gas reaches Fort Worth his company will be in it.

His statements only strengthen the prediction of Superintendent Lord that the Fort Worth Light and Power Company will beat the Texas Company in the race to Fort Worth with natural gas.

The Palo Pinto field is more than thirty miles nearer and the Fort Worth Light and Power Company has mains already laid for its manufactured gas supply in most parts of the city.

Mr. Scott takes the position that the company has no further part in the gas investigation recently inaugurated by the city commission with a demand of rate reduction to $1 a thousand cubic feet.

"We have already furnished them the statement they asked," said Mr. Scott. "We have also notified them that our books are ready for any additional investigation they may make. The books are at their service today, tomorrow or ten years from now, just whenever they desire them."

Mr. Scott held no communication with city officials Thursday tho he called at the office of Mayor Harris who was observing Thanksgiving Day. Most of his time was spent at the offices of the Company of Ninth Street, going over the affairs.

The arrival here of W.J. Mackey, attorney for the Navarro Gas Company, has given rise to the report that that company is also in the field to supply Fort Worth with natural gas. The Navarro and Texas companies have both secured options on a large part of the gas lands in the Texas fields. The companies are said to have about an equal share. Which has the more valuable gas yielding holdings will be determined by the tests.

HOLDING UP GAS COMPANY

C.M. Brown: "I'd be more thankful if the music of the saw and hammer was not so much fainter than two months ago. The lumber yards are quiet. There are reasons for this. One of the most startling is: There are over 500 applications for extension of gas mains and the Fort Worth Light and Power Company will not lay one single foot, not even for a millionaire property owner! Probably half of the applicants desire to build new houses but will not without gas connections, as everybody now wants a modern house or none at all. What's the matter with the gas company? Not a thing except the city has hold it up – in fact, has scared it out of ten year's growth."
[Newspaper clippings from The Telegram, included in Henry's 1908-11-26 letter.]

As it turned out, Henry's problems with the natural gas supply to Fort Worth was the result of the "*mighty unpleasant people*" of Standard Oil becoming involved in this Texas business. Henry had already tangled with Standard Oil in Wichita and wrote in his next letter to Bertha about these "*unpleasant people*", whether they are "*for or against you.*"

I have had a strenuous time these last two days and in classic lingo I am all fussed up. It looks very much as though the Standard Oil Co. was either behind or an actual factor in the movement to bring Natural Gas here. I have tackled the said Standard before and they are mighty unpleasant people to have around, either for or against you. I have been trying to save this property from loss but I am by no means sure I shall succeed and while I am in the midst of this muddle, Hugh Graves announces that Sam has failed to put up his share of the amount we agreed to raise to help the Coal Co. and that the latter is really crippled thereby. So I am going to church tomorrow to ask that my own sins and the sins of some others be blotted out.
[1908-11-28 (20180419A-4) Henry (Ft. Worth) to Bertha (64 Vandeventer Place, Stl)]

Henry was back in Ft. Worth in February 1909 and the situation had not improved.

I have been in a series of continuous meetings since my arrival and this is the first chance I have had to write. I was very glad to have your letter and to know that you had finished your journey safely and without great inconvenience. I found things in much of a mess here and the contrast between Buba with my best friend and Texas without her, is not consoling. It has been said by some sapient diviner of the truth that there can be no success without enthusiasm in one's work. If this be true, Fort Worth must fail because I have become so disgusted with the authorities here that I am in no fit condition to view anything in the town without aversion and disgust. Things here look blue and I am afraid we are to have much trouble ahead. And what between this snarl and

Sam[241] in St. Louis, I am not looking for what might be called a heavenly time these next three months. Sam has been riding for a bad fall and I am very much afraid he will get one. If you see him, try to be very careful in what you say to him for if the sale falls through, as I am morally sure it will, it is going to be a serious problem as to what is the next best step. I am trying to put my health in order for what is ahead but it is not behaving very handsomely and my spirits are therefore not buoyant. I ought to be and am ashamed to write such lamentations after having just been to paradise with you. But it's not ingratitude for past mercies but rather a sense of unequal strength for the struggle against the flesh – my aching brow and the devil - a group of Texas politicians.
[1909-02-03 Henry (Ft. Worth) to Bertha]

3. DALLAS

In 1890, Dallas was the largest city by population in Texas with 38,000 inhabitants. During the period from around 1880 through 1920, the Dallas economy evolved from being primarily farming and ranching to being a self-sustaining, industrial city. By 1920, Dallas became the center of inland cotton market and of the manufacture of cotton gin machinery.

Henry's principal business interest in Dallas was in one of the city's railroads and, so, Henry was a periodic visitor. Henry had to make one unexpected trip to Dallas during his planned trips to Waco, Fort Worth and Wichita in 1893 when he discovered a problem with his coal contracts and with his railroad men.

I have just returned from Dallas. It is eleven o'clock, so you will see that I have had a long, weary day of it. I tramped the town all day, looking up railroad men and coal agents whom I wished to see and I am pretty footsore and pretty weary and low in my mind generally and I need my darling here this very moment. But instead of being here, she is away and I shall not see her for a great many days! Three or four at least and so I am not having a good time, dearest.

Are you very, very sorry for me? If you are, that's some comfort even if I am forced to think of having your sympathy at arm's length instead of hearing you tell me you are sorry.

I had a successful trip, dearest. There's some comfort in the thought that I saved our company here at least a thousand dollars on the winter's coal supply. Don't you think that a fair day's work? I am preparing to finish up here tomorrow and expect to leave tomorrow night for Wichita. I shall be there until Saturday night and ought to be at home Sunday evening if nothing unforeseen happens to prevent my getting through the Wichita work within the time I have arranged to give it.
[1893-10-18 Henry (Ft. Worth) to Bertha (StL)]

Henry never seemed to be completely happy with the way his businesses were run by his managers.

I have just come from the meeting of the Rylea at which I was elected to preside over the destinies of one of the most tangled, badly managed properties it has been my ill luck to encounter. Now this is saying much, coming from one who has never been honored with any trusts other than broken down institutions. Look at my first charge – Carondelet, then Fort Worth and Pine Bluff and Waco, Wichita and now Dallas. Well, one of these days when I am too old to be pleased with any such work of favor, I may be requested to lend my valuable aid to something that is not utterly played out before it comes to me but now the forlorn hopes seem to be the only undertakings I am thought capable of conducting and this is the forlornest of the lot. Pine Bluff in its most magnificent days of desolation could not be compared to this. And such a shame too, dearest. More than six hundred thousand dollars have been sunk in roadways, street bridges, tunnels, engines, cars and such equipment, to run a road in exactly the wrong direction! I ran over the line yesterday: about four miles of the track is built in the air, à la New York elevated! And over this elaborate aerial system

---

[241] Henry's brother. At that time, Sam was the Vice President and General Manager of the Missouri & Illinois Coal Co. [The Book of St. Louisans]

about four passengers and the recently elected president were carried to take a bird's eye view of the country below.

...

I have been very busy all day and am very tired so I shall not be able to write many minutes. My foot which I twisted slightly yesterday has been giving me considerable amusement for about twenty-four hours and I am going to catch up some of the lost slumber which it cost me last night. I expect to go from here to Waco tomorrow night or Friday morning and I am trying to insure my return on the 19th with, I regret to say, small prospect of seeing you so soon. Do write, sweetheart. Texas is a poor place anyway and, without your letters, it is unbearable. Give the boy his Dad's blessing and make him tell you to be good and write.

[1894-03-06 Henry (Dallas) to Bertha (3337 Washington Ave, Stl)]

Henry exasperation with Texas was well summed up: *"Texas is a poor place anyway and, without your letters, it is unbearable."*

A decade later, in 1903, Henry was grousing about travel to Dallas.

On arriving at Dallas, my troubles began. I had arranged to remain there an hour and then come over here. My train was scheduled to reach Dallas at seven but was two hours late and, as I had the ill luck to strike a Dallas orgy in the shape of a street parade which brought millions of wild animals in from the surrounding country, all out going trains were simply crowed to suffocation with the aforesaid w. as. [i.e. wild animals]. So I tried the electric line, managed to get on the front platform of one car, the last to leave at eleven and sat on my suit case all the way over arriving at two A.M., more dead than alive and cross in proportion. It isn't necessary to describe the latter mood to you for I think you are familiar with my nervous? system and are in no need of additional samples of it.

[1903-04-16 Henry (Ft. Worth) Bertha (StL)]

Dallas Day Parade, 1905.

However, on the conclusion of the aforementioned trip, Henry remarked about some of the beautiful aspects of the state.

> *The fields are very pretty with their masses of Texas' duly legalized favorite flower, the buffalo clover, in full bloom. The fields were many of them blue with the mases of blossom and I wish you could be here to see them. I am too tired to dilate, however, on the beauties of anything just now for I am honestly fit for nothing but bed, whether I propose to go in the most direct fashion and I hope a night's rest will do the miracle of putting some life into this old and worn out frame for it needs revivifying, sadly.*

[1903-04-19 Henry (Waco) to Bertha (StL)]

4. WACO

> ### "WACO, TEXAS!"
>
> #### That's What We Say, But Waco Simply Says, "Great Scott!"
>
> WACO, Tex., May 8.—The plant and franchises of the Waco Electric Railway and Light Co. were sold at auction yesterday by order of court and bid in by Henry C. Scott of St. Louis for $60,100. He will consolidate the line with the Citizens' road and control the street railways of Waco.

Waco's economy suffered during the Civil War but recovered rapidly in the following years. Waco was on a spur of the Chisholm Trail used by cattlemen to drive steers to market and cattlemen and their employees often stopped in the town to buy supplies and for recreation. Similar to Ft. Worth, Waco had many saloons and gaming houses which catered to cowhands and drifters, and which helped Waco earn the nickname, "Six Shooter Junction." Prostitution was legally recognized, licensed, and regulated by the city until the early twentieth century. During this period, Waco developed a significant trade in cotton. But Waco also attracted a number of educational institutions and so was sometimes called the "Athens of Texas." Waco's first gas plant began operation in the 1880s, and, by 1891, some mule-drawn street cars were replaced by electric cars operated by the Waco Electric Railway and Light Company. By 1901, its successor, the Citizen Railway company, which was managed by Henry, was operating twenty electric trolleys.

a. Henry on the 1892 Waco Strike

The strike at Henry's Waco "Electric Railway and Light Company" business started in early August 1892, shortly after the Homestead Strike of July 1, 1892. The Homestead Strike, which took place at the Carnegie steel plant in Homestead Pennsylvania, marked a major change in the organization of American labor under union leadership. Previously, labor protests were generally unorganized, without clear leadership, and, not surprisingly, unsuccessful. Although the Homestead Strike resulted in the eventual demise of the Amalgamated Association of Iron and Steel Workers (which had organized the Homestead Strike), it nevertheless demonstrated the effectiveness of organized labor. Given the new organizing ability of unions in the 1890's, there was ample reason for Henry to be concerned about how to manage labor unrest in his businesses. Such was his concern and anxiety during 1892 the Waco strike that he wrote several times to Bertha, his fiancée at this time.

> *My reason for not writing yesterday you will think a good one, I am sure, for it grows out of the bother and rather taxing attention I have had to give to our property at Waco where a strike is in progress. I have not yet received full advice of the trouble but that it is a serious one I feel sure for*

our agent there in his last telegram advises me that we shall probably be without light tonight and the prospect of having that town in darkness for a single night is not a pleasant reflection!! I have been out engaging men here and I hope they, our officers at Waco, will keep up their courage and run the plants themselves if they cannot employ sufficient help. I could do no good by going down but it is pretty hard to sit here and wait for news of the trouble and not be able to help take care of it. Besides, if I went down, there would be no one here to send additional help when it is required so, beside making myself pretty miserable, I have done little else than look up engineers and mechanics for two days. I think I have walked forty miles these last two days. But I do not intend to annoy you with all this, dear. You can see that I am not losing my equanimity entirely for I have come up here [the University Club] to lunch because it is more comfortable than down town and I wanted to get the help and comfort which always comes from a talk with you, my own precious child.
[1892-08-12 (Friday) Henry (StL) to Bertha (Rye Beach)]

In another letter which was apparently written at the time of this 1892 Waco strike, Henry spoke of the toll that the strike was taking on him.

You will accuse me of neglecting you I know for I did not write yesterday. That miserable Waco strike threat is using up all my time and energies and I am at the office now consulting with detectives planning and stewing over the problems and trying to abort trouble. I hope I shall be able to prevent a strike for its consequences to both of our Waco properties would be most serious. I am keeping a stiff upper lip but the thing is wearing me some and I hope the strain won't last much longer.
[20180222-2 Henry to Bertha]

During such stressful times, Henry was always quick to tell Bertha how important her support was for him and how he always missed her.

If all Texas had been on a strike, I should not have minded it very much with the comfort and help of your letter this morning. That was a beautiful letter, dear, it was like the comfort of your voice when you are near me, dear, precious child, and it was as bright and full of hope as is the face of my darling, and the great comfort of it was that all you said was so true to what I know and love best in you, dear.

...

I am afraid the strike at Waco stuck the last nail in the coffin of my hope of seeing you before October, for I must give the work there all my attention until we are thoroughly well started again. You will see from the clipping [below] that our agents there are for the time being in command of the situation but I can't feel easy or content until I am quite sure there is no chance of the trouble being repeated and work of this kind takes my thought and attention from other duties which must receive attention too, as soon as the pressing needs of Waco are met. I may even have to go there although just now I think not. And, O, my darling, all this means I shall not see you for two months, as long a separation from now as has been endured since I last saw your dear face. Do you wonder that it sometimes is very hard to bear with patience, my dearest, my own love.
[1892-08-13 Henry (StL) to Bertha (Farragut House, Rye Beach)]

[The Newspaper clipping included in Henry's August 13, 1892 letter, above]
A STRIKE AT WACO TEX.
Special Dispatch to the Globe-Democrat.
WACO, TEX., August 12 – The electricians, engineers and firemen of the Waco Gas and Electric Light Company walked out last night. The pretense for the strike was that the light company had agreed to allow Electrician Wiggins and his brother the monopoly of the placing of rotary ventilating fans and afterward the light company began to put in these fans in competition with the Wiggins brothers. The light company managers contend that the Wiggens brothers, being their employees, put in fans and applied the Hobson motor instead of theirs and that this was a breach. The engineers and firemen went out in sympathy with the Wiggins brothers, the power house crew followed and then the employees of the Citizens' Electric Street Railway

Company struck in sympathy. This cut off the city's light and stopped the street cards on thirteen miles of track. It also stopped several factories depended on the electric power house for motive power, leaving 400 people idle. The striking crews were paid off and discharged and this afternoon new men took their places so that both the light and the street car plant are in full operation again.
[The August 12, 1892 Globe-Democrat newspaper clipping]

Since Henry was in St. Louis during this Waco trouble, he allowed himself to take a Sunday off to go the Country Club. Undoubtedly, Henry needed the break; but, in addition, he seemed to be showing good management skills in putting some trust in his "*boys at Waco*".

> *I came out here [The Country Club] last night, having literally run away from a lot of telegrams which came in all day from Waco and which worried me no little. I could not help any and I am really relieved to be where I can hear nothing more until tomorrow. I think my boys at Waco will control and master the trouble but if they feel that they really need me after tomorrow or if they have not secured all the necessary help to properly carry on the work, I shall go down there. It is much better to let the men, who have daily supervision of the work, take care of this difficulty for it gives them better control over their men but, if after having given them time to act they show they are unequal to the emergency, there will be nothing left but for me to try my hand which, you will agree with me, is not very well calculated to improve matters. I shall have an interesting time of it even if I do no good. So, on this account alone, I shall be compelled to go to Waco if the strike is not over by tomorrow. I shall telegraph you if I have to go away, dear, so don't stop writing here and that is all I shall say or think about Waco or the strike or any other thought that is unpleasant for I have so many beautiful things to think of today, my dearest.*
> [1892-08-15(-) Henry (StL) to Bertha (Farragut House, Rye Beach)]

Bertha was always sympathetic to Henry, even as his fiancée in 1892.

> *I have just received your Friday letter[242] so I know why I had none yesterday and, about the Waco trouble, whenever you are in trouble, dear, it makes me want to be at home so much. I can do nothing to help you here and perhaps I could not do very much if I were there. And yet I think if you could come to me as you did sometimes last winter when you were tired, I could give you some rest, dear. Or if instead of coming up to the University Club, our home were ready? It hurts me to hear you say I am away when you most need me for I do want to be there. As I cannot be, you must write me very fully of all that annoys you.*
> [1892-08-16 (Monday) Bertha (Rye Beach) to Henry (StL)]

Fortunately, the Waco strike ended after about a week's struggle, which resolution was "encouraged" by the hiring of replacement workers.

Electric Street Car Strike.

Waco, Tex., Aug. 12.—All the street car lines are tied up to-day by the strike. The companies, including the Waco gas and electric company, which are affected by the strike announce that they will fill the places of the strikers with new men and that everything will be running in a day or so.

This evening new crews were obtained for both power houses and to-night the light plant and the street cars are in full operation, greatly to the satisfaction of the public.

[The Galveston Daily News, August 13, 1892]

---

[242] 1892-08-12 (Friday) Henry (StL) to Bertha (Rye Beach) – quoted above.

Henry spoke of the strike's conclusion being of benefit to him. It was an occasion to get rid of *"our indifferent help"* in exchange for more accommodating laborers. Such was the nature of business and labor relations of the time.

> *The strike at Waco is over, I am very glad to say, and I can't help thinking the trouble will, in the end, be of material advantage to us for our arrangement with the new crew of mechanics is a much better one than we had with the old employees and, beside this, we have clearly shown our ability to operate our property independent of the association of so called skilled laborers, an advantage of no mean importance in this day of labor agitations and strikes. And I am very glad the strike was beaten by our officers at Waco for it will give them courage to face future difficulties of similar character if we are again compelled to deal with them.*
>
> *I had a very hopeful dispatch from our superintendent yesterday telling me to send no more men from St. Louis. That all the places were now well filled and that the "strike was a fine opportunity for getting rid of some of our indifferent help." So you will see that as usual, I had all my bother and worry for nothing, the conclusion people usually arrive at when they have distressed and taxed themselves about things that can neither be remedied nor removed by worry. When I am about a hundred years old, I will perhaps be able to use a little philosophy in such matters for I may be said to be gradually learning the virtue of "keeping cool" in times of emergency but, meanwhile, I shall probably take the next trouble as seriously to heart as I did this last. That is, if you are not with me, for I don't think I shall worry about many things when you are near, dear child.*
> [1892-08-16 (Tuesday) Henry (StL) to Bertha (Farragut House, Rye Beach)]

Henry's next letter spoke again of his *"new crew"*, his optimism for his Waco business and his gratitude for Bertha's support.

> *I have written you fully about the labor trouble. There is little else to say except that I have good news from the works and the new crew seems a great improvement on the old force. I like to tell you all about my little troubles – I seem to have only little worries for I am growing to measuring them against the great blessing of your love, dear child and today I feel ashamed that I should have carried a light burden so unwillingly when I had such joy in my heart because of you, my friend, my companion, my helpmeet in every thought and act of my life.*
> [1892-08-18 (Thursday) Henry (StL) to Bertha (Farragut House)]

Summarizing her views of strikes, Bertha wrote: *"Strikes are very disagreeable things in many ways, are they not, dear boy?"* [1892-08-18 Bertha (Farragut house) to Henry (StL)]

Bertha continued this subject in her next letter:

> *I am delighted to hear the Waco trouble is over. From the accounts I have been reading in the papers of other strikes, I was beginning to fear that it might be very serious for the striking fever seems to have seized the country. General Schofield and father sit up and discuss the Tennessee trouble with pretty sober faces.*
> [1892-08-19 (Friday) Bertha (Farragut House, Rye Beach) to Henry (StL)]

In December of 1892, months after the conclusion of the Waco strike, Henry had to return to Waco and wrote a more philosophical letter about his anxiety and feelings about the strike. In particular, Henry included toward the end: *"Wars of business are like the greater wars, very costly to the combatants. And the fellows in the field have the fighting and loss and are least rewarded."* Although Henry liked to win, he was able to see the larger picture in which he was just a part and, perhaps, just a small one.

> *I think I am inclined to be enthusiastic anyway this evening, dearest, for I really believe we have won our fight at Waco. I may be reckoning on victory too soon and may yet have considerable trouble but I hardly think it possible for those scamps did everything to get me to buy their property at far less than its cost and frankly admitted that they did not see how they could continue to operate*

against the ruinous competition we had inaugurated. Ruinous competition indeed! These fellows went to Waco, bribed the dishonest members of the council and obtained franchises we would have paid the city for, without any cost save the outlay of corruption money and then, with no thought of honestly competing with us, build works large enough to hamper and demoralize our business and calculated upon our paying them heavily to retire.

I am very glad they did not know how often they made me walk the floor in my anxiety over the troubles they were causing us or they might have pulled together and held out longer. Fortunately, they did not see behind a very determined manner and policy what a coward I really was, dear, or they might not be so hopeless now. But whether from good fortune or other causes, we certainly have the best of the struggle now and, if I can get our people in St. Louis to follow my plan out, I think there will be a funeral in Waco within a very few weeks which we will be able to claim credit for.

But I am beginning to boast, dear. Excuse me, please. The success too, if achieved, is a very little one, indeed and nothing to be proud of for our gain after all is small. Wars of business are like the greater wars, very costly to the combatants. And the fellows in the field have the fighting and loss and are least rewarded. And if I retire from Waco, after having won, I shall be in much the same position of a high private after hostilities are suspended. But it helps to win when you think you are right!

[1892-12-19 (Monday) Henry (Ft. Worth) to Bertha (Newton Centre)]

b. Waco's Better Side

Waco was not all bad. Henry had a number of distinguished acquaintances in Waco and Henry clearly enjoyed their company. On his return trip to Waco in December 1892, months after the Waco strike ended, Henry spoke of his dinner at Colonel Parrott's house in Waco (who introduced *"My wife, suh"),* and then his visit to Judge Clark's house. As Henry wrote much later in 1905 but was certainly applicable to Col. Parrott and Judge Clark, *"…at home he is like every other educated southern man: at his best".*

Robert B. Parrott (1848–1903) - Confederate soldier and business executive.[243]

My next item was dinner at Col. Parrott's. The Colonel would have made Colonel Carter green with envy if the latter had possessed the smallest amount of jealously for another who could complete with him in the extravagant mannerisms which made up the personality of that so called

---

[243] Historical Note: Robert Parrott, at age thirteen, entered the University of Virginia. In 1862, however, after only six months of classes, he dropped out to enter Confederate military service. He enlisted as a private in Lt. Col. John Singleton Mosby's Forty-third Virginia Cavalry Battalion and was soon elected second sergeant of Company F. He was captured at Rectortown, Virginia, on December 21, 1864, and was confined to Fort Warren in Boston harbor for the duration of the war. In October 1872 he moved to Waco, Texas. [Texas State Historical Association, https://www.tshaonline.org/handbook/entries/parrott-robert-b; also Find-A-Grave]

*typical southerner. Parrott's "My wife, suh. My dear, this is my esteemed friend, Colonel Scott",
was as good as a play and the old fellow's magnificent manner in dispensing his hospitality will
not soon be forgotten by his guest. Such a dinner! I think I have seen tables pretty bountifully
loaded down in old Virginia but this one fairly groaned with its burden. There were one or two
moments during that dinner in which I was somewhat reconciled to your absence for, if I have
caught your eye during some of the Colonel's orations, that genial old fellow would have lost all
of his good impressions of Colonel Scott for, as it was, I had to look very hard at the floor and try
to pick a quarrel with it more than once. After dinner, I declined the pressing invitation to drive
behind the Colonel's boys, "over the most magnificent city in the south, suh", and went for a long
walk with one of our boys.*

*Then, this evening, I spent at Judge Clark's. The Judge is President of the Gas Co and you may, if
you read the political dispatches of the last campaign, have heard of his nomination and defeat for
the governorship of the state. The Judge is only about forty and has been twice on the Supreme
Court and Attorney General of the state and as he is as gifted socially as he is in his professional
work and is besides a very good friend of mine, I enjoyed my last feat of the day immensely.*

The Rose that Henry sent in his 1892-12-18 letter to Bertha

*I am tempted to send a rose which I pulled from a bush in Colonel Parrott's yard today and which
has since been adorning my button hole. Will you accept it with my love, my darling?*
[1892-12-18 (Sunday) Henry (Waco) to Bertha (Stancote, Newton Centre MA)]

Henry obviously enjoyed his friendship with Judge Clark whose southern hospitality was something that a
Virginia man, such as Henry, appreciated.
*My train leaves in a few minutes for Wichita and I shall have time to tell you of my Sunday dinner
at Judge Clark's. You know the Judge is a widower and as his daughter is off at school, he is living
at home with no one for company except a rather attractive but dissipated son. I have never been
very enthusiastic about Judge C and we have had some rather heated business differences but at
home he is like every other educated southern man: at his best.*
[1905-11-12 Henry (Waco Tx) to Bertha (64 Vandeventer Pl, Stl)]

For all of his disparaging comments about Texas in general and Waco in particular, Henry, periodically,
spoke of it with some fondness. Perhaps because at those times his business was doing well.
*I wish you could be here with me. The hotel is poor but I think you could stand for a day or two
and the Cotton Palace is really superb. The lights at the World's Fair were hardly as beautiful
and the weather is simply magnificent. Talk of exhilarating climates. Give me Texas and a good*

hotel and I can guarantee care for any invalid. Business here is booming. Think of Waco's making more gas than Fort Worth. It seems incredible but it's true.
[1894-11-24 Henry (Waco) to Bertha (StL)]

Henry also pointed out other fine aspects of Waco. In his December 1892 trip to Waco, Henry spoke glowingly of the Waco Natatorium and hot springs.

Waco Texas Natatorium: The Waco Natatorium served as a center of activity in Waco and a downtown attraction for almost forty years. In the 1920s, Waco's artesian water supply began to run dry because of population growth and high demand for the water.

Let me give you the record of my day. I was up at seven and, after breakfast, I rode over the street railway system with our Superintendent. Then I went to the Natatorium. I don't believe I ever told you about the wonderful water supply of Waco. Well (I intend to use the adverb and not the noun "well" although discussing the water question), there is an artesian flow of hot water, strong enough to send the water sixty feet in the air or above the surface and as a consequence you merely drive down a well casing and you secure a stream of perfectly clear and pure hot water, strong enough, if the well is a sufficient size, to flood the whole town if allowed to run unchecked. This hot water supply has made Waco quite a health resort and the town is dotted over with swimming pools, some of which, like the one I visited today, are really quite gorgeous. This one was about a hundred feet square and made entirely of marble and tiling and I had great fun watching from the railing the swimming. The movements of the men could be as plainly seen as that of gold fish in the small glass tanks.
[1892-12-18 (Sunday) Henry (Waco) to Bertha (Stancote, Newton Centre MA)]

c. Waco Legal Disputes in 1897; Travel to Marlin TX

After a peaceful period, new Waco troubles presented themselves in 1897 which required Henry to appear in the Marlin Texas courthouse before a Texas judge whose "*integrity*" was uncertain. Apparently, Marlin was the seat of the court for Waco at this time.

The journey down was anything but delightful: hot, dusty and at times there was absolutely not a breath of air. Still, I got in with very few "scratches" and today I feel very well indeed, thanks to a good night's sleep.

We have a very vexing suit here, brought by a lot of adventures before a judge of whose integrity I am exceedingly uncertain, and I shall be most anxious until the case is heard. I am afraid I must remain here until Wednesday or Thursday so I shall probably not hear from you until my return and that will be more than a week's silence, dear child. I think Will Stribling was about right when he suggested that it was worth more than the loss of a debt to have to go to Texas to save it, but my keenest regret on this journey is that it paces me so far out of the way of any communication with you.

The climate here is not as hard to stand as one might imagine, for it is reasonably cool at nights and by keeping out of the sun I have generally kept well even in hotter weather than this. This has already become an exclusively egotistical letter but I venture to further remark that I have a good room, bath attached, so in that particular am as comfortable as one can be made here. And the Chinese restaurant still exists so I am not starving.
[1897-07-04 Henry (St. Charles Hotel, Waco) to Bertha (Jamestown RI)]

The next day, Henry believed that his legal disputes with the City of Waco may have been resolved. Although the disputes were clearly tiresome, Henry's remuneration for his efforts appeared to have been grand ($250,000 per year - in 1897!).

July 5th, 1897
Dear Bert,
I shall not write anything but a report that I am alive and well. Anything more would be simply tempting providence, for it is too unspeakable hot for anything like indoor work at night. I had a very successful day. We won on every point in our suit and I think will certainly close a contract with the City on Wednesday. I shall have to run over to Marlin tonight, about 30 miles distant, to present one feature of our case to the judge of that district who will hear us sitting in chambers. Wednesday I return here and if my plans succeed that day, I shall leave Wednesday evening for St. Louis and ought to reach home Saturday morning.

I have about concluded that it is worth $250,000.00 a year to manage the affairs of this company! Yours always,
Henry
[1897-07-05 Henry (Waco Gas Company) to Bertha (Jamestown)]

Henry travelled to Marlin Texas one day later for the court proceeding which would render a final ruling on the various Waco legal issues. This trip proved to be very unpleasant and not just because of the nasty legal matters.

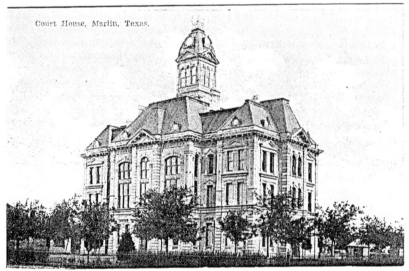

Marlin is a city in Falls County, Texas, United States. The population was 6,628 at the 2000 census but decreased by 10 percent to 5,967 in 2010. Since 1851, it has been the third county seat of Falls County. Marlin has been given the nickname "the Hot Mineral Water City of Texas".
The Court House that Henry visited looked like this (picture circa 1905).

Dear Bert,

This is the first letter I have ever written you from Marlin and I am very sure it will be my last one. By this I do not mean that I shall never write to you again, nor do I wish it understood that I intend to die. I will make my meaning clearer. I have made a solemn vow never to see this place again. Not all the wealth of the universe can make me break this vow for I am a firm man, I am.

We came down from Waco last night. By we, I mean Judge Clark and I. We tramped half a mile in the dust from the depot to this magnificent hotel. (I don't mean the dust was half a mile <u>deep</u>, but that <u>long</u>, at least I don't <u>think</u> it was half a mile deep.) We had telegraphed for rooms with southern exposure. The clerk, however, regretfully announced that his best rooms were all taken and would "the Judge and Col. Scott please make out for a night or two with rooms under the roof?" And next week we were promised cooler quarters. I thought of earning the right to distinction through the only course recognized by true Texans – by killing the clerk. But I spared him because of his great earthly sufferings. I spared him. And from the depths of my soul I pitied him for he will have to remain in this hotel all summer. I managed however to tell the clerk that I should not be able to avail myself of the dazzling prospect held out to us for business of the greatest importance called me away. I might even be compelled to leave today. I then proceeded to my attic but, being concerned that the hotel was on fire, I left hurriedly for the piazza which had happily been provided to cover just such emergencies and spent the remainder of the night in a rocking chair thinking of how cool it must be at Jamestown.

I am not as nearly dead as I imagined I would be today and a fine swim in a large pool they have here – like the one we saw at Waco – and some very good corn bread, which we bribed a waiter to make for us, have revived me and I have energy enough left to catch the first train to Waco.
[1897-07-06 Henry (The Arlington, Marlin TX) to Bertha (Jamestown)]

d. Waco Railroad Strike of 1903

It was a good thing that Henry was well compensated for his Waco business since Waco seemed to be synonymous with trouble. In the fall 1903, Henry's railroad workers went on strike.

Street Car Strike at Waco.

Waco, Tex., Sept. 27.—The strike on the local street car system went into effect this morning and not a car was moved today. The men demand the recognition of their union and an increase in wages.

[El Paso Times, September 28, 1903]

Henry wrote to Bertha of this new Waco trouble.

He that fights and runs away will live to fight another day. I proved this in my Sunday siege for, after my séance with the detectives, I went up to Gordon's, took dinner with him and went out to the country. And I feel now that I am able to put in one or two more licks on that Waco antagonist that will hurt if they hit, of which latter event I am not at all sure for I seem to have missed fire badly on two or three shots at that target. However, my desertion of the post of duty has put some life into my venerable body and I don't feel as I did that the deluge was engulfing me and that nothing was worthwhile.

I am afraid I placed you with my troubles, dear. That wasn't very generous or considerate, I am sure, but I am also sure that it was very natural that I should take my burden and "rest it" awhile while I talked to you of it. I never took any of my vexed things to you that the tangle did not seem easier, my dearest. Your letters were very dear, my sweetheart. After I got the first of the two I overtook myself in the midst of some rather bitter reflections on the iniquities of this wicked world, with the realization that the world was a very beautiful one to me, if there were some dark corners in it. And I caught myself up and went about that pesky Waco business with true enthusiasm. But there was more of you and less of Waco in the foreground all that day which I take it is sharp criticism on my business loyalty!

[1903-09-20(-) 20170725-3 Henry to Bertha]

Henry left by train from St. Louis for Waco on September 26. The Waco troubles – the Citizens Railway Strike — continued to bother Henry for some weeks. Henry sent a newspaper clipping from Waco to Bertha about the strike and wrote of his ongoing frustrations.

The enclosed clipping expresses the situation and the end of this mess is not yet. I had hopes yesterday that the men would come back to work and behave themselves but the outlook is not so good today and I feel much less confident of a happy outcome of the troubled. I toiled like a drayman all day yesterday and won over our own men but the appearance of an outside labor agitator has apparently undone all my missionary work and it looks now very much like a fight to test out our ability to manage our own affairs. I am not permitting the matter to worry me and am in good spirits which is a particular mark of "stick-at-itness" when it is remembered that all this little tempest is delaying my return to you.

I hope you had a pleasant journey west and that you and the chickens were not utterly used up by it. I think you really got more benefit out of your summer than you have for many years and, in spite of this trouble and the hard times generally that are making many a stout-hearted man anxious and which I am sorry to say I am not entirely proof against, I am made very happy, my dearest, in the thought that I shall find you when I return, well and much stronger than you have been in years. I don't see how any man could be very much cast down who has what I am looking forward to and with the thought of you and the young people to cheer me, you need not fear that this pesky affair will add to my gray hairs. [1903-09-29 Henry (Waco) to Bertha]

Bertha sympathized with Henry's struggles in Waco in her next letter: "*I should like [to] ... shout for you.*"
I am distressed over your struggle, sweetheart, and I wish Alice and I could be there in the thick of the fray. I should like to see you in fighting trim and shout for you if shouting would do any good. At any rate, I'd like to be there. You are pretty good to write to your wife in the middle of so much work and tumult as that.

[1903-10-01 (Wednesday) Bertha (64 Vandeventer Place, Stl) to Henry (Waco)]

The 1903 Waco strike seemed to worsen, "*becoming the subject of angry controversy with every light-headed idiot in the town.*"
This thing is getting monotonous. I have been here three days and, although I am glad I arrived when I did, I haven't much to show for the work and worry I have gone through. There are really only about thirty men involved in this mess but every imbecile in town is taking one side or the other and the result is that, what I had hoped and planned for a peaceable strike, is becoming the subject of angry controversy with every light-headed idiot in the town. There have been no disturbances as yet and I think there will be none but, as the miserable thing slowly takes its course, the people are getting daily more impatient and the last move of the men, a called mass meeting, is not calculated to keep down the ill feeling. I think tomorrow will be a tiring point in the trouble and I still hope the men will go back to their old places which have been kept open for them. If they don't go back by the end of the week, we shall discharge them all and then the slow process of reorganization will begin. I shall not wait for the company to secure all the force required before I leave here but of course will remain if we decide to start up within the next week. So you see, my return is uncertain.

[1903-09-30 Henry (Waco) to Bertha]

With no other option, Henry sought to resolve the strike by making a speech, "*an eloquent appeal*", to the striking workers. As Henry wrote to Bertha, "*I just hate to think of a conflict with them which will cost us the work of years and them their houses...*" After his speech, Henry hoped "*those idiots will go back to work*".

> *I have been having what is called, for want of a better name, a picnic. I got in last night at eleven, found the entire street railway force on a strike, was up until nearly two going over the situation, then started in this morning for a day of hard work which ended with a sort of conference called at the instance of citizens. I made a speech which one of my enthusiastic friends styled "an eloquent appeal" and I thought so myself when I learned afterwards that it turned the tide in our favor. I am not yet sure of its eloquence and will not be unless those idiots will go back to work.*
>
> *What makes it harder on me is that I have really become interested in some of the men and I just hate to think of a conflict with them which will cost us the work of years and them their houses and the comfort which they and their families seem so willing to throw away at the bidding of a lot of agitators who never did an honest lick of work in their lives.*
>
> *I was almost discouraged last night but today I came around all right and am preparing, if all peaceful efforts fail, to introduce Texas to a scrap that will be "a glorious sight to see for him who hath no friend or brother there."*[244]
> [1903-09-28(-) (Monday) 20170727-3 Henry (Waco) to Bertha]

Henry's quote in the preceding letter, "*a glorious sight to see...*", from Lord Byron's poem, undoubtedly reflected his despondency at that moment in preparing for a fight. The poem would often suit Henry as it "*describes the travels and reflections of a world-weary young man who, disillusioned ..., looks for distraction in foreign lands...*"

Bertha obviously enjoyed the newspaper clipping from Waco and the news about Henry's speech to the striking workers.

> *I thoroughly enjoyed the newspaper clipping. I wish you would send me more. If you can carry your side, it will be a tremendous victory for rational common sense against the foolish enthusiasm roused by the agitator. Why don't you read them Kipling's story of the labor agitator among the horses in the "The Day's Work". Of course, I don't mean that seriously but it ought to be printed in a pamphlet and scattered among them. It makes me ache all over to think how tired you must be and I am pretty tired too.*
> [1903-10-01 (3 letters) Bertha (64 Vandeventer Place, Stl) to Henry (Waco)]
>
> *I suppose you are in Waco still. I was awfully interested in your last clipping, the one about your being a favorite with the strikers. And I read part of it aloud to Maud this afternoon who says Carroll[245] was greatly interested in what you told him of the strike. I think you are covering yourself with glory only I wish I could be there. I would like to be somewhere else than this for more reasons than one. It is unbearably sultry, perspiration pours from every pore. The worst weather of the summer everyone says,...*
> [[1903-10-01 (3 letters — Saturday) Bertha (64 Vandeventer Place, Stl) to Henry (Waco)]]

---

[244] "*By Heaven! it is a splendid sight to see, For one who hath no friend, no brother there.*" Lord Byron (1788-1824) from "Childe Harold's Pilgrimage", Canto i, Stanza 40.
[245] Maud Reber Davis and Rev. Carroll Davis. Maud died one month later, age 40.

e. Other Waco Nuisances, 1907

Evil men always seemed to be lurking around Henry's businesses and the Waco public service business was exemplary. Reluctant to deal *"with the thieves"* with their vices, Henry philosophized, *"…my many weaknesses don't lie in this particular direction and I ought to hunt occupations in which the use of my own vices can be more in demand."*

> *I feel some encouragement over my work here and I think, although I am not sure, I have for the time being closed the assault upon our property. That I have not permanently cured the evil I am sure and I also am sure there is but one way to do this and that way I shall not adopt unless I become a much more demoralized man than I have the vanity to believe possible. One of our directors suggested yesterday "We can kill this sort of thing whenever it comes up very easily if we will only come to terms with the thieves" and he added slowly "but we won't do that, will we?" I was not sure whether he was asking me or himself the question but my experience here has made it plain that I am not fit to manage public service corporations. I don't mean that I am a whit better than the men who yield to this temptation and who are thus able to free themselves from such attacks but rather that my many weaknesses don't lie in this particular direction and I ought to hunt occupations in which the use of my own vices can be more in demand.*
> [1907-04-01(day-) Henry (Waco) to Bertha (StL)]

D. OTHER BUSINESS ENDEAVOURS
1. THE ST. CHARLES WATER WORKS

With two major rivers passing by St. Louis, there was always a plentiful supply of water for the city. But, regarding potable water, there was always the matter of the suspended mud and the transportation of such water to homes and businesses as reported in *"A History of the St. Louis Water Works"*.

> *The problem of clarifying the turbid waters of the Mississippi was a formidable one for the state of the art of that day. This is the reason Kirkwood favored slow sand filtration which was being practiced in Europe. He[246] said of the turbid western water that the sediment "though trifling in weight, renders the water very objectionable in appearance, very objectionable in its application to any of the Arts or manufacturers, and no acquisition certainly as regards health or cleanliness." He admits, however, that "Custom, as on the Western rivers, may reconcile persons to its presence". This reminds one of the story attributed to Mark Twain who said it was easy to recognize a stranger in the St. Louis area by offering him a glass of water. The stranger waits for the mud to settle, while the native stirs it up and drinks it immediately to secure to full power of its life-giving properties.*
> [*A History of the St. Louis Water Works*, (1764-1968), By William B. Schworm]

Surprisingly, some St. Louisans apparently spoke with pride about their "muddy" water.

> *The Missouri river imparts its peculiar muddy cast to the Mississippi at and below their junction and, although the appearance of the water is not clear and to a stranger is rather disagreeable, yet it is nevertheless about the best river water in the world. It is said to keep longer and to be sweeter on a sea voyage than the water of perhaps any other stream; indeed it may almost be said never to spoil."*
> *"The appearance of the water when first taken from the river or when the supply from the reservoir has not had time to settle is rather muddy and thick, from a great mixture of light sandy particles and strangers generally dislike it; but it soon settles on becoming stationary and then is very palatable, and persons soon become fond of it—preferring it to any other water.*
> [William B. Schworm, *A History of the St. Louis Water Works*, (1764-1968)]

---

[246] James Pugh Kirkwood who wrote a report on the St. Louis water issues in 1869.

It is not clear why Henry invested in the St. Charles water works project around 1900. It is possible that Henry viewed this as the civic duty of a St. Louis industrialist to forge a better future for the city. But Henry seemed to quickly regret ever becoming involved.

> *Here it is somewhat cooler but I should not use that term to describe it for it is 88° at this hour, half past ten. We have gotten accustomed to it apparently for I hear few complaints of the heat and I am well and sleep well which, considering that St. Charles inferno, is doing pretty well. I am religiously drilling myself not to let the St. Charles tangle annoy me and I succeed better than I even imagine I could which is my best testimony of good health but it is pretty hard to do at times, dear, and I am terribly humiliated over the affair. I mind the money because I shall feel the loss if it comes but I believe I mind my first real failure more and I begin to distrust my own judgment which is not good for a man who must work for his living. But I have so much to be thankful for, I have no right to complain and I really am not doing very much crying over the milk that's spilt or nearly so.*
> [20180320-2 (1900-) Henry to Bertha]

> *I have been in St. Charles all day and, although I am by no means sure that I have accomplished anything with that stiff-necked and rebellious people, I have received some comfort tonight in the thought that the day has not been entirely wasted on the theory that my brain must have developed some under the strain I subjected it to and that I shall therefore be better able to surmount future obstacles. That's small consolation but I am afraid it is all I can look forward to for of all the messes I have ever yet tried to unravel, this one takes the lead.*
> [20180319-2 (1900-) Henry to Bertha]

Henry wrote again to Bertha around 1901 about the continuing problems that he was confronting with the St. Charles water works.

> *I was much interested in what you said about St. Charles, only the force of your argument was partly lost from the fact that you only enclosed part of your letter. However, I have already tried your plan and, although I have not received a final report from the broker, I have not great hopes of success in that direction. It will be a hard blow if we lose the property for it represents a good part of seven years hard work for me but, if the loss comes, I shall certainly try not to grow unhappy over it. I feel very bitterly over the whole matter because I still believe my plans were all fairly well laid but I have never had worse luck in the manner of their execution which I was obliged to leave in the hands of others.*
> [20170821-3 (1901-) Henry to Bertha]

> *I am weary for a sight of you, dear, and I sometimes think if I could only see you for a day or two I could be perfectly content to come back and stick it out here until I could settle that blessed water company one way or the other. I think I shall have every other thing out of the way except St. Charles and that may be in such chaos that my presence will do no good. Were it possible I would turn the whole matter over to an agent to sell at whatever price he could obtain for it but I am afraid it has passed that stage.*
> [20170821-2 (1901-) Henry to Bertha]

Henry's frustration with the local St. Charles officials was clearly evident in the following letter to Bertha.

> *I spent all day in St. Charles and come back almost as much disgusted with the Deutch there as I have been with that tribe in St. Louis. I believe I told you that almost all the rioting in St. Louis was done by the Germans and that the large German paper was the most anarchistic and foul of all our bad press. Nagel was a director on that paper but I presume, of course, he has resigned.*

> *But to return to St. Charles, I met my most particular opponent there today and we had it up and down. He announced that if we didn't sell the water works to the city at the price he had stipulated,*

the city would build another works. I let him get well through and then told him if I didn't get my price and the city would not consent to arbitrate the value of the property, it could go ahead and build and the sooner the better, for if the city could stand two water plants, I could. I then told him there had been too much talk in this controversy and too little action and that I didn't care to discuss the matter any further with the city except upon the basis of learning the value of the works from disinterested parties. I expect I am in a fair way to have a huge row up there but I really believe I would rather lose the whole investment than submit to any more impositions from those miserable wretches. I am growing to despise the town and everyone in it. You see, I have become somewhat warmed up over the situation and I guess the water question and the bad weather – it is hot here tonight – have made me cross and unfit for further speech.
[1901-06—20170807-3 Henry (StL) to Bertha]

Henry even expressed the view that the St. Louis heat was much more bearable than the St. Charles mess.

It was one hundred in my office at six this afternoon yet, wonderful to relate, if it were not for that St. Charles worry which seems in a desperate plight, I should call myself perfectly well. I am afraid the time has gone by for me to sell the plant at any price and, if we lose the case in the Supreme Court, it will be a total loss beside the humiliation of my complete failure in the management. But for this attack upon it, of one of the prettiest little properties that a man ever owned, I don't know when I can go on for I am tied down here, but I hope not later than the first. I must get things settled before I leave or the rest would do me no good. I simply can't leave the thing when my presence may yet pull it out of the slough.
[1901-06—20180401-1 Henry (StL) to Bertha]

In the end, Henry was willing to accept defeat on the St. Charles water works but his attempts to sell out his interest was foiled.

We have had another setback at St. Charles and things look pretty blue up there but I hope for the best. My offer to sell was rejected so I am afraid there is nothing left but to fight it out to the bitter end, not a very comfortable prospect. But I really did not mean to go into details about things troublesome and, if I have fiery trial of one kind, they are much more than counterbalanced by my mercies, the chief of which latter is my dear wife.
[1901-07-03(-) (20170804-6) Henry to Bertha]

As Henry's next letter showed, Henry was more upset about losing and "*the shock to my sense of self-reliance*", than to the "*not inconsiderable*" loss of money.

The glorious fourth is practically over and I am very glad of it. I spent most of the day downtown but later got out to the Country at five and played gold. I can't get that miserable St. Charles matter off my mind. The loss of money which I think will not be inconsiderable is hardly more wearing than the shock to my sense of self-reliance I seem to have missed things terribly and whether I shall get out of it without a total loss of the property is most uncertain. [20180319-1 (1900-07-01-) Henry to Bertha]

By November 1901, Henry had given up on the St. Charles Water Works. The St. Louis Post-Dispatch published the following article which explained the $20,000 settlement which Henry was forced to accept after he had previously refused a settlement of $65,000. For someone who was never accustomed to losing, this was surely difficult for Henry.

[St. Louis Post-Dispatch, November 6, 1901]

2. ST. LOUIS, BROWNSVILLE & MEXICO RAILWAY

Henry had an interesting visit to Mercedes Texas and the King Ranch in 1908. Apparently, this trip was occasioned as a result of his investment in the St. Louis, Brownsville & Mexico Railway.

> King Ranch, located in South Texas between Corpus Christi and Brownsville near Kingsville, is the largest ranch in Texas. The King Ranch comprises 825,000 acres and was founded in 1853 by Captain Richard King and Gideon K. Lewis. It includes portions of six Texas counties, including most of Kleberg County and much of Kenedy County, with portions extending into Brooks, Jim Wells, Nueces, and Willacy Counties. The ranch does not consist of one single contiguous plot of land, but rather four large sections called divisions. The divisions are the Santa Gertrudis, the Laureles, the Encino and the Norias. Only the first two of the four divisions border each other, and that border is relatively short. The ranch was designated a National Historic Landmark in 1961. [Wikipedia]

Henry wrote a letter later that year on his business associate's stationary about his investment in the St. Louis, Brownsville & Mexico Railway, his visit to the King Ranch (*"A cunning little farm"*), and how the group had to stop the train at one point to shoot at some ducks.

> *On Jeff N. Miller stationary,*
> *Vice President & Gen'l Manger*
> *St. Louis, Brownsville & Mexico Railway*
>
> *On Train leaving Brownsville Tex*
> *Saturday, Feby 8th, 1908*
>
> *Dear Bert,*
> *We have been going some since we left Tuesday morning and this is the only moment I have had to write. We had a charming trip south. No dust, weather good, first class cook and the most sumptuous private car appointments. We have only had six people in our car – Mr. & Mrs. West, Mr. & Mrs. Bixby, Brookings and I so there is lots of room and we each have a large private room, toilet, etc. The Haursticks are in the other car with Col. and Mrs. Fordyce and, since we have been in Texas, we have stopped every night so the car has at night been like a comfortable hotel. We have our own train, engine, baggage car, two private cars and office car with stenographer, train dispatcher, etc.*
>
> *It is somewhat of a luxury to stop a whole train when a flock of ducks is sighted in order that the men may get off for the shooting. I got several shots yesterday morning and please tell the boys I*

missed every shot. Brookings killed a beautiful prairie chicken but, as he confessed to shooting it on the ground, the rest of us are not dismayed.

Yesterday, we took lunch on the King Farm. Mrs. King's daughter is an intimate friend of the Glenn (Simmons) girls. Another item for Hugh and George. The Ranch has only a million one hundred and sixty-five thousand acres (1,165,000) of land. It runs on the gulf coast for seventy-two miles and at the broadest point, runs back forty miles. A cunning little farm. The cattle sales last year numbered over a hundred thousand head and all these are the possessions of one woman, the widow of Captain King. You would have been charmed with the place and the free life.

Twenty two of us sat down to lunch and Mrs. Claybury, the daughter, said the table seated forty comfortably and there were often more for a meal, as they had no near neighbors (which did not surprise me when I learned the size of the place) and no visitor was permitted to leave the ranch without breaking bread at least once.

The grandchildren, boys and girls, are in the saddle every day and never off their own land. Bob[247], a boy of ten, had killed five deer, a number of turkeys and prairie chicken and countless ducks. I took his advice about "leading" flying game with some profit. He said "Mr. Scott, tell your boys if they will come down to see me, I will give them a fine time and go back to St. Louis with them for I like St. Louis and it is lonesome down here when visitors leave!"

Today we went over to Matamoras in Mexico and I am sending a few postals to show up the country to the children. I find I have only time to put this off at the next station so I must say goodbye. Address me hereafter: Point Isabel Club, Isabel P.O. Texas

Yours always,
Henry

The RR property looks splendidly and I am no longer anxious about the investment. But there is much to learn about it and I expect to be pretty busy for several days.
[1908-02-08 Henry (Brownsville TX) to Bertha (Rye Beach-)]

Henry wrote to Bertha the next day about his next stop in Mercedes Texas in a letter which is a window into another world.

> *Stationary of:*
> *Jeff N. Miller*
> *Vice president & Gen'l Manager*
> *St. Louis, Brownsville & Mexico Railway*
>
> *Mercedes, Texas[248]*

---

[247] Probably Kleberg, Robert Justus, Jr. [III] (1896–1974). Robert Justus Kleberg, Jr., rancher, the son of Alice Gertrudis (King) and Robert Justus Kleberg, was born on March 29, 1896, in Corpus Christi. He was the grandson of Richard King, founder of the King Ranch in South Texas. [Wikipedia]

[248] Mercedes is known as "The Queen City of the Valley" or "La Reina del Valle". The city of Mercedes was founded September 15, 1907, by the American Rio Grande Land & Irrigation Company, and was incorporated March 8, 1909. It is one of the oldest towns in the Rio Grande Valley, and the city celebrated its centennial in 2007.
The city was located in Capisallo Pasture, part of Capisallo Ranch owned by Jim Welles. This location was known as the Pear Orchard because of the vast numbers of prickly pear cactus growing there at that time.
General Zachary Taylor's headquarters was to the southeast of Mercedes near the river. There the old Rabb Ranch was famous for its stagecoach stop and riverboat landing for the riverboats that plied the Rio Grande carrying supplies to the settlements and military installations.

Sunday Feb 9th, 1908

Dear Bert,
I have had a strenuous day and I am afraid tomorrow will be still more so for I rode horseback today more than twenty miles and, as I am not in what might be termed athletic condition, I expect tomorrow to take breakfast standing. I am consoled, however, for as we came back to the hotel, one of the leaders of the cavalcade asked me if I learned to ride at West Point. One can stand considerable discomfort for a compliment like that and I think twenty miles pretty good for a tenderfoot anyway.

I wish the boys were with me for the country is the wildest and most interesting I have ever been in. Lots of game even for sportsmen who shoot no better than I do and the life is a most interesting one. Judge Boyle has two nephews down here and Tom Francis, Dave's son, is one of the cowboys ranchmen. Tell George they only shot <u>one</u> man last night but, as there are only three hundred people in the town, that is doing pretty well. The man was shot about two blocks from our car and Col. Fordyce says, as he was killed the first shot, it is obvious that he <u>was not</u> killed by any of our party and to prove his statement he offered to stand a block off and let the whole crowd shoot at him all day.

Doctor Fishel's younger son is also here and young Abels. The Jews are trying to spoil even the wilds. I am sleepy after my day in the sun so I must close.

Yours always,
Henry
[1908-02-09 Henry (Mercedes, Texas) to Bertha (StL)]

3. MEXICO GAS COMPANY

After his inspection of the St. Louis, Brownsville and Mexico Railway, Henry went with a business group to Cuernavaca[249] Mexico to consider managing the Mexico Gas Company. Perhaps, at a time when Henry was actively disposing of his various other business interests, he became nervous about having nothing to do? Although this business opportunity never bore fruit, the trip itself was interesting.

I hardly anticipated when the governor of Cuernavaca told us yesterday at the Country Club "I shall send my people word that you will visit our state tomorrow" that he meant we were to be the state's guests here but he did. We came out this morning from Mexico City in our car, hauled "special" over the most beautiful mountain route I have ever seen and were set down at this town at eleven this morning. The governor could not come with us as the Senate, of which he is a member, is in session at Mexico. But on our arrival we were met by a member of the Gov's staff who, through an interpreter whom I shall mention later, told us that city was our own and that the governor's carriage would take us over the town and to all places of interest.

With this pleasant surprise, we started out and had a most charming day. The city or town, for there are only ten thousand people, is a perfect jewel box of beautiful and quaint old churches and, being situated on a headland between two valleys at an elevation of 5028 feet and plentifully supplied with water, is almost buried in abundant masses of trees and plants and flowers. The

---

The old Toluca Ranch still stands east of the International Bridge at Progreso, the sister city to the south. This ranch was close to the river and a prized target for the bandidos during the days of Pancho Villa. It was built with many secret rooms and passages and heavy wooden shutters on the windows to protect its residents. [Wikipedia]

[249] Cuernavaca is the capital and largest city of the state of Morelos in Mexico. The city is south of Mexico City.

whole town is indeed a beautiful garden with brooks & mountain streams lacing it every few yards and such growth of flowers I believe are seen nowhere else.

There was embarrassment at the start because the governor's representative spoke not a word of English and in the small town no man could be found who would act as interpreter. Our host in despair finally appealed to an English girl and it is a red-letter day for us that she generously came to the rescue for she was one of the prettiest creatures I ever saw and her voice was like what the Mexicans call "the song of the moon." Miss Vera King is the daughter of an English gentleman who operates a small pottery plant just out of the town and I did not have to meet her parents afterwards, which I did to thank them, to know that her home training and education were above criticism. There was not a tree or plant or flower that she did not know in name and history and, as she threw herself into her work with manifest enjoyment (it is no easy task to satisfy a Spaniard when lost, that all is "buenos" with his cherished guests and yet find time to give said e.g. some idea of their surroundings) and raced from English to Spanish and back again, never missing a question or failing to answer one, her sweet voice was like a song.

It was apparent from the start that Signor Staff officer was madly in love with his interpreter for his eyes seldom left her face and I noticed he carefully assigned her and all the ladies to our carriage. I suppose I am impulsive, my dear, but old men of fifty have some privileges and I love a beautiful face so when I bade goodbye to our sweet guide, I kissed her on both checks and met no disapproval from her or from any member of our party. If you were here, I should have done the same thing but in that event, it would not be necessary to add that Miss Vera King is twelve years old. The Spaniard glared at me and said it should be a fight to the death between us but he is to kill me down here for I am specially invited to come again and "you will then bring the beautiful Senora Scott without whom travel and even fair Mexico can give no real pleasure".

We have not been playing all the time, my dearest, for good work has been done and if the Mexico Gas Co. is to be managed by your husband, you will soon be here to see this country yourself. But why drag in dull business to spoil the memory of sweet Vera King?
[1908-02-20 Henry (Cuernavaca Mexico) to Bertha]

4. A TRIP TO PANAMA[250]

The US acquired the rights over the Panama Canal Zone from the new government of Panama in November 1903 and February 1904 under two agreements. After two years of planning, the U.S. was ready to construct the canal. Due to the significance of this initiative to the Roosevelt Administration, the President encouraged a U.S. business delegation to visit Panama to review the project and provide legitimacy to the final decision on how to proceed. Secretary of War, Taft, spoke about the opportunity for a business delegation to visit Panama in his 1905 address to the Commercial Club of St. Louis in which Henry was a member.

I sincerely hope that the proposition to visit Panama will not be given up. Those who go will feel richly rewarded for the definite information that the eye will give them of the task which this government has undertaken, and which under the inspiration of energy breathed into the enterprise by the words and action of President Roosevelt, it will certainly perform.
[From the address of Honorable William H. Taft, Secretary of War, before the Commercial Club of Saint Louis, November 18th, 1905.]

---

[250] *A Trip to Panama*: the narrative of a tour of observation through the Canal Zone, with some account of visits to Saint Thomas, Porto Rico, Jamaica and Cuba, the Commercial clubs of Boston, Chicago Cincinnati and St. Louis, February 18th-March 14th, 1907. Author: Walter B Stevens Publisher: St. Louis [Printed by Lesan-Gould Co.] 1907.

The next year, President Roosevelt informed Congress in his Special Message, December 11th, 1906, that several business organizations were planning to go to Panama on a tour of observation.

I am informed that representatives of the Commercial Clubs of four cities Boston, Chicago, Cincinnati and St. Louis, the membership of which includes many of the leading business men of those cities, expect to visit the Isthmus for the purpose of examining the work of construction of the canal. I am glad to hear it and I shall direct that every facility be given them to see all that is to be seen in the work which the government is doing. Such interest as a visit like this would indicate will have a good effect upon the men who are doing the work, on one hand, while on the other hand, it will offer as witnesses of the exact conditions men whose experience as business men and whose impartiality will make the result of their observations of value to the country as a whole.
[President Roosevelt - Special Message to Congress, December 11th, 1906]

The following photograph was of the members of this St. Louis Club who joined in the voyage.

REPRESENTING THE COMMERCIAL CLUB OF ST. LOUIS.
Reading from left to right: Top row—Von Leitner (Captain), E. G. Cowdery, David R. Francis, Hanford Crawford, Chas. Gordon Knott, George M. Wright, Henry C. Scott, Walker Hill, George O. Carpenter, Robert Moore, J. D. Basson, Murray Carleton. Middle row—W. K. Bixby, Daniel Catlin, Oscar L. Whitelaw (President), Robert McKittrick Jones, Dan C. Nugent. Lower row—Chas. W. Knapp, Lewis D. Dozier, Homer P. Knapp, Rolla Wells, Walter B. Stevens (Press Representative), Collins Thompson (Official Stenographer).

Henry is standing, in the middle. (From: *A Trip to Panama*)

As the following excerpt from *A Trip to Panama* explains, this business delegation was not intended to provide any *"expert"* guidance regarding the canal project but merely to provide encouragement for the project through their reports to their respective business groups. (Most of commentary that follows is from *A Trip to Panama*.)

> *The Commercial Clubs looked forward to the trip to Panama as meaning much more than the interest in a three weeks' voyage with congenial companionship. In no sense did these gentlemen, who were going to the Isthmus at their own expense to observe conditions and the progress of the canal work, pose as experts. They did not expect to pronounce conclusions on the Gatun Dam or the Culebra Cut but as organizations they had stood in close relation to the selection of the Panama route and from the beginning they had been the mediums for the dissemination of much important information about the canal project.*

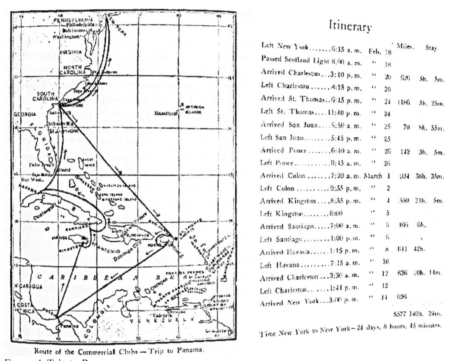

Route of the Commercial Clubs — Trip to Panama.
From: A Trip to Panama

Itinerary

			Miles.	Stay.
Left New York	6:15 a. m.	Feb. 18		
Passed Scotland Light	8:00 a. m.	" 18		
Arrived Charleston	3:10 p. m.	" 20	626	5h. 5m.
Left Charleston	8:15 p. m.	" 20		
Arrived St. Thomas	6:15 p. m.	" 24	1186	5h. 25m.
Left St. Thomas	11:40 p. m.	" 24		
Arrived San Juan	8:50 a. m.	" 25	70	8h. 55m.
Left San Juan	5:45 p. m.	" 25		
Arrived Ponce	6:40 a. m.	" 26	142	3h. 5m.
Left Ponce	9:45 a. m.	" 26		
Arrived Colon	7:20 a. m.	March 1	934	38h. 35m.
Left Colon	9:55 p. m.	" 2		
Arrived Kingston	8:55 p. m.	" 4	550	21h. 5m.
Left Kingston	6:10	" 5		
Arrived Santiago	7:00 a. m.	" 5	166	6h.
Left Santiago	1:00 p. m.	" 6		
Arrived Havana	1:15 p. m.	" 8	641	42h.
Left Havana	7:15 a. m.	" 10		
Arrived Charleston	3:30 a. m.	" 12	636	10h. 14m.
Left Charleston	1:44 p. m.	" 12		
Arrived New York	3:00 p. m.	" 14	626	
			5577	140h. 24m.

Time New York to New York—24 days, 8 hours, 45 minutes.

Approximately 80 of the various Commercial Club members left New York City on the Prinz Joachim Steamer on February 18, 1907. The "Prinz Joachim"[251] was selected by the Commercial Clubs since it *"was built for travel in the tropics, having large state-rooms and electric fans, and being otherwise equipped for voyages in the vicinity of the equator."* [from *A Trip to Panama*] The trip would take 24 days during which their ship made many stops.

---

[251] Prinz Joachim - Built by Flensburger, Schiffsb. Ges., Flensburg, Germany, 1903. 4,760 gross tons; 370 (bp) feet long; 45 feet wide. Steam quadruple expansion engine, single screw. Service speed 13 knots. Passenger cargo steamer; later refrigerator cargo ship. Built for Hamburg-American Line, German flag, in 1903 and named Prinz Joachim. Seized by U.S. authorities, in 1917 and renamed the Mocccasin. Managed by the US Shipping Board. Transferred to United States Navy, American flag, in 1918. Known as SP-1322. Carried food across Atlantic. Transferred to U.S. Shipping Board, in 1919 and renamed Porto Rico. Puerto Rico and West Indies to New York service. Chartered. in 1938. [Wikipedia]

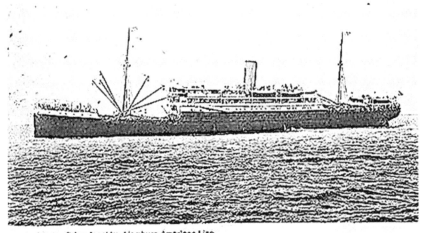

[Prinz Joachim in 1903]

During the voyage, David R. Francis, of St. Louis, made the following remarks to his shipboard companions.

> *I do not know of any better time to express what I feel about this excursion, upon which we are entering, than now at its inception. Four great cities of this country, represented on this occasion by organizations composed of the representative men of their respective cities, have concluded, of their own volition and at their own expense, to make an excursion of three or four weeks' duration in order to inspect the progress of the greatest work ever undertaken by the Government of the United States. It is very unusual that such men should enter upon such a mission. Divesting ourselves of partisanship, we have decided to go thousands of miles to inspect*
> *a work which was once undertaken and afterwards abandoned by one of the greatest nations on the globe[252], and which has now been undertaken by our own Government. We approach this duty, or this excursion, or whatever you may term it, with unprejudiced minds. We feel, however, that sense of proprietary responsibility which is inspired by our pride of American citizenship and our consequent desire to see our Government succeed in all of its undertakings. We may combine pleasure and recreation with our serious purpose on this excursion but I am sure that every member of each of the four Commercial Clubs is imbued with a determination to see and judge for himself. We all cherish a patriotic interest in this union of the two oceans and, however stupendous the undertaking, we would never have consented for another country to perform or attempt it again.*
> [From *A Trip to Panama*]

The delegation consisted of men and only men. *A Trip to Panama* described it as follows:

> *From stem to stern of the 373 feet, the "Prinz Joachim" was an Eveless Eden. Not a pound of femininity was represented in the 4789 tons of displacement. That is why the door-plate " Fur Damen " did not count on this trip. The members of the Clubs had unrestricted use of the ladies' saloon with piano, library and all. The only soprano sound heard on the " Prinz Joachim " was when the graphophone ground out some prima donna's selection. The conditions imposed by the Joint Committee went so far as to stipulate that the doctor must take along a male nurse. All of this may appear to be ideal from the masculine point of view. In practice, however, it meant business for the wireless telegraph man who worked his buzzing machine overtime sending "a few words to my wife, you know, just to let her understand I am all right." It meant also letter writing at all hours of the day and the mailing of hundreds of postcards at every stopping place. The day after the "Prinz Joachim" left Charleston, one of the happiest men in the party was President Whitelaw of the Commercial Club of St. Louis when he found upon his breakfast*

---

[252] France attempted to construct the Panama canal in the 1890's but abandoned the project.

table a bunch of roses with a card showing that Mrs. Whitelaw had done some telegraphing to a Charleston florist after President Whitelaw's departure from St. Louis. A member of the Boston Club exhibited with much pride a letter from his wife who is in Europe, the letter having followed him down the Atlantic seaboard and overtaken him in the West Indies.

In the evenings when the travelers gathered in the smoking room and the ladies' saloon, the graphophones were turned loose. The favorite records were those in treble as to tone and sentimental as to character. "Canned music", Mr. Wright, of St. Louis, called it, but everybody listened after dinner.

The life of the members of the Commercial Clubs on board the "Prinz Joachim" was not monotonous. Strenuous might apply to some features of it. There was golf on the boat deck, shuffle-board and ball on the promenade deck, and almost anything else in the way of entertainment on the saloon and upper decks. There was music by the German band. Graphophones at either end of the saloon deck supplied music and vaudeville as continuously as the boat's impressario found time to wind the machines.

...

... the question of supplies usually considered extras - mineral water, cigars, cigarettes, wines, liquors, playing cards, etc. which are issued as a rule on the order of the traveler and charged to him. The Committee decided that such supplies should be paid for from the common fund. Everything on board, with the single exception of service in the barber shop, was free. This decision proved to be so satisfactory in its operation that special mention of it seems justified.

Bertha, anticipating the long time that it would take her letters to arrive at the ship at various ports (and anticipating her own loneliness), wrote the following letter the day before Henry departed.

Dear Henry,

There isn't very much news to put in this letter as you are at the present moment at your office, having parted with but a few hours ago and as you are going to see me again tonight. I thought, however, you might like to get a message from your family in Panama, even if there were no news in it.

I mentioned to Mrs. Knox that mail sent today would reach Panama, which she had not noticed, and she jumped at the idea of writing, so I rather fancy Gordon will get a letter too. Maybe she has a vague idea that she is going to miss him[253] more than I am going to miss you, as if the children ever took or begin to take the place that belongs to only one person in the world. If you weren't a thousand miles or more away (I haven't calculated the distance yet) or, rather, if you weren't going to be those thousands of miles away when you get this, I wouldn't tell you that nor how horribly, horribly desolate the month ahead looks without anybody's coming home in the evening. Anybody that counts.

When you get this, I shall probably be either at church (maybe you have forgotten it's Lent) or hearing Hugh's spelling. So please see double. I don't believe you have found that difficult on this trip, but see enough for two and O, do, do come back strong and well enough for two. If you knew how much I have hoped for from this trip, you would take good care of yourself.

Give my love to Gordon and Robert and as Alice would say, "all my kind friends".

Yours always,

Bert [1907-02-18 Bertha (64 Vandeventer Place, StL) to Henry (Steamer "Prinz Joachim")]

---

[253] Ironically, her husband, Gordon Knox, died on this voyage so Edith Knox never saw him again.

While Bertha may have been worried lest Henry neglect his Lenten observances, Henry was an active participant in the first Episcopal Service on board as one of the two Committee Chairs for such events and as one of the choir members.

THE CHOIR
Lawrence Maxwell, Jr., Leader.

Reading from left to right: Standing—F. A. Geier, J. Parker Bremer, H. S. Warren (Surgeon), W. R. Lawrence, A. H. Chatfield, Benj. Carpenter, C. H. McCormick, H. C. Weber. Sitting—N. R. Davis, Robt. A. Rowe, Henry C. Scott, Lawrence Maxwell, Jr., Edward Goepper, Geo. M. Wight, Hanford Crawford.

The Prinz Joachim "Choir Boys" (Henry is seated, third from left)

The first Sabbath on board the "Prinz Joachim" will be remembered as one of the most notable days of the trip. The Joint Committee began preparations for the observance of the day by appointing a committee headed by Walker Hill and Henry C. Scott, of St. Louis. Associated with Mr. Hill and Mr. Scott to arrange appropriate observance of the day were Homer P. Knapp and George M. Wright, of St. Louis, Edward Goepper, President of the Commercial Club of Cincinnati, F. B. Carpenter, of Boston. Mr. Scott found a valuable auxiliary in the person of Lawrence Maxwell, Jr., of Cincinnati. Mr. Maxwell is remembered as Solicitor General in the second administration of President Cleveland. It was not so well known to members of the Commercial Clubs that Mr. Maxwell is an amateur musician of no ordinary qualifications. Mr. Scott pressed Mr. Maxwell into service with the result that the musical features of the service were something unusual in excellence. Mr. Maxwell arranged the scores and instructed the German band in the rendition of good American hymns. He trained a choir composed of Mr. Goepper, of Cincinnati, Dr. Warren, of Boston, Mr. Geicr and Mr. Davis, of Cincinnati, Mr. McCormick, of Chicago, Mr. Bremer and Mr. Lawrence, of Boston, Mr. Farwell, of Chicago, Mr. Rowe and Mr. Chatfield, of Cincinnati, Mr. Wright, Mr. Scott and Mr. Crawford, of St. Louis. Mr. Maxwell, played the piano and conducted his combined orchestra and choir. Mr. Scott and his committee selected with care hymns in which the congregation of the members of the Clubs could join with the choir. The words of the hymns were put in type by the ship's printer and a sufficient number printed on cards to supply all. Captain von Leitner and several officers of the ship attended the service.

At eleven o'clock the bugle sounded. There had been an air of quiet expectancy all of the forenoon. By common consent and without a suggestion from the Joint Committee, the usual amusements of week days were omitted. Members of the Clubs sat about the decks, looking at the flying fish, reading and conversing. At the sound of the bugle everybody moved in the direction of the dining saloon which had been prepared for the service. The band under the direction of Mr. Maxwell played a German hymn. When Mr. Walker Hill arose at the end of the room it was to face the entire membership of the Clubs on board. He invited all to join in the singing and gave out the hymn

> *"Come, Thou Almighty King,*
> *Help us Thy name to sing."*

The choir and orchestra led in perfect time. Quite generally the congregation made use of the card copies of the hymn. The singing was earnest and harmonious.

"Let us pray," said Mr. Hill, and every head was bowed. The Episcopal service was followed. Mr. Hill read the prayer in a manner which might be expected of one who was brought up in a city which has twenty-one Episcopal churches and whose family for several generations has been represented in the clergy. When he reached the Lord's Prayer the members of the Clubs repeated the whole in unison. The same was true when the Creed was reached. The choir and orchestra led in

> *"How firm a foundation, ye saints of the Lord,*
> *Is laid for your faith in His excellent word."*

The exercises lasted about three quarters of an hour. It goes without saying that, with such a body of American business and professional men, the most perfect decorum was observed. But it can be said with propriety that the spirit of reverence and interest in the service throughout was such as to make the occasion very impressive and such as to afford no small degree of satisfaction to the Joint Committee and to the special committee which had prepared the order of the day.

After the service the members sat about the decks in groups, reading or conversing. The first Sabbath of the Commercial Clubs was neither a dies non[254] nor was it like a week day. It was a day unto itself and to be most pleasantly remembered.

While the Prinz Joachim, was in Charleston, Henry was able to send a wireless message to Bertha and the family. This was the latest technology of the time. Bertha wrote back to Henry about receiving his telegram.

> *I envy you your southern skies! Your de Forrest-gram arrived. Speaking of southern weather and we are having the worst weather of the winter. That message was a most delightful surprise and father and I discussed the marvelousness of it but, to the younger generation, it is less wonderful than the old fashioned telegram to the elder generation. I asked the children to guess where I had heard from and Hugh guessed "wireless" with much promptness and seemed rather amused that I thought there was anything wonderful about it.*

[1907-02-24 Bertha (StL) to Henry (Steamer "Prinz Joachim", Cuba)]

The businessmen from the four clubs of Boston, Chicago, Cincinnati and St. Louis formed eight groups to analyze various aspects of the canal building:
1. Plan of Management
2. Sanitation and Hygiene Conditions
3. Social Conditions and Racial Conditions, including Ethical & Welfare Questions
4. Housing and Food
5. Climate as it Affects Americans
6. Efficiency of the Labor

---

[254] "Dies non": a day on which no legal business can be done, or which does not count for legal purposes.

7. Efficiency of the Plant, including Railroad
8. Progress of the Work

Henry was assigned to the Progress of the Canal Work group.

GROUP ON PROGRESS OF THE CANAL WORK
Reading from left to right: Sitting—J. T. Carew, L. W. Noyes, Robert Moore (Chairman), Thos. P. Egan, H. C. Frick.
Standing—Cyrus H. McCormick, Charles W. Durrell, Henry C. Scott, Harry L. Rice

Progress of the Canal Work Group. Henry is standing, second from right.

At the end of their inspection of the canal, each group prepared a report which was then presented to the entire group. (These businessmen liked to stay occupied and busy.)

Bertha undoubtedly knew that Henry would probably be lonely and sought to "bully him up".

> *Dearest beloved, there is only one sentence in your letter that did not ring true and that is where you hoped I would miss you as much as you would miss me. My dear, if on that trip with that crowd of men you should miss me as I miss you, you would not be as much of a man as I think you are. At least, I never could have fallen in love with that kind of man and I didn't.*
> [1907-02-24 Bertha (StL) to Henry (Steamer "Prinz Joachim", Cuba)]

In her next letter, Bertha wrote to Henry about his wireless transmission and the comments by the other wives.

> *I had a visit from Marion the other day who says all the other wives wish to know where Henry Scott got money enough to send his wife a Marconi gram, as none of them got any.*
> [1907-02-26 Bertha (StL) to Henry (Havana Cuba)]

The Businessmen were able to view the canal work from the Atlantic side (i.e. the Caribbean Sea) to the Pacific. The following was a picture of their stop at Bas Obispo.

A STOP AT BAS OBISPO

Reading from left to right: Laurence Miner, Edward F. Swift, James A. Green, F. P. Egan, N. H. Davis, C. L. Hutchinson, W. R. Lawrence, J. D. Rasson, James R. Chapin, L. B. Doerr, General Manager Bird, Passenger R. R., Consul General Shanklin, David R. Francis, Robert M. Rosner, H. L. Laws, A. H. Chatfield, Charles S. Deneeison, David B. Gamble, C. H. McCormick, William Worthington, J. A. Ault, W. D. Judick, Joseph B. Bassett. On the train—F. G. Cowdrey, Robert Moore, Robert Batcheller, George M. Wright, Charles H. Thorne, Lucius Wilson, L. W. Noyes, J. W. G. Cohen, Henry C. Scott.

And their most westerly stop was at "the Foot of Sosa Hill", near the Pacific.

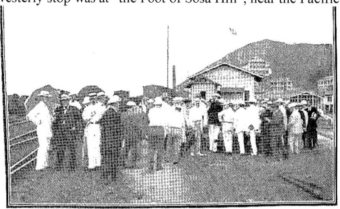

AT THE FOOT OF SOSA HILL

Viewing location of dams at Pacific terminus of Canal. On the extreme left are Henry C. Scott, Robert Moore, C. H. McCormick and John V. Farwell.

Viewing location of dams at Pacific terminus of Canal. Henry is at the far left.

It was unclear what the trip to Panama accomplished other than political cover for the Roosevelt Administration which wanted to build the canal. Nevertheless, Henry was an active participant in the mission and received the following kudos from Alfred Baker who was one of the representatives from Commercial Club of Chicago. (The recipient of the wire, G.L.E., is not known.)

> *I am overcome by your very flattering message which I did not receive until this morning. The only man on the trip who was really seriously worthy of our deepest feelings and commendation is our mutual friend Scott. He had an awful hard time and everyone had something good to say about him. I feel proud to have become acquainted with him through you and I wish you would tell him how much we all think of him.*
> [1907-03-20 Alfred L. Baker (AG Edwards & Sons) to G.L.E.]

Henry's letters from his Panama trip were not kept so the details of the trip from Henry's perspective were scarce. However, Henry did make the following comment about the Panama trip a month after his return while in Waco.

I had a curious experience today. A newspaper man held me up and insisted upon an account of Panama. As I am here trying to appease and smooth down these Texans, I could not afford to refuse the man. In fact, I have grown so meek through this trouble that, if the fellow had asked for my watch, I should have felt like giving it to him so I submitted to his questions for half an hour. The result will be, I think, the most remarkable account of that journey offered as yet to the public with the piquant sauce of that Texan's most ariginal dection [sic]. Unless I can get the thing cut down, I shall send you a copy and I think I shall be in duty bound to send a copy to Teddy for he wants all the really valuable Panama data!
[1907-03-31 Henry (Waco) to Bertha (StL)]

(It was unlikely that Henry had any direct communication with "Teddy", the President, since no letter from the President was kept. But, why not act like buddies?)

Two days into the trip to Panama, Gordon Knox, who was a close friend of Henry's from St. Louis, began to feel ill. Two days before their ship returned to Charlestown on March 10, Gordon's illness had become very serious.

The third Sabbath on board the " Prinz Joachim" came with the end of the cruise only two days away. Services were conducted by William Whitman of Boston. There was added solemnity when the prayer for the sick was read. In a near-by stateroom Charles Gordon Knox lay seriously ill, although at that time he was not thought to be in a critical condition. The choir sang impressively

> *" Nearer, my God, to Thee,*
> *Nearer to Thee."*

The exercises closed with the entire body singing

> *"Onward, Christian soldiers,*
> *Marching as to war."*

Gordon Knox died on March 11, 1907, one day before the official end of this voyage.

The record of voyage from *A Trip to Panama* provided the following news about Gordon Knox's death.
Charles Gordon Knox
WITH flags at half mast, the band silent, not a handkerchief waving from the promenade deck, not a loud word of greeting, the "Prinz Joachim" came to the dock at Charleston, early in the morning of March 12th. A few hours before the landing the unexpected death of Charles Gordon Knox, Secretary of the Commercial Club of St. Louis, had occurred.

Mr. Knox had participated actively in the earlier part of the three weeks' cruise of the Clubs in the West Indies. He was not thought to be critically ill until after the steamer left Havana for Charleston. When he started on the trip from St. Louis, February 18th, he was, apparently, in good health. Two days after the steamer left Charleston, February 20th, Mr. Knox told several of the members that he was not feeling well but he did not consult the physician accompanying the party, Dr. H. S. Warren, of Boston. He adopted such simple remedies as he thought the ailment called for. When the ship reached San Juan, Porto Rico, Mr. Knox was feeling so much better that he joined those of the party who elected to cross the island in carriages to Ponce, a distance of eighty-one miles. Mr. Knox rode in the carriage with Henry C. Scott, a fellow member of the Commercial Club of St. Louis. Mr. Knox spoke repeatedly of his enjoyment of this overland journey, long as it was. When he went on board the ship at Ponce, February 26th, he was not feeling so well, but he attended to business as an officer of the Club from St. Louis.

On Wednesday Mr. Knox discovered that he had considerable fever. He carried with him a testing thermometer and, on trying it, saw that his temperature was 104. This prompted him to call on Dr. Warren. The disease had not progressed to that stage which made a definite diagnosis possible. Dr. Warren gave his immediate and close attention to the patient. When the ship reached Colon, Mr. Knox was much improved. He greatly desired to make the trip across the Isthmus and was so certain he felt entirely equal to it that the Doctor consented. Mr. Knox took the trip without apparent discomfort. He was much interested in the Canal work.

In the division of members for systematic observation on the Isthmus, Mr. Knox was selected for chairman of the group on Housing and Food. He called together those who were to be associated with him and helped to plan the work before the arrival at Colon. This group made a thorough study of the housing policy and of the system of food supplies for the different classes of employees and labor.

When the party returned to the ship Saturday night, Mr. Knox was not so well. Shortly before the departure on the steamship, Dr. Warren asked Colonel Gorgas, the head of the medical department of the Canal Zone, to see the patient. He was apprehensive that typhoid fever was developing. Dr. Gorgas confirmed the opinion. From that time Mr. Knox was confined to his state-room with a trained nurse in charge. The disease progressed slowly. Mr. Knox repeatedly expressed entire confidence that he would pull through. He dictated the telegrams to his wife and friends. He insisted that he was in no danger and that nothing alarming should be sent about him.

Upon the arrival in Cuban waters the question of removing Mr. Knox from the ship to a hospital was considered. The situation was explained to the American officials. Governor Magoon took a personal interest in the matter. Dr. Jefferson R. Keane, the head of the American Medical Department in Cuba, saw Mr. Knox and make an examination of his condition. The patient was anxious to get home. Dr. Keane and the other physicians expressed the opinion that Mr. Knox was in no immediate danger and that it would be better for him to proceed to a cooler climate. Acting upon the best advice obtainable and in accordance with Mr. Knox's wishes, his friends decided to have him continue the voyage to Charleston, it being the purpose to have Mrs. Knox meet him there and to have him remain until able to proceed to St. Louis. At Havana, a second
nurse especially qualified for care of typhoid fever, was taken on board. There was nothing to indicate a critical condition until Monday, March 11th. In the forenoon, complications caused alarm. Mr. Knox had trouble in breathing. Later in the day the lungs cleared and the patient was better. At five minutes to seven o'clock in the evening, Mr. Knox was resting quietly and perfectly conscious. Mr. Scott said to him he would go to dinner. Mr. Knox replied, "All right." Ten minutes later Mr. Scott was summoned hastily by the nurse. At 7:30 p. m. Mr. Knox died.

It was the opinion of those most familiar with the case that Mr. Knox must have brought the germs the disease in his system when he came on board the ship at Charleston, Feby. 20th.

The death of Mr. Knox was announced to the members of the Clubs just before the close of the dinner Monday evening. Mr. Burnett, of Boston, conveyed the sad information in a few impressive words. The hush that followed was broken only when eight members, two from each Club, were named to express the sense of loss and the feeling of sympathy for the bereaved.

The memorial framed by the Committee was as follows :
The members of the Commercial Clubs of Boston, Chicago, Cincinnati and St. Louis, returning from Panama on board the S. S. "Prinz Joachim," do, by their Committee appointed for the purpose, express the deep sorrow which is felt by all over the death at sea of our fellow-member Charles

Gordon Knox, of St. Louis, on this the 11th day of March, 1907, as we are nearing our first home port of Charleston.

The respect and love felt for him by all who knew him, best testify to the high qualities of Mr. Knox. In his death the Commercial Clubs lose one of their most valued members, one who cherished and maintained by his unwavering devotion to duty, the high ideals of our Clubs. The hearts of all turn with deep sympathy to Mrs. Knox in her sad bereavement.

Mrs. Knox, who had been informed from time to time of her husband's illness, arrived in Charleston Tuesday morning shortly after the steamer docked. All arrangements had been planned to convey Mr. Knox to a hotel or to a hospital where he could remain until able to return to St. Louis, so confident were his friends up to the last day that he would reach Charleston and that he would recover.

Henry C. Scott and Robert McKittrick Jones, of St. Louis had been unremitting in their attention to the sick man. The details of the funeral were left with them, Mrs. Knox being prostrated by the shock. With Mr. Scott and Mr. Jones were associated L. D. Dozier, Dan C. Nugent and Murray Carleton to represent the Commercial Club of St. Louis at the funeral. A special car attached to the northbound train conveyed Mrs. Knox and the committee to Morristown, New Jersey, where the burial took place on Thursday, March 14th.

Mr. Knox was one of the most active members of the Commercial Club of St. Louis. He was a moving spirit in the arrangements for the Panama trip.

5. NATURAL GAS WELL IN SHREVEPORT LA

In 1909, Henry travelled to Shreveport LA to see one of the large natural gas wells. Writing on his arrival in Shreveport, Henry wrote with some excitement:

I am just starting for the gas fields and I am to have my first experience in actually seeing a monster natural gas well pouring by natures force enough gas from the bowels of the earth to supply a larger city than St. Louis. No machinery, no pumps, no resistance of any kind, only a twelve inch hole two thousand feet into the earth cased with a twelve inch tube. I expect to be "wisably" impressed and I shall retell my experience when I see you which I now hope will be Saturday morning.

[1909-10-27 Henry (Shreveport, LA) to Bertha (64 Vandeventer Pl, Stl)]

On the next day, Henry visited the gas wells and was very impressed.

I have had really a wonderful experience here. These gas wells are no myth as I found yesterday when, leaning too near a small leak to see if I could detect the difference in odor between the natural and artificial varieties, I was nearly asphyxiated. Think of a hole in the ground emitting eighty million cubic feet of perfectly pure clean fuel energy twenty-four hours without the aid of pumps, engines or any mechanical device. It is simply one of nature's marvels. One of the big wells caught fire and has now been burning for months unchecked because no means has been found, so great is the heat of checking it, and more gas is going to waste in each day than we made the whole of last year in Fort Worth. The heat has baked the surrounding country for a half mile and the flame which is a thousand feet high looks like an enormous torch. No scene in the Yellowstone could possibly be compared to it in grandeur! I am due in a few minutes to meet Governor Blanchard[255] of whom I wrote you when our bank crowd visited Marde Gras in New Orleans so I must stop.

[1909-10-28 Henry (Shreveport LA) to Bertha (StL)]

---

[255] Newton Crain Blanchard, the 34th Governor of Louisiana, served from 1904-1908.

6. SACRAMENTO IRRIGATION PROJECT

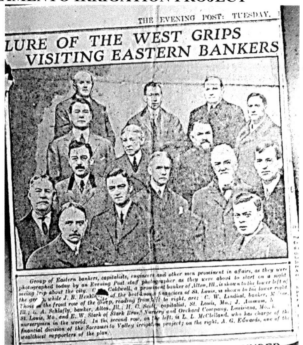

Henry with the "Eastern Bankers", in the center. [20180201 (1910-02-09) Sacramento Irrigation Project]

Henry was invited to join a group of bankers and businessmen to join a "sightseeing" trip to review the Sacramento irrigation project. Irrigation was key to the cultivation of the Sacramento Valley for its agriculture and the Sacramento and Joachim Valleys of Northern California were becoming major farming areas in the U.S. during the early 1900s. Consequently, any irrigation project in this area attracted a lot of interest. As the newspaper clipping from Tuesday, February 9, 2010, showed, Henry was in the midst of it, although it was not clear what this "delegation" accomplished.

7. THE SALE OF HENRY'S BUSINESS INTERESTS

From several comments that he made, it appeared that Henry started to sell off some of his business interests around 1908. Either by design or quirk of fate, Henry had disposed of most of his business interests by the time of his death.

> *I am going to write a short note only for, ..., I have an appointment with a dentist, have to attend a conference with Chicago people who are coming here to patch up an old account that has never been adjusted in that Wichita sale, a retort contract to sign up with its specifications for some gas retorts at Fort Worth and Waco, to make a contract for two miles of steel rails for Waco which little item in itself amounts to more than fifteen thousand dollars, so in spite of the fact that my friends say I have gone out of business and have nothing to do, I think I am pretty busy.*
> [1908-07-17 Henry (StL) to Bertha (Rye Beach)]

During the summer of 1910, Henry took additional action to sell off his remaining business interests. His stated goal was to have more time to spend with Bertha but at the near-term price of having to delay his trip east.

> *My own time of departure is still uncertain. The Fort Worth trade is working out gradually. As to the gas property, I received a check for four hundred thousand last Saturday but the electric property hangs fire and may not go at all. I could have that to "brew" during the summer but the coal strike in Texas and Oklahoma is keeping us out of fuel and that is a matter I may not either leave or delegate with safety. I have good reports from the operation and some confident*

prognostications but I think I know the typical miner and that he will lose out without a prolonged fight is, I am sorry to say, very unlikely. However, let us hope for the best, that is, if you really wish to see me.
[1910-06-28 Henry (StL) to Bertha (Rye Beach)]

It was clear from another letter that Henry was able to complete the sale of his Ft. Worth interests in 1910.
As for me, I am really flourishing. You know of course that I have been setting on the Fort Worth lid trying to effect that sale. Well, for the past week I have been delayed with telegrams with all sorts of suggestions for a change in price and terms and setting out that in this panic time the trade as arranged would not, could not, go through. It took some nerve to stand one's ground under the circumstances for business conditions are simply frightful. But I concluded that if I gave way at all, it would soon be a case of missing the sale or getting nothing for the property so I stood pat, let the other people do most of the telegraphing and played golf daily with Jack instead of sitting in the office waiting for the next telegram. The option was to expire today at three. At ten minutes before three, I received a telephone message from the Mercantile Trust Co. that one hundred & fifty thousand dollars has just been wired from New York to close the deal. And I almost collapsed for, when noon came and I had no word, I was reasonably sure that there would either be no trade or a new one "and sadly sank my spirits down and all the world looked very blue" to quote from B.W.D. But the trade is now closed and all the property at Fort Worth is sold.

The most pleasant feature of the whole transaction was a dispatch from Cullinan, the lawyer, confirming his draft and adding "because we could not secure modifications of the agreement, your efforts throughout the whole transaction to do what you could to accommodate us are none the less appreciated." That is a nice way to wind up a million dollar transaction and since a man may boast without limit to his wife without so much as hurting himself a jot with her, I don't mind adding that I am mighty proud of that transaction and especially the staying qualities that seem to have survived my attack and which served me so well these last few anxious days. If you will follow this story you may be led to believe that your husband is in fact a very fine man!
[20180317-5 (1910-) Henry to Bertha]

It is unclear why Henry felt that he needed to get his business affairs in order in 1910. While Henry had often expressed his desire to be with Bertha, he may also have been worried about his health and the fear that Bertha would be saddled with the unpleasant task of winding up of his business affairs. Or, perhaps, he was just tired of so much work and was ready for his rest. But what was clear, Henry meticulously sold off his business interests and simplified his estate.

CHAPTER 19 - SO FAR AWAY

It seems such a little while that we have ahead of us that it seems wrong to be separated, apart from the pain of it. I have missed you so this time that it was almost like another grief in my life to look for ahead and know that I must wait day after day with no cheer from your sweet face near me. ... we must some way fashion our lives that you may not be away from me so very, very long. There will be rejoicing in this lonely house as if you were here, almost, when I can write you...
[20180802-5 (2nd page only) Henry to Bertha]

I could not go to sleep for thinking how much I wanted to see you. I would like, it's very disgraceful to own up to it, but I would like very dearly to see you come across the bridge with your golf clubs over your shoulder and I believe I should even forgive you for playing golf all day if I could feel your hand in mine or your arms around me just once. It is raining tonight as usual but there is a salt tang to the air. There has been a sea turn and it would be nice to sit on the porch with warm wraps on and just talk. I would even let you do most of the talking ...
[1906-07-03 Bertha to Henry]

A. FIRST SEPARATION AS A MARRIED COUPLE

Henry's business matters soon imposed on the newly wedded couple. On April 15, 1893, shortly after their honeymoon ended and two weeks after moving into their new home on Washington Avenue, Bertha wrote: *"HCS left for Wichita, to go there and to Texas, our first separation. Miss Jennie Alexander came to spend the night with me. During that week, Nan Shepley, Minnie Scott, Frances Markham and Emma Lane staid with me, Frances Markham twice and I staid one night at the Shepley's."* [1893 Diary]

Henry was away until April 24th. Their first separation since their marriage was clearly uncomfortable for Bertha. Having lived so many years with her parents, being left alone was unusual for her. But, with Henry and his business interests, *"our first separation"* was followed by many more.

Their first separation gave rise to their first letters that we have since their marriage. Henry, writing from Wichita:

If I yielded to the temptation to talk about the blue side of life I should not send you a cheerful note this evening. For it is hard to be separated from you, sweetheart, but I think you do not wish me to grumble in my first letter to you, I mean to Mrs. Scott. So I shall merely account for myself before they call for me to go to the works.

...

I do hope you are not having a very lonely time, darling. Make Sam [Henry's brother] take good care of you. I left you in his charge and I shall never forgive him if he does not watch over you and save you from any bothers or worry over the house in matters where a man's help is required and do write me all about yourself and what you are doing every day and please take good care of my darling wife and, goodbye.
[1893-04-16 Henry (Hotel Carey, Wichita) to Bertha]

Henry wrote Bertha from Ft. Worth, his next stop after Waco on this first marriage separation. He was not having a particularly good time.

Just now I am almost rebelling of the thought of going back there, because I want to see you, my darling, and the need of you is so great that it is hard not to cut and run away from all these troublesome things, to find the perfect rich and happiness which you always give me when I am near you. Yes, and even when I am far away, my child, far far or near, your sweet life and the beautiful friendship and companionship you have given me is the greatest blessing and strongest influence on my life. Bert, I wonder if you realize how much you are to me. You can, I think, know somewhat of your helpfulness if you recall how easy it is for me to forget every worry even when I am most tired and worn, under the charm of my darling's sweet sympathetic companionship. Tonight I wish for you, yes, I need you, dear, for I am tired and very lonely.

Yours always,
Henry

PS If I don't encounter unlooked for difficulties, I think you can expect me Monday. Jubilate!
[1893-04-19 Henry (Ft Worth) to Bertha (StL)]

Perhaps to make Henry feel a little better, Bertha wrote the next day about the poor, rainy, weather and *"the grass which is flourishing like the wicked in the psalms"*.

You are missing the most abominable weather in creation. Cold, sleety rains and high wind. I had to go downtown yesterday afternoon to get some things for my luncheon and I started in a lull. When I got downtown, it was pouring water spouts. Why I did not catch my death of cold remains a mystery but apparently it agreed with me as it does with the grass which is flourishing like the wicked in the psalms. I think we shall have to cut hay on the Scott lawn very shortly.
[1893-04-20 Bertha (StL) to Henry (Ft. Worth)]

B. THE LETTERS: I NEED TO TALK WITH YOU ALWAYS

Bertha and Henry became very used to writing daily letters starting in the year before their marriage. Letter writing was their chief method of communication over this long pre-wedding separation and all of the separations that followed. Henry always seemed to think of Bertha when he was away.

I have had nothing to take my thoughts from an amount of most vexing and wearing difficulties until now when, for a little while, I can dismiss every unpleasant thought, so restful and happy are the moments I can spend with you."
[1892-08-09PM (Tuesday) Henry (StL) to Bertha (Farragut House, Rye Beach)]

I cannot write you about the pleasure your letter gave me. I could tell you, my darling, because no one could be made as happy as you have just made me without showing how his whole life went out in thankfulness for the happiness which I knew when your dear letter came. It is true you could have rested me had you been here. It is also true that you have that power now even while you are away from me. My love was beautiful and helpful from the first, dear, but it has grown stronger, much stronger, and your influence over my happiness is great enough to reach beyond the little distance that separates us and beyond the short time we have to live apart. O, my darling, you do not know how dear you grow to me every day!
[1892-08-18 (Thursday) Henry (StL) to Bertha (Farragut House)]

Not surprisingly, Henry was always excited to receive Bertha's letters.

The mail from the east was late this morning, dear, and, as I had not heard from you since Monday, you may imagine, as I knew nothing of the mail delay, that I was rather anxious. When the carrier came an hour later and handed in two letters, I felt like asking him to help himself to whatever he saw which he especially desired. I however restrained these generous impulses and turned to your letters which I greatly enjoyed, my own darling child.
[1892-09-07 (Wednesday) Henry (StL) to Bertha (Farragut House)]

That is a beautiful power you use in your letters. Your strong, pure, beautiful life is a rich gift in itself, dear, but the power you have of blessing others, of making their lives glad, does not come to many, dearest, and you have this. This helpful influence I shall call it, that not only makes one's

burdens seem light and easily born, but you make the whole world brighten to those who are near enough to know the beauty of your life.
[1892-09-23 (&24) (Thursday-Friday) Two letters - Henry (StL) to Bertha (The Ark, East Jaffrey)]

Bertha wrote about receiving a letter from Henry which was the "*first really long talk*" they had for a while.
I had your Sunday letter today almost the first really long talk I have had with you since you went away and I did enjoy it. I will tell you a secret. I have never missed you half so much before. Now, do not become too vain or I shall repent of having paid you a compliment. All sensible people would tell me it was a very unwise proceeding anyway.
[1892-12-08 (Wednesday) Bertha (Backbay, Boston) to Henry (StL)]

Due to the circumstances of Henry's travel locations, Henry's daily letters to Bertha might not arrive on a daily basis. As a result, Bertha would miss her daily chat with Henry which, she confessed, might make her "*a little wee bit foolish about you*".
Today as you had warned me, I had no letter, and I suppose I shall not get one for some days for, added to the fact that you will be two days without writing, there is all the extra distance from Wichita to count in and I miss my daily chat with you. Having no fresh one to read, I read over your last letter and it was a very dear letter, sweetheart. I believe tonight I am inclined to be a little wee bit foolish about you so I shall immediately stop talking nonsense which I know must bore you and go to graver matters.
[1892-12-14 (Tuesday) Bertha to Henry]

Obviously, Henry loved Bertha for such "*nonsense*" about their written talks, for in them, Henry heard "*the music of your sweet voice*".
... it may be that what you term as "nonsense" would have made me catch the music of your sweet voice far away as I am from you. Let me tell you a bit of "nonsense", dear. I have been thinking of you all day for, although it has been a busy one, I have not been working at the office but have been trying to make friends with some of the natives and I think I have had time to ask myself two or three times every hour in the day how you would have enjoyed sharing its experiences with me and , occasionally, I would selfishly conclude, "well, she couldn't have a very poor time if she were here for I would have enough happiness for two and I would be generous and divide with my darling if she needed this cheer."
[1892-12-18 (Sunday) Henry (Waco) to Bertha (Stancote, Newton Centre MA)]

At times, Bertha and Henry seemed to have engaged in a bit of a competition to write interesting and affectionate letters. On one occasion, when Bertha received two letters from Henry which she liked a great deal, she felt that Henry had "*heaped coals of fire on my head*" for such was her remorse for not writing better ones to him.
So, monsieur, you reproach me for not writing a more affectionate letter to Waco. I am sorry my letters have the misfortune not to please you. My dearest boy, if my letters were uninteresting, you heaped coals of fire on my head[256] for I have seldom had two letters I liked better from you. [1892-12-23 (Friday) Bertha (Newton Centre) to Henry (StL)]

Henry would also try to make Bertha feel guilty for choosing to be away from him, especially when there was no letter from Bertha at work: "*My cake is all dough for no letter waited for me here.*"
I have concluded that you do not really love me. I have been toiling through the grime and dirt to reach this deserted, smoky and unspeakably dejected town to earn a few dollars for our otherwise

---

[256] Romans 12:20. "if thine enemy hunger, feed him; if he thirst, give him drink: for in so doing thou shalt heap coals of fire on his head".

pauper babies and the one bit of sunshine I had counted upon to save me from the horrors of melancholia is denied me. My cake is all dough for no letter waited for me here.

It was the hottest, dustiest, journey I have taken in years and, when we neared St. Louis, I was too demoralized to even wash my disreputably grimy countenance before we "landed". When I finally reached the house, I betook me to the tub where I soaked and scoured in a manner which would have done justice to the cleansing process my unfortunate friend Wayman Allen was compelled to submit to. When I think of the small reward I returned to secure, I am inclined to not only charge a commission but for services as well. Now would this do for my bill?

20 days lost vacation @ 10.00 produces	*200.00.*
2 days D.T. (dirty trip) @ 100.00	*200.00.*
Acclimating process, including despair over smoke and dirt	*500.00*
Loss of pure air at R.B.(?)	*500.00*
No letter from BDS	*2,000.00*

Total charge	*3,400.00*
Add 10% for vain regret over return	*340.00*

	3,740.00

If they paid this bill, I should still consider I have been swindled. I suppose when you get this you will be sitting in a comfortable place on the porch with a wrap on, because it is a little cool! And will lazily reflect "Henry becomes more cross and unreasonably as he grows older." If you do indulge in any such reflections, don't betray them or I will not answer for the consequences. I have seen no one and don't wish to, so if you have any compassion, write me a love letter, even if it requires a supreme effort.
[20171212-2 (1900) Henry to Bertha]

When Henry received a letter from Bertha, his spirits would be renewed. In the following letter, Henry even spoke of leaving his work and going to her: "… *you are not so far away but that I may cease grieving for you and go to you, if I have but half the heart to do the things a man ought to do.*"

Your letter puts life and hope in me almost as if you had spoken to me, and I haven't heard you speak to me for nearly a lifetime. It is hard to know what to do when one's plan of life means such constant and such long separations. We plan and think we are solving life's problems with reasonable judgment and with fair profit to ourselves. We boast – if we are well enough and we don't to the world but we do to ourselves – that we do a share of work for ourselves and a little for others' sakes and we make our immediate surrounding comfortable to the danger point of luxury and, in spite of cares which no one should shirk and none may avoid, we know we are blest and that rewards are piled up far beyond our deserts, and then we send away and separate ourselves from the sound of all that makes life worthwhile and try to console ourselves in the inevitable misery of such folly with the thought that we are wise. I have no such conceit tonight, dearest.

I hate these long days and nights of loneliness and I know that it is not well for me to live apart from you. You say there are four weeks more to wait. I suppose I shall stand it. I have done so before and I may do so now but let no man tell me it is for my good! And, as it is not your wish, why do we who are free to come and go in other things, stand it? I wish you had followed your whim as you style it and had come to me. It would have taught me a lesson that I seem slow to learn – that you are not so far away but that I may cease grieving for you and go to you, if I have but half the heart to do the things a man ought to do. But I suppose I shall settle down quietly

tomorrow and count the work I have ahead of me and beg kind providence not to make the month more dreary or longer than the last two weeks have been.
[20171206-5 (1902) Henry to Bertha]

In his letters, Henry expressed his love for Bertha's letters, writing "*If I could make a crown for my darling, wrought of the love and trust and pride which I have in her, these letters of hers would be placed there as its jewels.*"

My darling, you are altogether the dearest, sweetest, child in the world, and I want you here tonight to hold you close to my heart that you may hear it beat because of the ecstasy, the thought of you gives me. I had three letters today, three messages from one whom I love far more that I thought it possible for anyone to care for another. If I could make a crown for my darling, wrought of the love and trust and pride which I have in her, these letters of hers would be placed there as its jewels.
[1893-01-26 (Wednesday) Henry (StL) to Bertha (Stancote, Newton, MA)]

Dearest,
You have no idea what a comfort it is to get away from other people and swap their society for yours, even if I must content myself with this long distance telephone. I have been dining with the Potters who called in Robert and Grace, Zack and Gordon, and me. I had a very good time but, when I left them, I felt I had made a very profitable exchange for a talk with another audience two days off. You will never credit me with the pleasure I get in writing to you and I little deserve it, for in most cases, when I write you, I have so little time that I can't make the items assemble themselves either decently or in order. But I do like to talk to you, even on paper, and, in seeking a reason for such a vagary, I have assumed that "it's because I love her so." Is that a good reason? It's the best I have.
[20180326-1 (1904-07-03-) Henry to Bertha]

You write very agreeable letters and I don't mind telling you I like them. I was cross and tired when your letter came this morning and it was like a tonic to a care sick patient. You make the world and life very beautiful, sweetheart, and I am so spoiled that I don't even think of looking elsewhere for help and what is I am afraid a ... confession, I don't rely on my own mean resources but can upon my wife for all the aid I so greatly need to keep up the fight.
[20180206-1 (1905-) Henry to Bertha

Henry would often get frustrated if Bertha's letters did not arrive on time and he would imagine various types of lapses of the part of the mail carriers which prevented such timely deliveries.

No letter today. I hardly understand this because your Sunday letter is the last I have had. Maybe it was lost in mailing for one of your letters was recently received in condition indicating that it had been dropped by your messenger in one of those puddles between the house and the post office. Who takes your letters to the office? Ask him or her why the letter was left in the road! I hope it will be found and sent along for I need it "so badly". I think I need you so badly too, dearest, for I am growing heart sick for a sight of you and, although I have no right to do so, I may run off from business any day and go to you and let the business be darned for a while anyway.
[1905(-) 201800730-5 Henry to Bertha]

In November 1905, Henry returned to Texas and complained of not receiving a letter from Bertha for 5 days. He wrote that he wondered whether he even had a family in St. Louis and a wife who put Henry on her "*list of duties*".

I don't know whether I have any wife or family for this is the fifth day I have been away without the slightest item to show that I left a family in St. Louis, to paddle around in the rain and slush of the wettest and forlornest Texas ever discovered by an obscure citizen of poor old Missouri. What is

the matter? I can't even guess for this time I know the Dorcas, the O.L.H. and the dispensary don't intervene. It can't be either church or state (of society) for the same reason. Doctor Monroe and his craft sent all of the above rivals to the rear for a time at least so what charges on your time are there that force you to neglect something with the inevitable result that your husband is removed from the list of duties as the chore that can best survive want of attention! You don't know it, maybe, but I require dusting and repairs and renovating as much as the other furnishings on your list and, if my cabinet maker don't get around and refit and thorough clean occasionally, I get rusty like the other things and feel rusty too which is worse for it doesn't hurt half as much to be shably as to know it and somehow I always know it, as you would realize if you could know just how a man's sensations are who has had wet feet for two days. I almost regret sending you a message from my old friend, Horatius Flaccus, "Vale, dulce puella, sed non longa vale spero." [257]
[1905-11-09 Henry (Ft. Worth) to Bertha (64 Vandeventer Pl., Stl)]

In the end, their correspondences were what they could most rely on when they were apart. As Henry wrote to Bertha: *"All I have to make this memory anything but a dream is the pleasure which a daily letter brings."*

No letter and I missed it very much for I am beginning to feel that, far back in the distant past, I was living in great happiness with a loving wife and four nice attractive tots which she had borne me as testimony of her love, and that really all I have to make this memory anything but a dream is the pleasure which a daily letter brings. I am getting homesick for a sight of you and our broad, dear child, and I think I can't stand it much longer if that Virginian would only hurry up and come here to take up his work I think I would cut the cabal business and pay you a visit even if I had to return in a few days even though I realize that this break and quick return to the heat would give me fits.
[20180209-1 (1905-) Henry to Bertha]

C. ANXIETY ABOUT BEING APART EARLY IN THEIR MARRIAGE

Bertha and Henry tried to get accustomed to being apart for weeks and even months during their married life together. But they never seemed to succeed. Bertha described one such occasion after their return to St. Louis from the Chicago World's Fair in May 1893. They were both in St. Louis at the time but, due to miscommunication, Bertha worried about Henry's absence the night before Country Club Day and wrote in her diary:

There was the Country Club Day for instance. The night before, Henry went off to leave [without] a note for me at Edith January's and I expected him back directly and sat and waited and waited and waited until one o'clock, by which time I had firmly made up my mind he was dead. And, when he did arrive, greeted him for the first time with a flood of tears. Discovered that he thought he had told me he was going to Judge Madill's to ask how Mrs. Madill was and had stayed talking to the Judge until twelve. Then thinking I would surely have gone to bed and, meeting Tom McKittrick and Louis Chauvenet, had gone with them to the Club. I felt like a goose. However, we went out early to the Country Club the next day and had a beautiful time, though it rained in the afternoon and stopped the polo – awful crowd going in.
[Bertha's diary, entry for May 1893]

For Bertha and Henry, being apart was always difficult and worrisome. Hence the daily letters and the reprimands if one of them did not abide by their daily correspondence commitment when away. And they frequently expressed their need for even a few words each day: *"I wish the time would come when I could get a letter from you. I don't like one bit being without hearing from you so long."* [1893-10-10 Tuesday Bertha (StL) to Henry (Waco)]

---

[257] "Goodbye, sweet girl, but not a long goodbye, I hope."

Bertha and Henry often wrote about the books that they were reading, another outlet to share their feelings. One such book was *The Mill on the Floss* by George Eliot, which Henry wrote made him "*blue*".

> *But you are a dear good girl for many reasons, sweetheart, and one of these is the thought that made you arrange "The Mill" for me. I finished it on the cars Sunday and got very blue over it and wanted to go home to be cheered up. It is a very sad story. I should not have read it if I had known how depressing it was. I think Maggie Tulliver's the saddest life I ever knew of. No wonder George Eliot loved her better than any of her creations.*
> [1893-10-11 Henry (Waco) to Bertha (StL)]

Bertha was also very moved by the *Mill*.

> *So the "Mill" made you blue, sweetheart. But weren't you interested? I confess I wept over it a little myself. And as long as it made you want to come home to be cheered up, I am quite satisfied.*
> [1893-10-08 Bertha (StL) to Henry (Fort Worth)]

In October 1893, Henry went on another business trip for two weeks to Waco, Fort Worth and then Wichita. Henry generally stayed in each place until his work was completed before moving on to the next. He would inevitably become frustrated if the work could not be completed expediently, preventing his return to Bertha and thus requiring that he "talk" to Bertha through his letters. "*You have been a dear girl, sweetheart, to write me such nice letters every day and I have only had time for very short, scrappy answers. I shall try to do better now that I have that abominable Waco snarl untangled.*" [1893-10-14 Henry (Ft. Worth) to Bertha (3337 Washington Ave, Stl)]

Henry was often very sentimental in his letters to Bertha, telling her of his love and how much, during their time apart, he missed her. These sentiments were certainly evident in the following letter that Henry wrote from Waco during his October 1893 business trip when he recalled, during their courtship, "*my taking your hand and keeping it in mine just a moment.*"

> *Last night, quite late, I sent you a short letter and today I am writing in a hurry before my train leaves for Fort Worth. Do you think me unkind because I give you so little of my time, dearest? You would not, I am very sure, if you knew how dearly I love you and how much I miss you all these days of banishment from the sweetest, dearest woman that ever lived. I have been thinking a great many times of you today. My work here is nearly done. It has been very well done too, dearest, for the outlook is more promising than it has been for years. And, as I have had less to worry me, I have had more time for bright thoughts and all my bright thoughts are of my darling. I haven't any glad moments but those which she gives me, have I?*
>
> *My memory in a dreamy fashion has been running back to all the early days of our first friendship and once or twice I have had very clearly before me an evening, I wonder if you will recall it, when I saw you at home the next time after the ball when you took back the stolen flower. Do you remember my taking your hand and keeping it in mine just a moment? If you do remember, you at least do not know all the pained confusion and doubt and happiness that I felt when I had said good night and left you. Well, I have been wondering why it is that this particular evening comes back to me so clearly now. Is it because as then I would rather have your hand in mine once more than all the world's treasure?*
> [1893-10-14 Henry (Waco) to Bertha (StL)]

Bertha very clearly remembered the incident when Henry took Bertha's hand. Undoubtedly shocking behavior for unmarried persons! Bertha very coyly replied to this affront in her next letter to Henry.

> *No, I have not forgotten that evening very shortly after the Bachelor's Ball, nor the fact that you took my hand. It was very wrong of you to have done so under the then existing circumstances. Shall I punish you by not allowing you to hold it when you return this time?*
> [1893-10-17 Bertha (StL) to Henry (Wichita)]

As it sometimes would happen, letters were delayed in the mail. After one such delay, Bertha scolded Henry for not writing as promised with: "*I don't care one bit about you…*" If she had had Henry's delayed letter, what a different letter she might have written.

> *You are a mean, hateful, unremembering, hard-worked boy! Why did you not write to me today? I don't care one bit about you and I was strongly tempted not to send you a letter but as I have never done that without feeling badly afterward, I decided for the sake of my own feelings, not one bit on your account, to write to you and, in consideration of the fact that I am writing, you will please excuse blots which are made anyway because I am using your old gold pen.*
>
> *…*
>
> *Yours always, but if I don't get a letter tomorrow, you need not expect one from me.*
> [1893-10-14 Bertha (StL) to Henry (Ft. Worth)]

Bertha's next letter included some repentance, for Henry's delayed letter and the "Jack roses".

Rosa 'Général Jacqueminot: 'Général Jacqueminot' also called 'General Jack' or 'Jack Rose'.

> *I am very glad I did not let my angry passions keep me from writing to you yesterday for, if I had, I should have been a very penitent individual when my beautiful box of Jaqueminot roses arrived this morning. I did not know you had sent the two boxes, sweetheart, I thought the man had simply sent the others out of date, but thank you very, very much for them and for your nice long letter which would have made me forgive you if nothing else had.*
>
> *…*
>
> *Haven't these eight months been beautiful, dearest? And the first year is the hardest!!*
> [1893-10-15 Bertha (StL) to Henry (Fort Worth)]

Henry accepted his scolding, after some protestation.

> *If you weren't the best child in the world and my beautiful wife besides, I should indulge in a wrathful protest over your condescension. You are inclined to forgive me for not writing when the very letter you – pardon the expression but it fits beautifully - are kicking about is in your hands. How can I prevent Uncle Sam's mails from delaying my letters! But I see, you imagine my dominion of control extends this far. Very flattering, I'm sure, this faith in my authority but learn, dear, innocent child, that my sway is limited to a very beautiful home in St. Louis where, by the way, I am only second in command, one or two miserable gas companies, and a somewhat capricious stenographer of whom you have heard much. But I forgive you. You are lovely, dear, not as much as I am, I know, but enough so to think I deserve a scolding and so I submit.*
>
> *…*

Yes these eight months have been beautiful my darling and the time ahead seems filled with happiness for me. God grant that it may bring joy and happiness to my darling.
[1893-10-16 Henry (Ft Worth) to Bertha (StL)]

While Bertha could be very sweet in her letters, she enjoyed ribbing Henry. After Henry misspelled "prittiest", Bertha posted: *"Dear, I forgot to mention in my letter answer to your letters yesterday that I would have appreciated that compliment to the "prittiest girl in the country" more if you had spelled "prettiest" right. Pardon me if I seem critical."* [1893-10-17 Bertha (StL) to Henry (Wichita)] Bertha could always keep Henry on his toes.

Toward the end of one of his business trips to Texas and Kansas in October 1893, Henry became hopeful of an earlier return home than originally expected. Henry was chagrined when his business took an unexpected turn for the worse. *"D---!!!"*

> *I am sufficiently provoked to be in a most vicious mood tonight, the reason being that I shall have to stay in this charming country until Thursday. Isn't that a delightful prospect? I shall probably see you about Tuesday, a whole week from now! Confound Fort Worth and Texas and Wichita and the lighting business and all this combination of worries that keep me from my darling. The immediate cause of my being delayed here is that I must go over to Dallas tomorrow to see about a change which has been made in our coal rates. As I shall be there all day and, as I have at least another day's work here, I shall not get away before Thursday night for Wichita, no matter how hard I try to finish up here. Join me in a malediction on all this hard, hard luck. D---!!!*
> [1893-10-17 Henry (Ft. Worth) to Bertha (StL)]

When the situation warranted, Bertha was very kind and more or less contrite. *"You are a dear boy to have written so regularly and I apologize for having scolded you but, if you did not deserve it, then you probably did some other time."* [1893-10-19 Bertha (StL) to Henry (Wichita)]

The importance of Bertha's letters to Henry found a full expression in the following letter when Henry wrote of holding her letters *"pretty tight in my hands"* as he reflected on their life together.

> *I have two nice, nice letters this morning and, after I read them, I was very happy and, after that on my way down to the works, I had these reflections. First, I agreed that I was tolerably happy and moderately fortunate. Then I found, let us say for the first time, that I owed all my happiness and all my good fortune to a very good friend of mine in Saint Louis and then I concluded I should be very grateful to that friend and as a better method of emphasizing these feelings which you can easily understand were but passing emotions and required further stirring influences to ensure their remaining with me and part of me for a short time, I took those two letters out of my packet and read them over and held them pretty tight in my hands and then I thought what an ungrateful fellow I was to send such scrappy letters in reply to real messages of cheer and love like those I had today. God bless you, my darling, for all your care and thought and love. Well, I am not going to write a love letter and, if these men in the office knew what I have been writing, all the force of my fierce attacks upon their delinquencies would be lost for all time.*
> [1894-11-24 Henry (Waco) to Bertha (StL)]

D. BUSINESS TRIPS IN 1895

> *"People who have been married five years are not expected to be so much in love with each other. At least, that is the opinion of all sensible people."[258]*

Henry's absences during his business trips were hard for Bertha. Bertha wrote of her loneliness for Henry in a letter to her friend, Muffy.

---

[258] 1892-07-13 Bertha (Jaffrey NH) to Henry (StL)

Henry left last night and I don't know when I have felt such a deserted feeling. I told him last night, the first time he left me for a week, I had to spend the night with me – Nan, Miss Jennie, Minnie, Maud, twice Frances & I staid one night at the Shepley's. Now Nan is married and gone, Minnie is married, France is gone, Maud & Miss Jennie in the country. Of course, I have my blessed son to keep me company now but his conversational powers are limited. Then nearly always since that first time, I have had you here and could go over and take either lunch or dinner with you and even Edith Knox has taken this occasion to be in Chicago.
[1895(-) 20180810-4 Bertha to Muffy]

On one occasion in 1895 when Henry's letter was not delivered on time, Bertha concluded that her *"marriage was a failure."*
When the mail came up with my breakfast this morning, there was no letter from you and I made up my mind that marriage was a failure but when the second post came in, I forgave you.
[1895-05-10 Bertha (StL) to Henry (Wichita)]

The separations were always challenging for Henry, *"like a throb of pain"*.
I want to see you so badly that I don't seem to be able to tell you, dearest. I have waked in the night once or twice lately and missed you so it was like a throb of pain; I will never let you go away for so long again.
[20180129-2 (1895-) Henry to Bertha]

I miss you more and more each day, dearest, and I sometimes think that if I were really any account, I would so arrange that we would not be separated for so long a time every summer. I realize more than I ever did before in my life how short the time is that we are to be together and it seems as if I were deliberately cheating myself in year after year letting you go away from me for so long a time.
[20170810-1 Henry to Bertha]

I hardly dare tell you how I have missed you, my darling. You will think I have done nothing but think of you and our separation. It has not been so horribly lonely during the day for I could, I believe, work just as hard as usual knowing that, if I did not get down to hard knocks, I would simply waste the days in vain regret at your absence. But the nights have been terrible and I have more than once been convinced that the greatest folly of my life is this plan of the long summer separations.
[20171222-1 (1895-) Henry to Bertha]

In his letters to Bertha, Henry often spoke of the great influence that Bertha was to his life and, in the following letter, worried that *"my ingratitude of your love may bear the evil consequence which it deserves."*
That was a beautiful letter you sent me today. I think, if I am vain on any subject, it is that I am capable of appreciating not only every line of your sermon but all the beautiful purpose that inspired it. You know without my saying it that every thought of mine, every act, every hope or inspiration that is in the least degree worthy, is due to you and, if I confess myself a failure, it will be the more humiliating that with such aid and comfort I am not equal to my task. It does seem a light task, dear, when I think of what you are in my life and I don't believe anything but the distorted thought which inevitably follows sickness would convince me even for a moment that my task is a hard one. Just now, the only fear I have for the future is that my ingratitude of your love may bear the evil consequence which it deserves.
[20180127-5 Henry to Bertha]

Days and even weeks prior to going east to be with Bertha during the summer of 1895, Henry became excited. Although Henry would worry about becoming "worthless" if he grew accustomed to spending too much time with Bertha, he wrote, *"for isn't every other thing in life very little beside this life of ours together?"*

> *I can hardly think I am to see you again with less than a week, sweetheart, and I think that I shall be fully rewarded for all the long dreary days of absence from you if I may meet you and find you half as well as you describe yourself as being. It hardly seems possible that we are to have a month together, sweetheart, with all the workaday cares locked up out of sight and nothing to do but make believe we are really fond of each other! I am already beginning to grudge the passing of every single day of that short time. No wonder the angels are happy; they know heaven never closes up and goes back to work! I expect it is well for me that I have to put a short limit upon my real married life with you, the vacation time, for otherwise I would be worthless for any other occupation and small blame to me either, dearest, for isn't every other thing in life very little beside this life of ours together?*
> [1895(-) 20180802-4 Henry to Bertha]

Bertha wrote Henry in September 1895 after having spent the summer in Jamestown that she was looking forward to seeing Henry but wondered what seeing him will be like, after all the time that they spent apart.

> *A week from today and we shall be together again! It does not seem possible somehow. Do you know, sweetheart, I really feel a little wee bit shy about meeting you – we have been apart so long. Do you think we shall have to get acquainted again, best friend? Well, it will not be long now before we find out. "The Lord watch between thee and me while we are absent one from another[259]."*
> [1895-09-12 Bertha (Jamestown RI) to Henry (StL)]

E. REMEMBERING THE DAY BEFORE NANCY WAS BORN

On July 4, 1896, when Henry was in Waco on business, he wrote to Bertha while she was in Jamestown, thinking about that day the year before when he and Bertha were caught in the rain on the Jamestown shore and thinking, *"that was a better fourth of July…"*

> *Dear, tomorrow will be sister's birthday[260]. I have been thinking very often of the fifth of July last year and I imagine you have not let it entirely escape you. I have thought too of that walk in the rain just a year ago this afternoon. It is quarter past six and at just this time a year back, we were lurching along the shore and fighting the storm. That was a better fourth of July for me my darling.*
> [1896-07-04 Henry (Waco) to Bertha (Jamestown, RI)

The 4th of July 1898 celebrations took on a more patriotic tone after the July 1st victory in the Battle of San Juan Hill in Cuba during the Spanish American war of 1898. Nevertheless (and not surprisingly), Henry wrote to Bertha when she was in Jamestown of his loneliness and of his fond recollection of their July 4th three years before and the birth of Nancy the next day.

> *I have had to work today. This glorious fourth so full of good news from the American armies in Cuba. But I am going out to the Country Club this evening and I hope to find someone to talk to for I have seldom been so utterly lonely. It is hardly a compliment in my present mood to say that I miss the best friend I have on earth but as she is not in much doubt of my great need of her, whether my mood be happy or sad, she will no doubt understand that today it is not putting it too strong to say that these separations are growing unbearable. We spent quite a different fourth three years ago, dearie, and I can hardly make the comparison with today without shedding tears. I hope you are as well as you were that day that we climbed along the rocks along the shore, you*

---

[259] Genesis 31:49, NIV: "It was also called Mizpah".
[260] For a brief time, Nancy Scott was called "sister", i.e. Hugh Scott's sister. Nancy Scott was born July 5, 1895.

thoroughly enjoying the walk, rough as it was, notwithstanding your encumbrance which materialized into fat Nancy the next day.
[1898-07-05 Henry (StL) to Bertha (Jamestown, RI)]

Henry spoke again of this July 4, 1895 walk in Jamestown in a letter to Bertha in 1907.
I suppose the fifth will be a fine day for Nancy Scott. Her birthday always recalls that beautiful June at Jamestown. I doubt if either of us were ever happier in our lives. Twelve years have not dimmed the peace and happiness of that month and I think I have no greater happiness in prospect than the ambition to be with you again and, in the same way, have for a season the world blotted out and apart from us. I am getting impatient to see you, my dearest, and may be that has something to do with the clog that has been put on my spirits, forever inclined to selfishly dwell upon what I wished for rather than the duty at hand. I seem, of late, to have little room in my thoughts for anything but selfish planning for my own happiness.
[1907-07-04 Henry to Bertha (20180416A-1)]

F. HE IS COMING, MY LOVE, MY SWEET
Henry planned to travel to Jamestown to visit Bertha in August 1898. Anticipating Henry's arrival, Bertha wrote to Henry quoting Tennyson, "*He is coming, my love, my sweet*", which amply described her feelings about seeing him so soon.
Give my love to your mother and Maggie. Perhaps a week from today, you will be with me! Anyway, goodbye to St. Louis and hurrah for a good time coming.
Goodbye,
Yours always,
Bert

> *"He is coming, my love, my sweet,*
> *Be it so airy a tread,*
> *My heart would know it & beat*
> *Had it lain for a century dead."* [261]

[1898-08-04 Bertha (Jamestown) Henry (StL)]

Henry wrote of their planned August 1898 Jamestown reunion, with Bertha "*bidding me come for there is joy in your heart...*"
I shall see you before a week has gone by and we will have our holiday together and have such a beauty, beauty time! I feel almost if I were starting off to be married over again and, as I sit here writing to you, I can see your dear face – it's a beautiful face, Bert – bidding me come for there is joy in your heart that we are to be united so soon. [1898-08-06 Henry (University Club, Stl) to Bertha (Jamestown, RI)]

Bertha and Henry's anticipation of reuniting after their various separations was always a cause for great joy which, perhaps, made the loneliness during such times more bearable. But it also seemed to make both of them more sentimental. Writing to Bertha about his feelings seemed to make Henry feel less lonely and

---

[261] Alfred Lord Tennyson, from "Maud", Stanza 11:
She is coming, my own, my sweet;
Were it ever so airy a tread,
My heart would hear her and beat,
Were it earth in an earthy bed;
My dust would hear her and beat,
Had I lain for a century dead,
Would start and tremble under her feet.

closer to Bertha when they were apart and better able to deal with the ills of life which *"are nothing when I open my selfish eyes to the happiness around me."*

> *I may not be able to keep three sermons, as you do, in my life but there will be one which will help me in the best and in the darkest hours. You are right, sweetheart, the ills which have come to me are nothing when I open my selfish eyes to the happiness around me. And your suggestion that all the joy of our lives might be interrupted by separation makes me very penitent that I have permitted trivialities to obscure even for an hour the great happiness which has come to me in your love. For you are my hope and joy, everything, dear, and without you there would be no place in my life for happiness or even usefulness for I could not live without you, my darling. I think my rough thought often drifts into dwelling upon life's little ills when you are near me because, as we are one, it is hard to understand that, though this be true, there is consideration due the better part of my life which the courser strain in me selfishly ignores. We are constantly trying and failing, sweetheart, but I shall not cease to try to help you more and to be more worthy of your love.*
> [1898(-) 20180127-3 (1897-07-22) Henry (StL) to Bertha (Jamestown)]

Even after four years of marriage, the feeling of loneliness during their separations did not grow any easier. As Bertha wrote to Henry in October 1897 while he was in Wichita, *"all the life of it is gone without you…"*. *"Each time you go away, it seems harder to bear."*

> *Dearest,*
>
> *I am going back to our early days and, though you have only been gone half an hour, I shall write to you now. I can't wait for tomorrow. The first time you left me after we were married, it was the April after our marriage. I remember very well how I felt when you left. I was ever so sorry to let you go – I wanted to go with you too but I had a lot of other things in my mind. I was going to give a lunch for Mary Reventlow and I was going to some entertainments other people gave for her and a lot of the girls were coming to stay all night with me for the first time in my own house and I was pretty full of the thrill of it all.*
>
> *Now, I have ever so much more in my life. I have those two babies upstairs and I have my beautiful new house to work and plan over and you know I love it. But all the life of it is gone without you. I don't know how to face the days ahead without you. I want you to talk to, to advise with, to sympathize with, even to be scolded by. That is a confession. Each time you go away, it seems harder to bear.*
>
> *I have nothing more to say.*
> > *"A little warmth, a little light*
> > *of love's bestowing, and so, goodnight."*
>
> *Yours always,*
> *Bert*
> [1897-10-01 Bertha (StL) to Henry (Wichita)]

What is sometimes striking in their letters is how much Bertha and Henry's sentiments toward each other seemed so very natural and ingenuous. After five years of marriage, Henry seemed to express the feelings of the youthful suitor who, upon receipt of his love's letter, held it to his lips as if holding her.

> *I have been thinking of your Saturday letter ever since I received it, dear, and if I make it clear how much happiness it gave me I am sure you would not be sorry you had sent it. It was a beautiful letter, sweetheart, and I shall not soon forget it. And let me tell you just what happened before I read it. It was an example of truth in telepathy which I was not quite prepared for. I found the letter on my desk – the first one – as I always do when it comes. And instead of following my usual habit of opening it at once, I turned it over in my hand once or twice, wondering what new message*

of love I should have for the day, when an impulse I can't even account for took hold of me and I held that little black edged envelop to my lips and held it there as I would have held you, closer, closer – yes, as I hold you when you are in my arms. You will think this sentimentality. I thought so after my silly performance, until I opened the letter and then it seemed plain that the little black rimmed package couldn't keep its silence and would have burst if it hadn't told!
[20180129-7 (1898-) Henry to Bertha]

Bertha and Henry sometimes mused over some benefits from their periodic separations. On one of his trips to Texas in 1898, Henry wrote, *"if in the hurry and worry of my business life I have failed to halt long enough at home to realize anyone of the new beautiful characteristics which my darling is every day giving me the charm of, I "catch up" completely if I am a day away from her."* [1898-03-25 (Friday Letter) Henry (Ft Worth, Waco) to Bertha (64 Vandeventer Place, Stl)]

Bertha was very moved by Henry's letter (above). Bertha also understood how these absences should not be viewed as simply cruel but as something more essential.
> *Thank you for you Friday letter, sweetheart, it has made the whole morning beautiful to me. Perhaps after all, there is something in a remark of Dumas which I read the other day though I resented it at the time. The woman said "absence is the most cruel thing in the world", and the man said, "if you destroyed it, you would also destroy love."*
> [1898-03-28 Bertha (StL) to Henry (Oriental Hotel, Dallas)]

On at least one occasion, Henry could be caught daydreaming of Bertha when they were apart. Henry wrote of one such time in July 1898 when he was with Edith and Gordon Knox. Edith said, *"Henry, Bert has the finest eyes I ever saw"* and there she asked me about something else which I evidently did not reply to promptly for she shouted her question the second time as if she had caught me dreaming. She was right and I was dreaming – of you, my darling.* [1898-07-10 Henry (StL) to Bertha (Jamestown)]

In the Spring of 1899, Henry was again traveling to Texas on business. This time, it was Bertha who felt some regret for not having been more appreciative of Henry.
> *I have about come to the conclusion that "I do not appreciate you, sah." I have been thinking a great deal about you as I have kept quiet these last two days and what a very hard time you have had this winter with all your business worries and your ill health and then your great sorrow[262]. And then I thought how very patient and cheery you had been with me and how low spirited and glooming and generally unpleasant I had been and I decided that you had a very poor kind of a wife and that you were anything but a poor kind yourself. There! I'll give you credit for your good qualities anyway if I do treat you badly.*
> [1899-03-28 (3 letters) Bertha (StL) to Henry (Ft. Worth)]

Also in that Spring of 1899, Henry wrote of being *"petulantly anxious"* to get to the office so that he could receive a word from Bertha.
> *I must tell you of a curious sensation I had every day just after you left. ... usually when I am not well, I just hate the thought of the office and am about as shy of it as is the burnt child of the fire. But, without knowing the reason, I became petulantly anxious to get to the office and, if anything turned up to detain me, I thought the world was coming to an end or, rather, the office. And I did not realize for several days that the cause of the changed attitude toward my work ... lay entirely in the small black-lined envelope which I found there each morning. I suppose you will say I should have realized the cause of my eagerness at once and may be it would be a higher tribute to you had I done so but the result certainly indicates that I am not entirely an unfit person for you to send that quotation to.*

---

[262] The *"great sorrow"* was probably the death of Henry's mother on November 12, 1898.

...

I am crazy to see you, dear, and I do want to see our tots, too. Hugh is evidently developing mentally. I hope his body is growing also. No such fears of Nancy! Or of that fat baby either, bless him. I am quite proud of your accts of him.

Jack Davis and I are going on together and I stay at the Waldorf so write me there. It is harder now that I am to see you so soon than at first with the long wait ahead. I think I have exhausted all my stock of happiness and comfort and, if the supply were not replenished soon, your patient would die.

[1899-03-29a Henry (Worth Hotel, Ft. Worth) to Bertha (64 Vandeventer Place, StL)]

Easter Sunday was on April 2, 1899 and Henry worried that he would not be able to return to his family in time. But his strong desire to return to St. Louis for Easter "*creates energy of movement which brings results of the most satisfactory volume.*"

Between hurry and scurry, I expect to scramble through with the Texas campaign in time to catch the Frisco fast train Saturday morning at Dallas which is due to reach St. Louis Sunday morning. If I succeed, good. If I don't --- ! I am not absolutely certain of my arrival for I have piles of work to do, but the thought of your spending Easter alone or my spending it alone, as you may care to put it, creates energy of movement which brings results of the most satisfactory volume and, if the steam holds out, there will be a vacuum instead of a white man's burden on my shoulders by tomorrow evening.

[1899-03-30 Henry (Waco) to Bertha (64 Vandeventer Place)]

Bertha spent the summer of 1899 in Jamestown with Hugh, Nancy and George; Henry joined them later that August. In the following letter while in Jamestown, Bertha reproached herself for not letting Henry see more clearly that the "*roughnesses*" in Henry's life were just as much part of hers.

Sometimes I wonder if perhaps I tell you too little of what you are in my life, you who are so much to me. I wonder if we do say too little of what is our innermost and deepest life and take it too much for granted that others understand how dear they are to us. You said something in one of your letters that hurt me. "You are so entirely one with me that I forget and bring you the roughnesses out of my life when I should not." Why should you not? There is nothing in your life, rough or hard or beautiful, that is not of keenest interest to me because it is your life and it hurts to be shut out of it. But I think on my part, "because we are so entirely one", I forget sometimes to tell you how much that close union is to me and how lonely, how very lonely I am without it. I love you so dearly, I depend on you so absolutely, and yet, instead of telling you so, I only sow my dependence on you by letting you bear all the brunt of every feeling of weariness or illness that I have and don't even say thank you.

[1899-07-30 Bertha (Jamestown RI) to Henry (StL)]

Perhaps from communicating so much by letter, Bertha and Henry were able to see each other in the words they sent. As Henry said, below, "*I could as clearly see your loving beautiful eyes as if you had been speaking to me.*"

Your letters bring with them the sweetest, happiest thoughts I am capable of knowing except when we are together. It seemed this morning almost as if you had come back to me, Bert, for as I read your letters, I could as clearly see your loving beautiful eyes as if you had been speaking to me. I do not intend, however, to be sentimental. I am told that after the first year of marriage, any such indulgence is not only quite out of the common experience but is distinctly inadvisable. Men have been known to spoil and lessen their influence over their wives through guilt of this blunder and I must not spoil you dearie and I do not care to change you in any way because I like you "best of all" just as you are.

[1900(-) 20170805-4 Henry to Bertha]

G. LA PATIENCE EST AMÈRE MAIS SON FRUIT EST DOUX

Although Henry was always impatient to see Bertha after any period of absence, he did write to Bertha of the virtue of patience. *"I can't send you as good French or as sweet a song as you send me but it is some balm to my lonely heart that "la patience est amère, mais son fruit est doux.""* [1900(-) 20180728-3 Henry to Bertha] A ripe sentiment in any language!

On his trip to Texas in January 1900, however, Henry's impatience to see Bertha was manifest.

> *I am writing just on my way to the train so don't be afraid of a long letter but I must really tell you – I can't keep it – how very much I love my dear child and how much I miss her. No man so entirely depended upon another as I do upon you, dear, and you ought to take care of yourself else you may not be able to take care of me. And I need your care, dear, more I sometimes think than the babies for they do not yet know what a world of happiness for others you can give out and I do, my darling.*
> [1900-01-31 Henry (Waco) to Bertha (64 Vandeventer Place, Stl)]

During the summer around 1900 when she was in Rye Beach, Bertha wrote of how little she could say in her letter knowing that, since she and Henry soon could speak face to face, *"everything must wait"*.

> *I can hardly believe that I shall only write you one more letter. And it strange, all summer I have had to close my letters only for need of sleep. I have felt as if I really could not get all I wanted to say into them and now I have nothing to say. I feel as if everything must wait until I can talk it over with you and that seems so beautifully near now. I wonder if the time will ever come when there are not perplexities to discuss. Zack [Lionberger] says we will be very much to be pitied if it does and I suppose he knows. It does not really matter much, I think, so long as we have each other to discuss them with. It is that lack that makes life impossible.* [1900(-) 20180528-4 Bertha (Rye Beach) to Henry]

Prior to his trip east in the August 1900, Henry complained that his work was making him blue.

> *...the work made me, trifling as it is, bluer than indigo. I thought how different things would be if you were here and then sat for a long time wondering if I should ever see you again. It seems about ten years since you ran away and left me and I feel more forlorn than I have since you went away. I would not be so disconsolate either if I were sure of seeing you by the fifteenth or sixteenth but I am not able to tell yet how soon I can get away or how long I may be delayed in New York or Philadelphia. If I am very late, why can't you come down to New York and meet me there? Do you think you could do that? Or maybe you would not mind coming all the way to Philadelphia? What do you say?*
> [1900-08-09(-) (Wednesday) Henry (StL) to Bertha (Rye or Dubin NH)]

And Henry's patience was always tried toward summer's end when he would take his vacation and travel east to see Bertha.

> *I can hardly think I am to see you again with less than a week, sweetheart, and I think that I shall be fully rewarded for all the long dreary days of absence from you if I may meet you and find you half as well as you describe yourself as being. It hardly seems possible that we are to have a month together, sweetheart, with all the workaday cares locked up out of sight and nothing to do but make believe we are really fond of each other! I am already beginning to grudge the passing of every single day of that short time. No wonder the angels are happy; they know heaven never closes up and goes back to work! I expect it is well for me that I have to put a short limit upon my real married life with you, the vacation time, for otherwise I would be worthless for any other occupation and small blame to me either, dearest, for isn't every other thing in life very little beside this life of ours together?*
> [1895(-) 20180802-4 Henry to Bertha]

So much for patience.

H. WORRIES ABOUT BERTHA'S HEALTH

Throughout their marriage, Henry worried about Bertha's health, especially when he was away on business and could not provide necessary care and strict instructions. After Bertha wrote to Henry that she suffered a *"stiffness around the muscles of my knee"*[263] which resulted from the cold weather and having gone out *"in low shoes"*, Henry scolded:

> *As I shall be in Dallas all day and on the train for two hours beside, I may not be able to write and I intended to write a long letter, scolding you for not getting your high shoes before the cold weather, the result of which carelessness, is the trouble in your knee. There. If the knee pains you at all now, send for Doctor Robinson. Please and please don't go out in the cold until you have the heavy shoes to wear. Min or Maggie can get them for you and you can send Brown with a note to one of the girls if you don't happen to see them. It is not very pleasant to think of your being unwell while I am away, dearest. It would be bad enough at any time but I give you fair warning, if you become unwell when I leave you, I will get out of all this outside work and then you will be sorry for, without the financial aid I derive from this work, you and I would very probably have to put to test our starvation qualities.*
>
> *…*
>
> *I had just gained all that any man could need to insure absolute "felicitas" when the dread of your approaching sickness interviewed to drive away this great joy with the sorrow it makes me feel when I think of your confinement and of your being kept so closely housed for so many days. If it were not for this thought and, if I were not away from you now, I should be the happiest man in the world. I think I am, anyway, sweetheart, and if I am not, I ought to be for am I not blessed with the sweetest companionship that ever gladdened a man's life?*
>
> [1893-10-17 Henry (Ft. Worth) to Bertha (StL)]

Bertha reassured Henry in her next letter about her knee. *"You need not have worried about my knee, dear old boy, it was a little stiff for two days and then I betook myself vigorously to camphorated Vaseline and it came out beautifully. I would not have mentioned it if I had thought you were going to worry. No indeed, I am splendidly well."* [1893-10-20 Bertha (StL) to Henry (Wichita)] Perhaps Bertha had wanted Henry to worry at least a little bit.

Henry also feared that Bertha was excessively taxing herself by taking long calls from friends and especially cousins. Henry had a solution for such people which would take full advantage of Narragansett Bay which surrounded Jamestown.

> *Speaking of nice people, it's pretty sad that you are to be beset by Bettie and Molly again. You know I have an idea about those two which, I think if applied, will do them lots of good and be a God send to their friends: let the St. Louis contingent announce the adoption of the rule that, during the summer, no one may pay a call lasting more than ten minutes. Penalty: death by drowning. Put my suggestion before your suffering friends and say that, if no one can be found to exact the penalty from the offenders, I will unwillingly accept the task, at least until the bay receives all that is mortal of our dear cousins, Molly & Bettie.*
>
> [1898-07-10 Henry (StL) to Bertha (Jamestown)]

In another letter, Henry wrote of his concern that Bertha was becoming overly tired in caring for their children.

> *Don't make company of them, dear, this will exhaust you and make it less pleasant for them and, as I am not to have you in New York, don't you think you ought to humor my especial wish that you*

---

[263] Bertha's letter, 1893-10-15 Sunday Bertha (StL) to Henry (Fort Worth)

lie down for two hours every day and try to get back your strength? If you knew what a real trouble it is to me to think that you may become the useless worn out individual that I have been for the past year, I am sure you would try to be very careful. We can't do very much for those blessed chicks, dear, if we have no health and it is because I am made so useless at times by sickness that I plead with you not to take liberties with your health. Putting it fairly, it is like taking from the babies what is theirs – your health and strength, to care for their blessed little souls and bodies. I am not sure you are right to continue nursing the baby. You may be right but I doubt if the food a mother gives is ever the best if the draft upon her is a tax. You know leading physicians all agree that milk given to the young should come only from the strong and we see enough evidences of weakly men and women every day, the children of delicate parents to know that all this is not fiction. But I did not mean to scold, dearie, and, if I have been cross, set it down as due to a naturally cranky disposition and don't mind. But you will admit that I give good advice and will act on it, even if I put my suggestions disagreeably?

[1898-07-26 Henry (StL) to Bertha (Jamestown)]

After Alice Scott was born in 1903, Henry reprimanded Bertha for spending too much of her energy on the baby.

So do be wise and as Dr. Mudd puts it, get in condition promptly lest your temporary setback become a normal condition which means chronic ill health. Dr. Mudd said the other night that not one woman in five was endowed with ordinary common sense in the matter of her own health and that half the female cases brought to him might be directly traced to the most flagrant disregard of the ordinary plain rules of healthful living. There! Now mind you, obey my orders and first relieve yourself of every tax, including Miss baby, that entails the slightest fatigue, then sit down and make me an exact report of what your trouble is as far as your feminine mind can grasp such really serious matters. If you don't and don't get on the invalid's discharged list promptly, I will not go to Rye one step until the time comes to bring you home. As my troubles at Waco bid fair to make my threat a reality anyway, for I must go down there soon and for a long visit of negotiation with the City, you may safely depend upon a literal fulfillment of my warning if you don't promptly return to the straight and narrow path of sanity and self-care.

[20180323-2 (1903-) Henry to Bertha]

In the course of his letters, it seemed that Henry tried every rhetorical argument he could muster to get Bertha's attention focused on her health, including the following: you will become old before your time.

I [don't] believe you really are taking better care of yourself. I don't think my suggestion of your duty to husband and children influenced you a particle but rather the picture of that decrepit old woman, old before her time, going round on two sticks, vainly trying to keep up with her young husband who, though seven years her senior, not having wasted his strength and substance in riotous living, was still young, strong and gay!

[1906-06-(-) 20180730-4 Henry to Bertha]

There is no evidence that Bertha followed Henry's strictures; but, one can imagine that she may have liked Henry's concerns and thoughts.

I. IF YOU WERE NOT AWAY

In his calmer moods, Henry would often ascribe his various ills to being apart from Bertha, such as in this letter written around 1910.

I hadn't time to write yesterday and your Wednesday letter has made me feel like a worm of the earth. I suppose when I am tired, I give you my woes in my exaggerated form for really I am not ill and only at times tired. I suppose as old age creeps on we feel less able to come buoyantly out of fatigue and then you know last winter was one of the very hardest of my life and maybe I am not

just feeling the effects. But I sleep well, play golf and do all the routine of your thoroughly healthy man and I am quite sure a little of your society and a little rest will make me as well and strong as I have ever been in my life. I am really provoked at my rather childish fussing over a trifle ... when I see everyday men who look and no doubt are much more worn with their daily tasks than I ever am. As to Jack Shepley, when you see me you will know without my protestations that he has been a really sick man and I a perfectly well one perhaps a trifle overtired and inclined at times to be cross about it. I think really, Bert, if it were not that you are away, I should be having nothing to worry about. And, as it is, my chief anxiety is for the time to lapse when we can be together again, for, my dearest, there really isn't any interest in life without you.
[1910(-) 20170724-1 Henry to Bertha]

"...my chief anxiety is for the time to lapse when we can be together again, for, my dearest, there really isn't any interest in life without you."

CHAPTER 20 – LIFE & TIMES

A. TRANSPORTATION

Tally Ho Coach, 1875

1. TRAVEL BY CARRIAGE

In an 1892 letter, Bertha described her ride on a Tally Ho Coach when she was in Kennebunkport ME.

> I enclose you a picture of the Tally Ho coach.[264] It was really taken of the expedition that went while I was up at Kennebunkport, so you need not look for me. But I want to give you an idea of how we looked when we went off last night. Only, as we went at night, the whole coach was hung with Japanese lanterns and it was most gorgeous to behold. We all wore large bouquets of goldenrod and scarlet geraniums so we made a most festive appearance when we arrived at the Wentworth.
>
> ...
>
> We had a glorious ride home, the moon was magnificent. It would have been impossible to have had a better night.
>
> [1892-08-08 (Wednesday) Bertha (Farragut house, Rye Beach) to Henry (StL)]

Around 1905, Henry's wrote about an amusing incident involving a Mrs. Copeland who was trying to board the stagecoach.

> I heard a good story on Mrs. Copeland today. The old lady was getting in a stagecoach somewhere east and, as may be imagined, the door proved to be small. The driver suggested "Get in sideways, madam." After another fruitless effort, she indignantly replied "I haven't any sideways."
>
> [20171218-1 (1905-) Henry to Bertha]

("I haven't any sideways"!!!)

2. TRAIN TRAVEL

Bertha may have best described train travel in the 1890s when she was on a trip to Florida – "After six hours, a journey becomes to me a thing rather to be endured than enjoyed." [1892-03-05 Bertha (Ponce de Leon, St Augustine FL) to Henry (StL)]

---

[264] Bertha's picture was not kept. The picture (above) is of an 1875 Tally Ho Coach from Long Island Museum, The Carriage Collection, Holland & Holland Builders, London, Great Britain. Internationally famous, the Tally-Ho Road Coach was a catalyst of the road coaching movement in America, which hit its stride in the 1880s.

During the summer, train travel could be very hot. *"Aren't those car trips very disagreeable, Henry? I should think they would be almost like a nightmare to you. And is it not very awfully warm in Wichita and those other horrid places?"* [1892-07-02 Bertha (Rye Beach) to Henry (Wichita)]

Likewise, Henry expressed his own, less than positive, views about train travel: *"... nothing takes the life out of me so completely as travelling."* [1892-08-15 (Monday) Henry (StL) to Bertha (Farragut House, Rye Beach)] *"If I had much railway travel to do, I should without doubt die young."* [1892-08-27 (Friday) Henry (StL) to Bertha (Farragut House)]

The decision as to which train to catch certainly mattered. In a 1892 letter, Bertha wrote about catching the "early train" on one occasion and regretting that decision.

> *You have to breakfast at six o'clock and, though I did not, I kept waking myself up all night in anticipation of this early rising and I am as cross as I can be in consequence. The other party who were going with us tell me they have had the same experience and I know mother was awake at half past three. If the family had taken my advice, they never would have attempted the early train. It is against all my principles and I know by experience that it upsets everybody's equilibrium for the whole day. I expect some vigorous contradictions from you about this but such has been my experience.*
> [1892-06-28 Bertha (The Ark, Jaffrey) to Henry (StL)]

Henry had his own ideas about the *"extremely convenient hour of six"* in the morning.

> *I had an idea that your party would take the most convenient train that left Jaffrey so your information about the selection of the early morning train neither greatly shocked nor surprised me. I am too well advised of your "system" in travelling to be greatly surprised at your varying from the usual rules that govern most people to the slight extent of starting out at the extremely convenient hour of six. I was thoroughly surprised at your permitting a thunderstorm to detain you. Why did you not take the night train down? It's true you might have landed in Boston at midnight but you would not have minded that. Ah, I see, there was no night train or you would have taken it, surely!*
> [1892-07-01 Henry (StL) to Bertha (Farragut House, Rye Beach)]

As Bertha's next letter revealed, she did not find Henry's comments about her *"system of travel"* at all amusing.

> *I did not think you were a bit funny in your remarks about our system of travel, not a bit! And you were most unjust as well. We usually travel in the most comfortable way. You were very playful about our going to Jaffrey so early and it was perfectly beautiful. As for starting on that early train, I am constitutionally opposed to that kind of thing but a great many people would have thought it very sensible as we should have arrived in Boston before two o'clock and had the whole day there.*
> [1892-07-05 Bertha (Rye Beach) to Henry (StL)]

Notwithstanding Henry and Bertha's generally negative views on train travel, Henry sometimes expressed his enjoyment of traveling with his companions and with the beauty of the scenery.

> *The homeward journey was not entirely uninteresting, although the heat today was at times excessive. But the Judge [Madill] was in one of his most attractive humors and the country was simply beautiful. We came in over the "Frisco" which, you know, runs through the hilly portion of this state and Kansas and which is at all times well worth seeing, but now the Ozarks are simply beautiful. You remember this is the route to Lebanon and Eureka and the road seems to be built on the back bone of the chief mountain range for one can see out of the car windows the whole*

surrounding country as far as the eye – but, dearest, I did not intend to afflict you with a description of Missouri scenery.
[20170828-4 (1892-08(-) (Tuesday) Henry to Bertha]

Similarly, Henry wrote in 1900 of the beautiful country through which his train was passing.
Yes, the rain has laid the dust and my seat in the parlor car of the Express on the shady side is a very easy and comfy one and the country we are racing by is more beautiful than Rye. No heat, brilliant sunshine and good country to look at and, better than all, a cry from the end of the car "dinner in the dining car."
[1900-08-15 Henry (Philadelphia) to Bertha (co Henry Leffingwell, Dublin NH)]

Periodically, Henry traveled in high style. Around 1900, perhaps on his friend Howard Elliott's car, Henry traveled on a Pennsylvania Limited, Pullman Vestibuled Train.

[Image of a Pullman Luxury Car, circa 1900]
I am not quite sure I am not still at the Waldorf for, apart from the train motion, one would not know this equipment from that of the chief of Gotham's hotels. I am travelling in state indeed and what with its compartment cars, electric lights, bathrooms, barber shop. Library, smoking room, café, dining car, valets, maids and bell boys, I haven't enough imagination to differentiate between this and any other first class hotel for it is all strictly first class down to the free stenographer who is not permitted to accept pay for his services.
[20180328-2 (1900-) Henry to Bertha]

Not unlike travel in any era, luggage was sometimes misplaced which could be a major inconvenience. Such was the case during Henry's trip to New York in 1894. He arrived with "*not even a clean change of underwear or an extra shirt!*"
After many delays, I have finally arrived. We reached Toledo four hours late and, as our connecting train did not wait for us, I prepared for an all-day siege in Toledo yesterday and did not count upon getting here until this evening. I found later that a special ran out of Toledo at two fifty yesterday which reached N.Y. at ten thirty this A.M. so, although I could not bring my baggage with me, I took this train and arrived on time, sans clothes of any kind, not even a clean change of underwear or an extra shirt! My trunk will arrive at five this afternoon and until it does, I shall stay in camp. I need hardly explain my reticence in going out. You have no doubt seen men's shirts after a railway journey has given them attention and can understand why I do not make haste to look up my friends. Not that I have not been often in a more disreputable plight for the journey east was

the least dusty and disagreeable, apart from the delay, that I have ever taken and I enjoyed the trip very much. But a shirt two days old is not an article which men as a rule are proud of and so I am waiting to be re-enforced before I make an attack upon the people I came to see.
[1894-09-17 Henry (New York) to Bertha (3337 Washington Ave, Stl)]

Bertha was sympathetic about Henry's shirt. However, whether Henry would be able to meet her in New York City, Bertha wrote: *"don't for an instant flatter yourself that I shall miss you…"*

I received your first letter this morning and I almost wept when I thought of your pathetic condition in New York and minus a clean shirt. Do go up and stay a couple of days with Mr. Tutt and rest yourself. I know your business can spare you a couple of days and don't for an instant flatter yourself that I shall miss you. I am having a beautiful time. I am going with my brother-in-law [Sam Scott] tonight to see the "Amazons" and I dine at your mother's frequently and my son takes breakfast with me.

…

Goodbye, my sweetheart and don't hurry home.
[1894-09-19 Bertha (StL) to Henry (Hotel Buckingham, NYC)]

Henry often communicated to Bertha about any transportation arrangements that he made for Bertha and arranging the sleeper car was *"de rigueur"*.

I engaged drawing room and a section and a half next to it for the morning of Sept. 27th (Wednesday). I enclose also folder showing the train (no. 7). You will if you go via New York take the Tuesday boat (26th) and try to be at the Cortlandt St. Ferry by 9:30 as this will give you ample time to pay for your sleeper which will be reserved for you until the train leaves. If you decide to go by Boston, let me know so I may cancel the sleeper reservation. It will be best for you to get your Rye tickets in Newport, via Pa Ry – 10 o'clock train – to enable you to ck your trunks through to St. Louis. If you decide to go by Boston, you must reserve your sleeper at once. I am inclined to favor the NY route as you reach St. Louis at 1:48 the next day, your arrangements for sleeper are already made and the route is more familiar. Then you are a little more than a day and night enroute & you can get your lunch at home the day of arrival.
[1899-09-13 Henry (NYC) to Bertha]

3. MEETING STRANGERS ON THE TRAIN

Since Henry was constantly traveling by train, it was not surprising that he met various fellow train travelers. The following train trip was remarkable since Henry decided to travel on an immigrant train and took great interest in the immigrants who were passengers with him. These immigrants were moving from Mississippi to Southern Texas to start a new life. *"The hard lives they had been leading had left its marks in the faces of these people…"* As Henry explained to Bertha, *"it was very good for me to know how selfish a man can become who does not sometimes see and know, as I have just done, the struggles and sorrows in the lives of others…"*

I have been on a most interesting excursion today. I had to go down to Gatesville about sixty miles south of Waco and, as I had the choice between remaining away until tomorrow and going on an immigrant train, I decided to go with the three car loads of Texas' newest citizens and, apart from the business part of my trip, I am very glad I had the day's experience. Hamlin Garland could have written a sketch of those unfortunates that would have enlisted as much interest as his "Jason Edwards".

I talked with two or three of the men and learned the history of the whole party. They came from northern Mississippi having been literally starved out by two years crop failure there and were on their way to southern Texas to occupy on lease the farms which the state is offering at nominal rentals to those who will occupy the land and cultivate the soil for a period of years. The hard lives they had been leading had left its marks in the faces of these people so plainly that not much knowledge of their history was required to convince all of their struggle with the world. The men were grim and sullen looking, some of them with that dazed helpless look in their eyes which often comes with defeat. And the women and even the little children looked so tired that I felt like asking them why they did not try to rest some on their journey.

You will wonder perhaps why I was glad of the chance I had to see the hardships of these people, dear. It was because I think some of those poor fellows were cheered considerably by what I told them of the country which they were to make their homes in. I know the country they are going to very well and realized what a contrast there was between its productiveness and that of those worn out lands in Mississippi and how happy these people would be when they found they had not been deceived by those who had induced them to come here. But the chief cause of my gratification in this experience is that it was very good for me to know how selfish a man can become who does not sometimes see and know, as I have just done, the struggles and sorrows in the lives of others who seem to have the hard side of life turned their way all the time. And beside its lesson of greater patience in my small vexations, it made me pretty anxious, dear, to do enough with my own life to be of some help to others and it is a great joy to me to know what a helper I shall have in my darling, in any good that I may ever be able to do.
[1892-12-17 (Saturday) Henry (Waco) to Bertha (Stancote, Newton Centre)]

Bertha's response to Henry's letter was also touching: *"I was very much interested too in your account of those poor emigrants. What terribly hard lives some people have. It does make one ashamed."* [1892-12-23 (Friday) Bertha (Newton Centre) to Henry (StL)]

Whether ladies should travel by train without an escort was a matter of concern to Henry. Probably in response to such a suggestion by Henry, Bertha responded that there was no reason for women not to travel *"over the whole continent"*. Bertha then proceeded to relate her story on the train.
Why a girl should not travel over the whole continent alone, I fail to see. There was another sole female travelling in the compartment next to me and we fraternized. I offered her some of my candy which forms the same bond as a man's offering another a cigar, you know.
[1892-10-26 (Wednesday) Bertha (Boston, MA) to Henry (StL)]

On a train to Waco in 1909, Henry showed his compassion for a *"stranger"* on the train who appeared lost and in great need of help. Henry movingly recounted the stranger's story.
I had an experience on the train coming down. At Hillsboro I saw an old man nervously enquiring about the train for Waco. He seemed distressed and unable to take care of himself so I spoke to him and told him I was on the Waco train and would direct him to it. He seemed very grateful but, as it was apparent he had other troubles than his timidity and ignorance of travelling, I went over to his seat and tried to divert him with small talk. He listened patiently for a while and then broke in: "Stranger I am in great trouble, the greatest of my life. I have a telegram that my thirty-five-year-old boy died in Waco today. I don't mean to bother people, stranger, but I am an old man and I don't see how I can stand the loss of my boy." I never have felt such sorrow for a stranger and I sat and talked with the poor old man until another passenger relieved me.
[1909-10-21 Henry (Hotel Metropole, Waco) to Bertha (64 Vandeventer Place, Stl)]

4. A TRAIN ACCIDENT IN 1902

On November 18, 1902, Henry was traveling from Houston to Beaumont Texas on an "Accommodation" train[265]. Henry described the harrowing experience of this train wreck but concluded his letter *"I am tired but likewise very thankful tonight..."*

---

[265] Accommodation Train: a train that stops at all or nearly all stations: a local train [Websters Dictionary]

Hotel Sabine
Port Arthur, Texas
Tuesday Evg 1902

My dearest,
I have had an experience today which will not be repeated in my future experiences, if I have
anything to do with the choosing. I left Waco last night and reached Houston this morning, too
late to take the regular train out to Beaumont. So about eight o'clock, I boarded an accommodation
and continued on the journey to Beaumont, about eighty miles distant, where I was to spend the
day. I was in a chair car which was the fourth car behind the locomotive, the other cars being a
mail car, baggage car and chair car, like ours.

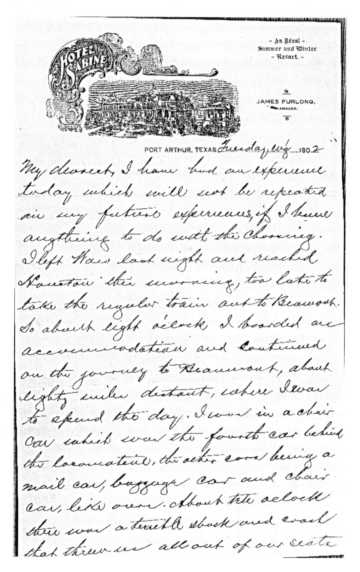

About ten o'clock, there was a terrible shock and crash that threw us all out of our seats, then a
second lunge forward and crash and a terrific explosion and, immediately after the explosion,
another plunge that broke up the chairs of the car as though they had been card board. I was
sitting on the inside seat. My companion in the seat next the window at the third plunge, seemed
to fly over the seat in front then shot back and was crumpled down in his seat. I remember he
looked as though a suit of clothes had been thrown over the back of the seat. I had been talking to

him just the moment before. I reached over and shook him and was relieved to see him look up at me. I told him he must get up & get out if he could and he then said he was not hurt much and thought he could climb through the window if one was open.

By that time, the car was on fire and had come to a stop, was so filled with smoke that, although I felt no heat, I had a mighty unpleasant premonition that I was going to boiled. I kicked out the glass of our window and a train gang knocked out the glass of several others. The doors, both of them, were so jammed they couldn't be opened so I partly dived and partly fell out of ours and landed just in front of the locomotive which was laying over on its side about five feet from our car, it having been three cars away before the accident, so you may imagine it was ... no small jinks to get that far back.

Well, when I got out, I looked back to see how my companions had fared. I saw a sight. The broken windows had cleared the car of steam & smoke so I could see and I think half of the people were still in the car with the locomotive near enough to be mighty dangerous company. I saw a young woman with a baby leaving from one window and I went to help her but before I go to her, a man caught hold of her and pulled her and the baby together out. I am ashamed to say I think the sight of that hissing engine made me slower to return and help than I would have done otherwise. Well, all the people got out and no one was harmed although the car was burning like a frame dwelling. The people in our car were none of them badly hurt, the little baby was slightly but not badly bruised, the man in the seat with me had his hands very badly cut and some of the others had ugly scrapes and cuts and bruises but not a single serious injury.

In the other car ahead there were one or two more serious injuries but none, I think, were dangerous. The engineer, poor fellow, was dreadfully hurt and I don't think there is much chance for him. I escaped without a scratch. I had on my gloves so I didn't even get any glass in... I can't get over the almost miraculous escape of all those people. The cars looked as if the seats had been broken up for kindling and I think the recent rains which have made a veritable marsh of this flat country so softened the ground that the impact was greatly reduced. Well, it is over and I got to Beaumont finally and safely, but it seems a long time since this morning.

I sent your father a telegram for we were promptly visited by a swarm of reporters taking the names of passengers and, as there were one or two Fort Worth and Waco acquaintance's aboard, I thought best to forestall the result of the appearance in any of the St. Louis papers of copies of the exaggerated and utterly unreliable messages which were being sent out to the Texas press. If I had known we would get through tonight, I would not have telegraphed until tomorrow. I sent you another dispatch tonight saying I would be home Saturday morning. I got four letters here tonight, dear, and I am more obliged to you than I can say. I am too tired to answer them tonight and as my letter tomorrow will not reach you until I do, I will answer them then.

I am tired but likewise very thankful tonight, my dearest.
Yours always,
Henry [1902-11-18(-) 20171210-1 Henry to Bertha]

Bertha wrote in her diary about this train wreck and she concluded with thanks, *"I humbly thank God for his great mercy to me."*
Nov. 18, 1902
Have lunch for sewing club. Afterward, receive telegram from Henry that he is safe but train wrecked. A few days later, receive letter containing description of his frightful experience. Engine exploded, train wrecked, car on fire, both doors jammed, escape through window. He himself

entirely unhurt but many injured, engineer dies later of his injuries. How terribly near sorrow can come to us. I humbly thank God for his great mercy to me.
[1893 Diary]

The Houston Post included a lengthy article about this wreck in the November 19, 1902 edition and the details were scary. But the most poignant part of the article were the last words spoken by the engineer, Joe Burts, who was trapped under the train engine and died of his injuries at the scene shortly after the wreck. (The reprinted article was difficult to read and best efforts have been made to record the words correctly here.)

ENGINEER BURTS' LAST WORDS
When ... 10 passed here it was running fifty miles an hour in order to make up time and when it struck the west .. Devers, as small station in the ... Pacific five miles west of here, it was derailed and turned over as ... the two cars following it, while the ... was torn into kindling wood and ... cars left the track.
It was a very pathetic scene when Engineer Joe Burts came to himself. He called for the conductor and Conductor McMahan went to him and as he gazed upon him, tears in his eyes, said: "what can I do for you, Joe?"
... said Mr. Burts, "I have been a soldier and fought in most of the battles in the Confederate army; where did they ..., I didn't run, did I? I was at my post, wasn't I?"
Conductor McMahan answered, "No, Joe, you didn't run; you were at your post."
"I have run this thing for thirty-five years," the dying man said, and he reached down in his pocket and drew the old morocco wallet that held his time card and handed it to the conductor saying: "Take this: I don't need it anymore."
The Conductor protested and Mr. Burts told him to keep it. "I am done for."
[The Houston Post, November 19, 1902, page 9]

5. AUTOMOBILES
During the early part of the 20th century, automobiles were being manufactured and were clearly the latest "thing" to own.

Jack Davis took dinner with Shepley & me and then brought us home in Dwight's automobile. My! How them things do travel!! Twenty minutes from the club to our house. I am covered with dust but I suppose the trip in was pleasant. I think I prefer the cars[266].
[20180326-2 (1905-) Henry to Bertha]

"My! How them things do travel!!"

B. NATURAL DISASTERS
1. THE 1892 ST. LOUIS TYPHOID FEVER OUTBREAK
Throughout the 19th and early 20th century, typhoid fever was a disease that periodically swept through communities around the U.S. Such was the case for St. Louis in 1892. Two and one-half months before their wedding date, Bertha was sufficiently concerned about the St. Louis outbreak to write a cautionary letter to Henry.

I saw by the paper that the typhoid fever was epidemic in St. Louis. Now, won't you please, please, please take care of yourself and don't be foolish and work too hard and over tire yourself – please.
[1892-11-27 (Sunday) Bertha (Boston) to Henry (StL)]

---

[266] Train cars.

AVOID THE GRIP of the TYPHOID HAND

CAPT. C. A. BALLOU

Henry wrote back to Bertha that Walter McKittrick, Hugh McKittrick Sr's son, who was 19 years old at this time, was critically ill from the disease. (Walter survived and lived until age 92.)

I have just returned from Mr. McKittrick's. I went over to see Will and was very sorry to find Walter, who has had typhoid, had had a relapse and was now in almost a critical condition. Mr. McKittrick seemed exceeding anxious and Will seemed to think that the strain on Mrs. McKittrick would probably make her ill. He said she had been in bed for two days which, I imagine, means that she is utterly worn out, for I think she would never have left Walter to the nurse for two days if she had been able to get about at all.

The cases of fever are less numerous but those who are ill now seem to be more dangerously stricken than even those who were attacked when there were many more cases. Miss Reber's brother has had a relapse and I am very much afraid there is no hope of his recovery. Dr. Mudd thinks he will hardly live through the night.

I did not mean to fill up my letter with only sad news, dearest. I thought though you would like to know about the ill ones in the homes of your friends and I hope I have said nothing to alarm you about the healthfulness of the town generally, for I can very positively tell you that there is much less sickness than there has been.

[1892-12-10 (Thursday) Henry (StL) to Bertha (Hotel Brunswick, Boston)]

2. THE MAY 1896 CYCLONE

Tornadoes were not uncommon in the Midwest and St. Louis had its share. But the May 27, 1896 St. Louis tornado or cyclone, as it was often called then, was historically monumental.

The 1896 St. Louis–East St. Louis tornado was an historic tornado that caused severe damage to downtown St. Louis, Missouri, East St. Louis, Illinois, and surrounding areas on Wednesday, May 27, 1896. One of the deadliest and most destructive tornadoes in U.S. history, this tornado was the most notable of a major tornado outbreak across the central United States which produced several other large, long-track, violent tornadoes and continued across the eastern United States the following day. The St. Louis tornado killed at least 255 people, injured over a thousand others, and caused more than $10 million in damage (equivalent to $307 million in 2019). More than 5,000 people were left homeless and lost all of their possessions. The hardest-hit areas of the city were the fashionable Lafayette Square and Compton Heights neighborhoods, as well as the poorer Mill Creek Valley. It remains the third-deadliest tornado in United States history.

The tornado struck this intersection in Soulard with particular force, causing many deaths at this location. A large crowd gathered at the site of Mauchenheimer's saloon, whose address had been 1300 South 7th Street. Across the street, Klute's Grocery, at 1305 South 7th, still stood. In the distance, the damaged church of St. Vincent de Paul, at Park Avenue and 9th Street, can be seen. [Wikipedia]

While a storm had been predicted for the latter days in May, many disregarded the warning or felt that the city of St. Louis would not be affected. Weather forecasters at the time lacked technology sufficient to predict tornadoes (then commonly called "cyclones") of this magnitude, but they were able to predict strong storm systems in general. The day started quietly, with people going about their daily business; the weather in the morning did not indicate any severe weather event. The local weather bureau predicted thunderstorms but nothing more serious. Around noon, the clouds began to appear more ominous and the barometric pressure dropped, alarming those who knew this was an indication of a tornado. Into the afternoon, the skies continued to darken, but the Weather Bureau Observatory was not overly concerned. Many residents, however, fled to their homes, anticipating severe weather. At 4:30 P.M. local time, the temperature dropped rapidly and black and greenish clouds approached the city; near 5:00 P.M., the sky reportedly became as dark as midnight. As the thunderstorm approached St. Louis, the western portion of the city was particularly affected. Winds were initially around 37 miles per hour (60 km/h), but they quickly increased to almost 80 miles per hour (130 km/h).
[Wikipedia]

From her home in St. Louis, Bertha described this event in her diary.
May 27, 1896
The cyclone. Take lunch at Janet's. The Knoxes, Nagels and ourselves had planned to take supper together at Koerner's, but such a heavy storm comes up, that we cannot go. At five o'clock, it is so dark and Nancy[267] is so frightened by the thunder that I draw down the blinds and light the gas. The gas goes out. In the street, the water reaches from our steps to the steps opposite, the pavement is entirely submerged. In a lull in the storm, Henry gets home and shortly afterward Madge Adams calls from her window to mine to know if I can telephone for a plumber for her, her cellar is flooded.

---

[267] Anne Warburton Scott – "Nancy" – who was 10 months old.

Discover our own to be in the same condition. Try to telephone. It won't work. We do not know until afterward that the power has all been turned off by order of the city. Henry goes to her assistance. He has brought home horrible tales of chimneys flying, roofs being torn off, etc. In his own office, the awning iron tore away and crashed through the window, the building shook, the floor looked as if it was parting under his feet and, in the height of the confusion, his type writer fainted away. At eleven o'clock, we hear an extra called, which we buy, but we have really no idea of the horror of it all until the next day.

May 28, 1896
Henry comes home at noon. There is no business doing and, after going to five stables in search of a carriage, we finally secure one and go over to the south side. What masses of ruin! We pass poles blown down, wires hanging in masses, then roofs of houses. Finally we come to where block after block of houses has been blown down, churches, schools, powerhouses, warehouses, masses of ruin, the streets in many places impassable. I hope and pray I may never see such a sight again. The worst are the blocks of little homes in German quarter with the broken-hearted looking women and men. The worst ruin is in the quarter around Lafayette Park. The park itself is absolutely laid waste. Nan Nagel's house opposite, in which I am specially interested, is unroofed and the west wall torn off.
[1893 Diary]

Two days later as Bertha wrote in her diary, the St. Louis Community started a collection for the people who were ravaged by this storm. Bertha assisted at a distributing station in the German section where her knowledge of German proved very useful.

May 29, 1896
Mrs. Tuttle comes to ask me to collect clothes and bedding for the tornado sufferers. Collect quantities. People give very liberally.

May 30, 1896
The Lanes and I drive down with what we have collected to St. Stephen's mission and to the police headquarters.

June 4, 1896
Stay all day at one of the distributing stations on Lafayette Ave where they give out clothes and bedding to the people who come. I find my German most useful – many can speak no English at all, many are Bohemian & speak through German interpreters. Nan Broadhead, Edith January, Josephine Poe, Myra, Emma and Josephine Lane, and Nan Broadhead are there also.
[1893 Diary]

C. POLITICS
1. THE 1892 ELECTION
As a Virginia native, Henry grew up as a southern Democrat. Therefore, presidential candidates, such as Democrat Grover Cleveland, were the type that he generally supported. In the following letter, Henry wrote of being in New York City with Gist Blair (who would be his best man in less than a year) and meeting Cleveland who won the presidency in that 1892 election.

I found Blair here and this morning I was inveigled into accepting an invitation we received from one of the prominent politicians of the west to call on Mr. Cleveland. One of the conclusions I reached after our visit you will not, I think, be glad to know. It is perfectly clear that Cleveland wishes the Democratic nomination and is permitting his friends to move actively in his interests, aiding them from time to time with his advice and, if his public utterances are in effect that the office "should neither be sought nor declined", he is much less dignified with his immediate

political following for not a word was said about the presidential preferences of different public men in the west that he did not treat the information as favorable to or unpromising to Democratic success in November and it was easy to draw the conclusion that the Democrats, with him, would win and without him would sustain defeat. Apart from this, he impressed me greatly. He had none of the affectations of the ordinary type of public men and his rough, weather beaten and careworn face was a very attractive one to me.
[20180421-1 (1892-03--) Henry (NYC) to Bertha]

The Silver Bill and "The Free Silver Movement" was an important topic during the 1890's. The Silver Bill was opposed by the Democrats and Henry who saw it as a *"most dishonest measure"*. Bertha was very interested in politics and didn't particularly appreciate Henry's letter regarding the Silver Bill that *"money is always a rather a difficult thing for a woman to understand."*

I am glad you like to have me take an interest in things political but very indignant that you should think I did not appreciate the danger of the silver bill. It was the object of my father's most intense hatred & I might say dread and he lost no opportunity of holding forth on the subject. I believe I understand it tolerably clearly though money is always a rather a difficult thing for a woman to understand. Now, don't take the opportunity to make a silly joke about that. I see perfectly the interpretation it is open to. [1892-04-04 Bertha (Port Comfort, VA) to Henry (Leland Hotel, NYC)]

Henry was pleased with Bertha's interest in politics and took the opportunity to send Bertha some Democrat propaganda to the Republican Drakes, all the while maintaining the view that *"women seldom extend their interest in politics to questions of strict finance."*

Oh, I am so glad to hear you are taking interest in political matters. Do you ever see the "Nation"? May I not send it to you while you are away? I think you told me once you took this paper but I am not sure. At any rate if you think a Democratic paper will not create too much excitement in your family, I would like to send it to you for one of the these days I want to take an humble part in some of the work which men ought to give some part of their time and attention to if they really wish to redeem government from the burdens put upon it by those who seek political prominence for "revenue only". And, as I try even now with the other things I have to do that sometimes are pretty taxing, not to let the movements in the political world escape me entirely and, as the subject greatly interests me, I am glad I shall be able to talk it over with you and not bore you. What is it you don't take interest in, child? I don't know, I'm sure.

You did not say why you were rejoiced over the quietus put upon the silver bill. I am a little afraid your pleasure came more from the fact that its disappearance from view meant improved prospects for the Democrats at the next election through a restored unity of interest in questions before the party rather than because the wildest and most dishonest measure that has been presented to the consideration of the Congress in a long time has happily disappeared from view, at least for the present. Or were you conscious of the harm in the bill itself? I imagine not, for women seldom extend their interest in politics to questions of strict finance.
[1892-03-28-3 (6 letters) Henry to Bertha]

In 1892, President Harrison was running for reelection. Notwithstanding that Harrison was a Republican and Henry was still a Democrat, Henry voiced his sympathy for the poor treatment of Harrison by his own party.

You ask me why Blaine resigned Ahem's (?) – that's easily enough answered – because he wanted to! Dare say I have no clear political opinions!! Seriously though, I am completely puzzled and I am only sure of one thing – that is Blaine does not wish and will not accept the nomination but is permitting his friends to use his name for the time being to defeat Harrison, a most unmanly and

contemptible proceeding. Little as I respect Harrison, I can't help sympathizing with him, for I don't think he is being fought fairly.
[1892-06-09 (Thursday) Henry (StL) to Bertha (The Ark)]

The 1892 election seemed to attract great interest and fueled in heated debates. Henry wrote of a *"veritable "scrap"* with Alfie Kennett, describing himself in the affair as having a *"truly yielding disposition"???* (A truly yielding disposition was not a characteristic generally ascribed to Henry.)

Alfie Kennett is one of the congenial spirits at the Club these days, and very good company he is. I became entangled with him on political questions yesterday and a veritable "scrap" was the result. He is a delightful fellow but mighty tenacious of his opinions and despite my truly yielding disposition, it was hard for me at times not to become provoked at his obstinacy. Politics are verily in the air these days - at the clubs, downtown, at the bank – everywhere. I won my first bet on Cleveland's nomination from a fool who could not understand that a man can express an opinion without sustaining it by wager and who forced me to let on what I told him was a certainty. And I think I shall have to stay away from the Club until after November or buy a record book and go regularly into the business as some of the men are doing. Or else, go there and listen and hold my tongue which you and I both know is impossible.
[1892-06-25 (Monday) Henry (StL) to Bertha (Farragut House, Rye Beach)]

Bertha wrote back about Alfie Kennett who was apparently a skilled and knowledgeable debater.

Your account of your argument with Mr. A. L. Kennett was very vivid. You see, I have heard you both argue and I know perfectly well which one argues with a cool ease that is enchanting and which one argues as if he wanted to knock his opponent down. As an arguer, to quote an expression you once used to me, Mr. Kennett can give almost any man I ever heard "cards and spades" and finish him up[268]. He is a mighty dangerous opponent for he never overlooks a point and he is pretty well up on his authorities. I may as well confess to you that when Alfred Kennett takes one side of a question, I generally assume at once that it is the best side and I would like to know what the question was you and he fought over.
[1892-07-01 (Friday) Bertha (Rye Beach) to Henry (StL)]

Henry was actively supporting Cleveland in the 1892 election[269] and was encouraged by the support given to Cleveland by the Republican Mugwumps[270].

I am really posted today on the news of the present time for, beside my family, I have had the kind offices of Gist and Joh Downing who came in to see me and whom I promptly pressed into service. The Cleveland canvass is progressing very satisfactorily. Whitney[271] is a clear-headed fellow and

---

[268] A liberal handicap: "I could give him cards and spades and still beat him at his own game."

[269] The United States presidential election of 1892 witnessed a re-match of the closely contested presidential election in 1888. In 1888, Cleveland won the popular vote over Harrison, but lost in the electoral college. In a re-match, Cleveland won both the popular and electoral vote, thus becoming the first and to date only person in American history to be elected to a second, non-consecutive presidential term. The 1892 campaign centered mainly on economic issues, especially the concept of a sound currency. Cleveland was a proponent of the gold standard, while the Republicans and Populists both supported bimetalism. Cleveland also ran on a platform of lowering tariffs (the Republicans were strongly protectionist) and opposed the Republicans' 1890 voting rights proposal. [Wikipedia]

[270] The Mugwumps were Republican political activists who bolted from the United States Republican Party by supporting Democratic candidate Grover Cleveland in the United States presidential election of 1884. They switched parties because they rejected the financial corruption associated with Republican candidate James G. Blaine. In a close election, the Mugwumps supposedly made the difference in New York state and swung the election to Cleveland. The jocular word *mugwump*, noted as early as 1832, is from Algonquian (Natick) *mugquomp*, "important person, kingpin" (from *mugumquomp*, "war leader"), implying that they were "sanctimonious" or "holier-than-thou," in holding themselves aloof from party politics. [Wikipedia]

[271] William Collins Whitney (July 5, 1841 – February 2, 1904) served as Secretary of the Navy in the first administration of President Grover Cleveland from 1885 through 1889. A conservative reformer, he was considered a Bourbon Democrat. In

is not likely to make many mistakes. Besides, he is a gentleman and he will not permit the use of the clap trap "machine" work which would be introduced in the campaign if the canvas were managed by any one of the stricter party leaders. I think the Mugwump element will show a much greater strength than in the '84 campaign for if there was good reason for their support of Cleveland then, the same argument is strengthened and made clearer now. The effect of class legislation upon the country, generally, cannot be defended as beneficial and the wasteful use of public money in the support of an army of worthless hangers-on can only be explained in the fact that voters are secured to the party which legislates in their interest. We think out here that the businessmen will as a rule support the Democratic ticket because of Harrison's support of the '91 silver bill and because of his encouragement of the wasteful use of the treasury's reserve whereby the ability of the government to redeem its obligations in gold has been seriously questioned.
[1892-07-04(-) 20170828-5 Henry to Bertha]

2. THE 1896 REPUBLICAN NATIONAL CONVENTION IN ST. LOUIS

As she wrote in her diary, Bertha was in attendance for the 1896 Republican National Convention in which William McKinley was nominated by the Republican Party and was part of the *"eighteen thousand people in the hall"* who sang *"that great battle hymn"*, *"Marching through Georgia"*.

June 19, 1896

Have splendid seats at the Convention for the second session which is supposed to be the exciting one – and very poor seats for the first one. The first session lasts all day, the delegates not going out to dinner. Nevertheless by standing on one foot and leaning way forward are able to hear parts of the speeches – nearly all of Chauncey M. Depew's[272] speech nominating Platt, which was very good. After much speaking and much voting, McKinley is declared nominated for President of the United States. The banner bearing his picture is hoisted into place. The cannon boom, the bands begin to play and the eighteen thousand people in the hall sing "Marching through Georgia"[273].

---

opposition to Tammany, Whitney was instrumental in bringing about the third nomination of Cleveland in 1892, and took an influential part in the ensuing presidential campaign. [Wikipedia]

[272] Chauncey Depew was considered for McKinley's Vice President and received 3 votes.

[273] "Marching Through Georgia"

by Henry Clay Work

> Ring the good ol' bugle, boys, we'll sing another song,
>   Sing it with the spirit that will start the world along,
> Sing it as we used to sing it 50,000 strong
>   While we were marching through Georgia.
>
> **CHORUS:** Hurrah, hurrah, we bring the jubilee!
>   Hurrah, hurrah, the flag that makes you free!
> So we sang the chorus from Atlanta to the sea
>   While we were marching through Georgia!
>
> How the darkies shouted when they heard the joyful sound!
>   How the turkeys gobbled which our commissary found!
> How the sweet potatoes even started from the ground
>   While we were marching through Georgia!--**CHORUS**
>
> Yes, and there were Union men who wept with joyful tears
>   When they saw the honored flag they had not seen for years.
> Hardly could they be restrained from breaking forth in cheers
>   While we were marching through Georgia!--**CHORUS**
>
> "Sherman's dashing Yankee boys will never reach the coast!"
>   So the saucy rebels said, and 'twas a handsome boast,
> Had they not forgot, alas, to reckon with the host
>   While we were marching through Georgia!--**CHORUS**

That is another experience to look back to. For when I finished, with that enormous throng of people singing that great battle hymn, I was trembling all over and then tears streaming down my cheeks. We go to our good seats and hear Garrett A Hobart of New Jersey nominated for Vice President, but it is tame and flat after all that has passed before. [1893 Diary]

The selection of the song, "Marching Through Georgia", to be sung at the 1896 Republican Convention pretty clearly indicated that McKinley and the Republican Party did not expect to win any southern state (and didn't). McKinley's opponent, William Jennings Brian, won the entire south and all the western states, except CA and OR which were won by McKinley. McKinley also won the virtually the entire Midwest and all of the northeast, virtually the reverse of what Democrats and Republicans win today.

3. THE WILLIAM JENNINGS BRYAN ERA

By 1896, Henry started to change his opinion of the Democrat party, perhaps due to the importance of his business interests and the protection of property which were generally Republican values. Hence, in the 1896 election between Bryan and McKinley, Henry voiced his support for McKinley.

> *I am amused to see your admiration of Bryan. I don't agree with you and I think the country would go to ---- if that idiot were elected. The Republicans, with all their schemes for making money out of the government, are far preferable for they at least believe in the protection of property.*
> [20171117-2 (1896 summer-) Henry (StL) to Bertha (Jamestown)]

William Jennings Bryan [Wikipedia]

Similarly, while he believed in National Unity, Henry became increasingly aware of how southern Democrat states felt about national holidays, such as the 4th of July, and he was not encouraged. While in Waco over the 4th of July in 1896, Henry described the celebration (or lack of one).

> *This town is illustrating the unreconstructed sentiments of Texas today. Not a flag flying from even the Government buildings. I have not heard the report of a single firecracker, there are no*

So we made a thoroughfare for freedom and her train,
  Sixty miles in latitude, 300 to the main.
Treason fled before us, for resistance was in vain
  While we were marching through Georgia!--**CHORUS**

fireworks offered for sale in the stores all of which are open as on any other day and there seems to be a tacit understanding to ignore the day. I spoke to the hotel man this morning about it and asked if Texans were averse to celebrating holidays. He replied "I should think not! This town is a perfect arsenal on Christmas." I am afraid I am becoming a very poor democrat these days. Don't be surprised if I someday claim allegiance to the State of Massachusetts.
[1896-07-04 Henry (Waco) to Bertha (Jamestown, RI)]

The 1904 Democratic National Convention was held in the Coliseum of the St. Louis Exposition and Music Hall from July 6-9, 1904. Not surprisingly, Henry found the time to attend.

I dissipated last night. I went to the Democratic convention and staid nearly all night! My, it was a sight! I had five seats and when fifteen thousand people began waving that many flags, I thought even the sane men present, and most of them were distinctly <u>not</u> sane, would go wild. I shall tell you about it all in my Sunday letter.
[1904-07-09 Henry (StL) to Bertha (Rye Beach)]

The next day, Henry was in attendance to hear William Jennings Bryan's "I Kept the Faith" speech. Henry described Bryan's speech: *"with tones like a bugle call"*.

You must really read the papers that describe the convention. The speeches, many of them were among the best I have ever heard and, really, Bryan's fight, humbug and blathers that he is, showed him to be a very brilliant and able debater. His voice is I think the best I have ever heard, perfectly clear and distinct and with tones like a bugle call.

I went down Friday night prepared to stay an hour and came home at four yesterday morning. The other men stayed until six! Of course, I was dead the next day but it really paid. I would give much if you had been here. One of the demonstrations, when the whole convention stood on chairs, waving flags, was a sight not to be forgotten.
[1904-07-10 Henry (StL) to Bertha]

4. POST BELLUM SOUTH

In 1892, Thomas Nelson Page published his essays entitled, *"The Old South"* which was a romanticized view of life in the Anti Bellum South. Henry and Bertha read this book as soon as it was published in 1892. (The author was already well known at this early point in his career). Henry wrote to Bertha about his views of the book.

As to the "Old South" [274], I dissented from Mr. Page's views almost throughout but I like the pictures he drew of the life in Virginia before the war and yes, I did like his discussion of the negro question very much and I entirely concur in his conclusions that the cotton states would be depopulated of whites if the negroes secured control of the state governments. I don't like the suppression of negro votes at all and I think I would solve the problem for myself by moving from a state where this practice was followed but I can't blame the people who are there and regard this as the only means of securing the quiet tenure of their property and the safety of their families.
[1892-07-28 (Thursday) Henry (StL) to Bertha (Farragut House, Rye Beach)]

In response to Henry's letter, Bertha wrote that she would have liked to *"have been alive then"* and added later, *"my sympathies have always been with the south..."*

I liked the "Old South" very much. I think if I had read it first, I should have sent it to you for I know just how it must have appealed to you. I read that picture of social life in Virginia before the war last night and it saddened me to think so beautiful a life should have passed out of existence as it has. I would like to have been alive then just to have known something of it and I know quite

[274] Thomas Nelson Page (April 23, 1853 – November 1, 1922) was a lawyer and American writer. Page's postbellum fiction, including *The Old South*, featured a nostalgic view of the South in step with what is termed "Lost Cause" ideology.

well that if I were one of the older generation of Southerners, I would never forgive the North. But then, my sympathies have always been with the south...
[1892-07-26 (Monday) Bertha (Rye Beach) to Henry (StL)]

5. A WOMAN'S ROLE
A "woman's role" in the 1890's was very different than today, as revealed in Bertha's letter (below).

> *I took tea with the Elliotts this evening, Miss Nan being their other guest and we had a very pleasant time. I would like for you to have heard some of the declarations of that strong-minded friend[275] of yours on the subject of woman's destiny. If you had fainted, I should not have been surprised. "Woman had no life of her own. She belonged to others, whether married or single. If married, her duty lay in pleasant places, but even if single, she could get some pleasure from those around her. Of course, to make her life most useful and happy, she ought to marry" etc, etc!*
[1893-01-23 (Sunday) Henry (StL) to Bertha (Stancote, Newton Centre)]

Bertha had warned Henry before they were married about her lack of knowledge of housekeeping (also, perhaps, lack of interest?). But, after 10 years of marriage, Bertha had assumed the role of keeping the house for the "*law and order*" Henry. In this, Bertha showed her "*disciplined Presbyterian side*" by putting the house in order upon returning from Rye Beach at the end of the summer of 1903.

> *On the whole, I believe I am glad you won't be at home. I have my whole domestic economy to arrange and I would rather get things into running order with you away and, Providence permitting, have you come back to a smooth, well ordered household. That is the well-disciplined Presbyterian side of me that wishes this. There is an undisciplined other side that has a vague feeling that, if I could see you on a desert island or worse still, in a kitchen, that other things would not count for much. But then I remember how dear is law and order to your own soul and I again feel glad that you will not be exposed to these trials and you must not miss my nice, smooth hair when I see you.*
[1903-09-28 (Saturday) Bertha (Rye, NH) to Henry (Waco)]

Although Bertha was clearly a very intelligent and strong-willed woman, she seemed to willingly accept the role that was given to her gender in those times. As she wrote in a letter to Henry in 1892, "*In the old days, a man captured his wife by main force and had the power of life and death over her. And the women were proud of it...*" [1902-07-19 Bertha (Rye Beach) to Henry (StL)] Bertha fully accepted and always showed pride in her role as Henry's wife.

6. DECORATION DAY (now Memorial Day)
Bertha wrote about seeing the Decoration Day parades while in Boston in 1892: "*They make a real memorial day of it here...*" This event in Boston reminded Bertha of when she was in Turin Italy on November 1, 1885, All Saints Day, and witnessed how the people strewed flowers on graves. (These details were not included in Bertha's 1885 Diary but she recalled them in this letter.)

> *Today has been Decoration Day and in consequence, every store has been closed and not even the mail delivered except once. The veterans passed here in procession this morning all carrying flowers. They make a real memorial day of it here. I wish they did at home – it seems to me sometimes as if we did not remember our dead enough. I never was so strongly impressed with that as once in Turin on All Saints Day the Cemeteries were thronged with all classes of people down to the peasants who came in from the country in costume and every one had flowers, some of the graves in the richest part of the cemetery had solid blankets of roses. One poor little place had nothing but a wreath of common white mosquito netting. I have always remembered that grave as one of the most pathetic things I ever saw. But I think it a beautiful custom.*
[1892-05-30(-) 20180308-1 Bertha (Backbay Boston) to Henry (StL)]

---

[275] i.e. Howard Elliott.

Henry responded to Bertha's admiration of Decoration Day in a philosophical way, first by admonishing the rebel South for making the day one of "*bitter memories*" and second by pointing out that it was no longer "*a very dignified tribute*" to the people who had actually served. Perhaps Henry felt some guilt for being one of the "*worthless people*" who never served in the military.

> *I am duly appreciative of the patriotic sentiments which Decoration Day aroused but I smiled at your attempt to make an impression on a Rebel whose people were the cause of this day being one of mourning and bitter memories. Seriously, though, I don't like the custom for it does not seem to me a very dignified tribute to the brave men who lost their lives in the country's service to make it a sort of parade day for all the worthless people in every community. The last men in the large cities whether rich or poor, are seldom found in the columns of these processions and they are usually filled up with the idle rabble who like the excitement and display.*
> [1892-06-04 Henry (StL) to Bertha]

7. THE 1900 ST. LOUIS STREETCAR STRIKE

[Wikipedia]

St. Louis had its share of labor unrest common to all major US cities around 1900 and the St. Louis Streetcar Strike of 1900 was a significant example.

> *The St. Louis streetcar strike of 1900 was a labor action, and resulting civil disruption, against the St. Louis Transit Company by a group of three thousand workers unionized by the Amalgamated Street Railway Employees of America. Between May 7 and the end of the strike in September, 14 people had been killed, and 200 wounded.* [Wikipedia]

A gathering of members of the citizens' posse that guarded the streetcars during the 1900 streetcar strike. Many of its members rode on the cars with their shotguns. [St. Louis Post Dispatch, May 8, 2020, "*A Bloody Street Car Strike …*"]

Bertha's diary contained several entries about the St. Louis Streetcar strike.

June 6, 1900 (St. Louis)
Arrive home. Children rapturous. Find people very anxious about the streetcar strike. It has continued four weeks now. Sheriff has called out his posse comitatus. Many men have done very funny things to avoid serving.

June 9, 1900
Henry comes home to take me to the Country Club and tells me he has volunteered under Major Cunningham in the posse. Secures many recruits at the Club.

June 10, 1900

… Riot in the afternoon, several men killed of the strikers.

June 11, 1900
Henry sworn in on the posse.

June 12, 1900
… Henry gets home 1:30 at night.

June 13, 1900

Am writing now, while waiting for him. He may be on guard all night tonight. I confess to feeling rather lonely, tho' Maggie and Preston were here to dinner.

June 25, 1900

As soon as Henry is released from posse duty in which he meets with no accident though much long and wearisome work, I go east.
[1893 Diary]

Henry was not shy about voicing his opinions on various business matters that affected St. Louis, including his view about the strike.

The town is in a state of disgust. The strike is on again. Alleged failure of the Transit Company to carry out its last agreement is the cause. I don't know how much truth there is in this but I haven't met a man who does not think it the height of stupidity for the streetcar company to permit another outbreak of the men.
[1900-07-10(-) Henry (StL) to Bertha]

"WELL, ANY WAY—WALKIN'S GOOD!"
Newspaper Cartoon – Streetcar strike [Wikipedia]

As Bertha wrote in her diary, Henry not only joined in the Posse Comitatus but enlisted additional volunteers from the Country Club. Henry was not a person to remain on the sidelines.

The Police Board swore in 2,500 citizens in a posse comitatus commanded by a local realty agent, John H. Cavender, who had played a similar paramilitary role in the bloody 1877 Saint Louis general strike."
[Wikipedia]

In assuming his duties on the posse, Henry was provided with a pistol to defend himself from the strikers. Henry kept this pistol loaded and close at hand for the remainder of his life.

D. RELIGION

Thorough her life, Bertha went to church nearly every Sunday and sometimes went two or three times, regardless of where she was, at home or on vacation. And Bertha was a very observant parishioner as revealed by her 1885 Diary account of going to St. Ignatius in NYC. Of the Church Rector: "Fine forehead, very weak mouth."

> *Go to St. Ignatius in the evening and hear a ritualistic Sermon and superb music. The scene in the chancel makes a really beautiful tableau. The clergyman has a fine forehead, very weak mouth and detestable delivery. Sermon chiefly remarkable for the glimpses of ritualism which it gave.*
> [1888-05 Diary, May 27, 1888]

Sometimes after a rousing discussion, Bertha would sometimes encapsulate her summary conclusions with a quotation. *"Pain surely makes one feel the need of prayer. "Lips cry 'God be pitiful' that ne'er said 'God be praised'."*[276] [1888-11 Diary, December 9, 1888]

After the announcement of Bertha and Henry's engagement, there was some kind-hearted banter about Bertha and Henry's different religions (Presbyterian and Episcopal). Henry wrote:

> *I met Ed Dameron for the first time since his return this evening and he insisted upon "celebrating" at the club, during which interesting performance, I learned that he had written you to send his blessing. He hopes you will not make a Presbyterian of me! And, by way of coincidency, advises the adoption of the Episcopal faith.*
> [1892-03-05(-) 20170828-3 Henry to Bertha]

While Bertha was in St. Augustine FL in 1892, traveling with her father and mother, she wrote the following unvarnished view of the three services that she attended on that Sunday.

> *I went to church three times yesterday. In the morning to the Presbyterian, in the afternoon, to the vesper service at the Roman Catholic where the music is very good, and in the evening to a little old Baptist Church down in darky town where we had a real old fashioned sermon from a colored brother with "Amens" thrown in by the congregation. The colored people are simply enchanting to me. I enjoyed that service and the singing there, much the best of any of the three.*
> [1892-03-14 Bertha (Hotel Ponce de Leon, St. Augustine FL) to Henry]

Bertha always seemed to be able to write what was on her mind. After reading George Eliot, Bertha wrote that Eliot's writing may be of more use in modern times than St. Paul's and she didn't mind if Henry lectured her about this.

> *I finished a sentence about George Eliot yesterday, very flatly, for I was seized with a fear in the middle that you would think me a very flippant young woman. Today, I think, I would rather be flippant than stupid. I was going to say that I thought some of her remarks were more use in our modern life and more to the point than a good many of St. Paul's. Now you can lecture on the*

---

[276] Quote from "The Cry of the Human" Elizabeth Barrett Browning, 1842.

impropriety of this remark if you choose. I shall continue to think so and I think I should enjoy a lecture.
[1892-07-01(-) 20170825-2 Bertha (East Jaffrey) to Henry (StL)]

Regarding a woman's role in the church, Bertha wrote *"St. Paul had real good sense when he advised the women to leave the managing of the church to the men."*

> *Daisy Jones is another of my best chums. A New York girl – tall, slender and the gentlest soul alive. I don't think Daisy is very clever, but she never would hurt anyone else's feelings and she cannot bear to have anyone else do it. And my last few days experience has made me feel that is the kind of woman the world needs. St. Paul had real good sense when he advised the women to leave the managing of the church to the men. I wonder if he had not learned that wisdom by bitter experience.*
[1892-08-03 (Wednesday) Bertha (Rye Beach) to Henry (StL)]

After Bertha and Henry moved into their "new" house at 3337 Washington Street, Bertha began to look for a pew to rent or sublet. *"I went down in the cars to church with Sister Leslie this morning and she invited me to sit in her pew not only for today but until I got a regular seat, if I so wished. Then Lute & I interviewed brother Gazzam on the subject of the Lindell pew and he promised to find out about it. Also, Nan Broadhead told me she was sure her family would sublet their pew and though not a very good one, it is better than the others we looked and not expensive."* [1893-04-18 Bertha (StL) to Henry (Ft. Worth)]

Bertha periodically worried about Henry's "soul" and whether Henry was attending to important matters of faith. *"That settles it. As soon as you come home, you begin going to church regularly, do you hear?"*
[1893-10-10 Monday Bertha (StL) to Henry (Waco)]

Henry maintained his own manner of observance which did not always include going to church on Sunday. In his papers, Henry kept the "Knight's Code" which provided the rules for the meetings of the K.H.C..

THE KNIGHT'S CODE

The Knight's Code (included with letters) – rules for K.H.C. meetings, etc
Motto of the K.H.C.
Live pure, speak true, right wrong, follow the Christ, else wherefore born?
> *(1) Meet every Saturday morning.*
> *(2) Always say the prayer together.*
> *(3) Elect President and Secretary on first Saturday of December, March, June and September.*
> *(4) Secretary to appoint one boy a week to write to F.H.S. /eLECT NEW*
> *(5) Elect new members by secret ballet, seven out of ten or eight out of twelve votes being necessary.*
> *(6) A member absent a whole month without excuse to be warned. Absent two months to be dropped.*
> *(7) Try to live up principles of K.H.C.*

I praise my God this day.
I give myself to God this day.
I ask God to keep me this day.

O dear Lord Jesus, who hast called us to follow Thee, grant by Thy help we may live pure, speak true and right wrong and ever continue loyal to Thee our Kind and our God. Amen

Bertha observed the passing of Bishop Brooks in January 1893 who was well known to the Drakes. Of his death, she wrote: *"it was just the time a man would choose to die and not have to face old age and the failure of all his powers."*

There are memorial services all over Boston today for Phillips Brookes: every denomination from Minot Savage, who represents the broadest Unitarianism to the narrowest old school Presbyterianism. The day of his funeral, from twelve to two, all the leading business houses, wholesale and retail, were closed and not by request. There was to have been a request made I believe but they found that spontaneously the houses had already resolved to do it. The stock exchange even was closed for an hour. Of course, there was no possibility of getting into Trinity church, the seats were all reserved, but I was sorry afterwards I did not go up to Copley Square.

BISHOP PHILLIPS BROOKS.

They said it was solidly packed with people and that the short service in the open air was most impressive. Bishop Potter simply recited the Lord's Prayer standing on the steps of the church and then copies of Luther's hymn, "A Mighty Fortress", had been distributed among the crowd and they sang it led by a cornet. The tributes of grief that came in from all sides were simply overwhelming: resolutions from working men's clubs, girls clubs, young men's unions – of all denominations. There did not seem to be a single part of the community he had not touched. One could not help contrasting his life and death with Blaine's[277]. It seems to be generally granted that he, the Bishop, died of overwork. The illness was not in itself severe if he had had the strength left to fight it. There does not seem to be anyone left to take his place but for himself I should think it was just the time a man would choose to die and not have to face old age and the failure of all his powers.
[1893-01-30 (Sunday) Bertha (Newton Centre) to Henry (StL)]

Throughout her life, Bertha supported the charitable work of many organizations, including the needle work guild which provided clothing for needy children. In November 1894, Bertha wrote to Henry of her purchase of clothing for 24 children for her donation costing $4.80. *"Then I went & bought your son some shirts that cost a dollar and ten cents apiece."* Bertha didn't elaborate to Henry what she was thinking and she knew that she didn't need to.

This morning I rocked my boy to sleep after his bath and he went sound sleepy very soon. And then I went downtown to buy our contribution to the needle work guild – twenty-four pairs of Canton flannel drawers for children two years old and twenty-four unbleached woolen shirts – entire outfit four dollars and eighty cents. Then I went & bought your son some shirts that cost a dollar and ten cents apiece.
[1894-11-20 Bertha (StL) to Henry (Fort Worth)]

---

[277] James Gillespie Blaine, the prominent Republican politician, died January 27, 1893, just days before Bishop Brook's passing.

Henry sometimes admitted to Bertha that he worked on the Sabbath.

> *I have been severely panicked for working on the Sabbath. I went down for the mail this morning, got your Wednesday letter, then went to the office 11AM and, to get the ox out of the mire, worked until 2:30, went to this [University] club for lunch and intended to go out to the country for some exercise but just as I started, it began to pour in torrents and now <u>everything</u>, except my ox, is in the mire and I have been sitting here for an hour cussing my luck in no uncertain language. I managed to get out to the country for golf yesterday and Gordon and I "went around" and then dined with the Joneses, Ben Adams and Tom.*

[1900(-) 20170902-2 Henry (University Club, Stl) to Bertha]

Even if Henry did not attend church regularly, he was able to express his Christian faith even if, as he wrote, he was not prepared for "*the change from earth to heaven…*"

> *… if men are true Christians, they are said not to resent the change from earth to heaven and, as you will know, I am an orthodox churchman and am thankful for God's blessings. You may judge my translation to the upper realm is not held as good ground for complaint, especially because like Remick, I was not too good or too well prepared not to be fully appreciative of all the new sensations which awaited me.*[278]

[1905(-) 20180730-1 Henry to Bertha]

Henry was able to attend church while away on many business trips. While in New York City in 1908, he attended a service and wrote to Bertha about "*a first-class sermon on the virtues of your sex.*"

> *Having nothing to do and concluding I would not go down to Morristown where I might have caused apprehension, I must to church! Heard a beautiful service and a first-class sermon on the virtues of your sex. My! How Doctor Grosvenor gave it to the men. I couldn't help thinking that the fat old ladies in front of me must be his best contributors and that the parson could thus flog the men with impunity. The church was the Holy Incarnation and a beautiful one.*

[1908-01-19 Henry (NYC) to Bertha (64 Vandeventer Place, Stl)]

On business trips, Henry was sometimes able to find "*consolation*" in a Texas church, as long as it was the right church.

> *No letter as yet and I have been away five full days and nights. Getting no consolation from you, I appealed to the church. I have been locked up for two days preparing for the ordeal tomorrow and, recognizing that a bad head is no preparation for any coming test of endurance, I jammed my notes into the desk and started off for a walk. As I sprinted along, reflecting over and finding some fault with my melancholy condition, I concluded that I could do no better than follow the example of other good Christians who, when other comforts fail and earthly helpers flee*[279]*, fall back upon the consolations which heaven offers. And so I looked around for the only true church.*
>
> *I did not succeed in finding it at first but I had plenty of time and finally succeeded, first having discovered more meeting houses than adequate to the real need of that sort of quick aid for the injured for a town of a million souls. I first passed an edifice with columns in front like the pantheon which I spotted as Methodist and wisely avoided. I was turned from the steps of a very respectable*

---

[278] Henry here expressed sentiments similar to what Bertha wrote in her 1902-07-09 letter to Henry in which she said: "*I think the matter with me is that I am like friend Demas in the Epistles who forsook Paul "having loved this present world". I should have gone along with Demas and found St. Paul uncongenial. I love this present world. Honestly, I love it more for your sake than for mine but I like it for my own well enough.*"

[279] Loosely quoting "Abide with Me", a Christian hymn by Scottish Anglican Henry Francis Lyte. The first verse:
Abide with me; fast falls the eventide;
The darkness deepens; Lord with me abide.
When other helpers fail and comforts flee,
Help of the helpless, O abide with me.

looking building by a shout of such volume that I could think of nothing but Camanchees and Baptists. And I got off the block in which I saw a church at the far corner that gave me the blues and, finally, when I despaired of finding the small and select object of my search, I luckily spied an old gentleman in clean but well-worn broad cloth, carrying in his hand a large prayer book and, knowing my man on the instant, followed him until I found my haven of rest for all weary souls who are also intelligent!

I was rewarded for being good. The church was simple but the service and music quite unusual and a man sang the Millard anthem[280] magnificently. I asked who he was and found him to be an English "cow-puncher". I have no sermon to preach as not much of one was preached to me by the Clergyman and none by my wife and as I must get back to shop, I am obliged to say goodbye.
[1908-03-15 Henry (Ft. Worth) to Bertha (64 Vandeventer Place, Stl)]

Being well situated, Henry received requests from various churches for donations. One such request was for the heating system in the rectory in St. George's church in Fredericksburg. After the appeal from Rev. R. J. McBryde[281] who wrote the following postscript to his letter to Henry in 1908, Henry wrote, "*I could not resist this appeal.*"

> P.S.
> *I know there has been a great shrinkage in values but stocks will rise. If the Democrats (& I am one) put forth a socialistic platform, they will be beaten out of their boots. It is hard to believe the Republican party will be overthrown. If they stay in power, the financial condition of the country will at once improve. The great crops & large resources of the country will bring prosperity after a while no matter what party is in power. But it is because of this uncertainty, I ask if you cannot help me now that you will try to help me in the fall, if you can. The Lord bless you & direct your steps!*
>
> *[In pencil, Henry wrote at the end of the letter]*
> *I suppose I had no business to yield but I could not resist this appeal.*
> *Henry*
> [1908-07-03 McBryde (Fredericksburg VA) to Henry]

Henry wrote a follow up letter to Bertha about his responding to this appeal from Rev. McBryde.

> *I enclose a letter from my old pastor. I don't know what you will think of my sending him money with all my present and prospective demands but I simply could not resist the appeal of that ill and sad old man. I wrote him the most cheerful letter I could devise and tried to remind him that one who lived in the affections of so many men in how he had guided and comforted, had a realm of happy retrospect which was certainly an earthly crown. And I thought of telling the dear old man what was in store for him in heaven. But the thought, that he might properly hold himself better capable of making accurate reckonings of the land of bliss than I, restrained me.*
> [1908-07-16 Henry (StL) to Bertha (Rye Beach)]

E. SLANG & ETIQUETTE

Although Bertha enjoyed using slang, she must have considered it sufficiently distasteful to give it up for Lent one year, with penalties for any infraction. "*Nan, Miss Jule & I resolve to give up slang during Lent and to pay a cent apiece for all we use.*" [1888-11 Diary, March 11, 1889]

---

[280] Possibly: Harrison Millard (1830– 1895), an American composer of "Abide with Me, 'Tis Eventide", the words by Presbyterian evangelist Martin Lowrie Hofford (1825–1888).
[281] Rev. Dr Robert James McBryde (1843-1916) was rector of St. George's Episcopal Church in Fredericksburg, VA.

Henry definitely considered slang to be ill-mannered and beneath the status of a cultivated person.

> *And please remember that "cut it short" is slang – so I could not possibly be quoted as you have attempted to.*
> [1892-06-28 (Sunday) Henry (StL) to Bertha (The Ark, East Jaffrey)]

Bertha wrote to Henry about a rude NY man who made her wonder if "*I am anything of a prude, that most disagreeable of all things…*"

> *This is what happened the other day. There is a New York man here, a married man, his daughter, Rosalie, is one of the younger set of girls here and I suppose he is about forty five but he does not look a day over thirty five and is a thorough man of the world and most attractive. He has been here several summers. The other day, we were all teasing Janie Selden about the way she snubbed people and Jane was defending herself and declaring she did not mean to. When he said, "come, better stop quarreling, kiss and make friend all round and begin with me, Miss Janie". And he took her hand. Rosalie said, "This is the time to show your powers, snub him now, Jane, he deserves it." "I don't know how", said Jane. "Exactly! You don't know how! Now I never should have thought of doing this to Miss Drake and I have known her a great deal longer than I have you." "Well, I should like to know why", cried the indignant Jane". "O, because she's engaged, I suppose". "Not at all, her protector isn't here. I should never have thought of doing it under any circumstances. No, I won't tell either of you why, you can puzzle it out for ourselves." And having succeeded in making us both this furious, which I think was what he wanted, he departed. And I have been wondering if I am anything of a prude, that most disagreeable of all things. The whole thing was the sheerest nonsense, done in a crowd, with his own daughter there and it never would have entered my head to have objected if he had taken my hand. Though, I acknowledge, I should not have liked it for I do not care for that kind of nonsense. But for that matter, Janie did not like it either. Will you please give me your opinion?*
> [1892-07-26 (Monday) Bertha (Rye Beach) to Henry (StL)]

Henry's response revealed his amusement (and pride) at Bertha's ability to handle rude men: "*I can smile at the suggestion that any man would think he could be undignified with you with impunity.*"

> *I did not like the incident you described in which "Rosalie's" father was not only, I think, rather undignified but heedless of the respect which an older man should carefully accept; certain usages which in themselves, perhaps, are not so important as they are the gauges of one's standard and I like the whole proceeding less because his daughter was present. I quite understood, though, his disinclination to attempt any such nonsense with you, dear, so don't attribute what I say to any fear that you may be made a part of his foolishness, although I by no means think you a prude because I can smile at the suggestion that any man would think he could be undignified with you with impunity.*
> [1892-07-28 (Thursday) Henry (StL) to Bertha (Farragut House, Rye Beach)]

Social events, such as the Great Imperial Ball in 1892 when Bertha and Henry were engaged, provided for chance meetings and "ruffled feathers", such as when Henry took offense when a Miss Kingsland suggested that her own eyes were like Bertha's.

> *The great Imperial is in the midst of its first ball of the year. I left it a few moments since in full swing, having very successfully proved to my entire satisfaction that at certain times that sort of excitement is decidedly jarring. I was not having a beautiful time to begin with but an interview with your friend, Miss Kingsland, started me in the direction of home more abruptly than one who has not had the good fortune of knowing Miss K. can possibly understand. As my short and very delightful talk with this young lady includes a sweeping complement to you, I may as well particularize.*

She was standing next to me in the square dance I was enjoying with Miss Emma Lane and, as I turned to speak to her, she began with "Mr. Scott, I don't believe you remember me, Miss Kingsland. Now, you ought to like me. There is a very good reason for your doing so." Perhaps my reply was not polite. If I was rude, my punishment was surely swift and terrible for her answer to my rather unenthusiastic "do explain, Miss Kingsland" was "why, I have been told that my eyes were like Miss Drake's!!" Do you wonder that I departed in undignified haste and will you please inform me what a man is to do when he is thus attacked by an exceedingly impertinent woman?
[1892-12-28 (Tuesday, Wednesday) Henry (StL) to Bertha (Stancote, Newton Centre)]

In the following letter, Henry diligently relays the latest news from a ball in February 1893, less than two weeks before Bertha and Henry's wedding. It was remarkable how much information Henry accumulated.

The ball after the play was fine. All the girls were there except the dearest of them all. Luty[282] was one of the very giddy ones and I had a beautiful dance with her. She was by far the prettiest girl there. I have never seen her look so well and Mr. Zack seemed mighty proud of her. Then your friend, Mrs. Knox, was one of the giddy ones and went in for the dancing as if it had been her first ball while Gordon stood around trying to make himself agreeable to people with indifferent success because his thoughts were all employed in deciding whether Mrs. Gordon was not "over doing it", as I heard him remark to one of the girls, as the only objection he could see to balls in general. Then my dear, let me break it to you gently: Miss Francis Markham and George Morey waltzed together four times. There can be no mistake in the count for it was verified by every man and woman in our party. I think it is just as well for you to prepare yourself for the evolution of your prize leader in the charities to an habitue of the ballroom, that is, if Brother George does not meanwhile convince her that a new line of charity, the "at home" kind, is her especial province and persuade her to take care of him and his flat. Brookings did not go near Mary all the evening which Miss Nan and Mrs. Dexter Tiffany agreed argues well for him. Miss Nan converted Mrs. Tiffany to this view by remarking with a distinct inclination of her head in my direction "I have seen men shy around and look forlorn before" and added "experience teaches that some men are not as sad as they sometimes would have you think them." What did she mean, dearest?
[1893-02-04 (Saturday) Henry (StL) to Bertha (Stancote)]

F. GOSSIP

Henry was generally very wary of gossipers, especially regarding engaged couples. Henry wrote the following letter when he was engaged to Bertha wherein he expressed disapproval of such "*tattlers*".

I sent a letter just received from Miss Janet [January]. I have not seen her since her engagement has come out, for she, Miss Edith [January], Mr. & Mrs. Tom [McKittrick], and Howard [Janet's fiancé] have gone off to Denver on Howard's car. The house they have taken, was, it seems, secured by Mrs. January before the engagement was announced and this seems to have made even the dumb talk. Just why I certainly can't see, but everyone, even that charming friend of mine, Mrs. Knox, seems inclined to ask "why this haste". For my part, I consider it nobody's business but the parties concerned, and I have gotten into trouble once or twice from speaking my mind rather strongly.

Dear, I begin to look with forgiveness on the tattlers who have interested themselves in our affair for by comparison we have been very gently treated. Mary put it very happily the other day in saying "well the town has so thoroughly informed itself about the two families of Mr. Elliott and Janet that, if in the history of either there has existed a fault or shortcoming, I think I have been told about it." It is perfectly disgusting and I almost reproach myself for being so attached to a place that is so filled up with vicious and ill-bred people. But I did not mean to write so much about these things, dear. [1892-06-15 (Tuesday) Henry (StL) to Bertha (East Jaffrey NH)]

---

[282] Louise (Shepley) Lionberger who was married to Isaac Henry ("Zack") Lionberger.

However, notwithstanding Henry's disapproval of gossiping, he was a participant as evidenced by Bertha's comment on Henry's "noble" efforts to obtain gossip.

> *O, I am so glad you are going out a little "in order to gather some items of news to interest me." Rarely have I read anything so nobly self-sacrificing, my gregarious friend. Your motives touch me deeply but you are hardly a success as a gossip writer yet. Why did you not tell me what you talked of at Mattie's, who else was asked to Hildegarde's, and who gave the circus party?*
> [1892-07-01x (Friday) Bertha (Jaffrey NH) to Henry (StL)]

Still, Bertha and Henry generally eschewed gossip. Bertha wrote:

> *And Henry, I now give you leave, if you ever see me developing into a gossiping mischief making old woman, to choke me. I said to Charlotte yesterday, if she ever saw any danger of my becoming a woman of that kind, I hoped she would quietly remove me from the earth by hitting me over the head with a club or any other way she chose. And Charlotte responded "I wouldn't dare. I'm afraid of Henry." But I assured her that under those circumstances, I thought she would earn your everlasting gratitude by so doing.*
> [1892-08-03 (Wednesday) Bertha (Rye Beach) to Henry (StL)]

Henry generally reacted defensively if Bertha accused him of being a gossip.

> *You do me an injustice to compare me with Zack and it humbles my pride no little to be compared with that gossip. I thought I kept secrets pretty well for I don't like gossip to begin with and, besides, I have a record in certain secrets of some of the girls we both know that entitles me, I think, to a pretty good reputation and so I am particularly astonished at Miss Janet's guarding her affairs from me. She certainly knows whether I am a leaky vessel or not. There! That is my reply to your charge that I can't keep a secret. I ought to add that such information, as I have given you about Jack and Miss Sarah, is legitimately yours as is anything I may have told me for the man or woman who thinks I do not possess the right to tell you what I please is an idiot and, in Zack's case, he knows very well that I hold no uncertain position on this subject. Secrets that you can't know would not interest me, dear. It's like receiving an invitation when you are not asked, too? There may come a time when I shall enjoy things without you, dear but you can be very sure that period is not very near at hand. And if it ever comes to me, I shall have to acknowledge to you that certain theories of mine have been very badly upset.*
> [1892-09-06 (Tuesday) Henry (StL) to Bertha (Farragut House)]

"*Secrets that you can't know would not interest me, dear. It's like receiving an invitation when you are not asked...*" Henry maintained that the only gossip or secrets to which he cared to hear were secrets which he could share with Bertha. Well said.

Although, protestations aside, Bertha and Henry did enjoy hearing the gossip.

> *Did you say you did not like gossip! O, for shame, my son, study thine own heart just a little wee bit better.*
> [1892-09-10 (Friday) Bertha (Rye Beach) to Henry (StL)]

"*O, for shame, my son, study thine own heart*" - is good advice to carry with us always.

CHAPTER 21 – SUMMERS IN THE EAST

A. THE MATRON

Bertha, surely, would never have referred to herself as a matron. But, after her marriage and the birth of Hugh Scott in 1893, her world had changed. Perhaps because of this and perhaps because of her new St. Louis circle of friends, Bertha would not spend her summers in Rye Beach again until the summer of 1900. Instead, Bertha went North with Henry to Niagara Falls, New York and Canada in 1893, then Meramec Highlands in Missouri in 1894, and Jamestown Rhode Island from 1895 through 1899. Although she never mentioned it, Bertha must have missed going to Rye Beach in those years.

B. JAMESTOWN 1895-1900

For six summers starting in 1895, Jamestown became the Scott's summer refuge. What can be surmised from Jamestown history, Shoreby Hill in Jamestown was incorporated and built by St. Louisans and became the summer retreat for Bertha and Henry's then circle of friends seeking a cooler summer climate.

1. SHOREBY HILL

A great many St. Louisans took up residences in Jamestown during the hot St. Louis summers and Shoreby Hill was where many congregated.

One of the "Cottages" on Shoreby Hill, Jamestown RI circa 1898.

Shoreby Hill is ... [a] type of summer community development: the planned "garden" suburb. A group composed mainly of St. Louis residents sought to establish an exclusive enclave of summer residences in Jamestown through their own development efforts. They formed the Jamestown Land Company as a Rhode Island corporation, with capital of $120,000. The Company's incorporators were St. Louis residents Ephron Catlin (president), James Taussig (secretary), Charles S. Taussig (James' son), Henry Scott and Charles Acton Ives of Newport (a prominent Newport lawyer and political figure). It was represented by its local agent Daniel Watson from Newport, a prominent figure in local real estate and the development of the Newport area as a summer resort.

[National Register of Historic Place, Shoreby Hill Historic District, Newport, Rhode Island, http://www.preservation.ri.gov/pdfs_zips_downloads/national_pdfs/jamestown/jams_shoreby-hill-hd.pdf]

Shoreby Hill was developed and built starting in 1895. By the summer of 1899, it was very much a St. Louis crowd that lived there, as Bertha commented in an 1899 letter to Henry.

It will soon become impossible to set your foot down in Jamestown without putting it upon a St. Louisan. Your friend Mr. Drew was up here for an hour this afternoon. He is very nice only he is another St. Louisan. I asked him to go sailing with us next Tuesday, entirely on your account. I supposed you would want me to show him some attention. He really is a charming man though.

[1899-07-31 Bertha (Jamestown RI) to Henry (StL)]

2. SUMMER OF 1895

Bertha wrote in her diary in May 1895 about closing up her St. Louis house and preparing for the summer in Jamestown where they would stay at one of the Emmons' Cottages. In her diary, Bertha provides the details of her daily activities which are included below, leaving out a little detail that she was pregnant with Nancy Scott who was born on July 5.

May 31, 1895
By this time I had begun to gradually dismantle my house, with a view to shutting it up entirely for the summer. We had taken the smallest of the Emmons Cottages at Jamestown, Rhode Island for the summer and I am going to take my dear cook, Lizzie Haase, with me to do all the cooking and house work, while I put the washing out. I am going to part with Joanna my housemaid and

Morgan, the man. From the latter, I part with deep regret. He is the finest servant I ever knew, when sober. From the former, I part with great joy. She has been subject to attacks of sick headaches all year which I did not find out until the week before we left to have been the effect of whisky. Sadie Taussig, when asked for a recommendation of her, said she was faithful, good natured and a hard worker but had "maddening limitations" & never was a truer word spoken. I presume now the aforesaid limitations had something to do with the other thing of which Sadie was probably as ignorant as I.

June 1, 1895
All the carpets come up. Entire house floors scrubbed from top to bottom. Everything nice and clean. Servants work like Trojans. Don't think much of Black Lizzie, though, whom I have in for the day.

June 2, 1895
Sunday, Henry and Charlie Taussig go out on their bicycles and have breakfast in the park. In the afternoon, Henry rides with Tom. It is very hot 93 1/2° and he does not want to go – but Tom is so blue about his father, he thinks it may cheer him up. We have spent morning in the cellar, the coolest place, tinkering with the bicycle. Lil McNair sends us in drinks

June 3, 1895
Pack all day.

June 4, 1895
Mary Lionberger and Sadie Taussig call. Evening – the Adams, Tom McKittricks and Gist all express surprise at everything being so utterly finished. Even my toothbrush, being a new one, is packed.

June 5, 1895
Morning, Edith Knox comes in to say goodbye and Hildegarde again. Afternoon, long visit from Nan, then a scramble over Henry's packing, the only thing not attended to, at his own special request. Annie and her daughter and the boy go to the park to meet us at Grandma Scott's. At six o'clock, lock up house, say good bye to Joanna and Morgan. Go to Grandma Scott's to dinner. Henry is delayed by non-arrival of transfer man for trunks. Minnie and Mr. Carter come in. All say good bye and we depart for station where Lizzie meets us. Hugh Scott delighted to go on choo-car but so excited that it is long before he sleeps. He, Lizzie and Annie are put in state room, a very nice one with dressing room attached, and I have a section and Henry a lower berth outside.

June 6, 1895
A very pleasant trip. We have to get out for breakfast though and Hugh Scott disgraces the family by crying for everything on the table.

June 7, 1895
Arrive in Boston. Go over to Old Colony Depot, take twelve o'clock train for Newport, buy luncheon in the station & eat it on the way. Met at Newport by father with a carriage. He drives us over to and on to the ferry and, at three-twenty, we arrive at Jamestown and take possession of the Emmons Cottage (the oldest of the three Emmons cottages, the highest on the hill) where mother meets us.

The AB Emmons lower cottage, built 1890, one of
3 cottages built 1889-96, JD Johnston design, circa 1900.

O the beauty of that view! And the comfort of that cottage!! What mother has not done to make it comfortable – my linen is all unpacked, the beds made, the curtains hung, the table spread, supper all ready, only waiting to be warmed. Then the stacks of things she has given us, dainty white embroidered covers on every table and bureau. A great big rug in the parlor and small rugs at every bedside and, in the hall, three beautiful student lamps and a lamp for a sick room, sofa cushions, a rocking chair, a dear little table with a tête à tête tea set, all the new magazines and novels. Words fail me, one has to be here to appreciate it all, besides all the cleaning she has had done, and did herself. Then when father first came down, there were no blankets in the house and he thought there were to be none, so they bought blankets and spreads for every bed, and Mr. Emmons supplied them afterwards. Father and mother go back to Newport on the six o'clock boat. We talk to them and explore the house until then.

Afterwards, we explore on our own account. It is the most comfortable house and just the right size for us. A big sitting room, with fire place, dining room opposite, large kitchen, with hard coal stove which at first is Lizzie's despair but afterwards she learns to manage it. A laundry, but as we put the washing out, the girls use that for a dining room. A large dining room pantry & a large kitchen pantry. A big room built on behind for wood, coal, etc.

Upstairs, four large bed rooms, daintily furnished, though inexpensively, pretty light papers, cottage furniture and matting. Mine has a fire place, and a little hall room opening into it. Every room has an enormous closet and there is a big linen closet. The house is thoroughly plumbed and there is a delightful bathroom with hot and cold water in abundance.

Third story – has three big rooms, garret rooms – one has been fixed for Lizzie, the other two unfurnished. We have a deep shady piazza in front and look straight out on a magnificent view of Newport Harbor. O, it is a heavenly, heavenly place.

June 8, 1895
Have a late breakfast. Then father and mother come over from Newport. We spend a lovely morning, talking gossip and showing off Hugh Scott. Mother says we all look better already. They leave on one o'clock boat and go back to Newport and then to Boston. We unpack, explore and get settled. We have our own bathing houses and our own wharf - that is the three Emmons cottages share the wharf.

Henry with Hugh Scott, in Jamestown

June 9, 1895
Sunday Morning. Henry and I take long tramp out to the Dumplings and look at the cottages, some very pretty ones but the walk is too long for me. Afternoon. Take charge of Hugh Scott and let the girls go off. Show him how to throw stones in the water. He is perfectly enchanted "Mah tones Heavy"

June 10, 1895
Go over to Newport on the ferry. Shop at various places. Buy household utensils on Mr. Emmons account as he told us to at Covell's, cheap baby carriage at Titus's, china pitcher at Allen's. Then take the famous ocean drive and see all the palaces, Vanderbilt's new one, etc. Afternoon – Henry comes in with the information that he has. Met Hallie Clarkson and her husband, Mr. Brinckerhoff. They are here on their bridal tour – and will go sailing with us this afternoon. Have a delightful sail and find them a delightful young couple. Take the "Hornet" with Captain Chandler to sail her.

June 12, 1895
Am paralyzed to find that the clothes I hung up to air are as wet as if soaked with water in a tub. A fog has come up in the night. We declined to go to Newport the Brinckerhoffs but they come for us in the afternoon to go sailing. I have let Hugh Scott go to Newport with Annie and Lizzie, give them money to take the ocean drive, etc. A heavy fog comes up before they get back and I am afraid they will see nothing & Hugh Scott will be drenched. But my fears are groundless. They had a beautiful time and he is as cheerful as possible.

June 13, 1895
Heavy fog. I had invited the Brinckerhoffs to tea but they appear at dinner time to say good-bye. The fog has driven them home.

June 14, 1895
Henry buys a row boat. Take Hugh Scott for his first row. He is a most intensely enchanted child. "Hugh 'Cott 'n yide boat with Mutter and Dat." "Boat way way out on big jikken of walker." And when he is brought back, wails of despair "Hugh 'Cott 'n yide boat on bid bid bat-tub with Mutter and Dat."

June 16, 1895
Henry rents the "Maud" (cat-boat) for a month. Take a first sail in her with Al Chandler as assistant.

June 17, 1895
Go sailing in the morning and am very sick.

June 18, 1895
Drive down to Conanicut Park and back.

June 19, 1895
Let the girls go to Newport and undertake the charge of Hugh Scott for the afternoon but find I am hardly strong enough. Morning, interview Dr. Berney.

June 20, 1895
On the water all day.

June 21, 1895
Long tramp, sail and row. Take dear Hugh Scott with us, rowing, he is so sleepy that he lies down in the bottom of the boat on a shawl with his head on my knee covered up with my afghan. Best little boy that ever lived.

June 22, 1895
Walk. Glorious sail in the afternoon.

Old Fort Dumpling, Jamestown RI[283]

June 23 (Sunday), 1895
Morning – fix curtains in boy's room, put some touches to Myra's in readiness for her coming over to the Dumplings and loaf there, watching the fog come up.
Afternoon – have the most glorious sail we have had yet. We have been here now two weeks and two days and I have been simply exultantly happy. Everything has been so beautiful. I have had Henry to myself, almost as much as when we were first married, and my precious Hugh Scott has been sweeter every day. Annie and Lizzie have been so nice, though, I am sure Lizzie, at least, has been homesick. Then father and mother meeting us with everything they had done to the dear house gave us such a delightful start. Then the weather has been glorious and we have all lived out of doors, every one of us rowing and looking stronger every day. If anything should happen – at all events this has been one of the most beautiful parts of my life. Unberufen[284].

---

[283] Fort Dumpling dating from the Revolutionary War, used to occupy a small site within Fort Wetherill. Fort Wetherill is a former Coast Artillery fort that occupies the southern portion of the eastern tip of Conanicut Island, located in Jamestown, Rhode Island. The fort sits atop high granite cliffs, overlooking the entrance to Narragansett Bay.
[284] Unberufen: i.e. "knock on wood"

Just here at half past nine at night, the doorbell rang and a telegram was brought by Al. I thought the ill luck had come but it was only from Myra Lane, delaying her visit until Tuesday.

June 24, 1895
Henry went to Newport. I spend morning fixing crib, find I have no pillow case but a plain one, when in the mail comes a lovely pale blue silk and lace pillow case from Gertrude McDonald. This makes my crib a real gem, with its snowy muslin sides, pale blue afghan and pillow case, and the ivory cross at the head. Afternoon – Magnificent sail.

June 25, 1895
Henry goes over to Newport to meet Myra Lane. I went on later boat, Dr. Berney drives me down to ferry. Have a glimpse of Susan Hale on ferry. Find Henry and Myra waiting for me with carriage, and we have a gorgeous drive around Newport, see all the pretty places and then take the ocean drive. We like "Bleak House" best of all, though not the grandest place by any means. Afternoon, it rains, build a fire and chat. Clears by six and have beautiful row. Evening, sit on piazza watching tall river boats pass.

June 26, 1895
Give Myra a sail. Splendid day for it. Run aground on the rocks near the red buoy, have to let down sail and push off. Afternoon – try to go to Narragansett. Find that the ferry is not running for probably only day this summer. They are dredging out the landing so we drive to Beaver Tail and around the Dumplings. Evening. Go for a walk and I twist my ankle and fall headlong.

Beavertail Lighthouse, Jamestown RI[285]

June 27, 1895
Henry takes Myra to Newport to see her off to Boston. We have enjoyed her visit so much. I stay at home and write letters. It rains.

June 28, 1895
Henry's bicycle arrives. He goes in bathing. Sail.

June 29, 1895
Row, take Hugh Scott. Afternoon – row and sail. Sail with all the reefs out – magnificent. Henry stays up till twelve o'clock writing letters.

---

[285] Beavertail Lighthouse, built in 1856, was and still is the premier lighthouse in Rhode Island, United States, marking the entrance to Narragansett Bay. The 64-foot (20 m) lighthouse lies on the southernmost point of Conanicut Island in the town of Jamestown, Rhode Island in Beavertail State Park, on a site where beacons have stood since the early 18th century.

June 30 (Sunday), 1895
Rain and fog. Loaf and write letters. Henry takes ride on his bicycle. Take a walk in the heavy Scotch mist.

July 1, 1895
Go sailing but it is too rough for me. Come in, all played out. Henry tries to give me a whisky and apollinaris, the latter bottle explodes in his hands cutting him badly. Afternoon. Annie, Lizzie and Hugh Scott go to Newport. Henry and I have a heavenly sail, first almost dead calm, then beautiful. Kill H.C.S. with a sardine supper.

July 2, 1895
Brilliant day. Sail in the morning. Get becalmed under a broiling sun. Sail nearly all the afternoon, the best we have had. Evening - Stern Henry puts Hugh Scott to sleep. Moonlight walk, with the scent of the new moon lay all about us – the last of our honeymoon time together. The others come tomorrow and I shall be sure to enjoy having them but I believe this last four weeks will always stand out to both of us as one of the happiest times of our lives.

July 3, 1895
Henry has gone over to Newport to meet his mother, Maggie and Mrs. Hurley. I arrange their room, etc. They arrive. Mrs. Scott looks utterly exhausted and very badly, says she was car sick all the way and Mrs. Hurley took the best possible care of her. Like the way Mrs. Hurley takes hold of things very much. She makes Mrs. Scott comfortable, unpacks satchel, etc. Evening. Maggie, Henry and I go for a beautiful row over to the fort and back. Afterward, I have a little talk Lizzie about her being homesick and she tells me one reason she came on is because she could not stand the idea of my being sick with a strange girl in the house who might go off and neglect things. Nice girl! She has been awfully homesick. Afternoon. Sadie Taussig and Laura Wells called.

July 4, 1895
It pours all day. Such a dismal welcome but we get our work, sit around and chat, and play with Hugh Scott. I am sorriest for Mrs. Hurley who has really no one to talk to. Henry said some man at the club offered to bet that it was the stupidest Fourth of July any of them had ever spent but no one would take him up. Afternoon. Henry and I have a magnificent walk in the storm, come in wringing wet but feeling splendidly. Mrs. Hurley takes good care of me. Evening – play whist.

July 5, 1895
Get up at half past four, sun is already up but watch some sunrise effects - Come down stairs. Write a note thanks to Emma Lane. Finish stitching around bottom of Gertrude. Put the parlor in order & write up the last two days of my diary.

Eleven o'clock AM on July 5, 1895, Anne Warburton Scott was born.

July 5, 1895 [written one year later]
It is a full year since I wrote the last entry in my diary at five o'clock in the morning. I have just written in the two lines above, which explain the pause immediately following at all events. Dr. Berney of Philadelphia and Dr. Hurst of the Pennsylvania University took care of me. Then followed a quiet time of course. Henry left me on July twelfth. The hardest parting we have ever had. It was a month before I went down stairs. Maggie read aloud to me and I dictated letters to her. Mrs. Hurley was a magnificent nurse, though a sad woman, having just lost her daughter.

Father came down for a day or two in August. Then about the eighteenth, Sam came on and we drove, walked and discussed the world freely. Henry did not come until Sept. 18 (this is going back to 1895 again.)

September 18, 1895
Henry came back, gives me a ruby and diamond ring.

September 19, 1895
The family, Sam, Mrs. Scott & Maggie went home.

September 21
Took the Taussigs sailing and had a dead calm. I forgot to say the Taussigs took me to the Newport tennis tournament.

Sept. 22, 1895
Glorious sail.

Sept. 26, 1895
Packer from Newport comes to pack & store our things. Leave for home on the night boat from Newport, the "Puritan", about five in the afternoon. Henry and I rush down for a last look at the surf breaking on the rocks. It looks as if a storm was coming and we have it on the sound that night. Anne and Hugh Scott both sick.

Sept. 27, 1895
Met in New York by mother & father. Mamma & I shop.

Sept. 28, 1895
Arrive at home. Lizzie's family are there and have a good supper waiting for us.
[1893 Diary]

3. SUMMER OF 1896

June 24, 1896
Myra Lane and I start east together with Hugh Scott, Nancy and Annie, Helen Lane and Laura. The two husbands see us off. We have a pleasant, though very fatiguing journey, and mother and father meet us in Boston on June 26th.

June 26, 1896
Father goes with us to Jamestown. We find the George Anthony cottage which we have rented for the season. Looking very neat and attractive, quite a sea view. The hotel where we take our meals, the Prospect House, is very well kept and has an excellent table. We select our table and have Katie for our waitress. Father stays with me ten days, we unpack all the things we have stored away and he helps me do everything, lay out the rugs, arrange the books, hang the curtains. We also take every excursion there is to be taken.

Carter's Inn, known at other times as Prospect House, St James Manor, built c1888, torn down c1923

June 29, 1896
Drive around Newport.

June 30, 1896
Drive to Conanicut Park.

July 1, 1896
Go sailing with Sadie Taussig.

July 2, 1896
Drive to Beaver Tail.

Aerial view of Beavertail Lighthouse

July 3, 1896
Go to Newport, buy things for the fourth and birthday presents for Nancy.

July 5, 1896
Go to Narragansett to see Edith Stockwell Moulton.

July 6, 1896
Engage Lilla Richardson to come to me and do the housework and help with this baby. This is thanks to Pater's present to me that I can do this. She proves a treasure in the end, though, she staggers me at first by giving her name as Miss Richardson.

July 7, 1896
Pater goes back to Rye, leaving me alone until July 11 when Mrs. Scott and Minnie arrive.

July 13
Had a magnificent sail with John, Marion, and quite a party.

John and Marion Davis's Jamestown house.

July 27, 1896
Sadie Taussig and I give a dinner at the light house. Drive the party over in a barge.

Aug. 10, 1896
Go to Newport – select presents for mother's birthday and express them to her.

Aug. 12, 1896
Annie has an attack of sciatica. I take part in tableaux. "The Lilies" is my tableau.

Aug. 13, 1896
Take care of children with Minnie's help all day. Take part in tableaux again in the Evening. Utterly exhausted. Heat intense.

Aug. 26, 1896
Go down on train with Miss Davis to meet Henry in New York. Meet Henry and go to the Waldorf. Go to Olympia in the evening.

Aug. 27, 1896
Shop. Take lunch on top of building in a little French restaurant looking up the harbor. Dine at Delmonico's. Go the Koster & Bial's.

Aug. 28, 1896
Take dinner at little German restaurant with delicious band.

Aug. 29, 1896
Dinner at Italian restaurant. Go to casino roof garden.

Aug. 30, 1896
Spend the day at Morristown with dear Uncle William. Henry unable to go. Have had a beautiful honeymoon time in N.Y.

Aug. 31, 1896
Take steamer Priscilla back to Newport. Arrive at Newport just in time to see Hugh Scott and Auntie Minnie going off on ferry.

September
Enjoying the whole month immensely, though there is too much rain.

Sept. 4, 1896
Go to Narragansett with the Taussigs & Maggie & Marion. We engage the "Hornet" and sail all the time. Edith January puts herself under our chaperonage. George Selfridge is there a great deal. Julius Foy sits at our table. The Francises are there. Governor Francis receives his appointment as Secretary of the Interior while there.[286]

USS Massachusetts

We go over the Battleship Massachusetts with him one day and receive the salute to a member of the cabinet of seventeen guns. We meet many pleasant people. The Bells of Philadelphia[287], the Pruyns of New York[288] who have the cottage next us, the Lemoines, etc. the last week glorious – sailing all day and every day.

Sept. 28, 1896
Start for home.

Sept 29, 1896
Reach New York. Have rainy fatiguing morning.

---

[286] David Rowland Francis (October 1, 1850 – January 15, 1927) was an American politician. He served in various positions including Mayor of Saint Louis, the 27th Governor of Missouri, and United States Secretary of the Interior. He was the U.S. Ambassador to Russia between 1916 and 1917, during the Russian Revolution of 1917. He was a Wilsonian Democrat. His biographer summarizes his personality:

> David R. Francis was a brash, opinionated, stubborn, smart, sometimes foolish, straight-talking, quick-acting, independent-minded, proud, self-made man who represented the United States in Russia for two and a half years, during the most tumultuous era in that country's history. Much of his activity has been shrouded in myth – some of that heroic, more of that comic and tragic. [Wikipedia]

[287] Possibly John Cromwell Bell (October 3, 1861 – December 29, 1935) was a distinguished Pennsylvania lawyer, serving as a District Attorney for Philadelphia and state Attorney General.

[288] Probably Robert Clarence Pruyn (October 23, 1847 – October 29, 1934), of Albany, New York, was an American inventor, banker, businessman, and politician.

Sept. 30, 1896
Reach Home

4. SUMMER OF 1897

On her summer pilgrimage to Jamestown in 1897, Bertha described the train trip on a private car – dusty but *"luxury unspeakable"*.

June 20, 1897
Minnie Carter, Hugh and Nancy, Ellen, Helen and I, leave on Janet Elliott's private car for Boston. Janet Elliott, little Janet and Edith, her nurse and Mrs. January are the others. Have a nice trip in spite of dust. Travelling on a private car is luxury unspeakable.

June 22, 1897
Arrive in Boston, say goodbye to Janet, take my party over to Providence depot, send the children into Public Garden. Minnie and I take walk down dear, dear old Boylston Street. Go back, get chicks, take lunch in station, arrive at Jamestown at half past four. Go straight to nice old Anthony Cottage, find everything just as I wanted it. Take tea at Prospect House. See the Pruyns, feel comfortable and happy.
[1893 Diary]

One of the big events for Bertha, Hugh and Nancy that summer was the arrival of the White Squadron into Narraganset Bay.

Aug. 4, 1897
The white squadron[289] come into harbor. [1893 Diary]

The Squadron of Evolution AKA The White Squadron

---

[289] The Squadron of Evolution—sometimes referred to as the "White Squadron"— was a transitional unit in the United States Navy, during the late 19th century. The squadron was composed of the protected cruisers USS Atlanta, USS Boston, USS Chicago, and dispatch boats USS Dolphin and USS Yorktown. Yorktown's sister ships USS Bennington and USS Concord joined the squadron in 1891. The "White Squadron" was the first group of modern American steel vessels (USS Atlanta, Boston, Chicago, and Dolphin) to be completed (1887–1888) after the naval decay following the Civil War. Congress had adopted a policy to modernize the navy in 1882 and required the use of steel in domestic manufacture. The White Squadron, named for the group's white-painted hulls, was the core of the "new Navy" of the 1890s, one capable of vying with major European powers for supremacy in the Pacific. The Boston participated in the Battle of Manila Bay (1 May 1898), which ended the Spanish-American War.

Bertha and her fellow St. Louisans would have been able to watch the White Squadron sailing into Narraganset Bay from Shoreby Hill where their cottages were located. Everyone would have dressed in their best and brought flags to wave as the ships passed Jamestown Island. It would have been quite a spectacle.

The arrival of the White Squadron was followed the next day by the arrival of the New York Yacht Club yachts. Some of this next day's luster was lost due to where the US Navy parked its ships – which blocked the view.

> *Aug. 5, 1897*
> *The New York Yacht Club come in. Evening – magnificent illumination of harbor. We go on steamer Beaver Tail and instead of going through the club, the captain anchors off the torpedo station. Crowd furious. Mrs. Johnson, "Well, at least, it is safe". Mrs. Kayser, "safe! You want to be safe! You stay home in your beds!"*
> [1893 Diary]

The summer of 1897 was "lovely".

> *Aug. 16, 1897*
> *...*
> *Pass a beautiful month sailing, golfing, buying furniture for new house from Newport. A lovely time to look back upon.*
> [1893 Diary]

Bertha and Henry contracted to have 64 Vandeventer Place, StL, built during 1897 and moved in on November 23, 1897. Given the large size of their new house, there was a considerable amount of shopping to do, especially for the new furniture. Bertha and Henry had a least one trip to New York City to acquire "necessities" during this year.

Henry was able to spend the entire month of August with Bertha and, from her diary entries, their time together was delightful, even if the wind did not always cooperate.

> *Aug. 23, 1897*
> *Newport tennis. Sail to Fort Adams in afternoon, are becalmed, Henry has to row all the way back.*
> [1893 Diary]

Fort Adams

Since Fort Adams was across the Narragansett Bay, south of Newport, Henry had a long row back to the Jamestown peer on that August 23rd day.

The tennis tournaments were held at the Newport "National Tennis Club" which was (and still is) magnificent. What is doesn't have with regard to space for a large crowd, it makes up for with old world charm.

National Tennis Club in Newport

The Men's 1897 Tennis Championship (now called the US open) was held from August 16th to August 23rd on the outdoor grass courts at the Newport Casino in Newport, Rhode Island. Bertha and Henry went to the tournament most of the days except Sunday (the 22nd) when they went to church.

Also that summer, the Newport Racing Club sponsored a yachting race held on September 4. The details of the race were covered by the New York Times: *"NEWPORT, Sept. 4. -- The second day's yacht racing under the auspices of the Newport Yacht Racing Association was held to-day and furnished one of the closest contests ever held between the two big sloops, Navahoe and Vigilant. Everybody expected the Vigilant to win, and she did, but it was by a narrow margin."*

Bertha described this yachting race in her diary:
> *Sept 4, 1897*
> *... Magnificent yacht race between the "Navahoe" and the "Vigilant". ... Follow the first course out to Beaver Tail. Are becalmed. Come home to dinner. See the finish of second course & start and finish of third course. Most magnificent sight I ever saw. Both ships under full sail and splendid stormy sunset.*
> [1893 Diary]

5. SUMMER OF 1898
Bertha wrote very little in her diary of her 1898 summer in Jamestown.
> *June 25, 1898*
> *Leave for Jamestown with Minnie. Nice Summer.*

6. SUMMER OF 1899
The summer of 1899, Bertha and her children, Hugh, Nancy and George, stayed at the Prospect House in Jamestown. The summer activities in 1899 included polo at Narraganset and sailing. Bertha explained all the details to Henry in her August 8th letter.

I have taken a buckboard for tomorrow afternoon to drive down and see the polo there [Narragansett] (it is there not at Newport) and am going to take Marion, John, Maggie and ourselves. I did not make the whole day excursion because it is too fatiguing and Hilda has to have her nap either morning or afternoon.

Buckboard - an open, four-wheeled, horse-drawn carriage with seating that is attached to a plank stretching between the front and rear axles. The "buckboard" is the front-most board on the wagon that could act as both a footrest for the driver and protection for the driver from the horse's rear hooves in case of a "buck".

...

Captain Chandler says he will have the "Hornet" for you on Saturday. From what I hear of Irwin Smith's sailing capacities, I guess there is nothing wrong with the Hornet's sail. As Knox Taussig says, "I wouldn't go sailing with Mr. Smith, not if I had two life preservers."
[1899-08-08 Bertha (Jamestown) to Henry (Waldorf Hotel, New York)]

Bertha wrote of Hildegarde McKittrick's visit during the 1899 summer – and more about their summer social activities.

Hildegarde leaves Wednesday morning. I think she has had a very nice time, people have been so exceedingly kind. She arrived Wednesday evening. Maggie's card party was that night. Thursday morning we had a string of visitors. Afternoon, went bathing – Hilda was crazy to have some sea bathing. Evening to Shoreby Hill to tea with Sadie. Friday morning Florence Boyle asked us to a musicale at the Bayview.

The Bayview Hotel

Friday afternoon, Mrs. Griffith had asked the endowment board to come have a cup of tea and discuss business, so Hildegarde went bathing & then drove down for me and the business being over, Mrs. Griffith asked her in to have some tea and she met Mrs. Selfridge and the others, saw that gorgeous view from the Griffith's porch, then we took Mary Pruyn and drove to Beavertail, after going around among the Dumpling cottages. Yesterday we went to Newport and saw all the shops on Bellevue Avenue in the morning and Fanita(?) took us the Ocean Drive in the afternoon.

This morning, all Shoreby came and sat on our porch so we could not even get to church & Florence Boyle staid to dinner. Tonight we take tea with Nellie Wickham. Marion takes us sailing tomorrow and Tuesday I am going to drive a big party over to see the polo at Newport. I have decided on doing nothing in the evening. There are so few men and Hilda and I got so tired. She & I may have some cards tomorrow night but I hardly think so. The tide is high in the morning this week so we can bathe in the morning.
[1899-08-10(-)A Bertha (Jamestown) to Henry (Waldorf Hotel, NYC)]

When Bertha and Henry were apart for weeks, they would both get excited on the days before they were to reunite. On one such occasion, on August 4, 1899, just prior to Henry's trip to Jamestown for a month, Bertha included a poem by Christina Rossetti in her letter to Henry which captured her feelings: "*the birthday of my life is come, my love is come to me.*"

My Heart is Like a Singing Bird
My heart is like a singing bird
Whose nest is in a water'd shoot;
My heart is like an apple-tree
Whose boughs are bent with thick-set fruit;
My heart is like a rainbow shell
That paddles in a halcyon sea;
My heart is gladder than all these,
Because my love is come to me.

Raise me a daïs of silk and down;
Hang it with fair and purple dyes;
Carve it in doves and pomegranates,
And peacocks with a hundred eyes;
Work it in gold and silver grapes,
In leaves and silver fleurs-de-lys;
Because the birthday of my life
Is come, my love is come to me.
[Poem by Christina Rossetti, copied by Bertha for Henry.
This poem was set to music by Sir Hubert Parry.]

7. FAREWELL TO JAMESTOWN
Bertha and Henry did not book the Prospect House for the next summer of 1900 since the proprietor, Mr. Tefft, would no longer "*take*" the hotel. So, the summer of 1899 was the Scott's last summer in Jamestown and thereafter they went to Rye Beach. They would often reminisce about Jamestown.

It is the most dazzlingly brilliant evening I have ever seen. The bay is a sheet of silver. I never saw anything so brilliant. The harvest moon in her full glory, the last I shall ever see in dear Jamestown, I fear. Mr. Tefft told me today that he had about decided positively not to take the hotel again and, under anyone else's charge, it would not be the same, tho'. I saw Mrs. Anthony today and took the refusal of our cottage for another year.

I went through the Champlin cottage, the one Beremir(?) Morrison-Fuller had, for which they ask six hundred and we thought it not as nice as ours. A little better furnished but small closets, no linen closet at all, a poor kitchen and a very small dining room. Small porch and about no back or side yard. So you see, we got a pretty good house for our money. [1899-09-19 Bertha (Prospect House, Jamestown RI) to Henry (StL)]

During her last stay in Jamestown, just after Henry left, Bertha wrote about its beauty and how difficult it would be to leave.

> *It is well in one way that you went home for, if you were here, I should never want to leave. ... But, O, everything is so beautiful. Maggie and I walked down to the Richards Rocks today and the sea was so dazzling in front and the golden rod made such a solid glory of the hill behind that it make one's heart ache with the beauty. And the air is almost like the Dublin air.*
> [20180222-1 (1899-) Bertha (Newport RI) to Henry (StL)]

Nancy Scott had a very special place in her heart for Jamestown, "*her native island*" where she was born, as Henry commented the next year in his letter when Bertha and the children were in Rye Beach.

> *I hope Nancy had a fine birthday. Ask her if she likes Rye as much as she did her native island. You know I think you and I, if we are spared the average life limit, will be very apt to take running trips occasionally to Jamestown because of our daughter's claim upon it. When we are rich - vain air castle - we must go there and take some of the cat-boat trips that helped make her such a lusty infant!*
> [1901-07-07 (20170804-5) Henry (StlCC) to Bertha]

Years later, Henry still reminisced about Jamestown.

> *I was thinking yesterday of ten years ago and Jamestown and I did not realize I think how vividly some marking points in our lives come back to us. That was a beautiful time together, sweetheart, and I have often looked back upon that June as one of the very happiest months in my life.*
> [20171218-2 (1908-08-) Henry to Bertha]

C. RETURN TO RYE BEACH, 1900

When Bertha returned to Rye Beach starting the summer of 1900, her focus had changed from her girlish exuberance of Rye Beach to her young children and, of course, to when Daddy would arrive.

1. DADDY'S ARRIVAL

When Bertha took the children to Rye Beach during the summer, the children were always excited for the arrival of "daddy".

> *The family have been planning for a month how they would "meet daddy at the station." If you want to bring a present to them and have time in Boston, they are all daft for a tether ball set. The McLures have one and George said this evening "mother, if you should get us a set, will you invite Mrs. McLure over to play with me because he invites me to play with her." I told them I would have to consult you about getting one.*
> [1902-07-30 Bertha (Rye Beach) to Henry (StL)]

2. THE SCOTT DOGS GO EAST

Bertha and Henry always seemed to have dogs with them and the dogs were very close companions of their children. On their vacations at Rye Beach, Henry would send their dogs east to join them. Generally, their dogs brought delight but, together with the joy they brought, there were also the sad partings.

> *We had a sad parting this morning. Hugh went out to give Rab his last breakfast and came in with quivering lips and a desperate effort to appear composed which his voice shook as he said, "If the man comes for Rab while we are at breakfast, may I be excused to see Rab off?" The man who came turned out fortunately to be a very nice kindly one and was so agreeable that it softened the actual parting but Hugh retired, looking as if he had lost his last friend and George, when asked if*

he would go to the farm, with tears in his eyes and a most sniffly voice, "I can't have Rab to go with me so I don't want to go anywhere." I felt quite affected myself.
[1903-09-28 (Friday) Bertha (Rye, NH) to Henry (Waco)]

The children have all gone over to play with Rab's brother. Whenever Hugh wakes out of a muse, it is to talk "dog." It is a very intense devotion.
[1903-09-28 (Saturday) Bertha (Rye, NH) to Henry (Waco)]

Frances, Bertha, and the dogs.

During Bertha and the children's 1904 summer in Rye Beach, Henry was tasked with sending their dog, Fido, east.

I have not shipped Fido. I have tried the express companies but I can get no guarantees that a puppy of that size will make the journey safely. Explain matters to George and, if he insists upon my sending the pup, I shall do so and take the chance.
[1904-07-01 Henry (StL) to Bertha (Rye Beach)]

Henry continued his attempts to make arrangements to ship Fido.

About Fido, I am still perplexed. The Expressmen will not advise shipping so small a puppy and, contrive as I will, I can get none of them to say but that he will reach Rye after all his earthly troubles are over. Still, I'll take the chance if you think best.
[1904-07-05 Henry (StL) to Bertha (Rye Beach)]

Henry was finally able to make the arrangements for shipping Fido to Rye Beach. Apparently, however, this left their other dog, Bobby, home alone and very lonely. Although Henry generally liked dogs, he did make exceptions.

I shipped off the puppy under guarantee of delicacy today having finally secured a guarantee from the American Express Co. to deliver him alive. Bobby still remains and howls nightly for the peace of our neighbors and my own joy. I shall slay Bobby before many moons and then "no more canines in the City, please." This is final. Mrs. Hitchcock threatens with the police, Wallace with his gun but no one has the decency to remove Bobby and that task is plainly left for me. I shall accept the responsibility and, unless I can give the cur away, I am going to do a bit of practice work with my posse pistol.
[1904-07-09 Henry (StL) to Bertha (Rye Beach)]

(The "posse pistol" that Henry mentioned in this letter was the pistol that had been given him when he served in the Posse Comitatus during the St. Louis Streetcar Strike in the summer of 1900.)

Henry wrote again to Bertha about shipping Fido to Rye Beach, suggesting that he could also ship Bobby.

You are going in for dogs in great fashion. I suppose you would like me to send on Bobby! You don't enthuse over the newest acquisition but his description sounds well. I think the uglier and more ungainly the pups of that variety are, the more "points" they are alleged to possess. The ticket on Fido's box evidently worked. The Expressman said "if the boys on the car take a fancy to the youngster, he'll not lack attention", so I tacked the sign on as an appeal

[20171206-6 (1904-07-) Henry to Bertha]

Apparently, Fido's arrival in Rye Beach met with great joy. Henry could only imagine Fido's welcome.

I should like to have seen Fido's reception and I am well paid for sending him in your description of the delight his arrival caused.

[1904-07-(-) 20180630-2 Henry (StL) to Bertha (Rye Beach)]

3. OTHER PETS

The Scott children did not limit their pets only to dogs. Bertha wrote to Henry about their other animal friends.

The Scott's seventy sixth pet has arrived. Hugh and Hayman caught a chipmunk in their box trap and such rapture and delight! It is well poor Hugh has it for I fear there is sad trouble ahead for him. I enclose Mr. Petter's letter about Marmion. I was sure all along that he was waiting for the two weeks to pass that must elapse after a dog has been exposed to distemper before he shows it.

[1906-09-24 Bertha (Rye Beach) to Henry (StL)]

4. THE 4TH OF JULY 1906

Bertha described her sleepless and eventful 4th of July 1906 at Rye Beach in her letter to Henry.

July 4th, 1906

Dear boy,

You were a boy once, so I suppose you will appreciate the tale I am about to relate.

When I finished my letter to you last night, it was about eleven forty, for I had sat up late after my card players went to write you, and, as I was taking my letter to the head of the cellar stairs, I heard a curious noise, suggestive of burglars. It proved to be my sons who had arranged for a midnight rendezvous to ring the church bell but, as it was pouring rain, nobody else had turned up. They had not intended to be caught for Hugh firmly intended, it seems, to stay up all night and was most indignant, though George owned up that he was glad to be ordered to bed. I went to sleep about one and at four fifteen, the Allens and Dwight Filley arrived and, as the boys had forgotten to readjust their strings, they let off a few gentle firecrackers to awaken them, also me. It was not raining then but by the time they reached the church, it was pouring in torrents and they couldn't get in and, just as I was falling asleep in the neighborhood of five thirty, George and Nancy returned looking as if they had swum the Atlantic Ocean. The older boys had gone into shelter somewhere but they & Wayman had not. Well, I called Ellen and between us we dried those heads, I had to rub George's with blankets it was so dripping, administered camphor, got off their wet clothes and insisted they go back to bed until breakfast time. And as it was storming terrifically, they did but they had breakfast awful promptly.

Do you wonder that tonight I feel a little wearied? It stopped raining and everybody had a successful fourth ending up in a blaze of glory for church Whittemore had ordered ten dollars' worth of fireworks and as his family did not come, Sarah and I bought them and the boys set them off under Russell's supervision. And all the children in the neighborhood – Lamberts, Otises, etc., came. They really were a beautiful lot and Russell said it was a pleasure to work with the boys, they were so absolutely obedient and did not rush into foolish risks. When the last display was over, the Allens responded with the most magnificent bonfire I have ever seen. And the boys say they believe it is the "slickest" fourth they ever had. I am delighted and I think I'll go to bed.

Lovingly,
Bert
[1906-07-04 Bertha (Rye Beach) to Henry (StL)]

5. THE LADIES FAIR, JULY 1906

Bertha wrote to Henry about the charity fair that the Rye Beach ladies organized.

It was of all days the most maddening for a fair – "open and shut." We met at half past nine to arrange our tables which were to have been on the porch but it was cold, damp, and windy with enough promise of rain to make it unwise also to have the tables for fancy goods on the green as intended. But the inside of the club was to be given up to bridge where each woman was to pay a dollar for the privilege of playing and we knew at least ten tables had been made up. Someone suggested that the Allen's might take the bridge at their house as it was their fair but at quarter of eleven, not an Allen had yet appeared. This was maddening. And I finally volunteered to capture an Allen which I did. Frances and they agreed to take the bridge and we went ahead. Mrs. Leland arranged the flowers for our little tables, six of them, wild roses, clover, iris, red rambler, hollyhock and water lily and Mrs. Clapp painted a mum card to correspond with the same flower to each table. They made a horseshoe around the central tea table where Mrs. Clapp, Maria and I sat and our pretty waitresses led by June Leland wore aprons with pink bows and caps with pink bows. But I am anticipating.

After arranging tables, Mrs. Clapp, Maria, Noca(?) Whittemore and I made a hundred sandwiches. I will mention in passing that I donated those sandwiches, two dozens of cake and all the lemonade, tea, cream and sugar. The other things were given by other people. As it was all donated, we did not charge high. It was too hard on the children. Lemonade 5 cents, cake 5 cents, two sandwiches 5, ice cream 15, tea 10. And we made fifty two dollars, dear, at our table. I call that very good work.

But the fair would have paid me if only for the intense happiness of Nancy Scott. She said it was the happiest day of her whole life. She and Edith were flower girls and wore wreaths! I ordered Nancy's from that somewhat dismal faced flower girl who, when I asked her if she could make a wreath for Nancy to wear to the fair, said solemnly, "O, yes, ma'am, we often make them for funerals." So Nancy wore a pale blue dress and a wreath of real forget-me-nots and carried a basket of flowers with a large pale blue bow on the handle and made six dollars and sixty cents. And Edith wore a white dress and a pink wreath and made nine dollars and forty cents. As Nancy explained, "Edith asked everybody she saw but I felt shy about speaking to people I did not know", with which I was well content.

The show had some amusing features as when Mr. Southworth bought the entire cake table (not ours but the one where they sold cakes whole) and then presented it to the boys. But the dearest thing at the whole show was precious, solemn-eyed Alice Scott, a little dazed but unutterably content, paying out endless five centses for a grab in the grab bag. Hugh showed his parentage for he bought cravats, one light blue and "one, I'm afraid you won't like, mother, it's pink." And dear George never found any ice cream, being unaware you sat at a table and ordered, and spent his entire substance on a scarf pin shaped like a trumpet. I gave them each two dollars to spend. Altogether, the children loved it and I remember to this day some fairs I went to as a child so it's worth something.

I suppose Frances cleared between four and five hundred for her charity. George Allen paid five dollars for five glasses of lemonade and refused to take change and Mr. Haarstick created an equally good impression by paying a quarter for a cup of tea and refusing to take change. Why not make a reputation economically if possible.
[1906-07-27 Bertha (Rye Beach) to Henry (StL)]

6. THE 1906 HORSE SHOW

Bertha kept a copy of the August 4, 1906 Ladies' Horse Show program which provided a glimpse into one of their diversions. Apparently, the "ladies" horse show was not only for women but also for girls, men and boys. The events included: jumping, saddle horses, best hunter, best Victoria (or suitable summer carriage), combination riding & driving. Nancy Scott was entered in Class 1 – best pony driven by a child and Hugh Scott (riding Ginger) and George Scott (riding Queen Bess) were entered in Class X – best saddle pony. (See below)

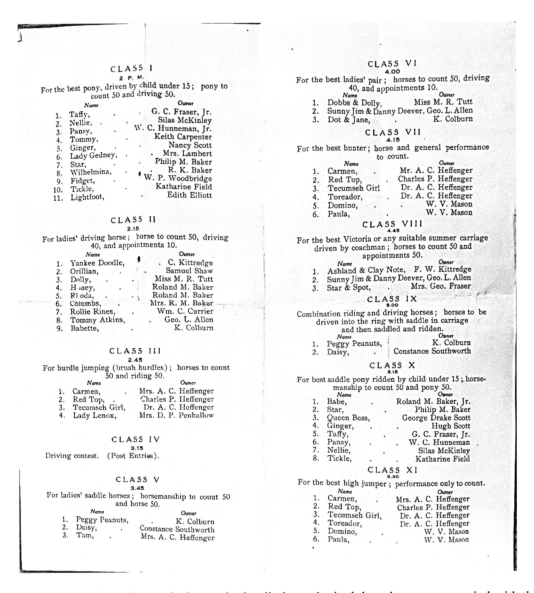

CLASS I
2 P.M.
For the best pony, driven by child under 15; pony to count 50 and driving 50.

Name	Owner
1. Taffy,	G. C. Fraser, Jr.
2. Nellie,	Silas McKinley
3. Pansy,	W. C. Hunneman, Jr.
4. Tommy,	Keith Carpenter
5. Ginger,	Nancy Scott
6. Lady Gedney,	Mrs. Lambert
7. Star,	Philip M. Baker
8. Wilhelmina,	R. K. Baker
9. Fidget,	W. P. Woodbridge
10. Tickle,	Katharine Field
11. Lightfoot,	Edith Elliott

CLASS II
2.15
For ladies' driving horse; horse to count 50, driving 40, and appointments 10.

Name	Owner
1. Yankee Doodle,	C. Kittredge
2. Orillian,	Samuel Shaw
3. Dolly,	Miss M. R. Tutt
4. Honey,	Roland M. Baker
5. Rhoda,	Roland M. Baker
6. Columbs,	Mrs. R. M. Baker
7. Rollie Rines,	Wm. C. Currier
8. Tommy Atkins,	Geo. L. Allen
9. Babette,	K. Colburn

CLASS III
2.45
For hurdle jumping (brush hurdles); horses to count 50 and riding 50.

Name	Owner
1. Carmen,	Mrs. A. C. Heffenger
2. Red Top,	Charles P. Heffenger
3. Tecumseh Girl,	Dr. A. C. Heffenger
4. Lady Lenox,	Mrs. D. P. Penhallow

CLASS IV
3.15
Driving contest. (Post Entries).

CLASS V
3.45
For ladies' saddle horses; horsemanship to count 50 and horse 50.

Name	Owner
1. Peggy Peanuts,	K. Colburn
2. Daisy,	Constance Southworth
3. Tam,	Mrs. A. C. Heffenger

CLASS VI
4.00
For the best ladies' pair; horses to count 50, driving 40, and appointments 10.

Name	Owner
1. Dobbs & Dolly,	Miss M. R. Tutt
2. Sunny Jim & Danny Deever,	Geo. L. Allen
3. Dot & Jane,	K. Colburn

CLASS VII
4.15
For the best hunter; horse and general performance to count.

Name	Owner
1. Carmen,	Mr. A. C. Heffenger
2. Red Top,	Charles P. Heffenger
3. Tecumseh Girl	Dr. A. C. Heffenger
4. Toreador,	Dr. A. C. Heffenger
5. Domino,	W. V. Mason
6. Paula,	W. V. Mason

CLASS VIII
4.45
For the best Victoria or any suitable summer carriage driven by coachman; horses to count 50 and appointments 50.

Name	Owner
1. Ashland & Clay Note,	F. W. Kittredge
2. Sunny Jim & Danny Deever,	Geo. L. Allen
3. Star & Spot,	Mrs. Geo. Fraser

CLASS IX
5.00
Combination riding and driving horses; horses to be driven into the ring with saddle in carriage and then saddled and ridden.

Name	Owner
1. Peggy Peanuts,	K. Colburn
2. Daisy,	Constance Southworth

CLASS X
5.15
For best saddle pony ridden by child under 15; horsemanship to count 50 and pony 50.

Name	Owner
1. Babe,	Roland M. Baker, Jr.
2. Star,	Philip M. Baker
3. Queen Bess,	George Drake Scott
4. Ginger,	Hugh Scott
5. Taffy,	G. C. Fraser, Jr.
6. Pansy,	W. C. Hunneman
7. Nellie,	Silas McKinley
8. Tickle,	Katharine Field

CLASS XI
5.30
For the best high jumper; performance only to count.

Name	Owner
1. Carmen,	Mrs. A. C. Heffenger
2. Red Top,	Charles P. Heffenger
3. Tecumseh Girl,	Dr. A. C. Heffenger
4. Toreador,	Dr. A. C. Heffenger
5. Domino,	W. V. Mason
6. Paula,	W. V. Mason

Bertha did not write about the results but undoubtedly her principal thoughts were occupied with the desire to ensure that her children participated.

7. RYE BEACH IN 1908

By 1908, it appeared that the crowd who went to Rye Beach was changing and not for the better in Henry's view.

> *...though it may inconvenience us to pull up stakes and leave Rye, there are compensations even for that in the riddance of a shoal of undesirable people who seem to be finding their way there in increasing crowds each year.*

[1908-06-08 (Sunday) Henry (StL) to Bertha (Rye Beach)]

And there was a major fire in Rye Beach that year. Bertha wrote to Henry about the fire which almost burned down Jack & Sarah Shepley's house next door to the Scott's house in Rye Beach.

> *Thursday night*
> *64 Vandeventer Place [stationary]*

Dear boy,

Thank the Lord for all his mercies and that the wind changed. Russell Sawyer's barn was struck by lightning this afternoon and burned to the ground. Everything, thanks to Elmer's coolness, was saved except his own things and the heavy rain fall and change in the wind saved our houses or no one knows where we would all be tonight. It was a frightful fire. Poor Russell had just got in all his hay, the men had worked eight days, and Russell himself was away when it started. Elmer let the ponies out first and they wheeled and went straight back into their stalls. Then he led them out, gave each one a terrific cut and they and Louis ran away and were caught and brought back later. Then they went for the carriages, Elmer and Eric and Mrs. Sawyer and Hugh. By this time the upper part was in a bright blaze, and then we all arrived together.

We were none of us except those four there at first but as soon as the flames shot out, help came from everywhere and Russell came tearing up in a buggy with a face white and set as a mask. He organized splendidly. By this time the rain was falling in sheets but of course everything had been dry as powder and the wind was blowing great flakes of cinders on Sarah's barn and our shed but specially toward the Shepley's. I thought Sarah would go crazy, she was like a frantic thing and she would not go in so I staid with her. Miss Engelhardt & Edith staid with father on the other side of the house and he never knew what was going on. Ed Sawyer was sent up on top Sarah's barn with a broom and Abbot Drake & another boy on top of our house to watch for any flake that might not be put out by the rain. But fortunately, it poured in floods.

I finally persuaded Sarah to stand in our shed, we were both soaked through, and George Allen came in and helped calm her down and then the men said the wind had changed. But of course, they staid on guard. It was magnificent to see but just dreadful. Russell is only partly insured and of course the hay is all gone and all the rent he expected to get from horses and automobiles. Elmer got everything out, horse harness, saddles & the oats and little Eric worked like a Trojan. Hugh said Eric was white as a sheet and dreadfully frightened but he went everywhere the men went and kept saying "if God means us to die, we'll die, and if he don't, we won't." That is the kind of stuff heroes are made of.

He lost all his belongings and he is dreadfully poor. I think we must do something for him and Elmer for they saved all our things and even put a cover over the new buggy in the floods of rain. Hugh brought out three carriages himself before the men got there and sent him out. The other boys did not get there in time. John Shepley had gone to Straw's Point & saw the flames from there and thought it was the house. George Allen said he was sure it was our house and he never knew how he got here.

This letter is rather incoherent but I can think of nothing but Russell & Mrs. Sawyer with all their promising summer so hurt. She was a perfect trump as long as she could walk but after it was all over, Edith found her crying quietly. Of course we turned over our little carriage house and Sarah her barn to the Sawyer's. Sarah's barn is a real practical help and of course the carriage house was built for carriages, but the four automobiles! I don't know what he'll do.

I haven't mentioned the storm itself which was perfectly frightful. There were two fires at Hampton. The embers are still burning quite brightly & we have watchmen tonight. Miss Engelhardt gave Sarah a sedative for her nerves and whisky for her wetting and we are not going to tell father till morning. You'll get this with my frivolous tennis letter but I don't feel frivolous tonight.

Yours always,
Bert!
[1908-06-04 Thursday (20180727-1) Bertha (Rye Beach) to Henry]

(Regarding *Little Eric*: "'*if God means us to die, we'll die, and if he don't, we won't.' That is the kind of stuff heroes are made of.*" Well said!)

Henry was none too happy that Bertha "*tried to play fire department*".[290]

> *When I had your account of how you tried to play fire department, I at first was wrathful at your forgetfulness of what you must have known was a dangerous experiment; but when I reached the stage of the wounded hand, I wanted to take the next train for Rye and try to comfort you as a dear injured child ought to be comforted. I am so sorry you darling child that you have had added to your other cares an injury which must have given you great pain for the time without any of the calming since that you were bravely enduring a serious hurt. You were most lucky too for I have known several serious explosions from that self-same experiment and that you and the house came out safely is cause for hymns of thanksgiving. If there had been gas enough over those hot coals, you would probably have been deposited at the Sawyers and the furnace itself in different parts of the house if the latter remained to tell the tale. I am glad the hurt hand is all right again but I am grieved that it was hurt at all.*
> [1908-06-10 Henry (StL) to Bertha (Rye Beach)]

Henry planned to meet Bertha in Boston during the middle of June 1908, although they may have met closer to Newport. Henry's sail from Newport/Jamestown gave him a farewell view.

> *I had a beautiful sail down the sound and the trip from Fall River to Newport was most interesting. The Newport harbor was filled as of old with smart yachts, one or two warships and millions of small craft. It was dark of course but numerous search lights from Fort Adams, the Torpedo station, our own Fort Dumpling and Beavertail lit up the whole harbor and both shores at times as if it had been daylight and, as the Conanicut Ferry puffed past us, I almost had a lump in my throat as I searched the decks of this old friend for a familiar face. Ah, I wanted my girl along so badly!*
> [1908-06-24 Henry (on train to Stl from Rye & NYC) to Bertha (Rye Beach)]

Bertha became very close to Russell and Mrs. Sawyer over the years that she went to Rye Beach. Russell wrote very poignantly to Bertha after Henry's death in 1911 to express his gratitude towards Henry.

> *You have my deepest heartfelt sympathy in your loss. It has been one of the greatest opportunities of my life to have known Mr. Scott so well; in a financial way he made it possible to start in business for myself and he has always been ready to aid me with advice and money. Socially, he made it possible for me to meet and associate with men above my path in life. It was always a pleasure and inspiration to me to stroll with him and get his ideals of the higher goals to strive for. If there is any way that I could show you or his children my appreciation of what he has done for me, I will be pleased to do so and trust that in small degree at least I might do as he would have wished.*
> [1911-03-23 H Russell Sawyer (Palmenton PA) to Bertha (StL)]

---

[290] Note: it is possible that the preceding fire was a different event than the one below. If so, the date of the previous fire is not correct and the true date is uncertain. Since the Sawyers were regulars at Rye Beach, this would be the location of the fire. Also, the "hurt hand" may have been communicated in another letter which was not kept.

D. THE RYE BEACH CHURCH, ST. ANDREW'S-BY-THE-SEA

St. Andrews, Rye, New Hampshire - 1910

In the late 1800's, Rye Beach and Little Boars Head were popular summer residences for wealthy families from New York as well as St. Louis, Chicago and other mid-western cities. Church services were important to these summer residents who united together to build this chapel. Until St. Andrew's was built, Episcopal services were held at the Casino, the social center for the nearby Farragut Hotel, beginning July 17, 1864. Generally, people brought their household staffs and lived in the hotels and boarding houses along the beach, the last of which are the Wentworth by the Sea and the Drake House. Some of these servants and employees of the hotels were African-Americans, who used St. Andrew's for their own worship services and meetings.
[History of St. Andrews by the Sea, https://standrews-by-the-sea.org/]

In a letter to Henry in August 1892, Bertha described the emotional toll that she endured in dealing with the new church altar in Rye Beach and the removal of a remembrance of someone's husband. But, while this was emotionally difficult, Bertha wrote of how she could always count on Henry, who was her "*stronghold*", to be able to weather such difficulties.

> *I cannot write you a long letter today. It is almost supper time now and I am invited out. Every bit of my spare time today has been given to trying to prevent trouble arising about the new church altar which displaced the hangings embroidered by someone in memory of her husband. It has been a very hard trying day for so many people have been hurt and wounded and I have been acting as a sort of go between trying to make both sides feel less unhappy about it and I am worn out. I would rather do hard manual labor. I do think women are the most unreasonable people in the world and they can say the cruelest things of one another. And to think of its being about the altar in a church, it makes it so much worse. Details would only bore you especially as I was not one of the immediate parties. I think what I would consider the downright scandal of an open row on such a subject has been prevented. But there is a great deal of hard feelings and all the pleasant atmosphere is jarred.*

> *I wonder if the others can get away to a place where they feel as much at rest as I do when I get back to the thought of you. If there is always one place where one can come and be sure of perfect understanding and sympathy, outside annoyances and disappointments can be faced easily. It is only when that fails that life does not seem worth living. You do not know what your sympathy is to me. I have had in one way a rather lonely life. One does not tell one's friends of one's troubles and I have had no sister and no brother near enough to my own age to come to. While my mother is too sympathetic, every slight disappointment of mine was a real grief to her so that, as soon as I grew old enough to see that, I have kept any annoyance of mine as much from her knowledge as possible. But you and I belong in the bothers as well as other times. I did not write all this because of what happened today. That wasn't my funeral except as it affected others. But I only wondered if those others wouldn't take life and especially the little worries of life more easily if they had a stronghold like mine.*

[1892-08-04- Bertha (Rye Beach) to Henry (StL)]

St. Andrew's-by-the-Sea

AN EPISCOPAL SUMMER CHAPEL

Rye Beach, New Hampshire
Serving the Seacoast since 1876

Bertha provided various volunteer services to the church which included directing the choir.

> *I believe I have told you that I run the chorus choir of this little Episcopal Church. That is, I beat up recruits for it, select the hymns, sing in it and get all the abuse that is usually showered on it. Our two best singers do not come until Tuesday, one of whom sings in a New York choir and whom we depend on to lead, so this morning there was only I and three very young girls and I had to lead. The music went sufficiently smoothly but father encouraged me afterwards by saying that you could not hear the choir at all in the back of the church. Fortunately, we have a splendid organist, Richard Hoffman. I do not know if you know him by name, but any New Yorker would. I staid to talk to him after church and then got the money from the clergyman & talked to him. I found Cherry Bent waiting for me to ask me to go home to dinner with her but I declined, though I walked home with her. Then there is an afternoon service.*
> [1892-07-07 Bertha (Farragut house, East Jaffrey) to Henry (StL)]

The comment by Bertha's father after less than optimal singing was priceless: *"father encouraged me afterwards by saying that you could not hear the choir at all in the back of the church"!!*

After more than a month, the choir singing improved to the point where Bertha pronounced it *"fine"*. After the service at the end of August, Bertha included a goldenrod from the church which she had been wearing in her letter to Henry.

> *I send you a spray of goldenrod left over from the church decorations. We had far too much so I have been wearing some, this spray among the rest. You ought to have heard the music this morning: no hitches this time. It was fine.*
> [1892-08-22 (Sunday) Bertha (Farragut House) to Henry (StL)]

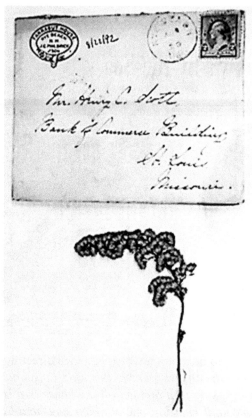

Bertha's August 22 Letter and the enclosed spray of goldenrod.

Henry was touched by Bertha's gesture.

> *The spray of golden rod made me feel as though you had put your hand in mine for you told me you had worn it.*
>
> [1892-08-27 (Friday) Henry (StL) to Bertha (Farragut House)]

Bertha and Henry both included flowers in many of their letters to each other, tangible mementos from the sender's heart.

CHAPTER 22 - HENRY'S HEALTH AND "HIS ENEMY"

O, ye gods, the relief it is not to wish you were dead every moment of your waking hours! I have had as mean an experience as I have ever had in my life and I hope it is not to be repeated in the near future for I don't think I could "beat it".
[1910-09-30 Henry (Stl) to Bertha (Morris Plains, NJ)]

... the art of saving yourself does not lie among your accomplishments.
[1892-07-28 Bertha (Rye Beach) to Henry (StL)]

Henry was ill at ease about many things in life, starting with growing up in Fredericksburg during the Civil War and seeing fortunes wiped out. Perhaps his work ethic originated in a post war fear which may have propelled him toward success in his business endeavors and the consummation of his dreams of a happy marriage to Bertha. Henry clearly experienced euphoric highs when everything seemed to go right. But, throughout his life, Henry suffered greatly from melancholia and depression. The deaths of friends and acquaintances were a constant reminder of illness, cruel fate and the running of the sands of time. Henry worried about his family's health and his own and, especially when he was blue, he imagined a variety of illnesses. Throughout, Henry was able to master of all of his worries except the one that he could not control: the uncontrollable darkness of depression which he referred to as "*my enemy*". And Henry seemed to understand that, against it, there was no remedy.

Bertha was warned by Henry's sister Mattie of his "*terrible moods of depression*" and Bertha could see firsthand Henry's sudden highs and lows as evidenced in many of Henry's letters, such as the following prior to their marriage.

Well, this morning I was blue as I have not been in a long time for I had a miserable night and, though I could not expect my attack to pass off and have me as well at first as I have been, I felt terribly abused and badly treated – and then, dearest, your letters came and I saw what an ungracious fellow I had been to let a few days sickness make me think for a moment that I was not the most fortunate, the happiest man on earth.
[1892-07-05 Henry (StL) to Bertha (Farragut House, Rye Beach)]

Henry's mood changes were also noticed by his friends. Bertha wrote to Henry of Jack Shepley's observations.

You cannot frighten me very much by threatening to make me go with you on those expeditions next year. I am only afraid that it is not the lack of my society but your own state of health which made you so blue when you were on this last trip. Jack Shepley said "I never saw a fellow in whom the state of his health made such a difference as it does in Henry. The days he doesn't feel all right he comes down looking as if he had been to his own funeral and the days he does, he fairly cuts pigeon wings[291] all over the place." This description applied with literal exactitude to two consecutive days I had just spent in his own society. Talk about people who live in vitreous domiciles. Jack said he would have written you and urged you again to come on but Jack told him he was sure it would be no use. If it would have been of use, I don't think I shall feel very much like forgiving Mr. Jack for I did want you so.
[1892-08-31 (Tuesday) Bertha (Rye Beach) to Henry (StL)

It is a testament to Bertha's strength of character that she was never consumed by Henry's darkness.

---

[291] Cut the pigeon('s) wing: To execute intricate dance steps gracefully.

A. PRE-MARRIAGE CONCERNS FOR HENRY'S HEALTH
1. "VACATION" AT THE GASCONADE

There was an indication that something was not quite right in 1891 when Henry went to stay for a week in The Gasconade, in Lebanon MO. The Gasconade was used as a vacation resort and work get-away, but also became known as a sanatorium due to its special waters.

> *Perhaps the most unique piece in Lebanon's history is the magnetic water. A worker digging a new city water well in 1889 found that his tools could pick up nails. The water had magnetized them. Bathing in the magnetic waters was said to have healing powers and visitors came to bathe in them and drink from the well. The Gasconade Hotel was built to accommodate them and no grander building has ever been seen in Lebanon.*
> [https://www.lebanonmissouri.org/108/History]

Bertha quipped in her first letter to Henry after he arrived at the Gasconade in 1891, "*To begin with, by being disagreeable as usual, I am very glad that you are gone. Yes, I really am. I do not want to see that tired look in your eyes again and do rest well.*" Bertha added, "*... you need not cut short your time at Lebanon and I hope you will not, dear, you need it more than you think. I do not mean to be unkind all through my letter but indeed I am very glad to know that you are resting.*" [1891-11-24 Bertha (StL) to Henry (Lebanon, MO)]

Bertha concluded this letter with, "*Your flowers have made my room perfectly beautiful. I love those roses almost better than any others. You sent them to me so often that spring two years ago, sent them to me when I started for Europe. You see, though you accused me of having a poor memory, there are some things I do not forget. Dear, there is not one of all the tender, considerate things that you have done for me that I have ever forgotten.*" [1891-11-24 Bertha (StL) to Henry (Lebanon, MO)]

Henry responded to Bertha's previous letter speaking about himself as a "*very annoying invalid*". Henry seemed to be particularly annoyed at the "*postponement*". Henry wrote, "*I have done very little in my life that was worth anything by waiting for "a more convenient season".*" It was clear that the postponement referred to their wedding which was to be put off for another year, "*a year [that] would be taken out of our lives...*" Perhaps these continual postponements was one reason why Henry needed convalescence?

> *Wednesday*
> *Your letter came this morning, my darling, as I knew it would. It was very sweet to hear from you dear. One would think, with a letter like that, any man would be too happy to write anything but words of thankfulness in return and yet, see – happy as I am, I intend to begin with criticism & not with expressions of gratitude.*

> *Your letter, dear, was a cleverly planned message to an interesting but very annoying invalid who had been persuaded against his will to go away for his health and who must be made to feel that everything was as it should be except the aforesaid health. This alone might, if not given proper attention, throw into confusion all these other less important matters which otherwise would move along most smoothly, etc. You were thinking too much of my well-being, dear, to see that you were making matters appear unnaturally bright in the existence of "a general quiet air of peace" but I love you all the more for your courage, my darling, coming as it does after I have been so gloomy with you because I could not accept your plan for the future, as best insuring the fulfilment of our wishes and as removing the dangers which ever attend postponements.*

> *It will not mend matters, though, to tell you I have reproached myself more than once for feeling discouraged. I might explain this partly by telling you I have done very little in my life that was worth anything by waiting for "a more convenient season". And so I rebelled more because it seemed to me a wrong way of grappling with difficulties rather than because I knew that in every sense more than a year would be taken out of our lives. But all this feeling is past now, dear, for I*

thoroughly understand that you need my aid and encouragement now as much as you will in the future and I know that I can aid you more by doing whatever lies in my power to sustain & strengthen your purpose than by merely telling you of my great love for you. I must have been worn a little or I should not have made so useless the opportunities I have had of talking with you since you came home.

Before you went away from me more than two years ago, we talked of almost everything, each with an understanding of the other's view that made our ideas clear and you don't know, my child, how sweet these moments were to me. Often I could catch your meaning before you spoke to me and, dear, I can do this now. For your beautiful eyes are so frank that I sometimes think they trust & sympathize with me more than their owner does.

I wish all the old thoughts to come back to us this winter. I wish to talk with you about the things we care for, about what we read. You think me a poor reader don't you? I am indeed, for I have had so little time to give myself that I am sadly late in reaching out for the many beautiful & useful thoughts that should have been sought and acquired from the "gray heads" of the book world. I thought, Sunday night, when you were furnishing Mr. B with you <u>views</u> on various subjects, what a stupid fellow you must have thought me lately because I seemed not to be able to think of, speak of or be interested in but one thought.

It is not quite as bad as that, dear, you are not the <u>only</u> but the <u>first</u> thought in my life. Because I can only think of you when I am near you, other things are not lost sight of. I think I have enjoyed nothing so much during my short stay here as the books I brought with me, more even than my very interesting friends or even "Tom Kick"[292] who, you remember, because of his loyalty under temptation which would have made desertion natural, is entitled to my unqualified affection. And by the way he has that, whether he deserves it or not, for he is a most irresistible youngster.

I am reading some of Andrew Lang's essays. They are very good and I am so sure you will agree with me that I shall send you my copy of the very excellent selections I am reading. I was proud to find that Lang preferred one of my favorites, Scott, to any other poet. You, I think, will regard this preference with contempt but that is the fault of your miscellaneous and rather too general reading. "This often destroys ones tastes for simple & direct style" says a certain philosopher.

We ride horseback here and this is another reason your absence is particularly hard to bear for I know how you would enjoy the exercise. I had a fine gallop with Miss Alma[293] this afternoon. She asked me in her quiet way if I was absent minded after recovering from my confusion. I tried to answer by recalling esteemed antecedents who were <u>thusly</u> troubled & from whom I had possibly inherited the weakness. Whether I succeeded in satisfactorily answering her question depends largely upon the girl's susceptibility.

It occurs to me to thank you for being so pleased over the fact that I am absent. I'm sorry I can't accommodate myself to the wishes of my friends by settling at Lebanon but, really, affairs most important must be attended to in St. Louis and I must return even if in so doing I disturb the peaceful & beautiful time you have had since my departure. You see, I am not writing like a worn-out pessimist for all my combativeness has returned after one day's rest.

---

[292] Thomas McKittrick - who was a good friend of both Henry & Bertha. His "desertion" may refer to his marriage to Hildegarde Sterling on May 9, 1888. (However, this appears to be the only time that he was referred to as "Tom Kick".) From Henry's letter, it appears that the Sterlings and Tom McKittrick also vacationed at the Gasconade when Henry was there.
[293] Possibly Alma Canfield Sterling who married William Townsend Porter (1862-1949) in 1893. Alma may have been Hildegarde Sterling McKittrick's cousin.

Your note was such cheer, my darling, that I would ask for another but that I prefer you should not write just because I wish it. I will not return until Saturday or possibly Sunday so you have time to write me, if the clubs can spare me a little of your time. I am glad you like my flowers. I hope those that come tomorrow will be pretty enough to win your praise.

Goodbye means God be with you, doesn't it dear?
Henry
[1891-11-25 Henry (The Gasconade, Lebanon MO) to Bertha (2807 Locust Str, StL)]

This letter, like so many, demonstrated Henry's playful yet serious writing: "*your beautiful eyes are so frank that I sometimes think they trust & sympathize with me more than their owner does.*" Given the delay in their marriage plans, Henry needed some encouragement.

Also, in this November 25th letter, Henry referred to his "*esteemed antecedents who were* <u>*thusly*</u> *troubled & from whom I had possibly inherited the weakness*". Henry's "*weakness*" probably referred to his bouts of depression and his "*esteemed antecedents*" may be a reference to the fact that his father, Hugh Scott, and his mother, Anne Clarkson, were cousins (they both shared William Payne as one of their grandfathers). This may have been the only letter in which Henry (or anyone else) referred to this intriguing aspect of his lineage. However, it seemed clear from this letter that Bertha had already been made aware of this and accepted it.

As far as Bertha was concerned, the matter of their marriage plans was put to rest for a time. Bertha wrote back about how glad she was that Henry expressed a "desire for *rational conversation*".
I was delighted to hear from you this morning and much pleased at the effect my first letter had for no one but an invalid and a most "annoying" one could have written the mournful note you sent me last Monday. Also, I am so glad to hear you express a desire for rational conversation. I was beginning to be afraid that you had either lost your taste for it or thought me incapable of it. I hardly know which is the worse alternative.
[1891-11-27(-) Bertha (StL) to Henry (Lebanon, MO)]

After his "rest" in Lebanon and his acceptance of their marital plans, Henry seemed to master his condition.
You don't know, dear, how sweet it is to be in your debt. I tried to tell you this last night but I know I failed & it was because I was too happy to put my thoughts into words. Do you know what I mean when I tell you that all my expressions seemed but a helpless interpretation of the sweet thoughts that came to me whenever I looked into your eyes. I don't need a trip to Lebanon now, dear, or any tonic save to be near you.
[20170805-1 (1892-) Henry to Bertha]

2. ARE YOU TAKING CARE OF YOURSELF?
Health was a frequent topic in Bertha and Henry's letters. Not only was Henry concerned for Bertha's health, Bertha often expressed her concern for Henry. And Henry often tried to deflect her concerns.
Dear, in your letter to my sister Maggie, you said something about my overworking and having been made unwell by it and, as a consequence, I have been advised with and counselled and warned until I have almost begun to think the household has concluded I would die young from fatigue. Now, if I ever become a lazy, worthless fellow, it will be your fault, child, and then you will be sorry.
[1892-03-28-2 (6 letters) Henry to Bertha]

Bertha often wrote to Henry that he was working too hard.
I am getting on famously but O, my dear, it does not make things easier to know that you have not been well. No, I will not shower an avalanche of reproaches on your head for overwork. I did

write a lecture to you on that subject last Saturday. I only want to ask you one question, dear friend, don't you think you owe a little care of yourself to me? If you knew how hard it is for me to hear of your being unwell when I am away and can do nothing for you, I think you would be more careful.

....

Now, dear friend, if you find that business makes it impossible for you to get away, you must not think that I don't understand perfectly that there are chains that cannot be set aside. I am not a very unreasonable woman but always, my dearest, Your friend,...
[20180125-3 (1892-) Bertha (-) to Henry]

When Henry reproached Bertha for suggesting to Henry's family that he was working too hard, Bertha was unrepentant.

I can well believe that you did not feel like being kind to me but rather like flinging coalscuttles at my head when your family descended upon you and begged you to take more care of yourself. But I am not one bit penitent, no one could be less so. I am perfectly delighted!!
[1892-04-01 Bertha (Richmond VA) to Henry (StL)]

Dear, there is a tone in your family's letters to me which sounds half reproachful as though they thought I ought not to let you get so weary and unwell. Are not you ashamed of yourself for giving them that bad impression of me? I hope you will find time to rest on that New York trip but I hardly trust you, though I have a vague remembrance of your once taking such a long nap on the cars that you passed the proper station.
[1892-04-04 Bertha (Port Comfort, VA) to Henry (Leland Hotel, NYC)]

In other letters before they were married, Bertha wrote to Henry that he was working too hard. She even threatened to make herself ill so that Henry would have to take a vacation to care for her.

When are you going to finish David[294]? Not soon I should imagine if you have to sit up until one o'clock to write to me. Dear, I wish you would not work so hard. It is not being good to me at all.
[1892-03-21 Bertha (Augustine) to Henry (StL)]

I do not want to hear again of your staying up all night or, yes, if you do it, I want to hear of it but I don't want you to do it. If I hear anymore of such things, I shall take pains to catch cold & become violently ill so that you will be obliged to come on and see me and so take an enforced rest.
[1892-04-22 (Friday) Bertha (New York) to Henry (StL)]

Bertha commented that even Henry's friend Crittenden McKinley felt that Henry was killing himself by "*overwork*", the 19th century equivalent to *karoshi*.

You are mistaken if you think you punished me for my curiosity by your long account of a day's doings. I read your letter through twice and then sat appalled at the amount of a work you get through in a "dull day". It reminded me of Crittenden McKinley's remark that you were killing yourself by overwork and I do not wonder that you so often end a letter because you are "rather tired". Is it necessary, dear? It does not seem to me other men work like this.

...

Dear, I suppose it all seems deadly dull when you are used to it and yet, I suppose it is because the difference between a man and a woman's life is so great. But it sounds to me so full of accomplished or rather accomplishing purposes and that must be interesting.
[1892-05-07 Bertha (Boston MA) to Henry (StL)]

---

[294] *The History of David Grieve* is a novel by Mary Augusta Ward.

I had no letter from you last night, dear, and of course I have imagined all sorts of causes after your last letter. I first thought you might have gone to Waco but I was pretty sure you would have telegraphed me. Then I was afraid you were sick from the overwork and heat and that fear I have not quite gotten over yet. I am waiting anxiously for tonight's mail. If it proves to be only that you were too tired to write, I shall be very glad you did not make the attempt, dear boy.
[20180218-1 (- -08-17) Bertha (Rye Beach) to Henry (StL)]

Bertha worried that Henry was often not completely truthful about his health and wished that Henry would think more about his own health than hers.

You have had a pretty hard time and I should not be at all inclined to accept your assurance of being entirely all right if your mother had not written me that she thought the trip had done you good. I consider her statement decidedly more reliable than yours.
[1892-06-06 Bertha (East Jaffrey) to Henry (StL)

I wish you would think a little more of your own health and less of mine. You must remember you owe something to me, dear friend.
[1892-06-27 Bertha (East Jaffrey) to Henry (StL)]

During June-July 1892, Bertha was with her parents in Jaffrey NH where she felt an *"exhilaration in being alive."* With this feeling in mind and Henry's assurance that he was once again himself, Bertha wrote to warn Henry against overwork.

I am so glad you feel like yourself once more. It is gorgeous to feel just that exhilaration in being alive. But don't overwork yourself in this mood. I enclose you a word of warning on that subject, which I tore off my calendar some time ago meaning to send you and forgot it. I especially sympathize with your enjoyment of your own well-being for today is one of my days for being glad I am alive. You never felt anything like the air today. My windows are all open and the room is fragrant with great bunches of lilacs.

> *"All the work that a man can do that can be rested by one night's sleep is good for him, but fatigue that goes into the next day is always bad." (Cut out from May 28, Saturday, Calendar: Mrs. Beecher Stowe)*

[1892-07-01(-) 20170825-2 Bertha (East Jaffrey) to Henry (StL)]

When Bertha would learn that Henry was unwell, she would scold Henry with – don't you *"dear"* me.

I am very angry with you indeed. You ought to be ashamed of yourself! You have been sick and miserable for a week and you told me the second day that "It was all over now, you wouldn't have mentioned it if you had not felt perfectly well and I was to be sensible and not worry, dear". And the "dear" was evidently an afterthought for you had made a period – and then turned it into a comma. And now it seems you have been unwell enough to worry your mother. I thought you could not be well from the tone of your letters but, remembering your promise to let me know, I had about come to the flattering conclusion that it was because you missed me so much! Now I am a very indignant person! I am glad you have three "attentive females" to take care of you but it makes me tremble to think of the future. A man who has been used to having three women to spoil him when he is ill, what will you do when you only have one, you spoiled boy! [1892-09-23 (Tuesday) Bertha (East Jaffrey) to Henry (StL)]

And Bertha would scold Henry again in a letter the next month.

I have just received your Tuesday letter and I am going to scold!! I am glad you are conscious of your iniquity in not telling me how unwell you were. Dear, that never helps me. It simply leaves me in doubt whenever you speak of not feeling entirely well, whether that means exactly what it seems to, or whether you are really ill. And this time, I tell you frankly it hurt me very much in another way. After you had asked me to stay and the plea the Bentons had urged had been that you would come up if I did stay, my vanity was decidedly wounded when you did not make the attempt especially when Mr. Benton said "Business!! Why, why, why! If that keeps him away now, Miss Bertie, what will it be afterwards!"

Yes, I know I was very unreasonable. But if you had only told me you were sick, while I should have been disappointed for myself and sorry for you, I should not have been as "mad as hops" and that was just about the way I did feel. For I saw no reason why, if you wanted to come, a train reaching St. Louis at six forty, even if there had been danger of its being one hour or so late, would not have taken you to your office in time. And I hope you can make out that complicated sentence. You see, dear old boy, you have spoiled me and I have become used to thinking that everything except very important matters must give way if you can give the time to me. And I would like to remain in that blissful estate of conceit for a little longer anyway.

I forgive you your concealment this time if you will promise me not to do it again. And not to get sick again while I am away either. And especially not to ride races when you are in that condition. I would not deliver this lengthy lecture if I were not sure you were perfectly well but I think since you are able to endure a dinner at the Joneses. You are evidently able to sit up and take nourishment. Perhaps at the close of that dinner, you were better able to understand why Nan and I were not thrilled over the prospect of having Robert and Grace act as our chaperons to the Country Club.
[1892-10-28) (Friday) Bertha (Backbay, Boston) to Henry (StL)]

However, when Bertha discovred that Henry's dour condition was due to "*sufferings*" sustained at a ball that he attended, she was unsympathetic.
I found two letters waiting too from which I gathered that you had been working too hard again of which I entirely disapprove. But you failed to rouse my sympathy when you talked of your sufferings at being obliged to stay at the Turner Ball. I have known you to heroically sacrifice yourself many times in that way, beloved friend, and I understand you far too well to waste any pity on you.
[1892-11-01 (Monday) Berth (Boston) to Henry (StL)]

One month before their wedding, Bertha's scolding took a new tack – "*You are my property and I don't want it injured*".
And then I meant to scold you for something else she [Edith Knox] mentioned in her letter, "They say he is the busiest young man in town," etc., a good deal more of the etc. Dear boy, please don't wear yourself out. You are my property and I don't want it injured. If looking after those carpets is going to take much time, let them go. I want to quote from a letter I received from a very wise man the other day, neighboring a hundred in age I should think. "I meant to have such a nice time in the south and here you are wearing yourself all out and I shall have to spend all my time taking care of you."

Now that cuts just as well one way as it does the other and, unless I get a letter promising me solemnly that you will take very good care of yourself & not wear yourself out, I shall go out and dig paths through the snow with no rubbers on!!! And let me assure you that would be no laughing matter – we have more or less of a snow storm every day.
[1893-01-18 (Sunday) Bertha (Newton Centre) to Henry (StL)]

But deep down, Bertha knew that Henry had one speed and it was full speed ahead. Bertha, recollecting what Henry's mother had said, wrote:
I could almost hear her sigh though when she added "but very busy, as usual."
[1893-01-21 (Saturday) Bertha (Newton Centre) to Henry (StL)]

3. DARING SAIL IN ST. PAUL

"O, and I must tell you of an adventure..." may not have been the best way for Henry to broach this news to Bertha, especially halfway through a relatively long letter.

> *O, and I must tell you of an adventure I had at the lake this morning. I got up early and after a hasty breakfast, went down to the lake to get a skipper and boat for a sail. The man in charge of the boats said all his men were engaged but that he had a small and pretty fast boat which he would give me to manage alone if I was "a first-class sailor." Now, I have not sailed a boat for a very, very long time but I satisfied the man I knew how, though I had never before seen a "craft" rigged like the one he pointed out to me and in a short time I had started out and there my troubles began. There was a very strong "choppy" breeze blowing off shore and, when I got well into the open, it blew a small gale and, by the time I had gone out about two miles from the landing, I agreed with myself that I had had enough sailing, enough glory for one day, and I tried to turn around. To say nothing of my very nearly upsetting the boat in turning, my return trip was anything but delightful and, after making several failures to tack and get clear of a cluster of islands between me and the harbor which was fast becoming what one of those hymns Miss Bent tells you I am so familiar with, "a dear haven of refuge", I concluded it would be wise to take in the sail and scull in. If you have never seen a single boatman struggle with a sail in a high wind, it will be useless for me to describe this delightful undertaking but I got the sail in finally and then began my struggle against the wind with one oar. I worked for two hours and, at the end of that time, was picked up and taken ashore, wet, humiliated and utterly disconsolate. My next sail will be in a boat of some such dimensions as the "Great Eastern" and I shall not be the only "first class sailor" on board!*
> [1892-08-24 Henry (St. Paul, MN) to Bertha (Farragut House, Rye Beach)]

Bertha was not too happy to hear about Henry's sailing adventure and scolded him, much in the same way that Henry would scold Bertha when she was in any danger.

> *On one subject though, I can say what I feel and that is your going sailing alone when you did not understand the vessel and were out of practice anyway, dear, it was not fair to me. I am not sure that Jack Shepley's warning will not be fulfilled and you requested to restrict yourself to "croquet and mumblety peg" if I am frightened that way again. I put you in his charge this morning when I said goodbye to him.*
> [1892-08-31 (Monday) Bertha (Rye Beach) to Henry (StL)]

Bertha, in her next day's letter, did not give up the topic of Henry's adventurous sail.

> *I have been reading your letters over too and I have not scolded you half enough for that venture. Some sail. Your life belongs to me now and you have no right to risk my life in such a way. Anyway, I have made up my mind and, if you are reckless again, I shall consider myself at liberty to swim over to the Shoals if I please and to drive the most dangerous horses on the place.*
> [1892-08-31 (Tuesday) Bertha (Rye Beach) to Henry (StL)]

Henry sometimes bristled at Bertha's reprimands. His rejoinder to Bertha's letter was that he was an excellent swimmer and was never in any danger. (Confidence or over-confidence?)

> *You did not really mean that I was imprudent at Minnetonka[295]? I mean as far as my safety was concerned, the worst that could have occurred would have been the loss of the boat and, if I had been sure it would have been found, I think I should have struck out for the shore without it very early in the struggle. I have been able to swim ever since I could talk and, although I am out of practice now, it would take a larger lake than Minnetonka to drown me.*
> [1892-09-02 (Friday) Henry (StL) to Bertha (Farragut House, Rye Beach)]

---

[295] Minnetonka is a suburban city in Hennepin County, Minnesota, United States, eight miles west of Minneapolis. The name comes from the Dakota Indian "mni tanka", meaning "great water".

B. ACCIDENTS

Henry suffered periodic accidents. Two such accidents were recorded by Bertha in her diary and third in a letter from Henry.

While they were in Jamestown during the summer of 1899, Bertha recounted in her diary one such "accident".

> *"Henry ordered an impertinent colored peddler off the place and the man cut his head open with a golf club. Two inches higher, it would have killed him. Do not like to think about it."*
> [1893 Diary, Aug. 30, 1899]

The news of Henry's injury was reported in the St. Louis Post Dispatch on August 30, 1899 (see below).

HE FOUGHT ST. LOUIS MEN

A Rhode Island Negro Picture Peddler Injures Henry C. Scott and John D. Davis.

Henry C. Scott, president of the Laclede Power Co. of St. Louis was assaulted by a negro, at his summer home in Jamestown, R. I., Tuesday, and seriously hurt. John D. Davis, also of this city, who went to Mr. Scott's assistance, was also hurt by the negro, but not badly.

The negro, who the police there say is a bad man, was peddling pictures. He insulted Scott, who ordered him off the premises. He declined to go and showed fight, when Scott attempted to put him off. Davis went to Scott's help, and was struck in the face.

Several others were bruised before the negro was taken into custody.

Scott was struck with a golf stick and knocked senseless. His scalp was laid open, and several of his fingers were bitten to the bone.

In another incident, Henry fell into an eight foot "repair pit" that had been left unprotected after a Country Club event in 1901.

> *Mrs. Catlin, Mrs. John D. David, Mrs. Geo. B. Leighton, Mrs. J.L. Mauran, Miss Lionberger & I give dinner dance to ninety people at the Country Club. It is a very brilliant and successful affair but the pleasure for me is dampened by Henry's fall. The chaperones drove out ahead, so I did not see Henry until he came out on the car with the other people. He then looks so ill that he startles me and tells me that the car did not come out on time – and going in to see what the trouble was, he fell forward into a repair pit, eight feet deep, striking fortunately on his breast bone or he would probably have killed himself. He stands bravely to his guns all evening but when we come home, tells me I must help undress him – and nearly faints in the bathroom. He is in bed until the following Monday and retards his recovery by insisting on going to the telephone. On Sunday, twenty-five people come to inquire how he is and during the week, his room has been banked with flowers.*
> [1893 Diary, Jan. 22, 1901]

Henry described another accident when something got imbedded in his eye.

> *I had a nasty experience today. I got a small piece of flint or steel imbedded in my eye and had an interesting time for a while. Doctor Shoemaker pulled the thing out but he had to use cocaine which made my head feel queer for a while but there was no pain after the bout with him. I didn't*

suppose one could have a shaft plainly sticking into the eye without disagreeable results after it was out but Shoemaker says there is rarely any after-inflammation. He impressed me much more highly with his capability than does our old friend, Green, and I wish your father had Dr. S or some other younger man. Dr. Smith says bluntly that Dr. G should never operate.
[1907-09 – Henry to Bertha (20180416A-6]

Through all of these accidents, Henry always kept his composure and stood *"bravely to his guns."*

C. MEDICATIONS

1. ALCOHOL

Henry was never a big drinker. From his letters, it was clear that he associated drinking with *"dissipation"*, although he did drink for "medicinal" reasons.

> *You accuse me of dissipation. I would like to know, my child, what symbols would better describe an orgy than a dose of strong coffee, a drink of whiskey and a "portion" of sulfonil to sleep off the effects. If you had added to your program a Turkish bath you would have perfectly pictured what George Wright calls "a quiet week's sojourn with Satan." I don't do that sort of thing! I take a drink occasionally on the advice of my physician but I believe in only making the good use of it which my German friend, Krauss, ascribed to beer and I don't make a pig of myself!*
> [1902-07-25 Thursday Henry (StL) to Bertha (Rye Beach)]

Bertha would sometimes joke with Henry about drinking, especially if he had a cold since his favorite cold remedy was a stiff drink.

> *I hope that cold of yours is not worse than you said it was. I don't think a cold office or a slip into an icy puddle are good things for you a bit. Were you able to get hold of your favorite remedy or is Kansas a prohibition state?*
> [1892-12-20 (Monday 1892-12-19) Bertha (Newton Highlands, MA) to Henry (StL)]

Henry usually found relief from his various ailments in trips to the country but sometimes this did not achieve its intended purpose. Some of these times, Henry found solace with Dr. Tuttle who seemed to be able to prescribe what was needed and who *"expressly prescribed a drink of whiskey with every meal! until I got away, after which he said the less I drank the better for me "but you need it now, Mr. Scott, and I think I can safely prescribe it for one who is in no danger of taking more than is good for him."* [1907-09-(-) (Sunday) (20180416A-14) Henry to Bertha]

Some of Henry's doctors were concerned about Henry's drinking, especially when he was rheumatic. Henry didn't particularly care for such advice but would go along with it for a while.

> *Doctor Smith told me today that I clearly had rheumatism. He says the soreness of muscle which gives me so much trouble and the stiff swollen joints at night are infallible signs and that I ought to give up all alcohol and diet, and drink gallons of water. I shall try giving up alcohol for a day or two to see if I am benefited but I don't propose to have rheumatism and have to give up everything besides. So if total abstinence for a day or so does no good, I shall return to my cups.*
> [1910-06-14 Henry (StL) to Bertha (Rye Beach)]

> *I hope the day in Boston was not very hot and wearing and that you went to the Touraine and got a good lunch including a Bronx![296] Speaking of intoxicants – pardon the term so shortly after the above recommendation, you will have a chastened and purified husband at Rye this summer*

---

[296] The Bronx Cocktail is essentially a Perfect Martini with orange juice added. It was ranked number three in "The World's 10 Most Famous Cocktails in 1934", making it a very popular rival to the Martini (#1) and the Manhattan (#2). Today, it remains a popular choice in some markets. Like the Manhattan, the Bronx is one of five cocktails named for one of New York City's five boroughs, but is perhaps most closely related to the Queens, which substitutes pineapple for the Bronx's orange.

provided he gets there at all for his doctor has sternly forbad for the time at least all alcohol and dear Henry has not had a single drink except that dreadful legend called mater for ten days nor has he smoked even a single cigarette. If he would next take up the Good Book, which his youngest daughter is so impressed with, I think it might be safely inferred that he was not long for this world for it has been said that the truly good die young.
[1910-06-25 Henry (StL) to Bertha (Rye Beach)]

2. MEDICINE

Henry was always enthusiastic when he thought that there was a new remedy for his problems. *"I have been rather disconsolate myself until today but thanks to Obly [his doctor], I am much better. This time the remedy is heroic sure enough. The pills are as big as rifle bullets but I would swallow footballs if it would do any good."* [1899-06-13 Henry to Bertha]

Concerning Henry's large pills, Bertha commented:
> *Your tale about the football pills reminds me of a story Dr. Birney told me about a patient of his, one of the islanders, to whom he prescribed suppositories and the woman told him the next day that she had tried her best but those pills were the biggest she ever had tried to swallow and she simply could not do it.*
>
> ...
>
> *Now goodbye, and please, please, dearie, take care of yourself and don't have to take too many footballs.*
> [1899-07-13 (3rd letter) Bertha (Jamestown) to Henry (StL)

Henry's concern over his health did prevent him from joking about the various medications his doctors prescribed to cure him.
> *I had a séance with Obly this week and perhaps his medicine has done me some good but I think the exercise is partly "to blame" for my feeling that I am willing to live a little longer. Robinson told me that my liver was torpid unto stagnation and gave me some little saveprove(?) that have certainly waked me up, for the first instalment almost lifted the roof of my cranium. You will be pleased to know that the doctor pronounces me free from malaria and he told me he could have saved me much of the anguish of mind that I endured last week in sad contemplation of my early departure from this fair world if I had come to him sooner which is his apology, I think, for the error of sending a patient to drink geyser water for his liver!*
> [1898-07-04(-) Henry (StL) to Bertha (Jamestown)]

In a letter to Bertha around the year 1910, Henry spoke of taking lithia[297] for several days with good results. *"Today has been the first day for days that I have been practically free from the annoyance and I have been blessing myself that I did not use earlier the Lithia tablets which I have now only tried for a day with such good results. I am nearly over the trouble and I feel better than I have for days."* [1910(-) 20170723-6 Henry to Bertha]

D. DEATH LURKING

At times, it seemed that death was all around and, throughout their lives, Bertha and Henry witnessed the death of many friends. After the death of Mrs. Lackland, Bertha wrote:
> *Poor old Mr. Lackland. I do feel very sorry for him. He was exceedingly dependent on her for all the brightness in his life and she was an exceedingly winning woman. Dear, does death seem any more terrible to you than it used, a separation like this means so much more to me than it ever did before.* [1892-08-08 (Saturday) Bertha (Rye Beach) to Henry (StL)]

---

[297] "Lithia" or Lithium has been used as a mood-stabilizing drug in the treatment of bipolar disorder in humans.

In 1893, Eliot & Helen Bridge[298] suffered the loss of two of their very young children during a two-week period from scarlet fever. Henry wrote, "*as I think of the sorrow in that home it makes me gloomy and depressed as I have not been for a long time.*"

> *I heard of the death of Eliot Bridge's oldest boy and I added a postscript to my letter telling you of it. I hear today that two of the other children are quite ill with the same disease that carried off this little fellow – scarlet fever. I hope very much that the little ones will pull through all right for there is something terrible to me in a child's death and I know what a sad blow the loss of their oldest boy will be to Eliot and his wife.*
> [1893-01-13 (Thursday) Henry (StL) to Bertha (Stancote Newton Centre)]

> *I had a pretty sad duty to perform this afternoon. Eliot Bridge's little girl [Helen] died yesterday and was buried today and, as I knew it would be hard for him to get pall bearers, I offered my services. I am really very sorry for Mrs. Bridge. This is the second little one she has lost within two weeks and, as I think of the sorrow in that home, it makes me gloomy and depressed as I have not been for a long time.*
> [1893-01-28 (Saturday) Henry (StL) to Bertha (Stancote, Newton Centre, MA)]

Bertha wrote in her diary of the particularly difficult Spring of 1894.

> *May 19, 1894, Mr. Lionberger died. There is no more to tell about the spring. It was a very sad one. Lu Seddon died, John Davis died. Edward Cunningham died. No one who was seriously ill recovered, at least so it seemed to us.*
> [1983 Diary]

Henry wrote to Bertha around 1900 the death of Mrs. West which, as he wrote, made him more aware of the uncertainty of life and the certainty that death can only be "*postponed*".

> *I suppose you have heard of Mrs. West's death. It was one of the most sudden I have ever known of and they say it will be a frightful thing for Tom West who has been ill all the spring and was just going away for a long rest. It makes life seem pretty uncertain when people are falling so near one. I begin to recall the statement Cox made about the war – that it did not cost a single life and that we who stayed at home could do no more than postpone.*
> [1900(-) 20171205-2 Henry (StL) to Bertha]

Charles Sumner Taussig, a friend of Henry's, died at the age of 40 on January 2, 1898. Henry wrote to Bertha of his sorrow for his wife, Sarah ("Sadie") Augusta Knox Taussig.[299]

> *Poor Sadie, I feel very, very sorry for her and I hardly see how she stands it. She couldn't, I know, if it were not for the children and it is a God's mercy that she can pin all her hopes to them. I don't like to think of it, dear. It makes me morbid when I think of Charlie.*
> [1898-01(-) 20170829-6 Henry to Bertha]

Bertha mentioned Sadie in a letter later that year and the reports of how difficult it was for her at the family dinner at her parent's (Edith and Charles Knox's) house.

> *We had our first meeting of Topics this morning at Lute's and had a delightful time. We all talked at once. I am almost afraid it was too much for poor Sadie. She looked pale and exhausted. Edith said she went through a very trying ordeal yesterday. That Mrs. Knox senior had them all to dinner &, against the advice of the whole family, insisted that Sadie should come. And Edith said Sadie's*

---

[298] Hudson Eliot Bridge (1858-1934) was married to Helen Lee Durkee (1860-1954). They had five children: Hudson Eliot Bridge Jr. (1887-1893), Laurence Durkee Bridge (1889-1979), George Leighton Bridge (1891-1968), John Dwight Bridge (1893-1974), and Helen Bridge (died 1/28/1893). Helen Bridge's death was two weeks after her eldest brother died on 1/12/1893.
[299] Sadie was the niece of Charles & Edith Sherman Knox.

struggle to be bright and brave was something so pathetic that it broke up the whole family. And perhaps it was the effect of that which made her look so badly. A sorrow like that makes other sorrows look so terrible beside it.
[1898-11-25 (3 letters) Bertha (StL) to Henry (Waco)]

Henry wrote to Bertha of Allan Simpkins' suicide in 1904. *"I have just been inexpressibly shocked at the news of the suicide of Allan Simpkins who shot himself early this morning."* The St. Louis Republic included the following comments in its article following his death.

Ralph Simpkins testified that his brother was 36 years old and married. He said that his brother had been in ill health for some time suffering from kidney trouble and that he had been despondent lately because of this and the fact that an application that he had made for insurance had been rejected.

...

Mr. Frank L. Ridgely [Mr. Simpkins' father-in-law] said: "I know of no cause other than that of ill health and the fact that he had been refused life insurance. There coupled with some slight business reverses, must have been the cause. His domestic life was perfect. I knew of no happier couple than he and his wife."
[The St. Louis Republic on July 2, 1904]

Perhaps the fact that Mr. Simpkins appeared to have a "perfect" domestic life was at the root of Henry's shock.

Henry was also shaken by Louis Chauvenet's[300] death in 1904, writing *"one of the most disheartening problems of my life has been that I don't seem to be able to really value friends until they are taken away."*

I am really heart sick. Louis Chauvenet died at four o'clock this morning. I was alarmed yesterday about him and wrote to Annie but it was a terrible shock when his office called me up this morning and they told me. I believe I have told you before that one of the most disheartening problems of my life has been that I don't seem to be able to really value friends until they are taken away. I think of Louis now as the kindly, sweet tempered, thoughtful gentleman – and he was every inch a gentleman – and wonder why I did not see more of him. It seems such a reckless waste of my opportunities.

Now that they are cut off, I wrote you about the card party out there as few nights ago and I think I told you I was really stimulated to learn bridge. The stimulus was that, booby as I was, I could do nothing so stupid as to provoke Louis' just wrath for we played together. You will smile at my recalling a trivial incident but it best illustrates my idea of a courteous, kindly fellow whom every one really liked.

Annie has telegraphed that the funeral will be Thursday, but I don't know whether it will be here or at Pittsfield. Will was to get there tomorrow, and I believe her brother Russell is near at hand so I presume we will know more tomorrow. I can't think of her. It seems a horribly unnecessary burden to lay upon a good woman and it does harm to speculate about the reason for it all. I sent her a telegram this morning which was all I could think it possible to do and I am going to meet Gordon now who possibly has heard more than he had this morning when I telephoned him. I can't write any more.
[20171206-4 (1904-08-02) Henry to Bertha]

---

[300] Louis Chauvenet was the brother of William Marc Chauvenet, "The Poet" (see Chapter 8.A). He died at age 51.

Upon returning from his trip east where he briefly met Bertha in Boston in 1908, Henry returned to his St. Louis work tired and depressed.

> *I returned safely yesterday and feeling rested if anything by my journey but today for some reason I am worthless and have the most melancholy fit of the depression I have experienced in months. I thought I took abundant care of my worthless self on the cars but my! How something has upset me! I must to poor Hutchin's funeral today with the other St. Luke's directors, of which board you remember, he was secretary and I almost envied the poor fellow who had finally escaped all of life's burdens and disappointments.*
> [1908-06-26 Henry (StL) to Bertha (Rye Beach)]

"*I almost envied the poor fellow who had finally escaped all of life's burdens and disappointments.*" Henry wrote this less than 2 years before his own death.

E. HENRY'S WORK

> *I am worked to death and no mistake about it. As our Chinese friends would put it, I am belly well but I am about as tired as men get who are not make sick by it.*
> [20171117-1 (1897-09-13-) Henry (StL) to Bertha (Jamestown)]

1. OVERWORKED & TIRED

In one letter to Bertha when he must have been very tired, Henry described daydreaming his way out of the office.

> *I was awakened from a dream in my office today and found one of the men standing in my office door eyeing curiously your letter open on my desk before me. "Mr. Scott, I have looked in twice to speak to you about this. Are you very busy? I can see you in the afternoon, but…" You can imagine how guilty I felt. I proceeded to show that young man I was not busy in a manner that puzzled him more than the vacant stare I had greeted him with before. I think I mistook him at first for one of the pieces of furniture in a home that was being prepared for its mistress and from his forlorn expression I know I could not place this piece anywhere to hide its ugliness and not mar the other things which were all so pretty. So I imagine I was on the point of throwing him or it out of the window to get rid of it when I came back to consciousness – I saw just what you wished me to see in that sweet home, my darling, but I cannot say the thought of all this happiness was entirely unmixed with pain. I was jealous of your friends, dearest, our real happiness seemed so far away with so many things intervening. I was glad too to have you write me about your school friends. You know, my child, how much I value any knowledge of your life. God knows I have seen little enough of you to make me wish to search out and know everything that has come into your life which you have treasured as a happy association.*
> [20170812-1 Henry to Bertha]

The constant demands of his work was not the only reason for Henry's tiredness. Perhaps more importantly, the incessant needs of his work prevented Henry from being with Bertha. Henry summed up his frustrations in the following letter writing, "*If I lived at the North Pole and was in this mess, I would know what to do. I'd just let the fires go out and freeze. But you can't freeze with the mercury at ninety-eight.*"

> *I hope to reach Rye by the fifteenth but I can't say. Things are simply looking devilish and I sometimes think it will be years before my nose gets a rest from the unfriendly grindstone. I can't buy a limp of coal except for daily supply and I simply can't bear things in that shape. It would be like going to Rye by way of jumping off the bridge. If that tangle was unraveled, I could go to Waco and mend things there temporarily – the City Election, the resale of which is so important – occurs on the eighteenth of August but I am tied here by that fire(?) stress and simply can't be away for two successive days. It is not as pleasant as sitting around at Rye with your wife and being glad for her dear sake you are alive! And it isn't as pleasant as anything between the covers of Mr.*

Webster's fat unabridged that I have noticed in that little guide to the young. In fact, pleasant is not a good word to describe my feelings just now. If I lived at the North Pole and was in this mess, I would know what to do. I'd just let the fires go out and freeze. But you can't freeze with the mercury at ninety-eight. The idea is absurd and it's better to go broke even than be ridiculous so don't even be annoyed about my catching cold, its quite hot enough for me sans fuel.

..

The world seems out of joint tonight and I am afraid I have written a very dull letter. I despise it too deeply to make sure of this. I can't look it over and decide between sending it to you or the waste basket. I know it isn't good enough to send but I couldn't make it good enough for that, but I love you even when I am as cross and out with things and am tonight and I hope that does make some difference.

[1903(-) 20170803-2 Henry to Bertha]

On a trip to Texas in April 1903, Henry wrote reflectively about the proper place for work in his life and for the "*lazy worthless idler*". He worried about getting to the point of hating his work.

I am surprisingly well today or amiable for that is a better term to express what I have not been for the last two weeks and I really think it is because the journey, hard as the latter part was, has rested me. I am beginning to think that either I have very small capacity for work and I think that is the really so, or that I have a lot of it to do, for looking back upon the last two weeks, I seem to have been rushing through things at a pace that shut out the possibility of any real thoughtful consideration of anything or else I was in a state of semi collapse from weariness and from the dread of the same mad rush ahead of me.

It is not the happiest way to live, Bert, and I ought to mend my life. Not to do less work for I don't wish that but to do better and more thoughtfully what is done at all and to have a little time to think of what I ought to do when I am really capable of mental effort. For weeks, I have been grudging even the lazy worthless idler his place in life and it ought not to be the natural bent of a man who has always had some work to do to hate work but I think I have been doing this more than I have myself suspected. This sounds a little like an announcement that until I fell from grace, I was a model in respect of my duties. I don't mean that, although I do know that there is an infinite difference between my point of view today or recently and, dating back only a few weeks, what it was then. At all counts, I am coming back to life slowly but I am very sure it was high time I left my work at home to take care of itself for a few days. My next will not be so blue-ful, so don't scold me for this.

[1903-04-16 Henry (Ft. Worth) Bertha (StL)]

Henry often wrote his longing for rest from work and to be where Bertha could cure him. But, in the following letter, Henry questioned if there was such an earthly rest.

My business seems to weigh on me today and I can't shake off the burden even to write you. I still keep well although I am not allowed to altogether forget each day what Doctor Robinson meant by one's nerves jumping. I think I could get entirely well in a paradise with nothing to do and you to play with always. Will you take me there some day to rest and cure me or is that heaven and not to be reached by either of us until the earthly span is met?

...

I know I am a grumpy old thing and am not very patient under the affliction of ill health and about the only thing I really want, if I can't be mended quickly, is to go somewhere with you and seek rest. I can't write more today and you are in luck that this tale of woe is no longer.

[1907-04-03 Henry (Ft. Worth) to Bertha]

On his May 1907 trip to Waco, Henry wrote of himself as *"a miserable ailing sinner"* for his own selfish concerns *"over a little upset condition which you in my place would have hardly let me know of."*

> *It is bad enough for me to have to wrestle with business cares but I certainly should save and shield you from all such anxiety and I really meant to but I seem to have failed pretty thoroughly. This last winter seems a nightmare to look back upon anyway, for I have been a miserable ailing sinner physically and I knew this very well but I can see that I have been neglectful as well and I am very sorry, dearie, but I have been too selfish to realize it before. You have had to carry every one's burdens and I have not only done nothing to lighten them by putting some joy into your life but I have been a poor companion with nothing but complaints and bitterness over a little upset condition which you in my place would have hardly let me know of.*
>
> *I hope you know that I am really very penitent and that I really love you and cherish you more than ever before and that I hope you will not hold my neglect as anything worse than the result of a vexed state of mind and body which I ought to have the strength to control.*
> [1907-05-08 Henry (Waco) to Bertha (StL)]

Henry blamed himself for feeling miserable while on business and burdening Bertha with sole care of their children. *"You are in no condition to be taking all the responsibility and care of our big family and I revile your worthless husband daily that he takes so small a share of such burdens."* (Henry 1907-07-?)

2. DREAMS OF LOAFING

Henry periodically dreamed of a life of loafing.

> *I think loafing is decidedly restful and I have concluded that about a hundred year's loaf would be good for me.*
> [20170724-5 Henry to Bertha]

Henry even wrote to suggest that a life on a farm could be the answer. Henry admired Bertha's friend, Colonel Leighton, not only for his bucolic life on his farm but also because he was strong enough to control intense feelings, something that Henry wished for himself. But a safe landing on such distant shore is a *"matter of decided uncertainty."*

> *... to return to Colonel Leighton, what you have written me about him has interested me greatly. He seems the type of man whose feelings are the more intense because he is strong enough to control them. I would like to see that stock form of George Leighton's. He is a lucky fellow to be able to select as pleasant occupation as the management of a place like that must be. When I was east last summer, I saw a number of forms of this character and I made a quiet promise to myself then that if my ship ever came into port, I should have a country place of that kind. Does this fancy alarm you? Be reassured in the fact that the said ship is far from port and is encountering uncommonly stormy weather and head winds which, though they cannot sink her, make her voyage a tedious one at times and the time of her safe landing a matter of decided uncertainty.*
> [1892-06-30(-) Henry (StL) to Bertha (Farragut House, Rye Beach)]

During the summer, Henry often saw his friends leaving on vacation to be with their wives and wondered if he shouldn't have gone into a different business.

> *I have seen so little of Jack Shepley that I don't know what he really thinks of Rye. I imagine he was not there long enough to get anything but a generally pleasant impression. He goes back tomorrow night and I am wishing for the time being that I belonged to a trust company[301].*
> [20180328-2 (1900-) Henry to Bertha]

---

[301] Jack Shepley worked for the St. Louis Union Trust Company and, apparently, was able to take frequent vacations.

Similarly, Henry was envious of Bud Dozier who was in Rye Beach during the summer of 1907.

> *I confess that your letter aroused the first envious thought I have ever had of Bud Dozier. To think of his being there and seeing and talking to my pretty wife while I am here wrestling with a lot of Texas scoundrels who are trying to destroy our properties is enough to arouse the envy, hatred, malice and all uncharitableness of better and milder mannered men than I. If it were not for the feelings aroused by that Dozier, I might send you a love message. And if I did, it might tell you something of the joy in my heart and the glad thankfulness that I am so soon to be near my darling once more.*
> [1907-07-11(-) Henry to Bertha (20180416A-4]

Although Henry wrote of wanting to be with Bertha on a trip abroad, such a trip never materialized. All Henry could do was to express jealousy for his friends who were so lucky.

> *Jack Shepley was out and told me the trip abroad had been definitely decided upon and he leaves here Saturday to join Sarah. I wonder if we will ever be that lucky, Bert. I have dreamed of a trip abroad with you until it has become the sum of my ambitious hopes and I believe I could settle down resignedly if not gracefully to the calm joys of middle age if we could only have that lark together. Well, let us hope for the good fortune, my dearest.*
> [20180329-1 Henry to Bertha]

Henry certainly enjoyed the outdoors and often wrote of the salutary impact on his health going out to the country (i.e. the St. Louis Country Club).

> *There is more virtue in one day in the fresh air than in all the nostrums and tonics of your best doctors. I had been cooped up all week working like a slave and that horrid pain at the nape of my neck was hitting it up like the trip hammer in a foundry by Friday.*
> [20170811-2 Henry to Bertha]

> *I am feeling better for the experience [of going to the country] but I wish some fairy goddess would give me a little more hopeful frame of mind. I have you and the chicks and what seems to me a competency enough reward for far better men than I ever have been or will be. But instead of offering up praises from the deep gratitude in my heart, I dwell upon the small troubles of my life until I wonder if this repeated weak indulgence has not permanently unfitted me for any real work for all time to come. There! You have a most enlivening confession to impress you with my joy on the nations holiday and I really enjoyed the day too which speaks all the worse for me.* [1907-07-04 (20180416A-1) (Thursday) Henry to Bertha]

In another letter around 1910, Henry's visit to the country brought relief and he was able to eat *"the only dinner that has had any taste to it since you left…"*

> *I am distinctly flourishing today and from a very bad beginning too. I couldn't sleep last night. I was awake at half past twelve then awake at two and heard the clock strike every hour except three until seven. I arose with the horrors thinking I would have a miserable day but, after a good hard turn at the office where my work seemed once more to be counting for something, I left at three with … John & Ray Davis, Bud Dozier & Murray Carlton for the Log Cabin Club, played 18 holes in the broiling sun, ate the only dinner that has had any taste to it since you left, played bridge and came in ready for bed and a line to you and feeling really as if life was worth living. I had almost concluded to decline Ray's invitation this morning and I am glad I did not for it has been the only day of real peace since you left.*
> [20180317-1 (1910-) Henry to Bertha]

3. THE WORK ETHIC

Henry worked very hard. From many of his letters, it seemed as if he thought that he alone needed to resolve every problem. And, Henry sometimes pointed to another reason: his own insecurity about his self-worth and the fear of not being successful. As Henry wrote, "*the world sooner or later places a man where he belongs.*"

> *Of all things disagreeable, I hold the overestimate of the world as to what I accomplish the least bearable and this is because of no humble mindedness, dear, but because the world sooner or later places a man where he belongs and, if he in the least has disappointed the people who have wildly theorized about him, he is never afterwards able to receive even fair credit for what he does. And it is clear that you must not be misled by such groundless rumors, my darling. I have really done very little in the direction of what is termed business success and I have no reason to look for more than the ordinary experience of the ordinary man. If better things come, dear, I shall have you to enjoy the greater blessings with me. If I only maintain what I have already acquired, I shall be perfectly happy if you, who make all my happiness, are content. But to expect not to work, not to have my share of the burdens that fall to the lot of the average man, would mean that I did not truly value the great blessing which has come to me in your love, my friend, my dearest helper, in every thought and hope of my life.*

[1892-07-22 Henry (Waco) to Bertha (Farragut House, Rye Beach)]

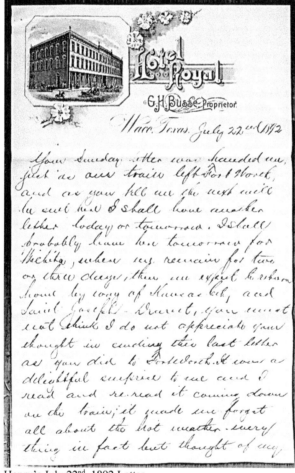

Henry's July 22nd, 1892 Letter

In response to Henry's letter (and many others like it), Bertha commended Henry's work ethic while still voicing concern for its ill effects. Bertha seemed prophetic when she wrote of Henry's inability to save himself and that he should let her be his "*best helper*".

> *You need not have defended yourself in the character of working man so vigorously, dear boy. Did you imagine for an instant that I would like to see you anything different? I am proud every day of*

my life that your work means to you, what it does. It is only sometimes when I hear of your seeming not well from the effects of it that I do dread it a little bit. For the art of saving yourself does not lie among your accomplishments. I wish I could really be your "best helper", more than I am now, but I like to have you call me so. When I feel that you look to me for that, my dear love, it helps me to be a better woman.
[1892-07-28 Bertha (Rye Beach) to Henry (StL)]

Even when Henry was "*cross and disagreeable*" and spurned the company of his friends because Bertha was away, he stood his post, "*floundering along, sticking like grim death to my work*".

I have missed you sadly this time and I hardly dare think of our meeting for I am cross and discontented enough as it is and, if I didn't go floundering along sticking like grim death to my work, I would be utterly unfit for association with anyone. As it is, I, whom you hold to be the most gregarious of men, shy off from people at times whom I know very well and like very well. I had an invitation today which ordinarily I would have jumped at but I preferred to dine alone to going to Delmar Gordon(?) with the Jack Davis', George Leighton, Gordon and the Jones. I suppose you would call it a bad liver but I think I am just cross and disagreeable. I sent Jack word I was busy and couldn't go so don't inform them I had no real reason except a bad disposition and a measly mean head piece which has not been behaving very decently of late. I am going to the country tomorrow and I expect to write you from there that my "grouch", as the boys style such lapses, has happily fled. Just now I am a miserable, dependent wretch and the woman I dearly love is not here to comfort me and bring me back to some interest in existence.
[1902-07-19 Henry (StL) to Bertha (Rye Beach)]

One summer when Bertha expressed her desire for Henry to start his vacation and come east to be with her, Henry wrote back that he could not do so "*without plunging you and the young people into poverty*".

I started to answer your last letter but I have concluded I shall not have time. I shall try to answer all your questions tomorrow. I ought to say now, however, that I have done none of the things you accuse me of "having ought to" for I haven't been near Garmi. I haven't been to the Fair for two weeks and, as for the girls, I haven't seen them since you left. I have been there three times but have in each case found them out so I am not feeling guilty on that score. I do feel as though I have neglected Garmi and I shall ask her to the Fair as you suggest.

I am not going to tell you definitely about my coming on for the very good reason that I don't know when I can get away. I may have doubt as to when I shall see you but I don't think I have any as to my willingness to see you as soon as I can without plunging you and the young people into poverty. My fuel contracts are giving me fits these days and I don't know when they will be closed up. As soon as they are arranged, I shall leave this lonely place and hie to the place where I can get what I most need of all earthly things, the companionship of my dear wife without whose cheer all thing business, society, even religion (I haven't been to church regularly since you left me) are utterly dull, stale and unprofitable.
[20180303-3 (1904-) Henry to Bertha]

In another letter, Henry wrote "*I have left undone what I ought to have done…*" There always seemed to be too much work for Henry to complete.

I have just finished my work for the day or, rather, not finished it for I have left undone what I ought to have done and more besides and, for the first time since you left, I seem to have time to write to you. I get slower and older pretty fast, I think, and what is to become of me if I don't change my ways is beyond my ken for there's work to do by the mile and good work too, such as many a man would give his eyes to be at. And I seem to move at it as if no time limit applied and other work was not howling to take the place of what is at hand. I am afraid I'm a worthless cuss and that someday you must needs scold me or give me over to idleness.

I had two letters from you today and, as they were the first for two days, I simply devoured them. You are really the nicest wife I ever had and I don't care who knows it. I think the real reason I am such a cross patch is that I am homesick for a sight of you. This, I fully understand, is not the talk befitting a married man of eleven years "stay" but I mean it and, if you were near me instead of in that far off Yankee land, you could not doubt the sincerity of my statement; I could prove it!
[1904-07-05 Henry (StL) to Bertha (Rye Beach)]

Periodically, Henry expressed his doubts about his ability to succeed in his work and be a worthy husband to Bertha.

I am simply broke off in the middle and must stop. Why did you marry a man so poor that he must work for a living and so stupid that he must work night and day not to be driven off the place?
[1904-07-26 Henry (StL) to Bertha (Rye Beach)]

Henry's sense of duty to his work often kept him alone during summers when Bertha and all of Henry's friends went away for their vacations.

The town is really deserted. Except Henry Potter with whom I julip tomorrow, Sadie, Jack and Edith, the folks have all tuck to the woods. Robert and Grace have gone to Poland Springs to join the Mallinckrodts! John and Ray are at Weque-West(?) also. Dozier is at Rye. Even my last golf chum, Harry Block, has gone to Clark. What will your poor boy do? No car, no friends, no golf. O, yes, he gotta plenta work, though, so I think he will keep free from guile.
[20180317-5 (1910-) Henry to Bertha]

4. BUSINESS & FINANCIAL FRUSTRATIONS

Henry's business and financial frustrations sometimes caused Henry to lose confidence in himself. On one such occasion, Bertha wrote Henry to try to cheer him up.

Another sad letter from you today. My dear old sweetheart, you certainly need Christian Science or something if you are beginning to fear your wife has lost faith in you. I have failed indeed if I have made you feel that when you have my whole heart and faith and trust, dear, and my pride too, Henry. Don't give way to these despondent moods. I know they mean lack of physical strength. Try and get that too or, rather, get that first and our old confidence in your self will come back.
[1899-07-13 (1st letter) Bertha (Jamestown) to Henry (StL)]

Around 1907, Henry grew sufficiency frustrated with his business activities that he began to consider selling everything.

I got your Tuesday & Thursday letters with their recount of your tedious and uncomfortable trip and I felt that the little return I am now securing from my active business is no compensation at all for leaving you to struggle alone with the family in its travels. One of the frantic impulses I have at times: to sell out the whole thing for what I can get for it, come over ..., but I suppose I must bide my time and find some one more eager and fit for trouble than I am before I can secure relief.
[1907-07-(-) (20180416A-10) (Sunday) Henry to Bertha (– 1907 envelope)]

Bertha understood Henry's anxiety over his business interests and, around 1909, wrote : "*I would rather go to Virginia and live a long happy life with you in the country...*"

Sunday afternoon
Dear Henry,
You said goodbye with such sad eyes that I thought I would write at once just to tell you that you have some friends in the world who do love you and a very nice family whose whole welfare is bound up with you and a perfectly lovely wife whose entire happiness is dependent on you. And please don't bind yourself to any struggle that means the sacrifice of your health and happiness.

Make any sacrifice. Tell him you'll shoulder his pipe contract if necessary. Make a <u>dead</u> loss of that part of your property if necessary but remember that if you lose your health and your nerves, your judgement will go with it and your most valuable asset will be gone. You won't be able to take care of the property that remains and as far as happiness is concerned which is what really matters. I would rather go to Virginia and live a long happy life with you in the country than see you drag out a harassed miserable existence here. So, my sweetheart, don't throw away what makes life worth having for that which does not make it worth having. And being Sunday, I will close with a text. "Wherefore do you spend your money for that which is not bread. <u>And you labor for that which satisfieth not?</u> "[302]
[20180802-2 (1909-) Bertha to Henry]

Although Bertha and Henry's financial condition was robust by 1907, nevertheless, Henry always seemed to be worried and closely watched their spending.

Your letters have both of them a note of trouble and I think I have been the direct cause. I really did not mean to cut down the allowance below your requirements and you have been far too considerate of me not to let me know how you have been pressed to meet expenses. I only kept to our old scheme because I thought under all the circumstances it was better for us not to "expand" until both my health and income were lodged upon more permanent basis. But you are right in your accounts and, in your request and as soon as I return, I shall deposit the $250.00 and as much more as you require for I can do this easily when it is really needed and you are positively not to have worries of this kind.
[1907-05-08 Henry (Waco) to Bertha (64 Vandeventer Pl, Stl)]

F. THE AILMENTS

Henry suffered from the fear of various illnesses, a fear that may have been abetted by the various theories that his doctors espoused. While a bad appendix was a particular concern to Henry and his doctors, there were also many other potential culprits including colds, a bad liver, rheumatism and his nervous system.

1. COLDS

Henry could pick up a cold anywhere, even in the summer heat of Waco. In the next three letters, Henry described the progress of one of his colds that beset him on a trip to Waco in May 1895.

Dear Bert,

This certainly has not been one of my fortunate journeys. We arrived today four hours late after a hot journey. The delay was caused by our own train which left the track about ten miles out of Waco, fortunately injuring no one but the fireman who got off with a few scratches but making the passengers take a very uncomfortable view of things in general for an hour or two. But a much worse misfortune has befallen me than a mere railroad accident. I have caught about the worst cold in the head I have ever had and I am too miserable and cross and unhappy to do anything.

The town is full of people who have come to see the May festival and I suppose, if I were well, I should enjoy the flowers and the street parades but as it is I can only wonder why it is that people have the heart to smile where such hideous plagues as bad colds are among the misfortunes of humanity.

I can't write any more. I am simply crushed with my misfortunes. Pray for my deliverance, my dear, and for my early return.

---

[302] Isaiah 55:2

Yours always,
Henry
[1895-05-06 Henry (Waco) to Bertha (3337 Washington Ave, Stl)]

Henry had his own remedy for colds: Quinine and *"old reliable"*.

I am not quite as "bused" tonight for my cold was knocked out of existence with a twelve-grain dose of quinine plus a strong portion of "old reliable", which combination pretty nearly put an end of me with the cold for this morning. I was almost blind but tonight my friends, who were all dead yesterday, are coming back and they are telling me it was all a joke about their being dead, etc.
[1895-05-07 Henry (Waco) to Bertha (3337 Washington Ave, Stl)]

There are evidently other cures for the cold other than quinine and old reliable. Henry's modified his view on the next day after taking into account the Texas *"cooking process"*.

The weather is good and hot and as my room happens to open on the north, I roast nightly. It is not surprising that my cold is cured. I now think it was not the quinine but he cooking process I have been undergoing that cured me. I am glad to say that I have been very well notwithstanding the heat so you need not be uneasy. It is good healthy hot weather and it won't hurt me but it makes me yearn for Jamestown and the sea.
[1895-05-08 (2 letters) Henry (Waco) to Bertha (3337 Washington Ave, Stl)]

2. FOOD POISONING

Henry wrote to Bertha in 1892 about being very sick for two days with food poisoning. Apparently, food poisoning was not uncommon then.

Sunday Evening

Dearest,

I have had a pretty trying time of it for a day or two. Yesterday I was sick in bed all day, the first time such a thing has happened to me in my recollection and all on account of that dinner of Crittenden's. Don't be alarmed, it was strictly a "dry" affair and I make particular note of this lest you may think me guilty of some of the remarkable performances of that Club affair, only I am sure it was the dinner that came within very little of making me bid the world an unwilling adieu for my brother tells me that Crittenden has been really ill since Thursday and is still quite sick. I have not inquired for the other members of the party but I am quite positive I shall learn they fared little better than I, as positive as I am that the cook put poison into something prepared for that dinner. I should not be astonished if the Elliott-January affair is forestalled by an awful tragedy! I can jest about it now, dear, for I am getting all right again but Friday and yesterday!!! I don't care to revive the memory of it; it is quite clear enough as it is.

You can rest quite securely in the confidence that there was good reason for my not writing yesterday or if you are in any doubt of my having exaggerated my unwellness I shall introduce you to Doctor McPheeters when you come home and have you hear his version of my attack for comparison with my own account. I am pretty well today, considering, although I can't say I should take especial pride in boasting to you as I have done that I am "rather stronger than the average man." I walked out today for a breath of fresh air against the protest of the family and after going about three blocks from home, I found it something of a problem to get home without assistance. If a long spell reduces one's vitality in the proportion that a two days attack does, I have profound admiration for the enduring power of some of the invalids I know. I conclude, however, the power of endurance is more taxed by the intensity than the duration of an attack, at least, it is much more comforting for me to think this since, otherwise, I would be compelled to admit that I did not or cannot endure suffering with becoming fortitude.

I did not intend to write a letter about so trivial a matter (as I now see it) but I thought I should explain why I did not write yesterday and, in doing this, the horrible suspicion occurred to me that an admission that I had been unwell would be held up to me for ages to come as a natural consequence of work or "overwork" as you put it, so I have anticipated any lecture you may have prepared to deliver by telling you of the real occasion of my attack. Kin, my brother reports, is not yet able to get about so please be good enough not to refer to the "last straw" theory as nothing could be more absurd than to suggest that Kin's health is impaired by overwork and, as my recovery has been the more rapid of the two, this idea would apply more properly to him than to me.

The family has taken compassion on me and today. I have been read to until I have concluded that the only way left open to me to recover the ground I have lost in the book world is to be an invalid for a while.

...

I did not expect to get a letter yesterday so I have not worried but I have missed your letter and, Bert, I have missed you, my darling, these wretched tiresome days more than ever before. If you had been here, I think it would have been easy to stand a little sickness and, without you, well, I am by no means sure you would approve of my impatience.

[1892-07-04(-) (Sunday) 20170828-5 Henry to Bertha]

Bertha was very concerned about the food poisoning incident. Bertha also wrote that she had a dream about Henry being ill which upset her – "*I don't think I could let you go.*"

I will never scold again about not having a letter from you. I am so grieved and worried about your being ill and, O, I do want to be at home so much. When I agreed to be away so long, I did not expect you to be ill and it is very hard to stand. I would have telegraphed to know how you were when I got your letter but I trust your promise to me, such as I made to you, to telegraph me if you really were seriously ill. I can hardly wait for tonight's mail and, if I get no letter or you do not say you are much better, I shall telegraph anyway.

Lucy McKinley is a fortunate woman in the fact that she is able to be there but I am very glad that, if you were made ill at the dinner, that old Crittenden [McKinley] was sick too and you missed all the good of your holiday and did not get out to the Country Club! I am so sorry, dear, I won't say a word about overwork for I don't think that was the cause of it from what you say but won't' you please not work very hard for a while now and please, please don't go to Texas until you are quite well.

Your letter came last night (your letters almost always come in the evening mail) and I did not get to sleep very soon after reading it. And when I did, I had the most curious dream. I dreamed that you and I had been spending a day together and we were exploring all the corners of a very curious large house. Finally we came to a deep sort of shaft with very narrow marble steps leading to the bottom and as slippery as glass. I was afraid and stepped back but you went nearer the edge and began to slip. As you slipped, the stairs, in the curious fashion of dream things, vanished and you were on the edge of this frightful abyss with nothing you could hold to but my hand. And then began the struggle, a fearful one to keep you from going while my own footing was not very secure. Now came the most curious part, for a dream, I mean. Ordinarily, this struggle would have gone on, I unable to cry for help or to move until it had waked me but this dream went on to the end. You finally slipped over the edge entirely but still holding my hand and I held you for what seemed like hours, both of us feeling that every moment your strength would give way and you would have to let go. Then I suddenly found I was able to call for help. (Before that, there had been an oppression on my chest that had kept me from uttering a sound.) And a man answered the call and helped you, with my assistance, back and, as soon as you were safe, all my strength suddenly went. I had been perfectly strong before and I went over the edge myself, crying all the time in a weak

sort of way. Then I was helped back and you and I went away together. The dream went on for long after that but it goes into a mist and I forget. Of course, it is easy enough to explain. I was reading that account of the people escaping from the "City of Chicago", climbing up that cliff which caused it but I cannot help feeling a little superstitious about it. I believe if you were ever to be really ill, dangerously, I mean, that I should bring you back. I don't think I could let you go. Well, you will laugh at me perhaps but I don't mind.
[1892-07-08 Bertha (Rye Beach) to Henry (StL)]

Henry joked about having bad food on another occasion. Henry wrote to Bertha about what he would have liked to do about it.

I forgot to tell you I had that restaurant burned down. I gave the order to have it done shortly after we were there and, in the press of other affairs, I forgot to mention it when the report that my directions had been enthusiastically carried out by the entire population of Newburyport came in. The proprietor was not lynched. It was concluded that he richly deserved this fate but a chinaman in the party suggested something long and lingering so he was given the dinner we left behind and died in great agony.
[20170804-1 Henry to Bertha]

3. PTOMAINE POISONING IN 1906

During the week of September 16, 1906 when Bertha was in Rye Beach, Henry had a bout with ptomaine poisoning which received a great deal of attention in their letters. Since Henry didn't want Bertha to be concerned, Henry delayed telling Bertha about this Sunday incident until the following Wednesday when he started feeling better.

I have had some interesting experiences! Sunday, for some reason unknown but which at the time I attributed to several soft drinks I had imbibed Saturday night because my standby seemed unwise in such hot weather. I felt rather aged and worn. I went however to dinner at Henry Potters and later went to the country with Gordon though I did nothing more strenuous there than write to you and loll around until we came home about ten o'clock. About twelve thirty I awoke with a bad stomachache and searched long and anxiously for that hot water bag which some considerate person had spirited away.

I had a pretty bad night but Monday I felt well enough to go down town but later in the day I had to give up and come home. You may know I was miserable for I looked up both John Salter and Dr. Clapton and sought their counsel most earnestly, Mudd being out of town. Today I am practically all right again except feeling a little battered and pathetic. I have missed you before in the twenty years I have known you but no woman could fail to appreciate a longing for her as greater as have been mine for you. These last two days, notwithstanding, I am practically all right. Although you can depend upon it, I am moving about carefully! I think this setback seals the fate of my joining you at Rye and you will have to make the arrangements and the trip home without me for, not to mention the time I have lost being sick on the very day I wished most to be well, I doubt if I could make the trip for some days with prudence for, short as was the attack, it has really left me weak and worthless. You are no doubt tired out with this long mail and I wish I had some more cheering news to send.
[20191023-1 (1906-09-18(-) Tuesday Henry (StL) to Bertha (Rye)]

Henry wrote to Bertha two days later about his recovery. Since his "*sore stomach*" prevented him from going downtown to work during this week, the disease was obviously serious.

For the first time since I have been sick, my "sperits" have failed to revive. This is not because I am not far better. I am really able to go downtown but I am advised that, after a sore stomach such as I have had, it saves time to be a little careful so I haven't been downtown as yet.

How I have missed you! I shall have to admit that Monday was pretty hard on me but after that I did not mind much and I got better so fast that I astonished myself even but I know from my weakness that I had a pretty hard rub and John Salter says "Mr. Scott, that fever was no joke."

I have had a regular reception in the evening. Gordon, Jack Shepley, Sam, Ray, the boys at the office and one or two business friends from downtown. Lion has also been over and Jack Davis came and spent the whole morning with me. So my friends are not all dead and they are very nice and kind but you have been away from me so long that I need you, dearest, and I am very, very thankful you are coming home next week. Bah, I have filled two pages with lamentations and I am stronger today than many a man who is down town working hard for a living.

[1906-09-21 Friday (20180402-2) Henry (StL)to Bertha (Rye)]

Bertha's concern for Henry's condition undoubtedly increased when they were apart. Being unable to care for him in person, Bertha was left to speculate about any ill-defined attack. In the following letter after hearing about Henry's illness, she reiterated her brother George's conclusion that Henry had appendicitis and should have an immediate operation.

You poor dear old boy! O, I am so sorry for you and I do so wish I was at home. It seems wicked for me to have been here enjoying these glorious days when you were alone at home, suffering. I did want to take the next train home when I got your letter and then I thought you would certainly have telegraphed for me if you had been worse. And I thought, if I got home and found you back at work and I having left everything at loose ends here, I should get but a Halsey Ives[303] welcome and shouldn't deserve much else.

The telegraph office is closed or I certainly should have telegraphed. And even now, if I don't get a letter tomorrow or if the one I do get isn't <u>perfectly</u> satisfactory, I am going over to Northampton to telegraph from there.

I went to Boston yesterday with Nancy to get some hats and things and I was too tired to write last night. That was when I received your pencil note in which you only apologized for writing in pencil and said you had a very occupied day and a curious experience in your "trade". Trade indeed. After I went to bed, I began to wonder about that pencil letter and I made up my mind that you had had an attack of appendicitis and had gone to St. Luke's hospital and had written this in bed the night before your operation. In the morning, I was less alarmed but still when I opened your letter, I was really not surprised, only very anxious and distressed that you had suffered so. No hot water bag! No Birney's indigestion medicine! No wife! No anything but hopeless misery. I have an awful feeling that you are not being properly taken care of and an equally awful one when I think of you in the hands of a trained nurse that I don't know. <u>Did you have one?</u> And how are you now? Answer the minute you get this letter so I'll know before you get home.

George says to tell you to please realize this matter is becoming serious and that you cannot put off that operation without very great danger of your life. Or if you pull through, of a slow, tedious, painful recovery, where, as between attacks, it is so simple. And, dearest, honestly, for my sake, you must go through with it. I am horribly anxious and alarmed now but I should never, never forgive myself if you put off that operation until you had to go through what Minnie did. I can hardly wait to get home and, next to that, I can hardly wait for tomorrow's mail. I do hope it will bring me better news. Your letter was as cheerful as you could make it but I read things between the lines and I want to come home.

[1906-09-22 (Friday) Bertha (Rye Beach) to Henry (StL)]

---

[303] Halsey Cooley Ives (27 October 1847 – 5 May 1911) was the founder of the Saint Louis School and Museum of Fine Arts. Ives was also a landscape painter, but is best remembered for the organization, administration, and popularization of art in Saint Louis, Missouri. It is not entirely clear what Bertha means by "*a Halsey Ives welcome*".

When Bertha received Henry's "Friday" letter (Henry's 1906-09-21 letter, above), she felt reproached and concerned.

> *Every letter that I get from you I feel more and more reproached at being away. I think too how very unsympathetic my first letters must have seemed. You see, I did not really know you were ill until Friday. Your first letter from the Country Club, saying you had had too many soft drinks. I answered by telling you that George said soft drink spelled appendicitis, but I did not take it or think of it seriously. Monday, you only spoke of a new trade experience. Tuesday came your full account, reaching me Friday, but even then you were altogether too careful about alarming me for, while you said you had suffered agonies, you also said you were over the attack and even then I supposed it was such an attack as you had had at William Lee's when you suffered horribly but were out the next day. Today's letter, Friday's, is the first in which you have admitted that you have not left the house and I am distressed and worried and grieved as I have not been before, though ever since Friday I have been worried. I cannot bear to think what a wretched miserable time you have had "without me" and I am awfully grateful to the people who have been good enough to sit up with you a bit. What makes it more bitter is that we could have had such a heavenly time here.*
> [1906-09-25 (Monday) Bertha (Rye Beach) to Henry (StL)]

Very soon, Henry's doctors arrived at a suitable diagnosis for his "*sore stomach*": ptomaine poisoning. (Undoubtedly, Henry was relieved that it was not his appendix!)

> *I think the mystery is solved. Ray crawled up the front steps this afternoon to see how I was faring and announced that he had been in bed since Monday! We retrospected together and recalled an oyster cocktail Saturday dinner at the Country Club. And then, when Gordon, who had been along and who having escaped, more clearly remembered his dinner and that we both had consumed our concoction, I knew what was the matter with both Ray and me. A clear case of ptomaine poison! Ray insists that he was sicker than I but I know he wasn't for starting with a chill on Monday and quite a fever afterwards, I had two miserable days.*
> [20170721-5 (1906-09--) Henry to Bertha]

When Bertha learned the true cause of Henry's illness, she was relived. However, she expressed disappointment that it wasn't Henry's appendix, a problem which could be resolved at once by an operation. (Bertha's brother George had his appendix removed in 1900 so they were acquainted with this operation.)

> *That was a nice long letter today, sweetheart, and I am glad you are better but do you know as long [as] you have had all the agony and misery, I am rather sorry it was not an appendicitis attack instead of ptomaine for the one would have served as a useful warning to hasten on the operation and this will only serve, as George says, for an excuse the next time you have a real appendicitis attack to be sure you have eaten something.*
>
> *...*
>
> *Father and George leave Tuesday. I am due to collapse on Tuesday and a nice time I expect to have packing and travelling. But I shall think of the vile time you had all alone last week and I shall feel it is a righteous judgment on me for having left you alone so long and not having come home a week ago at least. There is one thing certain. "I want to go home now, indeed I do" and I will never leave you again, so make your mind to it.*
> [1906-09-24 (Saturday) Bertha (Rye Beach) to Henry (StL)]

In Bertha's next letter, she expressed not only her bitterness for not returning to St. Louis sooner to care for Henry but also for having not written on the preceding day, realizing what a disappointment that would be to him.

> *Each letter that I receive makes me feel sadder and more self-reproached. Today came your Saturday's letter in which you for the first time admitted that you had been in bed all that week.*

You have softened matters very much to me for I supposed you had been up and about the house. You have been very good in trying not to make it seem as serious as it was to me but it has taken all the pleasure out of these last few days and I only want to get home. I should have thought you little sort of saintly in your suggestion that, if it remained hot, we might stay away longer if I had not known that in the bottom of your heart you were perfectly well aware that nothing would keep me here an instant longer than I was obliged to stay now.

One bitter regret I had from your letter, for you said you were going down the next day to get my letter and I knew you did not find any for that was the day I went to Boston. I was nearly dead when I came home, I was so tired and there was nothing in your letter to show that you had been sick. I should have written anyway. I got your confession the next day.

O, sweetheart, you will be amused at one thing I grieve over and that is that I have missed such a nice time with you for I know I should have had such a nice time and you would not have had a bad one after the first awful two days. If you could have been fairly comfortable, keeping perfectly still, I could have had such a nice, nice visit with you. I have some beauty books to read aloud and I know it would have been nicer than reading to yourself.

I am glad, as you did not have me, you had such a companion as Lady Burton. I have been wanting you to fall under her spell for some time. She repays study, does she not? And she is a far safer companion than Jane Fraser. Her note was highly interesting! She told me that when she wrote it, she handed it to the clerk to put it in the parcel and he deliberately read it and she thought from his expression that he was going to refuse to put it in. I understand that tale now, small blame to the worthy young man!

...

This is my last letter for I shall reach you as soon as one written tomorrow could. I know the one I shall get tomorrow, my last one, will be a reproach for my unwritten letter. It won't be half as bitter as my own. Will you be a little glad to see me? I want to see you so much that it would not be well to tell you how much, my dearest.

[1906-09-26 (Tuesday) Bertha (Boston) to Henry (StL)]

4. RHEUMATISM & THE LIVER

In a letter written around 1905, Henry wrote of having rheumatism.

The rheumaties or whatever the thing is has been giving me fits lately. I wake in the night with my hands so swollen that they hurt and the left side in a sort of inflamed and wounded state and "sleep departs from mine eyes and slumber from mine eyelids" as John How said during the strike. I am going on a diet and I hope it will keep, for the first of July is fast approaching and I simply must be in fit shape then for the Fort Worth matter comes to a head and I shall need every wit I possess. I could stand the nights if it were not that the sleeplessness is always followed by a bad head. There! You have a picture of my woes, darn them.

[20170721-9 (1905-) Henry (StL) to Bertha]

Other theories for Henry's ailments were also proffered, such Doctor Lambert's. *"Doctor Lambert's letter is just in. He thinks the trouble is probably liver and, if not, a mild attack of gall stones."* [1910-09-30 Henry (StL) to Bertha (Morris Plains, NJ)]

5. A PAIN IN MY RIGHT SIDE

I have had a mean time of it, sweetheart, but I think I am really better [to]day. I still have a bad head and at times a rather nasty pain my side but I could sit still for a minute or two today which

is far better than I could have done the week before. And, with the aid of sulfonal[304] which I procured from Grant today, I shall sleep tonight I am sure. It has been a nasty experience for it began the day before you left and has been progressing every day since until today when I fancy I can see some gain. I must really find out what the trouble is for life isn't worth much with your head going numb queer ways and a cannonball in your side that is like a tumor or boil whenever you move.
[20170721-3 Henry to Bertha]

Henry again mentioned the pain in his right side at the conclusion of a 1903 Texas trip and his views of surgeons: "carver[s] in anatomics".

My visit here has in a business way been a very satisfactory one and, as I am feeling very well except a slight pain in my right side that never entirely leaves me now, I am as content as I can be away from you. I think I must see Doctor Finney or some other carver in anatomics about that side for it gets sorer and sorer as time goes by and I am told we must attend to such things while we are in the bloom of youth and not put them off until old age comes and takes us off without the surgeons accessories.
[1903-04-21(-) Henry (Ft. Worth) to Bertha (StL)]

As mentioned elsewhere, Henry's doctors, including Bertha's brother George, frequently suggested that the pains that Henry suffered were due to a bad appendix. Such a diagnosis was not surprising considering that this was the new medical procedure of that time and one can imagine that everyone was doing it. Henry commented about this in his letters, sometimes jokingly.

Perhaps this will be the best time to have my appendix removed for, if I telegraph you, you say you would not miss the spree and I can thus kill three birds with one appendix which is an improvement on the number said to have been slain with the casual stone: I should rescue you from the gloom of Rye, myself from the loneliness of separation from you, and get rid of a troublesome and dangerous neighbor.
[1905(-) 20170831-3 Henry (StL) to Bertha (Rye)]

In spite of their suspicions, Henry's doctors had trouble making a definitive diagnosis. And, for Henry, his "dismal experiences" were clearly frustrating, writing: "I can't even tell what to do to make their recurrence less frequent."

I am much belter today although very tired which Tuttle thinks is natural considering the picnic I have been having. He frankly admits he does not know what has been the matter but, as he is taking a blood test for malaria, he may have something definite to report later. I wish the doctors knew something for it is awkward to feel that, having come out of one of the most dismal experiences, I can't even tell what to do to make their recurrence less frequent. But I am much better today and I promise to send no more mails that sound like hospital reports.
[1905(-) 20170806-3 Henry to Bertha]

Henry would sometimes use the word appendix when writing about the pain in his side.

I had another slight "appendix" turn today. I went to bed for it took a dose of Berney's medicine and, in two hours altho slightly disfigured, the pain all left me and I shall be all right tomorrow. A propos of appendices, Phil Scanlan had his taken out on Monday and is getting along nicely.
[1906(-) 20180709-1 Henry to Bertha]

Regardless of Henry and his doctors' apparent concern about his appendix, Henry always found a reason to either delay the procedure or to convince himself that there was nothing wrong with it.

---

[304] Sulfonmethane (Sulfonomethane, Sulfonal, Acetone diethyl sulfone) is a chemical compound introduced as a hypnotic drug but now superseded by newer and safer sedatives. It produces lengthened sleep in functional nervous insomnia.

I think I am right about the appendix business. There seems to be no change except for the better. My stomach becomes distended occasionally and there is also a slight burning sensation in the right side but less, I think, than formerly and I think, if I can get four or five weeks rest and have it out in October or November when I become thoroughly rested and strong, it will be far wiser than to go through it now in the heat when any day it may become insufferably hot. I am to see John Salter once more before I go away and I shall tell you what he says.
[1906-06-(-) 20180730-4 Henry to Bertha]

Henry mentioned in a 1906 letter that Dr. Mudd wanted to operate on his appendix.

I had another lecture from Dr. Mudd about the risk I am running etc., a night or two, although he knows I have not had a single return of my trouble for weeks. He wishes me to be operated on now and then go to Rye for a rest. But I have told him I couldn't even if I were not worked to death. I should not unless it seemed imperative [to] have it through now for I should get no real vacation and, as a result, be a wreck all winter. Besides, I am by no means sure I have appendicitis and I am not going through the operation until I am sure.
[1906-07-25 Henry (Chicago) to Bertha]

From 1906 to the end of Henry's life, the subject of appendicitis comes up with more regularity just as Henry's concern about undergoing such an operation. Henry seemed to be frequently reminded of this procedure as many of his friends and acquaintances had undergone this.

Marjory[305] is to be operated on for appendicitis Monday morning and they are much upset about it, except Marjorie who was out at the Country Club Saturday evening as blythe and chipper as possible and most drootedly attended by John Holliday who looked as if he were the one who was to go under the knife. They say they are engaged. If they are, I am mighty sorry for John. He really looked sick with dread of what was ahead.
[20171203-3 (1908) Henry (StL) to Bertha (Rye)]

To the end, Henry resisted the advice of many of his doctors to have his appendix removed and to submit to the surgeon's *"cutlery"*.

I think we must have another interview with Mudd when I return for, doubtful as I am that I have an unscrupulous and evil intending appendix, the trouble has been of late sufficiently insistent to make it wise to dislodge it. So you may as well anticipate my incarceration at St. Lukes if I can work even a short stay of hostelitics in Fort Worth. Don't speak of any such plan for I have resisted the medicine men so often that I don't wish to discuss giving myself over to their cutlery until I absolutely capitulate.
[1909-10-23 Henry (Waco) to Bertha]

G. MY ENEMY

*I feel dull despair bearing down upon me
with a ten-ton weight.* [20171218-1 Henry to Bertha]

It is difficult to ascertain how seriously Bertha or Henry viewed Henry's bouts of depression or even understood it. In some of their letters, there was a joking banter which can be used either to make fun of a comical situation or to avoid addressing something too serious to think about. And it may be wondered whether this condition may have influenced Bertha's parents regarding Henry's suitability, especially considering Henry's "intriguing" lineage. Bertha was certainly aware of Henry's "blues" and, in spite of his bravado at times, Henry sometimes referred to his blues as *"my enemy"*.

---

[305] Marjorie Thornburg Holliday (1886-1950), who was married to John H. Holliday (1879-1947).

During their engagement, Henry's sister, Mattie, broached the subject of Henry's blues to Bertha who then related the comments to Henry.

> *I am much pleased to hear you are learning not to take life so hard. I am afraid, though, you have not gotten far beyond the primer stage, not even with the first reader of that eminently necessary knowledge. If you could hear Mattie on the subject of "Henry's blues", I think you would be rather amused at the picture of yourself. She told me a great deal about your disposition in the time of my visit there, evidently wishing I should be under no illusions on the subject.*
> [1892-08-19 (Friday) Bertha (Farragut House, Rye Beach) to Henry (StL)]

Of his sister, Mattie's, warnings, Henry was generally dismissive.

> *I hadn't time yesterday to abuse Mattie for warning you against me so I think I shall do so now and, one of these days, I shall tell her she should have started in to frighten you earlier in the day when it might have done some good. She is as much of a Job's comforter[306] as that friend of yours who, in congratulating you on your engagement, told you of the unhappy marriages she had known of among her intimate friends. Mattie had some provocation for warning you, dear, for within the last two years, she has seen more than one of those "terrible moods of depression". Do I think of the future too hopefully, my darling, in anticipating that these blue days, which come when I was trying to give up and forget my darling, will cease now that I know we shall so soon be united never again to be parted?*
> [1892-09-20 (Tuesday) Henry (StL) to Bertha (The Ark, East Jaffrey)]

Notwithstanding Henry's optimism at her curative powers, Bertha wondered if she would be able to fulfill such expectations.

> *I wonder if I shall have the power over those blue fits that you credit me with. Mattie evidently did not think so when she warned me of "those terrible moods of depression Henry has, Bert."*
> [1892-09-17 (Friday) Bertha (Brunswick Hotel, Boston) to Henry (StL)]

Nevertheless, Bertha hoped that Henry would let her help to take care of him and that she would be able to actually help.

> *If the letter you received from me at Waco was a blue one, dearest, what am I to say about the one I received from there? You poor tired boy. I see very clearly in the future a succession of trips to Texas for me for it is perfectly evident you are not fit to be trusted alone. You catch cold, you overtire yourself and you let a lot of horrid little worries weigh upon you in a way that you would not do if I were there and you could come back for me to smooth out a few of those heavy lines about your eyes. Possibly I might not be of equal use in smoothing away the worries themselves. Strange as it may seem, I doubt whether you would consider any business advice valuable enough to accept but I think I could prevent your being absolutely sure that ruin and the poor house stared you in the face.*
> [1892-12-20 (Tuesday) Bertha (Newton Centre) to Henry (StL)]

Henry's frustration with his enemy was sometimes revealed in the stories that Henry concocted about how he would deal with it.

> *I didn't mind my head being taken off, although I am sorry you were not here to enjoy the neat and complete decapitation. It came off clean, being neatly shot off by the discharge of the first shell and rolled over the floor for hours until I finally rescued it and put it back in place where it has since done duty almost as if it had never been on the firing line or perished in a just cause. I think the reasons I was not resentful were (A) perfect consciousness of innocence and (B) the thought*

---

[306] "Job's comforter": A person who tries to console or help someone and not only fails but ends up making the other feel worse.

that a very sweet girl at the other end of the gun was tired and worn and, moreover, didn't really know it was loaded.
[20180406-1 Henry to Bertha]

Henry intuitively seemed to know that his enemy was not his appendix as many of his doctors believed. Although neither he nor his doctors understood the cause or its cure, it seemed apparent that the enemy was depression against which Henry struggled and feared over the course of his entire life. During periods of "remission" such as during one summer in 1903, Henry was upbeat: "*My enemy has not annoyed me at all for weeks.*"

I have come through the summer pretty well physically too. My enemy has not annoyed me at all for weeks, my ear is very much better, playing golf always once a week, for I always play on Sunday and sometimes twice, has kept me strong and fit for work and, for two weeks, I have been as contented as I could expect when every hour I recall that I haven't seen my darling for a thousand years and must wait and stand the separation for that many years more.
[1903-08-05 Henry (StL) to Bertha (Rye Beach)]

Unfortunately for Henry, the science of psychology and the study of depression was in its infancy during Henry's lifetime. Not knowing how to fight this invisible enemy was a constant source of anxiety.

I am getting along pretty well but I can't see why these depressions don't take flight. I am leading a regular life, take exercise three times a week and rest between times, but my nerves or temper gets on edge at small provocations and the "feel" of real happiness don't come around very often.
[1907-07-09(-) Henry to Bertha (20180416A-3]

I expected to get all my work up and instead I am almost useless. It is mean to bother you with all this woe but I am really at a loss what to do so please prescribe for me. I should go to a physician except that I have no confidence in the ability of any of them to tell me what the trouble is and I am getting more worthless daily without being able to do or take interest in anything. ... I am almost tempted to tear this up for much as I wish for you sympathy, I dread pouring out my woes like a child even to you.
[20170721-2 (Thursday) Henry to Bertha]

Toward the end of Henry's life, some of his doctors started to understand the true nature of Henry's ailment and to dismiss the idea that he suffered from appendicitis, galls stones, etc. And Henry would sometimes add some humor in his letters to Bertha whenever writing about his ailments.

Tell George that I found John Salter delightful and was much impressed with [his] convincing way of taking hold of things. I am glad it isn't appendicitis or gall stones or brights[307] but it was bad enough to have been all three and several other maladies thrown in for good measure. ... Lizzie was perfectly fine and trudged up the stairs to wait on me a thousand times. I can't say though she was quite as sympathetic as Ray's[308] cook was, for when Ray was at his worst, not knowing how ill he might become as he too was alone in his house, he suddenly remembered that Carroll[309] was in town so as fast as he could speak intelligibly, he told the cook to telephone the Reverend Davis he was ill and to come up to see him. The cook on receiving the message broke forth into a wail thinking, if Ray had sent for the Minister, he was preparing for death. And Ray said, sick as he was, he nearly went into convulsions.
[20170721-5 (1906-09--) Henry to Bertha]

---

[307] Bright's disease is a historical classification of kidney diseases that would be described in modern medicine as acute or chronic nephritis. It was characterized by edema, the presence of albumin in the urine and was frequently accompanied by high blood pressure (hypertension) and evidence of heart disease.
[308] Ray Davis
[309] Rev. Carroll Melvin Davis (1857-1932)

In particular, Dr. Tuttle[310] seemed to best understand that the problem was not some internal organ; Henry needed a "*new nervous system*".

> *I am afraid my letters greatly over did the picture of my woes. I was really sick for a few days but Tuttle pulled me around splendidly and I really mean what my telegram says and am perfectly well today. I am wroth with myself that I went through all that despair when apparently I could be so speedily mended and, next time I have a finger ache, off I go promptly to a doctor. Tuttle laughs at my liver or kidney or even that terrible appendix being out of gear and says, if he could give me a new nervous system, I would soon forget the possession of those other blessings.* [1907-07-11(-) 20180416A-4 (Thursday) Henry to Bertha (– 1907 envelope)]

"*...if he could give me a new nervous system.*" Although Dr. Tuttle seemed to be on the right track, his remedies, including a drink of whiskey, were "hit or miss".

> *I have been a miserable sufferer ever since you left. The trouble came to a sort of mild crisis last Friday and I just was obliged to go to bed. I sent for doctor Tuttle and he looked me all over, laughed at hints about my liver, kidneys et al, and, when I finally confessed that for two weeks I had at times been in such a bad way I could not tell what people who were around me were talking about, he said it was nothing whatever but a nervous let down and that he hoped I was wise enough to leave town as soon [as] I could pack up. He gave me some strong medicine that tastes like varnish and today I am on my feet and feeling very well. Tuttle says that great depression I have had and the headache and congestion are as typical of neurasthenia[311] as congestion in the lungs is of pneumonia. Well, I am better now ever with the hot weather than I have been since you left and I begin to feel that I am not going to be numb and dejected and unhappy for the remainder of my days. O, Tuttle expressly prescribed a drink of whiskey with every meal! until I get away, after which he said the less I drank the better for me "but you need it now, Mr. Scott, and I think I can safely prescribe it for one who is in no danger of taking more than is good for him." Really, his medicine or something has improved me wonderfully for I was on the point of writing you that I could not possibly go away because packing was too much of a job! I remember your contempt over this confession from Maggie but, really, last week I sympathized with her.* [(20180416A-14, 1907-09-(-) Henry to Bertha]

In spite of his mood swings, Henry tried to remain positive and trust that his condition would improve.

> *I am continuing to improve and today I ground out the best day's work since you left and I am beginning to realize and to gratefully be thankful that I have a dear wife and four nice children and that, even with my occasional visitations of physical woe, I am one of the very fortunate men in this world. I haven't seen doctor McConnell yet but I hope to do so in a day or two and, if all that bother don't cure my case, I am going to drift until I can get away and, if I am not well at Rye, I can hunt up Munro or some other man.* [Henry 1908, 21080316-1]

But, as Henry wrote in 1909, he wasn't sleeping and his gloom was "*rapidly transforming this fair earth in my view...*"

> *I am not having what you would call a heavenly time myself but your chapter of misfortunes seems even longer than my own. I hope you won't let things worry you for that state of mind makes life unbearable. I am having something of a picnic. I don't sleep well and the gloom that besets me as*

[310] Dr. George Marvin Tuttle of Washington University School of Medicine

[311] Neurasthenia is a term that was first used at least as early as 1829 to label a mechanical weakness of the nerves and would become a major diagnosis in North America during the late nineteenth and early twentieth centuries after neurologist George Miller Beard reintroduced the concept in 1869. The term was used to denote a condition with symptoms of fatigue, anxiety, headache, heart palpitations, high blood pressure, neuralgia, and depressed mood. Americans were said to be particularly prone to neurasthenia, which resulted in the nickname "Americanitis" (popularized by William James).

I helplessly contemplate this tangle is rapidly transforming this fair earth in my view... [20171119-2 1909-(-) Henry (Fort Worth) to Bertha]

In 1909 on a trip to Ft. Worth, Henry wrote of continuing to fight against his gloom.

Ah, my dearest, I have almost infinite capacity for happiness at times, the times when I am well and with you. But the siege of slight ailments are not fought with the spirit that should combat them and I feel much contempt for myself that I give in so easily. I make as I contemplate my sins one more fierce resolve to be good and you shall see the improvement when I return! The problem here has not grown much clearer but I hope tomorrow for word from my man fixing a meeting and I shall try to make it a means of some arrangement that will be an honorable adjustment of our difficulties if not a profitable one.
[1909-10-19 Henry (Ft. Worth) to Bertha]

Even when Henry tried to write a comforting letter to Bertha about his ailments, his underlying anxiety was still apparent: *"there were days when I would have pawned half my remaining days for the touch of your hand..."* It was not clear that such words had the desired calming effect on Bertha.

I cannot understand how my sick letters alarmed you so. I did not mean they should. But I was sick sweetheart and, altho' I tried not to be sorry for myself, there were days when I would have pawned half my remaining days for the touch of your hand. It was not exactly a collapse for I kept going but it was an experience, the return of which I shall hope may be a long way off in my remaining years. I think you caught added alarm because of Jack's letters to Sarah on top of mine and I wish I hadn't been selfish enough to talk to him for it couldn't have entertained him greatly and I am afraid it spoiled the girls visit in part.
[1910-06-27 Henry (StL) to Bertha (Rye Beach)]

Henry's attempt in his next letter may also have fallen short of providing the desired comfort.: *"...I am bitterly repenting all the anxiety I have given you because my head and side were acting badly for a few days. It was a very small burden after all for a man who has you to love and comfort him all the days of his life."* [1910-06-27 Henry (StL) to Bertha (Rye Beach)]

In his letters to Bertha written around 1910, Henry spoke of his ailment with Bertha's brother, George, and wrote of his annoyance with himself when he found that he could not rise above his physical concerns when his life was so beautiful.

Dear Bert,

I finished my last letter in such discomfort of mind and body that I scarcely recall what I wrote. I had to go to bed again yesterday and Tuttle slugged me last night with five grains of calomel in addition to the other stuff I have been taking regularly. This morning I was miserable and when I dressed, I went over and had a long talk with George who gave me more hope by his intelligent getting at the root of things than I have had since I have been ailing. George says there are better men here than I have yet seen and he wishes one of them to go over me thoroughly for he says the kidneys are now clearly not involved and, while he still believes I have chronic appendicitis, the liver inflammation or gall stones, either of which Lambert suspects, ought to be run down and clearly admitted or else eliminated. He knows as I do that these attacks have one cause and are getting more acute each time and, while he says if it were his responsibility, he would have the appendix out at once. He thinks in view of Lambert's strong leaning to "a strong tendency to the disturbance of the liver digestion", that his markers should be followed by someone else during one of my attacks and the trouble placed or looked for in the other directions.

I am so well tonight that, if you were here, I should have nothing more to ask in the way of comfort and happiness and yet I know that I may awake in the morning with all the old pain and horror and helplessness. I suppose I have not been as ill as I imagined or I could not in so short a time so fully regain my strength and spirits for the Lambert tonics. Altho' strong enough to work alone, would not do that if I had been seriously ill, but I do know that this last tussle was fully all that my strength would stand and that the breaking point once or twice was close at hand and so I know I must fend off future attacks if possible.

...

I must post this to make sure that it will reach you, so goodnight, sweetheart. Alice is sleeping quietly in my room having been brought down on account of the heat and, as I look at her sweet face and think of you and all our dear little people, I can't see how a few physical ills can so entirely rob me at times of peace. It must be that I am a poor fighter, sweetheart.

[20180317-2 (1910-) Henry to Bertha]

"...yet I know that I may awake in the morning with all the old pain and horror and helplessness." Henry's struggle with depression was clearly made worse by the fact that medical science of that age did not understand it or how to treat it. The fact that Henry found periodic comfort in labelling his disease rheumatism, a bad liver, bad appendix or even overwork, revealed his desperation to secure any answer to a then unanswerable question and to find a way to ultimately defeat *"my enemy"*.

CHAPTER 23 - ENDURING LOVE

My dear, I am never going to be married again, no matter what attractions are offered me. There is a New Year's resolution for you.

[Bertha, New Year's Day, just prior to their wedding]

[1893-01-01 (Sunday Bertha (Newton Centre) to Henry (StL)]

Flowers sent to Henry
[1892-09-13 (Monday) Bertha (Backbay, Boston) to Henry (StL)]

You have beautiful weather for your birthday and I am very glad for you. I hope the flowers I send will add a little to the sweet happy thoughts which should be yours this morning and that you will include me among those who wish for you in the coming year all the happiness you so richly deserve. Henry

[1890-04-30 Henry to Bertha]

Bertha kept these flowers (below) with Henry's letter.

In my life, I am thinking very much of you and I should not care to close my sleepy eyes feeling that my last act had been to slight even the least of your wishes or expectations. For I do love you very dearly, my child, and careless and heedless as I seem to be, there isn't anything in life that I care so much for as what you wish or expect of me. ... But tired and dejected as I am, I love you and shall love you always.

[20180222-5 Henry to Bertha]

A. WITHOUT YOU, THE SALT HAS LOST ITS SAVOR

Throughout their relationship, Bertha and Henry often expressed how diminished their lives were when they were apart. In a letter written around 1898, Henry reminisced about leaving Bertha for a short time at the Wickford boat in Jamestown Rhode Island. (The Wickford Boat serviced Narraganset Bay, Wickford being an onshore town North of Jamestown Island.) Although, at first, Henry expressed having a "*lovely feeling*", this gave way to the "*cold and dismal*". But, when Bertha returned, Henry wrote only of his happiness.

> *I don't think I was very much away from you from the time we met on the Wickford boat until I saw you last at seaport but it would make you smile if you could understand how clearly now I can remember the lovely feeling which possessed me whenever you were away from me for an hour. I was thinking last night of the tramp to the village I took that morning from Hildegarde's. I remember on my return how I trampled up the hill to the house, my blood tingling with the exercise and the brace in the air and my spirits way up, and how I went in, sat down, found the hall cold and dismal, changed to the porch where it was too hot, looked over the hills and didn't think they were very fine and concluded the confounded place wasn't good for me anyway! And that my first impression of it were foolish enthusiasms. Then you came back, and the mood changed to a deep set wish to live and die in a land where a man had nothing to do but be happy and well.*
>
> [20181231-2 (1898-) Henry to Bertha]

Henry and Bertha sometimes used the metaphor of the salt losing its savor or eating an egg without salt. Henry used this in the following letter to Bertha in August 1900 in which he spoke of missing Bertha and reproached her for not taking better care of him while he was in New York City.

> *First, let me say that I went to a real nice wicked place last night – the "Cadet Girl" at the Herald Theatre! It was one of those nice plays you like to take your wife to and grin over but which you don't exactly care to describe to your strictly religious friends. I am bound to say I had a good time but, to use a favorite metaphor of yours, it was a little like eating an egg without salt. I mean, the flavor wasn't there because you weren't. I mean, nothing else – not by no means!*
>
> *...*
>
> *It dawned a glorious day, one that makes even the native New Yorker love to walk down Fifth Avenue with joy in every step and breathing in God's blessed tonic every breath, a day in a thousand for any place. The children could have stayed out and never would have bothered Nan or anybody, bless them, and you could have been here, you bad unruly child, and I would have been perfectly happy instead of reproaching you all day for forgetting one of the solemn promises you made to the Rev. Sullivan that February morning in Newton Center, for I did positive tell you to come and take care of me and you did not come. Must I pursue you farther?*
>
> [1900-08-15 Henry (Philadelphia) to Bertha (co Henry Leffingwell, Dublin NH)]

Before Bertha and Henry were married, Bertha wrote about Dr. & Mrs. Will who, even though married for five years, still missed each other when they were apart. *"People who have been married five years are not expected to be so much in love with each other. At least, that is the opinion of all sensible people."* [1892-06-13 (Sunday) Bertha (Jaffrey NH) to Henry (StL)]

But after ten years of marriage when Bertha and Henry had moved into the new house on Vandeventer Place, Bertha's loneliness seemed to increase with each new separation. *"I did not miss you ten years ago as I do now."*

> *Sunday*
>
> *My Dear Henry,*
>
> *I am ashamed to say how much I miss you when you have been gone so short a time. For people who have been married nearly ten years, it is not quite the calm proper attitude toward life and each other. But I did not miss you ten years ago as I do now. All the life has gone out of everything,*

the salt has lost its savor[312]. I had no Sunday to look forward to and I cannot look forward to the evenings anymore.

I suppose one does spend a good deal of one's life in looking forward that might be better spent in enjoying what is going on. But really, it is the thought of your coming home at night that makes the pleasantness of the days. I listen always, all through the reading to the children for the sound of your key in the lock. At 3337 you used to shake the house when you came up the steps but you don't anymore. I grudge the time we have to be apart, sweetheart, I am disappointed sometimes when I am with father and the children and cannot come up to talk to you while you are dressing because those are among the few times we have to be alone together; it seems to me we are so much with other people. I should have loved this trip but I did not dare to go. I should never forgive myself if anything happened and I felt it was my own fault. Only come back as soon as you can for I can only end this letter as I began it. I miss you so much.

> *Yours Always,*
> *Bert*
> [1902-11-09 Bertha (StL) to Henry (Waco)]

(What a beautiful sentiment: "*it is the thought of your coming home at night that makes the pleasantness of the days.*")

Similarly, Henry wrote Bertha around the year 1900 that "*Even the beautiful Susquehanna isn't worth looking at if I can't talk about it to my best friend*".

We are running out of Harrisburg and I do wish so much you were with me, dear. The road is as smooth as can be and I am writing with the train at full speed. No dust or dirt, beautiful weather and the charming hills of western Pennsylvania but I haven't our companionship and that makes all the difference. Even the beautiful Susquehanna isn't worth looking at if I can't talk about it to my best friend. Bert dear, I don't think I ever so fully realized the beauty and unselfishness of your character as I did this last time we were together. You make my life seem a mean and selfish one, dear, for yours seems given up to me and the children and I wonder if you ever spare time for even momentary thought of yourself. You spoil me dreadfully and I oughtn't to let you do it but I am mean enough to permit, even when I realize all you give up for me and my whims. But I thank you and bless you for it all and for the happiness you bring me every day and how we are together.
[20180328-2 (1900-) Henry to Bertha]

In a conversation with a friend, Henry was reminded of his past travel to Switzerland and how beautiful it was. But it made him realize how much better that experience would have been if he had been with Bertha.

The continental trip aroused all my old longing for travel. That woman did exactly what I did in Switzerland around Geneva and I almost cried when she reflected, "if it is all so beautiful as I see it alone, what would be its beauty if I could see it with my hand in his." When will you let me take you to see it all, Bert? This is a cry from the bottom of my heart and we cannot, must not, let life go by without reaping that rich harvest.
[20180419-1 (1906-) Henry to Bertha]

Henry was able to arrange to be with Bertha in Rye Beach for a week in early July 1906. After their short time together, Bertha described her feelings immediately after Henry left, writing that nothing "*happened except somehow for all the light to go out of the sunshine.*"

Of course, enough time has not passed for anything to have happened except somehow for all the light to go out of the sunshine. It has been a glorious day, but the joy has gone out of the world. A cold gray path of duty lies ahead, duty without enthusiasm. It is perfectly disgraceful to admit after

---

[312] Luke 14:34

all these years that one man still has the power to write Ichabod[313] across the page when he leaves. Dearest, at the risk of being thought just a little sentimental, I must tell you what a radiantly happy week that was. All the clouds and the dullness went out of everything and life was worth the trouble of living it, a thousand times over. I cannot think of one minute that wasn't a joy. And now, it seems as if the contrast was exceeding bitter. Tonight, I feel tired and as if I were spending my money for that which is not bread and my labor for that which satisfieth not.[314]
[1906-07-16 Bertha (Rye Beach) to Henry (StL)]

While in Rye Beach in the summer of 1906, Bertha reminisced about the past when she experienced the beauty of Rye Beach with her hand in Henry's. Without his hand, Rye Beach *"was rather desolate… a gray sea, without a sail"*

The walk home with an autumn sunset, falling leaves, and the crimson marshes would have been exhilarating "with your hand in mine", but without it, it was rather desolate, not a human being in sight and a gray sea without a sail.
[1906-09-26 Bertha – Rye Beach]

Like Henry, Bertha shared her feelings of loneliness when Henry was away. But it was more than just loneliness: it was life wanting of joy.

You were done out of a letter yesterday for I expected by Saturday you would be on your way home and did not write. I almost cried when I got your letter saying you would not see your man before Monday or Tuesday. I was so sure you would be home Sunday. It is really awful to be so dependent on another person for all the joy in life and I will be perfectly frank, sweetheart, it gets worse. I did not use to miss you like this. Now, I miss you all the time. Don't speak of not talking out your troubles to me, I am afraid one of my selfish reasons for wanting you back is that I like to talk over my worries with you and load them off on your shoulders. It is a good thing they are broad, my dearest, for a good many people like to unload their worries on them.

And then, I like to talk over the nice things. It took half the flavor out of Mrs. Ewing's luncheon yesterday that you were not there to tell about it. I think I was asked because you have been so nice to her boy. You did not tell me anything about it but she told me you had been awfully nice to him and that she was very grateful. I had one of the nice seats too. Mrs. William Lee had the foot of the table and I had her right hand. It was a very nice crowd.
[1908(-) 20180801-1 Bertha (64 Vandeventer Place, Stl) to Henry]

On a business trip to New York in early 1908 which prevented his going away with Bertha, Henry expressed his frustration by saying that he was ready to reject any other pleasures that might be offered him since it would be like going *"to a feast with no appetite."*

This has been a pure and simple boresome affair and I am so cross and sad over the collapse of our honey-moon trip that, if anything in the way of joy and gladness offered, I should reject it for no other reason than that it seems silly to try to go to a feast with no appetite.
[1908-01-19 Henry (NYC) to Bertha (64 Vandeventer Place, Stl)]

---

[313] Ichabod (Hebrew: אִיכָבוֹד, ikhavod – no glory ,inglorious or where is the glory, is mentioned in the first Book of Samuel as the son of Phinehas, a malicious priest at the biblical shrine of Shiloh, who was born on the day that the Israelites' Ark of God was taken into Philistine captivity. His mother went into labour due to the shock of hearing that her husband and Eli, her father-in-law, had died and that the Ark had been captured. He is also named later as the brother of Ahitub.
In the Book of 1 Samuel, his name is said to be a reference to: the glory has departed from Israel, because of the loss of the Ark to the Philistines, and a lesser reference to the deaths of Eli and Phinehas. She repeats the phrase, "*The glory has departed from Israel, for the ark of God has been captured,*" to show her piety, and that the public and spiritual loss lay heavier upon her spirit than her personal or domestic calamity. Yairah Amit suggests that his name indicates "*the fate of this newborn child who would have no parents, no grandfather and not even God, because even the glory has departed from the place*".
[314] Isaiah 55:2.

B. ARRANGING TO MEET ON BUSINESS TRIPS
1. CAN WE MEET IN NEW YORK?
Periodically, when Henry's business took him east, he would plead with Bertha to come down from Rye Beach or Jamestown to visit him in New York or Boston, with the rhetoric of good weather and of the loneliness that comes from being *"cut off from our second self"*.

> *O, dearie, I do want you to come to New York! The weather is magnificent even here and I have watched the New York reports daily and have been delighted to see how cool it is there. I really could not do without you, Bert. You must come, sweetheart! And do you wish to come? Has it seemed a long time since we parted at Union Station and do you feel as I do that because we have to be separated very often, that fact does, in the least, enable us to be really happy a single day that we are alone? Alone is the only term that applies, dear, when we are cut off from our second self - and you will come! I know you will, for you love me, my darling.*
> [20171215-5 (1900-) Henry to Bertha]

Although Bertha joined Henry on a few of his business trips, generally she stayed at home with their children. But Bertha would sometimes write of her regret in not joining Henry on some of his business trips.

> *Your letter this morning made me feel more disappointed than ever that I had not gone with you. I almost wish you had taken the law into your own hands and said I had to, but that is a sort of selfish shirking of responsibility, is it not?*
> [1902-11-9 Wednesday Bertha to Henry Stl to Waco Texas]

Henry was generally able to go east for several weeks at the end of each summer for his vacation, as he did in 1903. His anticipation of seeing Bertha often brought out both joy and a feeling of loneliness and frustration with his *"confounded business."*

> *With much regret and with feelings which I am sure you will appreciate as natural in one who for so many years has devoted his entire time to business to the exclusion of all other demands upon him, I announce that I shall leave the confounded business on Saturday to join my wife. ... I have missed you sadly, dear. Sometimes more than I care to confess even to you, for it seemed weak to dwell as I did on our separation when there were such good reasons of it and when, with all my efforts, I seemed to accomplish so little to deserve the happiness waiting for me at the end of what would have seemed so short a period if there had been any other task involved than living apart from you.*
> [1903-08-05 Wednesday Henry (StL) to Bertha (Rye Beach)]

February 1905 brought Henry to New York and one more separation from Bertha who remained in St. Louis. Henry bemoaned the "poor *substitutes for your society which this country produces...*"

> *Things go slowly with me and both the days and nights are full long. I made a mistake not to bring you along, willy-nilly, for, although I haven't exactly been sitting up twirling my thumbs but have had to go over what one of my friends terms "space considable", I haven't had to go out of town yet and, if you had been here, I might have gotten some joy out of life in the evenings instead of keeping at the "gas bag" until I am sick of the whole subject and half inclined to run off and leave these people to repent at leisure their missing out of the greater enterprises of modern times. There's lots to do if I had the time and the one friend it is worth doing anything with in the line of pleasure. I declined a dinner invitation this evening partly because, like Hugh with his birds, I am waiting for my scheme to hatch out and don't dare leave it; but I think in great part because, if I can't get you for my sprees, I am not disposed to take the poor substitutes for your society which this country produces or any country can produce for that matter. There is lots to do. The opera, Ethel Barrymore, Mrs. Fiske, Mrs. Leslie Carter! Maud Adams, Francis Wilson and last, but not*

least, Mrs. Leffingwell's boots. My dear, it's no sort of discipline for a good man to be brought up by a good wife and then be neglected by her in time of need like this.
[1905-02-22 Henry (NYC) to Bertha (StL)]

2. THE NEW YORK TRIP OF 1908; GEORGE'S DEATH

On his July 1908 business trip to New York City, Henry wrote to Bertha in the hope of arranging a rendezvous there. Perhaps as encouragement, he sent Bertha the cartoon (below) from the paper.

"How About That Vacation!", Henry wrote.

I think you enjoyed the shoals more than the children but what must have been your meditations as the boat drew near Appledore[315] and your eager glance saw no kidnapper in the guise of a nice young man to rush off with you to the rocks in order that you might be given the chance to show him how a good woman loved him! The world is small, my dearest.

...

I am longing for your verdict on the New York meeting. I don't see how I can go there and attend properly to those stupid meetings and wait and wait and wait for you. I will have a horrid time if you don't come and, if you will after the business is over, we will go off alone somewhere where we can be for a little space alone and we will have another honeymoon to go down into history with the others of blessed memory, to keep our lives young and "gay with the fragrance of happiness." Take off your wedding ring and read its motto and come if you can, provided the weather man does his duty.
[1908-07-18 Henry (StL) to Bertha (Rye Beach)]

Due to her father's declining health, Bertha was uncertain about a trip to New York City, as she wrote to Henry on July 22. In her letter, Bertha regretted that her responsibilities prevented her from doing the things she would have most wanted, and said, *"When I am born again, ..., I want to be born in the tropics and without a conscience."* But, of course, Bertha without a conscience could hardly have been Bertha.

---

[315] The Appledore House on Appledore Island on the Isles of the Shoals was where Henry waited for Bertha to arrive by ferry and then proposed to her in August 1891.

Your urgent letters about New York make me just long to go, not by boat, no human power could make me take that outside sail from Boston to New York especially alone with no one to hold my head, but by train. And if father's bronchitis is better, I may come. I will telegraph the Plaza if there is any chance of my coming but today was a heavy, wet, foggy day, and he slept so badly last night and was so uncomfortable today that I should not be willing to have Miss Engelhardt alone or to be so far away myself. Ten hours is a long distance to be away. By Sunday, however, everything may have cleared up. The heavy, wet fog of course is trying but do not expect me, sweetheart. I am afraid I could not take my spree with the care free mind one ought to have to enjoy it. But I do want to come. I could not be away now though and leave him as uncomfortable as he is. It would not be right. Do you have to stay long? Can't you come up Monday night and I meet you in Boston Tuesday? I feel as if I did not tell you how I want you, I only say I can't do this or I can't do that. When I am born again, ..., I want to be born in the tropics and without a conscience.

[1908-07-22 (Wednesday) Bertha (Rye Beach) to Henry]

Henry so hoped that Bertha would be able to come to New York City during his business trip that he sent Bertha the telegraph message that he had received from the Hotel Plaza. Henry wrote on this message in red pencil, "*I call this a "red letter" dispatch – Sunday, my dearest.*"

Henry addressed the letter with a red pencil.

Henry's words at the bottom, "*a real red-letter dispatch*", were written in red pencil.

Unfortunately, due to the deteriorating condition of Bertha's father, Bertha was unable to go to New York. Bertha wrote to Henry on July 25th of her difficult decision to stay in Rye Beach.

> *I almost cried when I got your red-letter dispatch yesterday and then your letter following showing how fully you expected me to come. I sent a dispatch to St. Louis this morning because I did not want you to expect me in New York and then I worried and worried as to how to word it so that you would not think anything alarming had happened. Finally I decided that if I said I would meet you in Boston you would know nothing serious was wrong. And that is the case. If George were here, I would come but I have a feeling, a superstition you may call it but it is uncontrollable, that we must not both be out of reach. And ten hours is out of reach. Boston is as near on the cars as Exeter in a carriage. I had meant to leave the whole thing to discuss until you came on but I don't want you to feel that I am absolutely unreasonable in disappointing you. And I don't want you to think I am not disappointed. You know whether I enjoy a spree with you or not.*
>
> *...*
>
> *Perhaps you will understand better if I tell you that edema in its more advanced stages was Mrs. Shepley's trouble and you know if Nan had gone to Washington, she could not have gotten back.*
> [1908-07-25 (Saturday) Bertha (Rye Beach) to Henry]

In a note to herself later which Bertha penciled at the top of her letter written on July 26th: "*The end did come as Dr. Otis predicted. If I had gone to New York, father would have died while I was away. He died July 27.*" She wrote to Henry in this July 26th letter, trying to explain why she needed to stay with her father.

> *Dear old boy,*
>
> *I got your telegram yesterday and I could just see the reason you sent it. You thought I had gotten nervous and over wrought and that a trip and spree with you would cure it. You meant the very essence of kindness but you did a very unkind thing. I had visions of your rooms, ordered at the Plaza, the letters you had written for them to meet me and all your plans made in the security that I would not fail you. And I knew just how disappointing it would be and that probably too you would feel really vexed and irritated with me and think I might have made the effort and that I had sacrificed you to father and that, when there was not even a really good reason.*
>
> *Then father had a very bad evening, heavy asthmatic breathing, recalling some of your mother's struggles and I did not see how I could go until this attack was over. I went over and over this until two o'clock last night and woke with a sick headache this morning. Then Dr. Otis came and said that while the other conditions were better, the left lung had solidified more and this had increased the chances of anything sudden happening. I asked if he anticipated anything of the sort and he said "no, on the contrary, if we just have a north-west wind for a while and no fog, I expect that your father's breathing will be greatly relieved and he will be much better. At the same time, I do not think it fair to you to leave you in ignorance, that there is that possibility."*
>
> *Of course, I know as well as you, that Dr. Otis is an old pessimist but I should be simply unspeakably wretched if I were ten hours out of reach and especially with no other member of the family here. If George or even Minnie were here, I should feel differently.*
>
> *You are mistaken too in thinking I am nervous or overwrought. I have not felt as exultantly well for many years. Father has had so many nervous troubles too that you would be likely to think this another. This has not been and he has taken it very differently from the imaginary ones. And I am not nervous here, it is the idea of being out of reach that frightens me. I finally worked it out that you had sent the telegram because you wanted me to have a good time and that you would be bitterly disappointed yourself if I came, just longing to get back and only to please you. So please don't be angry about it, dear. I could not bear to start our vacation that way, after all our plans.*

Today is a glorious day and if father is no worse, I will come to Boston if you want me. I can get there at nine or ten, either one, but it may be that if you come by night, you can catch an early train to Rye and will not want me to come down. If you are to be there until 3:15, I want to come, if I can.

Yours always,
Bert

I am tired of always being the one to apologize and I wish you would do something to change the scale. Can't you find Tom and go on a tremendous spree with a blonde in black? I should be so glad to excuse it.
[1908-07-26 (Sunday) Bertha (Rye Beach) to Henry]

So Bertha did not go to New York or Boston that July to meet Henry. Bertha's father died July 27, 1908, the day after this letter was written.

C. MISSING BIRTHDAYS & SPECIAL OCCASIONS

Henry was often away from Bertha on various, special, occasions. On Bertha's thirty-sixth birthday when Henry was in Texas, Bertha wrote in her diary of her life and life's lessons to be learned.

April 30, 1902
Thirty-six years old but far older than last year. Henry is away but the children come into my room early in the morning with presents, including pearl crescent from Henry. He planned it all. It has been a strange year, with new lessons. I find I have been omitting the prayer in the Litany "In all time of our prosperity, Good Lord, deliver us". I am learning now to say, "Not my will, but thine be done", but when I have learned that lesson perfectly, life's lessons will be over.
[1893 Diary]

Henry often missed Nancy's birthday on July 5 since Bertha and the children were generally on summer vacation in the east. On Nancy's 13th birthday in 1908 when Bertha and the children were in Rye Beach, Henry reminisced about his walk with Bertha along the Jamestown shore on the day before Nancy was born and their great joy then.

I wonder if you have forgotten this day thirteen years ago. It seems to me every incident of that perfect summer has come back to me as though it had been yesterday. I can even see those huge boulders I helped you over in our walk and feel the soft sea air in my face as we stood on the shore and looked out on that beautiful bay. Nancy will be thirteen tomorrow and, if ever a baby came amid more peaceful surroundings or after more serene and happy season of preparation, I am unable to conceive such good fortune.

I love you very dearly, Bert dearest, as I think over that charming life we led together with that quaint island, spoiled in summer by the vulgar crowds that infect it, but really strong in its coast lines and peaceful and beautiful in its normal life of quiet and calm and its really beautiful outlook - our almost exclusive possession. And I wonder sometimes in my gloomy moments or when I am ill or have that unwholesome fancy of illness, which is even more than serious illness itself, whether we can ever be as carefree and happy again. Then I put away the idle thought as I realize that I only have such longings when I am away from you and realize that these recurrences are only the expression of my loneliness when I am away from you and my utter inability to be happy without you. And that there are as many happy years ahead as lay behind us if our lives are mercifully spared to us that long.
[1908-07-05 Henry (StL) to Bertha (Rye Beach)]

Henry's business trips often caused him to miss other family events, such as Alice's seventh birthday on February 20, 1910. Bertha wrote this letter to Henry while he was traveling on the Wabash Train No. 2 to Sacramento that, if he could not return in time, they would wait for him before opening the presents.

I woke up in the middle of the night last night and wondered if you were out in the teeth of the blizzard anywhere but the paper says the blizzard only went as far west as Colorado and I don't think you can be there quite yet. Mary Lionberger and Madge and I were out in the worst of it yesterday to hear Paul More lecture at the Wednesday Club and it was not worth it but I took Mrs. Lane home which was something, though she had to wade up to her knees through a snow drift to get into the house when she got there. It reminds me of the day before our wedding at Newton Centre.

I am afraid whatever happens, you will not get home on time. If you do, you will probably come into the middle of Alice's birthday party as Miss Alice Scott is receiving from 3:30 to 5:30 on Saturday though the presents are to be saved for the real birthday, Sunday, because "Dad will be home then."
[1910-02-16 Bertha to Henry (20180803-1)]

D. LOST WITHOUT YOUR INFLUENCE & CARE

After nearly a decade of marriage, Henry wrote of how much he was influenced by Bertha and how deeply he appreciated the *"true depths of your character"*.

Didn't we have a nice time, sweetheart? I don't know how I am ever going to pin my thoughts down to business after such a peep into paradise. I suppose one can get used to anything but just now I feel that it is simply an absurd task to put upon myself to remain here delving away when a few hours would take me to you and happiness greater than even an old married man like your husband ever dreamed of before. I loved to tell you when we first really grew to know each other how you never failed me and always met my ideals as if you couldn't do anything that was not the high mark of womanhood; but I was too new to the influence of your life then to realize that every day of your life you unfold to those who really love and prize your new resources and new beauty of character. And I was amazed this last beauty, beauty visit with you, to know how little with all my vain boasting of how well I knew you. I really had appreciated the true depths of your character. Don't put this aside as the tattle of a foolish boy, my dearest, for it is the talk and the religion of a mature man who is mighty sane on one subject if he is an idler and a dreamer of things in general.
[1900(-) 20180728-1 Henry to Bertha]

Bertha also spoke of how much she too was influenced by Henry and how much this had changed her. She wrote of a Mrs. Bell who said of Bertha that *"she had never seen anyone person change so entirely under the influence of another."*

I thought I was going to write you a business letter today about all the things that I wanted done at home but I have decided not to. I am going to write instead about a discovery I made this afternoon.

I have had ever since I got here a sort of numb, dull, feeling and I thought it was because I was so tired. This afternoon I thought I'm not tired, I am not nearly as tired as I have often been, it is simply a lack of interest and then I discovered the cause. It is disgraceful at my age but it is none the less true, I am simply homesick for you.

It seems to me I might have known it sooner. Do you remember Mrs. Bell at Jamestown saying that she had never seen anyone person change so entirely under the influence of another? O, it's true, sweetheart and it has always been so. I don't think really that I ever knew how to enjoy life until you taught me and I don't seem able to improve the lessons without the teacher. When it comes to unhappiness, I don't know, you haven't let much unhappiness come near me but I believe I can stand it better alone than with anyone. But I want you to be happy with, in fact, I don't know how to be happy without you. "What's this dull town to me? Robin's not here." And how am I going to wait another month to see you, I don't know. I am strongly inclined to do like Margaret Ives, descend upon you in the midst of summer, announcing that I cannot live without you.
[1904-07-06 Bertha (Rye Beach) to Henry]

Bertha's admission in this letter was striking: "*I don't think really that I ever knew how to enjoy life until you taught me.*"

In 1904, when Henry was lonely and depressed, Henry often wrote in a self-deprecating manner about his work efforts not having significance compared to Bertha's influence on him. Although Henry thought that other men might see it as weakness, that a man would be so influenced by his wife, Henry wrote, "*I don't mind people who laugh because another enjoys sunshine and shows it!*" In the end, Henry concluded that the only thing of value that he can give Bertha was his love of which Bertha was the source.

I am given, as you know, to fault finding. In spite of all my blessings, with rewards in my business far beyond either my deserts or achievements if my sporadic efforts may be so termed with friends, I have done so little to secure with the next, of babies dearer than my life and for above all with you, my comrade and friend, to make my life happier than I had ever dreamed I could be, I am given to deem my life a worthless one and to fretfully look ahead for chances, opportunities, advantages or whatever you may call them that may, as Judge Clark puts it, furnish some apology to the Almighty for my existence. I don't think you would imagine this if you had known the pleasure, the delight which your last letter gave me. It is, I am told, unmistakable weakness in a man to be "influenced" by his wife. Perhaps so, but somehow I don't mind people who laugh because another enjoys sunshine and shows it!
...
What experiences you women go through for men, Bert. And the best among us doesn't half appreciate your patience and courage and unselfishness. I try to, dearest, but I don't seem to develop much capacity for showing it. I know I have the best wife that ever a man was blessed with and yet, as far as I have ever been able to get in recognizing all I owe to her, is an occasional indulgence in idle wonder that she should seem content with a life partnership to which she is almost the sole real contributor. I can't give you back very much that is worthwhile but my love, dearest, but that must count for something and, since you are its inspiration, it can't be entirely worthless.

Yours always,
Henry

I dreamed of you last night and it was all so vivid that I was shocked this morning to find you were not with me.
[20180328-1 (1904-06-29-) Henry to Bertha]

In 1905, after she had been hospitalized at Carney Hospital in Boston for an illness, Bertha wrote of how much her recovery was due to Henry's diligence and care for her.

> *I was so dreadfully tired this morning that I sent you only a very short note, just to let you know all was well and I never said one word of all the gratitude I feel to you for all you have done these past weeks and just now. I could not have gotten well without you, dearest. All the progress I have made has been because I was happy, so perfectly happy in your love and care for me, my dearest, as I have never been even in all the beautiful years of our married life. I know it has been at the cost of great sacrifices and that you are paying now, soul and brain and body, for those beautiful days and it must have seemed sometimes as if you gave everything and I did not even appreciate it, but I did. It meant life and hope and courage to me. Everything I had came from you. And this last trip, dear, I know now that I could not have done it.*
> [1905-10-14 Bertha (Hotel Somerset, Boston) to Henry (StL)]

E. ABOUT LUCY BOISLINIÈRE

Henry wrote to Bertha in the summer of 1906 when Bertha is out of town that everything was dull, including his letters. So Henry wrote of an interesting story from his distant past in 1886 during a similar boring period of time when no one was around except Lucy Boislinière.

> *I thought I had given you every item of news since you left but you reproach me as if, for the lack [of] any real interest in my letters, you thought of discharging me and engaging another husband. Perhaps I have made a mistake in writing only of what actually happens since it has been dull here. But I thought you would understand that. You are out of town so how can things be other than dull? I wish I was as adaptable as I was eighteen years ago and I might furnish a few items of interest, for I very vividly recall that, as all the girls I knew best were out of town, I devoted myself one September to Lucy Boislinière and, although I didn't exactly make love to her, at least I hope I did not, I could have written an interesting letter about an evening I spent with her on the steps of the Second Baptist Church!*
>
> *You see, I am getting to be an old man and my habits have become somewhat staid and sot. But if you wish me to adapt more youthful pursuits, I shall try, only I shall hold you responsible for the results, it being agreed of course that first of all I must provide more interesting letters.*
> [20180206-7 (1906-07-01-) Henry to Bertha]

When Bertha received Henry's letter, she was missing Henry, maybe more than usual since she wrote that she wouldn't even mind if he played golf all day and then did most of the talking "*if I could feel your hand in mine*". And Lucy Boislinière? Bertha had no doubt that Henry would have "*made love to*" her.

> *Do you know, I really should like to see you, I mean, now. By August, I don't think I shall care much. But I wrote you I have been reading "Pam Decides"[316] aloud to Sarah and, as I said last year when I read "Pam", that woman understands what a good time a man and woman can have together who really care and she makes you feel it as almost no other authoress does that I know.*
>
> *At any rate, when I finished the book the other night, I could not go to sleep for thinking how much I wanted to see you. I would like, it's very disgraceful to own up to it, but I would like very dearly to see you come across the bridge with your golf clubs over your shoulder and I believe I should even forgive you for playing golf all day if I could feel your hand in mine or your arms around me just once. It is raining tonight as usual but there is a salt tang to the air. There has been a sea turn and it would be nice to sit on the porch with warm wraps on and just talk. I would even let you do most of the talking, the effect would not be so bad in the end.*

---

[316] Bettina Von Hutten, 1906. *Pam Decides* is a sequel to *Pam*.

I am quite convinced that you made love to Lucy Boislinière on the church steps because you never talked to any woman very long in the moonlight (or any other light) without making love to her. And tonight, there would be only one woman, convenient, so to speak, and she wouldn't mind.
[1906-07-03 Bertha to Henry]

Bertha painted a beautiful picture: "*I would like very dearly to see you come across the bridge with your golf clubs over your shoulder...*"

F. TIRED, FORLORN & BLUE

In the summer of 1904, Henry recounted the news of several recent deaths, news which was clearly not necessary to make him feel more "blue" since Bertha was away in Rye Beach. Henry lamented that, even though the time for their reunion became closer with each passing day, it counted for nothing since the remaining days seemed to become longer.

I don't know whether the bad news has been the cause of it or what is the trouble but I have had the blues all day and I don't think I am apt to write anything of interest so I shall say good night. I miss you tonight, my dearest, and, although some of the time has actually gone by, it is hard to realize that the time ahead is not farther off than ever. There is nothing in cutting down the number of days until we meet if each day gets longer proportionately.
[1904-07-19 Henry (StL) to Bertha (Rye Beach)]

After Henry returned from his trip to Panama in the spring of 1907, he had to immediately attend to his Texas businesses. On his trip to Waco in March, Henry wrote the following letter to Bertha when he was tired and forlorn, especially since he would have to miss Easter with Bertha and his family.

My train did not arrive until two this morning, just three hours late, so you may imagine I did not start out today on my search for trouble very early. I was tired of the journey and almost of life when I reached the hotel but today I am much rested. My head has ceased to ache and I am beginning to feel that not all the joy has gone out of life which, I have to confess, was my disgraceful frame of mind when I left home.

...

I grew blue today when I passed a stationary shop and saw the Easter cards. It made my lot seem indeed a sad one when I thought of being away from you next Sunday. I hope you will get this in time to know how I shall miss you then.
[1907-03-28 Henry (Waco) to Bertha (StL)]

Bertha's summers in Rye Beach were always a cause for Henry's being gloomy.

You have not been away very long but the summer seems to have gone with you and, our nice house which made me happy as soon as I entered it, has become a gloomy shelter with a bed in it that I can make use of to get man's allowance of needful sleep.
[1907-09- Henry to Bertha (20180416A-8]

Henry often included in his messages of missing Bertha with self-criticism.

I am awfully sorry you had such a cold dismal return trip to Rye and I feel very guilty in being the cause of your having to take the late train. Looking back on the summer, I seem to have led a very useless, selfish existence and I might have at least spared you inconvenience at the very last. I suppose it is because I am growing older but it fills me with bitterness, nevertheless, as I realize what a wonder and yet cross grained individual I have become. I don't think I can have always been so but perhaps this last flattering reflection is only my conceit and that I am no better and no worse than when I was young.

...

I can't help wishing I were back enjoying what my scotch friends would term that grand storm and also by way of accident seeing you and getting some of the bitterness of life, which seems to have beset me lately, rubbed out of my cross and disturbed spirit. I miss you but I suppose you know that without the telling.
[1907-10-01 Henry (420 Olive St, StL) to Bertha (Rye Beach)]

Similarly, Henry wrote.

This probably will reach you, as I shall post it tonight and I hope it will, for I want you to know how much I have missed you and how glad I shall be to have you at home. I have been in a sort of daze, which I at first attributed to the confusion after a long absence but I know now that the forlornity of home without you is what my apathy and utter heedlessness of everything around me really springs from. I have looked back at the summer and felt that I wasted all of that part of it that I really should have made good use of and although nothing seems in its right place or worthwhile and I need you very much because I feel blue and depressed and a very old man – all of which is fine comfort and cheer for you just starting on a busy journey!
[1907-10-06 Henry to Bertha]

When Henry felt that Bertha was not expressing enough about herself and her love for him, he did not shy away from expressing his feelings. *"Have you forgotten how to write love letters?"*

You seem to be working ... with the children and I hope therefore you are well. You write about everyone else but nothing of yourself. If you could know my eager search through your letters for some word or phrase which indicates how you are feeling, how your health and your spirits, which are always high when you are not overtaxed or ill, are, you would write more of yourself. And you never tell me these days that you miss me and that you still love me. Have you forgotten how to write love letters?
[1908-07-16 Henry (StL) to Bertha (Rye Beach)]

Bertha's response to Henry's plea was perfect. Regarding her feelings toward Henry, Bertha wrote *"I have not spoken of it any more than I have of living."*

Dearest,

Haven't I said I missed you? If I have not, it is because it is so much a part of me that I have not spoken of it any more than I have of living. I am never more than half myself when you are not here. You say I write about the children and not about myself. You see, I really don't take any interest in myself especially when the better part of me is gone. I have always told you that all the real joy of living I had came from you. When you are not here, I am a very good machine, for responsibilities and duties, that is all. And sometimes I think I am not even good at that.
[1908-07-18 Bertha (Rye Beach) to Henry]

Toward the end of 1908, Henry went back to Ft. Worth to look into his natural gas business interests which were being threatened by Standard Oil.

... [I] came home wishing I was an angel with no confounded franchise or natural gas troubles and nothing ahead but that peaceful but rather selfish and useless life of continuous song and peace making. Next to being an angel, I should prefer to be at home with you for somehow when I leave you these days I realize that I am not able to take care of myself or get anything out of life without you... I begin to think that it is time that women haven't the time to give their husbands much serious thought after their children come. Naturally this conclusion arouses mingled sorrow and indignation and I might like to say I can stand it but I can't for I believe I love you more and am more dependent upon you than I ever was in all our married life, which is speaking large since I have "depended" pretty absolutely all and every one of those sixteen years.
[1908-11-30 (20180419A-5) Henry (Ft. Worth) to Bertha (64 Vandeventer Place, Stl)]

G. THE FOLLY OF THEIR SEPARATIONS

Henry was sentimental and, he could also be prophetic: *"It seems such a little while that we have ahead of us..."* Nevertheless, when a summer separation was coming to its end, Henry wrote *"... when we do meet, there will be joy as of heaven for Yours always..."*

> *... for I do love you, dearest, and I don't like to live apart from you. It seems such a little while that we have ahead of us that it seems wrong to be separated. Apart from the pain of it, I have missed you so this time that it was almost like another grief in my life to look for ahead and know that I must wait day after day with no cheer from your sweet face near me. I have not liked it, my darling, and we must some way fashion our lives that you may not be away from me so very, very long. There will be rejoicing in this lonely house as if you were here, almost, when I can write you that I know when we shall meet and when we do meet, there will be joy as of heaven for*
>
> *Yours always,*
> *Henry*
> [20180802-5 (2nd page only) Henry to Bertha]

Although the St. Louis summer heat was a frequent topic when Bertha was east for the summer, Henry viewed the heat as little compared to the *"supremest folly"* of their separations.

> *Your Sunday letter sounded blue and the weather there is evidently worse than ours. I am very sorry for you, dear, for I thought you would have the comfort of decent weather at least. It does seem like folly to be running away a thousand miles to worse weather than you left behind and I take all the responsibility for your misfortune. If I hadn't been so wise, I would have you here and we would be having a nice time instead of this summer separation business which is the supremest folly of our rather senseless American life. If I thought you were resting and getting over being tired, I would be reconciled but I have almost come to think that you will never take time to rest, even to obey the commands of your devoted husband,*
> *Henry*
> [1904-06-24 Henry (StL) to Bertha (Rye Beach)]

When the summer of 1904 was coming to its end and Henry's vacation east imminent, Henry wrote that *"life isn't worth living without you"* and vowed that he would not consent to another separation.

> *I will telegraph you if I find it impossible to get away on Saturday. I can't think Mrs. Fortune is going to be so hard on me. In fact, I think I would rather go on now and loaf a week with you if I had to come back after that and remain here, for I simply can't get along without you, Bert, and I just have to see you because really, dearest, life isn't worth living without you and with you, ah, that is very different and I don't see what makes it possible for me to ever consent to your leaving me. I do not think I can even consent to another separation.*
> [1904-08-04 Henry (StL) to Bertha (Rye Beach)]

In 1910, Henry expressed the desire to retire from his work and spend his days with Bertha. In the following letter which may have been written the year before his death, Henry's wish to retire seemed to take on greater urgency.

> *I have missed you more this summer than I ever did before and I have made up my mind to retire next spring on the fortunes of several millions which I have accumulated so that I may never again be so long separated from my wife.*
> [20170822-3 (1910-) Henry to Bertha]

By the summer of 1910, Henry increasingly wrote about the shortness of life and questioned why he and Bertha should spent *"even a fraction of the mite of time which they may hope for here on earth"* separated and apart from each other. Somewhat ominously, Henry wrote of being rational during the daytime but being *"really very lonely at nights"*.

> *I am not ill. In fact, I am feeling particularly well. Even the granite boulder in my side seems to have disappeared today. But still I need that letter and just why this is, is strange since you know I need word from you most urgently when I am ill. If I were guessing, which I don't propose to do about so serious a matter, I might suggest that, whether I am ill or well, I need word from you. Ah, in sickness and in health, sweetheart, the need of you always is a very clear and pressing fact in my life and the other things that have come into it are nothing. I don't understand how married people who really care for reach other live apart in apparent contentment for months and ever years. It isn't fair to say that those who live together in apparent happiness and who rush off to educate their children to serve country or fill business obligations, leaving their mates for a large fraction of the time doled out in a short lifetime, are not really happy and what is better and more blessed dependent when united. I suppose these people are happy but if this is true, there must be many more aching hearts in the world than any of us realize.*
> [1910-06-28 Henry (StL) to Bertha (Rye Beach)]

> *It doesn't seem right for us to be apart for weeks anyway and it certainly would be wicked if one of us were not well. I am getting very well indeed. I haven't exactly forgotten the jolt of ten days ago but I am daily getting strong and hopeful, have a good appetite and no headaches. I don't sleep perfectly but that I can understand for I am really very lonely at nights. In the day I keep busy and my mind must work at the things I have to do but the nights bring thoughts of the utter folly of two people who really care deliberately planning their lives to be apart for even a fraction of the mite of time which they may hope for here on earth. When daylight comes, my reason returns to me but the solution of the problem in the day does not prevent its recurrence at night.*
> [1910-07-12 (1st letter) Henry (StL) to Bertha (Rye Beach)]

The despair in Henry's words is palpable: "... *the nights bring thoughts of the utter folly of two people who really care deliberately planning their lives to be apart for even a fraction of the mite of time which they may hope for here on earth...*"

H. BERTHA'S NOSTALGIA

The summer of 1910 was similar to virtually every past summer with Bertha spending June through mid-September at the Farragut House in Rye Beach N.H. (or in Jamestown R.I.) and Henry remaining in St. Louis to work for most of the summer. In her early years, Bertha went to the Farragut House in Rye Beach with her parents and would find the usual entourage of fellow vacationers which made for good camaraderie and childhood amusement. During their marriage, Henry was generally able to visit Rye Beach or Jamestown for several weeks. Starting in 1894, after Hugh Scott was born, Bertha enjoyed taking their son east, and, years later, Bertha would enjoy taking Nancy, George and Alice to Rye. But when this letter was written in 1910, many things had changed. Bertha's mother had died in 1898 and her father in 1908. Also, as they grew older, the children had less desire to go to Rye Beach and depended less on their mother as they used to. Some dear friends had died and, very simply, Bertha was feeling old. Perhaps, as for Shakespeare's *King Lear*[317], she wondered at her continuing relevance.

---

[317] Bertha expresses in her letter an anxiety about the change in her life from motherhood to an unknown future. In commenting on *King Lear*, Paula Marantz Cohen said of Lear:

> *If "King Lear" is a lesson in the unexpected results of child-rearing, it also dramatizes the vicissitudes of retirement. It captures the existential abyss that can open when a once-solid identity begins to melt, and purpose gives way to purposelessness. Lear is deprived of his retinue and thrown out into a storm, reduced to his most elemental self—a "poor bare, forked animal." ... Now on the downward curve of life, Lear faces the reality of death. Viewers and readers of the play can grasp this only when we reach the age when death, formerly hidden by the clutter of ambition and child-rearing, reveals itself.* [WSJ Opinion 2018-10-17]

My dearest,

Do you know I believe I am lonely? I want you. I took a leaf out of your book last night and staid awake and I did not have a nice time. You will be amused at the different gradations the blues took.

Did I write you that Douglas was dead? It was a very hot night and the dogs were restless on the lawn and I began to think of my beautiful golden dog with his loving eyes and eager, jealous rush to meet me and to realize that the loving, spirited thing was gone. None of the other dogs had that eager, personal devotion.

Then I went back over the years we had been here and it seemed as if it was a type of other things that were gone, my own youth among them and the people who needed me. The next generation does not need us, we need them. I mean for enjoyment; they may need us for counsel but that is different.

Lute[318] has gone out of the world, the loveliest nature I ever knew and the younger generation do not really miss her. We need them, not they us. And there are very, very few in the world anyway whom we really love or who love us. And why when life is so horribly short do we deliberately separate ourselves from the only one in the world who really counts. I went through a very selfish hour, sweetheart, but it was a very black one and I would have given everything I owned to have your arms around me. Finally I began to cry, and I cried and cried and cried. And then I went to sleep.

I woke up to the sound of most pathetic sobbing under my window. "O dear, O dear, I never can have it again and grandpa gave it to me and I kept it so carefully." Alice had left her shaker work basket on the porch table and Mae had chewed it up overnight. I explained to her that Grandpa did not like people to use things that were hopelessly soiled, worn out and faded (as in three years faithful use in St. Louis, it undoubtedly had become), and that he had much rather she had a clean, fresh one just like it to remember his by.

There are some loyal and loving souls in the world and by the time I had breakfast, the "blacks" of the night were gone and I was quite ready to face the much more real trouble that my cook was completely prostrated with a sick headache and was obliged to confess that she was subject to them. I thought there must be a fly in the ointment somewhere. The prospect of one of Margaret's dinners is a grief which requires real courage to face.

Then came four very, <u>very</u> nice letters, the nicest I have had this summer - only the idea of suggesting that I would take Hugh to the Touraine for lunch and order a Bronx - your severe regime must be slightly affecting your head. But you are a darling and I love you and to be perfectly honest, I don't quite see how I am going to live until the fifteenth and next year, I shall stay at home until after the fourth, anyway.

Yours always,
Bert
[1910-06-30(-) 20180318-1 Bertha to Henry]

Ironically, Henry died the next January, so Bertha did not get the chance to spend more of her summers with Henry.

---

[318] Mary Louise Shepley Lionberger ("Lute") died in 1910, age 46.

I. GOD BLESS YOU UNTIL WE MEET AGAIN

Henry wrote the following letter to Bertha toward the end of his life when he was feeling wistful and somewhat fatalistic. But, true to form, Henry closed his letter to Bertha: "*yours always*".

Saturday Afternoon

Goodbye, my darling, and think of me sometimes while I am away. It always makes it harder to leave you when I think how much I wished to say to you when we were last together and yet how little I seemed to say and this time it seems I have left unsaid more that I was anxious to talk to you about than ever before. You make the time fly so fast, dear, because you are so sweet and good to me and, dear, I never do. I think I never shall have time enough to tell you of my love for you.

Yesterday, I would not let myself think of how I should miss you and I even tried to fool you, my darling, because it seemed selfish to permit you to see there was anything but great joy in my heart. But I do miss you now, my child, and I can't take my thoughts from you, even for my work which is not light this last day, until I have said goodbye.

Dear, you have been very good to me all this week and you seemed more than ever before to know how dearly I love you. Do not think because I have not told you about your sweet thought of me that the least of your gentle kindnesses have been overlooked and are not remembered? Do you think I did not know why the music box played yesterday when I called for you, dear? Or that you have done these last few days any number of things because they made me glad? Someday, my darling, I may be able to show you how you thrill me with your sweet, gentle ways. I know I cannot do so now and I can only add, God bless you until we meet again.

Yours always,
H.C.S.
[1910(-) 20180716-1 Henry to Bertha]

"I can only add, God bless you until we meet again."

CHAPTER 24 – LATER YEARS

"I would rather have your hand in mine once more than all the world's treasure."
[1893-10-14 Henry (Waco) to Bertha (StL)]

Bertha Drake Scott

"I see a brightening light from far steal down a path beyond the grave! ... and shows the dear hand clasped in mine!" (Nathaniel Parker Willis)
[Poem quoted in Betha's 1893 Diary, April 30, 1901]

A. BERTHA'S MUSINGS ABOUT OLD AGE

Bertha was always aware of the passage of time and the "seasons" of one's life. In her poem, "La Gitana", which she wrote in 1918 after Henry had died, Bertha heard music that reminded her of past life and the scent of roses *"from the grave of days long past"*. And Bertha recalled Henry who often gave her roses, the one face she always saw.

> ### La Gitana[319]
> *Hush the music, hush the music,*
> *Do not let them play that strain,*
> *It brings dreams I thought long stifled*
> *Aching thrills of joy and pain.*
>
> *Is it real, that breath of flowers,*
> *That seems borne upon the blast*
> *Or the spirit scent of roses*
> *From the grave of days long past?*

---

[319] "La Gitana" ("The Gypsy" in Spanish) was written around 1900. It pulls us into the sunny, mystical world of Arabo-Spanish Gypsies. Bertha may have heard a recording of this piece by Fritz Kreisler (1875-1962) which has been described as "deeply alluring ... with its warm soulfulness and far-off nostalgia". [thelistenersclub.com]

Softer, sweeter, play the music,
How it all comes back to me.
With the violins' low plaining,
Like the throbbing of the sea.

Such a mist of lovely colors
Flash of jewels, foam of lace,
All a world of joy about me,
But I only see one face.

Only hear one voice, low pleading,
"Will you hold me as your friend?
I would rather have your friendship."
What! The music at an end!

Fades the picture, dies the fragrance,
Ah, how dim the world has grown.
And the darkness and the silence
I am left to meet – alone.

Bertha Drake Scott, February 9, 2018
[30 – 1918 - La Gitana]

Bertha first began to contemplate getting old when she was in her twenties and when her life changed from being a girl to a woman. During her last summer in Rye Beach as a single woman in 1892, Bertha wrote, *"I cannot help grieving over these last times – for it never will be quite the same again. A girl's life is a very happy carefree life and mine has been especially so..."* [1892-09-08 (Wednesday) Bertha (Rye Beach) to Henry (StL)]

On her 31st birthday, Bertha wrote in her diary of losing *"everything young"*.
April 30, 1897
I am thirty-one years old today and I feel forty. They tell me I will feel young again, that everyone goes through this when they are sad. I do not mean I am not happy but, since mother died and I have become the woman of the household, it seems to me as if everything young in me was gone. My little lad is sitting with me helping me to write. Henry wanted to know what I wanted for a present, and I begged him to have a good picture of himself taken so I have my first good picture of him.
[1893 Diary]

In 1901, shortly after her 35th birthday, Bertha quoted in her Diary, the words of Nathaniel Parker Willis, *"weary Heart, thou art halfway home"*.[320] But, while Bertha may have had this thought for a moment, she wrote immediately after, *"[I] Don't feel very weary."*

---

[320] "The Years of A Man's Life Are Three Score And Ten" from *The Sacred Poems* by Nathaniel Parker Willis (1806-1867).

On her tin (10th) wedding anniversary, Bertha wrote a prayer from the Book of Tobit in her diary that she and Henry would grow old together.

> *Feb. 14, 1903*
> *Our tin wedding day. Spend it very quietly, but feel more deeply than ever in my life, the great happiness God has given me in my married life. "Mercifully grant that we may grow old together."[321]*
> [1893 Diary]

But Bertha and Henry would not grow into old age together due to Henry's untimely death in 1911.

B. CONDOLENCES

Bertha received countless letters of condolence after Henry's death. The following are just a few.

Janet January (Elliott), her childhood friend, wrote the following.

> *My dear Berta,*
> *I know from experience that no sympathy can touch the boundaries of human grief. It only helps us to realize that we are not alone in joy or sorrow.*
> *Affectionately,*
> *J.E. January*

Hallie Chilton wrote:

> *I have just heard of your great sorrow and my heart aches with you. Words fail to tell you how deeply I feel for you and with you. I know how great is your loss and I pray strength may be given you to bear it.*
>
> *I can never forget how kind and lovely you and dear Henry were to me and I will always love you both although I seem to have no way of showing it. I had not heard of Henry's ill health and am sorry he had the suffering of insomnia to contend with. Only those who have experienced it can imagine what it is and the dreadful depression it produces.*
> [Hallie Hamilton Chilton 1911-01-18]

Bertha received the following note from her dear friend, Helen Ernst on March 26, 1911. Helen had been instrumental in making Bertha and Henry's engagement happen. (See Chapter 9) In the following letter, Helen wrote very poignantly.

---

[321] Quoting the Book of Tobit 8:4b-8

> *4. When the parents had gone out and shut the door of the room, Tobias got out of bed and said to Sarah, 'Sister, get up, and let us pray and implore our Lord that he grant us mercy and safety.'*
> *5. So she got up, and they began to pray and implore that they might be kept safe. Tobias began by saying,*
> *'Blessed are you, O God of our ancestors,*
> *and blessed is your name in all generations forever.*
> *Let the heavens and the whole creation bless you forever.*
> *6. You made Adam, and for him you made his wife Eve*
> *as a helper and support.*
> *From the two of them the human race has sprung.*
> *You said, "It is not good that the man should be alone;*
> *let us make a helper for him like himself."*
> *7. I now am taking this kinswoman of mine,*
> *not because of lust,*
> *but with sincerity.*
> ***Grant that she and I may find mercy***
> ***and that we may grow old together.'***
> *8 And they both said, 'Amen, Amen.'*

I can never, never tell you all that Henry has meant to me as well as all that he has been to me. I couldn't tell you when I was with you, even then. But you know, thank heaven, without being told, though I do long to be able to tell you someday. What breaks my heart is that I could never tell him, though I did try to, sometimes.

O my dear, my dear, I want to see you so, I miss you so. I am sick with grief for you, my darling, and there have been days and nights when my whole body, as well as my whole soul, has ached with love and pity for you. I haven't been able to face such grief and loss for you, everything has been black despair and dread to me, horrible dread. And then my knowing as I do now, what a wonderful soul you have, so brave, so steadfast, so unswervingly true, has made me feel too my own great loss of my dearly loved and trusted friend when I miss the very thought of all that time. O what a dull blind idiot I was all those years. I have come at last to understanding so much that has always been a sealed book to me, that has since so even when I went down into the depths.

O, the more I think about Henry, the more I remember little looks and words and ways that puzzled and distressed me at the time. The better I understand and every day, dear Bert, I love and honor him more truly, for his long brave struggle and conquest. I didn't suppose I needed to appreciate him more but now I do, I do.
1911-03-26 Enclosed Letter from Helen Ernst to Bertha

Helen's letter was a beautiful expression of her love and friendship for Bertha, and her faith that, after a brave struggle here, there will be the ultimate conquest over death.

C. ACCEPTANCE

During the months and years after Henry's death, Bertha thoughts often turned to Henry and these thoughts were both beautiful and painful. On her birthday, 3 months after Henry died, Bertha wrote in her diary[322]:

April 30, 1911
I am forty-five years old today – and my father and grandmother lived to be over eighty. Forty years more. It is only fifteen weeks since Henry died – what will the years be. Zack told me that writing what I could remember of the most beautiful times in my life would help me to get through the worst hours. I know it has helped me to bear the nights, just to think and try to recall in detail different trips together. For life has been so beautiful. I don't believe any two people in the world ever had a better time together. We always knew it, always wondered if it were possible if other people could really be as happy. Even in those black hours of despondency, when his health was failing – if we could just get off alone together.

I am going back. I have been reading George and Nancy this diary in the mornings and some time all the children may care to have it. And if I write it with some motive, it may be more likely to keep me at it. Just now it is difficult but I do want to keep those years clear if I can. Those first pages are so gay in this book but life grew steadily more beautiful to me always and to him, always when he was well. He said to me on that last trip to New York, last November "sweetheart, of all our sprees together, this has been the very best and we have had some very perfect ones." But I will go back, really, and write things as they happened – I have not written since my precious Alice was born.

Two months later, Bertha struggled to address her thoughts about Henry and their past lives together. As she wrote in her diary (below), "*There does not seem to be any reason, for the beauty or the joy of anything,*

---

[322] Except for the "1925 Diary" references later in this chapter, the "diary" refers to Bertha's "1893 Diary" unless otherwise specified.

if we are not to talk it over together." Still, Bertha continued to try to write about Henry and her past for several more months.

> *June 27, 1911 (Rye Beach)*
>
> *I have given up the idea of writing of just those hours together. I cannot, but the craving to write to Henry grows stronger. Here at Rye, I never realized how unconsciously everything that happened, I planned to write to him. I think he was never far from my thoughts and now, although I am used to being here alone in the early summer without him, the lack of that daily letter from him and to him, makes all life purposeless. There does not seem to be any reason for the beauty or the joy of anything if we are not to talk it over together, and that aching longing grows worse, not better, as the days go on. I thought yesterday when I grew quite mad with that desperate wish that I would just write the old letters daily and see if it would help but today I know it would be worse than useless. But I must talk about Henry – I must have some outlet or I cannot bear it. It is better to write and have a definite plan to follow than just to think and think – and I cannot talk to other people – so I am going to write, as far as I can remember it, from what Henry has told me, the incidents of his life for his children.*

Much of the pain that Bertha felt about losing Henry softened over time. The sorrow still remained but she seemed to find an inner peace which abided with her. One of the poems which Bertha kept with her diary and letters was written by Harold Monro, entitled "Solitude", which was a poem on the play *"The Distaff Side"*. This poem seemed to capture her feelings in this later part of her life.

SOLITUDE

Bertha's copy of the Harold Monro Poem

> *WHEN you have tidied all things for the night,*
> *And while your thoughts are fading to their sleep,*
> *You'll pause a moment in the late firelight,*
> *Too sorrowful to weep.*
>
> *The large and gentle furniture has stood*
> *In sympathetic silence all the day*
> *With that old kindness of domestic wood;*
> *Nevertheless the haunted room will say:*
> *'Someone must be away.'*

The little dog rolls over half awake,
Stretches his paws, yawns, looking up at you,
Wags his tail very slightly for your sake,
That you may feel he is unhappy too.

A distant engine whistles, or the floor
Creaks, or the wandering night-wind bangs a door

Silence is scattered like a broken glass.
The minutes prick their ears and run about,
Then one by one subside again and pass
Sedately in, monotonously out.

You bend your head and wipe away a tear.
Solitude walks one heavy step more near.
Harold Monro

D. POETRY

Bertha continued to write poetry and this poetry revealed both the acceptance of where her life had brought her and also the nostalgia for her past. In the following poem, Bertha was reminiscing over a picture which was taken around 1900. The picture had an assortment of old friends who apparently included Anne ("Nan") Shepley, Lucy Benton, Henry, Janet January, Edith January, and Maud Davis (i.e. whose initials she wrote at the beginning of the poem). Several of the people in the photograph had already died by the time this poem was written in 2018. As Bertha wrote, "*See the picture here of those Who shall go like last year's snows.*"

31 – 2018 – Lines to a Picture

- To A.S., L.B.B., H.S., J.J. E.J., M.D.

François Villon[323], poet, sage,
You have left one mournful page.
'Mid your songs with laughter mellow,
Naming o'er from days gone by.
Fair sweet women, but to sigh,
"Now where are they? Speak, who knows?
Ask where are the last year's snows."

Nothing's new beneath the sun
Goes the saying, when t'is done.
Each life is but like its fellow,
So the day shall come when we
Asking for some friend, shall see

---

[323] François Villon: born in Paris in 1431 and disappeared from view in 1463, is the best known French poet of the late Middle Ages. A ne'er-do-well who was involved in criminal behavior and had multiple encounters with law enforcement authorities, Villon wrote about some of these experiences in his poems. Villon was a great innovator in terms of the themes of poetry and, through these themes, a great renovator of the forms. He understood perfectly the medieval courtly ideal, but he often chose to write against the grain, reversing the values and celebrating the lowlifes destined for the gallows, falling happily into parody or lewd jokes, and constantly innovating in his diction and vocabulary; a few minor poems make extensive use of Parisian thieves' slang. Still Villon's verse is mostly about his own life, a record of poverty, trouble, and trial which was certainly shared by his poems' intended audience. [Wikipedia]

Strangers, answering cold, "who knows?
Can you find the last year's snows?

Aye, and when we too are gone,
Still the old song shall go on.
Not for us shall change the story,
Not by pleading, nor by will,
Can we hold this old world still.
Friends shall sigh, "Ah well, God knows,
They are gone with last year's snows."

Only art can live for aye,
Faces long since turned to clay.
Still smile at us in youth's glory
Kept by art from growing old.
We too claim that magic bold,
See the picture here of those
Who shall go like last year's snows.
[BDS April 23, 1918]

Bertha was often philosophical about suffering and grief. In 1888, Bertha wrote in her diary of visiting an ill friend, "*O, the suffering! It is a good thing for one to see the other side of the shield sometimes...*" [1888-05 Diary, October 9, 1888] Later in her life, Bertha wrote a poem, "*Weltschmerz*" (i.e. a feeling of melancholy and world weariness) in which she wrote of the "*shade*" and " being a necessary part of the deeper harmony which is essential to knowing life's light and joys.[324] "*[S]uch suff'ring is not vain.*"

Weltschmerz
We cannot know the light, save by the shade,
And love we cannot learn, except by pain.
Wouldst wish the lesson then unlearned, poor soul?
Ah no, ah no, such suff'ring is not vain.

The notes joy wakes ring but as zithers, light,
But when the Master grief has touched the keys,
A thousand echoes answer to the sound,
The world reveals its mighty harmonies.
[BDS Oct. 10, 1918]

Throughout her life, Bertha maintained her steadfast faith in her God. And even when she could not understand his works, she trusted in Him.

What Concerns Me
It does not concern me (if at all)
That Christ came to us through a Virgin Birth.
It does not much concern me that, the pall
Removed, dead Lazarus returned to earth.

And all this talk of blood that changed to wine

---

[324] This theme of light and dark, sunshine and rain, the outside and inside, etc., recurred often in Bertha's writing: see Chapter 6.B "A Prayer": "*Not always sunshine…*", Chapter 19.F, 1898-03-28 Bertha (StL), quoting Dumas "*absence is the most cruel thing ...*", and Chapter 7.A.7, 1888-05 Diary, October 9, 1888, "*The other side of the shield*". Bertha M also used this theme in Chapter 3.C quoting John Bunyan, "*Dark clouds bring waters when the bright bring none.*"

And bread that melted into flesh divine,
It does not much concern me! Nor that God
Will raise us living from the velvet sod.

Nor that Christ walked serene upon the sea,
The lake, the sacred book calls Galilee.
All life is such a miracle at best,
Do deeds then so much more surpass the rest?

But this concerns me. That He fought and won
And left His work magnificently done!
(20180817-1 Bertha Poem – *"What Concerns Me"*, Included in 1893 Diary by "Aunt" Alice in Bertha's printed Diary)

E. TRAVEL

After Henry's death, Bertha travelled extensively, often with her children and their spouses. Bertha listed her various trips in her diary.

EVENTS LISTED AT END OF DIARY

1913 – Graduation at Farmington & the Hill; Europe with the Whittemores; Rye Beach.

1914 – Europe; the World War; Rye Beach

1915 – California; the fair; El Mirasol, Rye Beach

1916 – Rye Beach, Miss James Cottage, Nancy met Tom Episcopal count(?)

1917 – America enters war, Paul Smith's in Adirondacks, Hot Springs

1918 – Hot Springs, Rye Beach, Nancy's marriage White Plains, Hugh sails for A.E.F.[325]

1919 - Hot Springs, boys return, Rye Beach

1920 – Rye Beach, little Nancy[326] christened

1921 – Rye Beach, afterward Athantie(?) City

1922 - Dinard, Paris

1923 – San Ysidro , Santa Barbara, California

1924 – San Ysidro, Santa Barbara, California

1925 - Switzerland, d'Ouchy, Lausanne, Winter: Egypt, San Moritz, Italy
    1925-07-15 L.R. Lemoine (1934 Locust St., Stl) to Bertha (Paris)

1926 – Came home from Europe, Rye Beach, Alice Joneses house.

1927 – Rye Beach, Alice's wedding, Hot Springs

1928 – Summer at the Mallinckrodt place, Pomfret.

1929 – Rye Beach, Winter: Palm Springs

1930 – San Ysidro California, Winter: Palm Springs. Built little house

1931 – Italy and Cherbourg, Normandy

1932 – Little house, Ozark Dam, Nancy visited me.

1933 – Little house, then Pomfret

1934 – Little house, then visit Minnie, then Nan, Nancy & Priscilla Boston.

1935 – Marion, Mrs. Cutler's cottage, Woodebuck(?)

1936 – St. Jean de Luz and Scotland

1937 – Marion & Boston

1938 – Santa Fe

---

[325] American Expeditionary Forces
[326] Nancy Boteler Scott, Bertha's granddaughter and Hugh and Anne's daughter.

Perhaps because Bertha was unable to travel extensively during her marriage due to Henry's work demands and her young children, she began to travel prodigiously in her later years when she was not so constrained. The difficulties of traveling at that time and her advancing age testify to her strength and vigor.

1. POSTCARDS

Bertha increasingly found it useful to send postcards to friends and family while on vacation. In 1922, while in Dinard, Brittany France, Bertha wrote a postcard to her daughter, Alice, who was in Paris at the time, commenting *"when you get local color, you also get much dirt. I have rarely known this rule to fail."*

Bertha's 1922 postcard from Dinard France

> *We have just had an enchanting trip to Quimper where Dr. Blumer had been to a French Medical Conference. It is in the heart of old Brittany, very little spoiled by tourists. All the peasants wear the costumes, women as well, men & every human being wears wooden shoes. We had the great luck of seeing a crowded market day & also a fete. But when you get local color, you also get much dirt. I have rarely known this rule to fail.*
> [1922-07-(-) Postcard Bertha (Dinard, France) to Alice (Paris)]

(Dr. Blumer was Nancy Scott Blumer's father-in-law.)

2. THE 1925 TRIP TO EUROPE & EGYPT

Bertha's 1925 world trip must have been grand. The trip began in July 1925 in New York City when Bertha set sail for France with Hugh, Anne, little Hugh and Nancy Boteler Scott (i.e. the Hugh Scott family), Alice Scott (Bertha's daughter), and Mary Cox (Bertha's maid). They were accompanied to the New York pier for their send off by Nancy Scott Blumer and her husband Tom, George Scott, Mary Keck? Scott (George's wife), George Jr. (their child), Dr. George Silas Drake Jr. and his wife Myrtle, Dr. & Mrs. Blumer (Nancy Scott's in-laws), and Harry and Nancy Block (Anne Block Scott's parents). Harry and Nancy Block met the Scotts in Switzerland toward the end of their trip and were able to spent time traveling with their daughter, Anne. And there were many friends and family which joined the party in New York City for their sendoff including Madge Scott and Minnie Carter, Henry's sisters. All of the details of this trip were recorded in the "1925 Bertha Diary".

RMS Olympic was a transatlantic ocean liner, the lead ship and namesake of the White Star Line's trio of Olympic -class liners. Unlike her younger sister ships, the Olympic enjoyed a long and illustrious career, spanning 24 years from 1911 to 1935. (The other two ships in the class, Titanic and Britannic, had short service lives: in 1912, Titanic collided with an iceberg in the North Atlantic on her maiden voyage and sank; in 1916, Britannic struck a mine and sank in the Kea Channel in Greece.) [Wikipedia]

The Scott family departed for France on July 10, 1925 on the RMS Olympic. Bertha wrote in her diary: *"We had sailed at midnight; beautiful moonlight sail down the harbor. Did not get up until luncheon time. Alice slept until three. We saw the deck and dining stewards last night, got an excellent little table for two and very well-placed deck chairs, middle of deck. Slept off and on all day."*

The Grand Staircase of Olympic. Olympic was designed as a luxury ship; her passenger facilities, fittings, deck plans and technical facilities were largely identical to those of her more famous sister ship, the Titanic, although with some small variations. [Wikipedia]

The RMS Olympic was, undoubtedly, a splendid vessel. (It is interesting, given the Olympic's similarity, that Bertha never mentioned the RMS Titanic.)

Things can and did go wrong, but often worked out in the end. Bertha wrote in her diary on July 10th, *"On return to cabin, saw baggage master who gave me four checks; had no record of Mary's trunk – heaven preserve us. I hope he finds it. Railway ticket missing, suitcase misplaced, steamer sailing date wrong. Fate seems. Afternoon read and wrote letters. He did find it."*

On July 16, six days after setting off from New York, the Olympic sailed into Cherbourg harbor, France. *"Rose early. Saw whole French fleet in Cherbourg harbor. Sailed past them with Admiral's boat beside us. All men at attention. Sea like glass. Landed*!" The Scotts immediately left Cherbourg for Paris, arriving in the evening.

The major event in Paris when the Scotts arrived was the Paris Exposition – the Exposition Internationale Des Arts Décoratifs.

EXPOSITION INTERNATIONALE DES ARTS DÉCORATIFS — PARIS 1925
2 - La Porte d'Honneur et le Pont Alexandre III - *Principal entrance and the Alexandre III bridge*

The International Exhibition of Modern Decorative and Industrial Arts (French: Exposition internationale des arts décoratifs et industriels modernes) was a World's fair held in Paris, France, from April to October 1925. [Wikipedia]

The Scotts stayed in Paris for four days and then took a train to Ouchy, Lausanne, Switzerland where they stayed in the Hotel Beau Rivage.

The Beau-Rivage Palace is a historical luxury five-star hotel in Lausanne, Switzerland. It is located in Ouchy, on the shores of Lake Léman. [Wikipedia]

July 21, 1925
Arrive Lausanne. Met by Anne, Hugh & little Hugh. Hugh with moustache. Drive to Ouchy. Hotel Beau Rivage. Most beautiful rooms in the palace half of hotel. Rose colored sitting room, white tiled bath, rooms quite worn out. Visit with family. Hugh has my ..., very sweet. Fiat car with chauffeur René. Alice, Mary Cox & I in pension, 150F a day. Swiss francs means $30, but in ... meals. Engaged rooms for Anne & children connecting, 80F a day more. Total 46.00
(Bertha frequently included details of the cost of her accommodations, including foreign currency exchange rates.)

The Scotts officially stayed in Ouchy until October 2, although they travelled extensively in the neighboring areas. Bertha noted in her diary that her son Hugh had his operation on August 12 and remained in the Clinique la Pensée with limited movement until September 12. Bertha wrote on August 12, the day of the operation: "*Hugh's operation. Dr. Feissly. Operation at 10 A.M. Stood it very well. Read aloud all afternoon. Hugh said afterward he could recall nothing. Took children to the forest & the zoo.*" It may be surmised that one principal reason for going to Ouchy was for Hugh's operation. The subject matter of the operation was not mentioned by Bertha.

While they were in Ouchy, the children (little Hugh and Nancy Boteler) were taken to Dr. Cerasol's school, the "Champs Soleil" which freed up the adults to visit various attractions including the nearby towns. In addition, Bertha wrote that Alice and Mary Cox travelled to London for two weeks, returning on August 10. "*Flew from London to Paris with the Striblings.*" (Air travel was then in its infancy.)

In addition to details of her day trips, Bertha included some comments of a more personal nature too. "*Drove with Alice to the Forêt. Lost my temper.*" (August 14) ""*Forgot what I did*". *Probably read to Hugh & played bridge.*" (August 15) "*Evening – sat on straight back chair until I nearly fell off it…*" (August 17)

On October 2, the Scotts traveled back to Paris and stayed at the Trianon Palais at Versailles.

Trianon Palace, Versailles (Waldorf Astoria)

October 2, 1925
Arrived Paris 11:40P.M. Met at once by Chasseur from Trianon Palais. Comfortable auto. Very pleasant drive through Paris. Hugh tremendously excited at being out in the "dark time" & Marie by her arrival in Paris. Arrive at Trianon Palais at 12:30. Most comfortable rooms & lovely outlook on the garden.

On October 6, Bertha wrote: "*Lunch at Westminster & then I go home. Hugh has taken little Hugh to see the little pictures at Versailles & he loved them. Anne & Alice returned from an afternoon at Chanel's frightfully depressed over prices.*" However, two days later, Bertha added: "*Alice and Anne had most successful afternoon at Kleb's, got all the rest of their evening dresses & a wrap for Anne.*" (Most successful afternoon!)

In additional to numerous days of shopping for clothes and the necessary fittings, there were visits to Chartres, Fontainebleau, Chateau Malmaison and the last horse race at Longchamps where "*Alice picked the winner in the sensational race of the day.*" [October 25]

They also went to various museums, visited with Albert Herter, an American painter, and saw his painting of the "Departure of the Infantrymen" on August 1914 from the Gare de l'Est, Paris. (As mentioned in Chapter 15, Nancy Boteler Scott's likeness was to be included in the painting.)

Also of note, on November 2, "*Hugh & I took little Hugh to see the Galleria des Battailles at Versailles. Monday & a holiday, it was not visible but Auguste got a particularly nice guide to agree to take us around after the other party left. WE had a wonderful time, particularly when he found he & Hugh had been at San Mihiel[327] together, one right, one left. Showed us many pictures not usually noticed.*" (What fortune that Hugh would run into one of his World War 1 compatriots in France!)

On November 3, the Scotts briefly went to Lyon and Avignon until finally arriving at their next temporary home in Cannes on the evening of November 5th. In addition to sightseeing around Cannes and environs, Bertha spent a fair amount of time with the Cook's agents regarding their trip to Egypt.

A Cook's poster from 1925

Obviously, getting their trip plans in order in those days was more complicated than today. "*Went to Cook's, found tickets had to go back to Paris to be changed.*" (November 17) But, by November 24, the Scotts were ready to sail for Egypt.

---

[327] The Battle of Saint-Mihiel was a major World War I battle fought from 12–15 September 1918, involving the American Expeditionary Forces (AEF) and 110,000 French troops under the command of General John J. Pershing of the United States against German positions. The U.S. Army Air Service played a significant role in this action.

Cook's agent arrives, says we must leave at ten. Scramble to get conveyance to boat, have to take taxis. Boat Messageries Maritimes' "The Sphinx". Rooms 16-18 & 60a for Mary. Excellent big rooms, very good table, poor deck steward, difficulty in getting our chairs placed. Very calm afternoon. Evening - bridge in salon where no one sits. [November 24]

On the trip to Egypt, Bertha was accompanied by her son Hugh, his wife Anne, Alice, and Mary Cox. The four-day voyage to Egypt was very rough.

November 26, 1925, Thursday

Thanksgiving Day. Waked feeling very ill but made the deck and went to lunch. Afternoon – Staid in exact center of boat in salon till my chair slid across the room with me. Changed to sofa – did the same. Dinner in state room. Very few in dining room where cold dinner is served owing to everything being upset in the kitchen.

Two days later, Bertha wrote: *"Steward said never had so much crockery broken on board."*

The Scotts' arrival in Alexandria was magnificent. Their boat arrived at the port in the evening of November 28th. Bertha wrote, *"at dinner time, sight land, have lovely sail into harbor, moon almost full."* On the next day, the Cook's man arrived to take care of everything. *"Cook's man arrives early & gets us with much skill through custom house & to a reserved compartment. Much thrilled over first view of Egypt, native costumes on docks, fakirs, etc."*

The Scotts spent more than two weeks in Egypt (November 28 through December 16). They started in Alexandria and visited Cairo, Giza, Luxor and spent a night camping in the desert. They rode camels, played tennis, sailed on the Nile and toured Egypt's famous sites.

The Great Pyramid. From the left: Anne, Hugh Scott Sr., Alice & Bertha.[328]

Bertha wrote the following about their December 5th trip to see the great pyramid and the sunset at day's end: *"I shall never see anything so beautiful again."*

December 5, 1925, Saturday
Morning – Anne, Mary Cox & I went to see Alice climb the great pyramid. Somewhat appalling to watch. Though accompanied by two guides. Alice quite exhausted. Hugh & Anne played tennis. Afternoon – saw Abdul's cousin's shop with the discoveries authenticated by the Egyptian museum. Then rode, Mary & I, in sand cart others on camels to have our photographs taken in front of the pyramids. There I also mounted a camel & so did Mary Cox. It is was not so bad as I expected but hardly enjoyable. Then, Alice on camel, Mary & I in sand car went beyond the second pyramid to the highest ridge to see the sunset on the desert. I shall never see anything so beautiful again.

On December 7, the Scotts visited the Temples of Luxor and Karnak, *"the two grandest things I ever saw."* Bertha's wrote the following detailed description of her visit to both temples.
Morning – Temple of Luxor. Afternoon – Temple of Karnak.
Oldest temple of Luxor, part built by Arnenophis III 1411-1375 B.C. (eighteenth dynasty). Wife Tiy, whose father & mother ... ... Dedicated to Amon Ra, ..., & Khous, their sun moon good. (small grantile chapel built by Thutmosis III, 1501-1447 B.C.) – Earlier date.
Interesting birth room with wall pictures of divine birth of Amenophis III . Great court built by him. Interesting chapel or holy of holies, rebuilt by Alexander the Great. Contains portraits of him & many representations of heavenly boat. Alexander adopted Egyptian religion certainly while in Egypt. Face & part of the temple built by Ramses II, the Great. Huge figure of Ramses, though much defaced, stand around the rear court. Some quite lovely ones of his wife with min. In front of temple was originally six statues, four standing & two sitting, & two pink obelisks. One has

---

[328] At least two photographs were taken on this day. In the 1994 booklet, "Anne Block Scott", my father included a photograph of this pyramid that also included Mary Cox, Bertha's maid, on a camel at Bertha's left.

been sent to Paris. We heard the muezzin call to prayer standing in the great court looking at the mosque which is really inside the temple. Date of Ramses III is 1292-1225 B.C. He is nineteenth dynasty.

Went to temple of Karnak. It is really many temples. Enter by some of the Sphinxes. Temple of Khous, the moon-god, son of Amon-Ra & Mut. Single column with lotus after column of Sphinxes & Great Pylon, ... begun by Seti. Finished by Ramses II with little white sphinx & tremendous statue of young Ramses II. Then ... court of Seti with one hundred & thirty-eight columns. Lotus bud & bill shaped cat, black granite, marvelous new statue in small temple of Thutmosis III. Wonderful temple of Ramses III with eight colossal figures of Ramses III as Osiris with hands crossed on breast. Chapel of Philip of Macedon. Chapel of Alexander the Great, much decorated with pictures of Alexander in armor making offerings to gods. A good deal of color museums in this chapel and also in many of the wonderful wall decorations. Lovely temple of Thutmosis III with protsdorie columns. Garden of Thutmosis III with bas reliefs of all the flowers and animals in his garden. Most marvelous bas reliefs all over the temple, especially those depicting Seti's wars & conquests. ... ...

On their last day in Luxor on December 9th, Bertha wrote about visiting the tomb of the Queens.

Went across the river to the tombs of the Queens, that of Queen Nefertari, wife of Ramses II. Wonderfully preserved with very clear wall paintings, one of herself in a white dress in a beautiful chair, playing draughts, small but most modern.

Tomb wall depicting Queen Nefertari (Wikipedia)

Two sons of Ramses III, one a boy of twelve with almost the best pictures we have seen. Saw two temples, Dir el Medina – very small, perfect, period of Ptolemies. Saw view from roof. Part was roofed over. Saw that ... tombs. Then Nudinet Abu – wonderful temple built by Ramses III. These great events, and small temple with porcelus like a cloistus, by use by Queen Hatshepsut & finished by Thutmosis III. Inner court, modelled on Rams.... Return just in time for lunch. ... has to tow boat to get it so current would help float it to hotel. After luncheon, buy photograph & postal cards & a uylyée which proves to be stained at the shop of a friend of Abdel. Rest. Then go to see sunset from temple at Luxor. Left Luxor with great regret. In dining car on train, had rather amusing neighbor who did tricks with apples.

On December 13th, the Scotts embarked on their desert bivouac, on camel, donkey and sand car.

Desert
Started on our marvelous desert trip. Alice on camel which behaved abominably. Anne & Hugh on white donkeys. Abdel on a gray donkey. Seven pack camels, five tents, eleven attendants. Mary Cox & I went different road in sand car & met them at Sakhara.

Lunch at Mariet's house. After luncheon, wonderful tomb of Ly. High priest of Fourth Dynasty, hippopotamus hunt on wall & beautiful boats. Tombs of sacred bulls. There adjourn to one beautiful tent illuminated with texts from Kezae. Regular beds, wonderful dining tent, delicious dinner with roast turkey. Marvelous sunset. Dancing & play of instruments.

The stepped Pyramid of Djoser at Saqqara. Saqqara is a vast, ancient burial ground in Egypt, serving as the necropolis for the Ancient Egyptian capital, Memphis. Saqqara features numerous pyramids, including the world-famous Step pyramid of Djoser, sometimes referred to as the Step Tomb due to its rectangular base, as well as a number of mastabas (Arabic word meaning 'bench'). Located some 30 km (19 mi) south of modern-day Cairo, Saqqara covers an area of around 7 by 1.5 km (4.35 by 0.93 mi). [Wikipedia]

December 14, 1925, Monday
Alice & Anne get up to see sunrise. Then we go to Memphis. See colossal figure of Ramses. Alabaster sphinx. Beautiful expedition. Then Alice & I returned in sand cart to Mena house & rested. Anne & Hugh rode their donkeys back. We met them for tea. Another marvelous sunset but night not so good. Mosquitos & tooth ache. Saw sunrise next day myself.

In addition to their last days of sightseeing, Bertha met with the Cooks' agent for their travel arrangements back to Europe and said their goodbyes to Abdel (their guide) in Cairo before going to Alexandria to meet their cruise ship. Bertha wrote on December 16, "*Bid good-bye to Abdel, who has bought us superb roses, with deepest regret – one of the most perfect gentlemen I ever knew.*"

The Scotts left Alexandria on December 17 on the SS Esperia.

SS Esperia, Sitmar Line (1929 Postcard)

Bertha wrote of their departure: "*Lovely little boat. Had most competent man from Cook's who managed everything. Saw last glorious sunset off Egypt. Mary's English valet & his English master are on board.*" (Mary Cox had met her "English Valet" on December 6th when they were in Cairo. From Bertha's account, the valet was an acquaintance of a mutual friend.)

The voyage on the Esperia from Alexandria to Genoa took five days from December 17th to the 21st, some of which were on seas that were "*pretty rough.*" On the way, they stopped in Syracuse and Naples, and saw Mt. Aetna and Mt. Stromboli, volcanoes which were active at the time. Bertha wrote of her visit to Syracuse on December 19th: "*First Christian church in Europe built by refugees from Antioch from which St. Paul preached. Wonderful view of Mt. Aetna in sunset. Less wonderful view of Stromboli in eruption.*"

Their stop in Naples on the 20th was somewhat disappointing. "*Stopped three hours at Naples but alas! Cold & gloomy, not my old, beautiful Naples. Finally found my old hotel & got everything straight but it was cold, gray & dismal.*" (Bertha may have been referring to her family trip to Naples in December 1885 when she was 19 years old and stayed at the Grand Hotel in Naples.)

It took four hours to travel from Genoa to Milan where the Scotts stayed for the night of December 21. Of their short stay there, Bertha wrote: "*Hugh & I sent to get an electric train for little Hugh & got it in a lovely store but failed to find a battery. Our knowledge of Italian was too slight for us to grasp the trouble about taxi cabs which is that they can only park in side streets.*"

On December 22nd, the Scotts left for St. Moritz where they remained until March 12, 1926, a stay of almost 3 months. It was not clear whether they originally intended to stay that length of time or whether their quarantine kept them longer. Regardless, Bertha's diary entries make it seem as if everything was according to plan. Bertha described their trip to St. Moritz.

December 22, 1925, Tuesday
Horrible early start at 6:30 A.M. to get train for St. Moritz. Anne & Hugh go ahead to hold seats & had hard time doing it. Changed cars and got luncheon baskets, etc. Then comes marvelous ride up the mountains through a driving snowstorm. Met Mr. & Mrs. Bulkley [Buckley?], from NY, he a Yale man who also introduced us to Mrs. Dean. Arrived San Moritz at five, two hours late, with another wonderful sunset on snowy hills. Beautiful rooms at Suvretta house.

Suvretta House, San Moritz

Evening – Children arrived wild with delight over their trip & arrival in the dark.

The 1925 Christmas at the Suvretta House was grand.

December 25, 1925, Friday
Had wonderful time with children over their stockings. Hughie most excited over his electric train & Nancy Boteler over pulling one thing after another out of her stocking. My own stocking a great surprise, filled with jokes & poems attached to each one, a rooster at the top, a package of picture postals, a purse with Cook's tickets, change & two pairs of glasses, a sand car & a small bear taking photographs. Then sleighed to a delightful service in a little English church. Home to Christmas dinner in the sitting room with the children. Fifty Christmas cards & holly & a small Christmas tree decorating the room. Read home letters aloud at table. After dinner, Hugh had terrible cold & went to bed. We read the rest of the letters aloud to him. Alice ... sprained her knee badly skiing but insisted on going to the Christmas dinner and ball. Had Christmas dinner in small dining room with tree and wonderful mottoes in shapes of skis & toboggans, preceded by a cocktail party & tree with souvenir knives for all in our salon. Bije & Bill Tuyhis, Mrs. Prentice, Lara & Mary Hamill & Miss Biggar. Hugh was not well enough to come down & dined with Anne upstairs. Alice went on with the Hamills to a dance at the "Palace".

While in St. Moritz, little Hugh and Nancy Boteler may have picked up ice skating for the first time. "*Hugh tries skating. Little Hugh skates quite well with Marie. Bought skates for Nancy Boteler who wants to skate alone, "Pas Touchez.*"[329] [December 29]

On New Year's Eve, the Suvretta House put on its annual Costume Ball for which everyone prepared with great seriousness. From Bertha's descriptions, the costumes were meticulously done and everyone was anxious to learn which costumes would win the various prizes.

Evening – The great costume ball. ... The party met in our room at ten. Hugh & Anne, beautiful old Russian costumes (Imperial guard & bride), Bije & Bill Spanish girl & clown, ... Shepherdess green, Mary Hamill Wattan shepherdess, Rose Miss Bijgar. Turkish. Sam, Red fig red ribbon & fly brush, Beatrice Toochy old fashioned costume with bonnet, Nancy Sellars black & white columbine.

Get to ball room just in time for grand march. Afterwards, thrilled when prizes given by Lady Watson are announced. "First prize for most artistically perfect lady's costume to the green shepherdess, Miss Scott." A lovely gold watch traveling clock in leather case. First prize, man's, Sir Harry Greer, American Indian. Second prize, lady's ... Most original lady's Woolworth Town.

---

[329] Nancy Boteler Scott was 2 ½ years at this time. I recall my father saying that Aunt Nancy become a very fine ice skater.

Most original gentleman's Johnny Walker. Perfectly matched pair, Cossacks white with black ... Afterward, Alice danced with Reed M. P. until supper. Very gay supper. Like Christmas paper ..., dancing & general confetti ... Auld lang syne at midnight.

After all these New Year's festivities, Bertha wrote on the next day, "*Everybody dead!*"

The Scotts spent much of their time in St. Moritz skiing, skating, sleigh riding, playing games, taking tea & socializing, and watching sports events, including ski jumping and hockey. Bertha mentioned seeing the January 7 hockey match between Cambridge & London Lions. (It is unclear why two English teams would have been in St. Moritz for a hockey match, but there it is.)

On January 23rd, the Scotts received the bad news that little Hugh had contracted scarlet fever and, as a consequence, he and all of the family members who had been exposed would have to be quarantined.

> *January 23, 1926, Saturday*
> *Waked in morning by news. Hughie has a rash. Dr. Flack came. Thought it German measles. Fears we cannot stay in hotel but will consult health department. Afternoon – Most beautiful ice carnival. Hugh & I watch from window. At five, Dr. Flack and Health Department doctor come and pronounced Hugh's illness scarlet fever. Said we must leave the hotel. Hugh went with the doctors to see Mr. Bon who said Hughie & whoever went with him must leave for hospital that night while the rest of us could stay until tomorrow morning, go to an apartment of his & come back after fumigation. Whoever goes to hospital must stay six weeks. I offered to rent a house but they say there is not one to be had. Anne begged me to see Mr. Bon myself so he came upstairs & was very nice. They telephoned various houses, all taken. Finally, the doctor (Flack) suggested the chalet at the "Misiriri". That we could have but it had been unheated for two weeks & there was a ball there that night. Mr. Bon allowed us to stay the night on condition we did not leave our rooms.*

> *January 24, 1926, Sunday*
> *Went down the backstairs of the "Suvretta" with Hughie and were driven in cloud sleigh to the "Misiriri" where we had the "Chalet". Baron Egen Von Schanky and his mother were our host and hostess. Spent seven happy weeks there.*

Bertha's capacity to see the bright side in unfortunate events seemed best exemplified by her words, "*spent seven happy weeks*" in the "Misiriri". (The name for their quarantine lodging sounded like something that little Hugh or Nancy Boteler could have made up.) Notwithstanding their quarantine, the adults were at least able to travel about, going sleighing and to ski jump parties, a visit to Sils Maria and to the Cresto Run, bobsledding and watching the horses race on the ice. And Anne Scott traveled to Genoa for 8 days in February on a visit with her parents (i.e. Harry and Nancy Block).

During their seven weeks at the "Misiriri", the Scotts developed a close friendship with the Baron and Baroness Barclay. As fortune had it, their youngest son also contracted scarlet fever and so they were all quarantined in the same lodging. When the Scotts finally departed from the "Misiriri" on March 12, the parting was emotional.

> *Last day at the "Misiriri". Gave the Baron and Baroness a travelling clock and ... lights with a poem written on the back of a group of Anne, Alice, Hugh and the Baron skiing. Everyone was near tears & the baroness wept outright.*

From St. Moritz, the Scotts went to Florence by way of Milan, arriving in Florence on March 13th, where they spent the next 6 days sightseeing. Following this stay, they went to Rome on March 20th, one week before Palm Sunday. During their Rome stay, Bertha recorded the various historical and beautiful places that they visited which read like a travel log. But of particular interest were the events during the days up through Easter.

March 28, 1926

Palm Sunday. Magnificent service in St. Peter's. Great procession carrying palms and olive branches. Pass through church. Knock on bronze doors with cross & march through them to high altar. Afternoon – Hear Mussolini speak to 50,000 people at 7th anniversary of founding of fasciati[330]. Great spectacle.

March 29, 1926, Monday

Hugh & I hurried out to buy rosaries to be blessed by the Pope. Audience with Pius XI at one o'clock. The women – Nancy Block, Mrs. Treat, Anne, Mary Cox and I wore black up to our throats and black veils (I, my Chantilly lace), Hugh finding his dress coat ruined by the flood, wore his dinner coat with a white tie and a low collar, having neglected to buy a high one. The audience was simple and dignified. His Holiness wore pure white and walked rapidly down the room. We all knelt & kissed his ring and at the door, he gave us his apostolic blessing. There were about fifty present in the throne room.

April 4, 1926
Easter Sunday

Early service at American Church. Buy loads of flowers. Calla lilies, forget me nots, pink tulips, carnations. Ten o'clock mass at St. Peter's. Afternoon – Drive to St. Peter's too early. Go to top of Janiculum Hill for our last view. Return. See procession in St. Peter's and hear service at Giulia Chapel in St. Peter's.

On April 7, the Scotts left Rome for Sorrento for two days.

Paid American Express for trunks. Recovered hundred dollar deposit. Said good-bye to Hugh. Alice, Mrs. Treat & I left for Naples. Have horrible cold & am afraid of abscess in tooth. Quite miserable. Dirty trip. Arrive Naples. Auto excellent with good driver waiting. Go to American Express and to pay for ticket to steamer. Then motor to Sorrento. First half of drive, dusty & unpleasant. Meet excited crowds of people and hear afterwards there was an attempt to assassinate Mussolini in Rome. Finally come out on lovely drive which ends driving under a marvelous wisteria in full bloom through an orange grove to Hotel Vittoria. Rooms with lovely porches on the sea. Paradise. Evening – I stay in bed but Mrs. Treat & Alice go see peasants in costume dance the tarantella.

The Scotts returned to Naples the evening before their steamer, the S.S. Duilio, was to leave on April 10 for home.

S.S. Duilio was the first Italian super ocean liner and one of the largest Italian merchant ships until 1925.

---

[330] Rome, March 28 (AP). -- Fascism's seventh birthday was enthusiastically celebrated today throughout the nation with imposing ceremonies attended by hundreds of thousands of "black shirts." Premier Mussolini and other members of the Cabinet reviewed one of the great parades and heard with approval the pledges of the Fascists to continue the task of making Fascism all-powerful.

The trans-Atlantic crossing took 10 days, arriving in New York City on April 20. Bertha simply concluded her diary, *"Landed in New York. Met by Nancy, Tom & Craig Biddle. Home!"*

F. GRANDCHILDREN

Bertha wrote in her diary on May 10, 1945, just six months before she died, of something that her dear friend, Helen Ernst had said to her soon after Henry's death in 1911: *"someday, your grandchildren will comfort you."*

Throughout Bertha's later years, the younger people were more and more central to her life and being. Her joy as a mother and grandmother may be felt in her poem that she wrote later in life entitled the *"Poppyland Express"*. In 1894, Bertha had read a poem of this title by Edgar Wade Abbott and sent a copy of it to Henry in a letter (*The Poppyland Limited Express*[331]). Bertha's own version was probably written when her children had grown much older. She wrote of how she missed the storied stops on the slow Poppyland *Express*.

Bertha's Poppyland Express
You spoke of the Poppyland Express
That morning in the rain,
But never a word that I ever heard
Of the Poppyland slow train.

It stops at stations along the way,
T'is a tiresome road to go,
For the stops are many, the halts are long,
And the progress very slow.

It stops at station "I want a drink",
And at "Give me another, please."
And at "Won't you tell me a fairy tale
If I promise not to tease?"

There's a woeful wait "I forgot my prayers."
And there's "Mother, please don't go,

---

[331]*"The Poppyland Limited Express"* - Edgar Wade Abbott, Buffalo News (ref: 20180803-2, poem kept by Bertha)

I really am trying to go to sleep
It's just that I can't, you know."

So with halts and stops, the train moves on
It verily seems to creep,
And the engineer has a look of cheer
When it reaches the haven "sleep."

Yet I've heard her say on the fast express
"Though the other is very slow,
T'was a stupid way, that we took today,
For I missed the stations so."
[20180803-2 Bertha's Poppyland Express]

Bertha with her grandchildren circa 1930. From left to right (best understanding): George D. Scott Jr., Hugh Scott Jr., Patricia Gross(?), Henry C. Scott, Francis L. Gross (the baby), Bertha, Nancy Scott Blumer Hovey (standing), Nancy B. Scott (standing), Joan Scott Gross(?), Bertha Scott(?).

As her children began to have their own families, Bertha became the loving grandmother that my father always treasured during his youth and early manhood.

On her 67th birthday, Bertha wrote in her diary:

April 30, 1933

Sixty-seven years old! I have been looking through my diary for records of other birthdays. I wish I had kept them more carefully. This has been a very nice one. At nine this morning, Nancy Boteler, Hughie, Bertha Drake and Karl Block came in with birthday presents most carefully selected. Bertha's, a most minute camera from the ten-cent store was especially adorable. Nan and I went to hear Dr. Moon preach the flower sermon, and this evening, George and Myrtle [Drake] are giving me a party. It has been a week of apple blossoms and lilacs, the loveliest spring in twenty years, and I have spent a great deal of time at my little house in the country. That is one of the wisest and happiest investments I ever made. No one really knows how I love being there, and the apple orchard and the lilac hedge! And most of all, Patricia and Francis [Gross] coming over.

How much has happened since I last wrote. Tom and Francis have both been born. I have had that lovely summer in France in 1931 with Nancy and the children and all the Blumer family. And last summer at the little house – such a very happy one! Nobody in the world ever had such a nice family! Forty years since I began to write this book; so many are gone that were in the first pages. This last year, the losses have begun to come among the young. Francis Drew's death was a great grief to me. Among our own friends, we know, it cannot be so very much longer but it does not seem natural for the young.

Bertha enjoyed writing poems to commemorate family dinners. One such occasion, probably around 1935, Bertha was joined by her children and their families.

You'll find no cards at your dinner places.
I fancy, I see relief in your faces.
I started my verses in plenty of time
But they timped & halted & would not rhyme
And the truth seems to in this congregation
I don't such to find any inspiration
So I went in despair to the muses mine
But they shook their heads & said "not for mine",
And then I looked up the grans three
But all they answered was "fiddle didee.
In short, I didn't know when to turn.
For t'was perfectly plain Gurins would not burn
At last the advice of one old timer
Was seek the ghost of Thomas the Rhymer
If all you need is a few old rhymes, he'll do it at once for a good dinner.
Tom was agreeable, somewhat conceited
If you only need rhymes, I can do this seated.
Politely, I faltered, what rhymes with Hugh?
I am willing to wait, while you think for a minute.
He snorted with scorn, the answer is pew.

But it isn't appropriate, he's never in it.
Then the next one in order, his wife's name is Anne
She's a dancer, I know. Can't you work in can-can?
And then of my daughters the oldest is Nancy
He answered "that's easy, she catches my fancy.
And as for her husband, whose name Tom Blumer
... in one, it rhymes with good humor.
Next in order, there are my two Georges

O, let them down easy, they're perfectly gorgeous.
And what ... you do with Mary & Myrtle.
If things go contrary, they make your heart humble.

Then you must know there's my son-in-law, Frances
On a small shooting trip, he takes all the chances.
And Myra and Alice who calls herself Pat,
Well, where in the world did she get that at?
Hold, don't give up yet, those children about
But they've the same names so that helps me out
O no, not all of them, here's Priscilla.
Here's a Christian dinner just take & fill her
And the ... my namesake, given name Bertha
I with glad to say that I think she's worth a -
I won't say what, but isn't that all
For speak I riding fast for a fall.
This isn't a hard one, what for Patricia.
I'd like to tell her, I wish I could kiss ya.
Can you think up one for Henry Clarkson
I could if I knew what street he parks on,
And now there only ones left, Joan & Peter
I can't think which I would own the sweeter.
But these won't into poems I pled
All you wanted was rhymes you said.
But these won't make poems for all of your pains
You asked me for rhymes but ... ... brains

If you can't use them to make a poem,
That's up to you, I'm going home.
So Thomas the rhymer faded away
And that's the reason why today
There are no poems at any one's plate.
But altogether conglomerate.
As here I hastily end my homily
With here's to the health of the entire family.
[1935(-) 20180811-1 Bertha]

Bertha also wrote an "Opening Address" in poetic form for a Christmas gathering in 1936.
Dear friends, we are gathered once more as you see.
And I know you're expecting a greeting from me,
Something quite musical, soft & mellifluous.
But shining with ... almost vociferous.
For I know that you think me both brilliant & wise,
I can see your assent by the look in your eyes.
And I grant that your judgment is good (like your piety),
Although I may possibly doubt your sobriety.
But though I am sure your opinion is justified
I am worried to find that my brain seems quite rustified
& if I could disclose the right mode of oiling it
I might make a spirit without danger of spoiling it.
But there ... with me a most horrible doubt
That it isn't the oil but the brain that's give out.
So I'll hastily wish you a glad merry Christmas
May the gifts you receive stretch(?) from North Pole to Inverness.
And is for your luck in the year thirty-seven
May it fairly pile up from St. Louis to heaven.
May you prosper in business whatever your callin',
..., Mussolini & Roosevelt & Stalin,
May your liquor & characters both much stronger
Having uttered which prayer, I will linger no longer.
But as chanced to a speaker of greater renown
That my audience should say amen & sit down.
[20180812-1 (1936-12-31-) Bertha – Opening Address]

G. HUGH JR.

When Hugh Jr. and Nancy were young adults, Bertha scheduled regular dinners with them and their friend Karl Block as often as weekly. My father spoke of how much he enjoyed these dinners.
The other most interesting thing I have done is having Hugh Jr., Nancy Boteler and Karl Block for dinner Friday nights. They are a very interesting group of young people. I enjoyed very much having Hugh with me three weeks when his mother, my dear Anne, was taken ill,... [April 30, 1933]

That Bertha was very fond of Hugh Jr. was clear. Some of Bertha's fondness for "little" Hugh must have formed during their 1925 trip to Europe and Egypt when Little Hugh was 4 years old. During this trip, Bertha wrote in her 1925 Diary of a memorable visit to the U.S. Consulate in Paris to obtain the appropriate papers prior to leaving for Egypt.

October 30, 1925
Go with Hugh & the children to American Counsel's. Little Hugh took the oath of allegiance. When Hugh told him it meant he would have to defend Old Glory, he said "Yes. Do I have to do it alone?" And the whole consulate laughed.

She said of Hugh Jr. in 1928 in her 1893 Diary, "*Little Hugh is my child self over again.*" [Nov. 29, 1928]

Although she encouraged Hugh to serve his country, nevertheless it must have been difficult for Bertha when Hugh Jr. actually enlisted with the American Field Service and was sent overseas during World War II. Bertha wrote the following in her 1893 Diary.

June 9, 1942
I should have entered earlier the fact that my grandson, Hugh Scott Jr. left Yale in his sophomore year to enter the American Field Service, having tried unsuccessfully for the Marines, Aviation, and Artillery, and been refused on account of defective eyesight. He then volunteered as an ambulance driver, and sailed with his unit (the 4th unit) on February seventeenth, 1942. We heard from him twice at sea, then at Capetown, then Cairo. The last letter said he could not say where he was, but from other information, think he is in Syria, near Damascus. I spent ten days with him in New York before he sailed. Previously, I had been in Boston where Nancy Blumer had an operation and returned there to stay with Priscilla while Nancy and Tom went south. In November, had been quite ill, myself, but recovered in time for Christmas Eve at Alice's to celebrate Hugh Sr.'s birthday. American entered the world war with the Japanese attack on Pearl Harbor, December 1941.

Sept. 21, 1942
We have heard from Hugh several times. He was in Syria, then sent to the desert where his convoy was bombed and he had heavy work, driving one night twelve hours without stopping. Then had a furlough in Alexandria, where he was entertained by Count Saab, the brother of Mr. Kraus's friend. His last letter was postmarked – Field Post and marked "On active service." We do not know where he is but somewhere in Africa. All his belongings had been lost, including his uniforms, some in a hasty departure at night which were probably taken by the Italians.

Letter several months –
Have learned since that he was with Montgomery up to the time he entered Tripoli. Then was in hospital[332].

April 11, 1943
Hugh Scott Jr. landed in New York after fifty-eight days at sea, touching at Arabia, three days at Bombay India, rounding the south of Africa, touching at Greenock, Scotland, but not allowed to go ashore.

April 12, 1943
We got his long-distance call, as he had been unable to reach us the night before. I have prayed every night and morning for his return, safe and uninjured, and my prayer has been answered in every way.

---

[332] Dad said that he had jaundice during his time in North Africa. With the heat and the effect of the disease, my Dad's description of the daily condition of his bedding need not be repeated.

February 1944
*Hugh received his commission as second lieutenant in the United States Marines at Quantico, VA.
He had taken a severe course in eye training to enable him to do this.*[333]

Although Dad did not say very much about his wartime experience, he did have a couple of very good stories that he related to us.

CHESS: While on a troop transport ship, Dad spoke about playing chess with his commanding officer who, instead of looking at the chess board, would stare out the porthole and call out his chess moves to Dad who, likewise, would tell the commander each of his moves. Evidently, the commander was a sufficiently good player to win most of his games, without looking at the board.

TENNIS: Dad was a good tennis player which served him well in the desert of North Africa. While with a British company, one of the officers apparently enjoyed playing tennis with my Dad, perhaps because he was better than most. Apparently, they would have the lines marked in the hard desert surface and have two Egyptians hold the net for them while they played. When the desert surface became too rough because of their footmarks in the hard sand, they would have the net moved to a new location and begin again.

DRINKING: While with a British company when Dad was one of the few Americans, there was a test of manliness in which Dad felt compelled to show the fiber of an American by way of a drinking contest. According to his story, each officer was given a bottle of scotch to consume, followed by another. Dad says that he recalls finishing the first bottle but has no recollection of what happened to the second one. Needless to say, Dad was out-of-commission for several days after that contest but noted that the Commander seemed to understand and left him alone until he fully recovered. Dad mused afterwards whether he was the only one who was actually drinking since he did not recall any of the others suffering the ill aftereffects of so much alcohol.

EYE SIGHT: Because of his bad vision, Dad was not assigned to front line combat but was given the role of ambulance driver, I suppose a suitable role for someone with bad vision(?!?!). While in that service, he described being strafed by German fighters, among other interesting stories. But my favorite story was, after the Germans had beaten General Montgomery in an early battle in Egypt, Dad recalled hearing a BBC report which said something like: "The British Ninth Army is now in full retreat after its defeat by the Germans; but, do not fear for the Tenth Army is now rushing to the rescue." Dad said that the Tenth Army was his ambulance corps.

H. BERTHA'S CHARITIES

Bertha was engaged in charitable work for her entire life. One of her favorite charities was the "Home of the Friendless". Her friendship to this charity was such that they hung her portrait in one of their meeting rooms.

> *Of work accomplished, I am Vice President of the "Home of the Friendless" now, Chairman of the
> Religious Committee and member of the Admission Committee – The Home has improved steadily
> of late years with new buildings and modern comforts. The Red Cross, which I am a director,
> organized a sewing unit to work for the unemployed, the government supplying the materials. Went
> once a week and spoke for it over the radio (very modern). They had rooms and power machines
> donated and made hundreds of thousands of garments before it was decided to employ the
> unemployed women and pay them. On all boards, one has the feeling that anyone else could do it
> as well or better but of course, if one gave way to that feeling, there would be no boards – and team*

---

[333] Dad said that he started to do eye exercises to strengthen his eyes even though many of his doctors believed that it was a mistake to do so. Miraculously, Dad's eyes improved so much that he didn't need glasses for much of the rest of his life.

work helps. Collected seven thousand dollars for the relief of the unemployed. That really was some use.

The most interesting thing was that Mr. Remick (the canon at Christ Church Cathedral) asked me to help him in an experiment to get some people who were out of work back to the country, both the man and his wife having originally come from the country. They were the Trask family, a man who lost his job when the factory in which he had worked for twenty years closed, his wife and four boys. We bought a farm in the Ozarks for eight hundred dollars and a pair of mules, a cow and some other necessary things. That was a year ago. They have had a hard struggle and have had to be helped a little but they are making good and are very happy, never want to come back to the city. [1893 Diary, April 30, 1933]

I. CLOSING THOUGHTS

I started to write of myself, but one's own life is so small a thing, but it has been well worth living it, and I would gladly live it over. [1893 Diary, April 30, 1942]

Bertha stopped making detailed and descriptive entries into her diary around 1900 and, after Henry died, she almost discontinued the diary altogether. From June 27, 1911 until the following entry on November 29, 1928, Bertha apparently did not have the heart to continue this diary; however, with this entry, she did return to her diary and wrote some beautiful entries which spoke of the new happiness and peace that she found since Henry's passing. *"The autumn of life is full of beauty."*

Nov. 29, 1928

Thanksgiving Day – and a very real one. Seventeen years since that last entry and I shall not try to write their history, only to tell of the great happiness that has come to me. In those last pages, I thought it could never come again and, of course, it is a different happiness. The grandmother of sixty-two cannot write as the young wife and mother did. But it is in a spirit of great happiness and peace. Four children who have all developed exactly as I wished and dreamed and as Henry would have wished. And all happily married – to the very people, of all others, I should have chosen. I cannot even say enough of my dear Tom and Anne, and Mary and Pip, or the joy they have brought to me. And as for my eight adorable grandchildren! There never were such perfect children. Blended likenesses, of course, I cannot quite trace my eldest grandchild, Nancy, with her high shiny loving sensitive nature. I hope life will deal gently with her. I think Priscilla comes from her father's side. Little Hugh is my child self over again. Nancy Boteler is Margaret Block[334]. Bertha too young to guess yet. Peter – the most like Henry of any of them. Henry Clarkson and Patricia too young too young to tell, but all of them so dear, and all with a winning charm, peculiarly individual. The autumn of life is full of beauty.

In those years after Henry's death, Bertha sometimes included in her diary what she considered major stories – such as the entries about Hugh Scott Jr.'s military movements. However, Bertha's diary entries especially after 1935 were increasingly introspective and philosophical. In 1935, Bertha wrote beautifully about *"God is love"*, and *"With that knowledge too comes an unshakable belief in immortality, for love cannot die."* Years before, Henry had written to Bertha with a similar sentiment after the death of a close friend, sometime around 1895.

Dear, I wish I could say or write something that would take away the distance you have been so depressed with. I think of your sorrow very often and I reproach myself that I seem to be of so little help to my darling in her sorrow. Do try to think, Bert, that we never lose the friends about whose lives beautiful memories linger with us.

[20170724-7 Henry to Bertha]

---

[334] Margaret Boteler Block Hill (1898-1936) was Anne Block Scott's sister.

In addition to Bertha's statement that *"love cannot die"*, Bertha also included the following in her 1935 entry – *"love is worth everything that it costs and nothing is of any value beside it."*

February Fourteenth, 1935

Forty-Two years ago, I began this book. It does not seem possible. Still less does it seem possible that I have lived twenty-four of those years without Henry. And yet he seems as vividly alive to me today, as he did then. I know now that you never lose those whom you really love. But it takes long to learn that lesson.

Last June was the fiftieth anniversary of the graduation of our class at the Mary Institute. I cannot realize that half a century had passed. People do not grow old to me. My friends always look to me as they did when first I knew them. I wonder if that is true of all older people. I do not feel old but I must seem so to other people. In writing the toast for the anniversary and the reminiscences for the "Chronicle", it was more with a sense of the shortness of the time that had passed than of the length of it. I feel I should have brought something out of those years.

What stands out most clearly? Nothing that is new, except as one's individual experience is new. First, that love is worth everything that it costs and nothing is of any value beside it. The people are happy who are able to love, and I think that comes before the joy of being loved but that comes second. And with the gift of human love and I mean not only of a man for a woman or a woman for a man but love of children, of parents, of friends. With that gift, comes, the more one understands it, the knowledge of God. Whoever wrote the great lines "God is love" grasped that truth. With that knowledge too comes an unshakable belief in immortality, for love cannot die. "Death is only an horizon, and an horizon is only the limit of our sight."[335] I am writing very poorly what has been said wonderfully by great men. When Kant was asked why he believed in immortality, he answered "Because my mind and spirit refuse to grasp that anything else can be possible". I have that feeling. But the thought of the future rarely troubled me. I have always lived intensely in the present. "I do not ask to see the distant scene, one step enough for me."[336]

---

[335] The earliest attribution of these words is to a prayer written by William Penn, 1644-1718.

> *We seem to give them back to Thee, 0 God who gavest them to us.*
> *Yet as Thou didst not lose them in giving,*
> *So do we not lose them by their return.*
> *Not as the world giveth, givest Thou 0 Lover of souls.*
> *What Thou givest Thou takest not away,*
> *For what is Thine is ours also if we are thine.*
> *And life is eternal and love is immortal,*
> ***And death is only an horizon,***
> ***And an horizon is nothing save the limit of our sight.***
> *Lift us up, strong Son of God that we may see further;*
> *Cleanse our eyes that we may see more clearly;*
> *Draw us closer to Thyself*
> *That we may know ourselves to be nearer to our loved ones who are with Thee.*
> *And while Thou dost prepare a place for us, prepare us also for that happy place,*
> *That where Thou art we may be also for evermore.*

[336] John Henry Newman (1801 – 1890) and Edward Henry Bickersteth, Jr. (1825 - 1906) – (excerpt from poem)

Lead, Kindly Light

> *Lead, Kindly Light, amidst th'encircling gloom,*
> *Lead Thou me on!*
> *The night is dark, and I am far from home,*
> *Lead Thou me on!*
> *Keep Thou my feet;* ***I do not ask to see***
> ***The distant scene; one step enough for me.***
> ...

What makes a happy life? As I said, first, love and the things that come from it. To be able to be of use is a great source of happiness, one of the greatest and, as one grows older, one eliminates many things one need to consider made for happiness –

> *"Wherefore do ye spend your money for that which is not bread and your labor for that which satisfieth not?"[337]*

Of course, we all have done a great deal of it, but one should learn what is bread and what is chaff. Reading I call almost essential to happiness, though I have known people happy without it. But I am speaking of myself. My friends in the book world are almost as dear, as those out of it. With me, books first, other beautiful things not nearly so necessary but all love of beauty is a help and the ability to see beauty and to hear it should most certainly be cultivated.

What gifts would I give my dear grandchildren if I were able to give them the gift of their wishes like a fairy godmother. First, an understanding heart – the ability not only to love but to understand is the greatest gift, I believe, that one can have. Second, the ability to lose oneself completely in the enjoyment of something beautiful. From my own experience, I should say in literature, but others would say art or music, but something. Third, the ability to accomplish successfully something useful. Given those three gifts, I should not fear for their happiness. I have not mentioned belief, because I feel that it comes to the understanding heart and so is included in that wish.

If one wishes to avoid unhappiness, there are plenty of negative maxims. Charles First wrote one in his list of rules for the guidance of his life which I have often thought of: "Never cherish a grievance". And George Eliot another: - Why not forgive? "A feeling of revenge is not worth so much that you should care to keep it."[338] Another maxim: "Always remember that you are as good as any other man but no better." All these have helped me. I think it is a pity that the present generation learns so little by heart. I think I should add that knowing wise sayings, great truths, even merely beautiful lines by heart, adds to the joy of living. I am not sure whether I am writing a lecture or a sermon but I feel tonight like writing out some of the things of which I often think. I have not written often in this book and, during some of the happiest years, I did not write at all. I may never have the desire to write again, so I am indulging it tonight. Among the things I have learned by heart and loved was Tennyson's "Grandmother" and, like her, I feel that:

> *"Age is a time of peace."[339]*

> *Meantime, along the narrow rugged path,*
> *Thyself hast trod,*
> *Lead, Saviour, lead me home in childlike faith,*
> *Home to my God.*
> *To rest forever after earthly strife*
> *In the calm light of everlasting life.*

[337] Isaiah 55:2
> *Wherefore do ye spend money for* that which is *not bread? and your labour for* that which *satisfieth not? hearken diligently unto me, and eat ye* that which is *good, and let your soul delight itself in fatness.*

[338] George Eliot, The Mill on the Floss:
> *"I don't mean your resentment toward them," said Philip, who had his reasons for some sympathy with this view of Tom, "though a feeling of revenge is not worth much, that you should care to keep it..."*

[339] Alfred Lord Tennyson, Grandmother (in 27 verses):
> XXV.
> *And age is a time of peace, so it be free from pain,*
> *And happy has been my life; but I would not live it again.*
> *I seem to be tired a little, that's all, and long for rest;*
> *Only at your age, Annie, I could have wept with the best.*

But I wonder if the future holds it. Just at present, the world is talking peace a great deal but like all older people, I do not feel they are approaching it from the right angle. Well –
> *"It is good to know God's greatness*
> *Flows around our incompleteness,*
> *Round our restlessness, His rest."*[340]

* * * * * * *

Bertha wrote the following poem when she was 70 years old, around 1936. As she witnessed more and more of her friends' passings, she wrote, perhaps in a more somber moment, *"You must accustom yourself to being alone"* with only the characters in your books.

> *You are more than seventy years old,*
> *You are fortunate that so many you love are left.*
> *But of those you have loved, more are gone.*
> *You must accustom yourself to being alone.*
> *Who then will companion you?*
> *Can you think long enough of those friends who never forsake you?*
> *Will Rosalind laugh with you?*
> *Will Mr. Pickwick thrust in his cheery visage?*
> *Will Ivanhoe and King Richard and Colonel Newcome*
> *Fill the vacant places?*
> *You have loved them truly*
> *And their hands are held out in friendship.*
> *You are glad to have them,*
> *But it is not enough.*
> [1936(-) 20180810-2 Bertha Poem]

On New Year's Eve, 1937, Bertha looked back at her prior New Year's Eves with Henry and reminisced about old friends, olden times, and what it was like to be young.

> *December 31, 1937*
> *I have just read over the New Year's Eves for 1899, 1900 and 1901. How long ago! How long ago! I thought then that I was growing old and how young that woman of thirty-six years ago seems! But I can still say that life is beautiful. Autumn is past now and winter is beginning. Of the gay crowd I wrote of then, how few are left. Each year now, a link is broken.*
> > *"We can but hope, our nursery joys*
> > *We know must have an end,*
> > *But love and friendship's broken toys*
> > *May God's good angels mend."*[341]

"Love and friendship's broken toys, May God's good angels mend"!

---

[340] Elizabeth Barrett Browning (1806 –1861) – "Rhyme of the Duchess"; reported in Josiah Hotchkiss Gilbert, Dictionary of Burning Words of Brilliant Writers (1895)
> *And I said in underbreath —*
> *All our life is mixed with death, —*
> *And who knoweth which is best?*
> *And I smiled to think God's greatness*
> *Flowed around our incompleteness, —*
> *Round our restlessness, His rest.*

[341] From "Our Sweet Singer", a poem by Oliver Wendell Holmes.

Three years before she died, Bertha's thoughts turned again towards her winter season, not with regret but with a deep sense of happiness in her life.

April 30, 1942

Seventy-six years old and autumn. The autumn of life is over, and winter has begun. Begun in a very lovely way today with a birthday party at Myrtle's and so many of my dear young people with me. Those things of which I have written as making for the greatest happiness are very fully with me. The love of children, the closeness of friends, the ability to enjoy beauty. I do not feel old, but I realize age in certain ways.

The world is plunged in a frightful war, such a war as one can see no meaning or reason for – and it has taken the young and strong and beautiful. One's heart aches for the youth of the world. They have gone, as they have gone before, to fight in a great cause and with a clear understanding of all the sacrifice and danger. No one would wish them to do otherwise. Their battle cry is Luther's "There I stand, I can do no other." But one resents that, on nations which wished to stand for peace, a cruel war has been forced, forced, because not to have fought was to surrender all the ideals for which the men who made our country gave their lives, all that we have held to be right and true and beautiful, and have wanted to hand on to our children and our children's children.

Perhaps, when it is all over, men will have a more real understanding of the rights of others - other men, other nations. I wonder, it has not been so before? But the world has steadily, during the centuries, grown wiser in spite of wars and revolutions. It does not seem so today but it did not during Napoleon's wars or the thousands of wars before that. So there is hope for a future. I wonder who of us will live long enough to see the good come out of the evil for, in the eventual triumph of right over wrong, I do most firmly believe.

I started to write of myself, but one's own life is so small a thing, but it has been well worth living it, and I would gladly live it over.

Bertha died November 4, 1945 when she was 79 years old. Her last diary entries written six months before she died expressed her gratitude for a wonderful life and her faith in a better one awaiting her. She rejected the idea of the futility of life but trusted in "*the grandeur of a purpose working to a great end that we cannot see ...*"

April 30, 1945

Seventy nine years old.

> *"My lot has fallen unto me in a fair land,*
> *Yea, I have a goodly heritage."*[342]

May 10, 1945

I was not able to finish writing any more and the text expressed my feelings as no other words could have done. Truly, a goodly heritage. After Henry had gone, that first summer of facing life alone, my dear friend Helen Ernst said to me "someday, your grandchildren will comfort you." I thought it sounded utterly futile and silly and I realize now a joy I never dreamed was possible in these magnificent young people. I can hardly say enough of my gratitude for what they have given me. It would take too long to give the whole history but each in turn has done some lovely thing and not once but many times. They have given me a wonderful sense of companionship which has kept me from feeling old. I realize that I am an old woman; in certain ways, I cannot deny it. I think I noticed my hands first – that they looked like an old lady's hands. I did not notice my face until someone said that the snap shots taken at my last year's birthday and the pictures taken at Priscilla's wedding were good likenesses, and then I looked in the glass and saw that it was a face

---

[342] Psalm 16-6

that was quite suitable for a grandmother. And very slowly, I began to realize that physically, I could not accomplish what I had done, I grew too tired to go on, or if I went on, too tired for the next thing to be done. And I suppose others see the change mentally - I myself, cannot see that, perhaps it will never be clear to me. But one thing is clear, during this war period, the work is being done by the younger people because they have the strength and the efficiency. One does mind that.

> *"But mine is a time of peace,*
> *And there is grace to be had."*

More and more, as one nears the end of life, one feels not, as many have said, the futility of it all but on the contrary, the grandeur of a purpose working to a great end that we cannot see but of which we are a part and a needed part as the rug makers in Persia, working on the wrong side do not see the perfect beauty of the pattern on the other side. Two days ago, the war in Europe came to an end. Why was that terrible war needed and why must the war with Japan go on? Hard to see and yet it has brought before the world as never before the need of destroying cruelty and of having an enduring peace. That lesson may have to be learned again but I think we are nearer learning it now. Nineteen hundred years we have been trying to learn Christianity and we have not learned it yet. Will it take nineteen hundred more? And what of our own little lives, which will have been long past? What lies ahead? There is only one answer: "Trust God, nor be afraid."

This was how Bertha ended her diary account of her life. The only diary entries that Bertha made after this one was one short entry which described some events from the previous year and a more lengthy entry to give her thanks and tribute to the various people who worked for her over her lifetime.

"Trust God, nor be afraid."

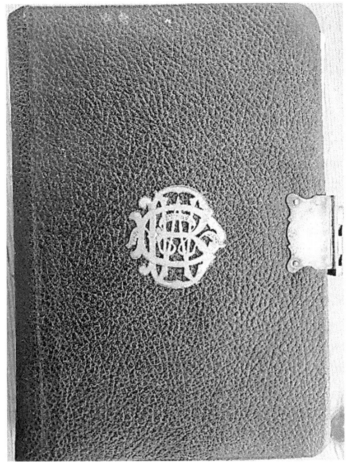
Bertha's 1893 Diary of her lifetime.

CHAPTER 25 – LAST WORDS

Bertha wrote the following poem years after Henry's death. It is fitting, now, to end this story of Bertha and Henry with her words.

For You

The things you loved I have not laid away
To moulder in the darkness year by year.
The songs you sang, the books you read each day
Are all about me, intimate and dear.

I do not keep your chair, a thing apart,
Lonely and empty, desolate to view.
But if one comes who's weary, sick at heart,
I seat him there and comfort him, for you.

I do not go apart in grief and weep
For I have known your tenderness and care.
Such memories are joys that we may keep
And so I pray for those whose lives are bare.

I may not daily go and scatter flowers
Where you are sleeping 'neath the sun & dew.
But if one lies in pain through weary hours,
I send the flowers there, dear heart, for you.

Life claims our best, you would not have me waste
A single day in selfish, idle woe.
I fancy that I hear you bid me haste
Lest I should sadly falter as I go.

Perchance so much that now seems incomplete
Was left for me in my poor way to do.
And I shall love to tell you when we meet
That I have done your errands, dear, for you.

Bertha Drake Scott
[20180810-1 Poem]

For You

The things you loved I have not laid away
To moulder in the darkness year by year
The songs you sang, the books you read each day
Are all about me intimate and dear—

I do not keep your chair a thing apart
Lonely and empty, - desolate to view —
But if one comes who's weary, sick at heart
Seat him there and comfort him - for you

I do not go apart in grief and weep
For I have known your tenderness and care,
Such memories are joys that we may keep
And so I pray for those whose lives are bare—

I may not daily go and scatter flowers
Where you are sleeping 'neath the sun & dew
But if one lies in pain through weary hours
I send the flowers there, dear heart - for you -

Life claims our best; you would not have me waste
A single day in selfish idle woe,
I fancy that I hear you bid me haste
Lest I should sadly falter as I go-

Perchance so much that now seems in vain
This life for me in my poor way to do-
And I shall love to tell you when we meet
That I have done your errands, dear - for you

Bertha's poem, "For You"